PERSONALITY
PSYCHOLOGY
DOMAINS OF KNOWLEDGE ABOUT HUMAN NATURE

Second Canadian Edition

Randy J. Larsen
WASHINGTON UNIVERSITY IN ST. LOUIS

David M. Buss
UNIVERSITY OF TEXAS AT AUSTIN

David B. King
UNIVERSITY OF BRITISH COLUMBIA

Carolyn E. Ensley
WILFRID LAURIER UNIVERSITY

PERSONALITY PSYCHOLOGY: DOMAINS OF KNOWLEDGE ABOUT HUMAN NATURE
Second Canadian Edition

ISBN-13: 978-1-26-006577-0
ISBN-10: 1-26-006577-4

3 4 5 6 7 8 TCP 24 23 22

Printed and bound in Canada.

Product Director: Rhondda McNabb
Portfolio Manager: Alex Campbell
Marketing Manager: Patti Rozakos
Content Developer: Melissa Hudson
Portfolio Associate: Tatiana Sevciuc
Senior Supervising Editor: Jessica Barnoski
Photo/Permissions Editor: Marnie Lamb
Copy Editor: Margaret Henderson
Plant Production Coordinator: Heitor Moura
Manufacturing Production Coordinator: Jason Stubner
Cover Design: Lightbox Visual Communications Inc.
Interior Design: Liz Harasymczuk
Cover Image: © Panther Media GmbH/Alamy
Page Layout: MPS Limited
Printer: Transcontinental Printing

Dedication

To Tommy and Ana.

RL

To my father and first personality teacher, Arnold H. Buss.

DB

To Chris, whose personality is the best part of my day; and to
Atticus and London, whose spirits are greatly missed.

DK

To my husband, Henry, my best friend and greatest supporter.

CE

Brief Contents

Contents

Contents

Chapter 7

Physiological Approaches to Personality   189

Chapter 8

Evolutionary Perspectives on Personality   227

PART III
The Intrapsychic Domain

Chapter 9

Psychoanalytic Approaches to Personality   263

Chapter 10

Psychoanalytic Approaches: Contemporary Issues   300

Chapter 11

Motives and Personality   331

PART IV
The Cognitive/Experiential Domain

Chapter 12

Cognitive Topics in Personality   371

Chapter 13

Emotion and Personality   402

About the Authors

Randy J. Larsen received his PhD in Personality Psychology from the University of Illinois at Champaign–Urbana in 1984. In 1992, he was awarded the Distinguished Scientific Achievement Award for Early Career Contributions to Personality Psychology from the American Psychological Association, and in 1987 he received a Research Scientist Development Award from the National Institute of Mental Health. He has been an associate editor at the *Journal of Personality and Social Psychology* and the *Personality and Social Psychology Bulletin,* and has been on the editorial boards of the *Journal of Research in Personality, Review of General Psychology,* and the *Journal of Personality.* Randy Larsen has served on several Scientific Review Groups for the National Institute of Mental Health and the National Research Council. He is a Fellow in the Association for Psychological Science and

Courtesy of Randy J. Larsen

the American Psychological Association. His research on personality has been supported by the National Institute of Mental Health, the National Science Foundation, the National Institute of Aging, the McDonnell Foundation for Cognitive Neuroscience, and the Solon Summerfield Foundation. In 2000 he was elected president of the Midwestern Psychological Association. He has served on the faculty at Purdue University and the University of Michigan. Currently Randy Larsen is chairman of the Psychology Department, and the William R. Stuckenberg Professor of Human Values and Moral Development, at Washington University in St. Louis, where he teaches Personality Psychology and other courses. He lives in St. Louis with his wife and two children.

David M. Buss received his PhD in 1981 from the University of California at Berkeley. He served on the faculties of Harvard University and the University of Michigan before accepting a professorship at the University of Texas at Austin, where he has taught since 1996. Buss received the American Psychological Association (APA) Distinguished Scientific Award for Early Career Contribution to Psychology in 1988, the APA G. Stanley Hall Award in 1990, and the APA Distinguished Scientist Lecturer Award in 2001. Books by David Buss include *The Evolution of Desire: Strategies of Human Mating* (Revised Edition) (Basic Books, 2003), which has been translated into 10 languages; *Evolutionary Psychology: The New Science of the Mind* (4th ed.) (Allyn & Bacon, 2012), which was presented with the Robert W. Hamilton Book Award; *The Dangerous Passion: Why Jealousy*

Courtesy of David M. Buss

Is as Necessary as Love and Sex (Free Press, 2000), which has been translated into 13 languages; and *The Handbook of Evolutionary Psychology* (Wiley, 2005). Buss has authored more than 250 scientific publications and has also written articles for *The New York Times* and the *Times Higher Education Supplement.* He appears in the ISI List of Most Highly Cited Psychologists Worldwide, and as the 27th Most Cited Psychologist in Introductory Psychology textbooks. He lectures widely throughout the United States and abroad and has extensive cross-cultural research collaborations. David Buss greatly enjoys teaching, and in 2001 he won the President's Teaching Excellence Award at the University of Texas.

David B. King received his PhD in 2013 from the University of British Columbia in Vancouver, Canada. During his doctoral training, he specialized in the field of *health psychology*, studying social factors in the daily stress of Canadian paramedics. He also holds a Master of Science degree in *statistical modelling* and a Bachelor of Science degree in *psychology*, both from Trent University. David's current research addresses the question of how stress unfolds within social contexts of varying size and complexity. Within dyads and small groups, he is interested in understanding how individuals cope with stress together and carry stress across roles and settings. On the sociocultural level, he explores how people cope with stress arising from disease outbreaks, pandemics, and other collective threats to health. In addition to his research, David has been teaching at the university level since 2012, leading

Courtesy of David B. King

courses in *personality*, *gender*, *health*, and *death and dying* in the Department of Psychology at the University of British Columbia. He remains dedicated to his goal of fostering critical thinking and student engagement in psychology, as well as improving science literacy more broadly in the community. David has authored multiple papers in peer-reviewed academic journals and is the co-author of one additional textbook, the Canadian edition of *Health Psychology: Biopsychosocial Interactions* (Sarafino, Smith, King, & DeLongis, 2015). He has also received multiple awards, including an Early Career Achievement Award from the American Psychological Association and a Postdoctoral Research Fellowship Award from the Social Sciences and Humanities Research Council of Canada. In his spare time, David enjoys writing, staying active, and spending time in nature with his husband, Chris, and his two rescue dogs from Mexico, Hunter and Scout.

Carolyn E. Ensley received her PhD in 1999 from the University of Waterloo in Waterloo, Canada. Carolyn's doctoral research examined dual-task interference and the role of attention in visual information processing. After completing her PhD, Carolyn began a post-doctoral fellowship for the Ontario government, which involved developing an assessment tool that could accurately predict the length of stay for psychiatric patients at inpatient facilities. The tool is now used at psychiatric facilities across Ontario. In 2004 Carolyn began teaching at Wilfrid Laurier University in Waterloo and since that time has developed and taught more than 60 courses covering a wide variety of topics in undergraduate psychology. Carolyn is an expert on evolutionary influences on personality and personality and psychological disorders. When not working, Carolyn enjoys reading, birding, gardening, and spending time with her husband, Henry, and her sons Jonathan, James, and Joshua.

Courtesy of Carolyn E. Ensley

Preface

We are pleased and excited to present the second Canadian edition of *Personality Psychology: Domains of Knowledge About Human Nature*. As with previous editions of the book, the second Canadian edition continues to adopt a framework of six important domains of knowledge about personality functioning, rather than organizing material around the traditional grand theories of personality. This innovative framework is one of the reasons *Domains of Knowledge* has remained a forerunner among personality texts, and it has proven equally valuable within a Canadian context. These six domains are the *dispositional domain* (traits, trait taxonomies, and personality dispositions over time), the *biological domain* (genetics, physiology, evolution), the *intrapsychic domain* (psychodynamics, motives), the *cognitive-experiential domain* (cognition, emotion, and the self), the *social and cultural domain* (social interaction, gender, and culture), and the *adjustment domain* (stress, coping, health, and personality disorders). Original authors Randy Larsen and David Buss believed that these domains of knowledge represented the contemporary state of affairs in personality psychology, and progress in the field since publication of the first American edition has continued to bear out that belief.

In line with the goals of previous editions, we envision our text as a reflection of the field of personality psychology, both generally and now specifically within a Canadian context. Our desire is to capture the excitement of what the science of personality is all about and how it remains relevant to Canadians. For the second Canadian edition, we did our best to remain true to that vision. We believe that the field of personality psychology has entered a golden age of sorts, and we hope that the changes we've made to this edition convey a discipline that is vibrant in a way it never has been before. After all, no other field is devoted to the study of all that it means to be human.

For the previous American edition on which the first Canadian edition was based, each chapter was streamlined through judicious trimming. This provided room for discussing new research and made the book a bit shorter and more economical. The book has since been edited and revised further to resonate with a Canadian readership. Key additions and revisions to the first and second Canadian editions are described below. We have updated the language of the text (to improve gender neutrality, to remove potentially stigmatizing language, and to ensure that examples are relevant within a modern context), added more salient cultural references, and paid special attention to current social issues that many Canadians consider important. In order to showcase Canadian contributions to personality research, we have included in each chapter a *Highlight On Canadian Research* box describing research by Canadian scientists. At the end of each chapter (as well as sections within), we have also added a few questions (referred to as "Concept Checks") to help students think more critically about the material.

Chapter 2: Personality Assessment, Measurement, and Research Design

- Research on social desirability and impression management, including a highlight of leading Canadian research by Del Paulhus.
- Updated practical examples of personality assessment and research methods.

Chapter 3: Traits and Trait Taxonomies

- An expanded look at the HEXACO model of personality developed by Canadian researchers, which is now featured as a main taxonomy following the Five Factor Model.
- A detailed discussion of the Honesty–Humility trait and new research supporting its inclusion as a sixth factor of personality.

- A new and expanded examination of the Dark Triad and Dark Tetrad models, including definitions of narcissism, subclinical psychopathy, Machiavellianism, and dispositional sadism. These additions better enable the reader's understanding of research findings on the dark traits discussed throughout the text.

Chapter 4: Theoretical and Measurement Issues in Trait Psychology

- Highlighted discussion of the work of Canadian researcher Sampo Paunonen, including expanded discussions of the hierarchical organization of traits.
- Information on personality testing in RCMP officers.
- New research on gender diversity in the Canadian workforce.

Chapter 5: Personality Dispositions over Time: Stability, Coherence, and Change

- New research on impulsivity in the section on sensation seeking, including findings on differential developmental trajectories of these traits.
- New content on increasing openness and creativity.
- New content on volitional personality change.
- Information on the Victoria Longitudinal Study addressing stability and change of personality traits over time.
- Updated research findings on historical changes in narcissism.

Chapter 6: Genetics and Personality

- Findings from a Canadian twin study on mental toughness.
- New material from behavioural genetics on the link between social values and personality.

Chapter 7: Physiological Approaches to Personality

- An overview of the famous Canadian case study of the brain injury of Patient K. C., including the contributions of the case to modern psychology.
- A highlighted discussion of Canadian research from the Centre for Gambling Research at the University of British Columbia.
- A closer look at fascinating research that demonstrates how the brain uses its own models of personality to predict behaviour.

Chapter 8: Evolutionary Perspectives on Personality

- Research on the adaptive rumination hypothesis, which proposes that depression is an evolved mechanism in humans.
- Information on how ADHD may have evolved as an adaptive trait.

Chapter 9: Psychoanalytic Approaches to Personality

- The discussion of a famous Canadian case of repression.
- Canadian research on dream analysis and dream interpretation.

Chapter 10: Psychoanalytic Approaches: Contemporary Issues

- The inclusion of an example of a Canadian court case that was influenced by false memories.
- Research on Erikson's psychosocial stages of development among Holocaust survivors from Canadian psychologist Peter Suedfeld.
- Updated research on attachment theory and narcissism.

Chapter 11: Motives and Personality

- Significant updates and corrections to the table of Murray's needs.
- Research on the effects of Canadian acculturation on intrinsic and extrinsic motivation for achievement.
- Updated research on Maslow's hierarchy of needs and self-actualization, including a brief discussion of self-transcendence.
- An expanded discussion of peak experiences, flow, and the autotelic personality.

Chapter 12: Cognitive Topics in Personality

- The inclusion of a clearer definition of *schema*.
- Information on learned helplessness among First Nations youth.
- New exercise on intelligence, numeracy, and information-processing within the context of analyzing data.

Chapter 13: Emotion and Personality

- Updated research on the basic emotion of pride from Canadian researcher Jessica Tracy.
- Updated research on money and happiness, including Canadian research on prosocial spending.
- A closer look at the link between money and happiness in a Canadian context.

Chapter 14: Approaches to the Self

- Updated research on the mirror recognition test in other species.
- Canadian research on the link between ambiguous text messaging and social anxiety.
- An expanded discussion of the distinction between shyness and social disinterest in childhood, based on Canadian research.
- Canadian research on implicit and explicit self-esteem.
- Canadian research examining self-concept and body dissatisfaction among First Nations schoolchildren.
- New discussion on self-concept differentiation and related research.

Chapter 15: Personality and Social Interaction

- More inclusive language when discussing relationships and families.
- Where available, research on gay and lesbian relationships, including new research on assortative mating among gay men.
- Canadian research on Internet trolling behaviour and its psychological underpinnings.

Chapter 16: Sex, Gender, and Personality

- Updated discussion of sex and gender (including additional definitions of key terms) to better align the text with a contemporary Canadian perspective.
- New section on gender identity.
- Updated research on sex differences throughout, with outdated research removed or replaced.
- Updated research on masculinity/femininity, gender stereotypes, and theories of sex differences.
- Information on the challenges faced by the transgender community, including a highlight box on Canadian research examining increased suicide risk resulting from discrimination.

Chapter 17: Culture and Personality

- New and comprehensive highlight box examining cultural identity (and related psychosocial factors) in Indigenous peoples of Canada, reviewed by David Newhouse, Chair of Indigenous Studies at Trent University.
- An expanded discussion of acculturation, including new Canadian research.
- Intriguing Canadian research on a third type of self-construal, the metapersonal type, and its link to environmental awareness and conservation behaviour.
- A detailed discussion of the limitations of Western, educated, industrialized, rich, and democratic (WEIRD) populations in research, as outlined by Canadian researchers.
- Information on the Cross-Cultural (Chinese) Personality Assessment Inventory and how it differs from conventional measures and models of personality.

Chapter 18: Stress, Coping, Adjustment, and Health

- New section on hardiness and resilience.
- Improved integration of research findings on the role of the Big Five traits in stress, coping, and health.
- Canadian research on the effects of acute social stress on children's emotional processing in the lab.
- Information on coping in a social context, including Canadian research on the role of neuroticism in relationship-focused coping.

Chapter 19: Disorders of Personality

- Reordering of clusters to align with the layout of the DSM-5.
- Inclusion of Cluster letters (A, B, or C) to better align with the DSM-5 and improve cross-referencing.
- Reviews of Canadian cases of antisocial personality disorder.
- Canadian research on ambiguous facial expressions and borderline personality disorder.
- A closer look at alexithymia, including a discussion of Canadian research on the topic.

Canadian Researchers/Psychologists Cited in *Personality Psychology, Second Canadian Edition*

Chapter 2: Personality Assessment, Measurement, and Research Design

- Brian Connelly, *University of Toronto Scarborough*
- Del Paulhus, *University of British Columbia*
- W. Q. Elaine Perunovic (Xun), *New Brunswick University*
- Michael Ross, *University of Waterloo*
- Ann Wilson, *Wilfrid Laurier University*

Chapter 3: Traits and Trait Taxonomies

- Michael Ashton, *Brock University*
- Kibeom Lee, *University of Calgary*
- Jessie Miller, *McMaster University*
- Del Paulhus, *University of British Columbia*

Chapter 4: Theoretical and Measurement Issues in Trait Psychology

- Norman Endler, *York University (deceased)*
- Ian Gellatly, *University of Alberta*
- Richard Goffin, *University of Western Ontario*
- Jacob Hirsh, *University of Toronto*
- Douglas Jackson, *University of Western Ontario*
- Adelheid Nicol, *Royal Military College of Canada*
- Thomas O'Neill, *University of Calgary*
- Sampo Paunonen, *University of Western Ontario (deceased)*
- Jordan Peterson, *University of Toronto*
- Deborah Powell, *University of Guelph*

Chapter 5: Personality Dispositions over Time: Stability, Coherence, and Change

- Roger Dixon, *University of Alberta*
- Lorraine Greaves, *BC Centre of Excellence for Women's Health*
- David Hultsch, *University of Victoria*
- Joy Johnson, *University of British Columbia*
- Carsten Wrosch, *Concordia University*

Chapter 6: Genetics and Personality

- Kerry Jang, *University of British Columbia*
- James Olson, *University of Western Ontario*
- Julie Schermer, *University of Western Ontario*
- Philip Vernon, *University of Western Ontario*

Chapter 7: Physiological Approaches to Personality

- Luke Clark, *University of British Columbia*
- Donald Hebb, *Dalhousie University (deceased)*
- Stefan Kohler, *University of Western Ontario*
- Shayna Rosenbaum, *University of Toronto*
- Robert Stelmack, *University of Ottawa*

Chapter 8: Evolutionary Perspectives on Personality

- Paul Andrews, *McMaster University*

Chapter 9: Psychoanalytic Approaches to Personality

- Teresa DeCicco, *Trent University*
- David King, *University of British Columbia*
- Peter Humphreys, *Trent University*

Chapter 10: Psychoanalytic Approaches: Contemporary Issues

- Don Dutton, *University of British Columbia*
- J. D. Haltigan, *University of Ottawa*
- Peter Suedfeld, *University of British Columbia*

Chapter 11: Motives and Personality

- Shaljan Areepattamannil, *Queen's University*
- John G. Freeman, *Queen's University*
- Frédéric Guay, *Université Laval*
- Don A. Klinger, *Queen's University*
- Richard Koestner, *McGill University*
- Marina Milyavskaya, *University of Toronto*
- Catherine F. Ratelle, *Université Laval*

Chapter 12: Cognitive Topics in Personality

- Mariangela Artuso, *York University*
- Janice Johnson, *York University*
- Suzanne Prior, *York University*
- Magdalena Smolewski, *Royal Roads University*
- Cynthia Wesley-Esquimaux, *Lakehead University*
- Susan Wingert, *University of Western Ontario*

Chapter 13: Emotion and Personality

- Lara Aknin, *Simon Fraser University*
- Elizabeth Dunn, *University of British Columbia*
- Andrew Spiers, *University of Alberta*
- Jessica Tracy, *University of British Columbia*
- Gordon Walker, *University of Alberta*

Chapter 14: Approaches to the Self

- Daniel Bailis, *University of Manitoba*
- James Battle, *Edmonton Public School Board*
- Tara Callaghan, *St. Francis Xavier University*
- Judith Chipperfield, *University of Manitoba*
- Robert Coplan, *Carleton University*
- Joseph Henrich, *University of British Columbia*
- Todd Jackson, *University of Windsor*

- Mila Kingsbury, *Carleton University*
- Tara Marshall, *University of Toronto*
- Diane Santesso, *University of Waterloo*
- Louis Schmidt, *McMaster University*
- Sidney Segalowitz, *Brock University*
- Romin Tafarodi, *University of Toronto*
- Shelagh Towson, *University of Windsor*
- Noreen Willows, *University of Alberta*
- Jennifer Wong, *Simon Fraser University*
- Joanne Wood, *University of Waterloo*

Chapter 15: Personality and Social Interaction

- Del Paulhus, *University of British Columbia*
- Louis Schmidt, *McMaster University*
- Paul Trapnell, *University of Winnipeg*

Chapter 16: Sex, Gender, and Personality

- Lucy Barney, *Provincial Health Services Authority of British Columbia*
- Greta Bauer, *University of Western Ontario*
- Lorraine Greaves, *BC Excellence for Women's Health*
- Natalie Hemsing, *BC Excellence for Women's Health*
- Jacob Hirsh, *University of Toronto*
- Joy Johnson, *University of British Columbia*
- Chizimuzo Okoli, *BC Excellence for Women's Health*
- Annie Qu, *BC Excellence for Women's Health*

Chapter 17: Culture and Personality

- Billie Allan, *University of Victoria*
- Marie Battiste, *University of Saskatchewan*
- Jacob Burack, *McGill University*
- Michael Chandler, *University of British Columbia (deceased)*
- Teresa DeCicco, *Trent University*
- Roxane de la Sablonnière, *Université de Montréal*
- Tara Flanagan, *McGill University*
- James Frideres, *University of Calgary*
- Joyce Green, *University of Regina*
- Steven Heine, *University of British Columbia*
- Laurence Kirmayer, *McGill University*
- Christopher Lalonde, *University of Victoria*
- Clarry Lay, *York University*
- Darrin Lehman, *University of British Columbia*
- Aislin Mushquash, *Lakehead University*
- Christopher Mushquash, *Lakehead University*
- Ara Norenzayan, *University of British Columbia*

- Janet Smylie, *Li Ka Shing Knowledge Institute*
- Sherry Stewart, *Dalhousie University*
- Mirella Stroink, *Lakehead University*
- Donald Taylor, *McGill University*
- Jessica Tracy, *University of British Columbia*
- Esther Usborne, *Université de Montréal*
- Sarah Wright Cardinal, *University of Victoria*

Chapter 18: Stress, Coping, Adjustment, and Health

- Frances Chen, *University of British Columbia*
- Anita DeLongis, *University of British Columbia*
- Susan Holtzman, *University of British Columbia–Okanagan*
- David King, *University of British Columbia*
- Hans Selye, *Université de Montréal (deceased)*

Chapter 19: Disorders of Personality

- Michael Bagby, *University of Toronto*
- Alexander Daros, *University of Toronto*
- Kevin Douglas, *Simon Fraser University*
- Alasdair Goodwill, *Ryerson University*
- Laura Guy, *Simon Fraser University*
- Robert Hare, *University of British Columbia*
- Paul Links, *Western University*
- Shelley McMain, *University of Toronto*
- James Parker, *Trent University*
- Anthony Ruocco, *University of Toronto*
- Graeme Taylor, *Western University*
- Amanda Uliaszek, *University of Toronto*
- Carolyn Watters, *Dalhousie University*

Acknowledgments

A project of this scope and magnitude requires the efforts of many people. We are greatly indebted to our colleagues who reviewed this and previous editions in their various stages. We sincerely appreciate their time, effort, and thoughtful feedback. We would also like to thank our team at McGraw-Hill, including Alex Campbell, Portfolio Manager, Melissa Hudson, Content Developer, Jessica Barnoski, Senior Supervising Editor, Marnie Lamb, Permissions Editor, and Margaret Henderson, Copy Editor. Thanks to David Newhouse, Chair of Indigenous Studies at Trent University, for providing invaluable feedback reviewing the Indigenous content in this edition. For their help and assistance on the first Canadian edition, we would like to give special thanks to Karolina Donasewicz and Juliane Dmyterko. Their time, effort, and feedback throughout the original Canadianization of this book proved invaluable to the project. David King feels especially indebted to their assistance in the initial research and editing process.

Award Winning Technology

McGraw Hill Connect

McGraw-Hill Connect® is an award-winning digital teaching and learning solution that empowers students to achieve better outcomes and enables instructors to improve efficiency with course management. Within Connect, students have access to SmartBook, McGraw-Hill's adaptive learning and reading resource. SmartBook prompts students with questions based on the material they are studying. By assessing individual answers, SmartBook learns what each student knows and identifies which topics they need to practice, giving each student a personalized learning experience and path to success.

Connect's key features also include analytics and reporting, simple assignment management, smart grading, the opportunity to post your own resources, and the Connect Instructor Library, a repository for additional resources to improve student engagement in and out of the classroom.

Instructor Resources for Larsen, Personality Psychology 2ce:

- Instructor's Manual
- Test Bank
- Microsoft® PowerPoint® Presentations

Power of Process

New to the second edition, Power of Process for Personality Psychology helps students improve critical-thinking skills and allows instructors to assess these skills efficiently and effectively in an online environment. Available through Connect, preloaded journal articles are available for instructors to assign. Using a scaffolded framework such as understanding, synthesizing, and analyzing, Power of Process moves students toward higher-level thinking and analysis.

Effective. Efficient. Easy to Use.

McGraw-Hill Connect is an award-winning digital teaching and learning solution that empowers students to achieve better outcomes and enables instructors to improve course-management efficiency.

Personalized & Adaptive Learning

Connect's integrated SmartBook helps students study more efficiently, highlighting where in the text to focus and asking review questions to give each student a personalized learning experience and path to success.

High-Quality Course Material

Our trusted solutions are designed to help students actively engage in course content and develop critical higher-level thinking skills, while offering you the flexibility to tailor your course to meet your needs.

Analytics & Reporting

Monitor progress and improve focus with Connect's visual and actionable dashboards. Reporting features empower instructors and students with real-time performance analytics.

Seamless Integration

Link your Learning Management System with Connect for single sign-on and gradebook synchronization, with all-in-one ease for you and your students.

Impact of Connect on Pass Rates

72.5%

Without Connect

85.2%

With Connect

SMARTBOOK

NEW SmartBook 2.0 builds on our market-leading adaptive technology with enhanced capabilities and a streamlined interface that deliver a more usable, accessible and mobile learning experience for both students and instructors.

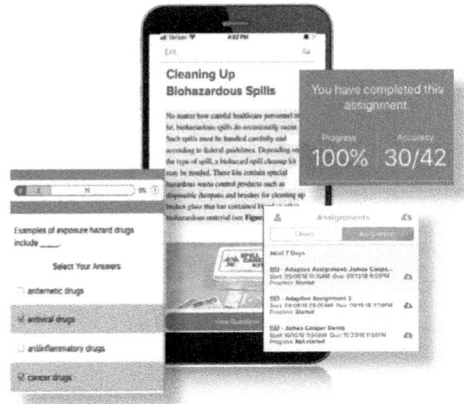

Available on mobile smart devices – with both online and offline access – the ReadAnywhere app lets students study anywhere, anytime.

SUPPORT AT EVERY STEP

McGraw-Hill ensures you are supported every step of the way. From course design and set up, to instructor training, LMS integration and ongoing support, your Digital Success Consultant is there to make your course as effective as possible.

Learn more about Connect at mheducation.ca

Introduction to Personality Psychology

Introduction

Those who carry humour to excess are thought to be vulgar buffoons, striving after humour at all costs, not caring about pain to the object of their fun; . . . while those who can neither make a joke themselves nor put up with those who do are thought to be boorish and unpolished. But those who joke in a tasteful way are called ready-witted and tactful . . . and it is the mark of a tactful person to say and listen to such things as befit a good and well-bred person.

Aristotle, in *The Nicomachean Ethics*, expressed these wise observations on the subject of humour and people who do and do not indulge in it. In this quote we see Aristotle behaving much as a personality psychologist. He is analyzing the characteristics of individuals who have an appropriate sense of humour, providing some details about what features are associated with a sense of humour. Aristotle adds to this description by comparing people who are extreme, having either too much or too little sense of humour. In his book on ethics, Aristotle described and analyzed many personality characteristics, including truthfulness, courage, intelligence, self-indulgence, anger proneness, and friendliness.

Each person is, in certain respects, like all other persons, like some other persons, and like no other person.
©FatCamera/Getty Images

We might conclude that Aristotle was an amateur personality psychologist. But aren't we all amateur personality psychologists to some extent? Aren't we all curious about the characteristics people possess, including our own characteristics? Don't we all use personality characteristics in describing people? And haven't we all used personality characteristics to explain behaviour, either our own or that of others?

When we say that a friend goes to a lot of parties because they are outgoing, we are using personality to explain their behaviour. When we refer to another friend as conscientious and reliable, we are describing features of their personality. When we characterize ourselves as thoughtful, intelligent, and ambitious, we are describing features of our personality.

Features of personality make people different from one another, and these features usually take the form of adjectives; for instance, John is lazy, Lina is optimistic, and Samir is anxious. Adjectives that can be used to describe characteristics of people are called **trait-descriptive adjectives**. There are nearly 20,000 such trait-descriptive adjectives in the English language. This astonishing fact alone tells us that, in everyday life, there are compelling reasons for trying to understand and describe those we interact with, as well as ourselves.

Notice that the adjectives describing personality refer to several very different aspects of people. Words such as *thoughtful* refer to inner qualities of the mind. Words such as *charming* and *humorous* refer to the effects a person has on other people. Words such as *domineering* are relational and signify a person's position, or stance, toward others. Words such as *ambitious* refer to the intensity of desire to reach our goals. Words such as *creative* refer both to a quality of mind and to the nature of the products we produce. Words such as *deceitful* may refer to the strategies used to attain one's goals, however socially problematic. All of these features describe aspects of personality.

 Exercise

Think of someone you know well—say, a friend, family member, or roommate. Consider the many characteristics that make this person unique. List the five adjectives you think best capture this person's personality. For example, if you were to describe this person to someone, what five adjectives would you use? Now, ask your target person to list the five adjectives *they* think make them most unique. Compare your lists. How similar or different are they?

Personality Defined

Establishing a definition for something as complex as human personality is difficult. The authors of the first textbooks on personality—Gordon Allport (1937) and Henry Murray (1938)—struggled with the definition. The problem is how to establish a definition that is sufficiently comprehensive to include all of the aspects mentioned in the introduction to this chapter, including inner features, social effects, qualities of the mind, qualities of the body, relations to others, and inner goals. Because of these complexities, some texts on personality omit a formal definition entirely. Nonetheless, the following definition captures the essential elements of personality: **Personality** *is the set of psychological traits and mechanisms within the individual that are organized and relatively enduring and that influence the individual's interactions with, and adaptations to, the intrapsychic, physical, and social environments.* Let's examine the elements of this definition more closely.

People are different from each other in many ways. The science of personality psychology provides an understanding of the psychological ways that people differ from one another.
Clockwise from top left: ©Ingram Publishing/SuperStock; ©Design Pics/Darren Greenwood; ©Shutterstock/Merla; ©Shutterstock/oneinchpunch; ©BananaStock/Alamy; ©A. Ramey/PhotoEdit; ©Shutterstock/Monkey Business Images; ©stevecoleimages/Getty Images; ©Kevin Peterson/Getty Images; ©Purestock/Superstock.

Personality Is the Set of Psychological Traits . . .

Psychological traits are characteristics that describe ways in which people are different from each other. Saying that someone is *shy* is to mention one way in which that person differs from others who are more outgoing. Traits also define ways in which people are *similar* to some others. For example, people who are shy are similar to each other in that they are anxious in social situations, particularly when there is an audience watching them.

Consider another example—the trait of talkativeness. This characteristic can be meaningfully applied to people and describes a dimension of difference among them. Typically, a talkative person is that way from day to day, from week to week, and from year to year. Certainly, even the most talkative person can have quiet moments, quiet days, or even quiet weeks. Over time, however, those with the trait of talkativeness tend to emit verbal behaviour with greater frequency than those who are low on talkativeness. In this sense, traits describe the **average tendencies** of a person. On average, a high-talkative person starts more conversations than a low-talkative person.

Research on personality traits asks four kinds of questions:

- How many traits are there?
- How are the traits organized?
- What are the origins of traits?
- What are the correlates and consequences of traits?

One primary question is *how many* fundamental traits there are. Are there dozens or hundreds of traits, or merely a few? The second research question pertains to the *organization,* or structure, of traits. For example, how is talkativeness related to other traits, such as impulsivity and extraversion? A third research question concerns the *origins* of traits—where they come from and how they develop. Does heredity influence talkativeness? What sorts of cultural and child-rearing practices affect the development of traits such as talkativeness? A fourth key question pertains to the *correlations and consequences* of traits in terms of experience, behaviour, and life outcomes. Do talkative people have many friends? Do they have a more extended social network to draw upon in times of trouble? Do they annoy people who are trying to study?

The four research questions constitute the core of the research program of many personality psychologists. Psychological traits are useful for at least three reasons. First, they help *describe* people and help understand the dimensions of difference among people. Second, traits are useful because they help *explain* behaviour. The reasons people act may be partly a function of their personality traits. Third, traits are useful because they can help *predict* future behaviour—for example, the sorts of careers individuals will find satisfying, who will tolerate stress better, and who is likely to get along well with others. Thus, personality is useful in *describing, explaining,* and *predicting* differences among individuals. All good scientific theories enable researchers to describe, explain, and predict in their domains. Just as an economic theory might be useful in describing, explaining, and predicting fluctuations in the economy, personality traits describe, explain, and predict differences among people.

And Mechanisms . . .

Psychological mechanisms are like traits, except that the term *mechanisms* refers more to the processes of personality. For example, most psychological mechanisms involve an information-processing activity. Someone who is extraverted, for example, may look for and notice opportunities to interact with other people. That is, an extraverted person is prepared to notice and act on certain kinds of social information.

Courage is an example of a trait that is activated only under particular circumstances.
©RubberBall/Alamy Stock Photo

Most psychological mechanisms have three essential ingredients: *inputs, decision rules,* and *outputs.* A psychological mechanism may make people more sensitive to certain kinds of information from the environment (input), may make them more likely to think about specific options (decision rules), and may guide their behaviour toward certain categories of action (outputs). For example, an extraverted person may look for opportunities to be with other people, may consider in each situation the possibilities for human contact and interaction, and may encourage others to interact with them. Our personalities contain many psychological mechanisms of this sort—information-processing procedures that have the key elements of inputs, decision rules, and outputs (see Figure 1.1).

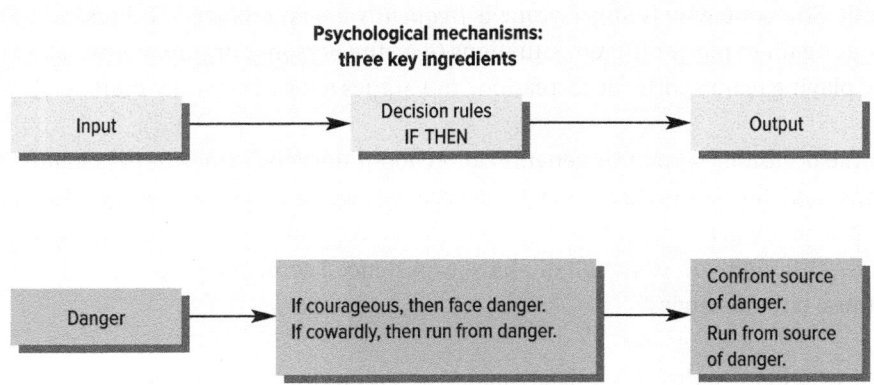

FIGURE 1.1 Psychological mechanisms have three essential ingredients. Our personalities contain many such mechanisms.

This does not mean that all of our traits and psychological mechanisms are activated at all times. In fact, at any point in time, only a few are activated. Consider the trait of courageousness. This trait is activated only under particular conditions, such as when people face serious dangers and threats to their lives. Some people are more courageous than others, but we will never know which people are courageous unless and until the right situation presents itself. Look around next time you are in class: Who do you think has the trait of courageousness? You won't know until you are in a situation that provides the potential for courageous behaviour.

Within the Individual . . .

Within the individual means that personality is something a person carries with themselves over time and from one situation to the next. Typically, we feel that we are today the same people we were last week, last month, and last year. We also feel that we will continue to have these personalities into the coming months and years. And, although our personalities are certainly influenced by our environments, and especially by the significant others in our lives, we feel that we carry with us the same personalities from situation to situation in our lives. The definition of personality stresses that the important sources of personality reside within the individual and, hence, are at least somewhat stable over time and somewhat consistent over situations.

That Are Organized and Relatively Enduring . . .

Organized means that the psychological traits and mechanisms for a given person are not simply a random collection of elements. Rather, personality is organized because the mechanisms and traits are linked to one another in a coherent fashion. Imagine the simple case of two desires—a desire for food and a desire for intimacy. If you have not eaten for a while and are experiencing hunger pangs, then your desire for food might override your desire for intimacy. On the other hand, if you have already eaten, then your desire for food may temporarily subside, allowing you to pursue intimacy. Our personalities are organized in the sense that they contain decision rules that govern which needs are activated, depending on the circumstances.

Psychological traits are also relatively **enduring** over time, particularly in adulthood, and are somewhat consistent over situations. To say that someone is angry at this moment is not saying anything about a trait. A person may be angry now but not tomorrow, or may be angry in this situation but not in others. Anger is more of a *state* than a trait. To say that someone is anger prone or generally hot tempered, however, is to describe a psychological trait. Someone who is anger prone is *frequently* angry, relative to others, and shows this proneness time and time again in many different situations (e.g., the person is argumentative at work, is hostile and aggressive while playing team sports for recreation, and argues a lot with family members).

There may be some occasions when this generalization about the consistency of personality from situation to situation does not hold. Some situations may be overpowering and suppress the expression of psychological traits. Individuals who are generally talkative, for example, may remain quiet during a lecture, at the movies, or in an elevator—although you undoubtedly have experienced someone who could not or would not keep quiet in any of these circumstances!

The debate about whether people are consistent across situations in their lives has a long history in personality psychology. Some psychologists have argued that the evidence for consistency is weak (Mischel, 1968). For example, honesty measured in one situation (say, cheating on a test) may not correlate with honesty measured in another situation (say, cheating on income taxes). We will explore this debate more fully later in the book. For now we will simply say that most personality psychologists maintain that although people are not perfectly consistent, there is enough consistency to warrant including this characteristic in a definition of personality.

The fact that personality includes relatively enduring psychological traits and mechanisms does not preclude change over time. Indeed, describing precisely the ways in which we change over time is one goal of personality psychologists.

And That Influence . . .

In the definition of personality, an emphasis on the **influential forces** of personality means that personality traits and mechanisms can have an effect on people's lives. Personality influences how we act, how we view ourselves, how we think about the world, how we interact with others, how we feel, how we select our environments (particularly our social environment), what goals and desires we pursue in life, and how we react to our circumstances. People are not passive beings merely responding to external forces. Rather, personality plays a key role in affecting how people shape their lives. It is in this sense that personality traits are forces that *influence* how we think, act, and feel.

The Individual's Interactions with . . .

This feature of personality is perhaps the most difficult to describe, because the nature of **person–environment interaction** is complex. In Chapter 15, we examine interactionism in greater detail. For now, however, it is sufficient to note that interactions with situations include perceptions, selection, evocations, and manipulations. *Perceptions* refers to how we "see," or interpret, an environment. Two people may be exposed to the same objective event, yet what they pay attention to and how they interpret the event may be very different. And this difference is a function of their personalities. For example, two people can look at an inkblot, yet one person sees two cannibals cooking a human over a fire, whereas the other perceives a smiling clown waving hello. As another example, a stranger may smile at someone on the street; one person might perceive the smile as a smirk, whereas another person might perceive the smile as a friendly gesture. It is the same smile, just as it is the same inkblot, yet how people interpret these situations can be determined by their personalities.

Selection describes the manner in which we choose situations to enter—how we choose our friends, hobbies, university or college classes, and careers. How we go about making these selections is, at least in part, a reflection of our personalities. How we use our free time is especially a reflection of our traits. One person may take up the hobby of parachute jumping, whereas another may prefer to spend time quietly gardening. We select from what life offers us, and these choices are partly a function of personality.

Evocations are the reactions we produce in others, often quite unintentionally. To some extent, we create the social environments that we inhabit. A child with a high activity level, for example, may evoke in parents attempts to constrain the child, even though these attempts are not intended or desired by the child. A person who is physically large may evoke feelings of intimidation in others, even if intimidation is not the goal. Our evocative interactions are also essential features of our personalities.

Manipulations are the ways in which we intentionally attempt to influence others. Someone who is anxious or frightened easily may try to influence their group to avoid scary movies or risky activities. Someone who is highly conscientious may insist that everyone follow the rules. Or a man who is very neat and orderly may insist that his partner pick up her things. The ways in which we attempt to manipulate the behaviour, thoughts, and feelings of others are essential features of our personalities. All of these forms of interaction—perceptions, selection, evocations, and manipulations—are central to understanding the connections between the personalities of people and the environments they inhabit.

And Adaptations to . . .

An emphasis on **adaptations** conveys the notion that a central feature of personality concerns adaptive functioning—accomplishing goals, coping, adjusting, and dealing with the challenges and problems we face as we go through life. Few things are more obvious about human behaviour than the fact that it is goal directed, functional, and purposeful. Even behaviour that does not appear functional—such as excessive worrying—may, in fact, be functional. For example, people who worry a lot often receive lots of support from others. Consequently, what appears on the surface to be maladaptive (worrying) may, in fact, have some rewarding characteristics for the person (eliciting social support). In addition, some aspects of personality processes represent deficits in normal adaptations, such as breakdowns in the ability to cope with stress, to regulate one's social behaviour, or to manage one's emotions. Although psychologists' knowledge of the adaptive functions of personality traits and mechanisms is currently limited, it remains an indispensable key to understanding the nature of human personality.

The Environment

The physical **environment** often poses challenges for people. Some of these are direct threats to survival. For example, food shortages create the problem of securing adequate nutrients for survival. Extremes of temperature pose the problem of maintaining thermal homeostasis. Heights, snakes, spiders, and strangers can all pose threats to survival. Human beings, like other animals, have evolved solutions to these adaptive problems. Hunger pangs motivate us to seek food, and taste preferences guide our choices of which foods to consume. Shivering mechanisms help combat the cold, and sweat glands help fight the heat. At a psychological level, our fears of heights, snakes, spiders, and strangers—the most common human fears—help us avoid or safely interact with these environmental threats to our survival.

Our social environment also poses adaptive challenges. We may desire the prestige of a good job, but there are many other people competing for the same positions. We may desire interesting friends and mates, but there are many others competing for them. We may desire greater emotional closeness with others, but may not know how to achieve closeness. The ways in which we cope with our social environment—the challenges we encounter in our struggle for belongingness, love, and esteem—are central to an understanding of personality.

The particular aspect of the environment that is important at any moment in time is frequently determined by personality. A person who is talkative, for example, will notice more opportunities in the social environment to strike up conversations than will someone who is low on talkativeness. A person who is disagreeable will occupy a social environment where people frequently argue with them. A person for whom status is very important will pay attention to the relative hierarchical positions of others—who is up, who is down, who is ascending, who is sliding. In short, from among the potentially infinite dimensions of the environments we inhabit, our "effective environment" represents only the small subset of features that our psychological mechanisms direct us to attend and respond to.

In addition to our physical and social environments, we have an intrapsychic environment. *Intrapsychic* means "within the mind." We all have memories, dreams, desires, fantasies, and a collection of private experiences that we live with each day. This intrapsychic environment, although not as objectively verifiable as our social or physical environment, is nevertheless real to each of us and makes up an important part of our psychological reality. For example, our self-esteem—how good or bad we feel about ourselves at any given moment—may depend on our assessment of the degree to which we are succeeding in attaining our goals. Success at work and success at friendship may provide two different forms of success experience and, hence, form different intrapsychic memories. We are influenced by our memories of these experiences whenever we think about our own self-worth. Our intrapsychic environment, no less than our physical and social environments, provides a critical context for understanding human personality.

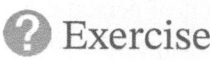 Exercise

Write a one-page essay about a good friend, someone you know well, in which you describe what is characteristic, enduring, and functional about that person. Include in this description those elements of the ways in which they interact with, or adapt to, the physical, social, and intrapsychic environments. Which traits or characteristics about this person do you think are most adaptive?

Three Levels of Personality Analysis

Although the definition of personality used in this book is quite broad and encompassing, personality can be analyzed at three levels. These three levels are well summarized by Kluckhohn and Murray in their 1948 book on culture and personality, in which they state that every human being is, in certain respects,

1. like all others (the human nature level);
2. like some others (the level of individual and group differences); and
3. like no others (the individual uniqueness level).

Another way to think of these distinctions is that the first level refers to "universals" (the ways in which we are all alike), the middle level refers to "particulars" (the ways in which we are like some people but unlike others), and the third level refers to "uniqueness" (the ways in which we are unlike any other person) (see Table 1.1).

Table 1.1 Three Levels of Personality Analysis	
Level of Analysis	**Examples**
Human Nature	Need to belong
	Capacity for love
Individual and Group Differences	Variation in need to belong (individual differences)
	Males are more physically aggressive than females (group difference)
Individual Uniqueness	Seiko's unique way of expressing their love
	Darren's unique way of expressing aggression

Human Nature

The first level of personality analysis describes **human nature** in general—the traits and mechanisms of personality that are typical of our species and are possessed by everyone or nearly everyone. For example, most humans have language skills which allow us to learn and use a language. All cultures on Earth speak a language, so spoken language is part of the universal human nature. At a psychological level, all humans possess fundamental psychological mechanisms—for example, the desire to live with others and belong to social groups—and these mechanisms are part of general human nature. There are many ways in which each person is like most or all other people, and by understanding those ways we may achieve an understanding of the general principles of human nature.

Individual and Group Differences

The second level of personality analysis pertains to individual and group differences. Some people are gregarious and love parties; others prefer quiet evenings reading. Some people take great physical risks by jumping out of airplanes, riding motorcycles, and driving fast; others avoid physical risks entirely. Some people enjoy high self-esteem and live life relatively free from anxiety; others worry constantly and are plagued by self-doubt. These are dimensions of **individual differences**, ways in which each person is like *some* other people (e.g., extraverts, sensation seekers).

Personality can also be observed by studying **differences among groups**. That is, people in one group may have certain personality features in common, and these common features make that group of people different from other groups. Examples of groups studied by personality psychologists include different cultures, different age groups, different political parties, and groups from different socioeconomic backgrounds. Another important set of differences studied by personality psychologists concerns those between males and females. Although many traits and mechanisms of humans are common to both sexes, there are a few that differ. For example, there is accumulated evidence that, across cultures, males are typically more physically aggressive than females. Males are responsible for most of the violence the world over. One goal of personality psychology is to understand why certain aspects of personality differ among groups, such as understanding how and why women are different from men and why people from one culture differ from those from another culture.

Personality psychologists sometimes study group differences, such as differences between men and women.
©Eric Audras/Getty Images

Individual Uniqueness

No two individuals, not even identical twins raised by the same parents in the same home in the same culture, have exactly the same personalities. Every individual has personal qualities not shared by any other person in the world. One of the goals of personality psychology is to support individual uniqueness and to develop ways to capture the richness of unique individual lives.

One debate in the field concerns whether individuals should be studied *nomothetically*—that is, as individual instances of general characteristics that are distributed in the population, or should be studied *idiographically,* as single, unique cases. **Nomothetic** research typically involves statistical comparisons of individuals or groups, requiring samples of subjects on which to conduct research. Nomothetic research is typically applied to identify universal human characteristics and dimensions of individual or group differences. **Idiographic** (translated literally as "the description of one") research typically focuses on a single subject, trying to observe general principles that are manifest in a single life over time. Often, idiographic research results in case studies or the psychological biography of a single person (Runyon, 1983). Sigmund Freud, for example, wrote a psychobiography of Leonardo da Vinci (1916/1947). An example of another version of idiographic research is provided by Rosenzweig (1986, 1997), in which he proposes to analyze individuals in terms of the sequence of events in their lives, trying to understand critical life events within the individuals' own histories.

The important point is that personality psychologists have been concerned with all three levels of analysis: the universal level, the level of individual and group differences, and the level of individual uniqueness. Each contributes valuable knowledge to the total understanding of the nature of personality.

A Fissure in the Field

Different personality psychologists focus on different levels of analysis. And there is a gap within the field that has not yet been successfully bridged. It is the gap between the human nature level of analysis and the analysis of group and individual differences. Many psychologists have theorized about what human nature is like in general. However, when doing research, psychologists most often focus on individual and group differences in personality. As a consequence, there is a fissure between the grand theories of personality and contemporary research in personality.

Grand Theories of Personality

Most of the grand theories of personality address the human nature level of analysis. That is, these theories attempt to provide a universal account of the fundamental psychological processes and characteristics of our species. Sigmund Freud (1915/1957), for example, emphasized universal instincts of sex and aggression; a universal psychic structure of the id, ego, and superego; and universal stages of psychosexual development (oral, anal, phallic, latency, and genital). Statements about the universal core of human nature lie at the centre of grand theories of personality.

Many of the textbooks used in teaching university courses in personality psychology are structured around grand theories. These books have been criticized, however, because many of those theories are primarily of historical interest. Only parts of them have stood the test of time and guide personality research today. Although the grand theories are an important part of the history of personality psychology, there is much interesting personality research going on today that is not directly relevant to the historical grand theories.

Contemporary Research in Personality

Most of the empirical research in contemporary personality addresses the ways in which individuals and groups differ. For example, the extensive research literature on extraversion and introversion, on anxiety and neuroticism, and on self-esteem all focuses on the ways in which people differ from one another. The extensive research on masculinity and femininity deals with the psychological ways in which men and women differ and the ways in which people acquire sex-typed social roles. Cultural research shows that one major dimension of difference concerns whether individuals endorse a collectivistic versus an individualistic attitude. Eastern cultures tend to be more collectivistic and Western cultures more individualistic (see Chapter 17).

One way to examine personality psychology would be to pick a dozen or so current research topics and explore what psychologists have learned about each. For example, a lot of research has been done on self-esteem—what it is, how it develops, how people maintain high self-esteem, and how it functions in relationships. There are many other interesting topics in contemporary personality psychology—shyness, aggression, trust, dominance, hypnotic susceptibility, depression, intelligence, attributional style, goal setting, anxiety, temperament, sex roles, self-monitoring, extraversion, sensation seeking, agreeableness, impulsivity, sociopathy, morality, locus of control, optimism, creativity, leadership, prejudice, and narcissism.

A course that just surveys current topics in personality research seems unsatisfactory. It would be like going to an auction and bidding on everything—soon you would be overwhelmed. Just picking topics to cover would not result in any sense of the connection among the aspects of personality. Indeed, the field of personality has been criticized for containing too many independent areas of investigation, with no sense of the whole person behind the separate topics of investigation. What holds personality together as a coherent field would be missing in such an approach.

You have probably heard the ancient legend of the three blind men who were presented with an elephant. They tried to figure out what the whole elephant was like. The first blind man approached cautiously; walking up to the elephant and putting his hands and then arms around the animal's leg, he proclaimed, "Why, the whole elephant is much like a tree, slender and tall." The second man grasped the trunk of the elephant and exclaimed, "No, the whole elephant is more like a large snake." The third blind man grasped the ear of the elephant and stated, "You are both wrong; the whole elephant more closely resembles a fan." The three blind men proceeded to argue with one another, each insisting that his opinion of the whole elephant was the correct one. In a sense, each blind man had a piece of the truth, yet each failed to recognize that his perceptions of the elephant captured only a narrow part of the truth. Each failed to grasp the whole elephant. Working together, however, the blind men could have assembled a reasonable understanding of the whole elephant.

The topic of personality is like the elephant, and personality psychologists are sort of like the blind men, examining only one perspective at a time. Psychologists often approach the topic of personality from one perspective. For example, some psychologists study the biological aspects of personality. Others study ways that culture promotes personality differences among people and among groups. Still other psychologists study how various aspects of the mind interact and work together to produce personality. And others study relationships among people and believe that social interaction is where personality manifests its most important effects. Each of these perspectives on personality captures elements of truth, yet each alone is inadequate to describe the entire realm of human personality—the whole elephant, so to speak.

Six Domains of Knowledge About Human Nature

The various views of researchers in personality stem *not* from the fact that one perspective is right and the others wrong, but rather from the fact that they are studying different domains of knowledge. A **domain of knowledge** is a specialty area of science and scholarship in which psychologists have focused on learning about some specific and limited aspects of human nature. A domain of knowledge delineates the boundaries of researchers' knowledge, expertise, and interests.

This degree of specialization is reasonable. Indeed, specialization characterizes many scientific fields. The field of medicine, for example, has heart specialists and brain specialists, focusing in great detail on their own domains. It is likewise reasonable for the field of personality psychology to have intrapsychic specialists, cultural specialists, and biological specialists. Each of these domains of personality has accumulated its own base of knowledge. Nonetheless, it is desirable to integrate these diverse domains to see how they all fit together.

The whole personality, like the whole elephant, is the sum of the various parts and the connections among them. For personality, each part is a domain of knowledge representing a collection of knowledge about certain aspects of personality. How are the domains of knowledge defined? For the most part, natural boundaries have developed in the field of personality psychology. That is, researchers have formed natural clusters of topics that fit together and are distinct from other clusters of knowledge. Within these identifiable domains, researchers have developed common *methods for asking questions*; have accumulated a foundation of *known facts*; and have developed *theoretical explanations* that account for what is known about personality from the perspective of each domain.

The field of personality can be neatly cleaved into six distinct domains of knowledge about human nature: personality is influenced by traits the person is born with and develops over time (*dispositional domain*); by biological events (*biological domain*); by processes within the person's own mind (*intrapsychic domain*); by personal and private thoughts, feelings, desires, beliefs, and other subjective experiences (*cognitive-experiential domain*); by social, cultural, and gendered positions in the world (*social and cultural domain*); and by the adjustments that the person must make to the inevitable challenges of life (*adjustment domain*).

Personality psychologists working within each domain often use different theoretical perspectives and focus on different facts. As a consequence, psychologists from different domains can sometimes appear to contradict one another. The psychoanalytic perspective of Sigmund Freud, for example, views the personality as consisting of irrational sexual and aggressive instincts, which ultimately motivate all human activity. The cognitive perspective on personality, in contrast, views humans as rational "scientists," calmly trying to anticipate, predict, and control the events that occur in their worlds.

On the surface, these perspectives appear incompatible. How can humans be both irrational and rational? How can humans be driven by desire yet be cool and detached in their quest for accurate prediction? On deeper examination, the contradictions may be more apparent than real. It is entirely possible, for example, that humans have both powerful sexual and aggressive motivations and cognitive mechanisms designed to perceive and predict events with accuracy. It is entirely possible that sometimes basic emotions and motivations are activated and at other times the cool cognitive mechanisms are activated. And it is possible that the two sets of mechanisms sometimes become linked with one another, such as when the rational mechanisms are used in the service of fulfilling fundamental desires. In short, although each theoretical perspective may be focused on a critically important part of human psychological functioning, each perspective by itself does not capture the *whole* person.

This book is organized around the six domains of personality functioning—dispositional, biological, intrapsychic, cognitive-experiential, social and cultural, and adjustment. Within each of these domains of personality, we focus on two key elements: (1) the *theories* that have been proposed within each domain, including the basic assumptions about human nature, and (2) the *empirical research* that has been accumulating within each of these domains. In an attempt to bridge the gap between theory and research in personality, we focus primarily on the theories that have received the greatest research attention and the topics within each domain for which there is the greatest cumulative knowledge base.

Dispositional Domain

The **dispositional domain** deals centrally with the ways in which individuals differ from one another. As such, the dispositional domain cuts across all the other domains. The reason is that individuals can differ in their habitual emotions, their habitual concepts of self, their physiological propensities, and even their intrapsychic mechanisms. However, what distinguishes the dispositional domain is an interest in the number and nature of fundamental dispositions. The central goal of personality psychologists working in the dispositional domain is to identify and measure the most important ways in which individuals differ from one another. They are also interested in the origins of the important individual differences and in how they develop and are maintained.

Biological Domain

The core assumption within the **biological domain** is that humans are, first and foremost, collections of biological systems, and these systems provide the building blocks for behaviour, thought, and emotion. As personality psychologists use the term, *biological approaches* typically refers to three areas of research within this general domain: genetics, psychophysiology, and evolution.

The first area of research addresses the genetic underpinnings of personality. Because of advances in behavioural genetic research, a fair amount is known about the genetics of personality. Some questions this research addresses include the following: Are identical twins more alike than fraternal twins in their personalities? What happens to identical twins when they are reared apart versus when they are reared together? Behavioural genetic research permits us to ask and provisionally answer these questions.

Identical twins Alvin (left) and Calvin (right) Harrison, age 26, celebrate their first and second place finishes in the 400-metre race in Brisbane, Australia, August 8, 2000. Psychologists study twins to determine whether some aspects of personality are influenced by genetics.
©Greg Wood/AFP/Getty Images

The second biological approach is best described as the psychophysiology of personality. Within this domain, researchers summarize what is known about the basis of personality in terms of nervous system functioning. Examples of such topics include cortical arousal and neurotransmitters, cardiac reactivity, strength of the nervous system, pain tolerance, circadian rhythms (whether you are a morning or a night person), and the links between hormones, such as testosterone, and personality.

The third component of the biological approach concerns how evolution may have shaped human psychological functioning. This approach assumes that the psychological mechanisms that constitute human personality have evolved over thousands of years because they were effective in solving adaptive problems linked to survival and reproduction. An evolutionary perspective sheds light on the functional aspects of personality.

Intrapsychic Domain

The **intrapsychic domain** deals with mental mechanisms of personality, many of which operate outside of conscious awareness. The predominant theory in this domain is Freud's theory of psychoanalysis. This theory begins with fundamental assumptions about the instinctual system—the sexual and aggressive forces that are presumed to drive and energize much of human activity. Considerable research reveals that sexual and aggressive motives are indeed powerful, and their manifestations in actual behaviour can be studied empirically. The intrapsychic domain also includes defence mechanisms, such as repression, denial, and projection—some of which have been examined in laboratory studies. Although the intrapsychic domain is most closely linked with the psychoanalytic theory of Sigmund Freud, there are modern versions as well. For example, much of the research on the power motives, achievement motives, and intimacy motives is based on a key intrapsychic assumption—that these forces often operate outside the realm of consciousness.

Cognitive-Experiential Domain

The **cognitive-experiential domain** focuses on cognition and subjective experience, such as conscious thoughts, feelings, beliefs, and desires about oneself and others. The psychological mechanisms involved in subjective experience differ, however, in form and content from one another. One important element of our experience entails the self and self-concept. Descriptive aspects of the self organize how we view ourselves: knowledge of ourselves, images of past selves, and images of possible future selves. Do we see ourselves as good or as evil? Are our past successes or past failures prominent in our self-views? Do we envision ourselves in the future as married with children or as successful in a career? How we evaluate ourselves—our self-esteem—is another facet of the cognitive-experiential domain.

A somewhat different aspect of this domain pertains to the goals we strive for. Some personality psychologists, for example, view human nature as inherently goal-directed, stressing the organizing influence of fundamental needs or strivings, such as the need for affiliation and the striving to influence others. Recent research within this tradition includes approaching personality through the personal projects; that is, the tasks that individuals are trying to accomplish in their daily lives. These can range from the commonplace, such as getting a date for Saturday night, to the grandiose, such as changing thought in Western civilization.

Another important aspect of subjective experience entails our emotions. Are we habitually happy or sad? What makes us angry or fearful? Do we keep our emotions bottled up inside, or do we express them at the drop of a hat? Joy, sadness, feelings of triumph, and feelings of despair all are essential elements in our subjective experience and are subsumed by the cognitive-experiential domain.

Social and Cultural Domain

One of the special features of this book is an emphasis on the **social and cultural domain** of personality. The assumption is that personality is not something that merely resides within the heads, nervous systems, and genes of individuals. Rather, personality affects, and is affected by, the social and cultural context.

At a cultural level, it is clear that groups differ tremendously from one another. Cultures such as the Yanomamö Indians of Venezuela are highly aggressive; indeed, a Yanomamö man does not achieve full status as a man until he has killed another man. In contrast, cultures such as the !Kung San of Botswana are relatively peaceful and agreeable. Overt displays of aggression are discouraged and bring social shame on the perpetrator. Personality differences among these groups are most likely due to cultural influences. In other words, different cultures may bring out different facets of our personalities in manifest behaviour. Everyone may have the capacity to be peaceful as well as the capacity for violence, as documented by the dramatic changes in violence and peacefulness over time (Pinker, 2012). Which one of these capacities we display may depend on what is acceptable in and encouraged by the culture.

At the level of individual differences within cultures, personality plays itself out in the social sphere. Whether we are dominant or submissive affects such diverse parts of our lives as the conflicts we get into with our partners and the tactics we use to manipulate others. Whether we tend to be anxious and depressed or buoyant and optimistic affects the likelihood of social outcomes, such as marital stability and divorce. Whether we are introverted or extraverted affects how many friends we will have and our popularity within the group. Many important individual differences are played out in the interpersonal sphere.

One important social sphere concerns relationships between men and women. At the level of differences between the sexes, personality may operate differently for men than for women. Gender is an essential part of our identities.

By studying people in different cultures, psychologists are learning how society shapes personality by encouraging or discouraging specific behaviours.
©blickwinkel/Alamy Stock Photo

Adjustment Domain

The **adjustment domain** refers to the fact that personality plays a key role in how we cope, adapt, and adjust to the ebb and flow of events in our day-to-day lives. Evidence, for example, shows that personality is linked with important health outcomes, such as heart disease. Personality is also linked with health-related behaviours, such as smoking, drinking, and risk taking. Some research has even demonstrated that personality is linked with how long we live.

In addition to health, many important problems in coping and adjustment can be traced to personality. In this domain, certain personality features are related to poor adjustment and have been designated as personality disorders. Chapter 19 is devoted to the personality disorders, such as narcissistic personality disorder, antisocial personality disorder, and avoidant personality disorder. An understanding of "normal" personality functioning can be deepened by examining the disorders of personality, much as in the field of medicine, in which an understanding of normal physiological functioning is often illuminated by the study of disease.

Personality relates to health by influencing health-related behaviours, such as smoking.
©Patrick Sheandell O'Carroll/Getty Images

 Exercise

Think of a behaviour pattern or characteristic that you find interesting in yourself or someone you know. Such characteristics as procrastination, narcissism, and perfectionism are good examples, but any personality characteristic that catches your interest is suitable. Then write six sentences about this characteristic, one to represent each of the six domains: dispositional, biological, intrapsychic, cognitive-experiential, social and cultural, and adjustment. Each sentence should make a statement or ask a question about the characteristic from the perspective of a particular domain. Which domain offers you the most insight about the characteristic?

The Role of Personality Theory

One of the central aims of this book is to highlight the interplay between personality theory and research. In each domain of knowledge, there are some prevailing theories, so we close this chapter with a discussion of theories. Theories are essential in all scientific endeavours, and they serve several useful purposes. A **good theory** is one that fulfills three purposes in science:

- provides a guide for researchers,
- organizes known findings, and
- makes predictions.

One of the most important purposes of theories is that they serve as a *guide for researchers,* directing them to important questions within an area of research.

A second useful function of theories is to *organize known findings.* In physics, for example, there is a bewildering array of events—apples fall from trees, planets exert attraction on each other, black holes pull in light. The theory of gravity neatly and powerfully accounts for all of these observations. By accounting for known findings, theories bring both coherence and understanding to the known world. The same applies to personality theories. Theories are viewed as powerful if they succeed in accounting for known findings, in addition to guiding psychologists to important domains of inquiry.

A third purpose of theories is to *make predictions* about behaviour and psychological phenomena that no one has yet documented or observed. Einstein's theory of relativity, for example, predicted that light will bend around large stars long before we had the technology to test this prediction. When researchers finally confirmed that light does, indeed, bend when going around stars such as our sun, that finding bore out the power of Einstein's theory.

Finally, we need to distinguish between scientific **theories and beliefs**. For example, astrology is a collection of beliefs about the relationship between personality and the position of the stars at birth. Some people hold that such relationships are true, even in the absence of supporting evidence. To date, psychologists have not found reliable factual support, using standard research methods and systematic observations, for the idea that the positions of the stars at a person's birth influence personality. As such, astrology remains a *belief,* not a scientific theory. Beliefs are often personally useful and crucially important to some people, but they are based on faith, not on reliable facts and systematic observations. Theories, on the other hand, are tested by systematic observations that can be repeated by others and that yield similar conclusions.

In sum, three key criteria of personality theories highlight the interplay of theory and research. They guide researchers to important domains of inquiry, account for known findings, and make predictions about new phenomena.

Standards for Evaluating Personality Theories

As we explore each of the six domains, it will be useful to bear in mind five **scientific standards for evaluating personality theories**:

- comprehensiveness
- heuristic value
- testability
- parsimony
- compatibility and integration across domains and levels

The first standard is **comprehensiveness**—does the theory do a good job of explaining all of the facts and observations within its domain? Theories that explain more empirical findings are generally superior to those that explain fewer findings.

A second evaluative standard is **heuristic value**—does the theory provide a guide to important new discoveries about personality that were not known before? Theories that steer scientists to making these discoveries are generally superior to theories that fail to provide this guidance. Plate tectonic theory in geology, for example, guided researchers to discover regions of volcanic activity that were unknown prior to the theory. Similarly, a good personality theory will guide personality researchers to make discoveries that were previously unknown.

A third important standard for evaluating theories is **testability**—does the theory provide precise predictions that can be tested empirically? Some theories—for example, certain aspects of Freud's theory of intrapsychic conflict—have been criticized on the grounds that they are difficult or impossible to test; other aspects of Freud's theory are testable (see Chapters 9 and 10). As a general rule, the testability of a theory rests with the precision of its predictions. Precise theoretical predictions aid progress in the science because they allow inadequate theories to be discarded (those whose predictions are falsified) and good theories to be retained (those whose predictions are empirically confirmed). If a theory does not lend itself to being tested empirically, it is generally judged to be a poor theory.

A fourth standard for evaluating personality theories is **parsimony**—does the theory contain few premises and assumptions (parsimony) or many premises and assumptions (lack of parsimony)? As a general rule, theories that require many premises and assumptions to explain a given set of findings are judged to be poorer than theories that can explain the same findings with fewer premises and assumptions. Although parsimony is important, bear in mind that this does not mean that simple theories are always better than complex theories. Indeed, simple theories often crash and burn because they fail to meet one or more of the other five standards described here; for example, they may fail to be comprehensive because they explain so little. It is our view that human personality is genuinely complex, and so a complex theory—one containing many premises—may ultimately be necessary.

A fifth standard is **compatibility and integration across domains and levels**. A theory of cosmology in astronomy that violated known laws of physics, for example, would be incompatible across levels and hence judged to be fundamentally flawed. A theory of biology that violated known principles of chemistry similarly would be judged to be fatally flawed. In the same way, a personality theory in one domain that violated well-established principles in another domain would be judged highly problematic. For example, a theory of the development of personality dispositions that was inconsistent with well-established knowledge in physiology and genetics would be judged to be problematic. Similarly, a theory of evolutionary influences on personality that contradicted what is known about cultural influences, or vice versa, would be problematic. Although the criterion of *compatibility and integration across domains and levels* is a well-established principle in most sciences (Buss, 2012; Tooby & Cosmides, 1992), it has rarely been used to evaluate the adequacy of personality theories. We believe that the "domains" approach taken in this book highlights the importance of the evaluative criterion of compatibility across levels of personality analysis.

In sum, as you progress through the six domains of personality functioning, keep in mind the five standards by which theories within each domain can be evaluated—comprehensiveness, heuristic value, testability, parsimony, and cross-domain compatibility (see Table 1.2).

Table 1.2 Five Standards for Evaluating Personality Theories

Standard	Definition
Comprehensiveness	Explains most or all known facts.
Heuristic value	Guides researchers to important new discoveries.
Testability	Makes precise predictions that can be empirically tested.
Parsimony	Contains few premises or assumptions.
Compatibility and integration	Consistent with what is known in other domains; can be coordinated with other branches of scientific knowledge.

Is There a Grand Ultimate and True Theory of Personality?

The field of biology contains a grand unifying theory—the theory of evolution by natural selection, originally proposed by Darwin (1859) and further refined in its neo-Darwinian form as inclusive fitness theory (Hamilton, 1964). This theory is comprehensive, guides biologists to new discoveries, has led to thousands of empirical tests, is highly parsimonious, and is compatible with known laws in adjacent scientific disciplines. Evolutionary theory provides the grand unifying framework within which most biologists conduct their work. Ideally, the field of personality psychology would also contain such a grand unifying theory. Alas, at the current time, it does not.

Perhaps Sigmund Freud, the inventor of psychoanalytic theory, provided the most ambitious attempt at a grand unifying theory of personality (see Chapter 9). And many grand theories have followed Freud's. But over the past several decades, most personality researchers have come to the realization that the field currently lacks a grand unifying theory. Instead, most have focused on more specific domains of functioning. It is precisely for this reason that our book is organized around the six domains—these represent the domains in which progress, scientific findings, and new discoveries are being made.

In our view, an ultimate grand theory of personality psychology will have to unify all six domains. It will have to explain personality characteristics and how they develop over time (dispositional domain). It will have to explain evolutionary, genetic, and physiological underpinnings of personality (biological domain). It will have to explain deeply rooted motives and dynamic intrapsychic processes (intrapsychic domain). It will have to explain how people experience the world and process information about it (cognitive-experiential domain). It will have to explain how personality affects, and is affected by, the social and cultural context in which people conduct their lives (social and cultural domain). And it will have to explain how people cope and function—as well as how adjustment fails—as they encounter the numerous adaptive problems they face over the inevitably bumpy course of their lives (the adjustment domain).

Although the field of personality psychology currently lacks a grand theory, we believe that work in these six domains will ultimately provide the foundations on which such a unified personality theory will be built.

Concept Check

What does it mean to say that personality consists of both traits and mechanisms? What does it mean to say that personality traits are organized and relatively enduring?

What are the three levels of analysis in personality research? Provide an example of each.

Name and describe the five standards for evaluating personality theories. What is a "good" theory?

Key Terms

trait-descriptive adjectives

personality

psychological traits

average tendencies

psychological mechanisms

within the individual

organized

enduring

influential forces

person–environment
   interaction

adaptations

environment

human nature

individual differences

differences among groups

nomothetic

idiographic

domain of knowledge

dispositional domain

biological domain

intrapsychic domain

cognitive-experiential domain

social and cultural domain

adjustment domain

good theory

theories and beliefs

scientific standards for
   evaluating personality
   theories

comprehensiveness

heuristic value

testability

parsimony

compatibility and integration
   across domains and levels

CHAPTER 2

Personality Assessment, Measurement, and Research Design

Introduction

Imagine that a federal election is looming. You are faced with a choice among numerous candidates and parties to vote for. The personalities of the candidates may prove to be critical to your decision. How will they hold up under stress? What are their attitudes toward climate change or immigration? Will they stand tough in negotiating with leaders from other countries? This chapter is concerned with the means by which we gain information about other people's personalities—the sources from which we gather personality data and the research designs we use in the scientific study of personality.

When deliberating among political parties, you might want to know what the party leaders say about their values and attitudes—through a *self-report*. You might want to know what others say about their strengths in dealing with foreign leaders—through an *observer report*. You also might want to place the party leaders in a

Much of the discussion surrounding political candidates involves their personalities.

(left): ©Victor Biro/Alamy Stock Photo; (right): ©The Canadian Press/Nathan Denette

more controlled situation, such as a debate, and see how each performs—to acquire *test data*. Furthermore, you might want to know about certain events in their lives, such as whether they have served in the Armed Forces, been arrested, or been caught in an embarrassing sexual scandal—*life history data*.

Each of these sources of data reveals something about the personalities of the party leaders, yet each alone is incomplete and may be biased. Party leaders may self-report a tough stance on climate change but then fail to follow through on it. Observers may report that one party leader is honest, yet they may be unaware of lies the party leader has told. A debate may show one party leader in a positive light, but perhaps another candidate happened to have a cold that day. And the public record of serving in the Canadian Armed Forces may not reveal the family connections that enabled the party leader to avoid combat. Each source of data provides important information. But each source, by itself, is of limited value. It offers an incomplete picture.

This chapter covers three topics related to personality assessment and research. The first concerns where we get our information—the sources of personality data and the actual measures that personality psychologists use. The second topic concerns how we evaluate the quality of those measures. The third topic pertains to how we use these measures in actual research designs to study personality.

Sources of Personality Data

Perhaps the most obvious source of information about a person is **self-report data (S-data)**—the information a person reveals about themselves. Clearly, individuals may not always provide accurate information for a variety of reasons, such as the desire to present themselves in a positive light. Nevertheless, the journals that publish the latest research in personality reveal that self-report is the most common method for measuring personality (Connelly & Ones, 2010).

Self-Report Data (S-Data)

Self-report data can be obtained through a variety of means, including interviews that pose questions to a person, periodic reports by a person to record the events as they happen, and questionnaires or surveys.

The questionnaire method, in which individuals respond to a series of items that request information about them, is by far the most commonly used self-report assessment procedure.

There are good reasons for using self-report. The most obvious reason is that individuals have access to a wealth of information about themselves that is inaccessible to anyone else, such as their habitual level of anxiety (e.g., Vazire, 2010). Individuals can report about their feelings, emotions, desires, beliefs, and private experiences. They can report about their self-esteem, as well as their perceptions of the esteem in which others hold them. They can report about their innermost fears and fantasies. And they can report about immediate and long-term goals. Because of this potential wealth of information, self-report is an indispensable source of personality data.

Self-report can take a variety of forms, ranging from open-ended "fill in the blank" questions to forced-choice true-or-false questions. Sometimes these are referred to as **unstructured** (open-ended, such as "Tell me about the parties you like the most") and **structured** ("I like loud and crowded parties: answer true or false") personality tests. A prime example of the open-ended form of self-report is called the Twenty Statements Test. In this test, a participant receives a sheet of paper that is essentially blank, except for the words "I am" repeated 20 times. There is a space after each of these partial statements, and participants are asked to complete them. For example, a person might say, in this order: *I am a woman; I am 19 years old; I am shy; I am intelligent; I am someone who likes quiet nights at home; I am introverted;* and so on. Personality instruments that use open-ended formats require coding schemes for classifying the responses they obtain. In other words, psychologists must devise a way to score or interpret the participant's open-ended responses. To get an idea of how outgoing the individual in our example is, the psychologist might count how many statements refer to social characteristics. We explore the Twenty Statements Test further in A Closer Look: Who Am I?.

 **A Closer Look**

Who Am I?

The Twenty Statements Test (TST) was published by a pair of sociologists. Manford Kuhn and Thomas McPartland were interested in attitudes people had toward themselves. In 1954, they published the "Who am I?" test. This test asked the participant to simply answer this question by completing the phrase "I am _____" 20 times. Kuhn and McPartland developed a way of scoring the test by analyzing the content of the person's responses. The order of each response was thought to be significant (e.g., something mentioned earlier might be more important to the self-definition than something mentioned later).

In the first decade of use by psychologists, the TST was applied mainly to clinical and personality research questions. For example, one study used the TST to see if the self-concepts of people in "unadjusted" marriages differed from the self-concepts of people in "well-adjusted" marriages (Buerkle, 1960). Results showed that those in adjusted marriages tended to mention their partner, their marriage, and their family more often in their self-definitions than those in unadjusted marriages. This finding implies that part of a successful marriage is incorporating the marriage role into one's definition of oneself.

In the 1970s, researchers turned a more critical eye on the TST. It is an open-ended questionnaire, so people with low verbal ability do not complete it as quickly or as thoroughly as those with high verbal ability, leading the test scores to be biased by intelligence differences in participants (Nudelman, 1973). However, if people are given enough time to complete the 20 questions—at least 15 minutes—then it appears that the intelligence bias is eliminated. The TST survived and emerged as a measure that the field deemed useful for assessing how people defined themselves.

In the 1980s, the TST was used in the study of timely personality topics, such as the influence of gender and other social roles in people's self-definitions. For example, one study compared married and single women (Gigy, 1980). Married women tended to respond to the "Who am I?" question by mentioning relationships *(I am a mother, I am a wife)*, acquired roles in family life *(I am the one who takes the children to school)*, and household activities *(I am the one who buys groceries)*. Clearly, marriage can mean a large change in self-concept, and studies such as this one document the link between social roles and how individuals see themselves.

There has been a trend toward using culture in self-definitions (Bochner, 1994). For instance, research by Ip and Bond (1995) found that responses to the TST by Asian participants included more references to themselves as members of social groups (e.g., "I am a member of the swim team") or occupants of social roles (e.g., "I am Sam's friend") than those by American participants. This tendency for individuals from Eastern cultures to include more references to other people in their self-concept than individuals from Western cultures has been confirmed in other research (e.g., Markus & Kitayama, 1991). Research using the TST has further demonstrated interesting aspects of self-concept when individuals with multiple cultural identities are primed to think about one identity or the other; or to respond in a particular language. One study found that Chinese-born Canadian university students described more interdependent aspects of themselves on the TST (i.e., those that were in line with a more collectivistic cultural orientation) when they were asked to write their responses in Chinese rather than in English (Ross, Xun, & Wilson, 2002). Results such as these show how culture and language may influence our self-concept. The Twenty Statements Test is a useful way to measure how people define themselves according to a variety of traits and attributes. It has proven especially effective at identifying the most important components of a person's identity—the ingredients that provide a person with a sense of self-esteem, meaning in life, and sense of belonging in the world of other people (Vignoles et al., 2006).

Structured personality questionnaires, in which the response options are provided, are more common than open-ended questionnaires. The simplest form of the structured self-report questionnaire involves a series of trait-descriptive adjectives, such as *active, ambitious, anxious, arrogant, artistic, generous, greedy, gregarious, open-minded, manipulative, methodical,* and *zany.* Individuals are asked to indicate whether each adjective describes them. The simplest format for presenting these terms is a checklist, such as the Adjective Check List (ACL) (Gough, 1980). In completing the ACL, individuals merely place a check beside adjectives that they feel accurately describe them and leave blank items that don't describe them. A more complex method involves requesting participants to indicate in numerical form the degree to which each trait term characterizes them, say on a 7-point rating scale of 1 (least characteristic) to 7 (most characteristic). This is called a **Likert-type scale** (after the person who invented it, Rensis Likert; Likert, 1932), and it is simply a way for someone to express with numbers the degree to which a particular trait describes them. The following is an example of a typical Likert-type scale:

ENERGETIC

1	2	3	4	5	6	7
Least characteristic						Most characteristic

A *personality scale* typically involves summing the scores on a series of individual rating scales like the one above. A personality scale for activity level, for example, might consist of adding up scores from rating scales on *energetic, active,* and *vigorous.*

? Exercise

DIRECTIONS: This list contains a series of adjectives. Please read them quickly and put an X in the box beside each one you consider to be self-descriptive. Try to be honest and accurate.

_____ absent-minded	_____ clever	_____ irrational
_____ active	_____ cold	_____ lively
_____ adaptable	_____ dependent	_____ shy
_____ adventurous	_____ determined	_____ sociable
_____ affectionate	_____ disorderly	_____ straightforward
_____ caring	_____ impersonal	_____ touchy
_____ cheerful	_____ impulsive	_____ trusting

More common than adjective checklists or scales, however, are self-report questionnaires that include statements. Examples of widely used self-report inventories are the NEO-FFI Personality Inventory (Costa & Mc-Crae, 2005) and the California Psychological Inventory (CPI) (Gough, 1957/1987). Sample items from the CPI are: *I enjoy social gatherings just to be with people; I looked up to my father as an ideal man; A person needs to "show off" a little now and then; I have a very strong desire to be a success in the world; I am very slow in making up my mind.* Participants read each statement and then indicate on an answer sheet whether they agree with the statement and feel that it is true of them or disagree with the statement and feel that it is false about them. Sample items from the NEO-FFI Personality Inventory are: *I like most people I meet; I laugh easily; I often get disgusted with people I have to deal with.* Participants indicate the degree to which they agree the item describes them, using a 1 to 5 Likert scale, with 1 anchored with the phrase *strongly disagree* and 5 anchored with *strongly agree.*

? Exercise

Choose a personality characteristic you would like to measure. Start by writing down a clear definition of that characteristic. For example, you might choose a characteristics such as friendly, conscientious, anxious, or narcissistic. Then write a short questionnaire, about five items long, to measure this characteristic. Your items can be statements or adjectives, and they can be open-ended, true–false, or on a Likert-response scale. Then give your questionnaire to other people. How easy was it to write items? Do you think your measure accurately assesses the trait?

Self-report measures, like all methods, have limitations and weaknesses. For the self-report method to be effective, respondents must be both willing and able to answer the questions put to them. Yet people are not always honest, especially when asked about unconventional experiences such as unusual desires, socially unacceptable behaviours, or less popular traits. Some people may also lack accurate self-knowledge. Because of these limitations, personality psychologists often use sources of data that do not rely on the honesty or insight of the participant. One such source is an observer or observers.

Application

Experience sampling—a wrinkle in self-report. One source of data in personality research is called experience sampling (e.g., Hormuth, 1986; Larsen, 1989; Mehl & Pennebaker, 2003). In this method, people answer some questions, perhaps about their moods or physical symptoms, every day for several weeks or longer. People are usually contacted electronically (paged) one or more times a day at random intervals to complete the measures. In one study, 74 university students reported on their moods every day for 84 consecutive days (Larsen & Kasimatis, 1990). The investigators were interested in discovering the links between the day of the week and mood. They found a strong weekly cycle in the moods of the university students, with positive moods peaking on Friday and Saturday and negative moods peaking on Tuesday and Wednesday (Monday was not the worst day of the week). The introverts turned out to have a much more regular weekly mood cycle than extraverts. That is, the moods of the introverts were more predictable from this seven-day rhythm than the moods of the extraverts. This difference was probably due to the fact that extraverts are less likely to wait for the weekend to do things that put them in a good mood—partying, socializing, or going out for a special meal with friends. Extraverts typically avoid routine in their daily lives, and introverts typically lead more predictable lives.

Although experience sampling uses self-report as the data source, it differs from more traditional self-report methods in being able to detect patterns of behaviour over time. Thus, experience sampling provides information not readily available using questionnaires taken at just one point in time. It's an excellent method, for example, for obtaining information about how a person's self-esteem may go up and down over time or how a person reacts to the stress of life day after day.

Observer-Report Data (O-Data)

In everyday life, we form impressions and make evaluations of others with whom we come into contact. For each individual, there are typically dozens of observers who form impressions. Our friends, families, teachers, and casual acquaintances are all potential sources of information about our personalities. **Observer-report data (O-data)** capitalize on these sources for gathering information about a person's personality.

Observer reports offer both advantages and disadvantages as sources of personality data. One advantage is that observers may have access to information not attainable through other sources. For example, observers can report about the impressions a person makes on others, one's reputation more generally, whether interactions with others are smooth or full of strife, and a person's relative status within a group hierarchy. Indeed, one study found that altruistic traits can be identified by observers with some accuracy by a mere 20-second exposure (Fetchenhauer et al., 2010). As noted by Santayana (1905/1980), "[The observer] sometimes reaches truths about people's character and destiny which they themselves are far from divining" (p. 154).

A second advantage of observer-reports is that multiple observers can be used to assess each individual, whereas in self-reports only one person provides information (Connelly & Ones, 2010; Paunonen & O'Neill, 2010). The use of multiple observers allows investigators to evaluate the degree of agreement among observers—also known as **inter-rater reliability**. Furthermore, statistical procedures, such as averaging the assessments of multiple observers, have the advantage of reducing the idiosyncratic features and biases of single observers. Typically, a more valid and reliable assessment of personality can be achieved when multiple observers are used.

Selection of Observers

A key decision point that researchers face when using observers is how to select them. Personality researchers have developed two strategies. One commonly employed strategy is to use professional personality assessors who do not know the participant in advance.

A second strategy for obtaining observational data is to use individuals who actually know the target participants. For example, close friends, partners/spouses, mothers, and roommates have all been used to provide personality data on participants (e.g., Buss, 1984; Connelly & Ones, 2010; Vazire & Mehl, 2008). The use of observers who have existing relationships with the participant has advantages and disadvantages when compared with professional assessors. One advantage is that such observers are in a better position to observe the target's natural behaviour. This may include witnessing more private actions of a person that professional observers typically do not. A partner or close friend has access to privileged information often inaccessible through other sources.

Observer reports can be used as one source of personality information.
©Bananastock/AGE Fotostock

Another advantage of using intimate observers is that **multiple social personalities** can be assessed (Craik, 1986, 2008). Each one of us displays different sides of ourselves to different people—we may be kind to our friends, ruthless to our enemies, loving toward a spouse, and conflicted toward our parents. Our manifest personalities, in other words, vary from one social setting to another, depending on the nature of relationships we have with other individuals (Lukaszewski & Roney, 2010). The use of multiple observers provides a method for assessing the many aspects of an individual's personality.

In the Department of Management at the University of Toronto, Scarborough, Brian Connelly has tried to understand and predict the role of personality in diverse organizational and occupational settings. And one of his primary methods has employed observer reports, specifically those obtained from acquaintances, friends, and family. His work has shown time and again that observer ratings of personality, including key traits such as extraversion, emotional stability, and agreeableness, appear to better predict performance behaviours at work when compared to self-report data on the same traits. Interestingly, personality ratings by strangers and acquaintances are often better predictors of behaviour than those by more intimate raters, but it depends on the trait in question (Connelly & Hülsheger, 2012; Connelly & Ones, 2010).

Although there are advantages in using intimate observers in personality assessment, there are drawbacks (Vazire, 2010). Because intimate observers have relationships with the target person, they may be biased in certain ways. A participant's mother, for example, may overlook the negative and emphasize the positive features of her child.

Naturalistic versus Artificial Observation

In addition to deciding what type of observers to use, personality researchers must determine whether the observation occurs in a natural or artificial setting. In **naturalistic observation**, observers witness and record events that occur in the normal course of the lives of their participants. For example, a child might be followed throughout an entire day, or an observer may sit in a participant's home. In contrast, observation can take place in contrived or artificial settings. Experimenters can instruct participants to perform a task, such as participation in a group discussion, and then observe how individuals behave in these constructed settings. For example, psychologists John Gottman and Robert Levenson have had married couples come in to their laboratory and discuss a topic on which they disagree. The psychologists then observe the couple having a small argument. The way in which a couple conducts an argument can predict the likelihood that the couple will remain together or get divorced (Gottman, 1994). Even the facial expressions displayed during these laboratory conflicts predict subsequent marital outcomes (Coan & Gottman, 2007; Gottman, Levenson, & Woodin, 2001).

Naturalistic observation offers researchers the ability to secure information in the realistic context of a person's everyday life, but at the cost of not being able to control the events and behavioural samples witnessed. Observation in experimenter-generated situations has the advantage of controlling conditions and eliciting the relevant behaviour. But this advantage comes at a cost—sacrificing the realism of everyday life.

In summary, there are many dimensions along which O-data differ, and personality researchers must take these into account, such as decisions about whether to use (1) professional assessors or intimate observers and (2) a naturalistic or an artificial setting. The strengths and weaknesses of the options must be evaluated with the goals of the investigation in mind. No single method is ideally suited for all assessment purposes.

Test Data (T-Data)

Beyond self-report and observer-report data sources, a third common source of personality-relevant information comes from standardized tests—**test data (T-data)**. Participants are placed in a standardized testing situation to see if different people react differently to an identical situation. The situation is designed to elicit behaviours that serve as indicators of personality variables (Block, 1977). A classic example is Henry Murray's (1948) bridge-building test. In this test, the person being assessed is given two assistants and a collection of wood, rope, and tools, and they then have the task of building a bridge over a small creek. The person being assessed cannot do the work alone, but must instruct the two assistants on how to build the bridge. Unbeknownst to the person being assessed, the two assistants are role-playing: one is acting clueless and has trouble understanding instructions; the other is a "know-it-all" who has their own ideas about how the bridge should be built and often contradicts the person being assessed. These two "helpers" are actually there to frustrate the person being assessed. Although the person being assessed thinks they are being observed on leadership skills, the person is actually being evaluated on tolerance of frustration and performance under adversity.

One fascinating example of the use of T-data is Edwin Megargee's (1969) study of manifestations of *dominance*. Megargee wanted to devise a laboratory test situation to examine the effect of dominance on leadership. He first administered the California Psychological Inventory Dominance scale to a large group of men and women. He then selected only men and women who scored either very high or very low on dominance. Megargee then took pairs of individuals into the laboratory, in each case pairing a high-dominant participant with a low-dominant participant. He created four conditions: (1) a high-dominant man with a low-dominant man; (2) a high-dominant woman with a low-dominant woman; (3) a high-dominant man with a low-dominant woman; and (4) a high-dominant woman with a low-dominant man.

Megargee then presented each pair with a large box containing many red, yellow, and green nuts, bolts, and levers. Participants were told that the purpose of the study was to explore the relationship between personality and leadership under stress. Each pair had to work as a team of troubleshooters to repair the box as fast as possible—by removing nuts and bolts with certain colours and replacing them with other colours. They were told that one person from the team had to be the *leader,* a position which entailed giving instructions. The second person was to be the *follower,* who had to go inside the box and carry out the menial tasks requested by the leader. The experimenter then told the participants that it was up to them to decide who would be the leader and who would be the follower.

The key variable of interest for Megargee was who would become the leader and who would become the follower. He simply recorded the percentage of high-dominant participants within each condition who became leaders. He found that 75 percent of the high-dominant men and 70 percent of the high-dominant women took the leadership role in the same-sex pairs. When high-dominant men were paired with low-dominant women, however, 90 percent of the men became leaders. But the most startling result occurred when the woman was high in dominance and the man was low in dominance. In this condition, only 20 percent of the high-dominant women assumed the leadership role.

Who takes the leadership role when people work together is often a function of personality.
©Sam Edwards/age Fotostock

Megargee audio-recorded the conversations while they were deciding who would be the leader. When he analyzed these tapes, he made a startling finding: the high-dominant women were *appointing* their low-dominant partners to the leadership position. In fact, the high-dominant women actually made the final decision about the roles 91 percent of the time. This finding suggests that women were *expressing* their dominance in a different manner than the men in the mixed-sex condition.

Megargee's study highlights several key points about laboratory studies. First, it shows that it is possible to set up conditions to reveal key indicators of personality. Second, it suggests that laboratory experimenters should be sensitive to manifestations of personality that occur in incidental parts of the experiment, such as the discussions among the participants. And, third, there are often interesting links between S-data obtained through questionnaires and T-data obtained through controlled testing conditions. Such links helped to establish the validity of both the questionnaire and the laboratory test of dominance.

Like all data sources, T-data have limitations. First, some participants might try to guess what trait is being measured and then alter their responses to create a specific impression of themselves. A second challenge is the difficulty in verifying that the research participants define the testing situation in the same way as the experimenter. An experiment designed to test for "obedience to authority" might be misinterpreted as a test for "intelligence," perhaps raising anxiety in ways that distort subsequent responses. Failure to confirm the correspondence between the conceptions of experimenters and those of participants may introduce error.

A third caution in the use of T-data is that these situations are inherently *interpersonal,* and a researcher may inadvertently influence how the participants behave. A researcher with an outgoing and friendly personality, for example, may elicit more cooperation from participants than a cold or aloof experimenter (see Kintz, et al., 1965). The choice of who runs the experiment, in short, including the personality and demeanour of the experimenter, may inadvertently introduce effects that alter the obtained results.

Despite these limitations, T-data remain a valuable and irreplaceable source of personality information. Procedures used to obtain T-data can be designed to *elicit behaviour* difficult to observe in everyday life. They allow investigators to *control the context* and to eliminate extraneous sources of influence. And they enable experimenters to *test specific hypotheses* by exerting control over the variables that are predicted to have causal influence. For these reasons, T-data procedures remain an indispensable set of tools for the personality researcher (Elfenbein et al., 2008).

Mechanical Recording Devices

Personality psychologists have been enterprising in adapting technological innovations. An example is the use of the "actometer" to assess personality differences in activity or energy level. The actometer is essentially a modified self-winding watch that can be strapped to the arms or legs of participants (typically, children). Movement activates the winding mechanism, registering the person's activity on the hands of the dial. Of course, day-to-day and even hour-to-hour fluctuations in mood, physiology, and setting limit the usefulness of any single sample of activity level. However, several samples can be recorded on different days to generate composite scores, reflecting, for each person, whether they are hyperactive, normally active, or sedentary (Buss, Block, & Block, 1980).

In one study, preschool children ages 3 and 4 wore actometers on the wrist of the nonfavoured hand for approximately two hours (Buss et al., 1980). The dial of each actometer was covered with tape, so the children would not be distracted. Indeed, in pretesting, the children who could observe the dial became preoccupied with it—sitting in one spot, shaking the device back and forth—a practice that interfered with the usefulness of the measure. Several separate recording sessions were held, and the actometer readings were aggregated to obtain a more reliable index of each child's activity level.

The experimenters then sought answers to three questions: (1) Does activity level measured with the actometer yield the same results as activity level measured through observation? (2) To what extent is activity level stable over time? (3) Do activity level measurements using this mechanical recording device relate to observer-based judgments of personality functioning? To answer these questions, the children's teachers provided observer evaluations using the children's version of the California Q-Sort—an instrument designed to produce a wide-ranging description of children's personality characteristics (Block & Block, 1980). Examples of items on the Q-Sort are: *is a talkative individual; behaves in a giving way toward others; is basically submissive; is guileful and deceitful, manipulative, opportunistic; has a high energy level.* These observations were made when the children were 3, 4, and 7 years old, whereas the actometer measures were recorded at ages 3 and 4.

It turns out that there was a strong correspondence between actometer measures of activity level and the observer-based measures. Activity level also turns out to be moderately stable over time. For example, actometer measures at age 3 showed a moderate correspondence with actometer measures at age 4. Is there any relationship between actometer measurements of activity level and observer-based judgments of personality? The highly active children, as assessed with the actometer, were judged by their teachers to be vital, energetic, and active. In addition, the highly active children were judged to be restless and fidgety. The active children were also seen by teachers as uninhibited, assertive, competitive, aggressive physically and verbally, attention-getting, and manipulative of others. Thus, actometer-based activity scores are linked to *other* personality characteristics, traits that have important consequences for social interaction.

In sum, various aspects of personality can be assessed through mechanical recording devices, such as the actometer (Wood et al., 2007). These forms of T-data have several advantages and disadvantages. They provide a mechanical means of assessing personality, unhampered by the biases that might be introduced when a human observer is involved. A second advantage is that they can be obtained in relatively naturalistic settings—such as a children's playground. Their primary disadvantage is that few personality dispositions lend themselves to being assessed by mechanical devices. There are no mechanical devices, for example, to directly measure introversion or conscientiousness. This highlights the often necessary dependence on S-data and O-data in personality research.

Activity level is stable over time and correlates with teacher ratings of vital, energetic, and active.
©Ariel Skelley/Corbis

Physiological Data

A critical source of personality data is physiological measurement. Physiological measures can provide information about a person's level of arousal, reactivity to various stimuli, and the speed at which one takes in new information—all potential indicators of personality. Sensors can be placed on different parts of a person's body, for example, to measure sympathetic nervous system activity, blood pressure, heart rate, and muscle contraction. Brain waves, such as reactivity to stimuli, also can be assessed. And even physiological changes associated with sexual arousal can be measured via instruments such as a penile strain gauge (Geer & Head, 1990) or a vaginal bloodflow meter (Hamilton, Rellini, & Meston, 2008).

In Chapter 7, we go into some detail on physiological measures. For our purposes here—examining alternative ways of measuring personality—we look at only one example of using physiological data as a source of personality information. Psychologist Christopher Patrick (1994, 2005) has been studying psychopathic behaviour, particularly men in prison who have committed serious crimes against other people. One theory about people with psychopathy is that they do not have the normal fear or anxiety response that most people have. Things that might make most people anxious may not make those with psychopathy anxious. To test this idea, Patrick used a technique called the "eyeblink startle reflex," which had previously been used in studies of fear.

When people are startled, as when a loud noise occurs, they show the startle reflex, which consists of blinking their eyes, lowering the chin toward the chest, and inhaling suddenly. If people are already anxious, they will exhibit the startle reflex faster than when feeling normal. It makes adaptive sense that they will be prepared to have a faster defensive startle if they are already in a fearful or anxious state. You can demonstrate this by showing people pictures of frightening or unpleasant scenes, such as a snake, a vicious dog, or spiders, which most people find make them a little anxious. If they are startled while looking at these scenes, they will startle faster than when looking at nonfeared objects, such as a house, a tree, or a table. Interestingly, Patrick found that people with psychopathy, who were in prison for violent crimes, did not exhibit the faster eyeblink response while viewing the anxiety-producing photographs. Perhaps people with psychopathy commit their crimes because they don't have the normal level of anxiety or guilt that prevents most of us from doing anything wrong. This is a good example of how physiological measures can be used to examine and understand various personality characteristics.

A more recent physiological data source comes from **functional magnetic resonance imaging (fMRI)**, a technique used to identify the areas of the brain that "light up" when performing certain tasks such as verbal problems or spatial navigation problems. It works by gauging the amount of oxygen brought to particular places in the brain. When a certain part of the brain is highly activated, it draws large amounts of blood. The oxygen carried by the blood accumulates in that region of the brain. The fMRI is able to detect concentrations of iron carried by the oxygen contained in the red blood cells and thus determine the part of the brain that is used in performing certain tasks. The colourful images that emerge from fMRI brain scans are often quite dramatic.

In principle, fMRI provides a physiological data source that can be linked with personality dispositions, intelligence, or psychopathology. In practice, however, the method has limitations on what it reveals. Because fMRI must compare the "activated" state with a "resting" state, it becomes critical to know what the resting state really is. If men's resting state turns more to sports and women's resting state turns more to social interactions, for example, it is possible that a comparison of a task such as looking at faces to the resting state would suggest that men and women are performing the task differently, when in fact the difference is due entirely to a sex difference in the resting state (Kosslyn & Rosenberg, 2004).

One of the key benefits of physiological data is that it is difficult for participants to fake responses, particularly on measures of arousal or reflexive responses, such as the eyeblink startle reflex. Nonetheless, physiological recording procedures share most of the same limitations as other laboratory test data. In particular, recording is typically constrained by a relatively artificial laboratory situation.

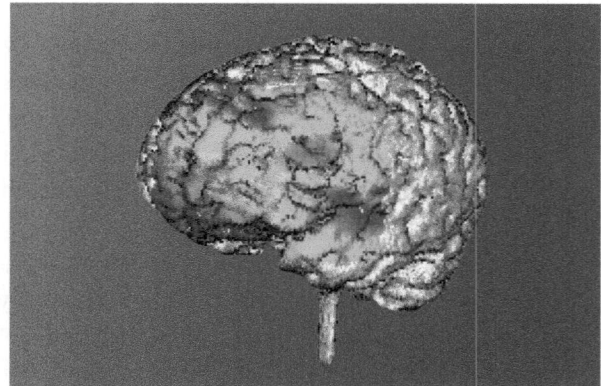

Measures of physiological responses, such as these fMRI brain scans, are a source of data in personality research.
©BSIP SA/Alamy Stock Photo

Projective Techniques

Another type of T-data is **projective techniques**, in which the person is given a standard stimulus and asked what they see. The most famous projective technique for assessing personality is the set of inkblots developed by Hermann Rorschach. The hallmark of any projective technique is that the person is presented with an ambiguous stimulus, such as an inkblot, and then asked to impose structure on this stimulus by describing what they see—for example, what is in the inkblot. The idea behind projective techniques is that what the person sees in the stimulus reveals something about their personality. Presumably, the person "projects" concerns, conflicts, traits, and ways of seeing or dealing with the world onto the ambiguous stimulus.

Projective techniques are considered T-data because all subjects are presented with a standard testing situation, all are given the same instructions, and the test situation elicits behaviours that are thought to reveal personality.

To the psychologist interpreting a person's responses to the inkblots, the content of those responses is important. Someone with a "dependent personality," for

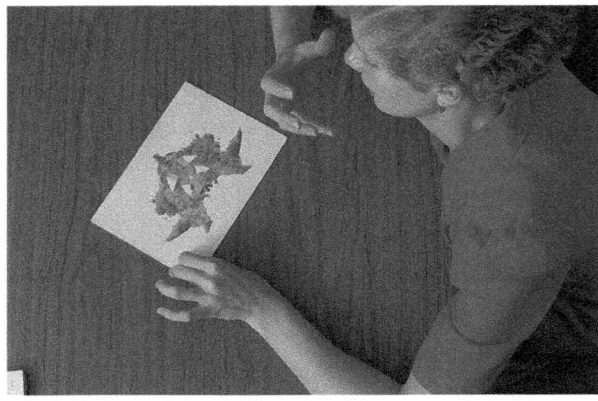

A person interpreting an inkblot may project their personality onto what is "seen" in the image.
©Will & Deni McIntyre/Science Source

example, might produce a high frequency of responses such as food, food providers, passively being fed, nurturers, oral activity, passivity, helplessness, and "baby talk" (Bornstein, 2005).

In sum, all projective measures present participants with ambiguous stimuli, asking them to provide structure by interpreting, drawing, or telling a story about the stimuli. Psychologists who advocate projective measures argue that they are useful for getting at wishes, desires, fantasies, and conflicts that the participants themselves may be unaware of and so could not report on a questionnaire. Others are critical of projectives, questioning their validity and reliability as accurate measures of personality (Wood, Nezworski, & Stejskal, 1996).

Life-Outcome Data (L-Data)

Life-outcome data (L-data) refers to information that can be gleaned from the events, activities, and outcomes in a person's life that are available to public scrutiny. For example, marriages and divorces are a matter of public record. Personality psychologists can sometimes secure information about the clubs a person joins, how many speeding tickets a person has received, and whether one owns a handgun. Whether a person gets arrested for a violent or white-collar crime is a matter of public record. Success at one's job, whether one is upwardly or downwardly mobile, and the creative products one produces, such as books published and music recorded, are often important outcomes in a person's life. These can all serve as valuable sources of information about personality.

The tendency to have frequent temper outbursts in childhood has been linked with negative adult outcomes, such as increased likelihood of divorce.
©Chris Knapton/Alamy

Personality psychologists often use S-data and O-data to predict L-data. An example that illustrates how O-data can be used to predict important life events is provided by Avshalom Caspi and his colleagues

(Caspi, Elder, & Bem, 1987). Based on clinical interviews with mothers of children ages 8, 9, and 10, researchers created two personality scales to measure ill-temperedness. One was based on the *severity* of temper tantrums; it noted physical behaviours such as biting, kicking, striking, and throwing things, and verbal expressions such as swearing, screaming, and shouting. The other scale assessed the *frequency* of these temper tantrums. Caspi and his colleagues summed these two scales to create a single measure of temper tantrums. This measure represents O-data because it is based on the mothers' actual observations. Then, in adulthood, when the participants were 30 to 40 years old, the researchers gathered information about life outcomes, such as education, work, marriage, and parenthood. They examined whether ill-temperedness, measured in childhood as O-data, predicted significant life outcomes two to three decades later, measured as L-data.

The results proved to be remarkable. For the men, early temper tantrums were linked with many negative outcomes in adult life. The men who had exhibited temper tantrums in childhood achieved significantly lower rank in their military service. They tended to have erratic work lives—changing jobs more frequently and experiencing more unemployment than those who had not been judged to be ill-tempered as children. Furthermore, such men were less likely than their even-tempered counterparts to have a satisfying marriage. Fully 46 percent of the ill-tempered men were divorced by age 40, whereas only 22 percent of the men in the low-temper-tantrum category were divorced by the age of 40.

For the women, early temper tantrums did not have a bearing on their work lives, in contrast to the men. However, the women who had had temper tantrums as children tended to marry men who were significantly lower than themselves in occupational status; fully 40 percent of the women who had showed temper tantrums as children displayed this outcome, compared with only 24 percent of the women who had been even-tempered as children. As with the men, childhood temper tantrums were linked with frequency of divorce for the women. Roughly 26 percent of the women who had had childhood tantrums were divorced by age 40, whereas only 12 percent of the even-tempered women were divorced by that age.

In addition to empirical studies that predict marriage and divorce outcomes, life-outcome data are used in other ways that affect our everyday lives. Our driving records, including speeding tickets and traffic accidents, are used by insurance companies to determine how much we pay for car insurance. Our histories of credit card usage are sometimes tracked by businesses to determine our behavioural preferences, which influence the advertisements we get exposed to on social network sites like Facebook. And more recently, advertisers will sometimes track the Web sites we visit and use e-mail spam and pop-up advertisements based on our patterns of Internet usage. Indeed, even a person's e-mail address can reveal personality. People who adopt e-mail addresses such as honey.bunny77@hotmail.com tend to be somewhat more extraverted than those who adopt other e-mail addresses (Back, Schmukle, & Egloff, 2008). Thus, driving records, credit card usage, and patterns of Internet usage have become modern sources of L-data. Do you think we can predict these patterns of publicly traceable data from personality variables, such as impulsivity (more driving accidents), status striving (credit card purchase of prestige possessions), and sex drive (more frequent visiting of pornographic websites)? Future studies of L-data will soon answer these questions.

In sum, L-data can serve as an important source of real-life information about personality. Personality characteristics measured early in life are often linked to important life outcomes several decades later. In this sense, life outcomes, such as work, marriage, and divorce, are, in part, manifestations of personality. Nonetheless, it must be recognized that life outcomes are caused by a variety of factors, including one's sex, race, and ethnicity and the opportunities to which one happens to be exposed. Personality characteristics represent only one set of causes of these life outcomes.

 Exercise

Think of a personality characteristic that you find interesting. For example, you might consider such characteristics as activity level, risk taking, temper, or cooperativeness. Using the four main data sources, think of ways that you might gather information on this characteristic. Give specific examples of how you could assess this characteristic using S-, O-, T-, and L-data as sources of information on people's level of this characteristic. Be specific in providing examples of how and what you might do to assess your chosen personality characteristic.

Issues in Personality Assessment

Now that we have outlined the basic data sources, it is useful to take a step back and consider two broader issues in personality assessment. The first issue involves using two or more data sources within a single personality study. What are the links among the various sources of personality data? The second issue involves the fallibility of personality measurement and how the use of multiple data sources can correct some of the problems associated with single data sources.

Links Among Various Data Sources

A key issue that personality psychologists must address is how closely the findings obtained from one data source correspond to findings from another data source. If, for example, a person rates herself as dominant, do observers, such as her friends and spouse, also view her as dominant? Do findings obtained from mechanical recording devices, such as an actometer, correspond to data obtained from observer reports or self-reports of activity level?

Depending on the personality variable under consideration, agreement across data sources tends to range from low to moderate. Ozer and Buss (1991) examined the relationships between self-report and spouse report for eight dimensions of personality. They found that the degree of agreement varied depending on the particular trait and on the observability of the trait. Traits such as extraversion showed moderate agreement across data sources. The trait of "calculating," on the other hand, showed low self–spouse agreement. Traits that are easily observable (such as extraversion) show a higher degree of self–observer agreement than do traits (such as calculating) that are difficult to observe and require inferences about internal mental states (see Vazire, 2010).

One of the central advantages of using multiple measures is that each measure has unique idiosyncrasies that have nothing to do with the underlying construct of interest. By using multiple measures from various data sources, researchers are able to average out these idiosyncrasies and home in on the key variable under study.

A major issue in evaluating linkages among the sources of personality data is whether the sources are viewed as alternative measures of the same construct or as assessments of different phenomena. A person self-reporting about their relative dominance, for example, has access to a wealth of information—namely, their interactions with dozens of other people in their social environment. Any particular observer—a close friend, for example—has access to only a limited and selective sample of relevant behaviour. Thus, if the friend rates a subject as highly dominant, whereas the subject rates themselves as only moderately dominant, the disagreement may be due entirely to the different behavioural samples on which each person is basing the ratings. Thus, lack of agreement does not *necessarily* signify an error of measurement (although it certainly might).

In summary, the interpretation of links among the sources of personality data depends heavily on the research question being posed. Strong agreement between two sources of data leads researchers to be confident that their alternative measures are tapping into the same personality phenomenon, as proves true with extraversion and activity level. Lack of strong agreement, on the other hand, may mean that the different data sources are assessing different phenomena, or it may indicate that one or more data sources have problems—an issue to which we now turn.

The Fallibility of Personality Measurement

Each data source has problems and pitfalls that limit its utility. This is true of all methods in science. Even so-called objective scientific instruments, such as telescopes, are less than perfect because minor flaws, such as a slight warping in the lens, may introduce errors into the observations. The fallible nature of scientific measures is no less true in personality research.

One powerful strategy of personality assessment, therefore, is to examine results that transcend data sources—a procedure sometimes referred to as *triangulation*. If a particular effect is found—for example, the influence of dominance on the assumption of leadership—does the effect occur when dominance is measured with self-report as well as with observer reports? If extraverts are more easily driven to boredom than introverts, does this show up when boredom is assessed with physiological recording devices as well as via self-report? Throughout this book, we pay special attention to findings that transcend the limitations of single-data-source assessment. If the same results are found with two or more data sources, then researchers can have greater confidence in the credibility of those findings.

 Concept Check

Compare and contrast the advantages and disadvantages of the four sources of personality data. If you were designing a study of your own, which two sources would you prioritize? Why?

Explain the importance of considering the degree of agreement among sources of personality data. Is it always necessary to have high agreement?

Evaluation of Personality Measures

Once personality measures have been identified for research, the next task is to subject them to scientific scrutiny so that researchers can determine how good the measures are. In general, three standards are used to evaluate personality measures: reliability, validity, and generalizability. Although these three standards are discussed here in the context of evaluating personality questionnaires, these standards are applicable to all measurement methods within personality research, not merely to those involving self-report personality questionnaires.

Reliability

Reliability can be defined as the degree to which an obtained measure represents the true level of the trait being measured. Assume for a moment that each person has some true amount of the trait you wish to measure and that you could know this true level. If your measure is reliable, then it will correlate with the true level. For example, if a person has a true IQ of 115, then a perfectly reliable measure of IQ will yield a score of 115 for that person. Moreover, a reliable measure of IQ will yield the same score of 115 each time it is administered to the person. A less reliable measure would yield a score, say, in a range of 112 to 118. An even less reliable measure would yield a score in an even broader range, between 100 (which is average) and 130 (which is borderline genius). Personality psychologists prefer reliable measures, so that the scores accurately reflect each person's true level of the personality characteristic.

There are several ways to estimate reliability. One is through **repeated measurement**. There are different forms of repeated measurement. A common procedure is to repeat a measurement over time—for example, at intervals of one month—for the same people. If the two tests are highly correlated, yielding similar scores for most people, the resulting measure is said to have high *test-retest reliability*.

A second way to gauge reliability is to examine the relationships among the items themselves at a single point in time. If the items within a test—viewed as a form of repeated measurement—all correlate well with each other, then the scale is said to have high *internal consistency reliability*. The reliability is internal because it is assessed within the test itself. The rationale for using internal consistency as an index of reliability is that psychologists constructing various measures assume that all items on a scale are measuring the same characteristic. If they are, then the items should be positively correlated with each other.

A third way to measure reliability—applicable only to the use of observer-based personality measures—is to obtain measurements from multiple observers. When different observers agree with each other, the measure is said to have high *inter-rater reliability*. When different raters fail to agree, the measure is said to have low inter-rater reliability.

It is important to demonstrate that a personality measure is reliable, whether through test-retest, internal consistency, or inter-rater reliability. One factor that can reduce measurement reliability, especially for self-report questionnaires, is response sets, to which we now turn.

Response Sets

When participants answer questions, psychologists typically assume that they are responding to the content of the questions. For example, when participants are confronted with the item "I have never felt like smashing things," psychologists assume that participants think of all the times when they were angry and then recall whether on those occasions they ever felt like smashing something. Psychologists also assume that participants make a deliberate and conscious effort to consider the content of the question and then answer "True" or "False" to reflect their behaviour honestly. This assumption may sometimes be incorrect.

The concept of **response sets** refers to the tendency of some people to respond to the questions on a basis that is unrelated to the question content. Sometimes this is also referred to as **noncontent responding**. One example is the response set of **acquiescence**, or yea saying. This is the tendency to simply agree with the questionnaire items, regardless of the content of those items. Psychologists counteract acquiescence by intentionally reverse-scoring some of the questionnaire items, such as an extraversion item that states, "I frequently prefer to be alone." **Extreme responding** is another response set, which refers to the tendency to give endpoint responses, such as "strongly agree" or "strongly disagree," and to avoid the middle part of response scales, such as "slightly agree" or "slightly disagree."

Personality psychologists worry about the effects of response sets on the reliability of measurement. If a participant is responding not to the content of the questions but on another basis, then the answers do not reflect the aspect of personality being measured. Response sets may invalidate self-report measures of personality, so psychologists have looked for ways to detect and counteract their effects.

The response set known as **social desirability** has received the greatest amount of research and evaluation by personality psychologists. Socially desirable responding is the tendency to answer items in such a way as to come across as socially attractive or likable. People responding in this manner want to make a good impression, to appear to be well adjusted, to be good citizens. For example, imagine being asked to answer "True" or "False" to the statement "Most of the time I am happy." A person might actually be happy only 45 percent of the time yet answer "True" because this is the well-adjusted thing to say in our culture. People like happy people, so the socially desirable response is "Yes, I am happy most of the time." This is an example of responding not to the content of the item but to the kind of impression a "True" or "False" answer would create, and it represents a response set.

There are two views regarding the interpretation of social desirability. One view is that it represents distortion and should be eliminated or minimized. The other view is that social desirability is a valid part of other desirable personality traits, such as happiness, conscientiousness, or agreeableness.

Viewing social desirability as distortion does not assume that the person is consciously trying to create a positive impression. A social desirability response set may not actually be an outright effort to distort responses and, so, is different from faking or lying. Some people may simply have a distorted view of themselves or have a strong need to have others think well of them. For this reason, most psychologists have resisted calling this response set "lying" or "faking" (cf. Eysenck & Eysenck, 1972, for a different opinion). Nevertheless, many personality psychologists believe that socially desirable responding introduces inaccuracies into test scores and should be eliminated or controlled.

Some rare individuals, like the late Mother Teresa of Calcutta, might score high on social desirability because they are in fact truly engaging in socially desirable behaviours, not because they want to create a good impression of themselves by lying on a personality questionnaire.
©Gavin Wickham/Corbis

One approach to the problem of socially desirable responses is to assume that they are erroneous or deceptive, to measure this tendency, and to remove it statistically from the other questionnaire responses. There are several social desirability measures available. Items from a popular measure developed by Crowne and Marlowe (1964) are shown in Table 2.1. Crowne and Marlowe thought of social desirability as reflecting a need for approval, and they published the social desirability scale in their book *The Approval Motive*. Looking at the items on their scale, you can see that they typically refer to minor transgressions that most of us have committed or inadequacies that many if not most of us suffer from. In addition, some items refer to almost saintlike behaviour. To the extent that a person denies common faults and problems and endorses a lot of perfect and well-adjusted behaviours, they will get a high score on social desirability. A person's score on social desirability can be used to statistically adjust their scores on other questionnaires, thereby controlling for this response set.

Table 2.1 Crowne/Marlowe Scale for Measuring Social Desirability

Instructions: Listed below are a number of statements concerning personal attitudes and traits. Read each item and decide whether the statement is true or false as it pertains to you personally.

	True	**False**
1. I'm always willing to admit it when I make a mistake.	_____	_____
2. I always try to practise what I preach.	_____	_____
3. I never resent being asked to return a favour.	_____	_____
4. I have never been irked when people expressed ideas very different from my own.	_____	_____
5. I have never deliberately said something that hurt someone's feelings.	_____	_____
6. I like to gossip at times.	_____	_____

Source: Crowne & Marlowe, 1964.

A second way to deal with the problem of social desirability is by developing questionnaires that are less susceptible to this type of responding. For example, in choosing questions to put on a questionnaire, the researcher may select only the items that have been found *not* to correlate with social desirability.

A third approach to minimizing the effects of socially desirable responding is to use a **forced-choice questionnaire** format. In this format, test takers are confronted with pairs of statements and are asked to indicate which statement in each pair is more true of them. Each statement in the pair is selected to be similar to the other in social desirability, forcing participants to choose among statements that are equally socially desirable (or undesirable). The following items from the Vando Reducer Augmenter Scale (Vando, 1974) illustrate the forced-choice format: Which would you most prefer (a or b)?

1. **a.** to read the book
   b. to see the movie
2. **a.** eat soft food
   b. eat crunchy food
3. **a.** continuous anesthesia
   b. continuous hallucinations
4. **a.** a job that requires concentration
   b. a job that requires travel

If one answers all *b*s, this scale measures the preference for arousing or strong stimulation. The two choices presented in each item are of approximately the same value in terms of social desirability. Consequently, participants must decide on an answer based on something other than social desirability. They should respond to the *content* of the item and hence provide accurate information about their personalities.

Although many psychologists view socially desirable responding as an error to be avoided or eliminated, others see it as part of an important trait. These psychologists consider social desirability to be a trait in itself, one that is correlated with positive traits such as happiness, adjustment, and conscientiousness. These psychologists suggest that being mentally healthy may, in fact, entail possessing an overly positive view of oneself and one's abilities. In her book *Positive Illusions,* social psychologist Shelly Taylor (1989) summarizes much research suggesting that self-enhancing illusions about oneself, the world, and one's future can promote psychological adjustment and mental health. Indeed, research finds that unrealistic beliefs about the self (positive illusions) are related to better physical health, such as slower progression of disease in HIV-positive men. If psychologists were to measure such positive illusions in the form of social desirability and remove them from other personality measures, they might, in effect, be throwing the baby out with the bathwater. That is, social desirability may be part of being high on adjustment and positive mental health.

To the extent that response sets, such as social desirability, are considered error, they can reduce measurement reliability (Paulhus & Vazire, 2007). That is, a personality questionnaire that is influenced by response sets would not reflect the true level of the trait being measured. Personality psychologists worry about response sets for this reason, especially for self-report questionnaires. Indeed, new measures of personality are often designed in ways that minimize participants' efforts to fake or present themselves in a socially desirable light (e.g., McDaniel et al., 2009). Questionnaires have also been developed and tested to measure social desirability specifically in research. We examine one such measure in Highlight On Canadian Research: The Balanced Inventory of Desirable Responding.

Highlight On Canadian Research

The Balanced Inventory of Desirable Responding

Canadian work on social desirability has attempted to disentangle self-deceptive optimism from impression management. Psychologist Delroy Paulhus of the University of British Columbia in Vancouver developed a social desirability inventory called the Balanced Inventory of Desirable Responding (BIDR; Paulhus, 1984, 1990). The BIDR contains two separate subscales, each designed to measure a different aspect of social desirability.

The Self-Deceptive Enhancement subscale was designed to tap self-deceptive overconfidence. This involves the tendency to exaggerate or inflate one's social and intellectual status (i.e., how a person compares to others) in a positive way. It ultimately leads to inaccurate but positive interpretations of oneself as fearless, overly dominant and confident, emotionally stable, intellectual, and even creative. On the BIDR, self-deceptive enhancement is measured using items such as "My first impressions of people usually turn out to be right," "I always know why I like things," and "I am fully in control of my own fate." According to Paulhus (2002), individuals with high scores on the Self-Deceptive Enhancement subscale are often seen to be high in *narcissism*, a trait involving an exaggerated sense of self and abnormally high self-admiration (to be discussed more in Chapter 10). They also tend to describe themselves as having almost "superhero" and saint-like qualities.

The Impression Management subscale was designed to measure the tendency to present oneself favourably and please others, as in the distortion interpretation of social desirability. This subscale is intended to be sensitive to self-presentation motives, such as those that lead someone to want to present a good impression to others. They are therefore reflective of more conscious motivations to respond in a socially desirable way. Impression management may specifically involve the promotion of one's assets, social responsibility, competence, fearlessness, and even physical prowess. The Impression Management subscale of the BIDR contains items such as "I don't gossip about other people's business," "I never swear," "I have done things that I don't tell other people about," and "I have never dropped litter on the street." Paulhus (2002) suggests that such impression management tendencies are especially common in occupational, legal, and even religious settings, where people are motivated to minimize their faults and make excuses for their shortcomings more frequently.

Regarding their link to key personality traits, Paulhus and colleagues have found positive correlations (in the moderate range) between self-deceptive enhancement and all five traits in the Five Factor model (to be explored further in Chapter 3), suggesting that a positive self-deceptive bias may play a role in all personality dimensions. Correlations are much weaker with impression management, where conscientiousness and agreeableness appear most highly correlated with the tendency to present oneself more favourably (Meston, Heiman, Trapnell, & Paulhus, 1998).

Weighing in on the debate regarding positive illusions, Paulhus is less supportive of the notion that positive illusions are purely adaptive. Although self-deceptive enhancement may indeed improve performance in certain situations, his research suggests that it is in interpersonal circumstances that positive illusions of oneself are maladaptive. In particular, Paulhus (1998) has shown that self-deceptive enhancement promotes self-esteem and positive first impressions, but has negative consequences for interpersonal transactions over time and may lead to distorted self-perceptions when compared to the perceptions of others. In the end, this is likely explained by the tendency for members of a group to detect some degree of self-deception in other members, resulting in negative judgment.

Although the Crowne/Marlowe Social Desirability Scale remains the most widely used measure of social desirable responding to date, it is often criticized for its dated language and its unidimensional nature (that is, it does not address the widely supported components or factors involved in socially desirable responding). The work of Del Paulhus and his colleagues has proven especially valuable to the evolution of this key dimension of personality. The 40-item BIDR has continued to demonstrate sound reliability and validity across populations (Paulhus 1990, 2002; Blasberg, Rogers, & Paulhus, 2014), and this is similarly true for abbreviated measures of the scale (Hart, Ritchie, Hepper, & Gebauer, 2015). More recently, evidence is emerging that overclaiming (i.e., exaggerating the extent of one's knowledge of facts and information) may be a distinct indicator of a positivity bias in research (Bensch, Paulhus, Stankov, & Ziegler, 2017).

Validity

Validity refers to the extent to which a test measures what it claims to measure (Cronbach & Meehl, 1955; Wiggins, 2003). Establishing whether a test actually measures what it is designed to measure is a complex and challenging task. There are five types of validity: face validity, predictive validity, convergent validity, discriminant validity, and construct validity. The simplest type of validity is **face validity**, which refers to whether the test, on the surface, appears to measure what it is supposed to measure. For example, a scale measuring manipulativeness might include the following face-valid items: *I made a friend just to obtain a favour; I tricked a friend into giving me personal information; I managed to get my way by appearing cooperative; I pretended that I was hurt to get someone to do me a favour.* Because most people agree that these acts are manipulative, the scale containing them is highly face valid.

A more important component of validity is **predictive validity**, which refers to whether the test predicts criteria external to the test (thus it is sometimes called **criterion validity**). A scale intended to measure sensation seeking, for example, should predict which individuals actually take risks to obtain thrills and excitement, such as parachute jumping or motorcycle riding. One study, for example, found that a measure of sensation seeking successfully predicted a variety of gambling behaviours, such as playing the lottery, betting on sporting events, playing video poker, and using slot machines—attesting to the predictive validity of the sensation-seeking measure (McDaniel & Zuckerman, 2003). A scale created to measure conscientiousness should predict which people actually show up on time for meetings and follow rules. Scales that successfully predict what they should predict have high predictive validity.

A third aspect of validity, called **convergent validity**, refers to whether a test correlates with other measures that it should correlate with. For example, if a self-report measure of tolerance corresponds well with peer judgments of tolerance, then the scale is said to have high convergent validity. Early in this chapter, we described a study of "activity level" in which mechanical recordings of activity level correlated highly with observer-based judgments of activity level—another example of convergent validity. Convergent validity is high to the degree that alternative measures of the same construct correlate or converge with the target measure.

A fourth kind of validity, called **discriminant validity**, is often evaluated simultaneously with convergent validity. Whereas *convergent validity* refers to what a measure *should* correlate with, *discriminant validity* refers to what a measure *should not* correlate with. For example, a psychologist might develop a measure of life satisfaction, the tendency to believe one's life is happy, worthwhile, and satisfying. However, there is another trait called social desirability, the tendency to say nice things about oneself; thus the psychologist might be concerned with the discriminant validity of the life-satisfaction measure and try to show that this measure is different from measures of social desirability. Part of knowing what a measure actually measures consists of knowing what it does not measure.

A final type of validity is **construct validity**, defined as a test that measures what it claims to measure, correlates with what it is supposed to correlate with, and does not correlate with what it is not supposed to correlate with. Thus, construct validity is the broadest type of validity, subsuming face, predictive, convergent, and discriminant validity. This form of validity is called construct validity because it is based on the notion that personality variables are **theoretical constructs**. If asked to "show your intelligence" or "show your extraversion," you would be hard-pressed to respond. That is because there is not any one thing you can produce and say, "This is my intelligence" or "This is my extraversion." Intelligence and extraversion, like almost all personality variables, are abstractions. Nevertheless, these theoretical constructs are useful to psychologists in describing and explaining differences among people. Determining whether actual measures can claim to be valid ways of assessing the constructs is the essence of construct validity.

How then do we know if a measure has construct validity? If a measure converges with other measures of the same construct, if it relates to other variables that a theory of the construct says it should, and if it does *not* relate to phenomena that the theory says it should not relate to, then we have the beginnings of construct validity. For example, say that a researcher has developed a questionnaire measure of creativity and is wondering about its construct validity. Do the questionnaire scores correlate with other measures of creativity gathered on the same sample, such as ratings of creativity provided by friends (convergent validity), or awards or grades obtained in fine arts classes (predictive validity)? Do the results correlate with behavioural tests in which participants are asked to name creative uses for common objects, such as a hammer and string?

Finally, if creativity is hypothesized to be different from intelligence, it will be important to prove that the measure of creativity does *not* correlate with measures of intelligence (discriminant validity). When a large number of known relations is built up around a measure, then we begin to believe that the measure is credible as a measure of a specific personality construct.

Generalizability

A third criterion for evaluating personality measures is **generalizability** (Cronbach & Gleser, 1965; Wiggins, 1973). Generalizability is the degree to which the measure retains its validity across various contexts. One context of interest might be different groups of *persons*. A personality psychologist, for example, might be interested in whether a questionnaire retains its predictive validity across age groups, genders, cultures, or ethnic groups. Is a particular scale equally valid when used on men versus women? Is a test equally valid for Indigenous and non-Indigenous people living in Canada? Is it equally valid among Canadians and Americans? Does the scale measure the same trait or quality among university students as among middle-aged adults? If the scale is widely applicable across these person and cultural contexts, then the scale is said to have high generalizability across populations of people.

Another facet of generalizability refers to *different conditions*. Does a dominance scale, for example, predict who becomes the leader in business settings as well as in informal, after-work settings? Does a scale designed to measure conscientiousness predict who will show up for class on time, as well as who will keep their bedrooms tidy? Scales have high generalizability to the degree that they apply widely across different people, situations, cultures, and times. It is important to note, however, that generalizability on this level is not necessarily required in all cases. It is only required to the extent that the measure or scale will actually be used in other contexts. Researchers who plan to use a scale in a new context for the first time must establish its validity in this context before making conclusions regarding their observations.

 Concept Check

Define reliability and validity, and explain why they are important considerations in the evaluation of personality measures.

Define generalizability. Is it always necessary to have a high degree of generalizability? Why or why not?

Research Designs in Personality

In this chapter, we have examined the *types of personality measures* and the *means for evaluating the quality* of those measures. The next step in personality research is to use these measures in actual *research designs*. Although the variations are nearly infinite, there are three basic research designs in the field of personality psychology: experimental, correlational, and case study. Each has strengths and weaknesses. Each provides information that complements the information provided by the others.

Experimental Methods

Experimental methods are typically used to determine causality—that is, to find out whether one variable *influences* another variable. A *variable* is simply a quality that differs, or can take different values, for different people. Height, for example, is a variable because individuals differ in height. Aggressiveness is a variable because individuals differ in their levels of aggressiveness. Personality characteristics, such as extraversion and agreeableness, are other examples of variables. In order to establish the influence of one variable on another, two key requirements of good experimental design must be met: (1) **manipulation** of one or more variables and (2) ensuring that participants in each experimental condition are equivalent to each other at the beginning of the study.

In the first requirement, manipulation, the variable thought to be the influence is manipulated as part of the experiment. For example, if a drug is hypothesized to influence memory, then some participants get the drug and other participants get sugar pills; then all participants have their memories tested. The second requirement, equivalence, is accomplished in one of two ways. If the experiment has manipulation among groups, then the **random assignment** of participants to experimental groups is a procedure that helps ensure that all groups are the same at the beginning of the study. However, in some experiments, manipulation is within each single group. For example, in the memory experiment, participants might get the drug and have their memories tested, then later take the sugar pills and have their memories tested again. In this case, each participant is in both conditions. In this kind of experiment (called a within-participant design), equivalence is obtained by **counterbalancing** the order of the conditions, with half of the participants getting the drug first and the sugar pill second, and the other half getting the sugar pill first and the drug second.

The meaning of each of these features will become clear through an example of a personality experiment. Perhaps you are curious about why some people like to study with music or a TV on, whereas others need total silence for studying. A personality theory predicts that extraverts prefer lots of stimulation and introverts prefer very little. Imagine being interested in testing the hypothesis that extraverts function best under conditions of high external stimulation, whereas introverts function best under conditions of low stimulation. To test this hypothesis, you could first give a group of participants a self-report questionnaire that measures extraversion–introversion. Then you could select only those individuals who score at either extreme—as very introverted or very extraverted—to participate in your experiment. Next you would take these participants into the laboratory and have them work on math and sentence comprehension problems under two different conditions—in one condition, a radio would be blaring in the background, and in the other there would be total silence. Half of each group (that is, half of the extraverts and half of the introverts) should be randomly placed in the noisy condition first and the quiet condition second. The other half should be placed in the quiet condition first and the noisy condition second. Then, you would measure the number of errors each group makes under each of the two conditions. If the personality theory you are testing is correct, you should get a pattern of results like that in Figure 2.1. The hypothetical results in Figure 2.1 show that the extraverts made few errors in the noisy condition and more errors when it was quiet. The introverts showed the opposite pattern—noise hampered their performance, whereas they functioned best under conditions of silence.

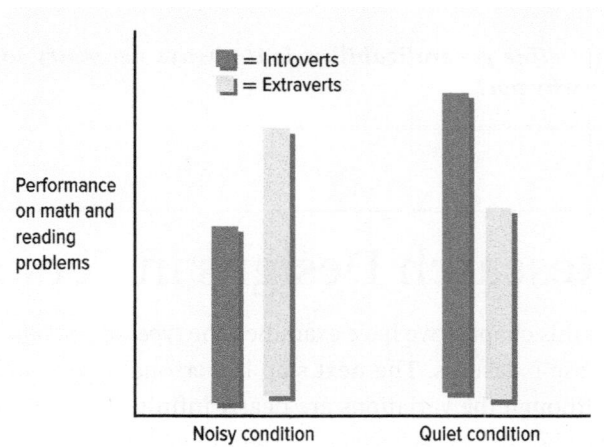

FIGURE 2.1 Performance on math and reading problems.

This study, although hypothetical, highlights the key features of good experimental design. The first is manipulation. In this case, the external condition (the *independent variable*) was manipulated—whether there was a lot of or a little ambient noise in the laboratory. The second feature is counterbalancing—half of the participants received the noisy condition first, and the other half received the quiet condition first. Counterbalancing is critical because there might be *order effects* as a consequence of being exposed to one condition first. Counterbalancing allows the experimenter to rule out order effects as an explanation for the results. The third feature is random assignment. Through random assignment, all individuals have an equal chance of being selected for a given condition. Randomization can occur by flipping a coin or, more commonly, by the use of a table of random numbers. Randomization ensures that there are no predetermined patterns linked with condition assignment that could account for the final results.

In experimental designs, it is desirable to establish whether the groups in the different conditions are *significantly* different. In the introversion–extraversion example, we want to know if the performance of introverts and extraverts in the noisy condition is significantly different. Is the performance of the introverts significantly different from that of the extraverts in the quiet condition? To answer these questions, we need to know five things: sample size, the mean, the standard deviation, the t-test, and the p-value (significance of the differences among the conditions).

The *mean* refers to the average—in this case, the average number of errors within each condition. The *standard deviation* is a measure of variability within each condition. Because not all participants make the same average number of errors, we need a way to estimate how much participants within each condition vary; this estimate is the standard deviation. Using these numbers, we can use a statistical formula—called the *t-test*—to calculate the difference between two means.

The next step is to see whether the difference is large enough to be called significantly different (the *p-value*). Although "large enough" is a somewhat arbitrary concept, psychologists have adopted the following convention: if the difference between the means would be likely to occur *by chance alone* (i.e., due to random fluctuations in the data) only 1 time out of 20 or less, then the difference is **statistically significant** at the $p < .05$ level (the .05 refers to 5 percent chance level, or 1 time in 20). A difference between means that is significant at the .05 level implies that the finding would be likely to occur by chance alone only 5 times out of 100. Another way to think about this is to imagine that, if the experiment were repeated 100 times, we would expect to find these results by chance alone only 5 times. If a difference is statistically significant, it is unlikely to be due to chance alone and is therefore likely to be a meaningful observation.

People who study alone in a library are likely to be introverted, whereas those who do their studying in groups tend to be extraverted.
(left): ©Shutterstock/Jacob Lund; (right): ©Design Pics/Leah Warkentin

In sum, the experimental method is effective at demonstrating *relationships among variables*. Experiments similar to the one described, for example, have established a link between extraversion–introversion and performance under conditions of high versus low noise. The procedures of manipulating the conditions, counterbalancing the order in which the conditions occur, and randomly assigning participants to conditions help to ensure that extraneous factors are cancelled out. Then, after calculating means and standard deviations, t-tests and p-values are used to determine whether the differences between the groups in the two conditions are statistically significant. These procedures determine whether personality influences how people perform.

Correlational Studies

A second major type of research design in personality is the correlational study. In the **correlational method** a statistical procedure is used for determining whether there is a relationship between two variables. For example, do people with a high need for achievement in university go on to earn higher salaries in adulthood than people lower on need for achievement? Correlational research designs attempt to identify the relationships between two or more variables, without imposing the sorts of manipulations seen in experimental designs. Correlational designs typically try to determine what goes with what in nature. We might be interested, for example, in the relationship between self-esteem, as assessed through S-data, and the esteem in which a person is held by others, as assessed through O-data. Or we might be interested in how achievement motivation relates to grade point average. A major advantage of correlational studies is that they allow us to identify relationships among variables as they occur naturally. To continue the example of extraversion–introversion and performance under noise conditions, we might measure people's preferences for studying with or without music in real life, then see if there is a correlation with their scores on a measure of introversion–extraversion.

The most common statistical procedure for gauging relationships between variables is the **correlation coefficient**. Consider the relationship between height and weight. We can take a sample of 100 university students and measure their height and weight. If we chart the results on a scatterplot, we see that people who are tall also tend to be relatively heavy and that people who are short tend to be less heavy. But there are exceptions, as you can see in Figure 2.2.

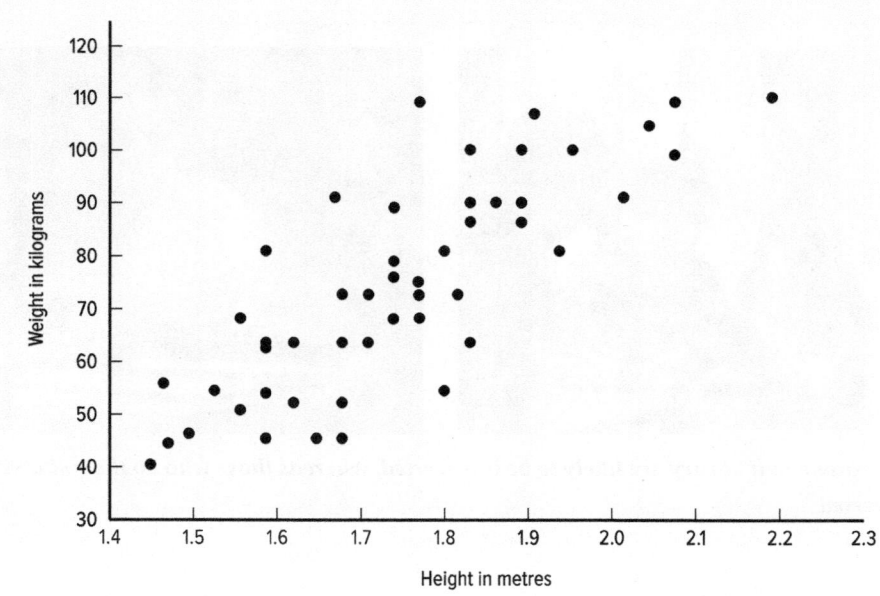

FIGURE 2.2 Fifty-five cases plotted, showing a strong positive correlation between height and weight. Each symbol (•) represents one person who was measured on both height and weight. Heavier people tend to be taller; lighter people tend to be shorter.

Correlation coefficients can range from +1.00 through 0.00 to −1.00. That is, the variables of interest can be positively related to each other (+.01 to +1.00), unrelated to each other (0.00), or negatively related to each other (−.01 to −1.00). Height and weight happen to be strongly positively correlated with each other—with a calculated correlation coefficient of +.60, for the data shown in Figure 2.2.

Consider a more psychological example. Suppose we are interested in the relationship between people's self-esteem and the amount of time they are unhappy. We might see a scatterplot as depicted in Figure 2.3. This scatterplot was obtained from a sample of university students using a standard questionnaire measure of self-esteem. As the second variable, a measure of unhappiness, the participants were asked to keep a diary for two months, noting for each day whether that day was generally good (felt happy) or generally bad (felt unhappy). Then the percentage of days for each participant being unhappy was calculated. As you can see, as self-esteem goes up, the percentage of time a person is unhappy tends to go down. In contrast, those with low self-esteem tend to be unhappy a lot. In short, there is a negative correlation between self-esteem and the percentage of time unhappy—in this case, approximately −.60.

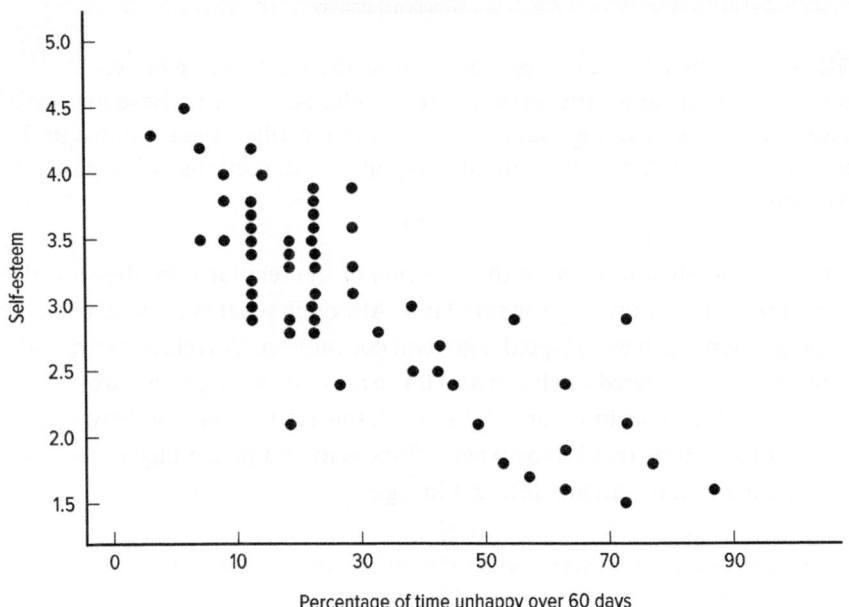

FIGURE 2.3 Fifty-eight cases plotted to illustrate the negative correlation between self-esteem and the percentage of time reported as being unhappy over two months. The correlation is −.60, indicating that people with higher self-esteem tend to be less unhappy than people with low self-esteem.

As a final example, suppose we are interested in the relationship between extraversion and emotional stability (the tendency to be calm and secure). The relationship is depicted in Figure 2.4. As you can see, there is no relationship between extraversion and emotional stability; as one variable goes up, the other may go up, down, or stay the same. In this case, the correlation coefficient is 0.00. This means that you can find people with all the different combinations of extraversion and emotional stability, such as those who are outgoing and sociable but also highly neurotic and unstable. In sum, relationships between variables can be positive, negative, or neither, as signified by positive, negative, or zero correlations.

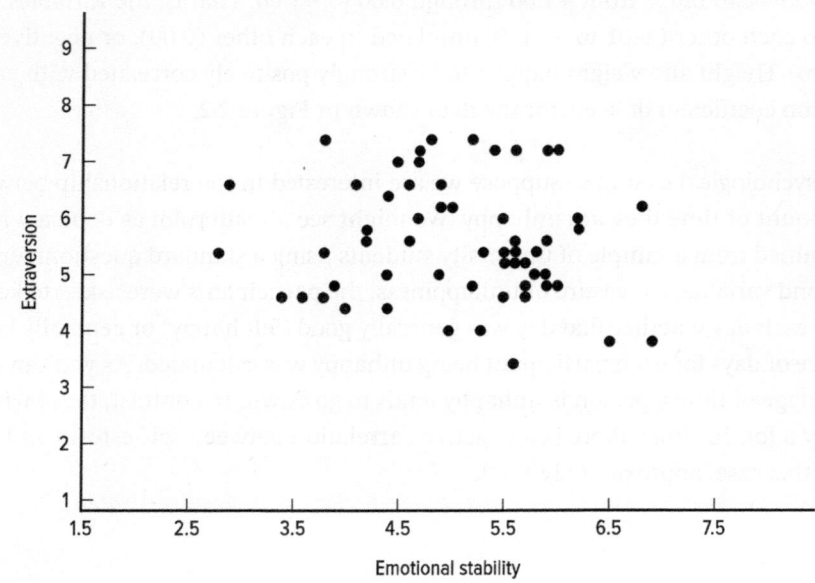

FIGURE 2.4 Fifty-seven cases plotted to show the relationship between emotional stability and extraversion. The correlation between these two variables is essentially 0.00, meaning that there is no relationship. Consequently, in the scatterplot, we see that people fall fairly equally in all sections of the plot, with no clear pattern.

Most researchers are not merely interested in the *direction* of the relationship; they are also interested in the *magnitude* of the relationship, or how large or small it is. Although what is considered large or small depends on many factors, social scientists have adopted a general convention. Correlations around .10 are considered small; those around .30 are considered medium; and those around .50 or greater are considered large (Cohen & Cohen, 1975). Using the examples in Figures 2.2 and 2.3, the +.60 correlation between height and weight is considered large, as is the −.60 correlation between self-esteem and percentage of time unhappy. These correlations have the same magnitude but are different in sign.

The concept of statistical significance can also be applied to correlation values. This is basically part of the statistical calculation, and it results in a numerical statement about how likely you are to find a correlation this size by chance, given the variables measured and the size of the sample. Here psychologists also require a probability of .05 or less before referring to a correlation as significant. If a correlation is significant, it is unlikely to be due to chance alone and is therefore likely to be meaningful.

It is important to keep in mind that one cannot infer causation from correlations. There are at least two reasons correlations can never prove causality. One is called the **directionality problem**. If *A* and *B* are correlated, we do not know if *A* is the cause of *B* or if *B* is the cause of *A*. For example, we know there is a correlation between extraversion and happiness. From this fact alone, we do not know if being extraverted causes people to be happy or if being happy causes people to be extraverted.

The second reason that correlations can never prove causality is the **third variable problem**. Two variables might be correlated because a third, unknown variable is causing both. For example, the amount of ice cream sold on any given day may be correlated with the number of people who drown on that particular day.

Does this mean eating ice cream causes drowning? Not necessarily, because there is most likely a third variable at work: hot weather. On very hot days, many people eat ice cream. Also, on very hot days many people go swimming who otherwise don't swim very much, so more are likely to drown. Drowning has nothing to do with eating ice cream; rather, these two variables are likely to be caused by a third variable: hot weather.

Case Studies

Sometimes a personality researcher is interested in examining the life of one person in-depth as a case study. There are advantages to the **case study method**. Researchers can find out about personality in great detail, which rarely can be achieved if the study includes large samples. Case studies can give researchers insights into personality that can then be used to formulate a more general theory to be tested on a larger population. They can provide in-depth knowledge of particularly outstanding individuals, such as Mahatma Gandhi or Martin Luther King Jr. Case studies also can be useful in studying rare phenomena, such as a person with a photographic memory or a person with multiple personalities.

Dodge Morgan was 54 when he completed a nonstop, solo circumnavigation of Earth by way of sailboat. An extensive case study of this fascinating man was conducted by psychologists William Nasby and Nancy Read and reported in their paper "The Voyage and the Voyager" published in the Journal of Personality, 1997, volume 65, pages 823–852.
Courtesy of Dodge Morgan

One case study occupied an entire issue of the *Journal of Personality* (Nasby & Read, 1997): the case of Dodge Morgan, who, at the age of 54, completed a nonstop solo circumnavigation of Earth by small boat. The case study is a highly readable account of this interesting man undertaking an almost impossible task. The focus is on how Mr. Morgan's early life experiences formed a particular adult personality, which led him to undertake the extreme act of going around the world alone in a small boat. The psychologists used Morgan's voyage log book, autobiographical material, interviews, and even standard personality questionnaires in conducting their case study. The report is noteworthy in that the psychologists also discussed the strengths and weaknesses of the case study method for advancing the science of personality psychology. The authors concluded that personality theories provide a language for discussing individual lives; analysis of individual lives, in turn, provides a means for evaluating personality theories on how they help us understand specific individuals.

Case study design can use a wide array of tools. One can develop coding systems to be applied to written texts, such as personal letters and correspondence. One can interview dozens of people who know the individual. One can interview the participant for hours and at great depth. One can follow the person around with a video camera and record, with sound and image, everyday actions and behaviours.

Case Study: An Attention-Seeking Boy

One of the strongest advocates of the case study method was Gordon Allport, one of the founders of the field of modern personality psychology. Allport firmly believed that important hypotheses about personality could come from examining single individuals in great depth. He also believed that one could test hypotheses about the underlying personality characteristics of a single individual using case study methods. The following example illustrates this sort of hypothesis formation and testing:

> *A certain boy at school showed exemplary conduct; he was orderly, industrious, and attentive. But at home he was noisy, unruly, and a bully toward the younger children....*

> *Now the psychologist might make the hypothesis: This boy's central disposition is a craving for attention. He finds that he gains his end best at school by conforming to the rules; at home, by disobeying them.*

> *Having made this hypothesis, the psychologist could then actually count the boy's acts during the day (being checked by some independent observer) to see how many of them were "functionally equivalent," i.e., manifested a clear bid for attention. If the proportion is high, we can regard the hypothesis as confirmed, and the p.d. [personality disposition] as established. (Allport, 1961, p. 368)*

Case Study: The Serial Killer Ted Bundy

Although Ted Bundy was convicted of killing three women, he was suspected of raping and killing as many as 36 women during his half-decade murder spree from Florida and Oregon all the way to the Canadian border in the 1970s (Rule, 2000). Case studies have been devoted to explaining what drove Bundy to rape and kill. Some traced it back to the fact that he felt a burning shame over never knowing his biological parents. Some tied it to his failed aspirations as a lawyer—where a status-striving motive was frustrated. Some traced it to the fact that he developed a deep-seated hostility toward women after being rejected by his fiancée—a woman who was considerably higher than him in socio-economic status and who he felt was impossible to replace. All case studies of Bundy revealed, however, that he shared many traits with other

Ted Bundy, a convicted serial killer, showed the personality characteristics of a classic psychopath.
©Bettmann/Corbis

serial killers. He had a "classic" psychopathic personality—characterized by grandiosity, extreme sense of entitlement, preoccupation with unrealistic fantasies of success and power, lack of empathy for other people, a long history of deceitfulness, repeated failures to meet normally expected obligations of school and work, and high levels of interpersonal exploitativeness and socially disruptive behaviour. Furthermore, Ted Bundy showed early traits and behaviours that are suggested to be associated with serial killers, the so-called homicidal triad: (1) torturing animals while young, (2) starting destructive fires, and (3) bedwetting. Case studies such as those of Ted Bundy can reveal unique aspects of his life (e.g., being rejected by a higher-status fiancée, failure to achieve status as an attorney), as well as the common personality dispositions that are often linked with serial killers (e.g., torturing animals, bedwetting; see also the case of Keith Hunter Jesperson, who confessed to raping and killing eight women, in Olson, 2002).

Despite the strengths of the in-depth case study method, it has some critical limitations. The most important one is that findings based on one individual cannot be generalized to other people. A case study is to the other research designs what a study of the planet Mars is to the study of planetary systems. We may find out a great deal about Mars (or a particular person), but what we find out may not be applicable to other planets (or other people). For this reason, case studies are most often used as a *source of hypotheses* and as a *means to illustrate* a principle by bringing it to life.

In order to apply statistical methods when studying a single person, it is possible to examine that person's behaviour as it compares to others. Del Paulhus provides a good example of such an approach in his analysis of Donald Trump's communication style. In order to make conclusions about this prominent public figure, Paulhus and colleagues compared the content of Trump's speeches to other Republican presidential candidates with whom he competed in 2015 (Ahmadian, Azarshahi, & Paulhus, 2017). Differences in qualities like informal language and grandiosity could be determined statistically, thereby gaining greater confidence in the conclusions made about this particular individual.

When to Use Experimental, Correlational, and Case Study Designs

Each of the three major types of research designs has strengths and weaknesses or, more precisely, questions that each is good at answering and questions that each is poor at answering. The experimental method is ideally suited for establishing causal relationships among variables. For example, it can be used to determine whether noisy conditions hamper the performance of introverts but not of extraverts. On the other hand, the experimental method is poor at identifying the relationships among variables as they occur naturally in everyday life. Moreover, it may be impractical or unethical to use the experimental method for some questions. For example, if a researcher is interested in the role of nutrition in the development of intelligence, it is unethical to conduct an experiment in which half of the participants are put on a starvation diet for several years as children to see if it affects their IQs as adults.

 Exercise

Think of a question about one aspect of personality. Most questions take the form of "Is variable *A* related to or caused by variable *B*?" For example, are extraverted individuals better than introverts at coping with stress? Are people with high self-esteem more likely to be successful than people with low self-esteem? Do narcissistic individuals have problems getting along with others? Write down your question about personality. Now think about how you might approach your question using an experiment, using the correlational method, and doing a case study. Briefly describe how you would use each of these three research designs to try to answer your question.

However, there are people who, for whatever unfortunate circumstances, have had several years of very poor nutrition. Thus a correlational study could be done on whether level of nutrition is related to the development of intelligence. The weakness of the experimental research design is precisely the strength of the correlational design. Correlational designs are ideally suited for establishing the relationships between two or more variables that occur in everyday life, such as between height and dominance, conscientiousness and grade point average, or anxiety and frequency of illness. But correlational designs are poor at establishing causality.

Case studies are ideally suited for generating hypotheses that can be tested subsequently using correlational or experimental methods. Case studies can be used to identify patterns in individual psychological functioning that might be missed by the more rigorous but artificial experimental approach and the limited correlational designs. Furthermore, case studies are wonderful in depicting the richness and complexity of human experience. Despite these strengths, case studies cannot establish causality, as can experimental methods, nor can they identify patterns of covariation across individuals as they occur in nature. Case studies also cannot be generalized to anyone beyond the single individual being studied. Together, all three designs provide complementary methods for exploring human personality.

 Concept Check

Describe the main differences between experimental and correlational methods in personality research.

What is the third variable problem? Provide an example of this problem as it might appear in personality research.

Summary and Evaluation

Personality assessment and measurement start with identifying the sources of personality data—the places from which we obtain information about personality. The four major sources of personality data are self-report (S-data), observer report (O-data), laboratory tests (T-data), and life history outcomes (L-data). Each of these data sources has strengths and weaknesses. In self-report, for example, participants might fake or lie. Observers in the O-data mode may lack access to the relevant information. Laboratory tests may be inadequate for identifying patterns that occur naturally in everyday life. Each source of personality data is extremely valuable, however, and each provides information not attainable through the other sources. Furthermore, new measurement techniques continue to be invented and explored; a recent example is fMRI, or functional magnetic resonance imaging, which detects locations and patterns of brain activity when individuals perform particular tasks.

Once sources of data have been selected for measuring personality, the researcher then evaluates their quality. Personality measures, ideally, should be reliable in the sense of attaining the same scores through repeated measurement. They should be valid, measuring what they are supposed to measure. And researchers should establish how generalizable their measures are—determining the people, settings, and cultures to which the measure is most applicable. Scales applicable only to university students, for example, are less generalizable than scales applicable to people of differing ages, economic brackets, ethnic groups, and cultures.

The next step in personality research involves selecting a particular research design within which to use the measures. There are three basic types of research designs. The first, the experimental research design, which involves controlling or manipulating the variables of interest, is best suited to determining causality between two variables. The second, correlational research design, is best for identifying relationships between naturally occurring variables but is poorly suited to determining causality. The third is the case study method, which is well suited to generating new hypotheses about personality and to understanding single individuals.

Perhaps the most important principle of personality assessment and measurement is that the decisions about data source and research design depend heavily on the purpose of the investigation. There are no perfect methods; there are no perfect designs. But there are data sources and methods that are better suited for some purposes than for others.

🛑 Concept Check

Imagine you are a researcher interested in studying the relationship between stress and aggressiveness. What specific methods would you employ to (a) measure these variables and (b) assess their degree of association?

What factors should you pay close attention to in this (or any) study in order to ensure confidence in your results and conclusions?

Could a case study prove useful in your investigation? Why or why not?

Key Terms

self-report data (S-data)

unstructured

structured

Likert-type scale

experience sampling

observer-report data (O-data)

inter-rater reliability

multiple social personalities

naturalistic observation

test data (T-data)

functional magnetic
    resonance imaging (fMRI)

projective techniques

life-outcome data (L-data)

reliability

repeated measurement

response sets

noncontent responding

acquiescence

extreme responding

social desirability

forced-choice questionnaire

validity

face validity

predictive validity

criterion validity

convergent validity

discriminant validity

construct validity

theoretical constructs

generalizability

experimental methods

manipulation

random assignment

counterbalancing

statistically significant

correlational method

correlation coefficient

directionality problem

third variable problem

case study method

PART ONE

The Dispositional Domain

The dispositional domain concerns those aspects of personality that are stable over time, are relatively consistent over situations, and make people different from each other. For example, some people are outgoing and talkative; others are more introverted and shy. The introverted and shy person tends to be that way most of the time (is stable over time) and tends to be introverted and shy at work, at play, and at school (is consistent over situations).

The study of traits makes up the dispositional domain. The term *disposition* is used because it refers to an inherent tendency to behave in a specific way. The term *trait* is used interchangeably with the term *disposition*. The major questions for psychologists working in the dispositional domain are these: How many personality traits exist? What is the best taxonomy, or classification system, for traits? How can we best discover and measure these traits? How do personality traits develop? How do traits interact with situations to produce behaviours?

In this domain, traits are seen as the building blocks of personality. A person's personality is viewed as being built out of a set of common traits. Psychologists have been concerned with identifying the most important traits, the ones out of which all differences among people can be formed.

The next step is to develop taxonomies, or classification systems. Taxonomies are very useful in all areas of science. Currently, the most popular taxonomy of personality has five fundamental traits: extraversion, neuroticism, agreeableness, conscientiousness, and openness to experience.

In the dispositional domain there is a unique conception of how people change yet remain stable at the same time. We will discuss how the traits that underlie behaviour can remain stable, yet the traits expressed in behaviour can change over a person's life span. For instance, a child may cry excessively in infancy, display a bad temper in childhood, and express highly anxious tendencies in adulthood. Underlying each of these traits may be a propensity towards neuroticism, one of the most common traits to describe human personality.

Lastly, we will review the ways in which personality psychologists have studied the development of dispositions as well as studies of how dispositions can change across the life span.

CHAPTER 3
Traits and Trait Taxonomies

The Dispositional Domain

Suppose that you walk into a party with a friend who introduces you to the host, an acquaintance of theirs. The three of you chat for 10 minutes and then you mingle with the other guests. Later, as you leave the party with your friend, she asks what you thought of the host. As you mull over the 10-minute interaction, what comes to mind? Perhaps you describe the host as *friendly* (they smiled a lot), *generous* (they told you to help yourself to the bountiful spread of food), and *poised* (they were able to juggle the many demands of their guests as they came and went). These words are all examples of *trait-descriptive adjectives*—words that describe *traits, attributes* of a person that are reasonably *characteristic* of the person and perhaps *enduring* over time. Just as you might describe a glass as *brittle* or a car as *reliable* (enduring characteristics of the glass and the car), trait-descriptive adjectives imply consistent and stable characteristics. For much of the past century, psychologists have focused on identifying the basic traits that make up personality and identifying the nature and origins of those traits.

Most personality psychologists hypothesize that traits (also called *dispositions*) are reasonably stable over time and at least somewhat consistent across situations. The host of the party just described, for example, might be friendly, generous, and poised at other parties later on—illustrating stability over time. And they might also show these traits in other situations—perhaps showing friendliness by smiling at people on elevators, showing generosity by giving homeless people money, and being poised by displaying confidence and composure when called upon in class. However, the actual degree to which traits show stability over time and consistency across situations has been the subject of considerable debate and empirical research.

People readily form impressions of others that can be described using a few traits of personality, such as whether the person is friendly, generous, and poised.
©Shutterstock/Pressmaster

Three fundamental questions guide those who study personality traits. The first question is, "How should we *conceptualize* traits?" Every field needs to define its key terms explicitly. In biology, for example, *species* is a key concept, so the concept of species is defined explicitly (i.e., a group of organisms capable of reproducing with each other). In physics, the basic concepts of mass, weight, force, and gravity are defined explicitly. Because traits are central concepts in personality psychology, they, too, must be precisely formulated.

The second question is, "How can we identify which traits are the *most important* traits from among the thousands of ways in which individuals differ?" Individuals differ in many ways that are both characteristic and enduring. Some individuals are extremely extraverted, enjoying loud and crowded parties; others are introverted, preferring quiet evenings spent reading. Some like R&B music, whereas others like classical rock. A crucial goal of personality psychology is to identify the most important ways in which individuals differ.

The third question is, "How can we formulate a *comprehensive taxonomy* of traits—a system that includes within it *all* of the major traits of personality?" Once the important traits have been identified, the next step is to formulate an organized scheme—a *taxonomy*—within which to assemble the individual traits. The periodic table of elements, for example, is not merely a random list of all the physical elements that have been discovered. Rather, it is a taxonomy that organizes the elements using a coherent principle—the elements are arranged according to their atomic numbers (which refer to the number of protons in the nucleus of a given atom). Within biology, to use another example, the field would be hopelessly lost if biologists were to merely list all of the thousands of species that exist, without relying on an underlying organizational framework. Thus, the individual species are organized into a taxonomy—all the species of plants, animals, and microbial species are linked systematically through a single tree of descent. Likewise, a central goal of personality psychology is to formulate a comprehensive taxonomy of all important traits. This chapter describes how personality psychologists have addressed these three fundamental questions of trait psychology.

What Is a Trait? Two Basic Formulations

As noted in the introductory chapter of this book, psychological traits are characteristics that describe ways in which people are different from each other. One important consideration is the way in which traits are formally conceptualized and measured by most psychologists: as *dimensions* on which people differ. For any given trait, some people are high, some people are low, and many others fall somewhere in the middle.

This is in contrast to a *categorical* approach, such as that taken by the Myers-Briggs Type Indicator (Myers et al., 1998), which attempts to describe people more strictly in terms of a limited number of personality types. Personality research has consistently demonstrated that traits indeed exist as dimensions, not types, distributed normally over a range of expressions. This issue is discussed at greater length in the next chapter.

When you describe someone as *impulsive, unreliable,* and *lazy,* what exactly are you saying? Personality psychologists differ in their assumptions about what these traits actually refer to. Some personality psychologists view these traits as *internal* (or hidden) *properties* of individuals that *cause* their behaviour. Other personality psychologists make no assumptions about causality and simply use these trait terms to *describe* the enduring aspects of a person's behaviour.

Traits as Internal Causal Properties

When we say that Deirdre has a *desire* for material things, that Dinesh has a *need* for stimulation, or that Dominick *wants* power over others, we are referring to something inside of each person that causes them to act in particular ways. These traits are presumed to be *internal* in the sense that individuals carry their desires, needs, and wants from one situation to the next (e.g., Alston, 1975). Furthermore, these desires and needs are presumed to be *causal* in the sense that they explain the behaviour of the individuals who possess them. Deirdre's desire for material things, for example, might cause her to spend a lot of time at the shopping mall, work extra hard to earn more money, and acquire many household possessions. Her internal desire *influences* her external behaviour, presumably causing her to act in certain ways.

Psychologists who view traits as internal dispositions do not equate traits with the external behaviour in question. This distinction is most easily explained using a food example. Sam may have a strong desire for a hamburger and a large order of fries. However, because Sam is trying to lose weight, they refrain from expressing their desire in behavioural terms—they look at the food hungrily but resist the temptation to eat it. Similarly, Dominick may have a desire to take charge in most social situations, even if he does not always express this desire. For example, some situations may have an already identified leader, such as in a class discussion with his psychology professor. Note that this formulation assumes that we can measure Dominick's need for power independently of measuring Dominick's actual behavioural expressions.

These examples are analogous to that of a glass, which has the trait of being brittle. Even if a particular glass never shatters (i.e., expresses its brittleness), it still possesses the trait of being brittle. In sum, psychologists who view traits as internal dispositions believe that traits can lie dormant in the sense that the *capacities* remain present even when particular behaviours are not actually expressed. Traits—in the sense of internal needs, drives, desires, and so on—are presumed to exist, even in the absence of observable behavioural expressions.

The scientific usefulness of viewing traits as causes of behaviour lies in ruling out other causes. When we say that Mona goes to a lot of parties *because* she is extraverted, we are implicitly ruling out other potential reasons for her behaviour (e.g., that she might be going to a lot of parties simply because her girlfriend drags her to them, rather than because she herself is extraverted). The formulation of traits as internal causal properties differs radically from an alternative formulation that considers traits as merely descriptive summaries of actual behaviour.

Traits as Purely Descriptive Summaries

Proponents of this alternative formulation define traits simply as *descriptive summaries* of attributes of persons; they make no assumptions about internality or causality (Hampshire, 1953; Saucier & Goldberg, 2001). Consider an example in which we ascribe the trait of *jealousy* to a young man named Zack. According to the descriptive summary viewpoint, this trait merely describes Zack's *expressed behaviour.* For example, Zack might glare at other guys when they talk to his girlfriend and ask her to spend all of her free time with them. The trait of jealousy, in this case, accurately *summarizes* the general trend in Zack's expressed behaviour, yet no assumptions are made about what causes Zack's behaviour.

Although it is possible that Zack's jealousy stems from an internal cause, perhaps deeply rooted feelings of insecurity, his jealousy might instead be due to *social situations.* Zack's expressions of jealousy might be caused by the fact that other guys are flirting with his girlfriend and she is responding to them (a situational cause), rather than because Zack is intrinsically a jealous person. The important point is that those who view traits as descriptive summaries do not prejudge the cause of someone's behaviour. They merely use traits to describe, in summary fashion, the trend in a person's behaviour. Personality psychologists of this persuasion (e.g., Saucier & Goldberg, 1998; Wiggins, 1979) argue that we must first identify and describe the important individual differences among people, then subsequently develop causal theories to explain them.

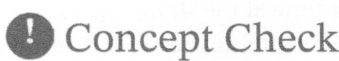 Concept Check

Distinguish between the formulations of traits as (a) internal causal properties and (b) purely descriptive summaries.

The Act Frequency Formulation of Traits—An Illustration of the Descriptive Summary Formulation

A number of psychologists who endorse the descriptive summary formulation of traits have explored the implications of this formulation in a program of research called the "act frequency approach" (Amelang, Herboth, & Oefner, 1991; Angleiter, Buss, & Demtroder, 1990; Buss & Craik, 1983; Church et al., 2007; Jackson et al., 2010; Romero et al., 1994).

The act frequency approach starts with the notion that *traits are categories of acts.* Just as the category "birds" has specific birds as members of the category (e.g., robins, sparrows), trait categories such as "dominance" or "impulsivity" have specific acts as members. The category of dominance, for example, might include specific acts such as the following:

- He issued orders that got the group organized.
- She managed to control the outcome of the meeting without the others being aware of it.
- They assigned roles and got the game going.
- She decided which programs they would watch on TV.

Dominance is a trait category with these and hundreds of acts as members. A dominant person, according to the act frequency approach, is someone who performs a large number of dominant acts relative to others. For example, if we videotaped Asha and a dozen of her friends over a period of three months and then counted up how many times each person performed dominant acts, Asha would be considered dominant if she performed more dominant acts than her friends. Thus, in the act frequency formulation, a trait such as dominance is a descriptive summary of the general trend in a person's behaviour—a trend that consists of performing a large number of acts within a category relative to other individuals.

Act Frequency Research Program

The act frequency approach to traits involves three key elements: act nomination, prototypicality judgment, and the recording of act performance.

Act Nomination

Act nomination is a procedure designed to identify which acts belong in which trait categories. Consider the category of "impulsive." Now think of someone you know who is impulsive. Then list the specific acts or behaviours this person has performed that exemplify impulsivity. You might say, "They decided to go out with friends on the spur of the moment, even though they had to study," "They immediately accepted the dare to do something dangerous, without thinking about the consequences," or "They blurted out their anger before they had time to reflect on the situation." Through act nomination procedures such as this one, researchers can identify hundreds of acts belonging to various trait categories.

Prototypicality Judgment

The second step involves identifying which acts are most central to, or *prototypical* of, each trait category. Consider the category of "bird." When you think of this category, which birds come to your mind first? Most people think of birds such as *robins* and *sparrows*. They do not think of *turkeys* and *penguins*. Even though penguins and turkeys are members of the category bird, robins and sparrows are considered to be more prototypical of the category—they are better examples, more central to what most people mean by "bird" (Rosch, 1975).

In a similar way, acts within trait categories differ in their prototypicality of the trait. Panels of raters judge how prototypical each act is as an example of a particular concept. For example, raters find the acts "*controlled the outcome of the meeting without the others being aware of it*" and "*took charge after the accident*" to be more prototypically dominant than the act "*deliberately arrived late for the meeting.*"

Recording of Act Performance

The third and final step in the research program consists of securing information on the actual performance of individuals in their daily lives. As you might imagine, obtaining information about a person's daily conduct is difficult. Most researchers have used self-reports of act performance or reports from close friends or partners. As shown in Table 3.1, you can provide your own responses to this measure of impulsive acts. Similar measures have been developed for conscientious acts (Jackson et al., 2010) and extraverted acts (Rauthmann & Denissen, 2011). In the same way, observational measures of dominant acts have been developed in the context of face-to-face groups (Anderson & Kilduff, 2009). Interestingly, traditional trait measures do a moderately good job of predicting manifest behaviour in everyday life (Fleeson & Gallagher, 2009).

Table 3.1 Self-Report of Impulsive Acts

Instructions: Following is a list of acts. Read each act and circle the response that most accurately indicates how often you typically perform each act. Circle "0" if you never perform the act; circle "1" if you occasionally perform the act; circle "2" if you perform the act with moderate frequency; and circle "3" if you perform the act very frequently.

Circle	Acts	
0 1 2 3	1.	I say what I think without thinking about the possible consequences.
0 1 2 3	2.	I react quickly and aggressively to verbal threats.
0 1 2 3	3.	I bought a new car without giving it much thought.
0 1 2 3	4.	I decide to live with somebody without due reflection.
0 1 2 3	5.	I make hasty decisions.
0 1 2 3	6.	I speak without thinking about what I am going to say.
0 1 2 3	7.	I am led by the feelings of the moment.
0 1 2 3	8.	I spend my money on whatever strikes my fancy.
0 1 2 3	9.	Having made definite plans, I suddenly change them and do something totally different.
0 1 2 3	10.	I do the first thing that comes into my head.

Note: From among the most prototypical impulsive acts. According to the act frequency approach, you would be judged to be "impulsive" if you performed a high overall frequency of these impulsive acts, relative to your peer group.

Source: Adapted from E. Romero et al., "The act frequency approach to the study of impulsivity," *European Journal of Personality, 8,* 119–134, Table 5, p. 125 © 1994 by John Wiley & Sons, Inc. Reprinted by permission of the publisher.

Evaluation of the Act Frequency Formulation

The formulation of traits as purely descriptive summaries, as in the act frequency approach, has been criticized on several grounds (see Angleitner & Demtroder, 1988; Block, 1989). Most of the criticisms have been aimed at the technical implementation of the approach. For example, the act frequency approach does not specify how much context should be included in the description of a trait-relevant act. Consider the following dominant act: *They insisted that the others go to their favourite restaurant.* To understand this act as a dominant act, we might need to know (1) the relationships among the people involved, (2) the occasion for going out to eat, (3) the history of restaurant going for these people, and (4) who is paying for the dinner. How much context is needed to identify the act as a dominant act?

Another criticism of the approach is that it seems applicable to overt actions, but what about *failures* to act and covert acts that are not directly observable? For example, a person may be very courageous, but we will never know this under ordinary life circumstances in which people have no need to display courageousness.

Despite these limitations, the act frequency approach has produced some noteworthy accomplishments. It has been especially helpful in making explicit the *behavioural phenomena* to which most trait terms refer—after all, the primary way that we know about traits is through their expressions in actual behaviour. As noted by several prominent personality researchers, "Behavioral acts constitute the building blocks of interpersonal perception and the basis for inferences about personality traits" (Gosling et al., 1998). Thus the study of behavioural manifestations of personality remains an essential and indeed indispensable part of the agenda for the field, despite the difficulties entailed by their study (Furr, 2009). The act frequency approach is also helpful in identifying behavioural regularities—phenomena that must be explained by any comprehensive personality theory (Furr, 2009). And it has been helpful in exploring the *meaning* of some traits that have proven difficult to study, such as impulsivity (Romero et al., 1994), conscientiousness (Jackson et al., 2010), and creativity (Amelang et al., 1991). It has also proven useful in identifying cultural similarities and differences in the behavioural manifestation of traits (Church et al., 2007). Initiating a conversation with a shy person, for example, is a greater reflection of extraversion in the Philippines than in North America, whereas smiling at a stranger is a greater reflection of extraversion in North America than in the Philippines.

Explorations of the act frequency approach have helped to identify the domains in which it provides insight into personality. One study, for example, examined the relationship between self-reported act performance and observer codings of the individual's actual behaviour (Gosling et al., 1998). Some acts showed high levels of self–observer agreement, such as "Told a joke to lighten a tense moment," "Made a humorous remark," "Took charge of things at the meeting." Acts that reflect the traits of extraversion and conscientiousness tend to show high levels of self–observer agreement. Acts that reflect the trait of agreeableness, on the other hand, tend to show lower levels of self–observer agreement. The more observable the actions, the higher the agreement between self-report and observer codings.

Other research has demonstrated that the act frequency approach can be used to predict important outcomes in everyday life such as job success, salary, and how rapidly individuals are promoted within business organizations (Kyl-Heku & Buss, 1996; Lund et al., 2006). Others have used the act frequency approach to explore topics such as *acts of deception* in social interaction (Tooke & Camire, 1991) and acts of "mate guarding" that predict violence in dating and marital relationships (Shackelford et al., 2005).

In sum, there are two major formulations of traits. The first considers traits to be internal causal properties of persons that affect overt behaviour. The second considers traits to be descriptive summaries of overt behaviour, with the causes of those trends in conduct to be determined subsequently. However traits are formulated, all personality psychologists must confront the next vexing challenge—identifying the most important traits.

 Concept Check

Consider the trait category of friendliness according to the act frequency approach. Which acts would you look for? Which acts would be prototypical of friendliness?

Identification of the Most Important Traits

Three fundamental approaches have been used to identify important traits. The first is the **lexical approach**. According to this approach, all traits listed and defined in the dictionary form the basis of describing differences among people (Allport & Odbert, 1936). Thus the logical starting point for the lexical strategy is the natural language. The second method of identifying important traits is the **statistical approach**. This approach uses factor analysis, or similar statistical procedures, to identify major personality traits. The third method is the **theoretical approach**, in which researchers rely on theories to identify important traits.

Lexical Approach

The lexical approach to identifying important personality traits starts with the **lexical hypothesis**: *all important individual differences have become encoded within the natural language.* Over time, differences among people that are important are noticed, and words are invented to talk about those differences. People invent words such as *dominant, creative, reliable, cooperative, hot-tempered,* or *self-centred* to describe these differences. People find these trait terms helpful in describing people and for communicating information about them. And so, usage of these trait terms spreads and becomes common within the group. The trait terms that are not useful to people in describing and communicating with others fail to become encoded within the natural language.

If we consider the English language, we find an abundance of trait terms codified as adjectives, such as *manipulative, arrogant, indulgent,* and *warm.* A perusal of the dictionary yields about 18,000 trait-descriptive adjectives (Norman, 1967). The key implication of this finding, according to the lexical approach, is clear: trait terms are extraordinarily important for people in communicating with others.

The lexical approach yields two criteria for identifying important traits—**synonym frequency** and **cross-cultural universality**. The criterion of synonym frequency means that if an attribute has not merely one or two trait adjectives to describe it but rather many words, then it is a more important dimension of individual difference. "The more important is such an attribute, the more synonyms and subtly distinctive facets of the attribute will be found within any one language" (Saucier & Goldberg, 1996, p. 24). Consider individual differences in "dominance." There are many terms to describe it: *dominant, bossy, assertive, powerful, pushy, forceful, commanding, domineering, influential, ascendant, authoritative,* and *arrogant.* The prevalence of many synonyms, each term conveying a subtle difference in dominance, suggests that dominance is an important trait and that different shades of dominance are important in social communication. Thus, synonym frequency provides one criterion of importance.

Cross-cultural universality is the second key criterion of importance within the lexical approach: "The more important is an individual difference in human transactions, the more languages will have a term for it" (Goldberg, 1981, p. 142). The logic is that if a trait is sufficiently important in all cultures in which its members have codified terms to describe the trait, then the trait must be universally important in human affairs. In contrast, if a trait term exists in only one or a few languages, then it may be of only local relevance. Such a term is unlikely to be a candidate for a universal taxonomy of personality traits (McCrae & Costa, 1997).

The Yanomamö Indians of Venezuela, for example, have the words *unokai* and *non-unokai,* which mean, roughly, "a man who has achieved manhood by the killing of another man" (*unokai*) and "a man who has not achieved manhood status by the killing of another man" (*non-unokai*) (Chagnon, 1983). In Yanomamö culture, this individual difference is of critical importance, for the *unokai* have elevated status, are widely feared, have more wives, and are looked to for leadership. In mainstream Canadian culture, by contrast, there is the generic *killer,* but there is no single word that has the specific connotations of *unokai.* Thus, although this individual difference is of critical importance to the Yanomamö, it is unlikely to be a candidate for a universal taxonomy of personality traits.

One problem with the lexical strategy concerns the fact that personality is conveyed through different parts of speech, including adjectives, nouns, and adverbs. For example, there are dozens of noun terms encoded within the English language to describe someone who behaves as if they know everything: *bigmouth, know-it-all, smart-aleck, smart-ass, smarty, smarty-pants, swellhead, windbag, wiseacre, wiseass, wise-guy,* and *wisenheimer.* Although they have not been explored much, personality nouns remain a viable source of potential information about important dimensions of individual differences.

The lexical strategy has proven to be a remarkably generative starting point for identifying important individual differences (Ashton & Lee, 2005). To discard this information "would require us needlessly to separate ourselves from the vast sources of knowledge gained in the course of human history" (Kelley, 1992, p. 22). The lexical approach represents a good starting point for identifying important individual differences but should not be used exclusively. Two other commonly used approaches are the statistical and theoretical strategies.

Statistical Approach

The statistical approach to identifying important traits starts with a pool of personality items. These can be trait words or a series of questions about behaviour, experience, or emotion. In fact, most researchers using the lexical approach turn to the statistical approach to distill self-ratings of trait adjectives into basic categories of personality traits. However, the starting point can also be self-ratings on a large collection of personality-relevant sentences (e.g., *I find that I am easily able to persuade people to my point of view*). Once a large and diverse pool of items has been assembled, the statistical approach is applied. It consists of having a large number of people rate themselves (or others) on the items, then using a statistical procedure to identify groups or clusters of items. The goal of the statistical approach is to identify the major dimensions, or "coordinates," of the personality map, much the way latitude and longitude provide the coordinates of the map of Earth.

The most commonly used statistical procedure is **factor analysis**. Although the complex mathematical procedures underlying factor analysis are beyond the scope of this text, the essential logic of this approach can be conveyed simply. Factor analysis essentially identifies groups of items that *covary* (i.e., go together) but tend not to covary with other groups of items. Consider, as a spatial metaphor, the office locations of physicists, psychologists, and sociologists on your campus. Although these may be spread out, in general the offices of the psychologists tend to be closer to one another than they are to the offices of the physicists or sociologists. And the physicists are closer to one another than they are to the sociologists or psychologists. Thus, a factor analysis might reveal three clusters of professors.

Similarly, a major advantage of identifying clusters of personality items that covary is that it provides a means for determining which personality variables have some common property. Factor analysis can also be useful in reducing the large array of diverse personality traits into a smaller and more useful set of underlying factors. It provides a means for organizing the thousands of personality traits.

Let's examine how factor analysis works in an example shown in Table 3.2. This table summarizes the data obtained from a sample of 1,210 subjects who rated themselves on a series of trait-descriptive adjectives. Among the adjectives rated were *humorous, amusing, popular, hard-working, productive, determined, imaginative, original,* and *inventive.*

Table 3.2 A Sample Factor Analysis of Personality Adjective Ratings			
Adjective Rating	**Factor 1 (Extraversion)**	**Factor 2 (Ambition)**	**Factor 3 (Creativity)**
Humorous	**.66**	.06	.19
Amusing	**.65**	.23	.02
Popular	**.57**	.13	.22
Hard-working	.05	**.63**	.01
Productive	.04	**.52**	.19
Determined	.23	**.52**	.08
Imaginative	.01	.09	**.62**
Original	.13	.05	**.53**
Inventive	.06	.26	**.47**

Note: The numbers refer to factor loadings, which indicate the degree to which an item correlates with the underlying factor (see text).

The numbers in Table 3.2 are called **factor loadings**, indexes of how much of the variation in an item is "explained" by the factor. Factor loadings indicate the degree to which the item correlates with, or "loads on," the underlying factor. In this example, three clear factors emerge. The first is an "extraversion" factor, with high loadings on *humorous, amusing,* and *popular.* The second is an "ambition" factor: *hard-working, productive,* and *determined.* The third is a "creativity" factor, with high loadings on *imaginative, original,* and *inventive.* Factor analysis is quite useful in identifying three distinct groups of trait terms that covary with each other but are relatively independent of (tend not to covary with) other groups. Without this statistical procedure, a researcher might be forced to consider the nine traits as all separate from each other. Factor analysis tells us that *hard-working, productive,* and *determined* all covary sufficiently that they can be considered a single trait, rather than three separate traits.

A cautionary note should be made about using the statistical approach for identifying important traits: you get out of it only what you put into it. If an important personality trait happens to be left out of a factor analysis, it will not show up in the subsequent results. Thus, it is critical that researchers pay close attention to their initial selection of items.

Factor analysis and similar statistical procedures have been extremely valuable to personality researchers. Perhaps their most important contribution has been the ability to reduce a large, cumbersome array of diverse personality adjectives or items into a smaller, more meaningful set of broad, basic factors.

Theoretical Approach

The theoretical approach to identifying important dimensions of individual differences starts with a theory that determines which variables are important. In contrast to the statistical strategy, which can be described as atheoretical in the sense that there is no prejudgment about which variables are important, the theoretical strategy dictates which variables are important to measure.

To a Freudian, for example, it is critical to measure "the oral personality" and "the anal personality" because these represent important, theory-driven constructs. Or, to a self-actualization theorist such as Maslow (1968), it is critical to measure individual differences in the degree to which people are motivated to self-actualize (see Williams & Page, 1989, for one such measure). The theory, in short, strictly determines which variables are important.

As an example of the theoretical strategy, consider the theory of **sociosexual orientation** (Simpson & Gangestad, 1991; Penke & Asendorpf, 2008a). According to the theory, men and women will pursue one of two alternative sexual relationship strategies. The first entails seeking a single committed relationship characterized by monogamy and tremendous investment in children. The second sexual strategy is characterized by a greater degree of promiscuity, more partner switching, and less investment in children. Because the theory of sociosexual orientation dictates that the mating strategy one pursues is a critical individual difference, Simpson and Gangestad have developed a measure of sociosexual orientation so that these traits can be assessed in the population. In this way, the theory provides the framework for the identification of key traits and their measurement.

 Exercise

Take a moment to think about yourself as an individual. What makes you who you are? In what ways are you similar to most or different from many? What makes you unique? In the spaces below, list five adjectives that you believe are most important to describe your personality. When you are finished writing down your words, rank them from 1 to 5 for their importance, with 1 representing your most important characteristic and 5 representing your least important.

Rank	Adjectives	Related Qualities
____	_____	_____
____	_____	_____
____	_____	_____
____	_____	_____
____	_____	_____

Take a look at the words. Are any of them related to one another or very similar in their meaning? If so, these words may represent a broader trait to describe your personality. For example, if you included the adjectives *friendly* and *sociable,* these could reflect a high level of *extraversion*. This kind of grouping is similar to the goal of the statistical approach, which uses factor analysis to determine characteristics that are more closely related. In this case, however, you're simply relying on the connections you make in your mind based on the meaning of the words. This is also similar to the concept of *synonym frequency,* part of the lexical approach, in so much that the presence of more synonyms for a particular word may mean a greater importance of the underlying trait. Take a look and see if this is true based on your original rankings.

Now, in the third column, write down any specific adjectives or characteristics that may be contained within the words you wrote in the second column. These may reflect even narrower traits or characteristics that make up your personality. As in most models of personality, traits are often organized hierarchically, with broad traits on one end and narrow traits on the other.

Evaluating the Approaches for Identifying Important Traits

In sum, the theoretical approach lets the theory determine which dimensions of individual differences are important. Like all approaches, the theoretical approach has strengths and limitations. Its strengths coincide with the strengths of the theory. If we have a powerful theory that tells us which variables are important, then it saves us from wandering aimlessly like a sailor without a map or compass. A theory charts the course to take. At the same time, its weaknesses coincide with the weaknesses of the theory. To the extent that the theory contains gaps or biases, the subsequent identification of important individual differences will reflect omissions and distortions.

The current state of the field of personality trait psychology is best characterized as "letting a thousand flowers bloom." Some researchers start with a theory and let their measurement of individual differences follow from that theory. Others believe that factor analysis is the only sensible way to identify important individual differences. Still other researchers believe that the lexical strategy, by capitalizing on the collective wisdom of people over the ages, is the best method of ensuring that important individual differences are captured.

In practice, many personality researchers use a combination of the three strategies. Norman (1963), Goldberg (1990), and Saucier (2009), for example, started with the lexical strategy to identify their first set of variables for inclusion. They then applied factor analysis to this initial selection of traits to reduce the set to a smaller, more manageable number (five or six). This solved two problems that are central to the science of personality (Saucier & Goldberg, 1996): the problem of identifying the domains of individual differences and the problem of figuring out a method for describing the order or structure that exists among the individual differences identified. The lexical strategy can be used to sample trait terms, and then factor analysis supplies a powerful statistical approach to providing structure and order to those trait terms.

 Concept Check

What are the three primary approaches used to identify the most important traits that make up human personality?

How are these approaches often used in combination?

Taxonomies of Personality

Over the past century, dozens of taxonomies of personality traits have been proposed. Many have been merely lists of traits, often based on the intuitions of personality psychologists. As personality psychologist Robert Hogan observed, "The history of personality theory consists of people who assert that their private demons are public afflictions" (Hogan, 1983). Indeed, two editors of a book on personality traits (London & Exner, 1978) expressed despair at the lack of agreement about a taxonomy of traits, so they simply listed the traits alphabetically. Clearly, we can develop a firmer basis for organizing personality traits. The taxonomies of traits presented in the rest of this chapter are not random samplings from the dozens available. Rather, they represent taxonomies that have solid empirical and theoretical justification.

Eysenck's Hierarchical Model of Personality

Of all the taxonomies of personality, that of Hans Eysenck, born in 1916, is most strongly rooted in biology. Eysenck was raised in Germany but moved to England at the age of 18, as Hitler's Nazi regime was rising in power. Although intending to study physics, Eysenck lacked the needed prerequisites, so almost by chance he began to study psychology at the University of London. He received his PhD in 1940 and after World War II became director of the psychology department at the Maudsley Hospital's new Institute of Psychiatry in London. Eysenck's subsequent productivity was enormous, with more than 40 books and 700 academic papers. Eysenck was the most cited living psychologist until he died in 1998.

Eysenck developed a model of personality based on traits that he believed were highly heritable (see Chapter 6) and had a likely psychophysiological foundation. The three main traits that met these criteria, according to Eysenck, were *extraversion–introversion* (E), *neuroticism–emotional stability* (N), and *psychoticism* (P). Together, they can be easily remembered by the acronym PEN.

Hans Eysenck at his London office.
Courtesy of Randy J. Larsen

Description

Let us begin by describing these three broad traits. Eysenck conceptualizes each of them as sitting at the top of its own hierarchy, as shown in Figure 3.1. *Extraversion,* for example, includes a large number of narrow traits—sociable, active, lively, venturesome, dominant, and so forth. These narrow traits are all subsumed by the broader trait of extraversion because they all covary sufficiently with each other to load on the same large factor. Extraverts typically like parties, have many friends, and seem to require having people around them to talk to (Eysenck & Eysenck, 1975). Many extraverts love playing practical jokes on people. They also tend to have a high activity level and display a carefree and easy manner.

Introverts, in contrast, like to spend more time alone. They prefer quiet time and activities such as reading. Introverts are sometimes seen as aloof and distant, but they often have a small number of intimate friends. Introverts tend to be more serious than extraverts and prefer a more moderate pace. They also tend to be well organized and prefer a predictable lifestyle founded on routine (Larsen & Kasimatis, 1990).

"You should get out more."

Introverts prefer to spend more time alone than do extraverts.
Richard Jolley/www.CartoonStock.com

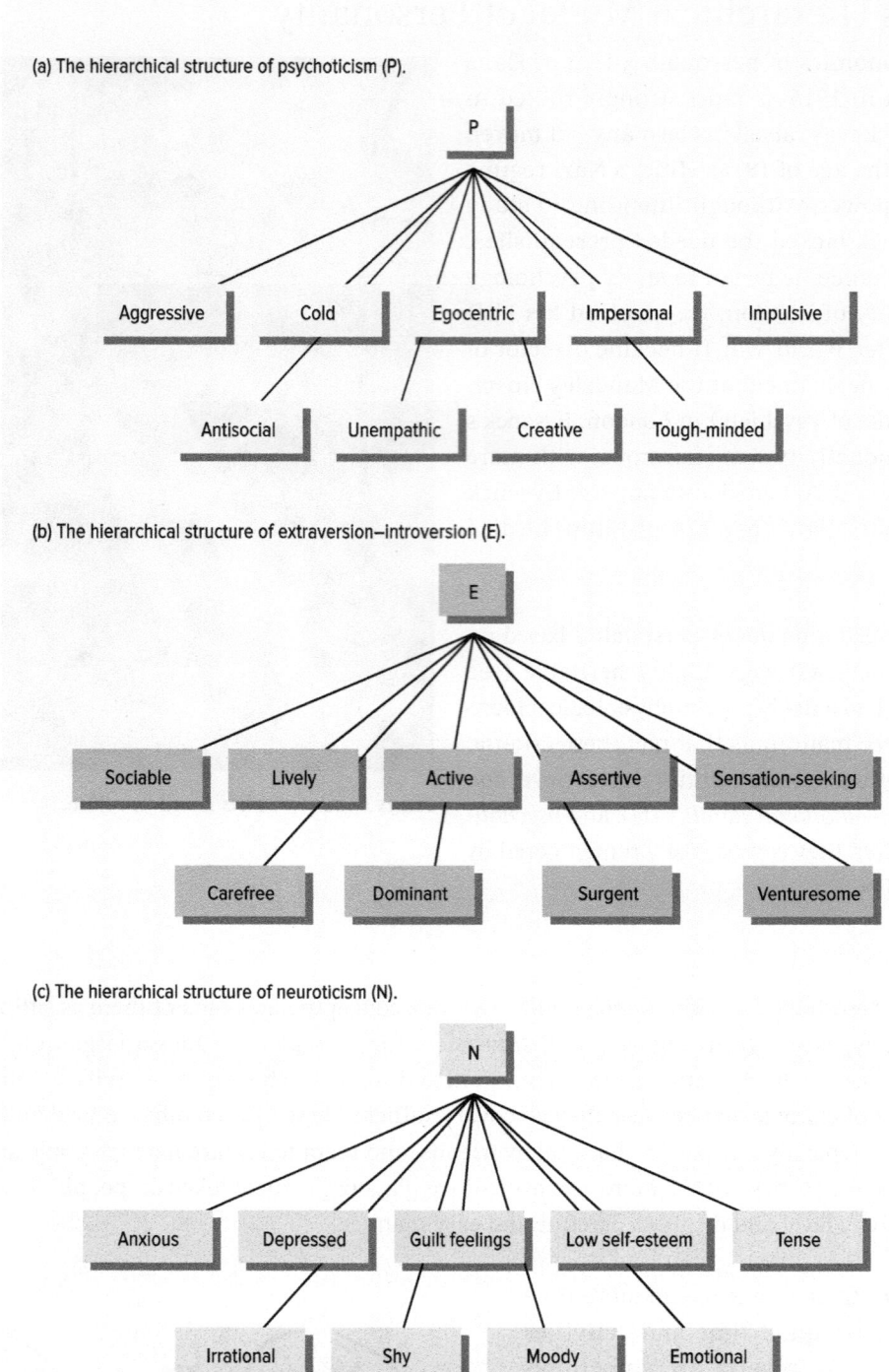

FIGURE 3.1 Eysenck's hierarchical structure of major personality traits. Each "super-trait" (P, E, and N) occupies the highest level in the hierarchy, representing broad personality traits. Each of these broad traits subsumes narrower traits in the hierarchy. (a) The hierarchical structure of psychoticism (P); (b) the hierarchical structure of extraversion–introversion (E); (c) the hierarchical structure of neuroticism–emotional stability (N).

The trait of *neuroticism* (N) consists of a cluster of more specific traits, including anxious, irritable, guilty, lacking self-esteem, tense, shy, and moody. Conceptually, narrow traits such as anxious and irritable might be viewed as very different from each other. Empirically, however, people who feel anxious also tend to get irritated. Thus, factor analysis has proven to be a valuable tool in showing that these two narrow traits are actually linked together, tending to co-occur in individuals.

The typical high scorer on neuroticism (N) tends to be a worrier. Frequently anxious and depressed, the high-N scorer has trouble sleeping and experiences a wide array of psychosomatic symptoms. Indeed, a study of 5,847 North American adults found that those high on neuroticism tend to be especially prone to the disorders of depression and anxiety (Weinstock & Whisman, 2006). One of the hallmarks of the high-N scorer is over-reactivity on the negative emotions. The high-N scorer experiences a greater degree of emotional arousal than the low-N scorer in response to the normal stresses of everyday life. They have more trouble returning to their baseline after an emotionally arousing event. Those high on neuroticism also stay angry longer after a perceived transgression and are less likely to forgive someone who they perceive has violated them (Maltby et al., 2008). They are more likely to be vigilant to threats, particularly social threats such as being socially excluded (Denissen & Penke, 2008b; Tamir, Robinson, & Solberg, 2006). The low-N scorer, on the other hand, is emotionally stable, even-tempered, calm, slower to react to stressful events, and returns to their baseline relatively quickly after an upsetting event.

The third large trait in Eysenck's taxonomy is *psychoticism* (P). As shown in Figure 3.1, P consists of the constellation of narrower traits that includes aggressive, egocentric, creative, impulsive, lacking empathy, and *antisocial* (meaning socially disruptive, not avoidant or anxious). Factor analysis proves valuable in grouping together narrower traits. It has shown, for example, that impulsivity and lack of empathy tend to co-occur in individuals. That is, people who tend to act without thinking (impulsivity) also tend to lack the ability to see situations from other people's perspectives (lack of empathy).

The high-P scorer is typically a solitary individual, often described by others as a "loner." Because they lack empathy, high-P scorers may be cruel or inhumane. Men tend to score twice as high as women on P. Often, such people have a history of cruelty to animals. The high-P scorer may laugh, for example, when a dog gets hit by a car or when someone accidentally gets hurt. High-P scorers show insensitivity to the pain and suffering of others, including their own kin. They are aggressive, both verbally and physically, even with loved ones. The high-P scorer has a strong inclination for the strange and unusual and may disregard danger in pursuit of novelty. They like to make fools of other people and are often described as having antisocial tendencies.

Empirically, the P-scale predicts a number of fascinating criteria. Those who score high on P tend to show a strong preference for violent films and rate violent scenes from films more enjoyable than those who score low on P (Bruggemann & Barry, 2002). High-P individuals prefer unpleasant paintings and photographs more than do low-P individuals (Rawlings, 2003). Men, but not women, who score high on Machiavellianism (a trait involving manipulative and deceptive tendencies, which is highly correlated with P) endorse promiscuous and hostile sexual attitudes—they are more likely than low scorers to divulge sexual secrets to third parties, pretend to be in love when they are not in love, lure potential sex partners with alcoholic drinks, and even report trying to force others into sex acts (McHoskey, 2001). Those who are low in P tend to be more deeply religious, whereas high-P scorers tend to be somewhat cynical about religion (Saroglou, 2002). Finally, high-P scorers are disposed to getting into dangerous activities, such as violence, theft, and vandalism (Carrasco et al., 2006; Pickering et al., 2003).

The labels Eysenck has given to these super-traits, especially P, have generated controversy. Indeed, some suggest that more accurate and appropriate labels for psychoticism might be "antisocial personality" or "psychopathic personality." Another point of controversy is Eysenck's inclusion of creativity as a narrow trait within P, which was founded on evidence suggesting that artists and creative people were not only higher in psychoticism, but also more likely to suffer mental illness. A meta-analysis by Acar and Runco (2012), however, found that research supporting this association was somewhat limited and depended on how both creativity and P were measured. Regardless of the label or its correlates, P has emerged as an important trait in normal-range personality research.

Let's look more closely now at two aspects of Eysenck's system that warrant further comment—its hierarchical nature and its biological underpinnings.

Hierarchical Structure of Eysenck's System

Figure 3.1 shows the levels in Eysenck's hierarchical model, with each super-trait at the top and narrower traits at the second level. Subsumed by each narrow trait, however, is a third level—that of *habitual acts*. For example, one habitual act subsumed by "sociable" might be talking on the phone; another might be taking frequent breaks to socialize with other students. Narrow traits subsume a variety of habitual acts.

At the very lowest level in the hierarchy are *specific acts* (e.g., *I talked with my friend during class* and *I took a coffee break to chat at 10:30 a.m.*). If enough specific acts are repeated frequently, they become habitual acts at the third level. Clusters of habitual acts become narrow traits. And clusters of narrow traits become super-traits at the top of the hierarchy. This hierarchy has the advantage of locating each specific personality-relevant act within a precise nested system. Thus, the fourth-level act *I danced wildly at the party* can be described as extraverted at the highest level, sociable at the second level, and part of a regular habit of party-going behaviour at the third level.

Biological Underpinnings

There are two aspects of the biological underpinnings of Eysenck's personality system that are critical to its understanding: *heritability* and *identifiable physiological substrate*. For Eysenck a key criterion for a "basic" dimension of personality is that it has reasonably high heritability. The behavioural genetic evidence confirms that all three super-traits in Eysenck's taxonomy—P, E, and N—do have moderate heritabilities, although this is also true of many personality traits (see Chapter 6).

The second biological criterion is that basic personality traits should have an identifiable physiological substrate—that is, that one can identify properties in the brain and central nervous system that are presumed to be part of the causal chain that produces personality traits. In Eysenck's formulation, extraversion is supposed to be linked with central nervous system arousal or reactivity. Eysenck predicted that introverts would be more easily aroused (and more autonomically reactive) than extraverts (see Chapter 7). In contrast, he proposed that neuroticism was linked with the degree of *lability* (changeability) of the autonomic nervous system, which explains the higher stress reactivity seen in high-N individuals. Finally, high-P scorers were predicted to be high in testosterone levels and low in levels of MAO, a neurotransmitter inhibitor.

In sum, Eysenck's personality taxonomy has many distinct features. It is hierarchical, starting with broad traits, which subsume narrower traits, which in turn subsume specific actions. The broad traits within the system have been shown to be moderately heritable. And Eysenck has attempted to link these traits with physiological functioning—adding an important level of analysis not included in most personality taxonomies.

Despite these admirable qualities, Eysenck's personality taxonomy has several limitations. One is that many other personality traits also show moderate heritability, not just extraversion, neuroticism, and psychoticism. A second limitation is that Eysenck may have missed some important traits in his taxonomy—a point argued by other personality psychologists, such as Raymond B. Cattell, and more recently by authors such as Lewis Goldberg, Paul Costa, and Robert McCrae.

Circumplex Taxonomies of Personality

People have been fascinated with circles for centuries. They have no beginning and no end, and they symbolize wholeness and unity. Circles have also fascinated personality psychologists as representations of the personality sphere. In the twentieth century, the two most prominent advocates of circular representations of personality were Timothy Leary (also known for his LSD experiments at Harvard) and Jerry Wiggins, who formalized the circular model with modern statistical techniques. (*Circumplex* is simply a fancy word for circle.)

Wiggins (1979) started with the lexical assumption—the idea that all important individual differences are encoded within the natural language. But he went further in his efforts at taxonomy by arguing that trait terms specify different *kinds* of ways in which individuals differ. One kind of individual difference pertains to what people do to and with each other—**interpersonal traits**.

Other kinds of individual differences are specified by the following types of traits: *temperament* traits, such as nervous, gloomy, sluggish, and excitable; *character* traits, such as moral, principled, and dishonest; *material* traits, such as miserly and stingy; *attitude* traits, such as pious and spiritual; *mental* traits, such as clever, logical, and perceptive; and *physical* traits, such as healthy and tough.

Because Wiggins was concerned primarily with *interpersonal* traits, he carefully separated these from the other categories of traits. Then, based on the earlier theorizing of Foa and Foa (1974), he defined *interpersonal* as interactions among people involving exchanges. The two resources that define social exchange are *love* and *status*: "interpersonal events may be defined as *dyadic interactions that have relatively clear-cut social (status) and emotional (love) consequences for both participants*" (Wiggins, 1979, p. 398, italics original). Hence, the dimensions of status and love define the two major axes of the Wiggins circumplex, as shown in Figure 3.2. These two dimensions, status and love, also correspond to the primary traits of **agency** and **communion**, respectively, originally described by Bakan (1966) as underlying many key aspects of social behaviour (Abele & Wojciszke, 2018; Wiggins, 1979).

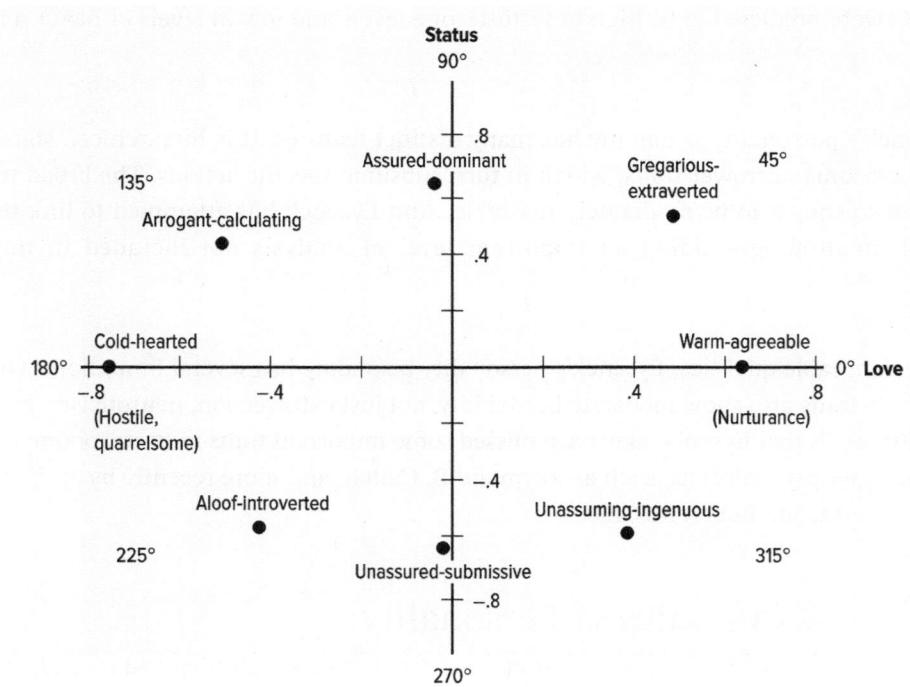

FIGURE 3.2 The circumplex model of personality.

Source: Adapted from "Circular Reasoning About Interpersonal Behavior," by J. S. Wiggins, N. Phillips, and P. Trapnell, 1989, *Journal of Personality & Social Psychology,* 56, p. 297. Copyright 1989 by the American Psychological Association. Reprinted with permission.

There are three clear advantages to the Wiggins circumplex. The first is that it provides an *explicit definition* of interpersonal behaviour. Thus it should be possible to locate any transaction in which the resources of status or love are exchanged within a specific area of the circumplex pie. These include not just giving love (e.g., giving a friend a hug) or granting status (e.g., showing respect or honour to a parent). They also include denying love (e.g., yelling at a boyfriend) and denying status (e.g., dismissing someone as too inconsequential to talk to). Thus the Wiggins circumplex model has the advantage of providing an explicit and precise definition of interpersonal transactions.

The second advantage of Wiggins's model is that the circumplex *specifies the relationships between each trait and every other trait within the model.* There are basically three types of relationships specified by the model. The first is **adjacency**, or how close the traits are to each other in the circumplex. The variables that are adjacent, or next, to each other within the model are positively correlated. Thus gregarious–extraverted is correlated with warm–agreeable. Arrogant–calculating is correlated with hostile–quarrelsome.

Jerry Wiggins developed measurement scales to assess the traits in the circumplex model.

Courtesy of Krista Trobst

The second type of relationship is **bipolarity**. Traits that are bipolar are located at opposite sides of the circle and are negatively correlated with each other. Dominant is the opposite of submissive, so the two are negatively correlated. Cold is the opposite of warm, so they are negatively correlated. Specifying this bipolarity is useful because nearly every interpersonal trait has another trait that is its opposite.

The third type of relationship is **orthogonality**, which specifies that traits that are perpendicular to each other on the model (at 90° of separation, or at right angles to each other) are entirely unrelated to each other. In other words, there is a zero correlation between such traits. Dominance, for example, is orthogonal to agreeableness, so the two are uncorrelated. This means that dominance can be expressed in a quarrelsome manner (e.g., *I yelled in order to get my way*) or in an agreeable manner (e.g., *I organized the group in order to get help for my friend*). Similarly, aggression (quarrelsome) can be expressed in an active/dominant manner (e.g., *I used my position of authority to punish my enemies*) or in an unassured/submissive way (e.g., *I gave him the silent treatment when I was upset*). Orthogonality allows one to specify with greater precision the different ways in which traits are expressed in actual behaviour.

The third key advantage of the circumplex model is that it *alerts investigators to gaps* in investigations of interpersonal behaviour. For example, whereas there have been many studies of dominance and aggression, personality psychologists have paid little attention to traits such as unassuming and calculating. The circumplex model, by providing a map of the interpersonal terrain, directs researchers to these neglected areas of psychological functioning.

In sum, the Wiggins circumplex model provides an elegant map of major individual differences in the social domain. The circumplex structure of interpersonal traits has been discovered in children as well as adults (Di Blas, 2007). It has been used to discover interpersonal sensitivities (Hopwood et al., 2011). For example, people tend to find others unpleasant who have personalities that are the polar opposite of their own. And it has been used to identify some maladaptive aspects of interpersonal functioning: Those who are submissive and agreeable, for example, may be overly accommodating (e.g., allowing themselves to be shortchanged at the store without saying anything) or passively aggressive (e.g., giving others the "silent treatment") (Hennig & Walker, 2008). Despite these positive qualities, the circumplex also has some limitations. The most important limitation is that the interpersonal map is limited to two dimensions. Other traits, not captured by these two dimensions, also have important interpersonal consequences. The trait of conscientiousness, for example, is interpersonal in that individuals high on this trait are very dependable in their social obligations to friends, mates, and children. Even a trait such as neuroticism or emotional stability may show up most strongly in interpersonal transactions with others (e.g., *He overreacted to a subtle interpersonal slight when the host took too long to acknowledge his presence,* and *He insisted that he and his partner leave the party*). A more comprehensive taxonomy of personality that includes these dimensions is known as the five-factor model.

The Five-Factor Model ("Big Five")

In the past few decades, the taxonomy of personality traits that has received the most attention and support from personality researchers has been the **five-factor model**—variously labelled the five-factor model, the Big Five, and even in a humorous vein the High Five (Costa & McCrae, 1995; Goldberg, 1981; McCrae & John, 1992; Saucier & Goldberg, 1996). The broad traits composing the Big Five have been provisionally named (I) *extraversion* or *surgency*, (II) *agreeableness,* (III) *conscientiousness,* (IV) *neuroticism* or *emotional instability,* and (V) *openness–intellect* or *openness to experience.* This five-dimensional taxonomy of personality traits has accrued some persuasive advocates (e.g., John, 1990; McCrae & John, 1992; Rammstedt, Goldberg, & Borg, 2010; Saucier & Goldberg, 1998; Wiggins, 1996), as well as some strong critics (e.g., Block, 1995; McAdams, 1992).

The five-factor model was originally based on a combination of the lexical approach and statistical approaches. The lexical approach started in the 1930s, with the pioneering work of Allport and Odbert (1936), who laboriously went through the English dictionary and identified 17,953 trait terms. Allport and Odbert then divided the trait terms into four lists: (1) *stable traits* (e.g., secure, intelligent), (2) *temporary states, moods, and activities* (e.g., agitated, excited), (3) *social evaluations* (e.g., charming, irritating), and (4) *metaphorical, physical, and doubtful terms* (e.g., prolific, lean).

The terms from the first category, 4,500 presumably stable traits, were subsequently used by Raymond Cattell (1943) as a starting point for his lexical analysis of personality traits. Because of the limited power of computers at the time, however, Cattell could not subject this list to a factor analysis. Instead, he reduced the list to a smaller set of 171 clusters (groups of traits) by eliminating some and lumping together others. He ended up with a smaller set of 35 clusters of personality traits.

Fiske (1949) then took a subset of 22 of Cattell's 35 clusters and discovered, through factor analysis, a five-factor solution. However, this single study of relatively small sample size was hardly a robust foundation for a comprehensive taxonomy of personality traits. In historical treatments of the five-factor model, therefore, Fiske is noted as the first person to discover a version of the five-factor model, but he is not credited with having identified its precise structure.

Tupes and Christal (1961) made the next major contribution to the five-factor taxonomy. They examined the factor structure of the 22 simplified descriptions in eight samples and emerged with the five-factor model: *surgency (extraversion), agreeableness, conscientiousness, emotional stability,* and *culture*. This factor structure was subsequently replicated by Norman (1963), then by a host of other researchers (e.g., Botwin & Buss, 1989; Digman & Inouye, 1986; Goldberg, 1981; McCrae & Costa, 1985; Rammstedt et al., 2010). The key markers that define the Big Five, as originally determined by Norman (1963), are shown in Table 3.3. Note that in this formulation, neuroticism is referred to by its opposite end, emotional stability.

Table 3.3 Norman's Markers for the Big Five

I. Extraversion or Surgency	IV. Emotional stability
Talkative–silent	Calm–anxious
Sociable–reclusive	Composed–excitable
Adventurous–cautious	Not hypochondriacal–hypochondriacal
Open–secretive	Poised–nervous/tense
II. Agreeableness	**V. Culture—Intellect, Openness**
Good-natured–irritable	Intellectual–unreflective/narrow
Cooperative–negativistic	Artistic–nonartistic
Mild/gentle–headstrong	Imaginative–simple/direct
Not jealous–jealous	Polished/refined–crude/boorish
III. Conscientiousness	
Responsible–undependable	
Scrupulous–unscrupulous	
Persevering–quitting	
Fussy/tidy–careless	

Source: Norman, 1963.

The past 25 years have witnessed an explosion of research on the Big Five. Indeed, the Big Five taxonomy has achieved a greater degree of consensus than any other trait taxonomy in the history of personality trait psychology. But it has also generated some controversy. We consider four key issues: (1) What is the empirical evidence for the five-factor taxonomy of personality? (2) What is the identity of the fifth factor? (3) What are the empirical correlates of the five factors? (4) Is the Big Five taxonomy really comprehensive, or are there major trait dimensions that lie beyond the Big Five?

What Is the Empirical Evidence for the Five-Factor Model?

The five-factor model has proven to be astonishingly replicable in studies using English-language trait words as items (Goldberg, 1981, 1990; John et al., 2008; McCrae & Costa, 2008). The five factors have been found by dozens of researchers using different samples. This model has been replicated in every decade for the past half-century. It has been replicated in different languages and in different item formats (Rammstedt et al., 2010).

In its modern form, the Big Five taxonomy has been measured in two major ways. One way is based on self-ratings of single-word trait adjectives, such as *talkative, warm, organized, moody*, and *imaginative* (Goldberg, 1990), and one way is based on self-ratings of sentence items, such as "My life is fast-paced" (McCrae & Costa, 1999). We will discuss these in turn.

Lewis R. Goldberg has done the most systematic research on the Big Five using single-word trait adjectives. According to Goldberg (1990), key adjective markers of the Big Five are as follows:

1. Extraversion (surgency): *talkative, extraverted, assertive, forward, outspoken* versus *shy, quiet, introverted, bashful, inhibited.*
2. Agreeableness: *sympathetic, kind, warm, understanding, sincere* versus *unsympathetic, unkind, harsh, cruel.*
3. Conscientiousness: *organized, neat, orderly, practical, prompt, meticulous* versus *disorganized, disorderly, careless, sloppy, impractical.*
4. Emotional stability (low neuroticism): *calm, relaxed, stable* versus *moody, anxious, insecure.*
5. Intellect or imagination (openness to experience): *creative, imaginative, intellectual* versus *uncreative, unimaginative, unintellectual.*

In addition to measures of the Big Five that use single trait words as items, the most widely used measure using a sentence-length item format has been developed by Paul T. Costa and Robert R. McCrae. It's called the NEO-PI-R: the neuroticism–extraversion–openness (NEO) Personality Inventory (PI) Revised (R) (Costa & McCrae, 1989). Sample items from the NEO-PI-R are neuroticism (N): *I have frequent mood swings*; extraversion (E): *I don't find it easy to take charge of a situation* (reverse scored); openness (O): *I enjoy trying new and foreign foods*; agreeableness (A): *Most people I know like me*; and conscientiousness (C): *I keep my belongings neat and clean.*

❓ Exercise

Your job is to develop a way to measure the Big Five traits in someone you know, such as a friend, a roommate, or a family member. Read the adjectives in Table 3.3 carefully until you have an understanding of each of the Big Five traits. Then, consider the different sources of personality data described in Chapter 2:

1. **Self-report—typically, asking questions on a questionnaire.**
2. **Observer-report—typically, asking someone who knows the subject to report what the subject is like.**

3. **Test data—typically, objective tasks, situations, or physiological recordings that get at manifestations of the trait in question.**
4. **Life-outcome data—aspects of the person's life that may reveal a trait, such as introverted people selecting careers in which there is little contact with others.**

Your job is to assess your target person on each of the Big Five traits, using a combination of data sources. You should first list, for each of the five traits, the way you measured that trait, such as the items on your questionnaire or interview or the life-outcome data. Then, in the second part of your report, indicate how high or low you think your examinee is on each of the five traits.

	Very low	Somewhat low	Average	Somewhat high	Very high
Extraversion					
Agreeableness					
Conscientiousness					
Emotional stability					
Openness–intellect					

You might be thinking at this point that five factors may be too few to capture all of the fascinating complexity of personality. And you may be right. But consider this. Each of the five global personality factors (broad traits) has a host of specific "facets" or narrow traits which provide a lot of subtlety and nuance. The broad trait of conscientiousness, for example, includes these six facets: competence, order, dutifulness, achievement striving, self-discipline, and deliberation. The broad trait of neuroticism has these six facets: anxiety, angry hostility, depression, self-consciousness, impulsivity, and vulnerability. These facets of each global factor go a long way toward adding richness, complexity, and nuance to personality description.

It is worth noting that the NEO-PI-R traits are presented in a different order (N, E, O, A, C) than the Goldberg order, and in a few cases the traits are given different names. Most importantly, emotional stability is referred to as *neuroticism*, which reflects a focus on the dimension's negative or reversed manifestation. Intellect, on the other hand, is referred to as *openness to experience*. Despite the differences in labelling, the underlying personality traits being measured are nearly identical to those found by Goldberg. This convergence between the factor structures of single-trait item formats and sentence-length item formats provides support for the robustness and replicability of the five-factor model (Rammstedt et al., 2010).

What Is the Identity of the Fifth Factor?

Although the five-factor model has achieved impressive replicability across samples, investigators, and item formats, there is still some disagreement about the content and replicability of the fifth factor. Different researchers have variously labelled this fifth factor as *culture, intellect, intellectance, imagination, openness,*

openness to experience, and even *fluid intelligence* and *tender-mindedness* (see Brand & Egan, 1989; De Raad, 1998). A major cause of these differences is that different researchers start with different item pools to factor analyze. Those who start with the lexical strategy and use adjectives as items typically endorse *intellect* as the meaning and label of the fifth factor (Saucier & Goldberg, 1996). In contrast, those who use questionnaire items tend to prefer *openness* or *openness to experience* because this label better reflects the content of those items (McCrae & Costa, 1997, 1999, 2008).

One way to resolve these differences is to go back to the lexical rationale to begin with and to look *across cultures* and *across languages.* According to the lexical approach, traits that emerge universally in different languages and cultures are more important than those that lack cross-cultural universality. What do the cross-cultural data show? In a study conducted in Turkey, a clear fifth factor emerged that is best described as *openness* (Somer & Goldberg, 1999). A different Dutch study found a fifth factor marked by *progressive* at one end and *conservative* at the other (De Raad et al., 1998). In German, the fifth factor represents *intelligence, talents,* and *abilities* (Ostendorf, 1990). In Italian, the fifth factor is *conventionality,* marked by the items *rebellious* and *critical* (Caprara & Perugini, 1994). Looking across all these studies, the fifth factor has proven extremely difficult to pin down, although *openness* and *intellect* best describe the most common content (John, Naumann, & Soto, 2008).

In summary, although the first four factors are highly replicable across cultures and languages, there is uncertainty about the content, naming, and replicability of the fifth factor (De Raad et al., 2010). Perhaps some individual differences are more relevant to some cultures than to others—intellect in some cultures, conventionality in other cultures, and openness in yet other cultures. Clearly, more extensive cross-cultural work is needed, particularly in African cultures and in more traditional cultures that are minimally influenced by Western culture.

What Are the Empirical Correlates of the Five Factors?

Over the past 15 years, a tremendous volume of research has been conducted on the empirical correlates of each of the five factors. This section summarizes some of the most recent interesting findings.

Extraversion. Extraverts love to party—they engage in frequent social interaction, take the lead in livening up dull gatherings, and enjoy talking a lot. Indeed, evidence suggests that **social attention** is the cardinal feature of extraversion (Ashton, Lee, & Paunonen, 2002). From the perspective of the extravert, "the more the merrier." Extraverts have a greater impact on their social environment, often assuming leadership positions, whereas introverts tend to be more like wallflowers (Jensen-Campbell & Graziano, 2001). Extraverted men are more likely to be bold with potential partners they don't know, whereas introverted men tend to be more timid (Berry & Miller, 2001). Extraverts tend to be happier, and this positive affect is experienced most intensely when a person acts in an extraverted manner (Fleeson, Malanos, & Achille, 2002; Oerlemans & Bakker, 2014). Extraversion also has an impact in the workplace. Extraverts tend to be more involved and enjoy their work (Burke, Mattheiesen, & Pallesen, 2006) and show more commitment to their work organization (Erdheim, Wang, & Zickar, 2006). Experiments also show that extraverts are more cooperative than introverts (Hirsh & Peterson, 2009), which might contribute to their positive work experiences. Extraverts tend to be physically stronger than introverts, in part because they engage in more vigorous and frequent physical activity (Fink et al., 2016; Tolea et al., 2012). But there are also downsides—extraverts like to drive fast and listen to music while driving, and as a consequence tend to get into more car accidents, and even road fatalities, than their more introverted peers (Lajunen, 2001). They are less likely than introverts to save money for retirement (Hirsh, 2015). When given a choice, extraverts prefer to spend leisure time on beaches and near oceans, whereas introverts enjoy the solitude of mountains (Oishi et al., 2015).

Agreeableness. Whereas the motto of the extravert might be "let's liven things up," the motto of the highly agreeable person might be "let's all get along." Those who score high on agreeableness favour using negotiation to resolve conflicts; low-agreeable individuals try to assert their power to resolve social conflicts (Graziano & Tobin, 2002; Jensen-Campbell & Graziano, 2001). The agreeable person is also more likely to withdraw from social conflict, avoiding situations that are unharmonious. Agreeable individuals like harmonious social interaction and cooperative family life. They are also highly prosocial and empathic, and enjoy helping others in need (Caprara et al., 2010). They value prosocial behaviours in others, but at the same time tend to judge harshly those who commit antisocial acts (Kammrath & Scholer, 2011). Agreeable children tend to be less often victimized by bullies during early adolescence (Jensen-Campbell et al., 2002). As you might suspect, politicians, at least in Italy, tend to score high on scales of agreeableness (Caprara et al., 2003). Those high on agreeableness seem to be good at reading other people's minds (Nettle & Liddle, 2008), an empathic ability that leads to more forgiveness of the transgressions of other people (Strelan, 2007).

At the other end of the scale of agreeableness lies aggressiveness. Wu and Clark (2003) found that aggressiveness was strongly linked to many everyday behaviours. Examples include hitting someone else in anger, blowing up when things don't work properly, slamming doors, yelling, getting into arguments, clenching fists, raising voices, being intentionally rude, damaging someone's property, pushing and hitting others, and slamming down the phone. So the next time you think about getting into an argument with someone, you might want to find out where they are on the agreeableness–aggressiveness disposition.

Agreeable individuals, in short, get along well with others, are well liked, avoid conflict, strive for harmonious family lives, and may selectively prefer professions in which their likeability is an asset. Disagreeable individuals are aggressive and seem to get themselves into a lot of social conflict.

Conscientiousness. If extraverts party it up and agreeable people get along, then conscientious individuals are industrious and get ahead. The hard work, punctuality, and reliable behaviour exhibited by conscientious individuals result in a host of life outcomes such as a higher grade point average (Conrad, 2006; Noftle & Robins, 2007; Poropat, 2009), greater job satisfaction, greater job security, and more positive and committed social relationships (Langford, 2003). Those who score low on conscientiousness, in contrast, are likely to perform more poorly at school and at work. The fact that highly conscientious individuals succeed in the work domain is likely due to three key correlates. They do not procrastinate, in contrast to their low-conscientiousness peers whose motto might be "never put off until tomorrow what you can put off until the day after tomorrow" (Lee, Kelly, & Edwards, 2006). Second, they tend to be perfectionists, setting high standards for themselves (Cruce et al., 2012; Stoeber, Otto, & Dalbert, 2009) and score high on achievement motivation (Richardson & Abraham, 2009). And those high in conscientiousness are exceptionally industrious, putting in the long hours of diligent hard work needed to get ahead (Lund et al., 2006). Those high on conscientiousness are more likely to stick with good plans for physical exercise (Bogg, 2008) and consequently are less likely to gain weight when they reach middle age (Brummett et al., 2006). High scorers on conscientiousness also display more passion and perseverance for long-term goals (Duckworth et al., 2007), including academic success in university (O'Connor & Paunonen, 2007). And they are more likely to do volunteer work when they retire from their jobs (Mike et al., 2014).

Low C is linked with risky sexual behaviours, such as failing to use condoms (Trobst et al., 2002) and being more responsive to other potential partners while already in an existing romantic relationship (Schmitt & Buss, 2001). Among a sample of prisoners, low-C scorers tend to have frequent arrests (Clower & Bothwell, 2001). The high-C individual, in sum, tends to perform well in school and work, avoids breaking the rules, and has a more stable and secure romantic relationship. But there does appear to be at least one downside to being highly conscientious—high scorers, compared to low scorers, experience a substantial drop in psychological well-being when they are unemployed for extended periods of time (Boyce et al., 2010).

Neuroticism (emotional instability). Life poses stresses and hurdles that everyone must confront. The dimension of neuroticism (or *emotional instability,* as it is often referred) taps into the way people cope with these stresses. Emotionally stable individuals, or those low on neuroticism, are like boats that remain on course through choppy waters. Emotionally unstable people, or those high on neuroticism, get buffeted about by the waves and are more likely to get knocked off course. The hallmark of neuroticism is variability of mood over time—such people swing up and down more than emotionally stable individuals (Murray, Allen, & Trinder, 2002).

Individuals high on neuroticism experience more fatigue over the course of the day (De Vries & Van Heck, 2002) and experience more grief and depression after the death of a loved one (Winjgaards-de Meij et al., 2007). Psychologically, these individuals are more likely to have dissociative experiences such as an inability to recall important life events, feeling disconnected from life and other people, and feeling like they've woken up in a strange or unfamiliar place (Kwapil, Wrobel, & Pope, 2002). Those high on neuroticism also tend to have more frequent suicidal ideation than those low on neuroticism (Chioqueta & Stiles, 2005; Stewart et al., 2008). Those high on neuroticism report poorer physical health, more physical symptoms, and fewer attempts to engage in health-promoting behaviours (Williams, O'Brien, & Colder, 2004). They also engage in health-impairing behaviours, such as drinking alcohol as a means of coping with, and attempting to forget about, their problems (Theakston et al., 2004).

Interpersonally, those high on neuroticism have more ups and downs in their social relationships. In the sexual domain, for example, emotionally unstable individuals experience more sexual anxiety (e.g., worried about performance) as well as a greater fear of engaging in sex (Heaven et al., 2003; Shafer, 2001). And with highly stressful events, such as an unwanted loss of a pregnancy, individuals high on neuroticism are more likely to develop posttraumatic stress disorder (PTSD), in which the psychological trauma of the loss is experienced profoundly and for a long time (Engelhard, van den Hout, & Kindt, 2003).

Neuroticism augers poorly for professional success. This may be partly due to the fact that emotionally unstable people are thrown off track by the everyday stresses and strains that we all go through. It may be partly due to their experience of greater emotional fatigue and burnout (Bakker, Van Der Zee, Lewig, & Dollard, 2006). But it may also be attributable to the fact that they engage in a lot of "self-handicapping" (Ross, Canada, & Rausch, 2002). Self-handicapping is defined as a tendency to "create obstacles to successful achievement in performance or competitive situations in order to protect one's self-esteem" (Ross et al., 2002, p. 2). Nonetheless, those high on neuroticism actually outperform their more emotionally stable counterparts in an office setting when changes in the work needs create an unusually busy work environment (Smillie et al., 2006). In sum, the affective volatility that comes with being high on neuroticism affects many spheres of life, from sexuality to achievement.

Personality characteristics predict who will climb mountains.
©OJO Images/Getty Images

Openness to experience (intellect-openness). Would you agree or disagree with the following statements? "Upon awakening during the night, I am unsure whether I actually experienced something or only dreamed about it," "I am aware that I am dreaming, even as I dream," "I am able to control or direct the content of my dreams," "A dream helped me to solve a current problem or concern" (Watson, 2003). If you tend to agree with these statements, you probably score high on openness to experience (sometimes referred to as "openness–intellect" or simply "openness" for short). Those who are high on openness tend to remember their dreams more, have more waking dreams, have more vivid dreams, have more prophetic dreams (dreaming about something that later happens), and have more problem-solving dreams (Watson, 2003).

Openness has been linked to experimentation with new foods, a liking for novel experiences, and even "openness" to having extramarital affairs (Buss, 1993). One possible cause of openness may lie in individual differences in the processing of information. Those high in openness have more difficulty ignoring previously experienced stimuli (Peterson, Smith, & Carson, 2002). It's as though the perceptual and information processing "gates" of highly open people are literally more "open" to receiving information coming at them from a variety of sources. Perhaps that is why high openness is linked with measures of creativity (Nusbaum & Silvia, 2011). Less-open people have more tunnel vision and find it easier to ignore competing stimuli. Those high in openness exhibit less prejudice against minority groups and are less likely to hold negative racial stereotypes (Flynn, 2005). They also are more likely to get tattoos and body piercings (Nathanson, Paulhus, & Williams, 2006; Tate & Shelton, 2008). High open people tend to be more politically liberal, especially when there is an external threat such as terrorism (Sibley et al., 2012). They excel in achievement in the arts (Kaufman et al., 2016) and show higher levels of musical sophistication (Greenberg et al., 2015). Openness also predicts more cross-sex friendships on social networks such as Facebook (Lönnqvist et al., 2014). In sum, openness has been correlated with a host of other fascinating variables from intrusive stimuli to possible alternative sex partners.

Combinations of Big Five variables. Many life outcomes, of course, are better predicted by combinations of personality dispositions than by single personality dispositions. Here are a few examples.

- *Good grades* are best predicted by conscientiousness (high) and emotional stability (high) (Chamorro-Premuzic & Furnham, 2003a, 2003b). One reason might be that emotionally stable and conscientious people are less likely to procrastinate (Watson, 2001).
- *Academic dishonesty* is more likely among those low in conscientiousness and low in agreeableness (Giluk & Postlethwaite, 2015).
- *Educational attainment and earnings* are predicted by high emotional stability, openness, and conscientiousness (O'Connell & Sheikh, 2011).
- *Risky sexual behaviours,* such as having many sex partners and not using condoms, are best predicted by high extraversion, high neuroticism, low conscientiousness, and low agreeableness (Miller et al., 2004; Trobst et al., 2002).
- *Alcohol consumption* is best predicted by high extraversion and low conscientiousness (Paunonen, 2003; Hong & Paunonen, 2009). A study of more than 5,000 workers in Finland found that low conscientiousness also predicts *increases* in alcohol consumption over time; that is, who ends up becoming a heavy drinker (Grano et al., 2004).
- *Substance abuse disorders,* such as illegal drug abuse, are linked to high neuroticism and low conscientiousness (Kotov et al., 2010).
- *Propensity to engage in disordered eating behaviours*, including anorexic and bulimic tendencies, is associated with high neuroticism and low extraversion (i.e., high introversion) among female university students in Canada (Miller, Schmidt, Vaillancourt, McDougall, & Laliberte, 2006).

- *Pathological gambling* is best predicted by a combination of high neuroticism and low conscientiousness (Bagby et al., 2007; Myrseth et al., 2009; MacLaren et al., 2011).
- *Aggression* against other people when angry is well predicted by neuroticism, but being high on agreeableness appears to cool the tempers that these emotionally unstable people sometimes experience (Ode, Robinson, & Wilkowski, 2008).
- *Mount Everest mountain climbers* tend to be extraverted, emotionally stable, and high on psychoticism (Egan & Stelmack, 2003).
- *Happiness* and experiencing positive affect in everyday life are best predicted by high extraversion and low neuroticism (Cheng & Furnham, 2003; Steel & Ones, 2002; Stewart, Ebmeier, & Deary, 2005; Yik & Russell, 2001).
- *Proclivity to engage in volunteer work,* such as campus or community services, is best predicted by a combination of high agreeableness and high extraversion (Carlo et al., 2005).
- *Workers who decline to become union members* are low on extraversion and high on emotional stability (Parkes & Razavi, 2004).
- *Forgiveness,* the proclivity to forgive those who have committed some wrong, characterizes individuals who are high on agreeableness and high on emotional stability (Brose et al., 2005; Steiner et al., 2012).
- *Leadership effectiveness* in business settings is best predicted by high extraversion, high agreeableness, high conscientiousness, and high emotional stability (Silverthorne, 2001).
- *Propensity to have children* is predicted by high extraversion (sociability) and high emotional stability (Jokela et al., 2009).
- *Favourable attitudes toward being touched by an intimate partner* are most strongly felt by those high in agreeableness and high in openness to experience (Dorros, Hanzal, & Segrin, 2008).

We should not be surprised that combinations of personality variables often do better than single variables in predicting important life outcomes, and we can expect future research to focus increasingly on these combinations.

Is the Five-Factor Model Comprehensive?

Critics of the five-factor model argue that it leaves out important aspects of personality. Almagor, Tellegen, and Waller (1995), for example, present evidence for seven factors. Their results suggest the addition of two factors: *positive evaluation* (e.g., *outstanding* versus *ordinary*) and *negative evaluation* (e.g., *awful* versus *decent*). Goldberg, one of the proponents of the five-factor model, has discovered that factors such as *religiosity* and *spirituality* sometimes emerge as separate factors, although these are clearly smaller in size (accounting for less variance) than those of the Big Five (Goldberg & Saucier, 1995).

Lanning (1994), using items from the California Adult Q-Sort, has found a replicable sixth factor, which he labels *attractiveness,* including the items *physically attractive, sees self as attractive,* and *charming.* In a related vein, Schmitt and Buss (2000) have found reliable individual differences in the sexual sphere, such as *sexiness* (e.g., sexy, stunning, attractive, alluring, arousing, sensual, and seductive) and *faithfulness* (e.g., faithful, monogamous, devoted, and not adulterous). These individual difference dimensions are correlated with the five factors: *sexiness* is positively correlated with *extraversion,* and *faithfulness* is positively correlated with both *agreeableness* and *conscientiousness.* But these correlations leave much of the individual variation unaccounted for, suggesting that these individual differences in sexuality are not completely subsumed by the five-factor model.

Paunonen and colleagues identified 10 personality traits that appear to fall outside of the five-factor model: Conventionality, Seductiveness, Manipulativeness, Thriftiness, Humorousness, Integrity, Femininity,

Religiosity, Risk Taking, and Egotism (Paunonen, 2002; Paunonen et al., 2003). Other researchers have confirmed that these traits are not highly correlated with the Big Five and that they highlight many interesting facets of personality at a more specific level than the "global" factors represented by the five-factor model (Lee, Ogunfowora, & Ashton, 2005).

Proponents of the five-factor model are typically open-minded about the potential inclusion of factors beyond the five factors, if and when the empirical evidence warrants it (Costa & McCrae, 1995; Goldberg & Saucier, 1995). Nonetheless, these researchers have not found the evidence for additional factors beyond the Big Five to be compelling. *Positive* and *negative evaluation,* some have argued, are not really separate factors but, rather, false factors that emerge simply because raters tend to evaluate all things as either good or bad (McCrae & John, 1992). With respect to the *attractiveness* factor found by Lanning (1994), Costa and McCrae (1995) argue that *attractiveness* is not ordinarily considered to be a personality trait, although the *charming* item that loads on this factor surely would be considered part of personality. The expansion of the five-factor model to the six-factor HEXACO model is another exciting new development in personality psychology, and illustrates important progress in this vibrant science. We explore this model further in the next section.

One approach to personality factors beyond the Big Five has been to explore **personality-descriptive nouns** rather than adjectives. Saucier (2003) has discovered eight fascinating factors within the domain of personality nouns such as: *Dumbbell* (e.g., dummy, twit), *Babe/Cutie* (e.g., beauty, darling, doll), *Philosopher* (e.g., genius, artist, individualist), *Lawbreaker* (e.g., pothead, drunk, rebel), *Joker* (e.g., clown, goof, comedian), and *Jock* (e.g., sportsman, tough, machine). A study of personality nouns in the Italian language revealed a somewhat different organization than that of the Big Five, discovering factors such as Honesty, Humility, and Cleverness (Di Blas, 2005). As Saucier concludes, "Personality taxonomies based on adjectives are unlikely to be comprehensive, because type-nouns have different content emphases" (Saucier, 2003, p. 695).

In addition to the possibility of discovering dimensions *beyond* the Big Five, some researchers have had excellent success in predicting important behavioural criteria from *within* the Big Five using the *facets* of the Big Five (Paunonen & Ashton, 2001a, 2001b). For example, in predicting course grades, Paunonen and Ashton (2001a) found significantly greater predictability from the facet subscales of *Need for Achievement* (a facet of conscientiousness) and *Need for Understanding* (a facet of openness) than from the higher-level factor measures of conscientiousness and openness themselves. Similarly, although job performance is well predicted by global measures of conscientiousness, even better prediction of job performance is attained by including the facet measures such as achievement, dependability, order, and cautiousness (Dudley et al., 2006). Paunonen and Ashton (2001a) conclude that "the aggregation of narrow trait measures into broad factor measures can be counterproductive from the point of view of both behavior prediction and behavior explanation" (p. 78).

The five-factor model has also drawn articulate critics, such as McAdams (1992) and Block (1995, 2010). Block, for example, argues that these five factors, although perhaps useful for laypersons in everyday life, fail to capture the underlying causal personality processes that interest researchers. Describing someone as high on neuroticism, for example, may be useful in social communication or global character descriptions, but it does not capture the underlying psychological processes involved in such things as feeling guilty, obsessing over worst-case scenarios, and worrying excessively when someone fails to respond to an e-mail message.

Proponents of the five-factor model respond to these criticisms by suggesting that the Big Five taxonomy has been proposed merely as a framework for the phenotypic attributes of personality that have become encoded within the natural language and makes no claims about the underlying personality processes (Goldberg & Saucier, 1995; John & Naumann, 2010). Debates such as these are the essence of the scientific enterprise and indicate a healthy and thriving field.

The HEXACO Model

In pursuit of additional personality factors beyond the Big Five, some researchers have revisited the lexical approach, examining large pools of trait adjectives in different languages (De Raad & Barelds, 2008). In an important development, Canadian researchers Michael Ashton (Brock University) and Kibeom Lee (University of Calgary) identified a sixth factor of personality not included in the popular five-factor model: **Honesty–Humility** (or "H" for short). While they were still graduate students at Western University, Ashton and Lee discovered that previous studies as well as their own converged on six rather than five factors. It was an early collaborative study of seven languages (Dutch, French, German, Hungarian, Italian, Korean, and Polish) that first demonstrated variants of the Big Five plus an additional factor (Ashton et al., 2004). What's more, this honesty–humility trait seemed to explain important aspects of human personality and behaviour not previously captured by the five-factor model, leading to the proposal of the **HEXACO model** of personality.

At one end of the honesty–humility factor lie trait adjectives such as *honest, sincere, trustworthy,* and *unselfish*; the other end is anchored by adjectives such as *arrogant, conceited, greedy, pompous, self-important,* and *egotistical*. Independent investigators have also found versions of this sixth factor in Greece (Saucier et al., 2005) and Italy (Di Blas, 2005). Those low on H tend to be egotistical and interpersonally exploitative, are more likely to sabotage others in their work environment, and are even more likely to engage in antisocial and criminal activity (Johnson et al., 2011; Zettler & Hilbig, 2010). Such people are also more likely to seek revenge against former romantic partners (Sheppard & Boon, 2012). The low end of honesty–humility captures several unpleasant interpersonal traits, most notably excessive self-admiration (narcissism), an exploitative and manipulative interpersonal style (Machiavellianism), and antisocial tendencies (subclinical psychopathy, i.e., psychopathic tendencies that exist within a normal range). This cluster of negative traits, called the "Dark Triad" of personality, appears to involve an important dispositional domain beyond the Big Five, such that these less desirable characteristics have been shown to predict key behavioural outcomes (Paulhus & Williams, 2002; Veselka, Schermer, & Vernon, 2012). We examine the "dark" traits, which now also include dispositional sadism, further in Highlight On Canadian Research: Exploring the "Dark" Side of Personality.

It is not simply in the proposal of a sixth trait that the HEXACO model differs significantly from earlier five-factor taxonomies. Other factors in the model, namely *emotionality* and *agreeableness,* include slight variations in their trait adjectives. Below is a summary of adjective markers that comprise each of the six factors in the HEXACO model as they have been identified across lexical studies (from Ashton & Lee, 2007). One of the key differences between the HEXACO model and other five-factor models is the inclusion of anger under agreeableness rather than emotionality, where most adjectives traditionally associated with neuroticism have been positioned.

1. **Honesty–Humility (H):** *sincere, honest, faithful/loyal, modest/unassuming, fair-minded* (versus *sly, greedy, pretentious, hypocritical, boastful, pompous*)
2. **Emotionality (E):** *emotional, oversensitive, sentimental, fearful, anxious, vulnerable* (versus *brave, tough, independent, self-assured, stable*)
3. **eXtraversion (X):** *outgoing, lively, extraverted, sociable, talkative, cheerful, active* (versus *shy, passive, withdrawn, introverted, quiet, reserved*)

4. **Agreeableness (A):** *patient, tolerant, peaceful, mild, agreeable, lenient, gentle* (versus *ill-tempered, quarrelsome, stubborn, choleric*)
5. **Conscientiousness (C):** *organized, disciplined, diligent, careful, thorough, precise* (versus *sloppy, negligent, reckless, lazy, irresponsible, absent-minded*)
6. **Openness to Experience (O):** *intellectual, creative, unconventional, innovative, ironic* (versus *shallow, unimaginative, conventional*)

Research supporting the HEXACO model points to an exciting expansion of the fundamental factors of personality within the dispositional domain, allowing psychologists to offer more accurate explanations for individual differences (Ashton & Lee, 2008, 2010; Ashton, Lee, & de Vries, 2014; Ashton, Lee, & Goldberg, 2004; Lee & Ashton, 2008). Most recently, this has included the successful prediction of values (Anglim et al., 2017) and aspects of psychopathology (Durand, 2017). So much evidence has accumulated that some argue the HEXACO model may be the most comprehensive cross-language taxonomy of personality to date.

 # Highlight On Canadian Research

Exploring the "Dark" Side of Personality

Canadian psychologist Del Paulhus (University of British Columbia) has dedicated much of his research career to better understanding the "dark" expressions of human personality. What does it mean to say that certain traits are *dark*? According to Paulhus and Williams (2002), dark traits are those which are socially malevolent and involve behavioural tendencies toward self-promotion, emotional coldness, deceitfulness, and aggressiveness.

Paulhus and his colleagues originally identified three dark traits that had long been associated with disruptions and transgressions in social relationships: *Machiavellianism, narcissism,* and *subclinical psychopathy*. Constituting a **Dark Triad** of personality (Paulhus & Williams, 2002), these interrelated traits are defined as follows:

- **Machiavellianism** is the tendency to be cunning, deceptive, exploitative, and manipulative in interpersonal relationships in order to advocate self-interest. Machiavellianism is discussed at greater length in Chapter 15.
- **Narcissism** is the tendency towards grandiosity, entitlement, and superiority, with frequent and excessive attention-seeking behaviour. It is distinct from *Narcissistic Personality Disorder* (explored further in Chapter 19).
- **Subclinical psychopathy** is the tendency towards high impulsivity and thrill-seeking behaviour, along with low empathy and anxiety, which together are associated with selfish and antisocial (or socially disruptive) behaviour. It is distinct from both *Antisocial Personality Disorder* and psychopathy (discussed in Chapter 19).

Links among these traits have been recognized by psychologists for quite some time. Empirical evidence supports overlap among all three traits, particularly in their uncooperative and socially problematic tendencies. Yet research by Del Paulhus has confirmed that the traits are distinct, despite commonly co-occurring in the population (Furnham, Richards, & Paulhus, 2013; Paulhus & Williams, 2002). When individuals are high on one of the traits, they have a greater likelihood of being high on the others.

In terms of their relationships to the Big Five and HEXACO models, research has demonstrated consistent associations among all three traits and both low agreeableness (Paulhus & Williams, 2002) and low honesty–humility (Hodson et al., 2018). Narcissism and subclinical psychopathy are also associated with higher extraversion, while Machiavellianism and subclinical psychopathy have been associated with lower conscientiousness (Paulhus & Williams, 2002) and higher neuroticism (Jakobwitz & Egan, 2006). Despite their overlap, research has supported a number of differences among the dark traits. High Machiavellianism is more highly correlated with a tendency to plagiarize essays (Nathanson, Paulhus, & Williams, 2006); high narcissism is associated with greater self-enhancement (Paulhus & Williams, 2002) and the tendency to become aggressive when threatened or criticized (Jones & Paulhus, 2010); and subclinical psychopathy is associated with a greater likelihood to bully others (Baughman et al., 2012) and carry out revenge fantasies (DeLongis, Nathanson, & Paulhus, 2011).

Dispositional sadism has been proposed as a fourth related yet distinct trait, forming what is referred to as the **Dark Tetrad** (Chabrol et al., 2009; Furnham et al., 2013). Dispositional sadism refers specifically to the tendency to gain enjoyment from hurting others. It can occur directly, as in actually causing pain or displeasure in others, or vicariously, through watching movies or playing video games. Despite a tendency towards unprovoked aggression in all four dark traits, those high in dispositional sadism are far more likely to work for the opportunity to hurt an innocent person. In experimental research, high sadism was associated with a greater tendency to voluntarily kill bugs (Buckels, Jones, & Paulhus, 2013).

More recently, the Dark Tetrad has also been found to predict trolling behaviour on dating apps (March et al., 2017) and cyberbullying and cyberstalking behaviours on social media platforms (Kircaburun et al., 2018), further verifying the malevolent nature of this cluster of traits.

🛈 Concept Check

What does it mean when personality psychologists describe trait taxonomies as hierarchical in nature? Consider the example of extraversion from the perspective of Eysenck's model specifically.

Compare and contrast the five-factor (Big Five) model with the HEXACO model, naming the broad traits or factors contained in each. How does the HEXACO model improve upon the Big Five?

What are the key "dark" traits identified by personality psychologists?

Summary and Evaluation

This chapter focused on three fundamental issues for a personality psychology based on traits: how to conceptualize traits, how to identify the most important traits, and how to formulate a comprehensive taxonomy of traits.

There are two basic conceptualizations of traits. The first views traits as the internal properties of persons that cause behaviour. In this conception, traits cause the outward behavioural manifestations. The second conceptualization views traits as descriptive summaries of overt behaviour. The summary view does not assume that traits cause behaviour; rather, it treats the issue of cause separately, to be examined after the behavioural summaries are identified.

There have been three major approaches to identifying the most important traits. The first is the lexical approach, which views all the important traits as captured by the natural language. The lexical approach uses synonym frequency and cross-cultural universality as the criteria for identifying important traits. The second approach, the statistical approach, adopts statistical procedures, such as factor analysis, and attempts to identify clusters of traits that covary. The third approach, the theoretical approach, uses an existing theory of personality to determine which traits are important. In practice, personality psychologists sometimes use blends of these three approaches—for example, by starting with the lexical approach to identify the universe of traits and then applying statistical procedures to identify groups of traits that covary and form larger factors.

The third fundamental issue—formulating an overarching taxonomy of personality traits—has yielded several solutions. Eysenck developed a hierarchical model in which the broad traits *extraversion, neuroticism,* and *psychoticism* subsume more narrow traits, such as activity level, moodiness, and egocentricity. Eysenck's taxonomy is based on a factor analysis but is also explicitly anchored in biological underpinnings, including a heritable basis for the traits and the identification of the underlying physiological basis for the traits.

Circumplex taxonomies of personality have been more narrowly targeted toward the domain of interpersonal traits as opposed to the entire personality sphere. Circumplex models are circular arrangements of traits organized around two key dimensions—status (dominance) and love (agreeableness).

The five-factor model of personality is a taxonomy that includes the circumplex in that the first two traits in the model—*extraversion* and *agreeableness*—are roughly the same as the circumplex dimensions of *dominance* and *agreeableness*. In addition, however, the five-factor model includes *conscientiousness, emotional stability,* and *openness–intellect.* The five-factor model has been criticized for not being comprehensive and for being inadequate for understanding underlying psychological processes. Recent evidence points to the exciting discovery of a sixth factor—*Honesty–Humility*—that necessitates an expansion of the Big Five. Some now argue for the cross-cultural robustness of a six-factor personality structure, the HEXACO model: Honesty–Humility (H), Emotionality (E), Extraversion (X), Agreeableness (A), Conscientiousness (C), and Openness to Experience (O). This development is likely the most important advance in personality taxonomy in the past 20 years.

 Concept Check

Imagine you are a researcher who is interested in studying key personality traits in a large population of students. Which model of personality would you rely on, and why?

If no such models of personality were at your disposal, how would you go about determining which traits are most important for describing the differences among us?

Key Terms

lexical approach	theoretical approach	synonym frequency
statistical approach	lexical hypothesis	cross-cultural universality

factor analysis

factor loadings

sociosexual orientation

interpersonal traits

agency

communion

adjacency

bipolarity

orthogonality

five-factor model

extraversion

social attention

agreeableness

conscientiousness

neuroticism (emotional instability)

openness to experience (intellect-openness)

combinations of Big Five variables

personality-descriptive nouns

Honesty–Humility

HEXACO model

Dark Triad

Macchiavellianism

narcissism

subclinical psychopathy

dispositional sadism

Dark Tetrad

CHAPTER 4

Theoretical and Measurement Issues in Trait Psychology

The Dispositional Domain

Sarah was a university student in her second year with a double major in math and computer science. She was a bit shy, especially around people her own age. Although she wanted to date more, she was very particular about the characteristics she looked for in a potential partner. She decided that a Web-based dating service might be an efficient way to find someone to date. She signed up with an Internet dating service and discovered that the first step was to complete an extensive personality questionnaire. She answered a lot of questions about her likes and dislikes, her habits, her traits, and what others thought of her. She even answered questions about the kind of car she owned. Following this, the site returned the personality profiles of a few people who, the site claimed, would be good matches for Sarah. One looked particularly interesting to her, so she spent a couple of hours with this person in online chat sessions. Sarah decided to call her potential match a couple of times on the phone. They had a lot in common, and they both seemed to enjoy the conversations, so they decided to take the next step and meet in person. When they made arrangements for a dinner date, Sarah was surprised to learn that they both lived in the same apartment complex. They may have seen one another, or even spoken, and not remembered it. But it took an Internet dating service, using a program that matched their personalities, for them to actually find one other.

There are many Internet-based dating services, and many of these use personality psychologists to help them do a better job of matching people. For example, the website eHarmony.com uses a 480-item personality questionnaire. The site also presents the applicant with a list of "bad behaviours" and asks them to check off those they "absolutely cannot stand" in someone they date. This dating service uses a combined matching system that relies on selecting matches on major personality traits and then deselecting based on what the applicant says he or she cannot tolerate in another. Other Internet dating services, such as chemistry.com, plentyoffish.com, or okcupid.com, also gather extensive personality data and engage in sophisticated matching routines. Personality psychologists have been accumulating evidence over the past half-century that personality similarity is a significant predictor of whether people will be attracted to each other (Izard, 1960) and whether they will be satisfied with their relationship once it is established (Decuyper, De Bolle, & De Fruyt, 2012).

Matching on personality traits sounds like a great idea, but it works only to the extent that people are telling the truth about themselves when they answer the questionnaires. People can represent themselves falsely in terms of physical characteristics (e.g., say they are petite when they are not, say they have thick, wavy hair when they are in fact bald), and they may represent themselves falsely in terms of their personality. They may, for example, try to cover up an aggressive, abusive personality. Consequently, some of these dating services are very concerned about safety and are using techniques from personality assessment to detect potential problem clients. For example, some sites ask about minor misbehaviours, such as "I never resent being asked to return a favour" or "I have, on occasion, told a white lie." People who deny a lot of these common faults raise a red flag because they are probably misrepresenting themselves on all the questionnaires.

Signing up for an Internet dating service often involves answering a personality trait questionnaire.
©Peter Scholey/Photographer's Choice/Getty Images

A key task for a first date is determining what you have in common with the other person— that is, how similar your personalities are.
©Image Source, all rights reserved

This use of personality testing brings into focus several questions about the measurement of traits. Do traits represent consistent behaviour patterns, such that we could make accurate predictions about a person's future based on their trait standings? How do personality traits interact with situations, particularly social situations? Are there ways to detect that someone is not telling the truth on a personality questionnaire? Are some people motivated to fake good or to fake bad on questionnaires?

Personality measures are also used in other selection situations, such as for jobs or for prison parole or for placement within an organization. What are some of the legal issues in using personality measures to make such decisions? Are there some common problems with selection procedures? Can an employer use a measure of "integrity" to screen out potentially dishonest employees? What about selecting people for admission into university, law school, or medical school on the basis of aptitude tests or other so-called intelligence tests? Although many of these questions seem abstract, they are important to how we think about personality traits and their measurement in business, industry, and education.

Theoretical Issues

Trait theories of personality offer a collection of viewpoints about the fundamental building blocks of human nature. As we saw in Chapter 3, there are differences among the various theories concerning what constitutes a trait, how many traits exist, and what the best methods are for discovering basic traits. Despite their differences, trait theories share three important assumptions about personality traits. These assumptions go beyond any one theory or taxonomy of personality traits and so form the basic foundation for trait psychology. These three important assumptions are

- meaningful individual differences,
- stability or consistency over time, and
- consistency across situations.

Meaningful Differences Among Individuals

Trait psychologists are primarily interested in determining the ways in which people are *different from each other.* Any meaningful way in which people differ from each other may potentially be identified as a personality trait. Some people like to talk a lot; others don't. Some people are active; others are couch potatoes. Some people enjoy working on difficult puzzles; others avoid mental challenges. Because of its emphasis on the study of differences among people, trait psychology has sometimes been called **differential psychology** in the interest of distinguishing this field from other branches of personality psychology (Anastasi, 1976). Differential psychology includes the study of other forms of individual differences in addition to personality traits, such as abilities, aptitudes, and intelligence. In this chapter, however, we focus mainly on personality traits.

Historically, the trait perspective has been concerned with accurate measurement. It takes a quantitative approach, which emphasizes how much a given individual differs from the average. Of all the perspectives and strategies for studying personality, the trait approach is the most mathematically and statistically oriented due to its emphasis on amount (Paunonen & Hong, 2015). You might be wondering how the vast differences among people could be captured and represented by a few key personality traits. How is it that the uniqueness of every individual can be portrayed by just a few traits? Trait psychologists are somewhat like chemists. They argue that by combining a few primary traits in various amounts, they can distill the unique qualities of every individual. This process is analogous to that of combining the three primary colours. Every visible colour in the spectrum, from dusty mauve to burnt umber, is created through various combinations of the three primary colours: red, green, and blue. According to trait psychologists, every personality, no matter how complex or unusual, is the product of a particular combination of a few basic and primary traits.

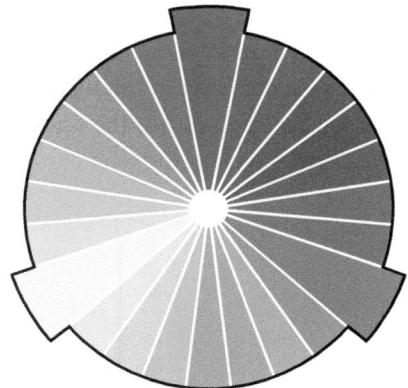

The Colour Wheel. The infinite hues of colour are created from a combination of three primary colours. Similarly, trait psychologists hold that the infinite variety of personalities are created from a combination of a few primary traits.

Consistency over Time

The second assumption made by all trait theories is that there is a degree of **consistency** in personality over time. If someone is highly extraverted during one period of observation, trait psychologists tend to assume that they will be extraverted tomorrow, next week, a year from now, or even decades from now. The view that many broad-based personality traits show considerable stability over time has been supported by a large number of research studies, which we review in Chapter 5. Traits such as intelligence, emotional reactivity, impulsiveness, shyness, and aggression show high test-retest correlations, even with years or decades between measurement occasions. Personality traits that are thought to have a biological basis, such as extraversion, sensation seeking, activity level, and shyness, also show remarkable consistency over time. Attitudes, however, are much less consistent over time, as are interests and opinions (Conley, 1984a, 1984b). Of course, people can change in important behavioural ways throughout adulthood, especially after encountering some important life "turning point," such as serving in the military (Allemand, Gomez, & Jackson, 2010).

Although a trait might be consistent over time, the way in which it manifests itself in actual behaviour might change substantially. Consider the trait of disagreeableness. As a child, a highly disagreeable person might be prone to temper tantrums and fits of breath holding, fist pounding, and undirected rage. As an adult, a disagreeable person might be difficult to get along with and hence might have trouble sustaining personal relationships and holding down a job. Researchers have found, for example, a correlation of −.45 between throwing temper tantrums in childhood and being able to hold a job as an adult 20 years later (Caspi, Elder, & Bem, 1987). This finding is evidence of consistency in the underlying trait (disagreeableness), even though the *manifestation* of that trait changes over time.

What about traits that decrease in intensity with age, such as activity level, impulsiveness, or sociopathy? How can there be consistency in a trait if it is known to change with age? For example, criminal tendencies usually decrease with age, so a 20-year-old with sociopathic tendencies becomes much less dangerous to society as they get older. The answer to this question lies in the concept of **rank order**. If all people show a decrease in a particular trait at the same rate over time, they might still maintain the same rank order relative to each other. Accounting for general change with age can be compared to subtracting or adding a constant to each participant's score on the trait measure. Figure 4.1 illustrates how a general decrease in impulsiveness with age might have no real effect on the correlation between measures obtained 20 years apart. People in general can show a decrease in impulsiveness as they get older, yet those individuals who were the most impulsive at an earlier age are still the ones who are most impulsive at a later age. We revisit the idea of rank order consistency, as well as the whole notion of stability and change, in Chapter 5.

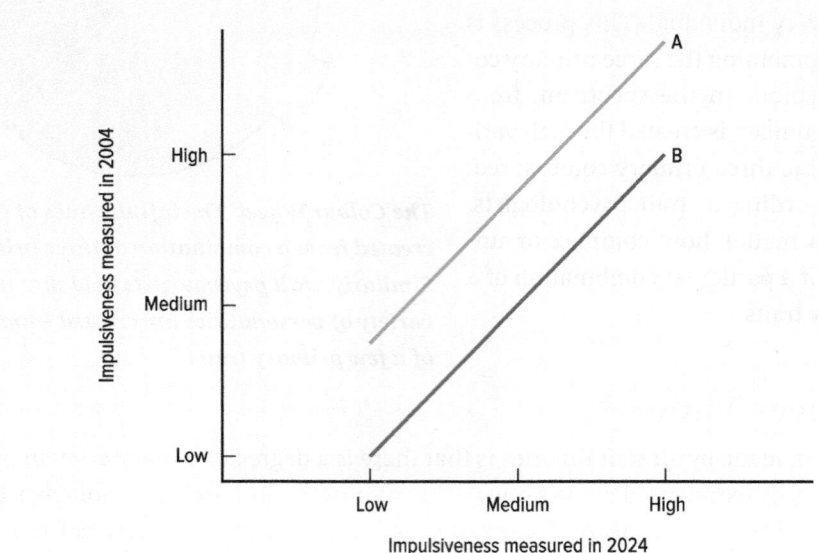

FIGURE 4.1 Hypothetical regression lines between impulsiveness measured 20 years apart. Line A represents an age change in impulsiveness, with all individuals scoring as less impulsive in later life. Line B represents no change in impulsiveness over 20 years. Both lines represent rank order consistency, however, and thus high test-retest correlations.

Consistency Across Situations

The third assumption made by trait psychologists is that traits will exhibit some consistency across situations. Although the evidence for consistency in traits *over time* is substantial, the question of consistency in traits *from situation to situation* has been more hotly debated (see Leikas, Lönnqvist, & Verkasalo, 2012). Trait psychologists have traditionally believed that people's personalities show consistency from situation to situation. For example, if a young man is "really friendly," he is expected to be friendly at work, friendly at school, and friendly during recreation activities. This person might be friendly toward strangers, people of different ages, and authority figures.

Even though someone is really friendly, there are, of course, situations in which the individual will not act friendly. Perhaps a particular situation exerts an influence on how friendly most people will be. For example, people are more likely to start conversations with strangers if they are at a party than if they are at a library. If situations mainly control how people behave, then the idea that traits are consistent across situations holds less promise as an approach to explaining behaviour.

The issue of cross-situational consistency has a long and checkered history in personality psychology. Hartshorne and May (1928) studied a large group of elementary school students at summer camp, focusing especially on the trait of honesty. They observed honest and dishonest behaviour in several situations. For example, they observed which children cheated while playing field games at summer camp and which children cheated during some written exams in school. The correlation between honesty measured in each of these two situations was rather low. Knowing that a child cheated one night while playing a game at summer camp tells us very little about whether this child is likely to copy from a neighbour during a test at school. Hartshorne and May reported similar low cross-situational correlations for the traits of helpfulness and self-control.

The Hartshorne and May study examined cross-situational consistency in academic and play situations in children. While they found little evidence for consistency in such traits as honesty, the study has been criticized for measuring behaviour on one occasion in each situation. Studies that aggregate measurements over several occasions in each situation find much higher levels of cross-situational consistency.
(left): ©Shutterstock/Syda Productions; (right): ©mbbirdy/E+/Getty Images

Forty years later, in 1968, Walter Mischel published a groundbreaking book entitled *Personality and Assessment*. In it, he summarized the results of the Hartshorne and May study, as well as the results of many other studies reporting low correlations between personality scores obtained in different situations. After reviewing many such findings, Mischel concluded that "behavioral consistencies have not been demonstrated, and the concept of personality traits as broad predispositions is thus untenable" (p. 140).

Mischel suggested that personality psychologists should abandon their efforts to explain behaviour in terms of personality traits and recommended that they shift their focus to situations. If behaviour differs from situation to situation, then it must be situational differences, rather than underlying personality traits, that determine behaviour. This position, called **situationism**, can be illustrated with the following examples. A young woman may be friendly at school with people she knows but reserved with strangers. Or a young man may want to achieve good grades at school but may not care whether he excels in sports.

Mischel's challenge to the trait approach preoccupied the field of trait psychology for the 20 years following publication of his 1968 book. Many researchers responded to Mischel's situationist approach by formulating new theoretical perspectives and gathering new data designed to rescue the idea of traits (e.g., A. H. Buss, 1989; Endler & Magnusson, 1976). Mischel, in turn, countered with new ideas and new data of his own, intended to reinforce his position that the trait concept was limited in its usefulness (e.g., Mischel, 1984, 1990; Mischel & Peake, 1982).

Although the dust is still settling from this long-running debate (for a summary of the current situation, see Benet-Martinez et al., 2015), it is safe to say that both trait psychologists *and* Mischel have modified their views as a result. Mischel has tempered his position that situations are always the strongest determinants of behaviour. However, he still maintains that trait psychologists have been guilty of overstating the importance of broad traits (Mischel & Shoda, 2010). Prior to Mischel's critique, it was common for trait psychologists to make statements about the predictability of people's behaviour from their scores on personality tests. Mischel points out that psychologists simply are not very good at predicting how *an individual* will behave *in particular situations*. Trait psychologists, too, have modified their views. Two of the most lasting changes that trait psychologists have embraced have been the notion of **person–situation interaction** and the practice of **aggregation,** or averaging, as a tool for assessing personality traits. Nevertheless, debate ensues, particularly in popular culture. We discuss a more recent example of situationism in A Closer Look: Situationism Today.

 A Closer Look

Situationism Today

The popular science writer Malcolm Gladwell (author of *Blink* and *David and Goliath*) released his book *Outliers* in 2008. (The term *outlier* comes from statistics and refers to an individual in a sample who is markedly different from all others in that sample.) In this book Gladwell tackles the issue of being exceptional: why some people are exceedingly successful in some area of life, such as sports, science, or business, whereas most others are only mediocre. This question embodies the very concept of individual differences and lies at the heart of personality psychology. It also is a useful example to illustrate the extreme situational perspective.

Gladwell takes the position that most exceptional people get that way because of special opportunities or life situations that give them some advantage. His view is that the successful among us were presented with a beneficial life situation and ran with it. For example, the founders of many major computer companies (e.g., Microsoft, Apple, Sun Microsystems) were all born between 1953 and 1956 and therefore were exposed to early prototype computers when they were geeky teenage boys with lots of time on their hands. They all spent countless hours with these early prototypes and grew up to be exceptionally successful in the computing industry.

Gladwell presents case after case like this, arguing that exposure to critical life situations, at the right time, is what matters most in understanding why some people are so successful. This is an entirely situational explanation, in that the cause of the success lies not in the person but in the situations to which she or he was exposed. In Gladwell's view, success is all about opportunity, timing, luck, and hard work. It has nothing to do with traits within the person, such as aptitude, intelligence, interest, motivation, or personality. Gladwell is a modern situationist, presenting a one-sided perspective on understanding exceptional success.

Two of the authors of the book you are currently reading were also both born between 1953 and 1956, just like Bill Gates, Steve Jobs, and Bill Joy. We were also exposed to primitive computers when we were geeky teenagers with lots of discretionary time on our hands. However, neither of us grew up to be corporate giants in the computing industry, even though we were exposed to the same kinds of life situations Gladwell argues were responsible for the exceptional success of these computing magnates. What explains this discrepancy? Well, we are both extremely interested in people, and we were both motivated to learn as much as we could about human nature when we were growing up. We must have had some innate ability in this field because we both went on to earn PhDs in psychology and to conduct award-winning research in the field of personality. Clearly, our interests, motivations, abilities, and personalities are very different from those of Bill Gates and Steve Jobs, even though we experienced many similar life situations. We might argue that it is precisely these personal characteristics that determined why we became personality psychologists and why Jobs and Gates became computing tycoons. This would be a strictly personality position, arguing that personal characteristics—ability, intelligence, interest, personality—entirely determine outcomes. Books presenting this perspective, which are as one-sided as Gladwell's, have also been written by nonscientists (e.g., *The Personality Code,* by Travis Bradberry, Putnam Press, 2007).

The real answer to understanding most life outcomes can be found in the interaction between personal characteristics and life situations: exceptional things happen when chance situations meet the prepared person. If someone had all the personal characteristics of Bill Gates or Steve Jobs, yet was from a poor, inner-city school that did not get those early prototype computers, they would most likely not go into this career. However, if someone had the exact same life experiences as Jobs and Gates, yet differed from them in basic interests, aptitudes, and personality (like us), then it is also likely that they would not go into computing as a career. It takes the right situations happening to people with the right personal characteristics to produce the exceptional outcome. Gladwell's book tells only half of the story, the situational half. The whole story is more complicated—and more interesting—than he portrays. For an integrated perspective on person–situation interaction, see Funder (2006).

Person–Situation Interaction

We first looked at the topic of person–situation interaction in Chapter 1. In this section, we examine this topic in a bit more detail, focusing on interactionism as a response to Mischel's challenge to trait consistency. As Mischel's debate with trait psychologists made clear, there are two possible explanations for behaviour, or why people do what they do in any given situation:

1. Behaviour is a function of personality traits, $B = f(P)$.
2. Behaviour is a function of situational forces, $B = f(S)$.

Clearly, there is some truth in both of these statements. For example, people behave differently at funerals than they do at sporting events, illustrating that situational forces direct behaviour in certain ways, as Mischel emphasized. Some people, however, are consistently quiet, even at sporting events, whereas other people are talkative and sociable, even at funerals. These examples lend support to the traditional trait position, which stresses that personality determines why people do what they do.

The obvious way to integrate these two points of view is to declare that both personality and situations interact to produce behaviour, or

$$B = f(P \times S)$$

This formula suggests that behaviour is a function of the *interaction* between personality traits and situational forces. Consider, for example, the trait of having a hot temper, a tendency to respond aggressively to minor frustrations. Acquaintances of a person high on this trait might be unaware of it as long as they did not encounter the person attempting to deal with a frustrating situation. The trait of having a short temper might be expressed only under the right situational conditions, such as in frustrating situations. If a person is frustrated by a situation (e.g., a vending machine takes the person's money but does not dispense the product) *and* the person happens to have a quick temper (personality forces), then they will become upset and perhaps strike out at the source of the frustration (e.g., kick the vending machine repeatedly while cursing loudly). Any explanation of why such people get so upset would have to take into account both particular situations (e.g., frustration) and personality traits (e.g., hot temper). This point of view is called person–situation interaction, and it has become a fairly standard view in modern trait theory. Another way to view this is in the form of "If ..., if ..., then ...." statements (Shoda, Mischel, & Wright, 1994). For example, "If the situation is frustrating, and if the person has a hot temper, then aggression will be the result." Norman Endler (1931–2003), a Distinguished Research Professor at York University, was one of the key researchers to advocate for the interactional perspective, specifically as it applied to anxiety, stress, and coping. His own model aimed to elucidate the relationships among coping processes and both personality and situational variables, highlighting the multiple adaptive functions of coping in controllable versus uncontrollable situations.

In the interactional view, differences among people are understood to make a difference only under the right circumstances. Some traits are specific to certain situations. Consider the trait of test anxiety. A student might be generally easygoing and confident. However, under a set of *very specific* situational conditions, such as when they have to take an important exam, they become very anxious. In these particular circumstances, someone who is otherwise easygoing might become distressed, anxious, and quite upset. This example illustrates how certain very specific situations can provoke behaviour that is otherwise out of character for the individual. This is referred to as **situational specificity**, in which a person acts in a specific way under particular circumstances.

Some trait–situation interactions are rare because the kinds of situations that elicit behaviour related to those traits are themselves rare. For example, you would find it difficult to identify which of your classmates are high in courageousness. It would take a certain kind of *situation,* such as a hostage situation at your school, for you to find out just who is courageous and who is not.

The point is that personality traits interact with situational forces to produce behaviour. Personality psychologists have given up the hope of predicting "all of the people all of the time" and have settled on the idea that they can predict "some of the people some of the time." For example, given the trait of anxiety, we might be able to predict who is likely to be anxious in some situations (e.g., evaluation situations, such as tests) but not anxious in other situations (e.g., when relaxed at home with family).

An interesting example of person–situation interaction is provided in a study by Debbie Moskowitz (1993). It has long been thought that the personality traits of dominance (the disposition to try to influence others) and friendliness (the degree to which a person is cordial and congenial) show large gender differences, with men being more dominant than women, and women being more friendly than men (Eagly, 1987). However, the study by Moskowitz showed that these traits interact with situational variables. Specifically, a person's level of dominance or friendliness may depend on who they are interacting with at the time; for example, whether the individual is interacting with a same-sex or opposite-sex person, and whether that person is someone known or a stranger. Moskowitz's (1993) study showed that women are more friendly than men, but only when they are interacting with other women; when interacting with opposite-sex strangers, women were not more friendly than men. As for dominance, the men were more dominant than women, but only when interacting with a same-sex friend; when interacting with strangers, the men were not more dominant than women. This study shows that who a person is interacting with will influence the expression of the personality traits of dominance and friendliness, and that this expression may or may not differ for men and women, depending on the social setting.

Some situations are so strong, however, that nearly everyone reacts in the same way. For example, in a study of emotional reactions to life events, Larsen, Diener, and Emmons (1986) were interested in finding out who tended to overreact emotionally to everyday events. Participants in this study kept a daily diary of life events for two months. They also rated their emotions each day. Based on a trait measure of emotional reactivity, these researchers were able to predict who would overreact to a minor or moderately stressful event, such as getting a flat tire, being stood up for a date, or having an outdoor event get rained out. When *really* bad things happened, such as the death of a pet, virtually everyone reacted with strong emotion. Researchers have coined the term **strong situation** to refer to situations in which nearly all people react in similar ways.

Certain strong situations, such as funerals, religious services, and crowded elevators, seem to support uniformity of behaviour. By contrast, when situations are weak or ambiguous, personality has its strongest influence on behaviour. The Rorschach inkblot cards are a classic example of a weak or ambiguous situation. A person being asked to interpret these inkblots is, in effect, being asked to provide structure by describing what they see in the inkblot. Many situations in real life are also somewhat ambiguous. When a stranger smiles at you, is it a friendly smile or is there a bit of a sneer in the smile? When a stranger looks you right in the eye and holds the stare for a bit too long, what does it mean? Many social situations, like these two, require us to interpret the actions, motives, and intentions of others. As with interpretations of inkblots, how we interpret social situations may reveal our personalities. For example, people with a Machiavellian character (i.e., the tendency to use others, to be manipulative and cold) often think others are out to get them (Golding, 1978). Especially in ambiguous social interactions, Machiavellian individuals are likely to see others as threatening.

Situational Selection

There are three other ways in which personality traits interact with situations. We discuss each of these in general terms here. The first form of interactionism is **situational selection**, the tendency to choose the situations in which one finds oneself (Ickes, Snyder, & Garcia, 1997; Snyder & Gangestad, 1982). In other words, people typically do not find themselves in random situations. Instead, they select the situations in which they will spend their time. Snyder (1983) states this idea concisely: "Quite possibly, one's choice of the settings in which to live one's life may reflect features of one's personality; an individual may choose to live his or her life in serious, reserved, and intellectual situations precisely because he or she is a serious, reserved, and thoughtful individual" (p. 510).

Researchers have examined whether specific personality traits predict how often people enter into specific situations (Diener, Larsen, & Emmons, 1984). These researchers had participants wear pagers so that the participants could be signalled electronically throughout the day. The participants wore the pagers every day for six weeks as they went about their normal routines. They were paged twice each day, resulting in a sample of 84 occasions for each participant. Each time the pager went off, the participants had to complete a brief questionnaire. One question inquired about the kind of situation each participant was in when the pager went off.

Personality plays a role in determining which situations a person chooses to enter. For example, whether one chooses team activities for recreation, such as basketball, or individual activities, such as long-distance running, is a function of one's level of extraversion. Studies show that extraverts prefer team activities and introverts prefer solitary activities for recreation.
©Shutterstock/Samuel Borges Photography

Over the 84 times when the participants were "caught," the researchers predicted that certain personality traits would predict how many times they were caught in certain situations. For example, the researchers found that the trait of need for achievement correlated with spending more time in work situations, the need for order with spending time in more familiar situations, and extraversion with choosing social forms of recreation (e.g., team sports, such as baseball or volleyball, rather than solitary sports, such as long-distance running or swimming).

The idea that personality influences the kinds of situations in which people spend their time suggests that we can investigate personality by studying the choices people make in life. When given a choice, people typically choose situations that fit their personalities (Snyder & Gangestad, 1982). The personality effect does not have to be large to result in substantial life-outcome differences. For example, choosing to enter into work situations just 10 percent more of the time (e.g., studying 10 percent longer, or working 10 percent more hours) may result in very large differences in real-life outcomes, such as achieving a degree or a higher salary. Think, for example, about how you choose to spend your free time and about whether your choices reflect your own personality, to a degree.

The relationship between persons and situations is bidirectional. So far, we have been emphasizing how personality affects situational selection. However, once in the situation, that situation can affect the person's personality. A study by psychologist Will Fleeson and colleagues (Fleeson, Malanos, & Achille, 2002) illustrates how situations can influence personality. It has long been known that the trait of extraversion is related to positive emotions. We discuss this more in Chapter 13, but for now it is important simply to know that a strong correlation exists between extraversion and frequently feeling high levels of positive emotions. In their study, Fleeson and colleagues had subjects come to the lab in groups of three to participate in a group discussion. They were randomly assigned to an "introverted" or an "extraverted" condition. Instructions for the extraverted condition emphasized that they should behave in a talkative, bold, and energetic manner for the group discussion. Instructions for the introverted condition emphasized that they should behave in a reserved, compliant, and unadventurous manner for the group discussion. They were then asked to have a discussion of either the 10 most important items needed after an airplane crash or to come up with 10 possible solutions to the parking problem on their campus.

During the discussion, observers rated how positive each participant appeared. Following the discussion, each participant self-reported how positive they felt during the discussion. For both of these variables—observed positivity and self-reported positive feelings—the participants in the extraverted condition were substantially higher than those in the introverted condition. Moreover, this effect did not depend on the person's actual levels of trait extraversion. This study shows that being in an extraverted situation (being with a group of energetic, talkative people) can raise a person's level of positive affect. The study clearly illustrates that, when it comes to person–situation interactions, situations can influence persons just as much as persons can influence situations.

Evocation

Another form of person–situation interaction discussed by Buss (1987) is **evocation**, the idea that certain personality traits may evoke specific responses from the environment. For example, people who are disagreeable and manipulative may evoke certain reactions in others, such as hostility and avoidance. In other words, people may create their own environments by eliciting certain responses from others. Consider the case of a male patient who had trouble sustaining relationships with women, such that he was divorced three times

(Wachtel, 1973). He complained to his therapist that every woman with whom he became involved turned out to be bad-tempered, vicious, and spiteful. He complained that his relationships started out satisfying but always ended with the women becoming angry and leaving him. Wachtel (1973) speculated that the *man* must have been doing something to *evoke* this response from the women in his life.

The idea of evocation is similar to the idea of transference, discussed in Chapter 9 on psychoanalysis. Transference occurs when a patient in psychoanalysis re-creates, with the analyst, any interpersonal problems being experienced with significant others. In doing so, the patient may evoke in the therapist the reactions and feelings that are typically evoked in other people. Malcolm (1981) reported on a male psychoanalyst who found one female patient to be particularly boring. The analyst could hardly stay awake during the therapy sessions because the patient and her problems seemed so dull and trivial to him. After experiencing this reaction for a few weeks, however, the analyst realized that the patient was making him feel bored, just as she made other men in her life feel bored. She made herself dull, he concluded, to avoid the attentions of men and drive them away. However, she was in therapy, in part, because she complained of being lonely. This case illustrates how people can evoke reactions in others—creating and re-creating certain kinds of social situations in their everyday lives.

Manipulation

A third form of person–situation interaction is manipulation, which can be defined as the various means by which people influence the behaviour of others. Manipulation is the intentional use of certain tactics to coerce, influence, or change others. Manipulation changes the social situation. Manipulation differs from selection in that selection involves choosing existing environments, whereas manipulation entails altering those environments already inhabited. Individuals differ in the tactics of manipulation they use. Researchers have found, for example, that some individuals use a charm tactic—complimenting others, acting warm and caring, and doing favours for others in order to influence them. Other people use a manipulation tactic sometimes referred to as the silent treatment, ignoring or failing to respond to the other person. A third tactic is coercion, which consists of making demands, yelling, criticizing, cursing, and threatening the other to get what one wants (Buss et al., 1987).

Aggregation

We've seen how their debate with Mischel led trait psychologists to appreciate that behaviour is an outcome of the interaction between personality traits and situations. Another important lesson learned by trait psychologists is the value of aggregation when it comes to measuring personality traits. Aggregation is the process of adding up, or averaging, several single observations, resulting in a better (i.e., more reliable) measure of a personality trait than a single observation of behaviour. This approach usually provides psychologists with a better measure of a personality trait than does using a single observation. Consider the concept of batting average, which is seen as a measure of a baseball player's batting ability (a trait). It turns out that batting average is not a very good predictor of whether or not a player will get a hit during any *single* time at bat. In fact, psychologist Abelson (1985) analyzed single batting occasions over the whole season. He found that batting average accounted for only .3 percent of the variance in getting a hit. This is a remarkably poor relationship, so why do people pay such close attention to batting average, and why do players with a good batting average earn so much more money? Because what matters is how a player performs *over the long run,* over an entire season. This is the principle of aggregation in action.

To draw an analogy between batting average and personality, let's say you decide to marry someone, in part, because of that person's cheerful disposition. Clearly, there will be days when your partner is not going to be cheerful. However, what matters to you is your partner's behaviour over the long term (i.e., how cheerful your partner will be in general) and not their mood on any given day or occasion.

Imagine taking an intelligence test that has only one item. Do you think this one-item test would be a good measure of your overall intelligence? You would be right if you concluded that a single question was probably not a very accurate or fair measure of overall intelligence. A related example might be if the instructor in your personality course were to decide that your entire grade for a course would be determined by asking you only one question on the final exam. Surely one question could not possibly measure your knowledge of the course material. Single questions or single observations are rarely good measures of anything.

Recall the Hartshorne and May (1928) study in which the researchers measured honesty by assessing whether or not a child cheated during a game on one occasion during summer camp. Do you think this one-item measure of honesty was an accurate reflection of the participants' true levels of honesty? It probably was not. This is one reason that Hartshorne and May found such small correlations among their various measures of honesty (that is, because they were all single-item measures).

Personality psychologist Seymour Epstein published several papers (1979, 1980, 1983) showing that aggregating several questions or observations results in better trait measures. Longer tests are more reliable than shorter ones (reliability was introduced in Chapter 2) and hence are better measures of traits. If we want to know how conscientious a person is, we should observe many conscientious-related behaviours (e.g., how neat or how punctual they are) on many occasions and aggregate, or average, the responses. Any single behaviour on any single occasion may be influenced by all sorts of extenuating circumstances unrelated to personality.

Imagine that a trait psychologist is developing a questionnaire to measure how helpful, caring, and conscientious respondents are. She includes the following item on the questionnaire: "How often in the past few years have you stopped to help a person whose car was stuck in the snow?" Imagine further that you live in a place where it rarely snows. You answer "never," even though you are generally a helpful person. Now imagine being asked a whole set of questions, such as how often you donate money to charity, participate in blood donation programs, and do volunteer work in your community. Your answers to that whole series of questions provides a better indicator of your true level of helpfulness than does your answer to any single question.

Psychologists "rediscovered" aggregation in the 1980s. Charles Spearman published a paper back in 1910, explaining that tests with more items are generally more reliable than tests with fewer items. Spearman provided a formula—now called the Spearman-Brown prophecy formula—for determining precisely how much a test's reliability will increase as it is made longer. Although this formula appeared in all the major textbooks on measurement and statistics, personality psychologists seemed to have forgotten about the principle of aggregation until Epstein (1980, 1983) published his reminders in the early 1980s. Since then, other researchers have provided ample demonstrations of how the principle of aggregation works to increase the strength of correlations between measures of personality and measures of behaviour. For example, according to a study by Diener and Larsen (1984), measures of activity level on one day correlated with activity level on another day at a correlation of only .08. However, when activity level was averaged over a three-week period and then correlated with activity level averaged over another three-week period, that correlation went up to .66. Clearly, aggregation provides a more stable and reliable measure of a person's average standing on a trait than any single observation can.

Aggregation is a technique designed to improve trait measures by adding items to a questionnaire or adding observations to obtain an overall score. Aggregation implies that traits are only one influence on behaviour. That is, at any given time, for any given behaviour, many factors influence why a person does one thing and not another. Aggregation also implies that traits refer to a person's average level. Traits are similar to the set-point concept in weight; a person's weight will fluctuate from day to day, but there is a set point, or average level, to which one typically returns. An otherwise cheerful person, for example, might be irritable on one occasion because they have a stomachache. If you were to observe this person on many occasions, however, you would be apt to conclude that, on average, they are generally cheerful.

This example illustrates that personality traits are average tendencies to behave in certain ways. Personality psychologists will *never* be very good at predicting single acts on single occasions. We may know, for example, that there is a strong negative correlation between conscientiousness and an aggregate measure of being late for class, yet, even if we know everyone's conscientiousness score in a class, are we able to predict on which particular day a specific person will be late? That's not likely. We can, for example, predict who is likely to be late over the whole semester, but we are not able to predict, from that person's personality scores alone, which *specific days* they will be late. Situational forces (e.g., a failed alarm clock or a flat tire) may determine why a person is late on any specific day. But personality may play a role in determining why a person is frequently late (e.g., low on conscientiousness). The useful concept of **density distribution of states** was introduced by Fleeson (2001). Each trait, such as extraversion, is associated with specific states, such as the state of talking with others, acting vigorously, or becoming enthusiastic. Within an individual, the states are distributed over time. The concept of "density distribution" refers to the idea that people high in a particular trait (say, extraversion) will have state distributions that are more dense with state manifestations of that trait (say, being more frequently talkative, vigorous, and enthusiastic). Sometimes even the most extraverted among us is quiet, calm, and peaceful. However, over time, the extraverted individuals will show more frequent or more dense distributions of state extraversion than introverted people. Indeed, Fleeson and Noftle (2012) have argued that studying people over time, and aggregating the frequency of particular behaviours and states, is one of the best ways to study personality. For a closer look at how to best predict behaviour as a function of personality, read Highlight on Canadian Research: The Goldilocks Zone of Personality Measurement.

Highlight on Canadian Research

The Goldilocks Zone of Personality Measurement

Sampo Paunonen (1952–2015) was a leading researcher and author on the complexities of trait theory and measurement. A professor of psychology at the University of Western Ontario, Paunonen's work spanned decades and included over 90 publications in peer-reviewed journals, making him one of Canada's most well-respected personality researchers. He was a proponent of the trait perspective of personality, and underscored the value of questionnaires specifically as means of measurement. Although his work addressed a number of issues associated with trait theory and measurement, one of his main areas of focus was the capacity for trait measurement to predict human behaviour.

In a chapter published in 2013, he and a colleague wrote the following: "To paraphrase Goldilocks, personality factor measures are too broad, personality behavior measures are too narrow, but personality trait measures are just right" (O'Neill & Paunonen, 2013, p. 299). What Paunonen and his co-author were referring to was the level of personality measurement that seems to most robustly predict behaviour—the *trait level*. Although lessons from person–situation interaction and aggregation tell us that personality psychologists cannot easily predict single instances of human behaviour, there is a "best" level of trait measurement at which we can make the most accurate predictions possible—what the authors referred to as a sort of Goldilocks zone.

This means that measurements of specific behavioural acts, which can be viewed as constituting the lowest possible level of the personality hierarchy, will not be broad enough to capture the range or richness of information to make adequate predictions about behaviour over time. In other words, taking too narrow an approach in measurement will offer an inadequate substrate on which to understand the totalities of human behaviour. This is true even if valid and reliable measures of behaviour exist. On the other hand, measuring personality factors at their highest position in the hierarchy, as in the broad traits contained in the five-factor model, will not offer the degree of specificity required to make accurate predictions about behaviour. The issue here is the variance that is observed at the unitary trait level; such variance is not captured by examination of the broad factor alone. The conclusion, then, is that it is measurement at the unitary trait level itself where the most accurate predictions of human behaviour can be made. At this level, personality psychologists describe more specific facets or narrower traits within broad factors on personality measures (Paunonen & Hong, 2015).

This has been illustrated empirically in a number of studies. In a sample of university students, Paunonen and Nicol (2001) compared the predictive value of broad personality factors versus narrower traits in a variety of behavioural criteria related to academic performance and participation in research, such as grade point average, questionnaire neatness, and tardiness. Most criteria were predicted with confidence by at least one broad factor in the five-factor model. Yet in nearly all of those cases, a narrower trait contained within one of the broad factors was an even better predictor of the behavioural criterion in question. For example, although conscientiousness was a significant predictor of students' grade point average, one of the facets of conscientiousness, *self-discipline*, was an even better predictor. As the authors noted, this is important information for both theory and research, as it indicates which facets of conscientiousness are playing a role in this particular behaviour and which are not. It might be assumed, for example, that the achievement motivation facet may be primarily driving grade point average, when in fact it is self-discipline. This even has practical implications, if we are interested in making recommendations to students as to the best strategies to engage in order to improve grade point average.

Paunonen accumulated a great deal of support for this position. Behaviours related to dating, attractiveness, and even religious activities were better predicted by narrower traits than their broader corresponding factors in multiple samples of university students (Paunonen, 1998). In cross-cultural research, narrower traits accounted for more variance in substance use behaviours (e.g., alcohol consumption and smoking) than broad traits (Paunonen et al., 2003). And similar patterns have been observed in work-related behaviours (Paunonen & Nicol, 2001). In all of these studies, Paunonen's conclusion was one of caution, as "aggregating personality traits into their underlying personality factors could result in decreased predictive accuracy due to the loss of trait-specific but criterion-valid variance" (1998, p. 538). This is a message that affects both measurement theory and research. Most poignantly, it suggests that there is an ideal level at which to measure personality if the goal is indeed to understand and explain human behaviour in practical terms.

 Concept Check

Define the concept of person-situation interaction, as well as specific notions of selection, evocation, and manipulation. Provide examples of each based on the same Big Five trait (of your choosing).

What is aggregation, and why is it important in personality measurement?

Measurement Issues

More than any other approach to personality, the trait approach relies on self-report questionnaires to measure personality. Although trait psychologists can use other measurement methods (e.g., projective techniques, behavioural observation), questionnaires are the most frequently used method for measuring traits (Craik, 1986). Personality psychologists assume that people differ from each other in the *amounts* of various traits they possess, so the key measurement issue is determining *how much* of a particular trait a person possesses.

Traits are often represented as dimensions along which people differ from each other. One of the most efficient ways to assess people's standing on any personality trait dimension is simply to ask them about their characteristics. If the right questions are asked, as the trait view holds, an accurate assessment of a person's standing on the trait dimension will be obtained.

Personality tests are frequently administered in large group settings. In such settings, some people may be careless or even fake their responses. Psychologists have developed ways of detecting faking and carelessness in the answers from individual test takers.
©Fuse/Getty Images

As compelling as this view of trait assessment is, it assumes that people generally are willing and able to report accurately on their behaviour. However, some people may be unwilling to disclose information about themselves or may be motivated for some reason to distort or otherwise falsify their self-reports, such as during an employment interview or a parole hearing. Trait psychologists have long concerned themselves with the circumstances that affect the accuracy, reliability, validity, and utility of trait measures. We will now consider some important measurement issues in trait research.

Carelessness

Some participants filling out a trait questionnaire might not be motivated to answer carefully or truthfully. For example, some colleges and universities require introductory psychology students to participate in psychology experiments, many of which involve personality questionnaires. These volunteer participants may not be motivated to complete the questionnaires carefully; they may rush through the questionnaire, answering randomly. Other participants may be motivated to answer correctly but might accidentally invalidate their answer sheets. For example, when participants are asked to put their answers on optical scanning sheets by filling in circles with a number 2 lead pencil, it is not uncommon for participants to inadvertently neglect to fill in a circle or two, which means that all subsequent answers are then incorrect as well. Another problem arises when, for some reason, the participant is not reading the questions carefully but is nevertheless providing answers. Perhaps the participant has difficulty reading, is tired, or even is hallucinating.

A common method for detecting these problems is to embed an **infrequency scale** within the set of questionnaire items. The infrequency scale contains items that all or almost all people will answer in a particular way. Using such items, if a person endorses more than one or two of these items in the "wrong" direction, then the test is flagged as suspicious. For example, on the Personality Research Form (Jackson & Messick, 1967), the infrequency scale contains items such as the following: "I do not believe that wood really burns," "I make all my own clothes and shoes," and "Whenever I walk up stairs, I always do so on my hands." These questions are answered "False" by over 95 percent of the people in samples from the United States and Canada. If a participant answers more than one or two of these as "True," we may begin to suspect that their answers do not represent valid information. Such a participant may be answering randomly, may have difficulty reading, or may be marking their answer sheet incorrectly.

Another technique used to detect carelessness is to include duplicate questions spaced far apart in the questionnaire. The psychologist can then determine the number of times the participant answered identical questions with different responses. If this happens often, the psychologist might suspect carelessness or another problem that invalidates the person's answers.

Faking on Questionnaires

Faking involves the motivated distortion of answers on a questionnaire. When personality questionnaires are used to make important decisions about people's lives (e.g., hire them for a job, promote them, decide that they are not guilty by reason of insanity, or allow prisoners to be paroled), then there is always the possibility of faking. Some people may be motivated to "fake good" in order to appear to be better off or better adjusted than they really are. Others may be motivated to "fake bad" in order to appear to be worse off or more maladjusted than they really are. For example, a worker suing a company for mental anguish caused by a poor working condition might be motivated to appear very distressed to the court-appointed psychologist.

Questionnaire developers have attempted to devise ways to detect faking good and faking bad. In constructing the 16 Personality Factor questionnaire, for example, Cattell, Eber, and Tatsouoka (1970) had groups of participants complete the questionnaire under specific instructions. One group of participants was instructed to fake good, to appear to be as well adjusted as possible. Another group of participants was instructed to fake bad, to try to appear as maladjusted as possible. The data for these two groups were then used to generate a "faking good profile" and a "faking bad profile." The data from real participants can then be compared with those in these two faking profiles, and the psychologist can calculate just how much a person's responses fit the profile of the groups asked to fake their answers. This approach offers psychologists an imperfect but nevertheless reasonable method for determining the likelihood that a person is faking responses to the questionnaire, as shown in Figure 4.2.

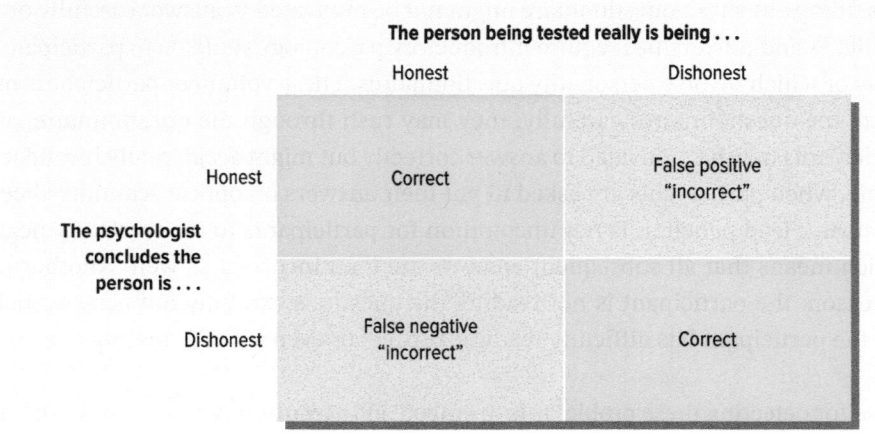

FIGURE 4.2 Two ways to make a mistake when deciding whether a person was faking responses to a personality questionnaire.

A recent study of military cadets applying for pilot training clearly illustrates that, when an important outcome is based on personality scores, people are motivated to "fake good" while answering the questions (Galic, Jerneic, & Kovacic, 2012). These researchers showed in three samples of military cadets applying to pilot school that the applicants' scores were more similar to scores obtained by individuals who were asked to fake the most desirable person's responses. They warn that whenever important decisions are based on responses to questionnaires, care must be taken to account for desirable responding, or "faking good," on the part of the test takers.

There are two ways for psychologists to make a mistake when seeking to distinguish between genuine and faked responses. They may conclude that a truthful person was faking and reject that person's data (called a **false negative**). Or they may decide that a person who was faking was actually telling the truth (called a **false positive**). Psychologists do not know for certain how well their faking scales perform when it comes to minimizing the percentages of false positives and false negatives. Because of this problem of undetected faking, many psychologists are suspicious of self-report questionnaire measures of personality.

Researchers Jacob Hirsh and Jordan Peterson of the University of Toronto have suggested removing the traditional Likert-type scale response options and use forced-choice responding (see Chapter 2) on personality measures, which may result in more robust predictive validity when faking is present (Hirsh & Peterson, 2008). In their forced-choice method, Hirsh and Peterson provide participants with lists of positive and negative items to describe themselves. Rather than rating the extent to which each word or phrase describes their personality, participants are asked to choose a certain number of representative descriptors from each list. Hirsh and Peterson (2008) suggest that this method avoids the inflation of responses that results from participants ranking themselves higher on positive dimensions and lower on negative ones.

Beware of Barnum Statements in Personality Test Interpretations

"We have something for everyone."

—*P. T. Barnum*

Barnum statements are generalities—statements that could apply to anyone—though they often appear to the readers of astrology advice columns to apply specifically to them. Astrology predictions are very popular in newspapers and magazines. For example: "You sometimes have doubts about whether you have done the right thing" or "You have a need for others to like or admire you" or "Although you are able to deal with confrontation in a pinch, you typically like to avoid it if you can." These are Barnum statements. People read such statements and think, "Yes, that's me all right," when in fact such statements could apply to anyone.

Personality test interpreters also sometimes offer interpretations that consist of Barnum statements. To illustrate this, one of the authors of this textbook completed an online version of the Myers-Briggs Type Indicator (MBTI), a very popular personality test. He then submitted his answers to three different online interpretation services to get feedback about his personality. Reading the results of the first interpretation, he felt it had it right: "You advance toward good and retreat from evil; you hate to miss out on what is going on around you; you always try to tell the truth to those around you; you strive to be authentic and genuine, and you communicate well with others." The second interpretation also sounded accurate: "You want to be liked and admired by others; you are interested in new ideas; you have a great deal of charm, and others genuinely like you; at times your attention span can be short; you dislike bureaucracy." The third interpretation, too, seemed to apply: "You are fun to be around; while you can be intellectual, serious, and all business, you are also capable of flipping the switch and becoming childlike, interested in fun; you enjoy learning new things and have good self-discipline."

These interpretations all sounded personally relevant. The only problem was that the answers to the questionnaire were filled in at random. That is, the author of this book did not read the questions, but merely clicked "true" or "false" randomly. How then did these test interpretations seem to apply so personally and directly? Read the interpretations again and you will see that they are Barnum statements. They could apply to just about anyone.

This example is not meant to suggest that the MBTI is not a good test. Rather, it is the personality feedback or test interpretations that can sometimes be less than accurate. Recall that these interpretations were obtained from free online services. So this example could also be an illustration of the advice, "you get what you pay for." Most reliable test interpretation services charge a fee for this service.

Reliable test interpretation services typically make statements that are quantitative or that provide information about a person's standing on a trait relative to others. So, for example, an interpretation might state: "Your scores on extraversion put you in the highest or most extraverted 10% of the population." Or the statement might refer to research results, such as: "Persons with extraversion scores such as yours were found to be extremely satisfied in careers that involved frequent social contact, such as salespersons, teachers, or public relations work." Also, reliable test interpretation services typically include checks for careless responding, as discussed earlier in this chapter. They typically provide an assessment of how suspicious one should be regarding the validity of the person's responses. None of the free test interpretation services used in this example provided such checks, and so none of them detected that the responses were random.

So far we have discussed some of the theoretical and measurement issues in trait psychology. Trait psychologists do not only concern themselves with these somewhat esoteric and academic issues. Trait psychology also has some real-world applications. We turn now to a consideration of the practical uses to which personality trait measures have been put.

 Concept Check

Discuss the key measurement issues that exist in personality research. Why are they so important to consider?

What are Barnum statements, and when are they an issue in personality research?

Personality and Prediction

Personality measures have a long history of use in industry and government. They are used in the federal and provincial prison systems to make decisions about inmates. They are also widely used in industry to match people with particular jobs, to help screen people for employment, and to select people for promotion. An employer may feel that emotional stability is a requirement for a specific job (e.g., police officer) or that the personality trait of honesty is especially important (e.g., for a sales associated in a jewellery store or a driver of a money delivery truck). Other jobs may require strong organizational or social skills, or the ability to work in a distracting environment. Whether someone does well in employment settings may be determined, in part, by whether the individual's personality traits mesh with the job requirements. In short, personality traits may predict who is likely to do well in a particular job, so it makes some sense to try to select people for employment based on measures of these traits.

Applications of Personality Testing in the Workplace

In an increasingly competitive business environment, many employers resort to employment testing to improve their workforce. Although cognitive ability testing (e.g., comprehension, reading speed) is the most commonly used form of psychological testing in the workplace, personality tests are being used more and more frequently.

The personality tests used in the workplace are primarily self-report measures of specific traits or dispositions. A very large number of personality measures are available. Some personality measures characterize people within the normal range of personality functioning; others focus on the identification of psychopathology or abnormal levels of functioning. Many personality tests, such as the Minnesota Multiphasic Personality Inventory (MMPI) or the California Personality Inventory (CPI), assess a large number of personality characteristics; others measure single traits in which the employer is specifically interested.

Employers use personality assessment in the workplace for three main reasons: personnel selection, integrity testing, and concerns over negligent hiring.

Personnel Selection

Employers sometimes use personality tests to select people who are especially suitable for a specific job. For example, an insurance company might use a measure of extraversion–introversion to select applicants high on extraversion for a sales job, so that their characteristics match successful incumbents in their sales department. Alternatively, the employer may want to use personality assessments to deselect, or screen out, people with specific traits. For example, a police department might use the MMPI or a similar test to screen out applicants who have high levels of mental instability or psychopathology. A number of personality tests and applications can aid employers in **personnel selection**.

Integrity Testing

Personality tests that assess honesty or integrity are probably the most widely used form of personality assessment in the business world. They are commonly used in the retail and financial service industries in selecting people for low-paying entry-level jobs in which the employee handles money or merchandise in an unsupervised setting. **Integrity tests** are designed to predict a tendency toward theft or other forms of counterproductive behaviours in work settings, such as absenteeism.

The annual economic losses to Canadian business from employee theft are estimated at $1.4 billion (Retail of Council of Canada, 2012). Moreover, a substantial proportion of annual business failures have been blamed on employee theft. Because of this, many employers are interested in any technique that could detect those employees most likely to commit theft on the job. Given that the use of polygraph tests (i.e., lie-detector tests) by the private sector is prohibited in some Canadian provinces (e.g., New Brunswick and Ontario) and throughout the United States, many companies have developed and promoted integrity tests to use in place of the polygraph (DeAngelis, 1991). Many of these tests are considered to be reasonably reliable and valid and so may be used legally for employment screening (DeAngelis, 1991). Integrity tests measure attitudes related to one or more of the following psychological constructs: tolerating others who steal, beliefs that many others engage in theft, rationalizations that theft may be acceptable, interthief loyalty, antisocial beliefs and behaviours, and admission to stealing in the past. These tests typically consist of two parts. The first part measures attitudes toward theft (e.g., beliefs concerning the frequency and extent of theft, whether or not theft should be punished and how severely, and ruminations about theft). The second part concerns admissions regarding theft and other wrongdoing. Applicants are asked to describe the frequency and amount of theft and other illegal or counterproductive activity they engaged in on past jobs. Test items that make up integrity tests are clearly assessing job-related content (e.g., "Will everyone steal at work if the conditions are right?"; "Do you believe you are too honest to steal at work?"; "Do you think it is humanly possible for the average person to be completely honest on the job?" etc.).

One review of integrity tests (Ones & Viswesvaran, 1998) concluded that the measures are reliable (have test-retest correlations in the range of 0.85) and valid (integrity test scores predict the following theft criteria: supervisors' ratings of employees' dishonesty, applicants who are likely to get caught stealing once hired, applicants who have a criminal history, and applicants who are likely to admit theft in an anonymous testing situation). In one study, a group of convenience stores started using an integrity test to select employees and experienced a 50 percent reduction in inventory shrinkage due to theft over an 18-month period. A more recent review (Berry, Sackett, & Wiemann, 2007) concludes that integrity tests are improving in terms of validity and resistance to faking and coaching, that they do not show adverse impact on protected groups (see following), and that they continue to be legal for use in employment settings. Moreover, new testing formats are being developed. Some use items that assess ethical decision-making in various scenarios while others look at how people justify the decisions that they make. Integrity testing is a very active area of applied personality psychology, where the principles of personality psychology are used to improve the workplace as well as worker productivity.

Concerns over Negligent Hiring

A third reason that employers may make use of personality testing is to avoid charges of negligent hiring. Should an employee assault a customer or a co-worker on the job, the employer may be held accountable should the matter be pursued in court. In such a case, the employer could be charged with **negligent hiring**; that is, hiring someone who is unstable or prone to violence. In such cases, the employer can be charged with negligently hiring an applicant with traits that posed a threat of injury to others. Such cases hinge on whether the employer should have discovered those traits ahead of time, before hiring such a person into a position where they posed a threat to others. Personality testing may provide evidence that the employer did in fact try to reasonably investigate an applicant's fitness for the workplace. On the other hand, employers should be cautioned that such personality tests are not used to discriminate on the basis of other variables, such as age or race. Ultimately, it is important that any selection procedure not produce any disparate impacts on specific groups.

Legal Issues in Personality Testing in Employment Settings

There are a number of legal issues surrounding the use of personality tests in employment settings. In any given case, these issues may or may not arise; however, like people, each case is unique, and each instance of personality testing may ultimately succumb to issues of a legal nature.

Right to Privacy

The first issue is one of privacy. Given that job candidates and prospective employees are relatively unaware of the implications or significance of their responses on personality tests, they are more likely to reveal their private thoughts and emotions. In turn, responses may be interpreted such that conclusions are drawn about behavioural tendencies, intelligence, or even mental health—all things that most of us would prefer to keep private. These are especially important considerations given that personality testing in an employment setting is not subject to the same ethical standards and procedures that we would find in a research or clinical setting, where confidentiality and privacy of participant responses are required. As a result, one's **right to privacy** may be violated, such that any one test may actually constitute an invasion of privacy, an act that is subject to liability in Canada if deemed highly offensive.

In some cases, psychological testing can be considered a form of medical examination if it provides evidence that would lead to a diagnosis or the identification of mental disorder or impairment. Consider the following example: A psychological test (like the MMPI) is constructed to diagnose mental illnesses, but a particular employer says they do not use the test to disclose mental illness. Instead, the employer says they use the test to disclose preferences and habits of job applicants. However, the test is also interpreted by a psychologist working for the company. In addition, the test is routinely used in clinical settings to provide evidence that would lead to a diagnosis of a mental disorder or impairment (for example, whether a person has paranoid tendencies or is depressed). The use of clinically oriented personality measures designed primarily to diagnose psychopathology, such as the MMPI, could provide even greater opportunities for employers to violate the privacy of job applicants. Consequently, employers should avoid the MMPI and similar measures for selection purposes. Tests of normal-range personality functioning (e.g., ratings on the five-factor model), and measures of integrity, have never been considered equivalent to a medical examination.

Discrimination

The second issue is the discriminatory hiring and/or promotion practices that may ensue as a result of personality testing. Job candidates may behave differently in uncertain testing situations, and this behaviour may be seen as more or less favourable by employers. On the other hand, responses to the tests themselves may be deemed as more or less desirable, such that individuals are discriminated against based on their personalities, their perceived intellectual capacities, or their mental health. If any of the traits or characteristics extracted from personality testing are then associated (either implicitly or explicitly) with certain social or minority groups who are already stigmatized (e.g.. women, LGBTQ individuals, or members of any ethnic minority), such tests may be used to discriminate against employees or job candidates on these bases. In such cases, personality and other employee screening measures could be used to perpetuate discrimination throughout an organization or an entire employment sector.

There have been numerous cases throughout Canada and the United States where employee screening measures have perpetuated discrimination both in hiring practices and on the job. One important case, and one with clear personality connections, was the case of *Price Waterhouse v. Hopkins,* decided in 1989 by the Supreme Court of the United States. Ann Hopkins was a senior manager at an accounting firm, who was being considered for promotion to partnership in the firm. Following its usual promotion practice, the firm asked each existing partner to evaluate Ms. Hopkins. Many of the evaluations came in as negative, criticizing her interpersonal skills and accusing her of being abrasive and too masculine for a woman (they felt she needed to wear more makeup, to walk and talk more femininely, etc.). She sued the company, charging that they had discriminated against her on the basis of sex, on the theory that her evaluations had been based on sexual stereotyping. The case eventually rose to the Supreme Court. Price Waterhouse acknowledged discrimination but maintained that sexual stereotypes were just one factor and argued that there were other reasons to deny partnership to Hopkins. They argued that even without any sex discrimination, they would have passed on Hopkins for the promotion.

The other legal issue (and the one that won the case for Hopkins) was that she had been passed over for partner because of gender stereotyping within the company. In essence, she argued, the voting partners compared her to a cultural stereotype of how a woman is supposed to behave in the workplace, and they decided that Hopkins did not fit that image. The American Psychological Association joined the case and provided expert evidence that such stereotypes do exist and that women who deviate from the cultural expectations are often penalized for violating these standards. The Supreme Court accepted the argument that gender stereotyping does exist and that it can create a bias against women in the workplace that is not permissible. By court order Ann Hopkins was made a full partner in her accounting firm. She went on to describe her long court case, both from a legal and personal perspective, in a book titled *So Ordered: Making Partner the Hard Way* by Ann Branigar Hopkins (Amherst: University of Massachusetts Press, 1996).

The **Employment Equity Act** of 1986 requires that federally regulated industries in Canada adopt proactive employment practices in order to improve the employment rates of four designated social groups: women, individuals with disabilities, Aboriginal peoples, and visible minorities. Inherent to the Employment Equity Act is the necessary removal of barriers to employment that place members of the four designated groups at a greater disadvantage. For example, buildings that are inaccessible by wheelchair may disadvantage individuals with disabilities and reduce their opportunities for employment. Employers should be especially careful when administering psychological testing to job applicants who belong to one of these four designated groups, as they may be especially vulnerable to forms of discrimination. To examine one line of research that bears implications for maintaining gender diversity through personality testing, see A Closer Look: The Five-Factor Model and Gender Diversity in the Canadian Workforce.

 A Closer Look

The Five-Factor Model and Gender Diversity in the Canadian Workforce

Deborah Powell, an organizational psychologist at the University of Guelph, was interested in studying gender differences in personality scores on the five-factor model and the potential implications for gender discrimination. Along with her colleagues, Richard Goffin of the University of Western Ontario and Ian Gellatly of the University of Alberta, she examined nearly 600 candidates applying for jobs at a large oil refinery in Western Canada (Powell, Goffin, & Gellatly, 2011). In addition to measuring hiring rates for these men and women, she also assessed both their broad traits (i.e., extraversion, neuroticism, agreeableness, conscientiousness, openness) and their facet-level traits (i.e., the narrower traits contained within the five broad traits) on a self-report measure of the FFM of personality.

Powell and colleagues were particularly interested in understanding the role of gender differences in trait scores, should they be observed, in the hiring decisions of the participating organization. On the broad trait level, the researchers found no significant differences between male and female applicants. As the authors noted, this reflects previous research with the FFM. Gender differences were, however, observed on the facet-level traits contained within extraversion (including dominance and affiliation) and conscientiousness (including industriousness).

When the researchers examined the facet-level traits that address the need to be part of a larger social group (what is known as *communion*), they found that women rated higher. In contrast, men rated higher on the facet-level trait that addresses the need to be autonomous (what is known as *agency*). These patterns reflect historical and stereotypical notions of women and men in the workplace. Interestingly, differential hiring rates were observed when women scored lower on agentic traits and men scored lower on communal traits, suggesting a bias in the desired qualities of male versus female applicants. When the employer was made aware of the lower degree of agency among female applicants, they were more likely to hire men; when the employer was made aware of the lower degree of communion among male applicants, they were more likely to hire women. Hiring preferences appeared to reflect differential expectations of male and female employees, but only when the employer was primed to consider these traits. When broad FFM scores were reported, no such differential selection occurred (Powell, Goffin, & Gellatly, 2011).

As noted by the authors, the use of FFM broad traits in the personality assessments of job candidates may be useful in promoting gender diversity in the workplace. However, reports of facet-level or narrow traits, especially those associated with traditional gender role expectations, should not be considered during hiring.

In addition to the Employment Equity Act, the **Canadian Human Rights Act** includes the following as prohibited grounds of discrimination: race, national or ethnic origin, colour, religion, age, sex, sexual orientation, marital status, family status, disability, and conviction for which a pardon has been granted. In all cases, employers should be cautious that psychological testing of any kind, including integrity testing, does not lead to discriminatory hiring or promotion practices that disadvantage any one group of individuals.

Disparate Impact

To prove a case of **disparate impact**, a plaintiff must show that an employment practice disadvantages people from a protected group. Most courts define disparity as a difference that is sufficiently large that it is unlikely to have occurred by chance. Tests of statistical significance are generally used to establish this. Once the court accepts that an adverse impact has occurred, the burden shifts to the employer to prove that the selection practice is job-related and consistent with business necessity. If a test is at its core job-related and consistent with the basic requirements of the occupational role, then in most cases the disparate impact claim is dropped by the court.

There have been relatively few disparate impact cases involving personality tests in North America because such tests generally do not disadvantage any protected group. Integrity tests may have the best record of any selection technique in demonstrating freedom from adverse impact. Moreover, integrity test publishers typically have extensive statistical evidence demonstrating the validity of integrity tests in predicting theft and job-relevant counterproductive behaviour, which would satisfy the employer's burden. Similar data supporting the job relevance for other personality tests also exist. In some cases, however, an organization may need to perform its own validity studies.

Race or Gender Norming

The Canadian Human Rights Act also forbids employers from using different norms or cutoff scores for different groups of people. For example, it would be illegal for a company to set a higher threshold for women than for men on their selection test. A few personality test publishers, including versions of the Myers-Briggs Type Indicator (MBTI), recommend different scoring practices based on **race or gender norming**. This involves the development of different standards based on data obtained from large samples of people. The application of these normative data in employment testing scenarios is clearly discriminatory, and employers should avoid tests of this sort in favour of personality tests with standard norms applied equally to all applicants.

Personnel Selection—Choosing the Right Person for the Job

Imagine giving a person a badge, a powerful car, and several guns, and then telling that person to drive around the community and uphold the law. It would be beneficial if you could somehow make sure that you were not giving all this power to the wrong person. Personality tests are frequently used to screen out the wrong individuals from the pool of applicants for police officers, including the Royal Canadian Mounted Police (RCMP). One of the most frequently administered tests is the revised Minnesota Multiphasic Personality Inventory (MMPI II), which was designed to detect various mental illnesses and related traits. The MMPI II has 550 items, and its primary use is to identify people with significant psychological problems. Individuals with elevated scores reflecting mental or emotional difficulties can be screened out of a pool of potential officers (Barrick & Mount, 1991).

Little was known about which personality traits contribute to the successful performance of the job of police officers until Hargrave and Hiatt (1989) examined the California Personality Inventory (CPI) in relation to police officer performance. In their study, they found that 13 percent of the cadets in training were found to be "unsuitable" by their instructors. Moreover, these unsuitable cadets differed from the "suitable" group on nine scales of the CPI, including the conformity and social presence scales. In another sample of 45 officers on the job who were having serious problems, Hargrave and Hiatt (1989) found that the CPI also discriminated this group from other police officers who were not having problems. These findings provided evidence that the CPI is useful in the selection of police officers, and it, along with other personality questionnaires, is being used for this purpose (e.g., Black, 2000; Coutts, 1990; Grant & Grant, 1996; Lowry, 1997; Mufson & Mufson, 1998).

Personality assessment of potential RCMP officers in Canada places greater emphasis on conscientiousness than other traits in the five-factor model. In particular, qualities associated with persistence, deliberation, and commitment to the job are highly valued. In addition to these traits, research on police officers generally emphasizes boldness and self-confidence, a heightened need for adventure, and a low need for support from others as valuable traits on the job. The personality traits associated with being a good police officer appear to be distributed equally among men and women (Krug, 1981).
©FPW/Alamy Stock Photo

The 16 Personality Factor (16 PF) questionnaire, based on the influential work of Raymond Cattell, is also being used in vocational advising and selection. The 16 PF profile that best matches police officers is one that emphasizes boldness and self-confidence, qualities that facilitate one's abilities to direct or control others and to achieve goals (Krug, 1981). A heightened need for adventure and a strong need to influence others are linked with the enjoyment of careers that provide challenges and opportunities to take charge. The police officer personality profile is low on the need for support from others, which suggests a very self-assured personality. All of these personality characteristics appear to combine into a "masculine" or instrumental profile. Nevertheless, the profile that matches the police prototype occurs equally often among men and women in typical North American samples (Krug, 1981). Psychologically, men and women appear about equally equipped with the personality traits that best match the police officer prototype.

In Canada, RCMP applicants are asked to complete the **Six Factor Personality Questionnaire (SFPQ)** (Jackson et al., 2000) as part of a larger selection battery that includes a polygraph (for more information on RCMP applicant screening, A Closer Look: Fit for the RCMP?). The SFPQ was developed and validated by a team of psychologists from the University of Western Ontario that included such names as Douglas Jackson and Sampo Paunonen. In addition to the standard broad traits of extraversion, agreeableness, and openness to experience, the SFPQ measures a broad trait of *independence* and divides conscientiousness into two distinct factors. In this model, many of the traits associated with emotional stability are included in the agreeableness factor, while independence measures one's tendencies toward autonomy and self-reliance. Conscientiousness is separated into the subscales of *industriousness* (involving diligence, persistence, and commitment to work) and *methodicalness* (involving preferences for order, precision, and deliberation), identifying traits that are particularly salient to the responsibilities of a police officer. Research has indicated that this revised six-factor structure may demonstrate greater validity in occupational settings compared to the Big Five measures, particularly in its ability to predict success at work (Jackson et al., 2000). Provincial and municipal police forces in Canada also administer personality tests to screen applicants, with the MMPI, the NEO-PI-R, and the 16 PF being popular choices.

 **A Closer Look**

Fit for the RCMP?

Individuals interested in joining the Royal Canadian Mounted Police (RCMP) must pass a series of tests and screening procedures before being considered for hiring. These tests range from physical and mental health measures to thorough background checks, polygraph interviews, and psychological assessments. One component, the RCMP Police Aptitude Battery (RPAB), consists of two examinations. The first part is the RCMP Police Aptitude Test (RPAT), designed to evaluate an applicant's potential aptitude for police work. It measures seven mental skills or abilities that are essential in fulfilling the duties and responsibilities of a police officer. Targeted abilities address various aspects of human intelligence, including composition (spelling, grammar, and vocabulary), comprehension, memory, judgment, observation, logic, and computation.

The second part of the RPAB consists of the Canadian-developed Six Factor Personality Questionnaire (SFPQ; Jackson et al., 2000), which is an extension of the five-factor model of personality. Developed and tested by a team of Canadian psychologists from the University of Western Ontario, the SFPQ extends the five-factor model by including a broad trait labelled *independence* and further dividing the conscientiousness trait into two subscales: *industriousness* and *methodicalness*. It is these two components of conscientiousness that are of particular interest to the RCMP applicant screening process, as they relate directly to some of the principled behaviours sought in new officers. In particular, these traits demonstrate a relationship with such qualities as integrity, honesty, and commitment to rules and procedures. The total SFPQ consists of 108 questions and takes approximately 45 minutes to complete. In terms of weighting, it comprises approximately 40 percent of the final aptitude battery score. Results are then analyzed and compared to other applicants; those with the most competitive scores (i.e., the most desirable traits and capacities) are deemed most eligible for the job. Like most personality tests that are used in employment settings, the RCMP's screening process has received its fair share of criticism; however, with such sizeable responsibilities, most would agree that some form of intensive screening is needed. Applicants who are selected for the job must undergo six months of intensive training in Regina, Saskatchewan, before beginning their two-year probationary period at their first post as a police officer.

Source: Royal Canadian Mounted Police, 2016.

Selection in Business Settings—The Myers-Briggs Type Indicator

Businesses confront critical decisions on which success or failure hinge. Different jobs pose different demands, and it's likely that personality plays a critical role in determining success in different positions. By far the most widely used personality assessment device in business settings is the **Myers-Briggs Type Indicator (MBTI)** (Myers et al., 1998). The test was developed by a mother–daughter team, Katharine Briggs and Isabel Myers, anchored in Jungian concepts (see Chapter 10). The test provides information about personality by testing for eight fundamental preferences. A sample item: "Do you usually value sentiment more than logic, or value logic more than sentiment?" This type of item is an example of a "forced-choice" format, in which individuals must respond in one way or another, even if they feel that their preferences might be somewhere in the middle. The eight fundamental preferences are shown in Table 4.1.

Table 4.1 Eight Fundamental Preferences Measured by the Myers-Briggs Type Indicator	
Extraversion	**Introversion**
Draws energy from the outside; involved with people; likes action and activity	Draws energy from internal world of thoughts and ideas
Sensing	**Intuition**
Prefers taking in information through all five senses; attends to what actually exists	Prefers information derived from a "sixth sense"; notices what's possible rather than what is
Thinking	**Feeling**
Prefers logic, organization, and clean objective structure	Prefers a person- and value-oriented way of processing information
Judging	**Perceiving**
Prefers living a well-ordered and controlled life	Prefers to live spontaneously, with room for flexible spur-of-the-moment activities

These eight fundamental preferences reduce to four scores—you are either extraverted OR introverted; sensing OR intuitive; thinking OR feeling; judging OR perceiving. These four scores are then combined to yield *types.* Indeed, each person is placed into one of the 16 types yielded by their four scores. For example, you could be an *ESTP* type: Extraverted, Sensing, Thinking, and Perceiving. This type, according to the MBTI authors, has a distinctive leadership style in business settings. ESTPs like to take charge when a crisis occurs; they are good at persuading others to adopt their point of view; they are assertive and lead the group to the most direct route to the goal; and they want to see immediate results.

Contrast this with another type, an *INFJ:* Introverted, Intuitive, Feeling, and Judging. This type, according to the authors of the instrument, has a fundamentally different leadership style. Rather than take charge and assert, INFJs are more likely to develop a *vision* for the organization; get others to cooperate rather than demand cooperation; work to inspire others rather than command others; and work solidly and with integrity and consistency to achieve business goals. One can readily imagine that different types of business leaders would be better in different organizational settings. In a time of crisis, for example, an ESTP might be better at organizing others to deal with immediate threats. On a plateau in business, an INFJ might be better at pausing to reflect on a long-term vision for the organization.

It is estimated that over 3 million people a year take the MBTI (Gardner & Martinko, 1996). Although it was developed for applications in education, counselling, career guidance, and workplace team-building, it is also widely used in personnel selection settings (Pittenger, 2005). Its wide use most likely comes from its intuitive appeal; people can readily understand the relevance of the personality traits supposedly measured by this test.

There are, however, several problems with the MBTI. The first problem is that the theory on which it is based—Carl Jung's theory of **psychological types**—is not widely endorsed by academic or research-oriented psychologists. For one thing, people don't come in "types," such as extraverted types and introverted types. Instead, most personality traits are normally distributed. Figure 4.3 illustrates the difference between data that would support a type model of introversion–extraversion (called a *bimodal distribution*) and the real data on introversion–extraversion, which are normally distributed according to a bell-shaped curve. Very few human characteristics follow a typological or bimodal distribution. Biological sex is one characteristic that does conform to a bimodal distribution; there are many female-type people, as well as many male-type people, and very few people in between. The distribution of extraversion–introversion is not like this at all; it has only one peak, right in the middle, suggesting that the majority of people are neither purely introverted nor purely extraverted, but are somewhere in between. Virtually all personality traits follow this normal distribution, so the concept of personality "types" is simply not justified.

One consequence of forcing a typology onto a trait that is normally distributed concerns the importance of cutoff scores for classifying people into one category or the other (e.g., as introverted or extraverted). Most users of the MBTI use the median score (the score at which 50 percent fall above and 50 percent fall below) from some standardization sample as the cutoff. The problem lies in the fact that a large percentage of people in any sample will be clustered right around the median score. If that median score moves a point or two in either direction, because of differences in sample characteristics used to determine the cutoff score, a very large number of people will be reclassified into their opposite category. In fact, a person with an introversion–extraversion score of 20 might be classified as an introvert in one sample (if it had a median of 21) and classified as an extravert in another sample (if it had a median of 19). So, the same individual score (a 20) will be interpreted very differently depending on the median used to perform the cutoff for classification. Despite this problem with cutoff scores and typologies, the majority of users of the MBTI continue to follow the scoring

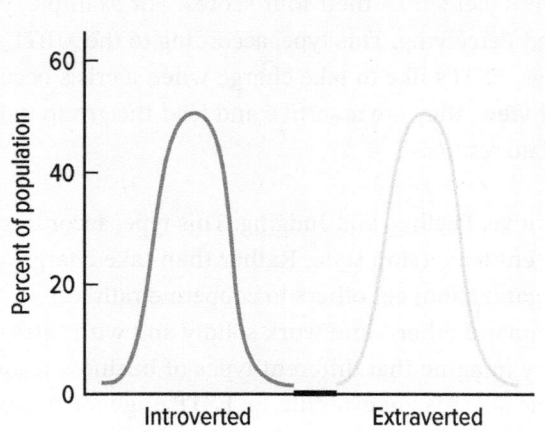

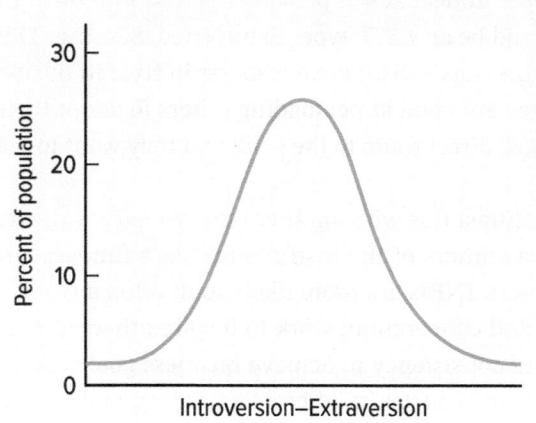

A Hypothetical data on the trait of introversion–extraversion if it followed a truly type-like distribution in the population. There would be a large number of introverts, a large number of extraverts, and few people in between.

B Typical data on the trait of introversion–extraversion, which follows a bell curve or normal distribution in the population. There are a large number of people in between the relatively rare extreme introverts and extreme extraverts.

FIGURE 4.3 Examples illustrating what the trait of introversion–extraversion would look like in terms of distributions in the population if it followed a type model (Panel A) or a normal distribution model (Panel B). Real data support the normal distribution model, not the type model.

system that classifies individuals into letter category groups, a practice that has been soundly criticized in the professional consulting literature (e.g., Pittenger, 2005).

Another related consequence of using a typology scheme for scoring the MBTI is that the scores will be unreliable. Reliability is often estimated by testing a group of people twice, separated by a period of time. With the MBTI, because cutoff scores are used to categorize people into groups, and because many people are very close to the cutoff scores, slight changes in people's raw scores on retesting can result in a large percentage being reclassified into different personality types. Indeed, a study of the test-retest reliability of the MBTI (McCarley & Clarskadon, 1983) showed that, across a five-week test-retest interval, 50 percent of the participants received a different classification on one or more of the type categories. These results are not surprising, and this is one reason most scientific personality psychologists do not recommend using typological scoring systems for any personality measure.

Another problem with typological scoring systems is that it assumes large between-category differences, and no within-category differences, among people. For example, all extraverted types are assumed to be alike, and introverted types are assumed to be very different from extraverted types. This, however, is not necessarily the case. Imagine two people who score as extraverted types, yet one of these is just one point above the median and the other is 31 points above the median. These two extraverted types are likely to be very different from each other (they differ by 30 points on the scale yet are given the same type category). Now imagine an introverted type who scored one point below the median, and an extraverted type who scored one point above the median. This introvert and this extravert are likely to be indistinguishable from each other (they differ by only 2 points on the scale yet are given different type categories). This is another reason psychologists who know about measurement issues avoid using type scoring systems for any personality test.

Dozens of validity studies of the MBTI have been published, mostly relating type categories to occupational preferences. These studies have been criticized, however, because most fail to report statistical details necessary to determine whether the differences are significant. For example, Gardner and Martinko (1996) review 13 studies that examined the distribution of MBTI types in managerial professions. All of these studies reported the frequencies of types in different categories, yet none reported scale score means that would have allowed strong statistical tests of mean personality differences among the different managerial categories. Moreover, other reviewers (e.g., Hunsley, Lee, & Wood, 2003) point out that no adequate tests have been done on the predictive validity of the MBTI (e.g., that the MBTI can predict *future* career choices or job satisfaction). Also, virtually no studies have been done examining the incremental validity of the MBTI (e.g., whether the MBTI can add meaningfully to the prediction of career choice or job satisfaction above and beyond that obtained with more traditional personality measures).

Every few years psychologists take a fresh look at the evidence for the MBTI and summarize what they find. In 1991, Bjork and Druckman reviewed the evidence and concluded: "At this time, there is not sufficient, well-designed research to justify the use of the MBTI in career counseling programs" (p. 99). A few years later, Boyle (1995) also reviewed the literature and found no strong scientific evidence supporting the utility of the MBTI. In 2003, Hunsley, Lee, and Wood reviewed the latest evidence and summarized their findings: "One can only conclude that the MBTI is insufficient as a contemporary measure of personality" (pp. 63–64). And in an even more recent review paper, Pittenger (2005) evaluated all of the scientific literature on the MBTI and concluded: "Using the MBTI to select employees, to assign employees to work groups or assignments, or for other forms of employment evaluation are [sic] not justified for the simple reason that there are no available data to recommend such decisions" (p. 219).

Given the highly negative reviews on the scientific merit of the MBTI, why does it continue to be a hugely popular tool in consulting and career counselling? There are probably several reasons. First, the popularity of the MBTI may reflect the success of the publisher's marketing campaign. In addition, the test comes with rather simple scoring and interpretation instructions, making it usable and understandable by people without advanced training in personality psychology. Moreover, the interpretations the test offers are readily translated into seemingly sensible predictions about work and interpersonal relations. Like the popularity of horoscopes, people like hearing about themselves and their futures, even if little or no scientific evidence exists for those descriptions and predictions.

Is there any legitimate use for the MBTI? Although it should definitely not be used as the single piece of evidence on which to base employment selections or career decisions, it may have a role in such areas as team-building, career exploration, or relationship counselling. The test can get people thinking about differences among people. People with vastly different personalities see the world differently, and if the test fosters an appreciation for this diversity, then it may be useful. The test might also be useful if it gets people thinking about the relationship between personality and behaviour. If we understand that how we act toward others, and they toward us, is influenced in part by our personalities, then this increases our ability to understand and relate well to others. For example, if teachers take the MBTI as part of a "teacher development workshop," they may think about their own teaching style or may gain an awareness that not all pupils are alike in how they relate to teachers. The test may even act as a catalyst for group exercises or team building that fosters *esprit de corps* among group members. For example, at a "corporate retreat" a group of managers may take the test and then explore ways that they can work better as a team given the differences in their personalities. So the test may indeed have some utility for getting people to think about personality, even though the test does not appear adequate as an instrument for selection.

Selection in Business Settings—The Hogan Personality Inventory

Because of the problems noted earlier, the Myers-Briggs Type Indicator test should probably not be used to select employees. Which tests are good alternatives? There are literally thousands of published personality tests (Spies & Plake, 2005) and hundreds of companies that use personality tests to help other companies select employees. We have chosen one of these companies and one of their personality tests to describe here, mainly because the procedures they use are based on a solid scientific foundation. The company is called Hogan Assessment Systems, and its main personality test is called the Hogan Personality Inventory.

The founder of this assessment company, Robert Hogan, was a professor of psychology at the University of Tulsa for many years. He had been teaching and doing research in personality psychology through the 1970s and 1980s, even becoming the head editor of the most prestigious scientific journal in personality psychology, the *Journal of Personality and Social Psychology*. During this time, Hogan's own research concerned efforts to identify aspects of personality important in contemporary business settings. He started with the Big Five model of personality but focused on how these traits might work in the business world. He developed a theory about the social aspects of personality that are important to business and concluded that the dominant themes in social life are the motive to get along with others and the motive to get ahead of others.

In most business settings, people work in groups, and every group has a status hierarchy. Hogan's theory states that, within such groups, people want three things: (1) acceptance, including respect and approval; (2) status and the control of resources; and (3) predictability (Hogan, 2005). Some of Hogan's research showed that business problems often occur when a manager violates one or more of these motives within a work group, for example by treating staff with disrespect, by micromanaging in a way that takes away the staff's sense of control, or by not communicating or providing feedback, thereby making the workplace unpredictable.

Hogan developed a questionnaire measure of personality, called the **Hogan Personality Inventory (HPI)**, that measures aspects of the Big Five traits that are relevant to the above three motives important to business. For the details on why and how this inventory was developed, see Hogan and Hogan (2002). The traits this inventory measures are described in Table 4.2. Hogan and his wife, Joyce Hogan, also a research psychologist, started using this inventory in research on the effectiveness of people working in a variety of businesses. They began to look at how specific job requirements fit with specific combinations of these personality traits. Soon they were doing validity studies, exploring how the personality test predicted how well people fit into specific business cultures. They also conducted outcome studies, to see how well the personality inventory predicted occupational performance in a wide variety of jobs. Across a large number of studies, the test achieved high levels of reliability and acceptable levels of validity for predicting a number of important occupational outcomes, including organizational fit and performance. Joyce Hogan and J. Holland (2003) provide a meta-analysis of 28 validity studies on the Hogan Personality Inventory, the results of which strongly support the validity of the personality scales for predicting several important job-relevant criteria.

Table 4.2   The Hogan Personality Inventory (HPI) Contains Seven Primary Scales and Six Occupational Scales

Primary Scales	Occupational Scales
Adjustment—self-confidence, self-esteem, and composure under pressure. The opposite of neuroticism.	***Service Orientation***—being attentive, pleasant, and courteous to customers.
Ambition—initiative, competitiveness, and the desire for leadership roles.	***Stress Tolerance***—being able to handle stress, remaining even-tempered and calm under fire.
Sociability—extraversion, gregariousness, and a need for social interaction.	***Reliability***—honesty, integrity, and positive organizational citizenship.
Interpersonal Sensitivity—warmth, charm, and the ability to maintain good relationships.	***Clerical Potential***—following directions, attending to detail, and communicating clearly.
Prudence—self-discipline, responsibility, and conscientiousness.	***Sales Potential***—energy, social skills, and the ability to solve customers' problems.
Inquisitiveness—imagination, curiosity, vision, and creative potential.	***Managerial Potential***—leadership ability, planning, and decision-making skills.
Learning Approach—enjoying learning, staying current on business and technical matters.	

In 1987, Robert and Joyce Hogan started their own company, Hogan Assessment Systems, to consult with businesses that wanted to use personality measures to select employees. Soon afterward, Robert Hogan left his position at the University of Tulsa to devote his full effort toward helping companies successfully use personality measures in business applications. The Hogans continue to use a scientific approach to improve and validate the use of their personality inventory in the business community. Their focus is mainly on determining the statistical personality profiles of people who perform well in specific job categories, and how these personality profiles fit with specific business cultures.

Why is the Hogan Personality Inventory (HPI) a better choice than the MBTI when it comes to employee selection? First, the HPI is based on the Big Five model, which has been modified specifically for applications to the workplace. The construction and development of the HPI followed standard statistical procedures, resulting in an inventory with a high level of measurement reliability (test-retest correlations range from .74 to .86). To date, there have been more than 400 validity studies of the HPI. These studies have examined the ability of the test to predict a wide variety of important business results in a large number of job categories, such as employee turnover, absenteeism, improved sales performance, customer service, employee satisfaction, customer satisfaction, and overall business performance. The test has been able to predict occupational success in a wide variety of job categories. Personality profiles on the HPI are available for over 200 different work categories that span the range of jobs in the U.S. economy. The company maintains a database from over a million people who have taken the HPI.

The HPI itself consists of true–false items and takes about 20 minutes to administer. None of the items are invasive or intrusive, and none of the scales show adverse impact on the basis of gender or race or ethnicity.

The test is also available in a number of foreign languages. Hogan Assessment Systems maintains a research archive and record-keeping practice for the HPI. If a company using the HPI is sued by a job applicant, Hogan Assessment Systems will provide reports and records on test development and validity necessary to defend the case. The selection procedures and validation research on the HPI have never been successfully challenged in court. The test authors are members of the American Psychological Association and the Society for Industrial and Organizational Psychology, both of which mandate professional levels of ethical, legal, and scientific standards with regard to assessment practices.

Because of all these positive qualities, including the research base and demonstrated effectiveness of the test, use of the HPI in business and industry has grown tremendously in the last 30 years. Hogan Assessment Systems has consulted with 60 percent of the Fortune 100 companies and has provided assessment services to more than a thousand other customers around the world. Currently, in any given month, between 300 and 500 companies utilize their services to select or develop employees.

While Hogan Assessment Systems provides other services, such as employee development, we will describe one case example of the use of the HPI in employee selection applications. A leading financial services company approached Hogan Assessment Systems to develop a preemployment assessment procedure to select financial consultants. The job requirements were analyzed and compared to known validity research on performance in related jobs, and a personality selection profile was determined. After new people were hired and on the job for a few years, the company evaluated the effectiveness of the selection procedure by comparing the performance of financial consultants hired before and after the selection procedure went into effect. They found that those financial consultants hired on the basis of their personality profiles earned 20 percent more in commissions annually, conducted 32 percent more volume in dollar terms annually, and made 42 percent more trades annually. Obviously, selecting those applicants with the "right stuff" was beneficial to this company. Other business examples of the use of the HPI in selecting employees can be found at www.hoganassessments.com.

It is clear that personality factors can play an important role in predicting who does well in specific employment settings. When it comes to using personality tests to select employees for specific positions, one should realize that not all personality tests do the job equally well. Clearly those assessment systems with a strong scientific base, grounded in an accepted theory of personality, with acceptable reliability and strong evidence of validity relative to the needs of the company will have the best potential for helping business users achieve positive results.

! Concept Check

Imagine you are a manager of a large retail store. You recently had to let go of two employees because they were stealing from the company. In your next round of hiring, what psychological tests can you administer in order to avoid hiring employees with similar problems?

Describe the unique approach that is taken by the Myers-Briggs Type Indicator (MBTI). What has research on the MBTI revealed about its utility for employee screening and selection?

Summary and Evaluation

This chapter described some important issues and concepts that the various trait theories have in common. The hallmark of the trait perspective is an emphasis on differences among people. Trait psychology focuses on the study of differences, the classification of differences, and the analysis of the consequences of differences among people. Trait psychology assumes that people will be relatively consistent over time in their behaviour because of the various traits they possess. Trait psychologists also assume a degree of cross-situational consistency for traits. Psychologists assume that people will be *more or less* consistent in their behaviour, depending on the particular trait being studied and the situations in which it is observed. Nevertheless, some situations are very strong in terms of their influence on behaviour. Some situations are so strong that they overpower the influence of personality traits. One important lesson is that traits are more likely to influence a person's behaviour when situations are weak and ambiguous and don't push for conformity from all people.

Most trait psychologists agree that personality trait scores refer primarily to average tendencies in behaviour. A score on a trait measure refers to how a person is likely to behave, on average, over a number of occasions and situations. Trait psychologists are better at predicting average tendencies in behaviour than specific acts on specific occasions. For example, from a person's high score on a measure of trait hostility, a personality psychologist could not predict whether this person is likely to get into a fight tomorrow. However, the psychologist could confidently predict that such a person is more likely to be in more fights in the next few years than a person with a lower score on hostility. Traits represent average tendencies in behaviour.

Trait psychologists are also interested in the accuracy of measurement. More than any other personality perspective, trait psychology has occupied itself with efforts to improve the measurement of traits, particularly through self-report questionnaire measures. Psychologists who devise questionnaires work hard at making them less susceptible to lying, faking, and careless responding.

A particularly important measurement issue is social desirability, or the tendency to exaggerate the positivity of one's personality. Currently, trait psychologists hold that one motive for socially desirable responding is the test taker's desire to convey a certain impression (usually positive). This behaviour is sometimes referred to as *impression management*. Many psychologists worry about social desirability as a response set, thinking that it lowers the validity of the trait measure. However, another view on social desirability is that socially desirable responding is a valid response by some people who simply view themselves as better or more desirable than most, or who actually have deceived themselves into thinking they are better off psychologically than they probably are. As is typical, trait psychologists have devised measures to identify and distinguish between these two types of socially desirable responding.

Finally, their interest in measurement and prediction has led trait psychologists to apply these skills to the selection and screening of job applicants and other situations in which personality might make a difference. There are legal issues employers must keep in mind when using trait measures as a basis for making important hiring or promotion decisions. For example, tests must not discriminate unfairly against protected groups, such as women and certain minorities. In addition, the tests must be shown to be related to important real-life variables, such as job performance. We considered a number of important legal cases in employment law that are relevant to personality testing. We also considered two specific instruments that are popular in employment selection settings. One instrument, the Myers-Briggs Type Indicator, is widely used but also widely criticized in the scientific literature for its low levels of measurement reliability and unproven validity. The other instrument, the Hogan Personality Inventory, can be considered a "best practice" case when it comes to the use of personality in employee selection.

Concept Check

Briefly summarize the historical debate between trait psychologists and situationists. How is this debate seen by psychologists today?

What are the main ethical concerns surrounding personality testing in employment settings, and how can they be overcome?

What concerns exist with personality testing more broadly?

Key Terms

differential psychology	density distribution of states	Employment Equity Act
consistency	infrequency scale	Canadian Human Rights Act
rank order	faking	disparate impact
situationism	false negative	race or gender norming
person–situation interaction	false positive	Six Factor Personality Questionnaire (SFPQ)
aggregation	Barnum statements	Myers-Briggs Type Indicator (MBTI)
situational specificity	personnel selection	
strong situation	integrity tests	psychological types
situational selection	negligent hiring	Hogan Personality Inventory (HPI)
evocation	right to privacy	

CHAPTER 5

Personality Dispositions over Time: Stability, Coherence, and Change

The Dispositional Domain

Think back to your days in high school. Can you remember what you were like then? Try to recall what you were most interested in, how you spent your time, what things were most important to you at that time of your life. If you are like most people, you probably feel that, in many ways, you are a different person now than you were in high school. Your interests have probably changed somewhat. Different things may be important to you. Your attitudes about school, family, and relationships have probably all changed at least a bit. Perhaps now you are more mature and have a more experienced view of the world.

As you think about what you were like then and what you are like now, you probably also feel that there is a core of "you" that is essentially the same

Even though people change and develop as they age, each person still has a sense of self as the same person from year to year. As we see in this chapter on development, when it comes to personality, some things change and some things stay the same.
©Andrea Laurita/Getty Images

over the years. If you are like most people, you have a sense of an enduring part of you, a feeling that you are "really" the same person now as then. Certain inner qualities seem the same over these several years.

In this chapter, we explore the psychological continuities and changes over time that define the topic of personality development. When it comes to personality, "Some things change; some things stay the same." In this chapter, we discuss how psychologists think about personality development, with a primary focus on personality traits or dispositions.

Conceptual Issues: Personality Development, Stability, Coherence, and Change

This section defines personality development, examines the major ways of thinking about personality stability over time, and explores what it means to say that personality has changed. The study of personality development has attracted increasing research attention, with an entire issue of the *Journal of Personality* devoted to the topic (Graziano, 2003).

What Is Personality Development?

Personality development can be defined as the continuities, consistencies, and stabilities in people over time *and* the ways in which people change over time. Each of these two facets—stability and change—requires definitions and qualifications. There are many forms of personality stability and, correspondingly, many forms of personality change. The three most important forms of stability are rank order stability, mean level stability, and personality coherence. We discuss each of these in turn. Then we examine personality change.

Rank Order Stability

Rank order stability is the maintenance of individual position within a group. Between ages 14 and 20, most people become taller, but the rank order of heights tends to remain fairly stable because this form of development affects all people pretty much the same, adding a few centimeters to everyone. The tall people at age 14 generally fall toward the tall end of the distribution at age 20. The same can apply to personality traits. If people tend to maintain their positions on dominance or extraversion relative to the others over time, then there is high rank order stability to those personality characteristics. Conversely, if people fail to maintain their rank order—if the submissive people rise up and put down the dominants, for example—then the group is displaying rank order instability, or **rank order change**. Rank order stability and change are commonly examined in research by looking at test-retest correlations. If a correlation between time points is high, it suggests that individuals' scores have remained relatively stable. On the other hand, low test-retest correlations would suggest rank order change.

 Exercise

To illustrate the phrase "Some things change; some things stay the same," consider your first years of high school and compare that with the period just after high school—typically, your college or university years. Identify three characteristics that have changed noticeably during that period. These characteristics might be your interests, your attitudes, your values, and what you like to do with your time. Then list three characteristics about you that have not changed. Again, these characteristics could reflect certain traits of your personality, your interests, your values, or even your attitudes about various topics. Write them down in the following format:

	What I was like when I started high school:	What I was like after high school:
Characteristics that have changed	1. _____	1. _____
	2. _____	2. _____
	3. _____	3. _____
Characteristics that have not changed	1. _____	
	2. _____	
	3. _____	

Mean Level Stability

Another kind of personality stability is constancy of level, or **mean level stability**. Consider political orientation. If the average level of liberalism or conservatism in a group remains the same over time, the group exhibits high mean level stability. If the average degree of political orientation changes—for example, if people tend to become increasingly conservative as they get older—then that population is displaying **mean level change**. Mean level stability and change are examined in research by comparing average levels (means) of a trait at different points in time. If the means do not differ significantly over time, then this provides evidence of mean level stability. If they do differ significantly, some degree of change has occurred on the population level.

Personality Coherence

A more complex form of personality development involves changes in the *manifestations* of a trait. Consider the trait of dominance. Suppose that the people who are dominant at age 8 are the same people who are dominant at age 20. The 8-year-olds, however, manifest their dominance by showing toughness in rough-and-tumble play, calling their rivals names, and insisting on monopolizing the computer games. At the age of 20, they manifest their dominance by persuading others to accept their views in political discussions, boldly asking someone out on a date, and insisting on the restaurant at which the group will eat.

This form of personality development—maintaining rank order in relation to other individuals but changing the manifestations of the trait—is called **personality coherence**. Notice that this form of personality coherence does not require that the precise behavioural manifestations of a trait remain the same. Indeed, the manifestations may be so different that there is literally no overlap between age 8 and age 20. The act manifestations have all changed, but something critical has remained the same—the overall level of dominant acts. Thus, personality coherence includes both elements of stability and elements of change—stability in the underlying trait but change in the outward manifestation of that trait. For a case study of personality stability, read A Closer Look: Mahatma Gandhi, A Case of Personal Stability.

The manifestation of disagreeableness may differ across the life span, ranging from temper tantrums in infancy to being argumentative and having a short temper in adulthood. Even though the behaviours are different at the different ages, they nevertheless express the same underlying trait. This kind of consistency is called personality coherence.

(top): ©Design Pics/Kristy-Anne Glubish; (bottom): ©AlexanderNovikov/Getty Images

---

 A Closer Look

Mahatma Gandhi, a Case of Personality Stability

Mohandas Karamchand Gandhi was born in 1869 into a family of modest means in India. His mother was devoutly religious, and she impressed young Mohandas with her beliefs and practices. The Gandhi family not only practised traditional Hinduism but also practised Buddhist chants, read from the Koran, and even sang traditional Christian hymns. Mohandas developed a personal philosophy of life that led him to renounce all personal desires and to devote himself to the service of his fellow human beings.

After studying law in England, and practising for a few years in South Africa, Gandhi returned to India. At that time, India was under British rule, and most Indians resented the oppression of their colonial rulers. Gandhi devoted himself to the ideal of Indian self-rule and to freedom from British oppression. When the British decided to fingerprint all Indians, for example, Gandhi came up with an idea he called passive resistance—he encouraged all Indians to simply refuse to go in for fingerprinting. During the period of 1919–1922, Gandhi led widespread but nonviolent strikes and boycotts throughout India. He coordinated campaigns of peaceful noncooperation with anything British—he urged Indians not to send their children to the British-run schools, not to participate in the courts, even not to adopt the English language. In their frustration, British soldiers sometimes attacked crowds of boycotting or striking Indians, and many Indians were killed. The people of India loved Gandhi. They followed him in droves, recording everything he did and said. He became a living legend, and the people referred to him as Maha Atma, or the Great Soul. We know him today as Mahatma Gandhi.

In 1930, Gandhi led the Indian people in nonviolent defiance of the British law forbidding Indian people from making their own salt. He started out with a few of his followers on a march to the coast of India, intending to make salt from seawater. By the time Gandhi had reached the sea, several thousand people had joined him in this act of civil disobedience. By this time, the British had jailed more than 60,000 Indians for disobedience to British law. The jails of India were bursting with native people put there by foreign rulers for breaking foreign laws. The British rulers were finally coming to some sense of embarrassment and shame for this situation. In the eyes of the world, this frail man Gandhi and his nonviolent followers were shaking the foundation of the British Empire in India.

Gandhi was not an official of the Indian government. Nevertheless, the British began negotiations with him to free India from British rule. During negotiations, the British played tough and put Gandhi in jail. The Indian people demonstrated and nearly a thousand of them were killed by the British, bringing shame on the colonial rulers in the eyes of the world. Gandhi was finally freed and a few years later, in 1947, Britain handed India its independence.

Gandhi negotiated a mostly peaceful transition from British rule to self-rule for the people of India. In his lifetime, he was one of the most influential leaders in the world. His ideas have influenced the struggles of many oppressed groups since.

In 1948, an assassin fired three bullets into Gandhi at point-blank range. The assassin was a Hindu fanatic who believed that Gandhi should have used his position to preach hatred of the Muslims of India. Gandhi instead preached tolerance and trust, urging Muslims and Hindus to participate together in the new nation of India. This most nonviolent and tolerant man became a victim of violence.

Mahatma Gandhi lived in a tumultuous period and led one of the largest social revolutions in human history. Despite the changing conditions of his life, his personality remained remarkably stable. For example, he practised self-denial and self-sufficiency throughout his adult life, preferring a simple loincloth and shawl to the suit and tie worn by most leaders of the world's great nations.
©Dinodia Photos/Hulton Archive/Getty Images

Even though Gandhi became the "Father of India," he remained essentially the same person throughout his adult life. Each day of his life, he washed himself in ashes instead of expensive soap, and he shaved with an old, dull straight razor rather than with more expensive blades. He cleaned his own house and swept his yard almost every day. Each afternoon he spun thread on a hand-wheel for an hour or two. The thread was then made into cloth for his own clothes and for the clothes of his followers. He practised the self-denial and self-sufficiency he learned early in his life. In most ways, his personality was remarkably stable over his life, even though he was at the centre of one of the most tumultuous social revolutions in history.

Personality Change

The notion of personality development in the sense of change over time also requires elaboration. To start with, not all change qualifies as development. For instance, if you walk from one classroom to another, your relationship to your surroundings has changed. But we do not speak of your "development" in this case because the change is external to you and not enduring.

And not all internal changes can properly be considered development. When you get sick, for example, your body undergoes important changes: your temperature may rise, your nose may run, and your head may ache. But these changes do not constitute development because the changes do not last—you soon get healthy, your nose stops running, and you spring back into action. In the same way, temporary changes in personality—due to taking alcohol or drugs, for example—do not constitute personality development unless they produce more enduring changes in personality.

If you were to become consistently more conscientious or responsible as you aged, however, this would be a form of personality development. If you were to become gradually less energetic as you aged, this also would be a form of personality development.

In sum, personality change has two defining qualities. First, the changes are typically *internal* to the person, not merely changes in the external surroundings, such as walking into another room. Second, the changes are relatively *enduring* over time, rather than being merely temporary.

 Concept Check

What is the difference between rank order and mean level stability? What about rank order and mean level change? Provide an example of each.

Define personality coherence, and provide an example.

Three Levels of Analysis

We can examine personality over time at three levels of analysis: the population as a whole, group differences within the population, and individual differences within groups. As we examine the empirical research on personality development, it is useful to keep these three levels in mind.

Population Level

Several personality psychologists have theorized about the changes that we all go through in navigating from infancy to adulthood. Freud's theory of psychosexual development, for example, contained a conception of personality development that was presumed to apply to *everyone* on the planet. All people, according to Freud, go through an invariant stage sequence, starting with the oral stage and ending with the mature genital stage of psychosexual development (see Chapter 9).

This level of personality development deals with the changes and constancies that apply more or less to everyone. For example, almost everyone in the population tends to increase in sexual motivation at puberty. Similarly, there is a general decrease in impulsive and risk-taking behaviours as people get older. This is why car insurance rates go down as people age, because a typical 30-year-old is much less likely than a typical 16-year-old to drive in a risky manner. This change in impulsivity is part of the population level of personality change, describing a general trend that might be part of what it means to be human and go through life.

Group Differences Level

Some changes over time affect different groups of people differently. Sex differences are one type of group differences. In the realm of physical development, for example, females go through puberty, on average, two years earlier than males. At the other end of life, men in Canada tend to die four years earlier than women. These are sex differences in development.

Analogous sex differences can occur in the realm of personality development. As a group, men and women suddenly develop differently from one another during adolescence in their average levels of risk taking (men become more risk taking). Men and women also develop differently in the degree to which they show empathy toward others (women develop a stronger awareness and understanding of others' feelings). These forms of personality development are properly located at the group differences level of personality analysis.

Other group differences include cultural or ethnic group differences. For example, in Canada there is a large difference in levels of extraversion and antagonism between European Canadian children and Asian Canadian

Some changes affect different groups of people differently. For example, European Canadian children tend to be, as a group, much higher in their levels of extraversion and antagonism than are Asian Canadian children. Consequently, European Canadian children have a higher risk for developing externalizing disorders, such as attention-deficit/hyperactivity disorder.

(left): ©Hero/Corbis/Glow Images; (right): ©Paul Bradbury/age fotostock

children. European Canadian children tend to be, as a group, much higher in both of these personality dimensions than are Asian Canadian children. Consequently, European Canadian children are higher in externalizing behaviours and at greater risk for developing externalizing disorders such as attention-deficit/hyperactivity disorder (ADHD) or conduct disorder, whereas Asian Canadian children are higher in internalizing behaviours and at greater risk for developing internalizing disorders such as depression or anxiety (Kotelnikova & Tackett, 2009).

Individual Differences Level

Personality psychologists also focus on individual differences in personality development. For example, can we predict, based on their personalities, which individuals will go through a midlife crisis? Can we predict who will be at risk for a psychological disturbance later in life based on earlier measures of personality? Can we predict which individuals will change over time and which ones will remain the same? These issues are located at the individual differences level of personality analysis.

 Concept Check

At what levels of analysis can we examine personality over time?

Personality Stability over Time

This section examines the research on the stability of personality over the lifetime. We first examine stability in infancy, then explore stability during childhood, and finally look at stability during the decades of adulthood.

Stability of Temperament During Infancy

Many parents of two or more children will tell you that their children had distinctly different personalities starting from the day they were born. For example, Albert Einstein, the Nobel Prize–winning father of modern physics, had two sons with his first wife. These two boys were quite different from each other. The older boy, Hans, was fascinated with puzzles as a child and had a gift for mathematics. He went on to become a distinguished professor of hydraulics. The younger son, Eduard, enjoyed music and literature as a child. As a young adult, however, he ended up in a Swiss psychiatric hospital, where he died. Although this is an extreme example, many parents notice differences among their children, even as infants. Do the intuitions of parents square with the scientific evidence?

By far the most commonly studied personality characteristics in infancy and childhood fall under the category of temperament. Although there is some disagreement about what the term means, most researchers define **temperament** as the individual differences that emerge very early in life, are likely to have a heritable basis (see Chapter 6), and are often involved with emotionality or arousability.

Mary Rothbart (1981, 1986; Rothbart & Hwang, 2005) studied infants at different ages, starting at 3 months of age. She examined six factors of temperament, using ratings completed by the caregivers:

1. *Activity level:* the infant's overall motor activity, including arm and leg movements.
2. *Smiling and laughter:* how much the infant smiles or laughs.

3. *Fear:* the infant's distress and reluctance to approach novel stimuli.
4. *Distress to limitations:* the child's distress at being refused food, being dressed, being confined, or being prevented access to a desired object.
5. *Soothability:* the degree to which the child reduces stress, or calms down, as a result of being soothed.
6. *Duration of orienting:* the degree to which the child sustains attention to objects in the absence of sudden changes.

The caregivers, mostly mothers, completed observer-based scales designed to measure these six aspects of temperament. Table 5.1 shows the cross-time correlations over different time intervals. If you scan the correlations in the table, you will notice first that they are all positive. This means that infants who tend to score high at one time period on activity level, smiling and laughter, and the other personality traits also tend to score high on these traits at later time periods.

Table 5.1 Stability Correlations for Temperament Scales						
	Months					
Scale	**3–6**	**3–9**	**3–12**	**6–9**	**6–12**	**9–12**
AL—activity level	0.58	0.48	0.48	0.56	0.60	0.68
SL—smiling and laughter	0.55	0.55	0.57	0.67	0.72	0.72
FR—fear	0.27	0.15	0.06	0.43	0.37	0.61
DL—distress to limitations	0.23	0.18	0.25	0.57	0.61	0.65
SO—soothability	0.30*	0.37*	0.41	0.50	0.39	0.29
DO—duration of orienting	0.36*	0.35*	0.11	0.62	0.34	0.64

*Correlations based on only one cohort.

Next, notice that the correlations in the top two rows of Table 5.1 tend to be higher than those in the bottom four rows. This means that activity level and smiling and laughter tend to show higher levels of stability over time than the other personality traits.

Now notice that the correlations in the right-most two columns are generally higher than those in the left-most columns. This suggests that personality traits tend to become more stable toward the end of infancy (from 9 to 12 months) compared with the earlier stages of infancy (from 3 to 6 months).

Like all studies, this one has limitations. Perhaps most important, the infants' caregivers may have developed certain conceptions of their infants, and it may be their conceptions rather than the infants' actual behaviours that show stability over time. Nonetheless, these findings reveal four important points. First, stable individual differences appear to emerge very early in life, when they can be assessed by observers. Second, for most temperament variables, there are moderate levels of stability over time during the first year of life. Third, the stability of temperament tends to be higher over short intervals of time than over long intervals of time—a finding that occurs in adulthood as well. And, fourth, the level of stability of temperament tends to increase as infants mature (Goldsmith & Rothbart, 1991; Rothbart & Hwang, 2005).

Stability During Childhood

Longitudinal studies, examinations of the same groups of individuals over time, are costly and difficult to conduct. As a result, there are few studies to draw on. A major exception is the Block and Block Longitudinal Study, which initiated the testing of a sample of more than 100 American children from the Berkeley-Oakland area of California when the children were 3 years old (see, e.g., Block & Robbins, 1993). Since that time, the sample has been followed and repeatedly tested at ages 4, 5, 7, 11, and into adulthood.

One of the first publications from this project focused on individual differences in activity level (Buss, Block, & Block, 1980). When the children were 3 years old, and then again at 4, their activity levels were assessed in two ways. The first was through the use of an **actometer**, a recording device attached to the wrists of the children during several play periods. Motoric movement activated the recording device—essentially a self-winding wristwatch. Independently, the children's teachers completed ratings of their behaviour and personalities. The behavioural measure of activity level contained three items that were directly relevant: "is physically active," "is vital, energetic, active," and "has a rapid personal tempo." These items were summed to form a total measure of teacher-observed activity level. This observer-based measure was obtained when the children were 3 and 4 and then again when they reached age 7.

Table 5.2 shows the correlations among the activity level measures, both at the same ages and across time to assess the stability of activity level during childhood. The correlations between the same measures obtained at two different points in time are called **stability coefficients** (these are also sometimes called test-retest reliability coefficients). The correlations between different measures of the same trait obtained at the same time are called **validity coefficients**.

Table 5.2 Intercorrelations Among Activity Measures

	ACTOMETER		JUDGE-BASED		
	Age 3	**Age 4**	**Age 3**	**Age 4**	**Age 7**
Actometer:					
Age 3	. . .	.44*	.61***	.56***	.19
Age 4	.43**	. . .	.66***	.53***	.38**
Judge-based:					
Age 3	.50***	.36**	. . .	.75***	.48***
Age 4	.34*	.48***	.51***	. . .	.38**
Age 7	.35*	.28*	.33*	.50***	. . .

$*p < .05.$ $**p < .01.$ $***p < .001$ (two-tailed). Correlations above the ellipses (. . .) are based on boys' data, those below the ellipses (. . .) are based on girls' data.

Source: Buss, Block, & Block, 1980.

Several key conclusions about validity and stability can be drawn from these findings. First, the actometer-based measurements of activity level have significant positive validity coefficients with the judge-based measurements of activity level. Activity level in childhood can be validly assessed through both observational judgments and activity recordings from the actometers. The two measures are moderately correlated at each age, providing cross-validation of each type of measure.

Second, notice that the correlations of the activity level measurements are all positively correlated with measurements of activity level taken at later ages. We can conclude that activity level shows moderate stability during childhood. Children who are highly active at age 3 are also likely to be active at ages 4 and 7. Their less-active peers at age 3 are likely to remain less active at ages 4 and 7.

Finally, the size of the correlations tends to decrease as the time interval between the different testings increases. As a general rule, the longer the time between testings, the lower the stability coefficients. In other words, measures taken early in life can predict personality later in life, but the predictability decreases over time.

These general conclusions apply to other personality characteristics as well. Aggression and violence have long been a key concern of our society from school shootings to suicide bombers. What causes some children to act so aggressively?

As it turns out, numerous studies of childhood aggression have been conducted by personality psychologists. Dan Olweus (1979) reviewed 16 longitudinal studies of aggression during childhood. The studies varied widely on many aspects, such as the age at which the children were first tested (2–18), the length of interval between first testing and final testing (half a year to 18 years), and the specific measures of aggression used (e.g., teacher ratings, direct observation, and peer ratings).

Figure 5.1 shows a summary graph of the results of all these studies. The graph depicts the stability coefficients for aggression as a function of the interval between first and final testing. Marked individual differences in aggression emerge very early in life, certainly by the age of 3 (Olweus, 1979). Individuals retain their rank order stability on aggression to a substantial degree over the years, a trend that has been similarly observed among bullies. (We explore personality stability in bullies and their victims further in A Closer Look: Bullies and their Victims, from Childhood to Adulthood.) Moderate levels of rank order stability have also been documented for major personality traits from early childhood to adolescence (Hampson et al., 2007), from middle

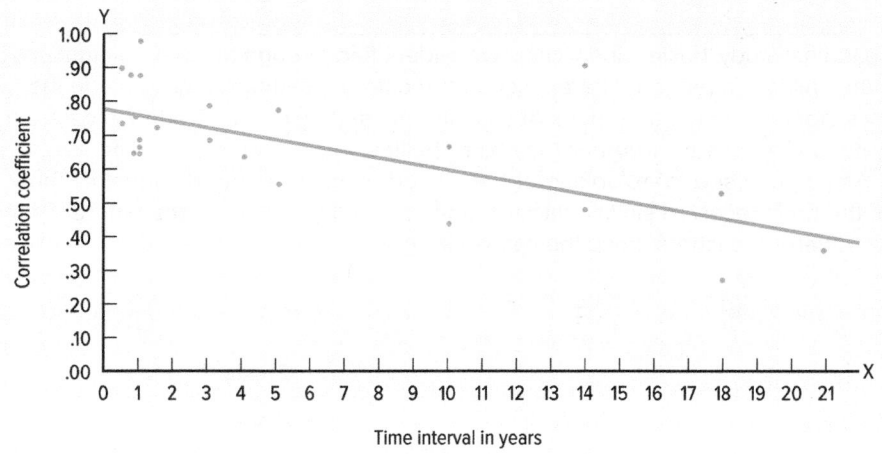

FIGURE 5.1 The figure shows the stability of aggression in males over different time intervals. Aggression shows the highest levels of stability over short time intervals such as from one year to the next. As the time interval between testings increases, however, the correlation coefficients decline, suggesting that aggressiveness changes more over long time intervals than over short time intervals.

childhood to adolescence (Tackett et al., 2008), and from adolescence to early adulthood (Blonigen et al., 2008). And, as we have seen with infant temperament and childhood activity level, the stability coefficients tend to decline as the interval between the two times of measurement increases.

In sum, we can conclude that individual differences in personality emerge very early in life—most likely in infancy for some traits and by early childhood for other traits, such as aggression. These individual differences tend to be moderately stable over time, so that people who are high on a particular trait tend to remain high. Indeed, childhood personality at age 3 turns out to be a good predictor of adult personality at age 26 (Caspi, Harrington, et al., 2003). Finally, the stability coefficients gradually decline over time as the distance between testings increases.

 # A Closer Look

Bullies and their Victims, from Childhood to Adulthood

The individual differences that emerge early in life sometimes have profound consequences, both for the life outcomes of individuals and for the impact on the social world. Norwegian psychologist Dan Olweus has conducted longitudinal studies of childhood bullies and victims of bullying (Olweus, 1978, 1979, 2001). In childhood, bullies tend to pick on and victimize other children. They trip their victims in the hallway, push them into lockers, elbow them in the stomach, demand their lunch money, and call them names.

Although victims of bullying do not have any external characteristics that appear to set them apart, they do have certain psychological characteristics. Most commonly, victims tend to be anxious, fearful, insecure, and lacking in social skills. They may also be emotionally vulnerable and even physically weak, making them easy targets who don't fight back. The victims tend to suffer from low self-esteem, lose interest in school, and often show difficulties establishing or maintaining friendships. They seem to lack social support that might buffer them against bullies. It has been estimated that 10 percent of all schoolchildren are afraid of bullies during the school day, and most children have been victimized by bullies at least once (Brody, 1996).

In one longitudinal study, bullies and victims were identified through teacher nominations in Grade 6. A year later, the children attended different schools in different settings, having made the transition from elementary school to junior high school. At this different setting during Grade 7, a different set of teachers categorized the boys on whether they were bullies, victims, or neither. The results are shown in Table 5.3. As you can see from looking at the circled numbers in the diagonal in Table 5.3, the vast majority of the boys received similar classifications a year later, despite the different school, different setting, and different teachers doing the categorizing.

Table 5.3 Longitudinal Classification of Boys in Aggressive Behaviours			
	Grade 7		
Grade 6	**Bully**	**Neither**	**Victim**
Bully	(24)	9	2
Neither	9	(200)	15
Victim	1	10	(16)

The bullying, however, does not appear to stop in childhood. When Olweus followed thousands of boys from grade school to adulthood, he found marked continuities. The bullies in childhood were more likely to become juvenile delinquents in adolescence and criminals in adulthood. An astonishing 65 percent of the boys who were classified by their Grade 6 teachers as bullies ended up having felony convictions by the time they were 24 years old (Brody, 1996). Many of the bullies apparently remained bullies throughout their lives. Unfortunately, we don't know the fate of the victims in this study, although research generally indicates increased anxiety, depression, and relationship problems, in addition to physical health problems, for those victimized by bullying (McDougall & Vaillancourt, 2015).

A study of 228 children, ranging in age from 6 to 16, found several fascinating personality and family relationship correlates of bullying (Connolly & O'Moore, 2003). A total of 115 children were classified as "bullies" based on both their own self-ratings and on the basis of at least two of their classmates categorizing them as bullies. These were then compared with 113 control children, who both did not nominate themselves as bullies and were not categorized as bullies by any of their classmates. The bullies scored higher on the Eysenck scales of extraversion, neuroticism, and psychoticism (see Chapter 3). Bullies, in short, tended to be more outgoing and gregarious (extraversion); emotionally volatile and anxious (neuroticism); and impulsive and lacking in empathy (psychoticism). In addition, the bullies, relative to the controls, expressed more ambivalence and conflict with their family members, including their brothers, sisters, and parents. Conflicts in the home, in short, appear to be linked to conflicts these children get into during school, pointing to a degree of consistency across situations.

Rank Order Stability in Adulthood

Many studies have been conducted on the stability of adult personality. Longitudinal studies span as many as four decades of life. Furthermore, many age brackets have been examined, from age 18 through older cohorts ranging up to age 84.

A summary of these data is shown in Table 5.4, assembled by Costa and McCrae (1994; see also McCrae & Costa, 2008). This table categorizes the measures of personality into the five-factor model of traits, described in Chapter 3. The time intervals between the first and last personality assessments for each sample range from a low of 3 years to a high of 30 years. The results yield a strong general conclusion: across self-report measures of personality, conducted by different investigators and over differing time intervals of adulthood, the traits of neuroticism, extraversion, openness, agreeableness, and conscientiousness all show moderate to high levels of stability. The average correlation across these traits, scales, and time intervals is roughly +.65.

These studies all rely on self-report. What are the stability coefficients when other data sources are used? In one six-year longitudinal study of adults using spouse ratings, stability coefficients were +.83 for neuroticism, +.77 for extraversion, and +.80 for openness (Costa & McCrae, 1988). Another study used peer ratings of personality to study stability over a seven-year interval. Stability coefficients ranged from +.63 to +.81 for the five-factor taxonomy of personality (Costa & McCrae, 1992). In sum, moderate to high levels of personality stability, in the individual differences sense, are found whether the data source is self-report, spouse-report, or peer-report.

Table 5.4 Stability Coefficients for Selected Personality Scales in Adult Samples

Factor/Scale	Interval	r
Neuroticism		
NEO-PI-N	6	.83
16 PF Q4: Tense	10	.67
ACL Adapted Child	16	.66
Neuroticism	18	.46
GZTS Emotional Stability (low)	24	.62
MMPI Factor	30	.56
Median:		.64
Extraversion		
NEO-PI-E	6	.82
16 PF H: Adventurous	10	.74
ACL Self-Confidence	16	.60
Social Extraversion	18	.57
GZTS Sociability	24	.68
MMPI Factor	30	.56
Median:		.64
Openness		
NEO-PI-O	6	.83
16 PF I: Tender-Minded	10	.54
GZTS Thoughtfulness	24	.66
MMPI Intellectual Interests	30	.62
Median:		.64
Agreeableness		
NEO-PI-A	3	.63
Agreeableness	18	.46
GZTS Friendliness	24	.65
MMPI Cynicism (low)	30	.65
Median:		.64
Conscientiousness		
NEO-PI-C	3	.79
16 PF G: Conscientious	10	.48
ACL Endurance	16	.67
Impulse Control	18	.46
GZTS Restraint	24	.64
Median:		.67

Note: Interval is given in years; all retest correlations are significant at $p < .01$. NEO-PI = NEO Personality Inventory, ACL = Adjective Check List, GZTS = Guilford Zimmerman Temperament Survey, MMPI = Minnesota Multiphasic Personality Inventory.

Source: Costa & McCrae, 1994. These stability coefficients are similar to those of all subsequent studies. A longitudinal study in Finland, for example, found that the five factors showed adult rank order stability ranging from .65 to .97 (Rantanen et al., 2007).

Studies continue to confirm the rank order stability of personality during the adult years. In one study, Richard Robins and his colleagues (Robins et al., 2001) examined 275 university students during their first year, and then again in their fourth year. Across the four years of university, the rank order stability obtained was .63 for extraversion, .60 for agreeableness, .59 for conscientiousness, .53 for neuroticism, and .70 for openness. A study of 2,141 German students tested over a two-year period from university to employment found stabilities of .70 for extraversion, .65 for agreeableness, .69 for conscientiousness, .65 for neuroticism, and .75 for openness (Ludtke, Trautwein, & Husemann, 2009). In sum, the moderate levels of rank order stability of the Big Five are highly replicable across different populations and investigators.

Similar findings emerge for personality dispositions that are not strictly subsumed by the Big Five. In a massive meta-analytic study of the stability of self-esteem—how good people feel about themselves—Trzesniewski, Donnellan, and Robins (2003) found high levels of continuity over time. Summarizing 50 published studies involving 29,839 individuals and four large national studies involving 74,381 individuals, they found stability correlations ranging from the .50s to the .70s. How people feel about themselves—their level of self-confidence—appears very consistent over time. Similar findings have been obtained with measures of prosocial orientation and interpersonal empathy (Eisenberg et al., 2002). In sum, personality dispositions, whether the standard Big Five or other dispositions, show moderate to considerable rank order stability over time in adulthood.

Researchers have posed an intriguing question about rank order personality stability in the individual differences sense: When does personality consistency peak? That is, is there a point in life when people's personality traits become so firm that they don't change much relative to those of other people? To address this question, Roberts and DelVecchio (2000) conducted a meta-analysis of 152 longitudinal studies of personality. The key variable Roberts and DelVecchio (2000) examined was "personality consistency," which was defined as the correlation between Time 1 and Time 2 measures of personality (e.g., the correlation between a personality trait at age 15 and the same trait at age 18).

Roberts and DelVecchio (2000) found two key results. First, personality consistency tends to increase with increasing age. For example, the average personality consistency during the teenage years was +.47. This jumped to +.57 during the decade of the twenties and +.62 during the thirties (see Vaidya et al., 2008, for similar results). Personality consistency peaked during the decade of the fifties at +.75. As the authors conclude, "trait consistency increases in a linear fashion from infancy to middle age where it then reaches its peak after age 50" (p. 3). As people age, personality appears to become more and more "set." For more on personality stability in old age, see Highlight on Canadian Research: Insights on Stability in Old Age from the Victoria Longitudinal Study .

Mean Level Stability in Adulthood

The five-factor model of personality also shows fairly consistent mean level stability over time, as shown in Figure 5.2. Especially after age 50, there is little change in the average level of stability in openness, extraversion, neuroticism, conscientiousness, and agreeableness.

Little change, however, does not mean no change. In fact, there are small but consistent changes in these personality traits, especially during the decade of the twenties. As you can see in Figure 5.2, there is a tendency for openness, extraversion, and neuroticism to gradually decline with increasing age until around age 50. At the same time, conscientiousness and agreeableness show a gradual increase over time—effects found in Switzerland, Germany, as well as in the United States (Anusic, Lucas, & Donnellan, 2012; Specht, Egloff, & Schmukle, 2011). The magnitude of these age effects is not large.

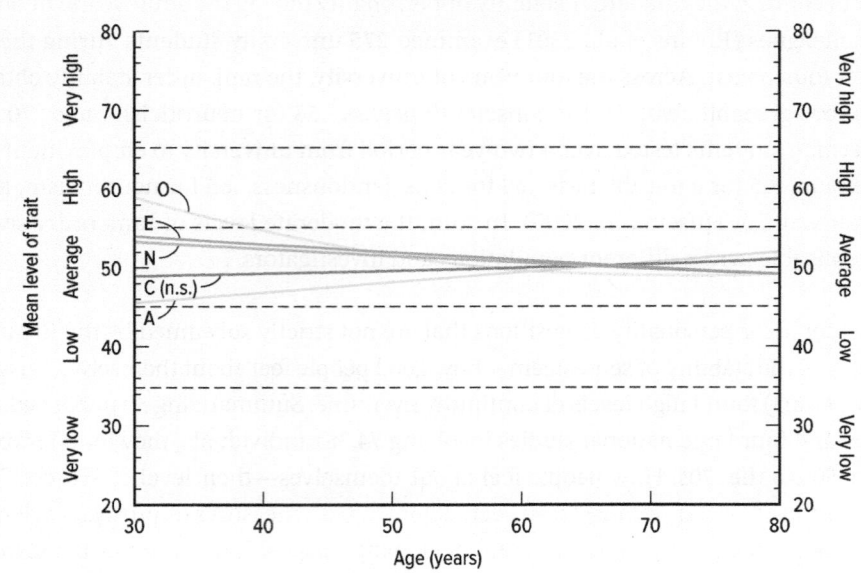

N = Neuroticism, E = Extraversion, O = Openness, A = Agreeableness, C = Conscientiousness

FIGURE 5.2 The figure shows the mean level of five traits over the life span. Although the average scores on each trait are quite stable over time, Openness, Extraversion, and Neuroticism show a gradual decline from age 30 to 50. In contrast, Agreeableness shows a gradual increase over these ages.
Source: Costa & McCrae, 1994.

Studies confirm that mean level personality traits change in slight, but nonetheless important, ways during adulthood. By far the most consistent change is a good one—people score lower on neuroticism or negative affect as they grow older. From first to fourth years in university, for example, students show a decrease in neuroticism corresponding to roughly half a standard deviation (d = −.49) (Robins et al., 2001). Students reported experiencing less negative affect and more positive affect over time (Vaidya et al., 2002). A study from adolescence to midlife also found a decrease in the experience of negative affect—individuals feel less anxious, less distressed, and less irritable as they move into midlife (McCrae et al., 2002). Emotional stability even increases from middle adulthood (ages 42–46) to older age (ages 60–64) (Allemand, Zimprich, & Hertzog, 2007). Similar findings were obtained in a longitudinal study of 2,804 individuals over a 23-year time span—negative affect decreased consistently as the participants got older (Charles, Reynolds, & Gatz, 2001).

A massive meta-analysis of 92 different samples found that both women and men gradually become more emotionally stable as they grow older, with the largest changes occurring between the ages of 22 and 40 (Roberts, Walton, & Viechtbauer, 2006). A study of 1,600 men found that those who got married showed above-average increases in emotional stability compared to their bachelor peers (Mroczek & Spiro, 2003). In sum, most people become less emotionally volatile, less anxious, and generally less neurotic as they mature— a nice thing to look forward to for people whose current lives contain a lot of emotional turmoil.

Some people, however, change more than others (Johnson et al., 2007; Neyer, 2006; Vaidya et al., 2008). Do people know how their personality may have changed? Researchers assessed the Big Five personality traits in a sample of students right when they entered university (Robins et al., 2005). Four years later they assessed them on the Big Five and then asked them to evaluate whether they believed that they had changed on each of these personality dimensions. Interestingly, people actually show some awareness of the changes— *perceptions* of personality change show moderate correspondence with *actual* personality change.

While neuroticism and negative affect decline with age, people score higher on agreeableness and conscientiousness as they grow older. One study found an increase in agreeableness of nearly half a standard deviation ($d = +.44$), and conscientiousness increased roughly one-quarter of a standard deviation ($d = +.27$) (Robins et al., 2001). The facets of conscientiousness that increase most with age are industriousness (working hard), impulse control, and reliability (Jackson et al., 2009). Similar findings have been discovered by other researchers: University students become more agreeable, extraverted, and conscientious from their first year to two and a half years later (Vaidya et al., 2002); agreeableness and conscientiousness increase throughout early and middle adulthood (Srivastava et al., 2003); positive affect increases from the late teen years through the early fifties (Charles et al., 2001). Some studies find increases in the trait of openness with age, although these are less robust than changes in traits such as emotional stability. One study found an increase in openness from adolescence to young adulthood (Pullman, Raudsepp, & Allik, 2006), whereas another study found this openness increase in a similar age group only for women (Branje, van Lieshout, & Geris, 2006). Perhaps a good summary of the mean level personality changes comes directly from the longitudinal researchers: "The personality changes that did take place from adolescence to adulthood reflected growth in the direction of greater maturity; many adolescents became more controlled and socially more confident and less angry and alienated" (Roberts, Caspi, & Moffitt, 2001, p. 670). Indeed, these personality changes have been dubbed the *maturity principle* (Caspi, Roberts, & Shiner, 2005).

Finally, the Big Five personality dispositions may be changeable through therapy. Ralph Piedmont (2001) evaluated the effects of an outpatient drug rehabilitation program on personality dispositions, as indexed by the Big Five. The therapy, administered to 82 men and 50 women over a six-week period, revealed fascinating findings. Those who went through the program showed a decrease in neuroticism, and increases in agreeableness and conscientiousness ($d = .38$). These personality changes were largely maintained in a follow-up assessment 15 months later, although not quite as dramatically ($d = 28$).

In sum, although personality dispositions generally show high levels of mean stability over time, predictable changes occur with age and perhaps also with therapy—lower neuroticism and negative affect, higher agreeableness, higher conscientiousness.

Highlight on Canadian Research

Insights on Stability in Old Age from the Victoria Longitudinal Study

One group of Canadian researchers has offered further insight into the degree of personality stability— and the potential for personality to change in later stages of adulthood. The Victoria Longitudinal Study is a multifaceted long-term study of human aging. Having commenced in the 1980s, the project is the ongoing collaboration of psychologists and researchers from the University of Victoria and the University of Alberta, as well as researchers from universities in the United States. The focus has not been on personality alone, but on the neurocognitive aspects of aging (including memory, sensory acuity, and executive function) and their influences on different facets of the aging process.

One of the studies that emerged from the Victoria Longitudinal Study involved a set of analyses on personality stability and change in old age. Remarkably, and in contrast to some previous suggestions in the research, Small and colleagues (2003) observed evidence of personality change in old age that could not be explained by measurement error or noise alone. The group of researchers analyzed personality traits and select sociodemographic variables in a sample of 223 adults between 55 and 85 years of age. Indeed, the findings suggested that personality change in this upper range of the life span may be possible after all.

In the study by Small and colleagues (2003), the Big Five personality traits and their facets were assessed using the NEO Personality Inventory by Costa and McCrae. The group of older adults responded to the NEO-PI at two points in time, with a response interval of approximately six years. Based on correlations between time points, mean level stability was high, with correlations ranging between approximately .70 for Agreeableness and Conscientiousness and approximately .80 for Extraversion, Neuroticism, and Openness. However, a multivariate analysis of variance indicated an overall effect of time. Statistically speaking, this suggested to the authors that a degree of change occurred over time and this change was significant.

This led the team of researchers to conduct further longitudinal analyses to determine exactly where the effect of time had occurred. Although the overall factor structure of the NEO-PI remained stable over time (supporting the model's reliability), significant individual differences in change from Time 1 to Time 2 were observed for all five factors. Most notably, personality change was related to age in some cases, in addition to other sociodemographic variables. For instance, older adults were more likely to show increases in Neuroticism over time. In analyses of gender, women specifically were more likely than men to show decreases in Neuroticism and increases in Agreeableness; they also reported higher levels of Openness. Older age was further correlated with lower scores on Extraversion, while Agreeableness was correlated with higher education and better health at baseline. Taken together, Small and colleagues interpreted these findings to indicate a significant degree of instability among all five factors of the NEO-PI in this sample of older adults.

According to these findings, it appears that significant personality changes in old age are indeed possible, even if other authors have made suggestions to the contrary. In their report, the researchers noted that such change in old age is not at all inconsistent with a life-span perspective on aging, which underscores the potential for unique life events (e.g., retirement, death of friends, death of spouse, increasing health challenges) to change various aspects of psychological functioning. The possibility of extending this to personality draws into question issues related to change, stability, and person–situation interaction; however, longitudinal analyses such as these offer a further degree of confidence in the potential for personality change in later life.

Critical life events have been known to affect personality in mid-life; given the ubiquity of change in even later stages of adulthood, a similar degree of change is in keeping with these observations. Further analyses from diverse samples of older adults are needed in order to determine the degree of change that is possible in later life. Nevertheless, ongoing research on aging continues to defy many of our preconceived notions (and previous findings) about the potential for change in old age.

❓ Exercise

Each person's personality is, in some ways, stable over time; however, in other ways, it changes over time. In this exercise, you can evaluate yourself in terms of what describes you now and how you think you will be in the future (Markus & Nurius, 1986). Following is a list of items. For each

one, simply rate it on a 1 to 7 scale, with 1 meaning "does not describe me at all" to 7 meaning "is a highly accurate description of me." Give a rating for each of two questions: (1) Does this describe me now? and (2) Will this describe me in the future?

Items	Describes Me Now	Will Describe Me in the Future
Happy		
Confident		
Depressed		
Unmotivated		
Travels widely		
Has lots of friends		
In good shape		
Speaks well in public		
Makes own decisions		
Manipulates people		
Powerful		
Unimportant		

Compare your answers to the two questions. Items you gave the same answers to indicate that you believe this attribute will remain stable over time. The items that change, however, may reflect the ways in which your personality will change over time.

You can view your possible self in a number of ways, but two are especially important. The first pertains to the *desired self*—the person you wish to become. Some people wish to become happier, more powerful, or in better physical shape. The second pertains to your *feared self*—the sort of person you do not wish to become, such as poor or rigid. Which aspects of your possible self do you desire? Which aspects do you fear?

 Concept Check

Describe some of the ways that personality remains stable over time. What traits seem to be more stable than others?

At what age does personality stability peak? Consider findings from the Victoria Longitudinal Study.

Personality Change

Global measures of personality traits, such as those captured by the five-factor model, give us hints that personality can change over time. But it is also true that researchers who have focused most heavily on personality stability have generally not explicitly designed studies and measures to assess personality change. It is important to remember that knowledge about personality change is sparse.

One reason for the relative lack of knowledge about change is that there might be a bias among researchers against even looking for personality change (Helson & Stewart, 1994). As Block (1971) notes, even the terms used to describe stability and change are laden with evaluative meaning. Terms that refer to absence of change tend to be positive: *consistency, stability, continuity,* and *constancy* all seem like good things to have. On the other hand, *inconsistency, instability, discontinuity,* and *inconstancy* all seem undesirable or unpredictable.

Changes in Self-Esteem from Adolescence to Adulthood

In a unique longitudinal study, Block and Robbins (1993) examined self-esteem and the personality characteristics associated with those whose self-esteem had changed over time. Self-esteem, which we explore in greater detail in Chapter 14, was defined in this study as as "the extent to which one perceives oneself as relatively close to being the person one wants to be and/or as relatively distant from being the kind of person one does not want to be, with respect to person-qualities one positively and negatively values" (Block & Robbins, 1993, p. 911). Self-esteem was measured by use of an overall difference between a *current* self-description and an *ideal* self-description: the researchers hypothesized that the smaller the discrepancy, the higher the self-esteem. Conversely, the larger the discrepancy between current and ideal selves, the lower the self-esteem.

The participants were first assessed on this measure of self-esteem at age 14, roughly the first year of high school. Then they were assessed again at age 23, roughly five years after high school.

For the sample as a whole, there was no change in self-esteem with increasing age. However, when males and females were examined separately, a startling trend emerged. Over time, the genders departed from each other, with men's self-esteem tending to increase and women's self-esteem tending to decrease. The males tended, on average, to increase in self-esteem by roughly a fifth of a standard deviation, whereas the females tended, on average, to decrease in self-esteem by roughly a standard deviation. This is an example of personality change at the group level—the two subgroups (women and men) changed in different directions over time.

In sum, the transition from early adolescence to early adulthood appears to be harder on women than on men, at least in terms of self-esteem. As a whole, females tend to decrease in self-esteem, showing an increasing gap between their current self-conceptions and their ideal selves. As a whole, males tend to show a smaller discrepancy between their real and ideal selves over the same time period.

Although changes in self-esteem from adolescence to adulthood are particularly robust, research by Sarah Liu and Carsten Wrosch of Concordia University in Montreal has shown that self-esteem continues to change in older adulthood. In a sample of men and women 60+ years of age, declines in self-esteem were associated with elevated levels of the stress hormone cortisol for those experiencing psychological distress. In addition to confirming ongoing changes to self-esteem in old age, the findings underscore the potential for increases in self-esteem to improve the physical health of seniors (Liu et al., 2014). As we discuss further in A Closer Look: Day-to-Day Changes in Self-Esteem, self-esteem can also fluctuate over shorter periods of time and is more variable for some than it is for others.

 **A Closer Look**

Day-to-Day Changes in Self-Esteem

Most personality psychologists who study self-esteem focus on a person's average level, whether the person is generally high, low, or average in terms of their self-esteem. A few studies have been done on changes in self-esteem over long time spans in people's lives—for example, in the years from adolescence to adulthood. However, with some reflection, most of us would realize that we often change from day to day in how we feel about ourselves. Some days are better than other days when it comes to self-esteem. Some days we feel incompetent, that things are out of our control, and that we even feel a little worthless. Other days we feel satisfied with ourselves, that we are particularly strong or competent, and that we are satisfied with who we are and what we can become. In other words, it seems that feelings of self-esteem can change, not just from year to year but also from day to day.

Psychologist Michael Kernis has become interested in how changeable or variable people are in their self-esteem in terms of day-to-day fluctuations. *Self-esteem variability* is the magnitude of short-term changes in ongoing self-esteem (Kernis, Grannemann, & Mathis, 1991). Self-esteem variability is measured by having people keep records of how they feel about themselves for several consecutive days, sometimes for weeks or months. From these daily records, the researchers can determine just how much each person fluctuates, as well as the person's average level of self-esteem.

Researchers make a distinction between level and variability of self-esteem. These two aspects of self-esteem turn out to be unrelated to each other and are hypothesized to interact in predicting important life outcomes, such as depression (Kernis, Grannemann, & Barclay, 1992). For example, variability in self-esteem is an indicator that the person's self-esteem, even if high, is fragile, and the person is vulnerable to stress. Consequently, we can think of level and variability as defining two qualities of self-esteem as in the figure below.

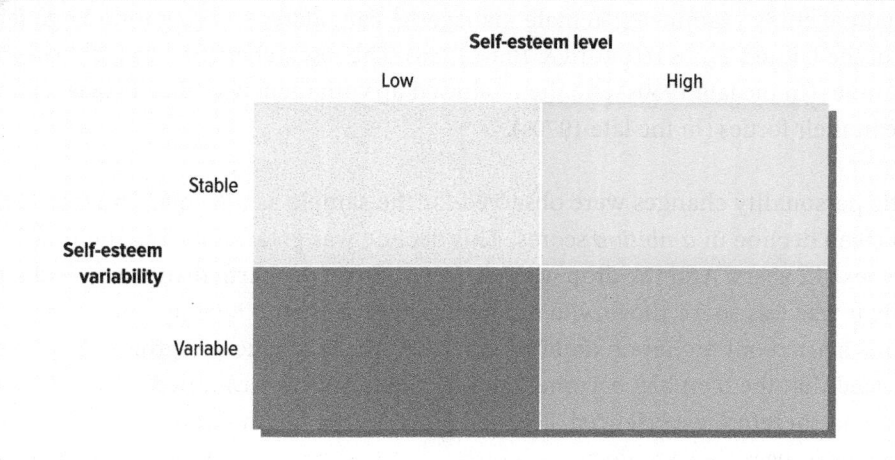

Kernis et al. (1991, 1992) have suggested that self-esteem variability is related to the extent to which one's self-view can be influenced by events, particularly social events. Some people's self-esteem is pushed and pulled by the happenings of life more than is other people's self-esteem. For example, for some people, self-esteem might soar with a compliment and plummet with a social slight, whereas others, who can better roll with the punches of life, might be more stable in their self-esteem, weathering both the slights as well as the uplifts of life without much change in their self-view. This stability versus changeability of self-esteem is the psychological disposition referred to as *self-esteem variability*.

Several studies have been conducted to examine whether self-esteem variability predicts life out-comes, such as depressive reactions to stress, differently than does self-esteem level. In one study (Kernis et al., 1991), self-esteem level was related to depression, but this relation was much stronger for those higher in self-esteem variability than for those lower in self-esteem variability. In other words, at all levels of self-esteem, the participants who were low in variability showed less of a relation between self-esteem and depression than did the participants who were high in variability. Similar results were obtained by Butler, Hokanson, and Flynn (1994), who showed that self-esteem variability is a good pre-dictor of who would become depressed six months later, especially when there was life stress in the intervening months. These authors also concluded that variability indicates that the person may have a fragile sense of self-value and that, with stress, they may become more chronically depressed than someone whose self-esteem is more stable.

Level of self-esteem (whether one is high or low) and variability in self-esteem (whether one is stable or variable from day to day) are unrelated to each other. This makes it possible to find people with differ-ent combinations, such as a person who has a high level of self-estem but is also variable.

Based on findings from studies like these, researchers have come to view self-esteem variability as a vulnerability to stressful life events (Roberts & Monroe, 1992). That is, variability is thought to result from a particular sensitivity in one's sense of self-worth. Psychologists Ryan and Deci (2000) have suggested that variable individuals are dependent for their self-worth on the approval of others. Variable people are very sensitive to social feedback, and they judge themselves primarily through the eyes of others. High-variability individuals show (1) an enhanced sensitivity to evaluative events, (2) an increased con-cern about their self-concept, (3) an overreliance on social sources for self-evaluation, and (4) reactions of anger and hostility when things don't go their way.

Autonomy, Dominance, Leadership, and Ambition

Another longitudinal study examined 266 male managerial candidates working for a large telecommunica-tions company in the United States (Howard & Bray, 1988). The researchers first tested these men when they were in their twenties (in the late 1950s) and then followed up with them periodically over a 20-year time span when they were in their forties (in the late 1970s).

Several dramatic personality changes were observed for the sample as a whole. The most startling change observed was a steep decline in *ambition* scores. This decline was greatest during the first 8 years but con-tinued over the next 12 years. And the drop was actually steepest for participants who had a postsecondary education, while it was less so for those who did not (though it should be noted that the more highly edu-cated participants started out higher on ambition than did the less educated group). Supplementary inter-view data suggested that the men had become more realistic about their limited possibilities for promotion in the company, and therefore experienced a corresponding drop in ambition. It is not that these men lost interest in their jobs or became less effective, as one might first assume. Indeed, their scores on *autonomy, leadership motivation, achievement,* and *dominance* all increased over time despite the drop in ambition (see Figure 5.3).

Sensation Seeking and Impulsivity

Conventional wisdom has it that people become more cautious and conservative with age. Studies of sensa-tion seeking confirm this view. The Sensation-Seeking Scale (SSS) contains four subscales, each containing items and phrases as a forced choice between two distinct options. First is *thrill and adventure seeking,* with items such as "I would like to try parachute jumping" versus "I would never want to try jumping out of a plane, with or without a parachute." The other scales are *experience seeking* (e.g., "I am not interested in experience for its own sake" versus "I like to have new and exciting experiences and sensations even if they are a little frightening, unconventional, or illegal"); *disinhibition* (e.g., "I like wild, uninhibited parties" versus "I prefer quiet parties with good conversation"); and *boredom susceptibility* (e.g., "I get bored seeing the same old faces" versus "I like the comfortable familiarity of everyday friends").

Sensation seeking increases with age from childhood to adolescence and peaks in late adolescence around ages 18–20; then it falls more or

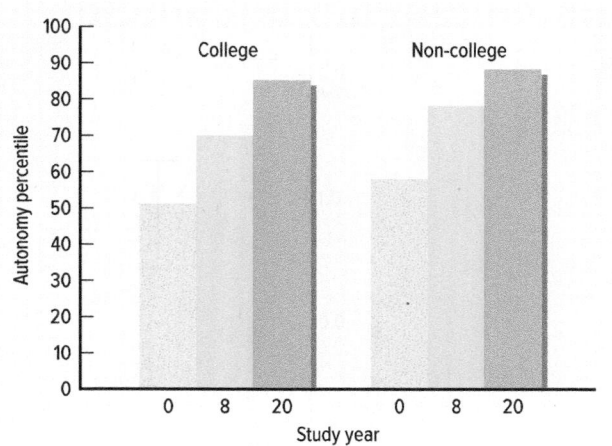

FIGURE 5.3 The figure shows change with age in autonomy scores of male managerial candidates. Both participants with and without postsecondary education tend to become more autonomous or independent as they grow older.

less continuously as people get older (Zuckerman, 1974). This age-related trend in sensation seeking scores has been replicated in North American samples and across many cultures (Chan et al., 2012; Steinberg et al., 2008). Parachute jumping and wild, uninhibited parties seem to be less appealing to older adults when compared to their younger counterparts.

Although they may seem similar on their surface, researchers have found evidence that sensation seeking and *impulsivity* are in fact distinct traits with divergent patterns of age-related change. A longitudinal study by Harden and Tucker-Drob (2011) confirmed this in a sample of 7,640 American youth who were studied between 1996 and 2004. Harden and Tucker-Drob defined impulsivity as the tendency to act on behavioural impulses without planning or consideration of consequences. Sensation seeking, on the other hand, was defined as the tendency to seek out experiences and situations that are novel, exciting, or rewarding. Both sensation seeking and impulsivity did indeed decline from late adolescence to early adulthood. However, the decline in impulsivity was much steeper and began earlier than the decline in sensation seeking. Unlike sensation seeking, impulsivity appears to be quite high in early adolescence, when sensation seeking is still low (see Figure 5.4).

Increasing Openness and Creativity

As discussed earlier, there is some evidence that openness to experience may change with age. Most findings point to a slight decrease at the mean level as people get older. But can openness also change as a result of life experiences, or even clinical interventions?

One study examining an intervention aimed at improving cognitive reasoning reported a significant increase in openness to experience among participants when compared to a control group. Jackson et al. (2012) were interested in the effects of a cognitive training program to improve inductive reasoning skills in older adults. The 16-week program, which also included the completion of weekly crossword and Sudoku puzzles, was associated with a significant increase in trait levels of openness to experience. Another study by MacLean et al. (2011) observed a similar effect of *psilocybin*, the active compound in the recreational drug magic mushrooms,

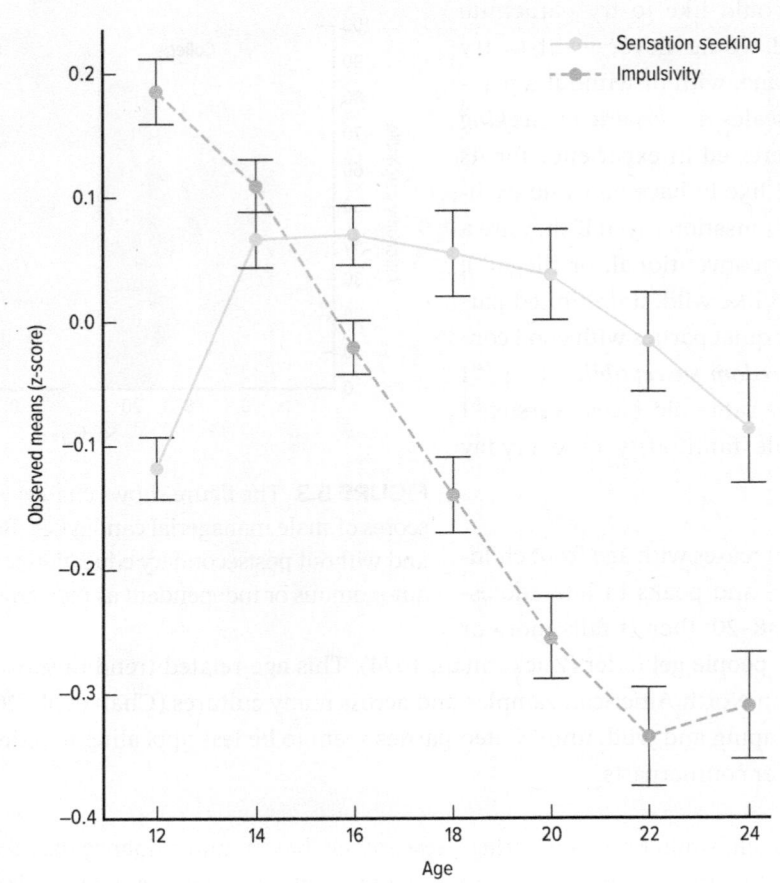

FIGURE 5.4 Age-related mean trends in impulsivity and sensation seeking from 12 to 24 years. Scores for impulsivity and sensation seeking are corrected for demographic and maternal characteristics and standardized.

Source: Harden, K.P., & Tucker-Drob, E. (2011). Individual differences in the development of sensation seeking and impulsivity during adolescence: Further evidence for a dual systems model. *Developmental Psychology, 47*(3), 739–746. © by American Psychological Association. Reprinted with permission.

on levels of openness. Significant increases in openness were seen in participants after they were given a high dose of psilocybin. In participants who also had mystical or spiritual experiences from the dose, openness remained significantly higher for over a year, suggesting the possibility of a lasting change.

Mindfulness-based meditation, a form of meditation aimed at increasing attention to present experiences, may also increase openness to experience and creativity specifically (Colzato et al., 2012; van den Hurk et al., 2011). What all of these studies point to is a possible impact of *experiences* on the openness trait. Whether such changes are temporary or long-lasting is an important question that needs to be answered in future research, but it seems that not all personality changes are tied to age or development.

Personality Changes Across Cohorts: Assertiveness and Narcissism

One of the interesting issues in exploring personality change over time is determining whether the changes observed are due to true personal change that all people undergo as they age, as can be determined by longitudinal studies of the sort just presented, or, conversely, changes in **cohort effects**—the social times in which they lived. Jean Twenge (2000, 2001a, 2001b) has been at the forefront in exploring personality change that is likely to be caused by cohort effects. She argues that North American society has changed dramatically over the past seven decades. One of the most dramatic changes centres on women's status and roles. During the depression era of the 1930s, for example, women were expected to be self-sufficient, but during the 1950s and 1960s, women assumed a more domestic role. Then from 1968 through 1993, women surged into the workforce and North American society increasingly adopted norms of sexual equality. For example, from 1950 to 1993, the number of women obtaining bachelor's degrees doubled roughly from 25 to 50 percent. And the number of women obtaining PhDs, medical degrees, and law degrees all more than tripled. Have these dramatic societal changes impacted women's personality?

Women's assertiveness scores rose from 1968 to 1993, pointing to a cohort effect.
©Image Source/Getty Images

Twenge (2001a) discovered that women's trait scores on *assertiveness* rose and fell dramatically, depending on the cohort in which the woman was raised. Women's assertiveness scores generally rose half a standard deviation from 1931 to 1945; fell by roughly that amount from 1951 to 1967; and then rose again from 1968 to 1993. On measures such as the California Psychological Inventory Dominance scale, for example, women increased +.31 of a standard deviation from 1968 to 1993. Men, in contrast, did not show significant cohort differences in their levels of assertiveness or dominance. Twenge (2001a) concludes that "social change truly becomes internalized with the individual . . . girls absorb the cultural messages they received from the world around them, and their personalities are molded by these messages" (p. 142).

Older people sometimes complain that the younger generation is too self-centred ("The kids these days!"). Is there any truth to these laments? Twenge and her colleagues (2008) explored this issue by analyzing the *narcissism* trait—which in the high range is associated with being self-centred, exhibitionistic, and self-aggrandizing, as well as unempathetic and entitled (Buss & Chiodo, 1991). Twenge and colleagues (2008) found that scores on narcissism increased in American college students by about a third of a standard deviation between 1982 and 2006. Yet these conclusions have been criticized by some (e.g., Donnellan, Trzesniewski, & Robins, 2009), with more recent research finding no evidence of an epidemic or reporting decreases in narcissism scores over time (some have declared the idea of a "narcissism epidemic" to be dead). Others still have found evidence that narcissism may indeed be increasing, and that levels of this trait may be impacted by social and cultural factors (Cai et al., 2012; Stewart & Bernhardt, 2010; Wilson & Sibley, 2011). Corresponding historical changes have also been documented, including a decline in empathy (Konrath et al., 2011) and an increase in materialism over a similar period of time (Twenge & Kasser, 2013).

Can sociocultural factors really shape such influential traits like narcissism? Although somewhat preliminary, the answer seems to be yes. In a fascinating study, Vater, Moritz, and Roepke (2018) examined levels of narcissism in a large population of German adults. They made comparisons between those who had grown up in West Germany (a largely individualistic culture more comparable to modern Western society) and East Germany (a largely collectivistic culture) prior to the fall of the Berlin Wall and the subsequent reunification of Germany in 1990. Grandiose narcissism, the kind involving superficial displays of superiority and attention-seeking, was significantly higher in individuals who grew up in former West Germany compared to those who grew up in former East Germany. Interestingly, no such difference was observed in narcissism among individuals who entered school after German reunification. Such findings point to the real possibility that sociocultural conditions unique to a generation can shape key aspects of personality.

Volitional Personality Change: Is it Possible?

One of the most challenging questions for researchers to answer is whether or not people can intentionally change their personality should they try to do so. Hudson and Fraley (2015) set out to examine this very question, noting that a number of previous surveys in psychology had indicated that most people want to change their personality in some way, often wishing to become more emotionally stable, extraverted, conscientious, and agreeable (reflecting what are commonly perceived as more socially desirable traits).

Hudson and Fraley conducted two experiments with undergraduate students in order to determine if such volitional change was possible. In both experiments, students set intentions regarding their desired changes on the Big Five traits. They were then coached to take realistic steps towards making those changes, including setting specific goals to implement change on a daily basis. Students who expressed goals to increase any Big Five trait at the start of the study tended to experience actual increases in that trait over the 16-week period. This was demonstrated by both self-report measures and relevant daily behaviours associated with the traits in question. Those who set the most practical intentions for implementation were the most likely to report successful change over time. Students tended to increase their level of agreeableness, conscientiousness, emotional stability, and extraversion when desired.

Although research on volitional personality change is still in its infancy (Hudson & Fraley, 2017), these findings suggest that self-improvement may be possible even when it comes to our most hard-wired traits. Exactly how much change, and whether or not such change is long-lasting, are important questions that will need to be addressed in future studies. Which traits would you change, if you could?

 Concept Check

Consider some of the ways that personality changes over time. What traits seem to change more than others?

How does self-esteem tend to fluctuate over time? Consider daily changes as well as normative changes over the lifespan.

Think about the notion of volitional personality change. Do you think that people can intentionally change their level on a trait if they try to do so?

Personality Coherence over Time: Prediction of Socially Relevant Outcomes

The final form of personality development we will examine is called personality coherence, defined as predictable changes in the *manifestations* or *outcomes* of personality factors over time, even if the underlying characteristics remain stable. In particular, we focus on the consequences of personality for socially relevant outcomes, such as marital stability and divorce; alcoholism, drug use, and emotional disturbance; and job outcomes later in life.

Marital Stability, Marital Satisfaction, and Divorce

In a longitudinal study of unprecedented length, Kelly and Conley (1987) studied a sample of 300 couples from their engagements in the 1930s all the way through their status later in life in the 1980s. At the final testing, the median age of the subjects was 68 years. Within the entire sample of 300 couples, 22 couples broke their engagements and did not get married. Of the 278 couples who did get married, 50 ended up getting divorced some time between 1935 and 1980.

During the first testing session in the 1930s, acquaintances provided ratings of each participant's personality on a wide variety of dimensions. Three aspects of personality proved to be strong predictors of marital dissatisfaction—the neuroticism of the husband, the lack of impulse control of the husband, and the neuroticism of the wife. High levels of neuroticism proved to be the strongest predictors. Neuroticism was linked with marital dissatisfaction of both the men and the women in the 1930s, again in 1955, and yet again in 1980.

Furthermore, the neuroticism of both the husband and the wife, as well as the lack of impulse control of the husband, were strong predictors of divorce. These three dimensions of personality accounted for more than half of the predictable variance in whether the couples split up. The couples who had a stable and satisfying marriage had neuroticism scores that were roughly half a standard deviation lower than the couples who subsequently got divorced.

Psychologists have identified personality variables that predict whether a marriage will turn out to be happy and satisfying or whether it will end in divorce. Although personality is not destiny, it does relate to important life outcomes, such as marital unhappiness and divorce.

(left): ©Ariel Skelley/Blend Images LLC; (right): ©Ingram Publishing

The reasons for divorce themselves appear to be linked to the personality characteristics measured earlier in life. The husbands with low impulse control when first assessed, for example, tended later in life to have extra-marital affairs—breaches of the marital vows that loomed large among the major reasons cited for the divorce. The men with higher impulse control appear to have been able to refrain from having sexual flings, which are so detrimental to marriages (Buss, 2003).

These results, spanning a 45-year period consisting of most of the adult lives of the participants, point to an important conclusion about personality coherence. Personality may not be destiny, but it leads to some predictable life outcomes, such as infidelity, marital unhappiness, and divorce. Later in this section, we explore the link between childhood temper tantrums and adulthood in A Closer Look: Adult Outcomes of Children with Temper Tantrums.

Interestingly, neuroticism also plays a role in another important life outcome—resilience after losing a spouse. A fascinating longitudinal study showed that one of the best predictors of coping well with the death of a spouse was the personality disposition of emotional stability (Bonanno et al., 2002). A total of 205 individuals were assessed several years prior to the death of their spouse and again 18 months after their spouse's demise. Those high on emotional stability grieved less, showed less depression, and displayed the quickest psychological recovery. Individuals low on emotional stability (high on neuroticism) were still psychologically anguished a year and a half later. Personality, in short, affects many aspects of romantic life: who is likely to get involved in a successful romantic relationship (Shiner, Masten, & Tellegen, 2002); which marriages remain stable and highly satisfying (Kelly & Conley, 1987); which people are more likely to get divorced (Kelly & Conley, 1987); and how people cope following the loss of a spouse (Bonanno et al., 2002).

Alcoholism, Drug Use, and Emotional Disturbance

Personality also predicts the later development of alcoholism and emotional disturbance (Conley & Angelides, 1984). Of the 233 men in one longitudinal study, 40 were judged to develop a serious emotional problem or alcoholism. These 40 men had earlier been rated by their acquaintances as high on neuroticism. Specifically, they had neuroticism scores roughly three-fourths of a standard deviation higher than men who did not develop alcoholism or a serious emotional disturbance.

Furthermore, early personality characteristics were useful in distinguishing between the men who had become alcoholic and those who had developed an emotional disturbance. Impulse control was the key factor. The alcoholic men had impulse control scores a full standard deviation lower than those who had an emotional disturbance. Other studies also find that those high on sensation seeking and impulsivity, and low on traits such as agreeableness and conscientiousness, tend to use and abuse alcohol more than their peers (Cooper et al., 2003; Hampson et al., 2001; Markey, Markey, & Tinsley, 2003; Ruchkin et al., 2002). Low levels of agreeableness and conscientiousness are also linked to substance abuse (prescription and illegal drugs) in mid-life (Turiano et al., 2012). In sum, neuroticism and impulsivity early in life are coherently linked with socially relevant outcomes later in life.

Religiousness and Spirituality

Another important life outcome pertains to religiousness and spirituality—the degree to which individuals embrace organized religion or seek to lead a spiritual life outside the context of organized religion. Personality traits in adolescence predict these outcomes in late adulthood. Adolescents who scored high on conscientiousness and agreeableness were more likely to score high on religiousness later in life (Wink et al., 2007). Openness to experience, in contrast, was the only personality trait in adolescence that predicted spirituality seeking in late adulthood. Personality in youth, in short, appears to influence spirituality and religiousness later in life, regardless of the early socialization practices to which people are exposed.

Education, Academic Achievement, and Dropping Out

Impulsivity also plays a key role in education and academic achievement. Early work by Smith (1967) indicated a correlation of −.47 between peer ratings of impulsivity before entry into university and subsequent GPA. Similar associations between impulsivity and academic performance have been reported by Kipnis (1971), in regards to performance on American standardized testing specifically. Impulsivity (or lack of self-control) continues to affect performance in the workplace. One longitudinal study looked at personality dispositions at age 18 and work-related outcomes at age 26 (Roberts, Caspi, & Moffitt, 2003). They found that those who were high on self-control at age 18 had higher occupational attainment, greater involvement with their work, and more financial security at age 26. Conversely, the impulsive 18-year-olds were less likely to progress in their work, showed less psychological involvement, and experienced lower financial security.

The personality trait of conscientiousness turns out to be the single best predictor of successful achievement in school and work. High conscientiousness at age 3 predicts successful academic performance nine years later (Abe, 2005). Observer-based assessment of children's conscientiousness at ages 4 to 6 predicts school grades nine years later (Asendorpf & Van Aken, 2003). Conscientiousness of children assessed between the ages of 8 and 12 predicts academic attainment two decades later (Shiner, Masten, & Roberts, 2003). Although other personality traits also predict successful academic performance, such as emotional stability (Chamorro-Premuzic & Furnham, 2003a, 2003b), and agreeableness and openness (Hair & Graziano, 2003), conscientiousness is the most powerful longitudinal predictor of success in school and work.

Work experiences also have an effect on personality change (Roberts et al., 2001). Those who attain high occupational status at age 26 have become happier, more self-confident, less anxious, and less self-defeating since they were 18 years old. Those who attain high work satisfaction also become less anxious and less prone to stress in their transition from adolescence to young adulthood.

What about people who attain financial success in the workplace? These individuals not only become less alienated and better able to handle stress, but they also increase their levels of social closeness—they like people more, turn to others for comfort, and like being around people. In sum, just as personality at age 18 predicts work outcomes at age 26 (e.g., self-control predicts income), work outcomes predict personality change over time. We see again that impulsivity is a critical personality factor that is linked in meaningful ways with later life outcomes.

Health and Longevity

How long people live and how healthy or ill they become during their years of life are exceptionally important developmental outcomes. It may come as a surprise that your personality actually predicts how long you are likely to live. The most important traits conducive to living a long life are *high conscientiousness, positive emotionality (extraversion), low levels of hostility,* and *low levels of neuroticism* (Danner, Snowdon, & Friesen, 2001; Friedman et al., 1995; Miller et al., 1996; Mroczek et al., 2009). There are several paths through which these personality traits affect longevity (Ozer & Benet-Martinez, 2006). First, conscientious individuals engage in more health-promoting practices, such as maintaining a good diet and getting regular exercise; they also avoid unhealthy practices such as smoking and becoming a "couch potato." Conscientious children in elementary school, for example, end up smoking less and drinking less alcohol when they are adults fully 40 years later (Hampson et al., 2006). Conscientiousness at age 17 also predicts refraining from engaging in legal (nicotine, alcohol) and illegal drug use three years later (Elkins et al., 2006). Those low on conscientiousness in adolescence are more likely to get addicted in young adulthood to drugs of all sorts. Moreover, conscientious individuals are more likely to follow doctors' orders and adhere to the treatment plans they recommend. Being low on conscientiousness (being impulsive, or low on self-control) during the preschool years predicted high levels of risk-taking during adolescence (Honomichl & Donnellan, 2012). Being impulsive (undercontrolled) in childhood predicted an increased likelihood of high blood pressure and stroke 40 years later (Chapman & Goldberg, 2011). And being impulsive also predicted unhealthy weight gain and weight fluctuations in later adulthood (Sutin et al., 2011).

Second, extraverts are more likely to have lots of friends, leading to a good social support network—factors linked with positive health outcomes. And third, low levels of hostility, a component of neuroticism, put less stress on the heart and cardiovascular system—a topic explored in greater detail in Chapter 18. High levels of neuroticism are also linked with poor health behaviours, such as smoking, although neuroticism predicts mortality even after statistically controlling for smoking (Mroczek et al., 2009). In sum, the personality traits of conscientiousness, positive emotionality (extraversion), and low hostility predict both positive health outcomes and longevity.

 **A Closer Look**

Adult Outcomes of Children with Temper Tantrums

In a longitudinal study spanning 40 years, Caspi et al. (1987) explored the implications of childhood personality for adult occupational status and job outcomes. He identified a group of behaviourally difficult and often explosive children, using interviews with their mothers as the data source. When the children were 8, 9, and 11, their mothers rated the frequency and severity of their temper tantrums. Severe tantrums were defined as behaviours involving biting, kicking, striking, throwing things, screaming, and shouting. From the sample, 38 percent of the boys and 29 percent of the girls were classified as having frequent and uncontrolled temper tantrums.

These children were followed throughout life, and the adult manifestations of childhood personality for men were especially striking. The men who as children had frequent and severe temper tantrums achieved lower levels of education in adulthood. The occupational status of their first job was also consistently lower than that of their calmer peers. The explosive children who had come from middle-class backgrounds tended to be downwardly mobile, and by midlife their occupational attainment was indistinguishable from that of their working-class counterparts. Furthermore, they tended to change jobs frequently, showed an erratic work pattern with more frequent breaks from employment, and averaged a higher number of months being unemployed.

Because 70 percent of the men in the sample served in the military, their military records could also be examined. The men who as children had been classified as having explosive temper tantrums attained a significantly lower military rank than their peers. Finally, nearly half (46 percent) of these men were divorced by the age of 40, compared to only 22 percent of the men without a childhood history of temper tantrums. In sum, early childhood personality shows coherent links with important adult social outcomes, such as job attainment, frequency of job switching, unemployment, military attainment, and divorce.

It is easy to imagine why explosive and erratic individuals tend to achieve less and get divorced more. Life consists of many frustrations, and people deal with their frustrations in different ways. Emotionally unstable and explosive individuals are probably more likely to yell at their boss, for example, or to quit their jobs during an impulsive moment. Similarly, they are probably more likely to vent their frustrations on their spouses or perhaps even to impulsively have an extramarital affair. All of these events are likely to lead to lower levels of job attainment and higher levels of divorce.

Predicting Personality Change

Can we predict who is likely to change in personality and who is likely to remain the same? In a fascinating longitudinal study, Caspi and Herbener (1990) studied middle-aged, heterosexual couples over an 11-year period. The couples were tested twice, once in 1970 and again in 1981. All the subjects had been born in either 1920–21 or 1928–29 and were part of a larger longitudinal project.

The question that intrigued Caspi and Herbener was this: Is the choice of a marriage partner a cause of personality stability or change? Specifically, if you marry someone who is similar to you, do you tend to remain more stable over time than if you marry someone who is different from you? They reasoned that similarity between spouses would support personality stability, because the couple would tend to reinforce one another on their attitudes, seek similar external sources of stimulation, and perhaps even participate together in the same social networks. Marrying someone who is unlike oneself, in contrast, may offer attitudinal clashes, exposure to social and environmental events that one might not otherwise seek alone, and generally create an environment uncomfortable to maintaining the status quo.

Using personality measures obtained on both husbands and wives, Caspi and Herbener divided the couples into three groups: those who were highly similar in personality, those who were moderately similar in personality, and those who were low in similarity. Then they examined the degree to which the individuals showed stability in personality over the 11-year period of midlife in which they were tested. The results are shown in Figure 5.5.

As you can see in Figure 5.5, the people married to spouses who were highly similar to themselves showed the highest personality stability. Those married to spouses least similar to themselves showed the highest degree of personality change. The moderate group fell in between. This study is important in pointing to a potential source of personality stability and change—the selection of spouses. It will be interesting to see whether future research can document other sources of personality stability and change—perhaps by examining the selection of similar or dissimilar friends, or by selecting university or work environments that show a good "fit" with one's personality traits upon entry into these environments (Roberts & Robins, 2004).

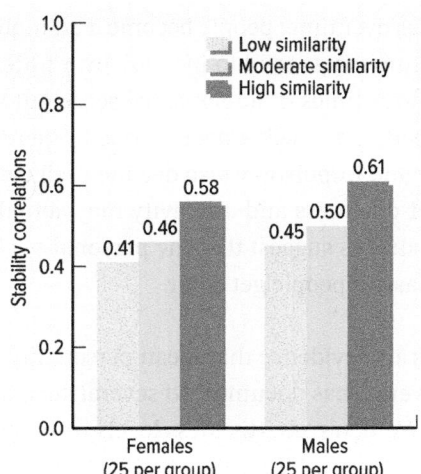

FIGURE 5.5 The figure shows the stability of personality over time as a function of the similarity (low, medium, or high) of the person to their spouse. Men and women who are married to someone similar to themselves in personality show the highest levels of personality stability over time.
Source: Caspi & Herbener, 1990.

 Concept Check

Define personality coherence and provide an example using one of the Big Five traits.

What are some of the predictable consequences of personality, and how do they support the notion of coherence?

Summary and Evaluation

Personality development includes both the continuities and changes in personality over time. There are three forms of personality stability: (1) rank order stability is the maintenance of one's relative position within a group over time; (2) mean level stability is the maintenance of the average level of a trait or characteristic over time; and (3) personality coherence is predictable changes in the manifestations of a trait. We can examine personality development at three levels of personality analysis: the population level, the group differences level, and the individual differences level.

There is strong evidence for personality rank order stability over time. Temperaments such as activity level and fearfulness show moderate to high levels of stability during infancy. Activity level and aggression show moderate to high levels of stability during childhood. Bullies in childhood tend to become juvenile delinquents in adolescence and criminals in adulthood. Personality traits, such as those captured by the five-factor model, show moderate to high levels of stability during adulthood. As a general rule, the stability coefficients decrease as the length of time between the two periods of testing increases.

Personality also changes in predictable ways over time. With respect to the Big Five, neuroticism generally decreases over time; people become a bit more emotionally stable as they age. Furthermore, agreeableness and conscientiousness tend to increase over time. All these changes suggest increased maturity, as the sometimes tumultuous times of adolescence settle out into the maturity of adulthood. From early adolescence to early adulthood, men's self-esteem tends to increase, whereas women's self-esteem tends to decrease. Sensation seeking and impulsivity also decline predictably with age, but along slightly different trajectories. And higher levels of openness and creativity may actually be cultivated by certain life experiences. On the other hand, several studies suggest that the personality characteristics of autonomy, independence, and competence tend to increase as people get older.

There is also evidence that mean personality levels can be affected by the social cohort in which one grows up. Jean Twenge has documented several such effects, most notably on women's levels of assertiveness or dominance. Women's assertiveness levels were high following the 1930s, in which women had to be extremely independent; they fell during the 1950s and 1960s, when women were largely homemakers and fewer became professionals. From 1967 to 1993, however, women's levels of assertiveness increased, corresponding to changes in their social roles and increasing participation in professional occupations.

And although limited, there is emerging evidence that efforts to change one's personality may result in actual change. This may depend on the individual, of course, as well as the kind of support and encouragement they have along the way.

Personality also shows evidence of coherence over time. Early measures of personality can be used to predict socially relevant outcomes later in life. High levels of neuroticism in both sexes and impulsivity in men, for example, predict marital dissatisfaction and divorce. Neuroticism early in adulthood is also a good predictor of later alcoholism and the development of emotional problems. Impulsivity plays a key role in the development of alcoholism and the failure to achieve one's academic potential. Highly impulsive individuals tend to get poorer grades and drop out of school more than their less impulsive peers. Children with explosive temper tantrums tend to manifest their personalities as adults through downward occupational mobility, more frequent job switching, lower attainment of rank in the military, and higher frequencies of divorce. People who are impulsive at age 18 tend to do more poorly in the workplace—they attain less occupational success and less financial security. Work experiences, in turn, appear to affect personality change. Those who attain occupational success tend to become happier, more self-confident, and less anxious over time.

Although little is known about what factors maintain these forms of personality stability and coherence over time, one possibility pertains to our choices of marriage partners. There is evidence that we tend to choose those who are similar to us in personality, and the more similar our partners, the more stable our personality traits remain over time.

How can we best reconcile the findings of considerable personality stability over time with evidence of important changes? First, longitudinal studies have shown conclusively that personality traits, such as those subsumed by the Big Five, show substantial rank order stability over time. These personality traits also show evidence of coherence over time. Bullies in middle school, for example, tend to become criminals in adulthood. Those with self-control and conscientiousness in adolescence tend to perform well academically and well in the workplace later in life. In the context of these broad brushstrokes of stability, it is also clear that people show mean level changes with age—as a group people become less anxious, less impulsive, lower in sensation seeking, more agreeable, and more conscientious. Some personality change affects only some individuals, such as those who succeed in the workplace. In short, although personality dispositions tend to be stable over time, they are not "set in plaster" in the sense that some change occurs in some individuals some of the time.

 Concept Check

Considering the majority of research, what general conclusions would you make regarding personality stability and change over time?

How does the notion of personality coherence offer insights into our understanding of stability and change?

Key Terms

personality development	mean level change	actometer
rank order stability	personality coherence	stability coefficients
rank order change	temperament	validity coefficients
mean level stability	longitudinal studies	cohort effects

PART TWO

The Biological Domain

The biological domain refers to those physical elements and biological systems within our bodies that influence or are influenced by our behaviours, thoughts, and feelings. For example, one type of physical element within our bodies that may influence our personalities is our genes. Our genetic makeup determines whether our hair is curly or straight, whether our eyes are blue or brown, and whether we have large, heavy bones or a slight build. Our genetic makeup influences how active we are, whether we are hot-tempered and disagreeable, and whether we like to be with others or prefer solitude. Understanding if and how genetics contribute to personality falls squarely within the biological domain.

Another area in which biology and personality intersect is in the physiological systems, such as the brain or peripheral nervous system, where subtle differences among people might contribute to personality differences. For example, some people might have more activity in the right half than in the left half of their brains. Empirically, we know that this imbalance of activation is linked with a tendency to experience distress and other negative emotions more strongly. Here, physical differences among people are associated with differences in emotional style. Because these differences represent enduring and stable ways that people differ from one another, these physiological features represent aspects of personality (see Chapter 7).

The literature in personality psychology contains many examples of physiological measures that are considered to be correlates of personality. The finding that shy children show elevated heart rates when in the presence of strangers compared to non-shy children is one such example (Kagan & Snidman, 1991). Would eliminating heart rate reactivity make the shy child less shy? Probably not. This is because the physiological response is a *correlate* of the traits in question rather than an underlying substrate that *produces* or *contributes* to the personality trait.

This is not to say that studying physiological correlates of personality is a worthless endeavour. On the contrary, physiological measures often reveal important *consequences* of personality. For example, the high cardiovascular reactivity of Type A individuals may have serious consequences for developing heart disease. For this reason identifying physiological measures that are correlates of personality is also a scientifically useful and important task.

On the other hand, there are several modern theories of personality in which underlying physiology plays a more central role in *generating* or forming the substrate of specific personality differences. In Chapter 7, we consider several of these theories in detail. Each shares the notion that specific personality traits are based on underlying physiological differences. Each theory also assumes that if the underlying physiological substrate is altered, the behaviour pattern associated with the trait will be altered as well.

The third biological approach we cover is based on Charles Darwin's theory of evolution. Adaptations that helped members of the species to survive and reproduce were passed on as evolved characteristics. For example, primates who could walk upright could colonize open fields, and their hands were freed for using tools. Evidence for the evolution of such physical characteristics is solid.

Psychologists are now considering evidence for the evolution of psychological characteristics. They are taking the principles of evolution, such as natural selection, and applying them to an analysis of psychological traits. For example, natural selection may have operated on our ancestors to select for group cooperation; those early humans who were able to cooperate and work in groups were more likely to survive and reproduce, and those who preferred not to cooperate were less likely to become an ancestor. Consequently, the desire to be part of a group may be an evolved psychological characteristic that is present in today's population of humans. Evolutionary perspectives on personality are discussed in Chapter 8.

Genetics and Personality

The Biological Domain

The Jim twins are identical twins separated at birth and raised in different adoptive families. They met for the first time when they were 39 years old, having been apart for their entire lives. One of the twins, Jim Springer, made the first phone call on February 9, 1979, after learning that he had a twin brother, Jim Lewis. They had an instant connection; three weeks after the phone call, Jim became the best man at his brother's wedding.

A record of the past is written in the genetic blueprint.
©SPL/Science Source

When they first met, the Jim twins displayed an astonishing set of similarities. Both weighed 82 kilograms. Both were 183 centimetres tall. They had each been married twice, and in each case their first wives were named Linda and their second wives named Betty. Each had a son named James. Their jobs were also similar—each worked part-time as a sheriff. Both smoked the same brand of cigarettes and drank the same brand of beer. Both suffered from the same kind of headache syndrome, and both had a habit of biting their fingernails. Both left love notes for their wives scattered around the house on a regular basis. And both had remarkably similar personality scores on standardized tests (Segal, 1999).

The Jim twins were not identical in all ways, of course. One was a better writer, the other a better speaker. They wore their hair differently; one combed his hair down over his forehead, and the other combed his hair back. But overall, the similarities were striking, especially since they had grown up from infancy in entirely different families. This is a single twin pair, and of course no conclusions can be drawn from one case. But the case of the Jim twins raises the intriguing question: "How exactly do genetics influence personality?"

The Human Genome

Genome refers to the complete set of genes an organism possesses. The human genome contains between 20,000 and 30,000 genes. All of these genes are located on 23 pairs of chromosomes. Each person inherits one set of each pair of chromosomes from the mother and one set from the father. One way to think about the human genome is to consider it as a book containing 23 chapters, with each chapter being a chromosome pair. Each one of the chapters contains several thousand genes. And each gene consists of long sequences of DNA molecules. One astonishing fact is that the nucleus of each cell within the body contains two complete sets of the human genome, one from the mother and one from the father. The only exceptions are red blood cells, which do not contain any genes, and female egg cells and male sperm cells, each of which contains only one copy of the human genome. Because the body contains roughly 100 trillion cells (a million times a million), each of which is smaller than the head of a pin, each of us has roughly 100 trillion copies of our genome within our bodies.

The Human Genome Project is a multibillion-dollar research endeavour that is dedicated to sequencing the entire human genome—that is, to identifying the particular sequence of DNA molecules in the human species. On June 26, 2000, scientists made headlines by announcing that they had completed the first draft of the complete human genome. Identifying the sequence of DNA molecules does not mean identifying all the functions of these DNA molecules. Scientists now have the "book" of life, but they must still figure out what role the genes play in the body, mind, and behaviour.

Some findings appear to be turning standard assumptions about the human genome on its head. Two findings are especially noteworthy. First, although the number of genes humans possess is similar to the number of genes estimated for mice and worms, the *manner* in which human genes get decoded into proteins turns out to be far more variable than in other species. These alternative forms of decoding create a tremendous variety of proteins—many more than seen in mice or worms—and may account for the complex differences we observe between rodents and humans (Plomin, 2002). Second, these protein-coding genes, making up roughly 2 percent of the human genome, are only part of the story. Many parts of the other 98 percent of the DNA in the human chromosomes used to be chalked up as **"genetic junk"** because scientists believed that these parts were functionless residues that served no purposes. Genetic researchers are discovering that this "junk DNA" is not junk at all. Rather, parts of these chunks of DNA have an impact on humans, potentially affecting everything from a person's physical size to personality (Gibbs, 2003; Plomin, 2002). These hidden layers of complexity in the human genome—given names such as "pseudogenes" and "riboswitches"—mean that we have a long way to go before understanding the complex and mysterious links between genes and human behaviour.

Most of the genes within the human genome are the same for each individual on the planet. That is why all normally developing humans have many of the same characteristics: two eyes, two legs, 32 teeth, 10 fingers, a heart, a liver, two lungs, and so on. A small number of these genes, however, are different for different individuals. Thus, although all humans have two eyes, some people have blue eyes, some have brown eyes, and a few even have violet eyes. Some of the genes that differ from individual to individual influence physical characteristics, such as eye colour, height, and bone width. Some genes that differ across individuals influence the behavioural characteristics that define human personality.

 Concept Check

What is a genome, and what is its role in individual differences?

Controversy About Genes and Personality

Perhaps no other area of personality psychology has been fraught with as much controversy as the study of behavioural genetics. Researchers in this field attempt to determine the degree to which individual differences in personality are caused by genetic and environmental differences. Scientific reports on behavioural genetic studies often make headlines and cover stories. On January 2, 1996, for example, *The Globe and Mail* caused a stir with reports of a scientific breakthrough: "Trait of Extroverts Traced to Gene." It reported the discovery of a specific gene for novelty seeking—the tendency to be extraverted, impulsive, extravagant, quick-tempered, excitable, and exploratory. A January 28, 2012, news article in the *National Post* proclaimed that, "Your Politics Are in Your Genes." And on March 3, 2015, the online news outlet *Elite Daily* published a story titled, "The Wanderlust Gene: Why Some People Are Born to Travel." Some popular media sources are proposing "designer babies," where parents select from a genetic checklist the characteristics they would like in their children. These ideas are controversial because they suggest that genetic differences among individuals, rather than differences in parental socialization or personal experience, are responsible for shaping the core features of human personality.

Part of the reason for the controversy is ideological. Many people worry that findings from behavioural genetics will be used (or misused) to support particular political agendas. If individual differences in thrill seeking, for example, are caused by specific genes, then does this mean that we should not hold juvenile delinquents responsible for stealing cars for joy rides? If scientists trace a behaviour pattern or personality trait to a genetic component, some people worry that such findings might lead to pessimism about the possibilities for change.

Another part of the controversy concerns the idea of eugenics. **Eugenics** is the notion that we can design the future of the human species by fostering the reproduction of people with certain traits and discouraging the reproduction of people without those traits. Many people are concerned that findings from genetic studies might be used to support programs intended to prevent some individuals from reproducing or, even worse, to bolster the cause of those who would advocate that some people be eliminated in order to create a "master race."

However, modern psychologists who study the genetics of personality are typically extremely careful in their attempts to educate others about the use and potential misuse of their findings (Plomin et al., 2008). Knowledge is better than ignorance, they argue. If people believe that hyperactivity, for example, is caused by parenting behaviours when in fact hyperactivity turns out to be primarily influenced by genes, then attempts to influence hyperactive behaviour by altering parental practices could cause frustration and resentment on the part of the parents. Furthermore, psychologists maintain that genetic findings need not lead to the evil consequences that some worry about. Finding that a personality characteristic has a genetic component, for example, does not mean that the environment is powerless to modify that characteristic. Let's now turn to the field of genetics and personality to discover what lies beneath the swirling controversy.

 Concept Check

What controversies surround the science of behavioural genetics?

Goals of Behavioural Genetics

To understand the primary goals of the field of behavioural genetics, let's look at a concrete example—individual differences in height. Some individuals are tall, such as basketball player Shaquille O'Neal (over 210 centimetres). Other individuals are short, such as actor Danny DeVito (around 150 centimetres). Geneticists focus on the key question, "What causes some individuals to be tall and others to be short?"

In principle, there can be a variety of causes of individual differences in height. Differences in diet while growing up, for example, can cause differences in height among people. Genetic differences can also account for some of the differences in height. One of the central goals of genetic research is to determine the percentage of an individual difference that can be attributed to genetic differences and the percentage due to environmental differences.

In the case of height, both environmental and genetic factors are important. Clearly, children tend to resemble their parents in height—generally, tall parents have taller than average children and short parents have shorter than average children. And genetic research has confirmed that roughly 90 percent of the individual differences in height are indeed due to genetic differences. The environment, which contributes 10 percent to individual differences in height, is far from trivial. In North America, average adult height has increased in the entire population by roughly 5 centimetres over the past century, most likely due to increases in the nutritional value of the food eaten by Canadian and U.S. citizens. This example brings home an important lesson: even though some observed differences among people can be due to genetic differences, this does not mean that the environment plays no role in modifying the trait.

In determining height, genetics accounts for 90 percent of the variation, and environmental factors, such as diet, account for 10 percent of the variation. The actor Danny DeVito (left) is about 60 centimetres shorter than basketball player Shaquille O'Neal (right).

(left): ©Joe Thomas/Getty Images; (right): ©David Keeler/Getty Images

 Exercise

Can you think of some human characteristics that you consider to be mostly under genetic influence? Consider, for example, individual differences in eye colour. Can you think of other characteristics that are not very much influenced by genetic factors? Consider, for example, individual differences in eating with forks versus eating with chopsticks. How might you go about proving that some individual differences are, or are not, influenced by genetic differences?

The methods used by behavioural geneticists examined in this chapter can be applied to any individual difference variable. They can be used to identify the causes of differences in height and weight, differences in intelligence, differences in personality traits, and even differences in attitudes, such as liberalism or conservatism.

Behavioural geneticists typically are not content simply with figuring out the **percentage of variance** due to genetic and environmental causes. *Percentage of variance* refers to the fact that individuals vary, or are different from each other, and this variability can be partitioned into percentages that are due to different causes. Behavioural geneticists also are interested in determining the ways in which genes and the environment interact and correlate with each other. And they are interested in figuring out precisely where in the environment the effects are taking place—in parental socialization practices, for example; in the teachers to whom children are exposed; or even in peer influences (Harris, 2007). We turn to these more complex issues toward the end of this chapter. First, we must examine the fundamentals of behavioural genetics: What is heritability, and what methods do geneticists use to get their answers?

 Concept Check

What are the goals of behavioural genetics?

What Is Heritability?

Heritability is a statistic that refers to the proportion of observed variance in a *group* of individuals that can be accounted for by genetic variance (Plomin et al., 2001). It describes the degree to which genetic differences among individuals cause differences in an observed property, such as height, extraversion, or sensation seeking. Heritability may be one of the most frequently misunderstood concepts in psychology. If precisely defined, however, it provides useful information in identifying the genetic and environmental determinants of personality.

Heritability has a formal definition: *the proportion of phenotypic variance that is attributable to genotypic variance.* **Phenotypic variance** refers to observed individual differences, such as in height, weight, or personality. **Genotypic variance** refers to individual differences in the total collection of genes possessed by each person. Thus a heritability of .50 means that 50 percent of the observed phenotypic variation is attributable to genotypic variation. A heritability of .20 means that only 20 percent of the phenotypic variation is attributable to genotypic variation. In these examples, the environmental component is simply the proportion of phenotypic variance that is *not* attributable to genetic variance. Thus, a heritability of .50 means that the environmental component is .50. A heritability of .20 means that the environmental component is .80. These examples illustrate the simplest cases and assume that there is no correlation or interaction between genetic and environmental factors.

The environmental contribution is defined in a similar way. Thus, the percentage of observed variance in a *group* of individuals that can be attributed to environmental (nongenetic) differences is called **environmentality**. Generally speaking, the larger the heritability, the smaller the environmentality and vice versa.

 Exercise

Discuss the meaning of the following statement: "All normally developing humans have language, but some people speak Chinese, others French, and others English." To what degree is variability in the language spoken due to variability in genes or variability in the environment in which one is raised?

Misconceptions About Heritability

One common misconception about heritability is that it can be applied to a single individual. It can't. It is meaningful to say that individual differences in height are 90 percent heritable, but it makes absolutely no sense to say, "Meredith's height is 90 percent heritable." You cannot say, for example, that the first 120 centimetres of her height are due to genes and the other 30 centimetres are due to the environment. For an individual, genes and environment are inextricably intertwined. Both play a role in determining height, and they cannot be separated. Thus, heritability refers only to differences in a sample or population, not to an individual.

Another common misconception about heritability is that it is constant. In fact, it is nothing of the sort. Heritability is a statistic that applies only to a population at one point in time and in a particular array of environments. If the environments change, then heritability can change. For example, in principle, heritability can be high in one population (e.g., among Swedes) but low in another (e.g., among Nigerians). And heritability can be low at one time and high at another time. Heritability always depends on both the range of genetic differences in the population and on the range of environmental differences in that population. To draw on a concept from Chapter 2, heritability does not always generalize across people and places.

A final common misconception is that heritability is an absolutely precise statistic (Plomin et al., 2001). Nothing could be further from the truth. Error or unreliability of measurement, for example, can distort heritability statistics. And because heritability statistics are typically computed using correlations, which themselves fluctuate from sample to sample, further imprecision creeps in. In sum, heritability is best regarded merely as an *estimate* of the percentage of phenotypic differences due to genetic differences. It is not precise. It does not refer to an individual. And it is not eternally fixed (see Johnson et al., 2011, for a more detailed treatment of what heritability means and its limits).

Nature–Nurture Debate Clarified

Clarifying the meaning of the term *heritability*—what it is and what it is not—allows us to think more clearly about the **nature–nurture debate**—the arguments about whether genes or environments are more important determinants of personality. The clarification comes from clearly distinguishing between two levels of analysis: the level of the individual and the level of a population of individuals.

At the level of an individual, there is no nature–nurture debate. Every individual contains a unique constellation of genes. And those genes require environments during one's life to produce a recognizable individual. At this moment, each person reading these pages is the product of an inseparable intertwining of genes and environment. It makes no sense to ask "Which is more important, genes or environment, in accounting for Sally?" At the individual level of analysis, there is simply no issue to debate. As an analogy, consider baking a cake. Each particular cake consists of flour, sugar, eggs, and water. It makes no sense to ask whether the finished cake is "caused" more by the flour or more by the eggs. Both are necessary ingredients, inextricably combined and inseparable in the finished cake. Genes and environment for one individual are like flour and eggs for one cake—both ingredients are necessary, but we cannot logically disentangle them to see which is more important.

At the level of the population, however, we can disentangle the influence of genes and environments. This is the level of analysis at which behavioural geneticists operate. It makes perfectly good sense to ask, "Which is more important in accounting for individual differences in trait *X*—genetic differences or environmental differences?" At the population level, we can partition the differences into these two sources: differences in genes and differences in environments. And for a particular population at a given point in time, we can make sensible statements about which is more important *in accounting for the differences*. Consider the cake example. If you have 100 cakes, it makes sense to ask whether the differences among the cakes in, say, sweetness are caused more by differences in the amount of flour used or by differences in the amount of sugar used.

Now consider physical differences among people. Individual differences in height, for example, show a heritability of roughly .90. Individual differences in weight show a heritability of roughly .50. And individual differences in mate preferences—the qualities we desire in a marriage partner—show very low heritabilities of roughly .10 (Waller, 1994). Thus, it is meaningful to say that genetic differences are more important than environmental differences for height. Genetic and environmental factors are roughly equal when it comes to weight. And environmental differences are overwhelmingly important for mate preferences.

The next time you get into a debate with someone about the nature–nurture issue, be sure to ask, "Are you asking the question at the level of the individual or at the level of individual differences within a population?" Only when the level of analysis is specified can the answers make any sense.

 Concept Check

What is heritability, and how does it help to clarify the nature–nurture debate?

Behavioural Genetic Methods

Behavioural geneticists have developed an array of methods for teasing apart the contributions of genes and environments as causes of individual differences. Selective breeding with animals is one method. Family studies provide a second method. A third, and perhaps the most well-known, method is that of twin studies. Adoption studies provide a fourth behavioural genetic method. We briefly discuss the logic of each of these methods, exploring where heritability estimates come from.

Selective Breeding—Studies of Humans' Best Friend

Artificial selection—as occurs when dogs are bred for certain qualities—can take place only if the desired characteristics are under the influence of heredity. **Selective breeding** occurs by identifying the dogs that possess the desired characteristic and having them mate only with other dogs that also possess the characteristic. Dog breeders have been successful precisely because many of the qualities they wish specific dog breeds to have are moderately to highly heritable.

Some of these heritable qualities are physical traits, characteristics that we actually see, such as size, ear length, wrinkled skin, and coat of hair. Other characteristics we might try to breed for are more behavioural and can be considered personality traits (Gosling, Kwan, & John, 2003). Some dogs, such as Doberman Pinschers, are, on average, more aggressive than most other dogs. Other breeds, such as the Labrador, are, on average, very sociable and agreeable. And others, such as the Chesapeake Bay retriever, have a strong desire to please their owners by retrieving objects. All of these behavioural traits—aggressiveness, agreeableness, and the desire to please—are characteristics that have been established in these animals through selective breeding.

If the heritability for these personality traits in dog breeds is literally zero, then attempts to breed dogs selectively for such traits will be doomed to fail. On the other hand, if the heritability of these personality traits is high (e.g., >80 percent), then selective breeding will be highly successful and will occur rapidly. The fact that selective breeding has been so successful with dogs tells us that heredity must be a factor in the personality traits, such as aggressiveness, agreeableness, and desire to please, that were successfully selected. For obvious reasons, we cannot do selective breeding experiments on people. Fortunately, however, there are other methods of behavioural genetics that can be used to study humans.

The Labrador retrievers (left) and the Chesapeake Bay retriever (right) have been selectively bred for certain characteristics. Both have webbed feet, for example, which make them strong swimmers and excellent water retrievers. They have also been selectively bred for certain "personality" characteristics. The Labrador was bred to be sociable and friendly, whereas the Chesapeake Bay dog was bred to be loyal to only one owner and suspicious of strangers. Consequently, the Chesapeake Bay retriever makes a good watch dog in addition to its skills as a sporting dog. The Labrador, however, is the most popular family dog in North America, most likely due to the unrestrained friendliness and cheerful disposition of this breed.

(left): ©Comstock Images/Alamy; (right): Courtesy of Randy J. Larsen

Family Studies

Family studies correlate the degree of genetic relatedness among family members with the degree of personality similarity. They capitalize on the fact that there are known degrees of genetic relatedness among family members. Parents are usually not related to each other genetically. However, each parent shares 50 percent of his or her genes with each of the children. Similarly, siblings share 50 percent of their genes, on average. Grandparents and grandchildren share 25 percent of their genes, as do uncles and aunts with their nieces and nephews. First cousins share only 12.5 percent of their genes.

If a personality characteristic is highly heritable, then family members with greater genetic

The family study method assumes that for traits with a large genetic component, the degree of similarity among relatives on that trait will be in proportion to the amount of genetic relatedness or degree of kinship among them.

©John Lund/Tiffany Schoepp/Blend Images LLC

relatedness should be more similar to each other than are family members with less genetic relatedness. If a personality characteristic is not at all heritable, then even family members who are closely related genetically, such as parents and children, should not be any more similar to each other than are family members who are less genetically related to each other.

Family members who share the same genes also typically share the same environment. Two members of a family might be similar to each other not because a given personality characteristic is heritable, but rather because of a shared environment. For example, certain brothers and sisters may be similar on shyness not because of shared genes, but because of shared parents. For this reason, results from family studies alone can never be viewed as definitive. A more compelling behavioural genetic method is that of twin studies.

Twin Studies

Twin studies estimate heritability by gauging whether identical twins, who share 100 percent of their genes, are more similar to each other than are fraternal twins, who share only 50 percent of their genes. Twin studies, and especially studies of twins reared apart, have received tremendous media attention. The Jim twins, described at the beginning of this chapter, are identical twins given up for adoption at birth. Because they were adopted into different families, they were unaware that they had a twin. When they met for the first time, to everyone's astonishment these men shared many behavioural habits—having the same favourite TV shows, using the same brand of toothpaste, owning a Jack Russell terrier dog, and so on. They also shared many personality traits, such as being highly conscientious and emotionally stable, as measured by valid personality scales. Is this coincidence? Perhaps, but these coincidences seemed to happen with unusual regularity in the course of studying twins (Segal, 1999).

Twin studies take advantage of a fascinating quirk of nature. Nearly all individuals come from a single fertilized egg, and humans—as contrasted with some other mammals, such as mice—typically give birth to a single child at a time. Occasionally, however, twins are born, occurring only once in 83 births (Plomin, DeFries, & McClearn, 1990). Twins come in two distinct types: identical and fraternal.

Twins come in two varieties: monozygotic and dizygotic. Can you identify which of these two pairs of twins is more likely to be monozygotic? Which pair is definitely dizygotic? What is the clue that helps you answer these questions?

(left): ©by golf9c9333/Getty Images; (right): ©Shutterstock/Romrodphoto

Identical twins, technically called **monozygotic (MZ) twins**, come from a single fertilized egg (or zygote—hence, *monozygotic*), which divides into two at some point during gestation. No one knows why fertilized eggs occasionally divide. They just do. Identical twins are remarkable in that they are genetically identical, like clones, coming from the same single source. They share literally 100 percent of their genes.

The other type of twin is not genetically identical to the co-twin; instead, such twins share only 50 percent of their genes. They are called fraternal twins, or **dizygotic (DZ) twins**, because they come from two eggs that were separately fertilized (*di* means "two," so *dizygotic* means "coming from two fertilized eggs"). Fraternal twins can be same sex or opposite sex. In contrast, identical twins are always the same sex because they are genetically identical. Dizygotic twins are no more alike than regular siblings in terms of genetic relatedness. They just happen to share the same womb at the same time and have the same birthday; otherwise, they are no more similar than are ordinary brothers and sisters. Of all the twins born, two-thirds are fraternal, or dizygotic, and one-third are identical, or monozygotic.

The twin method capitalizes on the fact that some twins are genetically identical, sharing 100 percent of their genes, whereas other twins share only 50 percent of their genes. If fraternal twins are just as similar to each other as identical twins are in terms of a particular personality characteristic, then we can infer that the characteristic under consideration is not heritable: the greater genetic similarity of identical twins, in this case, is not causing them to be more similar in personality. Conversely, if identical twins are substantially *more similar* to each other than are fraternal twins on a given characteristic, then this provides evidence that is compatible with a heritability interpretation. In fact, studies have shown that identical twins are more similar than fraternal twins in dominance, height, and the ridge count on their fingertips (Plomin et al., 2008), suggesting that heritability plays a causal role in influencing these individual differences. For dominance, identical twins are correlated +.57, whereas fraternal twins are correlated only +.12 (Loehlin & Nichols, 1976). For height, identical twins are correlated +.93, whereas fraternal twins are correlated only +.48 (Mittler, 1971). We explore heritability estimates for mental toughness, also based on twin research, further Highlight on Canadian Research: Behavioural Genetics and Mental Toughness.

There are several formulas for calculating heritability from twin data, each with its own problems and limitations. One simple method, however, is to double the difference between the MZ correlation and DZ correlation:

$$\text{heritability}^2 = 2(r_{mz} - r_{dz})$$

In this formula, r_{mz} refers to the correlation coefficient computed between pairs of monozygotic twins, and r_{dz} refers to the correlation between the dizygotic twins. Plugging in the correlations for height, for example, leads to the following heritability estimate: heritability of height = 2(.93 − .48) = .90. Thus, according to this formula, height is 90 percent heritable and 10 percent environmental (as the total has to add up to 100 percent). The basic logic of this method can be applied to any characteristic: personality traits, attitudes, religious beliefs, sexual orientation, drug use habits, and so on.

We must note an important assumption of the twin method. This assumption is known as the **equal environments assumption**. The twin method assumes that the environments experienced by identical twins are no more similar to each other than are the environments experienced by fraternal twins. If they are more similar, then the greater similarity of the identical twins could be due to the fact that they experience more similar environments rather than the fact that they have more genes in common. If identical twins are treated by their parents as more similar than fraternal twins are treated by their parents—for example, if the parents of identical twins dress them in more similar clothing than do the parents of fraternal twins— then the greater similarity of the identical twins might be due to more similar treatment.

Behavioural geneticists have been worried about the validity of the equal environments assumption and so have designed studies to test it. One approach is to examine twins who have been misdiagnosed as identical or fraternal (Scarr, 1968; Scarr & Carter-Saltzman, 1979). That is, some twins who were believed to be identical by their parents were really fraternal. And some twins whose parents believed them to be fraternal turned out to be identical. These mistakes in labelling allowed the researchers to examine whether fraternal twins who were *believed* to be identical were in fact more similar to each other than accurately labelled fraternal twins. Similarly, it allowed the researchers to examine whether the identical twins believed to be fraternal were in fact less similar to each other than identical twins correctly labelled as identical. The findings on a variety of cognitive and personality tests supported the validity of the equal environments assumption. The parents' beliefs and labelling of the twins did not affect their actual similarity on the personality and cognitive measures. This means that, however twins are labelled, the environments experienced by identical twins do not seem to be functionally more similar to each other than the environments experienced by fraternal twins.

Additional studies over the years have continued to support the equal environments assumption (e.g., Loehlin & Nichols, 1976; Lytton, Martin, & Eaves, 1977). Although it is true that identical twins do tend to dress more alike than fraternal twins, spend more time together, and have more friends in common, there is no evidence that these environmental similarities cause them to be any more similar in their personalities than they are to begin with (Plomin et al., 2008).

Highlight on Canadian Research

Behavioural Genetics and Mental Toughness

Mental toughness is a personality trait that has gained interest for its importance in academic and work achievement, athletics, and goal attainment. It combines elements of hardiness and confidence, and includes such characteristics as commitment to actions and goals, feeling in control of circumstances, and valuing change. Researchers from the University of Western Ontario examined the heritability of mental toughness in 219 pairs of adult monozygotic and dizygotic twins from across North America (Horsburgh et al., 2009). In addition to a validated self-report questionnaire to measure mental toughness (including four subscales of control, commitment, change, and confidence), participating twins also completed a measure of the five-factor model of personality, the NEO-PI-R, to understand the role of primary trait factors such as extraversion and neuroticism.

Heritability coefficients for the four subscales of mental toughness were .37 (commitment), .45 (confidence), .47 (challenge), and .49 (control), with the overall mental toughness score having a heritability coefficient of .54, suggesting that genes account for 54 percent of the variance in individual differences in mental toughness. This reflects common degrees of heritability observed in most personality traits, and suggests that the commitment and dedication with which people approach goals and challenges is at least partly genetically determined. In terms of the practical applications of these findings, the authors highlight the value of knowing which aspects of mental toughness are most highly influenced by environmental factors. Namely, the commitment component demonstrated the greatest degree of environmentality, and therefore may be most responsive to active improvement and training. This could have implications in educational or occupational settings, sport psychology, or clinical contexts in which self-esteem or other facets of psychological health could be positively impacted. Estimating the degree of heritability in newly identified personality traits is an important step in understanding their *etiology* or causes. If personality traits have a low degree of genetic influence, they may be more amenable to change. On the other hand, a high degree of genetic influence will likely mean greater stability in the trait over time.

Regarding the five-factor model, heritability coefficients ranged from .46 (conscientiousness) to .65 (openness to experience) in the current study, consistent with previous research. These additional analyses are of particular value when examining a new personality trait such as mental toughness: they indicate that the sample of twins examined in this study were relatively normal by statistical standards, as heritability estimates reflect those observed in other populations. This means that researchers can have greater confidence in the generalizability of their findings.

Horsburgh and colleagues (2009) also confirmed that mental toughness was significantly and positively correlated with all of the five factors except for neuroticism, which displayed a significant negative correlation with mental toughness. Further statistical modelling indicated that these observed phenotypic correlations between mental toughness and the Big Five were primarily attributable to common genetic effects (as well as common nonshared environmental effects, to be discussed later in this chapter). This means that significant correlations were observed between mental toughness and the Big Five traits due in part to some of the same genetic factors. This finding reflects the general observation that one-to-one relationships between genes and personality traits are rare. Indeed, many traits overlap in complex ways, with their unitary components often being explained by the same genes.

Adoption Studies

Adoption studies represent one of the most powerful behavioural genetic methods available. In an adoption study, one can examine the correlations between adopted children and their adoptive parents, with whom they share no genes. If one finds a positive correlation between adopted children and their adoptive parents, then this provides strong evidence for environmental influences on the personality trait in question.

Similarly, we can examine the correlations between adopted children and their genetic parents, who had no influence on the children's environments. If we find a zero correlation between adopted children and their genetic parents, again this is strong evidence for a lack of heritable influence on the personality trait in question. Conversely, if we find a positive correlation between parents and their adopted-away children, with whom they have had no contact, then this provides evidence for heritability.

Adoption studies are especially powerful because they allow us to get around the equal environments assumption, which must be made in twin studies. In twin studies, because parents provide both genes and environments to their children, and may provide more similar environments for identical than for fraternal twins, there is a potential compromise of the equal environments assumption. In adoption studies, however, genetic parents provide none of the environmental influences on their children, thus unconfounding genetic and environmental causes.

Adoption studies, however, are not without potential problems of their own. Perhaps the most important potential problem is the assumption of representativeness. Adoption studies assume that adopted children, their birth parents, and their adoptive parents are representative of the general population. For example, these studies assume that couples who adopt children are not any different from couples who do not adopt children. Fortunately, the assumption of representativeness can be tested directly. Several studies have confirmed that the assumption of representativeness holds for cognitive abilities, personality, education level, and even socioeconomic status (Plomin & DeFries, 1985; Plomin, DeFries, & Fulker, 1988).

Another potential problem with adoption studies is **selective placement**. If adopted children are placed with adoptive parents who are similar to their birth parents, then this may inflate the correlations between the adopted children and their adoptive parents. Fortunately, there does not seem to be selective placement, so this potential problem is not a problem in actual studies (Plomin et al., 2008).

One of the most powerful behavioural genetic designs is one that combines the strengths of twin and adoption studies at the same time, by studying twins reared apart. In fact, the correlation between identical twins reared apart can be interpreted directly as an index of heritability. If identical twins reared apart show a correlation of +.65 for a particular personality characteristic, then that means that 65 percent of the individual differences are heritable. Unfortunately, identical twins reared apart are exceedingly rare. Painstaking efforts have been undertaken to find such twins and study them (Segal, 1999). The effort has been well worth it, as such studies have yielded a bounty of fascinating results, to which we now turn. A summary of the traditional behavioural genetic methods, along with their advantages and limitations, is shown in Table 6.1.

Table 6.1 Summary of Traditional Behavioural Genetic Methods

Method	Advantages	Limitations
Selective breeding studies	Can infer heritability if selective breeding works	Are unethical to conduct on humans
Family studies	Provide heritability estimates	Violate equal environments assumption
Twin studies	Provide both heritability and environmentality estimates	Sometimes violate equal environments assumption
Adoption studies	Provide both heritability and environmentality estimates; get around the problem of equal environments assumption	Adopted kids might not be representative of population; problem of selective placement

 Concept Check

Compare the following methods used to determine heritability: family studies, twin studies, and adoption studies. What is the best approach?

In your own words, how do twin studies estimate the heritability of any given trait? In your response, be sure to define the equal environments assumption.

Major Findings from Behavioural Genetic Research

This section summarizes what is known about the heritability of personality. The results may surprise you.

Personality Traits

The most commonly studied personality traits in behavioural genetic designs are extraversion and neuroticism. Recall that extraversion is a dimension containing people who are outgoing and talkative at one end and people who are quiet and withdrawn at the other (introverted) end. Neuroticism is a dimension with one end characterized by people who are anxious, nervous, and emotionally volatile and at the other end calm and emotionally stable. Henderson (1982) reviewed the literature on more than 25,000 pairs of twins. He found substantial heritability for both traits. In one study involving 4,987 twin pairs in Sweden, for example, the correlations for extraversion were +.51 for identical twins and +.21 for fraternal twins (Floderus-Myrhed, Pedersen, & Rasmuson, 1980). Using the simple formula of doubling the difference between the two correlations yields a heritability of .60.

The findings for neuroticism were similar (Floderus-Myrhed et al., 1980). The identical twin correlation for neuroticism was +.50, whereas the fraternal twin correlation was only +.23. This suggests a heritability of .54. Twin studies have yielded very similar results, suggesting that extraversion and neuroticism are traits that are approximately half due to genetics. A large-scale twin study, conducted in Australia, found a heritability for neuroticism of 47 percent (Birley et al., 2006). Similar moderate heritabilities continue to be found for neuroticism and extraversion in more recent samples using diverse measurement methods (Loehlin, 2012; Moore et al., 2010).

The findings for extraversion and neuroticism from adoption studies suggest somewhat lower heritabilities. Pedersen (1993), for example, found heritability estimates based on comparisons of adoptees and their biological parents of about 40 percent for extraversion and about 30 percent for neuroticism. Correlations between adoptive parents and their adopted children tend to be around zero, suggesting little *direct* environmental influence on these traits.

Individual differences in *activity level* have also been subjected to behavioural genetic analysis. You may recall from Chapter 5 that individual differences in activity level, measured with a mechanical recording device called an actometer, emerge early in life and show stability in children over time. Activity level was assessed in an adult sample of 300 monozygotic and dizygotic twin pairs residing in Germany (Spinath et al., 2002). The researchers measured the physical energy each individual expended through body movements, recorded mechanically with motion recorders analogous to self-winding wristwatches. Movement of a person's limbs activates the device, which records the frequency and intensity of body activity. Activity level showed a heritability of .40, suggesting that a moderate proportion of the individual differences in motor energy are due to genetic differences.

Activity level is one among several temperaments that show moderate heritability. A study of 1,555 twins in Poland found 50 percent heritability, on average, for all temperaments, including activity, emotionality, sociability, persistence, fear, and distractibility (Oniszczenko et al., 2003). A study of Dutch twins at ages 3, 7, and 10 found even higher heritabilities for aggressiveness, ranging from 51 to 72 percent (Hudziak et al., 2003).

Behavioural genetic studies have also examined other personality dispositions. Using 353 male twins from the Minnesota Twin Registry, researchers explored the heritability of so-called psychopathic personality traits (Blonigen et al., 2003). These include traits such as Machiavellianism (e.g., enjoys manipulating other people), Coldheartedness (e.g., has a callous emotional style), Impulsive Nonconformity (e.g., indifferent to social conventions), Fearlessness (e.g., a risk taker; lacks anticipatory anxiety concerning harm), Blame Externalization (e.g., blames others for one's problems), and Stress Immunity (e.g., lacks anxiety when faced with stressful life events). All of these "psychopathic" personality traits showed moderate to high heritability. For example, for Coldheartedness, the r_{mz}

The trait of activity level—how vigorous and energetic a person is—shows a moderate degree of heritability.
©Shutterstock/Kzenon

was +.34, whereas the r_{dz} was −.16; for Fearlessness, the r_{mz} was +.54, whereas the r_{dz} was only .03. Using the method of doubling the difference between the MZ and DZ correlations suggests *substantial* heritability to all of these psychopathic-related personality dispositions (Vernon et al., 2008; Niv et al., 2012). The heritability of psychopathic personality traits, which predispose individuals to criminal activity, may be the key reason that a massive study from Sweden of more than a million individuals showed the heritability of violent crime to be roughly 50 percent (Frisell et al., 2012).

Interestingly, heritability of personality might not be limited to our own species. In a study of chimpanzees, Weiss, King, and Enns (2002) explored the heritability of dominance (high extraversion, low neuroticism) and well-being (e.g., seems happy and contented), as indexed by trained observer judgments. Individual differences in chimpanzee well-being showed a moderate heritability of .40, whereas dominance showed an even stronger heritability of .66. These findings suggest that the importance of genes in influencing personality may not be restricted to humans but instead may extend to other primates.

Behavioural genetic studies using more comprehensive personality inventories have been carried out in many different countries as personality research expands to include more and more cross-cultural work. A study of 296 twin pairs in Japan revealed moderate heritability for Cloninger's Seven-Factor model of temperament and character, which includes dispositions such as novelty seeking, harm avoidance, reward dependence, and persistence (Ando et al., 2002). A study of twins in Germany, using observational methodology, revealed a 40 percent heritability to markers of the Big Five (Borkenau et al., 2001). Similar findings for the Big Five personality traits have been documented in Canada and Germany using self-report measures (Jang et al., 2002; Moore et al., 2010).

One of the most fascinating studies to examine personality traits is the Minnesota Twin Study (Bouchard & McGue, 1990; Tellegen et al., 1988). This study examined 45 sets of identical twins reared apart and 26 sets of fraternal twins reared apart. The researchers found the correlations shown in Table 6.2 between identical twins reared apart. These findings startled many people. How could traditionalism, for example, which

Table 6.2   Correlations Between Identical Twins Reared Apart

Personality Trait	Twin Correlation
Sense of well-being	.49
Social potency	.57
Achievement orientation	.38
Social closeness	.15
Neuroticism	.70
Sense of alienation	.59
Aggression	.67
Inhibited control	.56
Low risk taking	.45
Traditionalism	.59
Absorption or imagination	.74
Average twin correlation	**.54**

reflects an attitude or a preference for the established ways of doing things, show such strong heritability? Traits that we intuitively think of as environmentally determined, such as self-esteem, have moderate heritabilities (Kamakura, Ando, & Ono, 2007). Even character traits that we sometimes think of as instilled by parents and teachers—compassion, integrity, courage, and tolerance—turn out to be strongly linked to traditional personality traits and show moderate heritabilities (Steger et al., 2007). And how could neuroticism have such a high heritability, given the traditional view that it is parents who make their children neurotic by their inconsistency of reinforcement and improper attachment? These behavioural genetic findings caused some researchers to question long-held assumptions about the origins of individual differences, a topic we consider later in this chapter under the heading "Shared versus Nonshared Environmental Influences: A Riddle."

Summaries of the behavioural genetic data for many of the major personality traits—extraversion, agreeableness, conscientiousness, neuroticism, openness to experience—yield heritability estimates of approximately 50 percent (Bouchard & Loehlin, 2001; Caspi, Roberts, & Shiner, 2005). A recent meta-analysis, for instance, identified an average heritability estimate of 48 percent across the Big Five traits (Vukasović & Bratko, 2015). Furthermore, it is clear that the heritability of personality is heavily responsible for the fact that personality traits remain fairly stable over time (Blonigen et al., 2006; Caspi et al., 2005; Johnson et al., 2005; Kamakura et al., 2007; Kandler et al., 2010; van Beijsterveldt et al., 2003). Overall, it is clear that major personality traits show a modest degree of heritability. The same studies, however, also suggest that a substantial portion of the variance in personality traits is environmental in origin.

Attitudes and Preferences

Stable attitudes are generally regarded to be part of personality: they show wide individual differences; they tend to be stable over time; and at least sometimes they are linked with actual behaviour. Behavioural geneticists have examined the heritability of attitudes. The Minnesota Twin Study showed that traditionalism—as evidenced by attitudes favouring conservative values over modern values—showed a heritability of .59. For comparative purposes, Canadian researchers have demonstrated a range of heritability coefficients for diverse categories of social values, from .36 for social enjoyment values to .63 for prosocial values (Schermer et al., 2011).

A longitudinal study of 654 adopted and nonadopted children from the Colorado Adoption Project revealed significant genetic influence on conservative attitudes (Abrahamson, Baker, & Caspi, 2002). Markers of conservative attitudes included whether participants agreed or disagreed with specific words or phrases such as "death penalty," "gay rights," and "censorship." Significant genetic influence emerged as early as 12 years of age in this study. Other studies confirm the moderate heritability of values (Renner et al., 2012). As for a highly salient trait like sexual orientation, it too appears to be partly heritable, though the research is more complex. We explore this further in A Closer Look: Sexual Orientation.

Genes also appear to influence occupational preferences. Occupational preferences are not mere whims, but can have important effects on a person's life work, wealth, and eventual social status. In a study of 435 adopted and 10,880 genetic offspring residing in Canada and the United States, Ellis and Bonin (2003) asked participants to respond to 14 different aspects of prospective jobs, using a scale ranging from 1 (not at all appealing) to 100 (extremely appealing). The 14 job aspects were high income, competition, prestige, envied by others, taking risks, element of danger, controlling others, feared by others, little supervision, independence, job security, part of a team, clear responsibilities, and help others. These occupational preferences were then correlated with seven measures of parental social status, including mother's and father's education level, occupational status, and income. A full 71 percent of the correlations were statistically significant for the genetic children, whereas only 3 percent were significant for the adopted children (suggesting that rearing environment does not create the effect). The authors conclude that "this study not only suggests that the genes influence various preferences related to occupations, but that these preferences have an effect on the social status attainment" (p. 929). In short, occupational preferences such as desire for competition and wealth can lead to choosing occupations in which more status and income are actually achieved. The jobs in which we spend a large portion of our lives and the prestige and income that comes from those jobs are at least partly influenced by the genes we inherit from our parents.

Not all attitudes and beliefs show these levels of moderate heritability, however. One study of 400 twin pairs yielded heritabilities of essentially zero for beliefs in God, involvement in religious affairs, and attitudes toward racial integration (Loehlin & Nichols, 1976). A study of adopted and nonadopted children confirmed that there is no evidence of a heritable influence on *religious* attitudes (Abrahamson et al., 2002). Another study also found extremely low heritability (12 percent) for religiousness, as measured by items such as "frequency of attending religious services," during adolescence (Koenig et al., 2005). In adulthood (average age of 33), however, the heritability of religiousness had increased to 44 percent. These and other findings suggest that genes have an increasingly important role in religiousness as people move from adolescence into adulthood (Button et al., 2011).

No one knows why some attitudes appear to be partly heritable. Are there specific genes that predispose people to be more conservative? Or are these heritabilities merely incidental byproducts of genes for other qualities? A study by researchers from the University of Western Ontario and the University of British Columbia suggested that for some attitudes, it was the heritability of personality traits that actually mediated the heritability of related attitudes (Olson et al., 2001). Future research in behavioural genetics will be able to address these questions and provide further answers to the mystery of why some attitudes appear to be partly heritable.

 ## A Closer Look

Sexual Orientation

Sexual orientation refers to whether a person is sexually and/or romantically attracted to other people of the same sex, the opposite sex, or both. Individual differences in sexual orientation tend to be relatively stable over time and can be associated with important life outcomes, such as the social groups with which one affiliates. Although it continues to be the subject of debate, some personality psychologists argue that sexual orientation falls within the scope of personality.

Is sexual orientation inherited? Psychologist Michael Bailey has conducted the most extensive studies of this issue. Bailey and his colleagues examined the twin brothers of a sample of gay men, as well as the adoptive brothers of another sample of gay men. Heritability estimates from all studies ranged from 30 percent to a strikingly high 70 percent. Similar heritabilities were found in a sample of lesbians and their adoptive sisters (Bailey et al., 1993).

These heritability findings come on the heels of another important discovery, which was published in *Science* magazine (LeVay, 1991). Brain researcher Simon LeVay discovered that gay and straight men differ in a specific area of the brain known as the hypothalamus. One area of the hypothalamus, the medial preoptic region, appears to be partially responsible for regulating male-typical sexual behaviour (LeVay, 1993, 1996). LeVay obtained the brains of gay men who had died of AIDS and compared them with the brains of straight men who had died of AIDS or other causes. He found that the size of the medial preoptic region of the hypothalamus—the region believed to regulate male-typical sexual behaviour—was two to three times *smaller* in the gay men, compared with that of the straight men. Unfortunately, given the extremely expensive nature of brain research, the samples in this study were quite small. Moreover, no one has yet replicated these findings.

Behavioural geneticist Dean Hamer has published some evidence that male sexual orientation is influenced by a gene on the X chromosome (Hamer & Copeland, 1994). However, this finding also needs to be replicated, and several researchers have debated its validity (e.g., see Bailey, Dunne, & Martin, 2000).

Obviously, this research area is controversial, and the findings are hotly debated. Moreover, the genetic studies of sexual orientation have attracted their share of critics. The studies have been challenged on the grounds that the samples, which were secured from advertisements in lesbian and gay publications, were unrepresentative (Baron, 1993).

Another weakness in past studies was a neglect of the correlates of sexual orientation. For example, childhood gender nonconformity is strongly related to adult sexual orientation. Gay men as adults recall having been more "feminine" boys, and lesbian women as adults recall being more "masculine" girls. This association is strong and has been established with many sources of data (e.g., using peer reports of childhood gender nonconformity). Regarding the importance of gender nonconformity in childhood, a leading researcher has remarked that "it is difficult to think of other individual differences that so reliably and so strongly predict socially significant outcomes across the life span, and for both sexes, too" (Bem, 1996, p. 323).

Bailey and his colleagues set out to clear up these weaknesses—unrepresentative samples and lack of accounting for childhood gender nonconformity—by conducting one of the largest twin studies of adult sexual orientation to date (Bailey, Dunne, et al., 2000). The participants were from a sample of almost 25,000 twin pairs in Australia, out of which approximately 1,000 MZ and 1,000 DZ twins participated. Their average age at time of participation was 29 years. The participants completed a questionnaire about childhood (before age 12) participation in a variety of sex-stereotyped activities and games. They also completed a detailed questionnaire on adult sexual orientation and activity, such as "when you have sexual daydreams, how often is your sexual partner male? how often female?"

The women were more likely than the men to have slight homosexual feelings without being exclusively homosexual, whereas the men tended to be either exclusively heterosexual or exclusively homosexual. Just over 3 percent of the men, but only 1 percent of the women, were predominantly or exclusively homosexual in sexual attraction and sexual fantasy. (It should be noted, however, that reporting on gender and sexuality questionnaires is known to be susceptible to gender stereotypes, such that men and women often respond in ways that reaffirm gender role expectations.)

Regarding whether sexual orientation runs in families, this study found lower rates than previous studies, at 20 percent concordance for the identical twin men and 24 percent concordance for the identical twin women. Concordance is the probability that one twin is gay if the other is also gay. Previous studies typically found concordance rates ranging between 40 and 50 percent. Bailey argues that previous studies overestimate genetic contributions due to selecting participants by advertising in gay and lesbian magazines.

In the Bailey, Dunne, et al., (2000) study, participants were randomly selected from a large pool of twins, so there was no selection bias. It seems likely that the real rate of genetic contribution to sexual orientation is lower than previously thought. Childhood gender nonconformity did, however, show significant heritability for both men (50 percent heritability) and women (37 percent heritability). This finding provides some support for Bem's (1996) theory that childhood gender nonconformity may be the inherited component of adult sexual orientation.

In summary, the findings from behavioural genetics and brain research point to the fascinating possibility that sexual orientation—an individual difference that is linked with the social groups one associates with, the leisure activities one pursues, and the lifestyle one adopts—may be partly heritable.

Drinking and Smoking

Drinking and smoking are often regarded as behavioural manifestations of personality dispositions, such as sensation seeking (Zuckerman & Kuhlman, 2000), extraversion (Eysenck, 1981), and neuroticism (Eysenck, 1981). Individuals differ widely in their smoking and drinking habits, and although consumers sometimes quit for good and abstainers sometimes start, these differences tend to be stable over time. Individual differences in drinking and smoking habits also show evidence of heritability. In one study of Australian twins, an MZ twin who smoked was roughly 16 times more likely than an MZ twin who did not smoke to have a twin who smoked (Hooper et al., 1992). The comparable figures for DZ twins were only a sevenfold increase, suggesting evidence of heritability. Similar findings were obtained in a sample of 1,300 Dutch families of adolescent Dutch twins (Boomsma et al., 1994). These studies also point simultaneously to the importance of environmental factors—a point taken up in the next section of this chapter.

Heritability studies of alcohol drinking are more mixed. Some studies find heritability for boys, but not for girls (Hooper et al., 1992). Other studies find heritability for girls, but not for boys (Koopmans & Boomsma, 1993). Most studies, however, show moderate heritability for both sexes, ranging from .36 to .56 (Rose, 1995).

Heritability studies of alcoholism, as opposed to everyday drinking habits, show even stronger heritabilities. Indeed, nearly all show heritabilities of .50 or greater (Kendler et al., 1992). In one study, the heritabilities of alcoholism were 67 percent in women and 71 percent in men (Heath et al., 1994). Interestingly, the same study found a genetic linkage between alcoholism and "conduct disorder" (antisocial behaviour), suggesting that the genes for both tend to occur in the same individuals.

Marriage

A fascinating study revealed that genes can even influence the propensity to marry or stay single (Johnson et al., 2004). The heritability estimate for propensity to marry turned out to be an astonishing 68 percent! One causal path through which this could work is through personality characteristics. Men who got married, compared to their single peers, scored higher on social potency and achievement—traits linked with upward mobility, success in careers, and financial success. These traits are also highly valued by women in selecting marriage partners (Buss, 2003). Thus, a genetic proclivity to marry occurs, at least in part, through heritable personality traits that are desired by potential marriage partners.

Genes also play an interesting role in marital satisfaction. First, individual differences in women's marital satisfaction are roughly 50 percent heritable (Spotts et al., 2004) (this study could not evaluate the heritability of a husband's marital satisfaction). Second, the personality characteristics of wives, notably dispositional optimism, warmth, and low aggressiveness, accounted for both their own marital satisfaction and their husband's marital satisfaction (Spotts et al., 2005). Thus, the marital satisfaction of both women and men seems partly to depend on the moderately heritable personality dispositions of the wives. Interestingly, husbands' personality did not explain as much of their own or their wives' marital satisfaction. Taken together, these results suggest that genes play a role in the quality of marriages, and even who gets divorced versus staying married (Jerskey et al., 2010), in part through heritable personality characteristics.

 Concept Check

Based on behavioural genetic research on key personality traits (such as the Big Five), what broad conclusions can be made regarding the degree of heritability of personality?

What evidence exists for the heritability of marriage, and what pathways are expected to be involved?

Shared versus Nonshared Environmental Influences: A Riddle

With all of the findings on the moderate heritability of so many personality characteristics, it is important not to lose sight of one important fact: the same studies that suggest moderate heritability also provide the best evidence for the importance of environmental influences. If many personality characteristics show heritabilities in the range of 40 to 60 percent, this means that the same characteristics show a substantial degree of environmentality—as much as 60 percent. This conclusion must be tempered, however, by the fact that all measures contain errors of measurement; some of the differences in personality might be attributable to *neither* environmental nor genetic differences, but rather to errors of measurement.

One critical distinction behavioural geneticists make is between **shared environmental influences** and **nonshared environmental influences**. Consider siblings—brothers and sisters in the same family. Some features of their environment are shared: the number of books in the home; the presence or absence of a TV, video game console, or computer; the quality and quantity of food in the home; the parents' values and attitudes; and the schools, church, synagogue, or mosque the parents send the children to. All of these are features of the shared environment. On the other hand, the same brothers and sisters do not share *all* features of their environment. Some children might get special treatment from their parents. They might have different groups of friends. They might occupy different rooms in the house. One might go to summer camp, whereas the others stay home each summer. All of these features are called nonshared because they are *experienced differently* by different siblings.

 Exercise

Make a list of five shared environmental influences you have in common with your siblings (or, if you are an only child, what things might be shared environmental influences if you had siblings). Then list five nonshared environmental influences. Which had the strongest influence on your personality, attitudes, or behaviour?

We know that the environment exerts a major influence on personality. But *which* environment matters most—the shared or the nonshared environment? Some behavioural genetic designs allow us to figure out whether the environmental effects come more from shared or from nonshared sources. The details of how this is done are too technical to examine in this book, but, if you are interested, you can check out Plomin and colleagues (2008) for more details.

The bottom line is this: for most personality variables, the shared environment has either little or no impact. Adoption studies show that the average correlation for personality variables between adopted siblings who share much of their environment, but who share no genes, is only .05. This suggests that even though these siblings grow up together—with the same parents, same schools, same religious training, and so on—whatever is happening in their shared environment (e.g., parenting, rearing practices, values education) is not causing them to be similar in personality.

Instead, most environmental causes appear to stem from the aspects of the environment that siblings experience differently. Thus, it's not the number of books in the home. It's not parental values or parental attitudes toward child rearing. In fact, it's not what most psychologists have long believed it is. Rather, the critical environmental influences on personality appear to lie in the unique experiences of individual children.

Which unique experiences are important? Well, here we run into a brick wall. Most theories of socialization over the decades have focused exclusively on the shared environment, such as poverty and parental attitudes toward child rearing. It is only recently that psychologists have begun to study nonshared environments.

There are two possibilities of what they will find. One possibility is a major breakthrough—a discovery of a critically important environmental variable that has been overlooked by psychologists who for years focused only on the shared environment. Different peer influences may be one good candidate (Harris, 2007). The other possibility is less satisfying. It is conceivable that there are so many environmental variables that exert an impact on personality that each one alone might account only for a tiny fraction of the variance (Willerman, 1979). If this is the case, then we are stuck with the discovery of many small effects.

Does this mean that the shared environment accounts for nothing? Have psychologists been entirely misguided in their thinking by their focus on shared effects? The answer is no. In some areas, behavioural genetic studies have revealed tremendously important shared environmental influences: attitudes, religious beliefs, political orientations, health behaviours, and to some degree verbal intelligence (Segal, 1999). As an example, adoptive siblings reared together but genetically unrelated correlated .41 (girls) and .46 (boys) in their patterns of smoking and drinking (Willerman, 1979). Thus, although smoking and drinking have a substantial genetic component, there is also a large shared environmental component.

Another study found that shared environments accounted for several personality clusters in the "adjustment" domain (Loehlin, Neiderhiser, & Reiss, 2003). These include antisocial behaviour (e.g., showing behaviour problems and breaking rules), depressive symptoms (e.g., moody, withdrawn), and autonomous functioning (e.g., being able to care for self in basic needs and recreational activities). And a study of adult twins using observational measurement—trait ratings of videotaped behaviours—suggests that shared environment might be more important in explaining Big Five personality traits than is typically revealed by studies using self-report (Borkenau et al., 2001). If this study is replicated by future research, it may have the far-reaching consequence of challenging the now conventional wisdom that shared environments have little effect on personality traits.

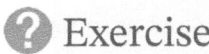

❓ Exercise

Discuss what you think might represent shared environmental influences that contribute to the tendency to smoke. That is, what in the environment might have influenced most people who smoke to start and maintain their smoking habit?

In summary, environments shared by siblings are important in some domains. But, for many personality traits, such as extraversion and neuroticism, shared environments do not seem to matter. Instead, it is the unique environment experienced by each sibling that carries the causal weight.

❗ Concept Check

Describe the difference between shared and nonshared environmental influences, and provide examples. What does the research have to say about the degree of influence from each?

Genes and the Environment

As important as it is to identify sources of environmental and genetic influence on personality, the next step requires an understanding of how genetic and environmental factors interact. More complex forms of behavioural genetic analysis involve the concepts of *genotype–environment interaction* and *genotype–environment correlation*.

Genotype–Environment Interaction

Genotype–environment interaction refers to the differential response of individuals with different genotypes to the same environments. Consider introverts and extraverts, who have somewhat different genotypes. Introverts tend to perform well on cognitive tasks when there is little stimulation in the room, but they do poorly when there are distractions, such as a radio blaring or people walking around. In contrast, extraverts do just fine with the stereo blasting, the phone ringing, and people walking in and out. But the same extraverts make a lot of errors in these cognitive tasks when there is little stimulation—when the task they are working on is boring or monotonous.

Extraversion–introversion is a perfect example of genotype–environment interaction, whereby individuals with different genotypes (introverts and extraverts) respond differently to the same environment (e.g., noise in the room). Individual differences *interact* with the environment to affect performance. You may want to take this into consideration when you arrange your studying environment. Before turning on the stereo, first determine whether you lie on the introverted or extraverted end of the continuum. If you are an introvert, you would likely do better studying in a quiet environment with few interruptions.

Studies have begun to identify other genotype–environment interactions. One examined the effects of abusive parenting on whether children developed antisocial personalities (Caspi, Sugden, et al., 2003). Abused children who had a genotype that produced low levels of the brain neurotransmitter monoamine oxidase A (MAOA) frequently developed conduct disorders, antisocial personalities, and violent dispositions. In contrast, maltreated children who had high levels of MAOA were far less likely to develop aggressive antisocial personalities. This study and replications of it (Kim-Cohen et al., 2006) provide excellent examples of genotype–environment interaction—exposure to the same environment (abusive parenting) produces different effects on personality, depending on the differences in genotype. Interestingly, this suggests that violent parents may create violent children *only* if the children have a genotype marked by low levels of MAOA. Similar G × E interactions have been discovered between the 5-HTT gene and childhood maltreatment in predicting persistent depression later in life. Only individuals with two short 5-HTT forms of the gene who had experienced maltreatment as children developed persistent depression (Uher et al., 2011). The empirical study of genotype–environment interactions represents one of the most exciting developments in the behaviour genetics of personality (Jang et al., 2005; Moffitt, 2005), psychological disorders (McGue, 2010), and health (Johnson, 2007).

Genotype–Environment Correlation

Just as interesting is the concept of **genotype–environment correlation**, the differential exposure of individuals with different genotypes to different environments. Consider, for example, a child who has a genotype for high verbal ability. Her parents may notice this and provide her with lots of books to read, engage in intellectual discussions with her, and give her word games and crossword puzzles. Parents of children with less verbal skill, who presumably have different genotypes than those with high verbal abilities, may be less inclined to provide this stimulation. This is an example of genotype–environment correlation; individuals with different genotypes (e.g., those with high versus low verbal abilities) are exposed to different environments (e.g., high versus low stimulation). In another example, parents might promote sports activities for athletically inclined children more than for less athletically inclined children.

Plomin, DeFries, and Loehlin (1977) describe three very different kinds of genotype–environment correlation: passive, reactive, and active. **Passive genotype–environment correlation** occurs when parents provide both genes and the environment to children, yet the children do nothing to obtain that environment. Suppose, for example, that parents who are verbally inclined pass on genes to their children that make them verbally inclined. However, because the parents are highly verbal, they buy a lot of books. Thus, there is a correlation between the children's verbal ability and the number of books in their home, but it is passive in the sense that the child has done nothing to cause the books to be there.

In sharp contrast, the **reactive genotype–environment correlation** occurs when parents (or others) respond to children differently depending on the child's genotypes. A good example is cuddlers versus noncuddlers. Some babies love to be touched—they giggle, smile, laugh, and show great pleasure when they are handled. Other babies are more aloof and simply do not like to be touched very much. Imagine that a mother starts out touching and hugging each of her two children a lot. One child loves it; the other hates it. Over the course of several months, the mother reacts by continuing to hug the cuddler but cuts down on hugging the noncuddler. This example illustrates the reactive genotype–environment correlation, which is achieved because people react to children differently based in part on the children's heritable dispositions.

Active genotype–environment correlation occurs when a person with a particular genotype creates or seeks out a particular environment. High sensation seekers, for example, expose themselves to risky environments: skydiving, motorcycle jumping, and drug taking. Highly intellectual individuals are likely to attend lectures, read books, and engage others in verbal discourse. This active creation and selection of environments has also been called "niche picking" (Scarr & McCartney, 1983). Active genotype–environment correlation highlights the fact that we are not passive recipients of our environments; we mould, create, and select the environments we subsequently inhabit, and some of these actions are correlated with our genotypes.

Modern views on the nature–nurture debate suggest more complex answers to the question of the origins of personality. One view is that genes and environments interact in determining personality.
©Ingram Publishing

These genotype–environment correlations can be positive or negative. That is, the environment can encourage the expression of the disposition, or it can discourage its expression. Adolescents who have personalities marked by positive emotionality (e.g., an upbeat, optimistic stance) tend to evoke high levels of helpful and affirmative regard from their parents, so that genotypes for positive emotionality are positively correlated with environments of high parental regard (Krueger et al., 2008). The positive link between personality and parenting, in short, is genetically mediated (South et al., 2008). Conversely, parents of highly active children may try to get them to sit still and calm down, and parents of less active children may try to get them to perk up and be more lively, in which case there is a negative genotype–environment correlation because the parents' behaviour opposes the children's traits (Buss, 1981). Another example of negative genotype–environment correlation occurs when people who are too dominant elicit negative reactions from others, who try to "cut them down" (Cattell, 1973). The key point is that environments can go against a person's genotype, resulting in a negative genotype–environment correlation, or they can facilitate the person's genotype, creating a positive genotype–environment correlation.

A study of 180 twins reared apart points to an intriguing potential example of genotype–environment correlation (Krueger, Markon, & Bouchard, 2003). The study assessed personality traits through the Multidimensional Personality Questionnaire (MPQ), which identifies three major factors of personality: Positive Emotionality (happy, content), Negative Emotionality (anxious, tense), and Constraint (controlled, conscientious). Then they evaluated each individual's *perceptions* of the family environments in which they were raised, which yielded two main factors: Family Cohesion (e.g., parental warmth, absence of family conflict) and Family Status (e.g., parents provided intellectual and cultural stimulation, active recreational activities, and financial resources). The intriguing results were that the correlations between personality and perceptions of family environment were genetically mediated. In other words, the perceived environment in which the individuals were raised was largely due to heritable personality traits. Specifically, experiencing a cohesive family upbringing was explained by genetic influence on the two personality traits of Constraint and lack of Negative Emotionality. In contrast, recalling a family environment high in cultural and intellectual activity was explained by the heritable personality trait of Positive Emotionality.

These results may be subject to several interpretations. One interpretation is that personality affects the subjective manner in which people remember their early environments. Perhaps calm, controlled individuals are more likely to forget about real family conflict that was present during their childhood, and so may simply recall greater family cohesion than actually existed. An alternative interpretation is in terms of genotype–environment correlation: Individuals with calm, controlled personalities (high Constraint, low Negative

Emotionality) may actually *promote* cohesion among family members—in essence, creating a family environment that further fosters their calm, controlled personality. Future studies of personality, parenting, and perceived family environments offer the promise of unravelling the complex ways in which genes interact and correlate with environments (Spinath & O'Connor, 2003).

Another promising avenue for exploring genotype–environment correlations is through peers (Burt, 2009; Loehlin, 2010). One study found a GE correlation for adolescent alcohol consumption based on the differential selection of peers, especially for females (Loehlin, 2010). Another found evidence for GE correlation between impulsivity, which leads to mild forms of rule breaking (e.g., drinking, smoking, vandalism), and popularity during adolescence (Burt, 2009). Thus, genes predispose some individuals to break rules, which in turn leads to greater popularity during adolescence—an example of reactive gene–environment correlation. Genes for impulsivity, in short, are correlated with a social environment of being popular—a correlation established, in part, through acts of rule breaking.

 Concept Check

Compare/contrast the concepts of genotype-environment interaction and genotype-environment correlation.

Molecular Genetics

The most recent development in the science of behavioural genetics has been the exploration of **molecular genetics**. The methods of molecular genetics are designed to identify the specific genes associated with personality traits. The details are quite technical, but the most common method, called the association method, is to identify whether individuals with a particular gene (or allele) have higher or lower scores on a particular trait than individuals without the gene (Benjamin et al., 1996; Ebstein et al., 1996).

The most frequently examined gene is called the **DRD4 gene**, which is located on the short arm of chromosome 11. This gene codes for a protein called a dopamine receptor. The function of this dopamine receptor, as you might guess, is to respond to the presence of dopamine, which is a neurotransmitter. When the dopamine receptor encounters dopamine from other neurons in the brain, it discharges an electrical signal, activating other neurons.

The most frequently examined association between the DRD4 gene and a personality trait has involved novelty seeking, the tendency to seek out new experiences, especially those considered risky, such as drug experiences, risky sexual experiences, gambling, and high-speed driving (Zuckerman & Kuhlman, 2000). Individuals with so-called long repeat versions of the DRD4 gene were found to be higher on novelty seeking than individuals with so-called short repeat versions of this gene (Benjamin et al., 1996). The researchers hypothesized that the reason for this association is that people with long DRD4 genes tend to be relatively unresponsive to dopamine. This causes them to seek out novel experiences that give them a "dopamine buzz." In contrast, those with the short DRD4 genes tend to be highly responsive to whatever dopamine is already present in their brains, so they tend not to seek out novel experiences, which might boost their dopamine to uncomfortable levels.

Although the association between DRD4 and novelty seeking has been replicated several times, there have also been several failures to replicate (Plomin & Crabbe, 2000). One study, for example, found that the DRD4 was *not* at all associated with measures of novelty seeking (Burt et al., 2002). A second study of preschool children found that DRD4 *was* significantly linked with mothers' reports of their children's problems with aggression (a possible precursor to novelty seeking) but was *not* significantly linked with observed behavioural measures of aggression (Schmidt et al., 2002). And a third study found that high novelty seeking was linked with a different allele of a *different* gene—the A1 allele of the D2 dopamine receptor gene (DRD2) (Berman et al., 2002).

Part of the problem is that the size of the association is small. The original researchers (Benjamin et al., 1996) estimate that the DRD4 gene explains only 4 percent of the variation in novelty seeking. It has also been speculated that there may be 10 other genes that are equally important in novelty seeking, none of which has yet been explored. And perhaps there are 500 genes that vary with other aspects of human personality (Ridley, 1999). It seems unlikely, therefore, that any single gene will ever be found to explain more than a small percentage of variation in personality. The most recent meta-analysis of the dopamine D4 receptor (DRD4) gene has found reliable links with novelty seeking and impulsivity (Munafo et al., 2008). As an illustration, one experiment found that men with the 7-repeat (7R) allele of the DRD4 gene were more likely to engage in financial risk taking than men lacking the 7R allele (Dreber et al., 2009), as shown in Figure 6.1.

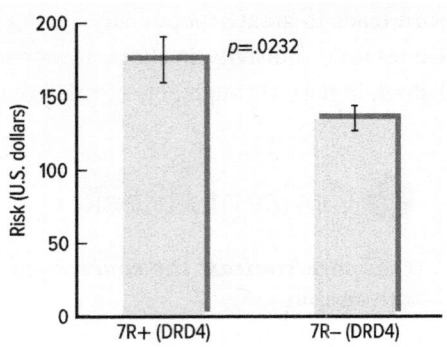

FIGURE 6.1 Men with DRD4 7R+ allele invest more money in a financial risk game.

Interestingly, the 7R allele of the DRD4 gene occurs at dramatically different rates in different geographical regions. It occurs at higher rates in North America than in Asia, and has been hypothesized to be favoured by evolutionary selection (see Chapter 7) when people migrate to new environments or inhabit resource-rich environments (Chen et al., 1999; Penke, Denissen, & Miller, 2007). Empirical evidence for this hypothesis comes from a study of the migration patterns of 2,320 individuals from 39 groups (Chen et al., 1999). Migratory populations showed a far higher proportion of the 7R allele of the DRD4 gene than did sedentary populations, which could be caused by selective migration of individuals carrying those genes, selective favouring of those genes in the new environments, or both. Evidence on sedentary and nomadic populations favours the hypothesis that the 7R allele of the DRD4 gene is more advantageous among nomadic than settled populations (Eisenberg et al., 2008). Men with the 7R allele may also have an advantage in highly competitive societies in resource competition and in direct competition for access to mates (Harpending & Cochran, 2002).

As exciting as the results are from these molecular genetic methods, it is important to exercise caution when interpreting them. In several cases, researchers have found an association between a particular gene and personality-related traits such as anxiety and attention deficit disorder, but subsequent researchers have failed to replicate these associations (Plomin & Crabbe, 2000; McGue, 2010; Turkheimer et al., 2014). Furthermore, some gene–personality links are found for one gender, but not for the other. For example, one study found that women with one copy of the A allele at OXTR rs2254298 experienced greater attachment anxiety than did women with two copies of the G allele (Chen & Johnson, 2012). Nonetheless, this gene–personality link was not found among men. Research over the next decade or two, however, should reveal the degree to which specific genes for specific personality traits can be found. A promising method known as genome-wide association studies (GWAS), which can rapidly examine the entire genome for links with personality, may yield faster scientific advances (Turkheimer et al., 2014). A GWAS study of Extraversion produced one promising candidate (van den Berg et al., 2016). But it appears possible that personality traits may be linked to such a large number of genes, each accounting for only tiny effects, that understanding the molecular genetics of personality may be many years in the future.

Finally, rather than looking for direct links between single genes and personality or behaviour, modern research in this area is beginning to explore gene–environment interactions using molecular genetic techniques (e.g., Caspi et al., 2003; South & Krueger, 2008). As noted above, stressful life events cause depressive symptoms, but *only* in people who carry the short version of the serotonin transporter (5-HTT) gene (Uher et al., 2011). For those carrying other variants of this gene, stressful life events did *not* produce depressive symptoms. This provides an illustration of the power of combining molecular genetic techniques with the important concept of gene–environment interaction.

 Concept Check

What specific genes have been found to be associated with personality?

Behavioural Genetics, Science, Politics, and Values

The history of behavioural genetic research has taken some fascinating twists and turns that are worth noting (see Plomin et al., 2008, for an excellent summary of this history). During the past century in North America, behavioural genetic research received what can be phrased as a "frosty reception." Findings that some personality traits were moderately heritable seemed to violate the dominant paradigm, which was environmentalism (and, especially, behaviourism). The prevailing **environmentalist view** was that personality was determined by socialization practices, such as parenting style. Furthermore, people worried about the potential misuse of findings emerging from behavioural genetics. Images of Nazi Germany sprang to mind, with the evil notions of a master race.

A large part of the controversy over genetic research on personality has centred around studies of intelligence, which has often been considered to be a personality variable. Many people have worried that findings from these studies will be misused to label some people intrinsically superior or inferior to others (e.g., see Herrnstein & Murray, 1994). Others worry that findings will be misused to give some people preferential treatment in education or job placement. Still others are concerned that standard tests of intelligence fail to capture many of the multiple facets of intelligence, such as social intelligence, emotional intelligence, and creativity. All of these are legitimate concerns, and they suggest that the findings from the field of behavioural genetics must be viewed with caution and interpreted responsibly, in terms of the larger picture of human nature and society.

In the past decade attitudes have shifted, and the field of psychology now considers the findings from behavioural genetics as fairly mainstream. Behavioural genetic studies tend not to generate the intense controversy that they did in prior decades. Indeed, findings from sophisticated behavioural genetic research on personality are now seen as critical in combating important individual and social problems, such as the effects of stressful life events on depression.

The links between science and politics, between knowledge and values, are complex, but they need to be confronted. Because scientific research can be misused for political goals, scientists bear a major responsibility for presenting findings carefully and accurately. Science can be separated from values. Science is a set of methods for discovering what exists. Values are notions of what people *want* to exist—to be desired or sought after. Although scientists clearly can be biased by their values, the virtue of the scientific method is that it is self-correcting. The methods are public, so other scientists can check the findings, discover errors in procedure, and hence over time correct any biases that creep in. This does not imply, of course, that scientists are unbiased. Indeed, the history of science is filled with cases in which values influenced the nature of the questions posed and the acceptance or rejection of particular findings or theories. Nonetheless, the scientific method provides a system for correcting such biases in the long run.

Summary and Evaluation

The behavioural genetic study of personality has a fascinating history. Early on, when behavioural genetic methods were being developed, the field of psychology was dominated by the behaviourist paradigm. In this context, findings from behavioural genetic research were not warmly received. Social scientists worried that findings from behavioural genetic research might be misused for ideological purposes.

Over the past two decades, the empirical evidence on heritability has become stronger and stronger, in part because of the convergence of evidence across behavioural genetic methods. There are four traditional behavioural genetic methods: selective breeding studies, family studies, twin studies, and adoption studies. Selective breeding studies cannot be ethically conducted on humans. Family studies are problematic because the genetic and environmental factors are often confounded. Twin studies have potential problems, such as violations of the equal environments assumption (the assumption that identical twins are not treated any more alike than fraternal twins) and the assumption of representativeness (the notion that twins are just like non-twins). Adoption studies also have potential problems, such as the nonrandom placement of adopted-away children in particular families. Empirical tests of these assumptions suggest that they are not violated much or are violated in ways that do not seem to make much difference. However, the most compelling evidence on the heritability of personality comes from looking across methods that do not share methodological problems. Thus, if the findings from twin studies *and* adoption studies converge on the same result, then we can have more confidence in the results than we can when only a single method is used.

The study of large samples of twins reared together, the study of smaller samples of identical twins reared apart, and sound adoption studies have added greatly to the credibility of behavioural genetic research. The empirical findings clearly show that personality variables, such as extraversion and neuroticism, as well as the other dimensions of the Big Five, have moderate heritability. Perhaps even more striking are the findings that drinking, smoking, attitudes, occupational preferences, and even sexual orientation appear to be moderately heritable. Equally important, however, is the finding that the same studies provide the best evidence for the importance of environmental influences. Overall, personality characteristics are 30 to 50 percent heritable and 50 to 70 percent environmental.

The environmental causes appear to be mostly of the nonshared variety—that is, the different experiences that siblings have even though they are in the same family. This finding is startling because nearly all theories of environmental influence—such as those that posit the importance of parental values and child-rearing styles—have been of the shared variety. Thus, behavioural genetic research may have provided one of the most important insights into the nature of nurture—the location of the most important environmental influences on personality. The next decade of personality research should witness progress in identifying the precise locations of these nonshared environmental influences. Separating perceived environments from objective environments will be an important part of this research program.

In interpreting the research findings, it is important to keep in mind the meaning of heritability and the meaning of environmentality. Heritability is the proportion of observed individual differences that are caused by genetic differences in a particular population or sample. It does not pertain to an individual; genetic and environmental influences are inextricably interwoven at the individual level and cannot be separated. Heritability does not mean that the environment is powerless to alter the individual differences. And heritability is not a fixed statistic—it can be low in one group and high in another, low at one time and high at another. Environmentality is the proportion of observed individual differences that is caused by environmental differences. Like heritability, environmentality is not a fixed statistic. It, too, can change over time and across situations. The discovery of a powerful environmental intervention, for example, could, in principle, dramatically increase environmentality while lowering heritability. The key point is that neither heritability nor environmentality is fixed in space and time.

In addition to providing estimates of heritability and environmentality, some behavioural genetic research examines the interactions and correlations among genetic and environmental variables. There are three major types of genotype–environment correlations: passive, reactive, and active. *Passive* genotype–environment correlation occurs when parents provide both genes and environment to their children in ways that just happen to be correlated—for example, parents who pass on genes for verbal ability and stock their houses with a lot of books. Books and verbal ability become correlated, but in a passive way because the children did not have to do anything for the correlation to occur. *Reactive* genotype–environment correlation occurs when parents, teachers, and others respond differently to some children than to others. Parents generally tickle and coo at smiley babies more than at nonsmiley babies, creating a correlation between genotypes for smiling and a cuddly social environment. The correlation occurs because parents react to babies differently. *Active* genotype–environment correlation occurs when individuals with certain genotypes seek out environments nonrandomly. Extraverted individuals, for example, might throw a lot of parties, thus surrounding themselves with a different social environment than that of the more reclusive introverts. The correlation occurs because individuals actively create it.

The more complex and interesting behavioural genetic concepts such as genotype–environment correlation have received relatively little research attention. One possible exception is the fascinating finding that individuals low on Negative Emotionality and high on Constraint recall their early family environment as being extremely cohesive. One interpretation is in terms of genotype–environment correlation: calm, non-neurotic individuals may actually promote calmness and cohesion in their family environment, thus creating an upbringing that further fosters their calm, controlled personality.

Molecular genetics represents the most recent development in the realm of personality psychology. The research techniques attempt to establish an association between specific genes and scores on personality traits. The DRD4 gene, for example, is linked with novelty seeking. One of the most promising new developments is combining molecular genetics with the search for *gene–environment interactions*—the ways in which people with different genes react differently to the same environment. Stressful environments, for example, appear to produce depressive symptoms, but primarily in people with the short version of the serotonin transporter (5-HTT) gene.

 Concept Check

In a single paragraph, offer a summary of the research findings on the heritability of human personality.

If you were tasked with designing a study to investigate the degree of heritability (as well as shared and nonshared environmental effects) associated with a newly identified personality trait, what would you do?

Key Terms

- genome
- genetic junk
- eugenics
- percentage of variance
- heritability
- phenotypic variance
- genotypic variance
- environmentality
- nature–nurture debate
- selective breeding
- family studies
- twin studies

- monozygotic (MZ) twins
- dizygotic (DZ) twins
- equal environments assumption
- adoption studies
- selective placement
- shared environmental influences
- nonshared environmental influences
- genotype–environment interaction

- genotype–environment correlation
- passive genotype–environment correlation
- reactive genotype–environment correlation
- active genotype–environment correlation
- molecular genetics
- DRD4 gene
- environmentalist view

Physiological Approaches to Personality

The Biological Domain

Elliot was a successful businessman, a proud father, and a good husband. At his firm, he was a role model for his younger colleagues. Personally, he was charming and pleasant. His social skills were such that he often was called on to settle disputes at work. Elliot was respected by others. His position in the community, his satisfying personal life, and his prosperity and professional status were all enviable.

One day Elliot began to have severe headaches. After a few days he went to his doctor, who suspected a brain tumour. This suspicion was confirmed when a small tumour was found growing not on his brain, but on the lining of tissue that covers the brain. The location was just above his eyes, behind his forehead. The tumour was, however, pushing against his brain and had damaged a small portion of the front of his brain, part of the prefrontal cortex, which had to be removed with the tumour.

The operation went smoothly and Elliot recovered quickly, with no apparent lasting damage—at least none that could be found with ordinary tests. Elliot's IQ was tested after the operation and was found to be superior, as it was before his operation. His memory was tested and was found to be excellent. His ability to use and understand language was also unaffected by the operation. His ability to do arithmetic, to memorize lists of words, to visualize objects, to make judgments, and to read a map remained unaffected. All of his cognitive functions remained normal or above normal, completely unaffected by the removal of a small portion of his prefrontal cortex.

Elliot's family, however, reported that his personality had changed. He began to behave differently at work as well. He could not seem to manage his time properly. He needed lots of prompting from his wife to get going in the morning. Once at work, he had problems finishing tasks. If he was interrupted in a task, he had difficulty starting back up where he had left off. Often he would become captivated by one part of a task and be sidetracked for hours. For example, in

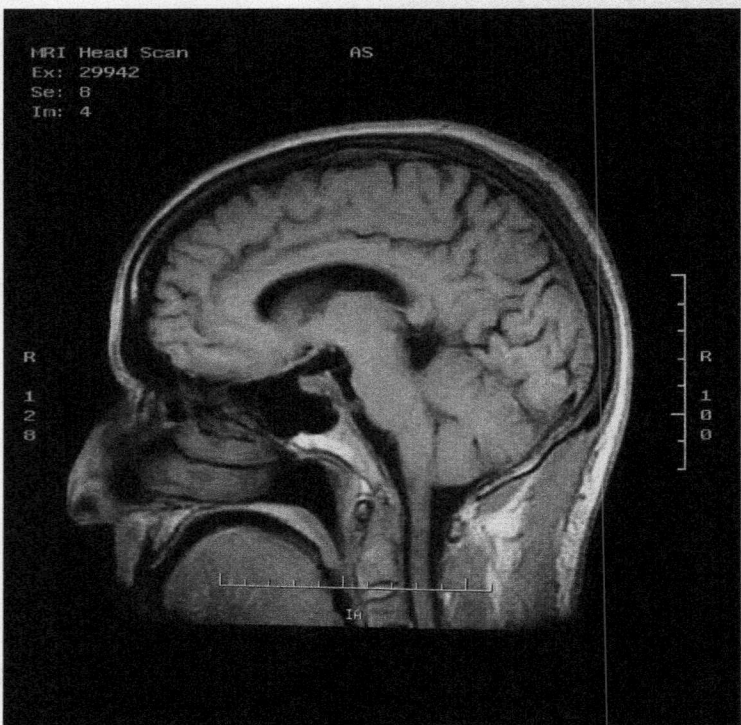

Brain imaging techniques have enabled researchers to learn more about the brain's role in behaviour and personality than previously thought possible.
©CGinspiration/Getty Images

refiling some books, which should have taken 15 minutes, he stopped to read one of the books and returned to his desk hours later. He knew his job but just had trouble putting all the actions together in the right order.

Soon Elliot lost his job. He tried various business schemes on his own and finally took his life savings and started an investment management business. He teamed up with a disreputable character, against the advice of many of his friends and family members. This business went bankrupt, and he lost all his savings. To his wife and children Elliot appeared to be behaving impulsively, and they had trouble coping with the difficulties he was getting into. A divorce followed. Elliot quickly remarried, but to a woman whom none of his friends or family approved of. This marriage quickly ended in another divorce. Without a source of income, and without a family to support him, Elliot became a drifter.

Elliot came to the attention of Dr. Antonio Damasio, a neurologist, who later wrote a book about Elliot's condition (Damasio, 1994). It seems that the small bit of brain matter destroyed by Elliot's tumour was essential in transmitting emotional information to the higher reasoning centres of the brain. Elliot reported that the only change he noticed in himself was that, after his operation, he did not feel any strong emotion—or much of any emotion for that matter.

The case of Elliot shows us that the body and the mind are intimately connected. Indeed, after Elliot's operation, the biggest change in him was in his personality—not in his memory, his reasoning, or his knowledge.

Studies have shown that traumatic brain injury can lead to large changes in personality (Tate, 2003). One of the most common changes in personality following brain injury is a diminished ability to inhibit or control one's impulses. This has been found in children who experienced brain trauma during birth (Christ et al., 2003), in adults with traumatic brain injuries (Kim, 2002), and in elderly people whose brains have been injured by stroke (Freshwater & Golden, 2002). This increased impulsivity and lack of self-control is most likely due to disruptions between the frontal lobes, which serve as the executive control centre of the brain, and other parts of the brain. As a result, individuals with extensive brain injury can retain most of their cognitive abilities, yet lose some degree of self-control (Lowenstein, 2002). Those with personality changes following traumatic brain injuries often have spontaneous outbursts, sudden changes in mood, and episodes of aggression, and can become quite disruptive to their families (Beer & Lombardo, 2007a). Indeed, this is the personality profile of one of the most famous brain injury patients, Phineas Gage, who was injured by an iron rod that was blasted through his brain while he was working as a railway builder in the mid-1800s (see A Closer Look: The Brain Injuries of Phineas Gage and Patient K. C.).

👁 A Closer Look

The Brain Injuries of Phineas Gage and Patient K. C.

Phineas Gage was a nineteenth-century rail worker, serving as foreman on a construction gang preparing the way for the Rutland and Burlington Railroad in Vermont. His work involved blasting large rocks with dynamite, and one day he was injured in a serious accident. Prior to his accident, Phineas was an industrious worker, highly agreeable and conscientious, and seen by his employers as one of their most capable and efficient foremen. On September 13, 1848, he was tamping dynamite into a hole in a rock using an iron rod. The dynamite accidentally ignited and the explosion shot the iron rod out of the hole like a bullet. Phineas was bending over the work area. The iron rod he was working with was 1¼ inches in diameter, 3-feet, 7-inches long, and weighed almost 14 pounds. It was tapered at one end almost to a point. The heavy iron rod came out of the tamping hole point first. It shot up through Gage's left cheek, just below the cheek bone, passed behind his left eye, and exited the top of his skull, landing approximately 75 feet away. Gage was knocked off his feet but did not lose consciousness. The iron rod destroyed a large portion of the front part of his brain. Remarkably, Gage survived this accident. He spent 10 weeks under a doctor's care, then returned to his home in New Hampshire. Even more remarkably, most of his intellectual

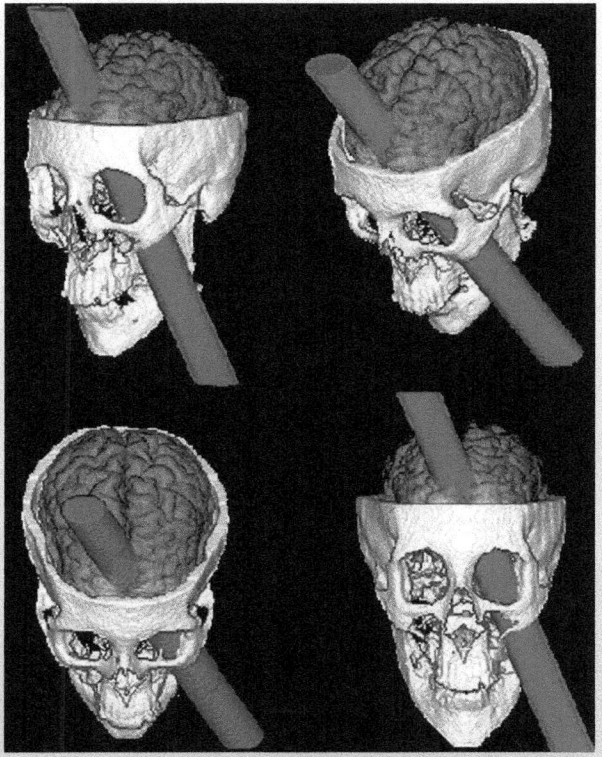

Reconstruction of the path of the iron rod through the brain of Phineas Gage.

Source: from H. Damasio, T. Grabowski, R. Frank, A.M. Galaburda & A.R. Damasio (1994), "The return of Phineas Gage: clues about the brain from the skull a famous patient," *Science,* 264: 1102–1105. Dornsife Cognitive Neuroimaging Center and Brain and Creativity Institute, University of Southern California.

functions remained intact. However, his personality changed dramatically. His doctor, John Harlow, described the new Phineas Gage as "obstinate, capricious, and vacillating, devising many plans of future operations which are no sooner arranged than they are abandoned, a child, yet with the passions of a strong man" (cited in Carter, 1999). He lacked the ability to direct himself nor could he devise plans to achieve goals. He was impulsive and aggressive. He started using profane language and disregarded social conventions, behaving impolitely toward those around him. Women were advised to avoid him. He never worked as a foreman again. Instead, he had various farm jobs, mostly caring for horses and cleaning stables. He died on May 21, 1860, almost 12 years after his devastating accident. His skull and the iron rod are on display at Harvard's Countway Library of Medicine. See Macmillan (2000) for a modern perspective on this famous case.

Fast forward over a century later, and the famous Canadian case of Kent Cochrane would provide further insights into our understanding of the brain, memory, and personality. Patient K. C., as he came to be known, was a Toronto-born man who experienced a series of traumas to the head during his lifetime. The first occurred when he was just 16 years old. While working on his aunt's farm in Montreal, K. C. lost consciousness when a bale of hay fell on his head. He later sustained a second head injury during college when his dune buggy collided with a larger vehicle. Neither of these accidents seemed to impact K. C.'s cognitive functioning, but it was his third accident that would have the greatest effect on his life. At the age of 30, while working at an engineering and manufacturing plant, he rode his motorcycle off the highway, losing consciousness. He was quickly rushed to the hospital where he underwent surgery to remove a blood clot from his brain. It was upon his rehabilitation and return to full consciousness that the full effects of his injury became apparent. MRI scans revealed severe injury to his medial temporal lobes, including almost complete hippocampal loss bilaterally. The main effect was seen on

Kent Cochrane, also known as Patient K. C., was a Toronto-born man who became the subject of over 20 neuropsychology papers due to a brain injury during a motorcycle accident in 1981.

©Carlos Osorio/Toronto Star/Getty Images

his episodic memory—K. C. was unable to commit any new experiences to either short- or long-term memory. The accident also affected K. C.'s personality in significant ways. Unlike Phineas Gage, he maintained his polite and easygoing nature; however, he was no longer as sociable, gregarious, or thrill-seeking as he once was. Following his injury, K. C. became far more subdued and tranquil in nature, in sharp contrast to his busy and exciting lifestyle before his injury. As reported in a review by Rosenbaum and colleagues in 2005, it was K. C.'s more conservative and unemotional persona that made him the ideal subject of research for nearly 30 years. His brain injury has been the case study of over 20 neuropsychology studies and publications and has played a pivotal role in our understanding of the brain, memory, and personality. Kent Cochrane passed away in 2014 in an assisted living facility in Toronto. See Rosenbaum et al. (2005) for a review of the research that has emerged from the case study of Patient K. C.

An advantage of the physiological approach is that physiological characteristics can be measured mechanically and reliably. The term *physiological characteristics* refers to the functioning of organ systems within the body. Examples of **physiological systems** are the nervous system (including the brain and nerves), the cardiac system (including the heart, arteries, and veins), and the musculoskeletal system (including the muscles and bones, which make all movements and behaviours possible). To get an idea of the importance of these physiological systems, imagine the result of removing any one of them. Without a brain, a person could not think or respond to the environment; without the musculoskeletal system, a person could not move or act on the environment; and without a cardiac system, the result is obvious. All of the physiological systems are important to the maintenance of life, and their study has resulted in the fields of medicine, anatomy, and physiology.

From the perspective of personality psychology, physiology is important to the extent that differences in physiology create, contribute to, or indicate differences in psychological functioning. For example, people differ from one another in how sensitive their nervous systems are to stimulation. Given exposure to loud noise, for example, some people find it quite irritating whereas other people are not bothered at all. A person who is particularly sensitive might frequent quiet environments (e.g., the library), avoid crowds (e.g., not go to loud parties), and limit the amount of stimulation in their environments (e.g., never play loud rock-and-roll music). The physiologically oriented personality psychologist would say that this person is introverted (a psychological characteristic) because they have an overly sensitive nervous system (a physiological characteristic). Thus, this approach assumes that differences in physiological characteristics are related to differences in important personality characteristics and behaviour patterns.

⊘ Application

Individual Differences in Digit Ratio. **Scholars have speculated on connections between bodily shapes and personality traits for centuries. Most such simple theories have been discredited (Stelmack & Stalkas, 1991), such as the system of phrenology that related bumps on the head to aspects of personality. However, one simple bodily difference that is receiving attention these days is the ratio of the index finger to the ring finger, commonly called the "digit ratio" index. This ratio is easy to calculate by measuring the index and ring fingers (see graphic), and there has been a wide variety of research on the correlates of digit ratio.**

One common and reliable finding is that females have a higher digit ratio than males. Females tend to have index fingers that are longer than their ring fingers, resulting in a digit ratio greater than 1.0, whereas males tend to have index fingers that are shorter than their ring fingers, resulting in a digit ratio less than 1.0. Why might this be so? Research with humans and animals (those with measurable digits, such as mice and monkeys) has confirmed that digit ratio is determined prior to birth through exposure of the fetus to testosterone in utero. Testosterone in utero also influences the development of the gonads and sexual development of the fetus. Consequently, the digit ratio after birth is thought to be a lifelong indicator of the amount of prenatal testosterone that the fetus was exposed to. The more testosterone exposure, the smaller the index finger relative to the ring finger (i.e., the smaller the digit ratio).

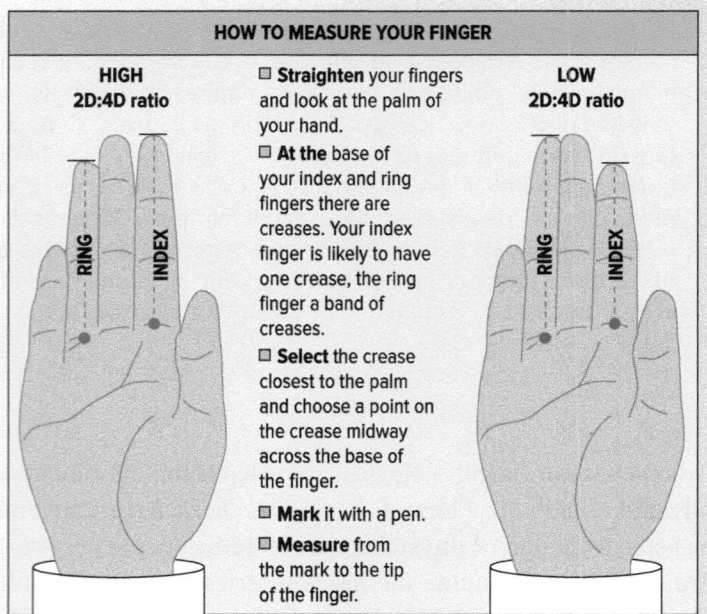

To calculate digit ratio, divide index finger length by ring finger length.

Source: Michael Hanlon, "What the Length of Your Index Finger Says About You," *Daily Mail*, December 3, 2010. Reprinted with permission.

Prenatal testosterone exposure is greater for male fetuses than female fetuses, and hence there is a lifelong difference between the sexes in digit ratio. However, even within a single sex, the differences in digit ratio appear related to the kinds of personality traits hypothesized to be related to testosterone. These traits are described by Wilson and Daly (1985) as the "young male syndrome" and include risk taking, a tendency toward violence, and competitiveness. Using terms more connected with personality psychology, some of which are discussed in this chapter, the relevant personality traits would have to do with impulsive sensation seeking, extraversion/assertiveness/ social dominance, and aggression. Although males do score higher on all three of these traits than females, research linking digit ratio to these traits is mixed.

A recent study by Wacker, Mueller, and Stemmler (2012) hypothesized that perhaps more specific traits related to aspects of the "young male" syndrome might correlate with digit ratio. Moreover, they thought this relationship might be stronger in males than females. In a study of over 200 young adult males, they administered a large number of personality scales related to the "young male" syndrome and used factor analysis to distill relatively pure and specific measures of these traits. They found a strong relationship between digit ratio and impulsive sensation seeking: males with longer ring fingers relative to their index fingers (lower digit ratio) scored higher in impulsive sensation seeking. This finding is consistent with a number of other studies that found lower digit ratio was associated with risk taking, such as participating in riskier lotteries (Garbarino, Slonim, & Sydnor, 2011), receiving more traffic violations (Schwerdtfeger, Heims, & Heer, 2010), and choosing riskier careers in finance (Sapienza, Zingales, & Maestripieri, 2009). Results with females tend to be less clear, though some studies have reported that, in females, a lower digit ratio (similar to the male digit ratio) is associated with higher levels of risk taking (Honekopp, 2011). One study of female rhesus macaque monkeys

found that females with lower digit ratios achieved a higher dominance status in their group (Nelson et al., 2010).

There is a vast amount of information on digit ratio on the Internet. Just enter this term in an Internet search and you will find many reports and articles. However, the research should be viewed skeptically, with an eye toward evaluating the quality of the studies reported. Looking at the best studies, we conclude that this bodily difference is very likely a lifelong signature of testosterone exposure prenatally and that it does correlate modestly with risk taking and sensation seeking as well as forms of social dominance in adulthood. There is a large gender difference in digit ratio, though within genders the correlates tend to be similar though somewhat weaker for women. We return to a discussion of testosterone in Chapter 16 when we cover sex and gender in personality psychology.

Another characteristic of the physiological approach to personality is simplicity or parsimony. Physiological theories often propose to explain a good deal of behaviour with a few constructs. Often the theories simply state that a physiological difference results in a given personality difference or a difference in an important behaviour pattern. Why, for example, do some people take up skydiving, race car driving, and other high-risk behaviours? One theory states that they do so because they have a deficiency of a certain chemical in their nervous systems. Despite the obvious simplicity of theories such as these, human nature is actually more complicated. For example, two people could be equally high on sensation seeking, yet one of them has satisfied this need in a socially approved manner (for instance, by becoming an emergency room doctor) whereas the other satisfies it in a socially unacceptable manner (for example, through various exciting but illegal behaviours, such as illegal gambling or drug use). Most physiologically oriented psychologists would *not* argue that "physiology is destiny." Most would agree that physiology is only one cause among many for explaining behaviour.

As you know from Chapter 1, Gordon Allport wrote one of the first textbooks on personality (1937) and in it he argued that "[t]he organization (of personality) entails the operation of both body and mind, inextricably fused into a personal unity" (p. 48). Because personality consists of both bodily and mental aspects, its study can be approached from either direction. In this chapter, we focus on several physiological systems that contribute to our understanding of personality.

A Physiological Approach to Personality

Most physiological personality psychologists today focus on measures of distinct physiological systems, such as heart rate or brain waves. The typical research question posed by contemporary psychologists concerns whether some people will exhibit more or less of a specific physiological response than others under certain conditions. For example, people who are introverted may avoid loud parties because they easily become overwhelmed by the social and physical stimulation at such parties. Notice that this statement specifies which particular environmental conditions (e.g., loud parties) affect which particular personality trait (e.g., introversion) to produce a particular physiological response (e.g., overstimulation, indicated by increased heart rate), which then promotes a specific behavioural response (e.g., avoidance). These connections are depicted in Figure 7.1.

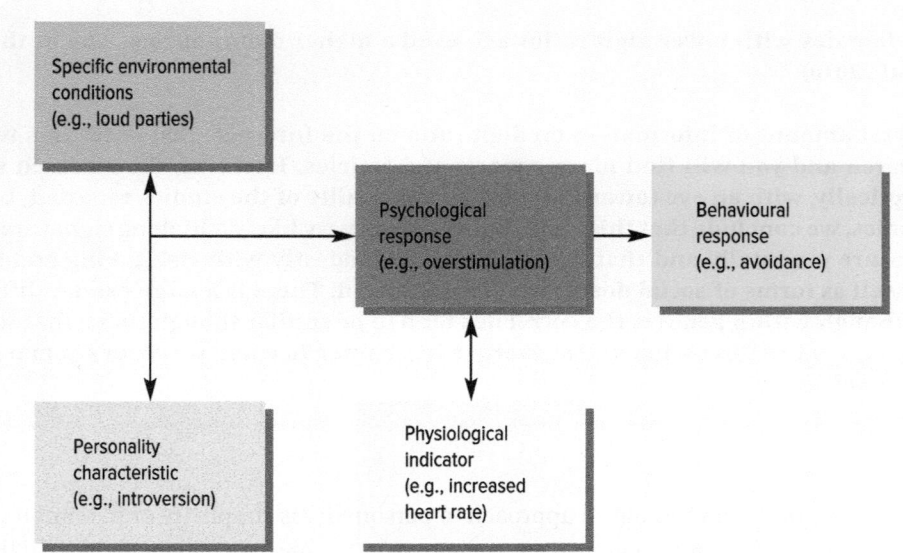

FIGURE 7.1 Connections among environmental conditions, personality traits, and responses build a theoretical bridge that links personality to specific situations in terms of evoking a certain psychological response, which can be identified and measured using specific physiological measures. A theory specifies which conditions or stimuli will interact with which personality traits to produce specific responses, which can be observed physiologically.

Specific statements—about which traits are connected to which psychological reactions under which conditions or in response to which stimuli—are now the way personality psychologists talk about physiology. Researchers must be able to build such a **theoretical bridge** between the personality dimension of interest and physiological variables in order to use physiological concepts to help explain personality (Levenson, 1983; Yarkoni, 2015). Let's turn now to a brief review of physiological variables, with an emphasis on how they are measured in personality research.

Physiological Measures Commonly Used in Personality Research

Most of the common physiological measures in personality research are obtained from **electrodes**, or sensors placed on the surface of a participant's skin. They are noninvasive in that they do not penetrate the skin, and these electrodes cause practically no discomfort. One drawback to such measures is that the participant is literally wired to the physiological recording machine (often called a polygraph), so movement is constrained. A new generation of electrodes will, however, overcome this limitation through the use of **telemetry**, a process by which electrical signals are sent from the participant to the polygraph through radio waves instead of by wires. This is already being used with astronauts whose physiological systems are monitored constantly on Earth. Three physiological measures of particular interest to personality psychologists are electrodermal activity (skin conductance of electricity), cardiovascular measures, and activity in the brain. Other biological measures, such as the amounts of hormones in the blood, are also of interest. We will discuss each of these in turn.

Electrodermal Activity (Skin Conductance)

The skin on the palms of the hands (and the soles of the feet) contains a high concentration of sweat glands. These sweat glands are directly influenced by the sympathetic nervous system, the branch of the **autonomic nervous system (ANS)** that prepares the body for action—that is, the fight-or-flight mechanism. When the sympathetic nervous system is activated (such as during episodes of anxiety, startle, or anger), the sweat glands begin to fill with salty water. If the activation is sufficiently strong or prolonged, the sweat may actually spill out onto the palms of the hands, causing the person to develop sweaty palms. Interestingly, all mammals have a similarly high concentration of sweat glands on the friction surfaces of their hands/paws.

Even before the sweat is visible, however, it can be detected by the clever application of a small amount of electricity because water (i.e., sweat) conducts electricity. The more water present in the skin, the more easily the skin carries, or conducts, electricity. This bioelectric process, known as **electrodermal activity** (*dermal* means "of the skin") or **skin conductance**, makes it possible for researchers to directly measure sympathetic nervous system activity.

In this technique, two electrodes are placed on the palm of one hand. A very low voltage of electricity is then put through one electrode into the skin, and the researcher measures how much electricity is present at the other electrode. The difference in the amount of electricity that is passed into the skin at one electrode and the amount detected at the other electrode tells researchers how well the skin is conducting electricity. The more sympathetic nervous system activity there is, the more water is produced by the sweat glands in the skin, and the better the skin conducts the electricity. The levels of electricity involved are so small that the participant does not feel anything.

Electrodermal responses can be elicited by all sorts of stimuli, including sudden noises, emotional pictures with charged content, conditioned stimuli, mental effort, pain, and emotional reactions such as anxiety, fear, and guilt (as in the so-called lie detector test, which uses skin conductance). One phenomenon of interest to personality psychologists is the observation that some people show skin conductance responses in the *absence* of any external stimuli. Imagine a participant sitting quietly in a dimly lit room who is instructed to just relax. Most people in this situation exhibit very little in the way of autonomic nervous system activity. However, some participants in this situation exhibit spontaneous electrodermal responses, even though there is nothing objectively causing these responses. Not surprisingly, the personality traits most consistently associated with nonspecific electrodermal responding are anxiety and neuroticism (Cruz & Larsen, 1995). A person who is rated as high in anxiety and neuroticism appears to have a sympathetic nervous system that is in a state of chronic activation. This is just one example of how electrodermal measures have been used by personality psychologists to ascertain differences in personality among people.

Cardiovascular Activity

The cardiovascular system involves the heart and associated blood vessels, and examples of measures of cardiovascular activity include blood pressure and heart rate. Blood pressure is the pressure exerted by the blood on the inside of the artery walls, and it is typically expressed with two numbers: diastolic and systolic pressure. The systolic pressure is the larger number, and it refers to the maximum pressure within the cardiovascular system produced when the heart muscle contracts. The diastolic pressure is the smaller number, and it refers to the resting pressure inside the system between heart contractions. Blood pressure can increase in a number of ways—for example, the heart may pump with larger strokes generating more volume or through a narrowing of the artery walls. Both of these actions occur through activation of the sympathetic nervous system in the fight-or-flight response. Blood pressure is responsive to a number of conditions, and personality researchers have been especially interested in blood pressure response to stress.

Another easily obtained cardiovascular measure is heart rate, often expressed in beats-per-minute (BPM). Heart rate can change beat by beat, so a technique with a degree of sophistication is needed to ensure accurate measurement. One approach is to measure the time interval between successive beats. If that interval is exactly one second, then the heart rate is 60 BPM. As the time interval between beats becomes shorter, the heart is beating faster, and vice versa. By measuring the intervals between successive heartbeats, the psychologist can get a readout of heart rate on a beat-by-beat basis. Heart rate is important because as it increases, it indicates that the person's body is preparing for action—to flee or to fight, for example. It tells us that the person is distressed, anxious, fearful, or otherwise more aroused than normal. Heart rate also increases with cognitive effort, as when people try to solve a difficult math problem. People differ from each other in heart rate responses, with some showing large increases and others only minor increases in response to the same stimuli or task.

Researchers have been interested in what happens to a person's cardiovascular system when they are challenged by having to perform a stressful task in front of an audience. One technique used to induce temporary stress is to have participants perform backwards serial subtraction (e.g., "take the number 784 and subtract 7, take the result and subtract 7, and keep doing so until you are told to stop"). Having to carry out a serial subtraction task is stressful, especially if the experimenter is standing there, writing down the answers and telling the participant to "work faster; come on, I know you can try harder." Not surprisingly, everyone's blood pressure and heart rate goes up during this task, but some people show much larger increases than others. This phenomenon has been called **cardiac reactivity** and has been associated with the **Type A personality**—a behaviour pattern characterized by impatience, competitiveness, and hostility. Evidence suggests that chronic cardiac reactivity contributes to coronary artery disease, which may be why the Type A personality trait, especially the hostility part of being Type A, is associated with a higher likelihood of heart disease and heart attacks. The relation between cardiovascular reactivity and Type A is one example of how physiological measures have been used in the study of personality.

Brain Activity

The brain spontaneously produces small amounts of electricity, which can be measured by electrodes placed on the scalp. This measure is called the electroencephalogram (EEG), and EEG recordings can be obtained for various regions of the brain while the participant is asleep, is relaxed but awake, or is doing a task. Such measures of regional brain activity can provide useful information about patterns of activation in various regions of the brain, which may be associated with different types of information-processing tasks (e.g., processing verbal versus spatial information, as in receiving directions from someone verbally or being shown a map of where to go). Personality psychologists have been especially interested in whether different regions of the brain show different activity for different people (e.g., introverts versus extraverts).

Another technique in measuring brain activity is called the evoked potential technique, in which the brain EEG is measured but the participant is given a stimulus, such as a tone or a flash of light, and the researcher assesses the participant's brain responsiveness to the stimulus. Several examples of how measurement of brain activity has contributed to our understanding of personality differences are presented in the section on brain asymmetry in this chapter.

The powerful brain imaging techniques currently being developed and perfected are another class of physiological measures useful in personality research. For example, positron emission tomography (PET) and functional magnetic resonance imaging (fMRI) are noninvasive imaging techniques used for mapping the structure and function of the brain. In fact, the 2003 Nobel Prize for medicine was awarded to two researchers—Paul C. Lauterbur and Sir Peter Mansfield—for their discoveries leading to the development of fast functional magnetic resonance imaging (fMRI). This powerful imaging tool, which was developed primarily for medical diagnosis, allows physicians and researchers to look inside the working brains of their patients and subjects. This tool can show which portions of the brain are active while the person is performing a particular task. For

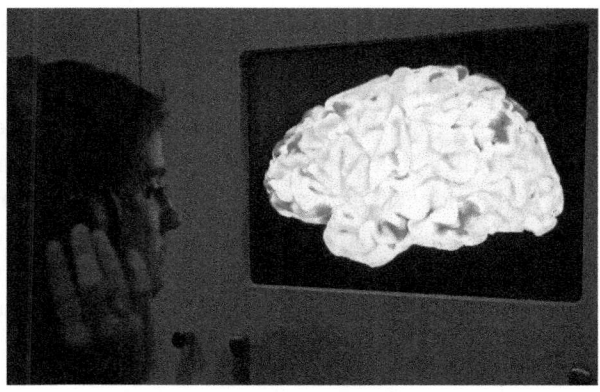

fMRI imagery tracks brain activity by monitoring glucose metabolism in the brain. When an area of the brain is used, it consumes energy in the form of glucose (Beer & Lombardo, 2007b).
©Miguel Medina/AFP/Getty Images

example, if we wanted to know what part of the brain is involved in memory, we would have a sample of people perform a memory task (such as remember a phone number for five minutes) while their brains were scanned by fMRI.

Powerful brain imaging techniques are now being applied to the study of personality (Herrington et al., 2006), creating a new subfield called personality neuroscience (DeYoung et al., 2009). An important study was published by Canli and colleagues (2001), in which they used fMRI to scan the brains of people as they looked at 20 negative pictures (e.g., spiders, people crying) and 20 positive pictures (a happy couple, cute puppies). They found specific brain changes associated with viewing the different emotion-inducing photographs. More important, however, they found that personality correlated with the degree of brain activation in response to the positive and negative images. Specifically, neuroticism correlated with increased frontal brain activation to the negative images, and extraversion correlated with increased frontal brain activation to the positive images. Correlations between personality and other brain structures were also found, and the pattern of findings is consistent with the notion that personality is associated with brain reactivity to emotional stimuli. Brain imaging tools are very likely to revolutionize what we know about the brain and personality over the next few years, making this a particularly exciting area of research (Beer & Lombardo, 2007b; Canli & Amin, 2002).

Other researchers are using imaging techniques to assess brain structure instead of function, to see whether personality correlates with the size of various areas of the brain. In a recent study, DeYoung and colleagues (2012) used the Big Five model of personality to generate predictions about which areas of the brain would be responsible for generating the behaviours or responses relevant to each trait. They then assessed brain structure in a large (for neuroscience studies; $N = 116$ subjects) sample of healthy young adults. They found support for many of their predictions about the volume of certain brain regions being associated with specific personality traits. For example, extraversion correlated with the volume of medial orbitofrontal cortex, a brain region involved in processing reward information. Neuroticism correlated with the volume of brain regions that have been associated with threat and punishment. Overall, they argue that their findings support a biologically based explanatory model of the Big Five personality traits. The article has, however, been widely criticized on several points. For example, the size of a brain region is not typically correlated with increased functioning of that region. The authors implicitly assumed that structure and function are related, whereas there is no evidence of this fact. Even the popular press criticized the article as a modern incarnation of phrenology, a discredited discipline that held that the size of various bumps on the head could be used to infer a person's personality. Although skepticism is healthy in science, at the very least we can say that this recent paper demonstrates one approach in the newly developed neuroscience of personality. Pioneering papers are often criticized, but over the long term their potential to guide the field is realized. In the long run, functional as well as structural information about the brain, combined with genetic information, other physiological measures, and even psychopharmacological techniques, may turn out to be useful in unravelling the connection between personality and bodily systems.

Other Measures

Although skin conductance, heart rate, and brain activity are the most commonly used measures in physiological studies of personality, other biological measures have also proven useful (see Table 7.1). One important class of measures includes biochemical analyses of blood and saliva. For example, from saliva samples, biochemists can extract indicators of how competently a person's immune system is functioning (Miller & Cohen, 2001). The quality of immune system functioning may go up and down with stress or emotions and thereby may relate to personality. Hormones, such as testosterone, that play a role in important behaviours can also be extracted from saliva samples. Testosterone has been linked to uninhibited, aggressive, and risk-taking behaviour patterns (Dabbs & Dabbs, 2000). Cortisol, a byproduct of the hormone noradrenaline, can be readily assessed from saliva samples. Researchers have found, for example, that shy children have high levels of cortisol in their systems (Kagan & Snidman, 1991), suggesting that they experience more stress than less shy children. Monoamine oxidase (MAO) is an enzyme found in the blood that is known to regulate neurotransmitters, the chemicals that carry messages between nerve cells. MAO may be a causal factor in the personality trait of sensation seeking. Other theories of personality are based directly on different amounts of neurotransmitters in the nervous system, and we briefly touch on these in the section on sensation seeking.

Table 7.1   Common Physiological Measures Used in Personality Research

Physiological Measure	Physiological System	Psychological Response System	Examples of Stimuli Used in Research
Electrodermal activity	Sweat gland activity controlled by sympathetic nervous system	Anxiety, startle, guilt, effort, pain	Noise, mental effort, emotional stimuli, painful stimuli
Cardiovascular activity	Blood pressure and heart rate controlled by autonomic nervous system	Fight-or-flight response, mental effort, stress	Stress, social anxiety, effort, high cognitive load
Electroencephalogram (EEG)	Brain's spontaneous electrical activity	Brain activation, alertness	Resting with eyes closed, reading

Evoked EEG	Brain's electrical activity in response to specific stimuli	Attention, recognition, cognitive processing	Brief sensory stimuli, emotional stimuli
Neuroimaging (e.g., fMRI, PET)	Brain's energy metabolism	Specific brain areas responsible for cognitive control, emotion, memory, pain, decision making, sensory processing	Wide variety of tasks that activate these psychological response systems
Antibodies	Immune system	Immune response to infection, stress	Virus, bacteria, stress
Testosterone	Hormone system (steroid)	Aggression, competitiveness, psychological drive and libido, muscle bulk	Tasks involving competition, aggression, attraction
Cortisol	Hormone system (adrenal)	Stress response	Life events, stress, anxiety stimuli
Serotonin, dopamine, MAO, etc.	Neurotransmitters	Transmission of specific nerve signals	Rewarding stimuli, emotions

 Concept Check

What physiological measures are commonly employed in personality research?

Physiologically Based Theories of Personality

Now that we have covered the basic physiological measures used in personality research, we turn to some of the theories that have generated interest and attention among personality psychologists. We begin with what is perhaps the most widely studied physiological theory of personality—the theory that proposes a biological explanation for why some people are introverted and others extraverted.

Extraversion–Introversion

Among the people you know, someone probably fits the following description: is talkative and outgoing, likes meeting new people and going new places, is active, is sometimes impulsive and venturesome, gets bored easily, and hates routine and monotony. Such a person would score as an extravert on an extraversion–introversion questionnaire. See Table 7.2 for items from a popular extraversion–introversion questionnaire—the Eysenck Personality Inventory.

Table 7.2 Items from the Eysenck Personality Questionnaire Extraversion Scale		
Extraversion Items		
For every question, circle just one response.		
YES	NO	Are you a talkative person?
YES	NO	Are you rather lively?
YES	NO	Can you usually let yourself go and enjoy yourself at a lively party?
YES	NO	Do you enjoy meeting new people?
YES	NO	Do you tend to keep in the background on social occasions? (reversed)
YES	NO	Do you like going out a lot?
YES	NO	Do you prefer reading to meeting people? (reversed)
YES	NO	Do you have many friends?
YES	NO	Would you call yourself happy-go-lucky?

Scoring directions: Reverse your answers to the items marked "reversed"; then count how many questions you endorsed with a "yes." The average university student scores about 6 on this questionnaire.

You probably also know someone who is just the opposite, someone who is quiet and withdrawn, who prefers being alone or with a few friends to being in large crowds, who prefers routines and schedules, and who prefers the familiar to the unexpected. Such a person would score in the introverted direction on an extraversion–introversion questionnaire. If you are wondering *why* introverts and extraverts are so different from each other, physiologically minded personality psychologists have an intriguing explanation: Eysenck's theory.

A classic example of a physiologically based theory of personality was put forward by H. J. Eysenck (1967) in his book *The Biological Basis of Personality*. Eysenck proposed that introverts are characterized by higher levels of activity in the brain's **ascending reticular activating system (ARAS)** than are extraverts. The ARAS is a structure in the brain stem thought to control overall cortical arousal. In the 1960s, the ARAS was thought of as a gateway through which nervous stimulation entered the cortex. If the gate were somewhat closed, then the resting **arousal level** of the cortex would be lower, and if the gate were more open, then the resting arousal level would be higher. Introverts, according to this theory, have higher resting levels of cortical arousal because their ARAS lets in too much stimulation. Introverts engage in introverted behaviours (are quiet and seek low-stimulation settings, such as libraries) because they need to keep their already heightened level of arousal in check. Conversely, extraverts engage in extraverted behaviours because they need to increase their level of arousal (Claridge, Donald, & Birchall, 1981).

Are you a talkative person? Do you like mixing with people? Do you like plenty of bustle and excitement around you? Answering no to such questions suggests an introverted personality.

©Kennan Harvey/Getty Images

Eysenck also incorporated Hebb's (1955) notion of "optimal level of arousal" into his theory. By optimal level of arousal, Hebb meant a level that is just right for any given task. For example, imagine going into a final exam in an underaroused state (e.g., sleepy, tired). Being sleepy and underaroused would be just as bad for your performance as going into the exam in an overaroused state (e.g., extremely anxious and agitated). There is an optimal level of arousal for taking an exam, one in which you are focused, alert, and attentive, but not aroused to the point of anxiety.

Do you like telling jokes and funny stories to your friends? Do you like mixing with people? Can you get a party going? Answering yes to such questions suggests an extraverted personality. Interestingly, Eysenck's extraversion–introversion theory is based not on a need to be with people, but rather on a need for arousal and stimulation.
©Shutterstock/Jacob Lund

If introverts have a higher baseline level of arousal than extraverts (i.e., level of arousal while at rest), then introverts are above their optimal level of arousal more often than extraverts. According to the theory, the generally overaroused condition of introverts leads them to be more restrained and inhibited. They avoid active social interactions that might aggravate their already overstimulated condition. Extraverts, on the other hand, need to get their arousal level higher and so seek out stimulating activities and engage in more unrestrained behaviours. The qualities that typically characterize introverts (e.g., quiet, withdrawn) and extraverts (e.g., outgoing, engaging) are understood to be attempts to regulate arousal downward (in the case of introverts) or upward (in the case of extraverts) to maintain an optimal level of arousal.

In the decades following publication of Eysenck's theory, many studies were conducted to test it (see reviews by Eysenck, 1991; Matthews & Gilliland, 1999; and Stelmack, 1990), including research by personality psychologist—and colleague of Hans Eysenck—Robert M. Stelmack of the University of Ottawa. If it is true that introverts are more cortically aroused than extraverts, then introverts should display enhanced responsiveness on measures of cortical activity, such as the electroencephalogram (EEG), as well as on measures of autonomic nervous system activity, such as electrodermal response. Studies designed to test this hypothesis typically have taken the form of comparing introverts with extraverts on physiological measures gathered under conditions of various degrees of stimulation (Gale, 1986). In conditions where participants were presented with either no stimulation or very mild stimulation, differences between introverts and extraverts turned out to be small or nonexistent. However, in studies that looked at nervous system responsiveness to moderate levels of stimulation, introverts showed larger or faster responses than extraverts, as predicted by Eysenck's theory (Bullock & Gilliland, 1993; Gale, 1983).

The fact that introverts and extraverts are not different at resting levels, but *are* different under moderate levels of stimulation, led Eysenck to revise his arousal theory (Eysenck & Eysenck, 1985). When he first stated his theory in 1967, Eysenck did not distinguish between resting, or *baseline,* levels of arousal and arousal *responses* to stimulation. A good deal of evidence now suggests that the real difference between introverts and extraverts lies in their **arousability**, or arousal response, not in their baseline arousal level. Extraverts and introverts do not differ in their level of brain activity while sleeping, for example, or while lying quietly in a darkened room with their eyes shut (Stelmack, 1990). However, when presented with moderate levels of stimulation, introverts show enhanced physiological reactivity compared with extraverts (Gale, 1987).

Imagine that an introvert and an extravert have to do a monotonous task, such as monitoring a computer display of the operating status of a nuclear power plant. The display does not change much, so the stimulation level is very low, and the situation is rather monotonous and boring. Eysenck's theory would predict that the introvert would remain more alert and perform better in this situation and that the extravert would be relatively underaroused and most likely bored to sleep. However, now imagine an emergency at the nuclear power plant, with sirens blasting, lights flashing, and people running and shouting. In such a high-arousal situation, it is likely that the extravert would perform better due to the introvert's tendency toward overarousal in response to stimulation.

❓ Exercise

The Lemon Juice Demonstration: **This demonstration is designed to illustrate that introverts are more reactive to stimulation than extraverts. Although some teachers have tried this in the classroom, it can be a bit messy and so might best be done as a thought experiment to illustrate the point of individual differences in reactivity. Here is how it would go: Take a double-tipped cotton swab and tie a thread exactly in its centre so that it hangs perfectly in balance (i.e., is horizontal). Swallow three times and put one end on your tongue for exactly 20 seconds. After removing the swab, place 4 drops of lemon juice under your tongue. Place the other end of the cotton swab on your tongue for 20 seconds. Remove the swab and let it hang by the thread. If you are an extravert it is likely that the swab will remain horizontal, indicating that you did not react strongly to the lemon juice by producing more saliva. If you are an introvert, it is likely that the swab will no longer balance horizontally and will instead be heavier on the end placed on the tongue following the lemon juice. This would indicate that you produced more saliva in response to the lemon juice. Eysenck conducted a similar experiment (Eysenck & Eysenck, 1967), as did Corcoran (1964).**

An important proposition of the theory is that, when given a choice, extraverts should prefer higher levels of stimulation than do introverts. Indirect evidence supports this prediction. For example, laboratory studies have shown that extraverts will press a button at a higher rate than introverts when the button pressing produces changes in the visual environment (such as change the channel on a TV, change the slide on a projector) (e.g., Brebner & Cooper, 1978). In a more naturalistic study, done in a university library, people studying in a noisy reading room scored as more extraverted than did students studying in the quieter rooms (Campbell & Hawley, 1982). Findings such as these suggest that, when given a choice, extraverts tend to seek greater levels of stimulation than introverts.

A clever study designed by psychologist Russell Geen (1984) tested the hypothesis that although introverts should choose lower levels of stimulation than extraverts, these two groups should nevertheless be equivalent in physiological arousal when performing under their chosen levels of stimulation. However, when extraverts are given the level of stimulation chosen by introverts, they should be underaroused and bored and should perform poorly on the task. When introverts are given the level of stimulation chosen by extraverts, they should be overaroused and distressed and perform poorly on the task. These complex predictions are explored further in A Closer Look: The Geen Study.

 **A Closer Look**

The Geen Study

Participants in the Geen (1984) study were selected on the basis of their answers to the extraversion scale of the Eysenck Personality Inventory (the items presented in Table 7.2 in the text). Thirty high-scoring participants formed the extraverted group, and 30 low-scoring participants formed the introverted group. Participants reported to the laboratory one at a time, whereupon they were told they would be participating in an experiment on the effects of noise on learning. Each participant was given a difficult paired-associates learning task, in which they guessed which word, from a pair of words, was selected by the experimenter according to some rule, and they had to learn the rule. The rules were "all words referring to animals," "all words that begin with a vowel," or "all words that are names of colours." During the time they were engaged in this task, the participants were having their heart rate and skin conductance measured.

Before starting the experiment, however, the participants were told they would have to perform the learning task while listening to random bursts of noise over headphones. One-third (10 introverts and 10 extraverts) were allowed to select the level of noise that they would hear over the headphones. Participants in this *choice* condition listened to the noise and turned a dial to adjust the volume of the noise. They were instructed to adjust the volume control upward until the intensity was "just right" for them in terms of working on the difficult task. Participants were told that they were not allowed to choose a perfectly quiet noise setting, although two participants (both introverts) inquired about this possibility before the complete instructions were given.

There were two control conditions in this study. In one control condition, called the *assigned-same* condition, one-third of the introverts and extraverts were subjected to the noise levels selected by previous introvert or extravert participants, respectively. In the other control condition, called the *assigned-other* condition, the final one-third of the introverts and extraverts experienced the noise levels selected by previous extraverts and introverts, respectively. Participants in this condition had to perform under the noise level selected by the most recently run participant from the *other* personality group. These two control conditions make this experiment an unusually strong one.

The results concerning the choice of noise intensity were as predicted, with extraverted participants choosing significantly louder levels of noise than introverts. The noise level chosen by the extraverts averaged 72 decibels, and the noise level chosen by the introverts averaged 55 decibels. The results for heart rate and skin conductance are displayed in Figure 7.2. When working under the noise levels selected by themselves or by someone from their personality group, there were no differences between introverts and extraverts.

Personality differences are seen, however, when we look at introverts working under conditions selected by extraverts and extraverts working under conditions selected by introverts. Under these conditions, the introverts showed evidence of greater arousal, compared with the extraverts. At the introvert-selected noise level, the extraverts were least aroused—in fact, probably bored. When subjected to the noisier, extravert-selected level of loudness, the extraverts' arousal level went up, but the introverts' went up to an even higher level. What the extraverts found just right, the introverts found overarousing.

As far as performance on the learning task was concerned, the introverts assigned to the noisy, extravert-selected volume had the poorest performance. Introverts in the noisy, extravert-selected condition took an average of 9.1 trials to learn the association, but only 5.8 trials to learn it in the quieter, introvert-chosen condition. This decrease in performance was probably due to the fact that the louder noise levels overstimulated the introverts. The extraverts, on the other hand, performed quite well under the noisy conditions, averaging only 5.4 trials to learn the association. Under the quieter, introvert-selected noise levels, the extraverts performed only somewhat worse, averaging 7.3 trials to learning.

This study is important because it clearly demonstrates that the extraverts preferred more intense stimulation than did the introverts. What the extravert finds just right is overarousing to the introvert and leads to poorer performance. Similarly, what the introvert finds just right leads to decreases in arousal and performance in the extravert. The best performance for both introverts and extraverts occurs when stimulation is provided at the appropriate level of intensity for each group.

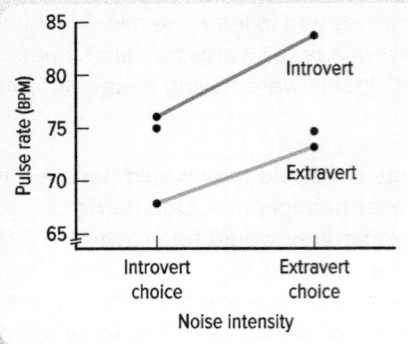 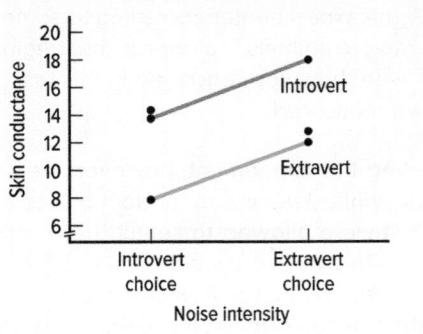

FIGURE 7.2 Results from Geen's study of preferred stimulation levels in introverts and extraverts. Unconnected dots are the assigned-same conditions.

Source: Geen, R. (1984). Preferred stimulation levels in introverts and extraverts: Effects on arousal and performance. *Journal of Personality and Social Psychology, 46*, 1303–1312. © by American Psychological Association. Reprinted with permission.

Sensitivity to Reward and Punishment

Jeffrey Gray has proposed an influential alternative biological theory of personality (Gray, 1972, 1990), called **reinforcement sensitivity theory**. Based on brain function research with animals, Gray has constructed a model of human personality based on two hypothesized biological systems in the brain. The first is the **behavioural activation system (BAS)**, which is responsive to incentives, such as cues for reward, and regulates approach behaviour. When the BAS recognizes a stimulus as potentially rewarding, it triggers approach behaviour. For example, as a child, you might have learned about an ice cream truck that made deliveries to your neighbourhood while playing music. When you heard that music (cues of reward), your BAS created the urge to run out into the street to find the ice cream truck (approach motivation). The other system in the brain postulated by Gray (1975) is the **behavioural inhibition system (BIS)**, which is responsive to cues for punishment, frustration, and uncertainty. The effect of BIS activation is to cease or inhibit behaviour or to bring about avoidance behaviour. You may have been scolded or punished by your mother for running into the street. The street becomes a punishment cue to the BIS, which causes you to inhibit your behaviour. A rough analogy is that the BAS is like an accelerator that motivates approach behaviour, whereas the BIS is like brakes that inhibit behaviour or help people stop what they are doing.

According to Gray, people differ from each other in the relative sensitivity of their BIS or BAS. A person with a reactive BIS is especially sensitive to cues of punishment, frustration, or novelty. They are vulnerable to unpleasant emotions, including anxiety, fear, and sadness. According to Gray, the BIS is responsible for the personality dimension of **anxiety**. A person with a reactive BAS, on the other hand, is especially sensitive to reward. Such a person is vulnerable to positive emotions and tends to approach stimuli. The ability of an individual with a reactive BAS to inhibit behaviour decreases as they approach a goal. According to Gray, the BAS is responsible for the personality dimension of **impulsivity**, the inability to inhibit responses.

Gray and others (Fowles, 1987, 2006) have framed this model of impulsivity and anxiety as an alternative to Eysenck's dimensions of extraversion and neuroticism. This alternative interpretation is presented in Figure 7.3. In Gray's model, the extraversion and neuroticism dimensions are rotated about 30 degrees from anxiety and impulsivity. Those who are highly extraverted and a bit neurotic are seen as the most impulsive. At the other end of the impulsivity dimension are individuals who are introverted and emotionally stable. Those who are a bit introverted and highly neurotic are seen as the most prone to anxiety. At the other end of the anxiety dimension are individuals who are extraverted and emotionally stable.

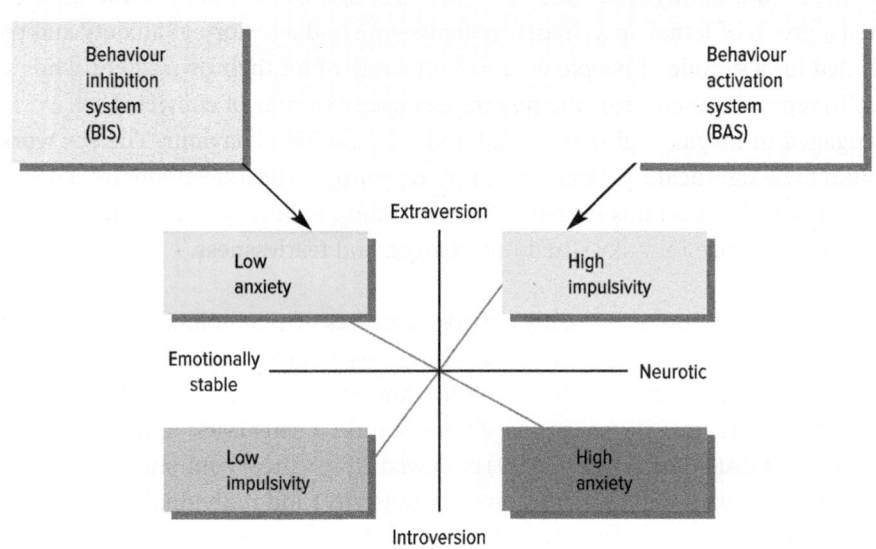

FIGURE 7.3 Relation between Eysenck's dimensions of extraversion and neuroticism, and Gray's dimensions of impulsivity and anxiety.

Some debate has focused on exactly where to locate BAS (impulsivity) and BIS (anxiety) in the conceptual space defined by Eysenck's dimensions of extraversion and introversion (Gomez, Cooper, & Gomez, 2000; Zuckerman et al., 1999). In fact, one of the authors of this book has had a series of exchanges with Gray and his colleagues about this issue (Pickering, Corr, & Gray, 1999; Rusting & Larsen, 1997, 1999). It appears that the relation between Gray's constructs and Eysenck's constructs is direct, with BAS being equivalent to extraversion and BIS being equivalent to neuroticism. In fact, the Canli and colleagues (2001) study cited earlier showed that the brains of extraverts (compared to introverts) were more reactive to pleasant, rewarding images, and the brains of individuals high on neuroticism were more reactive (than those low on neuroticism) to images associated with negative emotions. Many researchers view the BIS and BAS constructs as similar to neuroticism and extraversion in that both refer to dispositional tendencies to withdraw from punishment or to approach reward, respectively (e.g., Davidson, 2003; Knutson & Bhanji, 2006; Kosslyn et al., 2002; Sutton, 2002). Gray has revised his model and now locates BIS much closer to neuroticism and locates BAS much closer to extraversion (Pickering et al., 1999).

Gray believes that differences among people in sensitivity to reward and punishment are responsible for generating the varieties of behaviour associated with being anxious/neurotic and with being impulsive/extraverted. If we ask why some people are more susceptible than others to anxiety attacks, fears, worry, depressions, phobias, obsessions, or compulsions, Gray would argue that their susceptibility is due to an overly sensitive behavioural inhibition system. Such people tend to notice and are sensitive to punishment and other frustrations. Moreover, they are distressed by uncertainty and novelty. Then, if we ask why some people are more susceptible than others to positive emotions, to approach behaviours, to seeking out and interacting with others, Gray would argue that this is due to an overly sensitive behavioural activation system.

One team of researchers, stimulated by Gray's theory, constructed a questionnaire to measure BIS sensitivity—a tendency toward anxiety and fearfulness and the avoidance of uncertainty and risk (MacAndrew & Steele, 1991). The researchers identified a high and a low fearful group and determined which questions discriminated between the groups. Some examples of questions on this questionnaire include "I have been quite independent and free from family rule" and "I am entirely self-confident." For the high BIS group, the researchers selected a group of female psychiatric patients who had a history of anxiety and panic attacks. The low BIS group called for a sample of people who had little regard for their own safety, who took risks and disregarded danger. To represent this group, the researchers used a sample of convicted sex workers—individuals who regularly engaged in illegal, high-risk sexual and drug-taking behaviour. The sex workers and anxiety patients were found to be significantly different in their responses to the questionnaire. The sex workers scored lower than the anxiety patients on this measure. Such a finding indicates that the questionnaire has some validity as a measure of tolerance for risky situations, danger, and fearlessness.

A second research group making use of Gray's theory consists of psychologist Charles Carver and his colleagues (Carver, Sutton, & Scheier, 1999; Carver & White, 1994). Carver and White developed and validated a scale to measure individual differences in the strength of the BIS and BAS. Other researchers are adding to the validity evidence behind this scale. For example, Zelenski and Larsen (1999) found this scale to be one of the best measures of BIS and BAS. Carver et al. (1999) reviewed Gray's theory, emphasizing individual differences in approach or incentive motivation (extraversion or impulsivity) and individual differences in withdrawal or aversive motivation (neuroticism or anxiety). They showed how several programs of research can be integrated into the theme that humans appear to possess separate systems for responding to incentives and threats. For example, these systems show reliable individual differences, they relate to major affective dispositions, they may be lateralized in our cerebral architecture, and they may relate differently to learning by punishment and learning by reward. Carver and his colleagues consider these the "Big Two" personality dimensions. This review paper shows the remarkable integrating power of Gray's theory of personality.

Gray has primarily conducted research with animals. With animals, you can use drugs or surgery to eliminate certain areas of the brain, then test whether this affects the animal's ability to learn through punishment or reward. Gray's theory relates anxiety and impulsivity to the two principles of learning: reinforcement (both positive and negative) and punishment (and the loss of reinforcement). There is some evidence that these two forms of learning are under separate neural control. It appears likely that different brain mechanisms may be involved when a person or an animal learns through reinforcement or through punishment (Gray, 1991). Thus, there should be people with varying degrees of sensitivity (high, medium, or low) to punishment and to reward.

In a study of reward and punishment, participants were required to complete hundreds of trials of a difficult reaction time task (Larsen, Chen, & Zelenski, 2003). They had to name the colours of words that popped up on a computer screen, as quickly and accurately as possible. It is a difficult task, and people can get only about half the trials correct given that they have to respond in less than one second on each trial. One group was rewarded for each correct and fast response, and they earned $5 during the course of a 20-minute experiment. Another group was punished after incorrect or slow responses, and although they started the experiment with $10, proceeded to lose $5. As such, everyone finished the experiment with $5, but one group was rewarded on a trial-by-trial basis, whereas the other group was punished on a trial-by-trial basis. It turned out that BAS scores predicted better performance in the reward condition, with high BAS individuals working faster and becoming more accurate when they were working for reward. BIS scores, on the other hand, predicted performance in the punishment condition, with high-BIS individuals responding with better performance when they were being punished, compared to low BIS participants.

Much of the work carried out to test Gray's theory has focused on impulsivity (the inability to inhibit responses). Our jails are full of people who are deficient in the ability to control their behaviour, especially behaviour that may be immediately rewarding. For example, a 17-year-old male sees an expensive sports car parked on the street. As he looks at the car and thinks about how much fun it would be to drive, he notices that the keys are in the ignition. The owner appears nowhere in sight and the street is fairly deserted. He starts to reach for the door handle. The ability to stop this approach behaviour, even though it is immediately rewarding, separates the average person from the impulsive person.

Impulsive individuals can be characterized as having stronger approach than avoidance tendencies and are less able to inhibit approach behaviour, especially in the presence of desirable goals or rewards. You probably know people who often say things that get them into trouble or who hurt other people's feelings without even thinking. Even though they know they might hurt someone's feelings and feel bad themselves (i.e., are "punished" by feelings of remorse), why can't they control what they do and say?

According to Gray's theory, impulsive people do not learn well from punishment because they have a weak behavioural inhibition system. If this is true, then researchers should be able to demonstrate that in a task that involves learning from punishment, impulsive people do less well than nonimpulsive people. Studies have been conducted on impulsive university students, juvenile delinquents, psychopaths, and criminals in jail (Newman, 1987; Newman, Widom, & Nathan, 1985). The typical finding is that such individuals are, in fact, deficient in learning through punishment. Those who are impulsive, it seems, do not learn as well from punishment as from reward.

Let's say you have a roommate and you would like to teach them to clean their part of the apartment. You could try rewarding with candy and praise every time they picked something up. Or you could try punishing by yelling and scolding every time they left something out of place. If your roommate is an impulsive person, chances are that you would do better using the reward strategy than the punishment strategy. On the other hand, if your roommate is an anxious person, it might be more effective to use punishment than reward.

 Exercise

Think of a situation in which you are trying to teach someone something new. Discuss an example of how you might use a reward to teach that behaviour. Then discuss how you might use mild punishment to teach the same behaviour.

Sensation Seeking

Sensation seeking is another dimension of personality postulated to have a physiological basis. Sensation seeking is the tendency to seek out thrilling and exciting activities, take risks, and avoid boredom. Research on the need for sensory input grew out of studies on **sensory deprivation**. Let's begin, then, with a description of sensory deprivation research.

Imagine volunteering for a study in which you are put into a small room where there is no light, no sound, and only minimal tactile sensations. Imagine further that you agree to do this for 12 hours straight. What would this experience be like? Research suggests that at first you would feel relaxed, then bored, then anxious as you started to hallucinate and have delusions. Early research by Donald Hebb, a prominent Canadian psychologist from Nova Scotia, showed that in such a situation, university students chose to listen over and over to a taped

lecture intended to convince 6-year-olds about the dangers of alcohol. Other participants in these early sensory deprivation experiments who were offered a recording of an old stock market report opted to listen to it over and over again, apparently to avoid the unpleasant consequences of sensory deprivation (Hebb, 1955). People in sensory deprived environments appear motivated to acquire *any* sensory input, even if ordinarily such input would be perceived as boring.

Sensation-seeking behaviour is exhibited in a variety of activities, from speeding to skydiving and gambling. Gambling is perhaps one of the most problematic activities associated with sensation-seeking. We examine it further in Highlight on Canadian Research: Gambling, Personality, and the Brain—What's the Connection?

The theory of sensation seeking was proposed to explain why some people routinely seek out thrilling experiences, even though such experiences may come with certain risks.
©Purestock/SuperStock

 ## Highlight On Canadian Research

Gambling, Personality, and the Brain—What's the Connection?

Is there any evidence for an "addictive personality"? Are certain people more prone than others to get hooked on gambling? Before answering this question, we briefly review the scope of the problem according to psychiatric criteria in North America. Gambling disorder is classified as a behavioural addiction and is characterized by repetitive gambling behaviour that is persistent over time and that causes significant problems in the person's life, such as with family members or at school or work. The diagnosis of gambling disorder is made when at least four out of nine criteria are present for a 12-month period (American Psychiatric Association, 2013). These criteria include a preoccupation with gambling, the need to gamble with increasing amounts of money to obtain a level of excitement, making repeated and unsuccessful efforts to control or stop gambling, experiencing restlessness or irritability when attempting to control gambling, returning to gambling after losing money, lying to conceal gambling involvement, gambling to escape or manage negative moods such as anxiety, jeopardizing or losing a significant relationship, job, or opportunity because of gambling, and relying on others to relieve desperate financial situations caused by gambling. Having many characteristics in common with gambling disorder, one additional behavioural addiction that is warranting consideration by psychologists is Internet gaming disorder. Both manifest in ways that are similar to criteria for drug and alcohol addictions.

Pathological gambling behaviour often co-occurs with other addictions, including nicotine dependence, cannabis use, drug addiction, and alcohol dependence (Slutske, Caspi, Moffitt, & Poulton, 2005). In fact, those with pathological or problem gambling are two to four times more likely to develop alcohol dependence than nongamblers. This is an example of **comorbidity**, where two or more disorders simultaneously occur within the same individual.

We return now to the question of whether any specific personality traits are associated with problem gambling. Several correlational studies have found that measures of impulsiveness and sensation seeking correlate with problem gambling (McDaniel & Zuckerman, 2003; Vitaro, Arsenault, & Tremblay, 1997). From correlational data, we don't really know if the personality traits are causing the gambling or if gambling is causing people to become more impulsive and sensation seeking. In a 2005 longitudinal study, however, psychologist Wendy Slutske and colleagues (Slutske, Eisen, et al., 2005) found that problem gambling at age 21 was associated with the personality traits of risk taking and impulsivity at age 18. This study strengthens the conclusion that the personality traits of high impulsivity and risk taking (or sensation seeking) put a person at risk for developing problem gambling.

For some people, playing cards is a form of recreation. For others, however, it can result in compulsive gambling.
©Fotazdymak/Shutterstock

Luke Clark, one of the world's leading experts on gambling psychology, leads the Centre for Gambling Research at the University of British Columbia in Vancouver. Operating with complete independence from the British Columbia Lottery Corporation, Clark and his team are interested in understanding the cognitive, behavioural, and neuroscience aspects of gambling. A variety of cognitive neuroscience techniques in particular have been used to examine the neural circuitry that supports the decision-making processes involved in gambling behaviour. A number of findings have emerged from research in Clark's lab.

Genetic studies suggest that the risk for developing problem gambling and the risk for developing other addictions (e.g., alcohol) may be explained by largely overlapping genetic risk factors. These genetic factors may give rise to the specific personality traits related to low behavioural control (impulsivity and risk taking), and these traits may in turn be responsible for the comorbidity of pathological gambling and other addictive disorders (Chu & Clark, 2015). As discussed in Chapter 6, dopamine receptors on specific chromosomes have been shown to display an association with increased impulsivity, including that which is related to drug use and addiction. Similarly, among pathological gamblers, high mood-related impulsivity has been shown to be associated with variance in the availability of dopamine receptors (Clark et al., 2012). On the behavioural level, problem gambling is marked by impairments in inhibitory control, the capacity to voluntarily subdue or control strong or automatic responses to stimuli in the environment. In one study, Clark and his research team asked participants to play a simulated slot machine in the lab, with the possibility of winning real money. Inhibitory control was measured using a stop-signal task, during which participants had to randomly inhibit their responses to an experimental task when a signal was present. Subjective aspects of gambling were also measured via self-report. Researchers found that reduced inhibitory control, which is often implicated in drug addiction, was associated with more persistent gambling behaviours as well as increased subjective desires to continue playing even after near-wins (i.e., instances of loss that came very close to winning the jackpot; Devos et al., 2015).

Clark's research has demonstrated that the various gambling outcomes—wins, losses, near-wins, and near-losses—are especially relevant to our understanding of gambling behaviour and addiction. In one study, researchers monitored skin conductance (electrodermal activity) during a gambling task and observed that it varied according to these four types of outcomes. Skin conductance was shown to increase with the magnitude of the wins and losses. Furthermore, it appeared to be greatest during losses and near-losses (i.e., instances of winning that just very narrowly missed losses) compared to wins and near-wins, respectively. These findings support the notion that responses to losses are greater than similarly sized gains, and indicate that motivation toward loss aversion may be playing an important role in the addictive qualities of gambling (Wu et al., 2016). These and other studies by Clark and his team have highlighted a number of viable strategies for clinical interventions in pathological gambling, including specific methods to be employed by counsellors, therapists, and rehabilitation specialists. *For more information on Luke Clark and the Centre for Gambling Research, visit http://cgr.psych.ubc.ca.*

Hebb's Theory of Optimal Level of Arousal

Hebb developed the theory of **optimal level of arousal**, which was used by Eysenck in his theory of extraversion. Hebb's theory states that people are motivated to reach an optimal level of arousal. If they are underaroused relative to this level, an increase in arousal is rewarding; conversely, if they are overaroused a decrease in arousal is rewarding. For its time, Hebb's theory was controversial because most researchers thought that tension *reduction* was the goal of all motives, yet Hebb was saying that we are motivated to *seek out* tension and stimulation. How else can we explain the fact that people *like* to work on puzzles, enjoy mild frustration, and occasionally take risks or do something to arouse mild fears, such as going on a roller coaster ride. Hebb's belief that people need stimulation and sensory input is consistent with the results of sensory deprivation research. The nervous system appears to need at least some sensory input.

Zuckerman's Research

Early on in sensory deprivation research, Zuckerman and Haber (1965) noted that some people were not as distressed as others by the sensory deprivation experience. In these early experiments, some people found sensory deprivation extremely unpleasant. These participants requested lots of sensory material (tapes, reading material) during the experiment and quit the experiment relatively early. Zuckerman believed that such individuals had a particularly *high need for sensation* because they were the least tolerant of deprivation. He called them sensation seekers because they appeared to seek out stimulation, not just in the sensory deprivation experiment but in their everyday lives as well.

Zuckerman developed a questionnaire designed to measure the extent to which a person needs novel or exciting experiences and enjoys the thrills and excitement associated with them. He called the questionnaire the Sensation-Seeking Scale, and items from it appear in Table 7.3 (Zuckerman, 1978; Zuckerman & Aluja, 2015).

As it turned out, Zuckerman's questionnaire about preferences for stimulation in everyday life predicted how well people tolerated the sensory deprivation sessions. High sensation seekers found sensory deprivation to be particularly unpleasant, whereas low sensation seekers were able to tolerate it for longer periods of time. In the early 1960s, Zuckerman left the sensory deprivation laboratory and began to study the other unique

Table 7.3 Items from the Sensation-Seeking Scale

Several aspects of sensation seeking are reflected in the items on this scale.

Thrill and adventure seeking—reflected in items that ask about desire for outdoor sports or activities involving elements of risk, such as flying, scuba diving, parachute jumping, motorcycle riding, and mountain climbing—for example, "I sometimes like to do things that are a little frightening" (high) versus "A sensible person avoids activities that are dangerous" (low).

Experience seeking—reflected in items that refer to the seeking of new sensory or mental experiences through unconventional or nonconforming lifestyle choices—for example, "I like to have new and exciting experiences and sensations even if they are frightening, unconventional, or illegal" (high) versus "I am not interested in experience for its own sake" (low).

Disinhibition—reflected in items indicating a preference for getting "out of control" or an interest in wild parties, gambling, and sexual variety—for example, "Almost everything enjoyable is illegal or immoral" (high) versus "The most enjoyable things are perfectly legal and moral" (low).

Boredom susceptibility—reflected in items that refer to a dislike for repetition, routine work, monotony, predictable and dull people, and a restlessness when things become unchanging—for example, "I get bored seeing the same old faces" (high) versus "I like the comfortable familiarity of everyday friends" (low).

Source: All of the items on the Sensation-Seeking Scale, as well as scoring instructions, can be found in Zuckerman (1978).

characteristics associated with the personality dimension of sensation seeking. Notice that this theoretical explanation of sensation seeking is very similar to that Eysenck offered for extraversion. In fact, there is a moderately strong positive correlation between extraversion and sensation seeking. All of the items on the Sensation-Seeking Scale, as well as scoring instructions, can be found in Zuckerman (1978).

In the 40-plus years that Zuckerman and his colleagues and others have been doing research on sensation seeking, many interesting findings have emerged. A number of these findings are consistent with the idea that high sensation seekers have a need for high levels of stimulation in their daily lives (reviewed in Zuckerman, 1978). Police officers who volunteer for riot duty have higher sensation-seeking scores on Zuckerman's scale than officers who do not volunteer for riot duty. Skydivers score higher on sensation-seeking measures than non-skydivers. Among university students who volunteered to be in psychology experiments, the students with high sensation-seeking scores volunteered to participate in the more unusual studies (studies on ESP, hypnosis, or drugs) than in the typical studies (on learning, sleep, or social interaction). In studies of gambling behaviour, the participants with high sensation-seeking scores tended to make riskier bets. High sensation seekers also report having a larger number of sex partners, engaging in a wider variety of sex acts, and beginning to have sex at an earlier age than low sensation seekers. The list of correlates of sensation seeking is quite long, and you may consult various reviews to learn more about this personality trait (e.g., Zuckerman, 1984, 1991b).

According to Zuckerman, there is a physiological basis for sensation-seeking behaviour. Zuckerman's more recent work (1991b, 2006) focuses primarily on the role played by neurotransmitters in bringing about differences in sensation seeking. **Neurotransmitters** are chemicals in the nerve cells that are responsible for the transmission of a nerve impulse from one cell to another. As you may recall from your introductory psychology class, nerve cells are separated from one another by a slight gap, called a synapse. A nerve impulse must jump across this gap if it is to continue toward its destination. Neurotransmitters are the chemicals released by the nerves that allow nerve impulses to jump across the synapse and continue on their way.

The neurotransmitter must be broken down after the impulse has passed, or too many nerve transmissions would occur. As an analogy, think of the turnstile at a movie theatre or subway that lets in one person at a time. If it were left open, many people could run through, allowing too many people in. If it were stuck closed, however, no one could get through. The neurotransmitter system is similar in that the chemical balance in the synapse has to be just right in order for the correct amount of nervous transmission to get through and continue on.

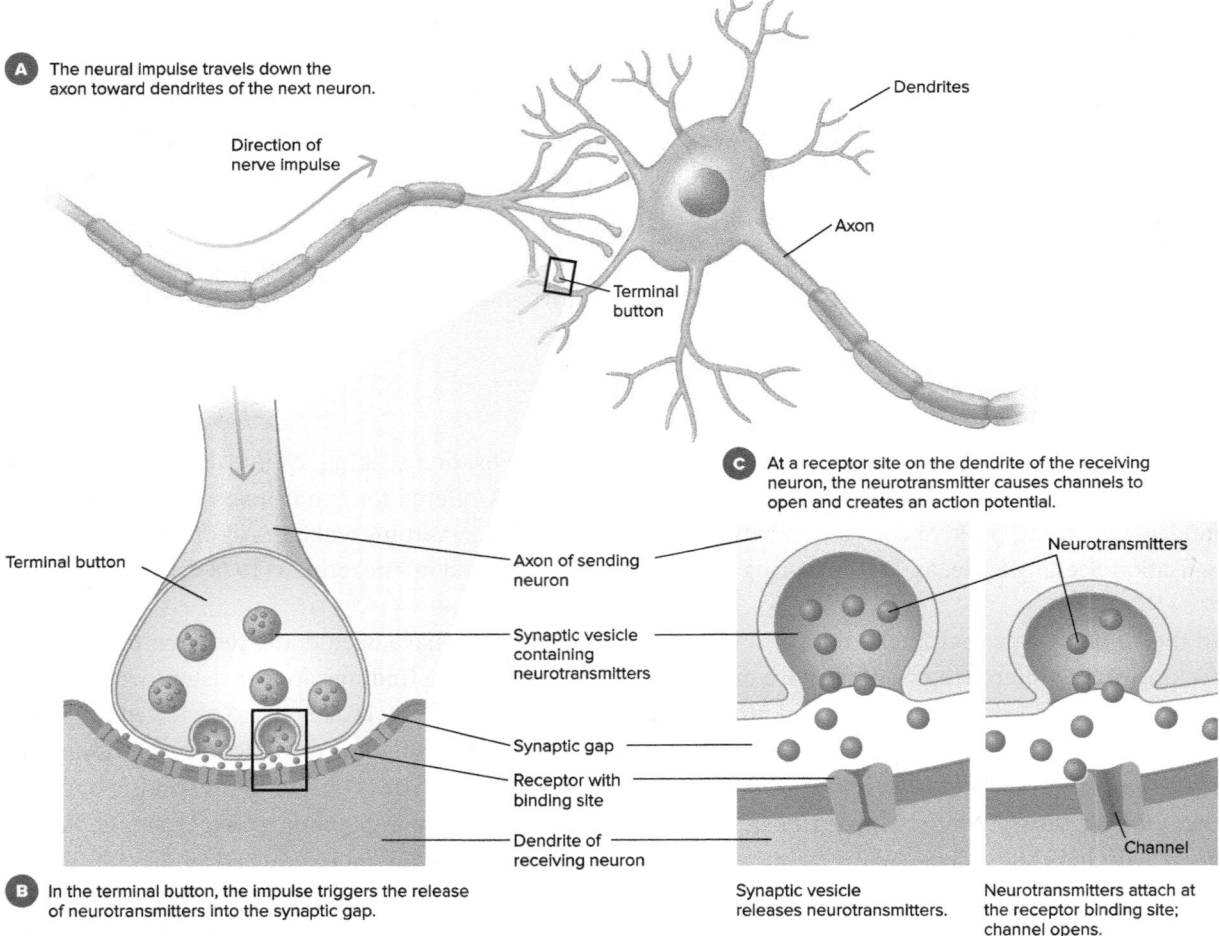

A The neural impulse travels down the axon toward dendrites of the next neuron.

Dendrites

Direction of nerve impulse

Axon

Terminal button

C At a receptor site on the dendrite of the receiving neuron, the neurotransmitter causes channels to open and creates an action potential.

Neurotransmitters

Terminal button

Axon of sending neuron

Synaptic vesicle containing neurotransmitters

Synaptic gap

Receptor with binding site

Dendrite of receiving neuron

B In the terminal button, the impulse triggers the release of neurotransmitters into the synaptic gap.

Synaptic vesicle releases neurotransmitters.

Neurotransmitters attach at the receptor binding site; channel opens.

Channel

Illustration of a synapse, the junction between two nerve cells. Synapses transmit electrical signals from one nerve cell to the next. When an electrical signal reaches a synapse, it triggers the release of chemicals called neurotransmitters (pink) from vesicles (purple). The vesicles burst through the membrane, and neurotransmitters cross a microscopic gap called the synaptic gap and bind to the receptor nerve cell, causing it to propagate an electrical impulse.

Certain enzymes, particularly **monoamine oxidase (MAO)**, are responsible for maintaining the proper levels of neurotransmitters. MAO works by breaking down the neurotransmitter after it has allowed a nerve impulse to pass. If an excessive amount of MAO were present, it would break down too much of the neurotransmitter, and nerve transmission would be diminished. If there were too little MAO present, an excessive amount of the neurotransmitter would be left in the synapse, allowing for too much nervous transmission to take place. Suppose that you had to do a fine movement with your fingers, such as pick up a dime off a flat surface. With too little MAO in your system, your fingers might be shaking and your movements jerky (too much nervous transmission). With too much MAO, however, your fingers might be clumsy because of dulled sensation and lethargic movement control. When MAO levels are just right, neurotransmitter levels are regulated appropriately, and the nervous system works properly to control the muscles, thoughts, and emotions.

High sensation seekers tend to have low levels of MAO in their bloodstream compared to low sensation seekers. Across studies, the correlation tends to be small to moderate but is consistently negative (Zuckerman, 1991b). If high sensation seekers tend to have low MAO levels, and low MAO means more neurotransmitter available in the nerve cells, then perhaps sensation seeking is caused by or is maintained by having high levels of neurotransmitters in the nervous system. MAO acts like the brakes of the nervous system, by decomposing neurotransmitters and thereby inhibiting neurotransmission. With low MAO levels, sensation seekers have less inhibition in their nervous systems and therefore less control over behaviour, thoughts, and emotions. According to Zuckerman's (1991a) theory and research, sensation-seeking behaviours (e.g., illicit sex, drug use, wild parties) are due not to seeking an optimal level of arousal, but to having too little of the biochemical brakes in the synapse.

Neurotransmitters and Personality

Whereas Zuckerman's theory concerns levels of MAO, which breaks down neurotransmitters, other researchers hypothesize that levels of neurotransmitters themselves are responsible for specific individual differences (Depue, 2006). Neurotransmitters are receiving a great deal of attention as possible sources of personality differences. One neurotransmitter, **dopamine**, appears to be associated with pleasure. For example, animals will work to obtain doses of dopamine, much as they would work to obtain food. As such, dopamine appears to function like a reward system and has even been called the feeling good chemical (Hamer, 1997). Drugs of abuse, such as cocaine, mimic dopamine in the nervous system, which accounts for the pleasure associated with taking them. However, such drugs deplete a person's natural levels of dopamine, leading to unpleasant feelings after the drug leaves the nervous system, creating a drive or urge to obtain more of the drug.

A second important neurotransmitter is **serotonin**. Researchers have documented the role of serotonin in depression and other mood disorders, such as anxiety. Specifically, drugs such as Prozac, Zoloft, and Paxil block the reuptake of serotonin, leaving it in the synapse longer, leading depressed people to feel less depressed. In one study, Prozac was given to nondepressed subjects. Over several weeks of observation, they reported less negative affect and engaged in more outgoing and social behaviour than did those in a control group (Knutson et al., 1998). In studies of monkeys, the monkeys that were higher in dominance and that engaged in more grooming had higher levels of serotonin. The monkeys low in serotonin were frequently fearful and aggressive (Rogness & McClure, 1996). In summarizing animal studies, Depue (1996) notes that low serotonin is associated with irritable behaviour.

A third important neurotransmitter, **norepinephrine**, is involved in activating the sympathetic nervous system for fight-or-flight. Not surprisingly, personality theories have been proposed based on the neurotransmitters dopamine, serotonin, and norepinephrine. Probably the most comprehensive is Cloninger's **tridimensional personality model** (Cloninger, 1986, 1987; Cloninger, Svrakic, & Przybeck, 1993), in which three personality traits are tied to levels of the three neurotransmitters. The first trait, **novelty seeking**, is based on low levels of dopamine. Recall that low levels of dopamine create a drive state to obtain substances or experiences that increase dopamine. Novelty, thrills, and excitement can make up for low levels of dopamine, so novelty-seeking behaviour is thought to result from low levels of this neurotransmitter.

The second personality trait identified in Cloninger's model is **harm avoidance**, which he associates with abnormalities in serotonin metabolism. Although various descriptions of the theory indicate increased or decreased serotonin levels are associated with increased harm avoidance, Cloninger himself (personal communication, October 2003) states that it is unwise to suggest a simple linear correlation between harm avoidance and absolute levels of serotonin. Very low levels of the principal serotonin metabolite 5-HIAA in cerebrospinal fluid are associated with risk of severe depression, but serotonin levels can also be elevated in states of anxiety or stress. The selective serotonin uptake inhibitors (like the antidepressants Prozac, Zoloft, or Paxil) result in increased levels of serotonin at synapses, which may increase anxiety initially but then lead to decreased vulnerability to overreact to stress, probably by down-regulating sensitivity to serotonin when it is released in response to stress. So we have to distinguish the acute role of serotonin, which is increased in states of acute stress, and the role of serotonin down-regulation over the life span, which is associated with lower levels of harm avoidance. People low in harm avoidance are described as energetic, outgoing, and optimistic, whereas people high in harm avoidance are described as cautious, inhibited, shy, and apprehensive. They seem to expect that harmful and unpleasant events will happen to them, so they are constantly on the lookout for signs of such threatening events. And like a dog that bites out of fear rather than anger, such a person can be irritable, snappy, and hostile.

The third trait in Cloninger's model is **reward dependence**, which Cloninger sees as related to low levels of norepinephrine. People high on this trait are persistent; they continue to act in ways that produce reward. They work long hours, put a lot of effort into their work, and often continue striving after others have given up.

Genes Work Through Neurotransmitter Systems to Influence Personality

Although we discussed behavioural genetics in more detail in Chapter 6, it is worth mentioning here that many researchers interested in personality and genetics are focusing on the genes involved in regulating our neurotransmitter systems. For example, if low levels of dopamine are related to novelty seeking, then perhaps the genes involved in dopamine transmission would be a good place to start in the search for the genetic basis of this personality trait. Keltikangas-Järvinen and her colleagues (2003) found evidence that the type 4 dopamine receptor gene (DRD4) was associated with heightened levels of novelty seeking, though other studies drew this finding into question (Azar, 2002). A meta-analysis suggested that very specific types of repeated genetic codes on the DRD4 gene were reliably associated with novelty seeking (Schinka, Letsch, & Crawford, 2002). These findings imply that many genes are involved in the creation of any single personality trait. So, although looking for one gene as the basis of a personality trait is like looking for the proverbial needle in the haystack, now the researchers are looking for many different needles in the same big haystack. That is, they are looking for multiple genes that interact in complex ways to influence neurotransmitter systems. A prominent researcher in this area, Dean Hamer, once commented, "After 10 years, it is quite clear to me that at least for most traits there are a very large number of genes involved" (quoted in Azar, 2002). As new technology for analyzing gene sequences is developed, the search will likely become more tractable. Nevertheless, any answers that are found in the future are likely to reveal complicated and multiple interacting genetic contributions, possibly requiring environmental triggers, for the expression of any biologically based personality trait.

Cloninger's theory has had some impact in psychiatry, where it has been used to help explain various types of addictions. For example, alcoholics do not all become addicted for the same reasons. Cloninger argues that some alcoholics began drinking due to high novelty seeking, that they drink to make up for low levels of dopamine, and that they drink primarily for the pleasure afforded by boosting dopamine. Other alcoholics began drinking because they are high in harm avoidance, and they drink to relieve the stress and anxiety they chronically feel. These drinkers are motivated primarily for the relief from anxiety that alcohol provides (Cloninger, Sigvardsson, & Bohman, 1988). Understanding people's motivations for abusing substances may play a large role in helping them overcome their addictions.

It is probably clear that Cloninger's model has much in common with Gray's, Eysenck's, and Zuckerman's. For example, novelty seeking seems a lot like the reward sensitivity associated with the BAS of Gray's theory. All of these theories have different explanatory bases for the traits (Depue & Collins, 1999). For example, Gray suggests that brain systems involved in learning through reward and punishment are important in determining these traits. Eysenck also implicates the brain and nervous system. Zuckerman focuses on the synapse and the neurochemicals found there. And Cloninger specifies particular neurotransmitters. All are perhaps describing the same behavioural traits but focusing on different levels of explanation within the body, ranging from the synapse to the brain.

Let's turn now to a consideration of two other personality dimensions that appear to have a biological base that is not related to physiological reactivity—morningness–eveningness and brain asymmetry.

Morningness–Eveningness

Perhaps you are the kind of person who likes to sleep late and stay up late, saving your important school-work for late afternoon or evening, when you are feeling at your peak. Or perhaps you are more of a morning person, regularly getting up early without the aid of an alarm clock. Moreover, perhaps you tend to do all your important work early in the day, when you are feeling at your best, and get to sleep fairly early in the evening. Being a morning type or an evening type of person appears to be a stable characteristic. Personality psychologists have become interested in such stable differences among people in preferences for different times of the day and have coined the term **morningness–eveningness** to refer to this dimension (Horne & Ostberg, 1976).

Differences between morning and evening types of individuals, sometimes called "larks" and "owls," appear to be due to differences in underlying biological rhythms. Many biological processes have been found to fluctuate around an approximate 24- to 25-hour cycle. These have been called **circadian rhythms** (*circa* means "around," *dia* means "day," or "24 hours"). Of particular interest have been circadian rhythms in body temperature and endocrine secretion rates. For example, on average, body temperature shows a peak around mid-evening (between 8 and 9 p.m.) and a trough in the early morning (around 6 a.m.). Figure 7.4 presents a graph of body temperature by time of day.

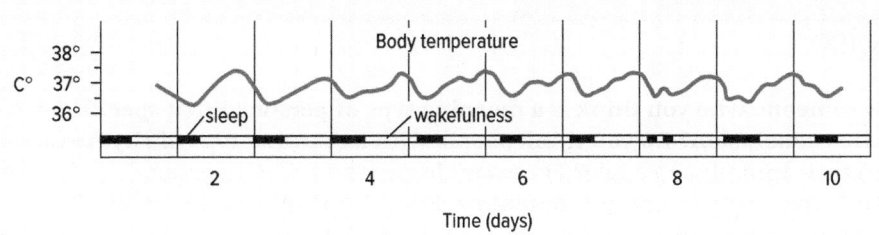

FIGURE 7.4 Circadian rhythm in body temperature.

Researchers use a temporal-isolation design to study such circadian rhythms. In this design, participants volunteer to live in an environment totally controlled by the experimenter with respect to time cues. There are no windows, so the participants do not know if it is day or night. There are no regularly scheduled meals, so the participants do not know if it is breakfast-, lunch-, or suppertime. Participants are given food whenever they ask for it. There is no access to live television or radio. Instead, the participants have a large collection of videotapes and audiotapes for entertainment. Volunteers live in this environment for several weeks or longer. Often, the participants are students who want to use the time in isolation as an opportunity to study for an important exam or who need to write a PhD thesis.

Imagine being a participant in such a study. You would go to sleep whenever you wanted, sleep as long as you wanted, eat whenever you felt like it, work or watch movies as the inclination struck, and so on. This is called **free running** in time, in which there are no time cues to influence your behaviour or biology. If you were in such a situation and your temperature were taken every hour, and if you were like the average person, you would find that your temperature followed an approximate 24- to 25-hour cycle, starting to rise before waking up and falling before going to sleep (Aschoff, 1965; Finger, 1982; Wever, 1979).

Note that 24- to 25-hour rhythms are the average; there are wide differences among people in the actual length of their biological rhythms (Kerkhof, 1985). Circadian rhythms in temporal-isolation studies have been found to be as short as 16 hours in one person and as long as 50 hours in another person (Wehr & Goodwin, 1981). While free running in a temporal-isolation experiment, the first person would complete a sleep-wake cycle every 16 hours, whereas the second person's sleep-wake cycle would last 50 hours.

Such wide differences among people are evident only in a temporal isolation situation. In real life, there are time cues all around us that fluctuate in a 24-hour rhythm—most notably, the light-dark cycle. These cues en-train us and make us fit into the 24-hour day. Even though people with short and long biological cycles entrain quite well to the 24-hour cycle, there nevertheless are differences between those people in terms of the timing of peaks and valleys in their biological rhythms. Imagine someone with a slightly long circadian rhythm (such as 26 hours) and someone with a slightly short rhythm (such as 22 hours). They both may entrain to the same 24-hour day, but the peak in body temperature might occur relatively late for the first person (perhaps at 10 p.m.), whereas the peak would occur relatively early for the second person (perhaps around 6 p.m.).

Individuals with short biological rhythms hit their peak body temperature and alertness levels earlier in the day and thus begin to get sleepy earlier than do those with longer circadian rhythms (Bailey & Heitkemper, 1991). A person with a 26-hour rhythm would have a harder time getting up at 6 in the morning, because their 26-hour biological rhythm still has 2 hours to go, even though the 24-hour clock is telling them to start a new day. A person with a 22-hour rhythm would have an easier time getting up early because they have completed a biological "day" in 22 hours and are ready to start another day even *before* the 24-hour clock is up.

❓ Exercise

Do you know someone who you think is a morning type of person? What specific evidence makes you come to this conclusion? Do you think people with a morning type of rhythm are different in other ways from evening-type people? For example, are there other personality characteristics associated with being a morning type? Benjamin Franklin is quoted as saying that "early to bed, early to rise, makes a man healthy, wealthy, and wise." Do you think it is possible that morning types are actually wiser or that they have better outcomes in life? How would you design a study to answer this question?

Research on individual differences in circadian rhythms provides the groundwork for understanding why some people are morning types and others are evening types. As you know, those with *shorter* biological rhythms tend to be morning people, and those with *longer* biological rhythms tend to be evening people. Horne and Ostberg (1976, 1977) developed a 19-item questionnaire to measure morningness–eveningness dimensions of personality, or what is sometimes referred to as *chronotype*. The items ask about preferences for activities earlier or later in the day. In a sample of 48 participants who took their body temperature every hour for several days, the researchers found that the scores on this questionnaire correlated –.51 with time of day that peak body temperature was reached. While the original study was done in Sweden, the negative correlation between self-reported preferences for activities in the morning and timing of peak body temperature has been replicated in the United States (Monk et al., 1983), Italy (Mecacci, Scaglione, & Vitrano, 1991), Spain (Adan, 1991, 1992), Croatia (Vidacek et al., 1988), and Japan (Ishihara, Saitoh, & Miyata, 1983).

These cross-cultural replications are consistent with the idea that preferences for morning or evening activities, and the time of day people are at their best, is a stable disposition with a biological basis. Scores on the Horne and Ostberg measure of morningness–eveningness are stable over time. Croatian researchers tested 90 university students on this measure and then tested them again seven years later, when they had finished university (Sverko & Fabulic, 1985). They found a significant positive correlation, suggesting that chronotype is fairly stable over time. There was, however, a general shift in the whole sample toward morningness, which might be expected in a group that moves from being university students to people having jobs. Although the 19-item Morningness–Eveningness Questionnaire (Horne & Ostberg, 1976) remains a gold standard in chronotype measurement, the brief Circadian Energy Scale (CIRENS) (Ottoni, Antoniolli, & Lara, 2011) is a valid alternative. Specific questions ask about the respondent's energy level at different times of the day, with a positive difference between morning and evening energy scores indicating that one is an evening person, and a negative difference indicating that one is a morning person.

Many studies have been done on the validity of the morningness–eveningness construct. In one study (Larsen, 1985), university students completed a report every day for 84 consecutive days, stating what time they felt at their best each day and what time they got up and went to bed each day. The Horne and Ostberg questionnaire correlated strongly with average rise and retire times, as well as with the time of day the participants reported feeling at their best. The morning people got up earlier, went to bed earlier, and reportedly felt at their best earlier, on average, than the evening people.

What would happen if people who had to live together, such as university roommates, were mismatched on morningness–eveningness? One person likes to stay up late and sleep late, whereas the other likes to get up early, even on weekends, as well as go to bed early. How happy do you think these people would be with their rooming situation? This was the topic of a study by Watts (1982), who selected first-year university students living on the campus of Michigan State University. The participants had to have only one roommate. The roommate pairs completed the Morningness–Eveningness Questionnaire (MEQ), and they rated various aspects of their roommate relationship. Watts found that, the greater the difference between the roommates' MEQ scores, the lower ratings they gave to the quality of their relationship. Roommates who were very different on morningness–eveningness said that they did not get along very well with each other, that they did not enjoy their relationship and were not good friends, and that they were unlikely to continue living together. Differences on other personality dimensions, such as achievement motivation and competitiveness, did not predict such dissatisfaction with the roommate relationship. It appears that differences in morningness–eveningness are especially related to interpersonal compatibility problems.

Other studies of morningness–eveningness have looked at cognitive performance at different times of the day in relation to this personality disposition. Monk and Leng (1986) measured performance on a serial search task and a logical reasoning task at different times of day for participants classified as morning or evening types by the Horne and Ostberg questionnaire. Between the hours of 8 and 11 a.m., the morning types performed their best. Between the hours of 5 and 11 p.m., the evening types showed their best performance. Such differences might be lessened through the use of stimulants, such as caffeine, as implied in the research of Revelle and colleagues (1980). Caffeine may help the performance of evening types most if taken in the morning, whereas it may help the performance of morning types most if taken in the evening. People can time their coffee consumption to give them the greatest benefit, given their morningness–eveningness disposition.

Being a morning type or evening type refers to preferences for time of day that may have a biological basis; however, sometimes situations occur that go against such preferences. Imagine a university student who is definitely an evening type, yet a class they need to take is offered only at 8 a.m., or a morning type of person who takes a job in a factory and is assigned to the late shift (4 p.m. to midnight). Going against one's natural circadian preferences is difficult, but not impossible. People do adjust to shift work and changes in sleep-wake schedule, and there is some evidence that evening types adjust to disruptions in sleep-wake cycles better than morning types (Ishihara et al., 1992). Such disruptions as transmeridian airline flights (which create jet lag) or working all night without sleeping (i.e., pulling an all-nighter) may be better tolerated by an evening type than a morning type of person.

In summary, the preference for being active and doing important or demanding work earlier or later in the day may be rooted in the length of a person's inherent biological circadian temperature rhythm. This is a good example of a physiological approach to personality because it highlights the notion of a behaviour pattern (i.e., preference for different times of the day) being based on an underlying physiological mechanism (i.e., circadian rhythms).

Brain Asymmetry and Affective Style

As you are probably aware, the left and right sides of the brain are specialized, with asymmetry in the control of various psychological functions. One type of asymmetry that is receiving research attention is the relative amount of activity in the front part of the left and right brain hemispheres. The brain constantly produces small amounts of electrical activity, which can be measured on the scalp with sensitive electrical recording equipment. A recording of such electrical activity is called an **electroencephalogram (EEG)**. Moreover, such electrical activity is rhythmic and exhibits waves that are fast or slow, depending on neurological activation in the brain. One particular type of brain wave, called an **alpha wave**, oscillates at 8 to 12 times a second. The amount of alpha wave present in a given time period is an inverse indicator of brain activity during that time period. The alpha wave is given off when a person is calm, relaxed, feeling a bit sleepy, and not attentive to the environment. In a given time period of brain wave recording, the *less* alpha wave activity present, the *more* we can assume that part of the brain was active.

EEG waves can be measured over any region or part of the brain. In emotion research, particular attention has been directed toward the frontal part of the brain, comparing the amount of activation in the right and left hemispheres. Study results suggest that the left hemisphere is relatively more active than the right when a person is experiencing pleasant emotions and vice versa, that the right frontal hemisphere is more active than the left when the person is experiencing unpleasant emotions. For example, in a study by Davidson and colleagues (1990), they showed film clips to the participants in an attempt to amuse some of the participants and disgust the others. The participants were also videotaped while they watched the funny or disgusting films. EEGs were taken while the participants looked at the films. When the participants were smiling at the amusing films, they had relatively more activation in their left than right frontal hemispheres. Similarly, when the participants were exhibiting a facial expression of disgust (lower lip pulled down, tongue protruding, nose wrinkled), their brains were more active in the right than left hemispheres.

Similar results have also been obtained in very young children. Instead of using films, Fox and Davidson (1986) used sweet and bitter solutions placed in the mouths of 10-month-old infants to produce pleasant and unpleasant affective reactions. The infants showed relatively more left- than right-brain activation to the sweet solution and more right- than left-brain activation to the bitter solution. In another study of 10-month-old infants, the infants' mothers left them alone in the testing room, whereupon a stranger entered the room (Fox & Davidson, 1987). In this standard anxiety-producing procedure, some infants become distressed but some do not; some infants cry and fuss but others do not. The researchers divided their sample of infants into those who cried during separation from their mothers and those who did not cry. They found that the criers exhibited more right-brain activation, relative with the left, compared with the noncriers. These results suggest that this tendency to become distressed or not (and the associated brain EEG asymmetry) is a stable characteristic of infants. Fox and colleagues (Fox, Bell, & Jones, 1992) studied a group of infants at age 7 months and again at age 12 months and found that the EEG measures of hemisphere asymmetry taken at those two time periods were highly correlated, suggesting stability over time in frontal brain asymmetry. Similar results have been found with adults, showing that measures of EEG asymmetry show test-retest correlations in the range of .66 to .73 across studies (Davidson, 1993, 2003). These findings suggest that individual differences in **frontal brain asymmetry** exhibit enough stability and consistency to be considered as indicative of an underlying biological disposition or trait.

Other studies suggest that EEG asymmetry indicates a vulnerability to pleasant or unpleasant affective states. Tomarken and colleagues (Tomarken, Davidson, & Henriques, 1990) and Wheeler and colleagues (Wheeler, Davidson, & Tomarken, 1993) examined the relation between individual differences in frontal asymmetry and reactions to affective film clips in normal participants. In these studies, EEG asymmetry was measured while the participants were resting. Then the participants were shown either happy and amusing films or disgusting and fearful films. For the dependent variable, the participants were asked to rate how the films made them feel. The hypothesis was that the participants with greater right-side activation at rest (measured before watching the films) would report more intense *negative* affective reactions to the fear and disgust films, compared with the participants with relatively more left-side activation. The opposite prediction was made for the participants with greater left-side activation—they should report stronger *positive* emotions in response to the happy and amusing films. The predictions were essentially supported, with frontal asymmetry measures taken *before* the films were seen predicting the participants' *subsequent* self-reported affective reactions to the films, with the right-side-dominant participants reporting more distress to the unpleasant films and the left-side-dominant participants reporting more pleasant reactions to the films.

Similar results have also been found with monkeys. Because monkeys cannot tell you how positive or negative they are feeling, researchers have used measures of cortisol to assess emotional reactivity. **Cortisol** is a stress hormone that prepares the body to fight or flee, and increases in cortisol mean that the animal has recently experienced stress. Davidson and his colleagues (reviewed in Kosslyn et al., 2002) have found that monkeys with greater right-sided activation had higher levels of cortisol. Identical results have been found with 6-month-old children. These researchers induced fear in the infants by having a male stranger enter the room, slowly approach the infant, and stare at the infant for two minutes. Those infants who had greater right-sided activation at baseline showed increased cortisol responses to the stranger. Also, those infants who showed the most right-sided activation during the stranger approach phase also displayed more crying and facial expressions of fear, and tried to escape more, compared to infants with less right-sided activation (Buss et al., 2003).

✐ Application

Assessing brain asymmetry without an EEG. An EEG is not the only way to obtain an index of asymmetry in brain activation. Research suggests that a person's characteristic level of left- or right-sided activation may be indicated by the direction in which their eyes drift as they concentrate on answering difficult questions. When answering a difficult question (e.g., "Make up a sentence using the words *rhapsody* and *pleasure*"), people's eyes drift one way or the other as they reflect on their answer (Davidson, 1991). Among right-handed individuals, eyes drifting to the right signify left-sided activation, and eyes drifting to the left signify right-sided activation. If you ask a person several difficult questions (e.g., "How many turns do you make from your house or apartment to the nearest store?") and note which way their eyes usually drift, you may get an indication of whether they tend to be right- or left-sided asymmetric. Of course, this quick measure is not as reliable as an EEG. It nevertheless may be a rough gauge of whether a person is left- or right-side asymmetric.

Perhaps you could make some observations of a few friends or acquaintances, asking them several difficult questions and observing which way they move their eyes as they think through their answers. Most people will not show completely consistent patterns of going one way or the other. That is why it is important to ask several questions and see which way they *usually* move their eyes. You will also need to decide whether they are more vulnerable to positive or negative emotions (see Figure 7.5). Those who glance frequently to the right are more likely to be left-hemisphere dominant and should be more vulnerable to the pleasant emotions (e.g., happiness, joy, enthusiasm). Individuals who frequently glance to the left while engaging in reflective thought are more likely to be right-hemisphere dominant and, by implication, should be more vulnerable to the negative emotions (e.g., distress, anxiety, sadness).

Certainly, many factors influence how people feel and which emotions they experience. The findings reviewed here suggest that the characteristic pattern of brain activation is one factor that may influence our affective lives by contributing to the likelihood that we will experience certain emotions.

FIGURE 7.5 These gaze patterns illustrate right and left gaze direction, associated with opposite brain hemisphere activation.

(both images): ©Cookie Studio/Shutterstock

A study by Sutton and Davidson (1997) showed that dispositionally positive people (assessed by Carver and White's [1994] BIS/BAS inventory) showed greater relative left frontal EEG asymmetry at baseline, in the absence of emotional stimulation. Sutton and Davidson (1997) explicitly draw on Gray's theory to organize the literature on affective dispositions and brain function, illustrating the utility of Gray's BAS and BIS concepts (e.g., approach motivation and withdrawal motivation, respectively) and their distinct activation. These results have been replicated using functional brain imaging techniques (Canli et al., 2001).

The importance of brain asymmetry research is that different portions of the brain may respond with pleasant or unpleasant emotions, given the appropriate affective stimulus. Fox and Calkins (1993) discuss this notion in terms of thresholds for responding. The concept of thresholds implies that individuals with a left- or right-sided pattern require less of the affective stimulus to evoke the corresponding emotion. The person who displays a right-frontal-activation pattern may have a lower threshold for responding with negative emotions when an unpleasant event happens. It may take less of a negative affective event to evoke unpleasant feelings for right-dominant individuals. For an individual who displays a left-frontal-activation pattern, the threshold for experiencing pleasant emotions in response to positive events is lowered. A person's affective lifestyle may have its origins in, or at least may be predicted by, the pattern of asymmetry in frontal brain activation.

An unlikely collaboration has emerged between the psychologist Richard Davidson, who runs the Laboratory for Affective Neuroscience at the University of Wisconsin, and Tenzin Gyatso, who is also known as the fourteenth Dalai Lama, the supreme leader of Tibetan Buddhism and winner of a Nobel Peace Prize. Davidson and other psychologists and researchers met with the Dalai Lama for five days in Dharamsala, India, in March 2000. Davidson measured the brain waves of one senior Tibetan monk, who turned out to have the most left-sided asymmetry that has ever been recorded. Was this a quirk, or is there something about the training of these monks that produces more left-sided brain activity?

To answer this question Davidson teamed up with Jon Kabat-Zinn, who founded the Stress Reduction Clinic at the University of Massachusetts Medical School. Dr. Kabat-Zinn uses a form of mindfulness meditation to teach people how to reduce stress. This form of meditation is loosely based on Buddhist meditation techniques. In this research, they obtained a sample of 41 workers employed in high-stress jobs in the biotechnology industry. Twenty-five of the workers were taught mindfulness meditation and practised it for eight weeks. A control group consisted of 16 workers from the same company in the same kinds of jobs. All subjects had their brain waves assessed before and after the eight-week period.

Before the mindfulness training, subjects tended toward a slightly right-sided asymmetry, suggesting chronic stress. After the training, these subjects, compared to the control group, showed a significant shift toward left-sided asymmetry. They also reported less stress, feeling more energized, more engaged in their work, and less anxiety. In a surprising finding, mindfulness meditation appeared to give the workers' immune systems a boost. This was determined by the amount of flu antibodies they produced in response to a flu shot, with the mindfulness meditators showing a more robust immune response to the flu shot (Davidson et al., 2003).

In 2005 the Dalai Lama attended the annual meeting of the Society for Neuroscience, where he charmed an audience of 14,000 with a talk presenting meditation as an empirical way to investigate the mind. Many neuroscientists argued that a religious leader should not be given time at a meeting of scientists, but most of those attending agreed with the Dalai Lama's view that scientific evidence will persuade more people than religious dogma. By encouraging scientific investigations of the brain, the Dalai Lama provides an interesting and current example of a physiological perspective on the mind.

Throughout this section, we have explored a number of physiologically based theories of personality. But did you know that your own brain acts a little like a personality theorist? There is evidence that your brain represents and categorizes people in order to predict their future behaviours. Read more on this fascinating research in A Closer Look: How the Brain Uses Personality Models to Predict Behaviour.

A Closer Look

How the Brain Uses Personality Models to Predict Behaviour

A collaborative study by researchers in the United Kingdom, Canada, and the United States revealed an interesting brain phenomenon using fMRI neuroimaging technology. Hassabis and colleagues (2014) were interested in understanding how the brain represents and categorizes people in order to predict their future behaviours. What they found was that the brain behaves much like a personality psychologist would—it creates its own models of personality in order to understand the behaviour of those it perceives. Researchers used fMRI scanning to detect the brain regions that were involved when participants imagined one of four protagonists acting in different scenarios. Protagonists' unique personalities were learned prior to fMRI scanning through a series of descriptive statements. Each protagonist was described as having either high or low levels of extraversion and agreeableness according to traits on the Big Five model.

Analyses of fMRI imaging indeed confirmed different areas of the brain being activated depending on the personality traits of the protagonists as they were imagined by participants to play out in different scenarios. What is most fascinating is that Hassabis and colleagues were able to accurately infer which protagonist participants were thinking of based entirely on activity in the prefrontal cortex. Brain activity was able to reveal exactly whom participants were thinking of. Specifically, activity in the lateral temporal and posterior cingulate cortex discriminated between degrees of agreeableness and extraversion, respectively. What the researchers concluded was that different brain regions actually code for different personality traits, and that activity in these regions combines to represent different individuals according to their complete personalities. In other words, the brain appears to develop its own model of personality as a way of representing and identifying other people. Given that this study confirmed this phenomenon in regards to extraversion and agreeableness, it may be that the brain's model of personality is actually in line with a five-factor or Big Five perspective. Future research is needed to confirm this with additional traits (Hassabis et al., 2014).

Concept Check

What physiological explanation has been offered to explain individual differences in extraversion-introversion?

In your own words, summarize Gray's reinforcement sensitivity theory.

How has sensation-seeking been explained according to physiological or biological mechanisms?

Summary and Evaluation

The study of personality can be approached biologically. Theorizing about the biological influences on personality has a long history, and there are two ways to think about how physiological variables can be useful in personality theory and research. One way to view physiological measures is as variables that may be correlated with personality traits. For example, in a sample of university students, there may be a negative correlation between resting heart rate and scores on a neuroticism questionnaire (perhaps due to the heightened level of chronic anxiety associated with neuroticism). Here a physiological variable is seen as a correlate of a personality dimension, as something that is associated with being neurotic. Does an elevated heart rate cause a person to become neurotic? Probably not. Instead, a pounding heart goes along with, or is a correlate of, being neurotic.

A second way to think about physiological approaches to personality is to view physiological events as contributing to or providing the physiological substrate for the personality characteristic. This chapter covered six such examples of theories about the biological underpinnings of specific personality dimensions: extraversion (and neuronal excitability or arousability), sensitivity to cues of reward and punishment (based on brain circuits of the BIS and BAS), sensation seeking (and level of MAO and hormones in the bloodstream), tridimensional personality theory (based on neurotransmitters), morningness–eveningness (and circadian rhythms in body temperature), and affective style (and hemispheric asymmetry in the frontal cortex of the brain). In these theories, the physiological variables are assumed to be more than just correlates of the personality traits; they are assumed to be substrates of the biological underpinnings for the behaviour pattern that defines the personality trait (see Table 7.4).

Table 7.4 Biological Theories of Specific Personality Traits	
RELATED TO PHYSIOLOGICAL REACTIVITY	
Personality Trait	**Biological Underpinnings**
Extraversion–introversion	Arousal level of brain (early theory)
	Arousability of nervous system
Sensitivity to reward and punishment	Behavioural activation system (BAS) responds to incentives and reward
	Behavioural inhibition system (BIS) responds to threat and punishment
Sensation seeking	Optimal arousal level (early theory)
	Monoamine oxidase (MAO) levels
Tridimensional personality model	
Novelty seeking	Dopamine
Harm avoidance	Serotonin
Reward dependence	Norepinephrine
NOT RELATED TO PHYSIOLOGICAL REACTIVITY	
Personality Trait	**Biological Underpinnings**
1. Morningness–eveningness	Length of circadian rhythm
	shorter = morning type
	longer = evening type
2. Affective style	Asymmetry in frontal brain activation
	left = tendency toward positive
	right = tendency toward negative

⚠ Concept Check

Based on your reading of Chapter 7, choose any one key personality trait and offer a physiological explanation for individual differences on that trait.

Which key personality traits are believed to be associated with physiological reactivity, and which are not?

Key Terms

physiological systems

theoretical bridge

electrodes

telemetry

autonomic nervous system (ANS)

electrodermal activity

skin conductance

cardiac reactivity

Type A personality

ascending reticular activating system (ARAS)

arousal level

arousability

reinforcement sensitivity theory

behavioural activation system (BAS)

behavioural inhibition system (BIS)

anxiety

impulsivity

sensation seeking

sensory deprivation

optimal level of arousal

comorbidity

neurotransmitters

monoamine oxidase (MAO)

dopamine

serotonin

norepinephrine

tridimensional personality model

novelty seeking

harm avoidance

reward dependence

morningness–eveningness

circadian rhythms

free running

electroencephalogram (EEG)

alpha wave

frontal brain asymmetry

cortisol

CHAPTER 8

Evolutionary Perspectives on Personality

The Biological Domain

Imagine living as our ancestors did a million years ago. You awaken at dawn and shrug off the coldness of night. A few warm embers are still glowing in the fire, so you stoke it with kindling. The others in your group gather around the fire as the sun breaks the horizon. Stomachs start growling. Your thoughts turn to food. Small groups set off in search of berries, nuts, and small game animals.

How much of human nature today is the result of behaviour patterns that evolved as our ancestors solved the problems of surviving and reproducing?
©The Natural History Museum/Alamy Stock Photo

After a long day of hunting and gathering, the members converge back at their temporary home site. As night begins to fall, the group again gathers around the fire. The day's hunting and gathering have been successful and the mood is warm and animated. Tales of the hunt are reenacted, the bounty of gathered goods admired. With bellies full, discussion turns to whether the group should move the next day or stay a bit longer. A successful hunter makes eye contact with his young lover, but she shyly looks away. Others notice this flirtation. Mating universally draws interest. As people grow sleepy and babies are put to sleep, the young lovers quietly slip away from the group to be alone. Their warm embrace echoes millions of past events as people partake of life's cycle.

Evolutionary psychology is a new and rapidly growing scientific perspective, and it offers important insights into human personality. In this chapter, we look at some of these insights in three areas: human nature, sex differences, and individual differences. We will see how theories of evolutionary psychology fit with the discoveries of personality psychologists and generate new lines of research. We begin by reviewing some basic information about the theory of evolution.

Evolution and Natural Selection

All of us come from a long and unbroken line of ancestors who accomplished two critical tasks: they survived to reproductive age, and they reproduced. If any one of your ancestors had failed at reproduction, you would not be here today to contemplate their existence. In this sense, every living human is an evolutionary success story. As descendants of successful ancestors, we carry with us the genes for the adaptations that led to their success. From this perspective, our human nature—the collection of adaptations that defines us as human—is the product of the evolutionary process.

Long before Charles Darwin, it was known that change takes place over time in organic structures. The fossil record showed the bones of long extinct dinosaurs, suggesting that not all species in the past are with us today. The paleontological record showed changes in animals' body forms, suggesting that nothing remains static. Moreover, the structures of species seemed extraordinarily well adapted to their environments. The long necks of giraffes enabled them to eat leaves from tall trees. The turtle's shell seemed designed for protection. The beaks of birds seemed suited for cracking nuts to get at their nutritious meat. What could account for change over time and apparent adaptation to environmental conditions?

Natural Selection

Darwin's contribution was not in observing change over time, nor in noticing the adaptive design of mechanisms. Rather, Darwin proposed a theory of the *process* by which adaptations are created and change takes place over time. He called it the theory of **natural selection**.

Darwin noticed that species seemed to produce many more offspring than could possibly survive and reproduce. He reasoned that changes, or *variants,* that better enabled an organism to survive and reproduce would lead to more descendants. The descendants would inherit the variants that led to their ancestors' survival and reproduction. Through this process, the successful variants were selected and unsuccessful variants weeded out. Natural selection, therefore, results in gradual changes in a species over time, as successful variants increase in frequency and eventually spread throughout the gene pool, replacing the less successful variants. Over time, these successful variants come to characterize the entire species; unsuccessful variants decrease in frequency and vanish from the species.

This process of natural selection, sometimes called *survival selection,* led Darwin to focus on the events that impede survival, which he called the **hostile forces of nature**. These hostile forces included food shortages, diseases, parasites, predators, and extremes of weather. Variants that helped organisms survive these hostile forces of nature led to an increased likelihood of successful reproduction. Food preferences for substances rich in fat, sugar, and protein, for example, helped organisms survive food shortages. An immune system teeming with antibodies helped organisms survive diseases and parasites. Fear of snakes and spiders helped them survive these dangers. These mechanisms, resulting from a long and repeated process of natural selection, are called adaptations, inherited solutions to the survival and reproductive problems posed by the hostile forces of nature.

Even after Darwin came up with his theory of natural selection, there remained many mysteries that puzzled him. He noticed that many mechanisms seemed contrary to survival. The elaborate plumage, large antlers, and other conspicuous features displayed by the males of many species seemed costly in terms of survival. He wondered how the brilliant plumage of peacocks could evolve, and become common, when it posed such an obvious threat to survival, acting as a blaring advertisement to predators. In response to anomalies of this sort, Darwin proposed a second evolutionary theory—the theory of sexual selection.

Sexual Selection

Darwin's answer to the mysteries of the peacock's tail and the stag's antlers was that they evolved because they contributed to an individual's mating success, providing an advantage in the competition for desirable mates. The evolution of characteristics because of their mating benefits, rather than because of their survival benefits, is known as **sexual selection**.

Sexual selection, according to Darwin, takes two forms. In one form, members of the same sex compete with each other, and the outcome of their contest gives the winner greater sexual access to members of the opposite sex. Two stags locking horns in combat is the prototypical image of this **intrasexual competition**.

The characteristics that lead to success in contests of this kind, such as greater strength, intelligence, or attractiveness to allies, evolve because the victors are able to mate more often and, hence, pass on their genes.

In the other type of sexual selection—**intersexual selection**—members of one sex choose a mate based on their preferences for particular qualities. These characteristics evolve because those that possess them are chosen more often as mates, and their genes thrive. Animals that lack the desired characteristics are excluded from mating, and their genes perish.

Success at same-sex competition leads to success at mating; traits that help to win these battles are passed on in greater numbers and hence evolve in the population.
©wingbeats551/Getty Images

Genes and Inclusive Fitness

Genes are packets of DNA that are inherited by offspring from their parents in distinct chunks. Genes are the smallest discrete units that are inherited by offspring intact, without being broken up. According to modern evolutionary biologists, evolution operates by the process of **differential gene reproduction**, defined by reproductive success relative to others. The genes of organisms that reproduce more than others get passed down to future generations at a greater frequency than do the genes of those that reproduce less. Survival is usually critical for reproductive success, so characteristics that lead to greater survival get passed along. Success in mating is also critical for reproductive success, and the qualities that lead to success in same-sex competition or to success at being chosen as a mate get passed along. Successful survival and successful mate competition, therefore, are both paths to differential gene reproduction. The characteristics that lead to the greater reproduction of genes that code for them are selected and, hence, evolve over time.

The modern evolutionary theory based on differential gene reproduction is called **inclusive fitness theory** (Hamilton, 1964). The "inclusive" part refers to the fact that the characteristics that facilitate reproduction need not affect the personal production of offspring. They can affect the survival and reproduction of genetic relatives as well. For example, if you take a personal risk to defend or protect your sister or another close relative, then this might enable her to better survive and reproduce. Because you share genes with your sister—50 percent on average in the case of siblings—then helping her survive and reproduce will also lead to successful gene reproduction.

A critical condition for such helping to evolve is that the cost to your reproduction as a result of the helping must be less than the benefits to the reproduction of your genes that reside in your relative. If helping your sister survive—for example, by jumping into rushing rapids to save her from drowning—puts your own life at risk, the odds of saving her must exceed twice the odds of your dying in order

Traits for helping can evolve through inclusive fitness.
©Bjorn Vinter/Getty Images

for evolution to select for mechanisms underlying this helping behaviour. Thus, inclusive fitness can be defined as one's personal reproductive success (roughly, the number of children you produce) *plus* the effects you have on the reproduction of your genetic relatives, weighted by the degree of genetic relatedness. Inclusive fitness can lead to adaptations that incline you to take some risk for the welfare of your genetic relatives, but not too great a risk. Inclusive fitness theory, as an expansion and elaboration of Darwin's theory, represented a major advance in understanding human traits such as altruism.

Products of the Evolutionary Process

All living humans are products of the evolutionary process, the descendants of a long line of ancestors who succeeded in surviving, reproducing, and helping their genetic relatives. The evolutionary process acts as a series of filters. In each generation, only a small subset of genes passes through the filter. The recurrent filtering process lets only three things pass through: adaptations; byproducts of adaptations; and noise, or random variations.

Adaptations

Adaptations are the primary product of the selective process. An adaptation can be defined as a "reliably developing structure in the organism, which, because it meshes with the recurrent structure of the world, causes the solution to an adaptive problem" (Tooby & Cosmides, 1992, p. 104). Known human adaptations include a taste for sweet and fatty foods, the drive to defend close relatives, and preferences for specific mates, such as those that are healthy.

Let's examine the components of the definition of adaptation. The focus on reliably developing structure means that an adaptation tends to emerge with regularity during the course of a person's life. The mechanisms that allow humans to see, for example, develop reliably. But this does not mean that vision develops invariantly. The development of the eye can be perturbed by genetic anomalies or by environmental trauma. The emphasis on reliable development suggests that evolutionary approaches are *not* forms of "genetic determinism." Environments are always needed for the development of an adaptation, and environmental events can always interfere with or enhance such development.

The emphasis on meshing with recurrent structures of the world means that adaptations emerge from, and are structured by, the selective environment. Features of the environment must be recurrent over time for an adaptation to evolve. The venomous snakes must be recurrently dangerous, ripe fruit must be recurrently nutritious, and enclosed caves must be recurrently protective before adaptations to them can emerge.

Finally, an adaptation must facilitate the solution to an adaptive problem. An **adaptive problem** is anything that impedes survival or reproduction, or anything whose solution increases the odds of survival or reproduction. Stated more precisely, all adaptations must contribute to fitness during the period of time in which they evolve by helping an organism survive, reproduce, or facilitate the reproductive success of genetic relatives.

The hallmark of adaptation is *special design*. That is, the features of an adaptation are recognized as components of specialized problem-solving machinery. Factors such as *efficiency* in solving a specific adaptive problem, *precision* in solving the adaptive problem, and *reliability* in solving the adaptive problem are key criteria in recognizing the special design of an adaptation. Adaptations are like keys that fit only specific locks.

The tines of the key (adaptation) show special design features, which mesh with the specific mirror-image elements within the lock (adaptive problem).

All adaptations are products of a history of selection. In this sense, we live with an ancient brain in a modern world, which is in some ways different from the world in which we evolved. For example, ancestral humans evolved in relatively small groups of 50 to 150, using both hunting and gathering as methods of acquiring food (Dunbar, 1993). In the modern world, by contrast, many people live in large cities surrounded by thousands or millions of people. Characteristics that were probably adaptive in ancestral environments—such as **xenophobia**, or fear of strangers—are not necessarily adaptive in modern environments. Some of the personality traits that make up human nature may be vestigial adaptations to an ancestral environment that no longer exists.

For most of our evolutionary past, humans lived in small, close-knit groups, usually of fewer than 100 people. This form of group living is relatively rare today.
©dbimages/Alamy Stock Photo

Byproducts of Adaptations

The evolutionary process also produces things that are not adaptations—such as **byproducts of adaptations**. Consider the design of a lightbulb. A lightbulb is designed to produce light—that is its function. But it also may produce heat, not because it is designed to produce heat, but rather because heat is an incidental byproduct, which occurs as a consequence of design for light. In the same way, human adaptations can also have **evolutionary byproducts**, or incidental effects that are not properly considered to be adaptations. The human nose, for example, is clearly an adaptation designed for smelling. But the fact that we use our noses to hold up our eyeglasses is an incidental byproduct. The nose was designed for smelling odours, not for holding up glasses. Notice that the hypothesis that something is a byproduct (e.g., by holding up eyeglasses) requires specifying the adaptation (e.g., the nose) of which it is a byproduct. Thus, both sorts of evolutionary hypotheses—adaptation and byproduct hypotheses—require a description of the nature of the adaptation.

Noise, or Random Variations

The third product of the evolutionary process is **evolutionary noise**, or random variations that are neutral with respect to selection. In the design of a lightbulb, for example, there are minor variations in the surface texture of the bulb that do not affect the functioning of the design elements. Neutral variations introduced into the gene pool through mutation, for example, are perpetuated over generations if they do not hinder the functioning of adaptations.

In sum, there are three products of the evolutionary process: adaptations, byproducts, and noise. Adaptations are the primary product of the selective process, so evolutionary psychology is primarily focused on identifying and describing human psychological adaptations. The hypothesis that something is a byproduct requires specifying the adaptation of which it is a byproduct. The analysis of byproducts, therefore, leads us back to the need to describe adaptations. And noise is the residue of nonfunctional variation that is selectively neutral.

 Concept Check

How does inclusive fitness theory explain the evolution of altruism?

What is an adaptive problem? What are some human traits that have developed to solve adaptive problems?

Use the lock and key analogy to explain why some adaptations are no longer useful when there is a change in the environment.

Evolutionary Psychology

The basic elements of the evolutionary perspective apply to all forms of life on Earth, from slime moulds to people. We will turn now to the application of this perspective to human psychology. This branch of psychology is referred to as evolutionary psychology.

Premises of Evolutionary Psychology

Evolutionary psychology involves three key premises: domain specificity, numerousness, and functionality.

Domain Specificity

Adaptations are presumed to be **domain specific** in the sense that they are designed by the evolutionary process to solve a particular adaptive problem. Consider the problem of food selection—choosing the right foods to eat from among a large array of possible objects in the world. A general decision rule, such as "eat the first thing you encounter," would be highly maladaptive because it would fail to guide you to choose the small subset of objects that are edible and nutritious. Such a general rule would result in the consumption of poisonous plants, twigs, dirt, or feces, which would interfere with successful survival. The mechanisms favoured by the evolutionary process are more specialized. In the area of food selection, domain specificity is seen in our preferences for calorically rich fat and in our evolved sweet tooth, which leads us to objects rich in sugar, such as ripe fruit and berries. General mechanisms cannot guide us to the small islands of successful adaptive solutions that are surrounded by oceans of maladaptive solutions.

Another reason for domain specificity is that different adaptive problems require different sorts of solutions. Our taste preferences, which guide us to successful food choices, do not help us solve the adaptive problem of choosing successful mates. If we were to use our food preferences as a general guide to the choice of mates, we would select strange mates indeed. Successful mate choices require different mechanisms. Domain specificity implies that selection tends to fashion at least somewhat specialized mechanisms for each adaptive problem.

Numerousness

Our ancestors faced many sorts of adaptive problems in the course of human evolution, so we have numerous adaptive mechanisms. If you look at a textbook about the human body, for example, you will discover a large number of physiological and anatomical mechanisms. We have a heart to pump our blood, a liver to detoxify poisons, a larynx to prevent us from choking, and sweat glands to keep the body thermally regulated.

Evolutionary psychologists suggest that the human mind, our evolved psychology, also contains a large number of mechanisms—psychological adaptations. Consider the most common fears and phobias. We tend to be scared of snakes, heights, darkness, spiders, cliff edges, and strangers. Just in the domain of fears, we have a large number of psychological mechanisms because the number of hazardous hostile forces of nature has been so large. We are also likely to have psychological mechanisms for the selection of mates, the detection of cheaters in social exchanges, the favouring of habitats, the rearing of children, and the formation of strategic alliances. Evolutionary psychologists expect there to be a large number of domain-specific psychological adaptations to correspond to the large number of distinct adaptive problems humans have recurrently confronted.

Functionality

The third key premise of evolutionary psychology is **functionality**, the notion that our psychological mechanisms are designed to accomplish particular adaptive goals. If you were a medical researcher studying the liver, you could not get very far in your understanding unless you understood the functions of the liver (e.g., filtering out toxins). Evolutionary psychologists suggest that understanding adaptive function is also critical to insight into our evolved *psychological* mechanisms. We can't understand our preferences for certain mates, for example, without inquiring about the function of such preferences (e.g., to select a healthy or fertile mate). The search for function involves identifying the specific adaptive problem for which the mechanism is an evolved solution.

Empirical Testing of Evolutionary Hypotheses

To understand how evolutionary psychologists test hypotheses, it is necessary to consider the hierarchy of levels of evolutionary analysis depicted in Figure 8.1. At the top of the hierarchy is evolution by selection. The theory has been tested directly in many cases. New species can be formed in the laboratory by its application, and dogs can be selectively bred using its principles. Because there has never been a single case in which evidence has indicated that the general theory is incorrect, most scientists take the general theory for granted and proceed with a more specific form of hypothesis testing.

At the next level down are middle-level evolutionary theories, such as the theory of parental investment and sexual selection. According to this theory, the sex (male or female) that invests more in offspring is predicted to be more discriminating or "choosy" about its mating partners. And the sex that invests less in offspring is predicted to be more competitive with members of its own sex for sexual access to the high-investing sex. From these hypotheses, specific predictions can be derived and tested empirically. In the human case, women bear the heavy parental investment burdens of internal fertilization and nine-month pregnancy. Women are the high-investing sex; thus, according to the theory, they should exert more selectivity in their choice of mates than should men, who require only the contribution of sperm in order to reproduce. Two specific predictions can be derived from this hypothesis: (1) women will choose as mates men who are willing to invest resources in them and their children, and (2) women will divorce men who fail to continue providing resources to them and their children.

Using this method of deriving specific testable predictions, researchers can carry out the normal scientific business of empirical research. If the data fail to support the predictions and hypotheses, then the middle-level

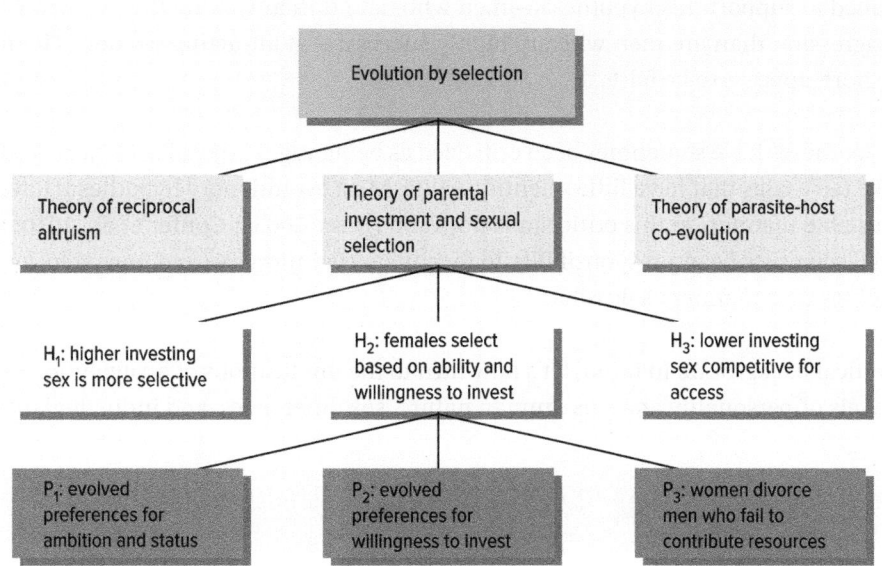

FIGURE 8.1 The evolutionary analysis hierarchy depicts the conceptual levels of evolutionary analysis. At the top of the hierarchy is natural selection theory. At the next level down are middle-level evolutionary theories from which specific hypotheses and predictions can be derived. Each level of the hierarchy is evaluated by the cumulative weight of the empirical evidence from tests of the predictions derived from it.

theory from which they were derived is called into question. If the findings support the predictions and hypotheses, then the middle-level theory from which they were derived increases in credibility.

The **deductive reasoning approach**, or the "top down," theory-driven method of empirical research, is one approach to scientific investigation. Another method, which is equally valid, is called the **inductive reasoning approach**, or the "bottom-up," data-driven method of empirical research. In the inductive reasoning approach, a phenomenon is first observed, and then the researchers develop a theory to fit the observations. Just as astronomers observed the galaxies in the universe expanding before they had a theory to explain why, psychologists notice and empirically document a number of phenomena before they have theories to explain them. In the domain of personality, for example, we might notice that men tend to be more physically aggressive than women. Although nothing in the theory of evolution by selection would have predicted this sex difference in advance, it is fair game for subsequent theorizing. The dual inductive and deductive approaches, of course, can apply to all theories in personality psychology, not just evolutionary theories.

Once a theory is proposed to explain the sex difference in aggression, however, we can ask, "If the theory is true, then what *further* predictions follow from it that we have not already observed?" It is in these further deduced predictions that the value and tenability of the theory rest. If the theory generates a wealth of new predictions, which are then confirmed empirically, we know that we are on the right explanatory track. If the theory fails to generate further testable predictions, or if its predictions fail to be confirmed empirically, then the theory is called into question. For example, one theory of sexual aggression against women has proposed that men who have experienced deprivation of sexual access to women are more likely to use aggressive tactics. This has been called the *mate deprivation hypothesis* (Lalumiere et al., 1996). The evidence so far, however, has failed to support this hypothesis—men who have difficulty attracting women are no more likely to use sexual aggression than are men who are highly successful at attracting women. The mate deprivation hypothesis, in short, appears to be false.

Evolutionary hypotheses have sometimes been criticized as being vague, speculative "just-so stories," implying that they are like fairy tales that have little scientific value. Most evolutionary hypotheses have been framed in a precise and testable manner, so this criticism is not valid (Buss, 2005a; Confer et al., 2010; Kenrick & Luce, 2004). Individual scientists bear a responsibility to formulate evolutionary (and nonevolutionary) hypotheses in as precise and testable manner as possible.

With this theoretical background in mind, let's now turn to the implications of an evolutionary perspective for the three key levels of personality analysis: human nature, sex differences, and individual differences.

 Concept Check

What does it mean when evolutionary psychologists say that they expect adaptations to be domain specific, numerous, and functional?

What do evolutionary psychologists do to avoid being criticized for having hypotheses that have little value?

Human Nature

In the history of psychology, "grand" theories of personality were proposed about the universal contents of human nature. Sigmund Freud's theory of psychoanalysis, for example, proposed that humans had the core motives of sex and aggression. Alfred Adler proposed that humans had the striving for superiority as a core motive. Robert Hogan suggests that humans are driven by the desire for status and acceptance by the group—getting ahead and getting along. Even the most radical behaviourist, B. F. Skinner, had a theory of human nature, consisting of a few domain-general learning mechanisms. Thus, all personality theories attempt to answer the question, If humans have a nature that is different from the nature of gorillas, dogs, or rats, what are its contents and how can we discover them?

The perspective of evolutionary psychology offers a set of tools for discovering the human nature component of personality. From this perspective, human nature is the primary product of the evolutionary process. Psychological mechanisms that are successful in helping humans survive and reproduce tend to out-replicate those that are less successful. Over evolutionary time, these successful mechanisms spread throughout the population and come to characterize a species. Let's examine a few evolutionary hypotheses about the contents of human nature.

Need to Belong

Hogan (1983) argues that the most basic human motivators are status and acceptance by the group. According to Hogan, the most important social problems early humans had to solve in order to survive and reproduce involved establishing cooperative relations with other members of the group and negotiating hierarchies. Achieving status and popularity likely conferred a host of reproductively relevant resources on an individual, including better protection, more food, and more desirable mates.

According to Hogan's theory, being ostracized from a group would have been extremely damaging. Therefore, it can be predicted that humans have evolved psychological mechanisms to prevent being excluded. Baumeister and Tice (1990) propose that this is the origin and function of **social anxiety**, defined as distress or worry about being negatively evaluated in social situations. They propose that social anxiety is a species-typical adaptation that prevents social exclusion. People who were indifferent to being excluded by others may have suffered in the currency of survival by lacking the protection of the group. They may also have suffered by failing to find mates. These individuals may have experienced lower reproductive success than those whose psychological mechanisms caused them to maintain inclusion in the group by avoiding doing things that elicit criticism.

If this hypothesis is correct, what testable predictions might follow from it? One set of testable predictions pertains to the *events* that elicit social anxiety (Buss, 1990). Groups can be expected to shun those who inflict costs on others within the group. Showing cowardice in the face of danger, displaying aggression toward in-group members, trying to lure away the mates of in-group members, and stealing from in-group members would all have inflicted costs on particular members of the group.

Baumeister and Leary (1995) present empirical evidence that the need to belong is a central motive of human nature. They argue that the group serves several key adaptive functions for individuals. First, groups can share food, information, and other resources. Second, groups can offer protection from external threat, or defence against rival groups. Third, groups contain concentrations of mates, which are needed for reproduction. And fourth, groups usually contain kin, which provide opportunities to receive altruism and to invest in genetic relatives.

Several lines of empirical research support Baumeister and Leary's theory about the need to belong. First, external threats have been shown repeatedly to increase group cohesion (Stein, 1976). In one study, World War II veterans were examined for enduring social ties (Elder & Clipp, 1988). Remarkably, their strongest social ties 40 years after the war were with comrades who had experienced combat together. This effect was intensified among the units in which some comrades had died, suggesting that the more intense the external threat, the greater the social bonding.

Humans evolved to live in groups. Consequently, an individual who is shunned by a group will feel anxious.
©SW Productions/Getty Images

The opportunity to acquire resources also seems to be a powerful context for triggering group cohesion. In one study, participants were randomly assigned to two groups (Rabbie & Horwitz, 1969). The assignment to groups alone produced no increase in group cohesion. When one group was given a prize—a transistor radio—based on the flip of a coin, however, both the rewarded group and the deprived group showed an increase in in-group preference. When resources are linked with group membership, people become increasingly bonded with their groups.

Further support for the importance of the need to belong as a fundamental human motive comes from a cross-cultural study on the effects of social interactions on self-esteem (Denissen et al., 2008). Those who spend a lot of time with others enjoy higher self-esteem. Day-to-day fluctuations in self-esteem are linked with quality and quantity of social interactions. And even at the level of nations, countries whose inhabitants frequently interact with friends and relatives enjoy higher self-esteem than countries with less frequent social interactions. These findings point to the notion that self-esteem functions, at least in part, as an internal tracking device that monitors social inclusion (Denissen et al., 2008).

Researchers have begun to make progress in identifying the underlying brain circuitry for the pain caused by social exclusion (Eisenberger, 2012; MacDonald & Leary, 2005; Panksepp, 2005). Social rejection or exclusion has often been described as literally painful. Brain research suggests that social exclusion is mediated by components of the physical pain system, such as the anterior cingulate cortex. The fact that people use words like *hurt, wounded,* and *damaged* when they are socially excluded may reflect the shared brain circuitry through which physically induced pain and socially induced pain are mediated.

Humans have always been intensely group living, and lack of a group almost surely would have meant death in ancestral environments, so it is not surprising that we have a strong need to belong—a part of our human nature.

Helping and Altruism

An evolutionary perspective provides a straightforward set of predictions about the human nature of helping and altruism (Burnstein, Crandall, & Kitayama, 1994). Burnstein and colleagues hypothesized that helping others is a direct function of the recipients' ability to enhance the inclusive fitness of the helpers. Helping should decrease, according to this hypothesis, as the degree of genetic relatedness decreases between the helper and the recipient. Thus, you should be more likely to help your sibling, who shares 50 percent of your genes, on average, than your nieces and nephews, who share only 25 percent of your genes, on average. Helping is expected to be lower still between individuals who share only 12.5 percent of their genes, such as first cousins. No other theory in psychology generates this precise helping gradient as a function of genetic relatedness or specifies kinship as one underlying principle for altruism.

Studies in the United States and Japan support these predictions. In one study, participants were asked to imagine different individuals asleep in different rooms of a rapidly burning building. The participants imagined that they had time to rescue only one of them. They circled the target they were most likely to help. As shown in Figure 8.2, the tendency to help is a direct function of the degree of genetic relatedness. This is especially true in a life-or-death context, as confirmed by independent researchers (Fitzgerald & Colarelli, 2009).

Genetic relatedness represents just the start of an evolutionary analysis of the altruistic component of human nature. Burnstein and colleagues (1994) predicted that people should help younger relatives more than older relatives because helping older kin would have less impact, on average, on their reproductive success than would helping a younger person. Furthermore, individuals of higher reproductive value (ability to produce children) should be helped more than individuals of lower reproductive value.

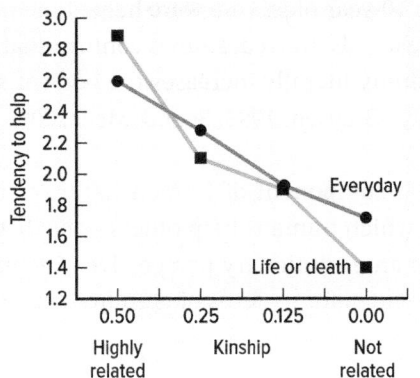

FIGURE 8.2 Tendency to help kin under life-or-death versus everyday conditions. Genetic overlap predicts the tendency to help, especially under life-or-death conditions.

Source: Adapted from "Some Neo-Darwinian Decision Rules for Altruism: Weighing Cures for Inclusive Fitness as a Function of the Biological Importance of the Decision," by E. Burnstein, C. Crandall, and S. Kitayama, 1994, *Journal of Personality & Social Psychology, 67,* pp. 773–789, Figure 2, p. 778. Copyright © 1994 by the American Psychological Association. Reprinted with permission.

In one study, 1-year-olds were helped more than 10-year-olds, who in turn were helped more than 45-year-olds (Burnstein et al., 1994). Least helped were 75-year-old individuals. These findings, replicated across both Japanese and American samples, provide further support for the hypothesis that life-or-death helping decreases as the kin member gets older. Interestingly, these results were strongest in the life-or-death situation, but showed a reversal in a trivial helping condition. For everyday helping, such as running a small errand for someone, the 75-year-olds were helped more than the 45-year-olds (see Figure 8.3).

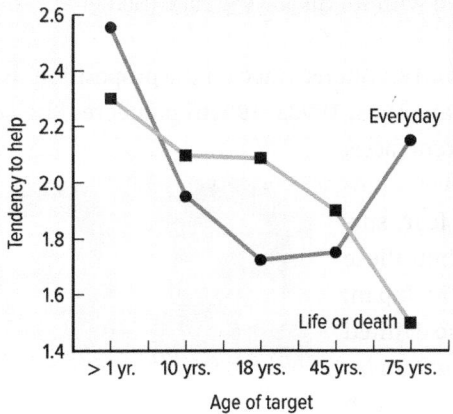

FIGURE 8.3 Tendency to help as a function of the recipient's age under life-or-death versus everyday conditions. When helping is relatively trivial, people tend to help those most in need, such as the young and the elderly. Under costly forms of help, however, the young are helped more than the old.

Source: Adapted from "Some Neo-Darwinian Decision Rules for Altruism: Weighing Cures for Inclusive Fitness as a Function of the Biological Importance of the Decision," by E. Burnstein, C. Crandall, and S. Kitayama, 1994, *Journal of Personality & Social Psychology, 67,* pp. 773–789, Figure 3, p. 779. Copyright © 1994 by the American Psychological Association. Reprinted with permission.

The tendency to help younger people depended on a critical survival context—famine conditions (Burnstein et al., 1994). When the participants imagined themselves living in a sub-Saharan African country that suffered widespread famine and disease, they reported a curvilinear relationship between age and helping. Infants in this condition were helped *less* than 10-year-olds, who were helped the most. But then helping began to drop, with the least helped being the 75-year-olds. Indeed, studies confirm that in real-life situations in which life is in danger, having kin in close proximity literally increases the odds of surviving compared to people in the same situation who lack in proximity (Grayson, 1993; Sear & Mace, 2008).

These studies suggest that a central component of human nature is helping other people, but in highly domain-specific ways. The ways in which humans help others—the distribution of helping acts across individuals—is highly predictable from an evolutionary perspective. The importance of genetic relatedness on helping others has even been documented for patterns of grandparental investment (Laham, Gonsalkorale, & von Hippel, 2005).

Universal Emotions

Evolutionary psychologists have taken three distinct perspectives on the study of emotions, such as fear, rage, and jealousy. One view is to examine whether facial expressions of emotion are interpreted in the same ways across cultures, on the assumption that universality is one criterion for adaptation (Ekman, 1973, 1992a, 1992b). If all humans share an adaptation, such as smiling to express happiness, that adaptation is likely to be a core part of human nature. A second evolutionary view is that emotions are adaptive psychological mechanisms that signal various "fitness affordances" in the social environment (Ketelaar, 1995). According to this perspective, emotions guide the person toward goals that would have conferred fitness in ancestral environments (e.g., the pleasure one feels having one's status rise within a group) or to avoid conditions that would have interfered with fitness (e.g., getting beaten up or abused). A third evolutionary perspective on social emotions is the "manipulation hypothesis," which suggests that emotions are designed to exploit the psychological mechanisms of other people. For example, expressions of rage might be designed to make a verbal threat more credible than the same threat made without displaying rage (Sell et al., 2009).

All these evolutionary perspectives on emotions hinge on the proposition that they are universal and universally recognized in the same way. Ekman (1973, 1992a, 1992b) pioneered the cross-cultural study of emotions. He assembled pictures of several different faces, each of which showed one of seven emotions: happiness, disgust, anger, fear, surprise, sadness, and contempt. When these pictures were shown to subjects in Japan, Chile, Argentina, Brazil, and the United States, all showed tremendous agreement on which emotions corresponded to which face. Subsequent research has confirmed the universal recognition of these emotional expressions in Italy, Scotland, Estonia, Greece, Germany, Hong Kong, Sumatra, and Turkey (Ekman et al., 1987).

Especially impressive is the study of the Fore of New Guinea—a cultural group with practically no contact with outsiders. They spoke no English, had seen no TV or

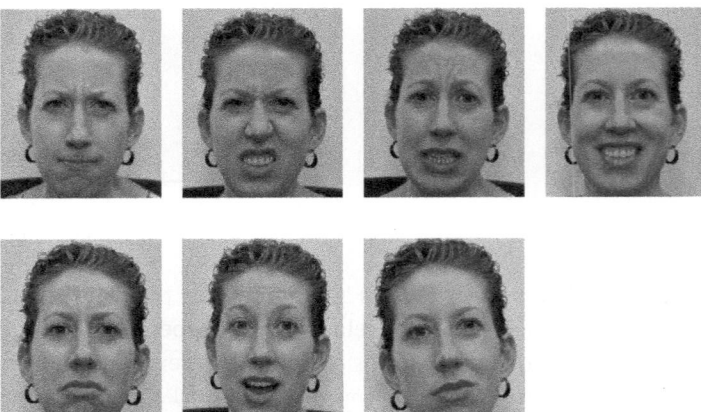

Photos of the seven emotional expressions that are correctly identified by people from many diverse cultures. Can you identify which photo is associated with the following emotions: happiness, disgust, anger, fear, surprise, sadness, and contempt?
(all images): ©Alison Derry/McGraw-Hill Education

movies, and had never lived with individuals of European ancestry. Nonetheless, the Fore also showed the universal pairing of emotions and faces. Subsequent research has also shown the universality of the facial expression of contempt (Ekman et al., 1987). Ekman's work suggests that emotions, as central components of personality, are universally expressed and recognized, thus fulfilling an important criterion for adaptation. They are good candidates for evolved components of human nature.

We have reviewed only a few hypotheses about the components of human nature from an evolutionary perspective: the need to belong, social anxiety about ostracism, the urge to help, and the universality of emotions. An evolutionary perspective may shed light on many other possible components of human nature, such as childhood fears of loud noises, darkness, spiders, and strangers; emotions such as anger, envy, passion, and love; the universality of play among children; retaliation and revenge for perceived personal violations; status striving; psychological pain on the loss of status and reputation; and perhaps many more. Human nature, however, represents only one level of personality analysis. We now turn to the second level—sex differences.

 Concept Check

Explain how evolutionary psychologists account for the existence of the need to belong, altruism, and universal recognition of facial expressions.

Imagine your friend has just ended a relationship and says that she feels like her heart is being torn in two. What evidence from evolutionary psychology could you use to validate your friend's claim?

Sex Differences

Evolutionary psychology predicts that males and females will be *the same* or *similar* in domains in which the sexes have faced the same or similar adaptive problems. Both sexes have sweat glands because both sexes have faced the adaptive problem of thermal regulation. Both sexes have similar taste preferences for fat, sugar, and salt, because both sexes have faced similar food consumption problems.

In other domains, males and females have faced substantially different adaptive problems over human evolutionary history. Females have faced the problem of childbirth; males have not. Females, therefore, have evolved particular adaptations that are lacking in males, such as mechanisms for producing labour contractions through the release of oxytocin into the bloodstream.

The sexes have also faced different information-processing *problems* in some adaptive domains. Because fertilization occurs internally within the female, for example, males have faced the adaptive problem of uncertainty of paternity in their offspring. Males who failed to solve this problem risked investing resources in children who were not their own. We are all descendants of a long line of ancestral males whose characteristics led them to behave in ways that increased their likelihood of paternity and decreased the odds of investing in children who were presumed to be theirs but whose genetic fathers were other males.

This does not imply that males were or are consciously aware of the adaptive problem of compromised paternity. A man does not think, "Oh, if my wife has sex with someone else, then my certainty that I'm the genetic father will be jeopardized, and this will endanger the replication of my genes; I'm really angry." Or if a man's wife is taking birth-control pills, he does not think, "Well, because Lisa is taking the pill, it doesn't really matter whether she has sex with other men; after all, my certainty in paternity is secure." Instead, jealousy is a blind passion, just as our hunger for sweets and craving for companionship are blind passions. The "wisdom" of jealousy is passed down to us over millions of years by our successful forebears (Buss, 2000a).

Females faced the problem of securing a reliable or replenishable supply of resources to carry them through pregnancy and lactation, especially when food resources were scarce (such as during droughts and harsh winters). We are all descendants of a long and unbroken line of females who successfully solved this adaptive challenge—for example, by preferring mates who showed the ability to accrue resources and the willingness to channel them toward particular females (Buss, 2003). Those who failed to solve this problem failed to survive, imperiled the survival chances of their children, and hence failed to become our ancestors.

Evolutionary-predicted sex differences hold that the sexes will differ in precisely those domains where females and males have faced different sorts of adaptive problems (Buss, 2009a, 2009b). To an evolutionary psychologist, the likelihood that the sexes are psychologically identical in domains in which they have recurrently confronted different adaptive problems over the long expanse of human evolutionary history is essentially zero (Symons, 1992). The key question therefore is not "Are males and females different psychologically?" Rather, the key questions about sex differences, from an evolutionary psychological perspective, are the following:

1. In what *domains* have females and males faced different adaptive problems?
2. What are the *sex-differentiated psychological mechanisms* of males and females that have evolved in response to these sex-differentiated adaptive problems?
3. Which social, cultural, and contextual inputs affect the magnitude of expressed sex differences?

This section reviews some of the key domains in which the sexes have been predicted to differ: aggression, jealousy, and mate preferences.

Sex Differences in Aggression

The earliest known homicide victim was a Neanderthal man who died 50,000 years ago (Trinkaus & Zimmerman, 1982). He was stabbed in the left front of his chest, indicating a right-handed attacker. As paleontological detective work has become increasingly sophisticated, evidence of prehistoric violence among our forebears has mushroomed (Buss, 2005b). Ancient skeletal remains contain cranial and rib fractures that appear inexplicable except by the force of clubs and weapons that stab. Weapon fragments are occasionally found lodged in skeletal rib cages. Humans apparently have a long evolutionary history of violence.

Of the 2610 homicides committed in Canada between 2010 and 2014, 89 percent were committed by males (Statistics Canada, 2015). Of these, 70 percent of the victims were also male. Although the exact percentages vary from

Males tend to engage in riskier tactics of competition, such as aggression and violence.
©Ollyy/Shutterstock.com RF

culture to culture, cross-cultural homicide statistics reveal strikingly similar findings. In all cultures studied to date, men are overwhelmingly more often the killers, and most of their victims are other men. Any reasonably complete theory of aggression must provide an explanation for both facts—why males engage in violent forms of aggression so much more often than females do and why males comprise the majority of their victims.

An evolutionary model of intrasexual competition provides the foundation for such an explanation. It starts with the theory of parental investment and sexual selection (Archer, 2009; Trivers, 1972). In species in which females invest more heavily in offspring than males do, females become the valuable limiting resource on reproduction for males. Males become constrained in their reproduction not so much by their own ability to survive but rather by their ability to gain sexual access to the high-investing females. In other words, in a species in which females can bear only a small number of offspring, such as the human species, females will express great care in their choice of mates, and males will be forced to compete for access.

Because female mammals bear the physical burden of gestation and lactation, there is a considerable sex difference in minimum obligatory parental investment. Therefore, males can have many more offspring than females can. Stated differently, the ceiling on reproduction is much higher for males than for females. This difference leads to differences in the *variances* in reproduction between the sexes. The differences between the haves and have-nots therefore become greater for males than for females. Among males, a few males will father multiple offspring, whereas some will have none at all. This is known as **effective polygyny**.

As a general rule, the greater the variance in reproduction, the more ferocious the competition within the sex that shows higher variance. An extreme case is the elephant seals off the coast of northern California, where 5 percent of the males sire 85 percent of all offspring produced in a given breeding season (Le Boeuf & Reiter, 1988). Species that show high variance in reproduction within one sex tend to be highly **sexually dimorphic**, highly different in size and structure. The more intense the effective polygyny, the more dimorphic the sexes are in size and form (Plavcan, 2012; Trivers, 1985). Elephant seals are highly size dimorphic: males are four times larger than females (Le Boeuf & Reiter, 1988). Chimpanzees are less sexually dimorphic: males are roughly twice as large as females. Humans are mildly dimorphic, with males roughly 12 percent larger than females, although some specific body components, such as upper body strength, show much larger sexual dimorphism (Lassek & Gaulin, 2009). Within primate species, the greater the effective polygyny, the more the sexual dimorphism and the greater the reproductive variance between the sexes (Alexander et al., 1979; Plavcan, 2012).

Effective polygyny means that some males gain more than their fair share of copulations, whereas other males are shut out entirely, banished from contributing to the ancestry of future generations. Such a system leads to ferocious competition within the high-variance sex. In essence, polygyny selects for risky strategies, including those that lead to violent combat with rivals and those that lead to increased risk-taking to acquire the resources needed to attract members of the high-investing sex.

Indeed, greater body size and strength in males is also likely due to a long history of females who select as mates males with these qualities (Buss, 2012; Plavcan, 2012). One study found that women who fear crime are especially likely to prefer long-term mates who are aggressive and physically formidable (Snyder et al., 2011). Another study found that men with more muscle mass had a larger number of sex partners and an earlier age of first sexual intercourse (Lassek & Gaulin, 2009). And a third study found that men who experienced aggressive victimization in adolescence at the hands of other males have fewer sex partners (Gallup et al., 2009).

This evolutionary account provides an explanation for facts revealed in the cross-cultural homicide record. Males are more often the perpetrators of violence because they are the products of a long history of effective polygyny. Throughout human evolution, male strategies have been characterized by risky intrasexual competition for females or for the social status and resources that attract females. The fact that males die, on average, five to seven years earlier than females is one of the many markers of this aggressive and risk-taking intrasexual strategy (Promislow, 2003).

Males are the victims of aggression far more than females because males are in competition primarily with other males. It is other males who block any given male's access to females. With increased aggression comes a greater likelihood of injury and early death. The patterns of aggression, in summary, are well predicted by the evolutionary theory of intrasexual competition (Buss & Duntley, 2006; Griskevicius et al., 2009). Even psychologists who argue that most psychological and behavioural sex differences are due to social roles concede that sex differences in aggression are most likely caused by a long evolutionary history in which females and males have confronted different adaptive problems in the context of mating and mate competition (Archer, 2009).

Sex Differences in Jealousy

Two main views exist on the interaction between jealousy and human evolution. One prominent view asserts that because fertilization occurs internally (and unseen) within females, over human evolutionary history, males have risked investing in children who were not their own. Few females, however, have ever been uncertain about which children were their own. From this perspective, a reproductively damaging act, from an ancestral male's point of view, would have been if his mate had had a pregnancy through sexual intercourse with another male. That is the act that would have jeopardized his certainty of passing on his genes. The concern for females, according to this view, is not whether their mate had sexual contact with another female, but whether their mate's behaviour puts her at risk for losing her mate's resources, time, and commitment. These reasons have led some evolutionary psychologists to predict that males and females should differ in the weighting they give to cues that trigger jealousy. Specifically, males are predicted to become more jealous than females in response to cues to a sexual infidelity, while females are predicted to become more jealous than males in response to cues to the long-term diversion of a mate's commitment, such as emotional involvement with someone else. To test these predictions, researchers such as David Buss from the University of Texas have presented a dilemma to research participants, which you can participate in as well. Take a look at the Exercise that follows.

 Exercise

Think of a serious, committed romantic relationship that you had in the past, that you currently have, or that you would like to have. Imagine that you discover the person with whom you've been seriously involved has become interested in someone else. Of the following, what would distress or upset you more?

1. **Imagining your partner forming a deep emotional attachment to that person.**
2. **Imagining your partner enjoying passionate sexual intercourse with that other person.**

When this hypothetical forced choice question has been presented to undergraduates, males have shown to be more distressed than females when imagining their partners having sexual intercourse with someone else (Buss et al., 1992). The majority of females, in contrast, have been more distressed when imagining their partners becoming emotionally involved with someone else. This does not mean that females are indifferent to their partners' sexual infidelities or that males are indifferent to their partners' emotional infidelities—far from it. Both events upset both sexes. However, when forced to choose which one is more upsetting, a large sex difference emerges. Thus far, researchers have replicated these sex differences in Germany, the Netherlands, and Korea (Buunk et al., 1996). Other researchers have replicated these sex differences in Korea and Japan (Buss et al., 1999). This theory centres around the assumption that males and females have evolved to have jealousy triggered by different types of events: sexual infidelity triggers jealousy in males while emotional infidelity triggers jealousy in females.

While all researchers do seem to find a consistent difference between the sexes using the forced choice paradigm described above, others have used a paradigm exemplified in the Exercise that follows.

 Exercise

Question 1: Think of a serious, committed romantic relationship that you had in the past, that you currently have, or that you would like to have. Imagine that you discover that the person with whom you've been seriously involved has become interested in someone else and that your partner is forming a deep emotional attachment to that person. How would you feel?

1	2	3	4	5	6	7
not upset						very upset

1	2	3	4	5	6	7
not angry						very angry

1	2	3	4	5	6	7
not jealous						very jealous

Question 2: Think of a serious, committed romantic relationship that you had in the past, that you currently have, or that you would like to have. Imagine your partner enjoying passionate sexual intercourse with that other person. How would you feel?

1	2	3	4	5	6	7
not upset						very upset

1	2	3	4	5	6	7
not angry						very angry

1	2	3	4	5	6	7
not jealous						very jealous

When researchers such as David DeSteno and Peter Salovey have used continuous rating scales to assess jealousy they have failed to find significant differences in the responses of males and females (DeSteno and Salovey, 1996). In addition, Christine Harris used a continuous rating scale and found that males and females are both equally distressed by sexual infidelity (Harris, 2002), a finding that is difficult to reconcile with the theory that the sexes evolved different jealousy triggers based on different reproductive strategies.

A second view of the origins of jealousy is the attachment-fertility view proposed by Miller and Fishkin (1997). According to this theory, the natural tendency for humans to have multiple dependent children at one time coupled with high rates of maternal mortality suggests that significant paternal involvement was key to reproductive success during the human evolution. This is contrary to views that suggest reproductive success was linked to a male's ability to control sexual access to mates they were sharing resources with. The attachment-fertility view suggests that large families and difficult living conditions meant that offspring were much more likely to survive if they had two parents providing support. The need for heavy paternal involvement led to selective pressure favouring males who could develop close emotional bonds with both their children and the mother of their children, and that jealousy evolved in both males and females in order to preserve these bonds. Miller and Fishkin's (1997) attachment-fidelity hypothesis is supported by Harris' (2003) meta-analysis of dozens of jealousy studies which revealed that males and females experience jealousy in a similar way, with both sexes more concerned about emotional than sexual infidelity.

Sex Differences in Mate Preferences

Evolutionary psychologists have also predicted that the sexes differ in the qualities they desire in a long-term mate. Because females bear the burdens of the heavy obligatory parental investment, they are predicted to place more value on a potential mate's financial resources and the qualities that lead to such resources. Males, in contrast, are predicted to place greater value on a female's physical appearance, which provides cues to her fertility. These predictions are only partially supported by research. In a sample of college students, the males ranked physical attractiveness an average of 4.04, whereas the females ranked it lower, giving it 6.26 (the highest possible rank would be a "1," whereas the lowest possible rank would be "13"). On the dimension of good earning capacity, the females ranked it 8.04, whereas the males ranked it 9.92 (Buss & Barnes, 1986). Thus, it is clear that both sexes place many qualities above looks and resources. In particular, "kind and understanding" (rank: 2.20) and having an "exciting personality" (rank: 3.50) are more valued by both sexes. Interestingly, people prefer the trait of "kindness" in mates when the kindness is directed toward them, but not necessarily when it is directed toward others (Lukaszewski & Roney, 2010). Personality, in short, plays a key role in what people want in a marriage partner. Nonetheless, in the study, the sexes differed in their rankings of looks and resources in the predicted direction. Indeed, these sex differences have been found across 37 cultures (Buss, 1989). Zambian, Chinese, Indonesian, and Norwegian males rank physical attractiveness as more important than do their female counterparts, just like the American samples. Similarly, worldwide, females rank a potential partner's good financial prospects to be more important than do their male counterparts. Perhaps even more important, the personality characteristics that contribute to financial success—ambition, industriousness, and dependability—are also highly valued by females worldwide. Indeed, whereas males prioritize physical attractiveness, females prioritize social status as a "necessity" in selecting long-term mates (Li et al., 2011).

 Exercise

Following is a list of characteristics that might be present in a potential mate or marriage partner. Rank them on their desirability in someone you might marry. Give a 1 to the most desirable characteristic in a potential mate, a 2 to the second most desirable characteristic in a potential mate, a 3 to the third most desirable characteristic, and so on down to 13 for the 13th most desirable characteristic in a potential mate.

_____ kind and understanding	_____ good housekeeper	_____ postsecondary graduate
_____ religious	_____ intelligent	_____ physically attractive
_____ exciting personality	_____ good earning capacity	_____ healthy
_____ creative and artistic	_____ wants children	
_____ easygoing	_____ good heredity	

In summary, personality plays a key role in mate preferences across the globe, and on a few dimensions there are universal sex differences in what people want in a marriage partner. Although the evolutionary hypotheses for these sex differences have received some support in cross-cultural research, competing hypotheses have been proposed to explain them, and these are currently being tested.

⏺ Concept Check

When does evolutionary psychology predict that males and females will be the same, and when does it predict that they will be different?

What key sex differences are supported by evolutionary psychology?

Individual Differences

There are a variety of ways in which individual differences can be explained from the vantage point of evolutionary psychology (Buss, 2009b; Buss & Hawley, 2011; Penke et al., 2007). The most common is explaining individual differences as a result of environmental differences acting on species-typical (human nature) psychological mechanisms. An analogy is the phenomenon of calluses that people sometimes develop on their hands and feet. Individual differences in calluses can be explained by proposing that different individuals are exposed to different amounts of repeated friction to their skin. All humans have essentially the same callus-producing mechanisms, so individual differences are the result of the environmental differences that activate the mechanisms to differing degrees. Evolutionary psychologists invoke a similar form of explanation to account for psychological individual differences. Individual differences in jealousy, for example, may be explained by differences in the degree to which individuals are exposed to evoking conditions, such as cues to a partner's infidelity or the presence of "mate poachers" (Buss, 2012).

Second, individual differences can emerge from *contingencies among traits* (Bouchard & Loehlin, 2001). For example, "a hair-trigger temper may be advantageous if one is big and strong but not if one is small and weak"

(p. 250). Rather than the trait's expression being contingent on the environment, however, its expression is contingent on other traits the person has—in this case, the size and strength of one's body.

A third source of individual difference stems from *frequency–dependent selection*: the process whereby the reproductive success (fitness) of a trait depends on its frequency relative to other traits in the population. For example, in a large population of people with a cooperative disposition, selection may favour those with a cheating disposition as long as they are not too common. As the frequency of cheaters gets more common, cooperators evolve defences to punish cheaters, and so the success of cheating goes down. Thus, heritable individual differences can be created through frequency–dependent selection.

A fourth source of individual differences comes from the fact that *the optimum level of a personality trait can vary over time and space.* Consider as an example differences over evolutionary time (or space) in the abundance of food, perhaps due to droughts or ice ages. In times of food scarcity, selection favours a risk-taking personality trait—one that prompts a person to risk encountering predators in order to venture widely to get food and prevent starvation. In times of food abundance, selection favours a more cautious personality disposition to reduce the risk of venturing widely in the environment. Variations over time and space in the optimum level of a trait can create heritable individual differences in personality that are maintained in the population. Even traits that we sometimes think of as problematic, like attention-deficit/hyperactivity disorder (ADHD), may have been maintained over time because they were adaptive in certain situations or environments. We explore this further in A Closer Look: Could ADHD Have Evolved as an Adaptive Trait?

 A Closer Look

Could ADHD Have Evolved as an Adaptive Trait?

Attention-deficit/hyperactivity disorder (ADHD) is a condition characterized by restlessness. People with ADHD are impulsive and tend to only be able to focus on tasks that they find highly interesting. Children with ADHD struggle in school and adults with ADHD often have difficulty with day-to-day life. Despite the fact that ADHD appears maladaptive, as it impairs school and work functioning in most people diagnosed with the condition, ADHD remains highly prevalent. ADHD affects about 2 to 5 percent of the world's population and the World Health Organization estimates that approximately 39 million people are currently living with the condition. But if ADHD is so maladaptive, why is it so prevalent? Researchers believe that ADHD may exist today because in humans' evolutionary past restlessness gave nomads specifically a survival advantage. Because nomads ultimately populated the globe, the traits that were adaptive to nomads are sometimes seen in modern humans. Because modern society is not well suited to restlessness, the once useful trait of restlessness is seen as maladaptive and labelled as ADHD.

Recent research has found that a gene known as *DRD4-7R* is linked to the traits that make up ADHD. About 20 percent of the human population carries this gene, and people with the gene tend to be more likely to take risks of all kinds, ranging from trying new activities to trying new sexual relationships, and prefer change and movement to staying in one place. Although not everyone with the *7R* gene develops ADHD, most people with ADHD have the *7R* gene. The *7R* gene is closely linked to human migration. In 1999 Chuansheng Chen and his colleagues at the University of California found that the *7R* mutation is more common among migratory cultures than settled ones. A similar study in 2011 found that the *7R* gene is more likely to be found in people whose ancestors migrated longer distances after leaving Africa (Matthews & Butler, 2011). Both of these studies support the notion that a nomadic lifestyle supports the *7R* variant.

A real-life example of the benefits of the *7R* gene can be observed in the Ariaal tribespeople in Kenya. The Ariaal are a nomadic community of about 10,000 individuals who first made contact with Westerners in the 1970s. Men in the Ariaal tribe who possess the *7R* gene are stronger and better fed than men in the group without *7R* (Eisenberg et al., 2008). The finding suggests that the *7R* gene may be associated with better fitness and higher status among nomadic people. Researchers speculate that a restless person may thrive in an ever-changing environment, and that because the *7R* gene is associated with restlessness, it is found among the most successful Ariaal. Thus modern-day issues ranging from "itchy foot syndrome" (a love for travel) to ADHD may be vestiges from a time when desiring constant change was highly adaptive (Dobbs, 2013).

Men from the nomadic Ariaal tribe in Kenya who have the 7R gene associated with risk taking are stronger than Ariaal men who do not have this gene, suggesting that the gene helps nomads thrive and survive (Eisenberg et al., 2008).
©Maria Stenzel/National Geographic Creative

In sum, the evolutionary framework identifies several sources of individual differences: (1) those that arise from individuals possessing universal adaptations whose expression is contingent on the environment; (2) those that arise from contingencies with other traits; (3) those due to frequency–dependent selection; and (4) those due to variation over time and space in the optimum value of a trait. Next, we explore some examples of these individual differences.

Environmental Triggers of Individual Differences

According to one theory, the critical event of early father presence versus father absence triggers specific sexual strategies in individuals (Belsky, Steinberg, & Draper, 1991). Children who grow up in father-absent homes during the first five years of life, according to this theory, develop expectations that parental resources will not be reliably or predictably provided. Furthermore, these children come to expect that adult pair bonds will not be enduring. Such individuals cultivate a sexual strategy marked by early sexual maturation, early sexual initiation, and frequent partner switching—a strategy designed to produce a larger number of offspring. Extraverted and impulsive personality traits may accompany and facilitate this sexual strategy. Other people are perceived as untrustworthy and relationships as transitory. Resources sought from brief sexual encounters are opportunistically attained and immediately extracted.

In contrast, individuals who experience a reliable, investing father during the first five years of life, according to the theory, develop a different set of expectations about the nature and trustworthiness of others. People are seen as reliable and trustworthy, and relationships are expected to be enduring. These early environmental experiences predispose individuals toward a long-term mating strategy, marked by delayed sexual maturation;

a later onset of sexual activity; a search for long-term, securely attached adult relationships; and heavy investment in a small number of children.

There is some empirical support for this theory. Children from divorced homes, for example, are more sexually promiscuous than children from intact homes (Belsky et al., 1991). Furthermore, girls from father-absent homes reach menarche (age of first menstruation) earlier than girls from father-present homes (Kim, Smith, & Palermiti, 1997). Nonetheless, these findings are correlational, so causation cannot be inferred. Men or women who are genetically predisposed to pursue a short-term mating strategy may be more likely to get divorced and more likely to pass on to their children genes for that strategy (Bailey, Kirk, et al., 2000). However, despite the current lack of conclusive data (Del Giudice & Belsky, 2001), this theory nicely illustrates an evolutionary approach to the emergence of consistent individual differences—in this case, the effects of different environments on species-typical mechanisms.

Heritable Individual Differences Contingent on Other Traits

Another type of evolutionary analysis of personality involves evaluating one's personal strengths and weaknesses. Suppose, for example, that men could pursue two different strategies in social interaction—an aggressive strategy marked by the use of physical force and a nonaggressive strategy marked by cooperativeness. The success of these strategies, however, hinges on an individual's size, strength, and fighting ability. Those who happen to be muscular in body build can more successfully carry out an aggressive strategy than those who are skinny or chubby. If humans have evolved ways to evaluate themselves on their physical formidability, they can determine which social strategy is the more successful to pursue—an aggressive strategy or a cooperative strategy. Adaptive self-assessments, therefore, can produce stable individual differences in aggression or cooperativeness. In this example, the tendency toward aggression is not directly heritable. Rather, it is **reactively heritable**: it is a secondary consequence of heritable body build (Tooby & Cosmides, 1990). There is some evidence to support this idea that body build enters into a man's decision of whether to pursue an aggressive strategy (Ishikawa et al., 2001). Body weight, which is highly correlated with strength, predicts aggression both among pro hockey players and among young men more generally (Archer & Thanzami, 2009; Deaner et al., 2012). Physically stronger males are also quicker to anger and are more likely to believe in the utility of warfare (Sell et al., 2012). Even more interesting when it comes to personality, the combination of physical strength and physical attractiveness predicted the trait of extraversion—a prime example of how a personality trait can be contingent on other traits (Lukaszewski & Roney, 2011). The notion of self-assessment of heritable qualities remains a fascinating avenue for understanding the adaptive patterning of individual differences.

According to reactive heritability, a man with a slim, wiry build is less likely than a stocky man to engage in aggressive behaviour.

©Radius Images/Alamy Stock Photo

We also consider the possibility that depression may be maintained in the population due to adaptive contingencies on other traits. See Highlight On Canadian Research: Depression as an Evolved Mechanism: The Adaptive Rumination Hypothesis.

🍁 Highlight On Canadian Research

Depression as an Evolved Mechanism: The Adaptive Rumination Hypothesis

Depression is characterized by a sad mood, the inability to derive pleasure from daily activities, and changes in sleeping and eating patterns. Depression exists in every culture around the world, and it is estimated that about one in three people will suffer from depression at some point in their lives. Paul Andrews of McMaster University and his colleague Anderson Thomson (2009) suggest that depression is common and widespread because depressive symptoms represent an evolved adaptation designed to help people cope with social problems. Andrews developed the analytical rumination hypothesis to explain how depression can be adaptive (see Figure 8.4). According to the analytical rumination hypothesis, depression is triggered by complex social problems that are related to fitness and survival. Once triggered, depression causes changes in multiple bodily systems that promote rumination on the triggering problem in an attempt to solve it. Affected systems include attention and interest in hedonic activity (such as sleeping and eating). Alterations in both of these systems are proposed to help ensure that an individual is not distracted from trying to solve the problem that triggered the depressive episode. Supporters of the analytical rumination hypothesis suggest that over evolutionary time, depressed rumination has helped individuals solve complex social problems and is thus adaptive. Andrews argues that over evolutionary time humans have faced many social dilemmas as they have struggled to balance the maintenance of cooperative bonds with the pursuit of self-interests. For example, ancestral humans

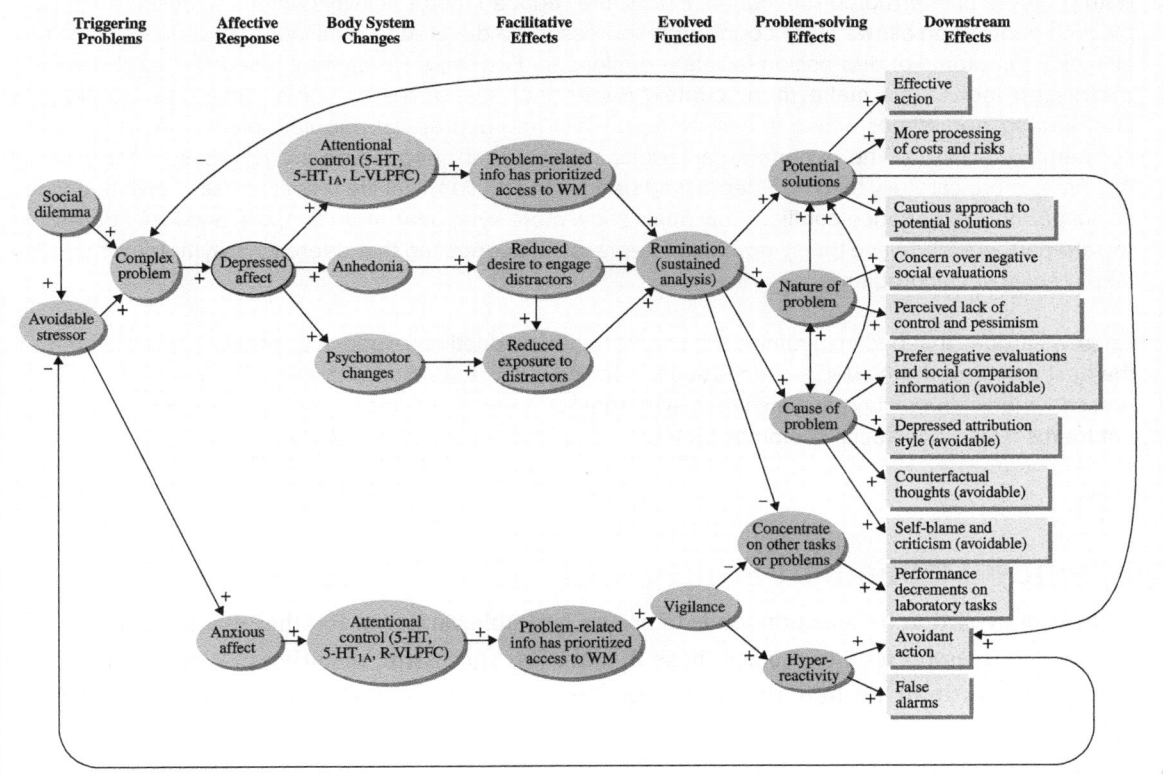

FIGURE 8.4 A diagram of the proposed causal relationships among the variables and constructs that are prominent in the analytical rumination hypothesis.

Source: Andrews, P. W., &, Thomson J. A., Jr. (2009). The bright side of being blue: Depression as an adaptation for analyzing complex problems. *Psychological Review, 116*(3), 620. © by American Psychological Association. Reprinted with permission.

would have benefited from food sharing but also benefited from competing with others when food was scarce. Andrews suggests that making the wrong decision when faced with a complex social problem could have significantly impacted fitness. If an individual was too cooperative they may not get adequate resources when food was scarce, while someone who never cooperated would not be able to secure a mate or benefit from the protection of a group. Individuals who gave careful consideration to social problems, Andrews argues, were those who were most likely to survive.

There is much support for Andrews's argument that depression is triggered by social stress. First, therapies that focus on problem solving are most effective at relieving the symptoms of depression. This suggests that a problem caused the symptoms in the first place. Second, depression is often linked to interpersonal conflict, and the symptoms of depression tend to be greatest when the conflict is with a close social partner. This suggests that depression is triggered by close interpersonal problems. Third, depressive symptoms are more common in women, and more common after puberty in populations all over the world. Andrews argues that this reflects the fact that female survival (more than male) is dependent on social support, both because of females' smaller size, and because females require social support during pregnancy, childbirth, and child rearing.

There is also much support to suggest that depressive symptoms facilitate problem solving. Neuroimaging studies have shown that depression activates the left ventrolateral prefrontal cortex (VLPFC), which increases the capacity of working memory. Anhedonia (which is a general loss of interest in eating, sexual activity, and socializing) and difficulty sleeping are both common symptoms of depression and both promote uninterrupted rumination. Finally, the reduced motor activity commonly observed in people with depression allows more cognitive resources to be devoted to rumination. Andrews argues that all major symptoms of depression facilitate rumination. Further, experimental research has shown that depressed individuals make more context-dependent responses to social dilemmas, sometimes cooperating, sometimes acting in self-interest, while non-depressed people typically opt only for the cooperative solution. The experimental results suggest that people who are depressed solve social dilemmas more carefully than non-depressed people. In addition, real-life research has shown that when social partners experience conflict, individuals show more sympathy, more support, and less aggression toward partners who have the symptoms of depression, suggesting that depressive symptoms may also help resolve social problems.

Andrews argues that because rumination seems to be an adaptive response to stressful social dilemmas, the best way to deal with depression is to allow an individual to ruminate. Andrews suggests that antidepressant medications may alleviate some symptoms of depression, but that because the medications do not themselves solve social dilemmas they can never actually cure depression.

Frequency–Dependent Strategic Individual Differences

The process of evolution by selection tends to use up heritable variation. In other words, heritable variants that are more successful tend to replace those that are less successful, resulting in species-typical adaptations that show little or no heritable variation. The universal human design is to have two eyes, for example.

In some contexts, two or more heritable variants can evolve within a population. The most obvious example is biological sex itself. Within sexually reproducing species, the two sexes exist in roughly equal numbers because of **frequency–dependent selection**. If one sex becomes rare relative to the other, evolution will produce an increase in the numbers of the rarer sex. Frequency–dependent selection causes the frequency of men and women to remain roughly equal.

Some propose that human individual differences in women's mating strategies have been caused by frequency–dependent selection (Gangestad & Simpson, 1990; Gangestad & Thornhill, 2008). They start with the observation that competition tends to be most intense among individuals who are pursuing the same mating strategy (Maynard Smith, 1982). This lays the groundwork for the evolution of alternative strategies.

According to Gangestad and colleagues, women's mating strategies should centre on two key qualities of potential mates: the parental investment a man could provide and the quality of his genes. A man who is able and willing to invest in a woman and her children can be an extraordinarily valuable reproductive asset. Similarly, independent of a man's ability to invest, women could benefit by selecting men who have high-quality genes, which can be passed down to her children. Men may carry genes for good health, physical attractiveness, or sexiness, which are then passed on to the woman's sons or daughters.

There may be a tradeoff, however, between selecting a man for his parenting abilities and selecting a man for his genes. Men who are highly attractive to many women, for example, may be reluctant to commit to any one woman. Thus, a woman who is seeking a man for his genes may have to settle for a short-term sexual relationship without parental investment.

These various selection forces, according to theorists, gave rise to two alternative female mating strategies. A woman seeking a high-investing mate would adopt a **restricted sexual strategy** marked by delayed intercourse and prolonged courtship. This would enable her to assess the man's level of commitment, detect the existence of prior commitments to other women or children, and simultaneously signal to the man her sexual fidelity and hence assure him of his paternity of future offspring.

A woman seeking a man for the quality of his genes, on the other hand, has less reason to delay sexual intercourse. A man's level of commitment to her is irrelevant, so prolonged assessment of his prior commitments is not necessary. This is referred to as an **unrestricted mating strategy**.

According to this theory, the two mating strategies of women—restricted and unrestricted—evolved and are maintained by frequency–dependent selection. As the number of unrestricted females in the population increases, the number of "sexy sons" in the next generation also increases. As the number of sexy sons increases, however, the competition among them also increases. Then, because there are so many sexy sons competing for a limited pool of women, their average success declines.

Now consider what happens when the number of restricted females seeking investing men increases in the population. Because there are now so many women seeking investment, they end up competing with each other for men willing to invest. Therefore, as the number of women seeking investment increases, the average success of their strategy declines. In short, the key idea behind frequency–dependent selection is that the success of each of the two strategies depends on how common each strategy is in the population. As a given strategy becomes more common, it becomes less successful; when it becomes less common, it becomes more successful.

There is some evidence for this theory (Thornhill & Gangestad, 2008). Individual differences in female mating strategy (restricted versus unrestricted) have been shown to be heritable. Women who pursue an unrestricted sexual strategy have been shown to place more value on qualities of men linked with good genes, such as physical attractiveness and good health (Greiling & Buss, 2000; Thornhill & Gangestad, 2008). There is also evidence that sexual strategy is somewhat flexible and responsive to aspects of the social situation.

Thus, people shift in the *restricted* direction of sociosexual desire when they enter a new relationship and become more *unrestricted* again when they break up with an existing romantic partner (Penke & Asendorpf, 2008a). Nonetheless, the dispositional components of sociosexual desire are reflected in the findings that unrestricted individuals tend to dissolve romantic relationships more quickly, become sexually involved with new partners more readily, and are more likely to be sexually unfaithful within existing mateships (Penke & Asendorpf, 2008a).

Another hypothesized example of personality differences originating from frequency–dependent selection centres on **psychopathy**—a cluster of personality traits marked by irresponsible and unreliable behaviour, egocentrism, impulsivity, an inability to form lasting relationships, superficial social charm, and a deficit in social emotions such as love, shame, guilt, and empathy (Cleckley, 1988; Lalumiere, Harris, & Rice, 2001). Psychopaths pursue a deceptive "cheating" strategy in their social interactions. Psychopathy is more common among men than women, but occurs in both sexes (Mealey, 1995). Psychopaths pursue a strategy of exploiting the cooperative proclivities of other people. After feigning cooperation, psychopaths typically defect, cheat, or violate the presumed relationship. This cheating strategy might be pursued by those who are unlikely to out-compete others in more mainstream or traditional social hierarchies (Mealey, 1995).

According to one evolutionary theory of this individual difference, a psychopathic strategy can be maintained by frequency–dependent selection. As the number of cheaters increases, and hence the average cost to the cooperative hosts increases, adaptations will evolve in cooperators to detect and punish cheating, thus lowering its overall effectiveness (Price, Cosmides, & Tooby, 2002). As psychopaths get detected and punished, the average success of the strategy declines. As long as the frequency of psychopaths is not too large, however, it can be maintained in a population composed primarily of cooperators.

There is some empirical evidence consistent with this theory of the evolution of this individual difference cluster. First, behavioural genetic studies suggest that psychopathy is moderately heritable (Willerman, Loehlin, & Horn, 1992). Second, psychopaths often pursue an exploitative sexual strategy, which could be the primary route by which genes for psychopathy increase or are maintained (Rowe, 2001). Psychopathic men, for example, tend to be more sexually precocious, have sex with higher numbers of women, have more illegitimate children, and are more likely to get divorced if they marry than nonpsychopathic men (Rowe, 2001). This short-term exploitative sexual strategy would increase in populations marked by high geographic mobility, in which the costs to reputation associated with this strategy are muted (Buss, 2012). This leads to the alarming idea that we may be witnessing an increase in psychopaths in modern times, as society becomes increasingly geographically mobile. Evidence supports the frequency–dependent theory of this individual difference cluster—that it is part of normal personality variation and is not due to "pathology" (Lalumiere et al., 2001). In sum, individual differences in this cluster of personality traits—unreliability, egocentrism, impulsivity, superficial social charm, and a deficit in empathy and other social emotions—may originate evolutionarily from frequency–dependent selection (see also Millon, 1990, 1999, for additional explorations of personality from an evolutionary perspective).

The most recent effort to explore individual differences from the perspective of frequency–dependent selection focuses on *life history strategy* (Figueredo et al., 2005a, 2005b, 2012; Gladden, et al., 2009; Rushton, 1985; Rushton, Cons, & Hur, 2008). According to this approach, individuals have evolved differences in the effort they allocate to reproductively relevant problems, such as survival, mating, and parenting. The core idea is that there are tradeoffs among these problems. Effort allocated to mating, for example, is effort taken away from parenting. On one end of the continuum, individuals favour what is called a *K-strategy*—greater effort is allocated to survival and heavy parenting over effort allocated to obtaining many mates (van der Linden et al., 2012). These high-K individuals are hypothesized to have formed strong attachments to their biological parents, avoid risk taking that would imperil survival, pursue long-term mating rather than short-term mating, and invest heavily in children. Low-K individuals, at the other end, are hypothesized to have formed weaker attachments to their biological parents, have a risk-taking personality, pursue short-term mating, and invest little in their children. Some empirical research supports the hypothesis that these variables do indeed covary or cluster together (Figueredo et al., 2005b; Gladden et al., 2009; Rushton et al., 2008; Templer, 2008). Others have criticized this theory on conceptual grounds (e.g., Penke et al., 2007).

In sum, we have examined several ways in which evolutionary psychologists study individual differences that might be adaptively patterned. First, different environments can direct individuals into different strategies, as in the case of father absence directing individuals toward a short-term sexual strategy. Second, there can be adaptive self-assessment of heritable traits, as is the case when individuals who are muscular in body build pursue a more aggressive strategy than those who are skinny or chubby. Third, two heritable strategies can be supported by frequency–dependent selection.

Fourth, the forces of selection can be different in different places, for example, or different times. This can result in evolved individual differences that are due to different evolutionary selection pressures in different local ecologies. We know, for example, that individual differences in the presence or absence of "sickle cells" in the blood, an adaptation to protect against mosquito-borne malaria, have been caused by different selection pressures in different local ecologies. Although no individual differences in personality have yet been empirically traced to this particular evolutionary source, it remains a viable theoretical possibility in the evolutionary arsenal of explanatory options.

 Concept Check

Match each trait to an evolutionary mechanism can well explain individual differences observed for that trait. Explain your answer.

1. *risk taking*

2. *jealousy*

3. *hair-trigger temper*

4. *cheating*

a. *differences in evoking conditions*

b. *variations in needs across time*

c. *frequency-dependent selection*

d. *a contingency with another trait*

The Big Five, Motivation, and Evolutionarily Relevant Adaptive Problems

Evolutionary psychologists have attempted to understand the importance of the Big Five personality dispositions within an evolutionary framework (Buss, 1991b, 1996; Buss & Greiling, 1999; Denissen & Penke, 2008a; Ellis, Simpson, & Campbell, 2002; Nettle, 2006). One approach views stable individual differences on the five-factor model as individual differences in "motivational reactions," or solutions, to particular classes of adaptive problems (Buss, 2009a; Denissen & Penke, 2008a, 2008b; Ellis et al., 2002; Nettle, 2006). Thus, agreeableness reflects differences in the proclivity to cooperate versus to act selfishly in conflicts over resources. Emotional stability reflects differences in sensitivity to the adaptive problem of social exclusion; high neuroticism, for example, can be beneficial in causing increased vigilance to social danger but at a cost of increased stress and depression (Nettle, 2006; Tamir et al., 2006). Extraversion reflects pursuit of a risk-taking social strategy marked by success in short-term mating versus adopting a more stable family life marked by long-term mating (Nettle, 2006). Conscientiousness reflects a long-term strategy of delayed gratification and tenacity of goal pursuit versus a more impulsive solution that involves grabbing immediate adaptive benefits.

Heritable individual differences on these dimensions can be maintained in the population because different levels are adaptive under different conditions; the optimum level *varies over time and space*. In technical terms, these personality differences are maintained by **balancing selection** (Penke et al., 2007), which occurs when genetic variation is maintained by selection because different levels on a trait dimension are adaptive in different environments.

A complementary evolutionary approach is to conceptualize major factors of personality as clusters of the most important features of the "adaptive landscape" of other people (Buss, 1991b, 2011). Humans, according to this perspective, have evolved "difference-detecting mechanisms" designed to notice and remember those individual differences that have the most relevance for solving social adaptive problems. Specifically, the five factors may provide important answers to questions such as these:

- Who is likely to rise in the social hierarchy and hence gain access to status and position in the social hierarchy? *(Dominance, Extraversion)*
- Who is likely to be a good cooperator and reciprocator, and who will be a loyal friend or romantic partner? *(Agreeableness)*
- Who will be reliable and dependable in times of need and work industriously to provide resources? *(Conscientiousness)*
- Who will drain my resources, encumber me with their problems, monopolize my time, and fail to cope well with adversity? *(Emotional Stability)*
- Who can I go to for sage advice? *(Openness, Intellect)*

In one study, Ellis and his colleagues (Ellis et al., 2002) developed a theoretical synthesis of the Big Five and evolutionary psychology, and conducted studies to see whether positioning on the five factors was correlated with these adaptively relevant individual differences. They included two additional individual differences that are relevant to romantic relationships: physical attractiveness (a sign of health and fertility) and physical prowess (a sign of the ability to protect a friend or romantic partner from danger). Using factor analysis, they discovered that the Big Five were indeed closely linked with solutions to these critical adaptive problems. In the context of romantic relationships, those who were high on agreeableness, for example, were also judged to be highly cooperative, devoted to their partners, and in love with their partners. Those who were high on extraversion were also judged to be socially ascendant, taking leadership roles in the group and showing proclivities to elevate themselves in social hierarchies. People highly responsible and efficient (signs of conscientiousness) were dependable in times of need, were well organized, and showed good potential for future earning.

This study is just the start of exploring the five-factor model within an evolutionary framework. But it does highlight the important point that individual differences of people who inhabit one's social environment are adaptively consequential. It's reasonable to hypothesize that humans have evolved psychological sensitivities to noticing, detecting, naming, and remembering precisely those individual differences that are most relevant to solving critical social adaptive problems—problems that are ultimately linked to survival and reproduction.

 Concept Check

Explain how a person's Big Five personality traits are linked to that person's ability to solve adaptive problems. What personality trait tends to be disliked and why?

Limitations of Evolutionary Psychology

Like all approaches to personality, the evolutionary perspective carries a number of important limitations. First, adaptations are forged over the long expanse of thousands or millions of generations, and we cannot go back in time and determine with absolute certainty what the precise selective forces on humans have been. Scientists make inferences about past environments and past selection pressures. Nonetheless, our current mechanisms provide windows for viewing the past. Our fear of snakes and heights, for example, suggests that these were hazards in our evolutionary past. Humans seem to come into the world prepared to learn some things quite easily (e.g., fear of snakes, spiders, and strangers) (Seligman & Hager, 1972). The intense pain we feel on being ostracized from a group suggests that group membership was critical to survival and reproduction in our evolutionary past. Learning more and more about our evolved mechanisms is thus a major tool for overcoming the limitation of sparse knowledge of the environments of our ancestors.

A second limitation is that evolutionary scientists have just scratched the surface of understanding the nature, details, and design features of evolved psychological adaptations. In the case of jealousy, for example, there is a lack of knowledge about the range of cues that trigger it, the precise nature of the thoughts and emotions that are activated when a person is jealous, and the range of behaviours, such as vigilance and violence, that are manifest outcomes. As more research is conducted, this limitation can be expected to be circumvented.

A third limitation is that modern conditions are undoubtedly different from ancestral conditions in many respects, so that what was adaptive in the past might not be adaptive in the present. Ancestral humans lived in small groups of perhaps 50 to 150 in the context of close extended kin (Dunbar, 1993). Today we live in large cities in the context of thousands of strangers. Thus, it's important to keep in mind that selection pressures have changed. In this sense, humans can be said to live in the modern world with an ancient brain.

A fourth limitation is that it is sometimes easy to come up with different and competing evolutionary hypotheses for the same phenomena. To a large extent, this is true of all of science, including personality theories that do not invoke evolutionary explanations. In this sense, the existence of competing theories is not an embarrassment but rather is an essential element of science. The critical obligation of scientists is to render their hypotheses in a sufficiently precise manner so that specific empirical predictions can be derived from them. In this way, the competing theories can be pitted against each other, and the hard hand of empirical evidence can be used to evaluate the competing theories.

Finally, evolutionary hypotheses have sometimes been accused of being untestable and hence unfalsifiable. The specific evolutionary hypotheses on aggression, jealousy, and so on presented in this chapter illustrate that this accusation is certainly false for some of them (see Buss, 2009a and 2012, for a list of others). Nonetheless, there is no doubt that some evolutionary hypotheses (like some standard "social" hypotheses) have indeed been framed in ways that are too vague to be of much scientific value. The solution to this problem is to hold the same high scientific standards for all competing theories. To be scientifically useful, theories and hypotheses should be framed as precisely as possible, along with attendant predictions, so that empirical studies can be conducted to test their merits.

 Concept Check

What is meant by the statement "humans live in a modern world with an ancient brain," and how does that limit the usefulness of evolutionary theories of personality?

Summary and Evaluation

Selection is the primary key to evolution, or change in life forms over time. Variants that lead to greater survival, reproduction, or the reproductive success of genetic relatives tend to be preserved and spread through the population.

Evolutionary psychology starts with three fundamental premises. First, adaptations are presumed to be domain specific; they are designed to solve specific adaptive problems. Adaptations good for one adaptive problem, such as food selection, offer little help in solving other adaptive problems, such as mate selection. Second, adaptations are numerous, corresponding to the many adaptive problems humans have faced over evolutionary history. Third, adaptations are functional. We cannot understand them unless we figure out what they were designed to do—the adaptive problems they were designed to solve.

The empirical science of testing evolutionary hypotheses proceeds in two ways. First, middle-level evolutionary theories, such as the theory of parental investment and sexual selection, can be used to derive specific predictions in a top-down method of investigation. Second, we can observe a phenomenon and then develop a theory about its function in a process known as bottom-up investigation. Using this method, specific predictions are then derived based on the theory about phenomena that have not yet been observed.

Evolutionary psychological analysis can be applied to all three levels of personality analysis: human nature, sex differences, and individual differences. At the level of human nature, there is good evidence that people have evolved the need to belong to groups; to help specific others, such as genetic relatives; and to possess basic emotions, such as happiness, disgust, anger, fear, surprise, sadness, and contempt. At the level of sex differences, men and women diverge only in domains in which they have faced recurrently different adaptive problems over evolutionary history. Examples include proclivities toward violence and aggression and specific mate preferences for qualities such as physical appearance and resources.

Individual differences can be understood from an evolutionary perspective using several approaches. First, individual differences can result from different environmental inputs into species-typical mechanisms. Second, individual differences can be contingent on other traits, such as when being large and strong inclines one to an aggressive disposition, whereas being small and weak inclines one to be less aggressive. Third, individual differences can result from frequency–dependent selection. Fourth, individual differences can be caused by variations over time or space in the optimum value for a trait.

The Big Five personality dispositions have begun to be examined through the lens of evolutionary psychology. One approach is to view individual differences as variations in strategic solutions to adaptive problems. Agreeableness, for example, reflects individual differences in adopting a strategy of cooperation versus acting selfishly when there are conflicts over resources. Emotional instability reflects high levels of vigilance to social threats, which can be adaptive under some circumstances but carries a cost of high levels of stress and fatigue. These adaptive individual differences can be maintained by balancing selection, which occurs when genetic variation is maintained by selection because different levels on a trait dimension are adaptive in different environments.

A second approach proposes that positioning on the five factors provides adaptively relevant information to solving key problems of social living: Whom can I trust for cooperation, devotion, and reciprocation (those high on agreeableness)? Who is likely to ascend social hierarchies (those high on extraversion)? Who will be likely to work hard, be dependable, and accrue resources over time (those high on conscientiousness)? Future evolutionary research will undoubtedly explore individual differences in the important social adaptive problems humans face in the context of group living.

Evolutionary psychology has several critical limitations at this stage of scientific development. The first is the lack of precise knowledge about the environments in which humans evolved and the selection pressures our ancestors faced. We are also limited in our knowledge about the nature, details, and workings of evolved mechanisms, including the features that trigger their activation and the manifest behaviour that they produce as output. Nonetheless, the evolutionary perspective adds a useful set of theoretical tools to the analysis of personality at the levels of human nature, sex differences, and individual differences.

 Concept Check

Provide an example of an aspect of human nature, a sex difference, and an individual difference that has been shaped by evolution.

Identify two major limitations of evolutionary psychology.

Key Terms

natural selection

hostile forces of nature

sexual selection

intrasexual competition

intersexual selection

genes

differential gene
reproduction

inclusive fitness theory

adaptive problem

xenophobia

byproducts of adaptations

evolutionary byproducts

evolutionary noise

domain specific

functionality

deductive reasoning
approach

inductive reasoning
approach

social anxiety

evolutionary-predicted sex
differences

effective polygyny

sexually dimorphic

reactively heritable

frequency–dependent
selection

restricted sexual strategy

unrestricted mating strategy

psychopathy

balancing selection

PART THREE

The Intrapsychic Domain

We now turn to the intrapsychic domain. This domain concerns the factors within the mind that influence behaviour, thoughts, and feelings. The pioneer of this domain was Sigmund Freud. Freud was a medical doctor and neurologist and was highly influenced by biology. He often applied biological metaphors to the mind—for example, proposing that the mind had separate "organ systems," which operated independently from each other yet that influenced each other. His goal was to analyze the elements within the mind and describe how the elements worked together. He named this enterprise psychoanalysis, which refers both to his intrapsychic theory of personality and his method of helping people change.

In this domain, we devote two chapters to psychoanalysis. In Chapter 9, we cover the foundations of classical psychoanalysis, primarily in terms of Freud's original ideas and formulations. We will present Freud's most influential ideas, including the notion that the human mind is divided into two parts, the conscious part and the unconscious part. Moreover, Freud proposed three forces in the human mind—the id, the ego, and the superego—and these forces were constantly interacting over taming the twin motives of sex and aggression, or the life and death instincts. We also present Freud's ideas on personality development and how he stressed the importance of childhood events in determining the adult personality.

Some of Freud's ideas, such as repression, unconscious processing, and recalled memories, have stood the test of time and are active research topics in personality today. However, many students of Freud have modified some of his ideas, so we devote Chapter 10 to a discussion of contemporary topics in psychoanalytic theory. These include the idea of personality development as continuing through adulthood rather than stopping in childhood as Freud originally proposed. Another key development in contemporary psychoanalysis concerns the importance of a child's attachments to caregivers in influencing his or her subsequent relationships.

The intrapsychic domain differs from all the other domains in that it is concerned with the forces within the mind that work together and interact with each other and the environment. To some extent, this domain is similar to the biological domain in that the biological domain also emphasizes forces within the person. However, in the intrapsychic domain, the concern is with aspects of *psychic* functioning. In the biological domain, we are concerned with aspects of *physical* functioning, such as the brain, genes, and the chemicals in the bloodstream.

A fundamental assumption of psychologists working in the intrapsychic domain is that there are areas of the mind that are outside awareness. Within each person, there is a part of him- or herself that even he or she does not know about. This is called the unconscious mind. Moreover, the unconscious mind is thought to have a life of its own, with its own motivation, its own will, and its own energy.

Another assumption within the intrapsychic domain is that most things do not happen by chance. That is, every behaviour, every thought, and every experience means something or reveals something about the person's personality. A slip of the tongue, for example, occurs not by accident, but because of an intrapsychic conflict. A person forgets someone's name not by accident, but because of something about the person whose name cannot be remembered. Or a person dreams of flying, not because dreams are random, but because of an unconscious wish or desire being expressed in the dream. Everything a person does, says, or feels has meaning and can be analyzed in terms of intrapsychic elements and forces.

We will also examine the life and ideas of one of Freud's more famous female students, Karen Horney. Freud's ideas have been criticized for neglecting women, and Horney was among the first to take women's issues seriously from a psychoanalytic perspective. She developed a feminist interpretation of Freud's ideas.

In Chapter 11, we examine work on motivational aspects of personality. Here psychologists emphasize the common motives that most people have to varying degrees. Individual differences in motives help psychologists answer the question "Why do people do what they do?" The three most common motives studied in this domain are the desire to achieve, the need to have close relationships with other people, and the motive to have power and influence over others. We present some of the basic findings on each of these three motives, as well as describe a projective technique that has been developed for assessing these needs. We also describe a contemporary notion that suggests that motives can be conscious or unconscious and that unconscious motives affect different kinds of behaviour than conscious motives.

Most of the research on motives emphasizes deficit motives—that is, motives that arise because something is lacking. There is, however, the notion that one particular motive is not based on a deficit, but rather is based on growth and change. This motive refers to the more abstract need to become who we are, to actualize our potential as the persons we were meant to be. The need to self-actualize can also operate outside awareness, and we may engage in certain behaviours not because we have thought everything through, but because it just feels like the right thing to be doing at the moment.

In Part Three of this book, we explore some of the major ideas and findings from the intrapsychic domain of personality. As you read, it is important to keep in mind that the intrapsychic domain, as well as all the other domains, refers to just one set of factors that influence personality. Personality is determined by many factors; like a jigsaw puzzle, it is made up of many parts. Let's now consider the part that dwells in the deeper reaches of the human mind.

Psychoanalytic Approaches to Personality

The Intrapsychic Domain

In 1983, a young woman (we'll call her *Sandra*) was referred to Dr. Voss, a psychologist at the Kitchener-Waterloo Hospital in Ontario, following a recent separation from her husband. Seeking help for her depression, the possibility of Sandra having experienced incest as a child was brought to the attention of Dr. Voss by

earlier psychiatric records. Although Sandra had
some general recollection of such childhood experiences, she resisted their discussion in therapy. It was
not until she remarried later that year that she began
exploring her past by attending local support groups.
In her subsequent meetings with a marital and family therapist, Dr. Pressman, Sandra would finally
begin realizing—and *remembering*—the full extent
of her incestuous abuse during childhood. What
Sandra would remember in therapy was a long history of sexual abuse perpetrated by her father, when
she was just a young girl.

*Events from childhood often form the topics for
discussion during therapy sessions.*
©Lisa F. Young/Alamy

Although she had always maintained some awareness of the abuse, Sandra had remained unaware of
the extent of her victimization, as well as the ways in which it had impacted her life as an adult. It was revealed in therapy that Sandra was sexually abused by her father from a very young age. He began having intercourse with her between the ages of 10 and 11, enticing her with treats while threatening her with the
possibility of her mother's suicide if she were to disclose her experiences. Sandra had reason to take these
threats seriously, given her mother's history of displaying irrational and violent behaviour. In spite of this,
Sandra did try to tell her mother several times, but she claimed her mother was unresponsive to her suggestions. When she was 16, she reached out to a high school guidance counsellor, which resulted in her referral
to a local psychiatrist. After interviewing both Sandra and her father, the psychiatrist concluded that the
claims had been falsified.

It ultimately took another decade for the events of her childhood to be fully realized by Sandra. With the help
of a support group and therapist in 1983, Sandra began to finally understand that the actions of her father
were in fact abusive. She also began to recall the details of the events, which she had previously blocked out by
imagining herself as an inanimate object during their occurrence, which Dr. Pressman described as a form of
dissociation. According to Dr. Pressman, Sandra had only a vague recollection of the events that took place in
childhood, and she had seen herself as largely responsible. The guilt that she felt from the experiences, as well
as the lack of adequate response from those to whom she disclosed, contributed further to the repression of
her memories. Once Sandra began to recall many of the details of her abusive past, she was finally able to
make the connection between those events and her depression in adulthood. At the age of 28, Sandra sued her
father for damages arising from the incest and for breach of a parent's fiduciary duty. Before the Supreme
Court of Canada, a jury found that the accused had indeed sexually assaulted his daughter, and assessed damages in the amount of $50,000. Although the judge in the trial determined that too much time had passed
since the events took place, the Ontario Court of Appeal disagreed and awarded the damages. The Court of
Appeal concluded that the new awareness of repressed memories constituted reasonable discoverability not
restricted by the statute of limitations.

Is it possible that a person can forget something as traumatic as the details of sexual abuse? Can a forgotten
memory lie dormant for years, only to be aroused later by an event, such as a chance phone call? Once aroused,
can such a memory cause a person to start having difficulties, such as feelings of depression and irritability,
without his or her knowing the cause of those difficulties? Some psychologists believe that people are
sometimes unaware of the reasons for their own problematic behaviours. When treating a person for a

psychological problem, some therapists believe that the cause of the problem resides in the person's unconscious, the part of the mind outside the person's immediate awareness. They contend that a memory of a past traumatic event can be completely forgotten yet nevertheless cause a psychological problem years later (Bass & Davis, 1988). Furthermore, such therapists believe that if they can help make this unconscious memory conscious—that is, if they can help the patient recall a forgotten traumatic memory—they can put the patient on the road to recovery (Baker, 1992).

This perspective on the causes and cures of psychological problems has its origin in a theory of personality developed by Sigmund Freud (1856–1939), commonly called psychoanalysis. In this chapter, we examine the basic elements of classical psychoanalytic theory and explore some of the empirical studies conducted to test certain aspects of the theory. We consider the scientific evidence for the repression of childhood memories, for the concept of unconscious motivation, and for other aspects of psychoanalytic theory. Whereas many of Freud's ideas have not stood the test of time, other ideas are still with us and are topics of contemporary research. Because this theory is so much the result of one person's thinking, let's first look at a brief biographical sketch of Freud.

Sigmund Freud: A Brief Biography

Although Freud was born in 1856 in Freiberg, Moravia (now part of the Czech Republic), his family moved to Vienna when he was 4 years old, and he spent virtually the remainder of his life there. Freud excelled in school and obtained his medical degree from the University of Vienna. Although he started out as a researcher

in neurology, he realized that he could make more money to support his wife and growing family if he entered into private medical practice. After studying hypnosis with Jean-Martin Charcot in Paris, Freud returned to Vienna and started a private practice, treating patients with "nervous disorders." During that time, Freud began developing the idea that portions of the human mind were outside conscious awareness. The unconscious is the part of the mind about which the conscious mind has no awareness. Freud sought to study empirically the implications of the unconscious for understanding people's lives and their problems with living. From his early contact with patients, Freud began to surmise that the unconscious mind operated under its own power, subject to its own motivations and according to its own logic. Freud devoted the rest of his career to exploring the nature and logic of the unconscious mind.

Freud's first solo-authored book, *The Interpretation of Dreams,* was published in 1900. In it, he described how the unconscious mind was expressed in dreams and how dreams contained clues to our innermost secrets, desires,

Sigmund Freud at age 82. He most likely insisted this photo be taken from the side in order not to show the ravages of his jaw and throat cancer, and after the many operations he underwent in an unsuccessful attempt to cure that disease. He died in 1939, less than a year after this photo was taken.
©Keystone/Archive Photos/Getty Images

and motives. The analysis of dreams became a cornerstone of his treatment. This book sold poorly at first but nevertheless attracted the attention of other medical doctors seeking to understand psychological problems. By 1902, there was a small group of followers (e.g., Alfred Adler) who met with Freud every Wednesday evening. At these meetings, Freud talked about his theory, shared insights, and discussed patients' progress, all the while smoking one of the 20 or so cigars he smoked each day. During this period, Freud was systematically building his theory and testing its acceptance by knowledgeable peers. By 1908, the membership of the Wednesday Psychological Circle had grown significantly, prompting Freud to form the Vienna Psychoanalytic Society (Grosskurth, 1991).

In 1909, Freud made his only visit to the United States, to present a series of lectures on psychoanalysis at the invitation of psychologist G. Stanley Hall, who was then president of Clark University. Rosenzweig (1994) describes Freud's trip to the United States in fascinating detail. In 1910, the International Psychoanalytic Association was formed. Freud's theories were gaining recognition around the world.

Freud and his work drew both praise and criticism. Whereas some accepted his ideas as brilliant insights into the workings of human nature, others opposed his views on various scientific and ideological grounds. To some, his treatment approach (the so-called talking cure) was absurd. Freud's theory that the adult personality was a result of how the person as a child coped with his or her sexual and aggressive urges was considered politically incorrect by the standards of Victorian morality. Even some of the founding members of his Vienna Psychoanalytic Society grew to disagree with developments in his theory. Nevertheless, Freud continued to refine and apply his theory, writing 20 books and numerous papers during his career.

Germany invaded Austria in 1938, and the Nazis began their persecution of the Jews there. Freud, who was Jewish, had reasons to fear the Nazis. The Nazi party burned his books and the books of other modern intellectuals. With the assistance of wealthy patrons, Freud, his wife, and their six children fled to London. Freud died the following year after a long, painful, and disfiguring battle with cancer of the jaw and throat.

Freud's London house continued to be occupied by his daughter, Anna Freud, herself a prominent psychoanalyst, until her death in 1982. The house is now part of the Freud Museum in London. Visitors can walk through Freud's library and study, which remain largely as he left them when he died. The study, which is where Freud treated his patients, still contains his celebrated couch, covered with an Oriental rug. It also contains the many ancient artifacts and small statues and icons that seemed to fascinate him and reveal his secret passion for archeology. Freud has been referred to as the original archeologist of the human mind.

Fundamental Assumptions of Psychoanalytic Theory

Freud's model of human nature relied on the notion of **psychic energy** to motivate all human activity. What were the forces that motivated people to do one thing and not another or that motivated people to do anything at all? Freud proposed a source of energy that is within each person and used the term *psychic energy* to refer to this wellspring of motivation. Freud believed that psychic energy operated according to the law of conservation of energy: The amount of psychic energy an individual possessed remained constant throughout life. Personality change was viewed as a redirection of a person's psychic energy.

Basic Instincts: Sex and Aggression

What was the basic source of psychic energy? Freud believed that there were strong innate forces that provided *all* the energy in the psychic system. He called these forces **instincts**. Freud's original theory of instincts was profoundly influenced by Darwin's theory of evolution. Darwin had published his book on evolution just a few years after Freud was born. In Freud's initial formulation, there were two fundamental categories of instincts: self-preservation instincts and sexual instincts. Curiously, these corresponded exactly to two major components of Darwin's theory of natural selection: selection by survival and selection by reproduction. Thus Freud's initial classification of instincts could have been borrowed from Darwin's two forms of evolution by selection (Ritvo, 1990).

In his later formulations, however, Freud collapsed the self-preservation and sexual instincts into one, which he called the life instinct. And due in part to his witnessing the horrors of World War I, he developed the idea of a death instinct. Freud postulated that humans had a fundamental instinct toward destruction and that this instinct was often manifest in aggression toward others. The two instincts were usually referred to as **libido** for the life instinct and **thanatos** for the death instinct. Although the libido was generally considered sexual, Freud also used this term to refer to any need-satisfying, life-sustaining, or pleasure-oriented urge. Similarly, thanatos was considered to be the death instinct, but Freud used this term in a broad sense to refer to any urge to destroy, harm, or aggress against others or oneself. Freud wrote more about the libido early in his career, when this issue was perhaps relevant to his own life. Later in his career, Freud wrote more about thanatos, when he faced his own impending death.

Although Freud initially believed that the life and death instincts worked to oppose one another, he later argued that they could combine in various ways. Consider the act of eating. Eating obviously serves the life instinct, entailing the consumption of nutrients necessary for survival. At the same time, eating also involves acts of tearing, biting, and chewing, which Freud thought could be seen as aggressive manifestations of thanatos. As another example, Freud viewed rape as an expression of extreme death instinct, directed toward another person in a manner that is fused with sexual energy. The combination of erotic and aggressive instincts into a single motive is a particularly volatile mixture.

Because each person possesses a fixed amount of psychic energy, according to Freud, the energy used to direct one type of behaviour is not available to drive other types of behaviours. Those who direct their death instinct into a socially acceptable channel, such as competitive sports, have less energy to expend toward more destructive manifestations of this instinct. Because psychic energy exists in a fixed and limited amount within each person, it can be directed and redirected in various ways.

Unconscious Motivation: Sometimes We Don't Know Why We Do What We Do

According to Freud, the human mind consists of three parts. The **conscious** mind is the part that contains all the thoughts, feelings, and perceptions that you are presently aware of. Whatever you are currently perceiving or thinking about is in your conscious mind. These thoughts represent only a small fraction of the information available to you.

You also have a vast number of memories, dreams, and thoughts that you could easily bring to mind if you so desired. What were you wearing yesterday? What was the name of your best friend in Grade 7? What is the earliest memory you have of your mother? This information is stored in the **preconscious** mind. Any piece of information that you are not presently thinking about, but that could easily be retrieved and made conscious, is found in the preconscious mind.

The **unconscious** is the third and, according to Freud, largest part of the human mind. The metaphor of an iceberg is often used to describe the topography of the mind. The part of the iceberg above the water represents the conscious mind. The part that you can see just below the water surface is the preconscious mind. And the part of the iceberg totally hidden from view (the vast majority of it) represents the unconscious mind. In Figure 9.1, we present a diagram of the iceberg metaphor, which illustrates the relationships among levels of consciousness and the three components of the psyche.

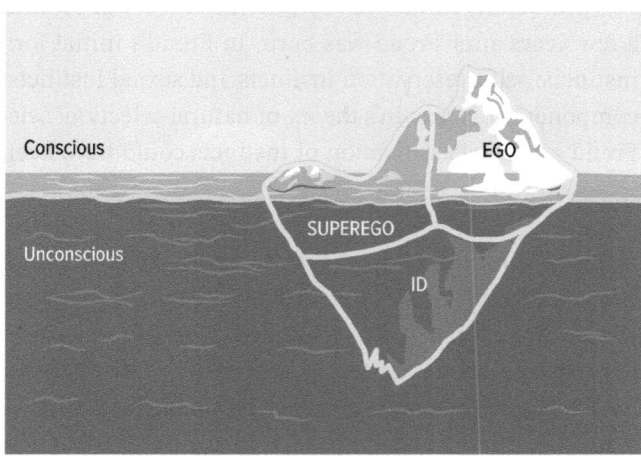

FIGURE 9.1 The iceberg metaphor is often used to describe the topography of the mind according to Freud. As you can see, the id is completely submerged, residing entirely in the unconscious mind. The superego is only slightly accessible by the conscious mind, while the ego is the part of personality that we are most aware of and that we most identify with. It represents the "tip of the iceberg."
Source: ©paul kline/Getty Images. Overlay art and text created by McGraw-Hill Education.

Society does not allow people to express freely all of their sexual and aggressive instincts. Individuals must learn to control their urges. One way to control these urges, according to Freud, is to keep them from entering conscious awareness in the first place. Consider a child who has gotten extremely angry with a parent. This child might have a fleeting wish that the parents die. Such thoughts would be very distressing to a child—so distressing that they might be held back from conscious awareness and banished instead to the unconscious, the part of the mind holding thoughts and memories about which the person is unaware. All kinds of unacceptable sexual and aggressive urges, thoughts, and feelings might accumulate in the unconscious during the course of a typical childhood.

❓ Exercise

Think back to the first house or apartment you lived in as a child. If you are like most people, you can probably remember as far back as your fourth or fifth year of age. Try to recall the structure of the house or apartment, the location of the rooms relative to each other. Draw a floor plan, starting with the basement if there was one, then the first floor, then the upstairs rooms (if the house had a second floor). On your floor plan, label each room. Now think about each room, letting the memories of events that happened in each of them come back to you. It is likely that you will recall some people and events that you have not thought about for a decade or more. You also might notice that many of your memories have an emotional quality; some memories are pleasant, whereas others are unpleasant. The memories that you can bring to conscious awareness are in your preconscious. You may have memories of events that occurred that do not come back to you during this exercise because they are in your unconscious.

Psychic Determinism: Nothing Happens by Chance

Freud maintained that nothing happens by chance or by accident. There is a reason behind every act, thought, and feeling. Everything we do, think, say, and feel is an expression of the mind—the conscious, preconscious, or unconscious mind. In his book *The Psychopathology of Everyday Life,* Freud introduced the idea that the little "accidents" of daily life are often expressions of the motivated unconscious, such as calling someone by the wrong name, missing an appointment, and breaking something that belongs to another. Once, a psychology professor referred to Sigmund Freud as "Sigmund Fraud." Such mix-ups can often be embarrassing, but, according to Freud, they represent the motivated activity of the unconscious. There is a reason for every slip of the tongue, for being late, for forgetting a person's name, and for breaking something that belongs to another. The reasons can be discovered if the contents of the unconscious can be examined.

Freud taught that most symptoms of mental illnesses are caused by unconscious motivations. Freud provided detailed case histories of 12 patients, as well as dozens of shorter discussions of specific patients. In these case studies, he found support for his theory that psychological problems were caused by unconscious memories or desires. For example, Freud wrote about the case of Anna O. Although Freud did not directly treat or even meet Anna O., her physician, Joseph Breuer, consulted with Freud.

At the time, Anna O. was a 21-year-old woman who had fallen ill while taking care of her sick father who eventually died of tuberculosis. Anna's illness began with a severe cough, and later included the loss of movement in her right side, disturbances of vision, hearing, and the inability to drink liquids. Dr. Breuer diagnosed Anna O.'s illness as hysteria and developed a form of therapy that appeared effective in relieving her symptoms. This form of therapy consisted of Breuer talking with Anna O. about her symptoms, and in particular about her memories of events that happened before the onset of the symptoms. For example, in talking about her severe cough, they talked about her memories of caring for her father, and the severe cough he had from his tuberculosis. As she explored these memories, and especially her feelings toward her father and about his death, her own cough lessened and disappeared. Similarly, when talking about her inability to drink liquids (she had been quenching her thirst with fruit and melons), she suddenly recalled the memory of seeing a dog drink from a woman's glass, an incident that completely disgusted her at the time but about which she had forgotten. Soon after describing this memory, she asked for a drink of water and immediately regained her ability to drink liquids.

To Breuer, and to Freud, hysterical symptoms did not occur by chance. Rather, they were physical expressions of repressed traumatic experiences. From the experience treating Anna O., Breuer concluded that the way to cure hysterical symptoms was to help the person recall the memory of the incident that had originally led to the symptoms. By the patient's recalling the traumatic incident (e.g., her father's death), an emotional catharsis or release can be achieved through the expression of any feelings associated with that memory. This then removes the cause of the symptom and hence the symptom disappears.

Freud adopted and refined the technique developed by Breuer for effecting the "talking cure." Freud believed that for a psychological symptom to be cured, the unconscious cause of the symptom must first be discovered. Often the process involves discovering a hidden memory of an unsettling, disagreeable, or even repulsive experience that has been repressed or pushed into the unconscious (Masson, 1984). Freud always acknowledged the importance of the case of Anna O. on his thinking, and gave credit to the careful observations of Dr. Breuer:

> *If it is a merit to have brought psychoanalysis into being, that merit is not mine. I had no share in its earliest beginnings. I was a student and working for my final examinations at the time when another Viennese*

physician, Dr. Josef Breuer, first made use of this procedure on a girl who was suffering from hysteria. (From Freud's lectures presented at Clark University in Massachusetts, 1909.)

Freud is uncharacteristically modest in the preceding quote. He adapted the notions of symptom formation and the talking cure from Breuer, and combined these with other ideas about the unconscious, about repression, about stages of development and many other notions, and, from these, he formulated a grand theory of personality that has yet to be rivaled by a single unitary theory of personality.

Although we examine contemporary perspectives on the unconscious further in Chapter 10, there are two lines of research that may support the notion of an active and influential unconscious. We discuss them next in A Closer Look: Examples of the Unconscious: Blindsight and Deliberation-without-Attention.

 # A Closer Look

Examples of the Unconscious: Blindsight and Deliberation-without-Attention

Following an injury or stroke that damages the primary vision centre in the brain, people will lose some or all of their ability to see. In this kind of blindness the eyes still work to bring information into the brain; it is just that the brain centre responsible for object recognition fails. People who suffer this kind of "cortical" blindness often display an interesting capacity to make judgments about objects that they truly cannot see. This phenomenon is termed **blindsight**, and it has fascinated psychologists since it was first documented in the 1960s (Leopold, 2012).

Imagine having a person with cortical blindness as a subject. You could hold a red ball in front of her open eyes and ask if she can see it. She would reply no, which is consistent with the fact that she is blind. Now you ask her to point to the red ball (which she has just denied seeing). What happens? She points directly to the red ball even though she does not have the ability to see it!

Blindsight is taken as evidence of the unconscious. Here one part of the mind knows about something that another part of the mind does not know about. There are many demonstrations of people with blindsight. For example, when an object is placed in front of a person with blindsight—that is, a person who does not know for sure whether it is there or not—that person can guess the colour of that object at levels much better than merely by chance. In other words, such a condition illustrates that information that is unconscious (whether an object is or is not in front of the person) is actually being processed somewhere in the mind (because the person knows the colour of objects that are presented).

An explanation for such "unconscious" perception has been offered in terms of nerve pathways from the eyes into the brain. The optic nerve carries information from the eye into the brain, and the majority of this information is transferred to the primary visual centre in the striate cortex. However, pathways split off of the optic nerve before getting to the visual centre and carry some of this visual information to other parts of the brain. These other centres may be involved in movement recognition or colour recognition or even emotional evaluation. If the vision centre were completely destroyed, the person would not recognize *what* the object was, but the person might know if it was moving or how they felt about it.

One of the most interesting and robust examples of blindsight concerns the perception of the emotional significance of something that one does not see. In one study, a person with blindsight underwent a conditioning procedure where a visual cue that the person could not see (a picture of a circle) was accompanied by an unpleasant shock, whereas other visual cues (pictures of squares, rectangles, etc.) were not paired with shock. Following a period of conditioning, the stimuli shapes were later "shown" to the blind subject, and the subject exhibited a fear response to the circle but not the squares or rectangles (Hamm et al., 2003). These researchers argue that emotional conditioning does not require a conscious representation in the mind of the subject. Other studies of people with cortical blindness demonstrate that, when "shown" pictures of facial expressions, they can "guess" the emotions expressed in the faces even when they cannot see the faces being presented. Obviously, a lot of emotional processing occurs at some level in the brain that does not involve the primary visual centre. People could have feelings about (i.e., like or dislike) something that they are not even aware of.

Another example of the unconscious at work concerns the phenomenon of **deliberation-without-attention**, or the "let me sleep on it" effect. The notion here is, if a person confronted with a difficult decision can put it out of their conscious mind for a period of time, then the unconscious mind will continue to deliberate on it outside of the person's awareness, helping them to arrive at a "sudden" and often correct decision sometime later. This is sometimes called "unconscious decision making."

The phenomenon of unconscious decision making was the topic of several clever studies recently published in the prestigious journal *Science* by a team of Dutch researchers (Dijksterhuis et al., 2006). These researchers hypothesized that, for simple decisions, conscious deliberation would work best, but when decisions were complex, involving many factors, then unconscious deliberation would work best. They presented subjects with the task of deciding on the best car out of four different cars. Subjects in the simple condition considered 4 attributes of the cars, whereas subjects in the complex condition considered 12 attributes of the cars. In all cases, one car was characterized by 75 percent positive attributes (i.e., the best car), two by 50 percent positive attributes, and one by 25 percent positive attributes. After reading all the information about the cars, half of the subjects were assigned to the conscious deliberation condition and the other half were assigned to the unconscious deliberation condition. In the conscious deliberation condition, subjects were asked to think about the information for four minutes before deciding on the best car. In the unconscious deliberation condition, subjects were distracted for four minutes by being asked to solve anagram puzzles, then immediately asked to decide on the best car.

As shown in Figure 9.2, in the simple decision condition, with only 4 attributes to consider on each car, subjects who consciously deliberated made the best decisions. However, when the decision was complex, involving 12 different attributes of the cars, subjects in the "unconscious" deliberation condition made the best decisions. The authors demonstrate similar effects in three additional studies. Even though the studies concern consumer items (e.g., cars), there is reason to believe that the unconscious deliberation effect might apply to any type of decision (e.g., what career path to pursue, whom to vote for, whom to marry, etc.). The authors (Dijksterhuis et al., 2006) argue that, with any decision, it would "benefit the individual to think consciously about simple matters and to delegate thinking about more complex matters to the unconscious" (p. 1007).

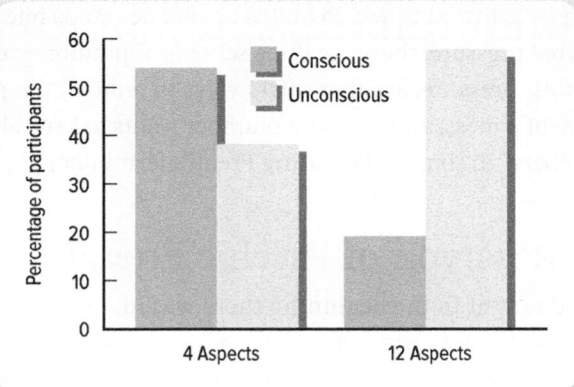

FIGURE 9.2 Percentage of participants who chose the most desirable car as a function of complexity of decision and mode of thought.

Research on deliberation-without-attention is not without it critics. Some have argued that the results do not prove that the subjects' "unconscious" actively arrives at the correct decision (Aczel et al., 2011). Others have argued that decisions are memory based, and thus offer an explanation for the findings that do not rely on anything like an "unconscious" (Lassiter et al., 2009). As you will see throughout this chapter, much that is connected with psychoanalysis is contentious and a matter of debate. Nevertheless, psychoanalytic ideas are stimulating research into novel and interesting phenomena.

 Concept Check

In your own words, describe Freud's organization of the mind, noting the relationships among the conscious and unconscious as well as the id, ego, and superego.

What is psychic determinism, and why is it important to Freud's ideas regarding the mind and human behaviour?

Structure of Personality

Psychoanalytic personality theory describes how people cope with their sexual and aggressive instincts within the constraints of a civilized society. Sexual and aggressive instincts often lead to drives and urges that conflict with society and with reality. One part of the mind creates these urges; another part has a sense of what civilized society expects; and another part tries to satisfy the urges within the bounds of reality and society. How is it that the mind can have so many parts, and how do these parts work together to form personality?

A metaphor may be helpful in answering this question. Think of the mind as a plumbing system, which contains water under pressure. The pressure is the metaphor for the psychic energy from the sexual and aggressive instincts, which builds up and demands release. According to Freud's theory, when it comes to this internal pressure, there are three schools of plumbing: one plumber suggests that we open all the valves at the slightest pressure, another offers ways to redirect the pressure so that the strain is relieved without making much of a mess, and the third plumber wants to keep all the valves closed. Let's discuss each of these "psychic plumbers" in some detail, using Freud's terminology.

Id: Reservoir of Psychic Energy

Freud taught in the beginning there was id, the most primitive part of the human mind. Freud saw the **id** as something we are born with and as the source of all drives and urges. Using the plumbing metaphor, the id is the plumber who wants to let off all pressure at the slightest hint of strain or tension. The id is like a spoiled child—selfish, impulsive, and pleasure-loving. According to Freud, the id operates according to the **pleasure principle**, which is the desire for immediate gratification. The id cannot tolerate any delays in satisfying its urges. During infancy, the id dominates. When an infant sees an attractive toy, it will reach for the toy and will cry and fuss if it cannot get it. Infants can sometimes appear unreasonable in their demands. Because the id operates according to the pleasure principle, it does not listen to reason, does not follow logic, has no values or morals (other than immediate gratification), and has very little patience.

The id also operates with **primary process thinking**, which is thinking without logical rules of conscious thought or an anchor in reality. Dreams and fantasies are examples of primary process thinking. Although primary process thought does not follow the normal rules of reality (e.g., in dreams, people fly and walk through walls), Freud believed that there were principles at work in primary process thought and that these principles could be discovered. If an urge from the id requires an external object or person, and that object or person is not available, the id may create a mental image or fantasy of that object or person to satisfy its needs. Mental energy is invested in that fantasy, and the urge is temporarily satisfied. This process is called **wish fulfillment**, whereby something unavailable is conjured up and the image of it is temporarily satisfying. Someone might be very angry, for example, but the target of the anger is too powerful to attack. In this case, engaging in wish fulfillment might produce an imagined fantasy of revenge for past wrongs. This strategy of wish fulfillment works only temporarily to gratify the id because the need is not satisfied in reality. A person must find other ways to gratify id urges or hold them in check.

Ego: Executive of Personality

The ego is the plumber who works to redirect the pressure produced by the id instincts into acceptable or at least less problematic outlets. The **ego** is the part of the mind that constrains the id to reality. According to Freud, it develops within the first two or three years of life (after the "terrible twos"). The ego operates according to the **reality principle**. The ego understands that the urges of the id are often in conflict with social and physical reality. A child cannot just grab a candy bar off the shelf at the grocery store or hit his sister whenever she makes him angry. Although such acts might reduce immediate tension in the child, they conflict with society's and parents' rules about stealing and beating up little sisters. The ego understands that such actions can lead to problems and that *direct* expression of id impulses must therefore be avoided, redirected, or post-

In the psychoanalytic theory of personality, conflicts between children and parents are normal, necessary, and an important part of personality development.
©Ingram Publishing/AGE Fotostock

poned. We explore the related notion of *ego depletion*, which occurs as a result of such attempts at self-control, in A Closer Look: Ego Depletion: Is Self-Control a Limited Resource?

The ego works to postpone the discharge of id urges until an appropriate situation arises. The ego engages in **secondary process thinking**, which is the development of strategies for solving problems and obtaining satisfaction. Often this process takes into account the constraints of physical reality about when and how to express a desire or an urge. For example, teasing one's sister is more acceptable than hitting her, and this can perhaps satisfy the id's aggressive urge almost as well. There may be some urges, however, that simply remain unacceptable according to social reality or conventional morality, *regardless* of the situation. The third part of the mind, the superego, is responsible for upholding social values and ideals.

 **A Closer Look**

Ego Depletion: Is Self-Control a Limited Resource?

In Freud's structure of the mind, the ego is that part that must deal with reality by resolving conflicts between inner and outer pressures. For example, a man walking through a "red-light" district in a city might feel the urge of his id to walk over to a sex worker, and he might simultaneously feel the urge from his superego to find a church. It is up to his ego, however, to start him moving in one direction or the other. Freud also taught that the mind is a closed energy system; the more energy used by one self-control activity, the less energy is available for other self-control activities. This implies that the psychic energy used to resolve a conflict among reality, the id, and the superego would leave less psychic energy available for resolving other conflicts.

Psychologist Roy Baumeister and his colleagues have subjected this basic notion—that psychic energy can be depleted by efforts toward self-control, leaving less energy available for subsequent self-control situations—to a series of experimental tests. In general, the findings are supportive of Freud's basic notion about the ego and psychic energy. Let's take a closer look at some of these studies.

In one study, participants signed up for a study on taste perception and were asked to skip a meal just prior to their session (to ensure that they would be hungry). Arriving at the laboratory, participants were left alone in a room; on the table was a bowl of radishes and a stack of freshly baked chocolate chip cookies (Baumeister, Bratslavsky, et al., 1998). One group of participants was instructed to "eat two or three radishes and avoid eating the cookies while waiting for the experiment to start." Another group was instructed to "eat two or three cookies and avoid eating the radishes." And a third group, the control group, was not exposed to any food while waiting. Following this waiting period, where presumably the "radish eating" group would have had to exercise self-control over the immediate gratification of eating some cookies, the participants then attempted to solve a geometrical puzzle that was, unbeknown to them, impossible to solve. Participants were told that they could quit working on the puzzle at any time. Results showed that participants in the radish condition gave up on the puzzle sooner than participants in either the cookie condition or the noneating control condition. Importantly, participants in the cookie condition did not differ from those in the no-food control condition in their persistence on the puzzle. Participants in the radish condition also reported being more tired after the puzzle task than those in the cookie or noneating conditions. These findings are consistent with the theory of **ego depletion**. In the radish condition, the participants' exertion of self-control in the face of temptation to eat cookies resulted in a decrease of psychic energy available to work on the difficult puzzle, leading them to give up sooner and report being more tired after the experiment.

To date, dozens of studies have been published on ego depletion (Baumeister, Vohs, & Tice, 2007). Most take the form of breaking research participants into two groups: one group performs a self-control task, and the second group performs a similar task that does not require self-control. Next, all participants go on to perform a second, unrelated self-control task. If self-control depletes a limited psychic resource, then performing the first self-control task should deplete this group's resource, leaving less available for the second self-control task and causing poorer performance on that task for this group compared to the group that did not perform the first self-control task. Many studies have looked at depletion effects on the self-control of cognitive effort; others have looked at the effects of ego depletion on more id-like self-control tasks, such as self-control of sexual impulses (Gailliot & Baumeister, 2007) and the self-control of aggressive and violent responding (DeWall et al., 2007; Stucke & Baumeister, 2006). For example, in one experiment on aggression the ego depletion group had to resist the urge to eat tempting food, whereas the control group could eat as much as they wanted. Later, in a second task, the ego depletion group reacted more aggressively to an insult than did the control group (Stucke & Baumeister, 2006). In a second study reported in Stucke and Baumeister, the ego depletion subjects had to watch an extremely boring movie without any expression of boredom (they had to control yawning), whereas the control group watched the same film but could yawn all they wanted. The ego depletion group later gave the experimenter poorer ratings on competence compared to the control group, even though they were told that poor ratings would harm the experimenter's career. In studies of sexual restraint, ego-depleted subjects were found to be less likely than a group that did not undergo ego depletion to stifle inappropriate sexual thoughts, and were more likely to consider engaging in sexual activity with someone other than their primary relationship partner (Gailliot & Baumeister, 2007).

All of us have to resist unacceptable impulses all the time: resist falling asleep in a boring class, eating forbidden foods, playing when we should be working, resting when we should be exercising, saying something that might hurt a relationship partner, engaging in inappropriate aggressive or sexual activities, or any one of a long list of problematic behaviours (such a list, based on studying people in their everyday lives resisting everyday temptations, can be found in Hoffman, Baumeister, et al., 2012, and in Hoffman, Vohs, & Baumeister, 2012). To resist these behaviours we call upon our powers of self-control, which Freud taught was the main function of the ego. The ego allows us to at least partially satisfy our desires by bringing our behaviour into line with long-term goals as well as with our values, morals, and social expectations. Freud also taught that the psyche is a closed energy system, such that the energy used to cope with a specific conflict would not be available to cope with another conflict that presented itself very close in time to the first. Results from a large number of studies are consistent with Freud's notion that psychic energy, when depleted by conflict, undermines people's ability to perform complex tasks and resist additional conflicts or threats.

Are we doomed to go through life with a chronically exhausted ego due to the serial temptations we encounter? Baumeister is optimistic about our self-control ability and has introduced a muscle metaphor of ego depletion (e.g., Baumeister et al., 2007). In this metaphor, self-control is like a muscle. If it is overused, it can become temporarily weak and unable to respond adequately to self-control challenges. However, even mildly tired athletes can summon strength for major exertion at decisive moments in a competition. Recent evidence is coming in that people can, with some effort or external motivation (e.g., cash incentives), increase their intentions to exert self-control and overcome multiple temptations. Moreover, like training a muscle, Baumeister believes that self-control can be trained through practice. People who practise mild but regular self-control in one area of life (e.g., dieting) exhibit better self-control in other areas of their lives (e.g., regular exercise). Moreover, Baumeister has identified conditions that can counteract the effects of ego depletion, including states of positive emotion and humour, forming plans for how to behave in tempting situations prior to entering them, and being guided by a strong set of social values. In Table 9.1 we list several of the key variables identified in the research on ego depletion.

Table 9.1 Key Variables Identified in Research on Ego Depletion

Responses That Require Self-Control

- Controlling thoughts
- Managing emotions
- Overcoming unwanted impulses
- Controlling attention
- Guiding behaviour
- Making many choices

Behaviours That Are Sensitive to Ego Depletion

- Eating among dieters
- Overspending
- Aggression after being provoked
- Sexual impulses
- Logical and intelligent decision making

Social Behaviours That Demand Self-Control

- Self-presentation for impression management
- Kindness in response to bad behaviour
- Dealing with demanding or difficult people
- Interracial interactions

Ways to Counteract the Harmful Effects of Ego Depletion

- Humour and laughter
- Other positive emotions
- Cash incentives
- Implementing intentions to cope with temptations with a specific plan
- Pursuing social values (e.g., wanting to help people, wanting to be a good relationship partner)

Superego: Upholder of Societal Values and Ideals

Around the age of 5, a child begins to develop the third part of the mind, which Freud called the superego. The **superego** is the part of the mind that internalizes the values, morals, and ideals of society. Usually, these are instilled into the child by society's various socializing agents, such as parents, schools, and organized religions. Freud emphasized the role of parents in particular in children's development of self-control and conscience, suggesting that the development of the superego was closely linked to children's identification with their parents.

To return to the plumbing metaphor, the superego is the plumber who wants to keep the valves closed all the time and even wants to add more valves to keep the pressure under control. The superego is the part of personality that makes us feel guilty, ashamed, or embarrassed when we do something "wrong" and makes us feel pride when we do something "right." The superego determines what is right and what is wrong: it sets moral goals and ideals of perfection and so is the source of our judgments that some things are good and some are bad. It is what some people refer to as *conscience*. The emotion of guilt is the main tool of the superego in enforcing right and wrong.

Like the id, the superego is not bound by reality. It is free to set standards for virtue and for self-worth, even if those standards are perfectionistic, unrealistic, and harsh. Some children develop low moral standards and consequently do not feel guilty when they hurt others. Other children develop very powerful internal standards, due to a superego that demands perfection. The superego burdens them with almost impossibly high moral standards. Such individuals might suffer from a chronic level of shame because of their continual failures to meet their unrealistic standards.

Interaction of the Id, Ego, and Superego

The three parts of the mind—id, ego, and superego—are in constant interaction. They have different goals, provoking internal conflicts within an individual. Consequently, one part of a person can want one thing, whereas another part wants something else. For example, imagine that a young woman is last in line at a fast-food counter. The man in front of her unknowingly drops a $20 bill from his wallet and does not notice. The woman sees the money on the floor in front of her. The situation sets off a conflict among the three parts of her personality. The id says, "Take it and run! Just grab it; push the person out of the way if you have to." The superego says, "Thou shalt not steal." And the ego is confronted with the reality of the situation as well as the demands from the id and the superego, saying "Did the clerk see the $20 fall? Do any of the other customers see the $20 on the floor? Could I put my foot over it without being noticed? Maybe I should just pick it up and return it to the person; perhaps he will even give me a reward." The young woman in this situation is bound to experience some anxiety. Anxiety is an unpleasant state, which acts as a signal that things are not right and something must be done. It is a signal that the control of the ego is being threatened by reality, by impulses from the id, or by harsh controls exerted by the superego. Such anxiety might be expressed as physical symptoms, such as a rapid heart rate, sweaty palms, and irregular breathing. A person in this state might also feel herself on the verge of panic. Regardless of the symptoms displayed, a person whose desires are in conflict with reality or with internalized morals will appear more anxious in such a situation.

A well-balanced mind, one that is free from anxiety, is achieved by having a strong ego. It is the ego that balances the competing forces of the id, on the one hand, and the superego on the other. If either of these two competing forces overwhelms the ego, then anxiety is the result.

 Concept Check

Define the main functions of the id, ego, and superego in daily life.

Consider an important or significant event that happened to you recently. Reflect on the details of that event, and speculate on how the id, ego, and superego may have interacted to influence the outcome.

Dynamics of Personality

Because anxiety is unpleasant, people try to resolve the conditions that give rise to it. These efforts to defend oneself from anxiety are called *defence mechanisms*, and they are used to defend against all forms of anxiety.

Types of Anxiety

Freud identified three types of anxiety: objective, neurotic, and moral anxiety.

Objective anxiety is fear. Such anxiety occurs in response to a real, external threat to the person. For example, being confronted by a large, aggressive-looking man with a knife while taking a shortcut through an alley would elicit objective anxiety (fear) in most people. In this case, the control of the ego is being threatened by an external factor rather than by an internal conflict. In the other two types of anxiety, the threat comes from within.

The second type of anxiety, **neurotic anxiety**, occurs when there is a direct conflict between the id and the ego. The danger is that the ego may lose control over an unacceptable desire of the id. For example, a woman who becomes anxious whenever she feels sexually attracted to someone, who panics at even the thought of sexual arousal, is experiencing neurotic anxiety. As another example, a man who worries excessively that he might blurt out an unacceptable thought or desire in public is also beset by neurotic anxiety.

The third type of anxiety, **moral anxiety**, is caused by a conflict between the ego and the superego. For example, a person who suffers from chronic shame or feelings of guilt over not living up to "proper" standards, even though such standards might not be attainable, is experiencing moral anxiety. A young woman with bulimia, an eating disorder, might run 5 kilometres and do 100 sit-ups in order to make up for having eaten a "forbidden" food. People who punish themselves, who have low self-esteem, or who feel worthless and ashamed most of the time are most likely suffering from moral anxiety from an overly powerful superego, which constantly challenges the person to live up to higher and higher expectations.

The ego faces a difficult task in attempting to balance the impulses of the id, the demands of the superego, and the realities of the external world. It is as if the id is saying, "I want it now!" The superego is saying, "You will never have it!" And the poor ego is caught in the middle, saying, "Maybe, if I can just work things out." Most of the time, this conversation is going on outside a person's awareness. Sometimes the conflicts among the id, ego, and superego are expressed in a disguised way in various thoughts, feelings, and behaviours. According to Freud, such conflicts often are expressed in dreams. They can also be elicited through hypnosis, free association (saying whatever comes to mind), and projective assessment instruments (e.g., the inkblot test).

Defence Mechanisms

In all three types of anxiety, the function of the ego is to cope with threats and to defend against the dangers they pose in order to reduce anxiety. The ego accomplishes this task through the use of various **defence mechanisms**, which enable the ego to control anxiety, even objective anxiety. Although intrapsychic conflicts frequently evoke anxiety, people can successfully defend themselves from conflict and never consciously feel the anxiety. For example, in conversion reaction, where a conflict is converted to a symptom, the conflict is expressed in the form of physical symptoms, an illness or weakness in a part of the body. Curiously, such people may be indifferent to the symptom, not anxious about losing feeling in a leg or having a headache that will not go away. The symptoms help them avoid the anxiety, and even the symptoms do not make them anxious. Defence mechanisms serve two functions: (1) to protect the ego and (2) to minimize anxiety and distress. Let's turn now to a discussion of one of the defence mechanisms that Freud wrote about extensively and that has received a good deal of attention from researchers in personality psychology.

Repression

Early in his theorizing, Freud used the term **repression** to refer to the process of preventing unacceptable thoughts, feelings, or urges from reaching conscious awareness. Repression was the forerunner of all other forms of defence mechanisms. Repression is defensive in the sense that, through it, a person avoids the anxiety that would arise if the unacceptable material were made conscious. From his clinical practice, Freud learned that people often tended to remember the pleasant circumstances surrounding an event more easily than the unpleasant ones. He concluded that unpleasant memories were often repressed.

Freud first developed the concept of repression as a global strategy that the ego uses to maintain forbidden impulses in the unconscious. The term is still used today to refer to "forgotten" wishes, urges, or events—recall the account of "repressed" traumatic memories with which the chapter opened. Later, Freud articulated several more specific kinds of defence mechanisms. All of these specific forms involved a degree of repression in that some aspect of reality is denied or distorted in the service of reducing anxiety and protecting the control of the ego over the psychic system. We explore recent research on repression in A Closer Look: Empirical Studies of Repression.

 **A Closer Look**

Empirical Studies of Repression

Although psychoanalysts have been interested in repression since Freud introduced the concept, empirical research on this topic has been relatively sparse until recent years (Holmes, 1990). Perhaps this has been due to the difficulty of defining repression in such a way that it may actually be measured for research purposes. Researchers have developed questionnaires to identify individuals who typically use repression as a mechanism for coping with threatening, stressful, or anxiety-producing situations.

Freud held that the essential aspect of repression was the motivated unavailability of unpleasant, painful, or disturbing emotions (Bonanno, 1990). He wrote that repression was a process whereby unpleasant emotions are turned away and kept "at a distance from the conscious" (Freud, 1915/1957, p. 147). Almost 65 years later, Weinberger, Schwartz, and Davidson (1979) were the first to propose that repression, as a style of coping with unpleasant emotions, can be measured by examining various combinations of scores on questionnaires of anxiety and defensiveness. These researchers administered a questionnaire measure of anxiety and a questionnaire measure of defensiveness to a group of subjects. The anxiety questionnaire contained items that inquired about whether one has strong symptoms of anxiety (e.g., heart pounding) when engaging in various behaviours, such as public speaking. The defensiveness questionnaire contained items inquiring about common faults, such as whether respondents had ever gossiped, had ever become so angry that they wanted to break something, or had ever resented someone's asking them for a favour. Clearly, almost everyone is guilty of these minor offences at one time or another. Therefore, subjects who consistently deny engaging in these somewhat undesirable behaviours score high on defensiveness. The researchers combined the subjects' anxiety and defensiveness scores, which resulted in the fourfold typology portrayed in Figure 9.3. Most of the subsequent research on repression involved comparing the repressor group to the other three groups on a dependent measure.

In the initial study, after subjects had completed the questionnaires, Weinberger and colleagues (1979) had the subjects engage in a phrase association task in which they match phrases in one list with phrases in another list that have similar meaning; several phrases contained angry and sexual overtones. As the subjects attempted to match the phrases, the researchers measured their physiological reactions. The researchers also measured the subjects' self-reported levels of distress immediately after their performance. They found that the repressors

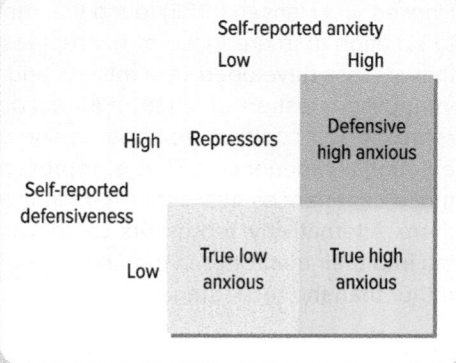

FIGURE 9.3 Finding repressors by measuring anxiety and defensiveness. The subjects who deny being anxious, but who are high on defensiveness, are most likely repressors.

reported the lowest levels of subjective distress yet were found to exhibit the highest levels of physiological arousal (heart rate, skin conductance). In short, repressors *verbally* say they are not distressed yet *physiologically* appear to be very distressed. Other researchers have obtained similar findings (e.g., Asendorpf & Scherer, 1983; Davis & Schwartz, 1987). These experimental results are consistent with Freud's view that repression keeps unpleasant experiences out of conscious awareness. Moreover, the results are consistent with Freud's ideas that such repressed unpleasant experiences still affect the individual, in spite of being outside of awareness (in this case, the repressed experiences affect the person's level of physiological arousal, even though the person is not consciously aware of being anxious).

Another way to examine repression is to ask subjects to recall childhood experiences associated with pleasant and unpleasant emotions. This is exactly what psychologists Penelope Davis and Gary Schwartz did in 1987. They asked their subjects to recall and describe childhood experiences that they associated with happiness, sadness, anger, fear, and wonder. The researchers' findings showed that the repressors, defined as high defensive–low anxious persons, did recall fewer negative emotional experiences than the other subjects and that the repressors were substantially older at the time of their earliest negative emotional memories. Somewhat surprisingly, the repressors also had limited access to positive memories. This finding illustrates what may be one of the costs of repression—pleasant as well as unpleasant emotional memories may be diminished or lost to conscious recall.

Penelope Davis (1987) expanded on the general idea that repressors have limited access to emotional memories. First, she found that the effect is strongest for memories about the *self.* The repressors in her study had no trouble remembering bad things that had happened to *other* people (e.g., siblings), but they did have limited recollection about unpleasant events that they themselves had experienced. Second, the effects of repression appeared to be strongest for the memories associated with feelings of fear and self-consciousness. Although Freud (1915/1957) wrote "the motive and purpose of repression was nothing else than the avoidance of unpleasure" (p. 153), according to Davis, the motive to repress is particularly strong for experiences associated with fear and self-consciousness. Why might this be the case? These emotions are often evoked in situations where the focus of attention is on the self in an evaluative or threatening way. In fear, for example, there is a threat to the very existence of the self. In self-consciousness, the threat of being negatively evaluated by others looms large, leading a person to feel exposed and vulnerable.

Hansen and Hansen (1988) found that repressors' memories are relatively less elaborate when it comes to emotion than are those of nonrepressors. That is, repressors have memories for emotional events that are less developed, less refined, and less rich than those of nonrepressors. These authors raise the intriguing question of what might account for this impoverished emotional memory on the part of repressors. It could come about in one of two ways. First, repressors may have limited *recall* of their emotional experiences. That is, repressors may have actually *had* varied emotional experiences and those experiences may actually be *in* their memories, but they just have trouble retrieving or recalling them. Alternatively, repressors could actually have blocked certain emotional experiences from entering into their memories in the first place. The effect of repression could have occurred at the *encoding* rather than the recall stage.

Although most studies of repression have examined memory for past events, a few studies (e.g., Hansen, Hansen, & Shantz, 1992) suggest that the effect of repression may occur not only as diminished *memory* for negative events but also in the person's actual reaction to negative events when they occur. This is what Freud would have predicted, that repressors actually do not experience negative emotions as strongly as nonrepressors do. We can ask whether repressors simply have poor memories for bad events or whether, when bad events happen, they actually experience less negative emotion than nonrepressors do, or both.

In a study by Cutler, Larsen, and Bunce (1996), repressors and nonrepressors kept daily diaries of 40 different emotions for 28 consecutive days. After reporting on their emotions every day for a month, the subjects were then asked to think back over the month and to rate how much of each emotion they recalled experiencing, on average, during the course of that month. The researchers thus had a measure of actual day-to-day emotion, recorded close to the time when the subjects experienced the emotions, as well as a measure of recalled emotion. This approach allowed the researchers to test whether the repressors reported less negative emotion, recalled less negative emotion, or both. The results showed that the repressors, compared with the nonrepressors, actually reported *experiencing* fewer and less intense unpleasant emotions on a day-to-day basis. The repressors' memories for unpleasant emotions, however, were only slightly less accurate than the memories of the nonrepressors. The effect of repression seems to occur during the *experience* of unpleasant events, whereby repressors somehow dampen their emotional reactions to bad events.

Freud said that the function of repression was to keep unpleasant experiences out of conscious awareness. We now know more specifically that the blunting effect of repression occurs primarily during the reaction to bad events. Repressors do not have bad memories; rather, somehow they keep unpleasant events from entering into their memories in the first place.

Other Defence Mechanisms

Freud's daughter Anna Freud (1895–1982), herself an accomplished psychoanalyst, played a large role in identifying and describing other mechanisms of defence (A. Freud, 1936/1992). She believed that the ego could muster some very creative and effective mechanisms to protect against blows to self-esteem and threats to psychic existence. A few of these defence mechanisms will be described in detail in this section.

A student of Freud's named Fenichel (1945) revised the idea of defence to focus more on how these mechanisms function to protect self-esteem. That is, people have a preferred view of themselves, and they will defend against any unflattering changes or blows to that self-view. Obviously, realizing that one has unacceptable sexual or aggressive wishes might be a blow to one's self-view, especially for people living in the Victorian era. However, in today's society there may be other events that threaten self-esteem, such as failure, embarrassment, and being excluded from a group. Most modern psychologists believe that people defend themselves against these threats to their self-esteem (Baumeister & Vohs, 2004). Much of the contemporary research on self-esteem maintenance can thus be thought of as having roots in the psychoanalytic concept of defence mechanisms (Baumeister, Dale, & Sommer, 1998). There is a questionnaire measure of defence mechanisms (Cramer, 1991) and empirical research is accumulating on their use. For example, in adolescence identification is a common defence mechanism (identification is covered in the next section, as it is the resolution of the phallic stage of psychosexual development), whereas later in life denial, covered next, becomes the most common defence mechanism (Cramer, 2012).

Denial When the reality of a situation is extremely anxiety provoking, a person may resort to the defence mechanism of **denial**. In contrast to repression, which involves keeping an *experience* out of memory, a person in denial insists that things are not the way they seem. Denial involves refusing to see the facts. A man whose partner has left him might still set an extra place at the dinner table and insist that they will be home at any time. Playing out this scenario night after night might be more acceptable than acknowledging that she is, in reality, gone. Denial can also be less extreme, as when someone reappraises an anxiety-provoking situation so that it seems less daunting. For example, a woman might convince herself that her husband *had* to leave her for some reason, that it really was *not* his fault, and that he *would* return if only he could. In this case, she is denying that her husband freely chose to leave her instead of acknowledging the whole reality of the situation.

A common form of denial is to dismiss unflattering feedback as wrong or irrelevant. When people are given a poor evaluation, say by a supervisor, some will reject the evaluation rather than change their view of themselves. They might blame their difficulties on bad luck or problems with the situation, anything but accepting personal responsibility and having to alter their view of themselves. Indeed, the tendency to blame events outside one's control for failure but to accept responsibility for success is so common that psychologists refer to this as the **fundamental attribution error**. It may be interpreted, however, as a specific form of denial.

Health psychologists are also interested in denial. How can a person smoke two packs of cigarettes a day and not worry about the health consequences? One answer would be to deny one's personal vulnerability, or to deny the evidence linking smoking to illness, or to deny that one wants to live a long and healthy life. Baumeister and colleagues (1998) review evidence that people often minimize the risks they see in various unhealthy behaviours.

Denial often shows up in daydreams and fantasies. Daydreams are frequently about how things might have been. To some extent, daydreams deny the present situation by focusing on how things could have been otherwise. In doing so, they may lessen or defend against the potentially anxiety-provoking circumstances of one's present situation. For example, a person who has done something embarrassing might daydream about how things might have gone had they not done that stupid, embarrassing thing.

Displacement In **displacement**, a threatening or an unacceptable impulse is channelled or redirected from its original source to a nonthreatening (or less threatening) target. Consider, for example, an employee who has an argument with their supervisor at work. They are really angry with the supervisor, but their ego keeps them in check because, after all, the supervisor is the boss and can make work life difficult, so they go home and take out their anger on their significant other. Although this approach may contribute to relationship problems, it will most likely avoid the difficulties associated with losing one's temper at one's boss. Sometimes displacement has a domino effect, whereby one person in a relationship berates another, who in turn yells at the children, who then abuse the family dog. Moreover, although displacement is often thought of as a defence mechanism involving the redirection of aggressive instincts, it can also involve sexual urges that are redirected from a less acceptable to a more acceptable target. For example, a woman may have a strong sexual attraction toward a man who is subordinate to her at work, but this man has no interest in her. Rather than harass the man, she may redirect this sexual energy toward her partner and rediscover that she is still attracted to him. Freud also noted that sometimes even fears are redirected through displacement and cited as an example the case of a boy who feared his father but who redirected that fear toward horses.

Although these examples seem to involve conscious awareness and a calculating choice of how to express the unacceptable emotion, the process of displacement takes place outside of awareness. *Deliberately* redirecting one's anger, for example, is not displacement, even though someone might do this to manage a situation. Real displacement is an unconscious means of avoiding the recognition that one has certain inappropriate or unacceptable feelings (e.g., anger or sexual attraction) toward a specific other person or a specific object. Those feelings then are displaced onto another person or object that is more appropriate or acceptable.

Researchers have tried to study the displacement of aggressive impulses. In one study, student participants were frustrated (or not, if they were in the control group) by the experimenter. Later they had the opportunity to act aggressively toward the experimenter, the experimenter's assistant, or another participant. The frustrated participants were more aggressive, but they were equally aggressive toward the experimenter, the assistant, or the other student (Hokanson, Burgess, & Cohen, 1963). The target did not matter. Other studies have replicated this finding. In one study subjects were angered, not by the experimenter, but by another participant, then given an opportunity to act aggressively toward that subject or toward a friend of that participant. Again, angered participants were more aggressive, but it did not seem to matter who the target was.

Baumeister and colleagues (1998) argue that angered people act aggressively and that there is no evidence that it is defensive. They suggest that, although displacement is an interesting concept, there is little empirical support for the idea that urges are like hydraulic fluid in a closed system, being shunted this way or that depending on displacement. Of course this does not mean that displacement of negative emotions more generally is impossible. Research on stress contagion, for example, has demonstrated that people frequently bring home tension from work and release it at home, in ways that often affect other people (e.g., Story & Repetti, 2006).

Rationalization Another common defence mechanism, especially among educated people (such as university students) is **rationalization**. It involves generating acceptable reasons for outcomes that might otherwise appear socially unacceptable. In rationalization, the goal is to reduce anxiety by coming up with an explanation for an event that is easier to accept than the real reason. For example, a student who receives a failing grade on a term paper might explain it away by insisting that the teacher did not give clear directions for how to write the paper. Or perhaps a woman whose girlfriend has broken up with her explains to her friends that she never really liked her that much to begin with. These reasons are a lot more emotionally acceptable than the alternatives that one is not as smart or as desirable as one thinks.

Reaction Formation In an attempt to stifle the expression of an unacceptable urge, a person may continually display a flurry of behaviour that indicates the opposite impulse. Such a tactic is known as **reaction formation**. For example, imagine the employee who is angry with their supervisor, described in the discussion of displacement. If, instead of displacing their anger, their ego unconsciously resorts to reaction formation, then they might go out of their way to be overly kind to their boss, to show the boss special courtesy and consideration.

An interesting example of reaction formation is provided by Cooper (1998), who discusses the concept of "killing someone with kindness." Consider a man who is angry with his girlfriend, but the anger is not conscious; he is not aware of how angry he really is. It is raining outside so he offers her his umbrella. She refuses to take it, but he insists. She keeps refusing, and he keeps insisting that she take it. Here he is replacing his hostility with apparent kindness. However, his aggression is coming out in his persistent insistence and his ignoring her wishes not to take the umbrella. According to psychoanalysis, this dynamic can often be found when defences are being used; people may try to cover up their wishes and intention and yet unwittingly express them.

The mechanism of reaction formation makes it possible for psychoanalysts to predict that sometimes people will do exactly the opposite of what you might otherwise think they would do. It also alerts us to be sensitive to instances when a person is doing something in excess, such as when someone is being overly nice to us for no apparent reason. Perhaps in such cases the person really means or feels the opposite of what is being displayed.

Projection Another type of defence mechanism, **projection**, is based on the notion that sometimes we see in others the traits and desires we find most upsetting in ourselves. We literally "project" (i.e., attribute) our own unacceptable qualities onto others. We can then hate them, instead of hating ourselves, for having those unacceptable qualities or desires. At the same time, we can disparage the tendencies or characteristics in question without admitting that we possess them. Other people become the target by virtue of their having qualities that we intensely dislike in ourselves. For instance, thieves are often worried about the prospect of others stealing from them and claim that others are not to be trusted. Or a woman denies having any interest in sexuality yet insists that all the men she knows "have nothing but sex on their minds." Married men who have affairs are more suspicious than other husbands that their partners are unfaithful. What a person intensely dislikes or gets upset with others is often revealing their innermost insecurities and conflicts. A person who always insults others by calling them "stupid" may, in fact, harbour some insecurity about their own intelligence.

In projection, we see in others those traits or desires we find most upsetting in ourselves. We can then disparage them for having the undesirable characteristic, without admitting that we have that very characteristic.

©Reza Estakhrian/Getty Images

In modern psychological research there is an effect, similar to projection, called the **false consensus effect**. This was first described by Ross, Greene, and House in 1977. It refers to the tendency many people have to assume that others are similar to them. That is, extraverts think many other people are extraverted, and conscientious individuals think many other people are conscientious. To think that many other people share your own preferences, motivations, or traits is to display the false consensus effect.

Baumeister and colleagues (1998) argue that having a false consensus about one's unflattering traits could be ego defensive. For example, to be the only person whose credit card is over the limit would imply that one is unique in this moral deficiency. But if one believes that many people are over their credit limits, or close to it, then this false consensus belief might be protective of one's self-concept. The adolescent who explains some misbehaviour with the phrase, "Gee, everyone else was doing it," is perhaps engaging in defensive false consensus, essentially saying, "I'm not so bad because everyone else is bad too."

Sublimation According to Freud, **sublimation** is the most adaptive defence mechanism. Sublimation is the channelling of unacceptable sexual or aggressive instincts into socially desired activities. A common example is going out to chop wood when you are angry rather than acting on that anger or even engaging in other less adaptive defence mechanisms, such as displacement. Watching football or boxing is more desirable than beating someone up. Mountain climbing or volunteering for combat duty in the army might be forms of sublimating a death wish. Freud once reportedly remarked about all the sublimated sexual energy that must have gone into building the skyscrapers of New York City. One's choice of occupation (e.g., athlete, mortician, or emergency room nurse) might be interpreted as the sublimation of certain unacceptable urges. The positive feature of sublimation is that it allows for some limited yet healthy expression of id tendencies, so the ego does not have to invest energy in holding the id in check.

Freud maintained that the greatest achievements of civilization were due to the effective sublimation of sexual and aggressive urges.

Defence Mechanisms in Everyday Life

Life provides each of us with plenty of psychological bumps and bruises. We don't get a job we badly wanted; an acquaintance says something hurtful; we realize something about ourselves that is not flattering. In short, we must face unexpected or disappointing events all the time. Defence mechanisms may be useful in coping with these occurrences and the emotions they generate (Larsen, 2000a, 2000b; Larsen & Prizmic, 2004). We all have to deal with stress, and to the extent that defence mechanisms help, so much the better (see Vaillant, 1994, for a discussion and categorization of defence mechanisms).

It is not too difficult, however, to imagine circumstances that are made worse by the use of defence mechanisms (Cramer, 2000, 2002). Others may avoid a person who projects a lot. A person who displaces frequently may have few friends. Moreover, the use of defence mechanisms takes psychic energy that is therefore not available for other pursuits. How do you know when the use of defence mechanisms is becoming a problem? The answer is twofold: you know a behaviour is becoming a problem if it begins inhibiting the ability to be *productive* or if it begins limiting the ability to *maintain relationships*. If either one of these areas in life is negatively affected—work or relationships—then you might wonder about a psychological problem. Moreover, there is much to be said in favour of directly confronting difficult issues and taking action directed at solving problems. Nevertheless, sometimes problems simply cannot be solved or a person does not have the energy or resources to directly confront a problem. Under these temporary circumstances, defence mechanisms may be very useful. When used occasionally, defence mechanisms most likely will not interfere with work or social life. According to Freud, the hallmark of mature adulthood was the ability to work productively and to develop and maintain satisfying relationships. Reaching mature adulthood, however, involves passing through several stages of personality development.

 Concept Check

Provide examples of the following defence mechanisms: denial, displacement, rationalization, reaction formation, and projection.

Which defence mechanism did Freud suggest was the healthiest ego defence? Provide a specific example.

Psychosexual Stages of Personality Development

Freud believed that all people passed through a set series of stages in personality development. Each of these stages involves a conflict, and how the person resolves this conflict gives rise to various aspects of personality. So in psychoanalytic theory, the source of individual differences lies in how the child comes to resolve conflicts in each of the stages of development. The end result, after going through all the stages, is a fully formed personality.

At each of the first three stages, young children must face and resolve specific conflicts. The conflicts revolve around ways of obtaining a type of sexual gratification. For this reason, Freud's theory of development is called the **psychosexual stage theory**. According to the theory, children seek sexual gratification at each stage by investing libidinal energy in a specific body part. Each stage in the developmental process is named after the body part in which sexual energy is invested.

If a child fails to fully resolve a conflict at a particular stage of development, they may get stuck in that stage, a phenomenon known as **fixation**. Each successive stage represents a more mature mode of obtaining sexual gratification. If a child is fixated at a particular stage, they exhibit a less mature approach to obtaining sexual gratification. In the final stage of development, mature adults obtain pleasure from healthy intimate relationships and from work. The road to this final stage, however, is fraught with developmental conflicts and the potential for fixation. Let's examine these stages and discuss the conflicts that arise, as well as the consequences of fixation at each stage.

The first stage, which Freud called the **oral stage**, occurs during the initial 18 months after birth. During this time, the main sources of pleasure and tension reduction are the mouth, lips, and tongue. You don't have to be around many babies to realize how busy they are with their mouths (e.g., whenever they come across something new, such as a rattle or toy, they usually put it into their mouths first). The main conflict during this stage is weaning, withdrawing from the breast or bottle. This conflict has both a biological and a psychological component. From a biological standpoint, the id wants the immediate gratification associated with taking in nourishment and obtaining pleasure through the mouth. From a psychological perspective, the conflict is one of excessive pleasure versus dependency, with the fear of being left to fend for oneself. Sometimes a child has a painful or traumatic experience during the weaning process, resulting in a degree of fixation at the oral stage. Adults who still obtain pleasure from "taking in," especially through the mouth, might be fixated at this stage (e.g., people who overeat or smoke). Problems with nail biting, thumb sucking, or pencil chewing might also occur. At a psychological level, people who are fixated at the oral stage may be overly dependent: they may want to be babied, to be nurtured and taken care of, and thus to have others make decisions for them. Some psychoanalysts also believe that drug addiction (because it involves pleasure from "taking in") is a sign of oral fixation.

There is another possible conflict of the oral stage that is associated with biting. This conflict can occur after the child grows teeth and finds that they can obtain pleasure from biting and chewing. Parents typically discourage a child from biting, particularly if the child bites other children or adults. Thus, the child has the conflict between the urge to bite and parental restrictions. People who fixate during this stage might develop adult personalities that are hostile, quarrelsome, or mocking. They continue to draw gratification from being psychologically "biting" and verbally attacking.

The second stage of development is the **anal stage**, which typically occurs between the ages of 18 months and 3 years of age. At this stage, the anal sphincter is the source of sexual pleasure. During this time, the child obtains pleasure from first expelling feces and then, during toilet training, from retaining feces. At first, the id desires immediate tension reduction whenever there is any pressure in the rectum. This is achieved by defecating whenever and wherever the urge arises. Parents, however, work to instill in the child a degree of self-control through the process of toilet training. Many conflicts arise around this issue of the child's ability to achieve some self-control. Some children achieve too little control and grow up to be sloppy and dirty. Other children have the opposite problem: they develop too much self-control and begin to take pleasure in little acts of self-control. Adults who are compulsive, overly neat, rigid, and never messy are, according to psychoanalysts, likely to be fixated at the anal stage. After all, toilet training usually presents a child with the first opportunity to exercise choice and willpower. When a parent puts the child on the potty seat and says, "Now, do your business," the child has the opportunity to say, "No!" and to withhold. This might signal the beginnings of being stingy, holding back, not giving others what they want, and being overly willful and stubborn.

The third stage, which occurs between 3 and 5 years of age, is called the **phallic stage**, because the child discovers that he has (or she discovers that she does not have) a penis. In fact, the major event during this stage is children's discovery of their own genitals and the realization that some pleasure can be derived from touching them. This is also the awakening of sexual desire directed outward, and according to Freud, it is first directed toward the parent of the opposite sex. Little boys fall in love with their mothers, and little girls fall in love with their fathers. But children feel more than just parental love, according to Freud's theory. A little boy lusts for his mother and wants to have sex with her. His father is seen as the competitor, as the one who is preventing the little boy from possessing his mother and receiving *all* of her attention. For the boy, the main conflict, which Freud called the **Oedipal conflict**, is the unconscious wish to have his mother all to himself by eliminating the father. (Oedipus is a character in Greek mythology who unknowingly kills his father and marries his mother.) Daddy is the competitor for Mommy's attention, and he should be beaten and driven from the home or killed. But killing or beating Daddy is wrong.

Part of the Oedipal conflict, then, is that the child loves, yet is competing with, the parent of the same sex. Moreover, the little boy grows to fear his father because surely this big and powerful person could prevent this all from happening. In fact, Freud argued that little boys come to believe that their fathers might make a preemptive strike by taking away the thing that is at the root of the conflict: the boy's penis. This fear of losing his penis, called **castration anxiety**, drives the little boy into giving up his sexual desire for Mommy. The boy decides that the best he can do is to become like the guy who has Mommy—in other words, like his father. This process of wanting to become like Daddy, called **identification**, marks the beginning of the resolution of the Oedipal conflict and the successful resolution of the phallic stage of psychosexual development for boys. Freud believed that the resolution of the Oedipal conflict was the beginning of both the superego and morality, as well as the male gender role.

For little girls, the situation is at once similar and different. One similarity is that the conflict centres on the penis, or actually the lack thereof, on the part of the little girl. According to Freud, a little girl blames her mother for the fact that she lacks a penis. She desires her father yet at the same time envies him for his penis. This is called **penis envy**, and it is the counterpart of castration anxiety. Penis envy is different in that the little girl does not necessarily fear the mother, as the boy fears the father. Thus, for girls, there is no strong motivation to give up her desire for her father.

Carl Jung, a colleague of Freud, termed this stage the **Electra complex** for girls. Electra was also a character in a Greek myth. Electra convinced her brother to kill their mother after the mother had murdered the father. Freud actually rejected the idea of the Electra complex, and he was vague about how the phallic stage is resolved for girls. He wrote that it drags on later in life for girls and may never fully be resolved. Because successful resolution results in the development of the superego, Freud believed that women must therefore be morally inferior to men. This aspect of Freud's developmental theory is not widely accepted today, and Freud has been strongly criticized for his beliefs about sex differences (e.g., Helson & Picano, 1990).

The next stage of psychosexual development is called the **latency stage**. This stage occurs from around the age of 6 until puberty. Little psychological development is presumed to occur during this time. It is mainly a period when the child is going to school and learning the skills and abilities necessary to take on the role of an adult. Because of the lack of specific sexual conflicts during this time, Freud believed that it was a period of psychological rest, or latency. Subsequent psychoanalysts have argued instead that much development occurs during this time, such as learning to make decisions for oneself, learning to interact and make friends with others, developing an identity, and learning the meaning of work. Because this is a more contemporary modification of Freud's theory, we examine it in Chapter 10.

The latency period ends with the sexual awakening brought about by puberty. If the Oedipus or Electra complex has been resolved, the person goes on to the next and final stage of psychosexual development, the **genital stage**. This stage begins around puberty and lasts through one's adult life. Here the libido is focused on the genitals, but not in the manner of self-manipulation associated with the phallic stage. This differs from the earlier stages in that it is not accompanied by a specific conflict. People reach the genital stage only if they have resolved the conflicts at the prior stages. It is in this sense that personality development, according to Freud, is largely complete at around the age of 5 or 6: the adult personality is dependent on how the conflicts that arise during infancy and childhood are resolved.

Freud's psychosexual stage theory is a theory about personality development, both normal and abnormal. In a nutshell, the theory states that we are all born with a drive for sexual pleasure (the id) but that the constraints of civilized society limit the ways we can satisfy that drive. We all go through a series of predictable clashes or conflicts between our desire for pleasure and the demands placed on us by our parents and by society in general. The nature of the conflicts and the stages we go through are universal, but the specific instances and outcomes are each unique. Parts of our personalities are shaped at each stage by the particular ways we resolve the conflict. If, for example, at the oral stage, a person did not receive enough gratification (was weaned early) or received too much gratification (was weaned too late), then they might continue to have inappropriate demands for oral gratification throughout the rest of their life (perhaps in the form of being a dependent personality or developing an eating disorder or developing an alcohol or drug problem).

Freud developed the metaphor of an army whose troops are called into battle during each stage of psychosexual development. If the resolution of a stage is incomplete, then some soldiers must be left behind to monitor that particular conflict. It is as if some psychic energy must stand guard, lest the psychosexual conflict break out again. The poorer the resolution at a particular stage, the more psychic soldiers have to be left behind. One consequence of this is that less psychic energy is available for the subsequent tasks of maturity. The more soldiers brought forward to the genital stage, the more psychic energy that can be invested in mature intimate and productive relationships and the better the adult personality adjustment. It is interesting to note that neither happiness nor life satisfaction was directly a part of Freud's conception of successful personality development. Successful personality development instead was defined by the ability to be productive and to maintain loving relationships.

 Concept Check

Name and briefly summarize the stages in Freud's theory of psychosexual development.

According to Freud, what is a fixation? What are the implications of a fixation for adult personality?

Personality and Psychoanalysis

Psychoanalysis, besides being a theory of personality, is also a method of psychotherapy, a technique for helping individuals who are experiencing a mental disorder or even relatively minor problems with living. Psychoanalysis can be thought of as a method for deliberately restructuring the personality. The connection between the psychoanalytic theory of personality and psychoanalytic therapy is very strong. Principles of psychoanalytic therapy are based directly on the psychoanalytic theory about the structure and functioning of personality. Freud developed his theory of personality while treating patients in therapy. Similarly, many modern psychoanalysts, even those in academic settings, maintain a practice of seeing patients. Most psychoanalysts have themselves undergone psychoanalytic psychotherapy, which Freud held to be a requirement for becoming a psychoanalyst.

Techniques for Revealing the Unconscious

The goal of psychoanalysis is to make the unconscious conscious. Mental illness, problems with living, and unexplained physical symptoms can all be viewed as the result of unconscious conflicts. Thoughts, feelings, urges, or memories have been forced into the unconscious because of their disturbing or threatening nature. Due to the dynamic nature of the human mind, these conflicts or restrained urges may slip out of the unconscious in ways that cause trouble. They often obtain expression as psychological or physical symptoms.

The first aim of psychoanalysis is to identify these unconscious thoughts and feelings. Once the patient can be made aware of this material, the second aim is to enable the person to deal with the unconscious urges, memories, or thoughts realistically and maturely. The major challenge facing the psychoanalyst is determining how to penetrate the unconscious mind of the patient. By its very definition, the unconscious mind is the part of which the person has no awareness. How can one person (the therapist) come to know something about another person (the patient) which that other person does not know? Freud and other psychoanalysts have developed a set of standard techniques that can be used to dredge up material from the unconscious minds of patients.

Free Association

If you were to relax, to sit back in a comfortable chair, to let your mind wander, and then to say whatever came into your mind, you would be engaging in **free association**. Chances are, you would say some things that would even surprise you, and you might be embarrassed by what comes out. If you were able to resist the urge to censor your thoughts before speaking, then you would have an idea of how a patient spends much of their time in psychoanalysis. The typical psychoanalytic session lasts 50 minutes and may be repeated several times a week; the sessions may continue for years. The goals of the sessions are to enable patients to identify unconscious material that might be causing unwanted symptoms and to help them cope with that material in an adult fashion.

By relaxing the censor that screens our everyday thoughts, the technique of free association allows potentially important material into conscious awareness. This takes some practice. Patients are encouraged to say whatever comes to mind, no matter how absurd, trifling, or obscene. The technique is a bit like looking for a needle in a haystack in that the psychoanalyst is likely to be subjected to a barrage of trivial material before stumbling on an important clue to an unconscious conflict.

In free association, the psychoanalyst must be able to recognize the subtle signs that something important has just been mentioned—a slight quiver in the way a word is pronounced, a halting sentence, the patient's immediate discounting of what they have just said, a false start, a nervous laugh, or a long pause. An effective psychoanalyst will detect such signs and intervene to ask the patient to stick with that topic for a while, to free associate further on that issue. Archeology is a good metaphor for this type of work, as the psychoanalyst is digging through all sorts of ordinary material in search of clues to past conflicts and trauma.

Dreams

Thinkers have always speculated about the meaning of dreams, and it has long been thought that dreams are messages from deep regions of the mind that are not accessible during waking life. In 1900, Freud published his book *The Interpretation of Dreams,* in which he presented his theory of the meaning and purpose of dreaming. He held that the purpose of dreaming was to satisfy urges and to fulfill unconscious wishes and desires, all within the protection of sleep. But aren't most dreams absurd and nonsensical? How, then, can they have anything to do with desires and wishes? For example, a person might have a dream about riding a white horse that suddenly begins to fly. Does this mean the person wishes to have a flying horse? No, Freud would argue, because the dream contains wishes and desires in *disguised* form. **Dream analysis** was a technique Freud taught for uncovering the unconscious material in a dream by *interpreting* the dream's content. Freud maintained that we must distinguish between the **manifest content** of a dream (what the dream actually contains) and the **latent content** (what the elements of the dream represent). He believed that the direct expression of desires and wishes would be so disturbing that it would waken the dreamer. The ego is still somewhat at work during sleep, and it succeeds in disguising the disturbing content of our unconscious. The wishes and unacceptable impulses have to be disguised in order to allow the person to keep sleeping, which is necessary, yet must be expressed in order to satisfy desires. Having a dream about killing one's father, for example, might be so disturbing that it would awaken a young boy who has an Oedipal fixation. However, a dream about a king who has a garden containing a fountain that is disabled by a small animal, so that it no longer shoots its plume of water up into the air, might make the same psychological point yet allow the sleeper to remain asleep.

Thus, although our dreams often appear to be ridiculous and incomprehensible to us, to a psychoanalyst, a dream may contain valuable clues to the unconscious. Freud called dreams "the royal road to the unconscious." The psychoanalyst interprets dreams by deciphering how the unacceptable impulses and urges are transformed by the unconscious into **symbols** in the dream. Parents may be represented as a king and queen. Children may be represented as small animals. Hence, a dream about a king whose fountain is broken by a small animal can be interpreted as wish fulfillment with an Oedipal overtone.

According to Freud, dreaming serves three functions. First, it allows for wish fulfillment and the gratification of desires, even if only in symbolic form. Second, dreams provide a safety valve by allowing a person to release unconscious tension by expressing their deepest desires, although in disguised form. And third, dreams are guardians of sleep. Even though a lot is going on in dreams, such as the expression of wishes and desires, the person remains asleep. Although tension is being released, no anxiety is being aroused, and the person sleeps without interruption.

In many of his writings, Freud provided interpretations or translations of common dream symbols. Not surprisingly, most symbols have sexual connotations. This may be because Freud was influenced by the Victorian era in which he lived, when most people were very inhibited about sexual matters. Freud believed that because people repressed their sexual feelings and desires, these inhibited urges came out in symbolic form in dreams. Many later thinkers have been critical of Freud's seeming preoccupation with sex, which they have attributed to the historical period during which he was developing his theory. Yet on the subject of dreams, scientific interest indeed continues today. We explore one line of research related to dream interpretation in Highlight on Canadian Research: Contemporary Approaches to Dream Interpretation.

 Highlight On Canadian Research

Contemporary Approaches to Dream Interpretation

Today, dreams continue to intrigue psychologists and researchers around the world. Although the Freudian perspective on dreams and their meaning is less endorsed by contemporary scientists, one of Freud's basic contributions regarding dream analysis continues to frame contemporary research on dreams. Namely, his differentiation between manifest and latent dream content has fostered research on more objective and self-driven methods of dream interpretation.

One such line of research has emerged at Trent University in Peterborough, Ontario. Created and validated by Teresa DeCicco, the storytelling method of dream interpretation (DeCicco, 2007) has proven a valuable tool for clinicians and researchers to facilitate independent and self-driven dream analysis (versus that which may be led by a therapist or clinician). In the storytelling method, individuals are instructed to write out a dream on paper and then circle or highlight some of the most meaningful words in the dream (or those words which stand out to the dreamer). This report of the dream and the key words contained within it constitute the *manifest* content of the dream. In order to access *latent* content, defined in contemporary terms as meaning, insight, or discovery that results from a dream, individuals are then instructed to engage in a word association activity based on the most salient words in the dream report. This involves writing down the very first word that comes to mind when reading each original word or phrase. These words, or *associations*, can provide insight or meaning about one's dream that may be of therapeutic value (Pessant & Zadra, 2004). However, in the storytelling method, individuals are further instructed to create a story or short narrative using the new words. Compared to a control group, DeCicco (2007) has demonstrated that this third step predicts discovery or insight above that which is gained by association alone. This is believed to be due to the greater coherence gained by the creation of a story, and therefore an increased likelihood of linking the dream to something important in the dreamer's life.

The value of such independent methods of dream interpretation lies in the modern view that dream meaning cannot be imposed upon an individual by another person, whether that person is a psychologist, therapist, or mystic. Psychologists can certainly help patients to gain insight and meaning from their dreaming experiences, but just like a dream dictionary, any outside opinion insufficiently accounts for all individual and contextual factors affecting the unconscious motivations behind a dream. In other words, only YOU can determine the meaning of your dreams or the insights gained therein—what is often referred to as *discovery* in contemporary work on dreams.

DeCicco and her colleagues have shown that the storytelling method is an effective means for gaining meaning and discovery from dreams in diverse populations. For example, in a sample of recovering alcoholics, the storytelling method proved a valuable tool in facilitating meaningful dream interpretations about sobriety and the recovery process (DeCicco & Higgins, 2009). Such meaningful and insightful dream interpretation has also been documented among Canadian soldiers returning from duty in Afghanistan (Dale & DeCicco, 2014) and among women with breast cancer (DeCicco et al., 2010). In both of these latter cases, meaning and insight were directly related to dreamers' current life experiences. In a study of dreams with sexual imagery as reported by Canadian university students, the storytelling method led 59 percent of participants to find insight regarding their romantic relationships, while only 20 percent of participants found meaning or insight regarding sex or sexuality specifically. The remaining 21 percent found meaning about fears, family issues, daily stress, and either work or school (King, DeCicco, & Humphreys, 2009). Findings such as these add support to Freud's concept of latent dream content, the idea that there may be more to dreams than meets the eye.

❓ Exercise

For a few days, keep a pencil and pad of paper by your bedside. Immediately on awakening each morning, write down anything you can remember about the dreams you had the night before. After a few days, read over your dream diary and look for themes. Do you see any recurring themes or elements in your collection of dreams? What are some of the common symbols in your dreams, and what do you think they represent? To help you answer these questions, try free associating to your dream content. That is, find a quiet place and relax. Start by describing your dream aloud, and then just keep talking, saying anything that comes to mind, no matter how foolish or trivial. After doing this exercise, have you learned anything about yourself or about what is important to you? If you find it difficult to gain insight this way, try highlighting the most salient or meaningful words in a dream and engage in word association, writing down the first thing that comes to mind next to each word. Do these new words offer any insight? Try creating a story or narrative out of these new words, as in the storytelling method (DeCicco, 2007). Reflect on the story. Does it relate to something important in your waking life?

Projective Techniques

You've undoubtedly seen drawings that can be interpreted in two or more ways (e.g., the picture of a vase that, when looked at differently, looks like two faces). Or maybe you've seen the children's games in which, within a larger drawing, there are hidden images that you are supposed to find. Imagine that you give a person a picture of something totally ambiguous, such as an inkblot, and ask them what they see. A person might see all sorts of things in the shapes created by the ink splatter: a rocketship, two fish swimming, a clown. The idea that what a person sees in an ambiguous figure, such as an inkblot, reflects their personality is called the **projective hypothesis**. People are thought to *project* their own personalities into what they report seeing in an ambiguous stimulus. A hostile and aggressive person might see teeth, claws, and blood in an inkblot. Someone with an oral fixation might see food or people eating. The inkblot technique, as well as other projective measures, is often criticized by research psychologists for the scant scientific evidence as to its validity or reliability (Wood, Nezworski, et al., 2003).

Another type of projective technique involves asking the person to produce something, such as a drawing of a person. What someone draws might be a projection of their own conflicts. Consider a young man who, when asked to draw a person, draws only a head. When asked to draw another person, but this time someone of the opposite sex, he draws another head. Finally, when asked to draw a picture of himself, he again draws only a head. We might presume that this person has an unconscious conflict about his body image. As with dreams and free association, the goal of projective techniques is to bypass the patient's conscious censor and reveal their unconscious conflicts and repressed urges and desires.

The Process of Psychoanalysis

With the help of free association, dream analysis, and projective techniques, the psychoanalyst gradually comes to understand the unconscious source of the patient's problems. The patient must also come to understand the unconscious dynamics of their situation. Toward this end, the psychoanalyst offers the patient interpretations of the psychodynamic causes of the problems. The patient is led to view problematic thoughts, dreams, behaviours, symptoms, or feelings as all having unconscious roots and as expressions of unconscious conflicts or repressed urges. The psychoanalyst might say, "Could it be that the reason you feel so sleepy when you go out with your boyfriend is that you are afraid of being sexually attractive to him?" The patient is confronted with an explanation of something she has been keeping from herself. Through many interpretations, the patient is gradually led to an understanding of the

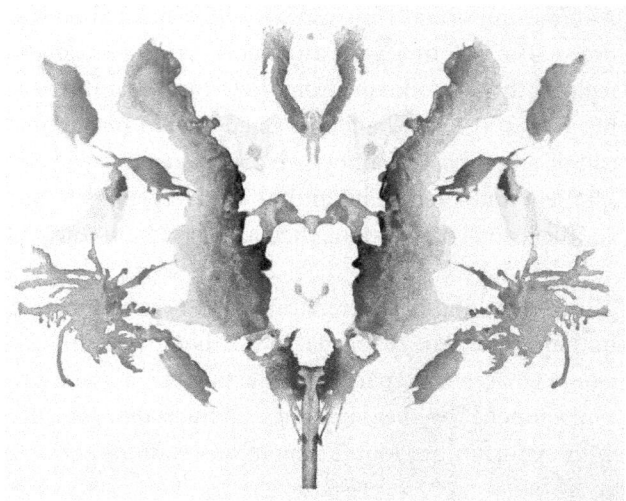

Projective techniques, such as the inkblots developed by the Swiss psychiatrist Hermann Rorschach, are popular methods for assessing unconscious aspects of personality, such as repressed desires, wishes, or conflicts.
©Science Museum/SSPL/The Image Works

unconscious source of her problems. This is the beginning of **insight**. Insight, in psychoanalysis, is more than a simple cognitive understanding of the intrapsychic basis of one's troubles, though this certainly is a part of insight. Insight refers to an intense emotional experience that accompanies the release of repressed material. When this material is reintegrated into conscious awareness, and the person experiences the emotions associated with that previously repressed material, then we say that some degree of insight has been achieved.

As you might imagine, none of this is easy. The patient, or at least the patient's ego, has expended much energy to repress the root of the problem in order to keep anxiety at bay. As the therapist pokes at the unconscious material through free association and dream analysis, and begins to offer interpretations, the patient typically feels threatened. The forces that have worked to repress the disturbing impulse or trauma now work to resist the psychoanalytic process, in a stage of psychoanalysis called **resistance**. As the patient's defences are threatened by the probing psychoanalyst, the patient may unconsciously set up obstacles to progress. The patient may come up with all sorts of clever ways to misdirect or derail the psychoanalyst. The patient may forget appointments, not pay the analyst's bill, or go very late to a session. Sometimes during a session, a patient in resistance might spend a great deal of time on trivial matters, thereby avoiding important issues. A patient might waste lots of time recalling the names of and other details about every classmate they knew in elementary school, a process that could take weeks of session time. Or a patient who is being pressed by the analyst and confronted with interpretations might become angry and insult the analyst.

When an analyst detects a patient's resistance, it is usually a welcome sign that progress is being made. Resistance signifies that important unconscious material is coming to the fore. The resistance itself then becomes an integral part of the interpretations the analyst offers to the patient. For example, the analyst might say, "Perhaps you are insulting me because you want to avoid discussing your relationship with your mother. Let's talk some more about what you are trying to avoid by starting an argument with me."

Another important step in most analyses is called **transference**. In this stage, the patient begins reacting to the analyst as if they were an important figure from the patient's own life. The patient displaces past or present feelings toward someone from their own life onto the analyst. For example, a patient might feel and act toward his analyst the way he felt or acted toward his father. The feelings that the patient transfers onto the analyst can be either positive or negative. For example, a patient may express her admiration for the analyst's powerful intellect and keen mind and offer the sort of adoration that a child is likely to have toward a parent. Old conflicts and old reactions then are played out during the therapy sessions.

The idea behind transference is that the interpersonal problems between a patient and the important people in their life will be reenacted in the therapy session with the analyst. Freud called this the "repetition compulsion," whereby the person reenacts interpersonal problems with new people, including the psychoanalyst. Transference may be one source of clues about the person's unconscious conflicts, and it provides the analyst with opportunities for offering interpretations about the patient's behaviour.

 Exercise

Transference can occur in everyday life as well as in psychoanalysis. The nature of our everyday interactions with others can be influenced by past relationship patterns. For example, a student might work hard on a paper to please a favourite professor. Earning less than a perfect grade on that paper—say, a B+—might cause distress, a tearful scene with the professor, or a temper tantrum. The surprised professor might wonder what this person is really reacting to. Perhaps the student is replaying a childhood pattern of reacting immaturely whenever they disappoint a person from whom they desperately seeks approval, such as a demanding parent.

Think of a time when you or someone you know overreacted to an event. Once you have identified such a situation, can you think of any similarities it has to past situations, particularly from childhood? Are there any reasons to suppose that you or someone you know who is overreacting is repeating a conflict from the past?

Movies and other modern media often portray psychoanalysis as resulting in a flash of insight, in which the patient is suddenly and forever cured. Real life is not so simple. A thorough psychoanalysis can take years, sometimes a decade or longer. The analyst provides interpretation after interpretation, illustrating to the patient the unconscious source of key problems. Along the way, the patient may exhibit resistance. Transference also typically becomes an issue for interpretation. Through long and laborious work by both patient and analyst, the patient gradually gains insight. The successfully analyzed patient then has available the psychic energy that the ego has formerly been expending in repressing conflicts. This energy may be directed into those twin pursuits Freud said were the hallmarks of adult personality development—to love and to work.

! Concept Check

Name and describe two key psychoanalytic techniques for revealing the unconscious.

In your own words, summarize the process of psychoanalysis.

Why Is Psychoanalysis Important?

Throughout much of the twentieth century, Freud's ideas had a profound influence on how the mind was understood to operate. His continuing influence can be seen in several areas. First, psychoanalytic ideas influence the practice of psychotherapy even today. The second largest division of the American Psychological Association is the Division of Psychoanalysis. The basic idea of the "talking cure" can be traced back to Freud. Even if a psychotherapist does not engage in classic psychoanalysis, many rely on a few psychoanalytic ideas, such as free association (saying whatever comes to mind as a part of therapy) or transference (that the patient will re-create interpersonal problems with the therapist) in their practice of therapy.

Another area of influence concerns the resurgence of interest in some Freudian ideas on the part of research psychologists. Research psychologists are showing a revival of interest in such topics as the unconscious (e.g., Bornstein, 1999), psychic energy (Baumeister et al., 2007), and defence mechanisms (Cramer & Davidson, 1998). Although they may not endorse the whole of Freudian theory, such researchers are nevertheless finding empirical support for several of his ideas, either in their original form or as they have been modified by others.

A third area of influence can be found in our popular culture, where many of Freud's ideas have been incorporated into everyday language and the logic of understanding our own and others' behaviour. For example, if someone says, "He cannot get along with his teacher because he has a conflict with authority," this comment draws on Freudian ideas. Or if someone explains a person's current problems as being the result of poor parenting, this is a Freudian interpretation. Or if you think a person is avoiding dating and putting all her time into needlepoint work because she is conflicted over sexuality, then you are following a Freudian theme. Many of Freud's ideas have made it into everyday explanations of behaviour and everyday forms of speech, such that you probably know more about Freud's theory than you actually realize.

A final reason Freud's ideas are important is that he laid the foundation for many of the topics and questions that psychologists are still addressing. He proposed a developmental sequence in the growth of personality. He devised a method to resolve internal conflicts. He proposed a structure of the basic elements of personality and described what he thought were the main dynamic relationships among these elements. He noted that the mind has regions about which it does not itself have awareness. All these ideas have continued to be areas of inquiry among contemporary psychologists.

Freud started one of the more interesting, influential, and even controversial approaches to understanding human nature. Consequently, no student of personality should skip over this theory, even if the theory does not play a large role in contemporary studies of personality. Pieces of it have survived and inform various parts of current personality research and theory, so it is worth taking a good look at Freud's classic theory as well as the contemporary modifications of it.

Evaluation of Freud's Contributions

Among contemporary personality psychologists, Freud's theory of personality remains controversial. Some personality psychologists (e.g., Eysenck, 1985; Kihlstrom, 2003a) suggest that psychoanalysis be abandoned. Others contend that psychoanalysis is alive and well (Weinberger, 2003; Westen, 1992, 1998). Opinions among personality psychologists differ dramatically on the accuracy, worth, and importance of psychoanalytic theory, and discussions about the merits of psychoanalysis often provoke passionate debate among those on both sides of the issue (Barron, Eagle, & Wolitsky, 1992).

The controversy surrounding psychoanalysis is covered in *Taking Sides: Clashing Views in Personality Psychology,* by Newman and Larsen (2011). Indeed, that book, or at least Chapter 11 in that book, would make excellent supplementary reading to the current chapter. At one extreme are the critics who hold that psychoanalysis is a stupendous con job by Freud and is totally and completely without merit. At the other extreme are the proponents who argue that it is the most complete theory of human nature to have arisen in recent centuries. Of course, like most controversies, the truth is probably somewhere between the extreme positions.

Proponents of psychoanalysis point to the major impact that Freud's theory has had on Western thought. Many psychoanalytic terms—id, ego, superego, Oedipal conflict—have entered our everyday language. In addition to their influence in psychology, Freud's writings have played a significant role in sociology, literature, fine arts, history, anthropology, and medicine, to name only a few disciplines. Within psychology, Freud's works are among the most frequently cited sources in the literature. Many subsequent developments in the discipline of psychology have borrowed or built on the foundation laid by Freud. Freud shaped modern personality psychology and set the course of advancement for perhaps half a century, and Freud's ideas on psychosexual development played a significant role in initiating the field of developmental psychology. His views on anxiety, defence, and the unconscious show up in modified forms across many areas of modern clinical psychology. The psychotherapy techniques he pioneered are frequently practised, even if sometimes in modified form. Although many modern therapists have done away with the couch, they still inquire about their patients' dreams, ask their patients to free associate, identify and interpret forms of resistance, and work through transference. Moreover, if we think Freud overemphasized sex and aggression, we need merely to look at the popular movies, books, and TV shows.

Critics of psychoanalysis also have strong arguments (e.g., Kihlstrom, 2003b). They maintain that Freud's theory is primarily of historical value, that it does not inform much of the contemporary research in personality psychology. If you were to look in the pages of mainstream personality journals that publish research, you would find very little that had direct relevance to classical psychoanalysis. Critics insist that without holding psychoanalysis up to scrutiny from outsiders, its merits cannot be fairly evaluated on scientific grounds. Freud himself did not believe in the value of experimentation or hypothesis testing in establishing the validity of psychoanalysis (Rosenzweig, 1994). The scientific method is self-correcting in that experiments are conducted to try to disprove theories. If psychoanalysis is not examined scientifically, is not subjected to tests of disproof, then it is simply not supported by scientific fact. Consequently, in the view of some psychologists, psychoanalysis is more a matter of belief than scientific fact.

Another criticism of psychoanalysis pertains to the nature of the evidence on which it was built. Freud relied primarily on the case study method, and the cases he studied were his patients. Who were his patients? They were primarily wealthy, highly educated, and highly verbal women who had lots of free time to spend in frequent sessions with Freud and lots of disposable income to pay his bills. His observations were made during the therapy sessions only. These are limited observations, obtained on a narrow segment of humanity. However, from these observations, Freud constructed a universal theory of human nature. In his writings, he provided as evidence not original observations, but his *interpretations* of those observations. Unlike scientists, who make their raw data available so that the results of their experiments can be checked and verified by others, Freud wrote about his interpretations of the patients' behaviour rather than reporting or describing their behaviour per se. If the actual raw observations were made available, it would be interesting to see if readers would come to the same conclusions that Freud did. Psychoanalysts today could tape therapy sessions for use as evidence. This is rarely done, however, as analysts argue that patients who know they are being taped do not respond naturally.

According to classic Freudian theory, human nature is powered by the twin motives of sex and aggression. These two motives are woven throughout much of contemporary literature, movies, and even video games.
©David McNew/Getty Images News/Getty Images

There are other specific disagreements with Freudian theory. For example, many believe that Freud's emphasis on sexual drives in his theory of childhood development is inappropriate, and perhaps reflects more of a preoccupation of Freud, and the times in which he lived than an actual topic of childhood development. Others disagree with the notion that personality development pretty much ends at around the age of 5, as Freud held. Those psychologists point to the sometimes profound changes in personality that can occur in adolescence and even throughout adulthood. In Chapter 10, we take up alternative conceptions of personality development that build on, but significantly extend, Freud's ideas. We examine other issues in contemporary psychoanalytic thought as well, including a modern view of the unconscious and the importance of relationships in determining personality development (Kihlstrom, Barnhardt, & Tataryn, 1992).

Some personality psychologists take issue with Freud's generally negative view of human nature. At heart, Freud's theory suggests that human nature is violent, self-centred, and impulsive. Freud suggested, in effect, that without the inhibiting influence of society, mediated by the superego, humans would self-destruct. Other personality psychologists suggest a more neutral or even positive core to human nature, which we cover in Chapter 11. Finally, Freud's view of women, when he wrote about them at all, implied that they were inferior to men (Kofman, 1985). He suggested that women developed weaker superegos than men (making them more primitive, with weaker moral character), that women's problems were more difficult to cure than men's, and even that women universally had an unconscious wish to become like men (the penis envy component of the Electra complex). Feminist writers have criticized Freud for confusing women's true capacities and potential with the role they were assigned in an oppressive, male-dominated society, an idea we discuss further in Chapter 10. For a strong feminist critique of Freud, see *Feminism and Psychoanalytic Theory* (Chodorow, 1989).

 Concept Check

What are the most common criticisms of Freud's contributions? Do you agree with these criticisms? Why or why not?

Summary and Evaluation

Freud proposed a theory of human nature that has become highly influential. The theory is unique in its emphasis on how the psyche is compartmentalized into conscious and unconscious portions. Freud's theory holds that there are three main forces in the psyche—the id, ego, and superego—which constantly interact in taming the two motives of sex and aggression. These motives may generate urges, thoughts, and memories that arouse so much anxiety that they are banished to the unconscious. Keeping these unacceptable thoughts, desires, and memories out of conscious awareness requires defence mechanisms, such as repression. Several of these defence mechanisms are topics of contemporary research by academic personality psychologists. Freud also theorized about a series of developmental stages that all individuals went through, with each stage involving a conflict over expressions of sexuality. How the person resolves these conflicts and learns to satisfy his or her desires within the constraints of a civilized society is the development of personality. That is, adults are different from each other because as children they learned different strategies for dealing with specific kinds of conflicts.

Freud also developed a theory and technique of psychotherapy, also called psychoanalysis. The goals of this form of therapy are to make the patient's unconscious conscious and to help the patient understand the traumatic basis of his or her problems. There has been a lively debate in the field about the value of psychoanalysis. However, as psychoanalytic ideas undergo more scientific examination, and as researchers undertake tests on psychoanalytic hypotheses using controlled laboratory experiments, they will undoubtedly learn more about the value and validity of Freud's theory.

The theory of personality proposed by Freud is one of the most comprehensive views on the working of human nature ever proposed; however, most modern personality psychologists do not totally and uncritically accept the entire theory as it was proposed, word for word, by Freud. Instead, most psychologists accept portions of the theory or agree with modifications to Freud's theory. For example, many psychologists agree that there is an unconscious mind that exists outside awareness, yet many disagree that it is motivated in the way Freud proposed. In Chapter 10, we discuss how this influences the debate over repressed memories.

 Concept Check

In your own words, summarize the main contributions of Sigmund Freud. Based on what you've read so far, which of these contributions seems to have been given the most credibility by psychologists today?

What are the main concerns that arise with Freud's original work? Do you believe that these concerns can be overcome at all? If so, how?

Key Terms

psychic energy	thanatos	unconscious
instincts	conscious	blindsight
libido	preconscious	deliberation-without-attention

id

pleasure principle

primary process thinking

wish fulfillment

ego

reality principle

secondary process thinking

superego

ego depletion

objective anxiety

neurotic anxiety

moral anxiety

defence mechanisms

repression

denial

fundamental attribution
  error

displacement

rationalization

reaction formation

projection

false consensus effect

sublimation

psychosexual stage theory

fixation

oral stage

anal stage

phallic stage

Oedipal conflict

castration anxiety

identification

penis envy

Electra complex

latency stage

genital stage

psychoanalysis

free association

dream analysis

manifest content

latent content

symbols

projective hypothesis

insight

resistance

transference

CHAPTER 10

Psychoanalytic Approaches: Contemporary Issues

The Intrapsychic Domain

One of the most famous legal cases involving repressed memory was that of Holly Ramona, a 23-year-old woman being treated through counselling for bulimia. During the course of therapy, which included sessions during which a hypnotic drug (sodium amytal) was administered, Holly Ramona began recalling incidents of sexual abuse that had occurred during her childhood. More specifically, in response to leading questions from her therapists, Holly began "recovering" memories of her father repeatedly raping her between the ages of 5 and 8. The therapist admitted telling Holly that, because sodium amytal is a "truth serum," if she recalled sexual abuse while under its influence, it *must* have really taken place. Holly's father, Gary Ramona, was severely affected by his daughter's accusations. When Holly went public with the allegations of incest, his wife divorced him, the rest of his

Gary Ramona, left, and his attorney walk to Napa County Superior Court on March 24, 1994, for the start of a trial accusing his daughter's therapist of implanting molestation memories using improper suggestion and drugs.
©Al Francis/AP Images

family left him, he lost his well-paying job as an executive at a large winery, and his reputation in the community was ruined. Mr. Ramona claimed he was innocent and accused his daughter's therapists of implanting false memories of incest in her mind.

In an unprecedented legal case, Gary Ramona decided to sue the therapists for the damage they had caused him and his family. He charged that his daughter's recovered memories of being raped by him were, in fact, created by the therapists through repeated suggestions that this was the cause of her bulimia and that she wouldn't get better until she actually remembered having been abused. Mr. Ramona held that implanting these false memories was a form of negligence on the part of the therapists, so he filed a malpractice suit against them. After a gruelling seven-week trial, the jury decided that the therapists were guilty of malpractice and awarded Mr. Ramona $475,000 in damages. The jury foreman was quoted in media sources as having said that the verdict was intended to "send a message about false child abuse memories." Mr. Ramona's attorney saw the verdict as a warning to other therapists, especially to those who believe that adult psychological problems are the result of repressed childhood traumas. One defendant, therapist Marche Isabella, described the verdict as a blow to the mental health profession, adhering to the position that "repressed memories are a reality."

The case of Michael Kliman in British Columbia may offer a similarly disturbing example of false memories resulting in very serious legal accusations. Mr. Kliman was an elementary school teacher and later vice-principal working in the city of Richmond when he was arrested and accused of sexually abusing two female students. The alleged abuse occurred when the students were in Grade 6, but charges were not brought against Mr. Kliman until the students were in their twenties. The claims appeared somewhat unusual from the beginning. In one of the cases, for example, the abuse was reported to have occurred in a specific room in the school that was not even built at the time. In the other case, allegations involved descriptions of abuse occurring in relatively open spaces, despite the lack of corroborating eyewitness testimony. The details of the accusers' stories also appeared to change over time. Nevertheless, in 1994, Mr. Kliman was found guilty of abuse and sentenced to serve time in prison.

It was revealed, however, that one of his accusers had received five years of intensive psychiatric treatment without any indication of childhood sexual abuse. Later, a different therapist claimed to "recover" repressed memories of abuse from one of the alleged victims. Mr. Kliman appealed, yet the second jury was unable to reach a unanimous decision. It was not until a third trial before the British Columbia Supreme Court that Mr. Kliman was found not guilty of allegations of abuse due to inconsistencies and improbabilities in the testimonies of his accusers. According to Elizabeth Loftus (2003), a leading expert on false memories who also testified in the Holly Ramona trial, this example is just one of the "problematic, if not downright dangerous" (p. 207) cases of memories being introduced into legal cases in Canada.

Why did these cases turn out so differently from the case of Sandra, described at the start of Chapter 9? The major difference between the two cases is that Sandra provided substantial corroborating evidence in support of her recovered memories.

But what do these cases tell us about the psychoanalytic idea of the motivated unconscious, the idea that the mind can bury memories of horrifying events and then, decades later, accurately retrieve those memories? By themselves, single cases do not prove anything for or against unconsciously motivated repression. People forget all sorts of things. Can you remember what you ate for dinner last Tuesday? With the right cues, however, could you be led to remember accurately? With other cues, could you be led to inaccurately remember what you had for dinner last Tuesday?

What is the difference between ordinary forgetting and motivated repression? Is there good scientific evidence for motivated repression? Could people be motivated to "remember" events that did not actually happen, as apparently was the case with Holly Ramona? To answer these questions we examine contemporary revisions to classical psychoanalysis, collectively known as the neo-analytic movement.

The Neo-Analytic Movement

As proposed by Freud, classical psychoanalysis is a detailed and comprehensive theory, developed in the early 1900s, of the totality of human nature. Many of Freud's ideas are out of date; however, contemporary psychoanalyst Drew Westen (1998) argues that they *should* be out of date; after all, Freud died in 1939 and "he has been slow to undertake further revisions" (p. 333) of his theory. Westen goes on humorously to note that "Freud, like Elvis, has been dead for a number of years but continues to be cited with some regularity" (p. 333). Whereas many of Freud's ideas have not stood the test of time, others have and have been incorporated into a contemporary version of psychoanalysis. Today, psychoanalysis is probably best thought of as a theory containing ideas variously inspired by Sigmund Freud but modified and advanced by others.

Westen (e.g., 1990, 1998) is one of the most active proponents of contemporary psychoanalysis. Writing on the scientific legacy of Freud, Westen notes that contemporary psychoanalysts no longer write much about ids, superegos, and repressed sexuality; nor do they liken treatment to an archeological expedition in search of forgotten memories. Instead, most contemporary psychoanalysts focus their attention on childhood relationships and adult conflicts with others, such as difficulties becoming intimate or readily becoming intimate with the wrong kinds of people (Greenberg & Mitchell, 1983). Westen (1998) defines contemporary psychoanalysis as being based on the following five postulates:

1. The unconscious still plays a large role in life, although it may not be the ubiquitous influence that Freud held it was.
2. Behaviour often reflects compromises in conflicts among mental processes, such as emotions, motivations, and thoughts (Westen & Gabbard, 2002a).
3. Childhood plays an important part in personality development, particularly in terms of shaping adult relationship styles.
4. Mental representations of the self and relationships guide our interactions with others (Westen & Gabbard, 2002b).
5. Personality development involves not just regulating sexual and aggressive feelings but also moving from an immature, socially dependent way of relating to others to a mature, independent relationship style.

This neo-analytic viewpoint has wider currency and better empirical support, in some cases, than Freud's original ideas. To start our coverage of contemporary issues in psychoanalysis, we begin with a discussion of repression and memory.

Repression and Contemporary Research on Memory

It is easy to find conflicting opinions among respected psychologists on the issue of motivated repression. One review of the clinical literature on motivated repression concluded "the evidence for repression is overwhelming and obvious" (Erdelyi & Goldberg, 1979, p. 384). Another review of the same literature concluded "the concept of repression has not been validated with experimental research" (Holmes, 1990, p. 97).

Elizabeth Loftus, a professor of psychology and world-renowned memory researcher, has perhaps conducted the most research on the authenticity of recovered memories. Loftus has been the one psychologist most connected to the repressed memory debate, and summarizes scientific status of the concepts of "repressed" and "recovered" memories of sexual abuse (Loftus, 2003). In her article titled "The Reality of Repressed Memories" (Loftus, 1993), she discusses many cases of individuals who suddenly recover memories of important events: some of these turn out to be true memories, whereas others are false or inaccurate accounts, which are later recanted. However, she argues that we should not conclude that *all* recovered memories are **false memories**, just because some, such as Holly Ramona's, have turned out apparently to be false. Similarly, we should not assume that *all* recovered memories are true, just because some, such as Sandra's that we explored in Chapter 9, have turned out to be true. Loftus believes that what is important is being aware of the processes that may contribute to the possible creation of inaccurate or false memories.

Professor Elizabeth Loftus testified in the Ramona trial and has contributed a good deal of scientific information to the debate over repressed memories.
©Don Shrubshell, Pool/AP Images

Loftus (1992, 1993, 2011) suggests that many variables contribute to the construction of false memories.

One factor that might influence people to have false memories is the popular press. Many books currently on the market purport to be guides for survivors of abuse; these are undoubtedly of some comfort to people who have been living with painful memories of abuse. For those who have no such memories, these books often provide strong suggestions that abuse could have happened, even if there is no memory of the abuse. For example, a popular book in this category is *The Courage to Heal* (Bass & Davis, 1988), which states:

> *You may think you don't have memories. . . . To say, "I was abused," you don't need the kind of recall that would stand up in a court of law. Often the knowledge that you were abused starts with a tiny feeling, an intuition. . . . Assume your feelings are valid. . . . If you think you were abused and your life shows the symptoms, then you were. (p. 22)*

What are some of the symptoms *The Courage to Heal* suggests indicate a person is likely to have been abused? The book lists, among other things, low self-esteem, self-destructive thoughts, depression, and sexual dysfunction. This book, and others like it, provides a strong message that even in the absence of a specific memory, many people should conclude that they have been abused. However, there are many causes of low self-esteem, depression, and sexual dysfunction. In addition, these symptoms are associated with many other psychological disorders, such as phobias and anxieties, and these disorders certainly can occur without a history of abuse.

This quote is a powerful suggestion that may lead some to conclude falsely that they must have been abused. A person who starts with this idea may embellish this suggestion by filling in details to make a convincing or consistent story of abuse. If one is led further along these lines by a questioning therapist, false memories may become more and more convincing. Loftus (1993) has demonstrated in the lab that subjects questioned in a leading manner after watching a video of a car accident can be led to conclude that one car ran a stop sign, even though there was no stop sign in the video. And with more leading questioning, subjects increase their confidence that one car is to blame because it ran the stop sign (Bernstein & Loftus, 2009). In A Closer Look: So, You Want to Have a False Memory, we demonstrate how easily false memories can be created in non-clinical situations.

 **A Closer Look**

So, You Want to Have a False Memory

Imagine you are a subject in a psychology experiment in which you are assigned to listen carefully to a list of 15 words, knowing that you will later be tested on these words. The words are *bed, rest, awake, tired, dream, wake, snooze, blanket, doze, slumber, snore, nap, peace, yawn,* and *drowsy.* Now cover the list of words and indicate whether or not each of the following words was on the list:

	On the List?	
	Yes	No
snooze	_____	_____
mother	_____	_____
bed	_____	_____
television	_____	_____
sleep	_____	_____
chair	_____	_____

If you are like most people, you checked yes following the word *sleep.* Indeed, many people are so certain that *sleep* was on the first list that they argue with the experimenter when they are told that, in fact, it was not. Thus, if you checked yes, indicating that sleep was on the list during the recall phase of the task, and you really remember seeing the word *sleep,* then you just had a false memory. Approximately 80 percent of normal subjects are induced to have this false memory; that is, they believe that *sleep* was on the original list (Roediger, Balota, & Watson, 2001; Roediger, McDermott, & Robinson, 1998).

The procedure you just completed was developed by psychologists Henry Roediger and Kathleen McDermott (1995). They devised the technique based on the **spreading activation** model of memory. This model of memory holds that mental elements (such as words or images) are stored in memory along with associations to other elements in memory. For example, *doctor* is associated with *nurse* in most people's memories, because of the close connection or similarity between these concepts. The mental association between these two concepts can be demonstrated easily; the speed of deciding that a letter string *(doctor)* is a word or not is faster if it is preceded by an associated concept *(nurse)* relative to an unrelated word *(table).* The explanation is that the activation of *nurse* in your memory spreads through an association network and activates other related concepts, such as *doctor,* allowing them to be recognized faster.

How does this explain the false memory for *sleep* in the exercise? Like any concept, *sleep* is stored in your memory in a network of associations to other words, such as *bed, rest, awake, tired, dream, wake, snooze, blanket,* and *doze.* This network of associations is depicted in Figure 10.1.

Activation from the multiple words on the first list spreads or primes the critical concept on the recall list *(sleep)* in the memory network of the person studying the list. The activation from all the words related to *sleep* (e.g., *bed, rest,* and *tired*) sums up and makes the concept of *sleep* more likely to be recalled or recognized later, even though the actual word *sleep* was not on the original list.

Researchers have also shown that the probability of a false memory in this task is a function of the number of words on the first list that are associated with the critical word (e.g., *sleep*). That is, the sum of the association strength from the list items to the critical item determines false recall of the critical item.

Association strength is determined by how frequently the critical word (e.g., *sleep*) is named when people are asked for the first word that comes to mind from some other word (e.g., *bed*). In fact, psychologists have determined lists of common associates to a whole variety of words, and the sum of association strength of the listed items to the critical item is what determines the probability of false recall (Roediger et al., 2001).

How is this material related to the psychoanalytic idea of false memories? First, this material highlights how most cognitive psychologists, even those with strong scientific values, believe that false memories can occur. It is accepted as fact that humans have a **constructive memory**; that is, memory contributes to or influences in various ways (adds to, subtracts from, and so on) what is recalled. Rather than referring to pristine and objective retrieval of facts from the past, human memory is fallible and open to error and corruption. Moreover, the corruption is most likely to occur when elements with strong associations to each other converge repeatedly in experience. In this condition, the person is likely to recognize or recall something associated to those elements, even if that new element never occurred. For example, during interrogation, imagine that a person is repeatedly asked about an event in many different leading ways. After some time, the person is asked something that is new but related to the first information. The person may then be more likely to recall this new event as happening, not because it did happen, but because it is associated with the previously presented information. This is how innocent mistakes of recognition on word lists might help us understand the larger and more dramatic false memories that have been documented in certain legal cases, such as that of Holly Ramona and Michael Kliman.

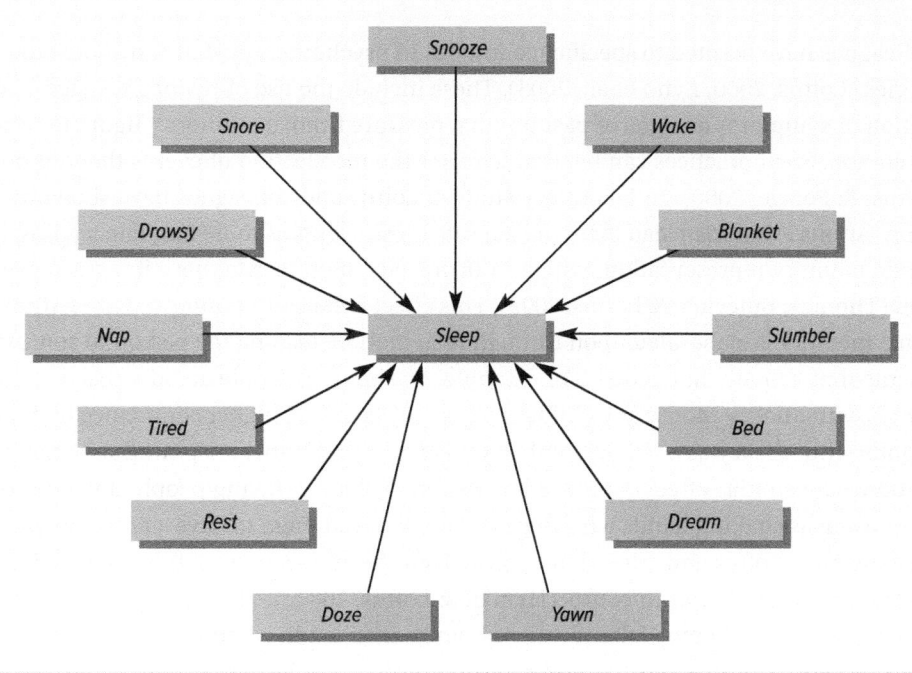

FIGURE 10.1 Hypothetical network of concepts related to the word *sleep*.
Source: Adapted from Roediger, Balota, & Watson, 2001.

Another factor that may contribute to false memories is the behaviour of some therapists. Loftus tells of a woman who wrote to her after the woman's therapist had concluded that her depression was caused by childhood sexual abuse. The patient stated that her therapist was certain of that diagnosis, even though the patient had no memory of the abuse. The patient further stated that she could not understand how something so terrible could have happened without her being able to remember the event. Loftus tells of another case of a man who went to a therapist because he was distraught over his father's suicide. The patient talked about painful events in his life, but the therapist kept suggesting that there must be something else. Not knowing what this "something else" was, the patient became even more depressed. Then, during a therapy session, the therapist stated that "you display the same kinds of characteristics as some of my patients who are victims of . . . ritualistic abuse" (cited in Loftus, 1993, p. 528).

A variety of techniques are used in therapy that encourage patients to reflect on their childhoods. Hypnosis is one technique used to get patients to recall freely childhood experiences within the protection of a relaxed, suggestion-induced, trancelike state. An extensive scientific literature, however, shows that hypnosis does not improve memory (Nash, 1987, 1988). This explains why hypnotizing witnesses is not allowed in courts of law; Canada was the first country to completely prohibit hypnosis in the court system in 2007. Hypnotized witnesses do not recall facts with any greater accuracy than nonhypnotized witnesses (Kihlstrom, 2003b; Wagstaff, Vella, & Perfect, 1992). In fact, hypnosis may be associated with increased distortions in memory (Spanos & McLean, 1986). In one case, a highly suggestible man was led under hypnosis to develop "memories" for crimes that had not even been committed (Ofshe, 1992). Under hypnosis, people are often more imaginative, more spontaneous, and more emotional and often report unusual bodily sensations (Nash, 2001). After being taken back to childhood through hypnosis, people have been known to recall being abducted by alien creatures with fantastic spaceships (Loftus, 1993).

Loftus and colleagues have pointed to specific techniques in psychotherapy that can contribute to the creation of false memories (Loftus, 2000; Lynn et al., 2003). These include the use of hypnosis, suggestive interviewing, the interpretation of symptoms as signs of past trauma, pressure from an authority figure to recall trauma, and dream interpretation. Such practices can be used to foster the recollection of events that did not actually happen (Tsai, Loftus, & Polage, 2000). In laboratory studies, Loftus and colleagues have shown that having individuals imagine various events can lead them to later rate those events as more familiar, leading subjects to have a more elaborate memory representation, which in turn leads them to rate those imagined events as likely to have happened (Thomas, Bulevich, & Loftus, 2003). This effect is called the **imagination inflation effect**, and it occurs when a memory is elaborated upon through imagination, leading the person to confuse the imagined event with events that actually happened. For example, by showing people an advertisement suggesting that they shook hands with Mickey Mouse as a child, those people later had higher confidence that they had personally shaken hands with Mickey as a child. Another study had participants imagining shaking hands with Bugs Bunny and produced a similar effect (Braun, Ellis, & Loftus, 2002). Having people imagine something, even something as unusual as shaking hands with Bugs Bunny, can lead them to have a false confidence that it actually may have happened. Loftus and others have pointed out the implications of this research for the admissibility of allegedly repressed memories in courts (Hyman & Loftus, 2002; Loftus, 2003). Loftus has also developed a misinformation paradigm whereby false memories can be instilled in laboratory settings by exposing subjects to misinformation when questioning them about some event. She has shown that this technique can alter memory for even very personally stressful events (Morgan et al., 2012), and that such false memories were found to persist over one and a half years later when subjects were followed up (Zhu et al., 2012).

Why would some therapists suggest false memories to their patients? Many therapists believe that effective treatment must result in a patient's overcoming repressed memories and reclaiming a traumatic past. They believe that the road to wellness requires bringing traumatic memories into consciousness and having the patient acknowledge and overcome them or at least deal with them in a mature, adult fashion. Therapists, like many other people, can also suffer from a **confirmatory bias**—the tendency to look only for evidence that confirms their previous hunch and to not look for evidence that might disconfirm their belief. If a therapist believes that childhood trauma is the cause of most adult problems, they will most likely probe for memories of childhood trauma. Compliant and suggestible patients are then often induced to spend long periods of time trying to imagine what events must have happened in their childhoods to produce their current difficulties. Meanwhile, the therapist relates stories of other patients with similar problems who were helped by recalling and coping with memories of childhood abuse. The therapist, as an "authority" on how to get better, stands ready to authenticate any possible memory of trauma that the patient might produce. These are the ideal conditions for constructing a shared reality that, even though both parties are confident of its authenticity, is not true.

Although false memories may indeed occur, this position must be balanced with some known facts about the rates of various forms of child abuse. After all, as Loftus (1993) has noted, not all memories of childhood trauma are false memories. Many are true. Recent surveys suggest that a remarkable amount of trauma is inflicted on children. For example, in 1998 there were approximately 135,600 reported child victims of maltreatment in Canada. Of these, 40 percent involved neglect, 31 percent involved physical abuse, 19 percent were for emotional maltreatment, 10 percent were sexual abuse cases, and approximately 9 percent involved medical neglect. From 1991–1999, an estimated 428 children died of abuse and neglect in Canada. Of these fatalities, 55 percent were under the age of 4 years. (All statistics are from a report by Statistics Canada, 2001.) Researchers have also specifically examined the extent to which childhood abuse leads to problems in adulthood. One study, a 1998 meta-analysis, caused a great deal of controversy over its provocative interpretation of results. We explore this further in A Closer Look: Does Childhood Sexual Abuse Cause Problems in Adulthood? Anatomy of a Controversy Started by a Scientific Paper (Rind et al., 1998).

 A Closer Look

Does Childhood Sexual Abuse Cause Problems in Adulthood? Anatomy of a Controversy Started by a Scientific Paper (Rind et al., 1998)

In 1998, a scientific paper appeared in the journal *Psychological Bulletin* titled "A meta-analytic examination of assumed properties of child sexual abuse (CSA) using college samples," and authored by psychologists Bruce Rind, Philip Tromovitch, and Robert Bauserman. The authors' goal was to determine whether child sexual abuse (CSA) causes intense or long-term psychological harm for both genders. They reviewed 59 studies on this topic, all conducted on college students. By meta-analyzing these studies, Rind and colleagues found that students with a history of CSA were, on average, slightly less well adjusted than students without a history of CSA. However, poor family environment also correlated with a history of CSA, making it impossible to argue that CSA in itself causes adjustment problems (independent from poor family environment). In general, the authors concluded that CSA does not appear to cause as much intense or long-lasting psychological harm as might be assumed.

This paper ignited a firestorm of controversy that took several years to play out. Most people assume that the sexual abuse of children is bad because of the long-term harm such abuse holds for children. Yet here was a study saying that it was difficult to document any substantial harm over the long run for childhood sexual abuse. Consequently, many people entered the debate because they were simply outraged over the conclusions that childhood sexual abuse was not so bad.

Other groups were outraged by the Rind and colleagues paper for other reasons. Psychologists with a psychoanalytic bent start with the critical assumption that psychological problems in adulthood often have their roots in childhood trauma. The Rind paper goes against this critical assumption by purportedly showing that the link between adult adjustment difficulties and history of sexual abuse in childhood is weak.

Organizations that endorse pedophilia (sexual contact between children and adults) applauded the Rind publication on their Web sites, citing this paper as supporting their moral position that sexual relations between children and adults is acceptable. In 1999 the publisher of the *Psychological Bulletin*—the American Psychological Association—issued a statement saying that they do not endorse pedophilia, and that "the sexual abuse of children is wrong and harmful to its victims." In 1999 the U.S. House of Representatives passed a resolution condemning the Rind and colleagues (1998) study, declaring that child–adult sex was inherently "abusive and destructive," and the resolution was passed unanimously in the Senate.

What can we say about the Rind and colleagues study in light of this controversy? The authors attacked a common assumption that CSA causes harm and leads to long-term problems. Most cultures around the world consider it wrong for adults to have sexual contact with children. However, Rind and colleagues argued that the "wrongfulness" of CSA may be in question because its "harmfulness" is in dispute. In other words, because the act may not produce harmful *consequences,* we might question whether CSA is actually *wrong.* Moreover, the authors were quite provocative in interpreting their results, for example arguing that discussions of CSA should not include such terms as *victim* or *perpetrator* or even *abuse* because these are moral, not scientific, terms.

The rebuttals of the Rind and colleagues paper fall into two categories: methodological and interpretational. On the methodological side, one important concern is that the data were based on college students. Such a sample would exclude victims of CSA that were so traumatized that they did not go on to attend college. Also, it could be that, for example, people with a history of CSA are more likely to drop out of college than people without such a history. By excluding non-college-attending individuals from their research, Rind and colleagues (1998) may have severely underestimated the effect of CSA on adult adjustment. Another methodological concern is the broad definition they used of CSA, which included acts ranging from forced sexual intercourse to being verbally propositioned. By including such "mild" abuses as being verbally propositioned (without sexual contact) in their definition of CSA, it could be that Rind and colleagues diluted the effects of real CSA on adjustment.

A final methodological concern involves the fact that most of the studies analyzed by Rind and colleagues relied completely on retrospective self-report of college students as the only source of data. A much better (though also much more difficult) approach would be a prospective design, where children identified as having been recently abused would be followed over the years until they are adults and then adjustment is assessed and compared with a control group that was not abused.

One can also disagree with how Rind and colleagues interpret their findings. For example, they argue that because poor family environment correlates with CSA, one cannot know that it is CSA that is causing the poorer adjustment outcomes. It could be that people from poor family backgrounds (those that have other forms of abuse or neglect, high levels of conflict, mental illness, etc.) are at risk of poor adjustment outcomes regardless of whether CSA occurs. However, Rind and colleagues never seriously consider whether poor family background is caused by, or is a consequence of, the child sexual abuse. Because most of the studies are based on retrospective self-report, we cannot know which of these possibilities is the correct interpretation for the relationship between poor family background and CSA (Lilienfeld, 2002).

Another interpretation issue concerns the meaning of "small" when the authors describe the relation between CSA and such adjustment outcomes as anxiety, depression, suicide, divorce, or paranoia. It is true that the effect sizes conform to the statistical definition of small (e.g., effect sizes less than .30).

However, even small effects can reflect very important consequences for people and impact large percentages of people. Moreover, individuals may exhibit elevated levels of one type of symptom, but the symptoms may differ from person to person, such that any one symptom may not be very elevated in the CSA population as a whole, even though individuals themselves suffer greatly. In certain ways, statistical effect sizes do not convey clinical significance and in this regard can be misleading.

A final interpretation issue concerns the fact that, because their data suggest that CSA is not intensely harmful, Rind and colleagues (1998) go on to allude that CSA is morally benign. However, this is a slippery slope. Such a position holds that in order for something to be wrong, it must be shown to be harmful. It replaces a moral standard with a scientific standard, and science can only document relations, not decide on what is right or wrong. Ultimately, the question boils down to how do we decide if something is wrong? Legally, the definition of most wrongs is given by society's norms, by what most people feel is wrong or inappropriate. Ultimately we need to rely on the wisdom of societal beliefs to help us determine what is wrong. When it comes to children, society generally believes that they are incapable of making rational and informed life decisions. For example, in North American society, children are not allowed to enter into financial contracts, to decide whether they want to attend school, to consent to medical procedures, to participate in research, or to consume tobacco or alcohol. In addition, add to this list the sociological belief that children cannot consent to sexual relations. The real moral basis for deeming sexual acts with children inappropriate is based on the social belief that children cannot give consent to sex because they have little knowledge about what is being consented to, and when it is an adult forcing the issue, they may not have the absolute freedom to accept or decline. This position is well summarized in a 1999 public letter written by the then American Psychological Association CEO Raymond Fowler to Congressman DeLay, holding "that children cannot consent to sexual activity with adults" and that such activity "should never be considered or labeled as harmless or acceptable (American Psychological Association, 1999)." Because society believes that children lack the maturity to make important life decisions, they need to be protected from those who would exploit their immaturity. In this sense, the data from the Rind and colleagues article are irrelevant to whether CSA is wrong. The huge controversy surrounding the article was not so much an attempt to censure unpopular results, though there were methodological problems with the study. Much of the controversy can be traced to the authors' use of science to replace morality, their confusing "harmfulness" with "wrongness."

Contemporary Views on the Unconscious

The idea of a motivated unconscious is at the core of classical psychoanalytic theory. Most contemporary psychologists also believe in the unconscious, although it is a different version of the unconscious than that found in classical psychoanalytic theory. Consider the views of psychologist John Bargh (2005), a social psychologist whose research on unconscious processes has had a large impact on psychology: "People are often unaware of the reasons and causes of their own behavior. In fact, recent experimental evidence points to a deep and fundamental dissociation between conscious awareness and the mental processes responsible for one's behavior" (p. 38). This can be illustrated with one of Bargh's own experiments in which college student subjects took part in what they thought was an experiment on language, where they were presented with many different words. Half of the participants were presented with words synonymous with rudeness; the other half were presented with words synonymous with politeness. After finishing the language experiment, they went to another experiment in another room and encountered a staged situation where it was possible to act in either a rude or polite way. Although the participants showed no awareness of the possible influence of the language experiment, they nevertheless behaved in the staged situation in a manner that was consistent with the kinds of words they were exposed to in the "previous" experiment (Bargh, 2005). Most psychologists believe that the unconscious can influence our behaviour, but not all agree with Freud that the unconscious can have its own autonomous motivation (Bargh, 2006a, 2008).

We can term these two differing views on the unconscious the **motivated unconscious** view and the **cognitive unconscious** view. Those with the cognitive unconscious view readily acknowledge that information can get into our memories without our ever being aware of the information (Kihlstrom, 1999). For example, in the phenomenon of **subliminal perception**, some information—such as the phrase "Buy a Coke"—is flashed on a screen so quickly that you don't recognize the actual words. That is, you would say that you had seen a flash but were not able to distinguish what was written. Indeed, you could not even guess that the word *Coke* was presented better than chance compared to guessing that some other nonpresented word, say *House*, was presented. However, if you were asked to judge whether a string of letters is a word or not a word, and the dependent variable were reaction time (how quickly you can make this judgment), then you would judge *Coke* as a word faster than words unrelated to Coke or soft drinks in general. Thus, subliminal information primes associated material in memory. **Priming** makes that associated material more accessible to conscious awareness than is material that is not primed. Results such as these using subliminal primes clearly demonstrate that information can get into the mind and have some influence, without going through conscious experience.

If someone were given the subliminal message "Buy a Coke," would they be more likely to spontaneously go out and do so? After all, this is consistent with the psychoanalytic idea of the motivated unconscious—that something in the unconscious can motivate behaviour. Can advertisers use subliminal messages to unconsciously motivate consumers? Similar questions arise concerning the influence of subliminal rock music messages that supposedly advocate suicide or violence. The vast majority of research on subliminal perception, however, suggests that unconscious information does not influence people's motivations. That is, the average teen exposed to subliminal messages of violence in a song is unlikely to go out and commit a violent act. Similarly, the average person subliminally exposed to the phrase "Buy a Coke" is unlikely to do so.

In the cognitive view of the unconscious, the content of the unconscious mind is assumed to operate just like thoughts in consciousness. Thoughts are unconscious because they are not in conscious awareness, not because they have been repressed or because they represent unacceptable urges or wishes. For example, we might say that buttoning a shirt is unconscious because we can do it without focusing any conscious attention on the act. Typing can also be unconscious for the person who is good at it. Other kinds of mental content, such as beliefs and values, might also be unconscious. Such elements are not in our unconscious because they are threatening; nor are they there to exert influence on our behaviour. And although unconscious material can influence subsequent thoughts or behaviour, as in the priming examples, these influences are not consistent with the motivated unconscious of classical psychoanalytic theory (Kihlstrom, 2003b; Nash, 1999). As such, the cognitive unconscious as viewed by contemporary psychologists is quite different from that put forward by Freud a hundred years ago. According to Freud, the unconscious was a torrid and fuming cauldron of anger and eroticism. It operated according to its own primitive and irrational rules, and it had broad, sweeping influence over our conscious behaviour, thoughts, and feelings. In contemporary psychology, the unconscious is peaceful, gentle, and much more rational than Freud's version. Moreover, although the unconscious is still viewed as having an influence on behaviour, thoughts, and feelings, that influence is seen as more bounded, rule governed, and specific, as in unconscious priming, than was taught by Freud (Bargh & Morsella, 2008, 2010). Nevertheless, the general idea that there is a lot happening "under the hood" (i.e., on an unconscious level) is relatively well supported by psychologists from diverse areas of study (e.g., social psychology) (Bargh, 2006b).

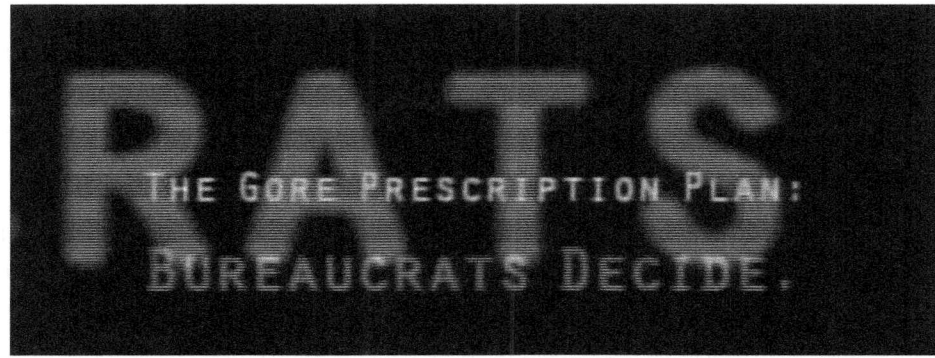

In the 2000 U.S. presidential election campaign, a Republican team released a commercial describing some of the questionable fundraising efforts of Al Gore, the Democratic opponent. During the commercial, the word RATS was subliminally presented, along with information about Gore. When the Gore campaign team discovered this, they responded with outrage and a public denouncement of this subliminal attempt to influence voter opinion on the part of the Bush campaign. The Bush campaign quickly pulled the commercial, with Bush himself denying he had had any role in ordering subliminal propaganda. The fact that both campaign teams believed that such subliminal messages would have a wide impact on voter motivation shows that many people believe in unconscious motivation. Researchers are debating the power of subliminal political advertisements to influence public opinion (Weinberger & Westen, 2007).
©Reuters/Newscom

 Concept Check

What are the five basic assumptions or ideas supported by contemporary psychoanalysis?

Summarize the contemporary perspectives on the unconscious. How does research on repression inform our understanding of the unconscious mind?

Ego Psychology

Another major modification to psychoanalysis concerns a shift in focus from id to ego. Freud's version of psychoanalysis focused on the id, especially the twin instincts of sex and aggression, and how the ego and superego respond to the demands of the id. We might characterize Freudian psychoanalysis as **id psychology**. Later psychoanalysts, including Freud's daughter Anna, felt that the ego deserved more attention, that it performed many constructive functions. One prominent student of Freud—Erik Erikson—emphasized the ego as a powerful, independent part of personality. Moreover, Erikson noted that the ego was involved in mastering the environment, achieving one's goals, and hence establishing one's identity. It is no wonder, then, that the approach to psychoanalysis started by Erikson is called **ego psychology**.

Establishing a secure identity is seen as the primary function of the ego. Identity can be thought of as an inner sense of who we are, of what makes us unique, and a sense of continuity over time and a feeling of wholeness. You have probably heard the term **identity crisis**. This term comes from Erikson's work, and it refers to the desperation and confusion a person feels when a strong sense of identity has not developed. Maybe you have even felt such feelings when you were uncertain about yourself, uncertain about who you were or how you wanted others to view you, what you valued and wanted out of life, and where you were going in terms of the direction of your life. A period of identity crisis is a common experience during adolescence, but for some people it occurs later in life or lasts for a longer period. The so-called midlife crisis, discussed more in Chapter 11, often begins with an identity crisis (Sheldon & Kasser, 2001).

One of Erikson's lasting contributions was developing the notion of identity as an important developmental achievement in everyone's personality. Identity has been thought of as a story that a person develops about himself or herself (McAdams, 1999, 2008, 2011). The story answers the following questions: Who am I? What is my place in the adult world? What are the unifying themes of my life? What is the purpose of my existence? McAdams (e.g., 2011) sees identity as a narrative story that a person constructs. Although a person may rearrange and reconstruct the plot of their life story, it nevertheless takes on importance as the person's unique story. According to McAdams, once the story has evolved to have coherent themes, the person may make very few changes to their story. However, certain events can cause large changes to identity and are incorporated into the narrative, such as graduation, marriage, birth of a child, turning 40, or retirement. Unexpected events can become a part of the story too, such as the death of a marriage partner, loss of a job, or unexpected wealth. A study by Cox and McAdams (2012) showed that even volunteering over spring break to work with people living in poverty can transform the narrative identity that college students write about themselves. McAdams (2008) describes how all of us construct a life story, and that part of becoming an adult is taking ownership of this story:

> People begin to construct narrative identities in adolescence and young adulthood and continue to work on these stories across the adult life course. . . . The stories we construct to make sense of our lives are fundamentally about our struggle to reconcile who we imagine we were, are, and might be in our heads and bodies with who we were, are, and might be in the social contexts of family, community, the workplace, ethnicity, religion, gender, social class, and culture writ large. The self comes to terms with society through narrative identity. (pp. 242–243)

Erikson's Eight Stages of Development

Whereas Freud taught that our personalities were formed by around the age of 5 years, Erikson disagreed and felt that important periods of development occurred throughout the life span. For example, Freud called the period from age 6 to puberty the latency period because he believed not much psychologically was going on. However, this is a period when children are starting to go to school; they are learning to work and to gain satisfaction from success and from accomplishments; they are learning to be sociable, to share, and to cooperate with peers; and they are learning about social structures, such as the fact that teachers are in charge and represent authorities. Erikson (1963, 1968) argued that much development occurred during the years that Freud thought were quiet. Indeed, Erikson believed that the development of personality lasted well into adulthood and even old age (Erikson, 1975). He outlined eight stages through which we all pass; **Erikson's eight stages of development** are illustrated in Figure 10.2.

Not only did Erikson disagree with Freud about the time span of development, but he also disagreed with Freud about the conflict, or crisis, that occurs at each stage. Whereas Freud felt that the crises were inherently sexual, Erikson believed that the crises were of a social nature. After all, he argued, the individuals with whom we have our first social relationships are our parents. Thus, there could be crises of learning to trust our parents, learning to be autonomous from them, learning from them how to act as an adult. He called these **psychosocial conflicts** rather than the psychosexual conflicts that formed Freud's developmental stages.

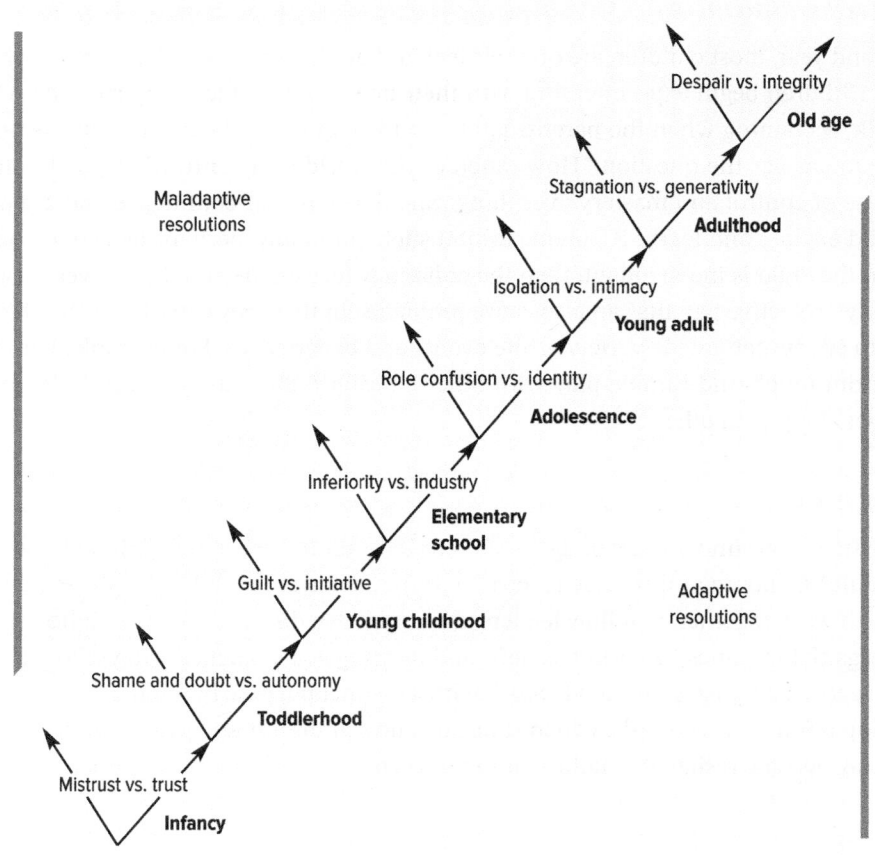

FIGURE 10.2 Erikson's eight stages of development.

Although Erikson disagreed with Freud on these two issues of development, he did agree with Freud on several other points. First, like Freud, Erikson kept a **stage model of development**, implying that people go through the stages in a certain order and that there is a specific issue that characterizes each stage. Second, Erikson believed that each stage represented a conflict, a **developmental crisis**, that needed to be resolved. Third, Erikson maintained the notion of fixation, meaning that if the crisis was not successfully and adaptively resolved, then personality development could become arrested and the person would continue to be preoccupied by that crisis in development. Let's now briefly consider each of the eight stages.

Trust versus Mistrust

When children are born, they are completely dependent on those around them. Their first questions would most likely be "Who's going to take care of me, and will they do a good job? Can I trust that they will feed me when I am hungry, clothe me when I am cold, comfort me when I cry, and generally take care of me?" If children are well taken care of, if their basic needs are met, then they will develop a sense of trust in their caregivers. This sense of trust, according to Erikson, forms the basis of future relationships, with such children growing up believing that other people are approachable, trustable, and generally good and loving. However, some infants are not well taken care of, for various reasons, and they never receive the love and care they need. Such infants may develop a sense that others are not to be trusted and may develop a lifelong pattern of mistrust in others, suspiciousness, and feelings of estrangement, isolation, or social discomfort when around others.

Autonomy versus Shame and Doubt

Around the second year, most children are on their feet and on the go. This is the stage many parents call the "terrible twos." Children begin experimenting with their new abilities, including running when the parents tell them to walk, screaming when the parents tell them to be quiet, and generally just testing their powers. They are trying to answer the question "How much of the world do I control?" A good outcome is when a child feels a sense of control and mastery over things and develops self-confidence and a sense of autonomy that lets the child explore and learn. If parents inhibit such autonomy, perhaps by being strict, restrictive, or punishing when the child is independent, then the child may feel shame and doubt over the goals being contemplated. Overly protective parents can also cause problems, in that they can hinder the child's natural urge to explore and to encounter a wide variety of life events and experiences. For example, parents who prevent their children from rough-and-tumble play with other children may cause their child to grow up doubting their ability to get along with others.

Initiative versus Guilt

Children at this stage—around 3 years of age—often imitate adults, dressing in adult clothes, playing adults, and acting as adults. Children at this stage receive their first practice in adult tasks during play. As adults, we must learn how to work together, to follow leaders, and to resolve disputes. When children play, they practise these skills by organizing games, choosing leaders, and forming goals. Then, during school activities they also take the initiative to accomplish goals and to work with a distinct purpose in mind. If all goes well, children at this stage develop a sense of initiative, which translates into ambition and goal seeking. If things do not go well, children may become resigned to failure or to not even take the initiative to pursue goals.

Industry versus Inferiority

It is good to have experiences of success, but we all have limits, and there is a lot of competition. Starting around age 4, children begin comparing themselves to each other, especially those their own age, and many (although not all) develop a sense of competence and achievement. If people have enough success experiences, then they believe in their strength and abilities and assume that if they just work hard enough, they can do most things they desire to do. This sense of industry—feeling as if they can work to achieve what they want—sets children on their way to being productive members of society. However, with enough failure experiences, children might develop a sense of inferiority, feeling that they don't have the talent or ability to get ahead in life.

Identity versus Role Confusion

During adolescence, people go through a whole series of drastic physical changes. This can be an especially difficult time of life, in which people emerge from childhood into adulthood, whether they are ready or not. Erikson gave this period special attention in his work, referring to identity achievement as one of the most important goals of development.

At this stage, adolescents begin to ask themselves the questions "Who am I?" and "Do others recognize me for who I think I am?" Many people do a lot of experimentation at this stage, trying on many different identities. One semester, a high school student might try on the role of athlete; the next semester, the role of punk rocker; the next semester, born-again Christian; and the next semester, Goth. Experimenting with identities is common at this time of life, with teenagers searching for identity in all sorts of ways and places. One student said he was going to Hawaii to "find himself." In actuality, no matter where you go, there you are, so the search for identity really has no special place. But many people at this stage join groups, drift around the country, commit themselves to various causes or ideals, or experiment with drugs, politics, or religion, all in an effort to find the true "me." Eventually, most people make some decisions about what is important and what they value and want out of life, and they acquire a sense of "who they are," achieving some degree of consistent self-understanding. People who fail in this stage develop role confusion and enter adulthood without a solid sense of who they are or what they think is the meaning of their lives. Such people bounce around among all sorts of roles and are generally unstable in their relationships, in their jobs, and in their goals and values.

People differ from one another in the extent to which they commit themselves to their values, careers, relationships, and ideologies (Marcia, 2002). Most people will pass through a period of **identity confusion**, which refers to not having a strong sense of who one really is. Some cultures institute a **rite of passage** ritual, usually around adolescence, which typically is a ceremony that initiates a child into adulthood. For example, some southwestern Native American tribes send adolescent males to be alone in the wilderness, fasting, until they have a vision. After such ceremonies, the adolescent is sometimes given a new name, bestowing a new adult identity. Secular Canadian culture does not provide common rite of passage rituals, though certain religions do, such as the Confirmation ritual in Roman Catholicism or Bar/Bat Mitzvah in Judaism.

In resolving the identity crisis, some people develop a **negative identity**, an identity founded on undesirable social roles, such as street gang member. Unfortunately, modern culture provides many undesirable role models. Because this is a time of life when youngsters are looking for models, most are very impressionable.

Identity is something that must be achieved. If a person commits to an identity they did not work for or that was handed to them, then that identity is likely to be shallow or changeable (Marcia, 1966). Indeed, Marcia (2002) holds that mature identity development involves going through a crisis and emerging with a firm sense of commitment to one's values, relationships, or career. If a person does not have a crisis, or if one forms an identity without exploring alternatives, such as accepting the values of parents, then this is called **identity foreclosure**. People in identity foreclosure are often moralistic and conventional, but when asked to back up their positions, they often cannot provide a good rationale for their beliefs and opinions.

A final concept relevant to identity development, especially to college students, concerns the notion of a **moratorium**. This refers basically to taking time to explore options before making a commitment to an identity. In some ways, college can be thought of as a socially approved period in which a young person is able to explore a variety of roles and responsibilities before taking any one set on "for real." One can change majors, change social groups, explore different relationships, meet people from diverse backgrounds, spend a semester studying abroad, and learn about a variety of fields of study before committing to any ideals and values. Erikson himself emphasized exploring alternatives before making a commitment to a particular identity (1968). He held that only after considering alternatives and spending time "shopping around" were people ready to make commitments and to spend the rest of their lives honouring those commitments. This is what it means to say that the development of an identity takes work (Newman & Newman, 1988).

Intimacy versus Isolation

Connecting with others, both in terms of friendships and intimate relationships, becomes a prime concern toward the latter half of the teenage years. People at this stage appear to have a need to develop relationships that are mutually satisfying and intimate. In such relationships, people grow emotionally and develop into caring, nurturing, and providing adults. For many people, this takes the form of making a commitment to one person through marriage. But many others find intimacy without the social contract of marriage. And of course marriage is no guarantee of intimacy, as it is certainly possible to have a marriage that is devoid of intimate feelings.

Isolation is the result of a failure to find or maintain intimacy. In Canada, the percentage of married people has dropped, from 61 percent in 1981 to 46 percent in 2011. In that same year, 11.5 percent of Canadians were divorced, but that number had risen from 5.1 percent in 1981. And nearly three-quarters of Canadians aged 25 to 29 reported having never been married (Milan, 2013). Certainly, being single has its benefits (DePaulo, 2006); however, most people report that a satisfying intimate relationship is something they desire. Failing to achieve this level of relationship is often a serious impairment to one's happiness and life satisfaction (Diener & Biswas-Diener, 2008).

Generativity versus Stagnation

At this stage, occupying most of the adult years, the main question concerns whether or not the person has generated something that they really care about in life. Often this takes the form of a career that one cares about. Other times, it is a family that has generated children that the parent cares about. Sometimes caring is achieved in a hobby or a volunteer activity that is particularly generative and that gives the person something to care about. The crisis at this stage is that when people step back and look at their adult years, they might get the feeling they are just spinning their wheels, stagnating. In other words, without anything to really care about, people may feel that their lives really don't matter, that they are just "going along to get along," and that they really don't care how it all works out. The people who don't really care about what they are doing, who are just going through the motions, are easily seen as phonies. For example, maybe you've had a teacher who really didn't care about the course material, who just came in, lectured blandly, and left. You have probably also had teachers who cared deeply about their topic, whose lectures were enlivened by their interest and enthusiasm, and who obviously drew satisfaction and meaning from their role as teacher or professor (see Professor Randy Pausch's "Last Lecture" on YouTube). This is the difference between generativity and stagnation.

Integrity versus Despair

This is the last stage of development, occurring toward the end of life, and even this stage contains a crisis, an issue to face. This occurs when we let go of the generative role; maybe we retire from the jobs we loved, maybe the children we loved and raised leave home and start their own lives, or maybe the hobbies or volunteer activities we found so meaningful are no longer possible for us. We start the process of withdrawing from life, pulling back from our adult roles, and preparing to face death. At this stage, we look back on our lives and pass judgment—"Was it all worth doing?" "Did I accomplish most of what I wanted to do in life?" If we can take some satisfaction in our lives, then we can face the inevitability of our passing with a measure of integrity (again, see Professor Randy Pausch's "Last Lecture" on YouTube for an example of integrity at the end of life). However, if we are dissatisfied with our lives, if we wish we had more time to make changes, to repair relationships, and to right wrongs, then we experience despair. People who have a lot of regrets at the end of their lives become bitter old people who have a lot of contempt and irritation. On the other hand, if people feel that their one go-around was acceptable, that they pretty much did it all up right and have no regrets, then they face their end with integrity.

Friedrich Nietzsche, a German philosopher, wrote a story in his book *Thus Spoke Zarathustra* (1891/1969) about a person walking on a mountain trail. Along the trail, a troll suddenly jumps out and kills the person. The person, however, is immediately reborn to the same parents, is given the same name, and lives the same life as before. Then one day, again the person is walking on a mountain trail and a troll suddenly jumps out and slays the person, who is reborn to the same parents, is given the same name as before, and lives the same life. And once again the person is walking along a mountain trail when a troll jumps out and slays the person. Once again the person is reborn, and so on. The point, Nietzsche says, concerns what a person would think about this eternal return of our lives. If you would not want to live your life over and over again, then perhaps you should make some changes in it now, as you are living it. The person who says, "Yes, I wouldn't mind another go-around of my life, even if it were all the same," is someone who would go through Erikson's last stage and achieve integrity. That is, if a person is satisfied with their life as a whole, then they can approach the ending of life with integrity.

Erikson's eight stages have been examined and applied in a variety of populations, including survivors of the Holocaust, a group that has been shown to be particularly resilient. For more on this research, which was led by Canadian psychologists, read Highlight On Canadian Research: Erikson's Stages of Development Among Holocaust Survivors.

Late in life there is still one more developmental stage, one more set of questions to be faced: "Was it all worthwhile? Did I accomplish most of what I wanted out of life?" How one answers these questions determines whether the remaining time is filled with bitterness and despair or satisfaction and integrity.
©Purestock/SuperStock

Highlight On Canadian Research

Erikson's Stages of Development Among Holocaust Survivors

Peter Suedfeld of the University of British Columbia has studied Erikson's stage theory of development within one of the most interesting samples available to psychologists studying trauma: survivors of the Holocaust. As has been well documented historically, the Holocaust was the Nazi attempt to wipe out the Jewish people during World War II. As psychology was in the prime of its early development during Adolf Hitler's Nazi regime, many mental health professionals at the time took interest in the psychological impact of the events that defined the Holocaust.

Relying on a combination of biographical interviews with survivors videotaped 30 to 50 years after the Holocaust, as well as audiotaped interviews recorded in 1946, Suedfeld and his colleagues (2005) conducted a series of qualitative analyses on the content of this material in order to identify specific themes in the survivors' lives. In particular, content was examined for its relevance to either positive or negative outcomes of each of Erikson's eight stages of development. For example, with Erikson's third stage of *initiative versus guilt*, a favourable outcome was determined based on the extent to which themes related to purpose and direction, competitiveness, and self-initiative were identified. For example, one survivor described being inspired by a poster about America and subsequently relocating to Canada as a result. An unfavourable outcome was determined by themes such as a sense of being fundamentally bad as a person and jealousy. For example, one survivor described the guilt that continued to consume her following the death of a loved one. The number of indicators of favourable and unfavourable outcomes was counted for each of Erikson's crises, resulting in frequency scores that could then be standardized and compared to determine which outcome was most likely at each stage and whether significant differences existed between samples.

Rather than taking a strictly sequential approach to the application of Erikson's model, Suedfeld's analyses examined outcomes related to all eight stages, despite the age of participants at the time the reports were obtained. Instead, Erikson's stages were used as a framework to understand the long-term psychosocial impact of the Holocaust on survivors, with a focus on adjustment in the eight resulting domains of life. The two time points at which information was collected also allowed researchers to compare outcomes for survivors at different stages of the life span. Since data were collected cross-sectionally at two points in time, however, the degree of change or growth over time could not be estimated. Longitudinal studies with repeated points of data collection would be required to accomplish this goal.

Across both samples, results suggested relatively positive outcomes according to Erikson's stages. In fact, for seven out of eight of the crises, both groups of survivors tended to describe favourable outcomes more often than not. The one exception was *trust versus mistrust*, in which more unfavourable outcomes of withdrawal, suspicion, and pessimism predominated. This finding is in line with the extreme betrayal experienced by the Jewish people—not only by their government, but by colleagues, neighbours, and even friends. Many other surprising findings emerged. For instance, despite the potentially high degree of shame that would be expected to occur among Holocaust survivors, the 1946 group of interviewees actually displayed no signs of *shame and doubt* while the more recent group did. Researchers explained this with the possibility that immediately following the events of World War II, survivors may have experienced an inflated sense of self-confidence that counterbalanced feelings of shame. Alternatively, given the correspondingly high degree of *autonomy* experienced early on, it's possible that this too provided protection against such negative feelings. The observation of high *industry* (versus *inferiority*) was explained by the active roles that these individuals took in their own survival, while the strong *identity* (versus *role confusion*) that appeared to persist was likely due to the strong family ties within Jewish families as well as feelings of pride associated with survivorship. Later favourable outcomes such as *generativity* were explained by the desire among survivors to create a more positive experience for their own children (Suedfeld et al., 2005).

Collectively, results from these analyses paint a much brighter picture of survivorship than may have previously been assumed. Although the Holocaust was undoubtedly one of the most horrific events in recent human history, it is important to recognize the human potential for resilience. Even immediately following the Holocaust, important aspects of development and personality appeared to remain intact.

Karen Horney and a Feminist Interpretation of Psychoanalysis

Karen Horney (pronounced Horn-eye) was another early proponent of ego psychology. She was a medical doctor and a psychoanalyst at a time when most doctors and practically all psychoanalysts were men, practising from the 1930s up to about 1950. She questioned some of the more paternalistic notions of Freudian psychoanalysis and reformulated some of the ideas to generate a more feminist perspective on personality development. For example, she reacted against Freud's notion of penis envy. Recall that Freud interpreted the phallic stage for women as a sexual conflict, starting when a little girl realizes she does not have a penis. Horney taught that the penis was a symbol of **social power,** or the ability to influence others, rather than an organ women actually desired. Horney wrote that girls realize, at an early age, that they are being denied social power because of their gender. She argued that girls did not really have a secret desire to become boys. Rather, she taught, girls desired the social power and preferences given to boys in the culture at that time. **Culture** is a set of shared standards for many behaviours. For example, whether a person should feel ashamed about promiscuous sexual behaviour is determined by a cultural norm. Moreover, culture might contain different standards for males and females, such that girls should be ashamed if they engage in promiscuous sex whereas boys should be proud of such behaviour, with it being culturally acceptable for them even to brag about such behaviour. This is known as the *double standard*.

Horney was among the first psychoanalysts to stress the cultural and historical determinants of personality, which we explore in more detail in Chapters 16 and 17. Horney noted that many gender roles were defined by culture. For example, she coined the phrase **fear of success** to highlight a gender difference in response to competition and achievement situations. Many women, she argued, felt that if they were to succeed they would lose their friends. Consequently many women, she thought, harboured an unconscious fear of success. She held that men, on the other hand, believed they would actually gain friends by being successful and hence were not at all afraid to strive and pursue achievement. This points to an important cultural influence on behaviour.

Horney stressed the point that, although biology determines sex, cultural norms are used to determine what is acceptable for a typical male and female in that culture. Partly because of Horney, today we use the terms **masculine** and **feminine** to refer to traits or roles typically associated with being male or female in a particular culture, and we refer to differences in such culturally ascribed roles and traits as **gender differences**, not *sex differences.* This distinction, so important to modern feminism, can be traced back to Karen Horney. It is unfortunate that Horney died in 1952 and did not see the progress made by the women's movement, of which she can truly be counted as an early leader.

Horney had very personal knowledge of the social and cultural forces that oppressed women in her era. Colleagues in the male-dominated profession of psychoanalysis were disapproving of her skeptical attitudes toward classical Freudian ideas. In 1941, the members of the New York Psychoanalytic Institute voted to remove Horney from her position as instructor there. Horney left immediately and went on to establish her own American Institute for Psychoanalysis, which was very successful. Indeed, she went on to develop a major reconceptualization of psychoanalysis, which stressed social influences over biology and gave special attention to interpersonal processes in the creation and maintenance of mental disorders and other problems with living. Her intriguing theories were laid out in a series of highly readable books (Horney, 1937, 1939, 1945, 1950).

Emphasis on Self and the Notion of Narcissism

Ego psychology generally emphasizes the role of identity, which is experienced by the person as a sense of self. Contemporary psychoanalysts Otto Kernberg (1975) and Heinz Kohut (1977) are important contributors to the psychoanalytic conception of the role of the self in normal personality functioning and in disorders. In normal personality functioning, most people develop a stable and relatively high level of self-esteem, they have some pride in what they have so far accomplished, they have realistic ambitions for the future, and they feel that they are getting the attention and affection from others that they deserve. Most of us have a healthy level of self-esteem; we consider ourselves worthwhile, we like ourselves, and we believe that others like us as well. And most of us engage in **self-serving bias**, which refers to the common tendency for people to take credit for successes yet to deny responsibility for failure.

Some take their self-serving bias too far, however, trying to increase their self-worth (and demonstrate it to others) in various problematic ways. For example, they may constantly try to appear more powerful than others, more independent, or more liked by others. As we first introduced in Chapter 3, this style of inflated self-admiration and constant desire to draw attention to oneself (and to keep others focused on oneself) is called **narcissism**. At the very high end, narcissism can be carried to extremes and become *narcissistic personality disorder* (see Chapter 19). However, narcissistic tendencies can be found in normal range levels, characterized as an extreme self-focus, a sense of being special, feelings of entitlement (that one deserves admiration and attention without earning it), and a constant search for others who will serve as one's private fan club. In order to lift themselves up and make themselves feel superior, people high in narcissism will often belittle and bully those around them. Alfred Adler referred to this as a *striving for superiority.*

There is a paradox, however, commonly called the **narcissistic paradox**: although people high in narcissism appear to be high in self-esteem, they actually have doubts about their value and worth as individuals. Adler suggested that it was this quality that led to the need to make others unhappy. Although narcissists (i.e., those high in narcissism) appear confident and sure of themselves, these people actually need constant praise, reassurance, and attention from others. Narcissists appear to have a grandiose sense of self-importance, but they are nevertheless very vulnerable to blows to their self-esteem and cannot handle criticism very well. In contemporary psychoanalysis, narcissism is seen as a disturbance in the sense of self that has many implications for creating problems with living and relating to others.

An example of one problem associated with narcissism is that when narcissists are criticized or challenged they may behave aggressively, trying to achieve some respect by attacking or belittling their critics. This tendency toward aggression and violence in response to criticism was illustrated in a laboratory study conducted by psychologists Brad Bushman and Roy Baumeister (1998). The subjects came to the laboratory and wrote a short essay on a topic given to them. Another person then commented on the essays they had just written, providing strong criticism of the subjects' opinions. Later in the experiment, the subjects were given the opportunity to play a computer game with their critic and were allowed to "blast" their opponent with loud bursts of noise during the game; that is, subjects could distract their opponents with irritating blasts of noise during the competition. The narcissistic subjects who had been insulted blasted the critic much more aggressively than did either the non-narcissistic or the narcissistic subjects who had not received criticism. This finding suggests that narcissism can lead to aggression when the high-narcissist is provoked or criticized. People with secure and normally healthy levels of self-esteem, however, do not become distressed and aggressive when insulted (Rhodenwalt & Morf, 1998).

 Exercise

A questionnaire measure of narcissism. The following items are from the Narcissistic Personality Inventory (NPI) (Raskin & Hall, 1979).

1. I think I am a special person.	True or False
2. I expect a great deal from other people.	True or False
3. I am envious of other people's good fortune.	True or False
4. I will never be satisfied until I get all that I deserve.	True or False
5. I really like to be the centre of attention.	True or False

In one interesting study of narcissism, it was found that the number of first-person pronouns a person used in an essay (*I, mine, me*) was correlated positively with narcissism scores (Emmons, 1987). In another study it was found that when given the opportunity to watch themselves on videotape or to watch a tape of someone else, the narcissists spent more time watching the tape of themselves (Robins & John, 1997). This study also showed that narcissists rate their performance on the videotape much more positively than it is rated by others, implying an inflated sense of their own abilities.

In sum, narcissism is not the same as having high self-esteem (Brown & Zeigler-Hill, 2004). Studies have confirmed the theoretical notions that narcissists are preoccupied with self, are vulnerable to criticism and blows to their self-worth, and respond to such challenges with anger and aggression. Although narcissists appear to have high self-esteem, their internal or private self-representations are fragile and vulnerable. Clearly, an important notion from contemporary psychoanalytic thought is that one's internal representation of self plays an important role in how one interacts with and reacts to the social environment. In the next section, you see how contemporary psychoanalysis also focuses on the internal representation of other people and how this influences social interactions.

 Concept Check

List Erikson's eight stages of development. How does Erikson's theory of development compare and contrast with Freud's theory of psychosexual development?

What were the main contributions of Karen Horney to ego psychology?

Define narcissism (as a trait) and discuss the narcissistic paradox.

Object Relations Theory

Other changes to Freud's original ideas have been so sweeping that one new approach drops the term "analytic" altogether: object relations theory. Recall that Freud emphasized sexuality in the development of personality. He viewed the adult personality as the result of how people accommodate the inevitable conflicts between their desires for sexual pleasure from various body parts and the constraints of parents, social institutions, and civilized society. Freud's emphasis on sexuality has been completely rethought by recent generations of psychoanalysts. This new movement—**object relations theory**—emphasizes social relationships and their origins in childhood.

Consider the Oedipal phase of development. Freud stressed the sexual attraction for the parent of the opposite sex, and the accompanying fear, rage, anger, and jealousy toward the parent of the same sex. Psychoanalysts after Freud looked at the same childhood situation and saw, instead, the importance of forming social relationships to the developing personality. Later analysts emphasized not sexuality but, instead, the development of meaningful social relationships as the task that occurs at this stage of development. After all, the first individuals with whom we have a meaningful relationship are our parents.

Although object relations theory has several versions, which differ from each other in emphasis, all the versions have at their core a set of basic assumptions. One assumption is that the internal wishes, desires, and urges of the child are not as important as the development of relationships with significant external others, particularly parents. A second assumption is that the others, particularly the mother, become **internalized** by the child in the form of mental objects. The child creates an unconscious mental representation of the mother. The child, thus, has an unconscious "mother" within, to whom the child can relate. This allows the child to have a relationship with this internalized object, even in the absence of the real mother—hence the term *object relations* theory.

The relationship object the child internalizes is based on the development of the relationship with the mother. If things are going well between the mother and the infant, the infant internalizes a caring, nurturant, trustworthy mother object. This image then forms the fundamentals for how children come to view others with whom they develop subsequent relationships. If the child internalizes a mother object who is not trustworthy, perhaps because the real mother has left the child alone too often or has not fed the child regularly, then the child might have difficulty learning to trust other people later in life. Children who are traumatically separated from their parents during childhood—who experience an attachment disruption—often become adults with distinct personality problems (Malone, Westen, & Levendosky (2011). The first social attachments that the infant develops form the templates for all meaningful relationships in the future. This is consistent with the classic psychoanalytic idea that the "child is father to the man," in the sense that what develops in childhood determines the outcomes in adulthood. However, in the neo-analytic case, it is early childhood experience with caregivers, especially attachment to the primary caregiver, that determines adult personality.

Early Childhood Attachment

Work on early childhood attachment has drawn on a couple of lines of research in developmental psychology. The first line of research was the work by Harry Harlow and others on infant monkeys. Harlow's well-known experiments involved taking infant monkeys away from their real mothers and raising them with models of mother monkeys made of wire or cloth. These fake mothers did not provide the grooming, cuddling, holding, or social contact of the real mothers. The infant monkeys raised with the fake mothers developed problems in adolescence and adulthood, growing into adults that were socially insecure, that were generally anxious, and that did not develop normal sexual relations as adults (Harlow, 1958; Harlow & Suomi, 1971; Harlow & Zimmerman, 1959). Moreover, the infant monkeys preferred their real mothers to the fake mothers, and they preferred the cloth mother to the wire mother when given the choice. Harlow concluded that **attachment** between infant and primary caregiver required physical contact with a warm and responsive mother and that it is vitally important to the psychological development of the infant.

Attachment to the mother or caregiver during the first six months of life appears to be crucial to all primates, including humans. Attachment in the human infant begins when they develop a preference for people over objects. For example, the child prefers to look at a human face rather than at a toy. Then the preference begins to narrow to familiar individuals, so that the child prefers to see familiar people (compared to strangers). And finally the preference narrows even further, so that the child prefers the mother or primary caregiver over anyone else.

The ways in which young children develop attachments to their parents and caregivers was the primary topic of research for British psychologist John Bowlby (1969a, 1969b, 1980, 1988). Bowlby focused on the attachment relationship with the mother and how that relationship meets the needs of the infant for protection, nurturance, and support. Bowlby studied what happens when this attachment relationship is temporarily broken, as when the mother has to leave the infant alone for a short time. He noticed that some infants seem to trust that the mother will return and

The strong bond between infant and primary caregiver, called attachment, is important in the development of all primates, including humans.
©Getty Images/iStockphoto

provide uninterrupted care—these infants are happy when the mother returns. Other infants, in contrast, react negatively to separation and become agitated and distressed when the mother leaves. They can be calmed only by the return of the mother. Bowlby said these infants experience **separation anxiety**. Bowlby also observed a third type of infants, who seem to become depressed when their mothers leave. Even when the mother returns, these infants seem to remain detached from, or angry at, their mothers.

Psychologist Mary Ainsworth and her colleagues developed a 20-minute procedure for studying separation anxiety—a procedure used for identifying differences among children in how they react to separation from their mothers. This is called the **strange situation procedure**. In this procedure, a mother and her baby enter the laboratory room, which is like a comfortable living room. The mother sits down, and the child is free to explore the toys and other things in the room. After a few minutes, a stranger, an unfamiliar but friendly adult, enters the room. The mother then gets up and leaves the baby alone with this unfamiliar adult. After a few minutes, the mother returns to the room and the stranger leaves. The mother is alone with the baby for several more minutes. All the while, the infant is being videotaped, so that their reactions can later be analyzed.

Across many studies, Ainsworth and her colleagues (e.g., Ainsworth, 1979; Ainsworth, Bell, & Stayton, 1972) found essentially the same three patterns of behaviour noted by Bowlby. One group of infants, called **securely attached**, endured the separation with only minimal anxiety and went about exploring the room, waiting patiently or even approaching the stranger and sometimes wanting to be held by the stranger. When the mothers returned, these infants were glad to see them, typically interacted with them for a while, then went back to exploring the new environment. They seemed confident the mothers would return, hence the term *secure*. This group of infants was the largest of the three (66 percent fell into this group).

The second group, called the **avoidantly attached** group, consisted of infants who avoided the mothers when they returned. The infants in this group typically seemed unfazed when the mothers left and typically did not give them much attention when they returned, as if aloof from their mothers. Approximately 20 percent of the babies fell into this category.

Ainsworth called the third category of infant response to separation the **ambivalently attached** group. The infants in this group were very anxious about the mothers' leaving. Many started crying and protesting vigorously before the mothers even got out of the room. When the mothers were gone, these infants were difficult to calm. On the mothers' return, however, the infants behaved ambivalently. Their behaviour showed both anger and a desire to be close to the mothers; they approached their mothers but then resisted by squirming and fighting against being held.

Mothers of babies in these three groups appear to behave differently. According to subsequent research, reviewed by Ainsworth and Bowlby (1991), mothers of securely attached infants provide more affection and stimulation to their babies, and are generally more responsive, than mothers of infants in the other groups. These studies have provided clear evidence that a caregiver's responsiveness to infants leads to a more harmonious relationship later in life between the child and parents. For example, in one study, responsiveness to infant crying in the early months of life was associated with less (not more) crying at 1 year of age. Although this finding was greeted with disbelief at first, especially by learning theorists, it eventually influenced recommendations for parenting practices (Bretherton & Main, 2000).

Mothers of babies from both the ambivalent and the avoidant groups tend to be less attentive to their children, less responsive to their needs. Such mothers appear to be less in tune or less engaged with their babies. Some children react to these less responsive mothers by becoming angry themselves (the ambivalent infants) or by trying to become emotionally detached (the avoidant infants). Fraley, Roisman, and Haltigan (2013) showed that maternal insensitivity assessed when the child was 3 years old was related to lower social competence and academic skills when the child was 15 years old. Although there may be alternative explanations for these findings, they are nevertheless consistent with the notion that the lack of maternal responsiveness can have negative childhood outcomes.

These early experiences and reactions of the infant to the parents, particularly the mother, become what Bowlby called **working models** for later adult relationships. These working models are internalized in the form of unconscious expectations about relationships. If children experience that they are not wanted, or that their mothers cannot be trusted to take care of them, then they may internalize the expectation that probably no one else wants them either. On the other hand, if children's needs are met, and they are confident that their parents really love them, then they will expect that others will find them lovable as well (Bowlby, 1988). These expectations about relationships, which are developed in our first contacts with our caregivers, are thought to become part of our unconscious and thereby exert a powerful influence on our adult relationships.

We might think that the "strange situation" paradigm is useful only for thinking about how children cope with the temporary separation from their caregivers. However, some researchers are studying an adult analogue of this paradigm, where married couples are temporarily separated by life circumstances (Cafferty et al., 1994). These researchers conducted a longitudinal study on members of the National Guard and other military reserve units who were separated from their spouses and deployed overseas during Operation Desert Storm. They found that attachment styles predicted individual differences in emotional reactions to the separation (securely attached individuals were not as distressed) and to postreunion marital adjustments (ambivalently attached individuals had the most difficulty). When adult marital relationships are temporarily disrupted, it may be that the individuals in those relationships will react and adjust in ways that resemble how they coped with their earliest separations, both of which may be influenced by the style of attachment they developed early in life with their primary caregiver.

Adult Relationships

Research on attachment has tested object relations ideas by examining whether the attachment style developed in childhood is related to later adult relationship styles. In 2010, an entire issue of the *Journal of Social and Personal Relationships* was dedicated to research on how childhood attachment styles are related to adolescent and adult relationships (Shaver & Mikulincer, 2012). In a study that started this line of research, psychologists Cindy Hazan and Philip Shaver (1987) showed that there are patterns of adult relationships that look similar to the secure, avoidant, and ambivalent childhood attachment patterns. In the adult **secure relationship style**, the person has few problems developing satisfying friendships and relationships. Secure people trust others and develop bonds with them. The adult **avoidant relationship style** is characterized by difficulty in learning to trust others. Avoidant adults remain suspicious of the motives of others, and they are afraid of making commitments. They are afraid of depending on others because they anticipate being disappointed, being abandoned, or being separated. Finally, the adult **ambivalent relationship style** is characterized by vulnerability and uncertainty about relationships. Ambivalent adults become overly dependent and demanding on their partners and friends. They display high levels of neediness in their relationships. They are high maintenance, in the sense that they need constant reassurance and attention.

Psychologist Philip Shaver and his colleagues have shown that there is a positive correlation between the parent–infant attachment style and the later relationship style developed in adulthood. In one study, for example, adults with an avoidant relationship style more frequently reported that their parents had unhappy marriages compared to adults with a secure relationship style (Brennan & Shaver, 1993). The adults with a secure relationship style, on the other hand, tended to report coming from a trusting and supportive family, with parents who were happily married. Those with an avoidant relationship style tended to report that their family members were aloof and distant, and that they did not feel very much warmth or trust either from or toward their parents.

❓ Exercise

Determining which adult attachment style a person has can be accomplished by having them report which style is most like them. Consider the following statements, and choose which is most descriptive of you:

1. **I am typically comfortable with others and find it easy to become close friends with people. I can easily come to rely on others and enjoy it when they rely on me. I don't worry about being left out or abandoned and find it easy to let others get close to me.**
2. **I am sometimes tense when I get too close to others. I don't like to trust other people too much, plus I don't like it when people have to depend on me for something. It makes me anxious when people get close or want me to make an emotional commitment to them. People often want me to be more personal and intimate than I feel like being.**
3. **In relationships, I often worry that the other person does not really want to stay with me or that they don't really love me. I often wish that my friends would share more and be more of a confidante than they seem willing to be. Maybe I scare people away with my readiness to become close and make them the centre of my world.**

The first description is associated with a secure relationship style, the second with an avoidant relationship style, and the third with an ambivalent relationship style. It is possible that you have different styles with different people, or that none of these descriptions applies perfectly to your relationships.

A dominant theme of attachment theory is that a person's romantic attachments in adulthood will be a reflection of attachment patterns in the past, especially with their earliest relationships (Shaver & Mikulincer, 2012). Representations of the earliest relationships can serve as prototypes for later relationships, with the early experiences retaining their influential role in attachment behaviours throughout the life span. The psychologist Chris Fraley has published meta-analyses of studies examining the long-term influence of attachment styles (Fraley, 2002a, 2002b). After reviewing a great deal of research and evaluating different models of change and stability, Fraley concludes that the data are consistent with a moderate degree of stability in attachment security from infancy to adulthood. His best estimate of the correlation between early attachment security and attachment security at any later point in time is approximately .39, which can be described as significantly larger than zero, but moderate in magnitude. In a study that followed people for a year and assessed adult attachment style, people's attachment style was found to be fairly stable over that time period, about as stable as each of the Big Five personality traits (Fraley et al., 2011). Fraley has published an online quiz that people can take to assess the similarity among their attachment styles with different people in their lives (see www .yourpersonality.net/relstructures/).

Adult relationship styles may be most important for understanding romantic relationships. What do people look for in a romantic relationship? What do people expect from their romantic partners? How do people cope

Object relations theorists believe that the characteristics and quality of adult relationships are determined, in part, by relationships experienced in early childhood.
(left): ©Purestock/SuperStock; (right): ©Alexander Benz/Purestock/SuperStock

with abandonment by and separation from their romantic partners either real or imagined? Research suggests that individuals with different attachment styles will answer these questions very differently from each other (e.g., Hazan & Shaver, 1987). Those with an avoidant attachment style tend to shun romance, believing that real love is rare and never lasts. They fear intimacy and rarely develop deep emotional commitments. They tend not to be very supportive of their partners, at least not emotionally.

Adults with an ambivalent attachment style tend to have frequent, but short-lived, romantic relationships. They fall in and out of love easily but rarely say that they are happy with their relationships. They develop a sort of desperation in their adult relationships and show fear of losing their partners. Their focus is often on keeping the other happy, and so they are quick to compromise, to change themselves for the sake of avoiding conflict with the other. As you might guess, ambivalent adults report that being separated from their partners is very stressful.

Adults with a secure attachment style can be separated from their partners without stress, just as secure attachment children can remain calm when their mothers leave the room. Secure adults are generally more warm and supportive in their romantic relationships, and their partners report more satisfaction with the relationship than do the partners of avoidant or ambivalent adults (Hazan & Shaver, 1994). Secure adults are also more likely to give emotional support to their partners when it is needed. Secure adults seek support when they need it more than do ambivalent or avoidant adults. In general, secure adults do a good job of navigating through the treacherous waters of adult romantic relationships. A study by Fraley and colleagues (Holland, Fraley, & Roisman, 2012) showed that the effects of attachment style on romantic relationships are more observable after the relationship has been developing for awhile, with stronger effects observed one year into the relationship than at the very start of the relationship. It takes a while to really get to know someone.

An interesting study by psychologist Jeff Simpson illustrates the working of attachment styles in adult relationships (Simpson et al., 2002). In this study heterosexual dating couples served as subjects. The couple was told that the male would undergo a stressful and unpleasant experience as part of the experiment. They were separated and the male was taken to a room where an experimenter recorded his pulse while saying the following:

> *In the next few minutes you are going to be exposed to a situation and set of experimental procedures that arouse considerable anxiety and distress in most people. Due to the nature of these procedures, I cannot tell you any more at this moment. Of course, I'll answer any questions or concerns you have after the experiment is over. (p. 603)*

The purpose of this statement was to make the male subject anxious. Moreover, he was taken to a darkened, windowless room that contained some polygraphs. The experimenter remarked that the equipment was "not quite ready yet" and that the subject would have to wait a few minutes before the "stress phase" could start. Meanwhile, the female was told that her partner was going to be involved in a "stress and performance session" that would start in 5 or 10 minutes. The couple was brought together to wait, and during this time they were unobtrusively videotaped for 5 minutes. After 5 minutes the experimenter entered the room and told the subjects the experiment was over, explained the purpose of the experiment, and told the subjects that they could erase the videotape if they so desired (none did).

The experimenters coded the videotape for a number of behaviours. Mostly they were interested in the degree to which the women offered support to their partners, and the degree to which the men asked for support from their partners. Prior to the start of the experiment, the experimenters used an interview method to assess childhood recollections of experiences with parents and other attachment figures. From these interviews the experimenters rated the degree to which each subject was avoidantly or securely attached to primary caregivers in early childhood.

Results showed that women who had avoidant attachment experiences with their parents were significantly less likely to offer support and encouragement to their male partners, even if the male asked for that. The securely attached women did provide support if the partner asked for it, but provided less if he did not ask for it. This is a contingent pattern of support, what some researchers consider ideal in relationships (George & Solomon, 1996). Regarding help seeking from the men, none of the attachment style variables predicted this behaviour in this study. However, this was not a very intense or long-lasting stressor. Studies of real, intense, and chronic stress (people under missile attacks, people undergoing combat training) have found that attachment styles do relate to help seeking (Mikulincer, Florian, & Weller, 1993; Mikulincer & Florian, 1995). Specifically, secure men and women seek support from others when distressed, whereas avoidantly attached individuals try to distance themselves from others, want to spend time alone when under stress, and distract themselves from the stressors. When stress is severe or chronic, it appears that a person's attachment style might relate to her or his pattern of support seeking.

Individual differences in attachment style may have implications beyond those for relationships. Any area of life that involves closeness, getting along with others, confiding in others, and exploring relationships might be negotiated differently by people with different attachment styles (Elliot & Reis, 2003). Attachment theory has been applied to understanding relationships between twins (Fraley & Tancredy, 2012), relationships with pets (Zilcha-Mano, Mikulincer, & Shaver, 2012), and even one's relationship with one's God (Granqvist et al., 2012). One study of adults examined attachment styles in relation to satisfaction with work, with family, with one's social role, and with stressful life events (Vasquez, Durik, & Hyde, 2002). These researchers found that those individuals with the secure attachment style showed the best adjustment across these domains. Individuals with avoidant/fearful attachment styles reported difficulties in many of the domains of family life and in several domains of work life. Other research from the University of British Columbia has shown that, among men, the avoidant/fearful attachment style was related to a collection of traits that is associated with abusiveness toward women (Dutton et al., 1994).

If a person develops a particular childhood attachment style, are they destined to live out the adult version of that style? This important question has been the topic of much theoretical debate and empirical research (Cassidy & Shaver, 1999; Simpson & Rholes, 1998). Attachment theorists believe that even the poorest childhood experiences with relationships can be overcome. Ainsworth and Bowlby (1991) argued that children were not necessarily damaged forever because of unfortunate parenting experiences in infancy. They felt that subsequent positive experiences could compensate for earlier negative relationships. Despite a bad start in life, people exposed to a loving, nurturant relationship in adulthood can revise their working models of object relations. If the relationship is positive and supportive enough, it is possible to internalize a new mental version of relationships that is more secure and trusting, with positive expectations about how people would relate to the person (Fraley, 2007).

 Concept Check

What is the main premise of object relations theory? Describe in your own words.

What are the three primary styles of attachment in childhood? How do these attachment styles relate to or predict behaviours in adult relationships?

Summary and Evaluation

In this chapter, we explored alternative versions of some of Freud's original ideas. We began with an evaluation of repressed memories, examining cases in which the recalled memories turned out not to be true, at least as determined in a court of law. These cases should not put doubt on the possibility of real cases of abuse and trauma causing memories to be forgotten or repressed. Indeed, such cases do exist and conform to the notion that traumatic experiences can be pushed out of consciousness. However, the material in this chapter is meant to lead you to a more balanced approach to the topic of repressed memories. Although repressed memories can occur, not all cases are truly of forgotten memories. Some memories can be implanted by well-meaning therapists and others interrogating a subject about an event. We also discussed how to discriminate real from false memories. The crucial element is corroboration, finding someone who can support the subject's version of the remembered event.

The view of repressed memories also highlights a more contemporary version of the unconscious. Although most modern cognitive psychologists believe in the unconscious, they do not believe in the motivated version of the unconscious proposed by Freud. Certainly, material can get into the mind without conscious experience, as through subliminal perception, but that material does not have the kind of sweeping motivational effects suggested by Freud.

Another reconstruction of Freud's theory concerns the emphasis on the role of the ego relative to the id. This is in stark contrast to Freud's emphasis on aggressive and sexual id urges as the twin engines powering psychic life. We discussed two proponents of ego psychology. The first, Erik Erikson, was well known for his alternative theory of personality development, which differed from Freud's in several important ways, including an emphasis on social tasks and an extension of development through the entire life span. A second important figure in ego psychology was Karen Horney, who was among the first psychoanalysts to consider the role of culture and social roles as central features in personality development. Horney also started a feminist reinterpretation of Freud's theories, which continues to this day. Ego psychology also generated an interest in the development of sense of self and the protection of self through various strategies.

Object relations theory is another major new development in this area, having been called the most important theoretical development in psychoanalysis since Freud's death. The term *object relations* is used to refer to enduring patterns of behaviour in relationships with intimate others, as well as to the emotional, cognitive, and motivational processes that generate those patterns of behaviour. The theory is about how relationship behaviours are determined by mental representations laid down in childhood through experiences with caregivers. This theory began with studies of attachment between children and primary caregivers—typically, mothers. This bond may set a pattern that continues into adulthood. Also important are the experiences the growing child has with the relationship observed between the parents. This is also internalized in the form of a mental representation for how people get along and what is appropriate behaviour in a relationship.

Parts and versions of Freud's psychoanalytic theory are alive and well today. However, instead of focusing on unconscious conflicts over id urges, contemporary psychoanalysts are more likely to focus on interpersonal patterns of behaviour and the emotions and motives that accompany those. Instead of seeing personality as the result of a sequence of sexual conflicts with the parents, contemporary psychoanalysts are more likely to see personality as the result of solving a series of social crises and the ensuing movement toward increasingly more mature forms of relating to others. And, finally, unlike much of classical psychoanalytic theory, which was based on one man's views, much of contemporary psychoanalytic theory is connected to empirical studies and corroborated observations of many people working to improve and expand on some of Freud's lasting contributions.

 Concept Check

Think back to Chapter 9. In consideration of ego psychology and object relations theory specifically, describe how Freud's original ideas have been interpreted and modified over time.

How have Freud's original ideas regarding childhood development specifically influenced contemporary thinking on adult relationships?

Key Terms

false memories	motivated unconscious	ego psychology
imagination inflation effect	cognitive unconscious	identity crisis
confirmatory bias	subliminal perception	Erikson's eight stages of development
spreading activation	priming	
constructive memory	id psychology	psychosocial conflicts

stage model of development

developmental crisis

identity confusion

rite of passage

negative identity

identity foreclosure

moratorium

social power

culture

fear of success

masculine

feminine

gender differences

self-serving bias

narcissism

narcissistic paradox

object relations theory

internalized

attachment

separation anxiety

strange situation procedure

securely attached

avoidantly attached

ambivalently attached

working models

secure relationship style

avoidant relationship style

ambivalent relationship style

Motives and Personality

Basic Concepts

The Intrapsychic Domain

Born and raised in Brantford, Ontario, Wayne Gretzky has been described as the greatest hockey player ever by his fans, fellow players, and sports writers and enthusiasts alike. Demonstrating a skill for the game even as a child, Gretzky signed with the World Hockey Association at the young age of 17. From there he went on to play for the Edmonton Oilers, where he set many scoring records and led his team to four Stanley Cup championships. In 1988 he was traded to the Los Angeles Kings, where he helped lead his team to the 1993 Stanley Cup Finals. He would play for two more teams, the St. Louis Blues and the New York Rangers, before retiring from the game in 1999. His number of trophies and MVP awards, as well as his 61 National Hockey League (NHL) records (including six All-Star records), have certainly earned him the nickname "The Great One."

How did Gretzky motivate himself to achieve so many unmatched NHL records, including the title of leading scorer in NHL history? His accomplishments were no easy feat. In addition to his physical stamina and well-honed skill, Gretzky's success is also owed to the unique strategies he adopted before and during each game. In fact, he is widely regarded as the smartest player in the history of hockey. According to a number of interviews, it was Gretzky's relentless study of the game and his regular contact with coaches that resulted in his seemingly instinctive hockey skills. Adding to this the training he received from his father at a young age, he became known as one of the most creative and intuitive players the game had ever seen.

As his talent became evident at a very young age Gretzky faced a great deal of jealousy from other players and their parents, to the extent that direct attacks on his self-esteem led him and his family to move to Toronto. But rather than allow the jealousy to bring him down, he used it as a source of motivation. When he was on the ice, The Great One was able to immerse himself in the mo-

The Canadian-born, record-breaking NHL hockey player Wayne Gretzky has been nicknamed "The Great One." Gretzky was known to use a few key strategies to motivate himself before and during a game.
©Focus On Sport/Getty Images

ment, concentrating on the intricacies of the game and thus avoiding unnecessary distraction. He would get himself so deeply "in the zone" that he could accurately predict the movement of the puck and move it precisely where he wanted. Beyond his methods, Wayne Gretzky was a dedicated high achiever in his sport, demonstrating a level of commitment and success that exceeded the norm. To sum up his motivation for the game in his own words, "I wasn't naturally gifted in terms of size and speed; everything I did in hockey I worked for." Following his retirement, he was immediately inducted into the Hockey Hall of Fame, and later helped the Canadian national men's hockey league win a gold medal during the 2002 Winter Olympics as their executive director.

We saw in Chapter 1 that personality psychologists ask, "Why do people do what they do?" Motivational psychologists phrase the question a bit differently—"What do people want?" All personality psychologists seek to explain behaviour. Personality psychologists interested in motivation, however, look specifically for a desire or motive that propels people to do the things they do (Cantor, 1990).

In this chapter we cover some of the major theories on human motivation, and we examine research findings related to these theories. Some theories that we will look at are quite different from each other, such as the theories of Henry Murray and Abraham Maslow. In fact, most texts in personality cover these two theories in different chapters. However, all the theories we examine have two features in common. First, they view personality as consisting of a few general motives, which all people have to various degrees. Second, these motives operate mainly through mental processes, either inside or outside of awareness, generating an intrapsychic influence on a person's behaviour (King, 1995).

Basic Concepts

Motives are internal states that arouse and direct behaviour toward specific objects or goals. A motive is often caused by a *deficit*, a lack of something; for example, a person is motivated by hunger after not eating for many hours. Motives differ from each other in both type and amount. Hunger differs from thirst, for example, and both of these differ from the motive to achieve and excel. Motives differ in intensity, depending on the person and the circumstances in which the motive arises. For example, the strength of the hunger motive varies considerably, depending on whether a person has merely skipped a meal or has not eaten for several days. Also, motives are often based on **needs**, states of tension within a person. As a need is satisfied, the state of tension is reduced. The need to eat creates the motive of hunger. The motive of hunger in turn causes the person to seek out food, to think about food constantly, and perhaps even to see food in objects not normally thought of as food. For example, a hungry person gazing at the sky might exclaim, "Wow, that cloud looks just like a sandwich!" Motives propel people to perceive, think, and act in specific ways that satisfy the need. Figure 11.1 illustrates the relation between needs and motives. As you will see in the section on self-actualization later in this chapter, some motives are not based on deficit needs, but rather are based on growth needs.

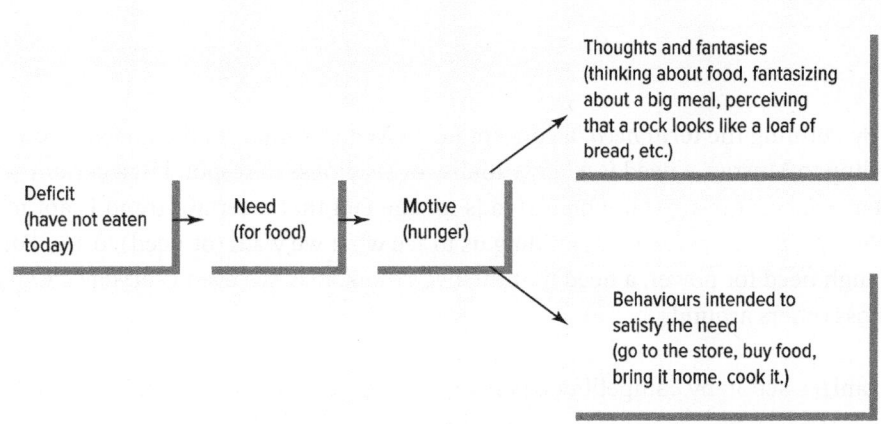

FIGURE 11.1 Deficits lead to a need, which leads to a motive to satisfy that need, either in reality, by fostering specific actions, or in fantasy, by creating thoughts that are satisfying.

Motives belong in the intrapsychic domain for several reasons. First, researchers who study motives have stressed the importance of *internal* psychological needs and urges that propel people to think, perceive, and act in certain predictable ways. Motives can be unconscious, in the sense that people do not know explicitly what they want. Just as people may not be fully aware of why they engage in particular fantasies, they may not be consciously aware of what compels them to act in certain ways. This similarity leads to another feature shared by psychologists interested in motives and other intrapsychic constructs—the reliance on projective techniques. Motive psychologists, like psychoanalysts, believe that fantasies, free associations, and responses to projective techniques reveal the unconscious motivation behind many thoughts, feelings, and behaviours (Barenbaum & Winter, 2003).

Motive psychologists also share some core ideas with dispositional psychologists, whose work we covered in Part 1 of this book. Like dispositional psychologists, motive psychologists stress that (1) people differ from one another in the type and strength of their motives; (2) these differences are measurable; (3) these differences cause or are associated with important life outcomes, such as success at work or relationship satisfaction; (4) differences among people in the relative amounts of various motives are stable over time; and (5) motives may provide one answer to the question "Why do people do what they do?" The motive approach can be thought of as a halfway point between the intrapsychic domain and the dispositional domain (Winter et al., 1998). We will discuss motives as we examine the intrapsychic domain because of the view that motives exist within the psyche and can operate outside of conscious awareness to affect everyday behaviours, thoughts, and feelings.

One of the first researchers to develop a modern theory of motivation was Henry Murray, a psychologist active in research from the 1930s through the 1960s. The path that ultimately led Murray to a career in psychology was decidedly untraditional. He went to medical school, became a physician, and interned in surgery. Murray then pursued research in embryology, followed by a PhD in biochemistry from Cambridge University. While studying in England, Murray went to Zurich during spring break in 1925, to visit the famous psychoanalyst Carl Jung. He met with Jung every day for three weeks, meetings from which he "emerged a reborn man" (Murray, reprinted in Shneidman, 1981, p. 54). Murray's encounter with psychoanalysis had a profound impact on him, leading him to abandon his medical practice and research and to turn his attention entirely to psychology. Murray was then trained in psychoanalysis and accepted a position at Harvard, where he remained until his retirement (Murray, 1967).

Need

Murray began by defining the term *need,* a concept he viewed as similar to the analytic concept of drive. In a nutshell, according to Murray, a need is a "potentiality or readiness to respond in a certain way under certain given circumstances. . . . It is a noun which stands for the fact that a certain trend is apt to recur" (Murray, 1938, p. 124). Needs organize perception, guiding us to see what we want (or need) to see. For example, someone who has a high need for power, a need to influence others, may see even everyday social situations as opportunities to boss others around.

A need also organizes action by compelling a person to do what is necessary to fulfill the need. A person who has a need to achieve, for example, often makes sacrifices and works hard at a desired task. Murray believed that needs referred to states of tension and that satisfying the need reduces the tension. According to Murray, however, it was the *process* of reducing tension that the person found satisfying, not the tensionless state per se. Murray believed that people might actually seek to increase tension (e.g., by going on a roller-coaster ride or viewing a horror movie) in order to experience the pleasure of reducing that tension (i.e., to end the roller-coaster ride or the horror movie).

In his model, Murray distinguished between primary needs (such as air, food, water, and sex, which he referred to as *viscerogenic* due to their satisfaction by physical means) and secondary or *psychogenic* needs, which are satisfied by mental or emotional means. Based on his research, he proposed a list of the fundamental psychogenic needs, some of which are described in Table 11.1. Each need is associated with (1) a specific desire or intention, (2) a particular set of emotions, and (3) specific action tendencies, and each need can be described with trait names. Consider the need for affiliation, which is the desire to develop and maintain associations with people. The primary set of emotions associated with this need are interpersonal warmth, cheerfulness, and cooperativeness, and the associated action tendencies are accepting people, spending time with others, and making efforts to maintain contact with others. The associated traits that characterize people with a strong need for affiliation are attributes such as agreeableness, friendliness, loyalty, and goodwill.

> **Table 11.1 A Brief Description of Several of Murray's Needs, Organized into Six Higher-Level Categories**

Materialistic Needs

- **Acquisition:** To gain possessions and property. To bargain or gamble. To work for money or goods.

- **Order:** To put things in orderly arrangement. To desire cleanliness, organization, balance, neatness, and precision.

Ambition Needs

- **Achievement:** To master, manipulate, or organize others, objects, or ideas. To accomplish difficult tasks. To overcome obstacles and excel. To surpass rivals by exercising talent.

- **Exhibition:** To be seen and heard, to be the centre of attention. To make an impression on others. To excite, fascinate, entertain, intrigue, amuse, entice, or amaze others.

- **Recognition:** To evoke praise, commendation, and respect. To boast and exhibit one's accomplishments. To seek distinction.

Needs to Defend Status

- **Infavoidance:** To avoid failure, shame, humiliation, ridicule. To refrain from attempting something beyond one's powers.

- **Inviolacy:** To prevent a depreciation of self-respect. To preserve one's good name. To be immune from criticism. To maintain psychological distance.

- **Defendance:** To defend oneself against blame or belittlement. To justify one's actions. To offer explanations and excuses.

Needs Related to Social Power

- **Autonomy:** To shake off restraint, break out of confines. To get free, to resist coercion and restriction. To avoid being domineered. To be free to act according to one's wishes.

- **Contrarience:** To act differently than others. To be unique. To hold unconventional views. To take the opposite side in arguments or debates.

- **Dominance:** To seek to influence or control the behaviour of others by persuasion, command, suggestion, or seduction. To restrain or prohibit others. To lead and direct.

Social Affection Needs

- **Affiliation:** To enjoy cooperation or reciprocal interaction with similar others. To draw near to others. To please and win affection of those you like. To remain loyal to friends.

- **Nurturance:** To take care of others in need, to give sympathy and gratify the needs of helpless others. To assist people in danger. To help, support, console, protect, comfort, nurse, feed, and heal others.

- **Succorance:** To receive aid from others. To have one's needs gratified by another, to be nursed, supported, protected, advised, indulged, loved, and consoled.

Exchange of Information Needs

- **Cognizance:** To explore one's environment. To ask questions and to satisfy one's curiosity. To look, listen, and inspect. To read and seek knowledge.

Murray believed that each person had a unique **hierarchy of needs**. An individual's various needs can be thought of as existing at different levels of strength—for instance, a person might have a high need for dominance, an average need for affiliation, and a low need for achievement. Each need interacts with the various other needs within each person. This interaction is what makes the concept of motive **dynamic**. The term *dynamic* is used to refer to the mutual influence of forces within a person—in this case, the interaction of various motives within a person. Consider someone with a high need for dominance. It would make a big difference in this person's overall behaviour if the need for dominance were accompanied with a high versus a low need for affiliation. If the high need for dominance were coupled with a high need for affiliation (e.g., a strong desire to develop and maintain relationships), then this person would most likely develop the social skills necessary to lead others effectively. If the high need for dominance were combined with a weak need for affiliation, in contrast, then this person might simply exercise power over others without regard to their feelings, seeming argumentative, disagreeable, and bossy.

Press

Another important contribution of Murray to personality psychology was a specific way of thinking about the environment. According to Murray, elements in the environment affected a person's needs. For example, a person with a high need for affiliation might be sensitive to the social aspects of a given environment, such as how many people are present, whether they are interacting, and whether they look approachable and outgoing. Murray used the term **press** to refer to need-relevant aspects of the environment. A person's need for affiliation, for example, won't affect that person's behaviour without an appropriate environmental press (such as the presence of friendly people). People with a high need for affiliation would be more likely to notice other people, and to see more opportunities for interaction with others, than someone with a low need for affiliation.

Murray also introduced the notion that there is a so-called real environment (which he called **alpha press**, or objective reality) and a perceived environment (called **beta press**, or reality as it is perceived). In any given situation, what one person sees may be different from what other people see. Consider what might happen if two people are walking down the street and a third person approaches and smiles at each of them. One person who is high on the need for affiliation might see the smile as a sign of friendliness and a nonverbal invitation to start a conversation. The other person who is low on the need for affiliation might see the same smile as a smirk and consequently become suspicious that the stranger is laughing at them. Objectively (alpha press), it was the same smile. Subjectively (beta press), it was a very different event for these two people, due to their differences in the need for affiliation. The need for affiliation can be distinguished from the need for intimacy. People high on the need for affiliation seek relationships, build social networks, and find approval from others very satisfying. They tend to prefer being part of a team rather than acting as an individual. The need for intimacy, on the other hand, refers specifically to the need for close, warm, and loving relationships with others.

Apperception and the TAT

Murray held that needs influenced how a person perceived the environment, especially when the environment is ambiguous (as when a stranger smiles at the person). The act of interpreting the environment and perceiving the meaning of what is going on in a situation is termed **apperception** (Murray, 1933). Because our needs and motives influence apperception, if we want to know about a person's primary motives, we might ask that individual to interpret what is going on in a variety of situations, especially ambiguous situations.

The simple insight that needs and motives influence how we perceive the world led Murray and his research associate Christiana Morgan to develop a formal technique for assessing these two constructs (Morgan & Murray, 1935). They called this the **Thematic Apperception Test** (or TAT, for short). The TAT consists of a set of black-and-white images that are ambiguous. The person is then asked to make up a story about what is happening in the picture. For example, in the drawing of a person on a windowsill, the person may be going in (to rob the house?) or going out (jumping to commit suicide?). Some pictures contain no people at all, such as a picture of a rowboat on the shore of a small creek. Such pictures are perhaps the most ambiguous: Who put the rowboat there? Are they coming or going? Why are they not in the picture right now? It is easy to make up a story because the picture is so ambiguous with respect to what is happening. (To see the TAT and try it yourself, visit the following website: http://www.utpsyc.org/TATintro/.)

In administering the TAT, participants are shown each picture and told to be creative and make up a short story, interpreting what is happening in the picture. They are encouraged to tell a story that has a beginning, a middle, and an end. The psychologist then codes the stories for the presence of various types of imagery associated with particular

This image was used by Morgan and Murray as one of the TAT pictures. Can you make up a story about the child in this picture? What do you believe he is thinking about? What happens next?

Farm Security Administration - Office of War Information Photograph Collection, Library of Congress, LC-USF34-055829-D

motives. For example, a subject might write the following about the TAT card of the boat on the shore: "The boat in the picture is being used by a young boy to take produce to market. The boy has stopped to gather some wild berries to take to the market to sell along with his farm produce. This boy works very hard and eventually grows up, puts himself through university, and becomes a famous scientist, specializing in the study of plants, primarily agricultural crops." This story has a lot of achievement imagery, so the subject who wrote it would be seen to have a high need for achievement.

Morgan and Murray published the TAT in 1935. Since then, many researchers have modified its administration (e.g., using fewer cards, selecting other drawings, and using a slide projector to show the pictures to large groups). Because the pictures in the original TAT are dated (e.g., clothing and hair are styles from the 1930s), newer versions of TAT-type pictures have been developed and found to function similarly to the original set in terms of soliciting need-relevant themes (Schultheiss & Brunstein, 2001). The essential features of the TAT and similar projective techniques are that (1) the subject is given an *ambiguous* stimulus, usually a picture, and (2) the subject is asked to describe and *interpret* what is going on.

Take the need for achievement motive, which can be scored by counting up the number of references in the person's story to wanting to do things better, anticipating success, feeling positive about succeeding, and overcoming obstacles (Schultheiss & Brunstein, 2001; Schultheiss & Pang, 2007). Studies of the TAT suggest that people do respond differentially to the themes of the picture—with, for example, high need for achievement people responding to the achievement pictures differently than low need for achievement people (Kwon, Campbell, & Williams, 2001; Tuerlinckz, De Boeck, & Lens, 2002).

Some personality researchers argue that projective tests in general, and the TAT in particular, are less useful as measures of personality than other methods, such as questionnaires and informant report. Some even argue that the term *test* should not be used to refer to projective methods (McGrath & Carroll, 2012). Nevertheless, the TAT continues to be used particularly to assess psychoanalytic constructs, such as defence mechanisms (Hibbard et al., 2010), attachment styles (Berant, 2009), and psychosexual stages (Huprich, 2008), as well as for needs and motives.

We can make a distinction between using the TAT to assess state levels of needs and trait levels of needs. **State levels** of a need refer to a person's momentary amount of a specific need, which can fluctuate with specific circumstances. For example, a person who is failing at a task (e.g., a player on a baseball team that is down 5 to 4 in the ninth inning) might experience a sharp increase in the state of achievement motivation. The assessment of state levels of needs can be useful in determining what aspects of a situation bring about changes in specific needs. The TAT has been shown to be sensitive to changes in state levels of various motives, particularly the needs for achievement, power, and intimacy (Moretti & Rossini, 2004). The assessment of **trait levels** of a need refers to measuring a person's average tendency, or their set point, on the specific trait. The idea is that people differ from each other in their typical or average amount of specific needs. The TAT and other such instruments have multiple pictures or items, and the amount of imagery related to a particular need is then averaged across the pictures to get at their trait level. The assessment of trait levels is most useful in determining differences among individuals in their average tendencies toward particular needs. Assessing trait levels of needs is the most frequent goal of personality psychologists who use such measures (Schultheiss, Liening, & Schad, 2008).

A newer form of assessing motives is the **Multi-Motive Grid**, which combines features of the TAT with features of self-report questionnaires (Schmalt, 1999). In this test, 14 pictures are selected to arouse one of the big three motives (achievement, power, or intimacy). The pictures are presented along with questions about important motivational states, and the person then answers those questions. The idea is that the photo will arouse the motive, which then will influence how the person will answer the questions. Although this technique is relatively new, initial results show promising levels of reliability (Langens & Schmalt, 2008; Sokolowski et al., 2000). Initial validity data are also promising, for example, showing that motive grid assessment of need for achievement predicted persistence and performance in laboratory tasks (Schmalt, 1999).

The TAT remains a popular personality assessment technique today, even though some researchers argue that it has low test-retest reliability (see, however, Smith & Atkinson, 1992). In addition, several researchers have reported extremely low correlations between TAT measures of certain needs and questionnaire measures of the same needs, leading them to question whether the TAT is a valid measure. This is a topic explored further in A Closer Look: TAT and Questionnaire Measures of Motives: Do They Measure Different Aspects of Motives?.

 A Closer Look

TAT and Questionnaire Measures of Motives: Do They Measure Different Aspects of Motives?

Psychologist David McClelland and his colleagues focused primarily on the TAT. Critics have argued that the TAT demonstrates poor test-retest reliability and that responses to one picture may not correlate with responses to other pictures—that is, the TAT has poor internal reliability (Entwisle, 1972). Moreover, when the TAT is used to predict actual motive-related behaviours (such as when TAT need for achievement scores are used to predict overall university grade point averages or performance on an achievement test), the correlations are frequently low and inconsistent (Fineman, 1977). Smith and Atkinson (1992) have reviewed the major criticisms of the TAT, as well as responses from its proponents.

These undesirable properties of the TAT have led some researchers to develop questionnaire measures of motives (Jackson, 1967). These questionnaires simply ask people directly about their motives and desires and about whether they engage in the kinds of behaviours that indicate high levels of the motives. These questionnaires turn out to have desirable measurement properties, such as adequate test-retest reliability and predictive validity (Scott & Johnson, 1972). A troubling finding, however, is that TAT measures of motives and questionnaire measures of the same motives are often uncorrelated (Fineman, 1977; for an exception see Thrash & Elliot, 2002). Many researchers therefore suggest that the TAT measure and other projective measures should be abandoned.

McClelland and his colleagues did not silently accept these criticisms (McClelland, 1985; Weinberger & McClelland, 1990; Winter, 1999). In response, McClelland argued that, when the TAT is properly administered and scored, the motive scores *do* show acceptable test-retest reliability. In addition, he asserted that the TAT predicts long-term real-life outcomes, such as business success, better than questionnaire measures do. He argued that the questionnaire measures are better at predicting short-term behaviours, such as how competitive a person will behave while playing a game in a psychology laboratory. McClelland argued that the TAT measure and the questionnaire measures are uncorrelated because they measure *two different types of motivation*. Let's discuss each in turn.

One type of motive is called **implicit motivation**. These motives are based on needs, such as the need for achievement (nAch), the need for power (nPow), and the need for intimacy (nInt), as they are measured in fantasy-based (i.e., TAT) measures. When the TAT is used to measure these three motives (which are explored further in the next section of this chapter), they are called implicit, because the individuals writing the stories are not explicitly telling the psychologist about themselves. Instead, they are telling stories about other people. The stories are thought to reflect the *implied* motives of the individuals writing the stories—their unconscious desires and aspirations, their unspoken needs and desires (Schüler, Sheldon, & Fröhlich, 2010). What people write in response to the TAT pictures is presumed to reflect their real, although unconscious, motivations (Hofer, Bond, & Li, 2010).

The other type of motivation is called explicit, or **self-attributed motivation**, which McClelland argued reflects primarily a person's self-awareness of conscious motives or "normative beliefs about desirable goals and modes of conduct" (McClelland, Koestner, & Weinberger, 1989, p. 690). These self-attributed motivations reflect a person's conscious *awareness* about what is important. As such, they represent part of the individual's conscious self-understanding (e.g., "I'm a person who doesn't really care about influencing others and being the boss [low self-attributed nPow], even though I want terribly to succeed in all my classes [high self-attributed nAch] and have a steady boy/girlfriend and lots of other friends [high self-attributed nInt]").

McClelland argued that implicit and self-attributed motives represent fundamentally different aspects of motivation and that they should predict different life outcomes. Implicit motives predict long-term, spontaneous behavioural trends over time. For example, compared with questionnaire measures, TAT-assessed need for achievement is the better predictor of long-term entrepreneurial success, and TAT-assessed need for power is the better predictor of long-term success as a business manager (Chen, Su, & Wu, 2012; McAdams, 1990). Self-attributed motives, on the other hand, are better predictors of responses to immediate and specific situations and to choice behaviours and attitudes (because they measure the person's conscious desires and wants). For example, questionnaire-assessed need for achievement is the better predictor of how hard a person will work to obtain a reward in a psychology experiment, and questionnaire-assessed need for power is the better predictor of a person's self-reported attitudes about social inequality (Koestner & McClelland, 1990; Woike, 1995).

The research literature supports a distinction between implicit and explicit motives, at least for achievement motivation (Spangler, 1992; Thrash & Elliot, 2002). Spangler examined more than 100 studies of need for achievement and performed a meta-analysis of these studies. Half the studies meta-analyzed by Spangler used TAT measures (implicit motives), and the other half used questionnaire measures (self-attributed motives) of the achievement motive. Spangler then looked carefully at the variables being predicted by achievement. He sorted the studies into those that looked at short-term responses to specific tasks (e.g., grades in university courses, performance on ability tests, and performance in laboratory achievement tests) and those that looked at long-term achievements (e.g., lifetime income, job level attained in an organization, number of publications achieved, and participation in community organizations). Spangler found that the TAT-based measure was a better predictor of the long-term outcomes than was the questionnaire measure, whereas the questionnaire was a better predictor of the short-term responses. Understanding the congruence of implicit and explicit measures of motives is receiving a good deal of attention from personality psychologists (e.g., Thrash, Elliot, & Schultheiss, 2007).

Spangler's meta-analysis suggests that both the TAT and questionnaire measures may play important roles in helping psychologists understand the short- and long-term effects of motives. If you want to know how someone will react to achievement demands today or tomorrow, you might be best advised to use a questionnaire or to just ask the person about their achievement needs. However, if you want to make a prediction about who in a group of people will earn the largest lifetime income or climb the highest in an organizational setting, you might be better off using the TAT measure of need for achievement.

 Concept Check

Distinguish among deficit, need, motive, and press. How are they related, and what role do they play in personality?

What is apperception? How is it measured by the TAT, and what are the implications of this measurement for needs and motives?

The Big Three Motives: Achievement, Power, and Intimacy

Although Murray proposed several dozen motives, researchers have focused most of their attention on a relatively small set. These motives are based on the needs for achievement, power, and intimacy. Let's review what we know about each of these fundamental human motives.

Need for Achievement

Behaviour that is motivated by the need for achievement has long interested psychologists. Because it has received the most research attention, we begin with this motive.

Doing Things Better

Following Murray at Harvard, psychologist David McClelland carried on the tradition of motive research. McClelland was best known for his research on the **need for achievement**, defined as the desire to do better, to be successful, and to feel competent. Like all motives, we assume that the need for achievement will energize behaviour in certain (achievement-related) situations. It is energized by the incentives of challenge and variety; it is accompanied by feelings of interest and surprise; and it is associated with the subjective state of being curious and exploratory (McClelland, 1985). People motivated by a high need for achievement obtain satisfaction from accomplishing a task or from the anticipation of accomplishing a task. They cherish the process of being engaged in challenging activities.

As the leader of two successful companies, Apple Computer and Pixar Animation, the late Steve Jobs was constantly striving to do things better. He is a good example of someone high in achievement motivation.
©Justin Sullivan/Getty Images

In terms of trait levels, high nAch individuals prefer moderate levels of challenge, neither too high nor too low. This preference makes sense given that the high nAch person is motivated to do better than others. A task that is almost impossible to accomplish will not be attractive because it will not provide the opportunity to do better if everyone does poorly. A task that is too easy will be easy for everyone; the high nAch person will not do better if everyone is successful. Theoretically, we expect high nAch individuals to have a preference for *moderately* challenging tasks. Dozens of studies have found support for this idea. One study examined children's preference for challenge in a variety of games (e.g., the ring-toss game, in which children attempt to toss rings around sticks that are placed at varying distances). Children high in nAch preferred a moderate challenge (e.g., tossed their rings at the sticks in the middle), whereas children low in nAch tried either the very easy levels of the games (closer sticks) or the levels at which success was almost impossible (McClelland, 1958). This relationship has also been demonstrated outside the laboratory. Young adults high in nAch have been found to choose university majors that are of intermediate difficulty and to pursue careers that are of moderate difficulty (reviewed in Koestner & McClelland, 1990).

❓ Exercise

Have a look at the TAT picture presented in the previous section. Write a short story about what is happening in this picture. However, instead of writing off the top of your head, try to write a story that would score high on the need for achievement. What themes would you put in such a story? What actions and outcomes might be interpreted as indicating high nAch? What you consciously try to put into such a story are the themes and acts that psychologists look for in the stories of people writing naturally. Some put plenty of such themes and acts into their stories quite naturally and so seem to see achievement-related behaviours all around. Others reveal that their stories and the characters therein act in very nonstriving, nonachieving ways. And this comes perfectly naturally to them when they make up a story about an ambiguous situation.

To summarize the characteristics of people high in nAch, (1) they prefer activities that provide some, but not too much, challenge; (2) they enjoy tasks in which they are personally responsible for the outcome; and (3) they prefer tasks for which feedback on their performance is available.

Increasing the Need for Achievement

Research on the achievement motive typically takes the form of correlating TAT need for achievement (nAch) scores with other measures thought to be related to achievement. Demonstrating the relationship between nAch and success in entrepreneurial activities is one example of this type of research. Starting and managing a small business appears to offer a high degree of satisfaction for the person with a strong need to achieve. It provides an opportunity to engage in a challenging pursuit, assume responsibility for making decisions and taking action, and obtain swift and objective feedback about the success of one's performance. Studies in several countries have found that men with a high nAch are more attracted to business occupations than are their peers who have a low nAch (McClelland, 1965). A study of farmers (who are, in effect, small business operators) showed those with a high need to achieve were more likely than low nAch farmers to adopt innovative farming practices and to show improved rates of production over time (Singh, 1978). A study comparing self-employed entrepreneurs to workers for large corporations found that the self-employed were significantly higher on need for achievement (Lee-Ross, 2015).

Research on entrepreneurial talent has not been limited to business activities. Some studies have examined the work habits of university students. Students with high nAch appear to be more deliberate in their pursuit of good grades: they are more likely to investigate course requirements before enrolling in a class, speak with a professor prior to exams, and contact the professor about the exam after it was given to obtain feedback about their performance (Andrews, 1967). In a very different subject sample, blue-collar workers with high nAch engaged in more problem-solving activities after being laid off than did unemployed workers lower in nAch: they started looking for a new job sooner and used a greater number of job-seeking strategies (Koestner & McClelland, 1990).

More recent studies on entrepreneurial orientation examined achievement motives in a group of students of small business (a major considered to have high entrepreneurial potential) and compared them to a group of students of economics (considered to have much less entrepreneurial potential). Results showed that small business students were significantly higher on achievement motivation than the economics students (Sagie & Elizur, 1999). A study by Langens (2001) also supports the notion that training for high need for achievement can promote success in business. It seems that people with high achievement motives are drawn to careers that have more potential risk and uncertainty, where success is a matter of personal responsibility and where emergency problem solving is routine.

There are also cultural differences in how the need for achievement is expressed. In North America, most high-achieving high school students strive for good grades for themselves. Many students, and their parents, go to great lengths to achieve. Cheating can be common, and some students do not view cheating as wrong. The psychologist Demerath (2001) even reports that some parents of high-achieving students sought to have them classified as special-education students, which would entitle them to extra time on standardized tests. When he went to Papua New Guinea, Demerath found a very different norm among students. There, school is seen as a noncompetitive place where it is important for all to do well. Doing well as an individual, especially if it is at the expense of others, is frowned upon. In fact, New Guineans call this "acting extra" and view it as a form of vanity. Given the cultural differences between New Guinea and North America, such differences in how the need for achievement is expressed make sense. People in Papua, New Guinea, make their living at farming and fishing, and they need to know that if they get sick or something happens and they cannot work their fields or nets, others will pitch in and help. In collectivist cultures, individual achievement is less valued than the person who helps their group achieve.

In addition to culture, the need for achievement also appears to vary according to whether one is intrinsically or extrinsically motivated in the first place. We examine research on this facet of motivation in Highlight On Canadian Research: The Effects of Canadian Acculturation on Intrinsic and Extrinsic Motivation for Achievement.

 # Highlight on Canadian Research

The Effects of Canadian Acculturation on Intrinsic and Extrinsic Motivation for Achievement

An additional facet of motivation studied by psychologists concerns the intrinsic versus extrinsic basis of motivations. Despite the traditionally unidimensional approach to motivation by many researchers, there is evidence to suggest that this facet adds valuable insight to our understanding of human behaviour.

Intrinsically motivated behaviours are those that are largely self-determined based on the inherent satisfactions directly associated with the behaviours themselves, such as enjoyment and interest. They are not contingent on reinforcements or responses in the environment that may be perceived as separable from the behaviours. In contrast, *extrinsically motivated behaviours* are those that are performed for more instrumental reasons (i.e., based on some kind of contingency in the environment). For example, one who is extrinsically motivated toward achievement may be seeking a reward or attempting to avoid punishment or guilt. Extrinsically motivated behaviours are often performed based on expected social responses, and are therefore less autonomous in nature.

In relation to academic achievement, previous research has demonstrated that intrinsic motivation is a stronger predictor of success as well as positive psychological outcomes compared to extrinsic motivation, which does not seem to predict success (Guay, Ratelle, & Chanal, 2008). Researchers Areepattamannil, Freeman, and Klinger (2011) from Queen's University were interested in understanding the effects of Canadian acculturation on the intrinsic and extrinsic motivation for achievement among Indian immigrant adolescents. *Acculturation* is the process by which individuals adopt new customs and behaviours upon moving to a new country or cultural context. Given the cultural differences between India and Canada, namely their collectivistic versus individualistic natures (respectively), the impact of acculturation on motivation in this group is an important factor in educational achievement and success.

To examine these questions, the researchers recruited 355 Indian immigrant adolescents in Grades 9 through 12 from provinces in central Canada. Intrinsic and extrinsic motivation were measured using a high school version of an academic motivation scale. A comparison sample of students living in India was also collected, in order to determine the extent to which Indian immigrant students were affected by their move to Canada. This sample included 363 adolescents in Grades 9 through 12. In both samples, approximately equal numbers of boys and girls were included.

Based on statistical comparisons between the two groups, Indian-Canadian adolescents were more intrinsically motivated than their Indian counterparts, while the Indian adolescents were more extrinsically motivated than the Indian-Canadian adolescents. This finding reflects key cultural differences mentioned earlier: the more individualistic Canadian culture may ultimately contribute to a less socially dependent and intrinsic motivation among Indian immigrants. Interestingly, academic achievement was also higher among Canadian-Indian students than among those living in India. At first glance, these findings appear to be in line with the notion that intrinsic motivation is a stronger predictor of academic success.

Indeed, that is what researchers found when they examined the associations among motivation styles and achievement in each sample. Areepattamannil and colleagues performed a regression analysis, allowing them to control for key variables like age and gender while also examining the combined influence of motivation styles on academic achievement (providing a more robust and accurate assessment of these associations). Controlling for age and gender, intrinsic motivation was a significant and positive predictor for both samples; however, it was a much stronger predictor for the Indian-Canadian sample compared to the Indian sample. Extrinsic motivation, on the other hand, was significantly associated with lower levels of academic achievement among Indian-Canadians; for the Indian sample, extrinsic motivation was not a significant predictor of achievement when controlling for all other variables.

Not only do these findings confirm the positive and negative roles of intrinsic and extrinsic motivation (respectively) in academic achievement, they also underscore the effects of Canadian acculturation on these key determinants of behaviour. Motivation appears to be more complex than once believed. Additionally, one's cultural context appears to shape the ways that people are motivated to succeed.

Determining Sex Differences

Much of the research on nAch, particularly that done in the 1950s and 1960s, was conducted on males only. Perhaps this was due to the fact that Harvard (where both Murray and McClelland did much of their research) was a primarily male institution at that time. Or it might have been due to the biased belief of that period that achievement was important only in the lives of men. Whatever the reason, little was known about achievement strivings in women until the 1970s and 1980s. Since then, some similarities and some differences have been found between men and women. Men and women high in nAch are similar in their preference for moderate challenge, personal responsibility for the outcome, and tasks with feedback. The major differences between such men and women occur in two areas: the life outcomes predicted by nAch and childhood experiences. Let's consider each of these in turn.

Research on men has focused primarily on achievement at work as a typical life outcome predicted by nAch. Research on women, however, has identified different

Jody Wilson-Raybould, Minister of Justice and Attorney General of Canada from 2015 to 2019, has been a high achiever her entire life. A member of the Wewaikai First Nation of B.C., Wilson-Raybould earned her law degree from the University of British Columbia and served as a provincial Crown prosecutor in Vancouver for four years. She subsequently held positions as councillor for the Wewaikai First Nation, board member for the Minerva Foundation for B.C. Women, first elected regional chief of the B.C. Assembly of First Nations, and a Member of the Canadian Parliament—all before joining Prime Minister Justin Trudeau's cabinet in 2015.
©The Canadian Press/Adrian Wyld

"achievement trajectories," depending on whether the women value having a family or value having both family and work-related goals. Among women who value both work and family, nAch is related more to achieving better grades and to completing university and starting a family later than it is among women low in nAch with career and family interests. Among women who are more exclusively focused on family, nAch is seen in the women's investment in activities related to dating and courtship, such as placing greater emphasis on physical appearance and talking with friends about their boyfriends more frequently (Koestner & McClelland, 1990). Such findings underscore the need for researchers to know the subjects' goals before they can make predictions about success in particular areas.

The second major difference between men and women has been in the childhood experiences associated with nAch. Among women, nAch is associated with a stressful or difficult early family life. The mothers of girls high in nAch were found to be critical of their daughters and to be aggressive and competitive toward them (Kagan & Moss, 1962). Mothers of high-achieving girls were also less nurturant and affectionate toward their daughters than mothers of less academically successful girls (Crandall et al., 1964). In contrast, the early lives of males high in nAch are characterized by parental support and care.

Several recent studies have examined sex differences in competitive achievement settings. In one study, the researchers had 40 men and 40 women solve simple addition problems as quickly as they could, paying them 50 cents for each correct answer (Niederle & Vesterlund, 2005). In one condition, the participants simply played against the clock, trying to solve as many problems as they could. In another condition the game was changed to a tournament, where subjects were divided into teams of two women or two men each, and they played against each other. The winning team received $2.00 for each problem they solved and the losing team received nothing. The researchers found that men and women performed equally well in both conditions: the tournament setting and the individual setting. The experimenters then had a third round, where each person could choose whether to play individually or in a tournament setting. Interestingly, only 35 percent of the women chose the tournament setting, whereas 75 percent of the men chose the tournament setting. The authors concluded that even in settings where women perform just as well as men, they are less likely to want to engage in direct competition with others. Women may be more selective in how they express their achievement strivings, especially when winning for oneself means that others lose.

Promoting Achievement Motivation in Children

Despite the sex differences in childhood antecedents of achievement, McClelland believed that certain parental behaviours could promote high achievement motivation in children. One of these parenting practices is placing an emphasis on **independence training**. Parents can behave in ways that promote autonomy and independence in their children. For example, a young child who is taught to feed themselves becomes independent of the parents during feeding time; a child who is toilet trained early no longer relies on their parents for assistance with this task. One longitudinal study found that strict toilet training in early childhood is associated with high need for achievement 26 years later (McClelland & Pilon, 1983). Training a child to be independent in various tasks of life promotes a sense of mastery and confidence in the child. This may be one way that parents can promote a need for achievement in their children. Research from McGill University has further demonstrated the promotion of autonomy and independence by parents supports goal achievement in young adults (Koestner et al., 2008).

A second parental practice associated with need for achievement is setting challenging *standards* for the child (Heckhausen, 1982). Parents need to let the child know their expectations. These expectations should not exceed the child's abilities, however, or else the child may give up. The idea is for parents to provide goals that challenge the child, support the child in working toward these goals, and reward the child when the goal is attained (see Table 11.2). Positive and frequent success experiences appear to be part of the prescription for developing a heightened need for achievement. For example, learning the ABCs is a challenging task for a 4-year-old; parents might encourage a young child to undertake this task, enthusiastically sing the ABC song with the child, and reward the child with praise and hugs when they recite the alphabet independently for the first time.

Table 11.2   Raising High Need for Achievement Children
• Set tough but realistic standards.
• Applaud successes and celebrate accomplishments.
• Acknowledge but don't dwell on failures; stress that failures are part of learning.
• Avoid instilling a fear of failure, and instead emphasize the motive to succeed.
• Stress effort over ability: instead of saying "You can do it because you are smart" say "You can do it if you really try."

Finally, a study has shown that individuals with a secure attachment style, as described in Chapter 10, typically develop a higher level of adult achievement motivation than those with avoidant or ambivalent attachment styles (Elliot & Reis, 2003). These researchers hypothesized that children with secure attachments were more likely to explore their environments and to thereby learn new skills. Over time, learning to be effective leads to higher achievement motivation and to valuing one's own competencies and seeing life's difficulties as challenges to be overcome rather than as opportunities to fail.

A developmental theory of achievement motivation has been proposed by the psychologist Carol Dweck (2002). This theory emphasizes the beliefs that people develop about their abilities and competencies. Briefly, the theory holds that the most adaptive belief system is that abilities are not fixed, but that they are malleable and can be developed through effort. Dweck (2002) argues that sometimes even "smart" people succumb to the belief that their abilities are fixed or given or genetically determined, that their current performance reflects their long-term potential, and that truly gifted individuals do not need effort to achieve. She argues that this set of beliefs is "dumb" in the sense that people who hold such beliefs will consequently have a low need for achievement. It is more adaptive, Dweck holds, to believe that abilities are changeable, that one's performance is a temporary indicator of where one is, not where one will ultimately be, and that one's true potential will be realized only through sustained effort. This new theory is having an impact on schools and other educational settings (Elliot & Dweck, 2005). Dweck (2006) has also written a popular book on how this new theory relates to achievement in sports, business, and relationships.

In a recent large-scale study, Dweck and her colleagues (Paunesku et al., 2015) showed that training students to view intelligence as a malleable and changeable quality, rather than viewing it as fixed or hereditary, lead to measureable increases in grades. We'll have more to say about Dweck's theory in the next chapter, when we discuss cognition and personality, but for now we'll simply say that believing one can become smarter with effort appears to be a prerequisite for actually becoming smarter (or at least achieving better grades).

Need for Power

Another motive of interest to psychologists is based on the need for power—the desire to have an impact on (and sometimes control) other people.

Impact on Others

Although McClelland was known primarily for his studies of the achievement motive, both he and several of his students went on to study other motives. One of his students, David Winter, focused a good deal of his research on the **need for power** (nPow). Winter (1973) defines the need for power as a readiness or preference for having an impact on other people. A more detailed definition is provided by Fodor (2009); people high on need for power have a need to impress, influence, or control other people, and to be recognized by others for their power-oriented actions. They achieve impact on others through various means, but most notably through forceful actions towards or against others, strong efforts to control others, or ostentatious displays of valued personal possessions. They want others to react to them, either with admiration, astonishment, or fear. One study investigated the hypothesis that high nPOW individuals would be faster at recognizing facial expressions of emotions in others (Donhauser, Rosch, & Schultheiss, 2015). Because of their desire to impact others, and because this impact is often registered in the faces of those around them, the high need for power person gauges the strength of their dominance by reading the emotions displayed by others. The researchers showed that the need for power indeed correlated with faster recognition of facial expressions of emotions in others. This is most likely how people with a high need for power monitor whether they are being successful in having an impact, by reading the emotions displayed by those around them.

As with the need to achieve, the need for power is assumed to energize and direct behaviour when the person is in opportune situations for exerting power. The TAT has likewise been the predominant assessment tool for research on nPow. The subjects' stories are scored for the presence of images related to themes of power. These include descriptions of strong or vigorous actions, behaviours that bring about strong reactions in others, and statements that emphasize the importance of a character's status or reputation.

Research Findings

Many studies have examined the correlates of individual differences in nPow (e.g., Kuhl & Kazén, 2008). The need for power correlates positively with having arguments with others, being elected to student office in university, taking larger risks in gambling situations, behaving assertively and actively in a small-group setting, and acquiring more of what Winter calls "prestige possessions," such as sports cars, credit cards, and nameplates for dormitory doors (Winter, 1973).

It appears that an individual high in nPow is interested in control—control of situations and other people (Assor, 1989). Men high in nPow have been shown to rate their ideal romantic partners as those who are under the men's control and dependent on them, perhaps because such relationships offer them a sense of superiority (Winter, 1973). Men high in nPow are also more likely to abuse or assault their partners (Mason & Blankenship, 1987). A person with a high need for power prefers as friends people who are not well known or popular, perhaps because such people do not pose a threat to the person's prestige or status (Winter, 1973).

Sex Differences

Research on the power motive has found no sex differences in average levels of nPow or in the kinds of situations that arouse the power motive. Men and women also do not differ in the life outcomes that are associated with nPow, such as having formal social power (e.g., holding office), having power-related careers (e.g., being a manager), or gathering prestige possessions (e.g., sports cars).

The largest and most consistent sex difference is that high nPow men, but not women, perform a wide variety of impulsive and aggressive behaviours. Men high in nPow are more likely than men low in nPow to have dissatisfying dating relationships, arguments with others, and higher divorce rates. Men high in nPow are also more likely to engage in the sexual exploitation of women, have more frequent sex partners, and engage in sex at an earlier age than do their counterparts who are lower in nPow. Men with a strong need for power also abuse alcohol more than those with a low need for power (feelings of power often increase under the influence of alcohol). None of these correlates have been found for women.

"Profligate impulsive" behaviours (drinking, aggression, and sexual exploitation) are less likely to occur if an individual has had **responsibility training** (Winter & Barenbaum, 1985). Taking care of younger siblings is an example of responsibility training. Having one's own children provides another opportunity to learn to behave responsibly. Among people who have had such responsibility training, nPow is not related to profligate impulsive behaviour (Winter, 1988). These findings have led Winter and others (e.g., Jenkins, 1994) to assert that socialization experiences, not biological sex per se, determine whether nPow will be expressed in these maladaptive behaviours.

Health Status and the Need for Power

As you might imagine, people high in nPow do not deal well with frustration and conflict. When high nPow people do not get their way or when their power is challenged or blocked, they are likely to show strong stress responses. McClelland (1982) called such obstacles **power stress** and hypothesized that people high in nPow were vulnerable to various ailments and diseases because of the stresses associated with inhibited power. In a study of university students, when power motives were inhibited or stressed the subjects' immune function became less efficient and they reported more frequent illnesses, such as colds and the flu (see McClelland & Jemmott, 1980). A later study of male prisoners found similar results, with prisoners high in nPow showing the highest levels of illness and the lowest levels of immune antibodies (McClelland, Alexander, & Marks, 1982). Other studies have demonstrated that inhibiting the power motive among people high in nPow is linked with high blood pressure. This relationship was also found in a longitudinal study, which revealed that the inhibited power motive measured in men in their early thirties significantly predicted elevated blood pressure and signs of hypertension 20 years later (McClelland, 1979).

An interesting laboratory study induced power stress by having people lead a group discussion without knowing that the group's members were coached ahead of time to disagree with the leader and to display a lot of conflict (Fodor, 1985). The group leader was assessed for muscle tension. Consistent with McClelland's theory, the greatest tension responses were found for those leaders in the group conflict condition who were high in nPow.

War and Peace and Power

In a fascinating line of research, Winter investigated nPow on a national level and related it to the broad areas of war and peace. Traditionally, nPow is measured by evaluating stories written in response to TAT pictures. However, nPow (as well as any motive) can be determined by assessing just about any written document, ranging from children's fairy tales to presidential speeches. Winter analyzed the content of 300 years of State of the Parliament speeches given by the prime ministers of England. Each of the speeches was rated for the presence of power images. He then used these image scores to predict warfare activity in these three centuries of British history. Winter found that wars were started when power imagery in the parliamentary speeches was high. Once under way, wars ended only after the levels of power imagery in the speeches ended. Similar analyses were done on the British–German communications during World War I, as well as on U.S.–Soviet communications during the Cuban missile crisis of the 1960s (Winter, 1993). In these cases, increases in power images preceded military actions, whereas decreases in power imagery preceded decreases in military threat.

Winter (2002) has conducted research on the motivational dimensions of effective leadership. He analyzed the motive profiles of various contemporary political leaders (e.g., President George W. Bush) to examine how their motives influenced their leadership style and success. Winter shows how different motives can have both strengths and weaknesses, but ultimately he comes up with a motivational prescription for effective leadership: the key is balance between motives, with power motivation balanced by affiliation, and achievement balanced by power concerns. Overall, the responsible leader should want to achieve much, be willing to exercise a good deal of power to attain those goals, yet want to maintain good relations with all other important people or governments.

Speeches delivered by national leaders can be analyzed for themes of power. Research has suggested that the presence of power imagery may predict the onset of war (Winter, 2002).
©The Canadian Press/Fred Chartrand

In an extension of this research, Winter and his students examined how power images in communications may lead to escalation in conflict (Peterson, Winter, & Doty, 1994). Subjects were asked to write replies to letters taken from real conflict situations. The letters the subjects were responding to were altered to create two versions: one with high power imagery and the other with low power imagery. Otherwise, the content of the letters remained the same. The subjects' responses were then analyzed for themes of power. Subjects responded to power imagery with power images of their own. Assuming that the other side would similarly respond with more power images, it is easy to see how conflicts might escalate to violence.

More recent studies of communications among governments involved in crises have revealed similar motive patterns (Langner & Winter, 2001). Analyzing official documents during four international crises, Langner and Winter found that making concessions was associated with affiliative motives expressed in the communications, whereas power images were associated with making fewer concessions. In a laboratory study, they found that power or affiliative motives could be primed by having the subjects read different communications from their negotiation partner and that these primed motives predicted the likelihood that they would make a concession during the negotiation. Such personality research may have wide implications for understanding how governments could respond to each other to avoid crises.

To summarize, the need for power is the desire to have an impact on others. It can be measured from the TAT and from other verbal documents, such as speeches and other forms of communication, by looking for evidence of themes related to status seeking, concerns about reputation, or attempts to make others do what one wants. For example, Winter (1988) provides an interesting analysis of former American president Bill Clinton, linking Clinton's motives to some of his problems as well as to his popularity. Krasno (2015) also analyzed the motives of president Bill Clinton, and found him to be particularly high on both the need for achievement as well as the need for intimacy.

Need for Intimacy

The last of the "Big Three" motives is based on the desire for warm and fulfilling relationships with others, and the need for human connection.

Intimacy

The third motive receiving a good deal of research attention is the need for intimacy (nInt). The researcher most closely associated with this motive is Dan McAdams, another McClelland student. McAdams defines the **need for intimacy** as the "recurrent preference or readiness for warm, close, and communicative interaction with others" (McAdams, 1990, p. 198). People high in nInt want more intimacy and meaningful human contact in their day-to-day lives than do those who are low in nInt.

Research Findings

McAdams and others have conducted a number of studies of nInt over the years in an effort to determine how people high and low in nInt differ from each other. As with the other motives, the TAT is often used to measure the strength of the intimacy motive. People high in nInt (compared to those who are low) have been found to (1) spend more time during the day thinking about relationships; (2) report more pleasant emotions when they are around other people; (3) smile, laugh, and make more eye contact; and (4) start up conversations more frequently and write more letters. We might think that the people high in nInt are simply extraverts, but the findings do not support this interpretation. Rather than being the loud, outgoing, life-of-the-party extravert, the person high in nInt is more likely to be someone with a few very good friends, who prefers sincere and meaningful conversations over wild parties. When asked to describe a typical time with a friend, people high in nInt tend to report one-on-one interactions instead of group interactions. When they get together with friends, people high in nInt are likely to listen to their friends and to discuss intimate or personal topics with them, such as their feelings, hopes, beliefs, and desires. Perhaps this is why people who are high in nInt are rated by their peers as especially "sincere," "loving," "not dominant," and "not self-centred" (McAdams, 1990).

A few studies have examined the relationship between nInt and well-being. In a longitudinal study, nInt measured at age 30 in a sample of male Harvard graduates was significantly related to overall adjustment (e.g., having a satisfying job and family life, coping well with life's stress, being free from alcohol problems) 17 years later (McAdams & Vaillant, 1982). Other studies have shown that nInt is associated with certain benefits and positive life outcomes for both men and women. Among women, nInt is associated with happiness and satisfaction with life. Among men, nInt is associated with less strain in life. Unlike the motives for power and achievement, for which no sex differences have been found as far as level of need is concerned, there does exist a consistent sex difference in need for intimacy—women have, on average, a higher need than men (McAdams, 1990; McAdams & Bryant, 1987).

To summarize, the need for intimacy is the desire for warm and intimate relationships with others. Individuals with a strong nInt enjoy the company of others and are more expressive and communicative toward others compared with people low in nInt. The intimacy motive is distinguished from extraversion in that individuals high in nInt prefer having a few close friends to being a member of a rowdy group. In contrast to the need for achievement and power, for which men and women show comparable levels, women's need for intimacy tends to be higher than men's.

The motives we have covered so far—the needs for achievement, power, and intimacy—all fall within the tradition of academic personality psychology. There is, however, another motivational tradition, one that is rooted more in clinical psychology than in academic personality research. This tradition has come to inform the field of personality psychology, and concepts from this tradition are present or implied in several areas of contemporary research. We turn now to the humanistic tradition within personality psychology.

Humanistic Tradition: The Motive to Self-Actualize

Earlier in this chapter, we discussed unconscious (implicit) motives. These are motives that a person is largely unaware of, yet they regularly guide and direct behaviour, life choices, and even responses to projective tests such as the TAT. Choices based on unconscious motives are, in most respects, made without free will.

An emphasis on conscious awareness of needs, choice, and personal responsibility is one of the characteristics of the **humanistic approach** to motivation. Humanistic psychologists emphasize the role of *choice* in human life, as well as the influence of *responsibility* on creating a meaningful and satisfying life. The meaning of any person's life, according to the humanistic approach, is found in the choices that person makes and the responsibility taken for those choices. In midlife, for example, some people conclude that they are not exercising much choice in their daily lives, that they have fallen into a rut in their careers, their personal relationships, or both. For example, the 2000 Oscar-winning movie *American Beauty* portrays the desperation of a man who has realized he is living a life he has not chosen and his extreme attempts to reclaim and take responsibility for his life. Some people respond to such a realization with drastic efforts to resume responsibility for creating their own lives. Career changes, relationship breakups, moves across the country, and other drastic choices are often symptoms of, and sometimes solutions to, the midlife crisis of responsibility for one's life.

A second major characteristic of the humanistic tradition is its emphasis on the human need for growth and the realization of one's full potential. Human nature, according to this view, is positive and life-affirming. This view stands in marked contrast to psychoanalysis, which takes a rather pessimistic view of human nature, one that views humans as seething cauldrons of primitive and destructive instincts. The humanistic tradition provides an optimistic counterpoint, one that stresses the process of positive growth toward a desired or even an idealized human potential. Such human potential is summed up in the concept of the self-actualization motive.

We will define self-actualization shortly. First, we must note a third characteristic of the humanistic tradition that distinguishes it from other motivational approaches. The humanistic tradition views much of motivation as being based in a need to *grow*, to become who one is meant to be. The other traditions, including those of Freud, Murray, and McClelland, view motivation as coming from a specific *deficit*, or lack of something. This is a subtle but important distinction, and it represents a historical break in motivation theory and research. All the motives we have discussed—achievement, power, and intimacy—are deficiency motives. In the humanistic tradition, the most human of all motivations—the motive to self-actualize—is seen as *not* based on a deficiency. Rather, it is a growth-based motive, a motive to develop, to flourish, and to become more and more what one is optimally suited to become. In the words of Abraham Maslow (1970), who coined the term in the 1960s, self-actualization is the process of becoming "more and more what one idiosyncratically is, to become everything that one is capable of becoming" (p. 46).

Abraham Maslow's Contributions

Abraham Maslow (1908–1970)
©Bettmann/Getty Images

Any discussion of the motive to self-actualize has to begin with Maslow's contributions (see Maslow & Hoffman, 1996). Several of his ideas form the foundation for theory and research in this area.

Hierarchy of Needs

Abraham Maslow (1908–1970) began with the concept of need but defined needs primarily by their goals. Maslow believed that needs were hierarchically organized, with more basic needs found toward the bottom of the hierarchy and the self-actualization need at the top (see Figure 11.2). He divided the hierarchy of needs into five levels.

Self-actualization

Esteem

Belongingness

Safety

Physiological

FIGURE 11.2 Maslow's hierarchy of needs in his theory of motivation. The needs are organized hierarchically into levels. Lower-level needs are more pressing (indicated by larger, bolder fonts) than are higher-level needs.

At the base of the hierarchy are the **physiological needs**. These include needs that are of prime importance to the immediate survival of the individual (the need for food, water, air, and sleep), as well as to the long-term survival of the species (e.g., the need for sex). At the next highest level are the **safety needs**. These have to do with shelter and security, such as having a place to live and being free from the threat of danger. Maslow believed that building a life that was orderly, structured, and predictable also fell under safety needs. Having your car inspected prior to a long trip might be seen as an expression of your safety needs.

With only two levels mentioned so far, we can make a few important observations. One is that we typically must satisfy the lower needs before we proceed to satisfy the higher needs. One of Maslow's enduring contributions is that he assembled the needs in a specific order, providing an understanding of how they relate to one another. Obviously, we have to have enough food and water before we will worry about earning esteem and respect from our peers. It is possible, of course, to find examples of people who do not follow the hierarchy (e.g., starving artists, who frequently go without adequate food to continue expressing themselves in their art). Maslow's theory, like most personality theories, is meant to apply to the average person or to describe human nature in general. Although there are always exceptions to the rule, people appear, on average, to work their way up Maslow's hierarchy from the lowest to the highest level. Maslow also taught that the need hierarchy emerges during the course of human development, with the lower-level needs emerging earlier in life than the higher-level needs.

A second observation is that needs lower in the hierarchy are more powerful or more pressing when not satisfied than the needs toward the top of the hierarchy. The higher-level needs are less relevant to survival, so they are less urgent when not satisfied than the lower needs. Another way to put this is that when people are working on satisfying their higher needs, their motivation is weak and easily disrupted. Maslow (1968) stated that "this inner tendency [toward self-actualization] is not strong and overpowering and unmistakable like the instincts of animals. It is weak and delicate and subtle and easily overcome by habit, cultural pressures, and wrong attitudes toward it" (p. 191).

People typically work at satisfying multiple needs at the same time. It is easy to find examples of people engaging in a variety of tasks that represent different needs in a given period of time (e.g., eating, installing a new lock on the front door, going to a family reunion, and studying for an exam to earn a better grade). At any given time, however, we can determine the level at which a person is investing *most* of their energy. The point is that, even if we are working primarily on self-actualization needs, we need to do certain things (e.g., buy groceries) to make sure the lower needs continue to be satisfied.

The plots of many movies, particularly adventure stories, involve people who find themselves in situations that force them to take a step downward on the hierarchy of needs—circumstances that require a sudden shift in focus to safety or even physiological needs. The series of *Alien* and *Die Hard* movies are examples of films that illustrate this phenomenon. In the film *The Edge,* actors Anthony Hopkins and Alec Baldwin take a few steps down the hierarchy of needs when their plane crashes in the wilderness and they are pursued by a large, hungry, and very persistent grizzly bear.

The third level in Maslow's hierarchy consists of **belongingness needs**. Humans are a very social species, and most people possess a strong need to belong to groups (families, friend groups, churches, clubs, teams, etc.) (Baumeister & Leary, 1995). Being accepted by others and welcomed into a group represents a somewhat more psychological need than the physiological needs or the need for safety. Some observers have argued that modern society provides fewer opportunities for satisfying our need to belong than it did in the past, when ready-made groups existed and people were automatic members (e.g., multigenerational extended families and small towns in which virtually everyone felt like a member of the community). Loneliness is a sign that these needs are not being satisfied; alienation from one's social group

In the movie **The Edge,** *the plot involves two high-esteem men who are suddenly knocked several steps down on Maslow's hierarchy of needs by a large and persistent grizzly bear.*
©Moviestore collection Ltd/Alamy Stock Photo

is another. The popularity of street gangs in dense urban areas may be a testament to the strength of belongingness needs. Gangs can provide group membership to people who might otherwise feel alienated or excluded by other members of society.

One reason that the need to belong is so basic comes from the theory of evolution. In our evolutionary past, belonging to a large social group was essential to survival. People hunted in groups, lived in groups, and moved around in groups. Belonging to a group allowed the individual members to share the workload and to protect each other, raise each others' young, and share important resources. Belonging to a group had survival value. Not only was each individual ensuring their own survival by living in a group, but all members of the group were invested in each other's survival because each member played an important role in the group. Today it is not necessarily the case that group living fosters survival; nevertheless, modern humans still have a strong desire to belong to specific groups, such as peer and work groups, clubs, and various interest groups.

The fourth level of Maslow's hierarchy contains **esteem needs**. There are really two types of esteem—esteem from others and self-esteem, the latter often depending on the former. We want to be seen by others as competent, strong, and able to achieve. We want to be respected by others for our achievements and our abilities. We also want this respect to translate into self-esteem; we want to feel good about ourselves, to feel that we are worthwhile, valuable, and competent. Much of the activity of adult daily life is geared toward achieving recognition and esteem from others and bolstering self-confidence.

The pinnacle of Maslow's hierarchy is the **self-actualization need**, the need to develop one's potential, to become the person one was meant to be and live according to one's **true self** (a topic that is explored further in Chapter 14). You might think this is difficult, as it assumes that one must first figure out who one was meant to be. However, self-actualizers seem to just know who they are and have few doubts about the direction their lives should take. They also tend to score higher on measures of general well-being (Bauer, Schwab, & McAdams, 2011). In his work, Maslow was able to identify a number of common characteristics of self-actualizers, which are reviewed later in Table 11.3. One of those characteristics included the tendency to have peak experiences, a topic we explore further in A Closer Look: From Peak Experiences to the Contemporary Notions of Flow and the Autotelic Personality.

In his final years, Maslow explored an additional, final level in his hierarchy of needs. He argued that people only fully achieve self-actualization by also giving themselves to some higher goal that extends beyond themselves, as in altruism and spirituality. He called this **self-transcendence**, and considered it the ultimate expression of the self (Maslow, 1971; Maslow & Hoffman, 1996). Though self-actualization is accompanied by a sense of meaning and purpose in life, even greater meaning and purpose can be achieved when people put their own needs aside (to a great extent) and commit themselves to a greater social cause. According to Koltko-Rivera (2006), self-transcendence is frequently overlooked in descriptions and summaries of Maslow's work, mainly for two reasons: (1) Maslow had insufficient time to publicize the amendment himself; and (2) there is an unwillingness in society (and in science) to give credit to spirituality in peoples' lives.

 **A Closer Look**

From Peak Experiences to the Contemporary Notions of Flow and the Autotelic Personality

According to Maslow (1964, 1968, 1970), a **peak experience** is a momentary feeling of extreme wonder, awe, and vision, sometimes called the "oceanic feeling." Peak experiences are characterized by feelings of euphoria, harmonization with one's environment, a deep sense of meaning and purpose, and interconnectedness; and very often by a disorientation in space and time, such that the individual loses an acute sense or awareness of their physical surroundings and the passing of time (Maslow, 1970). These are rare experiences that are very meaningful to those who have them, and they contribute to the self-actualization process by providing insight about one's true self and inner potential. As Maslow noted, individuals often describe these experiences (and their associated revelations) as possessing a mystical, spiritual, or overtly religious quality.

Maslow noted early on that such experiences were historically cited by religious mystics, saints, and monks (Maslow, 1964). Yet in his study of human nature, he found that peak experiences could be had by anyone, regardless of age, background, or vocation, in a variety of different environments and situations. For example, peak experiences could occur during sexual and romantic love, philosophical or intellectual insights, or child-bearing and birth, among many other possible circumstances (Maslow, 1970). He further noted that peak experiences tend to be associated with good psychological health; in addition to contributing to well-being, they are also more likely to occur in positive mental states (Maslow, 1964; 1970).

A concept closely related to peak experiences is *flow*, proposed by psychologist Mihaly Csikszentmihalyi (pronounced Me-high Cheek-sent-me-high), originally in 1975 (Csikszentmihalyi, 1975/2000). **Flow** is a subjective state that occurs when one is completely involved in something to the point of forgetting time, fatigue, and everything else but the activity itself. In states of flow, individuals are functioning at their fullest capacity. In more technical terms, they are neither under-stimulated (such that they are bored) nor overstimulated (such that they feel anxious or stressed). Although flow experiences are somewhat rare, they seem to occur more frequently under specific conditions; when there is a balance between the person's skills and the challenges of the situation, there is a clear goal, and there is immediate feedback on how one is doing (Csikszentmihalyi, 1975/2000; Csikszentmihalyi, Abuhamdeh, & Nakamura, 2005).

Like the peak experience, flow can be a powerfully motivating force and an indication that, at least for the moment, one is experiencing self-actualization (Csikszentmihalyi et al., 2005). It is important to note that in most respects, Maslow and Csikszentmihalyi are describing the same experience; Csikszentmihalyi has simply offered a definition that can be more easily subjected to scientific inquiry, and more easily operationalized and measured. Reminiscent of Maslow's own conclusions, Csikszentmihalyi (2000, 2005) suggests that flow can be experienced in a variety of situations and conditions, including physical activity and sport (e.g., running), artistic and creative expression (e.g., painting, writing, or playing music), or involvement in complex tasks (e.g., solving mathematical equations). Flow appears to be more likely to occur in activities in which the person is actively involved (e.g., one's own work) than those with more passive involvement (e.g., listening to a lecture, watching television).

In his early work, Maslow noted that after having a peak experience, some individuals may seek out similar experiences in the future (Maslow, 1964). Csikszentmihalyi (1997) made a similar observation, coining the term **autotelic personality** to describe someone who tends to enjoy life and does things for their own sake, rather than to achieve some later goal. These individuals have a general curiosity and interest in life and tend to be inclined to experience flow states, often seeking them out in work and other activities.

Research on flow and the autotelic personality has been expanded largely by measures developed to identify these concepts, such as the Flow State Scale (Jackson & Marsh, 1996) and the Autotelic Personality Questionnaire (Tse et al., 2018). One study examined experiences of flow in a group of 50 mountain climbers (Tsaur, Yen, & Hsiao, 2013), surveying them immediately after completing climbs of over 3000 metres. Transcendent experiences characterized by feelings of self-actualization were common, and these seemed to contribute to the experience of flow, which in turn increased feelings of happiness. As research on these fascinating aspects of human experience continues, we will undoubtedly expand our understanding of many of Maslow's original ideas about peak experiences and self-actualization.

Research Findings

Maslow developed his theory of human motivation based on highly subjective biographical analyses of select individuals, in addition to many of his own ideas, rather than on empirical research. He never, for example, developed a measure of self-actualization, though others did (Flett, Blankstein, & Hewitt, 1991; Jones & Crandall, 1986). How has his theory fared in the hands of researchers? Although not all the studies support Maslow's theory (e.g., Wahba & Bridwell, 1973), some studies support its main tenets (e.g., Hagerty, 1999).

One group of researchers tested the idea that lower-level needs in the hierarchy are stronger than the higher-level needs when deprived (Wicker et al., 1993). These researchers presented subjects with a variety of goals that mapped onto Maslow's theory: having enough to eat and drink, feeling safe and unafraid, being part of a special group, being recognized by others as an outstanding student, and being mentally healthy and making full use of one's capabilities. They then asked subjects several questions about each goal, including "How good would you feel if you attained it?" and "How bad would you feel if you did not attain it?" What the researchers found is that the negative reactions were strongest when subjects thought about not attaining the lower goals. Subjects were more upset when they contemplated their safety needs not being met than they were when they thought about not meeting their self-actualization needs. Just the opposite pattern was found for the positive reaction ratings. When subjects were asked about attaining goals, they reported more positive emotions in response to contemplating the attainment of goals higher in the hierarchy. For example, acquiring esteem from others makes one feel better about oneself than having enough to eat and drink. This study supports Maslow's hierarchical arrangement of motives, while highlighting differences in how people react to the attainment or frustration in the various need levels. Maslow's idea that the lower needs are "prepotent"—imperative for sheer survival—and therefore stronger than the higher needs when unfulfilled was supported. In addition, his belief that people value gratifying the higher needs more than they do the lower needs was also supported by the finding that people rated the attainment of higher goals as more satisfying than the attainment of lower goals.

Another study compared groups defined by where they stood on Maslow's hierarchy in terms of overall happiness (Diener, Horowitz, & Emmons, 1985). All of the subjects were asked, "What is it that most makes you happy?" The researchers assumed that the answer to this question would reveal each subject's level of need in Maslow's hierarchy. For example, one subject said, "A good meal and the ability to digest it," which was scored as being at the physiological level. The results showed no relationship between level of need and overall happiness (which was gauged in this study by a questionnaire measure). For happiness, it does not appear to matter what level of need a person is working on. People working on self-actualization needs are not any more likely to be happier than people working on other needs. Maslow also notes that happiness does not necessarily come with working on the self-actualizing need.

Many have criticized Maslow's hierarchy for being relevant only within an industrialized, Western cultural context that values individual achievement over the well-being of the group (Bouzenita & Boulanouar, 2016). Since we are dealing with human motivation, it is reasonable to expect that situational and cultural factors may influence people to satisfy needs to varying degrees. Edwin C. Nevis (1983), an American psychologist who taught organizational psychology in Shanghai, China, proposed an alternative hierarchy of needs for Eastern cultures who place greater importance on collective well-being and achievement. In this model, belonging needs reside at the bottom of the hierarchy and are the most pressing. Above the belonging needs are the physiological and then safety needs, with the self-actualization need at the top. There are no esteem needs, as it is suggested that these are only important in more independent cultures, while self-actualization is attained by meeting needs related to societal and communal development. Gambrel and Cianci (2003) discuss further support for this alternative, non-Western hierarchy in their review, though further research is needed to verify its accuracy. It nevertheless brings up an important concern around cultural variability in research on human needs and motivation.

Psychologist Doug Kenrick and colleagues (Kenrick et al., 2010; Krems, Kenrick, & Neel, 2017) have proposed a reinterpretation of Maslow's hierarchical model of fundamental human needs. It is a reformulation that merges Maslow's ideas with basic concepts from evolutionary psychology, offering a theoretical explanation for the evolutionary function of each particular need. At the bottom of the hierarchy, the basic needs related to physiological, safety or self-protection, affiliation, and esteem motives are all retained because they are important to survival, a major evolutionary goal. But, as we learned in Chapter 8, survival is only part of the evolutionary process. More important is reproduction, since survival without reproduction is an evolutionary dead end. So above the esteem needs, Kenrick et al. add the needs of mate acquisition, mate retention, and parenting, which resides at the very top of the hierarchy. Raising one's children so that they may, in turn, reproduce (thereby ensuring one's genes into future generations) is defined as the pinnacle of human success in this model. Maslow's ultimate need—the need to self-actualize—has no apparent function with respect to surviving and reproducing, and so Kenrick et al. leave that need out of their model. (This does not mean, of course, that it is of no significance to well-being or success more broadly.)

The journal that published Kenrick et al.'s revised model of needs also published four articles critical of this new model. One criticism (Kesebir, Graham, & Oishi, 2010) argued that a theory of human needs should be human-centred, and not animal-centred. After all, the Kenrick et al. model applies to rats and lizards as much as it applies to humans, ignoring what might be distinctively human about human nature. Others argued that self-actualization can be viewed as evolutionarily important, and should not be dropped off of the list of fundamental human needs (Peterson & Park, 2010). Others argued that purpose in life, other than ensuring one's genes into future generations, is missing from the Kenrick et al. model (Ackerman & Bargh, 2010). Recent research has demonstrated some support for this functional version of the hierarchy, further suggesting that status-seeking (associated with esteem needs) may be one of the most pressing of human motivations (Krems et al., 2017).

Characteristics of Self-Actualizing People

To learn more about self-actualization, Maslow conducted case studies of a number of people who he thought were self-actualizers. Maslow estimated about one percent of the population are growth motivated and are working on becoming all that they can become. Maslow's list of self-actualizing people he investigated included several living individuals whom he kept anonymous. He also studied several historical figures through their writings and other biographical information, including Albert Einstein, Eleanor Roosevelt, and Thomas Jefferson. Maslow then looked for common characteristics that could be identified in this group. From this study, he produced a list of 15 characteristics that he suggested are commonly found among self-actualizers (see Table 11.3). Most of the people Maslow studied were famous, and many had made great contributions to science, politics, or the humanities. When reading over the list of characteristics in Table 11.3, bear in mind that the theory does not say "you must make great contributions" to become self-actualized. Students of psychology often make this misinterpretation because of the special nature of the people studied by Maslow. It is possible for ordinary as well as extraordinary people to achieve self-actualization.

Table 11.3   Characteristics of Self-Actualizers from Maslow's Case Studies

1. *Efficient perception of reality.* They do not let their own wishes and desires colour their perceptions. Consequently, they are able to detect the deceitful and the fake.

2. *Acceptance of themselves, others, and nature or fate.* They realize that people, including themselves, make mistakes and have frailties, and they accept this fact. They accept natural events, even disasters, as part of life.

3. *Spontaneity.* Their behaviour is marked by simplicity and honest naturalness. They do not act like they are better (or know more) than others or strain to create an effect. They trust their impulses.

4. *Problem focus.* They have an interest in the larger philosophical and ethical problems of their times. Petty issues hold little interest for them.

5. *Affinity for solitude.* They are comfortable with being alone.

6. *Independence from culture and environment.* They do not go along with fads or feel compelled by social pressure. They prefer to follow their self-determined interests.

7. *Continued freshness of appreciation.* They have a "beginner's mind," for which every event, no matter how common, is experienced as if for the first time. They appreciate the ordinary and find pleasure and awe in the mundane.

8. *More frequent peak experiences.* A peak experience is a momentary feeling of extreme wonder, awe, and vision, sometimes called the "oceanic feeling." These are special experiences that appear to be very meaningful to those who have them.

9. *Genuine desire to help the human race.* All self-actualizers tend to have a deep and sincere caring for their fellow humans.

10. *Deep ties with relatively few people.* Although they care deeply about others, they have relatively few very good friends. They tend to prefer privacy and allow only a few people to really know them.

11. *Democratic values.* They respect and value all people and are not prejudiced in terms of holding stereotypes about people based on superficial characteristics, such as race, religion, sex, and age. They treat others as individuals, not as members of groups.

12. *Ability to discriminate between means and ends.* They enjoy doing something for its own sake rather than simply doing something for the goals the activity can fulfill.

13. *Philosophical sense of humour.* Most humour is an attempt to make fun of a perceived inferiority of a person or group of people. Self-actualizers do not think such jokes are funny. Instead, what they find funny are more intellectual jokes or examples of human foolishness in general.

14. *Creativity.* Creativity can be thought of as the ability to see connections among things—connections that no one has seen before. They are more likely to be creative because of their fresh perception of even ordinary things.

15. *Resistance to enculturation.* Cultures tell us how to behave, how to dress, and even how to interact with each other. Self-actualizers remain detached from culture-bound rules. They often appear different from and act differently from the crowd.

Recently, Scott Kaufman of the University of Pennsylvania developed and validated a self-report measure of 10 characteristics of self-actualizers originally described by Maslow, including efficient perception of reality, acceptance, authenticity, humanitarianism, creativity, and peak experiences. The questionnaire includes 30 items, all of which load on a single general self-actualization factor when subjected to factor analysis

(Kaufman, 2018). In line with Maslow's original theory, Kaufman found that those scoring high on characteristics of self-actualization were more motivated by growth, exploration, and love of humanity, while being less motivated to fulfill deficiencies in basic needs. Self-actualizers also tended to display higher well-being, reporting greater life satisfaction, more positive relations, greater environmental mastery, and purpose in life. In terms of the Big Five traits, self-actualizers tended to be higher in conscientiousness, openness to experience, extraversion, agreeableness, and emotional stability. Though further research is needed in order to demonstrate that the measure is reliable and valid, it also appears that self-actualization may be normally distributed in the population and unrelated to age (Kaufman, 2018).

❓ Exercise

Think of a person you know or someone you have met who impresses you. Try to identify someone who you think might be a self-actualizer. Review Maslow's list of the 15 characteristics he associated with self-actualized individuals (Table 11.3) and identify the characteristics that the person you've chosen seems to possess. Try to provide concrete examples from the person's life to illustrate the characteristics.

You might also consider the following famous people. Do you believe any of these individuals would be described as self-actualizers by Maslow? Why or why not?

- **Steve Jobs, co-founder and former CEO of Apple.**
- **Malala Yousafzai, activist for girls' education and Nobel Peace Prize laureate.**
- **Kylie Jenner, reality television and social media star.**
- **Wayne Gretzky, former professional hockey player.**
- **Laverne Cox, transgender American actress and LGBTQ activist.**
- **Tenzin Gyatso, 14th Dalai Lama and Buddhist spiritual leader.**
- **Donald Trump, 45th president of the United States.**
- **Stefani Joanne Angelina Germanotta (also known as Lady Gaga), American singer, songwriter, and actress.**

Carl Rogers' Contributions

Maslow focused on the characteristics of self-actualizing individuals, but psychologist Carl Rogers (1902–1987) focused on the ways to foster and attain self-actualization. During the four decades of his productive career, Rogers developed a theory of personality and a method of psychotherapy (client-centred therapy). Like Maslow, Rogers believed that people were basically good and that human nature was fundamentally benevolent and positive. He felt that the natural human state was to be fully functioning, but under certain conditions people become stalled in their movement toward self-actualization. His theory explains how people lose their direction. Moreover, he proposed techniques for helping people get back on track toward achieving their potential. His general approach to self-actualization—the person-centred approach—has been expanded and applied to groups, to education, to corporate organizations, and even to government (see Rogers, 2002, for his posthumously published autobiography).

At the core of Rogers' approach is the concept of the **fully functioning person**, the person who is on their way to self-actualization. The fully functioning person may not actually *be* self-actualized yet, but they are not blocked or sidetracked in moving toward this goal. Several characteristics describe the fully functioning person. Such individuals are open to new experiences, and they enjoy diversity and novelty in their daily lives. Fully functioning individuals are also centred in the present. They do not dwell on the past or their regrets. Neither do they live in the future. Fully functioning individuals also trust themselves, their feelings, and their own judgments. When faced with a decision, they don't automatically look around to others for guidance (e.g., "What would make my parents happy?"). Instead, they trust themselves to do the right thing. Fully functioning individuals are often unconventional, setting their own obligations and accounting to themselves.

How does someone become fully functioning? This is where Rogers' theory of the development of the self comes into play. An entire chapter of this book is devoted to an exploration of the self, and much of the work covered in Chapter 14 can be traced back to Carl Rogers, who strongly believed that there was one primary motive in life—the motive to self-actualize, to develop the self that was meant to be.

Journey into Selfhood: Positive Regard and Conditions of Worth

According to Rogers, all children are born wanting to be loved and accepted by their parents and others. He called this inborn need the desire for **positive regard**. Parents frequently make their positive regard contingent on conditions, such as the conditions expressed in the statements "Show me you are a good child and earn all A grades on your report card" and "I will really like it if you earn the star role in your school play." In another example, parents push children into sports, and the children might stay in the sports not because they like sports, but to earn the love and positive regard of their parents. Of course, it is good for parents to have expectations for their children, but not to make their love contingent on the child's meeting those expectations.

The requirements set forth by parents or significant others for earning their positive regard are called **conditions of worth**. Children may become preoccupied with living up to these conditions of worth rather than discovering what makes them happy. They behave in specific ways to earn the love, respect, and positive regard of parents and other significant people in their lives. Positive regard, when it must be earned by meeting certain conditions, is called **conditional positive regard**.

Children who experience many conditions of worth may lose touch with their own desires and wants. They begin living their lives in an effort to please others. They become what others want them to become, and their self-understanding contains only qualities that others condone. They are moving away from the ideals of a fully functioning person. What matters most is pleasing others. "What will *they* think?"—not "What do I really want in this situation?"—is a question such people ask themselves repeatedly.

As they reach adulthood, they remain preoccupied with what others think of them. They work primarily for approval from others, not out of their own sense of self-direction. They are dependent on others for positive regard and are constantly

Carl Rogers (1902–1987)
©Michael Rougier/The LIFE Picture Collection/Getty Images

looking for the conditions of worth, which must be satisfied. They hide their weaknesses, distort their short-comings, and perhaps even deny their faults. They act in ways that make everybody, except themselves, happy. They have been working to please others for so long that they have forgotten what they want out of life. They have lost self-direction and are no longer moving toward self-actualization.

How can one avoid this outcome? Rogers believed that positive regard from parents and significant others should have no strings attached. It should be given freely and liberally without conditions or contingencies. Rogers called this **unconditional positive regard**—when the parents and significant others accept the child without conditions, communicating that they love and value the child because the child just is. Parents need to show unconditional acceptance of the child, even when providing discipline or guidance. For example, if a child has done something wrong, the parent can still provide correction in combination with unconditional positive regard: "You have done something bad. *You* are not bad, and I still love *you*; it's just that the thing you have done is bad, and I don't want you to do that anymore."

With enough unconditional positive regard, children learn to accept experiences rather than deny them. They don't have to engage in efforts to distort themselves for others or alter their behaviours or experiences to fit a mould or model of what others want. Such individuals are free to accept themselves, even their own weaknesses and shortcomings, because they have experienced unconditional **positive self-regard**. They are able to give themselves unconditional positive regard and accept themselves for who they are. They trust themselves, follow their own interests, and rely on their feelings to guide them to do the right thing. In short, they begin to take on the characteristics of a fully functioning person and begin to actualize the selves that they were meant to be.

Promotion of Self-Actualization in Self and Others

People who are not moving forward in terms of self-actualization experience frequent episodes of anxiety. **Anxiety**, according to Rogers, is the result of having an experience that does not fit with one's self-conception. Imagine a young person who worked hard all through elementary school and high school to earn good grades in an effort to make their parents happy. Part of their self-concept is that they "are smart and get good grades." Then they enter university and obtain less than perfect grades in some of their courses. This experience is alien; it does not fit with their self-concept as a person who is smart and gets good grades, so it makes them anxious. "What will *they* think," referring to their parents, "when they find out about these grades?" This new experience is a threat to their self-image, and that self-image is vitally important to this individual because in the past it brought them the positive regard of their parents. Rogers believed that people needed to defend themselves against anxiety, to reduce the discrepancy between their self-concept and their experiences. A fully functioning person could change their self-concept to incorporate the experience (e.g., "Perhaps I'm not so smart after all, or perhaps I don't always need to get perfect grades").

A less functional response to anxiety is to alter the experience by using a defence mechanism. Rogers emphasized the defence mechanism of **distortion**. People who engage in distortion modify their experience rather than their self-image to reduce the threat. For example, a person might say, "The professors in these classes are unfair," or "The grades really don't reflect how well I did," or in another way distort the experience. Or perhaps the person decides to take only "easy" classes, in which they are likely to earn high grades. Their decisions about which classes to take are based not on their own interests and desires (as would be the case for a self-actualizing reason) but on which classes are more likely to result in better grades to make their parents happy (a condition-of-worth reason). Taking classes merely to obtain easy grades is at odds with their self-concept of someone who is smart, and they may become anxious over the fact that so many of their experiences do not fit exactly with the way they would like to see themselves.

One study found a relationship between the self-actualizing tendency and emotional intelligence (Bar-On, 2001). **Emotional intelligence** is a relatively new construct that has five components: the ability to know one's own emotions, the ability to regulate those emotions, the ability to motivate oneself, the ability to know how others are feeling, and the ability to influence how others are feeling. This may be an especially adaptive form of intelligence, which we describe in more detail in Chapter 12 on cognitive approaches. In the Bar-On (2001) study, the self-actualizing tendency was defined as working on actualizing one's talents and skills, and it was found that emotional intelligence correlated with this tendency. The author argues that emotional intelligence may be more important for self-actualizing than IQ, or mere cognitive intelligence. People may get off the path toward self-actualization, not because they lack IQ or education but because they have gotten out of touch with their emotions.

Application

Paul Gauguin is most famous for his paintings of South Pacific islanders using lush colour, the denial of perspective, and the use of flat, two-dimensional forms. His powerfully expressive yet stylistically simple paintings helped form the basis of modern art. Gauguin was not always an artist, however. In 1872, Gauguin started a very successful career as a stockbroker in Paris. His marriage to his Danish wife Mette produced five children, and they led a content, upper-middle-class life in Paris. Gauguin always wanted to paint, however. He felt he could be a great painter, but his job as a stockbroker consumed all of his time (Hollmann, 2001).

In 1874, Gauguin attended the first Impressionist painting exhibition in Paris. He was entranced with this style of painting. He had a strong desire to become a painter, but instead he put all of his energy into his stockbroker's job and used the proceeds to purchase some paintings by Monet, Pissarro, and Renoir. This was the closest he could come, he felt, to realizing his potential as an artist.

Fortunately or unfortunately, the bank that employed Gauguin began having difficulties in 1884. Gauguin began to take time away from work and started painting. His income went down, and he had to move his family from expensive Paris to the town of Rouen, where the cost of living was lower. As Gauguin devoted more time to painting and less time to stockbrokering, his income went even lower and his marriage started to suffer. Neither Paul nor his wife were happy with their current situation, but for different reasons; Paul wanted more of the new life of painting he was discovering, and his wife wanted more of the old life and for him to return to the Paris life of stockbrokers, banks, and the upper middle class.

After a period of some marital discord, Paul Gauguin left his wife and five children and, with absolute sincerity and clarity of purpose, began to realize his potential as an artist. He fell in with the likes of van Gogh, Degas, and Pissarro, who mentored him in impressionism. In 1891, he decided to flee civilization in search of a new way of life, one that more matched his painting style: primitive, bold, and sincere. He sailed to Tahiti and the islands of the South Pacific, where, except for a brief visit back to France, he remained until his death in 1903 (Gauguin, 1985). In Tahiti, his paintings of indigenous people grew more powerful and distinctive, and on a large scale he achieved his potential as one of the modern world's greatest artists.

The ethical questions in Gauguin's life concern the competing responsibilities that are so evident; he had one life as a responsible banker and stockbroker, complete with a loving wife and five dependent children. On the other hand, Gauguin felt (correctly) that he had the potential to become a truly outstanding artist. Should he have been true to this inner calling, or should he have been true to his responsibilities as husband, father, and provider for his family? How should we judge his decision to abandon his family to pursue his self-actualization? What role does his success as an artist have in our judgment? What if, for example, he had abandoned his family and then failed miserably as an artist? What should get priority in life when there is a conflict between one's immediate responsibilities and one's inner calling to become someone else? These are the difficult ethical questions of choice and responsibility that sometimes confront people on their way toward self-actualization.

Rogers' approach to therapy is designed to get a person back on the path toward self-actualization. Rogers' therapy, sometimes called **client-centred therapy**, is very different from Freudian psychoanalysis. In client-centred therapy, the client (a term Rogers preferred over *patient*) is never offered an interpretation of their problem. Nor is a client given any direction about what course of action to take to solve the problem. The therapist makes no attempts to change the client directly. Instead, the therapist tries to create the right conditions in which the client can change and grow.

There are three **core conditions** for client-centred therapy (Rogers, 1957). These conditions must be present in the therapy context in order for progress to occur. A film of Carl Rogers conducting a therapy session with "Gloria" is widely available and is sometimes used in training therapists. In this film, Rogers expertly sets up these three conditions in his conversation with Gloria (see the analysis of

A painting by Paul Gauguin titled Self-portrait with Yellow Christ, *from a private collection. The life of Paul Gauguin raises several complicated questions about responsibility, choice, and self-actualization.*

Gauguin, Paul (1848–1903). Self-portrait with Yellow Christ. 1890–1891. Oil on canvas, 38.0 × 46.0 cm. Musee d'Orsay, Paris, France. Image credit © Erich Lessing/Art Resource, NY.

this film by Wickman & Campbell, 2003). The first core condition is an atmosphere of *genuine acceptance* on the part of the therapist. The therapist must be genuinely able to accept the client. Second, the therapist must express *unconditional positive regard* for the client. This means that the therapist accepts everything the client says without passing judgment on the client. Clients trust that the therapist will not reject them if they say the "wrong" thing, or if something unflattering comes out in the course of therapy. The atmosphere is safe for clients to begin exploring their concerns.

The third condition for therapeutic progress is *empathic understanding*. The client must feel that the therapist understands them. A client-centred therapist attempts to know the client's thoughts and feelings as if they were their own. **Empathy** is understanding the other person from their point of view (Rogers, 1975). The therapist conveys empathic understanding by restating the content and feelings for the client. Instead of interpreting the meaning behind what the client says (e.g., "You have a harsh superego, which is punishing you for the actions of your id"), the client-centred therapist simply listens to what the client says and reflects it back.

It is analogous to looking in a mirror; a good Rogerian therapist reflects back the person's feelings and thoughts, so that the person can examine them in full and undistorted detail. The client comes to understand themselves better by making the therapist understand. The therapist expresses this understanding by restating the content ("What I heard you say is . . .") and by reflecting back the person's feelings ("It sounds as if you are feeling . . ."). This may sound simple, but it is a very effective approach to helping people understand themselves and helping them change how they think about themselves.

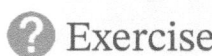 Exercise

Empathic listening is a technique of conversation that can be rather easily developed. You might practise with a friend. Find someone to role-play with you, and ask the person to start by describing a small problem in their life. Your job is to role-play a client-centred approach to the conversation. That is, you will try to do the two activities involved in reflecting back: first, try to just restate the content of what your friend says. That is, repeat what the person has said, exactly as you understand it (e.g., "What I hear you saying is . . ."). The second reflecting-back action is to restate your friend's feelings. That is, take any feelings the friend mentions and state them back to them exactly as you understand those feelings (e.g., "It seems you are feeling . . . about this situation"). The friend will correct you or elaborate on the situation or feelings. After a few minutes, switch the roles and have your friend be the empathic listener while you describe a small problem. If done correctly, you should feel that your friend is really understanding you and that you are encouraged to explore your problem situation and your feelings about that situation.

Ever since Rogers published his classic article describing empathy as one of the necessary conditions for therapeutic change (Rogers, 1957), many psychologists have attempted to understand the nature of empathy. Are some people natural-born empathizers, or is empathy a skill that can be acquired and improved with training? A study of 839 twin pairs suggests that the ability to take the perspective of another person is not significantly heritable (Davis, Luce, & Kraus, 1994). This finding implies that people are not necessarily born with a predisposition to be good at the empathic understanding of others' points of view. Other studies have demonstrated that empathy can be taught effectively. For example, in one study the researchers measured empathic ability both before and after training in peer counselling (Hacher et al., 1994). They found that the training program, which emphasized listening skills, produced significant increases in overall empathy scores. The training especially helped university and high school students improve their abilities to take the perspectives of other people and understand the others' concerns.

Application

The metaphor of a mirror is a useful one that can help us appreciate how the client-centred techniques work. Imagine that you want to adjust your outward appearance, so you look in a mirror to examine your appearance and see how the adjustment looks. Similarly, if you want to change your inner self, you can use the positive atmosphere and empathic understanding of a client-centred therapist to examine yourself and to contemplate changes. The following example demonstrates the technique of reflecting back:

Client: **I just don't know which classes to take next year. I wish someone could make those decisions for me.**

Therapist: You are looking for someone to tell you what to do.

Client: Yes, but I know that's impossible [sigh]. Nobody can decide what's right for me if even I don't have a clue.

Therapist: You find it exasperating that you are having so much trouble deciding on a class schedule.

Client: Well, none of my friends have this much trouble making decisions.

Therapist: You feel that your situation is not normal; it's not like the experience of your friends.

Client: Yeah, and it makes me mad. I should just be able to pick four or five courses and stick with my decision, but I can't seem to. I know it's silly.

Therapist: You think it is a trivial thing, yet it makes you angry that you cannot seem to make the decision.

Client: Well, you know, it really is trivial, isn't it? I know I can always change classes if they don't work out. I guess I just need to try them out.

Therapist: You see some options, that you can get out of a class if it isn't right for you.

The therapist never directs the client or offers an interpretation of the problem. This is why Rogerian therapy is sometimes called nondirective therapy—the focus is on the client's understanding of the situation, not the therapist's interpretation. The client works to clarify the therapist's understanding and, in so doing, increases their self-understanding. The client may come to accept that they have been denying or distorting experiences, such as taking classes for grades rather than for their own intrinsic interest. In helping the therapist understand why she is having so much trouble deciding on a class schedule, the person in the example may come to the realization that she has been taking classes primarily to make her parents happy. In an accepting atmosphere, she may come to this unflattering realization, and she might go on to explore how she can change her self-concept to accept this new understanding.

In another study, empathic ability increased with practice (Marangoni et al., 1995). University students watched videotapes of three individuals undergoing an interview about a personal problem (e.g., a recent divorce or the difficulties of being both a wife and a career woman). The researchers' hypothesis was supported; the subjects with more empathy were more accurate in their hunches about what the videotaped person was thinking and feeling, compared with the subjects who had less empathic ability. Moreover, the more practice the subjects had, the better they became at discerning what the videotaped individual was thinking and feeling. Finally, some subjects were simply better than others at empathic understanding. Even though everyone's performance could improve with practice, some subjects were consistently better than others. Trying to understand the characteristics that make someone particularly adept at empathic understanding is an important topic for future research. A recent paper (Weisz & Zaki, 2017) reviewed a number of studies which have demonstrated that empathy can indeed be learned. But there are additional key considerations to be made in regards to empathy interventions, including situational factors and individual differences in people's motivations (Weisz & Zaki, 2017).

Rogers' theory is important to personality psychology for a number of reasons. His theory concerns the development of the self over the life span and includes specific processes that can interrupt or facilitate that development. He offers a new perspective on the importance of early experiences, similar to secure attachment, but which he calls unconditional positive regard. As in psychoanalysis, he assigns an important role to anxiety as a signal that things are not going well with the psychological system. Also as in classical psychoanalysis, he offers a system of psychotherapy for helping people overcome personal setbacks on the road toward actualizing their full potential. His work has had a large impact on the practice of psychotherapy over the last half century (see Patterson, 2000).

Concept Check

Imagine that you wake up to a fire in your home, and you have only moments to escape. What would you take with you, if you could? Come up with a list of five items. How do these items satisfy various needs on Maslow's hierarchy? Are there any needs that have not been satisfied?

If you had a friend who was interested in self-actualizing, what advice would you give them? What traits or characteristics would you suggest they try to develop? Consider the work of both Maslow and Rogers.

Summary and Evaluation

Motives can be used to explain why people do what they do. Motive explanations are unique in that they imply a goal that pulls people to think, act, and feel in certain ways. Many motives grow out of deficits. For example, someone motivated to achieve must feel that they have not yet achieved enough in life. The three motives discussed in detail—achievement, power, and intimacy—are all deficit motives. The fourth major motive—the motive to self-actualize—is not a deficit motive, but rather a growth motive because it refers to the desire to become more and more what one is destined to become.

Henry Murray was among the first to catalogue the variety of human needs. He assumed that individuals differed in the strength of these needs and that the intensity of the needs also fluctuated over time and in different situations. Murray's emphasis was on how individuals differ from each other in terms of the basic needs, such as how some people have a more intense and lasting need for achievement than do other people.

Individual differences in the need for achievement have received a good deal of systematic attention from researchers. The need for achievement is the need to do things better and to overcome obstacles in the quest to attain one's goals. Those with high levels of the need for achievement differ from those low in this need in many important ways, such as the preference for moderate levels of challenge, the tendency to do well in situations where they have control and responsibility, and the interest in receiving feedback on their performance.

The need for power, another deficit motive, has also received research attention. This motive is the desire to have an impact on other people, to make other people respond, and to dominate others. Individuals who have a high need for power seek out positions in which they can influence others and acquire possessions that have all the markings of power, such as sports cars and expensive stereo equipment. They prefer friends who are not particularly powerful or popular. Men with a high need for power may sometimes engage in social influence tactics that are irresponsible or unethical.

The need for intimacy is the motive to acquire warm and communicative relationships. People high in this need tend to think about, and spend more time with, other people. Communication and self-disclosure characterize their interactions, and they prefer one-to-one interactions to large group activities.

The TAT is a projective technique for assessing levels of motivation in people. The technique is based on the idea that what people see is influenced by their needs. For example, a lonely person might see all situations as opportunities to be with people. The TAT was validated by showing that arousing a need in a person influences the person to write TAT stories consistent with that aroused need. Recent reviews of the literature suggest that the TAT assesses implicit motives, and it might be best suited for predicting long-term consequences of motives rather than short-term behaviours. Newer measures of motives, including the Multi-Motive Grid, are being developed.

The need to self-actualize represents a distinct tradition in the psychology of motivation, fundamentally different from the tradition that emphasizes deficit motivation. This humanistic approach emphasizes taking responsibility for decisions and making efforts to move and grow in a positive direction. The humanistic tradition assumes that human nature is positive and life-affirming and that most people would become fully functioning human beings if left to their own devices.

Abraham Maslow developed a hierarchical theory of motivation, the pinnacle of which is self-actualization, ranging from lower-level needs (physiological needs and safety needs) to higher-level needs (need for esteem and self-actualization). Maslow also studied the characteristics of self-actualizing people and developed a list of the traits and behaviour patterns that are common among the small percentage of the population working on becoming more of who they were meant to be.

Psychologist Carl Rogers theorized about obstacles to self-actualization and the therapeutic techniques that help people overcome those obstacles. Client-centred therapy is designed to help people regain their potential for growth and positive change. The therapist creates an atmosphere of unconditional positive regard and communicates empathic understanding to the client in order to enhance therapeutic effectiveness. It is clear from research that empathy is a skill that can be learned, supporting Rogers' theory.

❗ Concept Check

Consider your current life circumstances, your daily activities, and your goals. What needs and motives seem to be dominant in your life? Do any of these needs and motives align with those discussed by Murray, McClelland, or Maslow?

Define the concept of self-actualization. How did Maslow and Rogers offer different perspectives on this concept?

Key Terms

motives

needs

hierarchy of needs

dynamic

press

alpha press

beta press

apperception

Thematic Apperception Test

state levels

trait levels

Multi-Motive Grid

implicit motivation

self-attributed motivation

need for achievement

independence training

need for power

responsibility training

power stress

need for intimacy

humanistic tradition

physiological needs

safety needs

belongingness needs

esteem needs

self-actualization need

true self

self-transcendence

peak experience

flow

autotelic personality

fully functioning person

positive regard

conditions of worth

conditional positive regard

unconditional positive regard

positive self-regard

anxiety

distortion

emotional intelligence

client-centred therapy

core conditions

empathy

The Cognitive/ Experiential Domain

Part 4 covers the cognitive/experiential domain, which emphasizes an understanding of people's perceptions, thoughts, feelings, desires, and other conscious experiences. The focus here is on understanding experience, especially from the person's point of view. However, distinctions can be made in terms of the kinds of experiences that people have.

One kind of experience that people have concerns cognitive experiences; what they perceive and pay attention to, how they interpret the events in their lives, and their goals and strategies and plans for getting what they want in the future.

People differ from each other when it comes to cognitively interpreting or making sense out of life events. We introduce a theory based on the idea that people construct their experiences by applying personal constructs to their sensations. A related theory concerns how people decide on the causes of life events. Often people interpret events by making attributions of responsibility for those events. That is, "Why did this happen?" and "Whose fault is this?" Personality psychologists have extensively studied how people make attributions of responsibility, and how there may be stable individual differences in the tendency to blame oneself for bad events.

Cognitive experiences can also be studied in terms of the plans and goals that people formulate for themselves and for the strategies they develop for reaching their goals. People anticipate different futures and strive for different goals. Understanding people's goals and how their goals are expressions of personality as well as social standards also forms a part of the cognitive/experiential domain of knowledge about human nature.

A topic related to cognitive experience, and included in this part of the book, is intelligence. Currently there are several controversies about the concept of intelligence. For example, what is the best definition of intelligence—the accumulation of what a person has learned or the ability to learn new information? Is intelligence one quality, or are there several different kinds of intelligence?

A second broad but important category of experience—one that is associated with but distinct from cognition—is emotion. Psychology has seen a sharp rise in research on emotion in the past few decades. We can ask a straightforward question about emotional lifestyle: Is a person generally happy or generally sad? What makes a person anxious or fearful? Why is it that some people become enthusiastic so easily? What makes people angry, and why can some people control their anger, whereas others cannot?

Emotional experiences are often thought of as states that come and go; now you are anxious, now you are not, or now you are angry, now you are not. However, emotions can also be thought of as traits, as the frequent experiences of specific states. For example, a person may become anxious frequently or have a lower threshold for experiencing anxiety. And so we might talk of anxiety proneness as a personality trait—the tendency to easily and frequently become anxious.

When it comes to emotions as traits, we can divide the main topics into variables that refer to the content and variables that refer to the style of emotional life. When it comes to content, we are referring to the kinds of emotions a person is likely to experience. The content of emotional life can be divided into pleasant and unpleasant emotions. In terms of pleasant emotions, the typical personality-relevant trait is happiness. Psychologists have recently become very interested in happiness.

When it comes to unpleasant emotion traits, the research can be divided into three different dispositional emotions: anger, anxiety, and depression. Depression is a syndrome that is experienced by a large portion of the population, and it is of great importance in terms of public mental health implications. Trait anxiety has many different names in the personality literature, including neuroticism, negative affectivity, and emotional instability. Anger proneness is also a traitlike tendency, but this one refers to the tendency to easily or frequently become angry, a characteristic personality psychologists are keenly interested in.

People also differ from each other in the style of their emotional lives. Emotional style refers to how their emotions are typically experienced. Some people, for example, tend to experience their emotions at a higher intensity than others. For such high affect-intensity people, a positive event makes them very, very happy, and a negative event makes them very, very unhappy. Consequently such people experience wider emotional swings from day to day or even within a day.

A third major category of experience is distinct from cognition and emotion yet is very important to the average person. This category of experience refers to experiences of the self. These experiences are unique in that individuals can focus on themselves as an object, pay attention to themselves, come to know themselves. The experience of self is unlike all of our other experiences, because in the experience of the self the knower and the known are one and the same. Psychologists have paid a great deal of attention to this unique object of our experience, self-knowing, and research and theorizing on the self has a long and rich tradition in personality psychology.

There are some useful distinctions among types of self-experiences. First there are descriptive aspects of the self: who are we, what are the important images we have of our past self, and what are the images of possible future selves? A second main component of the experience of self is evaluative: Do we like or dislike who we are? This is called self-esteem, and it is a central organizing force in much of what we do. And a third component of our self experience concerns the social roles we inhabit, the social selves we show to others, which we call identity. For example, many university students show one identity to their parents and another identity to their companions at school. And people sometimes go through identity crises, especially during transitions in life, such as starting university, getting married, or starting a new job.

Cognitive Topics in Personality

The Cognitive/Experiential Domain

On February 4, 1999, just past midnight, Amadou Diallo, a 22-year-old immigrant from West Africa, was standing on the front stoop of his home after putting in a full day at work. An unmarked car carrying four plain-clothes police officers cruised by. The police officers were investigating crimes that had plagued that particular area, including a series of gunpoint rapes. Mr. Diallo's neighbourhood was one of the most dangerous in New York City. As they passed Mr. Diallo, he backed into a dark doorway. On noticing this, the officer driving put the car into reverse and backed up to a point directly in front of Mr. Diallo.

Mourners in New York City after the shooting of Amadou Diallo. Protests erupted over the killing of an unarmed African male by the police. The court ruled that what occurred the night Mr. Diallo was shot was a series of terrible accidents, errors in perception and cognition on the part of the police officers.
©Paul Fusco/Magnum Photos

As Mr. Diallo stood in the doorway, the plainclothes officers exited their vehicle, and two approached Mr. Diallo saying, "Police Department. We'd like to have a word with you." At this point, Mr. Diallo started to back into the vestibule and the two officers then added the commands, "Stay where you are," and "Keep your hands where we can see them."

Mr. Diallo reached his right hand into his front pocket. He turned toward the officers while pulling a black object out of his pocket and going into a crouching stance, bringing his hands toward each other. One officer yelled, "Gun!" Two officers fired. The closest officer, trying to back away from Mr. Diallo, fell backward down the steps. The other officers thought he had been shot.

In the next four seconds, the police officers fired a total of 41 bullets, 19 of which struck Mr. Diallo, killing him almost instantly. When the officers approached Mr. Diallo's body, they found him holding not a gun, but his wallet.

The details of this tragic and controversial case were made public during the subsequent trial of the police officers. The jury concluded that what occurred that night was a series of terrible accidents, errors in perception and cognition that had catastrophic results. The officers "saw" a gun, they "thought" one of their own had been shot, and they "thought" Mr. Diallo was returning gunfire, when in fact it was their own ricocheting bullets. Their behaviour then followed these cognitive errors. Many police academies now analyze the Diallo case during the training of new officers to understand what factors contributed to such misunderstandings and to avoid similar misperceptions in the future. The final chapter in this case closed in January 2004 when the City of New York settled a civil rights lawsuit by paying Mr. Diallo's family $3 million and offering an apology for the tragic misunderstanding.

The case of Mr. Diallo illustrates the connection between cognitive factors and behaviour. People perceive and think and then act. Sometimes this all happens very quickly; sometimes we take our time thinking things through. We are processing information all the time and using this information to guide our actions. Most of the time, our information processing is fairly accurate, resulting in appropriate actions. Sometimes errors of information processing occur, and mistakes are made. Psychologists are very interested in understanding how humans process information. Personality psychologists take this interest a step further; they are interested in how people differ from each other in processing information. They are interested in different styles of perceiving and thinking and in different strategies people use to solve problems. It is possible, for instance, for two people to look at the same object and see two very different things. Such differences in how people think are the focus of **cognitive approaches** to personality.

Many years ago, a study was done on what people think about when they are exposed to emotion-provoking stimuli (Larsen, Diener, & Cropanzano, 1987). The researchers showed people slides of emotion-provoking scenes, then asked the participants what they thought about when they looked at each slide (a technique called *thought sampling*). For example, one picture was of a mother holding a child who was bleeding from a severe head wound. In this study, the researchers were interested not in what the participants felt but in what they thought about—in the information that went through their minds—when exposed to such emotional scenes. One participant said, "My brother once had a bad gash on his head just like that, and I remember all the blood, and how upset my mother became, and my brother screaming and my mother trying to stop the bleeding, and me feeling helpless and confused." The next participant looked at the same picture and said, "Head wounds bleed quite a bit because, in the head, there is a high concentration of blood vessels close to the surface of the skin. I was thinking about the major artery groups in the head when I looked at that photo." The first person who looked at the picture engaged in what is called **personalizing cognition**. That is, the scene prompted him to recall a similar event from his own life. The second subject looked at the same picture and engaged in what is called **objectifying cognition**. That is, the scene prompted her to recall objective facts about the distribution of blood vessels in the human head. The difference between these two people is a difference in cognition.

Cognition is a general term referring to awareness and thinking, as well as to specific mental acts such as perceiving, attending to, interpreting, remembering, believing, judging, deciding, and anticipating. All these mental behaviours add up to what is called **information processing**, or the transformation of sensory input into mental representations and the manipulation of such representations. If you have ever wondered whether other people think about things the same way you do, then you are a budding cognitive personality psychologist. Perhaps you have wondered if other people see colours the same as you do. Is the perception of green, for example, the same for everyone?

An interest in cognitive topics, ranging from perception to problem solving, represents an information-processing approach to personality. This approach to personality grew rapidly during the 1970s and 1980s, during which time psychology in general saw a large upsurge in interest in cognition. It is perhaps no coincidence that an emphasis on information processing in personality psychology took hold during an era commonly known as the Information Age. Humans, in some ways, are like computers, in that we spend a great deal of our time processing information. Unlike computers, however, humans are not always accurate or unbiased in how they process information. Moreover, unlike computers, humans differ greatly from each other in terms of their information processing—in how they perceive, think about, and construe themselves, the world, and other people. Cognitive differences in how people process information represent one domain of human nature that has been investigated in some detail by personality psychologists.

In this chapter, we cover three levels of cognition that are of interest to personality psychologists. The first level is **perception**, or the process of imposing order on the information our sense organs take in. You might think that there are few, if any, differences in how people perceive the world because our sensory and perceptual systems are all the same and what we perceive is an accurate representation of what is out there. But this is not true; two people can look at the same situation and actually see very different things.

Consider Figure 12.1. If you look at this illustration, you can see it in three dimensions. That is, instead of being a two-dimensional, flat drawing, you perceive it as having depth, as coming out of the page. This is because your perceptual system interprets cues of depth as representing a three-dimensional object. Another aspect of this figure—known as the Necker cube—is that you may perceive the cube as extending out and upward to the right of the base, whereas others perceive the cube as extending outward and downward toward the left. Thus, not everyone sees the same object, even though the drawing is objectively the same. An especially interesting feature of the Necker cube is that most people can

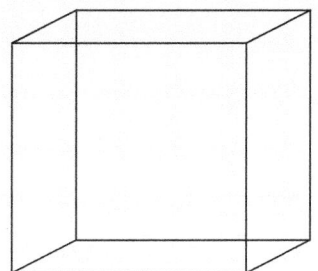

FIGURE 12.1 The Necker cube.

actually see the cube reverse directions. If you stare at the cube long enough, you will see the two different three-dimensional cubes, and you should be able to see the two cubes flip back and forth, from up and rightward to down and leftward.

Imagine how people might differ in what they see when they look at the much more complicated social world. Even at the level of perception, what we see in the world can be quite different from person to person. Moreover, these differences in what people see may be related to their personalities. It is this reasoning that underlies the rationale for such projective assessment techniques as the Rorschach inkblots. As we discussed in Chapters 2 and 9, what people see in the inkblots can be a function of their personalities. When looking at the same inkblot, one person might see a family of butterflies landing on a garden of flowers, and another person, looking at the same inkblot, might see a dog that has been hit by a car, with blood splattered all over the street. Do you think these two people might have dramatically different personalities?

The second level of cognition of interest to personality psychologists is **interpretation,** or the making sense of, or explaining, various events in the world. Interpretation concerns giving meaning to events. When you are confronted with an event and you are asked, "What does this mean?" or "How did this happen and how will it turn out?" you are likely to engage in the act of interpretation. For example, suppose you have a small mishap while driving your car, driving up a curb and scratching your fender. Someone might ask you, "Why did this happen?" You quickly and automatically make an interpretation and offer it to your inquisitor as a fact: "The street there is poorly laid out. It's too narrow and the curve is too sharp, and lots of people jump the curb there. It's the fault of the road department." However, maybe you offer a different interpretation, equally certain that it represents a fact: "I'm really a clumsy driver; I just can't handle the car. Maybe I should quit driving."

These are two of many possible interpretations, and which ones people offer may reveal aspects of their personalities. This notion of differences in interpretation underlies the rationale for such projective techniques as the Thematic Apperception Test (TAT), discussed in Chapter 11.

The third level of cognition that is of interest to personality psychologists is people's **conscious goals,** the standards that people develop for evaluating themselves and others. People develop specific beliefs about what is important in life and which tasks are appropriate to pursue. These tasks may be age specific and culture specific, such as establishing independence from one's family in early adulthood in Western cultures. Individuals transform these cultural beliefs about which life tasks are appropriate and important into personal desires or goals. A final topic in cognitive approaches is intelligence. Because this is a large and controversial topic in psychology, the student of personality should have some grasp of the basic issues and concepts in this area.

Personality Revealed Through Perception

Most people assume there is reality out there and that the representation we have of it in our minds is a precise duplicate, a flawless perception of the facts. This is simply not true; the perceiver contributes to the mental representations such that, even in perception, there are differences among people in what they see when they look at a scene. In this chapter, we expand on this notion and cover two topics that explore individual differences in perception. These topics show how perceptual differences can be stable, consistent, and meaningfully related to other areas of life.

Field Dependence

Have you ever heard the phrase that someone "can't see the forest for the trees"? This usually refers to the fact that someone cannot look beyond the details to get the big picture about a situation, that they cannot disengage their perception from the particular details to get a grasp of the general gist of the situation. Psychologist Herman Witkin studied such differences in perceptual style for almost 30 years. He came to call this topic *field dependence versus field independence*. Witkin's first book was titled *Personality Through Perception* (Witkin et al., 1954), and this title captures the idea that personality can be revealed through differences in how people perceive their environment.

Witkin was first interested in the cues that people use in judging orientation in space. If you see an object that is tilted, how do you know it is the object, and not your body, that is tilted? To make such judgments, some people rely on cues from the environment surrounding the object (are other things tilted as well?), whereas other people rely more on bodily cues that tell them that *they* are upright and therefore it must be the object that is tilted. To investigate this individual difference, Witkin devised an apparatus called the **Rod and Frame Test (RFT)**. Using this apparatus, the participant sits in a darkened room and is instructed to watch a glowing rod surrounded by a square frame, which is also glowing. The experimenter can adjust the tilt of the rod, the frame, and the participant's chair. The participant's task is to adjust the rod by turning a dial, so that the rod is perfectly upright. To do this accurately, the participant has to ignore cues in the visual field in which the rod appears (i.e., the square frame surrounding the rod, which the experimenter tilts). If the participant adjusts the rod so that it is leaning in the direction of the tilted frame, then that person is said to be dependent on the visual field, or **field dependent**. Other people disregard the external cues and, instead, use information from their bodies in adjusting the rod to upright. Such participants are said to be independent of the field, or **field independent**; they appear to rely on their own sensations, not the perception of the field, to make the judgment.

The Rod and Frame Test is a difficult and time-consuming way to measure field dependence/independence, so Witkin sought new ways to measure this perceptual difference (Witkin et al., 1962). One clever way of measuring field dependence/independence is to create a complex figure that contains many simple figures or shapes. You may have seen children's puzzles that consist of a large drawing with several smaller, hidden figures within it. The goal of such puzzles is to find as many of the hidden figures within the larger drawing as possible. An example of a hidden figures test is given in Figure 12.2. Witkin devised a similar test, called the Embedded Figures Test (EFT), which can be used to measure field dependence without relying on the cumbersome Rod and Frame Test. Some people, when given the EFT, have trouble locating the simple figures embedded within the more complex surrounding figure, apparently being bound up in the "forest" and unable to see the "trees." These people are said to be field dependent. Other people quickly spot many or all of the embedded figures and, so, are able to see objects independently from the background. Such people are said to be field independent. Performance on the EFT correlates strongly with performance on the RFT (Witkin, 1973). Moreover, scores on measures of field independence/dependence are stable over time. Witkin and others have extended research on field dependence/independence by investigating its consequences for various domains of life, such as education and social relations.

Field Dependence/Independence and Life Choices

Are differences in perception related to other differences in personality functioning? Just before his death in 1979, Witkin wrote several papers summarizing his research in two broad domains in which field dependence/independence appears to have consequences: education and interpersonal relations.

Can you find these
Hidden Pictures?

cap

high-heeled
boot

moon

screwdriver

eel

parrot

kangaroo

eyeglasses

mitten

horseshoe

shark

squirrel

FIGURE 12.2 An Embedded Figures Test, in which the objective is to find as
many of the smaller figures hidden in the larger figure as possible.

In one large study, 1,548 students were followed from their entry into university until several years after
graduation. Choice of major in university was found to be related to field independence/dependence:
the field-independent students tended to favour the natural sciences, math, and engineering, whereas

the more field-dependent students tended to favour the social sciences and education (Witkin, 1977; Witkin et al., 1977).

A second major area of research reviewed by Witkin and Goodenough (1977) concerns the interpersonal correlates of field independence/dependence. Field-dependent people, as might be predicted, tend to rely on social information and frequently ask other people for their opinions. They are attentive to social cues and, in general, are oriented toward other people. They show a strong interest in others, prefer to be physically close to other people, gravitate to social situations, and get along well with others. Field-independent people, on the other hand, function with more autonomy and display a more impersonal or detached orientation toward others. They are not very interested in others' opinions, keep their distance from others, and show a preference for nonsocial situations.

Current Research on Field Dependence/Independence

After Witkin's death, little research was done on field independence/dependence for about a decade. However, starting in the 1990s, new research began to appear in the literature (Messick, 1994). One new area of research concerns how people react to situations that are rich in sensory stimulation and whether field-independent people can focus on a task and screen out distracting information from the field. For example, one study of 100 police officers examined their ability to disregard noise and distractions in simulated, though naturalistic, shooting situations. Similarities can be drawn between this study and the Diallo case presented at the beginning of this chapter. That night, the officers were trying to focus on Mr. Diallo. However, the light was dim, other people were around, the four officers needed to be aware of each other and aware of the commands being given, and so on. In short, they were in a stimulus-rich environment. Field-independent individuals are predicted to be better at ignoring distracting information and focusing on the important details of the event. The researchers conducting the study of 100 police officers in simulated high-stimulation settings (Vrij, van der Steen, & Koppelaar, 1995) made exactly this prediction—that the more field-independent officers would perform better by noticing details more accurately, would be less distracted by the noise and activity, and would be more accurate in deciding when to shoot. Results showed that the field-independent officers per-

formed better on the shooting task under these high-stimulation conditions and were able to give a better description of the witnessed event, compared with the field-dependent officers. Presumably, the field-independent officers could better focus on the target without being distracted by the noise and activity going on in the field around them. In another study, when presented with complex photographs of people, field-independent individuals were better at noticing and decoding the facial expressions in the photographs, compared with field-dependent individuals (Bastone & Wood, 1997).

The trait of field independence predicts better performance in simulated shooting tasks among police officers (Vrij et al., 1995). The field-independent officers presumably are better able to focus on the suspect without being distracted by the activity and noise going on around them.
©Image Source/Moodboard

Another area of high stimulation is in hypermedia- and multimedia-based computer instruction, such as educational materials on the World Wide Web, which come with sound and streaming video. Field dependence is related to different preferences for Web-based instruction (Clewley, Chen, & Liu, 2011).

This form of instruction involves the presentation of information in multiple media formats (text on a computer screen, graphics, video, sound) while students navigate through this maze of sensory information at their own pace.

In a study of Grade 8 students, the researchers found that the field-independent students learned more effectively than the field-dependent subjects in a hypermedia-based instructional environment. Presumably, the field-independent students more easily found the thread that ran through the various media presentations of information. The experimenters concluded that field-independent students are able to get the points embedded within the various sources of media faster and are able to switch between educational media or sensory fields

The trait of field independence may correlate with the ability to learn in hypermedia-based instructional environments, where the flow of information is fast in a stimulus-rich environment.
©Getty Images

faster, compared with field-dependent students (Weller et al., 1995). Many studies of this perceptual style suggest that it leads to different styles of learning—for example, field-independent individuals are good at selective attention in stimulus-rich environments (at processing specific information while blocking out what is not important), whereas field-dependent individuals tend to process information in chunks and are good at seeing connections among categories of information (Nicolaou & Xistouri, 2011; Oughton & Reed, 1999; Richardson & Turner, 2000).

Some interesting research has also been done on the relation between field dependence and the ability to "read" or decode emotional facial expressions. On the one hand, because field-dependent people tend to be more socially oriented, we might think they should do especially well in reading emotional expressions. On the other hand, if we think of facial expressions as complex arrays of information, then maybe the field-independent people would be better at analyzing and interpreting such patterns. In a study on this topic, psychologists Linda Bastone and Heather Wood (1997) had subjects indicate the emotion expressed in 72 different faces. However, to make the task difficult, some emotion displays showed only the eyes, and some showed only the mouth. The field-independent subjects were significantly better at interpreting facial expressions than the field-dependent subjects, but only when the tasks were difficult. This finding reinforces the notion that field-independent individuals are good at tasks that require finding and interpreting patterns and making generalizations.

Another area that requires skill at seeing patterns, organizing information, and making generalizations is learning a second language. Psychologists interested in second language acquisition have examined the role of personality, and several studies have identified field-independent individuals as making better progress than field-dependent individuals when learning a second language. One study looked at Canadian university students learning English as a second language (Johnson, Prior, & Artuso, 2000). The study concluded that field-independent people have an easier time acquiring a second language, most likely because they are better able to perceive patterns within a complex stream of information (e.g., a foreign language).

Is it better to be field independent or field dependent? Like most personality dimensions, there are pros and cons associated with both tendencies (and remember, we are describing points along a continuum, not two categories of people). Field-independent people are skillful at analyzing complex situations and extracting information from the clutter of background distractions. Field-independent people also tend to be more creative (Miller, 2007). However, they are somewhat low on social skills and prefer to keep their distance from others. Field-dependent people, on the other hand, have strong social skills, gravitate toward others, and are more attentive to the social context than are field-independent individuals (Tamir & Nadler, 2007). It appears that each of these contrasting perceptual styles is adaptive in particular situations, making it impossible to state which orientation is more valuable (Collins, 1994).

Pain Tolerance and Sensation Reducing/Augmenting

The way in which people perceive their surroundings and navigate through information—whether they tend to focus on the whole or tend to notice the particulars—is a perceptual style. What about other individual differences in perception? One commonly noticed difference among people is in **pain tolerance**, in which people undergo the same physical stimulus (e.g., having to get an injection from the doctor) but react quite differently from each other in terms of the pain they report experiencing. You probably know people who cannot tolerate the slightest pain, who complain about minor discomforts, and who are distressed by even the *thought* of having an injection. Perhaps you know other people who can easily tolerate pain, who don't notice, or at least don't complain about, little discomforts, and who don't even wince when given an injection. This difference among people in their pain tolerance attracted the interest of psychologist Aneseth Petrie, whose book *Individuality in Pain and Suffering* describes her research on and theory of individual differences in tolerance for sensory stimulation (Petrie, 1967).

Petrie's Research

Petrie studied people in hospitals undergoing painful operations, as well as normal subjects in whom she induced pain—through applying heat or by piling weights on the middle joint of her subjects' fingers. In these studies, she was able to quantify how well each subject could tolerate pain. She developed a theory that people with low pain tolerance had a nervous system that amplified, or augmented, the subjective impact of sensory cues. In contrast, people who could tolerate pain well were thought to have a nervous system that dampened, or reduced, the effects of sensory stimulation. For these reasons, her theory came to be called the **reducer/augmenter theory**. This term refers to the dimension along which people differ in their reaction to sensory stimulation; some appear to reduce sensory stimulation, whereas some appear to augment stimulation.

Petrie believed that individual differences in pain tolerance originated in the nervous system. A few studies have examined nervous system reactivity directly in relation to augmenting/reducing. For example, researchers reported that reducers show relatively small brain responses to flashes of lights (Spilker & Callaway, 1969) as well as smaller brain responses to bursts of noise (Schwerdtfeger & Baltissen, 1999) in comparison with augmenters. In this last study, conducted in Germany, reducers also reported that the noise was less loud, compared with augmenters, though the noise was, in fact, identical for all the participants.

The brain-evoked response increases with increasing stimulus intensity, but the rate of change differs for different individuals, with augmenters showing a steeper rate of change with increasing stimulus intensity (Schwerdtfeger & Baltissen, 2002). Moreover, the brain-evoked potential augmenting/reducing measure shows high test-retest reliability, similar to other personality traits (Beauducel et al., 2000). Individual differences in brain augmenting/reducing have also been studied in other animals, including cats and rats (Siegel, 1997). In fact, rats that have been bred to be sensation seeking or sensation avoiding have been shown to display brain-evoked responses that indicate reducing and augmenting, respectively (Siegel & Driscoll, 1996). Given that this individual difference in sensory reactivity can be observed in other mammals, it is not surprising that studies also show that this individual difference arises in infancy in humans (Evans, Nelson, & Porter, 2012; Fox & Polak, 2004).

Reducers should be motivated to seek strong stimulation to compensate for their lower sensory reactivity, related to optimal level of arousal, discussed in Chapter 6. Supporting this prediction, reducers have been found to drink more coffee, smoke more, and have a lower threshold for boredom, compared with augmenters (Clapper, 1990, 1992; Larsen & Zarate, 1991). Reducers also have been found to more frequently consume psychoactive drugs and listen to music at a louder level compared to augmenters (Schwerdtfeger, 2007). Other studies have shown that reducers tend to start smoking at an earlier age and to engage in more minor delinquencies as adolescents, compared with augmenters (Herzog, Williams, & Weintraub, 1985). One study found that smokers were more reducing than augmenting (Patton, Barnes, & Murray, 1993), and a study of individuals with alcohol dependence were more in the reducing direction (Milin, Loh, & Wilson, 1992). Findings such as these are consistent with the notion that reducers may use substances to artificially obtain a lift in their arousal level to compensate for their reduced sensory reactivity.

Many researchers see a strong similarity between the augmenting/reducing construct and other personality constructs related to individual differences in how people respond to stimulation, such as those covered in Chapter 6 (e.g., sensation seeking), as well as Eysenck's theory of extraversion, covered in Chapters 3 and 6. For our purposes here, the reducer/augmenter research illustrates how personality psychologists have studied individual differences in perception, the most basic form of cognition. Let's turn now to a consideration of how people differ from one another in a higher level of cognition—interpretation.

 Concept Check

Based on research findings, describe the key differences between individuals who are field dependent and those who are field independent.

Consider individual differences in pain tolerance. What is the main difference between reducers and augmenters?

Personality Revealed Through Interpretation

Trial lawyers are familiar with the fact that two or more people can witness the same event yet offer differing interpretations of that event. Trials often hinge on having the jury arrive at a particular interpretation of the facts, such as whether the suspect *intended* to harm someone, whether the suspect had *planned* the crime ahead of time, or whether the suspect is capable of *appreciating the consequences* of their behaviour at the time of the criminal act. Many defence lawyers do not dispute that their clients committed their acts, but rather argue that the clients did not possess the required intention to be found guilty of a crime.

Everyday life may not be as dramatic as the cases that make their way to courtrooms. Nevertheless, we often find ourselves interpreting everyday events: Why did I get a poor grade on my test? Can I really do anything to lose weight? Whose fault is it that I can't seem to get along with my girlfriend/boyfriend? Such interpretations often concern responsibility or blame—such as whose fault it is when someone gets a poor grade. Other times, such interpretations inquire about expectations for the future—such as whether someone can lose weight. Both of these kinds of interpretations—about responsibility and about expectations for the future—have been studied by personality psychologists. However, before covering these topics, let's examine the theory that started the cognitive revolution in personality psychology: the work of George Kelly.

Kelly's Personal Construct Theory

Psychologist George Kelly (1905–1967), who spent most of his career at Ohio State University, played an important role in starting the cognitive tradition within personality psychology. Although a clinical psychologist, Kelly believed that all people are motivated to understand their circumstances and to be able to predict what will happen to them in the near future. He viewed psychoanalysis as effective because it provided people with a system for explaining psychological problems (e.g., "You are depressed because you have a hostile and sadistic superego, probably as the result of an improper anal stage resolution"). Kelly believed that the content of explanations was not as important as the fact that people believed them and could use them to understand their circumstances. Kelly felt that a primary motivation for all people was to find meaning in their life circumstances, and to use this meaning to predict their own future, to anticipate what is likely to happen next (Fransella & Neimeyer, 2003).

Kelly's view of human nature was that of humans as scientists. He felt that, just like scientists, people in general engage in efforts to understand, predict, and control the events in their lives. When people do not know why some event happened (e.g., "Why did my girlfriend break up with me?"), they experience greater distress than if they had an explanation. Thus, people seek explanations for the events in their lives just the way scientists seek explanations for phenomena in the laboratory.

Scientists employ **constructs** to interpret observations. A construct does not exist in itself; it is a word that summarizes a set of observations and conveys the meaning of those observations. Gravity, for example, is a scientific construct. We cannot show you gravity, but we can demonstrate the effects of gravity by observing other things, such as an apple falling from a tree. There are lots of constructs that could be applied to people: smart, outgoing, arrogant, shy, deviant. Like scientists interpreting the physical world, we use constructs all the time to give meaning to, or to interpret, the social world.

The constructs a person routinely uses to interpret and predict events are called, in Kelly's theory, **personal constructs**. Kelly's idea was that people have a few key constructs that they habitually apply in interpreting their world, particularly the social world. No two people have the same personal construct system, and so have their own unique interpretation of the world. For Kelly, personality consisted in differences in the way people construe the world, particularly the social world. These differences were the result of differences in the personal constructs that people habitually employed. What do you tend to notice when you meet a person for the first time? For you, it might be important how athletic versus nonathletic a person is, and this plays a large role in how you first construe the person. Another person, however, might apply the construct of intelligent versus nonintelligent to the same target person. As a result, that person will have a different construal of the target person than you have because you are each viewing the target person through the unique "lens" of your preferred construct systems (Hua & Epley, 2012).

Conceptually, a personal construct is similar to the notion of a **cognitive schema** (*schema* is singular; *schemata* or *schemas* is plural). A schema is a mental concept that helps a person to process incoming information, organize that information, and interpret daily experiences. According to Kelly, personal constructs are bipolar, which is not necessarily the case for all schemas. That is, personal constructs consist of some characteristic understood against its opposite, or what the person takes to be its opposite. So, a few typical constructs might be smart–not smart, cooperative–uncooperative, tall–short, and boring–interesting. People develop characteristic sets of constructs that they frequently use in interpreting the world. A person might apply smart–not smart to most people they meet and use this construct to parse their social world into groups. Moreover, they then behave differently toward people in the smart category compared to the not-so-smart category. However, it is the person's own construal that puts the acquaintances into those categories to begin with. Personal constructs are used to create the social groupings.

In many ways, Kelly was ahead of his times. He was postmodern before postmodernism became popular. **Postmodernism** is an intellectual position grounded in the notion that reality is constructed, that every person and certainly every culture has a version of reality that is unique, and that no single version of reality is any more privileged than another (Gergen, 1992). Kelly's emphasis on how personal constructs serve to create each person's psychological reality puts him in the postmodern camp (Raskin, 2001).

Kelly presented a highly complex but systematic theory of personality and personal constructs, which the interested student can pursue in Kelly's own work (e.g., 1955) or in recent summaries of his work (e.g., Fransella, 2003). We present some of the basic ideas here. His most basic idea was the *fundamental postulate,* which refers to the statement that "a person's processes are psychologically channelized by the ways in which he anticipates events" (Kelly, 1955, p. 46). To this fundamental postulate, Kelly added a number of corollaries. For example, if two people have similar construct systems, they would be psychologically similar (the commonality corollary). Some couples might be quite different in many ways, but if their personal construct systems are similar, then they are likely to get along quite well because they interpret the world similarly.

Like many personality theorists, Kelly also devoted a special place in his theory to the concept of anxiety. For Kelly, anxiety was the result of not being able to understand and predict life events. In his terms, anxiety is the result of our personal constructs failing to make sense of our circumstances. People are anxious when they don't understand what is happening to them and when they feel that events are unpredictable, outside of their control. How do constructs fail? Sometimes they are too rigid and impermeable to new experiences. Something comes along that they just cannot understand. Imagine a woman who, after raising the children and shipping them off to university, decides she wants to work. Her husband, whose conception of a good marriage is one in which "the wife does not have to work," cannot understand this experience. His construct of good versus bad marriage cannot make sense out of his wife's newfound desire for employment. Another way that constructs fail is if they are too permeable, if the person applies them too liberally. If a person categorizes everyone she encounters as either smart or not smart, and once categorized refuses to change her mind about them even in the face of contradictory information, then her construct is too rigidly applied. A person knows that her construct system is in trouble when she starts having experiences that she cannot understand ("I just can't understand why you are leaving") or cannot anticipate ("That caught me by surprise").

Kelly's ideas about how people construct their experiences based on construct systems that they "carry" through life was part of a cognitive revolution within personality psychology. Several self-report methods exist for the assessment of a person's personal construct system (e.g., Caputi, 2012; Hardison & Neimeyer, 2012). Another example of this cognitive emphasis can be seen in a development in learning theory, which occurred about the same time that Kelly was formulating his theory. We turn now to this other important development in the cognitive approach to personality.

Locus of Control

Locus of control is a concept that describes a person's perception of responsibility for life events. More specifically, *locus of control* refers to whether people tend to locate that responsibility internally, within themselves, or externally, in fate, luck, or chance. For example, when you see a person who gets good grades, do you think it is because she is just plain lucky or because of her personal efforts? When you see someone in poor health, do you think it is because of fate, or is it because he does not take care of himself? Your answers to such questions may reveal your standing on the personality dimension of locus of control—the tendency to believe that events are or are not under one's personal control and responsibility.

Locus of control research started in the mid-1950s, when psychologist Julian Rotter was developing his social learning theory. Rotter was working within traditional learning theory, which emphasizes that people learn because of reinforcement. Rotter expanded these notions to suggest that learning also depended on the degree to which the person *valued* the particular reinforcer—its reinforcement value. Rotter's insight was that not all reinforcements are equal. Some reinforcers—for example, social praise and appreciation—are not valued by some people, and such people will not respond well to them. People also differ in terms of their *expectations* for reinforcement. Some people expect that certain behaviours will result in obtaining a reinforcer. In other words, they believe that they are in control of the outcomes of life. Other people fail to see the link between their behaviour and reinforcement. This is Rotter's "expectancy model" of learning behaviour. Interestingly, the expectation part involves characteristics that the individual brings to each situation. That is, *the expectancy of reinforcement* refers to characteristics that distinguish specific individuals. For example, suppose a person expects that acting in an assertive and demanding manner will get her what she wants. She wants a raise at work, so she expects that if she is assertive and demanding toward her boss, she will get her raise. Another person may have the opposite expectation, that acting in such a manner will be counterproductive, so he believes that being assertive will not produce the desired raise. These two individuals have different expectations for the outcome associated with the same assertive behaviour pattern. She thinks she can do something to obtain a raise; he thinks he must just wait for the boss to make the decision. Differences in the subsequent behaviour of these two people—for example, she is demanding and he is submissive at work—may be due to differences in their expectations of whether a certain behaviour (assertiveness) will bring reinforcement (the desired raise).

Rotter published a questionnaire measure of internal versus external locus of control in 1966. Some items from that questionnaire are presented in Table 12.1.

Rotter emphasized that a person's expectations for reinforcement held across a variety of situations, what he called **generalized expectancies** (Rotter, 1971, 1990). When people encounter a new situation, they base their expectancies about what will happen on their generalized expectancies about whether they have the ability to influence events. For example, if a young man generally believes that he can do little to influence events, then in a new situation, such as entering university, he would have a generalized expectancy that things are outside of his control. He may, for example, assume that his grades will be due to luck or chance or fate, not to anything that he can actually control.

Such a generalized expectancy that events are outside of one's control is called an **external locus of control**. An **internal locus of control**, on the other hand, is the generalized expectancy that reinforcing events are under one's control and that one is responsible for the major outcomes in life. People high on internal locus of

Table 12.1   Sample Items from the Locus of Control Scale

Yes	No	
_____	_____	1. Do you believe that most problems will solve themselves if you just don't fool with them?
_____	_____	2. Do you believe that you can stop yourself from catching a cold?
_____	_____	3. Are some people just born lucky?
_____	_____	4. Most of the time do you feel that getting good grades means a great deal to you?
_____	_____	5. Are you often blamed for things that just aren't your fault?
_____	_____	6. Do you believe that if somebody studies hard enough he or she can pass any subject?
_____	_____	7. Do you feel that most of the time it doesn't pay to try hard because things never turn out right anyway?
_____	_____	8. Do you feel that if things start out well in the morning, it's going to be a good day no matter what you do?
_____	_____	9. Do you feel that most of the time parents listen to what their children have to say?
_____	_____	10. Do you believe that wishing can make good things happen?

Source: Copyright © 1966 by American Psychological Association. Adapted with permission. Rotter, B. (1966). Generalized expectancies for internal versus external control of reinforcement. *Psychological Monographs, 80,* 1–28.

control believe that outcomes depend mainly on their own personal efforts, whereas people who have a more external locus of control believe that outcomes largely depend on forces outside of their personal control. Although problems can arise when a person with an internal locus of control confronts circumstances that truly are outside of one's control (Heidemeier & Göritz, 2013), an internal locus of control is, in general, conducive to well-being.

Internal locus of control has been found to be predictive of a variety of real-world outcomes. For example, people who displayed an internal locus of control at age 10 were found to have a reduced risk of obesity at age 30 compared to people with an external locus of control (Gale, Batty, & Deary, 2008). In another study of university students, those with an internal locus of control completed their degrees in a more timely manner than students with an external locus of control (Hall, Smith, & Chia, 2008). Another interesting study showed that adults with a more internal locus of control had higher credit ratings than those with a more external locus of control (Perry, 2008). In many ways, internal locus of control is associated with a tendency toward being more in charge of one's life, ranging from better control over one's weight to better control over one's spending habits and hence credit rating.

Research on *generalized* locus of control has waned in recent years. Instead, researchers have become interested in specific areas of life, where people might be internal in one area and external in another. This approach is referred to as **specific expectancies**, in which the emphasis is on locus of control in discrete areas of life. One specific area of life concerns locus of control expectations for health and whether people believe that their health depends on their own actions (Wallston & Wallston, 1978; Wallston et al., 1989).

Another specific area concerns expectations about academic outcomes in young children and the extent to which children expect that their behaviour in the classroom influences whether the teacher praises them and gives them good grades (Crandall, Katkovsky, & Crandall, 1965). Another scale was developed to examine locus of control expectations in marriage and whether people believe that their actions can influence the quality and outcome of their marital relationships (Miller, Lefcourt, & Ware, 1983). In all of these areas—health, academic behaviour, and marriage—the general finding is that people with an internal locus of control tend to be more active in taking charge, and they take more responsibility for the outcomes in these areas, compared to more externally oriented individuals.

❓ Exercise

Can you think of situations in which having an internal locus of control is a disadvantage? Under what circumstances would a person with an internal orientation experience relatively more stress than someone with an external orientation? What characteristics or situations would match the expectations of the person with an external locus of control? When might it be healthy to have an external locus of control?

Some situations are truly beyond our control and cannot be influenced by us, no matter what we do. For example, a loved one may be dying from an incurable disease. This is not anyone's fault, and there is nothing anyone can do to prevent the outcome. However, even in such situations some people, particularly close relatives, can feel that they are somehow to blame. In such situations, an internal locus of control might be a handicap to personal coping with the outcome.

Another example is the "survivor syndrome" often reported by people who have lived through a tragedy in which many others were severely injured or killed, such as in war or an airplane crash. Often, survivors report feeling that "if only" they had done something differently, they could have helped others make it to safety. They often report some feelings of personal responsibility for the outcome, even though the event was horrifically outside of their control.

In an interesting case study, a 29-year-old man who sailed around the world solo in 260 days (Kjaergaard, Leone, & Venables, 2015) was found, as you might have guessed, to have a very internal score on a locus of control measure, quite literally the captain of his fate. Another activity where people's control over outcomes is sometimes at risk is stage acting, and a study of professional actors found that those with a more external locus of control suffered more from stage fright than actors with a more internal locus of control (Goodman & Kaufman, 2014).

When it comes to locus of control, the general finding is that an internal perspective is the more adaptive one, to see oneself as being in control of one's fate. However, what about situations that require giving up control? For example, the willingness to use autonomous cars requires that a person give up control of the driving to a machine, to turn over one's fate to a computer. Some people may be reluctant to try an autonomous car. A recent study showed that people with an internal locus of control were more unwilling to try autonomous vehicles than those with an external locus of control (Choi & Ji, 2015). Like with other personality traits, we can never say that one extreme of the dimension is entirely good or entirely bad; one can always find strengths and weakness associated with either high or low levels of any particular trait. As computers and machines do more and more for us, it may be adaptive to relinquish control for some aspects of our lives, and people with a more external locus of control may be more willing or more able to do so.

Learned Helplessness

We now turn to another individual difference in how people interpret the world—**learned helplessness**. Research on this topic also had its start in learning theory, similar to Rotter's start. Work on learned helplessness began when psychologists were studying avoidance learning in dogs and subjected the dogs to foot shocks from which the dogs could not escape. During the first few shocks, the dogs would pull at their harnesses, jump and twist, and try to escape. Eventually, however, they seemed to accept the shocks and did not try to escape anymore. The dogs, apparently knowing that they could not escape, would passively accept the shocks.

The dogs were then put into a different cage, a cage where they *could* escape the foot shocks by simply jumping over a small barrier into a different part of the cage. However, the dogs that had received inescapable shocks earlier did not even try to escape in this new situation. It was as if they had learned that their situation was hopeless, and they gave up seeking to avoid their painful circumstance. Other dogs that had not been shocked earlier quickly learned to avoid the shocks by jumping over the barrier. The researchers were surprised that the learned helplessness dogs did not even try to escape, and so they turned off the shock after one minute.

Next, the researchers tried lifting the dogs over the barrier to the safe part of the cage. After being shown how to reach safety, the dogs quickly learned to jump over and avoid the shocks. However, without such coaching, the learned helplessness dogs simply accepted their painful fates without attempting to remove themselves from the unpleasant situation.

Numerous studies document the learned helplessness phenomenon with humans (Seligman, 1992, 1994). Using unpleasant noise rather than shock, researchers set up the following learned helplessness situation. Participants are told that they will be given problems to solve and that they can avoid or turn off the blasts of unpleasant noise by solving the problems (for example, by pressing buttons in a correct order) (Garber & Seligman, 1980; Hiroto & Seligman, 1975). Some participants (the learned helplessness subjects) are given problems without solutions. Consequently, for these participants, the unpleasant blasts of noise are inescapable—nothing they can do will control the irritating and aversive blasts of noise. But do these participants generalize their helplessness to new situations?

Participants are then taken to a new situation and given a new set of problems to solve. This time there is no unpleasant noise. The researchers tell the participants that they are simply interested in how the participants will work on these new problems. Participants who were exposed to the learned helplessness condition in the earlier trials usually perform much worse on the subsequent problems. It is as if they are saying, "What's the use in trying to solve these problems? They are too difficult." Such participants appear to generalize their experiences of helplessness from one problem-solving situation to another.

In the real world, learned helplessness can result from a variety of difficult or challenging experiences, including trauma. Canadian researchers have studied this phenomenon in specific populations who have experienced historical trauma, including Indigenous peoples of Canada. We explore this further in Highlight On Canadian Research: Trauma, Learned Helplessness, and Locus of Control Among Indigenous Peoples of Canada.

Highlight on Canadian Research

Trauma, Learned Helplessness, and Locus of Control Among Indigenous Peoples of Canada

Prior to the arrival of European settlers to Canada, Indigenous populations (including First Nations, Métis, and Inuit peoples) were independent and self-governing, making their own decisions about how to live their lives, from their religion to the education of their children. A number of events took place when Europeans arrived, including the loss of land and forced assimilation into the European way of life. Although some communities were more severely impacted than others, these events were highly stressful and traumatic in nature. The long-term impact of these events has been described as *intergenerational trauma*. This is the idea that the historical trauma experienced by earlier generations has had lasting effects that are still felt by members of these communities today. In this way, trauma can be viewed as a collective experience that makes certain groups more vulnerable to stress. The extent of the impact has been far-reaching, including high poverty and unemployment rates, increased violence and homicide, shorter life expectancy, and higher infant mortality. Regarding the psychological impact specifically, Indigenous communities in Canada display higher rates of depression, alcohol and substance use, and suicide (Tjepkema, 2002). The underlying factors involved in these differences are complex, but many have been linked to the cultural displacement that began with European settlement.

Cynthia Wesley-Esquimaux, Chair on Truth and Reconciliation at Lakehead University in Thunder Bay, Ontario, has dedicated much of her career to understanding the effects of the historical trauma experienced by Indigenous people in Canada on their feelings of learned helplessness and locus of control. Indeed, it appears that these two variables offer a number of insights into the problems currently facing Indigenous communities. In her model of historical trauma transmission, Wesley-Esquimaux argues that one pathway through which past trauma influences subsequent generations involves the passing of learned behavioural patterns between generations. Symptoms of trauma exhibited by parents, such as family violence or abuse, create traumatic experiences for their children, disrupting their social and psychological adjustment. This is in addition to the ongoing subjugation and oppression of Indigenous people in Canada via lack of support services, inadequate infrastructure, and ongoing discrimination and ethnically motivated violence in many communities.

One outcome of historical trauma described by Wesley-Esquimaux is learned helplessness. As she notes, failure in the past is likely to cause expectations of failure in the future, leading to a sort of collective form of learned helplessness in which internal attributions are made in nearly all experiences of failure. This contributes to the lower rates of self-esteem and higher rates of depression reported in these communities. Socially, Wingert (2011) suggests that people feel more invisible, and thus have a difficult time actively preserving their own culture. The second impact is on locus of control, such that internal locus of control is diminished and the person lacks the intrinsic motivation for achievement and success. As previous research has indicated a link between external locus of control and suicidal thoughts, this may be one explanation for the increasing rates of suicide and attempted suicide in Indigenous communities in Canada (Wesley-Esquimaux & Smolewski, 2004).

Although we'll explore issues related to the role of culture in personality further in Chapter 17, Wesley-Esquimaux proposes an interesting (and in this case, alarming) way in which culture shapes cognitive aspects of personality. Indeed, if historical experiences have led a culture to adopt a pessimistic attributional style, it is reasonable to expect that new generations will adopt similar cognitive styles. Given that feelings of helplessness are *learned*, both personal experience as well as the historical experiences of one's people likely contribute to this detrimental cognitive framework.

In real life, learned helplessness can result whenever people are stuck in an unpleasant situation that is apparently outside of their control. For example, imagine a woman who tries everything she knows to get her husband to stop abusing her. She tries being nice to him, and it works for a while, but soon he is abusive again. She threatens to leave, and this works for a while, but he starts abusing her again. No matter what she does, nothing seems to solve the problem. A woman in such circumstances may develop learned helplessness. She may give up even trying to solve the problem: "What's the use," she may say, "nothing I do seems to help, so maybe I just have to take it."

However, people in learned helplessness don't have to "take it." They need an outside perspective and a new source of optimism. They need someone who can see the situation objectively and who can recommend strategies for solving the problem. Whenever a problem situation looks as if it has no solution or is inescapable, that is the time to ask others for help, to seek an outside opinion (Seligman & Csikszentmihalyi, 2000).

The original model of learned helplessness began with experiments on dogs and was generalized to humans through experimental studies. Humans are more complex than dogs, at least when it comes to thinking about the events in their lives, analyzing situations, and forming new expectancies for behaviour. What factors determine whether feelings of helplessness in one situation will spill over to other situations? Under what circumstances do people become motivated to take control of their lives? What factors influence people to decide that they do or do not have the ability to take control of a situation? In seeking answers to these questions, psychologists began to study what was going on in the minds of people who underwent learned helplessness conditioning (Peterson, Maier, & Seligman, 1993). Current research is examining the neurobiology of learned helplessness in humans (Hammack, Cooper, & Lezak, 2012) and animals (Bredemann, 2012).

Today, we can also understand learned helplessness in terms of *explanatory style*, which involves different ways of interpreting and explaining the causes of events. We discuss this next in A Closer Look: Reformulated Learned Helplessness: Explanatory Style.

 **A Closer Look**

Reformulated Learned Helplessness: Explanatory Style

The reformulation of learned helplessness theory focuses on the cognitions, or thoughts, a person has that may lead to feelings of helplessness. More specifically, the focus is on the *explanations* that people give for events in their lives, particularly the *unpleasant events* (Peterson et al., 1993). Imagine that you had submitted a paper in your class and that you received a surprisingly low grade on that paper. A common question you might ask yourself is "What *caused* the low grade on my paper?" Your explanation for the cause of the low grade might reveal something about your explanatory style. When things go wrong, who or what typically gets the blame? Psychologists prefer the term **causal attribution** to refer to a person's explanation of the cause of an event. To what cause would you attribute your paper's low grade? Was it because you happened to be in a rush and submitted a quickly written paper? Was it because you are simply a poor writer? Was it because the professor who graded it was unduly harsh in her grading? Or was it because your dog ate your original paper, so you quickly wrote another, which was not nearly as good as the one your dog ate? All of these explanations are causal attributions for the event.

Psychologists use the term **explanatory style** to refer to tendencies some people have to frequently use certain explanations for the causes of events. Explanations for the causes of events can be broken down along three broad dimensions. First, explanations for events can be either *internal* or *external.* The poor paper grade could be due to something pertaining to *you* (internal, such as your lack of skill) or something pertaining to the *environment* (external, such as the professor's being unduly harsh). Some people blame themselves for all sorts of events and are constantly apologizing for events that are outside their control. The more internal your explanation, the more likely you are to blame yourself for unpleasant events, even those events over which you have little or no control.

A second dimension concerns whether the cause of the event is *stable* or *unstable.* For example, if you were temporarily set back by your dog eating the original version of your paper, then that would be an unstable cause (assuming your dog does not eat all of your papers). However, an explanation that concerns your lack of writing skill is a more or less *permanent,* or stable, characteristic. When bad events happen, some people tend to think that the causes of such situations are permanent, that the causes are stable and long-lasting.

The third important dimension of causes of events concerns whether the cause is *global* or *specific.* A specific cause is one that affects only the particular situation (e.g., writing papers), whereas a global cause affects many situations in life (all areas involving intellectual skills). For example, you might have explained the cause of your poor paper grade like this: "I am just unable to write; I can hardly put a noun and a verb together to form a sentence." This is a global explanation and might imply that you would be expected to do poorly in whatever task required writing.

Whenever someone offers an explanation for an event, that explanation can be analyzed in terms of the three dimensions: internal–external, stable–unstable, and global–specific. Most people use different combinations of explanations—sometimes blaming themselves, sometimes blaming external causes, sometimes blaming specific causes, and so forth. However, some people develop a consistent explanatory style. For example, suppose someone consistently blames herself whenever *anything* goes wrong. After arriving at her destination on a plane that was late, the woman apologizes to her friend who picked her up at the airport, saying, "I'm sorry I'm late," when, in fact, *she* was not at all responsible for being late. She might say to her friend instead, "I'm sorry that *the plane I was on was late* and that you had to be inconvenienced. Next time I'll use a different airline." This might be a more appropriate external explanation for the real cause of being late.

The explanatory style that most puts a person at risk for feelings of helplessness and poor adjustment is one that emphasizes internal, stable, and global causes for bad events. This has been called the **pessimistic explanatory style.** This style is in contrast to the **optimistic explanatory style**, which emphasizes external, temporary, and specific causes of events. For example, one scenario on the Attributional Style Questionnaire (Peterson, 1991) asks you to imagine being on a date that goes badly, in which both you and your date have a lousy time. You are then asked why this might happen to you. If your explanation involves an external attribution to an unstable and highly specific cause (e.g., "I happened to choose a movie that neither one of us liked, then we went to a restaurant where the service was poor, and afterward my car got stuck in the mud"), then you are scored as more optimistic than someone who offers an internal, stable, and global interpretation (e.g., "I just have trouble relating to people, I cannot keep a conversation going, and I am completely shy when it comes to the opposite sex") (see Figure 12.3).

Is explanatory style a stable characteristic? One study examined explanatory style over the life span (Burns & Seligman, 1989). A group of participants, whose average age was 72 years, completed a questionnaire on explanatory style and provided diaries or letters written in their youth, an average of

52 years earlier. The diaries and letters were content analyzed for explanatory style. The correlation between these two measures of explanatory style for negative life events that were generated five decades apart was .54, indicating a significant amount of stability in explanatory style.

	Internal/external	Stable/unstable	Global/specific
Optimistic style	External: "My girlfriend broke up with me because her parents forced her."	Unstable: "My girlfriend broke up with me because she needs all her time right now to devote to the charity drive, which only lasts one month."	Specific: "My girlfriend broke up with me because she found out I dated Julie last weekend."
Pessimistic style	Internal: "My girlfriend broke up with me because I'm from a low-class family, I'm not going to college, and I have very little ambition in life."	Stable: "My girlfriend broke up with me because I'm shorter than her, and she wants someone who is taller."	Global: "My girlfriend broke up with me because I'm an inconsiderate, two-timing, unfaithful jerk who couldn't keep a relationship going if his life depended on it."

FIGURE 12.3 The three dimensions underlying explanatory style, with their pessimistic and optimistic versions.

Because an optimistic explanatory style correlates with beneficial effects in many areas of life, including earning better grades in college (Maleva et al., 2014), programs have been developed to train people to have a more optimistic explanatory style. For example, one program for college students (Gerson & Fernandez, 2013) is a three-session program that teaches students to adopt an optimistic explanatory style, and has been shown to increase student reports of optimism, resilience, and thriving in college. The majority of research on explanatory style focuses on how people adapt to traumatic events, with the general finding that an optimistic style is associated with better response. For example, researchers examined survivors of the 2004 tsunami that devastated two-thirds of the coast of Sri Lanka (Levy, Slade, & Ranasinghe, 2009), and found that a pessimistic explanatory style was associated with more symptoms of post-traumatic stress disorder.

An interesting extension of the concept of explanatory style is to extend it from individuals to groups. For example, recent studies have examined the explanatory style of sports teams (Carron, Shapcott, & Martin, 2014) and the explanatory style of business organizations (Smith, Caputi, & Crittenden, 2013). Results generally mirror those found with individuals, that team optimism was associated with better outcomes (higher percentage of winning, business success).

What are some of the correlates and consequences of pessimistic versus optimistic explanatory styles? In Chapter 13, we discuss the role of explanatory style in depression, and in Chapter 18 we return to the topic of explanatory style, again in some detail, with reference to health.

Concept Check

How would you summarize Kelly's Personal Construct Theory? Come up with three examples of personal constructs based on your own experiences, and speculate on their role in everyday life.

What is locus of control, and how is it seen to vary between people?

Name and define the three dimensions involved in explanatory style. How can they be used to define optimism and pessimism?

Personality Revealed Through Goals

So far in this chapter, we have considered aspects of personality related to how a person perceives and interprets the world. We turn now to a third aspect of cognition, a person's goals and how these are related to personality. Such goals may range from minor ones, such as buying groceries for the week, to the more lofty, such as reducing world hunger. The focus in this approach is on intention, on *what people want to happen,* on what they want to achieve in their lives. People differ in their goals, and these differences are part of and reveal their personalities.

Different psychologists have offered different terms, such as personal strivings (Emmons, 1989), current concerns (Klinger, 1977a, 1977b), personal projects (Little, 1999), and life tasks (Cantor, 1990). All of these constructs emphasize what people believe is worth pursuing in life, as well as the kinds of goal-directed behaviours they enact to achieve these desires. Other personality theories in this section emphasize self-guides, or the standards that people strive to meet (Higgins, 1996), their understanding of their own abilities and motivations (Dweck, Chiu, & Hong, 1995), or internal abilities related to goals, including people's expectations, beliefs, plans, and strategies (Mischel, 2004).

Personal Projects Analysis

A **personal project** is a set of relevant actions intended to achieve a goal that a person has selected. Psychologist Brian Little (e.g., Little, 2007, 2011) believes that personal projects make natural units for understanding the workings of personality because they reflect how people face up to the serious business of navigating through daily life. Most people, if asked, are able to make a list of the important projects that they work on in their daily lives, such goals as to lose weight, do homework, make new friends, start and maintain an exercise program, send away for graduate school applications, develop a better relationship with God, or find some principles to live by. People typically have many goals that come and go in their day-to-day lives—one project is more important today, and a different one is important tomorrow—as well as other projects that are more ongoing.

Little developed the Personal Projects Analysis method for assessing personal projects. Participants first generate a list of their personal projects, as many or as few as they deem relevant. Most participants list an average of 15 personal projects that are currently important in their daily lives. Next, participants rate each project on several scales, such as how important the project is to them, how difficult it is, how much they enjoy working on it, how much progress they have made on it, and the negative and positive impacts it has had in their lives (Little & Gee, 2007).

Personal Projects Analysis has a number of interesting implications for understanding personality. Researchers have investigated the relation between the Big Five personality traits (discussed in Chapter 3) and aspects of personal projects. Little (1999) reports several interesting relationships. For example, people who score high on the trait of neuroticism are also likely to rate their personal projects as stressful, difficult, likely to end in failure, and outside of their control. Such people are also likely to state that they have made little progress toward achieving their goals. Apparently, part and parcel of being high on the neuroticism dimension is experiencing difficulty and dissatisfaction in accomplishing one's personal projects (Little, Lecci, & Watkinson, 1992).

Researchers have also been interested in which specific aspects of personal projects are most closely related to overall reports of life satisfaction and happiness. Little (1999, 2007) summarizes research suggesting that overall happiness is most related to feeling in control of one's personal projects, feeling unstressed about those projects, and being optimistic that projects will end successfully. These aspects of personal projects have also been found to predict well-being in an elderly sample (Lawton et al., 2002). These aspects of Personal Project Analysis (low stress, high control, high optimism) do indeed predict overall levels of happiness and life satisfaction (Palys & Little, 1983). Such findings have led Little to conclude that "bringing our personal projects to successful completion . . . seems to be a pivotal factor in whether we thrive emotionally or lead lives of . . . quiet desperation" (Little, 1999, p. 25). Recent work on personal projects is presented in an edited volume by Little, Salmela-Aro, and Phillips (2007).

Cognitive Social Learning Theory

A number of modern personality theories have expanded on the notion that personality is expressed in goals and in how people think about themselves relative to their goals. Collectively these theories form what has been called the **cognitive social learning approach** to personality, an approach that emphasizes the cognitive and social processes whereby people learn to value and strive for certain goals over others.

Albert Bandura and the Notion of Self-Efficacy

Albert Bandura was trained in classical behavioural psychology, popular in the 1940s, which viewed humans, and all organisms, as passive responders to the external environment, completely determined by external reinforcements. Bandura helped change this view by emphasizing the active nature of human behaviour. He argued that people have intentions and forethought; they are reflective and can anticipate future events; they monitor their behaviour and evaluate their own progress; plus they learn by observing others. Because he expanded on classical learning theory by adding cognitive and social variables, the movement he helped start is called *cognitive social learning theory*. Bandura referred to these distinctly human cognitive and social activities under the rubric of the self-system. The self-system exists for the self-regulation of behaviour in the pursuit of goals (Bandura, 1997).

In Bandura's theory, one of the most important concepts is that of **self-efficacy**, which refers to the belief that one can execute a specific course of action to achieve a goal. For example, a child learning to bat a baseball may believe she can hit most balls pitched to her. We would say she has high self-efficacy beliefs for batting. A child who doubts his hitting ability, on the other hand, has low self-efficacy beliefs in this area. As it turns out, high self-efficacy beliefs often lead to effort and persistence on tasks, and to setting higher goals, compared to people with low self-efficacy beliefs (Bandura, 1989). As another example, university students who have higher self-efficacy beliefs about their studies are more persistent in their academic work and perform better in their classes than students with lower self-efficacy (Multon, Brown, & Lent, 1991).

Self-efficacy and performance mutually influence one another. Self-efficacy leads to better performance; then better performance leads to further increases in self-efficacy. As such, high self-efficacy is most important when starting out on some particular task. If the task is complex, it can be broken down into parts or subgoals, which can be accomplished. For example, in learning to dive from a diving board, a child can practise jumping in from the side of the pool, then going in head first from the side of the pool, then going on the diving board and jumping, then finally diving from the diving board. Accomplishing each subgoal along the way can increase overall self-efficacy. Self-efficacy can also be influenced by **modelling**, by seeing others engage in the performance with positive results.

Carol Dweck and the Theory of Mastery Orientation

We introduced the work of psychologist Carol Dweck in Chapter 11. Her early research focused on helpless and mastery-oriented behaviours in schoolchildren (Deiner & Dweck, 1978, 1980). She noted that some students persist in the face of failure, whereas others quit as soon as they encounter difficulties or their first failure. She started investigating the cognitive beliefs, particularly beliefs about ability, that lie behind these behaviour patterns. For example, she discovered that students' implicit beliefs about the nature of intelligence had a significant impact on the way they approach challenging intellectual tasks: Students who view their intelligence as an unchangeable and fixed internal characteristic (what Dweck calls an "entity theory" of intelligence) tend to shy away from academic challenges, whereas students who believe that their intelligence can be increased through effort and persistence (what Dweck calls an "incremental theory" of intelligence) seek them out (Dweck, 1999, 2002; Dweck, Chiu, & Hong, 1995).

It may sound like such a small thing, simply believing that intelligence is a fixed trait that cannot change, yet this belief is associated with putting less effort into school, with giving up earlier on academic challenges, and with lower academic success. Dweck's research illustrates the power of this belief in many studies of school children and college students (see Dweck & Master, 2009). Having the opposite mindset—that intelligence is malleable and is something that can be changed with effort—is associated with better academic motivation and higher grades (Romero, Master, Pauneku, Dweck, & Gross, 2014). Moreover, Dweck and colleagues have designed and tested several school-based interventions to change student's beliefs about their own intelligence, with students who have been trained to view intelligence as malleable subsequently putting more effort into academic performance and doing better in terms of grades (reviewed in Rattan et al., 2015).

Dweck's theory also has implications for how the praise of teachers and parents may unwittingly lead children to accept an entity view of intelligence. Praising a child for their intelligence may reinforce the notion that success and failure depend on something beyond the child's control. Comments such as "I'm so happy you got an A+ on your biology test, Mary! You are such a smart girl!" are interpreted by the child as "If good grades means that I'm intelligent, then poor grades must mean I am dumb." Or when trying to comfort a student, a teacher might say, "It's okay—not everyone can be good at math." This can reinforce an entity theory of math ability in the child, leading her to have lower motivation and lower expectations for her own math performance (Rattan, Good, & Dweck, 2012). When children with an entity view of intelligence do perform well, they have high self-esteem, but self-esteem diminishes as soon as they hit academic challenges that make them falter. Children who are admired for their effort are much more likely to view intelligence as changeable, and their self-esteem remains stable regardless of how hard they have to work to succeed. According to Dweck, it is much better to praise children for their effort ("Congratulations, your effort really paid off!") rather than for their ability ("Congratulations, you are really smart!"). Children who are praised for their effort learn to associate success with effort, not ability, and therefore become more confident that they can meet challenges through effort and hard work (Gunderson et al., 2013). Children with a view of intelligence and ability as changeable are more likely to work through frustrations and setbacks and reach their full academic potential (Dweck, 1999, 2002).

E. Tory Higgins and the Theory of Regulatory Focus

Psychologist E. Tory Higgins has also developed a motivational theory concerning goals, called *regulatory focus theory* (Higgins, 2012). His theory adds the notion that people regulate their goal-directed behaviours in two distinct ways that serve two different needs. One focus of regulation is called **promotion focus**, in which the person is concerned with advancement, growth, and accomplishments. Behaviours with a promotion focus are characterized by eagerness, approach, and "going for the gold." The other focus of regulation is called **prevention focus**, in which the person is concerned with protection, safety, and the prevention of negative outcomes and failures. Behaviours with a prevention focus are characterized by vigilance, caution, and attempts to prevent negative outcomes.

When examined from a trait perspective, promotion focus correlates with such traits as extraversion and behavioural activation (which we discussed in Chapter 7). Prevention focus correlates with such traits as neuroticism and harm avoidance and (negatively) with impulsivity (Grant & Higgins, 2003). However, the concepts of prevention and promotion focus are more concerned with motivation and goal behaviours than the standard personality traits with which they correlate. For example, in a study of decision making and goal striving, subjects participated in a decision task that involved the possibility of making either errors of "commission" (making an incorrect choice) or errors of "omission" (not making a correct choice). Participants high in promotion focus were less likely to make errors of omission; that is, they appeared motivated to not miss any possible opportunities for being correct, even if some choices were incorrect. Participants high in prevention focus, on the other hand, were less likely to make errors of commission; that is, they appeared motivated to make sure they did not make incorrect responses (Higgins et al., 2001). Higgins and his colleagues are investigating several other ways that people high in prevention focus differ from those high in promotion focus, such as the kinds of information each finds persuasive, or in terms of how they react to life events (e.g., Scholer & Higgins, 2011).

Walter Mischel and the Cognitive-Affective Personality System (CAPS)

As discussed in Chapter 4, psychologist Walter Mischel had a huge impact on personality psychology when he wrote a book in 1968, titled *Personality and Assessment,* that was highly critical of the evidence for personality traits. Recall that he argued that people's behaviour was more strongly influenced by the situations they were in than by the personality traits they brought to those situations. In more recent years, Mischel has proposed a theory that personality variables (though not necessarily traits) do have an influence on behaviour, mainly by interacting with and modifying the psychological meaning of situations.

In Mischel and Shoda's cognitive-affective personality system (CAPS), they reconceptualize personality not as a collection of traits, but as an organization of cognitive and affective activities that influence how people respond to certain kinds of situations (Mischel, 2000, 2004; Shoda et al., 2013, 2015; Smith & Shoda, 2009). The emphasis is more on personality processes than on static traits. These cognitive and affective processes consist of such mental activities as construals (how one views a situation), goals, expectations, beliefs, and feelings as well as self-regulatory standards, abilities, plans, and strategies. According to this theory, each individual is characterized by a relatively stable network of such mental activities. Individuals acquire their specific set of these mental abilities through their learning history, their particular culture and subculture, their genetic endowment, and their biological history.

The CAPS theory argues that people differ from each other in the distinct organization of their cognitive and affective processes. As people move through the different situations in their lives, different cognitive and affective processes will be activated and mediate the impact of specific situations. For example, if a situation engenders frustration (e.g., being blocked from a goal), and the person has a specific cognitive-affective system (e.g., high expectations for success, the belief that aggression is permissible to obtain what you want), then that person may respond with hostility. So, it is not the case that aggressive people would be aggressive in all situations (the trait view) but that aggressive people are sensitive to certain kinds of situations (e.g., frustration), and only then will they behave aggressively.

Mischel presents a contextualized view of personality as expressed in **"if . . . then . . ." propositions**: If situation A, then the person does X; but if situation B, then the person does Y. Personality leaves its signature, Mischel argues, in terms of the specific situational ingredients that prompt behaviour from the person. To illustrate his approach, Mischel (2004) presents data gathered at a summer camp for delinquent children. All of the children had impulse control problems and had been aggressive in the past. The children were observed over many days and in many different situations in the summer camp. The researchers were interested in verbal aggression. They broke down the situations into five categories: when the child was "teased by a peer," "warned by an adult," "punished by an adult," "praised by an adult," and "approached by a peer." The children showed distinct profiles of verbal aggression across these different situations. For example, some children were aggressive only after being warned by an adult. Other children were aggressive only when approached by a peer. Mischel points out that verbal aggression was not consistent across all five situations and that specific "if . . . then . . ." profiles could be discerned for each child. These profiles were consistent, however, in the sense that kids who were aggressive when warned by an adult behaved that way repeatedly (Mischel, Shoda, & Mendoza-Denton, 2002).

Mischel's theory offers an important new way to think about personality, a way that emphasizes cognitive and affective processes that influence a person's behaviours relative to specific situational characteristics in terms of "if . . . then . . ." propositions (for another example, see Smith et al., 2009). We present this theory in the chapter on cognitive approaches because it emphasizes the internal processes that people engage in to regulate their behaviour. It is interesting that Mischel still argues that situations exert the most control over people's behaviour but now believes that it is the psychological situation—that is, the meaning of the situation from the individual's perspective—that organizes behaviour (Mischel, 2004; Mischel & Shoda, 2010).

Concept Check

Define self-efficacy, and explain how it is related to performance. When is self-efficacy most important?

What are the two primary ways in which people regulate their goal-directed behaviours according to Higgins?

Intelligence

No discussion of individual differences in cognition and information processing would be complete without at least some mention of intelligence. Intelligence has been defined in many ways, and there may be many different kinds of intelligence. One definition of intelligence is associated with educational attainment, how much knowledge a person has acquired relative to others in their age cohort. This is an **achievement view of intelligence**. Other definitions view intelligence less as the product of education and more as an ability to become educated, as the ability or aptitude to learn. This is the **aptitude view of intelligence**. Traditional measures of intelligence—so-called IQ tests—often have been used and interpreted as aptitude measures. For much of the past century, IQ tests were used to predict school performance and to select individuals for educational opportunities. They are still used in this fashion today. For example, one study on university undergraduates found that general intelligence predicted 16 percent of the variability in grades, which translates into a correlation of about .40 between IQ and grades. Interestingly, need for achievement, which we discussed in Chapter 11, accounted for 11 percent of the variability in grades, beyond the variability accounted for by IQ (Lounsbury et al., 2003).

Early in the study of intelligence, most psychologists thought of this characteristic in traitlike terms, as a property of the individual. And individuals were thought to differ from each other in amount, in how much intelligence they possessed. Moreover, intelligence was thought of as a single broad factor—often called g for **general intelligence**. As tests were developed, however, researchers began to identify separate abilities—such as verbal ability, memory ability, perceptual ability, and arithmetic ability. Many standardized tests in Canada and the United states, such as the Canadian Test of Basic Skills (CTBS), the Graduate Record Examination (GRE), or the Scholastic Aptitude Test (SAT), provide multiple scores, typically a verbal score and a mathematical score, among others. These different domains are examples of differential kinds of intelligence. Although there is controversy over whether these tests measure intelligence or simply academic achievement, they have proven useful in selecting people who are likely to do well in higher education settings.

Other intelligence tests yield even more than two scores. For example, the Wechsler Intelligence Scale for Children–Revised (revised in 1991, originally published by Wechsler, 1949) yields 11 subtest scores, 6 of which require or depend on verbal ability and 5 of which are nonverbal, such as finding missing elements in a picture and assembling a puzzle. Also, the test yields two broad scores to represent verbal and performance intelligence. Psychologists use the multiple scores to evaluate a person's strengths and weaknesses, as well as to understand how the individual uniquely approaches and solves problems.

 Exercise

One interesting question related to intelligence and information-processing is how debate over a topic or issue can persist in the face of compelling evidence. In other words, how can people continue to disagree on a subject when there is clear evidence for one side over the other? For example, there is overwhelming scientific evidence that climate change is primarily caused by human activity. How, then, do people ignore the evidence and continue to be in denial? From a cognitive psychology point of view, there must be some kind of psychological mechanism(s) underlying this behaviour.

According to Kahan and colleagues (2017), it may have something to do with politics. In their research on *numeracy*, the ability to reason and analyze using numbers, they found that more intelligent participants (i.e., those higher in numeracy) tended to make more accurate judgments about scientific data when presented with quantitative information or data. This is what we would expect to see. However, when information was presented about issues that were more political in nature, such as gun ownership, participants higher in numeracy were more likely to support whatever side of the debate they were already on. It seems, according to Kahan et al. (2017), that more intelligent people are more likely to confirm their pre-existing beliefs by choosing to dismiss information, at least when it revolves around a polarized or highly debated topic. They seem to use their analytical capacity to maintain their worldview.

Such a finding is as shocking as it is relevant. In a world where public officials freely attack the media, decrying "fake news" when things don't go their way, it is of paramount importance to understand how people come to their own conclusions regarding socially relevant information. Can you think of a topic or issue about which you feel very strongly? Perhaps it's climate change, public education, or marriage. Now consider this: Have you ever dismissed information or evidence that was contrary to your beliefs a little too quickly? Alternatively, can you think of someone you know who is probably high in numeracy (or overall intelligence), and who has overlooked or dismissed scientific evidence when it didn't quite fit with their beliefs?

A widely accepted definition of intelligence, proposed by Gardner (1983), is that it is the application of cognitive skill and knowledge to solve problems, learn, and achieve goals that are valued by the individual and the culture. With intelligence defined this broadly, it is obvious that there are many kinds of intelligence, perhaps several more beyond the traditional verbal, mathematical, and performance distinctions. Howard Gardner has proposed a theory of **multiple intelligences**, which includes seven forms, such as interpersonal intelligence (social skills, ability to communicate and get along with others) and intrapersonal intelligence (insight into oneself, one's emotions, and one's motives). Gardner also includes bodily or kinesthetic intelligence—describing the abilities of athletes, dancers, and acrobats—and musical intelligence (Gardner, 1999). Other experts are adding to the growing list of forms of intelligence, such as the concept of emotional intelligence, proposed by psychologists Peter Salovey and Jack Mayer (1990) and popularized by journalist Dan Goleman (1995). The concept of emotional intelligence, defined generally as the capacity to perceive, manage, and regulate one's emotions (in addition to understanding the emotions of others), has received a great deal of attention from researchers (see Zeidner et al., 2003, for a review).

Gardner's concept of multiple intelligences is controversial. Some intelligence researchers feel that these separate abilities are correlated enough with each other (implying that they tend to co-occur in the same individuals) to justify thinking of intelligence as g, a general factor (e.g., Herrnstein & Murray, 1994; Petrill, 2002; Rammsayer & Brandler, 2002). Other experts acknowledge a few broad distinctions, such as the verbal and mathematical intelligences that are so much a part of North American and Western school systems. Yet another group of experts, including many educators, are examining the implications of the multiple intelligences notion. Some universities are considering using "noncognitive" measures of personality characteristics, like persistence, initiative, and conscientiousness, in addition to the standardized tests, to inform admissions decisions (Hoover, 2013). Some schools are making curriculum changes designed to develop and strengthen various forms of intelligence in their students. For example, some schools are teaching units in emotional intelligence. Other schools offer classes for those high on nonverbal intelligence. Other schools are fostering character education, which can be thought of as a form of civic intelligence. These modern educational efforts are the direct outcomes of research being conducted by personality psychologists exploring the basic nature of intelligence.

We cannot leave the concept of intelligence without looking at the **cultural context of intelligence**. What is defined as "intelligent behaviour" will obviously differ across cultures. For example, among the people who live on the islands of Micronesia, the ability to navigate the ocean and other maritime skills are considered superior forms of intelligence. Among Inuit who hunt along the shores in their canoes, the ability to develop a cognitive map of the complex shoreline in Nunavut is a valued ability. Many psychologists define culture, in part, as the shared notions about what counts as efficient problem solving (Wertsch & Kanner, 1992). These skills then become part of the way successful people think in that culture. Western cultures, for example, emphasize verbal skills, both written and oral, as well as the mathematical and spatial skills necessary in a technologically advanced culture. Other cultures, however, might guide their members to develop different problem-solving skills, such as developing a sense of direction or a knowledge of animal behaviour.

Because of these considerations, we should always view intelligence as comprising the skills valued in a particular culture. However, Western culture—along with its economic, social, and political systems—is proliferating into countries around the world. Will the world become a monoculture? If so, will there become one form of intelligence, which is universally valued? Or will cultures maintain separate identities and define differences in what counts as intelligent behaviour? For example, currently most people in Europe speak more than one language, and many speak three or more because of the problem-solving advantage a multilingual person has in Europe. Many Europeans consider Americans to be linguistically challenged or, less charitably, verbally unintelligent because most Americans know only one language.

Interestingly, average IQ scores have risen steadily the past several decades, at the rate of approximately one IQ point every 4 or 5 years within populations (Flynn, 2007, 2012). This rise in population IQ scores is known as the *Flynn effect,* named after the person who first documented this observation (Flynn, 1984). Various explanations have been put forward for rising population IQ scores, such as better nutrition around the world. Flynn's (2007, 2012) own explanation focuses on access to, and improvements in, quality of education over those decades. However, despite steady increases in average IQ over the last half of the twentieth century, psychologists have observed a decline in population IQ scores over the last decade, starting around 1998, in specific countries (Teasdale & Owen, 2008) as well as worldwide (Lynn & Harvey, 2008), a phenomenon called the *reverse Flynn effect.*

This decline in population IQ worries intelligence researchers because the average IQ in a country is correlated with many indicators of national well-being, including gross domestic product (the wealth of the nation, Gelade, 2008; Hunt & Wittmann, 2008), educational attainment, and technological advancements (Rindermann, 2008). Lower population IQ has also been associated with the prevalence of juvenile delinquency, adult crime, single parenthood, and poverty (Gordon, 1997). Each decline of one IQ point is associated with a reduction of income of about $425 per year (Zagorsky, 2007). Lynn and Harvey (2008) attribute this decline in national IQ scores around the world to increasing fertility rates, generalizing from the often-replicated observation that IQ and fertility are negatively correlated (i.e., people with lower IQ scores tend to produce more offspring than people with higher IQ scores) (Shatz, 2008; Vining, 1982).

A new variable in intelligence research is called **inspection time**, which refers to the time it takes a person to make a simple discrimination between two displayed objects. For example, two lines appear on a computer screen and the subject's task is to say which one is longer. The time it takes the subject to inspect the two lines, measured in milliseconds (thousandths of a second), before making the discrimination is the measure of inspection time. This variable is highly related to standard measures of general intelligence (Osmon & Jackson, 2002). Inspection time correlates with other measures of perceptual speed and reaction time to make decisions (Jensen, 2011), and these mental speed abilities contribute to higher IQ scores (Johnson & Deary, 2011). Inspection time is also a sensitive leading indicator of the cognitive decline that occurs with old age for some people (Gregory, Nettelbeck, Howard, & Wilson, 2008). Another similar measure is the ability to discriminate auditory intervals that differ only in the range of a few milliseconds, which also is related to general intelligence (Rammsayer & Brandler, 2002). A recent review of 172 studies of the relationship between IQ and speed of information processing (Sheppard & Vernon, 2008) concluded that measures of intelligence are correlated with mental speed, with smarter people being generally faster on a wide variety of mental tasks. Findings such as these suggest that brain mechanisms specifically involved in information processing are more efficient in individuals scoring high on intelligence measures.

There are many debates about intelligence that are beyond the scope of an introductory personality text. If you are interested, we recommend looking at advanced sources, such as the journal *Intelligence,* or to books, such as Neisser's (1998) or Herrnstein and Murray's controversial *The Bell Curve* (1994) and the direct responses to the controversy created by *The Bell Curve*—such as Fraser (1995), Jacoby and Glauberman (1995), and Lynn (2008). Other alternatives to the Herrnstein and Murray position include works by Sternberg (1985), Gardner (1983), and Simonton (1991). You should know that there are several current debates about intelligence, including whether it can be measured accurately, whether measures of intelligence are biased to favour people from the dominant majority group in the culture, the extent to which intelligence is heritable and the implications of heritability, whether different racial groups differ with respect to intelligence, and whether race differences should be interpreted as social class differences. These issues are politicized and have many implications for social and government policy, and so are generating much heated debate. Personality psychologists are playing an important role by doing the research necessary to provide a scientific approach to these issues.

 Concept Check

What are two different ways of defining intelligence as reviewed in this section?

Why has the study of intelligence (and IQ specifically) proven so controversial?

Summary and Evaluation

Cognitive topics in personality psychology are a broad class of subject matter. People differ from each other in many ways, in how they think as well as in how they perceive, interpret, remember, want, and anticipate the events in their lives. In this chapter, we organized the coverage into four broad categories: perception, interpretation, goals, and intelligence.

We began by examining some ways in which personality is related to perceptual differences among people. Field independence/dependence concerns the ability to see the trees despite the forest. This individual difference in perceptual style has to do with the ability to focus on the details despite the clutter of background information. This style of perceiving may have important implications for learning styles and career choices.

The second perceptual difference we discussed was sensory reducing/augmenting. This dimension originally referred to the tendency to reduce or augment painful stimuli and was first related to individual differences in pain tolerance. It is now more generally used to refer to individual differences in sensitivity to sensory stimulation, with some individuals (augmenters) being more sensitive than others (reducers). This individual difference may have important implications for the development of problem behaviours associated with seeking stimulation, such as smoking or other forms of drug abuse.

Another aspect of cognition is how people interpret events in their lives. This approach to personality has its roots in the work of George Kelly. His personal construct theory emphasizes how people construct their experiences by using their constructs to make sense out of the world. Another general difference among people is in locus of control, the tendency to interpret events either as under one's control or as not under one's control. Many researchers now apply the locus of control concept in particular life domains, such as health locus of control or relationship locus of control.

Learned helplessness is the feeling engendered when a person experiences an inescapable aversive situation. The feeling of helplessness may also generalize to new situations so that the person continues to act helplessly and fails to seek solutions to problems. The theory of learned helplessness was reformulated to incorporate how people think about events in their lives, particularly unpleasant events. Psychologists have focused on specific dimensions of people's explanations, such as whether the cause is internal or external to the person, whether it is stable or unstable, and whether it is global or specific. A pessimistic explanatory style is internal, stable, and global.

Personality can also be revealed by how people select projects and tasks to pursue in life. If you know what a person really wants out of life, then you probably know that person fairly well. Our goals define us, and the strategies with which we pursue those desires illustrate the active aspects of personality in our daily lives.

Cognitive social learning theory was introduced and several specific examples of this approach were described. All of the example theories incorporate the concept of goals and related cognitive activities, such as expectancies, strategies, and beliefs about one's abilities. These theories are important new additions to the psychology of personality because they emphasize how the psychological situation is a function of characteristics of the person (e.g., their self-efficacy beliefs).

Intelligence was also discussed in this chapter, along with different views on intelligence (as academic achievement versus an aptitude for learning). We reviewed the historical development of intelligence as starting with the view of this as a single and general trait up to today's trend toward a multiple intelligences view. We also noted that culture influences which skills and achievements contribute toward intelligence and presented some results on a biological interpretation of intelligence. In addition, we briefly reviewed some of the controversies that are being debated in the area of intelligence.

! Concept Check

What is the primary focus of the cognitive domain of psychology? Consider its role in personality research specifically.

Provide specific examples of individual differences in cognitive perception and interpretation. In other words, what are a few key cognitive variables on which people differ?

Key Terms

cognitive approaches

personalizing cognition

objectifying cognition

cognition

information processing

perception

interpretation

conscious goals

Rod and Frame Test (RFT)

field dependent

field independent

pain tolerance

reducer/augmenter theory

constructs

personal constructs

cognitive schema

postmodernism

locus of control

generalized expectancies

external locus of control

internal locus of control

specific expectancies

learned helplessness

causal attribution

explanatory style

pessimistic explanatory style

optimistic explanatory style

personal project

cognitive social learning approach

self-efficacy

modelling

promotion focus

prevention focus

"if ... then ..." propositions

achievement view of intelligence

aptitude view of intelligence

general intelligence

multiple intelligences

cultural context of intelligence

inspection time

Emotion and Personality

The Cognitive/Experiential Domain

Imagine you are travelling to visit a friend who lives in a city that you've never visited before. You've taken a train to this city and are walking to your friend's apartment from the station. The train was late, so it is dark as you begin to make your way in the unfamiliar neighbourhood. The directions you were given seem a little vague and, after 20 minutes of walking, you are beginning to think they are incorrect. It is late and there are not many people on the street. You are certain that the directions are wrong, your cellphone battery has died, and now you just need to find a phone to call your friend. You decide to take a shortcut through an alley and head back to the train station. The alley is dark, but short, and it will get you back to the train station faster, so you start down the alley. You are alert, a bit on edge, as you are really out of your element. You look over your shoulder and notice that someone has followed you down the alley. Your heart is pounding. You turn and look ahead, and you see that someone has entered the alley in front of you as well. You suddenly feel trapped and you freeze. You are in a real predicament, as your way is blocked in both directions. Your breathing is rapid and you feel confused and light-headed. Your mind is racing, but you are not sure what to do as the two people are closing in on you from both directions. Your palms are sweating and you feel the tension in your neck and throat, as if you might scream any second. The two people are getting closer and closer to you. You feel nervousness in your stomach as you look first in front, then behind. You want to run but cannot decide which way to go. You are paralyzed with fear; you stand there, trembling, not knowing whether you can run away or whether you will have to fight for your life. Suddenly, one of the people calls out your name. You realize it is your friend, who has come with his roommate to look for you between the train station and the apartment. You breathe a sigh of relief, and quickly your state of fear subsides, your body calms, your mind clears, and you greet your friend with an enthusiastic, "Am I glad to see you!"

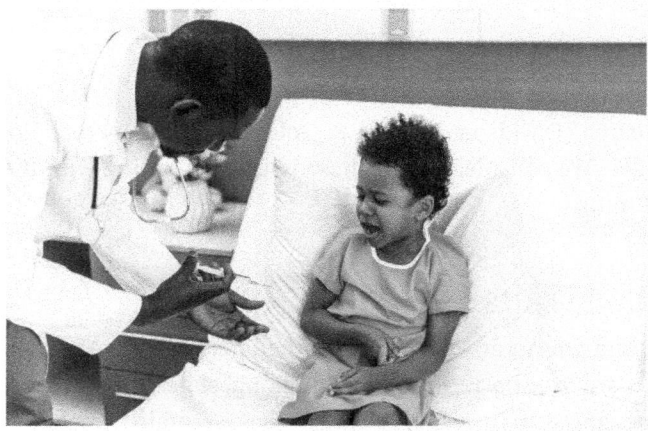

The emotion of fear is characterized by a distinct facial expression. Fear also has a distinctly unpleasant subjective feeling. There are also the associated changes in physiology, such as heart rate increases and increases in blood flow to the large muscles of the legs and arms. These changes prepare the frightened person for the intense action tendency associated with fear, for example, to flee or to fight.

©lightfieldstudios/123RF

In this example, you experienced the emotion of fear. You also experienced the emotion of relief, and perhaps even elation, at being rescued by your friend. **Emotions** can be defined by their three components. First, emotions have distinct subjective feelings, or affects, associated with them. Second, emotions are accompanied by bodily changes, mostly in the nervous system, and these produce associated changes in breathing, heart rate, muscle tension, blood chemistry, and facial and bodily expressions. And third, emotions are accompanied by distinct **action tendencies**, or increases in the probabilities of certain behaviours. With the emotional feeling of fear, there are subjective feelings of anxiety, confusion, and panic. There are also associated changes in bodily function, such as heart rate increases, decreased blood flow to the digestive system (making for stomach queasiness), and increased blood flow to the large muscles of the legs and arms. These changes prepare you for the intense activity sometimes associated with fear. The activity, or action tendency, associated with fear is to flee or to fight.

Why are personality psychologists interested in emotions? People differ from each other in their emotional reactions, even to the same events, so emotions are useful in distinguishing among individuals. For example, imagine losing your wallet, which contains a large sum of money, your credit card, and all your identification, including your driver's licence. What emotions do you think you would feel—anger, embarrassment, hopelessness, frustration, panic, fear, shame, guilt? Different people would have different emotional reactions to this life event, and understanding how and why people differ in their emotional reactions is part of understanding personality.

Other theories of emotion emphasize the functions that emotions play, such as generating short-term adaptive actions that help us survive. For example, the emotion of disgust has the adaptive value of prompting us to quickly spit out something that is not good for us. Interestingly, the expression of disgust, even when the feeling is evoked by a thought or something that is only psychologically distasteful, is to wrinkle the nose, open the mouth, and protrude one's tongue as if spitting something out.

In his 1872 book *The Expression of the Emotions in Man and Animals,* Charles Darwin proposed a **functional analysis** of emotions and emotional expressions. His analysis focuses on the "why" of emotions and expressions, in particular in terms of whether they increase the fitness of individuals (see Chapter 8 of this textbook). In his book he describes his observations of animals, his own children, and other people, linking particular expressions with specific emotions. He recognized that evolution by natural selection applied not only to anatomic structures but also to the "mind," including the emotions and their expressions. How do emotions increase evolutionary fitness? Darwin concluded that emotional expressions communicate information from one animal to another about what is likely to happen. The dog baring its teeth and bristling the hair on its back is communicating to others that he is likely to attack. If others recognize this communication, they may choose to back away, thereby avoiding the attack. Many modern emotion theorists accept this functional emphasis, but most personality psychologists approach emotion with an interest in how and why people differ from each other in terms of emotions.

Issues in Emotion Research

Several major issues divide the field of emotion research (Davidson, Scherer, & Goldsmith, 2003). Psychologists typically hold an opinion on each of these issues. We consider two of these issues, beginning with the distinction between emotional states and emotional traits.

Emotional States versus Emotional Traits

We typically think of emotions as states that come and go. A person gets angry, then gets over it. A person becomes sad, then snaps out of it. **Emotional states** are *transitory*. Moreover, emotional states depend more on the situation a person is in than on the specific person. A man is angry *because* he was unfairly treated. A woman is sad *because* her bicycle was stolen. Most people would be angry or sad in these situations. Emotions as states are transitory; they have a specific cause, and that cause typically originates outside of the person (something happens in the environment).

We can also think of emotions as dispositions, or traits. For example, we often characterize people by stating what emotions they *frequently* experience or express: "Tanya is cheerful and enthusiastic," or "Mohammed is frequently angry and often loses his temper." Here we are using emotions to describe dispositions, or persistent emotional traits, that a person has. Emotional traits are consistencies in a person's emotional life. Traits, as you'll recall from Chapter 3, are patterns in a person's behaviour or experience that are at least somewhat consistent from situation to situation and that are at least somewhat stable over time. Thus, **emotional traits** are patterns of emotional reactions that a person consistently experiences across a variety of life situations. This pattern of emotional experiences is stable over time and characteristic for each person. To continue with the case of Mary, we might expect her to be cheerful at home, at school, and at work. Moreover, by referring to cheerfulness as an emotional trait, we would expect that she was cheerful last year and will most likely be cheerful next year, barring any major changes to her personality.

Categorical versus Dimensional Approach to Emotion

Emotion researchers can be divided into two camps based on their answers to the following question: What is the best way to think about emotions? Some suggest emotions are best thought of as a small number of primary and distinct emotions (anger, joy, anxiety, sadness). Others suggest that emotions are best thought of as broad dimensions of experience (e.g., a dimension ranging from pleasant to unpleasant). Those who think that primary emotions are the key are said to take the **categorical approach**. Hundreds of terms describe different categories of emotions. Averill (1975), for example, compiled a list of 550 terms that describe different feeling states. This is similar to the situation with basic trait terms, in which psychologists started with thousands of trait adjectives and searched for the fundamental factors that underlie those many variations, concluding that there are probably about five primary personality traits that underlie the huge list of trait adjectives.

Emotion researchers who take the categorical approach have tried to reduce the complexity of emotions by searching for the primary emotions that underlie the great variety of emotional terms (Levenson, 2003). They have not reached the kind of consensus that is found in the personality trait domain, however. The lack of consensus found in this area of psychology results from different criteria that researchers use for defining an emotion as primary. Primary emotions are thought to be the irreducible set of emotions, combinations of which result in the huge variety of experienced emotions. This is similar to the primary trait issue discussed in Chapter 3. Various researchers have proposed criteria for determining which emotions are primary emotions. Ekman (1992a) requires that a primary emotion have a distinct facial expression that is recognized across cultures. For example, sadness is accompanied by frowning and knitting the brow. This facial expression is universally recognized as depicting the emotion of sadness. Similarly, clenching and baring the teeth is associated with anger and is universally recognized as anger. In fact, people who are blind from birth frown when sad, clench and bare their teeth when angry, and smile when they are happy. Because individuals who are blind from birth have never seen the facial expressions of sadness, anger, or joy, it is not likely that they learned these expressions. Rather, it seems likely that the expressions are part of human nature. Based on these criteria of distinct and universal facial expressions, Ekman's list of primary emotions contains disgust, sadness, joy, surprise, anger, and fear.

Happiness can be thought of as a state or as a trait. People high in trait happiness experience frequent happiness states, or have a lower threshold for becoming happy. Moreover, happiness is recognized around the world through the expression of smiling. People from all cultures smile when they are happy.

(top left): ©Bartosz Hadyniak/Getty Images; (top right): ©Amos Morgan/Getty Images; (bottom left): ©Shutterstock/zeljkodan; (bottom right): ©Thurtell/Getty Images

Other researchers hold different criteria for counting emotions as primary. For example, Izard (1977) suggests that the primary emotions are distinguished by their unique motivational properties. That is, emotions are understood to guide behaviours by motivating a person to take specific adaptive actions. Fear is included as a primary emotion on Izard's list because it motivates a person to avoid danger and seek safety. Interest is similarly a fundamental emotion because it motivates a person to learn and acquire new skills. Izard's criteria result in a list of 10 primary emotions. In Table 13.1 we present additional lists of primary emotions based on various criteria. Jessica Tracy has also studied *pride* and suggests that it, too, is a primary emotion. Read Highlight On Canadian Research: Finding Pride: Evidence for a New Discrete Emotion?

Theorists	Basic Emotions	Criteria
Ekman, Friesen, & Ellsworth, 1972	Anger, disgust, fear, joy, sadness, surprise	Universal facial expression
Frijda, 1986	Desire, happiness, interest, surprise, wonder, sorrow	Motivation to take specific actions
Gray, 1982	Rage, terror, anxiety, joy	Brain circuits
Izard, 1977	Anger, contempt, disgust, distress, fear, guilt, interest, joy, shame, surprise	Motivation to take specific actions
James, 1884	Fear, grief, love, rage	Bodily involvement
Mower, 1960	Pain, pleasure	Unlearned emotional states
Oatley & Johnson-Laird, 1987	Anger, disgust, anxiety, happiness, sadness	Little cognitive involvement
Plutchik, 1980	Anger, acceptance, joy, anticipation, fear, disgust, sadness, surprise	Evolved biological processes
Tomkins, 2008	Anger, interest, contempt, disgust, fear, joy, shame, surprise	Density of neural firing

Table 13.1   A Selection of Theorists Who Provide Lists of Primary Emotions

Source: Adapted from Ortony & Turner, 1990.

 # Highlight On Canadian Research

Finding Pride: Evidence for a New Discrete Emotion?

Although the emotions in Table 13.1 are numerous and varied, there may be one important discrete emotion missing from the list: *pride*. Jessica Tracy of the University of British Columbia has dedicated much of her career to understanding, validating, and measuring this particularly boastful emotion. But what is *pride*, according to Tracy's research? And does it indeed qualify as a distinct, universal emotion?

As the Director of the Emotion and Self Lab at UBC, Jessica Tracy and her colleagues have worked hard to establish pride as a discrete emotion with its own recognizable and unique expression. As discussed in her 2004 paper in *Psychological Science*, Ekman's originally proposed set of six primary emotions with universal facial expressions is highly limited in its inclusion of positive emotion. In fact, happiness is the only positive emotion on the list, despite Darwin's (1872) description of pride as one of the most distinct and evident emotions in human beings. In her early work, along with her colleague Richard Robins at the University of California–Davis, Tracy reported findings from three separate experiments, each validating pride as a discrete emotion. In the first experiment, researchers administered a forced-choice response format in which participants successfully identified pride among photographs of various emotional expressions, including pride, happiness, and surprise, at a frequency that was greater than chance. In experiment 2, an open-ended format was used in which any word could be offered by participants to describe photos of pride, happiness, and surprise. All photos of pride expressions were indeed identified as pride or pride-related (e.g., proud, self-confident) at a frequency greater than chance.

In their final experiment, Tracy and Robins (2004) manipulated specific features and bodily movements associated with pride in order to determine which components resulted in the most frequent identification of pride in photographs shown to participants. Two photos were identified as pride with a greater frequency than the rest. In each of these photos, expressions included a slight smile, the head tilted back with the chin up, and a fully visible expanded posture with either hands on hips or arms raised. The first expression (hands on hips) was identified as pride by 87 percent of judges. A similar expression of pride is shown in the image below.

In their definition of pride, Tracy and Robins (2007a) have distinguished between two key facets of the emotion that are especially important when predicting behaviour: *authentic* and *hubristic* pride. Authentic pride is based on achievement and contributes to a genuine sense of self-esteem. On the other hand, hubristic pride is associated with self-aggrandizing aspects of narcissism and may contribute to aggression and hostility. The former is far more likely to lead to prosocial behaviour, while the latter is associated with low agreeableness. Al-

According to research by Tracy and Robins (2004), this expression represents one of the two most common displays of pride, which appears to be a discrete and culturally universal emotion.
Source: Tracy, J.L., & Robins, R.W. (2007). The prototypical pride expression: Development of a nonverbal behavior coding system. *Emotion*, 7(4), 789–801. © by American Psychological Association. Reprinted with permission.

though Tracy and Robins have developed scales to measure both aspects of pride, their research has indicated that the distinct facial and bodily expressions that define pride are the same for both authentic and hubristic forms (Tracy and Robins, 2007b). This suggests that the internal representations of this emotion have a degree of complexity that exceeds their outward expression. In recent research, authentic pride has been associated with higher achievement (Weidman et al., 2016) as well as *humility*—specifically, *appreciative humility*, which is derived from personal success and more likely to involve celebrating others (in contrast to self-abasing humility, which is associated with failure and shame; Weidman et al., 2018).

Perhaps the most interesting area of support for pride as a discrete emotion comes from Tracy and Robins' (2008) cross-cultural research. As proposed by Ekman (1992a), an important criterion for the identification of primary emotions is their recognition across cultures. In the 2008 paper, results were presented that confirm the recognition of pride expressions in both the United States and Italy. The second study presented in the paper further confirmed the reliable recognition of pride in an isolated, preliterate tribe in Burkina Faso, West Africa. The Burkinabe participants, according to Tracy and Robins (2008), were unlikely to have been exposed to the emotion via cross-cultural transmission, offering further evidence for pride as a universal emotion.

Another approach to understanding the complexity of emotion has been based on empirical research rather than on theoretical criteria. In the **dimensional approach**, researchers gather data by having subjects rate themselves on a wide variety of emotions, then apply statistical techniques (usually factor analysis) to identify the basic dimensions underlying the ratings.

There is remarkable consensus among researchers on the basic dimensions that underlie self-ratings of affect (Judge & Larsen, 2001; Larsen & Diener, 1992; Watson, 2000). Most of the studies suggest that people categorize emotions using just two primary dimensions: how pleasant or unpleasant the emotion is, which psychologists refer to as **valence**, and how high or low on arousal the emotion is. When these two dimensions are arrayed as axes in a two-dimensional coordinate system, the adjectives that describe emotions fall in a circle around the two dimensions, as shown in Figure 13.1.

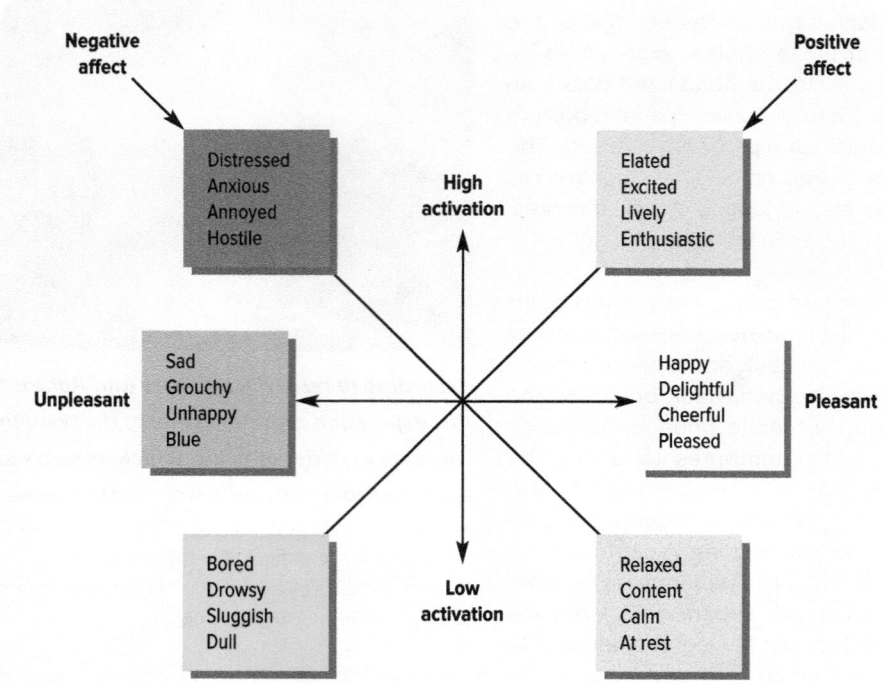

FIGURE 13.1 The dimensional approach to emotion, showing two primary dimensions: high activation to low activation and positive valence (pleasantness) to negative valence (unpleasantness).

This model of emotion suggests that every feeling state can be described as a combination of pleasantness/unpleasantness (valence) and arousal. For example, a person can feel unpleasant feelings in a very high-arousal way (nervous, anxious, terrified) or in a very low-arousal way (bored, fatigued, tired). Similarly, a person can feel pleasant feelings in a high-arousal way (excited, enthusiastic, elated) or in a low-arousal way (calm, relaxed). Thus the two dimensions of pleasantness and arousal are seen as fundamental dimensions of emotion.

The dimensional view of emotion is based on research studies in which subjects rate their emotional experiences. Emotions that occur together, which are experienced as similar to each other, are understood as defining a common dimension. For example, the emotions of distress, anxiety, annoyance, and hostility are very similar in terms of experience and thus seem to anchor one end of a dimension of negative affect. The dimensional approach to emotion refers more to how people *experience* their emotions than to how they *think about* their emotions. In contrast, the categorical approach relies more on conceptual distinctions among emotions: the primary emotions are those that have distinct facial expressions or distinct motivational properties. The dimensional approach, on the other hand, suggests that what we experience are various degrees of pleasantness and arousal and that every emotion we are capable of experiencing can be described as a combination of pleasantness and arousal (Larsen & Fredrickson, 1999; Larsen & Prizmic, 2006).

Some researchers prefer the categorical perspective, finding it useful to think about emotions as distinct categories rather than dimensions. For example, the emotions of anger and anxiety, although similar in terms of being high-arousal negative emotions, are nevertheless associated with different facial expressions, feelings, and action tendencies. Personality psychologists with a categorical perspective would be interested in how people differ from each other with respect to primary emotions, such as anger and anxiety. For example, are there individual or group differences in anxiety, sadness, or aggression? There are also personality psychologists who prefer to think about how people differ with respect to the primary dimensions of emotion. For example, who are the people who have a good deal of pleasantness in their lives? Who are the people who have frequent bouts of high-arousal unpleasant emotions? In this chapter, we cover the research and findings from both of these perspectives.

 Concept Check

Compare emotional states to emotional traits. When can emotional states become traitlike?

What is the main difference between the categorical and dimensional approaches to emotion research? To illustrate the difference, consider how the emotion of pride would be defined by each approach.

Content versus Style of Emotional Life

Another distinction that is useful to personality psychologists is that between the content of a person's emotional life and the style with which that person experiences and expresses emotion. **Content** is the specific kind of emotion that a person experiences, whereas **style** is the way in which an emotion is experienced. For example, saying that someone is cheerful is to say something about the *content* of the person's emotional life, because this refers to the specific kind of emotions a person frequently experiences. However, to say that someone is high on mood variability is to say something about the *style* of their emotional life—that this person's emotions change frequently. Each of these facets of emotion—content and style—exhibits traitlike properties (stable over time and situations and meaningful for making distinctions among people). Content and style provide an organizational theme for discussing personality and emotion. We first discuss the content of emotional life, focusing on various pleasant and unpleasant emotions. We then consider emotional style, focusing on individual differences in the intensity and variability of emotional life.

Content of Emotional Life

Content of emotional life means the typical emotions a person is likely to experience over time. For example, someone characterized as an angry or hot-tempered person should have an emotional life that contains a good deal of anger, irritability, and hostility. Someone whose emotional life contains a lot of pleasant emotions we might characterize as happy, cheerful, and enthusiastic. Thus the notion of content leads us to consider the *kinds* of emotions that people are likely to experience over time and across situations in their lives. We begin with a discussion of the pleasant emotional dispositions.

Pleasant Emotions

In lists of primary emotions, happiness or joy are typically the only pleasant emotions mentioned (though some theorists include interest as a pleasant emotion). In trait approaches to emotion, the major pleasant disposition is happiness and the associated feelings of being satisfied with one's life. We begin with these concepts.

Definitions of Happiness and Life Satisfaction Over 2,000 years ago, Greek philosopher Aristotle wrote that happiness was the supreme good and that the goal of life was to attain happiness. Moreover, he taught that happiness was attained by living a virtuous life and being a good person. Some modern researchers similarly emphasize *eudaimonia*, the creation of a life of meaning and purpose, as the route to happiness (e.g., King & Hicks, 2012). Other scholars and philosophers have offered other theories on the sources of human happiness. For example, unlike Aristotle, eighteenth-century French philosopher Jean-Jacques Rousseau speculated that the road to happiness lies in the satisfaction of one's desires and the hedonistic pursuit of pleasure. In the late nineteenth century, the founder of psychology in America, William James, taught that happiness was the ratio of one's accomplishments to one's aspirations. One could achieve happiness, James thought, in one of two ways: in accomplishing more in life or by lowering one's aspirations.

Although philosophers and psychologists have speculated about the roots of happiness for centuries, the scientific study of happiness is relatively recent (see Eid & Larsen, 2008, for a review). Psychologists began the serious study of happiness (also called *subjective well-being*) in the mid-1970s. Since then, scientific research on the topic has grown by leaps and bounds. In recent years, hundreds of scientific articles on happiness have been

published annually in the psychological literature (Diener & Seligman, 2002). Indeed, a journal started in the year 2000, titled *Journal of Happiness Research*, publishes six volumes a year dedicated to the science of happiness. Another journal, the *Journal of Positive Psychology*, also publishes many scientific studies on happiness.

One way to define **happiness** is to examine how researchers measure it. Several questionnaire measures are widely used in surveys and other research. Because happiness is a subjective quality—it depends on an individual's own judgment of their life—researchers *have* to rely on questionnaires. Some of these questionnaires focus on judgments about one's life, such as "How satisfied are you with your life as a whole these days? Are you very satisfied, satisfied, not very satisfied, or not at all satisfied?" Other questionnaires focus on emotion, particularly on the balance between pleasant and unpleasant emotions in a person's life. An example of this type of questioning was proposed by Fordyce (1978), in which the subject is asked the following questions:

William James defined happiness as the ratio of one's accomplishments to one's aspirations.
©SPL/Science Source

What percent of the time are you happy? _____

What percent of the time are you neutral? _____

What percent of the time are you unhappy? _____

Make sure your percents add up to 100.

Among university students, data indicate that the average person reports being happy 65 percent of the time, neutral 15 percent, and unhappy 20 percent (Larsen & Diener, 1985). The percent happy scale is one of the better measures of happiness in terms of construct validity (see Chapter 2). For example, it predicts a wide range of other happiness-related aspects of a person's personality, such as day-to-day moods and peer reports of overall happiness (Larsen, Diener, & Lucas, 2002).

Researchers conceive of happiness as having two complementary components. One is more cognitive and consists of judgments that one's life has purpose and meaning and has been called the life-satisfaction component. The other component is affective and consists of the ratio of a person's positive emotions to their negative emotions averaged over time. This has been called the hedonic component and really refers to the balance of positive to negative emotions in a person's life over time. The two components—life satisfaction and hedonic balance—tend to be highly correlated. Although we can think of cases where a person could be high on one and low on the other (e.g., a starving artist who feels her life has a great deal of purpose and meaning, yet is suffering greatly day to day to produce her art), the fact is that most people who have a life of meaning and purpose also have more positive than negative emotions in their life. Consequently, most psychologists refer to the general construct of happiness to talk about this characteristic.

Can it be that happy people are just deluding themselves, that most people are really miserable and happy people just don't know it or are denying it? It would be easy to lie on a questionnaire and to portray oneself as being happy and satisfied. This is the idea of social desirability, as discussed in Chapter 4. It turns out that measures of happiness *do* correlate with social desirability scores. In other words, people who score high on social desirability also score high on self-reported happiness scales. Moreover, social desirability measures also correlate with non-self-report happiness scores, such as peer reports of happiness. This finding suggests that having a positive view of oneself is part of being a happy person. Said differently, part of being happy is to have **positive illusions** about the self, an inflated view of one's own characteristics as a good, able, and desirable person (Taylor, 1989; Taylor et al., 2000). We explore this topic further in Chapter 14.

Despite the correlation of self-report measures of happiness with social desirability, other findings suggest that these happiness measures are valid (Diener, Oishi, & Lucas, 2003). These findings concern the positive correlations found between self-report and non-self-report measures of happiness. People who report that they are happy tend to have friends and family members who agree (Sandvik, Diener, & Seidlitz, 1993). In addition, studies of the daily diaries of happy people find that they report many more pleasant experiences than do unhappy people (Larsen & Diener, 1985). When different clinical psychologists interview a sample of people, the psychologists tend to agree strongly about which are happy and satisfied and which are not (Diener, 2000). And, in an interesting experiment, Seidlitz and Diener (1993) gave the participants five minutes to recall as many happy events in their lives as possible and then gave them five minutes to recall as many unhappy events in their lives as possible. They found that the happy people recalled more pleasant events, and fewer unpleasant events, than did the unhappy people.

Questionnaire measures of happiness and well-being also predict other aspects of people's lives that we would expect to relate to happiness (Diener, Lucas, & Larsen, 2003). For example, compared with unhappy people, happy people are less abusive and hostile, are less self-focused, and report fewer instances of disease. They also are more helpful and cooperative, have more social skills, are more creative and energetic, are more forgiving, and are more trusting (Myers, 1993, 2000; Myers & Diener, 1995; Veenhoven, 1988). In summary, self-reports of happiness appear to be valid and trustworthy (Larsen & Prizmic, 2006). After all, who but the individuals themselves are the best judge of their subjective well-being? See Table 13.2 for a sample "life satisfaction" questionnaire.

What Good Is Happiness? It has long been known that happiness correlates with many positive outcomes in life, such as marriage, longevity, self-esteem, and satisfaction with one's job (Diener et al., 1999). These correlations between desirable outcomes in life and happiness are often interpreted to mean that success in some area of life (e.g., a good marriage) will make a person happy. As another example, the small

Table 13.2 Satisfaction with Life Scale

Below are five statements with which you may agree or disagree. Using the scale below, indicate your agreement with each item by placing the appropriate number on the line preceding that item. Please be open and honest in your responses.

Strong Disagreement	Moderate Disagreement	Slight Disagreement	Slight Agreement	Moderate Agreement	Strong Agreement
1	2	3	4	5	6

1. _____ In most ways my life is close to my ideal.
2. _____ If I could live my life over, I would change almost nothing.
3. _____ I am satisfied with my life.
4. _____ So far I have gotten the important things I want in life.
5. _____ The conditions of my life are excellent.

correlation between personal wealth and happiness is often interpreted as meaning that having money can make one (slightly more) happy. The majority of researchers in this area have gone on the assumption that successful outcomes foster happiness and that the causal direction goes from being successful leading to increased happiness.

However, a group of researchers (Lyubomirsky, King, & Diener, 2005) questioned this assumption about the causal direction going from success to happiness. They suggested that there may be areas of life where the causality goes in the opposite direction, from happiness to success. For example, it could be that being happy leads one to get married, or to have a better marriage, instead of having a good marriage leading one to become happy.

In an extremely large meta-analysis of the happiness and well-being literature, Lyubomirsky and colleagues (2005) reviewed many studies that might be used to disentangle the causal direction between happiness and several different outcomes. Two kinds of studies are most useful in assessing causal direction. One type of study is longitudinal, in which people are measured on at least two occasions separated in time. If happiness precedes success in life, then we have some evidence that the causal direction might go from happiness to the outcome. A second type of study is experimental, in which happiness is manipulated (people are put in a good mood) for half the sample (the other half is the control group), and some outcome is measured. If the outcome is higher in the group undergoing the happiness induction than in the control group, then we have some evidence that the causal direction might go from happiness to the outcome.

Lyubomirsky and colleagues (2005) found that longitudinal studies provided evidence that happiness leads to, or at least comes before, positive

Does having a good relationship cause a person to be happy? Or does being happy cause one to have a good relationship?
©Ariel Skelley/Blend Images LLC

outcomes in many areas of life. They found that happiness preceded many important positive outcomes, including fulfilling and productive work, satisfying relationships, and superior mental and physical health and longevity. Experimental studies also provide evidence that happiness can lead to several positive outcomes, including being more helpful and altruistic, wanting to be with others, increases in self-esteem and liking of others, a better functioning immune system, more effective conflict resolution skills, and more creative or more original thinking.

Although happiness has been shown to lead to many positive outcomes in life, the situation with some outcomes might be more complex and involve **reciprocal causality**, which refers to the idea that causality can flow in both directions. For example, we know that happy people are more likely to help others who are in need. Also, from the experimental literature, we know that helping someone in need can lead to increases in happiness. This kind of reciprocal causality may apply to many areas of life, including having a satisfying marriage or intimate relationship, having a fulfilling job, or having high self-esteem.

What Is Known About Happy People In an article titled "Who Is Happy?" psychologists David Myers and Ed Diener (1995) reviewed what is known about happy people. For example, are women happier than men, or are men the happier gender? In Canada and the United States, women are diagnosed with depression twice as often as men. This might suggest that men are happier than women. However, men are at least twice as likely as women to become alcoholics. The use of alcohol may be one way men medicate themselves for depression, so the real rate of depression may be more similar for men and women. Researchers need to examine actual studies of happiness to address the gender difference question. Fortunately, an excellent and thorough review of the studies on gender and happiness has already been done. Haring, Stock, and Okun (1984) analyzed 146 studies on global well-being and found that gender accounted for less than 1 percent of the variation in people's happiness. This finding of practically no difference between men and women appears across cultures and countries as well. Michalos (1991) obtained data on 18,032 university students from 39 countries. He found that roughly equal proportions of men and women rated themselves as being satisfied with their lives. Diener (2000) also reports gender equality in overall happiness.

Is happiness more likely among young, middle-aged, or older people? We often think that certain age periods are more stressful than others, such as the midlife crisis or the stress of adolescence. This might lead us to believe that certain times of life are happier than others. Inglehart (1990) addressed this question in a study of 169,776 people from 16 nations. It was found that the circumstances that make people happy change with age. For example, financial security and health are important for happiness later in life, whereas for younger adults success at school or work and satisfying intimate relationships are important for happiness. However, in looking at overall levels of happiness, Inglehart concluded that there was no evidence to suggest that any one time of life was happier than any other.

Is ethnicity related to happiness? Are some ethnic groups happier than others? Many surveys have included questions about ethnic identity, so a wealth of data exist on this question. Summarizing many such studies, Myers and Diener (1995) conclude that ethnic group membership is unrelated to subjective well-being. For example, African Americans report roughly the same amount of happiness as European Americans and in fact have slightly lower levels of depression (Diener et al., 1993). Crocker and Major (1989) suggest that people from disadvantaged social groups maintain their happiness by valuing the activities they are good at, by comparing themselves with members of their own group, and by blaming their problems on events that are outside of their control. However, in Canada researchers at the University of Alberta have suggested that British

Canadians have higher levels of life satisfaction compared with Chinese Canadians (Spiers & Walker, 2009). In this case, researchers suggested that differences in how these groups define happiness may have made the measures employed less accurate.

What about national differences in well-being? Are people from certain nations happier than people from other nations? The answer here seems to be yes. An impressive study by Diener, Diener, and Diener (1995) examined well-being scores obtained using probability surveys in 55 nations. The nations sampled in this study represented 75 percent of Earth's population. The results are portrayed in Table 13.3, where the nations are rank-ordered on the well-being measure. Looking at the rankings, what do you think might account for the differences among the countries that were high and low on well-being?

Table 13.3 Country Scores of Average Subjective Well-Being

Country	Subjective Well-Being	Country	Subjective Well-Being
Iceland	1.11	Bangladesh	−.29
Sweden	1.03	France	−.38
Australia	1.02	Spain	−.41
Denmark	1.00	Portugal	−.41
Canada	.97	Italy	−.44
Switzerland	.94	Hungary	−.48
U.S.A.	.91	Puerto Rico	−.51
Colombia	.82	Thailand	−.62
Luxembourg	.82	South Africa	−.63
New Zealand	.82	Jordan	−.77
N. Ireland	.78	Egypt	−.78
Norway	.77	Yugoslavia	−.81
Finland	.74	Japan	−.86
Britain	.69	Greece	−.89
Netherlands	.68	Poland	−.90
Ireland	.57	Kenya	−.92
Brazil	.57	Turkey	−1.02
Tanzania	.51	India	−1.13
Belgium	.51	S. Korea	−1.15
Singapore	.43	Nigeria	−1.31
Bahrain	.36	Panama	−1.31
W. Germany	.18	E. Germany	−1.52
Austria	.15	U.S.S.R.	−1.70
Chile	.13	China	−1.92
Philippines	.10	Cameroon	−2.04
Malaysia	.08	Dominican Republic	−3.92
Cuba	.00		
Israel	−.18	**Average**	**0.00**
Mexico	−.28	**Standard deviation**	**1.00**

Source: Diener, Diener, & Diener, 1995.

The researchers were able to assemble a broad array of other environmental, social, and economic information on each of these countries, and they tested whether any of these variables correlated with average national happiness. At the national level, the poorer countries appeared to possess less happiness and life satisfaction than the countries that were wealthier. The nations also differed in the rights they provided their citizens. The researchers found that the countries that provided few civil and political rights tended to have lower well-being than did the countries where civil rights and individual freedoms were well protected by laws. Other national variables, such as population density and cultural homogeneity, showed only minor correlations with well-being. Diener and colleagues (1995) concluded that differences in the economic development of nations may be the primary source of differences in the subjective well-being of societies. Researchers who have conducted similar but smaller-scale national surveys have offered similar findings (Easterlin, 1974; Veenhoven, 1991a, 1991b).

Such findings might lead us to think that money or income makes people happy. People often think that if they made a bit more money or if they had a few more material goods, they would be happier. Some believe that if they win the lottery they will be happy for the rest of their lives. Researchers have found that there is no simple answer to the question about whether money makes people happy (Diener & Biswas-Diener, 2002, 2008). We explore this topic further in A Closer Look: Does Money Make People Happy?

 **A Closer Look**

Does Money Make People Happy?

Pop singer Madonna, also known as the "Material Girl," has sung the praises of materialism. North Americans are often thought of as materialistic. In fact, in surveys, the goal of being very well off financially is often rated as the top goal in life by first-year university students, surpassing other goals, such as being helpful to others, realizing potential as a person, and raising a family (Myers, 2000). This attitude is summarized by a bumper sticker seen on an expensive car towing a large boat, which read, "When the game is over, the person with the most toys wins." Does having more make one a winner? Does money lead to happiness?

Looked at in terms of national data, the answer seems to be that wealthier countries do indeed have higher average levels of life satisfaction than poorer countries. Myers and Diener (1995) report that the correlation between a nation's well-being score and its gross national product (adjusted for population size) is +.67. However, national wealth is confounded with many other variables that influence well-being, such as health care services, civil rights, women's rights, care for the elderly, and education. This is a classic example of how potential third variables might explain why two variables are related (see discussion of this problem in Chapter 2). For example, wealthier countries may have higher well-being *because* they also provide better health care for their citizens.

To counteract this research problem, we must look at the relationship between income and happiness within specific countries. Diener and Diener (1995) report that, in very poor countries, such as Bangladesh and India, financial status is a moderately good predictor of well-being. However, once people can afford life's basic necessities, it appears that increasing one's financial status matters very little to one's well-being. In countries that have a higher standard of living, where most people have their basic needs met (such as in Europe or North America), income "has a surprisingly weak (virtually negligible) effect on happiness" (Inglehart, 1990, p. 242).

This finding of a lack of relation between income and happiness contradicts the views of many politicians, economists, and policymakers. Moreover, it seems to run counter to common sense, as well as data on poverty and poor life outcomes. For example, people in the lowest levels of the economy have the highest rates of depression (McLoyd, 1998). Economic hardship takes a toll on people, increasing stress and conflict in people's lives (Kushlev, Dunn, & Lucas, 2015). Poverty is associated with elevations in a variety of negative life outcomes, ranging from infant mortality to increased violent crimes, such as homicide (Belle et al., 2000). How can poverty be associated with such unfortunate circumstances, yet income not be related to happiness? The answer, it seems, lies in the notion of a threshold of income, below which a person is very unlikely to be happy, at least in North America (Csikszentmihalyi, 2000). Once a person is above this threshold, however, the notion that having more money would make one happier does not seem to hold (Diener & Biswas-Diener, 2002).

Myers and Diener (1995) make the analogy between wealth and health: the absence of either health or wealth can bring misery, but their presence is no guarantee that happiness will follow. An interesting experiment to test this assertion for wealth would be to take a sample of people and randomly assign them to two groups. In Group 1, you give each member $1 million. In Group 2, you give each member $1. Then you see whether, six months later, the people in Group 1 (the new millionaires) are happier than the people in Group 2. Of course, this experiment would be impossible to conduct, right? Wrong. With the advent of lotteries in North America, many people become millionaires overnight. Brickman, Coates, and Janoff-Bulman (1978) conducted a study of lottery winners, comparing their happiness levels with those of people from similar backgrounds who had not won large amounts of money. Within six months of winning, the newly rich lottery winners were found to be no more happy than the subjects in the control group. Apparently, winning the lottery is not as good as it sounds, at least not in terms of making a person permanently happy. External life circumstances have a surprisingly small effect on happiness and subjective well-being (Lucas, 2007).

What can we conclude about money and happiness? Probably the most reasonable conclusion is that below a very low income level, a person is very unlikely to be happy. Being able to meet the basic needs of life (e.g., the needs on Maslow's hierarchy that are discussed in Chapter 8, including food, shelter, and security) appears crucial. However, once those needs are met, research suggests that there is little to the notion that further wealth will bring increased happiness. Support for this idea is provided in a study by Diener, Ng, Harter, and Arora (2010) that is based on a huge sample that is representative of almost everyone on planet Earth. Elizabeth Dunn and her colleagues at the University of British Columbia, for example, reported a correlation of +.25 between household income and happiness (Aknin, Norton, & Dunn, 2009), but this study was based on data from the United States. Other American research by Diener and colleagues (1995) has found an even lower correlation of .12 between personal income and happiness. In a German sample, that correlation was found to be .20 (Lucas & Schimmack, 2009). Although these correlations are not negative, they are hardly large enough to think that having a huge income, in itself, will make you happy. In fact, analyses of data from the 2003 Statistics Canada General Social Survey revealed no significant correlation whatsoever between income and perceived happiness (Jehn, 2014). What wealthy people choose to do with their money may have more to do with their potential happiness than does the mere fact of having a lot of money. For example, Dr. Lara Aknin from Simon Fraser University in Burnaby, British Columbia, has demonstrated that spending money on others can have a greater positive impact on happiness than spending the same amount on oneself (Dunn, Aknin, & Norton, 2008). The effect of prosocial spending on happiness appears to be even greater when givers are aware of their positive impact (Aknin et al., 2013).

Research on the objective circumstances of a person's life—age, sex, ethnicity, income, and so on—shows that these matter very little to overall happiness, yet we know that people differ from each other and that, even through life's struggles and disappointments, some people are consistently happier than others. Costa, McCrae, and Zonderman (1987) found, in a study of 5,000 adults, that the people who were happy in 1973 were also happy 10 years later, in spite of undergoing many changes in life. What else might explain why some people are consistently happier than others?

? Exercise

Recall and describe in writing a recent time when you purchased something for someone else. After writing a brief description of this, think of a time when you spent an equivalent amount of money on something for yourself. Now consider which of these two events produced the higher level of happiness in you? If you are like the participants in research reported in *Science* by Dunn, Aknin, and Norton (2008), you will find that spending one's money on other people has a larger effect on happiness than spending money on oneself. Why do you think this might be so? The effect is so reliable that these authors even found that participants randomly assigned to spend money on others experienced greater happiness than participants randomly assigned to spend money on themselves.

Personality and Well-Being In 1980, psychologists Paul Costa and Robert McCrae concluded that demographic variables, such as gender, age, ethnicity, and income, accounted for only about 10 to 15 percent of the variation in happiness, an estimate confirmed by others (Myers & Diener, 1995). This leaves a lot of the variance in subjective well-being unaccounted for. Costa and McCrae (1980) proposed that personality might have something to do with disposing certain people to be happy and so looked into that research. The few studies existing at that time suggested that happy people were outgoing and sociable (Smith, 1979), emotionally stable, and low on neuroticism (Wessman & Ricks, 1966).

Costa and McCrae used such information to theorize that there may be two personality traits that influence happiness: extraversion and neuroticism. Moreover, Costa and McCrae made specific predictions about exactly how extraversion and neuroticism influenced happiness. Their idea was both simple and elegant. They began with the notion that happiness was the presence of relatively high levels of positive affect, and relatively low levels of negative affect, in a person's life over time. Extraversion, they held, influenced a person's positive emotions, whereas neuroticism determined a person's negative emotions.

Costa and McCrae (1980; McCrae & Costa, 1991) found that their model was supported by further research. Extraversion and neuroticism predicted the amounts of positive and negative emotions in people's lives and hence contributed greatly to subjective well-being. In fact, extraversion and neuroticism accounted for up to three times as much of the variation in happiness among people compared with *all* of the common demographic variables (e.g., age, income, gender, education, ethnicity, religion) put together. It appears that having the right combination of personality traits (high extraversion and low neuroticism) may contribute much more to happiness than gender, ethnicity, age, and all the other demographic characteristics. Their model of well-being is portrayed in Figure 13.2.

Since Costa and McCrae's original study in 1980, more than a dozen studies have replicated the finding that extraversion and neuroticism are strong personality correlates of well-being (summarized in Rusting & Larsen, 1998b). All of these studies have been correlational, however, usually taking the form of administering personality and well-being questionnaires, then examining the correlations (Lucas, Le & Dyrenforth, 2008).

Correlational studies cannot determine whether there is a direct causal connection between personality and well-being, or whether personality leads one to live a certain lifestyle and that lifestyle in turn makes one

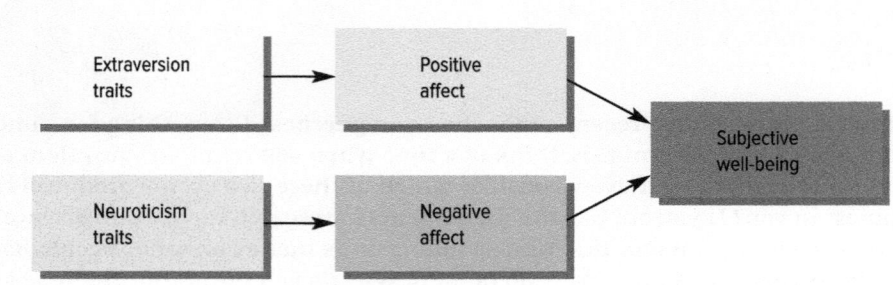

FIGURE 13.2 The influence of extraversion and neuroticism on subjective well-being by making a person susceptible to positive and negative affect.
Source: Adapted from Costa and McCrae, 1980.

happy. For example, being neurotic may lead one to be a worrier and complainer. Other people dislike being around someone who worries a lot and is always complaining, so people may avoid the person who is high on neuroticism. Consequently, that person may be lonely and unhappy; however, that unhappiness may be due to the fact that the person drives people away by complaining all the time. The person's neuroticism leads them to create certain life situations, such as making others uncomfortable, and these situations in turn make the person unhappy (Hotard et al., 1989).

We can contrast this with a different view of the causal relation between personality and well-being, in which personality is viewed as directly causing people to react to the same situations with different amounts of positive or negative emotions, hence directly influencing their well-being. A neurotic person may respond with more negative emotion, even to the identical situation, than a person low in neuroticism. These two different models of the relation between personality and well-being—the direct and the indirect models—are portrayed in Figure 13.3. In the indirect model (Panel B), personality causes the person to create a certain lifestyle, and the lifestyle, in turn, causes the emotional reaction. In the direct model (Panel A), even when exposed to identical situations, certain people respond with more positive or negative emotions, depending on their level of extraversion and neuroticism.

Larsen and his colleagues (e.g., Larsen, 2000a; Larsen & Ketelaar, 1989, 1991; Rusting & Larsen, 1998b; Zelenski & Larsen, 1999) have conducted several studies of whether the personality traits of extraversion and neuroticism have a direct effect on emotional responding. In these studies, the participants underwent a **mood induction** in the laboratory. In one study, the subjects listened to guided images of very pleasant scenes (a walk on the beach) or very unpleasant scenes (having a friend dying of an incurable disease). In other studies, the participants' emotions were manipulated by having them look at pleasant or unpleasant photographs. Prior to the laboratory session, their personality scores on extraversion and neuroticism were obtained by questionnaire. The researchers were then able to determine if extraversion and neuroticism scores predicted responses to the laboratory mood inductions. Across several studies, the best predictor of responsiveness to the positive mood induction was the personality variable of extraversion. The best predictor of responses to the negative mood induction was neuroticism. It seems that it is easy to put an extravert into a good mood, and easy to put a high-neuroticism person into a bad mood. Moreover, these laboratory studies suggest that personality acts like an amplifier of life events, with extraverts showing amplified positive emotions to good events and high-neuroticism subjects showing amplified emotions to bad events. These findings are important because they suggest that personality has a direct effect on emotions and that, even under controlled circumstances, people respond differently to the emotional events in their lives, depending on their personalities.

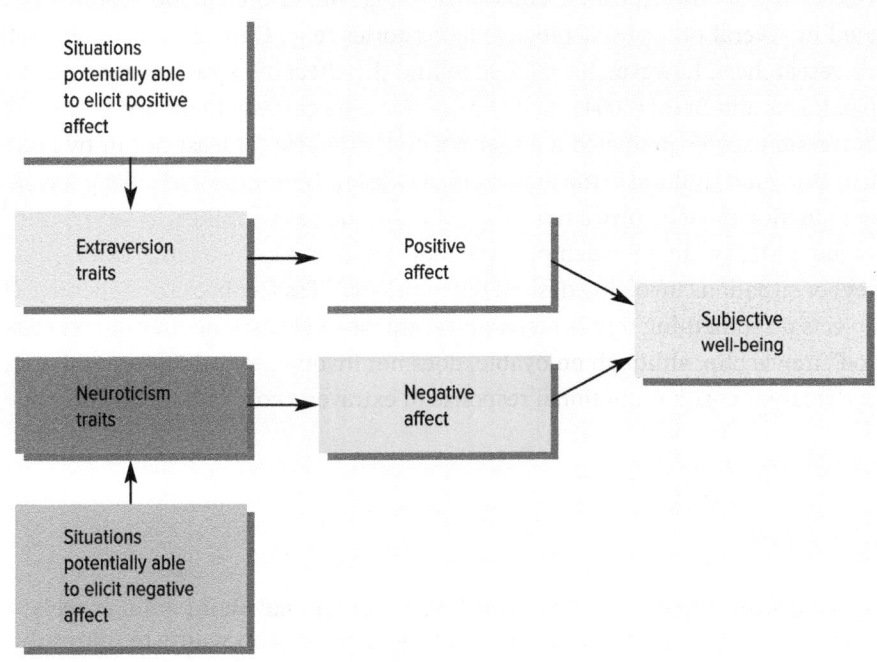

Panel A

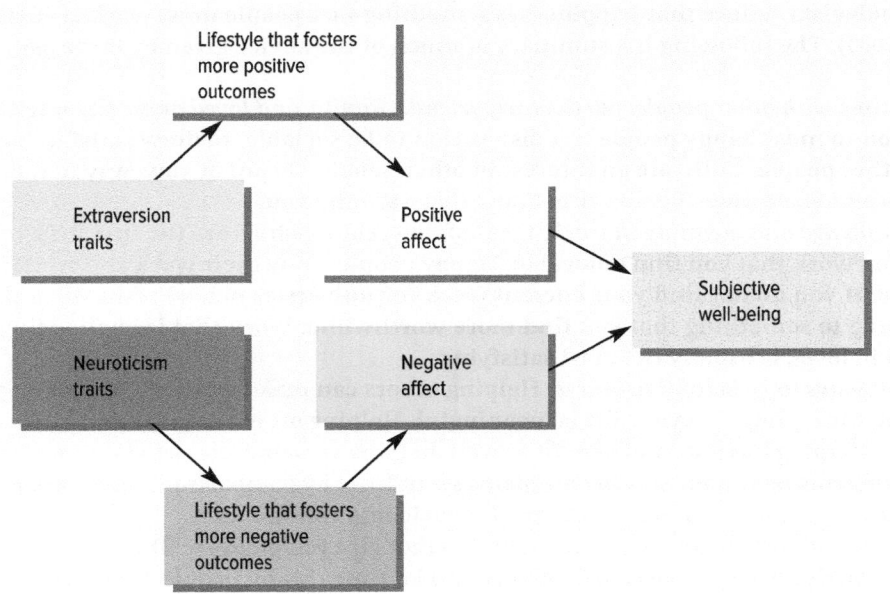

Panel B

FIGURE 13.3 Two models of the relationship between personality variables and subjective well-being. Panel A: Model showing a direct effect of personality on emotional life, where life events are amplified by the personality traits, resulting in stronger positive or negative emotions for high extraversion or neuroticism subjects, respectively. Panel B: Model of the indirect relation between personality and emotional life. Here personality causes one to develop a lifestyle, and that lifestyle in turn fosters positive or negative affect for the high extraversion or neuroticism individuals, respectively.

The finding that extraverts get more positive emotional "bang" out of the emotion-inducing "buck" (or event) has been replicated in several other psychological laboratories (e.g., Gomez, Cooper, & Gomez, 2000; Gross et al., 1998). Some researchers, however, have failed to find the effect of extraversion on positive affective reactivity. For example, Lucas and Baird (2004) used clips of stand-up comedy to induce positive emotions and did not find that extraversion scores predicted a larger positive response (at least not in two out of four studies, whereas the fourth study did find the extraversion effect). Recently, Smillie and colleagues (2012) argued that the positive affect induction must involve a rewarding stimuli, such as winning a lottery or finding some money. Smillie and colleagues (2012) went on to demonstrate that, across five experiments, extraverts are more reactive to rewards (money) or situations involving desired outcomes (success feedback) or appetitive stimuli (delicious food). Having subjects do something that is merely pleasant, such as imagine they are relaxing at the beach or watch a "feel-good" movie clip, although enjoyable, does not involve rewards or appetitive stimuli and hence does not produce the larger positive emotional response in extraverts compared to introverts.

Application

A program to increase happiness. **Psychologists know a great deal about what correlates with happiness, but what can they recommend for the average person who wants to maintain or increase levels of trait happiness? Buss (2000b) has identified several strategies for improving one's chances of being happy. In addition, Fordyce (1988) (see also Swanbrow, 1989) has developed a practical program for applying what is known about happiness in everyday life. And Larsen (2000a; Larsen & Prizmic, 2004) proposes a collection of strategies for coping and improving one's emotional life. Most psychologists believe that happiness is something that people must work at (Csikszentmihalyi, 1999, 2000). The following is a summary of much of the advice given by these psychologists:**

1. *Spend time with other people, particularly friends, family, and loved ones.* **The one characteristic common to most happy people is a disposition to be sociable, to draw satisfaction from being with other people. Cultivate an interest in other people. Go out of your way to spend time with friends and loved ones. Try to get to know those around you.**
2. *Seek challenge and meaning in work.* **If satisfying relationships are the first priority, the second is having work that you find enjoyable. Happy people enjoy their work and work hard at what they do. If you do not find your current work (or university major) rewarding, then consider switching to something that you find more worthwhile. Work that is challenging, but within your skill level, is usually the most satisfying.**
3. *Look for ways to be helpful to others.* **Helping others can make you feel good about yourself and give you the feeling that your life is meaningful. Helping others thereby provides a boost in self-esteem. Helping has a second benefit as well; helping someone else can take your mind off your own problems or can make your problems seem little by comparison. There are plenty of worthy causes and plenty of organizations that welcome volunteers.**
4. *Take time out for yourself; enjoy the activities that give you pleasure.* **Don't wait to find time for your favourite hobby or activity. Instead, make time. Many people learn to keep a calendar while in university to schedule work and other obligations. Use it to schedule fun things as well. Set aside time to read a book, take in a movie, exercise regularly, or do whatever else you enjoy. Think about what gives you pleasure, and build time into your busy schedule for those activities.**
5. *Stay in shape.* **Exercise is positively associated with emotional well-being. Exercise need not be intense or all that frequent to provide the emotional benefit. Playing team sports, dancing, biking, swimming, gardening, or even walking, if done at a brisk pace, is about all it takes. It doesn't seem to matter what the activity is, as long as you move around enough to keep in shape.**

6. *Have a plan, but be open to new experiences.* Having an organized life allows a person to accomplish much. However, sometimes the most fun moments in life are unplanned. Be open to trying different things or having different experiences—try going somewhere you have never been, try doing a routine activity a little differently, or try doing something on the spur of the moment. Be flexible, rather than rigid, and try to avoid getting stuck in any ruts.

7. *Be optimistic.* Put on a smiling face, whistle a happy tune, look for the silver lining in every cloud. Sure, it sounds too good to be true, but acting happy and trying to look on the bright side of things can go a long way toward making you feel happy. Try to avoid negative thinking. Don't make pessimistic statements, even to yourself. Convince yourself that the cup *really is* half full.

8. *Don't let things get blown out of proportion.* Sometimes when something bad happens, it seems like the end of the world. Happy people have the ability to step back and see things in perspective. Happy people think about their options and about the other things in their lives that *are* going well. They think about what they can do to work on their problems or what to avoid in the future. But they *don't* think it is the end of the world. Often asking yourself "What's the worst that can come of this?" will help put things in perspective.

Just wishing for happiness is not likely to make it so. Psychologists agree that people have to work at being happy; they have to work at overcoming the unpleasant events of life, the losses and failures that happen to everyone. The strategies in the previous list can be thought of as a personal program for working on happiness.

Unpleasant Emotions

Unlike pleasant emotions, the unpleasant emotions come in several distinct varieties. We discuss three important unpleasant emotions that are viewed by psychologists as having dispositional characteristics: anxiety, depression, and anger.

Trait Anxiety and Neuroticism Recall that people who exhibit the trait of neuroticism are vulnerable to negative emotions. As discussed in Chapter 3, **neuroticism** is one of the Big Five dimensions of personality, and it is present, in some form, in every major trait theory of personality.

Different researchers have used different terms for neuroticism, such as emotional instability, anxiety-proneness, and negative affectivity (Watson & Clark, 1984). Adjectives useful for describing people high on the trait of neuroticism include moody, touchy, irritable, anxious, unstable, pessimistic, and complaining. Hans Eysenck (1967, 1990; Eysenck & Eysenck, 1985) suggested that individuals high on the neuroticism dimension tend to overreact to unpleasant events, such as frustrations or problems, and that they take longer to return to a normal state after being upset. They are easily irritated, worry about many things, and seem to be constantly complaining. You may have heard the phrase "She is not happy unless she has something to worry about." Well, it is unlikely that worrying

People high on the personality trait of neuroticism tend to worry frequently. They may worry about their health, their social interactions, their work, their future, or just about anything. Worrying and complaining takes up a great proportion of their time.
©Shutterstock/tab62

actually makes a person happy. But the fact that some people worry almost all the time might suggest that worrying fulfills a need for them. Some people worry about their health ("Is this nagging cough really a sign that I have lung cancer? Could this headache really be a brain tumour?"). Others worry about their social relations ("When that person smiled at me, was it really a smirk?"). And still others worry about their work ("Why can't I seem to get as much work done as my friends do?").

In addition to worry and anxiety, the person high on the neuroticism dimension frequently experiences episodes of irritation. An interesting way to illustrate this is to ask people to list all the things that have irritated them in the past week. Perhaps seeing someone spit in public is irritating to many people. Or seeing someone with a pierced nose and eyebrows might be mentioned as irritating. Or seeing a couple kissing in public might be mentioned. If people were to write down all the things that irritated them, you would find that people high on neuroticism would have much longer lists than people low on neuroticism. Individuals high on neuroticism are frequently annoyed, even by the smallest transgressions ("I went to the store and someone was parked in the fire lane. That really irritates me. Then my mathematics professor wore the same suit and tie for two days in a row. What a jerk; he can't even change his tie each class."). The person high on neuroticism is a complainer, and others quickly learn that such a person will complain about practically anything—"That person driving in front of us changed lanes without using his turn signal; what a complete idiot!"

Eysenck's biological theory As briefly discussed in Chapter 3, Eysenck (1967, 1990) argues that neuroticism has a biological basis. In his theory of personality, neuroticism is due primarily to a tendency of the **limbic system** in the brain to become easily activated. The limbic system is the part of the brain responsible for emotion and the fight-or-flight reaction. If someone has a limbic system that is easily activated, then that person probably has frequent episodes of emotion, particularly emotions associated with flight (such as anxiety, fear, and worry) and with fight (such as anger, irritation, and annoyance). High-neuroticism people are anxious, irritated, and easily upset, so the theory goes, because their limbic systems are more easily aroused to produce such emotions. They are also prone to get irritated easily, sometimes to the point of anger.

Because the limbic system is located deep within the brain, its activity is not easily measured by EEG electrodes, which are placed on the surface of the scalp. Newer brain imaging technologies, such as MRI or PET, are allowing personality researchers to test this theory directly (DeYoung, 2010). Nevertheless, Eysenck (1990) has made several logical arguments in favour of a biological basis for neuroticism. First, many studies have shown a remarkable level of stability in neuroticism. For example, Conley (1984a, 1984b, 1985) found that neuroticism showed a high test-retest correlation after a period of 45 years. Although this does not prove a biological basis for neuroticism, stability is nevertheless consistent with a biological explanation. A second argument is that neuroticism is a major dimension of personality that is found in many different kinds of data sets (e.g., self-report, peer report) in many different cultures and environments by many different investigators. Again, although this ubiquity does not prove a biological basis, the fact that neuroticism is so widely found across cultures and data sources is consistent with a biological explanation. And a third argument in favour of a biological explanation is that many genetic studies find that neuroticism shows one of the higher heritability values. Trait negative affect shows relatively high levels of heritability, whereas trait positive affect shows a significant shared environment component (Goldsmith, Aksan, & Essex, 2001). That is, a predisposition to be neurotic appears to be somewhat inherited. Most behaviour geneticists believe that what is heritable in the heritability of emotion traits is individual differences in neurotransmitter function, such as in dopamine transport or serotonin reuptake (Canli, 2008).

Other biologically based research on emotion traits examines which areas of the brain are active when processing emotion information, such as looking at sad pictures or thinking about something that makes one anxious or angry (Sutton, 2002). Most of the studies reveal that emotion is associated with an increased activation of the anterior cingulate cortex (Bush, Luu, & Posner, 2000; Whalen, Bush, & McNally, 1998). The **anterior cingulate** is located deep inside and toward the centre of the brain, and it most likely evolved early in the evolution of the nervous system. DeYoung and colleagues (2010) measured the volume of brain tissue in different regions of the brain. Neuroticism was correlated with the volume of brain regions associated with the evaluation of threat and punishment and the production of negative emotions.

Other researchers have focused on the biological basis of the self-regulation of negative emotions. For example, Levesque, Fanny, and Joanette (2003) had subjects watch a sad film. Half of them were told to do whatever they could to stop or prevent the sad feelings and to not show any emotional reactions during the film. Subjects who were successful at this exhibited increased activity in the right ventral medial **prefrontal cortex**, part of the so-called executive control centre of the brain. Other studies also have identified this area as highly active in the control of emotion (Beauregard, Levesque, & Bourgouin, 2001). When specifically told to try to dampen their emotional responses to unpleasant images, the amount of activity in the prefrontal area correlated positively with neuroticism. This suggests that the high neuroticism individuals were putting in extra effort to regulate their negative emotions (Harenski, Kim, & Hamann, 2009).

Cognitive theories Another way to look at neuroticism is as a cognitive phenomenon. Some personality psychologists have argued that the cause of neuroticism lies not so much in the biology of the limbic brain but in the psychology of the person's overall cognitive system. These theorists have argued that neuroticism is caused by certain styles of information processing (such as attending, thinking, and remembering). Lishman (1972), for example, found that high-N (neuroticism) subjects were more likely to recall unpleasant information than were low-N subjects. There was no relation between neuroticism and the recall of pleasant information. After studying lists of pleasant and unpleasant words, high-N subjects also recalled the unpleasant words *faster* than the pleasant words. Martin, Ward, and Clark (1983) had subjects study information about themselves and about others. When asked to recall that information, the high-N subjects recalled more negative information about themselves but did not recall more negative information about others. There appear to be very specific information-processing characteristics associated with neuroticism: it appears to relate to the preferential processing of negative (but not positive) information about the self (but not about others). Martin and colleagues (1983) state that "high-N scorers recall more self-negative words than low-N scorers because memory traces for self-negative words are stronger in the high-N scorers" (p. 500).

As a related explanation for the relation between neuroticism and selective memory for unpleasant information, researchers use a version of the spreading activation concept, which was discussed in Chapter 10. Recall that this notion suggests that material is stored in memory by being linked with other, similar pieces of material. Many psychologists hold that emotional experiences are also stored in memory. Moreover, some individuals—those high in neuroticism—have richer networks of association surrounding memories of negative emotion. Consequently, for them, unpleasant material is more accessible, leading them to have higher rates of recall for unpleasant information.

One type of unpleasant information in memory concerns memory for illnesses, injuries, and physical symptoms. If high-N subjects have a richer network of associations surrounding unpleasant information in memories, then they are also likely to recall more instances of illness and bodily complaints. Try asking a high-N person the following question: "So, what's your health been like the past few months?" Be prepared for a long answer, with a litany of complaints and many details about specific symptoms. Study after study has established a link between neuroticism and self-reported health complaints. For example, Smith and colleagues (1989) asked subjects to recall whether they had experienced each of 90 symptoms within the past three weeks. Neuroticism correlated with the self-reported frequencies of symptoms, usually in the range of $r = .4$ to .5. This means that roughly 15 to 25 percent of the variation in health symptoms could be attributed to the personality variable of neuroticism.

Larsen (1992) examined the sources of bias in neurotics' reports of physical illnesses. He asked participants to report every day on whether they experienced any physical symptoms, such as a runny nose, cough, sore throat, backache, stomachache, sore muscles, headache, loss of appetite, and so on. The participants made daily reports for two months, providing the researcher with a day-by-day running report of physical symptoms. After the daily report phase was complete, Larsen then asked the participants to recall, as accurately as they could, how many times they reported each symptom during the two months of daily reporting. This unusual research design allowed the researcher to calculate the subjects' "true" total number of symptoms, as reported on a daily basis, as well as their remembered number of symptoms. It turned out that both of these scores were related to neuroticism. That is, the high-N participants reported more daily symptoms, *and* they recalled more symptoms, than did the stable low-N subjects. Moreover, even when controlling for the number of day-to-day symptoms reported, neuroticism was *still* related to elevated levels of recalled symptoms.

High-neuroticism people recall and report more symptoms, but are they more likely than stable low-N individuals to actually *have* more physical illnesses? This is a tricky question to address, as even medical doctors rely on a person's self-reports of symptoms to establish the presence of physical disease. The answer is to look at objective indicators of illness and disease and to see if those are related to neuroticism. Major disease categories, such as coronary disease, cancer, or premature death, appear to have little, if any, relation to neuroticism (Watson & Pennebaker, 1989). Costa and McCrae (1985) reviewed this literature and concluded that "neuroticism influences perceptions of health, but not health itself" (p. 24). Similar conclusions were reached by Holroyd and Coyne (1987), who wrote that neuroticism reflects "a biased style of perceiving physiological experiences" (p. 372).

Research on the immune system, however, is showing that neuroticism does appear to be related to diminished immune function during stress (Herbert & Cohen, 1993). In a fascinating study by Marsland and colleagues (2001), subjects underwent vaccination for hepatitis B, and their antibody response to the injection was measured (this is a measure of how well the immune system responds to antigens in a vaccine). It was found that the subjects low in neuroticism mounted and maintained the strongest immune response to the vaccine. This finding suggests that people high in neuroticism may, in fact, be more susceptible to immune-mediated diseases.

The immune system plays a role in many diseases, suggesting that neuroticism may affect health through compromising the body's ability to fight off foreign cells. In a study of neuroticism and lung cancer, Augustine and colleagues (2008) found that age of onset of lung cancer was negatively related to neuroticism. This finding held even after statistically controlling for the age of subjects when they started smoking and the number of cigarettes smoked per day prior to contracting lung cancer. Smoking history and amount smoked were strongly related to earlier onset of lung cancer, but neuroticism was an additional risk factor for earlier onset of this disease. Examining differences between persons one standard deviation above and below the mean on neuroticism showed that the high-N subjects contracted lung cancer an average of 4.33 years earlier than the low-N subjects. The authors speculate that neuroticism is related to the speed of cancer progression due to its impact on the immune system. The chronic stress associated with neuroticism can lead to depletion of the immune system (Irwin, 2002), which in turn can make a person less able to fight off the progression of cancer.

Psychologists have proposed a theory that high-neuroticism subjects pay more attention to threats and unpleasant information in their environment (e.g., Dalgleish, 1995; Matthews, 2000; Matthews, Derryberry, & Siegle,

2000). High-N subjects are thought to have a stronger behavioural inhibition system, compared to low-N individuals, making them particularly vulnerable to cues of punishment and frustration and prompting them to be vigilant for signs of threat. These researchers argue that high-N subjects are on the lookout for threatening information in their environment, constantly scanning for anything that might be menacing, unsafe, or negative.

Researchers have incorporated a version of the Stroop effect into investigations of attentional bias and neuroticism. The Stroop effect (Stroop, 1935) describes the increased time it takes to name the colour in which a word is written when that word names a different colour, relative to when it is a matching colour word or a patch of colour. For example, if the word *blue* is written in red ink, then it takes longer to name the colour of the ink (red) than it would take if the word *red* were written in red ink. Researchers agree that the relevant dimension (colour of ink) and the irrelevant dimension (name of the word) produce a conflict within the attentional system. If a person's attentional system can efficiently suppress the irrelevant dimension (the word), then they should be faster in naming the colour than someone who cannot suppress the word information.

The Stroop task has been modified to study individual differences in attention to emotion words. In the so-called emotion Stroop task, the content of the words is typically anxiety- or threat-related, such as *fear, disease, cancer, death, failure, grief,* or *pathetic* (Larsen, Mercer, & Balota, 2006). The words are written in coloured ink, and the subject is asked to name the colour of the ink and ignore the content of the words. Emotional interference is assumed when the time it takes to name the colours of the threat words is longer than the time it takes to name the colours of neutral words (Algom, Chajut, & Lev, 2004). Applied to neuroticism, the idea is that high-N people have an attentional bias such that certain stimuli (the threat words) are more salient, or attention-grabbing. The threat words should be more difficult for them to ignore when naming the colour. Therefore, neuroticism should correlate with response time to name the colours when the words refer to threat (e.g., *disease, failure*).

A thorough review of this literature was published by Williams, Mathews, and MacLeod (1996). These researchers reviewed more than 50 experiments that used a version of the emotion Stroop task. Many of the studies show that high-N groups (or participants with anxiety disorder) are often slower to name colours of anxiety- and threat-related words, compared with the colour naming of control, nonemotion words. The explanation given for this effect is that the emotion words capture the attention of the high-N participants, but not of the low-N participants.

In summary, neuroticism is a trait that relates to a variety of negative emotions, including anxiety, fear, worry, annoyance, irritation, and distress. Those high in neuroticism are unstable in their moods, are easily upset, and take longer to recover after being upset. There are both biological and cognitive theories about the causes of negative emotions in neuroticism, and each has some supportive evidence in the scientific literature. One particularly well-known finding concerns the tendency of people high in neuroticism to complain of health problems. In addition, high-N individuals are thought to be on the lookout for threatening information; they pay more attention to negative cues and events in life, however minor, compared with more emotionally stable individuals.

Depression and Melancholia **Depression** is another traitlike dimension. In this chapter, we cover only a small part of what is known about depression. There is a huge body of literature on the topic of depression, as is befitting a psychological disorder that is estimated to strike 8 percent of the people in Canada at some time in their lives (Canadian Mental Health Association, 2016). There are entire books on depression, graduate courses devoted to this topic, and clinicians who specialize primarily in the treatment of depression. There are thought to be many varieties of depression (e.g., Rusting & Larsen, 1998a), and researchers are attempting to categorize the kinds of depression and are looking for ways to help people who suffer from the debilitating effects of depression. See Table 13.4 for the symptom criteria of Major Depressive Disorder, a depressive condition described in the *Diagnostic and Statistical Manual of Mental Disorders,* 5th edition (DSM-5; American Psychiatric Association, 2013). In lower intensity and/or lower frequency, these symptoms also describe important aspects of everyday, subclinical experiences of depression.

Table 13.4   Major Depressive Disorder

Diagnostic Criteria

A. Five (or more) of the following symptoms have been present during the same 2-week period and represent a change from previous functioning; at least one of the symptoms is either (1) depressed mood or (2) loss of interest or pleasure.

Note: Do not include symptoms that are clearly attributable to another medical condition.

   1. Depressed mood most of the day, nearly every day, as indicated by either subjective report (e.g., feels sad, empty, hopeless) or observation made by others (e.g., appears tearful). (**Note:** In children and adolescents, can be irritable mood.)

   2. Markedly diminished interest or pleasure in all, or almost all, activities most of the day, nearly every day (as indicated by either subjective account or observation).

   3. Significant weight loss when not dieting or weight gain (e.g., a change of more than 5% of body weight in a month), or decrease or increase in appetite nearly every day. (**Note:** In children, consider failure to make expected weight gain.)

   4. Insomnia or hypersomnia nearly every day.

   5. Psychomotor agitation or retardation nearly every day (observable by others, not merely subjective feelings of restlessness or being slowed down).

   6. Fatigue or loss of energy nearly every day.

   7. Feelings of worthlessness or excessive or inappropriate guilt (which may be delusional) nearly every day (not merely self-reproach or guilt about being sick).

   8. Diminished ability to think or concentrate, or indecisiveness, nearly every day (either by subjective account or as observed by others).

   9. Recurrent thoughts of death (not just fear of dying), recurrent suicidal ideation without a specific plan, or a suicide attempt or a specific plan for committing suicide.

B. The symptoms cause clinically significant distress or impairment in social, occupational, or other important areas of functioning.

C. The episode is not attributable to the physiological effects of a substance or to another medical condition.

Source: Reprinted with permission from the *Diagnostic and Statistical Manual of Mental Disorders, Fifth Edition,* (Copyright ©2013). American Psychiatric Association. All Rights Reserved.

Diathesis-stress model One way to view depression is through a **diathesis-stress model**. This model suggests that there is a preexisting vulnerability, or diathesis, that is present among people who later become depressed. In addition to this vulnerability, a stressful life event must occur in order to trigger the depression, such as the loss of a loved one, a career failure, or another major negative life event. Neither element alone—the diathesis or the stress—is sufficient to trigger depression. Rather, they must occur together—something bad or stressful must happen to a person who has a vulnerability to depression.

Beck's cognitive theory Many researchers have emphasized certain cognitive styles as one type of preexisting condition that makes people vulnerable to depression (Larsen & Cowan, 1988). One of these researchers is Aaron Beck (1976), who has written extensively on his cognitive theory of depression. He suggests that the vulnerability lies in a particular cognitive schema, or mental framework for interacting with the world, as mentioned in Chapter 12. The cognitive schema involved in depression, according to Beck, distorts the incoming information in a negative way, a way that makes the person depressed.

According to Beck, three important areas of life are most influenced by the depressive cognitive schema. This **cognitive triad** includes information about the self, the world, and the future. Information about these important aspects of life is distorted in specific ways by the depressive cognitive schema. For example, after doing poorly on a practice exam, a depressive person might say to himself, "I am a total failure." This is an example of the *overgeneralizing* distortion applied to the self. Overgeneralizing is taking one instance and generalizing to many or all other instances. The lay term for this is "blowing things out of proportion." The person might have failed at one exam, but that does not mean he is a total failure. The same overgeneralizing style can be applied to the world ("If anything can go wrong, it will") and the future ("Why bother trying, when everything I do is doomed to fail?"). In Beck's (1976) theory, there are many other cognitive distortions, such as making *arbitrary inferences* (jumping to a negative conclusion, even when the evidence does not support it), *personalizing* (assuming that everything is your fault), and *catastrophizing* (thinking that the worst will always happen). These cognitive elements are portrayed in Figure 13.4.

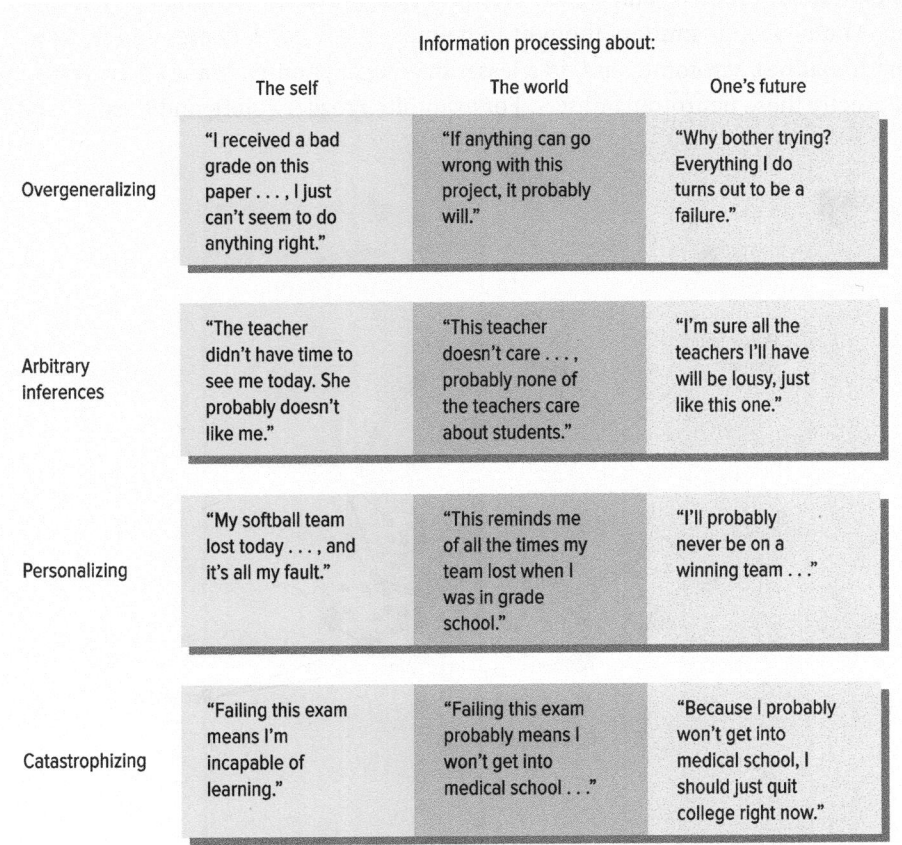

FIGURE 13.4 Beck's cognitive model of depression, showing how distortions are applied to processing information about the self, the world, and one's future. These cognitive distortions promote depression.

According to Beck's influential theory (1976), depression is the result of applying these cognitive distortions to the information from daily life. These distortions are applied quickly and outside of immediate awareness, resulting in a stream of automatic negative thoughts, which deeply affect how the person feels and acts ("I'm no good. The world is against me. My future is bleak."). The person who thinks they are a total failure will often act like a total failure and may even give up trying to do better, creating a **self-fulfilling prophecy**. Moreover, depressive feelings lead to more distortions, which in turn lead to more bad feelings, and so on, in a self-perpetuating cycle. Beck devised a form of therapy for changing people's cognitive distortions. In a nutshell, this involves challenging the person's distortions, such as by asking, "Does it really mean that you are a *total failure* because you flunked just this one exam?"

Biology of Depression Nerve cells in the brain communicate with each other by way of chemical messengers called neurotransmitters (Chapter 6). These neurotransmitters are broken down and delivered from one neuron across a gap—called the synapse—to another neuron (Figure 13.5). The first neuron is called the presynaptic neuron, and the second neuron is called the postsynaptic neuron. If the neurotransmitter reaches the postsynaptic neuron in sufficient strength, the nerve signal continues on its way toward completing the action for which it is intended; for instance, changing the channel on the remote, reading another sentence in a book, casting a flirting glance at someone you like. When someone is depressed, it is thought that there are imbalances in the levels of neurotransmitters in the brain. Depressed individuals often describe feeling slowed down, as if they don't have energy to do what they want to do. The **neurotransmitter theory of depression** holds that this emotional problem may be the result of neurotransmitter imbalance at the synapses of the nervous system. The neurotransmitters thought to be most involved in depression include norepinephrine (also called noradrenaline), serotonin, and, to a lesser degree, dopamine. Many of the drugs used to treat depression target exactly these neurotransmitters. For example, Prozac, Zoloft, and Paxil inhibit the reuptake of

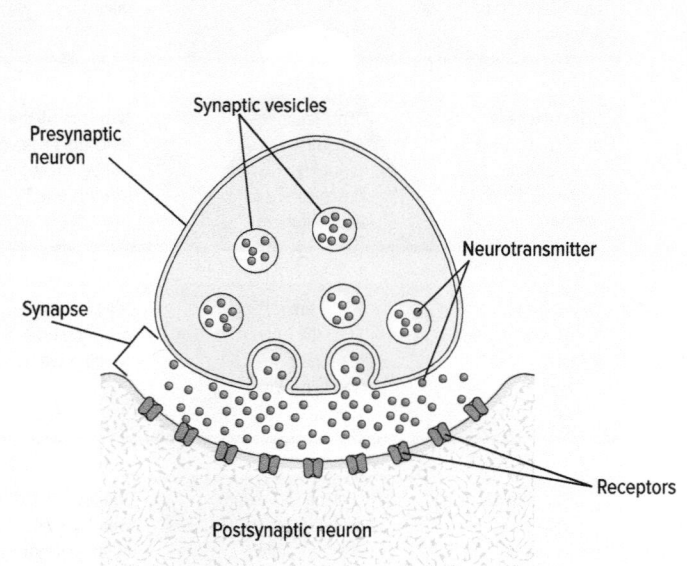

FIGURE 13.5 Diagram of synapse between two neurons illustrating how neurotransmitters must be released, cross the synapse, and bond with the receptors on the postsynaptic neuron in order for a nerve impulse to pass on its way to completion.

serotonin in the synapse, resulting in increased levels of this neurotransmitter in the nervous system. The medication Tofranil works to maintain a better balance between levels of both serotonin and norepinephrine. Not all people with depression are successfully treated with these kinds of medications, suggesting that there may be varieties of depression, some more biologically based, others more reactive to stress or cognitively based. Recent studies suggest that exercise might be usefully applied to the treatment of depression, at least for some people (Dubbert, 2002). The use of exercise in counselling people with depression is described by Dixon, Mauzey, and Hall (2003).

Anger Proneness and Potential for Hostility Another important negative emotion is anger and feelings of hostility. Psychologists have long been interested in what makes people hostile and aggressive. Social psychologists, for example, have examined conditions under which the average person will become aggressive (Baron, 1977). One finding is that most people are willing to strike out against someone who has treated them unfairly. Here the emphasis is on how certain situations, such as being treated unfairly, are likely to evoke aggression in *most* people. Personality psychologists agree that some circumstances tend to make most people angry, but their interest is more in terms of individual differences in anger proneness. They begin with the position that some people are characteristically more hostile than others in response to the same kinds of situations, such as frustration. **Hostility** is defined as a tendency to respond to everyday frustrations with anger and aggression, become irritable easily, feel frequent resentment, and act in a rude, critical, antagonistic, and uncooperative manner in everyday interactions (Dembrowski & Costa, 1987).

The scientific objectives, from the personality psychologist's perspective, are (1) to understand how hostile people became that way, what keeps them that way, and in what other ways they differ from nonhostile people and (2) to examine the consequences of hostility in terms of important life outcomes.

One consequence of hostility is its relation to coronary heart disease. We cover this topic in more detail in Chapter 18 on Type A behaviour and health. It turns out that chronic hostility is the component of the Type A behaviour pattern that most contributes to heart disease. Hostility as a personality trait can be measured with questionnaires that ask about the frequency and duration of anger episodes, whether anger is triggered by minor events (e.g., having to wait in line), or how easily one is bothered or irritated in everyday life (Siegel, 1986). For most people, even those high on the hostility dimension, the trait produces mostly feelings and urges that are uncomfortable and that create a negativistic and brooding outlook. For some these urges spill over into acts of aggression.

Anger is an emotion that causes some people to lose control. Most of the violent inmates in our prisons have trouble with the self-regulation of this potent emotion. Researchers have long speculated that there may be biological differences, particularly in brain function, between violent and nonviolent individuals. The psychologist Adrian Raine has spent many years examining some of the most violent and aggressive members of our society (e.g., Brennan & Raine, 1997; Raine, 2002). In one study of especially violent murderers, Raine, Meloy, and Bihrle (1998) found that these people showed decreased activity in the prefrontal areas of their brains, those areas mentioned earlier

Would a person with a long history of extreme violence be able to change completely into a gentle, loving father and pillar of his community?
©YAKOBCHUK VIACHESLAV/Shutterstock

that are associated with normal emotional regulation. Psychologist Jonathan Pincus has also specialized in the study of violent criminals. In a review of his work, Pincus (2001) presents information on the lives of numerous serial killers, and in virtually all cases these murderers suffered from some damage to their brains, either through violence, accidental injuries, or excessive drug or alcohol abuse. In addition, practically all of these murderers came from severely abusive families. Pincus presents data that the presence of brain damage in violent criminals is most often in the prefrontal areas. Again, these are the areas involved in self-control. Interestingly, this is the area that was severely damaged in the case of Phineas Gage, discussed in Chapter 6.

In large studies not every violent or sadistic person is found to have brain abnormalities. However, the rates of brain abnormalities are much higher in violent people than in those without a history of violence. For example, in a study of 62 criminals in Japan the researchers divided the inmates into those convicted of murder and those convicted of nonviolent offences. Brain abnormalities were much more frequent among the murderers than among the nonviolent offenders (Sakuta & Fukushima, 1998). In a study done in Austria, a group of high-violence offenders were compared with a group of low-violence offenders. In the high-violence group, 66 percent were found to have brain abnormalities, whereas in the low-violence group only 17 percent were found to have the same brain abnormalities (Aigner et al., 2000). In a study of sexual offenders, criminals were divided into those who physically harmed their victims (e.g., committed murder or sadistically violent acts) and those who did not physically harm their victims (e.g., exposed themselves). In the group of violent sex offenders, 41 percent were found to have brain abnormalities, a rate significantly higher than in the nonviolent sex offenders (Langevin et al., 1988). In a particularly strong longitudinal study, a group of 110 hyperactive and 76 normal boys had their brain activity assessed when they were between 6 and 12 years of age. They were followed up between the ages of 14 and 20 years, with special attention to arrest records. Those adolescent boys with a history of delinquency turned out to have had unusual brain patterns in childhood compared to those adolescents without subsequent delinquency (Satterfield & Schell, 1984).

More recent studies (e.g., Hawes et al., 2016) document the trajectory of having poor anger management in childhood leading to higher rates of violence and aggression in adulthood. Such findings highlight the importance of developing anger control strategies which, for most people, naturally develop in childhood. Could it be that the brain abnormalities often seen in violent adults involve those brain regions that are responsible for self-control and the management of emotions, especially anger?

The kind of brain damage most often observed in hostile aggressive individuals involves areas in the frontal lobe and, to a lesser extent, the temporal lobe. These areas are important in regulating impulses, particularly aggressive impulses, and fear conditioning. The damage may be developmentally caused or caused by injury. For example, sniffing glue or inhaling butane gas, which can induce intoxication similar to alcohol, can cause the kind of brain damage that has been related to antisocial behaviour (Jung, Lee, & Cho, 2004). Another example is a case report where a man developed a cyst in his brain. Prior to this development he was not a violent person. However, after the cyst grew, and presumably caused damage to his brain, he strangled his wife to death after she scratched his face (Paradis et al., 1994). The kind of brain abnormalities found in violent people appears to involve decrements in the person's ability to inhibit or control aggressive impulses.

Style of Emotional Life

So far in this chapter, we have discussed people's emotional lives in terms of emotional content, or the various characteristic emotions that define how one person is different from others. Now we turn to a discussion of emotional style. As a quick distinction, we might say that content is the *what* of a person's emotional life, whereas style is the *how* of that emotional life.

Affect Intensity as an Emotional Style

When we think about how emotions are experienced, probably the major stylistic distinction is one of intensity. You know from experience with your own emotional reactions that emotions can vary greatly in terms of magnitude. Emotions can be weak and mild, or strong and almost uncontrollable. To characterize a person's emotional style, we must inquire about the typical intensity of their emotional experiences. For emotional intensity to be useful to personality theory, we must establish that it describes a stable characteristic useful for making distinctions among individuals.

Affect intensity can be defined by a description of people who are either high or low on this dimension. Larsen (2009) describes *high affect intensity* individuals as people who typically experience their emotions strongly and are emotionally reactive and variable. High affect intensity subjects typically go way up when they are feeling up and go way down when they are feeling down. They also alternate between these extremes more frequently and rapidly than do low affect intensity individuals. Low affect intensity individuals, on the other hand, typically experience their emotions only mildly and with only gradual fluctuations and minor reactions. Such individuals are stable and calm and usually do not suffer the troughs of negative emotions. But they also tend not to experience the peaks of enthusiasm, joy, and other strong positive emotions.

Note that these descriptions of high and low affect intensity individuals make use of the qualifying terms *typically* and *usually*. This is because certain life events can make even the lowest affect intensity person experience relatively strong emotions. For example, being accepted into one's first choice of schools can cause intense positive emotions in almost anyone. Similarly, the death of a loved pet can cause strong negative emotions in almost everyone. However, because such events are fairly rare, we want to know what people are usually or typically like: how they characteristically react to the normal sorts of everyday emotion-provoking events.

Figure 13.6 presents daily mood data for two subjects from a study by Larsen and Diener (1985). These subjects kept daily records of their moods for 84 consecutive days. Note that Subject A's emotions were fairly stable and did not depart too far from her baseline level of mood over the entire three-month reporting period. Actually, she had a bad week at the beginning of the semester, which is denoted by the several low points at the left side of the graph. Otherwise, things were pretty stable for this subject.

Subject B, on the other hand, exhibited extreme changes in mood over time. This subject was hardly ever near his baseline level of mood. Instead, Subject B appears to have experienced both strong positive and strong negative affect frequently and to alternate between these extremes frequently and rapidly. In other words, this high affect intensity person exhibited a good deal of variability in his daily moods, fluctuating back and forth between positive and negative affect from day to day. Interestingly, Subject B was in the student hospital three times that semester, once for an infection and twice for feeling run down.

Assessment of Affect Intensity and Mood Variability

In early studies of affect intensity (e.g., Diener, Larsen, et al., 1985), this characteristic of emotional life was assessed using a daily experiential sampling method. That is, data were gathered much like that presented in Figure 13.6, panels A and B. Researchers would then compute a total score for each subject to represent how intense or variable that person was over the time period.

This longitudinal method of measuring affect intensity is straightforward and face valid, and it represents the construct of affect intensity quite well. However, it takes several weeks or longer of daily mood reporting to

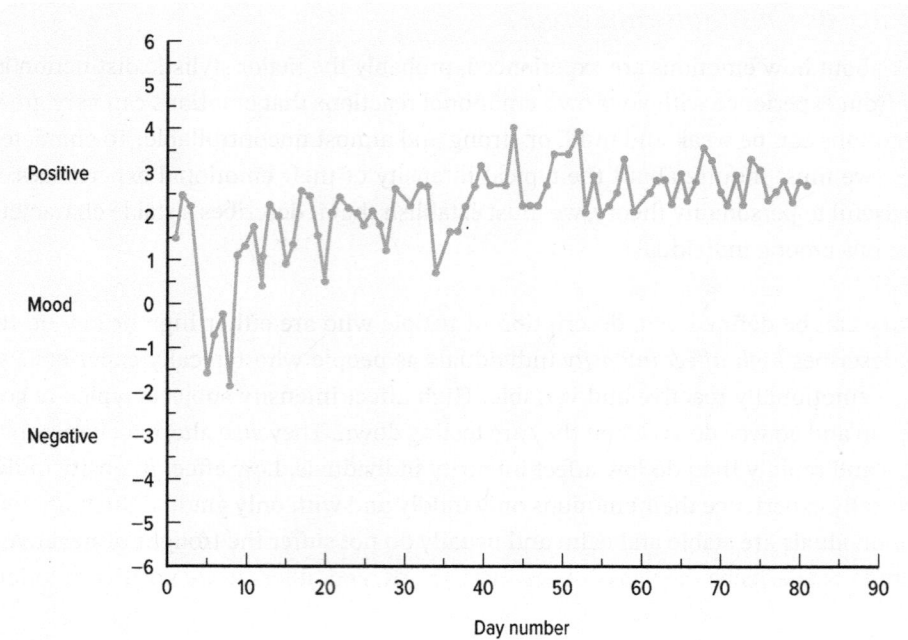

Panel A

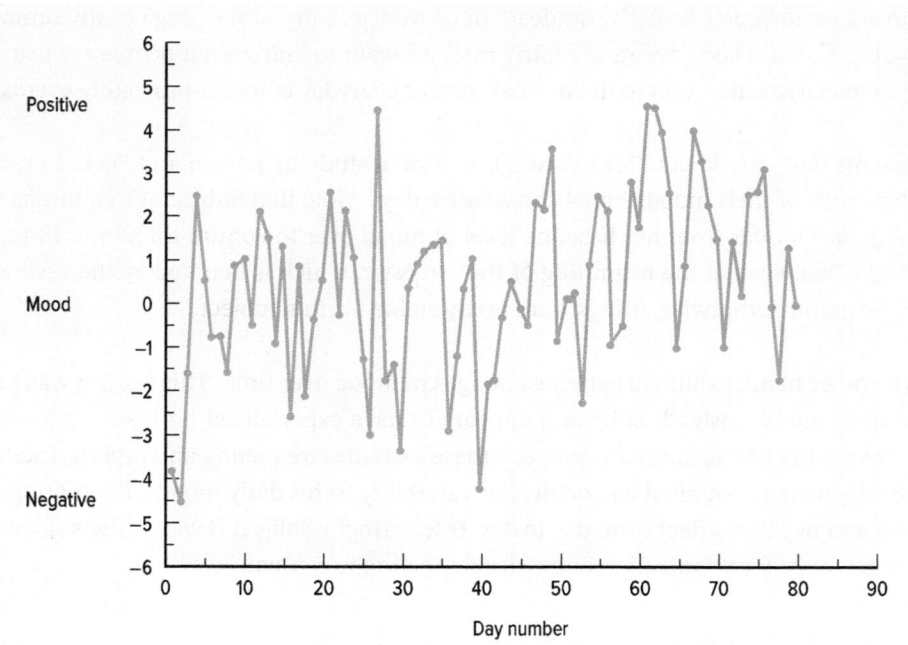

Panel B

FIGURE 13.6 Data from individual subjects who kept a mood diary every day for three consecutive months. Panel A: data from Subject A. Panel B: data from Subject B, who has much more intense moods and larger day-to-day mood swings than Subject A.

Source: Adapted from Larsen, 1991.

generate a reliable composite affect intensity score for each individual. Consequently, a questionnaire measure of affect intensity has been developed that allows a relatively quick assessment of a person's emotional style in terms of intensity. Table 13.5 lists 20 items from this questionnaire, called the Affect Intensity Measure (AIM) (Larsen & Diener, 1987).

Table 13.5 AIM Questionnaire

Instructions: The following statements refer to emotional reactions to typical life events. Please indicate how *you* react to these events by placing a number from the following scale in the blank space preceding each item. Please base your answers on how *you* react, *not* on how you think others react or how you think a person should react.

Never	Almost Never	Occasionally	Usually	Almost Always	Always
1	2	3	4	5	6

1. _____ When I accomplish something difficult, I feel delighted or elated.
2. _____ When I feel happy, it is a strong type of exuberance.
3. _____ I enjoy being with other people very much.
4. _____ I feel pretty bad when I tell a lie.
5. _____ When I solve a small personal problem, I feel euphoric.
6. _____ My emotions tend to be more intense than those of most people.
7. _____ My happy moods are so strong that I feel as if I were in heaven.
8. _____ I get overly enthusiastic.
9. _____ If I complete a task I thought was impossible, I am ecstatic.
10. _____ My heart races at the anticipation of an exciting event.
11. _____ Sad movies deeply touch me.
12. _____ When I'm happy, it's a feeling of being untroubled and content, rather than being zestful and aroused.
13. _____ When I talk in front of a group for the first time, my voice gets shaky and my heart races.
14. _____ When something good happens, I'm usually much more jubilant than others.
15. _____ My friends might say I'm emotional.
16. _____ The memories I like the most are of those times when I felt content and peaceful, rather than zestful and enthusiastic.
17. _____ The sight of someone who is hurt badly affects me strongly.
18. _____ When I'm feeling well, it's easy for me to go from being in a good mood to being really joyful.
19. _____ "Calm and cool" could easily describe me.
20. _____ When I'm happy, I feel as if I'm bursting with joy.

Copyright © 1984, Randy J. Larsen, Ph.D.

An important aspect of the affect intensity trait is that we cannot really say whether it is bad or good to be low or high on this trait. Both positive and negative consequences are related to scoring either high or low. High-scoring people, for example, get a lot of zest out of life, enjoying peaks of enthusiasm, joy, and positive emotional involvement. On the other hand, when things are not going well, high-scoring people are prone to strong negative emotional reactions, such as sadness, guilt, and anxiety. In addition, because high-scoring individuals have frequent experiences of extreme emotions (both positive and negative), they tend to suffer the physical consequences of this emotional involvement. Emotions activate the sympathetic nervous system, making the person aroused. Even strong *positive* emotions activate the sympathetic nervous system and produce wear and tear on the nervous system. High-scoring people tend to exhibit physical symptoms that result from their chronic emotional lifestyles, such as muscle tension, stomachaches, headaches, and fatigue. An interesting finding is that, even though they report more of these physical symptoms, high-scoring individuals are not particularly unhappy or upset by them (Larsen, Billings, & Cutler, 1996). Interviews with high-scoring people usually show that they have no desire to change their level of emotional intensity. They seem to prefer the emotional involvement, the ups and downs, and the physiological arousal that accompanies their highly emotional lifestyle (Larsen & Diener, 1987).

Low affect intensity individuals, on the other hand, are stable and do not typically get upset very easily. Even when negative events happen, they maintain an even emotional state and avoid the troughs of negative affect. The price such people pay for this emotional stability, however, is that they fail to experience their positive emotions very strongly. They lack the peaks of zest, enthusiasm, emotional engagement, and joy that energize the lives of high affect intensity individuals. Low affect intensity individuals, however, do not pay the price of the physical and psychosomatic symptoms that go along with the high affect intensity personality.

Research Findings on Affect Intensity

In a daily study of mood, Larsen, Diener, and Emmons (1986) had subjects record the events in their daily lives. Sixty-two subjects recorded the best and the worst events of the day for 56 consecutive days, resulting in almost 6,000 event descriptions. The subjects also rated these events each day in terms of how subjectively good or bad the events were for them. The same event descriptions were rated later by a team of raters for how objectively good or bad they would be for the average university student. Results showed that the subjects high on the affect intensity dimension rated their life events as significantly *more severe* than did the low affect intensity subjects. That is, events that were rated as only "moderately good" by the objective raters (such as receiving a compliment from a professor) were rated as "very good" by the high affect intensity subjects. Similarly, events that were rated as only "moderately bad" by the objective raters (such as losing a favourite pen) tended to be rated as "very bad" by the high affect intensity subjects. Thus, the high affect intensity subjects tended to evaluate the events in their lives—both good and bad events—as having significantly more emotional impact than did the low affect intensity subjects. High affect intensity individuals are thus more emotionally reactive to the emotion-provoking events in their lives, both the good and the bad events.

An aspect of these findings worth emphasizing is that high affect intensity individuals are more reactive to *both* positive and negative events in their lives. This may be due to the fact that affect intensity correlates positively with both extraversion and neuroticism. These aspects of affect intensity make high-scoring individuals look like neurotic extraverts; they respond with strong positive emotion to good events and with strong negative emotion to bad events. However, if we assume that good and bad events happen fairly randomly in life, then we should expect the daily emotions of high affect intensity individuals to go up and down randomly with those events. In other words, high affect intensity individuals should exhibit more **mood variability**, or more frequent fluctuations in their emotional lives over time. Larsen (1987) found that individuals high on the affect intensity dimension do, in fact, exhibit more frequent changes in their moods and that these changes tend to be larger in magnitude than are the mood changes of low affect intensity individuals.

The concept of affect intensity, containing as it does the notion of mood variability, is a general and broad characteristic of emotional life. Affect intensity has been found to relate to a variety of standard personality variables. For example, Larsen and Diener (1987) reported that affect intensity relates to the personality dimensions of high activity level, sociability, and arousability. High affect intensity individuals tend to have a vigourous and energetic lifestyle, tend to be outgoing and enjoy being with others, and tend to seek out stimulating and arousing things to do in their daily lives. During an interview, a high affect intensity subject reported that, to her, the worst thing in life was to be bored. She reported that she often did things to liven up her life, such as playing practical jokes on her roommates. Although such activities sometimes got her into trouble, she felt that it was worth it to obtain the stimulation. Another high affect intensity subject described himself as an "intensity junkie," hooked on the need for an emotionally stimulating lifestyle. A recent review of what is known about individual differences in affect intensity can be found in Larsen (2009).

Interaction of Content and Style in Emotional Life

People differ from each other in terms of the relative amounts of positive and negative emotional *content* in their lives over time, as well as in terms of the *stylistic* intensity of their emotional experiences. In trying to understand emotional life as an aspect of personality, it appears that the *hedonic balance*—the degree of pleasantness in a person's life over time—represents the content of emotional life. For example, Larsen (2000b) reported that the average university student had a positive hedonic balance on 7 out of 10 days. That is, out of every 10 days, 7 of them contained predominantly positive emotions, and 3 of them contained a predominance of negative emotions. However, there were wide individual differences, so that some people had as few as 20 percent positive days, whereas others had as many as 95 percent positive days. This hedonic balance between positive and negative affect, between the good and bad days in a person's life over time, best represents the content of emotional life (Zelenski & Larsen, 2000).

Affect intensity represents the style of emotional life and refers to the magnitude of a person's typical emotional reactions. Together, these two characteristics—content and style—provide a good deal of descriptive and explanatory power. An interesting aspect of these two dimensions is that hedonic balance and affect intensity are unrelated to each other (Larsen & Diener, 1985). This means that there are people who have frequent positive affect of low intensity and others who have frequent positive affect of high intensity. Similarly, there are people who have frequent negative affect of low intensity and others who have frequent negative affect of high intensity. In other words, hedonic balance interacts with affect intensity to produce specific types of emotional lives that may characterize different personalities. The effects of this interaction of hedonic balance and affect intensity in creating emotional life are illustrated in Figure 13.7.

In Figure 13.7, you can see that individuals high and low on the affect intensity dimension typically experience the content of their emotional lives in very different ways. A person low in affect intensity has an emotional life that is characterized by its enduringness, evenness, and lack of fluctuation. If such a person also happens to be a happy person (more positive than negative emotional content in life), then they experience this happiness as a tranquil sort of enduring contentment. If they happen to be an unhappy person (less positive than negative emotional content in life), then their emotional life consists of a chronic and somewhat annoying or irritating level of negative affect over time. On the other hand, a person high on the affect intensity dimension has an emotional life characterized by abruptness, changeableness, and volatility. If this kind of person also happens to be a happy person, then they experience this happiness as enlivened and animated spikes of enthusiasm and exhilaration. If this high affect intensity person is, instead, an unhappy person, then they experience troughs of a variety of negative emotions, such as anxiety, guilt, depression, and loneliness.

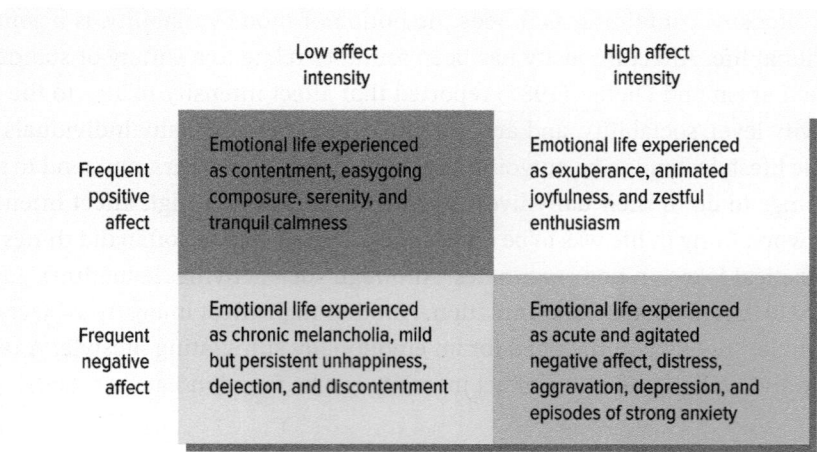

	Low affect intensity	High affect intensity
Frequent positive affect	Emotional life experienced as contentment, easygoing composure, serenity, and tranquil calmness	Emotional life experienced as exuberance, animated joyfulness, and zestful enthusiasm
Frequent negative affect	Emotional life experienced as chronic melancholia, mild but persistent unhappiness, dejection, and discontentment	Emotional life experienced as acute and agitated negative affect, distress, aggravation, depression, and episodes of strong anxiety

FIGURE 13.7 Quality of emotional life as a function of content (hedonic balance) and style (affect intensity).

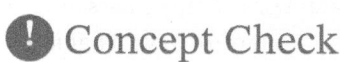 Concept Check

Aside from anxiety, what are two other common negative emotions that can come to define personality over time? Name and define the corresponding traits.

What does the "style" of emotional life refer to?

Summary and Evaluation

Emotions can be thought of either as states or as traits, and both of these are patterns of experience, physiological changes, and changes in behaviour, or action tendencies. Emotional states are short-lived and are typically caused by an event in the environment. As traits, however, emotions are consistent and stable patterns of experience in a person's life, where these patterns are due mostly to the person's personality. In this chapter, we looked at emotions as traits. For example, people differ from each other in how often they are angry, happy, or depressed. Such differences can be useful in describing aspects of personality.

Emotional content is the types of emotional experiences that a person is likely to have. If we know, for example, the typical content of a person's emotional life, then we know the kinds of emotions they are likely to experience over time.

Emotional content can be broadly divided into the pleasant and the unpleasant emotions. In the pleasant emotion category are happiness and the associated judgment of life satisfaction. On most people's lists of primary emotions, there is only one major pleasant emotion, whereas there are many varieties of unpleasant emotions. From a trait perspective, under pleasant emotions we discussed dispositional happiness. Some people are happier than others, and psychologists are developing theories and gathering data to understand why people differ on happiness and how people might increase their level of trait happiness.

Under the content approach to dispositional unpleasant emotions, we discussed three dispositions: anxiety, depression, and anger. Trait anxiety has many names in the personality literature, including neuroticism and negative affectivity. This trait emotion appears to have distinct cognitive components and is related to ongoing health, especially self-reported health. Depression is also defined as a syndrome of associated experiences and behaviours, and we examined several cognitive theories of depression. Anger proneness and hostility were also discussed as a trait affect, and we examined the health and well-being implications of this disposition. Anxiety, depression, and anger are currently topics of intense interest for neuroscientists, and data are accumulating on the brain centres involved in the experience, as well as the regulation, of each of these emotions.

Emotional style is the typical way in which a person experiences emotions. We focused on the stylistic component of affect intensity, or the typical magnitude with which people experience emotions. People who score high on the affect intensity dimension have larger emotional reactions to the events in their lives, are reactive to both pleasant and unpleasant events, and are more variable in their day-to-day moods. Content and style interact within individuals to produce distinct varieties of emotional lives.

 Concept Check

Define emotion. Considering this chapter in its entirety, briefly summarize the role of emotions in personality.

What are the main individual differences seen in the content and style of people's emotional experiences?

Key Terms

emotions	style	depression
action tendencies	happiness	diathesis-stress model
functional analysis	positive illusions	cognitive triad
emotional states	reciprocal causality	self-fulfilling prophecy
emotional traits	mood induction	neurotransmitter theory of depression
categorical approach	neuroticism	
dimensional approach	limbic system	hostility
valence	anterior cingulate	affect intensity
content	prefrontal cortex	mood variability

Approaches to the Self

The Cognitive/Experiential Domain

"Know thyself!" was the advice given by the Greek Oracle at Delphi. Do you know yourself? Who are you? How would you answer this question? Would you define yourself first as a student, as a son or daughter, or as someone's spouse or significant other? Or would you define yourself by listing your various characteristics: "I am smart, optimistic, and confident"? Or would you instead give a physical description, perhaps stating your sex, height, and hair colour? No matter how you respond to this question, your answer is an important part of your **self-concept**, your understanding of yourself and all of your qualities and characteristics. Moreover, some people are quite satisfied with who they are, whereas others are less satisfied with their self-concept. How you feel about who you are is your **self-esteem**. On top of this, you have a **social identity** as you present yourself to others. Sometimes social identity does not match self-concept, and the selves we present to others are not the selves we know ourselves to be, leading some of us to feel fake or inauthentic in our relationships.

In this chapter, we explore how psychologists have approached the notion of the self. We do this by considering the three main components of the self: self-concept, self-esteem, and social identity. At the most fundamental level, it is our capacity for **self-awareness** as human beings that creates the potential for the inner psychological experience of the self. We are self-conscious creatures, insomuch that we can think about ourselves and recognize ourselves as separate from other individuals and the world around us. William James, American psychologist and philosopher, distinguished between the "I" and the "me" in his theory of the self, noting that we can simultaneously think of ourselves as active observers and as objects of our observation. The "I" reflects our capacity for self-awareness, the ability to observe and evaluate ourselves. This gives rise to the "me," or what becomes our self-concept (Cooper, 1992).

There are many aspects to the self: the way we see and define our selves, or our self-concept; the evaluation we make of that self-concept, which is called self-esteem; and our social identities, which are the outward reflections we show other people.
©Jack Hollingsworth/Getty Images

Why might we want to learn about the self? To most people, their sense of self is their anchor, their starting point for interpreting everything around them. For example, when you look at a group photo on a friend's Facebook page, whom in the group do you look at first? If you are like most people, you will say that you look at yourself first. And when looking at the photo of yourself, you immediately engage in an evaluation. You might think the picture is not a good representation, that it does not show you in the best light. Maybe you think that you have a nicer smile than that and that you are, in fact, a happier person than this picture portrays. Or you might think that you have put on a few pounds lately, that you are heavier than your friends in the photo. Maybe you dislike the fact that you have gained weight, and a small blow to your self-esteem occurs when you look at the photo. Or maybe you wonder how certain other people would view this photo of you. Would your parents like to see you this way? For example, would they approve of the self you portray in this group photo of your friends?

Our sense of self is changing all the time. In infancy, we first distinguished ourselves from the world around us and began the lifelong process of constructing, evaluating, and presenting to others our sense of who we are. During this process, we constantly undergo challenges and changes to our self-concept. High school and college or university are years in which many people struggle with defining their self-concept, and it is a time when people are especially sensitive to events that challenge their sense of self. Once people have a fairly stable sense of who they are, they begin to use that sense of self to evaluate their experiences. Only events that are important to one's sense of self will have any strong impact either way, as very good or very bad. For example, if doing well in school is not part of your self-concept (maybe you are in university for other reasons), then doing poorly on an academic assignment will not affect you much.

People do not always like or value what they see when they turn inward and assess their self-concept. That liking or value is self-esteem. For example, two people may both tend to save money rather than spend it, to not leave tips at restaurants, and to always buy the cheapest things. The first person may view herself as frugal and conservative, and she evaluates these to be positive characteristics. She has positive self-esteem, at least as far as these attributes go. The second person may see himself as stingy, ungenerous, and without compassion.

He views these characteristics as negative. Consequently, he has low self-esteem, at least as far as these attributes go. Both have the same self-concept, of being thrifty and hoarding their money, but differ in how they evaluate those characteristics and hence in their self-esteem.

Finally, social identity is the self that is shown to other people. This is the relatively enduring part of ourselves that we use to create an impression, to let other people know who we are and what can be expected from us. For instance, your driver's licence, which is often used for social identification purposes, contains information about your social identity: your family name, your first name, your date of birth, your address, your physical description, such as height, weight, and eye colour. These characteristics differentiate you from other people and form some of the more visible and socially available aspects of your identity. Other, less available aspects of your social identity include how you like to be perceived by others and the impression that you want others to have of your personality. Maybe you are the kind of person who wants to be taken seriously, so it is important to you to have a very businesslike social identity. Maybe you are the kind of person who wants to be liked by most people, so you strive to have a social identity as a friendly and agreeable person.

The three main components of the self—self-concept, self-esteem, and social identity—are all vitally important in our day-to-day lives. Personality psychologists have studied these aspects of the self and have generated a good deal of knowledge about them. We begin this chapter with a focus on the descriptive component of the self—the self-concept.

Descriptive Component of the Self: Self-Concept

Knowledge of the self does not happen all at once. It develops over years, starting in infancy, accelerating in adolescence, and reaching completion in old age. Self-concept is the basis for self-understanding, and it forms the answer to the question "Who am I?"

Self-Concept Development

The first glimmer of a self-concept occurs in infancy, when the child learns that some things are always there (e.g., the physical body) and some things are there only sometimes (e.g., food or nourishment). The child makes a distinction between its own body and everything else: it discovers that boundaries exist between what is "me" and what is "not me." Gradually, the infant comes to realize that it is distinct from the rest of the world. This distinction forms the rudimentary sense of self, an awareness of one's body.

An important method for determining the development of self-awareness is *the mirror recognition test.* Psychologists have devised a clever technique for studying whether a human or other primate can recognize its own reflection in a mirror. They place a small mark on the face or head that cannot be seen without a mirror. Then, when faced with a mirror, they look to see if the child or primate uses the reflection to touch (or try to remove) the mark on its own face. Such behaviour suggests an understanding of one's own reflection.

Chimpanzees and orangutans exhibit self-recognition with mirrors at a relatively high frequency and typically find the mark after about two to three days with the mirror (Gallup, 1977a; Gallup et al., 2002). Studies of lower primates, such as the macaque monkey, have found that they do not exhibit spontaneous self-recognition with mirrors, even after 2,400 hours of exposure to a mirror (Gallup, 1977b); however, it seems that they can be *taught* to recognize their reflections, which may indicate a rudimentary capacity for self-awareness (Chang et al., 2017). Animals that have passed some form of the mirror test of self-recognition now include all of the great apes (bonobos, chimpanzees, gorillas, orangutans, and humans) (Gallup et al., 2002; Westergaard & Hyatt, 1994), Asian elephants (Plotnik et al., 2006), bottlenose dolphins (Marten & Psarakos, 1994), orcas (Delfour & Marten, 2001), and one species of magpie, a relative of the crow (Prior, Schwarz, & Güntürkün, 2008). Similar research with mirrors has even suggested that ants (Cammaerts & Cammaerts, 2015) and

Self-recognition in the mirror test is one criterion for determining whether a species has self-awareness.
©David Allan Brandt/Getty Images RF

cleaner wrasse fish (Kohda et al., 2019) may recognize their own reflections, though further research is needed to verify this.

In children, self-recognition with mirrors occurs on average at age 18 months (Lewis & Ramsay, 2004). There is, however, some variability in age of onset of self-recognition, with 15 months being the earliest documented case, and age 24 months being the point at which all or almost all children demonstrate self-recognition. Cultural variations in the mirror test have also been observed. A team of Canadian and American researchers, for instance, found that although samples of children from Western countries demonstrated spontaneous recognition of and orientation toward a mark placed on their foreheads, children from Kenya demonstrated a significant absence of response. When children from Fiji, Saint Lucia, Grenada, and Peru were also examined, they too demonstrated less frequent spontaneous self-recognition compared to Canadian and American children (Broesch et al., 2011). As the researchers suggest, the cross-cultural validity of the mirror test may be limited, as such findings do not indicate either a lack of self-concept or cognitive delays in non-Western children.

Interestingly, pretend play appears to require self-recognition (Lewis & Ramsay, 2004). A child pretending to feed a doll imaginary food or a child drinking an imaginary liquid from a cup must know that what they are doing is not real. Pretending behaviour requires that the child distinguish "this is what I pretend to be doing" from "this is what I actually am doing." In a study of children aged 15 to 21 months, only those children who exhibited self-recognition to a mirror were capable of pretend play (Lewis & Ramsay, 2004). Moreover, children do not begin using personal pronouns (I, me, mine) until they gain self-recognition abilities in the mirror test. Self-recognition is therefore an important developmental achievement that allows the child to go on to more complex manifestations of self-awareness, such as engaging in pretend play and representing the self in language with personal pronouns.

Although very young children can be fascinated with their reflections, it takes a while for children to be able to recognize themselves where they are included in photographs of a group. Children need to be about 2 years old before being able to pick themselves out of a photograph of a crowd (Baumeister, 1991). Around this time, the second year of life, children begin to grasp the idea that other people have expectations for them. For example, this is about the time when children can follow rules set up by parents. Children learn that some behaviours are good and other behaviours are bad, and they evaluate their own behaviour against these standards. They will smile when they do something good and frown when something bad occurs. They clearly are developing a sense of themselves relative to standards. This is the beginning of self-esteem.

Among the first aspects of the self that people learn to identify and associate with themselves are gender and age. This occurs between roughly 2 and 3 years of age, when children typically begin to call themselves "a boy" or "a girl" and to refer to other children as boys or girls. A rudimentary knowledge of age also develops, with a child often learning to hold up the number of fingers that designate age. Children at this age also expand their self-concept to include reference to a family. "I'm Sarah's brother," a child might say.

From age 3 to about 12, children's self-concepts are based mainly on developing talents and skills. Children think of themselves as being able to do this or unable do that, such as recite the alphabet, tie their own shoes, read, walk to school by themselves, or tell time. Starting with the school years, ages 5 or 6 onward, children increasingly begin to compare their skills and abilities with those of others. They are now either better than or worse than other children. This is the beginning of **social comparison,** which most people engage in to varying degrees for the rest of their lives (Baumeister, 1997). Social comparison is the evaluation of oneself or one's performance in terms of a comparison with a reference group. "Am I faster, smarter, more popular, more attractive, and so on than my friends?" is the question that children repeatedly ask themselves during this period of development.

Also during this time, children learn that they can lie and keep secrets. This is based on the realization that there is a hidden side to the self, a side that includes private attributes, such as thoughts, feelings, and desires. The realization that "Mommy doesn't know everything about me" is a big step. The development of an inner, **private self-concept** is a major but often difficult development in the growth of the self-concept. It may start out with children developing an imaginary friend, someone only they can see or hear. This imaginary friend may actually be the children's first attempt to communicate to their parents that they know there is a secret part, an inner part, to their understanding of the self. Later, children develop the full realization that only they have access to their own thoughts, feelings, and desires and that no one else can know this part of themselves unless they choose to tell others.

As children grow from childhood to adolescence, their self-concept changes from one based on such concrete characteristics as physical appearance and possessions to one that is based on more abstract psychological terms. In early adolescence, it becomes common to hear references to likes and dislikes, as well as more abstract personality and social characteristics (e.g., "I am a human being," "I try to be helpful"). By late adolescence, individuals tend to emphasize interpersonal characteristics, such as typical mood states, ideologies, and opinions and beliefs (e.g., "I am a moody person," "I am an atheist").

A final unfolding of the self-concept, occurring during adolescence, involves **perspective taking**: the ability to take the perspectives of others, or to see oneself as others do, to step outside of oneself and imagine how one appears to other people. This is why many teenagers go through a period of extreme self-consciousness during this time, focusing much of their energy on how they appear to others. You might vividly recall this period of your life, the strong emotions involved in episodes of **objective self-awareness**, of seeing yourself as an object of others' attention. Remember going to gym class in your funny gym uniform, or that first trip to the beach in your new swimsuit? Often, objective self-awareness is experienced as shyness, and for some people this is a chronic problem.

Because shyness is such a common challenge for people, especially during the adolescent years, we provide more information on this topic in A Closer Look: Shyness: When Objective Self-Awareness Becomes Chronic.

We will mention here that, because shy people are anxious over interacting with others, they often avoid opportunities to socialize. One way to avoid face-to-face interaction is to socialize online, where the interaction is more controllable, proceeds more slowly, and provides limited information exchange (e.g., no nonverbal information, etc.). Researchers have found that young adults with social anxiety (shyness) are more likely to use the Internet excessively (Weinstein et al., 2015) and in ways that are problematic (e.g., Carli & Durkee, 2016). Social anxiety among young adults has been further associated with excessive use of Facebook, to the point of interfering with school work (Lee-Won, Herzog, & Park, 2015), and excessive online gaming (Lee & Leeson, 2015). While there are certainly socially beneficial ways to use the Internet and social media, most of us have had the experience of being ignored by someone who is preoccupied with their smart phone.

In the development of the self, children learn to compare themselves to others. "I'm faster than you" is a phrase commonly heard whenever a group of young children gather. This is the beginning of social comparison, whereby people define and evaluate themselves in comparison to others.
©Getty Images/iStockphoto

Shy individuals are at risk of developing these preoccupations, presumably because it gives them a means to avoid direct socializing.

A Closer Look

Shyness: When Objective Self-Awareness Becomes Chronic

Many famous and accomplished people have described themselves as *shy*, including singers Barbra Streisand and Bob Dylan (Stocker, 1997). This may at first seem paradoxical. How could a person whose career is based on performance and fame be shy? But what shy people have in common is that they desire friendships and social interactions while simultaneously being held back by their insecurities and fears. Consequently, they typically avoid the spotlight, avoid face-to-face interaction, and ruminate excessively after conversations, worrying about whether they said the right things, made a good impression, or sounded stupid. The inner experience of a shy person in an interaction is quite different from that of someone else in the same interaction who is not shy.

Shy people are not necessarily introverts (Cheek, 1989; Cheek & Krasnoperova, 1999). Introverts prefer to be alone or in small groups; they are more likely to enjoy the peace and quiet of solitude. Shy people, on the other hand, want to have contact with others, to be socially involved, and to have friends and be part of the group. But self-doubt and self-consciousness associated with shyness prompt individuals to pass up opportunities to socialize (Henderson & Zimbardo, 2001a, 2001b; see www.shyness.com). They handicap themselves; by not entering groups, not speaking to unfamiliar people, and not approaching others, they deny themselves the opportunities to learn and practise the very social skills they need to overcome their shyness (see Table 14.1). It is this conflicted nature of shyness—desiring social interaction which is impaired due to the associated anxiety—that has led Robert Coplan and his colleagues at Carleton University to refer to it more precisely as *conflicted shyness*. Like others before him, Coplan has underscored the important distinction between conflicted shyness and *social disinterest*, a preference for social isolation that is not motivated by anxiety or fear (Coplan et al., 2004). Unlike shyness, the latter is unrelated to internalizing problems such as depression (Coplan, Ooi, & Nocita, 2015).

| | Table **14.1**   Example Items from the Henderson/Zimbardo Shyness Questionnaire | | | | |

Instructions: Rate each item using a number from the following scale to indicate how characteristic that statement is of you.

Not at all characteristic 1	Somewhat characteristic 2	Often characteristic 3	Very characteristic 4	Extremely characteristic 5

1. I am afraid of looking foolish in social situations.
2. I often feel insecure in social situations.
3. Other people appear to have more fun in social situations than I do.
4. If someone rejects me I assume that I have done something wrong.
5. It is hard for me to approach people who are having a conversation.
6. I feel lonely a good deal of the time.
7. I tend to be more critical of other people than I appear to be.
8. It is hard for me to say "no" to unreasonable requests.
9. I do more than my share on projects because I can't say no.
10. I find it easy to ask for what I want from other people.

Source: Adapted from "The Henderson Zimbardo Shyness Questionnaire: A New Scale to Measure Chronic Shyness," by L. Henderson and P. Zimbardo, 2000, The Shyness Institute, 644 Cragmont Ave., Berkeley, CA 94708. Copyright © 2000 by The Shyness Institute. All rights reserved. Reprinted with permission of The Shyness Institute.

Psychologist Jerome Kagan has been studying shyness for decades (Kagan, 1981, 1994, 1999). In his studies of infants, he found that about 20 percent of 4-month-old babies exhibit signs of shyness—they flail their arms and legs and cry when presented with an unfamiliar object or person. Following up these infants for several years, Kagan found that most of them exhibited signs of shyness as young children. For example, in play situations they often did not move very far from their parents, and some even clung to their parents, not leaving their sides at all when there were unfamiliar children around. Following them a few more years, Kagan found that roughly half of the shy children were transformed and were no longer shy in later childhood. In looking at parenting practices, Kagan found that the parents of these formerly shy children had encouraged their children to socialize, while the parents of the children who remained shy often had given in to the children's reluctance to join groups (Kagan, 1999). Other research has shown that parents who are too controlling and protective toward their children often have children who are shy and anxious (Wood et al., 2003). Regardless of causal underpinnings, Coplan's work with Canadian preschoolers suggests that parents can reliably differentiate between conflicted shyness and social disinterest. In other words, parents seem to be aware of the motivations behind their children's solitary behaviour (Coplan et al., 2004).

Psychologists studying shyness sometimes prefer the term *social anxiety*, which is defined as discomfort related to social interactions, or even to the anticipation of social interactions (Chavira, Stein, & Malcarne, 2002). Socially anxious people appear to be overly concerned about what others will think and describe feeling nervous or awkward when talking to new people. After a conversation, they often conclude that they said something wrong, sounded foolish, or looked stupid (Ritts & Patterson, 1996). Sometimes the social anxiety is so strong that it shows in various outward signs, such as a trembling voice or jittery movements. Shy people can be so overcome with anxiety that it hinders their ability to carry on a conversation. Other people interacting with a socially anxious person often interpret their behaviour as unfriendliness, rather than as shyness (Cheek & Buss, 1981).

Shy people also tend to interpret social interactions negatively; they are more likely to interpret a comment as a criticism than as a helpful suggestion. For example, DePaulo and colleagues (1987) had students work in groups, then write reports on each other's performance. They were then individually interviewed about what they thought the others had said about them. It turns out that the shy participants thought that the others liked them less and that the others thought they were less competent. It seems that shy people are not only reluctant to enter into social interaction but also expect that others will dislike them. These expectations may lead them to avoid interactions or cut conversations short, losing the very opportunities they need to overcome their shyness. According to Canadian researchers at the University of Windsor, however, shy people do not appear to hold unrealistically high standards for themselves, nor do they perceive others as expecting perfection from them (Jackson, Towson, & Narduzzi, 1997).

What makes shy people so socially anxious? Kagan believes that some of it is due to genetics. After all, it shows up in some infants very early in life. However, some of this social anxiety must also be learned. What most researchers believe is that shy people have learned to put too much stock in other people's judgments of them. This is called *evaluation apprehension*, the idea that shy people are apprehensive about being evaluated by others. For example, shy people believe that a person with whom they are talking will think they are dull, silly, or childish. They fear that others will evaluate them negatively. As a consequence, just the thought of going out on stage or leading a group meeting fills them with dread. And so they avoid such situations. When forced into interaction, they try to limit it or cut it short. They avoid eye contact, which indicates to others that they prefer to end the conversation. When forced into conversation, they try to keep it impersonal and nonthreatening. They do a lot of agreeing, nodding their heads, without getting too involved in the conversation. They try not to give too much in the way of opinions or personal information, which can be evaluated by others. In sum, researchers believe that at the root of shyness is a fear of being evaluated negatively by others (Leary & Kowalski, 1995), which translates into a lack of confidence in social interactions and feeling that they lack the social skills necessary to navigate social situations (Cheek & Melchior, 1990).

Psychologists studying the brain have suggested that shy individuals have a more reactive **amygdala**, which is a section of the limbic or emotional system of the brain that is most responsible for fear. A study by Kagan and colleagues followed up a group of adults who, at age 2 years, had been assessed for shyness. They found that the adults who were shy as children showed a greater fMRI response within the amygdala to novel versus familiar faces, compared to the nonshy adults (Schwartz et al., 2003). In another interesting study, researchers assessed cortisol (the stress hormone described in Chapter 6) on the first and fifth days of school among 35 students in Grade 1 (Bruce, Davis, & Gunnar, 2002). They found that most children showed an elevated cortisol response on the first day of school. However, the shy children showed an elevated and extended cortisol response even on the fifth day of school. There is also evidence that shy individuals are hypervigilant and more reactive to both social and nonsocial stimuli, especially that which is ambiguous or threatening. For example, Canadian researchers recently offered evidence suggesting that shy children, especially those high in conflicted shyness (high shyness, high sociability), displayed a hypervigilance and hypersensitivity for auditory stimuli in the environment as indicated by electrocortical activity (Tang, Santesso, Segalowitz, & Schmidt, 2016).

Stocker (1997) reviewed much of what is known about helping shy individuals overcome their difficulties. She offers seven concrete steps a shy person can take:

1. *Show up.* Shy people want to avoid the situations that make them anxious. However, if you want to overcome shyness, you've got to enter those uncomfortable situations.
2. *Give yourself credit.* Stop being your own worst critic. In scorning or deriding their own social performance after the fact, shy people are often very hard on themselves.

3. *Take baby steps.* It is useful to take big goals and break them into smaller steps. Instead of wanting to "become an engaging conversationalist," maybe try to set some smaller goals, like joining a group or social club.
4. *Give unto others.* Shy people, because they are nervous, are focused on themselves during conversations. Shift your attention to others; look at them when they talk, listen carefully to what they say, and ask them questions.
5. *Exude warmth.* The nervousness that shy people feel is often interpreted by others as unfriendliness or tension. Try to create a more positive nonverbal impression by smiling, making eye contact, and staying relaxed.
6. *Anticipate failure.* Overcoming shyness is a learning process. It will take practice, and small failures will happen.
7. *Join the crowd.* Nobody is perfect all the time. There are many people who are not perfect conversationalists. When you really listen to other people's small talk, you'll realize that it really is just that—small talk, nothing more.

In summary, self-concept is a distinct knowledge structure made up of many different elements and stored in our memories much as we might store a cognitive map of our hometown. Part of developing a sense of self lies in being able to see yourself through the eyes of others and, while this perspective can be a valuable skill to have, it can sometimes make a person feel uncomfortable and lead to shyness.

Self-Schemas: Possible Selves, Ought Selves, and Undesired Selves

So far, we have considered some of the main steps in the development of a self-concept. Once formed, self-concept provides a person with a sense of continuity and a framework for understanding the past and present, in addition to guiding future behaviour. In adults, self-concept is a structure made up of building blocks of knowledge about who one is, a multidimensional collection of knowledge about the self: "Am I a responsible person? How do I treat others? Do others consider me to be attractive? Am I athletic? Am I more or less assertive in social situations?"

Self-concept is like a network of information contained in one's memory, which organizes and provides coherence to the ways in which we experience the self (Markus, 1983). Self-concept also guides how people process information about themselves (Markus & Nurius, 1986). For example, people more easily process information that is consistent with their self-concept; if you see yourself as highly sociable, then you will quickly agree with statements such as the following: "I am outgoing" and "I am friendly."

The term **self-schema** refers to a specific knowledge structure, or cognitive representation, of self-concept. Self-schemas are the networks of associated building blocks of one's self-concept. For example, a person might have a schema about what it means to be warm and loving, and this schema might include such attributes as friendliness, tender-mindedness, and compassion. Someone with a warm and loving self-schema would then apply this to understanding their personal experiences, using it to make sense of the past and to organize current, personally relevant information. Such a self-schema would guide this person to pay attention to certain kinds of information, such as evidence that they are indeed friendly, kind, and compassionate. In conversations, for example, they might enjoy hearing others comment on their friendliness or saying something about their compassion. Self-schemas are cognitive structures that are built on past experiences and guide the processing of information about the self, particularly in social interaction.

Self-schemas usually refer to past and current aspects of the self. However, there are also schemas for future selves, which people are able to imagine. The term **possible selves** describes the many ideas people have about who they might become, who they hope to become, or who they fear they will become (Markus & Nurius, 1987). People often have specific desires, anxieties, fantasies, fears, hopes, and expectations about their own future selves. Although possible selves are not based on actual past experiences, they nevertheless are part of the overall self-concept. That is, possible selves are some of the building blocks of the general self-concept. For example, are you the kind of person who could envision yourself becoming a scientist—that is, is this a possible self for you? Buday, Stake, and Petersen (2012) showed that possessing such a possible self as a scientist in high school predicted whether the participants were actually in a science career 10 years later. Other researchers have shown that future career selves in college and university predicted proactive career behaviours (e.g., visiting the job centre on campus, signing up early for career fairs, and so forth (Strauss, Griffin, & Parker, 2012). One's future work self can be a strong motivating force for engaging in behaviours that prepare one for specific careers. Even older individuals who are retired can have possible selves, such as future images of themselves as healthier or slimmer (Bolkan, Hooker, & Coehlo, 2015).

Because they play a role in defining self-concept, possible selves may influence a person's behaviour in certain ways. For example, a high school student may have no idea what it would be like to be an astronaut. Nevertheless, because this is one of their possible selves, they have many thoughts and feelings about this image of being astronaut. Information about astronauts, the space agency, aviation science, and so forth has personal significance, and they seek it out at every opportunity. Thus this possible self will influence the person's here and now in terms of current decisions (e.g., to take an extra math course). Possible selves are like bridges between our present and our future: they provide a working model of the self at a later point (or points) in time (Oyserman & Markus, 1990). Such a working model can, however, lead to problem behaviours, as when the possible self is a poor role model. A study of Grade 8 students found that those who could imagine themselves as problem drinkers (i.e., had a "problem drinker" possible self) were more likely to have experienced problematic alcohol use as Grade 9 students (Lee et al., 2015).

Possible selves allow us to stay on schedule, and to work toward self-improvement. Behaviours that stem from possible selves (desired or undesired) can activate a host of intense feelings and emotions. For example, to a person who does not have a possible self with coronary artery disease, missing a few days of an exercise program will not be as distressing as it is to a person who has such a possible self.

Psychologist Tory Higgins (1987, 1997, 1999) has elaborated on the possible selves notion by distinguishing the **ideal self**, which is what individuals themselves want to be, from the **ought self**, which is their understanding of what others want them to be. The ought self is built on what people take as their responsibilities and commitments to others—what they ought to do. The ideal self is built on one's own desires and goals—what one wants to become. Higgins refers to the ought and the ideal selves as **self-guides**, standards that one uses to organize information and motivate appropriate behaviour. The self-guides get their motivating properties from emotions. Higgins argues that these two types of possible selves are at the root of different emotions. If one's self-concept does not fit one's ideal self, then one will feel sad, despondent, and disappointed. If, on the other hand, one's self-concept does not fit one's ought self, then one will feel guilty, distressed, and anxious.

Self-guides also influence our motivation by changing what we pay attention to (Higgins, Shah, & Friedman, 1997). The ideal self guides us to focus our attention on achievement and goal accomplishment, what Higgins calls a promotion focus (as we reviewed in Chapter 12). Alternatively, a prevention focus is motivated by the ought self-guide, shifting our attention to avoiding harm and seeking safety. Achieving goals associated with the promotion focus results in pleasure, and achieving goals associated with the prevention focus is associated with relief. Some people are more intent on a promotion focus; they guide their behaviour according to which goals they want to achieve. Other people are more prevention focused; they guide their behaviour according to what they do not want to happen.

Is There a "True" Self?

As you will recall from Chapter 11, Abraham Maslow described self-actualization as involving the need to become the person one was meant to be, and to live according to one's *true* self. But what do we mean when we say "true" self? Is there such a thing, and if so, what is it exactly?

You may have spent time in your life trying to "figure yourself out." Or you may have travelled somewhere in order to "find yourself." In fact you may still feel like you don't really know who you are, or that there are things you still have to learn about yourself. Such experiences reflect this idea that there is a true version of you somewhere deep inside, waiting to be realized. William James (1891), who wrote extensively on the topic of the self and its various manifestations, defined the true self as the most real and authentic self. If we consider the work of Maslow (1968, 1971), we might also infer that the true self involves living according to one's potential—doing what is right for you based on your intrinsic skills, abilities, and interests. People can feel more or less like their true selves depending on a variety of factors and in many different kinds of situations. For example, you may feel closest to your true self when you're volunteering at the crisis centre and helping people in need. Perhaps there is something about that role that just feels right and natural to you. Your friend, on the other hand, may feel closest to his true self when he's dancing to music with his favourite people and able to let himself go. Feeling like your true self is the subjective experience of feeling *authentic*.

Authenticity has been suggested to involve four main factors (Kernis & Goldman, 2006). The first is *awareness* of strengths, weaknesses, and motives. When people are authentic, or living according to their true selves, they have a great deal of personal insight about who they are and what they want, and this allows them to interact with the world more efficiently. They have a relatively accurate self-concept. The second is *unbiased processing*, which is the tendency to perceive reality accurately, and to process information in a realistic way. The third factor is *behaviour*. When people are authentic, their behaviours and responses to the world are in line with their true emotions, values, and beliefs. In other words, they don't present themselves or behave in ways that are deceptive or otherwise inconsistent with who they actually are. Finally, authenticity involves engaging in *authentic relationships* in which people feel like they can be themselves. When people are being their true selves, they're not trying to please others or act differently depending on what others want. There is a degree of self-confidence involved in being authentic with others. Indeed. authenticity generally involves self-confidence, self-acceptance, and strong beliefs about who one is (Kernis & Goldman, 2006).

Consider a friend who has had a difficult time choosing a major to study in university. She has gone back and forth and changed majors a couple of times, and isn't confident about what she wants to do. In new social situations, however, you've found that this friend tends to act overly confident about her career path, in a way that almost seems dishonest. In fact you've been noticing a lot of behaviour from this friend that seems inconsistent with the person you thought you knew. She seems to be worrying more and more about what others think of her, and doesn't seem to have a clear sense of who she is or what she really wants in most situations.

These behaviours are indicators of a lack of authenticity. Each on its own could be the result of any number of psychological factors, but together they suggest that a person is not in touch with their true self.

Living according to one's true self can also be thought of in terms of living according to one's *ideal* self, rather than one's *ought* self. This is largely consistent with Maslow and Rogers' work in the humanistic domain. The feeling of being authentic and living according to one's true self has been associated with higher levels of extraversion, agreeableness, openness, conscientiousness, and emotional stability (Fleeson & Wilt, 2010); as well as high honesty–humility (Maltby et al., 2012). Though it is an abstract concept, the true self describes a very real human experience that seems to have meaningful consequences in one's life. For example, it has recently been associated with better health and well-being at work (Emmerich & Rogotti, 2017).

 Concept Check

In your own words, describe the development of self-awareness and self-concept from infancy to adolescence.

Provide an example of a self-schema. How are self-schemas related to self-concept?

Evaluative Component of the Self: Self-Esteem

The first glimmer of self-esteem occurs when children identify standards or expectations for behaviour and live up to them. For example, parents have expectations for toilet training. When children finally master these expectations, it is a source of pride and self-esteem, at least until larger challenges are encountered. In later childhood, the next shift in the source of self-esteem occurs when children begin to engage in social comparison; children compare themselves to others, and if they are doing better than others, then they feel good about themselves. And later, people develop a set of internal standards, part of what they hold to be important to their self-concept. Behaviour or experiences inconsistent with these internal standards can lead to decreases in self-esteem. In all cases, self-esteem results from an evaluation of oneself.

Evaluation of Oneself

Self-esteem is a general evaluation of self-concept along a good–bad or like–dislike dimension: Do you generally like yourself and feel you are a worthwhile, good person? Do you feel that others respect you? Do you feel you are basically a decent, fair person? Do you take pride and satisfaction in what you have done, in who you are, and in who you would like to become? Self-esteem is the sum of your positive and negative reactions to all of the aspects of your self-concept. It involves both cognition (as in *thinking* positively or negatively about yourself) and emotion (as in *feeling* good or bad about yourself).

Most of us have a mixed reaction to ourselves; we have to take the bad with the good, and we acknowledge that we have both strengths and weaknesses. How we feel about ourselves can change from day to day and even from hour to hour. When we do something that is not consistent with our self-concept, such as hurt someone's feelings, but we do not think of ourselves as uncaring, then we may experience a dip in self-esteem. Such fluctuations, however, occur around our average level of self-esteem. Most personality psychologists are interested in our average level of self-esteem, our characteristic standing on the self-esteem dimension. Average levels of self-esteem fluctuate across the life span in predictable ways. The average low point in self-esteem usually occurs in adolescence, followed by a gradual rise through midlife for most people (Donnellan et al., 2012). Increases in self-esteem over time tend to accompany other positive life events, such as the development of intimate relationships and career success (Wagner et al., 2013).

Personality researchers have begun to acknowledge that people can evaluate themselves positively or negatively in different areas of their lives. For example, you may feel pretty good about your intellectual abilities, but perhaps you are shy around people to whom you are attracted. Consequently, you may have high academic self-esteem but lower self-esteem when it comes to dating or feeling attractive to others. Global self-esteem may be a composite of several individual areas of self-evaluation. Each of these subareas can be assessed separately, and researchers can examine self-esteem about various areas of life or about life in general. For example, research from Indigenous communities in Canada has shown that overweight and obese children tend to report lower global self-esteem and feelings of self-worth; yet feelings of self-worth were even lower within the physical appearance and attributes domains (Willows et al., 2013).

Although there are distinct areas of life in which people can feel more or less confident about themselves—such as friendships, academics, and appearance—self-esteem measures of these content areas are moderately correlated. This means that people who tend to have high self-esteem in one area also tend to have high self-esteem in the other areas. Sometimes researchers find it useful to examine specific areas of self-esteem, such as appearance self-esteem in people at risk for eating disorders. However, the majority of researchers find it useful to think of self-esteem as the person's global or average evaluation of their whole self-concept. Table 14.2 includes examples of the kinds of questions that are commonly used by researchers in global self-esteem assessments. By reading and answering the questions for yourself you will get an idea of what self-esteem means as a construct in psychological research. High scores on global self-esteem are obtained by answering items 1–3 as "Yes" and items 4–6 as "No."

Table 14.2 Examples of Questions that Might Appear in a Global Self-Esteem Assessment		
1. Do you feel like you have a lot of positive traits and qualities?	Yes	No
2. Do you feel like you can do things as well as most people you know?	Yes	No
3. Overall, do you feel pretty happy and satisfied with yourself as a person?	Yes	No
4. Do you sometimes feel worthless as an individual?	Yes	No
5. Do you often feel like you have nothing to be proud of?	Yes	No
6. Do you feel like a failure in life?	Yes	No

The questions in Table 14.2 all measure *explicit* self-esteem, which means that they ask people about their conscious feelings about themselves. But self-esteem can also be measured on the *implicit* or unconscious level. We examine this in A Closer Look: "But How Do You Really Feel?" Measuring Implicit Self-Esteem.

👁 A Closer Look

"But How Do You Really Feel?" Measuring Implicit Self-Esteem

Recall the material in A Closer Look: TAT and Questionnaire Measures of Motives from Chapter 11, which discussed research comparing people's explicit and implicit levels of particular motives. Implicit motivation referred to the person's unconscious desires and aspirations, their unspoken needs and wants. Researchers measured this with the TAT and then compared their level of implicit motivation to their explicit level of that same motivation, with particular attention to subjects who were discrepant (i.e., reported high levels of some motive, yet on the TAT showed low levels of that motive). A similar situation has arisen in the literature on self-esteem, with researchers developing an implicit measure of self-esteem to get at a person's unconscious view of their self-worth and to contrast this to the explicit level they report on a questionnaire measure of self-esteem.

Greenwald and Farnham developed an implicit measure of self-esteem in the year 2000. It consists of a task done on the computer and does not rely on self-reports of how positively people see themselves. Instead, the task, called the Self-Esteem Implicit Association Test (SE-IAT), measures how quickly and consistently people associate positive words to themselves compared to how quickly and consistently they associate negative words to themselves. The task is described in detail in Greenwald and Farnham (2000).

Before actually undertaking the task, the participant is asked to generate 18 "me-type" items and 18 "not-me-type" items. Me-type items are things such as first and last name, phone number, birth month, birth year, and the postal code in which one lives. Not-me-type items are things like a province where one does not live, a street name that one does not live on, and so forth. The researcher also has two lists of words; one list contains positive words (e.g., smart, nice, joy, lucky, etc.) and the other list contains unpleasant words (e.g., stupid, despised, filth, poison, etc.).

When the task begins, the researcher presents pairs of words on the computer screen, with each pair containing either a me-type item or a non-me-type item paired with either a positive or a negative word. The participant is instructed to categorize each pair, as quickly as they can, according to some rule, such as "If a me item is paired with a positive word, press the left key, and if a not-me item is paired with a positive word, press the right key." Participants are presented with many pairs of words and categorize each pair as quickly as they can according to the rule. The time it takes them to perform the categorization is measured by the computer in milliseconds.

An implicit self-esteem score is calculated by taking the average time it takes to categorize me-pleasant word pairs and subtracting the average time it takes to categorize me-unpleasant word pairs. A person with a small number is someone who is fast at categorizing me with pleasant words and relatively slow at categorizing me with unpleasant words, and we say that they have high implicit self-esteem. Such individuals easily associate positive attributes to themselves. We say the measure is "implicit" because it does not rely on some conscious understanding or some spoken verbalization of how positively they see themselves. Rather, it relies on the strength of associations they have in their cognitive system between positive concepts and their self-concept, relative to the strength of associations they have between negative concepts and their self-concept.

Researchers have compared implicit to explicit measures of self-esteem. Explicit measures are questionnaires, such as that presented in Table 14.2, where the person self-reports how good they feel about themselves. Because the method of measuring implicit self-esteem was developed in 2000, a good deal of research has accumulated on people with discrepant levels. One particularly interesting line of research examines individuals who have high explicit self-esteem (they say they feel pretty good about themselves) yet have a low level of implicit self-esteem (they more quickly associate negative than positive words to themselves). This discrepancy in how one "really" feels about themselves is correlated with narcissism (Jordan et al., 2003). That is, on the outside, narcissists appear to have high self-esteem, but on the inside they are insecure about their self-esteem. Other researchers have replicated this finding of a discrepancy between outward and inward self-esteem, and have shown that people who exhibit an abundance of explicit self-esteem but a dearth of implicit self-esteem have a kind of fragile self-concept and are overly sensitive to the opinions of others and other threats to their self-esteem (Gregg & Sedikides, 2010).

Other studies have examined discrepancies where explicit self-esteem is low (the person says they don't feel very good about themselves) yet implicit levels remain high (unconsciously they remain positive). This kind of discrepancy is associated with emotional problems, such as depression and feeling worthless (Leeuwis et al., 2015). These authors also found that being victimized by a bully can bring about declines in explicit self-esteem yet leave implicit levels intact. Another study found that psychotherapy (25 sessions of either cognitive therapy or psychoanalysis) elevated both implicit and explicit self-esteem (Ritter et al., 2013).

As research accumulates (e.g., Laws & Rivera, 2012), we will gain a better understanding of the dynamics of inner and outer manifestations of how people feel about themselves. Starting with a measure of some new concept, and then proceeding to ask questions about that new concept, is exactly how science progresses in personality psychology. As suggested by researchers at the University of Toronto, one important point of concern is the degree to which implicit self-esteem (as measured by the IAT) is completely independent from explicit self-esteem (Tafarodi & Ho, 2006). Is implicit self-esteem best defined as an indirect representation of self-esteem more generally, or is it a subterranean form of self-esteem that is altogether free from conscious reflection?

Research on Self-Esteem

Much of the research on self-esteem concerns how people respond to evaluation. Being evaluated is a very common occurrence, especially during the school years. Homework is evaluated, tests are given, and children receive regular reports on their performance. Even outside school, a lot of play in childhood also involves evaluation, such as occurs with competitive games. In adulthood, the games change but the evaluation continues. At most jobs, there is usually some form of evaluation done on a regular basis, and the workers receive feedback on their performance at least in the form of the size of the raise they get that year. There is also competition and evaluation in many other areas of adult life, such as career and finances, relationships, and children, where people often compare how they are doing with their neighbours. Because self-esteem is linked to evaluation, much of the research on this topic concerns how people react to criticism and negative feedback.

Reactions to Criticism and Failure Feedback

Many laboratory studies have been conducted on how people high and low on self-esteem react to failure and criticism. In general, participants are taken into the laboratory and instructed to complete an important task. For example, they may be given an intelligence test and told that norms are being developed and that they should try to do the very best they can because they are representing their school in this norming project. Usually this gets the participants very involved and motivates them to want to perform well. The researcher then scores the test when the subjects are finished, and the researcher is critical of the participants' performance, saying that they did very poorly. The research question is "How are high and low self-esteem individuals affected by this criticism and personal failure?" The research has looked mainly at how failure feedback affects subsequent performance on similar tasks, and whether failure affects high and low self-esteem individuals differently (Brown & Dutton, 1995; Stake, Huff, & Zand, 1995). The participants are offered the opportunity to work on a similar intelligence test after the failure feedback. The researcher then looks at how hard the participants try, how well they do, and whether they give up on the subsequent difficult tasks. The findings suggest that, following failure, those with low self-esteem are more likely to perform poorly and to give up earlier on subsequent tasks. For high self-esteem individuals, on the other hand, failure feedback seems to spur them into action on subsequent tasks, and they are less likely to give up and more likely to work just as hard on the second task as they did on the first (Brown & Dutton, 1995).

Why is it that failure seems to incapacitate low self-esteem individuals but seems to encourage those with high self-esteem into renewed effort? Researchers think that people readily accept feedback that is consistent with their self-concept, so for low self-esteem individuals, failure feedback on the first task is consistent with their self-concept, and it confirms their views that they are the kind of people who fail more than succeed. And so, when confronted with the second task, low self-esteem individuals, who have just had their negative self-view confirmed with failing on the first task, believe they will also fail on the second task, and so do not try so hard or just give up. For those with high self-esteem, however, failure is not consistent with their existing self-concept, so they are more likely *not* to accept this feedback. Also, it is likely that they will discount the feedback, perhaps thinking that failure on the first task must have been an accident or a mistake. Consequently, they are motivated to try just as hard the second time, and to not give up, because they do not see their self-concept as the kind of people who fail. Psychologist Roy Baumeister and his colleagues (e.g., Baumeister & Tice, 2006; Baumeister, Tice, & Hutton, 1989) argue that high self-esteem individuals are concerned with projecting a successful, prosperous, and thriving self-image. Low self-esteem people, on the other hand, are most concerned with avoiding failure. It is a difference of emphasis: people with high self-esteem fear not succeeding; people with low self-esteem fear failure.

Research is also uncovering interesting associations among electronic forms of communication (e.g., texting, social media use) and both self-esteem and social anxiety. Such aspects of personality appear to influence how various electronic message are actually perceived and interpreted. We explore one interesting line of research in this area in Highlight On Canadian Research: Social Anxiety and Texting: When We Don't "Get" the Message.

Highlight on Canadian Research

Social Anxiety and Texting: When We Don't "Get" the Message

As we discussed earlier in this chapter, shy or socially anxious people have a tendency to interpret social interactions more negatively and are much more likely to interpret a comment as criticism. But does this finding extend to electronic forms of communication, such as text messages? Researchers Mila Kingsbury (University of Ottawa) and Robert Coplan (Carleton University) have tackled this very question. In a sample of over 200 Canadian undergraduate students, Kingsbury and Coplan (2016) examined how ambiguous text messages were interpreted according to levels of social anxiety. Given that previous research has indicated a significant interpretation bias among those with social anxiety such that ambiguous stimuli are interpreted more negatively, the researchers expected a similar phenomenon would emerge with text messages in which the sender's intention was unclear.

Previous research examining interpretation biases has used short stories or vignettes describing ambiguous social interactions. After reading a vignette, participants must choose among a few possible interpretations. An example of a negative interpretation might be, "They are saying negative things about you." In their 2016 study, however, Kingsbury and Coplan needed a new method for studying electronic communications. They developed a series of ambiguous text messages describing common social scenarios based on previous measures of interpretation bias in face-to-face contexts. For each hypothetical text message, a "screen shot" or image of the message as it would appear on a smartphone was developed. As an example, one of the text messages read, "I heard about last night." Each ambiguous text message was followed by two possible interpretations of the sender's intention, one negative and one benign, which participants were asked to rate on a scale of 1 to 5 according to how they interpreted each message.

Kingsbury and Coplan first validated this new measure of interpretation bias in a group of graduate students, confirming that it produced similar results as face-to-face studies of the same phenomenon. They subsequently administered the new measure of interpretation bias to a sample of male and female undergraduate students, along with a self-report questionnaire assessing symptoms of social anxiety. They further manipulated the gender of the text message sender, in order to examine the role that gender may play in such biases.

In both graduate and undergraduate samples, the researchers confirmed a negative interpretation bias among those reporting the highest level of social anxiety. Indeed, it seemed that social anxiety led people to interpret their text messages more negatively, especially when the intent of those messages was unclear. In their sample of undergraduates, gender also appeared to play a significant role, such that ambiguous text messages from women were more often interpreted negatively by those with high social anxiety. Among male participants specifically, social anxiety predicted interpretation biases only when the sender was described as female. For female participants, however, no opposite-gender interaction was observed between sender and recipient. Interestingly, there was something about male–male friendships that lessened the impact of social anxiety on interpretation bias, yet this same effect did not occur for females. Kingsbury and Coplan interpreted these findings to reflect the greater degree of closeness experienced in all-female friendships. This closeness may lead socially anxious women to interpret ambiguous messages from other women more negatively. Young men, on the other hand, are known to be more tolerant of minor missteps by same-gender peers; for them, social anxiety is more likely to lead to a negative interpretation bias when the sender of the text message is a young woman (Kingsbury & Coplan, 2016).

Although this study provides important insights into social anxiety within a largely unexplored social medium, it is important to note that messages from strangers tend to produce more anxiety overall compared to those from known individuals. Nevertheless, the work by Kingsbury and Coplan may be one piece of a much larger picture emerging on the disadvantages of electronic forms of communication, which are inherently more ambiguous than face-to-face social interactions. A large body of research is also emerging on the negative implications of Facebook and other social media for both social anxiety and self-esteem. For instance, research from the Department of Psychology at the University of Waterloo found that individuals with low self-esteem posted more negative content on Facebook. What's worse, this content was "liked" less by readers (Forest & Wood, 2012).

Self-Esteem and Coping with Negative Events

Other research on high self-esteem individuals has examined the strategies these people use to get through life. Unpleasant events happen to everyone. People with high self-esteem appear to maintain their positive evaluation through the ups and downs of everyday life. Have high self-esteem people somehow figured out how to cope more effectively with these challenges of life? How do high self-esteem people overcome the disappointments, shortcomings, losses, and failures that are a normal part of being human?

One strategy identified by Brown and Smart (1991) is that, following failure in one area of life, the high self-esteem person will often focus on other areas of life in which things are going well. Larsen (2000a; Larsen & Prizmic, 2004) identifies this strategy as one of the most effective but least used strategies for overcoming feelings of failure. For example, imagine you are a research psychologist and you are evaluated in this job by the number of research articles you publish each year. Imagine then that one of your articles is rejected by a publisher. This represents a small failure in your life. If you were a low self-esteem person, this failure would have a large effect, confirming your view that you are generally a failure in most things that you do, that this is just one more instance of how you are unworthy and inadequate. On the other hand, if you were a high self-esteem person, you would likely remind yourself that you are still a good teacher, a good faculty member at your university, and a good spouse and a good parent to your children; that you still play a good game of squash; and that your dog still loves you. Larsen and Prizmic (2004) have suggested that in order to cope with such failures, people should make a list of all the things in their lives that are going well and keep this list in their wallets. Then, if a failure occurs in one area of life—for instance, at work—they can take this list out and review it, just as a high self-esteem person might do naturally. This can help people cope with the inevitable bumps, bruises, and failures of everyday life. For someone with low self-esteem, however, coping with failure may be especially challenging. Tafarodi and colleagues (2003) have shown that self-esteem affects memory, such that individuals with low self-esteem more frequently attend to and remember negative experiences associated with failure.

The idea of compartmentalizing the self is consistent with the research on **self-complexity** initiated by psychologist Patricia Linville (1987). She holds the view that we have many roles and many aspects to our self-concept. However, for some of us, our self-concept is rather simple, being made up of just a few large categories. This can be seen when people believe they have no sense of purpose without their career, or they are "nothing" without their partner, meaning that their whole self-concept is wrapped up in a single social role or relationship. Other people have a more multifaceted and complex self-concept with many parts: relationships, family, work, hobbies, friends, and so forth. For people with high self-complexity, a failure in any one aspect (such as a relationship that ends) is buffered because there are many other aspects of the self that are unaffected by that event. However, if a person is low in self-complexity, the same event might be seen as devastating because they define themselves mainly in terms of this one aspect.

Although self-complexity technically refers to the state of one's self-concept, it has implications for self-esteem—namely, by supporting more positive global evaluations of the self during stress. An early review of the self-complexity research concluded that under conditions of objective and identifiable stress, higher self-complexity is weakly but significantly associated with well-being (Rafaeli-Mor & Steinberg, 2002). The relationship between self-complexity and successful coping has since been replicated by other researchers (e.g., Martins & Calheiros, 2012; McConnell et al., 2009). Some have even proposed programs for expanding self-concept with the goal of improving a person's functioning in the face of threats to self-esteem, such as failures or losses (Walton, Paunesku, & Dweck, 2012). The old phrase "Don't put all your eggs into one basket" seems to apply to self-concept as well.

Research has also supported the health benefits of a having a high **collective self-esteem**, which is defined as an individual's global self-evaluation as a member of a social group or category. Worthiness, personal value placed on one's membership, and public respect within a group make up this concept, originally proposed by Crocker and Luhtanen (1990). Research has demonstrated that having a high collective self-esteem is related to psychological well-being. For instance, Bailis, Chipperfield, and Helgason (2008) found that collective self-esteem predicted improved health and fewer chronic conditions over a six-year period in a sample of community-dwelling older adults in Manitoba.

Protecting versus Enhancing the Self

Imagine you are a graduating university student; you have majored in computer science and have a lot of expertise in Web-based programming. You are being recruited by a trendy Internet start-up company for a job managing its information technology department. You know there is a lot of potential for you in this company. In fact, it could make you a millionaire within a few years if the company were to go public. However, you also know that it will be a lot of hard work. You will have to put in many hours and dedicate yourself almost entirely to the company for several years. You know you will also need to have some luck to get the right team together, to have some successes on your first few projects. It is a high-stakes but also a high-risk position. You know you have a lot of skill in this area, but you also know it is quite possible for you to fail miserably. What would you do? Would you take this job?

Some people may decline this opportunity and prefer to wait for a more likely success because they are motivated to protect their self-concept. That is, they are concerned with *not failing,* and, in situations in which failure is a good possibility, they prefer not to take the risk. In other words, for some people, not failing is much more important than succeeding wildly. It turns out that people low in self-esteem are like this, in that they are motivated to protect their self-concept by avoiding failure much more than they are motivated to enhance it with success (Baumeister & Tice, 2006; Tice, 1993).

Support for this notion has been found in several studies. For example, in one study (Taylor et al., 2000) the participants took an intelligence test and then were given their scores, plus the scores of the other participants. The participants were led to believe they had done much better (false success feedback) or much worse (false failure feedback) than the others. They then had the opportunity to receive more feedback on how they compared with the others, feedback that was likely to be in the same direction as their test scores. The low self-esteem participants asked for more feedback only when they knew it would be good news, when they were sure that they already were doing above average. When they thought they were below average, the low self-esteem individuals did not want any more feedback. This is consistent with the idea that low self-esteem people are motivated to protect their self-concept; they wanted more feedback only if they were certain it would be positive. The high self-esteem people, on the other hand, did not avoid more feedback after learning they were below average.

Early work by Canadian psychologist James Battle confirmed that students with low self-esteem display lower perceived ability, and not surprisingly, lower academic performance (Battle, 1979). Low self-esteem individuals sometimes put a lot of energy into evading any new negative information about themselves. One strategy is to simply expect to fail; then, when it happens, it is not anything new. **Defensive pessimism** is a strategy in which a person facing a challenge, such as an upcoming test, expects to do poorly. Defensive pessimists are motivated by their fear of failure, but they take this gloomy outlook because the impact of failure can be lessened if it is expected in advance. For example, a little boy who strikes out at bat is not so upset with himself if he expects to strike out in the first place. Psychologist Julie Norem, who has done most of the research on defensive pessimism, sees a positive side to this characteristic: defensive pessimists use their worry and pessimism in a constructive way, to motivate themselves to work on the thing they are pessimistic about. She gives the example of a man who must give a public speech (Norem, 1995). Even though he has done a lot of public speaking, and all of his speeches have gone well, he nevertheless is anxious and convinces himself that this time he is surely going to make a fool of himself. Thus, he decides to work extra hard on this speech; he rehearses and rehearses, prepares and prepares. When it comes time to give the speech, he does great, as usual. By reflecting on the worst outcome, defensive pessimists work through ways to keep that worst case from happening. The downside to defensive pessimism is that the negativity of defensive pessimists annoys others (Norem, 1998, 2001).

Sometimes people go to great lengths to set up their failure. This is called self-handicapping (e.g., Tice & Baumeister, 1990). **Self-handicapping** is a process in which a person deliberately does the things that increase the probability that they will fail (Tice & Bratslavsky, 2000). For example, a young woman may have a pessimistic attitude toward her upcoming exam, so she uses this as an excuse for not studying. However, not studying for the exam provides a handicap, an excuse to fail. By not studying, she increases the chances that she will fail, but it also gives her an excuse for that failure. When she fails, she can then say that she was simply unprepared, not that she is unintelligent or lacks the ability to do well in her classes. For low self-esteem people, failing is bad, but failing without an excuse is worse.

All in all, high self-esteem has been associated with a variety of positive outcomes and experiences, while low self-esteem has been associated with less-desirable outcomes. In many cases, however, the assumptions that have been made about self-esteem have been somewhat inaccurate, with many of the implications of self-esteem exaggerated or overemphasized. We discuss some important conclusions and considerations in self-esteem research in A Closer Look: The Six Myths of Self-Esteem.

 ## A Closer Look

The Six Myths of Self-Esteem

Most people naturally try to enhance and protect their self-esteem, believing that it is important to psychological health. In many Western nations, particularly Canada and the United States, there has been a growing concern over developing self-esteem, based largely on the belief that it is related to all manner of good things in life. Task forces on self-esteem have been implemented, and many elementary and high schools include curriculum designed to foster a "feel-good" version of self-esteem (e.g., to feel good about yourself). But this has raised many concerns among psychologists, who fear that too much emphasis may be placed on self-esteem, while too little emphasis will be placed on such things as achievement and self-efficacy.

The Association of Psychological Science set up a task force charged with reviewing the scientific literature on self-esteem, particularly with respect to objective behaviours and outcomes. The report was published in 2003 (Baumeister et al., 2003). We have taken this report and distilled the findings into a series of myths about self-esteem that are not supported by scientific research.

Myth One: High self-esteem is correlated with all manner of positive characteristics, such as being physically attractive, smart, kind, generous, etc. It is true that, for example, when both self-esteem and physical attractiveness are assessed using self-report (e.g., rate how attractive you are, rate your self-esteem), then strong correlations are typically found. However, when objective measures of attractiveness are used, such as having raters rate photographs of people in terms of attractiveness, then the correlation between self-reported self-esteem and other-rated physical attractiveness drops to zero. These kinds of findings have been obtained with a variety of other positive characteristics. For example, high self-esteem people may rate themselves as smart or high in kindness or generosity as well, yet others do not necessarily see them as being this way. In a sense, individuals high in self-esteem may have an inflated or unrealistic view of their positive characteristics, a view that is not necessarily supported by those who know the person well.

Myth Two: High self-esteem promotes success in school. The issue here is really one of causality and causal direction: does self-esteem cause people to achieve success or does achieving success lead to self-esteem? Many of the educational movements imply that if only we could raise children's self-esteem then we would help them on their way to achieving success in life. Consequently teachers are sometimes taught to praise students all the time, even if they are not successful. However, there is very little empirical science to support the idea that self-esteem leads to academic success. For example, Baumeister and colleagues (2003) reviewed a study that tested more than 23,000 high school students, first in Grade 10 then again in Grade 12. They found that self-esteem in Grade 10 only weakly predicted academic achievement in Grade 12. Academic achievement in Grade 10 correlated higher with self-esteem in Grade 12. Many studies show similar results, and none of them indicate that improving self-esteem offers students much benefit. In fact, some studies show that artificially boosting self-esteem (through unconditional praise, for example) may actually lower subsequent performance (Baumeister et al., 2003).

Myth Three: High self-esteem promotes success on the job. The same basic issues about causality apply here; does self-esteem promote success on the job, or vice versa? When people rate their own job performance, there is often a modest correlation with self-esteem, but when job performance is assessed objectively (e.g., supervisor ratings), the correlations drop to close to zero.

Myth Four: High self-esteem makes a person likable. Again, if we use self-reports of popularity (e.g., How much do other people like you?), then these self-ratings of likability do correlate with self-esteem (i.e., high self-esteem individuals regard themselves as being popular and believe they have many friends). However, these self-perceptions do not reflect reality. Baumeister and colleagues (2003) reported a study of high-school students who were asked to nominate their most-liked peers. The person in the class receiving the most votes was ranked as most popular, the person with the second-most votes was ranked as second most popular, and so on. When self-esteem scores were correlated with the objective peer-ranking of popularity, that correlation was approximately zero. Similar findings have been found with college students. In another study reported by Baumeister and colleagues (2003), college students self-reported their own interpersonal skills in several domains (e.g., initiating relationships, self-disclosure, being assertive when necessary, providing emotional support to their friends, and managing interpersonal conflict). The researchers also had each subject's roommate report what the subject was like on each of the above interpersonal skill domains. Although the subjects' self-esteem scores correlated with all of the self-reported interpersonal skill domains, the correlations between self-esteem and the roommates' ratings were essentially zero for four out of five of the interpersonal skills. The only interpersonal skill area that the roommates noticed that was associated with self-esteem was the subject's ability to initiate new social contacts and friendships. This does seem to be the one area in which the confidence associated with self-esteem really matters. People who think that they are desirable and attractive should be good at striking up conversations with strangers. In most other areas of interpersonal skills, however, self-esteem is not associated with having an advantage over other people.

Myth Five: Low self-esteem puts a person at risk for drug and alcohol abuse and premature sexual activity. The scientific studies reviewed by Baumeister and colleagues (2003) do not support the idea that low self-esteem predisposes young people to more or earlier sexual activity. If anything, people with higher self-esteem are less inhibited, more willing to disregard risks, and more prone to engage in sex. There is, however, evidence that unpleasant sexual experiences and unwanted pregnancies appear to lower self-esteem. As for alcohol and illicit drugs, preventing these behaviours has been a major rationale for those calling for programs to promote self-esteem. The data, however, do not conclusively show that low self-esteem causes, or even correlates with, the abuse of illicit drugs or alcohol. For example, in a longitudinal study, no correlation was found between self-esteem at age 13 and drinking or drug abuse at age 15. All in all, the results are not conclusive to make any statements about self-esteem protecting people from the dangers of risky behaviour.

Myth Six: Only low self-esteem people are aggressive. For decades many psychologists thought that low self-esteem was an important factor underlying aggressive behaviour. Under their tough exteriors, aggressive people were thought to suffer from insecurities and self-doubt. However, recent research has shown that aggressive people often have quite favourable views of themselves. In fact, extremely high self-esteem can blend into narcissism, which has been associated with bouts of anger and aggression when the narcissist does not get their way. If self-esteem is threatened or disputed by someone or some event, especially among high self-esteem individuals, then they may react with hostility or violence. People with a highly inflated view of their own superiority, those with narcissistic tendencies, may be the most prone to violent reactions. After a challenge to self-esteem (e.g., getting beaten at a game), people might protect their self-concept by directing their anger outward, attacking the victor. Baumeister and colleagues (2003) reviewed the literature on bullying and concluded that bullies are often very self-confident and less socially anxious than average. The general pattern in these studies and those on adults is that even high self-esteem, especially when it blends into narcissism, can be associated with interpersonal aggression. Canadian research by Jennifer Wong and colleagues at Simon Fraser University recently confirmed not only higher self-esteem, but also lower depression and better mental health among adolescents who were identified as bullies (Koh & Wong, 2015). In her work, Wong suggests an evolutionary role of bullying that maintains status and promotes survival, which offers one explanation for its link to high self-esteem.

After crushing these myths about self-esteem, we can ask the question: So, what good is self-esteem? As described elsewhere in this chapter, self-esteem improves persistence in the face of failure. People high in self-esteem perform better in groups than those with low self-esteem. Also, having a poor self-image is a risk factor for developing certain eating disorders, especially bulimia. Low self-esteem is related to depression, with evidence suggesting that low self-esteem can lead to depression rather than the other way around (Sowislo & Orth, 2013). And high self-esteem is related to social confidence and taking the initiative in making new friends. It is most likely the case that successes in academics, in the interpersonal domain, or in one's career lead to both happiness and self-esteem. Consequently, efforts to artificially boost children's self-esteem (through unconditional praise, for example) might fail. Rather, we should encourage and praise children when they put effort into learning or achieving the skills necessary to succeed in various areas of life.

Positive Illusions about the Self As noted in Chapter 13, part of being happy is having *positive illusions* about the self; having an inflated view of one's own characteristics as a good, able, and desirable person. There is some evidence that this is part of emotional well-being (Taylor, 1989; Taylor et al., 2000). But is it possible to have excessively positive illusions about the self? After all, as we discussed earlier in this chapter, authenticity involves some degree of self-awareness, which seems at odds with this idea of seeing oneself differently than one actually is.

It may be a matter of degree and time. Most people seem to think of themselves as better than average, and as slightly better than other people judge them to be (Brown, 2012; Makridakis & Moleskis, 2015). In line with this, there is evidence that people often demonstrate higher levels of implicit self-esteem when compared to explicit reports (Falk & Heine, 2015). In the short-term, higher positive illusions about the self may be associated with higher psychological well-being and better adjustment to stress (Makridakis & Moleskis, 2015; Taylor et al., 2000). However, in the long-term, the negative consequences of high positive illusions appear to be numerous. They include unrealistic and overly optimistic judgments of events, poor planning, gambling and financial loss, high risk-taking in business and in health, and on the broader social scale, even war (Makridakis & Moleskis, 2015). In a longitudinal study of American college students, greater self-enhancement and use of positive illusions was also associated with decreasing levels of self-esteem and well-being over time, as well as with increasing disengagement from academic studies (Robins & Beer, 2001).

It seems that positive illusions may be beneficial when considering short-term outcomes like performance evaluation and the maintenance of positive emotional states. Yet over time, there is evidence that positive illusions increase the likelihood of negative outcomes, by leading people to take too many risks (which results in increased failure) or by leading people to disengage from goals and tasks as they are unable to live up to their unrealistic expectations (Makridakis & Moleskis, 2015; Robins & Beer, 2001). Interestingly, but not surprisingly, the use of positive illusions has also been associated with narcissism (Robins & Beer, 2001). Although there are still questions to be answered in the research, it seems that maintaining highly positive illusions of the self may be quite problematic over time.

Self-Esteem Variability

Most of the research on self-esteem concerns the average level, or what people's evaluations of themselves are like on average. But we also know from Chapter 5 that people fluctuate on their self-esteem from day to day and even from hour to hour. **Self-esteem variability** is an individual difference characteristic; it is the magnitude of short-term fluctuations in ongoing self-esteem (Kernis, Grannemann, & Mathis, 1991). In this section, we stress two main points. First, researchers make a distinction between level and variability of self-esteem. These two aspects of self-esteem are unrelated to each other. Moreover, level and variability in self-esteem are hypothesized to be based on different psychological mechanisms and are often found to interact in predicting important life outcomes (Kernis, Grannemann, & Barclay, 1992).

A second point is that self-esteem variability is related to the extent to which one's self-evaluation is changeable. That is, some people's self-esteem is pushed and pulled by the events of life much more than other people's self-esteem. Psychologist Michael Kernis, who has written extensively about this characteristic, believes that self-esteem variability is high in some people because they

- have an enhanced sensitivity to social evaluation events.
- have an increased concern about their self-view.
- are overly reliant on social sources of evaluation.
- react to evaluation with anger and hostility.

Several studies have been conducted to examine whether self-esteem variability moderates the relation between self-esteem level and other variables, such as depression (Gable & Nezlak, 1998). In one study (Kernis et al., 1991), self-esteem level was related to depression, but this relation was much stronger for those higher in self-esteem variability. Based on such findings, researchers have come to view variability as a susceptibility to depression (Roberts & Monroe, 1992). That is, depression is thought to be a result of a person's vulnerability to the self-deprecating events of everyday life (Butler, Hokanson, & Flynn, 1994). Other studies are exploring the health correlates of chronic self-esteem variability, finding that this characteristic is frequently associated with various health risk factors (Ross et al., 2013). All in all, variability in self-esteem is turning out to be as consequential as average level of self-esteem.

Concept Check

Define self-esteem. What does it mean to measure self-esteem (a) implicitly and (b) explicitly?

In your own words, discuss three common myths regarding self-esteem. In each case, what is a more accurate summary of the research?

Social Component of the Self: Social Identity

Social identity is the self that is shown to other people. This is the part of ourselves that we use to create impressions, to let other people know who we are and what they can expect from us. Social identity is different from self-concept because identity contains elements that are socially observable, publicly available outward expressions of the self. Gender and ethnicity are aspects of social identity. They may figure into a person's self-concept to varying degrees, but gender and ethnicity are parts of one's social self, because they involve information that is available to others.

Identity has an element of continuity because many of its aspects, such as gender and ethnicity, are constant. People are recognized as being the same from day to day, week to week, and year to year. If you were asked for your "identification," you might produce a passport or a driver's licence. These documents contain socially available facts about you, such as your height, weight, age, and eye colour. They also contain your family name and your address. All of these pieces of information are aspects of your identity, and they provide others with a brief sketch of who you are.

The Nature of Identity

Identity has two important features: continuity and contrast. **Continuity** means that people can count on you to be the same person tomorrow as you are today. Obviously, people change in various ways, but many important aspects of social identity remain relatively stable, such as gender, surname (though some people elect to change this when they marry), language, ethnicity, and socioeconomic status.

Some aspects of identity can change but do so gradually, lending some sense of continuity (e.g., education, occupation, and marital status). Other aspects of identity refer to behavioural patterns that are public, such as being an athlete, a party animal, or even a jerk. These labels, often imposed upon us, also contribute to a sense of continuity (Baumeister & Muraven, 1996).

Contrast means that your social identity differentiates you from other people. An identity is what makes you unique in the eyes of others. The combination of characteristics that make up your identity differentiates you from everyone else. For example, there may be other students who speak the way you do and work where you do, but you are the only one who likes a particular type of music and has your ethnic background and eye colour. Some characteristics are more important to social identity for some people than others. We now turn to how people develop identity by selecting what they choose to emphasize about themselves in their social identities.

Identity Development

Although anything that provides a sense of sameness can potentially become part of identity, people have some latitude to choose what they want to be known for. For example, a student may try out for the swim team, thereby choosing the identity of an athlete. Another might break a lot of rules, thereby choosing the identity of a delinquent. People also differ from each other in the strength of their identities. Some people feel a strong sense of reputation, whereas others feel adrift in their social relations, not knowing who they are expected to be. In fact, most people go through a period, usually in high school or university, in which they experiment with various identities. For many people, this is an uncomfortable time. They may feel socially insecure or sensitive while developing their social identity.

As mentioned in Chapter 10, the term *identity* was popularized in the 1960s by the psychoanalyst Erik Erikson (1968). He believed that identity resulted from efforts to separate oneself from one's parents, to stop relying on one's parents to make decisions about what values to hold and what goals to pursue in life. Erikson believed that achieving an identity took effort and work and that there was always a risk that an identity achieved could come undone, resulting in what he called role confusion. People need to continually work on achieving and maintaining their identity, Erikson taught.

Identity can be achieved in several ways, according to Erikson (1968). Many people struggle with identities, particularly during late adolescence and early adulthood. Experimenting with various identities can be compared to trying on different hats to see which one fits. In trying on identities, a young man in college or university might one semester be an athlete and the next semester join the debate and chess clubs; the following semester, he starts hanging out with a different crowd and frequently skips classes. People actively struggle to find a social identity that feels *authentic*, one they are comfortable with. Usually, after a period of experimentation, most people settle into a comfortable social identity and attain some stability.

For other people, the route to identity is not through experimentation. Instead, some people attain an identity by accepting and adopting a ready-made social role. Typically, such people adopt an identity that is practised and provided by their parents or significant others. For example, they may take over the family business, buy a house in their hometown, and attend the same place of worship as their parents. Such people appear stable and mature in their identities and have mature values, plans, and objectives even when they are teenagers. Another identity adoption example is arranged marriages, in which the parents decide whom their children will marry and the children accept this decision.

These kinds of instant identity adoptions can be risky, however, as they may be achieved with a certain amount of rigidity, making the person closed to new ideas or lifestyles. Such people may be inflexible and stubborn in their social roles, especially when they are under stress. Nevertheless, for many people, this route to identity is an acceptable and reasonably healthy alternative.

Identity Crises

A person's identity is challenged from time to time. The answer to the question "Who do others think I am?" can change. For example, when a man gets divorced, his social identity changes from "I am married" to "I am divorced and newly single." Or a woman gives up a career as a business executive to pursue a vocation in small-scale farming, so her identity changes from "I am an executive" to "I am a farmer." Other challenges to identity include events that change one's reputation, change one's family life, or change one's social status.

Erikson (1968) coined the phrase *identity crisis*, meaning the feelings of anxiety that accompany efforts to define or redefine one's own individuality and social reputation. For most people, the process of going through an identity crisis is an important and memorable phase of life. Sometimes it happens early, in adolescence; sometimes it happens later, in midlife. And some people have identity crises multiple times in their lives. Psychologist Roy Baumeister suggests that there are two distinct types of identity crises: identity deficit and identity conflict (Baumeister, 1986, 1997).

Identity Deficit

An **identity deficit** arises when a person has not formed an adequate identity and thus has trouble making major decisions: Should I go to university or not? If I go to university, what major should I choose? Should I join the military service? Should I get married? A person without a secure, established identity would have trouble making such major decisions because they have no inner foundation. When facing a tough decision, many people turn inward to find the answer. In doing so, many people arrive at a course of action right away, because they know their own values and preferences very well; they know what "a person like me" would do in such situations. When people who have an identity deficit turn inward, however, they find little in the way of a foundation on which to base such life choices.

Identity deficits often occur when a person discards old values or goals. For example, college and university students often reject old opinions in favour of new ideas and new values to which they are exposed at the post-secondary level. In fact, some college and university courses are designed to encourage students to doubt or challenge their previous assumptions about themselves or the world. But rejecting old beliefs and assumptions can create a void or an identity deficit, which is accompanied by feelings of emptiness and uncertainty. Such feelings prompt people to search for new beliefs, for new values and goals. People who are trying to fill this identity deficit may try on new belief systems, explore new relationships, and investigate new ideas and values. They may be alternately depressed and confused at one point in time and then euphoric about the possibilities in their lives.

People in identity deficit are particularly vulnerable to the propaganda of various social groups. They are often very curious about other belief systems, so they are vulnerable to influence from other people. Because of their feelings of emptiness and their search for new values and ideas, they tend to be very persuadable during this period. As Baumeister (1997) points out, recruiters for cults are often especially successful at enlisting people who are undergoing identity deficit crises. Recent research also suggests that both the need to feel unique and the need to be part of a group are related to believing in conspiracy theories, such as the belief that climate change is a hoax or that vaccines cause autism (Hart & Graether, 2018). It is reasonable to expect individuals with an identity deficit to also believe in such conspiracies.

❓ Exercise

Do you see yourself as having the same traits and characteristics from one social role to another? Or do you tend to see yourself differently depending on the situation you're in and the people you're interacting with? Although self-complexity seems to be an adaptive quality (as discussed in the previous section of this chapter), seeing oneself very differently across social roles may be less adaptive.

In a study by Donahue and colleagues (1993), participants were asked to rate their personality traits according to how they saw themselves in different social roles. Self-reports were then compared to determine the degree of difference across roles for each individual, what the authors referred to as self-concept differentiation. Greater differentiation of the self across social roles was associated with depression and low self-esteem, leading the authors to conclude that a more differentiated identity reflected psychological fragmentation and a lack of a strong sense of self. While having a self-concept that is rich and complex appears to be adaptive (as in self-complexity), instability in self-concept across social roles, also referred to as *multiple selves*, seems to be maladaptive. This finding, which is in line with our understanding of authenticity and living according to one's true self, has now been demonstrated in numerous studies (Pilarska & Suchańska, 2015).

Consider how you see yourself when you are with your friends, and then compare that to how you see yourself when you are with your family, or at work. This may give you a sense of your degree of self-concept differentiation. Many prominent psychologists (including Carl Rogers and Abraham Maslow) have stressed the importance of having a stable sense of self and presenting oneself consistently across social roles.

Identity Conflict

An **identity conflict** involves an incompatibility between two or more aspects of identity. This kind of crisis often occurs when a person is forced to make an important and difficult life decision. For example, a person who immigrates to Canada may have an identity conflict between wanting to assimilate into the majority culture and wanting to maintain their ethnic identity. A similar identity conflict arises in working individuals who also want to have a family. A person with a strong commitment to building a family might experience an identity conflict if they are offered a promotion at work that involves longer hours or frequent out-of-town travel. Whenever two or more aspects of identity like this clash, there is a potential for an identity conflict crisis.

Identity conflicts are "approach–approach" conflicts, in that the person wants to reach two mutually contradictory goals. Although these conflicts involve wanting two desirable identities, not much pleasure is experienced during identity conflicts. Identity conflicts usually involve intense feelings of guilt or remorse over perceived unfaithfulness to an important aspect of the person's identity. People in an identity conflict may feel as if they are letting themselves and others down.

Overcoming an identity conflict is often a difficult and painful process. One course of action is to put aside a part of one's identity, to abandon a formerly important aspect of the self. Some people are able to strike a balance in their lives. For example, a university professor may accept a lighter teaching load to have more time with his family; or a business executive may telecommute to her job two days a week in order to spend more time with her partner. Some people partition their lives in ways that prevent such conflicts from arising. For example, some people keep their work lives and their private lives entirely separate.

Resolution of Identity Crises

Identity crises—both deficits and conflicts—commonly occur during adolescence, though not all adolescents experience identity crises. Those who do find that resolution involves two steps (Baumeister, 1997). First, they decide which values are most important to them. Second, they transform these abstract values into desires and actual behaviours. For example, a person might arrive at the conclusion that what is really important is to have a family. The second step is to translate this value into actions, such as finding the right relationship with someone who also wants a family; working hard to maintain this relationship; preparing a career with which to support a family; and so forth. As the person begins working toward these goals, they assume a secure identity and are unlikely to experience an identity crisis, at least during this early phase of life.

A second phase of life in which identity crises commonly occur is during middle age. For some people, this is a period in which they experience dissatisfaction with their existing identities, perhaps at work or in a marriage. Whatever the reason, people undergoing a midlife identity crisis begin to feel that things are not working out as they wished. They may feel that their lives are inauthentic. People in the midlife identity crisis begin to doubt that they made the right choices early in life, and they reconsider those commitments: "If only I had done . . ." is a frequent complaint. It is a period of regret over time spent pursuing goals that turned out to be unsatisfying or impossible. Many people in this predicament decide to abandon their goals and experience an identity deficit because they give up the principles that have guided their lives so far.

People who undergo midlife crises often act as adolescents again. That is, an identity crisis often looks the same whether it occurs at adolescence or at midlife: the person experiments with different lifestyles, forms new relationships and abandons old ones, and gives up previous ambitions and responsibilities. In midlife crises, people often change their careers, their relationships, their religions or value systems, where they live, or any combinations of these. Sometimes they simply change their priorities—for example, a person might keep their job and their relationship, but decide to spend more time with their partner and less time working. A midlife identity crisis can be just as much of an emotional roller-coaster as an adolescent identity crisis.

To summarize, your social identity consists of the social or public aspects of yourself, the impression that you typically create in others. Many of your more visible characteristics—such as gender, ethnicity, and occupation—contribute to your identity. In Chapters 15 and 16, we explore gender identity and cultural identity in greater depth. Other characteristics, including those that make up reputation, also play a role in the formation of identity. Your identity is what gives you and others a sense of continuity, of being the same person tomorrow as today. It also makes you unique in the eyes of others.

 Concept Check

Define social identity, and explain the key features of continuity and contrast. Why is social identity so important?

Name and define two types of identity crises. How are they similar, and how are they different?

Summary and Evaluation

This chapter presented an outline of what personality psychologists know about the self. This knowledge is neatly divided into three broad areas: self-concept, self-esteem, and social identity. These aspects of the self are important to understanding personality. The notion of a self makes sense in terms of our everyday lives and our experience. We frequently use terms such as *selfish, self-worship, selfless, self-conscious,* and *self-esteem* in everyday life. In the evolution of language, we developed a rich vocabulary for talking about the self. This reflects people's general preoccupation with themselves. Another reason psychologists are interested in the self is that it plays an important role in organizing a person's experiences of the world. What a person deems important, for example, are the things that are relevant to their self-concept. Moreover, people behave differently when they are self-involved than when they are not, so the concept of the self is important for understanding how people construe their world, their experiences, and their actions. The self is a major organizing force within the person.

Self-concept is a person's self-understanding. The self-concept has its start in infancy, when the child first makes a distinction between its body and everything else. This glimmer of self-concept goes on to develop, through repeated experiences of self-awareness, into a collection of characteristics that the child uses for self-definition, such as gender, age, and membership in a particular family. Children acquire skills and talents and start comparing themselves with others and refining their self-concept. They also develop a sense of privacy and a sense of their ability to keep secrets, so they begin to develop a private self-concept, things they know about themselves that no one else knows. Cognitive schemata then develop around aspects of the self; these knowledge structures are collections of characteristics associated with the self-concept. People also develop views of themselves in the future, their possible selves, which include both desirable (ideal self) and undesirable features. All in all, the self-concept is the person's answer to the questions "Who have I been, what am I like now, and who do I want to be in the future?" Authenticity further describes the feeling of living according to one's "true" self, the real or most natural version of the self.

Self-esteem is the evaluation a person makes of their self-concept along a good–bad dimension. People differ from each other in terms of whether they see themselves as worthwhile, valuable, and good. Research on self-esteem has emphasized how people respond to failure, and findings suggest that high self-esteem people persevere in the face of failure, whereas low self-esteem people often give up following failure. High self-esteem people seem particularly good at deflecting the bumps and bruises of everyday life. One strategy they seem particularly adept in using is, when something bad happens in one area of their lives, to remind themselves that other areas in their lives are going well. This puts negative events in perspective and helps them cope. Extremely high self-esteem, associated with narcissistic tendencies, can sometimes result in aggressive responses to threats to that self-esteem. Researchers have shown that narcissistic individuals often retaliate following negative feedback. Another clinical problem associated with self-esteem is extreme shyness. Shyness does have some biological correlates, but it is also associated with an overcontrolling parenting style. Shyness can often be changed through treatment efforts. Another area of research shows that high self-esteem people are often concerned with enhancing their self-concept, whereas low self-esteem people are often concerned with protecting what they have from insult. Finally, in terms of self-esteem variability, variable individuals seem especially sensitive to evaluative life events, such as social slights and public failures.

The final aspect of the self discussed in this chapter was social identity, as a person's outward manifestation or the impression they give others. Identity develops over time through relations with others. For many people, the development of an identity follows a period of experimentation, but for others it happens more easily by adopting ready-made social roles. There are periods in life when some people undergo identity crises and have to redefine their social identities. Developing an identity is a lifelong task, as identity changes with the changing social roles that come with age.

Erikson coined the term *identity crisis* to refer to the anxiety that comes with having to redefine one's social reputation. There are two kinds of crises: identity deficit, not forming an adequate identity; and identity conflict, in which two or more aspects of identity come into conflict. Despite crises and challenges, most people develop a solid identity, and other people know them for their unique characteristics.

Concept Check

Think back on this chapter in its entirety. What are the main aspects of the self as studied by psychologists? Offer a brief definition of each.

Which aspects of the self are private, and which are observable by others?

What is the "true" self? What does it mean to be authentic? Consider these ideas in your own life, and come to some conclusions about what they mean for you.

Key Terms

self-concept

self-esteem

social identity

self-awareness

social comparison

private self-concept

perspective taking

objective self-awareness

amygdala

self-schema

possible selves

ideal self

ought self

self-guides

authenticity

self-complexity

collective self-esteem

defensive pessimism

self-handicapping

self-esteem variability

continuity

contrast

identity deficit

self-concept differentiation

identity conflict

PART FIVE

The Social and Cultural Domain

In the social and cultural domain, the emphasis is on personality as it is affected by and expressed through social institutions, social roles and expectations, and relationships with other people in our lives.

We saw in Chapter 3 that several taxonomies of traits emphasize interpersonal traits, such as dominance versus submissiveness, or love versus hate. Indeed, most of the important trait adjectives in language are important for describing how people behave with others. Interpersonal traits have long-term outcomes in our lives. For example, whether a person is controlling or easygoing affects such different aspects of one's life as relationship satisfaction, conflicts and challenges at work, and the strategies used to achieve various goals. Whether a person tends to be nervous or optimistic affects the likelihood of diverse social outcomes, such as divorce or success in a particular career. Many of the most important individual differences and personality traits are played out in our interpersonal relationships.

We describe three key processes whereby personality affects social interactions. The first process is *selection,* in which people may choose specific social environments according to their personalities. A second process is *evocation,* in which our traits naturally evoke responses in others, such as distress or happiness. A final process whereby personality affects social interactions is *manipulation*, which involves intentional efforts to influence others. What are the strategies that people use to get what they want from others?

One important interpersonal context concerns sex and gender, which are essential parts of our social identity. Differences between men and women in terms of personality have long been of interest to personality psychology. Some researchers prefer to minimize the differences between men and women, emphasizing that sex differences are small and that the variability within a sex exceeds the variability between the sexes. Other researchers focus on the differences between the sexes and emphasize that some are large and are found across cultures. Men tend to score higher on aggressiveness, whereas women tend to score higher on measures of trust and nurturance.

Where do such differences come from? Much of what we call gender may have its origins in culture; that is, in how society makes up different rules and expectations for men and women. Other theories emphasize differences between men and women that may be due to hormones. Testosterone levels, for example, differ greatly between men and women, and testosterone has been reliably associated with the personality traits of dominance, aggression, and sexuality. Another theory is evolutionary and suggests that men and women faced different challenges and have evolved solutions to these different challenges. Whatever their origins, sex differences have long been of interest to personality psychologists and are clearly part of the social and cultural domain because they refer to and are played out in interpersonal relations.

A second socially relevant difference among people derives from their culture, the system of social rules, expectations, and rituals in which a person is raised. For example, in one culture it might be expected that a crying baby is always picked up and comforted by its parents, whereas in another culture crying babies are left to cry. Could it be that being raised in these two different cultures results in differences in adult personality? Indeed, do people in different cultures have different personalities?

An important goal of personality psychology is to understand how cultures shape personality and how specific cultures are different from or similar to one other. Besides identifying ways in which people from different cultures differ, cultural personality psychologists have also looked for similarities among cultures. One example of a cultural universal appears to be the expression of specific emotions. Another aspect of personality that appears to show cultural universality is described by the five-factor model of personality.

In this part of the book, we focus on the broader social-interpersonal, gender-related, and cultural aspects of personality.

Personality and Social Interaction

The Social and Cultural Domain

Kate and Genevieve sipped coffee while discussing their dates from the previous evening. "Andrew seemed like a nice guy, at least at first," Kate noted. "He was really polite, asked me what kind of food I liked, and he seemed genuinely interested in getting to know me. But I was a little turned off by the way he talked to our server. He was pretty rude and demanding. He also insisted on ordering my dinner for me, and he ordered something I didn't like very much. Then over dinner he talked about himself the whole time. At the end of the night, he tried to invite himself back to my place, but I told him that I was tired and had to work early the next day." "Did he try to kiss you or anything?" asked Genevieve. "Yeah, he started to give me a good-night kiss, but then he started getting a little aggressive, and I had to push him away. So he walked off all angry. He really wasn't that nice of a guy after all. Anyway, how did your date with Jen go?"

In the course of this conversation, Kate revealed a wealth of information about her date, Andrew—information that figures prominently in the social decisions we make. Andrew displayed aggressiveness, both toward the server and toward Kate during the good-night kiss. He displayed self-centredness, focusing on himself during the course of the dinner. He showed a lack of empathy, as illustrated by his uncaring attitude toward the feelings of the server and his abrupt sexual aggressiveness. The thin veneer of politeness quickly gave way over the evening, revealing an abrasive interpersonal disposition.

Profiles at online dating Web sites often mention personality characteristics that the person is seeking in a partner (e.g., caring, sense of humour, affectionate). Personality plays an important role in social interaction.
©David J. Green/Alamy Stock Photo

This episode illustrates several key ways in which personality influences social interaction. Personality interacts with situations in three ways: through selection, evocation, and manipulation of the situation. These three mechanisms can be applied to an understanding of how personality affects interpersonal situations. First, the personality characteristics of others influence whether we *select* them as our dates, friends, and even marriage partners. In this episode, Kate was turned off by Andrew's aggressive and self-centred personality characteristics. People's personality characteristics also play a role in the kinds of interpersonal situations they select to enter and stay in. For example, someone with a personality different from Kate's might actually be attracted to a guy like Andrew and could put up with his self-centredness.

Second, the personality qualities of others *evoke* certain responses in us. Andrew's aggressive displays upset Kate, evoking an emotional response that would not have been evoked if he had been kinder and more caring. Behaviours related to personality can evoke many responses in others, ranging from aggression to social support, and from relationship satisfaction to infidelity.

Third, personality is linked to the ways in which we try to influence or *manipulate* others. Andrew first tried the charm tactic. Then he pulled out the boasting tactic. Finally, he used coercion, trying to force himself on Kate. Someone with a different personality might use different tactics such as reason or reward.

These three processes—selection, evocation, and manipulation—are key ways in which personality interacts with the social environment. Individuals in everyday life are not exposed to all possible social situations; individuals with certain personality dispositions seek out and avoid social situations selectively. Personality also influences how we evoke different reactions from other people and how others in turn evoke different responses from us, sometimes quite unintentionally. And personality affects how we purposely influence, change, exploit, and manipulate the others with whom we have chosen to be associated.

Selection

In everyday life, people choose to enter some situations and to avoid others. These forms of situation selection can hinge on personality dispositions and how we view ourselves. Such choices range in importance from the seemingly trivial ("Should I attend this party tonight?") to the profound ("Should I take this job offer and move across the country?"). Social selections permeate daily life; they are decision points that direct us to choose one path and avoid another. These decisions, which determine the nature of our social environments and social worlds, are often based on the personality characteristics of the selector.

Mate selection provides a dramatic example of this mechanism. When you select a long-term partner, you place yourself into close and prolonged contact with one particular other. This alters the social environment to which you are exposed and in which you will reside. By selecting a partner, you are selecting the social acts you will experience and a network of friends and family.

In terms of personality characteristics, who do people seek as potential partners? Are there common personality characteristics that are highly desired by everyone? Do we look for potential partners who have personalities similar to our own or different from our own? And how is the choice of a partner linked to the likelihood that a couple will stay together over time?

Personality Characteristics Desired in a Partner

What do people want in a long-term partner? This was the focus of an international investigation of 10,047 individuals located on six continents and five islands from around the world (Buss et al., 1990). A total of 37 samples were chosen from 33 countries, representing every major racial group, religious group, and political system. Samples ranged from the coastal-dwelling Australians to the South African Zulu people. The economic status of the samples varied from middle- and upper-middle-class college/university students to lower socioeconomic groups, such as the Gujarati Indians and Estonians. Fifty researchers were involved in the data collection. Standard questionnaires were translated into the native language of each culture and then were administered to the samples by native residents of each culture. This study, the largest conducted on what people want in a long-term partner, revealed that personality characteristics play a central role in selection. In the Exercise that follows, you can complete this questionnaire yourself and see how your selection preferences compare with those of the worldwide sample.

 Exercise

INSTRUCTIONS: Evaluate the following factors in choosing a mate or partner. If you consider the factor to be

indispensable, give it	**3 points**
important, but not indispensable, give it	**2 points**
desirable, but not very important, give it	**1 point**
irrelevant or unimportant, give it	**0 points**

1. **Good cook and housekeeper**
2. **Pleasing disposition**
3. **Sociability**

4. **Similar educational background**
5. **Refinement, neatness**
6. **Good financial prospect**
7. **Chastity (no prior intercourse)**
8. **Dependable character**
9. **Emotional stability**
10. **Desire for home and children**
11. **Favourable social status**
12. **Good looks**
13. **Similar religious background**
14. **Ambition and industriousness**
15. **Similar political background**
16. **Mutual attraction or love**
17. **Good health**
18. **Education and intelligence**

Now compare your ratings with the ratings given by the international sample of 10,047 men and women shown in Table 15.1.

As you can see in Table 15.1, mutual attraction or love was the most favoured characteristic, viewed as indispensable by almost everyone in the world. After mutual attraction or love, personality characteristics loom large in people's mate selection preferences—dependable character, emotional stability, and pleasing disposition. You may recall that these are quite close to the labels given to three of the factors in the five-factor model of personality (see Chapter 3). Dependability is close to conscientiousness. Emotional stability is identical to the fourth factor on the five-factor model. And pleasing disposition is quite close to agreeableness. Other personality factors rated highly include sociability, refinement and neatness, and ambition and industriousness.

Note that the respondents' top choices, except for love, were personality characteristics. Thus, personality factors play a central role in what people worldwide are looking for in a long-term partner—findings that have now been documented over many decades of research (e.g., Fletcher et al., 2004; Kamble et al., 2014; Lei et al., 2011; Souza et al., 2016). Moreover, the priority placed on personality traits such as Agreeableness, Conscientiousness, and Emotional Stability occur regardless of sexual orientation; they are as strong among non-heterosexual men and women as they are among heterosexual men and women (Valentova et al., 2016). Low scores on these personality traits tend to be relationship "dealbreakers" (Jonason et al., 2015).

Assortative Mating for Personality: The Search for the Similar

Over the past century, two fundamentally competing scientific theories have been advanced for who is attracted to whom. **Complementary needs theory** postulates that people are attracted to those who have different personality dispositions than they have (Murstein, 1976; Winch, 1954). People who are dominant, for example, might have a need for someone whom they can control and dominate. People who are submissive, according to complementary needs theory, choose a mate who can dominate and control them. One easy way to think about complementary needs theory is with the phrase "opposites attract."

In contrast, **attraction similarity theory** postulates that people are attracted to those who have similar personality characteristics. People who are dominant might be attracted to those who are also dominant

Table 15.1	Summary of Ratings by Sex Using Entire International Sample					
	RATINGS BY MALES			**RATINGS BY FEMALES**		
Ranked Value	**Variable Name**	**Mean**	**Std. Dev.**	**Variable Name**	**Mean**	**Std. Dev.**
1.	Mutual attraction or love	2.81	0.16	Mutual attraction or love	2.87	0.12
2.	Dependable character	2.50	0.46	Dependable character	2.69	0.31
3.	Emotional stability and maturity	2.47	0.20	Emotional stability and maturity	2.68	0.20
4.	Pleasing disposition	2.44	0.29	Pleasing disposition	2.52	0.30
5.	Good health	2.31	0.33	Education and intelligence	2.45	0.25
6.	Education and intelligence	2.27	0.19	Sociability	2.30	0.28
7.	Sociability	2.15	0.28	Good health	2.28	0.30
8.	Desire for home and children	2.09	0.50	Desire for home and children	2.21	0.44
9.	Refinement, neatness	2.03	0.48	Ambition and industriousness	2.15	0.35
10.	Good looks	1.91	0.26	Refinement, neatness	1.98	0.49
11.	Ambition and industriousness	1.85	0.35	Similar education	1.84	0.47
12.	Good cook and housekeeper	1.80	0.48	Good financial prospect	1.76	0.38
13.	Good financial prospect	1.51	0.42	Good looks	1.46	0.28
14.	Similar education	1.50	0.37	Favourable social status or rating	1.46	0.39
15.	Favourable social status or rating	1.16	0.28	Good cook and housekeeper	1.28	0.27
16.	Chastity (no previous experience in sexual intercourse)	1.06	0.69	Similar religious background	1.21	0.56
17.	Similar religious background	0.98	0.48	Similar political background	1.03	0.35
18.	Similar political background	0.92	0.36	Chastity (no previous experience in sexual intercourse)	0.75	0.66

because they like someone who "pushes back." People who are extraverted might like partners who are also extraverted so that they can party together. One easy way to remember this theory is with the phrase "birds of a feather flock together." Although there have been many proponents of both theories over the past century, the results are now in. They provide overwhelming support for the attraction similarity theory and no support for the complementary needs theory (Buss, 2016). Although some individual differences exist, the research shows that people are generally drawn to those who share their traits and characteristics.

One of the most common findings in the mate selection literature—that people are partnered with people who are similar to themselves—is a phenomenon known as **assortative mating**. For nearly every variable that has been examined—from single actions to ethnic status—people seem to select mates or partners who are similar to themselves. Even for physical characteristics such as height, weight, and, astonishingly, nose breadth and earlobe length, couples show positive correlations. Even the perceived personality of individuals based on faces—that is, personality trait assessment based solely on judgments of photographs—shows evidence of assortative mating (Little, Burt, & Perrett, 2006). Couples who have been together the longest appear most similar in personality, a finding that results from the initial selection process and from dissimilar couples breaking up more frequently (e.g., Humbad et al., 2010).

Although research on assortative mating in gay and lesbian couples is lacking, a few studies have suggested a slightly smaller degree of similarity in basic characteristics compared to straight couples (e.g., Verbakel & Kalmijn, 2014). According to recent analyses of large population data from the Netherlands, gay male couples are less homogenous in terms of age and education than different-sex couples, while lesbian couples are less homogenous in age only (Verbakel & Kalmijn, 2014); yet there remains evidence for some degree of assortative mating even in same-sex partnerships. In terms of personality traits specifically, a study of gay and straight couples in Brazil and the Czech Republic found that men in both types of relationships preferred similar traits to roughly the same degree (Štěrbová et al., 2017). However, when the researchers examined the actual traits of both populations (rather

People often are attracted to others who are similar to themselves. This refers to the concept of assortative mating.
©Rido/Shutterstock

than preferences), they found that straight partners resembled each other on Extraversion, Openness, and Conscientiousness, while gay partners resembled each other only on Extraversion. It seems that in gay coupling, preferences translate into actual mate choice less often. One important factor in such differences may be the size of the mating pool, with gay and lesbian individuals having fewer potential partners to choose from.

Are the positive correlations observed between partners caused by the active selection of significant others who are similar? Or are the positive correlations merely byproducts of other causal processes? Sheer proximity, for example, could, in principle, account for some of the positive correlations. It is known that people tend to marry those who are close by. Notions of romantic love aside, the "one and only" typically lives within driving distance. And because people in close proximity may have certain common characteristics, the positive correlations found between partners may be merely a side effect of mating with those who are close by rather than the active selection of partners who are similar. Cultural institutions, such as colleges and universities, may promote assortative mating by preferentially admitting those who are similar with respect to certain variables, such as intelligence, motivation, and social skills.

To test these competing predictions, Botwin and colleagues (Botwin, Buss, & Shackelford, 1997) studied two samples of subjects: straight dating couples and straight newlywed couples. The participants were asked to express their preferences for the personality characteristics in a potential mate on 40 rating scales, which were scored on five dimensions of personality: Extraversion, Agreeableness, Conscientiousness, Emotional Stability, and Intellect–Openness. The next step was to assess personality dispositions on these dimensions, using the same 40 rating scales. Three data sources were used for this second stage: self-reports; reports by their partners; and independent reports by interviewers. Correlations with mate preferences were computed between two sets of personality ratings: the ones made by the subject (self) and the average of the peer and interviewer ratings of the subject (aggregate).

As shown in Table 15.2, these correlations were consistently positive. Those who scored high on Extraversion wanted to select an extraverted person as a partner. Those who scored high on Conscientiousness desired a conscientious partner. The conclusions from this study, of course, must be qualified by one important consideration—perhaps the preferences people express for the personalities of their ideal partners might be influenced by the partners they already have. If an emotionally stable person is already partnered to an emotionally stable person, perhaps the choice is justified by claiming that they are truly attracted to the person chosen. This could result in positive correlations between one's own personality and the personality people express for a desired partner. Nonetheless, studies of individuals who are not partnered already find the same pattern of results—people prefer those who are similar to themselves (e.g., Buss, 2012), supporting the attraction similarity theory.

Table 15.2 Personality Correlated with Partner Preferences among Straight Couples								
	DATING COUPLES				**MARRIED COUPLES**			
	MEN		**WOMEN**		**MEN**		**WOMEN**	
Trait	**Self**	**Aggregate**	**Self**	**Aggregate**	**Self**	**Aggregate**	**Self**	**Aggregate**
Extraversion	.33*	.42**	.59***	.35**	.20*	.15	.30**	.25**
Agreeableness	.37*	.17	.44***	.46***	.30**	.12	.44***	.31**
Conscientiousness	.34**	.45***	.59***	.53***	.53***	.49***	.61***	.53***
Emotional Stability	.29*	.36**	.52***	.30*	.27**	.21*	.32***	.27**
Intellect–Openness	.56***	.54***	.63***	.50***	.24*	.31**	.48***	.52****

$*p < .05$; $**p < .01$; $***p < .001$

Note: Each correlation in the table refers to the relationship between the personality trait of the individual and the corresponding personality trait desired in a partner. Thus, under Men, Self-Report column, the .33* indicates that men who are highly extraverted tend to prefer partners who are also extraverted. The fact that all the correlations in the table are positive, many significantly so, indicates that people generally want mates who are similar to themselves in personality.

These data provide evidence that positive correlations on personality variables between partners in committed relationships are due, at least in part, to direct social preferences based on the personality characteristics of those doing the selecting. Subsequent studies have confirmed that people actively prefer romantic partners who are similar to themselves on Extraversion, Agreeableness, Conscientiousness, Emotional Stability, and Intellect–Openness. However, most people consider the "ideal" romantic partner personality to be someone who is higher on Extraversion, Conscientiousness, Agreeableness, and Emotional Stability than they are (Figueredo, Sefcek, & Jones, 2006). In sum, personality characteristics appear to play a pivotal role in the social mechanism of selection.

Do People Get the Partners They Want? And Are They Happy?

A fact of human life is that we do not always get what we want, and this is true of partner selection. You may want a partner who is kind, understanding, dependable, emotionally stable, and intelligent, but such desirable partners are always in short supply compared with the numbers of people who seek them. Therefore, many people end up partnered with individuals who fall short of their ideals. It is reasonable to predict, therefore, that individuals whose partners deviate from their ideals will be less satisfied than those whose partners embody their desires.

Table 15.3 shows the correlations between the preferences that individuals express for the ideal personality characteristics of their partners and the partners' actual personality characteristics (Botwin et al., 1997, p. 127). Across three of the four subsamples—women who are dating, women who are married, and men who are married—there are modest but consistently positive correlations between the personality desired in a partner and the actual personality characteristics displayed by the partner. The correspondence between what one wants and what one gets is especially strong for Extraversion and Intellect–Openness. In short, as a general rule, people seem to find the partners they want in terms of personality.

Table 15.3 Personality Partner Preferences and Personality of Partner Obtained among Straight Couples								
	DATING COUPLES				**MARRIED COUPLES**			
	WOMEN'S PREFERENCES		**MEN'S PREFERENCES**		**MEN'S PREFERENCES**		**WOMEN'S PREFERENCES**	
Partner's Personality	Self	Aggregate	Self	Aggregate	Self	Aggregate	Self	Aggregate
Extraversion	.25	.39**	.28*	.24	.39***	.49***	.31***	.32**
Agreeableness	.28*	.32	.24	.02	.20*	.40***	.03	.25
Conscientiousness	.28*	.29*	.24	.26	.36***	.46***	.13	.24
Emotional Stability	.36**	.12	.40**	.10	.27**	.37**	.07	.12
Intellect–Openness	.33**	.41**	.40**	.11	.24**	.39***	.14	.39****

$^*p < .05; ^{**}p < .01; ^{***}p < .001$

Are people who get what they want happier with their relationships than people who do not? To examine this issue, Botwin and colleagues (1997) created difference scores between the preferences each individual expressed for the ideal personality of a partner and assessments of the partner's actual personality. These difference scores were then used to predict satisfaction with the relationship, after first controlling for the main effects of the spouse's personality. The results were consistent—one's partner's personality had a substantial effect on relationship satisfaction. Specifically, people were especially happy with their relationships if they were partnered with people who were high on the personality characteristics of Agreeableness, Emotional Stability, and Intellect–Openness. But the difference in scores between the partner's personality and one's ideal for that personality did *not* predict relationship satisfaction. In other words, the key to happiness is having a partner who is agreeable, emotionally stable, and open, regardless of whether the partner departs in specific ways from what one wants (Luo et al., 2008).

The correlations between the participants' relationship satisfaction scores and the partners' personality scores, obtained through the partners' self-reports, are shown in Table 15.4. Having a partner who is *agreeable* is an especially

Table 15.4   Facet of Relationship Satisfaction and Partner's Self-Reported Trait Ratings among Straight Couples

Relationship Satisfaction	PARTNER'S SELF-REPORTED TRAIT RATINGS				
	E	A	C	ES	I–O
Men's relationship satisfaction					
General	.12	.32***	.06	.27**	.29**
Partner as someone to confide in	−.05	.27**	.07	.11	.05
Sexual	−.08	.31**	.32***	.25**	.04
Partner as source of encouragement and support	.03	.29**	.11	.26**	.18
Love and affection expressed	.07	.31**	.14	.21*	.26**
Enjoyment of time spent with spouse	.11	.30**	.13	.28**	.08
Frequency of laughing with spouse	.19*	.23*	.19	.11	.24**
Partner as source of stimulating conversation	.06	.12	−.04	.21*	.17
Women's relationship satisfaction					
General	.07	.37***	.20*	.23*	.31***
Partner as someone to confide in	.06	.25**	.15	.24**	.27**
Sexual	.08	.19*	.14	.09	.13
Partner as source of encouragement and support	.04	.47***	.06	.20*	.31***
Love and affection expressed	−.04	.29**	.14	.28**	.33***
Enjoyment of time spent with spouse	.06	.27**	.06	.33***	.18
Frequency of laughing with spouse	−.02	.27**	−.02	.10	.08
Partner as source of stimulating conversation	.23*	.24**	.25**	.18	.45***

*$p < .05$; **$p < .01$; ***$p < .001$

Note: E = Extraversion; A = Agreeableness: C = Conscientiousness: ES = Emotional Stability; I–O = Intellect–Openness.

strong predictor of being happy with one's relationship for both men and women. People partnered with agreeable individuals are more satisfied with their sex lives and view their partners as more loving and affectionate, a source of shared laughter, and a source of stimulating conversation. People partnered with disagreeable individuals are the most unhappy with the relationship and perhaps are most at risk of separation or divorce.

The other personality factors that are consistently associated with relationship satisfaction are conscientiousness, emotional stability, and intellect–openness. Straight men whose wives score high on conscientiousness are significantly more sexually satisfied with their marriage. Straight women whose husbands score high on conscientiousness are generally more satisfied as well as happier with their partners as sources of stimulating conversation—a finding replicated in a study of 125 long-wed couples (Claxton et al., 2012). Both men and women whose partners score high on emotional stability are generally more satisfied, view their partners as sources of encouragement and support, and enjoy spending time with their partners. Low emotional stability scores are linked with relationship dissatisfaction among dating university students and among older adults in committed relationships (Slatcher & Vazire, 2009). Indeed, a meta-analysis of 19 samples found that emotional stability and agreeableness were the strongest predictors of satisfaction in intimate romantic relationships (Malouff et al., 2010). High neuroticism in one or both members of the couple leads to relationship dissatisfaction (Schaffhuser et al., 2014). On a positive note for those partnered with individuals low on emotional stability, one study found that having frequent sexual intercourse seems to protect couples from the negative marital consequences of neuroticism (Russell & McNulty, 2011).

Another link between personality and relationship satisfaction emerges over the years following the first year of marriage. As a general rule, in the newlywed year, people rate their partners high on agreeableness, conscientiousness, extraversion, and intellect–openness (Watson & Humrichouse, 2006). Over the ensuing two years, however, ratings of partners' personalities become increasingly negative on these dimensions, illustrating a "honeymoon effect." And those who show the most marked negative ratings of their partner's personality over time show the largest decreases in marital happiness. One speculation is that couples in progressively unhappy marriages actually display progressively more unpleasant personalities, such as lower levels of agreeableness, but only *within* the marital context itself. Those who maintain positive illusions about their partner's personality, in contrast, maintain high levels of satisfaction (Barelds & Dijkstra, 2011). Another key predictor of marital satisfaction is mate value—whether one succeeds in selecting a mate whose personality embodies qualities most people want. Those partnered with high mate-value individuals tend to be happier in their relationship than those partnered with lower mate value individuals (Conroy-Beam et al., 2016).

In summary, the personality of one's partner plays an important role in marital satisfaction. Those who select partners high on agreeableness, conscientiousness, emotional stability, and intellect–openness show the greatest happiness with their relationships. Those who select partners low on these personality factors are the most unhappy with their relationships. Differences from each person's individual ideal, however, do not appear to contribute to relationship or marital satisfaction. An important caveat in the research findings to date is that they are primarily based on straight couples. More research is needed on assortative mating and personality in gay and lesbian partnerships.

Personality and the Selective Breakup of Couples

We have examined two ways in which personality plays a role in the partner selection process. First, there appear to be universal selection preferences—personality characteristics that everyone desires in a potential partner, such as dependability and emotional stability. Second, beyond the desires shared by everyone, people prefer partners who are similar to themselves in personality—dominant people prefer other dominant people, conscientious people prefer other conscientious people, and so on. But there is a third role that personality plays in the process of selection—its role in the selective breakup of relationships.

According to one theory of conflict between the sexes, breakups should occur more when one's desires are violated than when they are fulfilled (Buss, 2016). Following the **violation of desire** theory, we would predict that people partnered with others who lack desired characteristics, such as dependability and emotional stability, will more frequently end the relationship. We would also predict, based on people's preferences for those who share their personality attributes, that the couples who are dissimilar on personality will break up more often than those who fulfill desires for similarity. Are these predictions borne out in the research findings?

Across a wide variety of studies, *emotional instability* has been the most consistent personality predictor of relationship instability and dissolution, emerging as a significant predictor in nearly every study that has included a measure of it (Karney & Bradbury, 1997; Kelly & Conley, 1987). One reason is that emotionally unstable individuals display high levels of jealousy—they worry more about a partner's infidelity, try to prevent social contact between their partner and others, and react more explosively when their partner does in fact engage in sex with others (Dijkstra & Barelds, 2008). Low impulse control, or low conscientiousness (i.e., being impulsive and unreliable), particularly as exhibited by men, also emerges as a good predictor of relationship dissolution and dissatisfaction in straight relationships (Claxton et al., 2012; Kelly & Conley, 1987). A study of 52 nations found that the personality traits of low agreeableness and low conscientiousness (high impulsivity) were linked with higher rates of sexual infidelity in romantic relationships (Schmitt, 2004). Interestingly, extraversion and dominance are linked with higher levels of sexual promiscuity (Markey & Markey, 2007; Schmitt, 2004), although these personality traits are *not* related to relationship satisfaction or breakups.

Being partnered with someone who lacks the personality characteristics that most people desire—dependability, emotional stability, and pleasing disposition—puts one most at risk for breakup. People actively seek partners who are dependable and emotionally stable, and those who fail to choose such partners are at greater risk of breaking up. Other studies also point to two other influences of personality on relationship satisfaction or dissatisfaction. One is *similarity in overall personality profile,* rather than similarity in individual personality traits (Luo & Klohnen, 2005). The second is closeness of match between an *individual's conception of an ideal mate* and their partner's actual personality (Zentner, 2005). Both personality profile similarity and congruence between ideal and actual partner are linked with positive relationship outcomes, such as marital quality.

In summary, personality plays two key roles in mate selection. First, as part of the initial selection process, it determines the partners to whom we are attracted and the partners whom we desire. Second, personality affects satisfaction with one's partner and therefore determines the selective breakup of couples. Those who fail to select partners who are similar, agreeable, conscientious, and emotionally stable tend to break up more often than those who succeed in selecting such partners.

Shyness and the Selection of Risky Situations

Several other domains of selection have also been explored by personality researchers. One important domain pertains to the effects of the personality disposition of shyness. **Shyness** is defined as a tendency to feel tense, worried, or anxious during social interactions or even when anticipating a social interaction (Addison & Schmidt, 1999). Shyness is a common phenomenon, and more than 90 percent of the population experience shyness at some point during their lives (Zimbardo, 1977). Some people, however, seem to be dispositionally shy—they tend to feel awkward in many social situations and so tend to avoid situations in which they will be forced to interact with people.

The effects of shyness on the selection of situations have been well documented. During high school and early adulthood, shy individuals tend to avoid social situations, resulting in a form of isolation (Schmidt & Fox, 1995). Shy women are also more likely to avoid going to the doctor for gynecological exams, and hence they put themselves at greater health risk (Kowalski & Brown, 1994). They are less likely to bring up the awkward issue of contraception with their partners before sexual intercourse, and so put themselves in potentially dangerous sexual situations (Bruch & Hynes, 1987).

Shyness also affects whether a person is willing to select risky situations in the form of gambles (Addison & Schmidt, 1999). In an experiment led by Louis Schmidt of McMaster University in Hamilton, Ontario, shy people were identified through the Cheek (1983) shyness scale. This scale contains items such as "I find it hard to talk to strangers" and "I feel inhibited in social situations." On entry into the laboratory, each participant received the following instructions: "During this part of the experiment, you have a chance to win some money by picking a poker chip out of this container. There are 100 poker chips in this box that are numbered from 1 to 100. . . ." The participants were given a choice to pick a gamble that they would most likely win (95 percent odds of winning) but from which they would receive only a small amount of money (e.g., 25¢), or to pick a riskier gamble, perhaps with only a 5 percent chance of winning but from which, if they won, they would receive $4.75. The experimenters also recorded the heart rate of the participants during their choice of gambles.

Researchers found that shy women differed substantially from their non-shy counterparts in choosing the smaller bets that were linked with a higher likelihood of winning. The non-shy women, in contrast, chose the riskier bets with a lower likelihood of winning but with a larger payoff if they did win. During the task, the shy participants showed a larger increase in heart rate, suggesting that fearfulness might have led them to avoid the risky gambles (Addison & Schmidt, 1999).

Shy individuals often feel tense or anxious in social situations and avoid entering situations in which they would be forced to interact with others.
©BananaStock/Getty Images

These studies illustrate the importance of the personality disposition of shyness in the selection of, or avoidance of, certain situations. Shy women tend to avoid others, creating social isolation, and to avoid choosing risky gambles. Perhaps paradoxically, they also avoid going to the doctor for gynecological exams and avoid obtaining condoms, thus putting themselves at greater health risk than less shy women. Shyness, in short, appears to have a substantial impact on the selective entry into, or avoidance of, situations.

Other Personality Traits and the Selection of Situations

Other personality traits have been shown to affect selective entry into, or avoidance of, certain situations (Ickes et al., 1997). Those who are more empathic, for example, are more likely to enter situations such as volunteering for community activities (Davis et al., 1999). Those high on psychoticism seem to choose volatile and spontaneous situations more than formal or stable ones (Furnham, 1982). Those high on Machiavellianism prefer face-to-face situations, perhaps because these offer a better chance to ply their social manipulative skills to exploit others (Geis & Moon, 1981). People high on extraversion tend to select more friends; however, people high on agreeableness tend to be selected more often by others as friends (Selfhout et al., 2010). High sensation seekers have been found to more frequently choose to enter risky situations (McCoul & Haslam, 2001). In a study of 112 straight men, those who scored high on sensation seeking were more likely than their low-scoring peers to have unprotected sex more frequently ($r = .21$, $p < .05$). Even more striking, high sensation seekers had sexual intercourse with many more different partners than low sensation seekers ($r = .45$, $p < .001$).

Personality researchers are also interested in how people choose to use online social environments like Facebook and Twitter as a function of their personality traits. A large international study of over 20,000 adults from around the world found that high extraversion, agreeableness, conscientiousness, and neuroticism were all associated with more frequent social media use, including for the purposes of social interaction and reading news (Gil de Zúñiga et al., 2017). Perhaps not surprisingly, extraversion has been the trait most consistently associated with higher social media use for social and relational purposes, while openness to experience has been inconsistent across studies (Correa et al., 2010; Gil de Zuniga et al., 2017). In sum, personality affects the situations to which people are exposed through their selective entry into, or avoidance of, certain kinds of activities, even those which unfold on our electronic devices.

 Concept Check

Describe three specific ways in which personality traits influence selection processes in relationships, from partner selection to relationship satisfaction and dissolution.

How is shyness associated with the selection of risky situations?

Evocation

Once we select others to occupy our social environment, a second class of processes is set into motion—the evocation of reactions from others. **Evocation** may be defined as the ways in which features of personality elicit reactions from others. Recall from Chapter 3 the study of highly active children. Compared with their less active peers, highly active children tend to elicit hostility and competitiveness from others. Both parents and teachers tend to get into power struggles with these active children. The social interactions of less active children are more peaceful and harmonious. This is a perfect example of the process of evocation at work—a personality characteristic (in this case, activity level) evokes a predictable set of social responses from others (hostility and power struggles). Another example comes from the evocation of trust and cooperativeness by those high on honesty–humility (Thielmann & Hilbig, 2014). Perhaps because high scorers tend to trust other people, they evoke trustworthy expectations in those with whom they interact.

Aggression and the Evocation of Hostility

It is well known that aggressive people evoke hostility from others (Dodge & Coie, 1987). People who are aggressive expect that others will be hostile toward them. One study has shown that aggressive people chronically interpret ambiguous behaviour from others, such as being bumped into, as intentionally hostile (Dill et al., 1999). This is called a **hostile attributional bias**, the tendency to infer hostile intent on the part of others in the face of ambiguous behaviour from them.

Because they expect others to be hostile, aggressive people tend to treat others in an aggressive manner. People who are treated in an aggressive manner often aggress back. In this case, the aggressive reactions of others confirm what the aggressive person suspected all along—that others have hostility toward them. But what the aggressive person fails to realize is that the hostility from others is a product of their own making—the aggressor evokes it from others by treating them aggressively. A recent review of the research on children and adolescents found that *reactive aggression* (the kind that involves reacting in anger and frustration) is more closely associated with the hostile attribution bias than *proactive* or premeditated aggression (Martinelli et al., 2018).

Evocation of Anger and Upset in Couples

Personality can play a role in evoking conflict in close relationships in at least two ways. First, a person can perform actions that cause an emotional response in a partner. A dominant person, for example, might act in a condescending manner, habitually evoking upset in the partner. Or a person low in conscientiousness might neglect household chores and responsibilities, which might upset their partner. In short, personality characteristics can *evoke emotions* in others through the actions performed.

A second form of evocation occurs when a person elicits actions from another that in turn upset the original elicitor. An aggressive man, for example, might elicit the silent treatment from his partner, which in turn upsets him because his partner won't speak to him. A condescending wife might undermine the self-esteem of her husband and then become angry because he lacks self-confidence. People's personality traits can upset others either directly by influencing how they act toward others or indirectly by eliciting actions from others that are upsetting.

To examine these forms of evocation, it is necessary to design a study that assesses the personality characteristics of both persons involved. In one study, the personality characteristics of husbands and wives were assessed through three data sources: self-report, spouse-report, and independent reports by two interviewers (Buss, 1991a). An instrument assessed multiple sources of anger and upset in close relationships (Buss, 1989). A short version of this instrument is shown in the Exercise in this section.

❓ Exercise

INSTRUCTIONS: We all do things that upset or anger other people from time to time. Think of a close romantic partner or close friend with whom you have been involved. Following is a list of things this person might have done that evoked anger or upset in you. Read the list, and place a check by the things your partner or close friend has done in the past year that have irritated, angered, annoyed, or upset you.

_____ 1. **They treated me as if I were stupid or inferior.**
_____ 2. **They demanded too much of my time.**
_____ 3. **They ignored my feelings.**
_____ 4. **They slapped me.**
_____ 5. **They saw someone else intimately.**
_____ 6. **They did not help clean up.**
_____ 7. **They fussed too much with his/her appearance.**
_____ 8. **They acted too moody.**
_____ 9. **They refused to have sex with me.**
_____ 10. **They talked about members of the opposite sex as if they were sex objects.**
_____ 11. **They got drunk.**
_____ 12. **They did not dress well or appropriately for a social gathering.**
_____ 13. **They told me that I was ugly.**
_____ 14. **They tried to use me for sexual purposes.**
_____ 15. **They acted selfishly.**

These acts represent items from the larger instrument of 147 acts that one can do to upset or anger a member of the opposite sex. The acts correspond to the following factors: (1) condescending,

(2) possessive/jealous, (3) neglecting/rejecting, (4) abusive, (5) unfaithful, (6) inconsiderate, (7) physically self-absorbed, (8) moody, (9) sexually withholding, (10) sexualizing of others, (11) abusive of alcohol, (12) dishevelled, (13) insulting of partner's appearance, (14) sexually aggressive, and (15) self-centred. It turns out that the personality of the person we are close to is a reasonably good predictor of whether that person will perform these upsetting acts.

Statistical analyses were conducted to determine which personality traits predicted that the partner would become upset. The results were similar for men and women.

The husbands high on dominance tended to upset their partners by being condescending—treating their wives' opinions as unintelligent or inferior and placing more value on their own opinions. The husbands who scored low on conscientiousness, in contrast, tended to upset their wives by having extramarital affairs. By far the strongest predictors of evoked anger and upset, however, were the personality characteristics of disagreeableness and emotional instability. Disagreeable husbands evoked anger and upset in their wives in the following ways: being condescending, such as treating them as if they were inferior; neglecting and rejecting them, such as failing to spend enough time with them and ignoring their feelings; abusing them, such as slapping, hitting, or spitting; committing infidelity; abusing alcohol; insulting their appearance, such

The strongest predictors of a wife's anger and relationship dissatisfaction in heterosexual marriages are the personality traits of disagreeableness and emotional instability on the part of the husband.
©SrdjanVrebac/Shutterstock

as calling them ugly; and exhibiting self-centredness. Indeed, low agreeableness of the husband was a better predictor of evoking upset in the wife than any other personality variable in the study.

The more emotionally unstable husbands also evoked anger and upset in their wives. In addition to being condescending, abusive, unfaithful, inconsiderate, and abusive of alcohol, these husbands also upset their wives by being moody (acting irritable) as well as jealous and possessive. For example, the emotionally unstable men tended to upset their wives by demanding too much attention, monopolizing the wife's time, being too dependent, and flying into jealous rages.

Several other studies have confirmed the important role of agreeableness and emotional stability in evoking or diminishing conflict in interpersonal relationships. In one study that used both hypothetical and daily diary assessments of conflict, those high in agreeableness tended to evoke less interpersonal conflict (Jensen-Campbell & Graziano, 2001). One reason might be that highly agreeable individuals tend to use "compromise" in dealing with conflict when it arises, whereas those low in agreeableness are less willing to compromise and are more likely to use verbal insults and physical force to deal with conflict. The importance of low agreeableness in evoking conflict extends to a wide variety of interpersonal relationships, including those in the workplace (Bono et al., 2002).

These links between personality and conflict show up at least as soon as early adolescence—young teenagers low in agreeableness not only evoke more conflict, but are also more likely to become victimized by their peers in high school (Jensen-Campbell et al., 2002). More agreeable individuals tend to use more effective conflict resolution tactics, a path leading to harmonious social interactions (Jensen-Campbell et al., 2003). They also tend to evoke trust and cooperation in laboratory-based economic games (Zhao & Smillie, 2015). Those high in neuroticism also appear more likely to experience greater conflict in their relationships, whereas those high in positive emotionality (a close cousin of agreeableness) experience less conflict in all of their relationships (Robins, Caspi, & Moffitt, 2002). Indeed, studies from the United States, Australia, the Netherlands, and Germany reveal that *agreeableness* and *emotional stability* are the traits most consistently conducive to evoking satisfaction in relationships (Barelds, 2005; Donnellan, Larsen-Rife, & Conger, 2005; Heaven et al., 2003; Neyer & Voigt, 2004; White, Hendrick, & Hendrick, 2004). The Application box provides principles to make a successful marriage.

Application

Psychologist John Gottman has been conducting research on marriage and relationship dynamics for three decades. His main question has been "What distinguishes the happily married couple from the dissatisfied, unhappy couple?" After studying thousands of marital pairs, some of whom have been happily married for years and others of whom were applying for divorce, he has found many ways that the happy and unhappy couples differ. He distilled his research findings in an applied book on how to make marriage work (Gottman & Silver, 1999). His seven principles of positive relationships are summarized below. Several of these principles concern behaviours related to evoking responses in the partner.

1. **Develop an empathic understanding of your partner (see Chapter 11 for a discussion of empathy). Get to know their "world," their preferences, and the important events in their life. As an example, once a day try to find out one important or significant event for your partner: what they are looking forward to or what important event happened to them. Trivial as it sounds, try asking, "How was your day?" each day.**
2. **Remain fond of each other and try to nurture your affection for your partner. Remember why you like this person, and tell them about it. As an example, keep a photo album together and go over it once in a while, reminding yourself of the fun times you had together and how much you enjoy being with this special person.**
3. **In times of stress, turn toward, rather than away from, each other. Also during the good times, do things together. In other words, don't take your partner for granted, and never ignore him, even in day-to-day life. Pay attention, stay connected, touch each other, and talk frequently.**
4. **Share power, even if you think you are the expert. Let your partner influence you. Ask them for help once in a while. Ask for their opinion. Let them know that their views matter to you.**
5. **You will undoubtedly have arguments. However, try to argue only about the solvable problems. When arguing:**
   - **Start gently**
   - **Proceed with respect**
   - **If feelings get hurt, stop and try to repair those hurt feelings**
   - **Be willing to compromise**
6. **Realize that some problems may never be solved. For example, perhaps one of you is religious and the other is not, and both intend to stay this way. Avoid gridlock on such unsolvable problems and don't let them become permanent topics of argument. Agree to disagree on certain issues.**
7. **Become a "we" instead of "I" and "I." Make the relationship important and consider it as well as your own wants and desires. Think about what is best for "us" rather than only what is best for "me."**

Source: Adapted from Gottman & Silver, 1999.

Personality can also evoke responses from others in a wide variety of social contexts outside of romantic relationships. Extraverted people tend to crack more jokes, evoking greater laughter from others than do introverts (Eysenck & Eysenck, 1985). Agreeable people tend to evoke more social support from their parents (Gallo & Smith, 1999). And narcissistic people report receiving more likes and comments on their Facebook posts, likely the result of their tendency to evoke a positive response from others (Marshall et al., 2015). One's personality, in short, can create the social environment to which one is exposed through the process of evocation.

Evocation of Likability, Pleasure, and Pain

One of the most important effects a person can have on the social world is the evocation of likability. Being liked by others is linked with higher levels of adjustment, mental health, and even academic performance (Wortman & Wood, 2011). Some personality traits consistently evoke likability in others—those linked with agreeableness, the sociable component of extraversion, and the honesty–humility factor (Wortman & Wood, 2011). People with these qualities evoke pleasure in others, leading to their liking (Saucier, 2010). Being extraverted increases likability even on online social networks (Stopfer et al., 2013). In contrast, people low on agreeableness and honesty–humility evoke pain in others. They cause others to be offended, annoyed, irritated, and even frightened and intimidated. Personality, in short, creates a footprint on one's social world by evoking liking, pleasure, or pain in other people.

Evocation Through Expectancy Confirmation

Expectancy confirmation is a phenomenon whereby people's beliefs about the personality characteristics of others cause them to evoke in others actions that are consistent with the initial beliefs. The phenomenon of expectancy confirmation has also been called *self-fulfilling prophecy*. Can mere beliefs have such a powerful role in evoking behaviour from others?

In a study of expectancy confirmation, Snyder and Swann (1978) led individuals to believe that they would be dealing with a hostile and aggressive individual and then introduced the two individuals. They found that people's beliefs led them to act in an aggressive manner toward the unsuspecting target. Then the behaviour of the unsuspecting target was examined. The intriguing finding was that the unsuspecting target actually acted in a more hostile manner, behaviour that was evoked by the person who was led to expect hostility. In this example, beliefs about the personality of the other actually created the behaviour that confirmed those initial beliefs (Snyder & Cantor, 1998).

Expectancies about personality may have widespread evocation effects in everyday life. After all, we often hear information about a person's reputation prior to, or following, actual encounters with the person. We hear that a person is smart, socially skilled, egocentric, or manipulative. These beliefs about the personality characteristics of others may have far-reaching effects on evoking behaviour that confirm our initial beliefs. It is sometimes said that, in order to change your personality, you must move to a place where people don't already know you. Through the process of expectancy confirmation, people who already know you may unwittingly evoke in you behaviour that confirms their beliefs, thereby constraining your ability to change.

Expectancy confirmation has also been noted as one mechanism through which stigmas can have a negative impact on individuals who are stigmatized. People's negative stereotypes about certain groups of people can lead them to interact with members of those groups in ways that elicit behaviours in line with the original stereotypes (Major & O'Brien, 2005). Of course for members of any minority group, moving to a new place may not be enough to escape the effects of this phenomenon.

 Concept Check

Define the hostile attributional bias and compare it to the concept of expectancy confirmation. Are they the same or similar? How so?

Describe one specific example of evocation within the context of relationships.

Manipulation: Social Influence Tactics

Manipulation, or social influence, includes all the ways in which people intentionally try to change the behaviour of others. No malicious intent need be implied by the term *manipulation*, although such intent is not excluded either. A parent might influence a child not to cross the street from between parked cars, but we would not call this behaviour malicious. Indeed, part of social living is that we influence others all the time. Thus, the term *manipulation* is used here descriptively, with no negative connotation.

From an evolutionary perspective (see Chapter 8), natural selection favours people who successfully manipulate objects in their environment. Some manipulable objects are inanimate, such as the raw materials used to build shelters, tools, clothing, and weapons. Other manipulable objects are alive, including predators and prey of different species and mates, parents, children, rivals, and allies of the same species. The manipulation of other people can be summarized as the various means by which we influence the psychology and behaviour of other people.

The process of manipulation can be examined from two perspectives within personality psychology. First, we can ask, "Are some individuals consistently more manipulative than others?" Second, we can ask, "Given that all people attempt to influence others, do stable personality characteristics predict the sorts of tactics that are used?" Do extraverted people, for example, more often use the charm tactic, whereas introverts use the silent treatment tactic?

A Taxonomy of Eleven Tactics of Manipulation

A **taxonomy** is simply a classification scheme—the identification and naming of groups within a particular subject field. Taxonomies of plants and animals, for example, have been developed to identify and name all the major plant and animal groups. The periodic table is a taxonomy of elements in the known universe. The Big Five personality traits that we examined in Chapter 3 is a taxonomy of major dimensions of personality. In this section, we look at the development of a taxonomy of tactics of manipulation—an attempt to identify and name the major ways in which people try to influence others in their social world.

A taxonomy of tactics of manipulation was developed through a two-step procedure: (1) nominations of acts of influence and (2) factor analysis of self-reports and observer-reports of the previously nominated acts (Buss, 1992; Buss et al., 1987). The act nomination procedure (see Chapter 2) was as follows: "We are interested in the things that people do to influence others in order to get what they want. Please think of your [romantic partner, close friend, mother, father, etc.]. How do you get this person to do something? What do you do? Please write down specific behaviours or acts that you perform in order to get this person to do things. List as many different sorts of acts as you can."

After this list was generated, the researchers converted it into a questionnaire that could be administered via self-report or observer report. You can see for yourself how this was done by taking the test in the Exercise in this section to find out what tactics of social influence you use. (Note that you may consider a friend or family member instead of a romantic partner.)

 Exercise

INSTRUCTIONS: When you want your [romantic partner, close friend, sibling, or parent] to do something for you, what are you likely to do? Look at each of the following items and *rate how likely you are to do each when you are trying to get this person to do something*. None of them will apply to all situations in which you want your [romantic partner, close friend, sibling, or parent] to do something, so rate how likely you are, in general, to do what is described. If you are extremely likely to do it, write a "7" in the blank next to the item. If you are not at all likely to do it, write a "1" in the blank next to the item. If you are somewhat likely to do it, write a "4" in the blank. Give intermediate ratings for intermediate likelihood of performing the behaviours.

_____ 1. I compliment them so that they will do it.
_____ 2. I act charming so they will do it.
_____ 3. I try to be loving and affectionate when I ask them.
_____ 4. I give them a small gift or card before I ask.
_____ 5. I don't respond to them until they do it.
_____ 6. I ignore them until they do it.
_____ 7. I am silent until they do it.
_____ 8. I refuse to do something they like until they do it.
_____ 9. I demand that they do it.
_____ 10. I yell at them until they do it.
_____ 11. I criticize them for not doing it.
_____ 12. I threaten them with something if they do not do it.
_____ 13. I give them reasons they should do it.
_____ 14. I point out all the good things that will come from doing it.
_____ 15. I explain why I want them to do it.
_____ 16. I show them that I would be willing to do it for them.
_____ 17. I pout until they do it.
_____ 18. I sulk until they do it.
_____ 19. I whine until they do it.
_____ 20. I cry until they do it.
_____ 21. I allow myself to be debased so that they will do it.
_____ 22. I lower myself so that they will do it.
_____ 23. I act humble so that they will do it.
_____ 24. I act submissive so that they will do it.

You can find out your scores by simply adding up your scores in clusters of four: items 1–4 = charm tactic; items 5–8 = silent treatment tactic; items 9–12 = coercion tactic; items 13–16 = reason tactic; items 17–20 = regression tactic; items 21–24 = self-abasement tactic. The tactics you tend to use the most are those with the highest sums. The tactics you use the least are those with the lowest sums. This is an abbreviated version of the instrument used in the studies by Buss (1992).

A large number of participants completed versions of an expanded instrument, consisting of 83 acts of influence or tactics. Factor analysis was then used to identify clusters of acts of influence, or tactics. In all, 11 tactics were discovered through this procedure, as shown in Table 15.5.

Table 15.5 Taxonomy of Eleven Tactics of Manipulation	
Tactic	**Sample Act**
Charm	I try to be loving when I ask them to do it.
Coercion	I yell at them until they do it.
Silent treatment	I don't respond to them until they do it.
Reason	I explain why I want them to do it.
Regression	I whine until they do it.
Self-abasement	I act submissive so that they will do it.
Responsibility invocation	I get them to make a commitment to doing it.
Hardball	I hit them so that they will do it.
Pleasure induction	I show them how much fun it will be to do it.
Social comparison	I tell them that everyone else is doing it.
Monetary reward	I offer them money so that they will do it.

Note: These tactics then formed the basis for subsequent analyses, such as whether there are sex differences in the tactics of manipulation and whether personality traits are associated with the tactics of manipulation that people use.

Source: Buss (1992).

Personality Predictors of Tactics of Manipulation

The next interesting question is whether people with certain personality traits are more likely to use certain tactics of manipulation, or whether manipulation is part of one's personality. One personality trait that describes people who are more manipulative in general is *Machiavellianism*, which we examine more closely in A Closer Look: The Machiavellian Personality. But many other traits have been associated with the tendency to be manipulative. In one study, a sample of more than 200 participants (Buss, 1992) rated each act of influence on the degree to which they used it in each of four relationships: spouse, friend, mother, and father. Then, correlations were computed between the personality traits of the participants and their use of each tactic of manipulation.

 A Closer Look

The Machiavellian Personality

The term *Machiavellian* originates from an Italian diplomat, Niccolò Machiavelli, who wrote a classic treatise, *The Prince,* in 1513 (Machiavelli, 1513/1966). Machiavelli observed, in his diplomatic role, that leaders come and go, rising and falling as they gain and lose power. *The Prince* is a book of advice on acquiring and maintaining power, which Machiavelli wrote to ingratiate himself with a new ruler after the one he had served had been overthrown. The advice is based on tactics for manipulating others and is entirely lacking in traditional values, such as trust, honour, and decency. One passage in the book, for example, notes that "men are so simple and so much inclined to obey immediate needs that a deceiver will never lack for victims for his deceptions" (p. 63). Machiavellianism, a trait first introduced in Chapter 3, eventually came to be associated with a manipulative strategy of social interaction and with a personality style that uses other people as tools for personal gain.

Two psychologists—Richard Christie and Florence Geis—developed a self-report scale to measure individual differences in Machiavellianism (Christie & Geis, 1970). The following are some sample items from the test, with the Machiavellian direction noted in parentheses:

- *The best way to handle people is to tell them what they want to hear* (true).
- *Anyone who completely trusts anyone else is asking for trouble* (true).
- *Honesty is the best policy in all cases* (false).
- *Never tell anyone the real reason you did something unless it is useful to do so* (true).
- *Most people who get ahead in the world lead clean, moral lives* (false).
- *The biggest difference between most criminals and other people is that criminals are stupid enough to get caught* (true).
- *It is wise to flatter important people* (true).

Niccolò Machiavelli, after whom the trait of Machiavellianism was named, wrote a book on strategies for manipulating others.
©BeBa/Iberfoto/The Image Works

As you can see from these items, the high scorer on the Machiavellianism scale (called a "high Mach") is manipulative, has a cynical world-view, treats other people as tools to be used for personal ends, does not trust other people, and lacks empathy. The low scorer on the Machiavellianism scale (called a "low Mach") is trusting, empathic, believes that things are clearly either right or wrong, and views human nature as basically good.

High and low scorers represent two alternative strategies of social conduct (Wilson, Near, & Miller, 1996). The high Mach represents an exploitative social strategy—one that betrays friendship and uses other people opportunistically. Theoretically, this strategy works best in social situations when there is room for innovation, rather than those that are highly constrained by rules. Political consulting or the world of an independent entrepreneur might be relatively unconstrained, allowing much latitude for the high Mach to operate. The more structured world of universities, on the other hand, might allow fewer opportunities for the high Machs to ply their skills.

The low Mach, in contrast, represents a strategy of cooperation sometimes called tit-for-tat. This strategy is based on reciprocity—you help me, and I'll help you in return, and we will both be better off as a result. This is a long-term social strategy, in contrast to the short-term strategy of the high Mach.

The success of the high Mach should depend greatly on the context. As demonstrated by Shultz (1993) in a study of stockbrokers, Machiavellianism is not a social strategy that works well all the time or in all settings. Social situations with many rules do not allow high Machs to con others, tell lies, and betray those who trust them with impunity. In these situations, the high Machs get caught, sustain damage to their reputations, and often are fired. In more fluid occupational contexts, high Machs succeed because they can wheel and deal, move quickly from one situation to another, and exploit the opportunities available in these less rule-bound settings.

Machiavellianism is a social strategy in which practitioners are quick to betray others (Wilson et al., 1996). In one laboratory study, participants were given an opportunity to steal money in a worker-supervisor situation (Harrell & Hartnagel, 1976). The participants played the role of workers. They were supervised by a person who acted trustingly and who stated that they did not need to monitor the workers closely. A full 81 percent of the high Machs stole money, as contrasted with only 24 percent of the low Machs. Furthermore, the high Machs who did steal took a larger amount of money than those few low Machs who stole, they tended to conceal their theft, and they lied more often to the supervisor when questioned about the theft.

Not only do high Machs lie and betray others' trust more than low Machs, but there is also evidence that they make more believable liars (Exline et al., 1970; Geis & Moon, 1981). In one study, high and low Machs were instructed to cheat on a task and then to lie to the experimenter about having cheated (Exline et al., 1970). The experimenter then became increasingly suspicious and questioned the participants about whether they had cheated. The high Machs were able to maintain greater eye contact than the low Machs. Fewer of the high Machs than the low Machs confessed. Finally, the high Machs were judged to be better liars than the low Machs.

The manipulative tactics used by the high Machs extend to the romantic and sexual domains. High Machs, compared to their low Mach peers, are more likely to feign love in order to get sex (e.g., "I sometimes say 'I love you' when I don't really mean it to get someone to have sex with me"), get a partner drunk in order to induce the partner to have sex, and express a willingness to use force to achieve sex with an unwilling partner (McHoskey, 2001). High Machs are more likely to cheat on their romantic partners and to be sexually unfaithful with other people. Interestingly, these links between Machiavellianism and specific tactics of manipulation are stronger for male than for female samples.

The Machiavellian strategy has many advantages, but it also has costs. By betraying, cheating, and lying, the high Mach runs the risk of retaliation and revenge by those who were exploited. Furthermore, the high Mach is more likely than the low Mach to incur damage to their reputation. Once people acquire reputations as exploitative, other people are more likely to avoid them and refuse to interact with them. In his work on the "dark triad" of personality (previously discussed in Chapter 3), Canadian researcher Del Paulhus has confirmed that although Machiavellianism overlaps with both *narcissism* and *subclinical psychopathy*, it remains a distinct construct with its own unique behavioural characteristics (Paulhus & Williams, 2002). Recent research has suggested that high Machs are higher in *fluid intelligence*, which involves the ability to solve new problems (Kowalski et al., 2018). This may explain why high Machs are able to successfully manipulate many situations.

This discussion of the Machiavellian strategy also illustrates the three key processes by which personality affects social interaction, bringing us back full circle to the three central processes of personality and social interaction. First, the high Mach tends to *select* situations that are loosely structured, untethered by rules that would restrict the deployment of an exploitative strategy. Second, the high Mach tends to *evoke* specific reactions from others, such as anger and retaliation for having been exploited. Third, the high Mach tends to *manipulate* other people in predictable ways, using tactics that are exploitative, self-serving, and deceptive.

Those scoring relatively high on dominance (a narrow trait within extraversion) tended to use coercion, such as demanding, threatening, cursing, and criticizing, in order to get their way. The highly dominant people also tended to use responsibility invocation, getting others to make commitments to a course of action and saying that it was their duty to do it.

Those scoring low in dominance (relatively submissive individuals) used the self-abasement tactic as a means of influencing others. They lowered themselves, for example, or tried to look sickly to get others to do what they wanted. Interestingly, these submissive individuals also tended to use the hardball tactic—deception, lying, degradation, and even violence—more often than their dominant counterparts.

The two primary tactics of influence used by highly agreeable people are pleasure induction and reason. Agreeable individuals tell and show others how enjoyable the activity will be, explain the rationale for wanting others to engage in particular behaviours, and point out all the good things that will come from doing them. A study of how children manipulate their parents regarding their choice of a mate revealed that highly agreeable children used the reason tactic, and also convinced their parents to trust them (Apostalou et al., 2015).

Those who are disagreeable, in contrast, frequently use coercion and the silent treatment—results also found in a Croatian study (Butkovic & Bratko, 2007). Not only do they threaten, criticize, yell, and scream in order to get their way, they also give the stony silent look and refuse to speak until the other person complies. Low-agreeable individuals are also likely to seek revenge on people whom they have perceived to have wronged them in some way, supporting the general use of cost-inflicting rather than benefit-bestowing tactics of manipulation (McCullough et al., 2001). Low-agreeable individuals tend to be more selfish in their use of collective resources, whereas high-agreeable individuals exercise more self-restraint when the group's resources are scarce or threatened (Koole et al., 2001).

The "silent treatment" is a manipulation strategy often employed by people high on the trait of disagreeableness.
©Image Source/Getty Images

The personality disposition of conscientiousness is associated with only one tactic of social influence: reason. Conscientious individuals explain why they want the other person to do something, provide logical explanations for wanting it done, and explain the underlying rationale for doing it. One study found that low-conscientious individuals are more likely to use criminal strategies in gaining resources, as indicated by arrest records and recidivism (being rearrested after being let out of prison) (Clower & Bothwell, 2001).

Emotionally unstable individuals (i.e., those high on neuroticism) use a wide variety of tactics to manipulate others—hardball and coercion, but also reason and monetary reward. The tactic most commonly used by emotionally unstable people, however, is regression. These people pout, sulk, whine, and cry to get their way (see Butkovic & Bratko, 2007). In a sense, this kind of behaviour comes close to the core definition of emotional instability—the display of volatile emotions, some positive and some negative. But the fascinating part of these findings is that the emotional volatility is strategically motivated—it is used with the purpose of influencing others to get what they want.

What tactics do people high on openness to experience use? Not surprisingly, these smart and perceptive people tend to use reason above all other tactics. They also use pleasure induction and responsibility invocation, however—findings that are not as intuitively obvious. Can you guess which tactic those *low* on openness use? They tend to use social comparison—saying that everyone else is doing it, comparing the partner with someone else who would do it, and telling others that they will look stupid if they do not do it.

A recent study examined the links between the "dark triad" personality traits (narcissism, psychopathy, and Machiavellianism) and tactics of social influence (Jonason & Webster, 2012). Those scoring high on these dark traits tended to manipulate others through a wide variety of tactics—coercion, hardball, reciprocity, social comparison, monetary reward, and even charm. High dark triad scorers were especially prone to using the hardball tactic, as illustrated by their tendency to bully other people with whom they are involved socially (Baughman et al., 2012). High dark triad scorers also tend to engage in more trolling behaviour online. We explore this further in Highlight on Canadian Research: The Personalities of Internet Trolls: Manipulative or Sadistic?.

In summary, these results provide strong evidence that personality dispositions are not static entities residing passively in the heads of people. They have profound implications for social interaction—in this case, for the tactics people use to manipulate others in their social environment.

 ## Highlight on Canadian Research

The Personalities of Internet Trolls: Manipulative or Sadistic?

If you've ever clicked the *Comments* button on a Facebook news post, waded into the depths of an ongoing Twitter debate, or read user responses to a controversial online article, you've undoubtedly encountered an Internet troll in your lifetime. These tricksters of the World Wide Web cause quite a bit of mayhem, posting controversial, disruptive, and often deceptive commentary in order to get a rise out of their next online victim. It appears that their motivation is just that—to upset other online users (or to make them appear foolish), often by touching on highly sensitive social or political issues. Although the behaviour of these individuals is manipulative, the intent is not nearly as clear as other antisocial behaviour seen online, such as cyberbullying.

In order to better understand this disturbing social behaviour, Canadian researchers in Manitoba and British Columbia studied the personality profiles of Internet trolls. Paul Trapnell (University of Winnipeg) and Del Paulhus (University of British Columbia), along with a graduate student, Erin Buckels (University of Manitoba), examined the associations among Internet trolling behaviour and other key personality traits, including narcissism, Machiavellianism, psychopathy, and dispositional sadism. As previously noted, these traits comprise the Dark Tetrad, which is an expansion of the Dark Triad (Chabrol et al., 2009; Furnham et al., 2013).

Across two large samples of Internet users, including Canadian psychology students and users from the United States, Buckels, Trapnell, and Paulhus (2014) administered online questionnaires measuring the aforementioned "dark" traits, a measure of the Big Five personality factors, and a unique survey on Internet trolling behaviour. This included questions about trolling behaviour, amount of time spent posting comments on the Internet, and degree of enjoyment gained from trolling activities.

Controlling for overall Internet usage, frequency of Internet commenting was positively and significantly correlated with all factors in the dark tetrad, including all subtypes of dispositional sadism. Enjoyment gained from trolling was also positively correlated with sadism, Machiavellianism, and psychopathy, while narcissism was unrelated to such enjoyment. An important finding was the lack of any significant correlation among these dark personality traits and enjoyment gained from other online activities, such as chatting, debating, or making friends.

The overall measure of Internet trolling devised for the study, however, suggested a very clear personality profile for Internet trolls. They appear to be especially high in sadistic tendencies, with the highest correlations emerging for all subtypes of sadism (correlations ranging from $r = .55$ to .65). They also appear to be relatively high in psychopathy ($r = .55$). This is in comparison to relatively low correlations among the composite Internet trolling survey and Machiavellianism ($r = .34$) and narcissism ($r = .18$). More interesting, perhaps, was the finding that the enjoyment gained from trolling emerged as the primary mechanism by which sadism predicts trolling behaviour. In other words, the Internet provides an opportunity for sadists to "have fun" by disrupting conversation, provoking emotional responses, and manipulating online discourse.

Regarding the Big Five personality traits, only two significant correlations were observed. Not surprisingly, Internet trolls are significantly higher in extraversion and significantly lower in agreeableness, supporting an overall socially problematic personality profile (Buckels et al., 2014). No correlations were observed with any of the remaining Big Five traits.

In their discussion, the team of researchers suggested that their findings were in line with a growing body of research linking excessive technology and Internet use with antisocial tendencies. One important outstanding question in regards to trolling, of course, is whether antisocial tendencies lead to the use of technology or result from it. The findings from Buckels, Trapnell, and Paulhus suggest the former, at least when it comes to Internet trolling behaviour specifically. It seems that in this sadistically manipulative use of technology, the Internet simply offers an ideal setting in which anonymity enables preexisting behavioural tendencies and motives.

The Dark Tetrad traits have since been found to predict trolling behaviour on dating apps like Tinder (March et al., 2017) and cyberbullying and cyberstalking behaviours on social media (Kircaburun et al., 2018)

 Concept Check

How are the traits of dominance and agreeableness specifically associated with manipulation tactics?

Define Machiavellianism, and summarize the manipulative strategies associated with this dark trait.

Panning Back: An Overview of Personality and Social Interaction

The most important message from this chapter is that personality does not reside passively within individuals, but rather profoundly affects each person's social environment. The three processes by which personality can influence an individual's social environment—selection, evocation, and manipulation—are highlighted in Table 15.6.

These fundamental mechanisms operate in the physical as well as the social environment. Let's consider selection first. In the physical domain, an introvert is more likely to choose to live in a rural habitat, whereas an extravert is more likely to choose city living with all the opportunities for social interaction city life provides. In the social domain, an extravert is more likely to select a partner who is also extraverted, whereas an introvert is more likely to choose an introverted partner so that they can read books quietly side by side.

For the process of evocation, a loud, heavy person who treads heavily is more likely to evoke an avalanche while climbing a snowy mountain. In the social domain, narcissistic people evoke admiration from their followers

Table 15.6 Causal Mechanisms That Create Links Between Personality and Environment: Examples from the Physical and Social Domains

Mechanism	Physical Environment	Social Environment
Selection	Introvert selects rural habitat	Extravert chooses extraverted partner
	Avoidance of cold climates	Emotionally stable person chooses stable roommate
Evocation	Person who treads heavily elicits an avalanche	Disagreeable people evoke relationship conflict
	Clumsy person creates, elicits more noise and clatter	Narcissistic people evoke admiration from followers
Manipulation	Conscientious person creates clean, neat, uncluttered room	Disagreeable person uses the silent treatment
	Person high on openness creates stylish, colourful room with varied collection of books and artwork	Narcissists transfer blame to others

and contempt from those who dislike their unbridled self-centredness. For the process of manipulation, personality affects how people mould and modify the rooms in which they live (Gosling et al., 2002). Conscientious individuals, for example, keep their rooms tidy, neat, and free of clutter. Those low on conscientiousness have more dirt, clutter, and mess in their rooms. Those high in intellect–openness decorate their rooms with stylish and unconventional objects and have many books and CDs that are highly varied in genre. Those low on intellect–openness have fewer and more conventional decorations, a narrower range of books, and a more delimited collection of CDs. In the social domain, disagreeable individuals are more likely than stable individuals to use the silent treatment as a tactic of manipulation. Those high in intellect–openness tend to use reason and rationality to get their way. And narcissists try to transfer blame for their failures onto others. We examine narcissism and its associations with all three mechanisms of social interaction (selection, evocation, and manipulation) in A Closer Look: Narcissism and Social Interaction.

Personality, in short, affects the partners and friends a person chooses as well as the environments a person decides to enter or avoid (selection); the reactions elicited from others and from the physical environment (evocation); and the ways in which one's physical and social environments are altered once inhabited (manipulation). These three processes are shown in Figure 15.1.

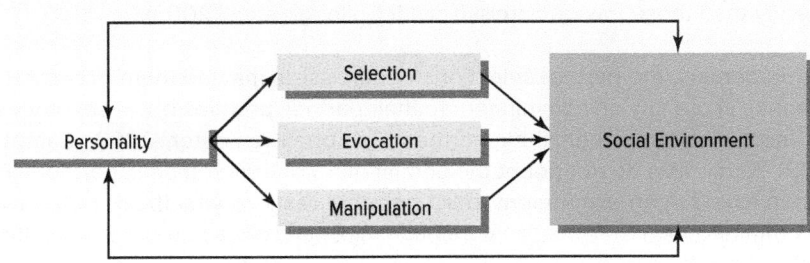

FIGURE 15.1 Personality and social interaction.

Further research is needed to determine whether the causal arrows in the figure run in both directions. Does the choice of a partner who is similar in personality, for example, create a social environment that reinforces that personality and makes it more stable over time (Neyer & Lehnart, 2007)? Does the conflict evoked by disagreeable people create a social environment in which they receive a lot of negative feedback, hence maintaining their disagreeable personality? Does the wide variety of manipulative tactics used by emotionally unstable individuals—from hardball to threats to sulking, whining, and pouting—create a social environment that is indeed rocked with greater turmoil, thus maintaining the personality disposition of neuroticism? Research within the next decade will undoubtedly answer these questions.

 A Closer Look

Narcissism and Social Interaction

Narcissism is a personality dimension that involves, at the upper end, high levels of self-absorption and conceitedness, placing one's own wants and needs above those of others, displaying unusual grandiosity, showing a profound sense of entitlement, and lacking empathy for other people's feelings, needs, and desires (see Chapters 3, 10 and 14; Raskin & Terry, 1988). Those high on narcissism tend to be *exhibitionistic* (e.g., flaunting money to impress others), *grandiose* (e.g., talking about how great they are), *self-centred* (e.g., taking the best piece of food for themselves), and *interpersonally exploitative* (e.g., using others for selfish ends) (Buss & Chiodo, 1991). Interestingly, female celebrities such as women on reality TV shows tend to be more narcissistic than average (Young & Pinsky, 2006). It is also true that narcissistic individuals tend to think they are very attractive, but empirical evidence suggests that they are only slightly more attractive than average (Bleske-Rechek, Remicker, & Baker, 2008; Holtzman & Strube, 2010). Personality psychologists have documented the impact of narcissism on social interaction, providing a fascinating illustration of the influence of personality on social selection, evocation, and manipulation.

In terms of *selection*, narcissists tend to choose people who admire them, who will reflect the extraordinarily positive view they hold about themselves. They don't want people around who will view them as anything other than as extraordinary, beautiful, or brilliant (Buss & Chiodo, 1991). In fact, because narcissists view themselves as "exceptional performers," they tend to select social situations in which they perceive that their "opportunity for glory" will be enhanced, and avoid situations in which their self-perceived magnificence will not be noticed by others (Wallace & Baumeister, 2002). Although they tend to appoint themselves to positions of power (Buss & Chiodo, 1991), they strenuously avoid social situations that don't afford the chance to show off their brilliance (Wallace & Baumeister, 2002). Life, however, sometimes has a way of crashing in, and narcissists are sometimes rejected. When they are rejected, narcissists tend to lash out with great anger at those they perceive to have wronged them (Carpenter, 2012; Horton & Sedikides, 2009; Jones & Paulhus, 2010), perhaps because their self-esteem is a bit fragile in response to failure (Zeigler-Hill et al., 2010). Interestingly, narcissists are highly selective in their social perceptions—they view themselves as victims of interpersonal transgressions far more frequently than those low on narcissism (McCullough et al., 2003).

In the relationship domain, the partner selections of narcissists may be more precarious than those of others because they score low on commitment to their partner, perhaps because they view themselves as "better" or more desirable than their partner (Campbell & Foster, 2002; Campbell, Rudich, & Sedikides, 2002). Narcissists do not doubt the commitment of their romantic partners (Foster & Campbell, 2005). When asked in an experiment to list possible reasons why their current romantic partner might be less committed than they are to the relationship, narcissists had great difficulty even completing the task! After the task, narcissists (compared with those low on narcissism) indicated substantially lower levels of their own commitment to their romantic partner and a greater willingness to accept a dating invitation from someone else. Narcissistic entitlement has also been linked to *an inability to forgive others,* a quality that could also impair the functioning of romantic relationships (Exline et al., 2004).

Narcissists also *evoke* predictable responses from others in their social environment. Because they are exhibitionistic and thrust themselves into the centre of attention, narcissists sometimes split people in their evocations—some view them as brilliant, entertaining, and "not boring," whereas others view them as selfish and boorish (Campbell et al., 2002). They sometimes evoke anger in others because of their self-aggrandizing actions, such as pulling rank on others to make a point. Narcissists evoke reactions from others through their behaviour and dress. They tend to create Facebook pages that are more self-promoting (Buffardi & Campbell, 2008; Ong et al., 2011), including posting sexy images of themselves (DeWall et al., 2011). Narcissists post more "selfies," update their online profile photos more often, and spend more time on Instagram (Marshall et al., 2015; Moon et al., 2016; Sorokowski et al., 2015; Weiser, 2015). They are more likely to wear expensive and flashy clothes; and if they are female, they wear more makeup and show more cleavage—actions that may evoke sexual overtures in others (Vazire et al., 2008).

Finally, narcissists use a predictable set of tactics of *manipulation.* They are highly exploitative of others and would be described as "users." They use friends ruthlessly for their wealth or connections. When in positions of power, they use their positions to exploit subordinates and show no hesitation in pulling rank to humiliate someone else in front of others. They react to failure by derogating other people, possibly in an attempt to transfer the blame for their failure onto others (Park & Colvin, 2015; South, Oltmanns, & Turkheimer, 2003). In the mating domain, they engage in manipulative game-playing and are more likely to use sexually coercive and aggressive tactics (Blinkhorn et al., 2015; Haslam & Montrose, 2015). They also lash out in anger and aggression against others when confronted with their own failure. The entitlement and exploitativeness components of narcissism are especially good predictors of aggression (Reidy et al., 2008). In sum, the personality dimension of narcissism shows many links to the social selections they make, the reactions they evoke from others, and the tactics of manipulation they use to enhance their self-centred goals.

 Concept Check

What remains unclear about the relationship between personality and social interaction?

Summarize the ways in which high narcissism is associated with various forms of social interaction.

Summary and Evaluation

The personality characteristics we carry with us affect the ways in which we interact with other people occupying our social world. The reciprocal influences of personality and social interactions have brought the fields of personality psychology and social psychology closer together (Swann & Selye, 2005).

This chapter described three key processes by which personality affects social interaction. First, we *select* people and environments, choosing the social situations to which we expose ourselves. In selecting a partner or mate, for example, people worldwide look for partners who are dependable, are emotionally stable, and have a pleasing disposition. Furthermore, we tend to select partners who are similar in personality to ourselves, a process known as assortative mating. Complementary needs theory—the idea that opposites attract when it comes to human mating—has received no empirical support. Those who fail to get what they want—for example, ending up with partners who are emotionally unstable or disagreeable—tend to be unhappy with their relationships and tend to split up or divorce more often than those who succeed in choosing what they want.

The process of selection extends beyond the choice of romantic partners. The personality trait of shyness, for example, is linked with avoiding gynecological exams, entering risky sexual situations by failing to bring up the topic of contraception, and avoiding risky situations that involve gambling money. Similarly, high sensation seeking heterosexual males tend to choose risky sexual situations, such as having unprotected sex and sex with a larger number of partners.

Second, we *evoke* emotions and actions in others. These evocations are based, in part, on our personality characteristics. In a study of the ways in which men and women anger and upset their romantic partners, the strongest predictors of anger and upset are low agreeableness and low emotional stability. Those low on agreeableness, for example, tend to create a lot of conflict in their social situations, including with friends and romantic partners, and they tend to be socially victimized during their high school years. Furthermore, in a phenomenon known as expectancy confirmation, our beliefs about the personality characteristics of others sometimes evoke in others precisely the behaviours we expect. A belief that someone is hostile, for example, tends to elicit hostile behaviour from that person.

Manipulation is the third process and is defined as the ways in which people intentionally influence and exploit others. Humans use many tactics for influencing others, including charm, silent treatment, coercion, reason, regression, and self-abasement. Men and women use these tactics approximately equally with the exception of regression, which is used slightly more often by women. Personality characteristics play a key role in which tactics we use to influence others. Emotionally unstable people, for example, tend to use regression and the silent treatment. They also tend to use reason and monetary reward, though, suggesting some nonintuitive links between personality and tactics of manipulation. People high on intellect–openness tend to use reason, but they also use the social comparison tactic.

One personality trait linked with manipulation tactics is called Machiavellianism. The high Mach tends to tell people what they want to hear, to use flattery to get what they want, and to rely heavily on lying and deception. In the mating domain, for example, high Machs are more likely to feign love in order to get sex, use drugs and alcohol to render a potential sex partner more vulnerable, and even express a willingness to use force to get sex. High Machs also betray the trust of others, sometimes feigning cooperation before defecting. They are also more likely than low Machs to steal and then to lie about stealing when they are caught. The success of the high Mach seems to depend heavily on context. In loosely structured social situations and work organizations, high Machs can wheel and deal, using their manipulative, conning strategies to great effect. In more tightly structured, rule-bound situations, however, low Machs outperform high Machs.

All three processes have been documented with the personality disposition of narcissism. Narcissists tend to select others who admire them and avoid those who are skeptical of their claims of greatness. They selectively enter social situations in which there are opportunities for glory and avoid situations in which their brilliance will not be seen by others. Narcissists evoke admiration and respect from those who fawn over them, while evoking anger and disgust from those who are victims of their scorn and conceit. In terms of manipulation, narcissists are highly interpersonally exploitative, using friends for wealth or connections and transferring blame to others when things go wrong. Examining all these processes with respect to narcissists creates a fascinating portrait of the ways in which personality is strongly connected with the social interactions we create and the social environments we inhabit.

In summary, personality is predictably and systematically linked with social interaction through the ways in which we select our partners and social worlds, the ways in which we evoke responses from people we have initially chosen, and the ways in which we influence those people to attain our desired ends.

 Concept Check

Consider one of the Big Five traits, and provide an example of each of the three primary mechanisms of social interaction.

Consider an individual high in the Dark Triad traits. How might they be inclined to (a) choose certain social situations, (b) elicit responses from others, and (c) intentionally manipulate and affect those around them?

Key Terms

complementary needs theory   violation of desire   hostile attributional bias

attraction similarity theory   shyness   expectancy confirmation

assortative mating   evocation   taxonomy

Sex, Gender, and Personality

The Social and Cultural Domain

"Despite the advances of feminism, escalating levels of sexism and violence—from undervalued intelligence to sexual harassment in elementary school—cause girls to stifle their creative spirit and natural impulses, which ultimately destroys their self-esteem" (Pipher, 1994, bookjacket). This is a quotation from the book *Reviving Ophelia,* which remained on the best-seller list for an astonishing 135 weeks (Kling et al., 1999). The sentiment expresses widespread belief that women experience lower self-esteem than men do and that this difference in adult personality is caused by destructive events during development.

Although we cannot know with certainty why *Reviving Ophelia* remained popular for so long, several possibilities warrant consideration. First, many people are fascinated with psychological **sex differences**: average differences between women and men in personality or behaviour. Second, many people are concerned with the political implications of findings of sex differences. Will such findings be used to foster gender stereotypes, or worse, to oppress women? Third, people are concerned with the practical implications of sex differences in their everyday lives. Will knowledge of sex differences help people to understand and communicate better with others and reduce conflict between people?

Some differences in personality between adult men and women are hypothesized to result from environmental events that occur during adolescence.
©Iakov Filimonov/Shutterstock

This chapter focuses centrally on scientific issues, but it also discusses the broader debate about the scientific findings. Are men and women basically different or basically the same when it comes to personality? Have the differences been exaggerated because of stereotypes about what men and women are like? Which theories provide compelling explanations for sex-linked features of personality? As used in this book, the phrase *sex differences* simply refers to an average difference between women and men on certain characteristics, such as height, body fat distribution, or personality characteristics, with no prejudgment about the cause of any difference. In other words, the findings presented here reflect statistical trends or patterns. Importantly, they do not allow us to make conclusions or assumptions about individual people.

We begin by briefly outlining the history of the study of sex differences in personality. This background information will show how complex this topic can be. Indeed, we will see that the very definition of **gender**, or the social and cultural interpretation of what it means to be a man or a woman, can change over time. This is in contrast to **sex**, which refers to whether an individual is biologically considered male, female, or **intersex** according to specific anatomy or physiology. Although the terms are often used interchangeably in everyday conversation, their conceptual distinction is important to psychologists. These constructs, gender and sex, are independent of one another. They are also independent of **sexual orientation**, which refers to one's sexual or romantic attraction to the same or opposite gender.

Next, we look at some of the techniques psychologists use to describe sex differences identified in research. We examine sex differences in traits such as assertiveness, criminality, and sexuality, and we use these differences to explore the fascinating topic of **gender stereotypes**: beliefs about how men and women differ or are supposed to differ, in contrast to what the actual differences are. Finally, we explore theories that attempt to explain the reasons for these sex differences. Although many differences between men and women are reviewed, it is important that such differences not be exaggerated or focused on in a way that reinforces gender stereotypes in everyday life. On most psychological traits and variables, women and men are more similar than they are different. As concluded by Costa, Terracciano, and McCrae (2001), individual variation within each gender is far greater than the differences observed between genders.

As you will notice throughout this chapter, psychologists and researchers have traditionally studied differences between straight (heterosexual) males and females whose internal sense of gender is the same as the one they were assigned at birth (we refer to such individuals as *cisgender*). Historically, there has been little attention paid to participants' **gender identity**: the deeply felt, inherent sense of being a man, a woman, or an alternative gender which may or may not correspond to a person's sex characteristics (American Psychological

Association, 2018). One's gender identity may or may not "match" the sex assigned to them at birth, as in the case of someone who identifies as *transgender*. This is a major limitation of past research, which has primarily viewed gender as a binary construct determined by physical attributes. Today we see gender as being more fluid and variable than once conceived.

The Science and Politics of Studying Sex and Gender

Few topics generate as much controversy as the study of sex differences; "public debates about the nature of women and men are frequently in the spotlight, whether in media reports on the latest sex difference findings or in highly publicized legal cases involving single-sex educational institutions or sexual harassment" (Deaux & LaFrance, 1998, p. 788). Some worry, for example, that findings of sex differences might be used to support certain political agendas, such as excluding women from leadership or work roles. Some argue that findings of sex differences merely reflect gender stereotypes rather than real differences. Indeed, some psychologists have even advocated ending research on sex differences because findings might conflict with egalitarian ideals (Baumeister, 1988).

Others argue, however, that both scientific psychology and social change will be impossible without coming to terms with whatever sex differences do exist. Feminist psychologist Alice Eagly (1995), for example, argues that sex differences do exist, they are consistent across studies, and they should not be ignored merely because they are perceived to conflict with certain political agendas. Indeed, Eagly argues that those who try to minimize these differences or pretend that they do not exist hamper feminist and egalitarian agendas by presenting a dogma that is out of touch with reality. Still others, such as Janet Hyde, argue that sex differences have been exaggerated and that there is so much overlap between the sexes on most personality traits that the differences are minimal (Hyde, 2005; Hyde & Plant, 1995). We will examine these contrasting positions in more detail. One important consideration, however, is that whatever differences have been observed between males and females, they are surely the result of a complex interaction among biology, evolution, and social factors, making it impossible to conclude that any one difference is entirely innate or unchangeable over time.

History of the Study of Sex Differences

Before 1973, relatively little attention was paid to sex differences. Indeed, in psychological research, it was common practice to use participants of only one sex, most often males. And even when both males and females were studied, few researchers actually analyzed or reported whether the effects differed by sex.

All of this changed in the early 1970s (Eagly, 1995; Hoyenga & Hoyenga, 1993). In 1974, Eleanor Maccoby and Carol Jacklyn published a classic book, *The Psychology of Sex Differences,* in which they reviewed hundreds of studies and drew several key conclusions about how men and women differed. They concluded that women were slightly better than men at verbal ability. Men were slightly better than women in mathematical ability (e.g., geometry, algebra) and spatial ability (e.g., ability to visualize what a three-dimensional object would look like if it were rotated in space by 90 degrees). In terms of *personality* characteristics, they concluded that only one sex difference existed: men were more aggressive than women. With other aspects of personality and social behaviour, they concluded that there was not enough evidence to determine whether men and women actually differed. Overall, they concluded that sex differences were few in number and trivial in importance.

The Psychology of Sex Differences set off an avalanche of research on the topic. The book itself was criticized on various grounds. Some argued that many more sex differences existed than were portrayed by Maccoby and Jacklyn (Block, 1983). Others challenged the conclusion that men were more aggressive than women (Frodi, Macauley, & Thome, 1977). Furthermore, the methods by which the authors drew their conclusions, although standard practice at that time, were crude by today's standards.

Following the publication of *The Psychology of Sex Differences,* psychology journals changed their reporting practices. They started to require authors to calculate and report sex differences. Furthermore, protests that many of the findings in psychology were based primarily on studies of men led to calls for the greater inclusion of women as participants. There followed an explosion of research on sex differences. Literally thousands of studies were conducted on the ways in which men and women differed.

Since Maccoby and Jacklyn's early work, researchers have developed a more precise quantitative procedure for examining conclusions across studies, and thus for determining sex differences, called *meta-analysis*. Recall that meta-analysis is a statistical method for summarizing the findings of large numbers of individual studies. Gaining popularity in the mid-1980s, meta-analysis allows researchers to calculate with greater objectivity and precision whether a particular difference—such as a sex difference—is consistent across studies and likely reflects the real world. Furthermore, it allows researchers to estimate how large the difference actually is—called the **effect size**.

Calculation of Effect Size: How Large Are the Sex Differences?

The most commonly used statistic in meta-analysis is the effect size, or *d* statistic. The *d* statistic is used to express a difference in standard deviation units (see Chapter 2). A *d* of 0.50 means that the average difference between two groups is half a standard deviation. A *d* of 1.00 means that the difference between the groups is one full standard deviation. A *d* of 0.25 means that the difference between the groups is one-quarter of a standard deviation. An effect size can be calculated for each study of sex differences and then averaged across studies to give a more precise and objective assessment of whether the sexes differ and, if so, by how much.

Most meta-analyses have adopted a convention for interpreting effect sizes (Cohen, 1977):

d Score	Meaning
0.20 or –0.20	Small difference
0.50 or –0.50	Medium difference
0.80 or –0.80	Large difference

When comparing men to women, assume that positive *d* scores, such as 0.20 or 0.50, indicate that men score higher than women. Negative *d* scores, such as –0.20 or –0.50, indicate that women score higher than men. For example, a *d* score of –0.85 means that women score much higher on a particular trait.[1]

To get a feel for various effect sizes, let's examine a few findings outside the realm of personality. On average, who can throw a ball farther, males or females? Although there are great individual differences within each

---

[1] Note, however, that signs may be reversed in other publications of findings. See specific papers for guidance.

sex, males can, on average, throw farther than females. The *d* is approximately 2.00 (Ashmore, 1990). This means that the sexes differ, on average, by two full standard deviations, which is considered quite large. Which sex has a higher grade point average in college? The *d* for grade point average is –0.04, which is very close to zero. This means that the sexes are essentially the same in their grade point average.

Which sex scores higher in verbal ability? It turns out that females are slightly better than males, but the *d* is only –0.11. Are males better at math? The *d* here also turns out to be quite small, only 0.15. These findings are in line with a vast literature that now documents that men and women are essentially the same (or do not differ by much) on most measures of cognitive ability (Hyde, 2005; Hyde, 2014). About the only well-documented exception to this conclusion pertains to spatial rotation ability, such as the spatial ability involved in throwing a spear (or football) so that it correctly anticipates the trajectory of a moving object, such as an animal or a receiver. The *d* for this sort of spatial ability is 0.73, which comes close to the standard for "large" (Ashmore, 1990).

It is important to keep in mind that even large effect sizes for average sex differences do not necessarily have implications for any particular individual. Even with a *d* of 2.00 for throwing distance, some females can throw much farther than the average male, and some males cannot throw as far as the average female.

When it comes to who can throw a ball farther, the effect size for the difference between males and females is 2.00, in favour of males. Although this is a large difference in average ability, there will nevertheless be some females who can throw farther than most males because the distributions still overlap.
©Corbis/Glow Images

This overlap in the distributions of the sexes must be kept in mind when evaluating effect sizes (see Figure 16.1). This is also why it is important to not make assumptions about any single individual based on these effect sizes.

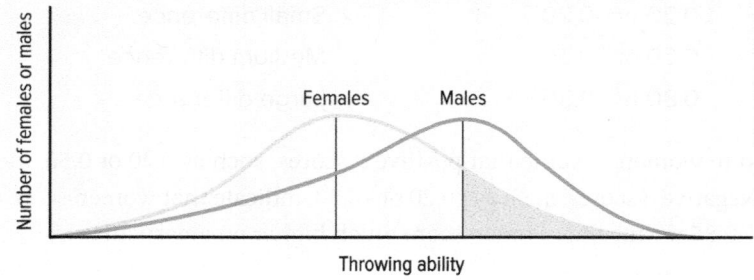

FIGURE 16.1 Overlap between the sexes in context of a mean difference. Even when one sex greatly exceeds the other in a particular ability, there is a large area of overlap. Females whose throwing ability falls in the shaded area exceed the throwing ability of the average male.

Minimalists and Maximalists

A central focus of the debate on sex differences follows from a consideration of effect sizes—on whether sex differences are small and relatively inconsequential or substantial and important. Those who describe sex differences as small and inconsequential take the **minimalist** position and offer two arguments. The first is that, empirically, most findings of sex differences show small magnitudes of effect (Deaux, 1984; Hyde, 2005; Hyde, 2014; Hyde & Plant, 1995). Minimalists tend to emphasize that the distributions of men and women on any given personality variable show tremendous overlap, which reflect their small magnitude of effect (review Figure 16.1). A second argument advanced by minimalists is that whatever differences exist do not have much practical importance for behaviour in everyday life. If the sex differences are small and don't have consequences for people's lives, then perhaps we should concentrate on other psychological issues that are more important.

In contrast, those who take the **maximalist** position tend to argue that the magnitude of sex differences is comparable to the magnitude of many other effects in psychology and should not be trivialized (Eagly, 1995). Some sex differences tend to be small in magnitude, others are large in magnitude, and many are in the moderate range, according to this view. Furthermore, Eagly notes that even small sex differences can have large practical importance. A small sex difference in helping behaviour, for example, could result in a large sex difference in the number of lives each sex aids over the long run. As you read through this chapter, you should keep in mind the range of positions psychologists have taken on sex differences, from the minimalist stance to the maximalist stance.

 Concept Check

What are some of the concerns surrounding the scientific study of sex differences?

Compare the minimalist and maximalist views on sex differences.

Sex Differences in Personality

We begin by examining sex differences in temperament in children. How do males and females differ early on in life? We then move on to the five-factor model, which provides a useful framework for our discussion of key sex differences in personality in adulthood. Finally, we explore sex differences in other domains of personality, such as sexuality, aggression, and depression, as well as the tendencies for men and women to interact in certain ways in group settings.

Temperament in Children

The importance of sex differences in temperament is aptly summarized by the authors of a meta-analysis: "The question of gender differences in temperament is arguably one of the most fundamental questions in gender differences research in the areas of personality and social behaviour. Temperament reflects biologically based emotional and behavioural consistencies that appear early in life and predict—often in conjunction with other factors—patterns and outcomes in numerous other domains such as psychopathology and personality" (Else-Quest et al., 2006, p. 33). These authors conducted the largest meta-analysis ever undertaken of sex differences in temperament in children between the ages of 3 and 13.

The sex differences they discovered ranged from substantial to negligible. **Inhibitory control** showed the largest sex difference, with a $d = -0.41$, which is considered in the moderate range. Inhibitory control refers to the ability to control inappropriate responses or behaviours. A more recent study found very large differences on the trait of impulsivity, with boys being less able to control their impulses ($d = -0.72$) (Olino et al., 2013). As the authors summarize, "these findings may represent an overall better ability of girls to regulate or allocate their attention" and suppress socially undesirable behaviour (Else-Quest et al., 2006, p. 61). **Perceptual sensitivity**—the ability to detect subtle stimuli from the environment—also showed a sex difference favouring girls ($d = -0.38$). Girls, on average, appear to be more sensitive than boys to subtle and low-intensity signals from their external world. Inhibitory control is related to the later development of the personality trait of Conscientiousness. Interestingly, the sex difference appears to fade, because adult men and women do not differ much in conscientiousness.

Surgency, a cluster including approach behaviour, high activity, and impulsivity, also showed a significant sex difference ($d = 0.38$), with boys scoring higher than girls. Perhaps the combination of high surgency and low inhibitory control accounts for the fact that boys tend to experience more disciplinary difficulties in school in the early years of their lives. Some subcomponents of surgency showed slightly smaller sex differences, such as activity level ($d = 0.33$) and high-intensity pleasure ($d = 0.30$), which is consistent with the finding that boys are more likely than girls to engage in rough-and-tumble play.

The combination of low inhibitory control and high surgency may account for another reliable gender difference—a difference in the domain of *physical aggressiveness.* Using an act frequency measure based on codings of actual behaviour, Zakriski, Wright, and Underwood (2005) found a $d = 0.60$, indicating that boys were more physically aggressive than girls (approximate age 13). In contrast to inhibitory control and surgency, girls and boys showed virtually no difference in a variable called **negative affectivity**, which includes components such as anger, difficulty, amount of distress, and sadness. A more fine-grained analysis of negative emotions, however, reveals that girls are higher on fearfulness ($d = -0.34$), whereas boys are higher on anger expression ($d = -0.34$) (Olino et al., 2013).

In summary, meta-analysis of temperament in children between the ages of 3 and 13 suggests a few gender differences of moderate magnitude. Girls show more inhibitory control and higher fearfulness. Boys show higher levels of surgency, higher levels of activity, more impulsivity, and more anger in the domain of emotional expression. These are average sex differences, however, which means that the distributions overlap considerably.

Five-Factor Model

The five-factor model of personality provides a convenient framework for organizing a number of key findings about sex differences in personality. We have included findings from two large cross-cultural studies (see Table 16.1), one presenting effect sizes based on self-report data (S-Data) and the other presenting effect sizes based on observer-report data (O-Data). Being able to compare the two allows us to get a sense of how men and women see themselves and how they tend to be seen by others in their respective culture.

Table 16.1 Effect Sizes for Sex Differences in Facets of the Five-Factor Model

Dimension	Effect Size (based on S-Data from 25 cultures)	Effect Size (based on O-Data from 50 cultures)
Extraversion		
Gregariousness	−0.14	−0.26
Warmth	−0.23	−0.29
Activity	−0.11	−0.16
Assertiveness	0.27	0.24
Excitement Seeking	0.38	0.25
Agreeableness		
Trust	−0.17	−0.16
Tender-mindedness	−0.28	−0.29
Modesty	−0.19	−0.26
Altruism	−0.25	−0.33
Conscientiousness		
Order	−0.10	−0.24
Openness to Experience		
Feelings	−0.31	−0.42
Ideas	0.16	0.31
Neuroticism		
Anxiety	−0.43	−0.54
Depression	−0.29	−0.29
Self-Consciousness	−0.23	−0.31

Note: Positive numbers mean men tend to score higher than women, and negative numbers mean women tend to score higher than men.

Extraversion

Many studies have found a small to moderate difference between men and women at the factor level of extraversion, with women demonstrating higher levels than men (Costa et al., 2001; McCrae et al., 2005b; Weisberg et al., 2011). In a study that included a large Canadian sample, the difference between men and women was small but significant ($d = -0.08$) (Weisberg, et al., 2011). Others still have found no significant difference at the factor level, including one of the largest American studies of sex differences in personality to date (Kajonius & Johnson, 2018).

Much more insight can be gained by comparing men and women on the facet or narrow trait level of the five-factor model. Women score slightly higher on gregariousness and activity level than men, but the difference is quite small (Costa et al., 2001; McCrae et al., 2005b). Women across cultures and age groups have also consistently displayed higher levels of warmth (Costa et al., 2001; De Bolle et al., 2015; McCrae et al., 2005b), but again effect sizes have been relatively small. Men, on the other hand, tend to display somewhat higher levels of assertiveness and excitement seeking (Costa et al., 2001; Feingold, 1994; McCrae et al., 2005b; Weisberg et al., 2011). Historically, men have demonstrated much higher levels of assertiveness compared to women, though this difference may not appear until young adulthood (deBolle et al., 2015). A related finding, emerging from a study of 127 samples in 70 countries ($N = 77,528$), is that men place a greater importance on the *value of power* than do women (Schwartz & Rubel, 2005). That is, on average, men tend to value social status and dominance to a greater degree. In line with these findings, a number of studies suggest that men interrupt others in conversation more than women do in mixed-sex groups (Hoyenga & Hoyenga, 1993).

The sex difference in agreeableness appears to be greater, with women more agreeable than men on average. Cross-cultural studies have revealed small to medium effect sizes at the factor level (De Bolle et al., 2015; Costa et al., 2001; McCrae et al., 2005b). This difference has been confirmed in large Canadian and American populations of men and women, with effect sizes for agreeableness ranging from –0.48 (Weisberg et al., 2011) to –0.58 (Kajonius & Johnson, 2018), respectively. We'll examine two facets of agreeableness in greater detail, though others are presented in Table 16.1. **Trust** is the proclivity to cooperate with others, giving others the benefit of the doubt, and viewing one's fellow human beings as basically good at heart. **Tender-mindedness** is a nurturant proclivity—having empathy for others and being sympathetic with those who are downtrodden. Women tend to describe themselves as more trusting than men and they tend to be seen this way by others. Women are also more tender-minded than men (e.g., caring, giving), with an effect size of –0.28 based on cross-cultural self-report data (Costa et al., 2001). However, previous meta-analyses have found effect sizes as high as –0.97 for tender-mindedness (e.g., Feingold, 1994), which would suggest a much more substantial sex

difference. A large study of gender and personality in the United States concluded that women are also significantly higher on morality, altruism, and modesty compared to men, with effect sizes ranging from –0.40 to –0.57 (Kajonius & Johnson, 2018). On the Dark Triad traits of narcissism, Machiavellianism, and subclinical psychopathy (all of which are associated with low agreeableness), men also tend to be higher (Schmitt et al., 2017).

Studies show that women naturally smile more than men. Researchers disagree, however, on what this sex difference means; some suggest smiling is a sign of agreeableness, whereas others hold that smiling is a form of submissiveness or a way to ease tension in social situations.

©Realistic Reflections

Another finding related to agreeableness pertains to *smiling*. Meta-analyses have shown that women smile more often than men, with an effect size of −0.60 (Hall, 1984). If smiling reflects an agreeable personality disposition, we can conclude that women are more agreeable than men. However, some researchers view smiling as a sign of submissiveness rather than agreeableness (Eagly, 1995). It's possible that smiling reflects agreeableness in some contexts and submissiveness in others.

It also seems that sex differences in agreeableness may vary according to situational factors. Women seem to be more cooperative than men in mixed-sex social interactions. In contrast, men are slightly more cooperative than women in same-sex social interactions (Balliet et al., 2011). This highlights the importance of considering contextual determinants of sex differences, as some differences between men and women may be the result of situational demands.

Aggressiveness falls at the opposite end of agreeableness. It will likely not surprise you that males are more physically aggressive than females, on average, and this difference is evident at a young age (Björkqvist, 2018). This shows up in personality tests, in aggressive fantasies, and in actual measures of behaviour (Hyde, 1986). In general, the effect sizes for aggression are largest for projective tests, such as the TAT ($d = 0.86$), the next largest for peer report measures of aggression ($d = 0.63$), and the smallest for self-report measures of aggression ($d = 0.40$). Fantasy measures of aggression, which assess how often people imagine aggressing against others, show large sex differences, with an effect size of 0.84.

These sex differences can have profound consequences for everyday life. The effect size for violent crimes is especially striking. Worldwide, men commit roughly 90 percent of all homicides, and most of the victims of these homicides are other men (Buss, 2005b; Daly & Wilson, 1988; Statistics Canada, 2015). This trend is the same in Canada, where approximately 90 percent of homicides and 78 percent of all violent crimes are committed by men (Statistics Canada, 2009). Men commit more violent crimes of all sorts, ranging from assaults to gang-related violence. Interestingly, the largest sex differences in violent crimes show up just after puberty, peaking in adolescence and in the early twenties. After age 50, violent crimes start to decline, and men and women become much more similar to each other in criminal aggressiveness.

These findings are not limited to North America. In all cultures for which there are data, the vast majority of killings and other violent crimes are committed by young men (Daly & Wilson, 1988; Pinker, 2012). Psychologically, a key reason for this sex difference is that women are much more sensitive to punishment than men ($d = -.33$), whereas men seem more inclined to take risks, sometimes oblivious to the punishments they may receive (Cross, Copping, & Campbell, 2011). These culturally universal findings lend credence to theories that offer evolutionary explanations for some sex differences (see Chapter 8). It is important to keep in mind, however, that these forms of aggression refer to physical violence. Other forms of aggression, including that which is relational in nature (e.g., verbal insults, gossiping about others), show either no sex differences or a tendency for women to score higher (e.g., Hess et al., 2010; Ostrov & Godleski, 2010).

Conscientiousness

Although cross-cultural research has suggested a small sex difference at the factor level of conscientiousness, with women scoring slightly higher than men (e.g., McCrae et al., 2005b), others have suggested that it is necessary to examine the facets of conscientiousness in order to detect any meaningful differences (Weisberg et al., 2011). One facet of conscientiousness that has been scrutinized for sex differences is order. Women score slightly higher than men on order, with an effect size of only –0.10 based on cross-cultural self-report data (Costa et al., 2001). The difference appears to be greater, however, when looking at observer-report data ($d = -0.24$), suggesting that people tend to see women in their lives as being more ordered that they tend to see themselves. Nevertheless, the effect is small enough to conclude that men and women are very similar on this dimension. Research findings by Kajonius and Johnson (2018) are in line with this conclusion, demonstrating no significant differences on any of the facets of conscientiousness. Nevertheless, it is possible that very small effects can have large cumulative effects over time. For example, a small difference in order between marriage partners may result in a large number of arguments about housecleaning over the course of a year.

Openness to Experience

Research has consistently demonstrated little meaningful difference between men and women at the factor-level of openness to experience. Even when a small effect is observed, it tends to be non-significant (Costa et al., 2001; Kajonius & Johnson, 2018; McCrae et al., 2005b; Weisberg et al., 2011). While it may seem safe to conclude that men and women are identical on this dimension of personality, research by Weisberg and colleagues (2011) has suggested that women score higher on the openness component specifically while men score slightly higher on intellect specifically. Indeed, further differences emerge as we examine the facets of openness. As presented in Table 16.1, women score higher on the feelings facet ($d = -0.31$) while men score higher on the ideas facet ($d = 0.16$), and this pattern is further supported by observer-report data (McCrae et al., 2005b). Interestingly, cross-cultural analyses by De Bolle et al. (2015) found that adolescent girls reported higher openness to experience compared to adolescent boys; in particular, they were consistently higher on the feelings and aesthetics facets.

Neuroticism

Looking back at Table 16.1, the largest sex difference is seen with neuroticism and the anxiety facet specifically. North American and cross-cultural research has consistently reported that women score higher on neuroticism compared to men, with effect sizes typically in the moderate range at the factor level (Costa et al., 2001; Kajonius & Johnson, 2018; McCrae et al., 2005b; Weisberg et al., 2011). This difference is also apparent in adolescence, though to a smaller degree (De Bolle et al., 2015). Regarding facets of neuroticism, multiple studies confirm that the greatest sex difference is observed with anxiety. According to data collected from men and women around the world, women report experiencing more anxiety ($d = -0.43$) (Costa et al., 2001) and they tend to be described as more anxious by others ($d = -0.54$) (McCrae et al., 2005b). Recent conclusions by Kajonius and Johnson (2018) are in agreement with these findings, suggesting an effect size of −0.56 for anxiety. In fact research on adult populations from multiple cultures suggest that women are slightly to moderately higher on most facets of neuroticism, including anxiety, self-consciousness, vulnerability, and *depression*. We examine sex differences in this last facet of neuroticism further in A Closer Look: Sex Differences in Depression.

Regarding anger/hostility and impulsiveness, findings have been inconsistent, with some suggesting men are higher (Costa et al., 2001; McCrae et al., 2005b). We explore sex differences in emotional experiences further in the next section.

 A Closer Look

Sex Differences in Depression

Depression is marked by characteristics such as low self-esteem, pessimism (expecting the worst to happen), and the perception that one has little control over one's life. It's one of the most common psychological maladies of modern humans, and there is evidence that the rate of depression is increasing (Albert, 2015). Adult men and women differ in the incidence of depression and in the nature of their depressive symptoms, but the sexes don't start out different. In childhood, there are no sex differences in depression. After puberty, however, women show a depression rate two to three times that of men (Hoyenga & Hoyenga, 1993; Albert, 2015). Roughly 25 percent of all women have at least one depressive episode in their lifetime. In contrast, only 10 percent of all men will have a depressive episode. The largest sex differences in depression show up between the ages of 18 and 44. After that, the sexes start to converge.

The following list contains some of the critical aspects of sex differences in depressive symptoms (Hoyenga & Hoyenga, 1993):

1. Depressed women more often than depressed men report excessive eating and weight gain as symptoms (although loss of appetite is the most common symptom of depression in both sexes).
2. Women are more likely to express their emotions when depressed and to confront their feelings directly; men are more likely to become aggressive when depressed.
3. Depressed women are more likely than men to seek treatment; depressed men are more likely to miss work.
4. Nervous activity (e.g., fidgeting) is more common in depressed women than in depressed men; inactivity is more common in depressed men than in depressed women.
5. Among depressed university students, men are more socially withdrawn, more likely to use drugs, and more likely to experience aches and pains; women are more likely to experience hurt feelings and a decline in self-esteem.
6. Men are more likely to die by suicide, perhaps because men are more likely to use violent means; women are more likely to make nonfatal suicide attempts.

One clue to the sex difference in the nature and rate of depression comes from a large-scale study of 1,100 community-based adults (Nolen-Hoeksema, Larson, & Grayson, 1999). The researchers speculated that women's greater vulnerability to depressive symptoms may stem from factors such as having less power in the workplace, a relative lack of control over important areas of their lives, work overload, and lower status in heterosexual relationships. Because they may be more limited in their capacity for control, women may start to *ruminate*. **Rumination** involves repeatedly focusing on one's symptoms or distress (e.g., "Why do I continue to feel so bad about myself?" or "Why doesn't my boss like me?" or "What if I had taken that other job when it was offered?"). Because rumination fails to lead to effective solutions, according to this theory, women continue to ruminate, and rumination is a key contributor to women's greater experience of depressive symptoms. Women ruminate substantially more than men, and rumination in turn contributes to the perseverance of the depressive symptoms.

Another theory is that the greater incidence of depression in women is caused by humans in the modern world living in isolated nuclear families, stripped of the extended kin and other social supports that characterize more traditional societies (Buss, 2000b). We might also consider our previous discussion regarding lower self-esteem in young girls and women. Some of the same underlying factors may be playing a role in depression as well, such as internalized notions of beauty and incongruence between actual and ideal body types (Gilligan, Lyons, & Hammer, 1990). Whatever the origins, sex differences in depression represent one of the largest and most consequential differences in personality.

Basic Emotions: Frequency and Intensity

Emotions are central to personality, so much so that we devoted an entire chapter to them (Chapter 13). Research conducted on a cross-cultural scale has revealed precisely where the sexes differ in their experiences of emotions and where the sexes are essentially the same. The most extensive study examined 2,199 Australians and an international sample of 6,868 participants drawn from 41 different countries (Brebner, 2003). Eight fundamental emotions were examined, four "positive" emotions (Affection, Joy, Contentment, Pride) and four "negative" emotions (Fear, Anger, Sadness, Guilt). Participants used rating scales to indicate (1) how frequently they experienced each emotion and (2) the intensity with which they experienced each emotion. The basic findings are summarized in Table 16.2.

Table 16.2 Sex Differences in Experience of Emotions		
Emotion	**Frequency**	**Intensity**
Positive Emotions	0.20	0.23
Affection	0.30	0.25
Joy	0.16	0.26
Contentment	0.13	0.18
Pride	ns	ns
Negative Emotions	0.14	0.25
Fear	0.17	0.26
Anger	0.05	0.14
Sadness	0.16	0.28
Guilt	ns	0.07

Note: Entries in the table are effect sizes (*d*). The designation "ns" indicates that the sex difference was not significant. Positive values indicate that women report experiencing the emotion more frequently or intensely than do men.
Source: Brebner (2003).

There are small but statistically significant differences in the experience of emotions. All point to women experiencing both positive *and* negative emotions more frequently and intensely than men. In the positive domain, affection and joy show the largest sex differences. Pride, in contrast, shows no sex difference in either frequency or intensity. In the negative domain, women experience fear and sadness more than men, especially in the reported intensity of the experience. Guilt, in contrast, shows a minimal sex difference in intensity and no difference in frequency—perhaps contradicting the stereotype that women are more guilt prone than men. These effect sizes are generally small, however, and it is possible that other variables (e.g., situational factors) may play a role.

One of the most common complaints that women express about men is that they don't express their emotions enough (Buss, 2003). Men, in contrast, often complain that women are too emotional. The results point to one possible reason for these complaints—perhaps men don't *express* their emotions because they don't *experience* emotions as frequently or as intensely as do women. On the other hand, it is possible that social norms regarding emotional expression lead men to either restrict their expression or under-report their emotional experiences when asked.

Other Dimensions of Personality

Several dimensions of personality are related to, but not directly subsumed by, the five-factor model of personality. We will examine three: self-esteem, sexuality and emotional investment, and the people–things dimension.

Self-Esteem

A topic of major interest to women and men is self-esteem, or how good we feel about ourselves. This is reflected in the many popular books on the topic, such as *10 Simple Solutions for Building Self-Esteem*

(Schiraldi, 2007). Although researchers have explored many facets of self-esteem, such as esteem of one's athletic abilities and esteem of one's social skills, by far the most frequently measured component is **global self-esteem**, defined as "the level of global regard that one has for the self as a person" (Harter, 1993, p. 88). Global self-esteem can range from highly positive to highly negative and reflects an overall evaluation of the self (Kling et al., 1999).

Global self-esteem is associated with many aspects of functioning and is central to mental health. Those with high self-esteem appear to cope better with the stresses and strains of daily life. In laboratory studies, when faced with negative feedback about one's performance, those with high self-esteem perform better on cognitive tasks. Those with high self-esteem tend to take credit for their successes but deny responsibility for their failures (Kling et al., 1999).

Meta-analyses have yielded an interesting pattern regarding sex differences (Feingold, 1994; Kling et al., 1999). The overall effect size is relatively small ($d = 0.21$), with males scoring slightly higher than females in self-esteem (Kling et al., 1999). But the degree of difference in self-esteem between males and females appears to change with age. Young children (ages 7–10) show only a slight sex difference in self-esteem ($d = 0.16$). As children approach adolescence, however, the gap between the sexes widens. At ages 11–14, d was 0.23. And the sex difference peaks during the ages of 15–18 ($d = 0.33$). Females seem to suffer from lower self-esteem than males as they hit their mid- to late teens. The good news is that in adulthood the self-esteem gap starts to close. During the ages of 19–22, the effect size shrinks to 0.18. During the ages of 23–59, the sexes converge even further, with a d of 0.10. And during older age, from 60 and up, the d is only -0.03, which means that the males and females are virtually identical in self-esteem. These gendered patterns in self-esteem development have been observed in more recent Internet-based research (e.g., Robins et al., 2002), including a large study of nearly a million people from 48 different countries (Bleidorn et al., 2016). A significant gender gap was observed in nearly every country examined, with males consistently reporting higher self-esteem than females.

The magnitudes of these effects are relatively small, even during adolescence when the gap between the sexes is the widest. Nonetheless, even small differences in self-esteem can be extremely important to day-to-day well-being, so this sex difference should not be dismissed. It is therefore important for psychologists to better understand the causes of low self-esteem in young girls and women. Carol Gilligan (American psychologist and feminist) has suggested that during adolescence, girls begin internalizing the stereotypical notions of how they should look and behave. Since these idealized standards are impossible to satisfy completely, self-esteem is impacted negatively. Greater bodily changes with puberty may exacerbate the incongruence between actual and ideal body type, lowering self-esteem even further (Gilligan, Lyons, & Hammer, 1990).

Sexuality and Emotional Investment

Two recent reviews concluded that there exist large sex differences in the desire for sexual variety (Petersen & Hyde, 2010; Schmitt et al., 2012). Men are more likely to have more permissive attitudes toward casual sex ($d = .45$) and view pornography more often ($d = .63$). Men more than women also desire a larger number of sex partners, have more frequent sexual fantasies, and are more willing to accept offers of sex from strangers (Hald & Hogh-Olesen, 2010).

Can straight men and women "just be friends"? It turns out that compared to straight women, straight men have more difficulty being friends with the opposite sex. Straight men are more likely than women to initiate friendship with someone of the opposite sex because they are sexually attracted to them; more likely to actually become sexually attracted to their opposite-sex friends; and more likely to dissolve such friendships if they do not result in sex (Bleske-Rechek & Buss, 2001).

Men are also more likely than women to be sexually aggressive, particularly in terms of pressuring others to have sex (Buss, 2003). Nonetheless, not all men are sexually aggressive. Some studies have shown that men who indicate "hostile masculinity" (domineering and degrading attitudes towards women) and men who lack the personality disposition of empathy are most likely to report using sexual aggression (Wheeler, George, & Dahl, 2002). Furthermore, men who are narcissistic are especially likely to express rape-supportive beliefs and to lack empathy for rape victims (Bushman et al., 2003). Although the sexes can be said to differ overall in sexual aggression, it appears to be fairly limited to a subset of men—those who are narcissistic, lack empathy, and display hostile masculinity. Such a crucial caveat underscores the importance of not generalizing research findings to all individuals.

If men score higher in desire for sexual variety, women typically score higher in "emotional investment," a cluster of items including *loving, lovable, romantic, affectionate, cuddlesome, compassionate,* and *passionate* (Schmitt & Buss, 2000). A study of 48 nations found an average effect size of −.39 (Schmitt et al., 2009). The authors interpreted this sex difference as stemming from the evolution of sex differences in attachment, with women showing higher levels of emotional attachment both to children and to romantic partners (Schmitt et al., 2009). Women between the ages of 18 and 39 also report greater life longings for family and romantic partners (Kotter-Gruhn et al., 2009).

People–Things Dimension

Another dimension of personality has been labelled the **people–things dimension** (Lippa, 1998; Little, 1972a, 1972b). This refers to the nature of vocational interests. People who score toward the "things" end of the dimension prefer vocations that deal with impersonal objects—machines, tools, or materials. Examples include carpenters, auto mechanics, building contractors, tool makers, and farmers. Those scoring toward the "people" end of the dimension prefer social occupations, which involve thinking about others, caring for others, or directing others. Examples include teachers, social workers, nurses, and counsellors.

There are strong sex differences in these occupational preferences. The correlation between sex and the people–things dimension is .56, or a *d* of roughly 1.35, which means that men are more likely to score at the things end of the dimension, and women are more likely to score at the people end (Lippa, 1998). A study of more than half a million people found a *d* of 0.93, which is considered quite large (Su, Rounds, & Armstrong, 2009). When girls are asked to describe themselves spontaneously, they are more likely than boys to make references to their close relationships. They are more likely to value personal qualities linked to group harmony, such as sensitivity to others. And they are more likely to identify their personal relationships as central to their identity as a person (Gabriel & Gardner, 1999).

The people–thing distinction is similar to the empathizing–systemizing distinction. **Empathizing** refers to tuning in to other people's thoughts and feelings. **Systemizing** is the drive to comprehend how things work, how systems are built, and how inputs into systems produce outputs (Baron-Cohen, 2003). Women score higher on empathizing, while men score higher on systemizing, which may partially explain sex differences in occupational preferences—women more than men prefer teaching and helping professions; men more than women gravitate toward construction and engineering (Wright et al., 2015). But as we explore later in this chapter, social factors such as reinforcement should also be considered as possible causes underlying such differences. It may be that the sexes differ in occupational preferences simply because they are reinforced for said preferences.

> **!** Concept Check
>
> *Summarize the research findings on sex differences associated with the five-factor model. Which traits show the greatest sex differences?*
>
> *Consider the sex differences observed for self-esteem and depression. What might be a common factor underlying both trends?*

Masculinity/Femininity, Gender Stereotypes, and Gender Identity

As we've seen, women and men tend to differ in a few dimensions: assertiveness, tender-mindedness, and anxiety, as well as in aggressiveness, sexuality, and depression. But do these differences mean that there is such a thing as a "masculine" or "feminine" personality? This section explores conceptions of masculinity and femininity and how our understanding of these topics has changed over time.

In the 1930s, personality researchers began to notice that men and women differed in their responses to a number of personality items on large inventories. For example, when asked whether they preferred to take baths or showers, women indicated that they preferred baths, whereas men indicated that they preferred showers. Based on these sex differences, researchers assumed that the differences could be described by a single personality dimension, with *masculinity* at one end and *femininity* at the other end. A person who scored high on masculinity was assumed to score low on femininity, and vice versa. Researchers assumed that all people could be located on this single masculinity–femininity dimension. Items that showed large sex differences, such as "I enjoy reading *Popular Mechanics*" (men scored higher), and "I would enjoy the work of a librarian" (women scored higher), were used to construct a single scale of masculinity–femininity. But does a single scale with masculinity at one end and femininity at the other end really capture important individual differences that exist among people? Can't someone be both masculine *and* feminine? This question led to a new conception of sex-linked personality differences—*androgyny*.

Masculinity, Femininity, and Androgyny

In the early 1970s, with the rise of the feminist movement, researchers like Sandra Bem and Janet Spence began to challenge the assumption of a single masculinity–femininity dimension. These new researchers instead suggested that masculinity and femininity are independent dimensions. Thus, one can be high on both masculinity and femininity, or low on both dimensions. Alternatively, one can be stereotypically masculine: high on masculinity, low on femininity; or one can be stereotypically feminine: high on femininity, low on masculinity. This shift represented a fundamental change in thinking about masculinity, femininity, and sex roles.

Two major personality instruments were published in 1974 to assess people using this new conception of sex roles (Bem, 1974; Spence, Helmreich, & Stapp, 1974). On each survey, the **masculinity** dimension contained items reflecting assertiveness, boldness, dominance, self-sufficiency, and instrumentality. Those who agreed with personality trait terms connoting these qualities scored high on masculinity. The **femininity** dimension contained items that reflected nurturance, expression of emotions, and empathy. Those who agreed with personality trait terms connoting these qualities scored high on femininity. Those who scored high on both dimensions were labelled **androgynous,** to reflect the notion that a single person could possess both masculine and feminine characteristics. Table 16.3 shows the four possible scores these instruments can yield.

Table 16.3 Conception of Sex Roles Developed in the 1970s		
	Low Masculinity	**High Masculinity**
Low Femininity	Undifferentiated	Masculine
High Femininity	Feminine	Androgynous

The researchers who developed these questionnaires viewed the androgynous person as the most highly developed. Androgynous individuals were presumed to embody the most valuable elements of both sexes, such as the assertiveness to take positive steps in one's job and interpersonal sensitivity to the feelings of others. Furthermore, androgynous individuals were presumed to be liberated from the shackles of traditional notions of sex roles. Before proceeding with our analysis, however, pause for a few minutes to determine where you are located on these measures. To find out, complete the Exercise below.

❓ Exercise

INSTRUCTIONS: Forty items follow. Each one contains a pair of statements describing contradictory characteristics; that is, you cannot be both at the same time, such as very artistic and not at all artistic. The letters form a scale between the two extremes. Select the letter that describes where you fall on the scale. For example, if you think that you are not at all aggressive, you would choose A. If you think you are very aggressive, you would choose E. If you are in between, you would choose C, or possibly B or D. Be sure to make a choice for every item. Mark your choice by drawing an X through the letter that you select.

1.	Not at all aggressive	A.....B.....C.....D.....E	Very aggressive
2.	Very whiny	A.....B.....C.....D.....E	Not at all whiny
3.	Not at all independent	A.....B.....C.....D.....E	Very independent
4.	Not at all arrogant	A.....B.....C.....D.....E	Very arrogant
5.	Not at all emotional	A.....B.....C.....D.....E	Very emotional
6.	Very submissive	A.....B.....C.....D.....E	Very dominant
7.	Very boastful	A.....B.....C.....D.....E	Not at all boastful
8.	Not at all excitable in a major crisis	A.....B.....C.....D.....E	Very excitable in a major crisis
9.	Very passive	A.....B.....C.....D.....E	Very active
10.	Not at all egotistical	A.....B.....C.....D.....E	Very egotistical
11.	Not at all able to devote self completely to others	A.....B.....C.....D.....E	Able to devote self completely to others
12.	Not at all spineless	A.....B.....C.....D.....E	Very spineless
13.	Very rough	A.....B.....C.....D.....E	Very gentle

14. Not at all complaining	A.....B.....C.....D.....E	Very complaining
15. Not at all helpful to others	A.....B.....C.....D.....E	Very helpful to others
16. Not at all competitive	A.....B.....C.....D.....E	Very competitive
17. Subordinates oneself to others	A.....B.....C.....D.....E	Never subordinates onself to others
18. Very home-oriented	A.....B.....C.....D.....E	Very worldly
19. Very greedy	A.....B.....C.....D.....E	Not at all greedy
20. Not at all kind	A.....B.....C.....D.....E	Very kind
21. Indifferent to others' approval	A.....B.....C.....D.....E	Highly needful of others' approval
22. Very dictatorial	A.....B.....C.....D.....E	Not at all dictatorial
23. Feelings not easily hurt	A.....B.....C.....D.....E	Feelings easily hurt
24. Doesn't nag	A.....B.....C.....D.....E	Nags a lot
25. Not at all aware of feelings of others	A.....B.....C.....D.....E	Very aware of feelings of others
26. Can make decisions easily	A.....B.....C.....D.....E	Has difficulty making decisions
27. Very fussy	A.....B.....C.....D.....E	Not at all fussy
28. Gives up very easily	A.....B.....C.....D.....E	Never gives up easily
29. Very cynical	A.....B.....C.....D.....E	Not at all cynical
30. Never cries	A.....B.....C.....D.....E	Cries very easily
31. Not at all self-confident	A.....B.....C.....D.....E	Very self-confident
32. Does not look out only for self, principled	A.....B.....C.....D.....E	Looks out only for self, unprincipled
33. Feels very inferior	A.....B.....C.....D.....E	Feels very superior
34. Not at all hostile	A.....B.....C.....D.....E	Very hostile
35. Not at all understanding of others	A.....B.....C.....D.....E	Very understanding of others
36. Very cold in relations with others	A.....B.....C.....D.....E	Very warm in relations with others
37. Very servile	A.....B.....C.....D.....E	Not at all servile
38. Very little need for security	A.....B.....C.....D.....E	Very strong need for security
39. Not at all gullible	A.....B.....C.....D.....E	Very gullible
40. Goes to pieces under pressure	A.....B.....C.....D.....E	Stands up well under pressure

The popularity of this new conception of sex roles was a testament to the influence of feminism in North America. With the rise of the women's movement, traditional ideas about the roles of men and women were cast aside. Women started entering the workforce in record numbers. Some men opted for more nurturant roles. John Lennon, of former Beatles fame, decided to stay at home and raise his son, Sean, while his wife, Yoko Ono, went to work, overseeing a massive financial empire (Coleman, 1992). Many people applauded Lennon for taking on this new liberated role. This political movement reinforced the idea that men could benefit from becoming more nurturant, caring, and empathic. At the same time, women could benefit from becoming more assertive as they entered many professions traditionally reserved for men. The psychological trend toward changing the conceptualization and measurement of sex roles reflected this larger political movement.

The new androgynous conception of sex roles, however, was not without its criticisms. One such criticism pertained to the items on the inventories and their correlations with each other. Researchers seemed to assume that masculinity and femininity were single dimensions. Other researchers argued, however, that both constructs were actually multidimensional, containing many facets. Furthermore, research has not supported the original notion that androgynous people are more highly developed; this is a term that is less commonly used in contemporary research.

In response to such shortcomings, many of these original researchers have changed their views. Janet Spence, for instance, no longer believes that her questionnaire assesses sex roles (Swann, Langlois, & Gilbert, 1999). Instead, she claims that her scales actually measure the personality characteristics of *instrumentality* and *expressiveness*. **Instrumentality** consists of personality traits that involve working with objects, getting tasks completed in a direct fashion, showing independence from others, and displaying self-sufficiency. **Expressiveness**, in contrast, is the ease with which one can express emotions, such as crying, showing empathy for the troubles of others, and showing nurturance to those in need. This reconception of masculinity and femininity is important because it removes any implicit association with gender, recognizing that any person may exhibit any combination of these traits regardless of their sex or gender. Other alternative labels for masculinity and femininity include *competence* and *warmth* (respectively) and *agency* and *communion* (respectively), though subtle differences in their definitions do exist (Kachel et al., 2016).

Sandra Bem, an original proponent of the concept of androgyny, also changed her views on sex roles, later believing that her original measure (the Bem Sex Role Inventory; Bem, 1974) assesses **gender schemas**, or cognitive orientations that lead individuals to process social information on the basis of sex-linked associations (Hoyenga & Hoyenga, 1993). Bem suggested that the inventory specifically assesses the extent to which individuals live according to, and see the world through, gender schemas. For example, if a male scores high on the masculinity dimension and low on the femininity dimension, he would be said to be imposing a gender-based lens on his reality and living according to gender role expectations. According to this perspective, it is not necessarily ideal to be *androgynous*, but rather it is ideal to be *gender-aschematic*: to not use gender at all in one's processing of social information. There remains some debate over exactly what the Bem Sex Role Inventory is measuring. Some suggest that it is simply assessing a person's tendency to adopt gender role expectations and behaviours, while providing little insight about their use of gender schemas (Hoffman & Borders, 2001).

Many researchers are interested in exploring the real-life consequences of masculinity and femininity, including outcomes associated with either conforming or not conforming to traditional gender roles (Kachel et al., 2016). One study, for example, found that these dimensions affect sexual behaviour and relationships (Udry & Chantala, 2004). Adolescent couples containing a highly masculine male and a highly feminine female tend to have sex sooner than other pairings. Couples in which both members are average for their sex tend to break up compared with other pairings. In a Canadian study, self-report indicators of masculinity and femininity were associated with smoking behaviour in Indigenous adolescents (Greaves et al., 2012). Boys with higher ratings of affectionate femininity were more likely to smoke, suggesting that gender nonconformity in this group may contribute to increased incidence of smoking.

There also seems to be an impact on how individuals interact with others. For instance, research has found that when straight men identify with idealized notions of masculinity (such as those which prescribe men to seek status, exhibit toughness, and avoid feminine behaviours), they are more likely to express sexist and homophobic attitudes and reject people who do not conform to gender role expectations, such as men who are stay-at-home dads and women who are career-focused (Thompson et al., 1992). This finding supports Sandra Bem's earlier contention that an individual who scores very high on masculinity (but low on femininity) is more likely to impose a gender-based lens on reality.

Gender Stereotypes

Much of this chapter has been concerned with the ways in which men and women differ. An important related topic pertains to the *beliefs* about how the sexes differ, regardless of whether these beliefs are accurate reflections of the sex differences that empirically exist. The beliefs and assumptions we hold about men and women are referred to as gender stereotypes. They are based largely on our gender schemas, which are shaped early in life through a variety of learning and socialization processes (Bem, 1981).

The distinctions between what behaviour is appropriate for a woman and what behaviour is appropriate for a man in our culture—social roles—have changed dramatically in the past few decades.
©Design Pics/Darren Greenwood

Gender stereotypes have three components (Hoyenga & Hoyenga, 1993). The first is *cognitive* and deals with the ways in which we form **social categories**. Broadly speaking, we have different thoughts and beliefs about men and women, and we make assumptions about people based on whether we believe they belong to one gender or the other. We may further categorize all men as "playboys," "career men," or "family men" (or any number of other subcategories), depending on more specific traits. Likewise, we may categorize all women into "career women," "homemakers," or "promiscuous women." These are not necessarily meaningful ways of categorizing people, but they do reflect some of the stereotypes and attitudes that people hold. The second component of gender stereotypes is *affective*. You may feel hostile or warm toward someone simply because they are a man or a woman, or because you place that person in a particular subcategory. The third component of gender stereotypes is *behavioural*. For example, you may discriminate against someone simply because of the person's sex or gender, or because they belong in some other social category within gender. We explore these various aspects of gender stereotypes in the following sections, in order to illuminate how social categorizing shows up in everyday life.

Content of Gender Stereotypes

Although some variations exist from culture to culture, it is remarkable that the content of gender stereotypes—the attributes that we believe men and women possess—is highly similar across cultures. In the most comprehensive set of studies yet conducted, Williams and Best (1982, 1990) studied gender stereotypes in 30 countries around the world. Across cultures, men were commonly viewed as more aggressive, autonomous, achievement-oriented, dominant, exhibitionist, and persevering than women. Compared to men, women were commonly seen as more affiliative, deferent, nurturant, and self-abasing. These broad gender stereotypes have a common theme. Women in all 30 countries tend to be perceived as more *communal*—oriented toward the group and relationships with others. Men, in contrast, are perceived to be more *agentic* or *instrumental*—asserting their independence from the group. These stereotypes correspond in many ways to the actual sex differences that have been reviewed previously in this chapter. Nonetheless, there is evidence that people overestimate the magnitude of sex differences in personality, showing exaggerated beliefs about the size of the differences that actually exist (Krueger, Hasman, et al., 2003; Wood & Eagly, 2010).

Stereotypic Subtypes and Subgroups

In addition to broad gender stereotypes, studies show that most people have more finely differentiated stereotypic views of each gender. Six and Eckes (1991) examined the structure of their participants' cognitive categories of men and women and came up with several subtypes. Men were viewed as falling into five subtypes. The playboy subtype, for example, included men who were cool, casual, "players," and macho. The career man subtype included men who were social climbers and managers. Stereotypes of women fell into a smaller number of subtypes, the first being the "classically feminine" subtype, which included housewives, secretaries, and maternal women. In the modern world these family-oriented women might be categorized into "soccer moms." A second subtype was the short-term or overtly sexual woman, and a third was the confident and intelligent

Dr. Roberta Bondar, the first Canadian woman in space, illustrates a relatively recent gender stereotype—women who are assertive and career-minded.
Canadian Space Agency

career woman. Dr. Roberta Bondar, Canada's first female astronaut, might be a good illustration of this third category—she holds degrees in zoology, neuroscience, medicine, and experimental pathology, and served as NASA's head of space medicine for over a decade.

Remember, these are just stereotypes. They are not meaningful ways of categorizing people. The key point is that, cognitively, most people do not hold only a single gender stereotype. People typically develop *subtypes* when they encounter men and women who do not fit their existing gender stereotypes. They see these individuals as exceptions to the rule, place them in separate subcategories, and are then able to maintain their original stereotypes. People also form stereotype *subgroups*, which result from the ongoing differentiation and organization of men and women into smaller groups based on similar characteristics (Richards & Hewstone, 2001).

Prejudice and Gender Stereotypes

Categories of gender, and the stereotypes associated with them, are not merely cognitive constructions that rattle around inside people's heads. They have real-world consequences, including prejudiced behaviour and discrimination on the basis of gender.

These damaging effects can be found in many important activities: in legal decisions, medical treatment, car purchases, and job hunting (Hoyenga & Hoyenga, 1993; Wood & Eagly, 2010). For example, there is evidence from Canada and the United States that men are more likely to be recommended for coronary bypass surgery than women, even when they show the same amount of heart damage (Johansen et al., 1998). Canadian women are much more likely to experience workplace harassment than men, including sexual harassment (Hango & Moyser, 2018). And although the gap has decreased over time, Canadian women still earn 8 percent less than Canadian men (after controlling for gender differences in industry, occupation, education, age, job tenure, etc.), a difference that is often attributed to gender biases and prejudices (Morissette et al., 2013). Although prejudices can occur in either direction, Canadian women are 24 percent more likely to report experiencing discrimination than men; young women specifically (ages 25 to 45) are 54 percent more likely than men in the same cohort (Godley, 2018).

These examples of gender-based discrimination are believed to occur because of persisting negative attitudes and feelings about women and their role in society. They therefore depend on both cognitive and affective components of gender stereotypes. But discrimination can also occur when women and men violate gender role expectations and stereotypes. Consider the common stereotype that women are emotionally expressive (Shields, 2002). In a review of research on gender and emotions, Brescoll (2016) cited evidence that women in leadership roles are evaluated more negatively if they express emotions associated with dominance, such as anger and pride, and also when they express no emotions at all. In this example, it seems that any deviation from the stereotype—either the wrong kind of emotion or no emotion at all—results in social penalties. Another study found that preschool children receive less favourable evaluations by adults when they display qualities and behaviours that are inconsistent with gender stereotypes (Sullivan et al., 2018). It is important to consider how such prejudice and discrimination might impact key developmental outcomes at such a young age.

Hostile sexism, the kind of discrimination that is based on overtly negative stereotypes of women as inferior to men, has been associated with particularly negative evaluations of both women and men who violate traditional gender role expectations. Negative stereotypes about women do not only affect women; they also affect men who may be perceived as possessing feminine qualities or who occupy social roles traditionally held by women (Glick et al., 2015). Though more research is needed, the social pressure that men experience to adhere to strict definitions of masculinity has been shown to lead to problematic outcomes for men in heath, career, and relationships (Moss-Racusin & Good, 2015). You may have also heard of *toxic masculinity*. It is an expression used to underscore the negative consequences of strict and traditional definitions of masculinity, including those which prescribe social dominance, physical and emotional toughness, and superiority over women.

In the end, gender stereotypes can have important consequences for both women and men, regardless of age or background. Sandra Bem's suggestion that we try to be *gender-aschematic*—that we not use gender when processing social information—may be good advice.

Gender Identity

In this chapter, we've explored many gender-related traits and characteristics that involve observable behaviours. But what about aspects of the inner self, like self-concept and identity? How are they related to gender?

As noted in the introduction of this chapter, gender is the social or cultural notion of what it means to be a man or a woman. It comes with all kinds of ideas about what men and women should be like, how they should dress and act, and the activities they should engage in. Gender is a reflection of our stereotypes about men and women, or more accurately, our stereotypes are a reflection of our social and cultural definitions of "man" and "woman." They are inextricably intertwined. As gender is inherently a social category, it is also part of our self-concept and social identity from a very early age. It is one of the first characteristics we think of when we consider who we are as individuals. This deeply-felt, inherent sense of being a man, a woman, or neither is referred to as *gender identity*. For most people, their self-concept and identity regarding their gender are in line with how other people see them, and in line with the gender they were assigned at birth. These individuals are referred to as *cisgender*. For others, self-concept and identity regarding their gender do not align with social expectations or assumptions, such that they may find the gender labels imposed upon them to be inappropriate; or they may have a gender identity that does not align with their primary or secondary sex characteristics. These individuals are often referred to as *transgender* or just *trans* for short (though some may identify with other terms, such as *gender neutral*, *genderqueer*, *non-binary*, or *two-spirit*, highlighting the very personal and internal nature of gender identity).

Despite challenges, many trans individuals are able to maintain a healthy and happy life, especially when a supportive social network is present (Bauer et al., 2015). Others experience significant distress. According to the American Psychiatric Association's (APA) current *Diagnostic and Statistical Manual of Mental Disorders* (DSM-5; APA, 2013), *gender dysphoria* is a condition in which one's sex or gender assigned at birth causes significant distress or impairment in one or more life domains. Although not all self-identifying transgender people meet the criteria for this diagnosis, some do. And this continues to be a point of contention within the trans community. Some trans individuals support the APA's inclusion of gender dysphoria in the DSM-5, as it aids in the delivery of both mental and physical health services to members of the community. Others argue that it simply perpetuates stigma and discrimination surrounding gender nonconformity, notably with the suggestion that such nonconformity may reflect psychological disorder.

There is evidence that our gender identity, whether it aligns with biological sex or not, is at least partly the result of internal, biological factors (Polderman et al., 2018). Cleveland and colleagues (2001) found that sex-typed behaviours and attitudes themselves tend to show moderate heritability within sex. By extension, gender identity appears to be present early in life, and in some cases, even children describe themselves in terms that are inconsistent with the gender they are assigned at birth. Cases of transgender children are often met with skepticism, however, with many questioning whether they are confused or simply engaging in imaginative thinking. To shed light on these questions, Olson and colleagues (2015) studied 32 transgender children (ages 5 through 12) who were presenting themselves according to their identified gender (i.e., not as the gender assigned to them at birth). Using a variety of implicit and explicit association tests aimed at measuring gender identity and gender role preferences, the transgender children in this sample displayed patterns of gender cognition that were consistently in line with their expressed gender. In other words, they seemed to genuinely identify with the opposite gender (their expressed gender) and displayed no signs of confusion over who they were (Olson et al., 2015).

Although further research is needed in order to understand the biological and psychological factors underlying gender identity, it is estimated that 1 in 200 Canadian adults (0.5 percent) are transgender, with about two-thirds living as their experienced gender. Due to their lack of conformity to gender stereotypes and gender role expectations, transgender individuals experience frequent discrimination that is often accompanied by verbal and physical abuse (Bauer et al., 2015). We examine the impact of stigma associated with being transgender further in Highlight on Canadian Research: Gender Identity and Discrimination: Increased Suicide Risk among Transgender Canadians.

⊕ Highlight on Canadian Research

Gender Identity and Discrimination: Increased Suicide Risk among Transgender Canadians

Being *transgender* (or *trans*) means that a person's gender identity differs from the sex or gender assigned to them at birth. It is estimated that approximately 180,000 Canadians identify as transgender today (Bauer et al., 2015). Many (but not all) trans people dress, behave, or alter their physical body in order to express the gender they more closely identify with psychologically, often in ways that differ from the stereotypical behaviours associated with their assigned sex at birth. In line with our previous discussion on gender stereotyping, such violation of gender stereotypes results in a great deal of backlash from other members of society.

Many Canadians and much of the international community still respond to trans people in prejudiced and discriminatory ways. The discrimination experienced by the trans community can be quite severe. In an online survey of over 1,000 transgender individuals, the stigma associated with being transgender was associated with increased job discrimination, higher rates of depression, and barriers to addiction services (Bockting et al., 2013). Relationship difficulties and social exclusion are also common experiences for transgender youth and adults, resulting in smaller social networks, inadequate social support, and social isolation. Not surprisingly, these factors limit the ability of trans people to function optimally in society, which is why many in Canada are unemployed or live in poverty (Goldberg et al., 2003). Other poor health outcomes include depression, anxiety, stress, and higher rates of suicide. It is this last outcome that has been of particular concern to researchers.

In 2009–2010, a large research project was launched in the province of Ontario to investigate a variety of factors associated with discrimination in the transgender community. The Trans PULSE Project, a community initiative, collected data from 433 transgender individuals over the course of one year. Findings regarding suicide were especially alarming. Within a subset of 380 trans people aged 16 years and older, 35 percent reported having seriously considered suicide in the past year, while 11 percent had actually attempted suicide (Bauer et al., 2015). It is worth noting that this last statistic is in contrast to approximately 1.6 percent of the general population of Canada who report attempting suicide each year. Although it should be alarming that attempted suicide rates are nearly seven times higher in the trans community, what is more disconcerting is the potential number who have actually died by suicide. These individuals are not included in these statistics, and suicide rates are difficult to estimate in this population due to the frequent lack of disclosure regarding gender identity and/or the tendency for family members to misidentify gender to authorities.

A recent study of 923 transgender youth from across Canada found evidence of higher risks of psychological distress, self-harm behaviour, depression, suicidal ideation, and attempted suicide in this population (Veale et al., 2017). Only a small minority of the youth in this study reported good mental health, underscoring the unique pressures and challenges associated with gender nonconformity. Transgender boys and men (i.e., those living as boys and men who were not assigned the male sex at birth) were at a particularly high risk of self-harm behaviour, as were those who identified as neither gender (i.e., non-binary). The authors of this study concluded that the mental health disparities experienced by trans youth in Canada are significant, highlighting the need to identify more effective coping resources and systems of support for this population.

In research conducted by Greta Bauer (University of Western Ontario) and colleagues (2015), lower personal experience with transphobia was associated with a 66 percent reduction in suicidal ideation. *Transphobia* refers to intense dislike, discrimination, or violence directed at transgender people. This suggests that the abnormally high rates of discrimination experienced by this group are playing a significant role in the observed rates of attempted suicide. Analyses further indicated that factors related to social inclusion can reduce suicidal ideation, such as gender-specific parental support, identity documents that are in line with one's gender identity, and social support more generally, including support in the form of protection against transphobia. Clearly a number of changes are required on the societal level to more adequately support trans Canadians of all ages. As it stands now, the federal government and all provinces and territories in Canada include gender identity and gender expression as prohibited grounds for discrimination. Perhaps more needs to be done to challenge the very stereotypical notions of men and women that persist in the general population.

 Concept Check

Define masculinity, femininity, and androgyny. How are these terms understood by psychologists today?

What are gender stereotypes? Discuss two ways that traditional gender stereotypes can result in negative consequences for people.

Theories of Sex Differences

So far in this chapter, we have seen that there are some differences in personality between the sexes but also many similarities. We have also seen that people hold stereotypes of sex differences that may go beyond the actual differences—stereotypes that can have lasting consequences for people's day-to-day lives. This section examines the major theories that have been proposed for explaining how sex differences arise. These include traditional theories of socialization and more complex theories of social roles and other notions of "gendered environments," hormonal theories, and, most recently, theories anchored in evolutionary psychology.

Socialization and Social Roles

Socialization theory, the notion that boys and girls become different because boys are reinforced by parents, teachers, and the media for being "masculine" and girls for being "feminine," is probably the most widely held theory of sex differences in personality. The theory can be summarized as follows: Boys are given baseball bats and trucks. Girls are given dolls. Boys are praised for engaging in rough-and-tumble play. Girls are praised for being cute and obedient. Boys are punished for crying. Girls are comforted when they cry. Over time, according to socialization theory, children adopt behaviours deemed appropriate for their sex.

Both socialization and social learning theories hold that gender roles have their roots in early sex-differentiated learning experiences—in short, boys are encouraged in one direction and girls are encouraged in another direction.
©Bill Aron/PhotoEdit

In Bandura's (1977) **social learning theory**, a variant of socialization theory, boys and girls also learn by observing the behaviours of others, called *models,* of their own sex. Boys watch their fathers, male teachers, and male peers. Girls watch their mothers, female teachers, and female peer models. Boys see their fathers work. Girls see their mothers cook. Over time, even in the absence of direct reinforcement, these models provide a guide to behaviours that are "masculine" or "feminine."

What empirical evidence has been offered to support socialization and social learning theories of sex differences? Early studies of socialization practices found that North American parents tended to encourage dependency more in girls than in boys (Block, 1983). They encouraged girls to stay close to home, whereas boys were permitted or even encouraged to roam. But some parenting practices have changed over time. A recent meta-analysis of observational studies of parenting behaviours in Western nations found no overall difference in the extent to which parents supported the autonomy of boys versus girls (Endendijk et al., 2016). It seems that parents encouraged autonomy more in boys in the 1970s and 1980s, but this shifted in the 1990s, such that parents began encouraging autonomy more in girls.

Research in the 1970s and 1980s also suggested that fathers engaged in more physical play with their sons than with their daughters (Fagot & Leinbach, 1987). This differential treatment of boys and girls appears to persist today, at least to some extent, with research continuing to document more frequent rough-and-tumble play between fathers and their sons (e.g., Flanders et al., 2009). There is also evidence that parents provide "gendered toys" to their children. Early research found that boys tended to receive a greater variety of toys, more cars and trucks, more sports equipment, and more tools, while girls received more dolls, pink clothing and furnishings, strollers, swings, and household appliances. (Rheingold & Cook, 1975). Research has continued to find evidence that parents provide boys with stereotypical masculine toys and girls with stereotypical feminine toys (Blakemore & Centers, 2005). Parents today also tend to view gender-typical toys as more desirable for their children than gender-atypical toys (Kollmayer et al., 2018).

Cross-cultural evidence of the differential treatment of boys and girls exists as well. It has been shown, for example, that boys in most cultures are socialized to be more competitive than girls (Gneezy & Rustichini, 2004; Low, 1989). An interesting study compared two tribal societies in rural India, one *patriarchal* (in which males are socially dominant and control many prominent aspects of society) and one *matrilineal* (in which women compete more than men and kinship is defined by maternal lines). Girls were observed to be less competitive than boys only in the patriarchal society, while no such difference was found in the matrilineal society. In the patriarchal society, it was around puberty that the difference in competitiveness emerged (Andersen et al., 2013). Such a comparative analysis provides us with evidence that in terms of competitiveness, social factors likely play a greater role than more innate differences between sexes.

Girls in most cultures also tend to be assigned more domestic chores than boys, while boys are permitted in most cultures to stray farther from home than girls (Hoyenga & Hoyenga, 1993). In a large study of socialization practices across cultures, Low (1989) found that in 82 percent of the cultures the girls were trained to be more nurturant than the boys. In the majority of the cultures studied, the girls were also socialized to be more sexually restrained than the boys—the parents tried to teach their daughters to delay having sexual intercourse (Perilloux Fleischman, & Buss, 2011), whereas the boys were encouraged to have sexual intercourse (Low, 1989). These patterns of parenting have also been reported more recently in college and university populations (Perilloux, Fleischman, & Buss, 2008), explained under what has been called the "daughter-guarding hypothesis."

One potential difficulty, however, pertains to the direction of effects—whether parents are socializing children in sex-linked ways or whether children are eliciting their parents' behaviour to correspond to their existing sex-linked preferences. Perhaps the interests of the children drive the parents' behaviour rather than the other way around. Parents may start out by giving a variety of toys to their children; however, if boys show no interest in dolls and girls show no interest in trucks, then over time parents may stop purchasing masculine toys for their daughters and feminine toys for their sons. The theory that the causal arrow runs one way—from parents to children—is at least open to question.

Research on toy preferences has given us some insight into this matter. Are differences in toy preference between boys and girls due entirely to differences in socialization? Or are parents buying toys based on their children's inherent preferences? Jadva and colleagues (2010) reported observational findings from a study of 120 male and female infants who were exposed to different kinds of toys. Male infants were indeed more likely to look at toy cars, while in comparison, female infants were more likely to look at dolls. However, when examining preferences within each sex, it was found that overall, both boys and girls preferred to look at dolls at 12 months. The frequency was simply lower in boys than it was in girls. Both boys and girls also preferred the colour red over blue. The authors concluded that the avoidance of dolls in older boys and the preference for pink in older girls may be largely acquired via socialization (Jadva et al., 2010). Yet some differences were still observed at a very young age, which may indicate a partial role of other, more innate influences. In support of this latter consideration, other research has found evidence of sex-linked preferences in boys and girls as young as 3 to 8 months (Alexander et al., 2008).

A theory closely related to traditional socialization theories is **social role theory** (Eagly, 1987; Eagly & Wood, 1999; Wood & Eagly, 2010). According to social role theory, sex differences originate because men and women are distributed differently into different occupational and family roles. Men, for example, are expected to assume the breadwinning role. Women are expected to assume the homemaker role. Over time, children presumably learn the behaviours that are linked to these roles. Girls learn to be nurturing and emotionally supportive because these qualities are linked with the maternal role. Boys learn to be tough and aggressive, qualities expected of the breadwinner.

There is some evidence supporting social role theory (Eagly, 1987, 1995). Men and women in North America have tended to assume different occupational and family roles, with women found more often in domestic and child-care roles, and men more often in occupational roles. Even in Canada, women continue to perform more housework than men at all ages (Horne et al., 2018). An event-sampling procedure explored how men's and women's behaviour varied as a function of the social role to which they were assigned—a supervisor role, a co-worker role, or the role of someone being supervised by someone else. Social role assignment had a large impact on the dominant behaviours that were expressed. The men and women assigned to the supervisor role displayed significantly more dominance, whereas those assigned the supervisee role displayed significantly more submissiveness (Moskowitz, Suh, & Desaulniers, 1994). When the roles were reversed, the people who formerly displayed dominance displayed submissiveness when they were put in a supervisee role, whereas the people who formerly were submissive became more dominant when they were assigned to the supervisor role.

Social role theory is becoming increasingly testable as family and occupational dynamics change. In straight relationships, women are assuming breadwinning roles more often than in the past, and men are assuming greater responsibility for domestic duties. In same-sex relationships, there seems to be greater equality in housework allocations, presumably because of greater equality in relationships and less importance placed on displays of sex-typical behaviour (Geist & Ruppanner, 2018). If social role theory is correct, sex differences should diminish as society continues to become more egalitarian. Interestingly, the largest test of this prediction, a study of 17,637 individuals in 55 different cultures, has found precisely the opposite pattern (Schmitt et al., 2008). The most gender-egalitarian countries—those with the most equal access to education and knowledge and the greatest levels of economic wealth—have shown the largest, not the smallest, sex differences in personality. This surprising result appears to contradict the social role theory of sex differences in personality (see also Schmitt et al., 2017). Costa and colleagues (2001) found a similar pattern in their cross-cultural analyses. They suggested a number of possible explanations, including that personality traits and their sex differences may be seen as less important in collectivistic cultures. Alternatively, it may be that certain differences are more freely expressed in more developed parts of the world.

An interesting study from Sweden, often described as one of the world's most gender-equal countries, found that Swedish teenagers are still more likely to choose gender-typical career paths (Tellhed et al., 2017). In these analyses, belief in ability to succeed in a given career and concerns over fitting in were the most important factors explaining young people's choices, in addition to personal preferences for wanting to help others versus gaining status (the latter of which was exhibited more by males). The authors concluded that the persistence of pervasive gender stereotypes, despite greater gender equality, may have contributed to the strong sex-linked preferences. Indeed, gender schemas and stereotypes likely play a role in the distribution of males and females into different social roles (by influencing behaviour, decision-making, and social responses to the sexes). There is evidence, for example, that exposure to role models who contradict gender stereotypes (e.g., female doctors, male nurses) can at least temporarily influence the career aspirations of children and adolescents, such that they are more likely to aspire to counter-stereotypical careers (Olsson & Martiny, 2018).

More research is needed, however, in order to better understand the origins of sex-linked roles, as well as factors underlying the differential socialization of males and females. Why do parents want their boys and girls to grow up differently? Why do men and women passively accept the roles they are assigned? And why do women assume domestic roles more than men? Ideally, a comprehensive theory of the origins of sex differences should be able to account for the origins of sex-linked socialization practices.

Hormonal Theories

Hormonal theories of sex differences argue that men and women differ not because of the external social environment, but rather because the sexes have different underlying hormones. Physiological differences, not differential social treatment, cause boys and girls to diverge over development. Thus, some studies have sought to identify links between hormones such as testosterone (present in greater amounts in men) and sex-linked behaviour.

There is some evidence that hormonal influences on sex differences begin in utero. The hormonal bath that the developing fetus is exposed to, for example, might affect both the organization of the brain and consequently the gendered interests and activities of the individual. Some of the best evidence for this comes from a condition called congenital adrenal hyperplasia (CAH), in which the female fetus has an overactive adrenal gland. This results in the female being hormonally masculinized. Young girls with CAH show a marked preference for male-typical toys, such as Lincoln logs and trucks (Berenbaum & Snyder, 1995). As adults, CAH females show superiority in traditionally masculine cognitive skills, such as spatial rotation ability and throwing accuracy, as well as preferring traditionally masculine occupations (Kimura, 2002). These findings suggest that fetal exposure to hormones can have lasting effects on gender-related interests and abilities.

Men and women do differ in their levels of circulating hormones. Women's level of circulating testosterone typically falls between 200 and 400 picograms per millilitre of blood at the lowest part of the menstrual cycle and between 285 and 440 at the highest part of the menstrual cycle (just prior to ovulation) (Hoyenga & Hoyenga, 1993). Men, in contrast, have circulating testosterone levels ranging from 5,140 to 6,460 picograms per millilitre of blood. Following puberty, there is no overlap between the sexes in their levels of circulating testosterone. Men typically show more than 10 times the level of women.

These sex differences in circulating testosterone are associated with some of the traditional sex differences found in behaviour, such as aggression, dominance, and career choice. In women, high levels of testosterone are associated with pursuing a more male-stereotypical career and having greater success within the chosen career (Hoyenga & Hoyenga, 1993). Among lesbian women, testosterone has been associated with erotic role identification; more self-described "masculine" lesbian partners having higher levels of testosterone than

Testosterone is associated with dominance and aggressiveness, as well as with the massive buildup of muscular tissue. Here, Canadian Olympic weightlifter Christine Girard performs at the World Weightlifting Championships in 2011. She would later set a record at the 2012 summer games in London, being the first Canadian woman to win a medal, lifting a total weight of 236 kg. Controversially, Olympic athletes are tested to make sure their testosterone levels are within normal ranges for their sex.

©Bertrand Guay/AFP/Getty Images

more "feminine" partners (Singh et al., 1999). Higher testosterone levels are associated with greater dominance and aggressiveness in both sexes. Female prison inmates who had more frequent disciplinary infractions also had higher testosterone (Dabbs & Hargrove, 1997). And Dabbs and colleagues (Dabbs, Hargrove, & Heusel, 1996) found that members of college fraternities who were more rambunctious had higher average levels of testosterone than those in fraternities who were better behaved.

Sexual desire is also associated with levels of circulating testosterone, but only in women (van Anders, 2012). Women's testosterone levels peak just prior to ovulation, and women report a spike in their sexual desire at precisely the same time. At this time, women report more female-initiated sexual intercourse and more desire for sexual intercourse (Sherwin, 1988). One study found that just thinking about sex increases testosterone in women, but not in men (Goldey & van Anders, 2012). The links between hormones and sexuality are much more complicated than scientists initially believed (van Anders, 2012; van Anders et al., 2015).

These findings do not prove that the differences between men and women in sexuality, dominance, aggression, and career choices result from differences between the sexes in testosterone levels. Correlation does not mean causation. Indeed, there is some evidence in nonhuman primates that rises in testosterone levels *follow* rises in status and dominance within the group rather than lead to them (Sapolsky, 1987). Furthermore, sexual arousal itself can result in an increase in testosterone level (Hoyenga & Hoyenga, 1993). A study on sports fans found that those whose team had just won an event had higher levels of testosterone than those fans whose team had just lost (Bernhardt et al., 1998). These results suggest that the link between hormones and behaviour is bidirectional (Edwards, Wetzel, & Wyner, 2006). Higher testosterone may result from, as well as cause, behavioural changes (van Anders et al., 2015).

An additional limitation of hormonal theories of sex differences in personality is one shared with socialization theories—namely, neither of these theories identifies the *origins* of the differences. Precisely why do men and women differ so dramatically in their levels of circulating testosterone? Is this merely an incidental effect of being male versus being female? Or is there a systematic process that causes men and women to differ in testosterone precisely because testosterone differences lead to behavioural differences in dominance and sexuality? One theoretical perspective that argues for this possibility is evolutionary psychology.

Evolutionary Psychology Theory

According to the evolutionary psychology perspective (see Chapter 8), men and women differ only in some domains of personality and show large similarities in most domains. The sexes are predicted to be similar in all the domains in which they have faced similar *adaptive problems* over human evolutionary history. The sexes are predicted to differ only in the domains in which men and women have confronted different adaptive challenges over human evolutionary history (Buss & Schmitt, 2011).

Adaptive problems are problems that need to be solved in order for an individual to survive and reproduce, or whose solution increases overall reproductive success. For example, both sexes have similar taste preferences for sugar, salt, fat, and protein. That's why fast-food restaurants are so popular—they package food with fat and sugar that both men and women desire. Food preferences reflect a solution to an important adaptive problem—getting calories and nutrients to survive.

In the domains of mating and sexuality, according to evolutionary psychologists, men and women have confronted somewhat different adaptive problems (Buss, 1995b). In order to reproduce, women must carry and gestate a fetus for nine months. Men, in contrast, can reproduce through a single act of sex. As a consequence, women historically faced the adaptive problem of securing resources to carry them through harsh winters or droughts, when resources might be scarce and a woman's mobility might be restricted by the burden of pregnancy. The costs of making a poor choice of a mate, according to this logic, would have been more damaging to women than to men. Because of the heavy investment women require for reproduction, they are theorized to have evolved exacting mate preferences for men who showed signals of the ability and willingness to invest in them and their children.

This line of reasoning predicts that men will be more sexually motivated as well as more aggressive with other men about pursuing opportunities for sexual access to women. Because of women's heavy investment, they become the extraordinarily valuable reproductive resource over which men compete. Women, on the other hand, are predicted to be more selective about sex partners—being more discerning about who they are willing to have sex with. A woman who had made a hasty or poor mate choice in the past would have been faced with the difficulties of bearing and raising a child without the help of an investing man. A strategy of casual sex, in short, was more reproductively beneficial to ancestral men than to ancestral women.

Some of the empirical evidence for sex differences indeed corresponds to these predictions. Men clearly have a greater desire for sexual variety than women do (Buss & Schmitt, 1993, 2011; Symons, 1979). Men desire a larger number of sex partners, seek sex after a shorter time period has elapsed in knowing a potential partner, and have more fantasies about casual sex than do women (Schmitt et al., 2012). Furthermore, men tend to take more risks to secure the resources and status that women find desirable in marriage partners (e.g., Byrnes, Miller, & Schafer, 1999; Wilson & Daly, 2004). Thus, the findings that men are more aggressive, more willing to take physical risks, and more interested in casual sex are precisely the findings predicted by evolutionary psychology (Archer, 2009).

Despite this support, evolutionary psychology theory, like the other theoretical perspectives, leaves unanswered questions: What accounts for individual differences within each sex? Why are some women keenly interested in casual sex? Why are some men meek, dependent, and nurturing, whereas others are callous and aggressive? Some of these questions are beginning to be answered. It turns out, for example, that some women benefit greatly from pursuing a short-term sexual strategy, which can result in obtaining more and better resources, switching to a mate who is better than her regular mate, and possibly securing better genes for her offspring (Buss, 2003; Gangestad & Cousins, 2002; Gangestad & Thornhill, 2008). Ultimately, a comprehensive theory of sex differences must account for these differences within each sex, as well as the average differences between the sexes.

An Integrated Theoretical Perspective

The theoretical accounts we have examined seem very different, but they are not necessarily incompatible. Indeed, to some extent, they operate at different levels of analysis. Evolutionary psychology suggests *why* the sexes differ, but it does not specify *how* they became different. Hormonal and socialization theories specify *how* the sexes became different but do not specify *why* the sexes are different.

An integrated theory of sex differences would take all of these levels of analysis into account because they are clearly compatible with each other. Parents, for example, clearly have an interest in socializing boys and girls differently, and these socialization differences are, to some degree, universal (Low, 1989; Perilloux et al., 2008). Furthermore, there is evidence that both men and women change their behaviour as a function of the roles they adopt. Both sexes become more dominant when in supervisory roles; both become more submissive when being supervised. Socialization, in short, must play a role in any integrated theory of sex differences although some evidence contradicts social role theory.

Men and women clearly differ in circulating testosterone levels, and these differences are linked with differences in sexuality, aggression, dominance, and career interests (Edwards et al., 2006; Hoyenga & Hoyenga, 1993). Nonetheless, we cannot ignore the causal possibility, for which there is some evidence, that being in a dominant position actually causes testosterone to rise. Thus, social roles and hormones may be closely linked, and these links may be necessary for an integrated theory of sex differences.

These proximate paths—socialization and hormones—might provide the answers for *how* the sexes differ, whereas evolutionary psychology provides the answers for *why* the sexes differ. Are there evolutionary reasons that parents encourage greater aggressiveness and dominance in boys but more nurturance in girls? Are there evolutionary reasons for surges in testosterone when a person ascends a dominance hierarchy? At this point in the history of the science of sex differences, there are no answers to these questions. Nonetheless, it's a good bet that all three levels of analysis—current social factors, hormonal and other physiological influences, and evolutionary processes—are needed for a complete understanding of gender and personality.

 Concept Check

Define socialization theory in your own words. What two specific variants of socialization theory have been offered to explain sex differences? Briefly define each.

What additional insights can be offered by hormonal and evolutionary theories of sex differences?

Summary and Evaluation

The study of sex, gender, and personality has provoked heated debate over the past several decades. Perhaps in no other area of personality psychology do politics and values get so intermingled with science. Some researchers, called minimalists, emphasize the great similarities between the sexes, pointing out that the effect size differences are small and the distributions overlapping. Other researchers, called maximalists, emphasize that sex differences are real and replicable and stress the effect size differences rather than the overlap of the distributions.

When we take a step back, it is possible to gain a more accurate understanding of sex, gender, and personality. The past few decades have witnessed an explosion of research on sex differences, along with the development of meta-analytic statistical procedures, which allow for firm conclusions grounded in empirical data.

Some sex differences are real and not artifacts of particular investigators or methods. Some sex differences have remained relatively constant over generations and across cultures. Nonetheless, the magnitudes of sex differences vary tremendously. When questions about sex differences are posed, therefore, we must always ask the question "In what domains?"

The domains that show large and small sex differences are now fairly clear. Men score consistently higher on the personality attributes of assertiveness, aggressiveness (especially physical aggressiveness), and casual sexuality. Women consistently score higher on measures of anxiety, trust, and tender-mindedness (nurturance). Women are more likely than men to experience both positive emotions (e.g., affection, joy) and negative emotions (e.g., fear, sadness), although the magnitude of these differences is not large. Men are also more likely to be sexually aggressive, although these findings appear to be limited to a subset of men—those who are narcissistic, lack empathy, and show hostile masculinity. Women tend to score higher on emotional investment—a cultural universal likely linked to attachment and bonding in romantic and other social relationships. Although no sex differences are reported in depression rates prior to puberty, at around age 13 women tend to show higher rates of depression than do men. This sex difference has been tied to theories suggesting that women ruminate more than men and theories linked to the importance of physical appearance in the domain of mate competition. Men tend to score toward the things end of the people–things dimension, whereas women tend to score more toward the people end. Within each of these domains, however, there is overlap. Some women are more assertive, aggressive, and things-oriented than the majority of men. Some men are more anxious, tender-minded, and people-oriented than the majority of women.

In the 1970s, much attention was focused on the concept of androgyny. However, it became clear as more empirical evidence was gathered that masculinity and femininity were not independent, as the androgyny researchers had asserted. Those who score high on masculinity, or instrumentality, tend to score low on femininity, or expressiveness, and vice versa. Furthermore, many of the original androgyny researchers now believe that these dimensions capture the essence of sex differences. Men tend to be more instrumental. Women tend to be more expressive. Nonetheless, there is much overlap, and many women are highly instrumental and many men are expressive.

Another important topic centres on gender stereotypes, or beliefs that people hold about each sex, regardless of their accuracy. Cross-cultural research has revealed some universality of gender stereotypes. In all cultures, men are believed to be more aggressive, autonomous, dominant, achievement-oriented, and exhibitionistic, and women are believed to be more affiliative, deferent, nurturing, and self-abasing. These stereotypes about the sexes correspond in many ways to the actual sex differences that have been discovered. The stereotypes that people hold about men and women can have a number of negative consequences, from prejudice to discrimination and even sexual harassment. Such outcomes are likely for those who do not conform to traditional gender stereotypes.

Gender identity reflects an important aspect of the self, one that is defined as a person's inherent, deeply-felt sense of being a man, a woman, or neither. Although most people identify with the gender assigned to them at birth, some do not. Due to their violation of gender norms and stereotypes, transgender individuals experience frequent discrimination.

Traditional theories of sex differences have emphasized social factors—socialization by parents, observational learning from social models, and social roles. There is some support for the importance of the social environment. Cross-cultural studies have revealed that boys are universally socialized more than girls to be achievement strivers, and girls are universally socialized to be more restrained than boys, especially in the sexual domain.

More recently, studies of hormones such as testosterone suggest that social factors do not tell the whole story. Testosterone, for example, has been implicated in the personality factors of dominance, aggression, and sexuality. Because men and women differ substantially in their levels of circulating testosterone, it is possible that some of the personality differences are caused by hormonal differences.

According to evolutionary psychologists, men and women differ in domains in which the sexes have faced different adaptive problems over human evolutionary history. In other domains, the sexes are the same or highly similar. Aggression and orientation toward casual sex are two domains in which the sexes should differ, according to this theory, and these predictions are empirically supported. What is needed is an integrative theory of sex, gender, and personality that takes into account all of these factors: social factors, physiological factors, and evolutionary factors.

! Concept Check

Consider some of the differences in personality that have been observed between men and women. In your own life, where do you see evidence of these differences being exaggerated? How could you imagine such differences being used for political purposes?

What would you say to someone claiming that all men are the same and all women are the same?

Considering all of the theoretical explanations for observed sex differences, what is the most likely conclusion in the end?

Key Terms

sex differences	perceptual sensitivity	masculinity
gender	surgency	femininity
sex	negative affectivity	androgynous
intersex	trust	instrumentality
sexual orientation	tender-mindedness	expressiveness
gender stereotypes	aggressiveness	gender schemas
gender identity	global self-esteem	social categories
effect size	people–things dimension	socialization theory
minimalist	empathizing	social learning theory
maximalist	systemizing	social role theory
inhibitory control	rumination	hormonal theories

Culture and Personality

The Social and Cultural Domain

The Yanomamö people of Venezuela set up temporary shelters, from which they forage for food and hunt for game. When these shelters become depleted of food, they push on and settle elsewhere. On one particular day, the men gather at early dawn, preparing to raid a neighbouring village. The group is tense. The men in the raiding party risk injury, and a fearful man might turn back, excusing himself from the raid by telling the others that he has a thorn in his foot. Men who do this too often risk damaging their reputation (Chagnon, 1983).

Not all Yanomamö men are the same. There are at least two discernible groups that differ profoundly in personality. The lowland

The indigenous Yanomamö tribes are among the last truly traditional societies on Earth, living a hunter-gatherer existence in the isolated jungles of Venezuela.
©John Maier/The Image Works

534

Yanomamö men are highly aggressive. They do not hesitate to hit their wives with sticks for "infractions" as minor as serving tea too slowly. They often challenge other men to club fights or axe fights. And they sometimes declare war on neighbouring groups, attempting to kill the enemy men and capture their wives. Yanomamö men shave the tops of their heads to reveal the scars from club fights, sometimes painting the scars red to display them as symbols of courage. Indeed, one is not regarded as a true man until one has killed another man—acquiring the honour of being called an *unokai*. The men who are unokai have the most wives (Chagnon, 1988).

In the highlands reside a different group of Yanomamö. These people are more peaceful and dislike fighting. The high levels of agreeableness can be seen on their faces. These Yanomamö do not raid neighbouring villages, do not engage in axe fights, and rarely engage in club fights. They stress the virtues of cooperation. Unfortunately, though, food resources are more plentiful in the lowlands, where the aggressive Yanomamö dominate.

How can we understand cultural differences in personality between the highland and lowland Yanomamö? Did those who were temperamentally more disposed to aggression drive those who were more agreeable up to the highlands and away from the food resources? Or did the two groups start out the same, and only subsequently did cultural values take hold in one group different from those that took hold in the other? These questions form the subject matter of this chapter. What is the effect of culture on personality? What is the effect of personality on culture? And how can we understand patterns of cultural variation amid patterns of human universals?

Personality psychologists explore personality across cultures for several important reasons (Allik & Realo, 2009; Church, 2000; Paunonen & Ashton, 1998). One is to discover whether concepts of personality in one culture, such as North American culture, are also applicable in other cultures. A second is to find out whether cultures differ, on average, in the levels of particular personality traits. Are Japanese, for example, really more agreeable than North Americans, or is this merely a stereotype? A third reason is to discover whether the factor structure of personality traits varies across cultures or is universal. Will the five-factor model of personality discovered in North American samples, for example, be replicated in Germany, Egypt, and the Philippines? A fourth reason is to discover whether certain features of personality are universal, corresponding to the human nature level of personality analysis (see Chapter 1).

In this chapter, we explore which features of personality are common to everyone but differentially elicited only in some cultures; which features of personality are transmitted so that they become characteristic of some local groups, but not others; and which features of personality are common to everyone in all cultures. We start by examining just how different cultures can be.

Cultural Violations: An Illustration

Consider the following events:

1. One of your family members eats beef regularly. (your beef-eating family member)
2. A young married woman goes alone to see a movie without informing her husband. When she returns home, her husband expresses anger towards her and tells her that she's not allowed to do things like that on her own. (the angry and controlling husband)

3. A man goes to the hospital after being seriously hurt in an accident. The hospital refuses to treat him because he has no identification and cannot afford to pay. (the refusing hospital)

Now examine each event and decide whether you think the behaviour on the part of the person or institution in parentheses is wrong. If so, is it a serious violation, a minor offence, or not a violation at all?

If you are a Brahman Hindu, you are likely to believe that the first event—eating beef—is a serious violation but that the second event—the angry and controlling husband—is not (Shweder, Mahapatra, & Miller, 1990). If you are a Canadian, however, the odds are that your views are the reverse: unless you are vegan or vegetarian, you likely see nothing wrong with eating beef, but you view it as inappropriate for anyone in a relationship to be that controlling. Both Brahman Hindus and Canadians, however, agree that the hospital that denies treatment to the badly injured man is committing a serious violation.

This example highlights a fascinating question for personality psychologists. Some aspects of personality (including attitudes, values, and self-concepts) are highly variable across cultures. But other aspects of personality are universal—features that are shared by people everywhere. The central questions addressed by this chapter are "How do people from different cultures differ in personality, and how are people from all cultures the same?"

 Concept Check

Consider someone you know whose cultural background is different from your own. Can you think of one similarity between your two cultures? What about a key difference?

What Is Cultural Personality Psychology?

Before proceeding further, it is useful to briefly define culture. Let's start with an observation: "Humans everywhere show striking patterns of local within-group similarity in their behaviour and thought, accompanied by profound intergroup differences" (Tooby & Cosmides, 1992, p. 6). Within-group similarities and between-group differences can be of any sort—physical, psychological, behavioural, or attitudinal. These phenomena are called **cultural variations**.

Consider the example of eating beef. Beef eating is common among Canadians but is rare and viewed with abhorrence among Hindus. Among Hindus in India, the values and behaviours are shared for the most part. But they differ from the widely shared Canadian attitudes toward beef eating. This difference—a local within-group similarity and between-group difference—is an example of a cultural variation.

Attaching the label of "culture" or "cultural variation" to phenomena such as these is best treated as a description, not an explanation. Labelling attitudes toward beef eating as "cultural" certainly describes the phenomenon. It tells us that we are dealing with a within-group similarity and a between-group difference. But it doesn't explain what has *caused* the cultural difference or *why* the groups differ.

Cultural personality psychology generally has three key goals: (1) to discover the principles underlying the cultural diversity; (2) to discover how human psychology shapes culture; and (3) to discover how cultural understandings in turn shape our psychology (Fiske et al., 1997).

Cultural Differences in Personality

Certain traits are common to all people, but others display remarkable variation. Cultural variants are the personality attributes that vary from group to group. Psychologists apply two major approaches to explaining and exploring differences in personality across cultures: evoked culture and transmitted culture. We will also consider whether cultures have distinctive personality profiles.

Evoked Culture

Evoked culture is defined as cultural differences created by differing environmental conditions activating a predictable set of responses. Consider the physical examples of skin calluses and sweat. There are undoubtedly cultural differences in the thickness and distribution of calluses and in the amount people sweat. The traditional !Kung Bushmen of Botswana, for example, tend to have thicker calluses on their feet than most North Americans because they walk around without shoes. These differences are aspects of evoked culture—different environments have different effects on people's callus-producing mechanisms. People who live near the equator, for example, are exposed to more intense heat than those who live in more northern climates, such as Canada. The observation that residents of the Democratic Republic of the Congo sweat more than residents of Canada is properly explained as an environmentally evoked difference that operates on sweat glands, which all humans possess.

Note that two ingredients are necessary to explain cultural variations: (1) a universal underlying mechanism (in this case, sweat glands possessed by all people), and (2) environmental differences in the degree to which the underlying mechanism is activated (in this case, differences in ambient temperature). Neither ingredient alone is adequate for a complete explanation.

The same explanatory logic applies to other environmentally triggered phenomena shared by members of one group, but not by other groups. Drought, plentiful game, and poisonous snakes are all environmental events that affect some groups more than others. These events activate mechanisms in some groups that lie dormant in others. In the next section, we discuss several psychological examples of evoked culture and show how they may result in differences in personality traits among groups.

Evoked Cooperation

Whether someone is cooperative or selfish is a central part of personality, but these proclivities may differ from culture to culture. A concrete example of evoked culture is the patterns of cooperative food sharing found among different bands of hunter-gatherer tribes (Cosmides & Tooby, 1992). Different classes of food have different variances in their distribution. High-variance foods differ greatly in their availability from day to day. For example, among the Ache tribe of Paraguay, meat from hunting is a high-variance resource. On any given day, the probability that a hunter will come back with meat is only 60 percent. On any particular day, therefore, one hunter will be successful, whereas another hunter will come back empty-handed. Gathered food, on the other hand, is a lower-variance food resource. The yield from gathering depends more on the skill and effort a person expends than on luck. Under high-variance conditions, there are tremendous benefits to sharing. You share your meat today with an unlucky hunter, and next week he or she will share meat with you. The benefits of engaging in cooperative food sharing increase under conditions of high variance. In this example, the benefits of sharing are also increased by the fact that a large game animal contains more meat than one person, or even one family, can consume. Thus, some of the meat would spoil if it were not shared with others.

Inuit families sharing freshly caught whale meat. In Inuit culture, sharing food with other members of the community is a highly valued tradition. The benefits of such cooperative food sharing are high in their environment and further strengthen important social bonds.
©H. Mark Weidman Photography/Alamy Stock Photo

Kaplan and Hill (1985) found that, indeed, within the Ache tribe, meat is communally shared. Hunters deposit their kill with a "distributor," a person who allocates portions to various families, based on family size. In the same tribe, however, gathered food is not shared outside the family. In short, cooperative sharing seems to be evoked by the environmental condition of high food variance.

Halfway around the world, in the Kalahari Desert, Cashden (1980) found that some San groups are more egalitarian than others. The degree of **egalitarianism** is closely correlated with the variance in food supply. The !Kung San's food supply is highly variable, and they share food and express egalitarian beliefs. To be called a "stinge" (stingy) is one of the worst insults, and the group imposes strong social sanctions for stinginess and gives social approval for food sharing. Among the Gana San, in contrast, food variance is low, and they show great economic inequality. The Gana San tend to hoard their food and rarely share it outside their extended families.

Environmental conditions can activate some behaviours, such as cooperation and sharing. Everyone has the capacity to share and cooperate, but cultural differences in the degree to which groups do share and cooperate depend, to some extent, on the external environmental conditions, such as variance in the food supply.

Early Experience and Evoked Mating Strategies

Another example of evoked culture comes from the work of Jay Belsky (2000; 2012), who argues that harsh, rejecting, and inconsistent child-rearing practices, erratically provided resources, and marital discord foster a personality of impulsivity and a mating strategy marked by early reproduction. In contrast, sensitive, supportive, and responsive child rearing, combined with reliable resources and spousal harmony, foster a personality of conscientiousness and a mating strategy of commitment, delayed reproduction, and relationship stability. Children in uncertain and unpredictable environments, in short, seem to learn that they cannot rely on a single partner and, so, opt for a sexual life that starts early and inclines them to seek multiple mates. In contrast, children growing up in stable homes with parents who predictably invest in their welfare opt for a strategy of long-term partnering because they expect to attract a stable, high-investing mate. The evidence from children of divorced homes supports this theory. Such children tend to be more impulsive, tend to reach puberty earlier, engage in sexual intercourse earlier, and have more sexual partners than do their peers whose parents have not divorced.

The sensitivity of personality and mating strategies to early experiences may help explain the differences in the value placed on chastity across cultures. In China, for example, marriages are lasting, divorce is rare, and parents invest heavily in their children over extended periods (Lei et al., 2011). In Sweden, many children are born to single mothers, divorce is more common, and fewer fathers invest consistently over time. These cultural experiences may evoke in the two groups different mating strategies, with the Swedes more than the Chinese tending toward short-term mating and more frequent partner switching (Buss, 2016).

Although more evidence is needed to confirm this theory, this example illustrates how a consistent pattern of individual differences can be evoked in different cultures, producing a local pattern of within-group similarities and between-group differences. All humans presumably have within their mating menu a strategy of short-term mating, marked by frequent partner switching, and a strategy of long-term mating, marked by enduring commitment and love (Buss, 2016). These mating strategies may be differentially evoked in different cultures, resulting in enduring cultural differences in mating and relationship strategies.

Honours, Insults, and Evoked Aggression

Why are people in some cultures prone to aggression at the slightest provocation, whereas people in other cultures resort to aggression only reluctantly as a last resort? Why do people in some cultures kill one another at relatively high rates, whereas people in other cultures kill one another at relatively low rates? Nisbett (1993) proposed a theory to account for these cultural differences—a theory based on the notion of evoked culture.

Nisbett proposed that the economic means of subsistence of a culture affects the degree to which the group develops a **culture of honour**. In cultures of honour, insults are viewed as highly offensive public challenges, which must be met with direct confrontation and physical aggression. The theory is that differences in the degree to which honour becomes a central part of the culture rests ultimately with economics—specifically, the manner in which food is obtained. In herding economies, one's entire stock could be lost suddenly to thieves. Cultivating a reputation as willing to respond with violent force—for example, by displaying physical aggression when publicly insulted—presumably deters thieves and others who might steal one's property. In more settled agricultural communities, the cultivation of an aggressive reputation is less important because one's means of subsistence cannot be rapidly undermined.

Nisbett tested his theory by using homicide statistics from different regions within the United States and experiments in which subjects from the northern and southern United States were insulted. Interestingly, the southerners (historically using animal herding for subsistence) did not endorse more positive attitudes toward the use of violence in general, compared with the northerners (historically using farming or agriculture for subsistence). The southerners, however, were indeed more likely to endorse violence for the purposes of *protection* and in response to *insults*. Furthermore, the homicide rates in the South were far higher than those in the North, particularly for murders triggered by efforts to defend one's reputation.

Nisbett found a similar pattern in the laboratory, where the northern and southern participants were insulted by an experimenter. In this study, the experimenter intentionally bumped into the participants and then said "asshole." Subsequently, the participants were asked to complete a series of incomplete word stems, such as "h____." The southerners who had been insulted wrote down more aggressive words, such as *hate,* than did the northerners who had been insulted, suggesting that the insults had evoked in the southerners a higher level of aggression. When southerners and northerners were threatened in a laboratory setting, southerners had higher elevations of testosterone and responded with greater aggression (Nisbett & Cohen, 1996).

Presumably, all humans have the capacity to develop a high sensitivity to public insults and a capacity to respond with violence. These capacities are evoked in certain cultures, however, and presumably lie dormant in others.

Cultural Differences in Conformity and Authoritarianism

Pressures to conform with social norms are widespread. Individuals sometimes pay a steep social price for deviating from the group. Children are expected to obey parents and are sometimes punished if they rebel. On the other hand, uniqueness and novelty are sometimes celebrated, and those who resist the tyrannical dictates of a culture are sometimes seen as heroes. Could cultural differences in **conformity** be an example of evoked culture?

One hypothesis stems from evolutionary psychology, and suggests that the prevalence of disease-causing pathogens causes cultural pressure to conform (Murray et al., 2011). The logic is that infectious diseases historically posed a great threat to human survival. Consequently, humans have evolved defences to protect against disease-causing pathogens. These include physiological defences such as the immune system. They also include a "behavioural immune system" that functions to prevent contact with disease-causing agents. These may include avoiding people with open sores, people who cough, or those who otherwise show signs of disease. When the threat of pathogen infection becomes especially salient, people become more introverted, avoiding contact with others (Murray et al., 2011).

Similarly, conformity to group norms may also help to avoid diseases. Deviating from cultural norms of food preparation, for example, may increase one's risk of a food-borne disease. In an innovative set of four studies, Murray and colleagues (2011) found that people in cultures with a high prevalence of pathogens tended to be substantially more conformist than those with a lower pathogen prevalence. And in cultures with low pathogen prevalence, there was substantially greater tolerance for nonconformity. Some additional evidence for this relationship has been offered by Horita and Takezawa (2018). Conformity may indeed be a prime example of evoked culture—one that rests on a universal evolved psychology that is differentially activated by environmental differences in pathogen prevalence.

In a parallel line of research, Murray and colleagues (2013) found a similar relationship between pathogen prevalence and **authoritarianism**, a personality trait involving submission and blind allegiance to authority (overlapping largely with conformity). It is reasonable to consider an adaptive advantage associated with both conformity and allegiance to authority when disease threats are present, as individuals with these traits would better avoid new and unusual situations that might increase disease exposure. In line with this, higher historical pathogen prevalence has also been associated with lower levels of extraversion and openness to experience, in addition to more restricted sexuality, across cultures (Schaller & Murray, 2008).

The concept of evoked culture provides one model for understanding and explaining cultural variations in personality traits, such as conformity, cooperativeness, or aggression. It rests on the assumption that all humans have the same potentials or capabilities. The aspects of these potentials that get evoked depend on features of the social or physical environment.

Transmitted Culture

Transmitted culture consists of ideas, values, attitudes, and beliefs that exist originally in at least one person's mind that are transmitted to other people's minds through their interaction with the original person (Tooby & Cosmides, 1992). The view that it is wrong to eat beef, for example, is an example of transmitted culture. This value presumably originated in the mind of one person, who then transmitted it to others. Over time, the view that eating beef is a serious violation came to characterize Hindus. Although we do not know much about how culture is transmitted or why certain ideas spread but others do not, the discovery of large cultural differences in seemingly arbitrary values provides circumstantial evidence for the existence of transmitted culture. Whereas people in some cultures view the eating of beef as wrong, people in other cultures view the eating of pork as wrong. Others see nothing wrong with eating beef or pork, and still others eat no meat at all.

Cultural Differences in Moral Values

Cultures differ in their beliefs about what is morally right and wrong. As an example, consider whether you agree or disagree with the following statement: "It is immoral for adults to disobey their parents" (Rozin, 2003, p. 275). If you are a Hindu Indian, the odds are great that you will agree with this statement (80 percent of the Hindu women and 72 percent of the Hindu men). If you are a Canadian or an American, however, the odds are strong that you will disagree (only 13 percent of American women and 19 percent of American men agree, for example).

Views of moral behaviour—what is right and what is wrong—are important psychological principles that guide behaviour. Though morals and beliefs are generally more malleable than personality traits, they often exhibit some degree of stability and influence behavioural tendencies over time. When it comes to judgments regarding certain situations and behaviours, cultures can differ considerably from one another. One way to examine group differences in moral values is to present people with different moral dilemmas and compare their responses. To explore a classic moral dilemma commonly studied by psychologists, complete the following Exercise.

❓ Exercise

The following scenario is a variation of the popular "trolley dilemma" used by researchers to examine individual and group differences in moral values and beliefs. Read it and consider what you would do.

You are walking on a path that runs alongside nearby train tracks. You suddenly see a runaway train on the tracks ahead, moving noticeably faster than normal. There are also people working on the main track ahead of the train, but the train doesn't seem to be slowing down. It's moving so fast that anyone in its path will be killed.

There are five people working on the main track, directly in the train's path. It is obvious that they will not be able to get off the track in time to avoid being hit. If nothing is done, they will surely be killed. You notice that the main track has a side track leading off to the right. You are standing next to a lever that controls a switch that can change the path of the train. If you pull the lever, the train will be redirected onto the side track, and the five people on the main track will be saved. However, there is a single person working on the side track, also unable to move out of the way. If the train goes onto the side track, then the person on that track will surely die. In this scenario, you have two options:

(1) Do nothing, in which case the five people on the main track will die but the one person on the side track will live.

(2) Pull the lever and divert the train onto the side track, in which case one person will die but the five people on the main track will live.

Think about it for a moment, remembering that there is no right or wrong answer. Would you pull the lever? Yes or no?

Psychologists have been studying responses to variations of this classic moral dilemma for years, and they've found some interesting patterns across cultures. The majority of people surveyed, regardless of culture, say that they would choose to pull the lever, leading one person to die rather than five (Henrich et al., 2010). However, most research on the train (or trolley) dilemma is from rich, developed, Western countries. Do people from other cultures make similar judgments?

Gold and colleagues (2014) compared British and Chinese responses to a variation of the train dilemma, in which a bystander has the ability to save five people and sacrifice one. While British participants chose to pull the lever 76 percent of the time, Chinese participants chose to do so only 64 percent of the time. Previously, Ahlenius and Tännsjö (2012) found that only 52 percent of Chinese respondents agreed that it is morally permissible to pull the lever in the train dilemma, compared to 81 percent of Americans who endorsed doing so (though this earlier research had some methodological concerns).

What could explain the difference between Chinese and Western judgments of the train dilemma? There are a few possible explanations, but there is one that relates directly to transmitted culture: *Chinese fatalism* (Gold et al., 2014). This includes the general belief that one should allow events to run their natural course without active interference, reflecting a broader set of beliefs about destiny and fate that are deeply ingrained in Chinese culture. This belief, handed down through generations, marks an important cultural difference that could reasonably affect people's moral judgments of events, including misfortunes. Transmitted culture maintains beliefs and values such as Chinese fatalism over centuries, and in turn, cultural differences in behaviour and decision-making can result.

As Gold and colleagues (2014) note, however, it is also possible that such cultural differences in moral reasoning in the train dilemma could be due to the impact of self-construal (individualism and collectivism) on cognitive processes, including decision-making. Interestingly, cultural differences in individualism and collectivism also appear to be maintained by transmission.

Cultures clearly differ in their views of what is right and wrong, sometimes in seemingly arbitrary ways. Among the Semang of Malaysia, for example, it is considered sinful to comb one's hair during a thunderstorm, to watch dogs mate, to tease a helpless animal, to kill a sacred wasp, to have sexual intercourse during the daytime, to draw water from a fire-blackened vessel, or to act casually or informally with one's mother-in-law (Murdock, 1980).

There may also be universals in what is considered right and wrong. Both Brahman Indians and North Americans, for example, agree about the following wrongs: ignoring an accident victim, breaking a promise, kicking a harmless animal, committing brother-sister incest, and stealing flowers (Shweder et al., 1990). Most cultures consider it wrong to kill without cause. Most cultures consider it wrong to commit incest (Lieberman & Lobel, 2012). But even these seeming universals are violated in some cultures. Among certain subcultures, for example, killing is viewed as justified if one has been publicly insulted (Nisbett, 1993). In certain royal dynasties, to take another example, incest between brother and sister was actively encouraged as a way to preserve the family's wealth and power. Statements about universality are relative in the sense that there are always some cultural or subcultural exceptions.

The key point is that many moral values are specific to particular cultures and are likely to be examples of transmitted culture. They appear to be passed from one generation to the next, not through genes but through the teachings of parents and teachers or through observations of the behaviour of others within the culture. Now we turn to another possible example of transmitted culture—the self-concept.

Cultural Differences in Self-Construal

As discussed in Chapter 14, the way in which we define ourselves—our self-concept—is a core aspect of human personality and a determining factor in behaviour. Research has shown that aspects of self-concept can differ substantially from one culture to the next. In particular, our grounds for self-definition, and the extent to which the self is defined independently of others or interdependently with others, vary significantly depending on culture. Psychologists refer to this aspect of the self as **self-construal**.

Markus and Kitayama (1991, 1994, 1998) propose that each person has two fundamental "cultural tasks," which have to be confronted. The first is communion, collectivism, or **interdependence**. This cultural task involves how you are affiliated with, attached to, or engaged in the larger group of which you are a member. Interdependence includes your relationships with other members of the group and your embeddedness within the group. The second task—agency, individualism, or **independence**—involves how you differentiate yourself from the group. Independence includes your unique abilities, your personal internal motives and personality dispositions, and the ways you separate yourself from the group.

These traits appear to explain the breadth of self-construal or self-concept within a mainly sociocultural context. People from different cultures differ profoundly in how they balance these two tasks. Western cultures such as Canada and the United Kingdom, according to this theory, are characterized by independence and an independent self-construal. They are typically described as **individualistic** in their orientation. Conversations emphasize individual choices (e.g., "Where do you want to eat tonight?"). The system of salaries puts a premium on individual merit—your salary is specifically pegged to *your* performance.

In contrast, many non-Western cultures such as Japan and China are characterized by interdependence and an interdependent self-construal. They are typically described as **collectivistic** in their orientation. These cultures emphasize the fundamental interconnectedness among those within the group. The self is meaningful, according to this view, only with reference to the larger group of which the person is a part. The major cultural tasks in these cultures are to fit in and to promote harmony and group unity. Personal desires are to be constrained rather than expressed in a selfish manner (e.g., "Where do *we* want to eat tonight?"). Conversational scripts emphasize sympathy, deference, and kindness. Pay is often determined by seniority rather than by individual performance.

To illustrate the contrasting orientations of independence and interdependence, consider the following descriptions, the first from a North American student and the second from a Japanese student, in response to the instruction "describe yourself briefly":

> *I like to live life with a lot of positive energy. I feel like there is so much to do and see and experience. However, I also know the value of relaxation. I love the obscure. I play ultimate Frisbee, juggle, unicycle, and dabble on*

the recorder and concertina. I have a taste for the unique. I am very friendly and in most situations very self-confident. (Markus & Kitayama, 1998, p. 63)

I cannot decide quickly what I should do, and am often swayed by other people's opinions, and I cannot oppose the opinions of people who are supposed to be respected because of age or status. Even if I have displeasure, I compromise myself to the people around me without getting rid of the displeasure. Also, I am concerned about how other people think about me. (p. 64)

Notice the different themes that run through the self-descriptions of these two individuals. The North American student tends to use global and largely context-free trait descriptions, such as *friendly, self-confident,* and *happy.* The Japanese student tends to use self-descriptions that are embedded in a social context, such as responding to elders or those who are higher in status and even using the social group as a method of calming down. These illustrate the themes of independent and interdependent self-construal. Independence, or individualism, is characterized by a self-concept as autonomous, stable, coherent, and free from the influences of others. Interdependence, or collectivism, is characterized by a self-concept as connected, interpersonally flexible, and committed to being bound to others (Markus & Kitayama, 1998).

Is there empirical evidence that the way in which we define ourselves—something so fundamental to personality—depends on the culture in which we reside? Using the Twenty Statements Test, researchers have discovered that North American participants tend to describe themselves using abstract internal characteristics, such as *smart, stable, dependable,* and *open-minded* (Rhee et al., 1995). Asian participants, in contrast, more often describe themselves using social roles, such as "I am a daughter" or "I am Jane's friend" (Ip & Bond, 1995).

Another study administered a variation of the Twenty Statements Test to samples of Chinese adolescents who immigrated to Canada and Chinese adolescents born in Canada (Lay & Verkuyten, 1999). The study was designed to examine the role of culture in self-concept and self-esteem, but with one additional question of interest: Do Canadians with Chinese heritage have a self-concept that is different, and more "Canadian," than Chinese residents who have immigrated here?

The results were conclusive. The Chinese adolescents who immigrated to Canada were more likely to label themselves as "Chinese" rather than "Chinese Canadian" compared to Canadian-born adolescents, suggesting that they were more likely to see themselves as separate from Canadian culture. Those born in China were also more likely to make reference to their ethnicity in the questionnaire. In line with interdependence and a collectivistic cultural orientation, the personal self-esteem of immigrated participants was closely tied to positive evaluations of their ethnic group, or what is referred to as *collective self-esteem.* In other words, the well-being of the

A family who recently immigrated from China uses a dog sled as a toboggan at the winter festival in Cannington, Ontario. After entering a new culture, acculturation is the process of adopting the ways of life and beliefs common in that culture.
©Jill Morgan/Alamy Stock Photo

group played an important role in the self-esteem of foreign-born participants. For those born in Canada, personal self-esteem was independent of collective self-esteem. Overall, findings support an emphasis on internal characteristics among Canadian-born Chinese and on group membership among Chinese who have immigrated to Canada (Lay & Verkuyten, 1999). Even within ethnic groups, cultural context over the lifespan has a major influence on the development of self-concept, probably from a very early age.

Another study asked Japanese and North American university students to complete the Twenty Statements Test in four social contexts: alone, with a friend, in a classroom with other students, and in a professor's office (Cross et al., 1995). The Japanese university students tended to describe themselves in all four conditions using preferences (e.g., "I like frozen yogurt") and context-dependent activities (e.g., "I like to listen to music on the weekends"). The North American students, as in previous studies, more often used abstract, context-independent trait terms, such as *friendly* and *assertive*. Furthermore, the Japanese students, but not the North American students, tended to characterize themselves differently in different contexts. In the professor's office, for example, Japanese students described themselves as "good students," but they did not mention this role in the other three contexts. The North American students' responses tended to be more constant across different contexts.

A similar study examined how frequently Japanese and European American students endorsed a variety of attributes as descriptive of themselves (Markus & Kitayama, 1998). A full 84 percent of the Japanese students described themselves as *ordinary,* whereas only 18 percent of the American students used this self-description. Conversely, 96 percent of the Americans described themselves as *special,* whereas only 55 percent of the Japanese described themselves with this term (see Table 17.1).

Table 17.1 Most Frequently Endorsed Attributes ("I Am")

EUROPEAN AMERICANS		JAPANESE	
Attribute	**Percentage of Responses**	**Attribute**	**Percentage of Responses**
Responsible	100%	Happy	94%
Persistent	100	Fun-loving	94
Cooperative	98	Relaxed	92
Special	96	Direct	92
Happy	95	Assertive	90
Unique	95	Laid-back	86
Fun-loving	93	Calm	86
Sympathetic	93	Free-spirited	86
Hardworking	93	Undisciplined	84
Ambitious	93	Ordinary	84
Reliable	93		
Independent	93		

Source: Adapted from Markus & Kitayama (1998), p. 79, Table 1.

This theme of standing out and being unique versus fitting in and going along with the group is seen in the folk sayings of North American and Japanese cultures. In North American culture, people sometimes say "The squeaky wheel gets the grease," signifying that standing out and asserting oneself as an individual is the way to pursue one's interests. In Japan, it is sometimes said that "the nail that stands out gets pounded down," which suggests that the North American social strategy would fail in Japan. These themes even show up in language usage. Those with an interdependent/collectivist orientation tend to use "we," whereas those with an independent/individualistic orientation tend to use "I" (Na & Choi, 2009).

These cultural differences may be linked to the ways in which people process information. Japanese, compared with North Americans, tend to explain events in a **holistic** way—with attention to relationships, context, and the links between the focal object and the field as a whole (Nisbett et al., 2001). North Americans, in contrast, tend to explain events in an **analytic** way—with the object detached from its context, attributes of objects or people assigned to categories, and a reliance on rules about the categories to explain behaviour. When watching animated scenes of fish swimming around, for example, the Japanese made more statements than did the North Americans about contextual information, linking the behaviour of the fish to their surroundings (Masuda & Nisbett, 2001). Thus, the cultural differences in the personality attributes of independence–interdependence may be linked to underlying cognitive proclivities in the ways in which individuals *attend to,* and *explain,* events in their world.

What happens when people leave one cultural context to live in another? Do they shift their perspective and develop self-concepts more similar to those of the adopted culture? For example, in the study of Chinese adolescents who immigrated to Canada, would we expect their self-concept to become more similar to that of Canadians over time, compared to those living in China? This process of adapting to the ways of life in one's new culture is called **acculturation**.

In examination of the acculturation phenomenon, one study administered the Twenty Statements Test to samples of Asians in Seoul, Korea; to Asian Americans in New York City; and to European Americans in New York City (Rhee et al., 1995). Researchers were further interested in the extent to which identity with one's culture affected acculturation. In other words, did having a strong American identity enhance acculturation, compared to maintaining a strong Asian identity? Indeed this seemed to be the case. The Asian Americans living in New York who did not self-identify as Asian described themselves using highly abstract and autonomous self-statements, similar to the responses of European Americans residing in New York. In contrast, New York–dwelling Asians who identified themselves as Asian used more socially embedded self-descriptions that were far more similar to Chinese respondents. They often referred to themselves by describing their role status (e.g., student) and their family status (e.g., son). Moreover, they were more likely to include contextual information in their self-descriptions.

It is also reasonable to consider that acculturation may produce changes in self-reported levels of the Big Five traits. To investigate this, Güngör and colleagues (2013) collected Big Five ratings of Japanese Americans and compared them to two groups: European Americans and residents of Japan. Correlations among the groups on individual Big Five traits were then examined, along with responses to a questionnaire that specifically asked about degree of involvement in American culture. The findings support an effect of acculturation on the Big Five traits. Higher participation in American culture was associated with personality profiles that were more American and less Japanese. On average, Japanese Americans became lower in both neuroticism and conscientiousness and higher in openness as they reported greater participation in American culture.

In sum, there is empirical support for the claim that people in different cultures have different self-concepts. Presumably, these different self-concepts are transmitted through parents and teachers to children. Additionally, there is some support for the idea that people change their self-concept upon moving to a new culture, in such a way that they become more similar to that new culture over time. For some members of a given society, self-concept and identity as they pertain to culture can be very different from those of the general population. Considerations regarding self-concept and cultural identity in Indigenous Canadians specifically are explored further in Highlight on Canadian Research: Cultural Identity Clarity in Indigenous Peoples of Canada.

Criticisms of the Interdependence–Independence and Collectivist–Individualist Concepts

Several authors have criticized the theory that Western self-construal is independent, whereas Asian self-construal is interdependent, both on theoretical and evidentiary grounds. Matsumoto (1999) and Church (2009) contend that the evidence for the theory comes almost exclusively from North America and East Asia (notably, Japan) and may not generalize to other cultures. Furthermore, there is far more overlap in the self-concepts of people from different cultures than Markus and Kitayama imply. Many individuals in collectivist cultures, for example, do use global traits (e.g., *agreeable, fun-loving*) when describing themselves. Many in individualist cultures use relational concepts (e.g., "I am the daughter of . . .") when describing themselves. The cultural differences are more a matter of degree.

On theoretical grounds, Church (2000) notes that "attempts to characterize cultures of individuals in terms of such broad cultural dichotomies may be overly simplistic" (p. 688). Views of the self in all cultures appear to incorporate both independent and interdependent self-construals, and self-concepts in all cultures vary somewhat across social contexts.

A meta-analysis of dozens of studies suggests even more caution in generalizing about cultural differences in individualism and collectivism (Oyserman, Coon, & Kemmelmeier, 2002a). It found that although European Americans tended to be somewhat more individualistic (valuing independence) and less collectivistic (valuing interdependence) than those from *some* other cultures, the effect sizes proved to be small and qualified by important exceptions. European Americans were *not* more individualistic than either African Americans or Latinos, for example. Nor were European Americans less collectivistic than Japanese or Koreans—two cultures presumed to anchor one end of the interdependence continuum. Indeed, the Chinese, rather than the Japanese or Koreans, stood out as being unusually collectivistic and nonindividualistic in self-concept. Still other studies have found little support for the influence of transmitted culture on self-concept. One study of two individualistic (United States, Australia) and two collectivistic (Mexico, Philippines) cultures found that (1) people in all four cultures described themselves in trait terms with a high level of frequency; and (2) people in all four cultures mentioned *personal* rather than *social* or *collective* identity to be more important to their sense of self (del Prado et al., 2007).

Furthermore, characterizations such as independent–interdependent have been criticized on the grounds that they are too general (Chen & West, 2008), combining different kinds of social relationships and ignoring the context-specificity in which they are expressed (Fiske, 2002). Canadians, for example, may be individualistic and independent while playing computer games, but interdependent while with their families or participating in social events.

Despite these criticisms, there are real differences across cultures, and these must be explained. Most researchers have assumed that cultural differences in dimensions such as independence–interdependence are instances of transmitted culture—ideas, attitudes, and self-concepts that are passed from one mind to another within a culture, down through the generations. Others have proposed a different explanation involving evolutionary psychology and evoked culture (Oyserman, Coon, & Kemmelmeier, 2002b). They hypothesize that humans have evolved psychological mechanisms for *both* types of self-concepts and can switch from one mode to another, depending on fitness advantages. Specifically, when one's group is low in mobility, is limited in resources, and has many relatives in close proximity, it has paid survival dividends to be highly collectivistic and interdependent. One's genetic relatives, often the recipients of these collectivist proclivities, tend to benefit. On the other hand, when mobility is high and people move frequently from place to place, when resources are relatively abundant, and when few genetic relatives live close by, it has paid survival dividends to adopt a more individualistic and independent proclivity. This hypothesis is best summed up by its authors: "Thus, an evolutionary perspective suggests both the 'basicness' of independent and interdependent processing as well as the likelihood that all social systems are inhabited by individuals who can do both and draw on one or the other depending on their immediate contexts" (Oyserman et al., 2002b, p. 116). Future research will explore this fascinating fusion of evolutionary psychology and cultural psychology (e.g., Henrich, 2015).

A Third Type of Self-Construal?

Canadian researchers Mirella Stroink of Lakehead University and Teresa DeCicco of Trent University have proposed a third type of self-definition: a **metapersonal self-construal**, which involves the representation of the self within a much broader context, such as the global community, humankind, the planet, or the cosmos. Those high in metapersonal self-construal may see themselves not simply as a sibling or a parent, for instance, but rather as a member of the human race. Similarly, a metapersonal definition of the self may involve one's place in the universe or one's connection to other living beings. According to DeCicco & Stroink (2007), this is similar to William James's (1902/1999) earlier notion of a *spiritual self*, in which the boundary between the self and the environment vanishes and one experiences a feeling of unity with all things. It is further characteristic of many Eastern views, including those attributable to Buddhist philosophy.

The implications of this particular self-concept were revealed in a 2007 study in which metapersonal self-construal demonstrated a significant association with environmental concern and pro-environmental behaviour. It appears that the interpretation of oneself as connected to all things results in a *biospheric value orientation*, which focuses on the inherent value of the environment beyond the rights of any one species (Arnocky, Stroink, & DeCicco, 2007). In a follow-up study by Davis and Stroink (2016), the link between metapersonal self-construal and both a biospheric value orientation and pro-environmental behaviours was confirmed. In a sample of Canadian university students, biospheric values again mediated the relationship between metapersonal self-construal and greater tendencies towards conservation and environmental concern. Feelings of connectedness to nature, a new variable investigated by Stroink and her team, appeared to play a similar role. It too seems to result from a higher metapersonal self-definition and in turn contributes to pro-environmental behaviour. As suggested by Hanley and colleagues (2017), a metapersonal self may further reflect a *selfless* self-concept, in which identity is anchored in elements of existence that extend beyond the individual.

 Highlight on Canadian Research

Cultural Identity Clarity in Indigenous Peoples of Canada

Canada is often referred to as a *cultural mosaic*, consisting of people with diverse cultural backgrounds from around the world. Its policy of multiculturalism, established in 1971, has attempted to maintain diversity in languages, cultural attitudes, and traditions. What does this mean for personality, including self-concept and identity? In general, Canada scores fairly high on individualistic cultural orientation, similar to other Western nations like the United States—though the United States is higher still (Hofstede, 2001). On average, Canadians tend to describe themselves in relatively independent terms, yet there are significant differences by region and subculture. The province of Quebec, for example, is more collectivistic than other provinces, presumably due to its French heritage (MacNab et al., 2007).

Despite great diversity in beliefs and practices among First Nations, Inuit, and Métis cultures, Indigenous peoples of Canada also tend to be *collectivistic* in their cultural orientation, and by extension, more *interdependent* than non-Indigenous Canadians (O'Neill, 2017). Indeed, this tends to be the case for Indigenous cultures around the world (Fryberg & Markus, 2003). The Canadian Constitution originally defined three groups of Aboriginal peoples in Canada, now referred to as *Indigenous* peoples:

- *First Nations (originally referred to as Indian)*, which include over 600 recognized cultures or bands across Canada (with a population of over 977,000 according to Statistics Canada, 2016).
- *Inuit*, a unique cultural group who live in the Northern territories of Canada, as well as Alaska, Greenland, Russia, and Denmark (with a Canadian population of 65,000 according to Statistics Canada, 2016).
- *Métis*, who are descendants of unions between early European settlers and Indigenous people and live primarily in Manitoba and the Prairies (with a population of over 587,000 according to Statistics Canada, 2016).

Though First Nations, Inuit, and Métis cultures are diverse, they share common historical experiences of European settlement and colonialism (Green, 2009). European colonization of what is now Canada began in the 17th century. It involved a number of highly stressful and traumatic events for existing Indigenous populations, many of whom had lived on the continent for over 10,000 years. Critical events included the outlawing of Indigenous gatherings, ceremonies, and other cultural practices; forced community relocation to designated reserves, on which approximately half of First Nations people still live; mandatory residential school attendance for Indigenous children, who were forcibly separated from their families and forbidden to speak their own language; social, medical, and legal forms of discrimination that persist today; intentional malnourishment, medical testing, and withholding of medical care; and the introduction of new diseases that resulted in the deaths of thousands (Allan & Smylie, 2015; Indigenous and Northern Affairs Canada, 2010). It is estimated that Indigenous people in Canada experienced a 60 percent reduction in effective population size due to factors associated with European colonization (Lindo et al., 2016).

These events had lasting effects on the health and well-being of Indigenous cultures, undermining not only mental health but also cultural identity (Kirmayer, Brass, & Tait, 2000; Taylor & de la Sablonnière, 2014). **Cultural identity** refers to a person's sense of belonging to a particular culture or group. Today, there is evidence that Indigenous communities in Canada maintain a collectivistic orientation despite living within a broader individualistic cultural context (Medd, 2010). Indigenous identity is one which emphasizes connections among individuals and between the individual and the community; indeed, the primary source of identity for most Indigenous people today is their community, band, or nation, in which the individual is seen as embedded. This is typically prioritized over personal identity or identity within a Canadian context. Indigenous identity is further rooted in a sense of belonging to a particular time and place, highlighting the importance of both history and community, as well as land and nature, in self-concept (Frideres, 2008; Green, 2009; Wright Cardinal, 2017). Such qualities reflect a self-construal that is both highly interdependent and metapersonal in nature (DeCicco & Stroink, 2007).

On both individual and community levels, the ability to maintain a clear sense of cultural identity has nevertheless been severely challenged, not only due to the historical events associated with colonization but also persisting experiences of discrimination in Canada (Allan & Smylie, 2015; Taylor & de la

Sablonnière, 2014; Usborne & Taylor, 2010). As highlighted by Chandler, Lalonde, and Sokol (2000), In-digenous people literally had their culture criminalized; today, it continues to be highly stigmatized and marginalized by non-Indigenous Canadians (Allan & Smylie, 2015). The ongoing mistreatment of Indigenous peoples in Canada can be seen in events such as the Sixties Scoop, a period lasting from the 1950s to the 1980s in which approximately 20,000 Indigenous children were removed from their homes and placed in government care (Wright Cardinal, 2017); and more recently, the more than 1,000 Indigenous women and girls across Canada who have gone missing or were murdered since 1980 at a rate that is considerably higher than what is seen in the general population (National Inquiry into Missing and Murdered Indigenous Women and Girls, 2019). Collectively, such experiences have compro-mised clarity of both self-concept and cultural identity (Lalonde, 2006; Taylor & de la Sablonnière, 2014; Usborne & Taylor, 2010). According to Taylor and de la Sablonnière (2014), it is not simply a mismatch between Indigenous and European cultures that has resulted in this lack of clarity. Rather, it is the direct and pervasive attack on Indigenous identity that is to blame. Such direct efforts to restrict, degrade, and extinguish Indigenous culture have resulted in community dysfunction as well as numerous challenges for Indigenous individuals, including a lack of clearly defined values, difficulties setting goals, and a sense of hopelessness about the future (Taylor & de la Sablonnière, 2014).

As noted by Chandler and colleagues (2000), the notion of *self-continuity* is also core to one's self-concept. It is the understanding of ourselves as individuals persisting through time, despite any momen-tary variation, and it is an essential part of our identity within social and cultural contexts. For Indigenous people living in Canada (and elsewhere), culture and identity are often prescribed narratively through the sharing of stories. This means that Indigenous cultures rely heavily on their oral histories in order to understand who they are. If we consider the impact of colonization on Indigenous cultures, namely the concerted efforts that were made to oppress and silence cultural traditions and languages, it is not surprising that self-continuity, and continuity of cultural identity specifically, have been limited among First Nations, Inuit, and Métis peoples (Chandler et al., 2000; Lalonde, 2006). Denial of culture and language prevents subsequent generations from accessing the full richness of their traditional knowledge and relations (Battiste, 1998).

What are the consequences of having a cultural identity that is unclear and unstable over time? Researchers (Chandler et al., 2000; Lalonde, 2006) have drawn a connection to the higher rates of suicide among Indigenous youth in Canada, noting that the overall rate of suicide among First Nations people specifically is three to five times higher than the national average. They suggest that a lack of self-continuity and identity clarity compromises mental health and increases the likelihood of suicidal ideation. The heightened sense of hopelessness associated with an unclear cultural identity has been further associated with increased drinking and alcohol abuse in Indigenous youth (Mushquash et al., 2014). In their research on Indigenous communities across Canada, Usborne and Taylor (2010) found that cultural identity clarity was consistently related to self-esteem and psychological well-being; and it was mediated by self-concept clarity. In other words, having a strong sense of cultural identity is needed in order to have clarity about who one is as an individual. This, in turn, facilitates self-esteem and well-being. On the other hand, those who do not have a clear cultural identity are less likely to have a clear self-concept, and in turn experience lower self-esteem and well-being. This underscores the importance of cultural identity for selfhood.

As concluded by Burack and colleagues (2019), Indigenous youth tend to display higher levels of success and well-being when they report feeling connected meaningfully to their Indigenous culture. Taylor and Usborne (2010) similarly recommend interventions aimed at clarifying and strengthening cultural identity in order to promote the well-being of Indigenous individuals. In support of this approach, research on the Naskapi First Nation of Quebec found reduced physical and relational aggression among youth who had stronger cultural identities (Flanagan et al., 2011). Research by Christopher Lalonde at the University of Victoria has further demonstrated that as Indigenous communities regain control of their cultural heritage and independence, they experience significant improvements to mental and social well-being. Examining suicide data over a 14-year period, Lalonde (2006) reports that Indigenous communities that engage in a greater number of efforts to reclaim their culture (including regaining title to traditional lands, re-establishing self-government, gaining control of education and community services, and creating community facilities dedicated to promoting cultural events) experience decreases in youth suicide, improved educational outcomes, and fewer children being placed in care—all of which reflect improved community resilience. As underscored by Taylor and de la Sablonnière (2014), Indigenous communities have indeed demonstrated resilience in the face of profound trauma, and in spite of ongoing threats to cultural identity. Such collective resilience must be further cultivated in order for Indigenous communities and their members to overcome the many challenges that persist (Taylor & de la Sablonnière, 2014).

Cultural Differences in Self-Enhancement

Self-enhancement is the tendency to describe and present oneself using positive or socially valued attributes, such as *kind, understanding, intelligent,* and *industrious.* Tendencies toward self-enhancement tend to be stable over time (Baumeister, 1997). Many studies have documented that North Americans tend to maintain a generally positive evaluation of themselves (Fiske et al., 1997). One study showed that the self-concepts of North American adults contain more than four times as many positive attributes as negative ones (Herzog

et al., 1995). The Japanese tend to make far fewer spontaneous positive statements about themselves. The Japanese score lower than North Americans on translations of self-esteem scales (Fiske et al., 1997). Japanese respondents tend to give more negative descriptions of themselves, such as "I think too much" and "I'm a somewhat selfish person" (Yeh, 1995). Even the positive self-descriptions of the Japanese respondents tend to be in the form of negations, such as "I'm not lazy." North American respondents would express a similar sentiment with the phrase "I'm a hard worker."

Similar cultural differences have been discovered between Korean and North American respondents (Ryff, Lee, & Na, 1995). Korean respondents are more likely to endorse negative statements about themselves, whereas North American respondents are more likely to endorse positive statements. Differences in self-enhancement also show up in parents' self-descriptions of the quality of their parenting practices (Schmutte, Lee, & Ryff, 1995). North American parents describe their parenting practices in generally glowing terms; Korean parents give mostly negative self-evaluations.

Toshiyuki Tanaka, an umpire in the Japanese baseball league, during an interview. In his culture, harmony is valued over conflict. To keep the peace during a heated game, Tanaka often plays the role of diplomat. He rarely penalizes a team or ejects a player or coach from the game, events that are fairly common in North American baseball. Moreover, Tanaka sometimes admits it when he makes a mistake, which is practically unheard of among North American umpires.
©Itsuo Inouye/AP Images

Another study found that Chinese individuals showed less of a tendency to self-enhance than Americans, but only one some traits and not others (Church et al., 2014).

Cultural differences in self-enhancement extend to evaluations of one's group compared with evaluations of other groups. Heine and Lehman (1995) asked Japanese and Canadian students to compare their own university with a rival university within their own culture. Among the Canadian respondents, there was a strong tendency toward in-group enhancement, with the rival university evaluated negatively by comparison. Among the Japanese respondents, there was no favouritism in the evaluation of one's own university in comparison with the rival university. Japanese and Asian-Canadians also tend to be more self-critical than Euro-Canadians (Falk et al., 2009), again suggesting cultural differences in self-enhancement.

There are a few explanations for cultural differences in self-enhancement. One is that people surveyed are engaging in impression management (see Chapter 4). Perhaps deep in their hearts, Asians truly evaluate themselves positively, but to express these views publicly would damage their reputation. Alternatively, it is possible that North Americans do evaluate themselves more negatively, but they feel pressured to present themselves more positively than they actually are. In others words, it is possible that Asians are more "accurate" in their self-evaluations. A second explanation is that these cultural differences accurately reflect people's deep experiences. Asians, according to this view, truly evaluate themselves more negatively than do North Americans. This may be due to profound differences in values, or perhaps differences in perception and cognition associated with differences in self-construal. For example, higher individualism and the need to assert one's independence may be associated with more positive self-evaluations. This is supported by evidence from multiple studies demonstrating a positive relationship between individualism and narcissism (e.g., Vater et al., 2018), a trait that involves the tendency to be boastful.

Cultural differences are matters of degree; people in all cultures appear to display a self-enhancement bias to some extent (Kurman, 2001). In a study of three cultures—Singaporeans, Druze Israelis, and Jewish Israelis—Kurman (2001) asked participants whether they considered themselves to be below average or above average for the sex and age group on six traits: intelligence, health, and sociability (agentic traits); and cooperation, honesty, and generosity (communal traits). Although the Singaporeans showed slightly more self-enhancement than the other two cultures, it applied only to the agentic traits, and people in *all* cultures showed a self-enhancement bias. On the communal traits, 85 percent of the participants in all three cultures viewed themselves as "above average" for their age and sex group. On the agentic traits, although the Druze and Jewish Israeli samples showed a self-enhancement level of 90 percent and 87 percent, respectively, the Singaporeans showed a self-enhancement level of nearly 80 percent. Thus, people across cultures show a self-enhancement bias, so the cultural differences must be interpreted within the context of this overall similarity.

Personality Variations Within Culture

Another dimension of transmitted culture pertains to **within-culture variations**, although these have not received the same degree of attention as cross-cultural variations. Within-culture variations can arise from several sources, including differences in growing up in various socioeconomic classes, differences in historical era, or differences in the racial context in which one grows up.

There is some evidence, for example, that social class within a culture can have an effect on personality (Kohn et al., 1990). Lower-socioeconomic parents tend to emphasize the importance of obedience to authority, whereas higher-status parents tend to emphasize self-direction and nonconformity to the dictates of others. According to Kohn, these socialization practices stem from the sorts of occupations that parents expect their children to enter. Higher-status jobs (e.g., manager, start-up company founder, doctor, lawyer) often require greater self-direction, whereas lower-status jobs (e.g., factory worker, gas station employee) more often require the need to follow rules and permit less latitude for innovation. In studies of American, Japanese, and Polish men, those from higher social classes in all cultures tend to be more self-directed, show lower levels of conformity, and have greater intellectual flexibility than men from lower social classes. Interestingly, those from lower classes tend to be more generous and charitable than those in the upper classes, giving more even though they have less (Piff et al., 2010).

These findings are correlational, so the direction of effects cannot be assumed. Perhaps people with personalities marked by self-direction and intellectual flexibility gravitate toward the higher social classes. Or perhaps the socialization practices of higher-social-class parents produce children with personalities that are different from the personalities of lower-social-class children. In either case, this example highlights the importance of within-culture differences. Figure 17.1 shows the distribution of individualism–collectivism in two cultures. The shaded part shows the overlap among cultures. Even though cultures can differ in their average levels of self-construal, many individuals within the one culture can be higher (or lower) than many individuals in the other culture.

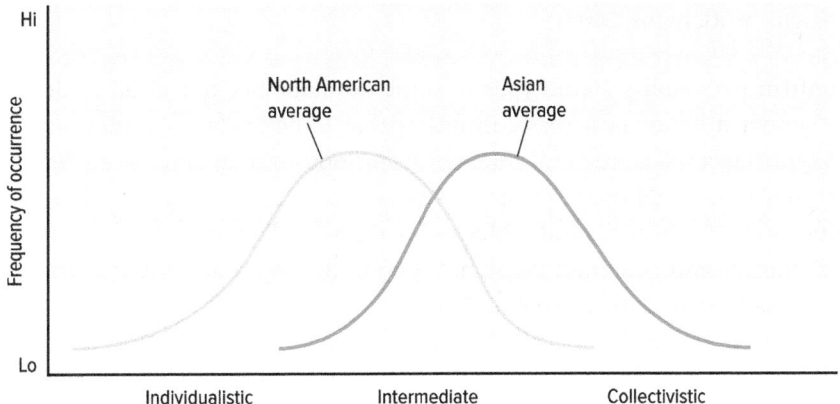

FIGURE 17.1 Individualism versus collectivism in North American and Asian cultures. The distribution of two groups may be significantly different from each other in terms of the group mean yet have a high proportion of overlap. This means that many individuals from one group are higher (or lower) than many members of the other group, in a pattern opposite that of the mean difference. Asians score higher on collectivism than North Americans do, yet there will always be some North Americans who score higher than some Asians (those in the shaded area) on this measure.

Another type of within-culture variation pertains to the effects of **historical era** on personality. People who grew up during the Great Depression of the 1930s, for example, might be more anxious about job security, adopting a more conservative spending style. Those who came of age during the sexual revolution of the 1960s and 1970s might show a greater openness to experimentation. Those growing up in the age of the Internet spend more time interacting with others in distant places, expanding social horizons in ways that might influence personality. Today many people find partners through online dating sites, a phenomenon virtually absent a generation ago (Buss, 2016). Disentangling the effects of historical era on personality is an extremely difficult task because most currently used personality measures were not in use in earlier eras. One recent exception examined changes in average personality scores over a period of 25 years in the Netherlands (Smits et al., 2011). Researchers found small but consistent increases in extraversion, agreeableness, and conscientiousness, and small decreases in neuroticism.

Do Cultures Have Distinctive Personality Profiles?

People have long been fascinated with the question of whether cultures have distinctive personality profiles. Are people from the Mediterranean region of Europe really more emotionally expressive, or is this merely an incorrect stereotype? Are people from Scandinavia really more calm and stoic, or is this merely an incorrect stereotype? Most studies reveal that stereotypes about national personality rarely correspond to average levels of actual assessed personality (Allik, 2012).

Robert McCrae and 79 colleagues from around the world studied the personality profiles of 51 different cultures, using 12,156 participants (McCrae et al., 2005a). They translated the Revised NEO Personality Inventory into the appropriate language for each culture and then examined the aggregate Big Five personality scores for each culture. The largest difference they found across cultures centred on Extraversion. North Americans and Europeans scored higher than Asians and Africans on this broad trait. A few examples will illustrate these differences. With the cross-cultural average set to 50, the average Extraversion score was 52.3 for North Americans, 53.8 for Australians, 53.7 for the English, and 52.2 for Belgians. In contrast, the average Extraversion scores were 46.5 for Ugandans, 47.0 for Ethiopians, and 46.6 for People's Republic Chinese. Some have questioned the validity of these findings because they rely exclusively on self-report (Ashton, 2007; Perugini & Richetin, 2007).

Recent studies confirm personality stereotypes in some domains but not in other domains. For example, stereotypes about gender differences across cultures appear to be fairly accurate (Lockenhoff et al., 2014). Women are stereotyped as a bit more agreeable, conscientious, and anxious in a study of 26 cultures, and findings from both self-report and observer-report studies bear this out. On the other hand, many national character stereotypes appear to be inaccurate (McCrae et al., 2013). Some Chinese people stereotype Malays as "friendly, but lazy," but the empirical findings do not support this. A study of 26 countries found little support for national character stereotypes (McCrae et al., 2013).

It is important to bear in mind that observed cultural differences in average personalities are relatively small. Most of the differences in personality occur *within* cultures, not between cultures. Indeed, the most striking finding from the study by McCrae and colleagues (2005a) is how similar the 51 cultures actually are in their overall scores on the five-factor model.

Despite evidence of cross-cultural similarities in average levels of traits, some differences may nevertheless exist that warrant concern regarding the cross-cultural generalizability of psychological research. Concerns primarily revolve around the characteristics of countries where most psychological research is conducted, and whether findings can reasonably be generalized to other parts of the world. We discuss this next in A Closer Look: Cross-Cultural Generalizability and Limitations on WEIRD Populations in Psychological Research.

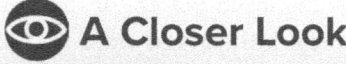 ## A Closer Look

Cross-Cultural Generalizability and Limitations of WEIRD Populations in Psychological Research

In psychological research, even that which is not of cross-cultural significance, the generalizability of any set of findings to other groups of people is always of major concern. Researchers are (or should be) interested in the degree to which conclusions may be applied to other people, either those similar to or different from the study's participants. This is a necessary step in determining the implications of a study.

In the past couple of decades, concerns have arisen over the tendency for much of the psychological and behavioural research in the world's top academic journals to be based on samples drawn entirely from Western, educated, industrialized, rich, and democratic (WEIRD) societies. Conclusions stemming from research using these "weird" samples are often assumed to extend to the human race more generally—even to other cultures. In other words, many conclusions regarding the fundamental nature of human behaviour are based on what is essentially a small subset of the human population. Cultural psychologists Joseph Henrich, Steven Heine, and Ara Norenzayan of the University of British Columbia were interested in understanding just how big of a concern this was for researchers. In 2010, in a paper published in the journal *Behavioral and Brain Sciences*, they conclude that indeed, WEIRD samples are pretty *weird*.

First, Henrich and colleagues (2010) outline some of the obvious problems and assumption associated with research findings based on WEIRD samples. One of these problems is the amount of published research that originates in North America. Unlike other scientific disciplines, approximately 70 percent of all psychology citations come from the United States. Despite human behaviour being a phenomenon in which we would expect the greatest variation, there is the least amount of variation in scientific research (compared to say, chemistry, where only 37 percent of citations are American in origin). The second problem lies in the assumptions contained within the published findings. Researchers routinely assume that their findings are universal in nature. This is done both explicitly (for example, by assuming that a cognitive bias is characteristic of all people) and implicitly (for example, by not addressing a study's limitations on generalizability).

Henrich and his colleagues then summarize the various ways in which research has not supported the generalizability of WEIRD populations. For instance, although more research is needed to understand the scope of the problem, studies have indeed documented significant differences in cognitive and social processes between members of industrialized and small-scale societies. Many differences in key behavioural characteristics have also been documented between Western and non-Western cultures, including many noted in this book (such as analytic vs. holistic reasoning). Considering the tendency for most psychology citations to be based on American samples specifically, there arises a further concern over whether research from the United States generalizes to other Western populations, such as Canadians. Indeed, despite the similarities that do exist, Americans stand out in a few important ways. For example, they tend to be the most individualistic people in the world, even within a Western context. As so much of the research using WEIRD populations is conducted using undergraduate students, generalizability may be further restricted in this regard. Studies have confirmed that in tests of a number of psychological phenomena, college and university students differ significantly from non-student members of the population.

This is a long list of potential limitations to the generalizability of WEIRD populations. Although problems seem to exist even within a purely Western context, the greatest limitation by far is in the cross-cultural applicability of the research. In addition to better addressing these concerns in their published findings, researchers should be making a greater attempt to investigate psychological and behavioural phenomena cross-culturally. What is characteristic of one narrow and "weird" demographic is by no means characteristic of the entire human race.

 Concept Check

Discuss the difference between evoked and transmitted culture, and offer one cultural difference in personality that is believed to have resulted from each of these mechanisms.

According to research, do cultures tend to differ much overall in their personality profiles?

Cultural Similarities in Personality

A third approach to culture and personality involves the identification of features of personality that appear to be universal, or present in most or all human cultures. As described in Chapter 1, these universals constitute the human nature level of analyzing personality.

Cultural Universals

In the history of the study of personality and culture, the study of **cultural universals** has long been in disfavour. For most of the twentieth century, the focus was almost exclusively on cultural differences. This emphasis was fuelled by anthropologists who reported on seemingly exotic cultures. Margaret Mead, for example, purported to discover cultures entirely lacking in sexual jealousy, cultures in which sex roles were reversed and adolescence was not marked with stress and turmoil (Mead, 1928, 1935). On sex roles, for example, Mead purported to discover "a genuine reversal of the sex-attitudes of our culture, with the woman the dominant, impersonal, managing partner, the man the less responsible and the emotionally dependent person" (Mead, 1935, p. 279). Human nature was presumed to be infinitely variable, infinitely flexible, and not constrained by a universal human nature: "We are forced to conclude that human nature is almost unbelievably malleable, responding accurately and contrastingly to contrasting cultural conditions" (p. 280).

Over the past few decades, the pendulum has swung toward a more moderate view. Anthropologists who visited the islands Mead had visited failed to confirm Mead's findings (e.g., Freeman, 1983). In cultures in which sexual jealousy was presumed to be entirely absent, it turned out that sexual jealousy was the leading cause of spousal battering and spousal homicide. In cultures such as the Chambri, where the sex roles were presumed to be reversed, anthropologists instead found that men were considered to be in charge (Brown, 1991; Gewertz, 1981). Furthermore, the Chambri considered men to be more aggressive than women and women to be more submissive than men. Behavioural observations of social interactions among the Chambri confirmed these conceptions (Gewertz, 1981). All available evidence back to 1850, including some of Mead's recorded observations (as opposed to the inferences she made), suggest that the Chambri's sex roles are, in fact, strikingly similar to those of Western cultures. Brown (1991) has a list of practices and attitudes that are good candidates for cultural universals—see Table 17.2 (see also Pinker, 1997).

In this section, we consider three examples of cultural universals: beliefs about the personality characteristics of men and women, the expression of emotion, and the possible universality of the five-factor model of personality traits.

Table 17.2 Culturally Universal Practices and Attitudes
Incest avoidance
Facial expressions of basic emotions
Favouritism toward in-group members
Favouritism toward kin over non-kin
Collective identities
Division of labour by sex
Revenge and retaliation
Self distinguished from others
Sanctions for crimes against the collectivity
Reciprocity in relationships
Envy, sexual jealousy, and love

Sources: Brown, 1991; Pinker, 1997.

Beliefs About the Personality Characteristics of Men and Women

In the most massive study undertaken to examine beliefs about the personality characteristics of men and women, Williams and Best (1990) examined 30 countries over a period of 15 years. These included western European countries such as Germany, the Netherlands, and Italy; Asian countries such as Japan and India; South American countries such as Venezuela; and African countries such as Nigeria. In each country, university students examined 300 trait adjectives (e.g., *aggressive, emotional, dominant*) and indicated whether each trait is more often linked with men, women, or both sexes. The responses of the subjects within each culture were then summed. When the results came in, the big shock was this: many of the trait adjectives were highly associated with one or the other sex, and there proved to be tremendous consensus across cultures. Table 17.3 shows sample trait adjectives most associated with men and with women across cultures.

Table 17.3 Pancultural Traits Linked with Men or Women			
Traits Associated with Men		**Traits Associated with Women**	
Active	Loud	Affected	Modest
Adventurous	Obnoxious	Affectionate	Nervous
Aggressive	Opinionated	Appreciative	Patient
Arrogant	Opportunistic	Cautious	Pleasant
Autocratic	Pleasure-seeking	Changeable	Prudish
Bossy	Precise	Charming	Sensitive
Coarse	Quick	Dependent	Sentimental
Conceited	Reckless	Emotional	Softhearted
Enterprising	Show-off	Fearful	Timid
Hardheaded	Tough	Forgiving	Warm

Williams and Best (1994) scored each of these adjectives on the following dimensions: *favourability* (How desirable is the trait?), *strength* (How much does the trait indicate power?), and *activity* (How much does the trait signify energy?). These dimensions originate from older classical work in the field that discovered three universal semantic dimensions of *evaluation* (good–bad), *potency* (strong–weak), and *activity* (active–passive) (Osgood, Suci, & Tannenbaum, 1957). Overall, the traits ascribed to men and women are equally favourable. Some "masculine" traits, such as *serious* and *inventive,* were viewed as favourable, whereas others, such as *arrogant* and *bossy,* were viewed as unfavourable. Some "feminine" traits, such as *charming* and *appreciative,* were viewed as favourable, whereas others, such as *fearful* and *affected,* were viewed as unfavourable.

How can we interpret these cultural universals in beliefs about the personality characteristics of men and women? One way is that these beliefs represent stereotypes based on the roles men and women assume universally. Williams and Best (1994) argue that society assumes that men are stronger than women and therefore assigns men to roles and occupations such as soldier and construction worker.

A second possibility is that the traits ascribed to men and women in all 30 cultures reflect observations of natural sex differences in personality. Studies of the five-factor model, for example, do find that women score lower on emotional stability. As we reviewed in Chapter 16, men are, on average, more physically aggressive than women. Although this may lend support to the idea that universal beliefs about men and women stem from innate differences between the sexes, it is difficult to completely factor out social influences. Any innate differences that do exist are likely reinforced and exaggerated by stereotypes.

Expression of Emotion

It is commonly believed that people in different cultures experience different emotions. As a consequence, personality psychologists have argued that different cultures have different words to describe emotional experiences. The Tahitians, some have argued, do not experience the emotions of grief, longing, or loneliness, so they have no words in their language to express these emotions. For example, when a Tahitian boy dies in combat, according to legends reported by anthropologists, the parents smile and experience no grief, unlike the profound sadness felt by people in the modern Western world who experience similar events. Cultural variability in the presence or absence of emotion words has been interpreted by some personality psychologists to mean that cultures differ in the presence or absence of actual experiences of these emotions.

However, are emotions really this culturally variable? Or are there cultural universals in the experience of emotions? Psychologist Steven Pinker summarizes the evidence in this way: "Cultures surely differ in how often their members express, talk about, and act on various emotions. But that says nothing about what their people feel. The evidence suggests that the emotions of all normal members of our species are played on the same keyboard" (Pinker, 1997, p. 365).

The earliest evidence of cultural universals in emotions came from Charles Darwin. In gathering evidence for his book on emotions, *The Expression of Emotions in Man and Animals,* Darwin (1872/1965) asked anthropologists and travellers who interacted with peoples on five continents to give detailed information about how the natives expressed various emotions, such as grief, contempt, disgust, fear, and jealousy. He summarized the answers he received: "The same state of mind is expressed throughout the world with remarkable uniformity; and this fact is in itself interesting as evidence of the close similarity in bodily structure and mental disposition of all the races of mankind" (Darwin, 1872/1965, pp. 15, 17).

Darwin's methods, of course, were crude by today's scientific standards, but subsequent research has confirmed his basic conclusions. Psychologist Paul Ekman created a set of photographs of people expressing six basic emotions and then showed them to people in various cultures (Ekman, 1973). Some cultures in his study, such as the Fore foragers of New Guinea, had had almost no contact with Westerners. The Fore spoke no English, had seen no TV or movies, and had never lived with Caucasians. He also administered the tests to people in Japan, Brazil, Chile, Argentina, and the United States. Ekman asked each subject to label the emotion expressed in each photograph and to make up a story about what the person in the photograph had experienced. The six emotions—happiness, sadness, anger, fear, disgust, and surprise—were universally recognized by people in the various cultures. These findings have been subsequently replicated in other countries, such as Italy, Scotland, Estonia, Greece, Germany, Hong Kong, Sumatra, and Turkey (Ekman et al., 1987). Further research by Ekman and his colleagues has expanded the list of universal emotions to include contempt, embarrassment, and shame (Ekman, 1999).

In addition to finding that people of different cultures effortlessly recognized the emotions expressed on the faces in the photographs, Ekman reversed the procedure. He asked the Fore participants to act out scenarios, such as "Your child has died" and "You are angry and about to fight," and then photographed them. The emotions expressed in these photographs were easily recognized by facial expressions and were strikingly similar to the expressions of the same emotions seen in the photographs of the Caucasian participants. Further evidence for the universality, and possible evolutionary origins, of these basic emotions comes from the finding that children who are blind from birth display the same facial expressions of emotions that those with full sight display (Lazarus, 1991). As you'll remember from Chapter 13, other candidate emotions such as pride (Tracy & Robins, 2004) have accumulated similar cross-cultural support.

Pinker notes that whether a language has a word for a particular emotion or not matters little if the question is whether people *experience* the emotion in the same way: Tahitians are said not to have a word for grief; however, "when a Tahitian woman says 'My husband died and I feel sick,' her emotional state is hardly mysterious; she is probably not complaining about acid indigestion" (Pinker, 1997, p. 367).

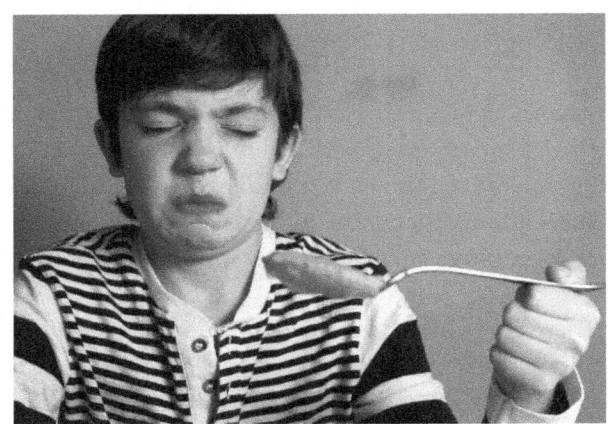

Disgust appears to be an emotion universally experienced by all humans, regardless of culture.
©Shutterstock/Lapina

Another example is the German word *Schadenfreude:* "When English-speakers hear the word *Schadenfreude* for the first time, their reaction is not, 'Let me see . . . pleasure in another's misfortunes . . . what could that possibly be? I cannot grasp the concept; my language and culture have not provided me with such a category.' Their reaction is, 'You mean there's a word for it? Cool!'" (Pinker, 1997, p. 367). People universally may experience the emotion of pleasure in an enemy's misfortunes in the same way, even if all cultures do not have a single word in their language to capture it.

The view that language is not necessary for people to experience emotions may be contrasted with what has been called the **Whorfian hypothesis of linguistic relativity**, which contends that language *creates* thought and experience. In the extreme view, the Whorfian hypothesis argues that the ideas that people can think and the emotions they feel are constrained by the words that happen to exist in their language and culture (Whorf, 1956).

The difference between *experiencing* an emotion and *expressing* that emotion in public may be critical to resolving this debate. Ekman (1973) performed an ingenious experiment to explore the difference between the experience of emotion and its expression in public. He secretly videotaped the facial expressions of Japanese and North American students while they watched a graphic film of a primitive puberty rite involving genital mutilation. In one condition, an experimenter wearing a white lab coat was present in the room. In the other condition, the participants were alone. When the experimenter was present (a public context), the Japanese students smiled politely during the film, but the North American students expressed horror and disgust. If this were the only condition run, we might conclude that Japanese and North American students experience the emotion of disgust differently. However, when the students were filmed when they were alone in the room watching the film, both the Japanese and North American faces showed equal horror. This result suggests that Japanese and North American students *experience* this emotion in the same way, even if they differ in their expression of it in a more public setting.

More recent cross-cultural work has confirmed the universality of some basic forms of emotional expression. One study compared non-verbal emotional vocalizations (e.g., "yuck," "huh") of the "basic emotions" of anger, disgust, fear, joy, sadness, surprise among Namibian and Western participants (Sauter et al., 2010). These vocal expressions were bi-directionally recognized—Namibians correctly identified the emotion that corresponded with the nonverbal vocalizations uttered by Westerners and vice-versa. These findings lend further support to the notion that some emotions are universal across cultures.

Five-Factor Model of Personality

A fascinating question is whether there is a universal structure of personality, such as the five-factor model, or whether different factorial models exist in different cultures. To examine this issue, it is helpful to outline the conceptual positions that have been advanced.

According to some psychologists, even the concept of personality lacks universality. Hsu, for example, argues that "the concept of personality is an expression of the Western ideal of individualism" (Hsu, 1985, p. 24). Shweder, a well-known cultural psychologist, argues that "the data gathered from . . . personality inventories lends illusory support to the mistaken belief that individual differences can be described in language consisting of context-free global traits, factors, or dimensions" (Shweder, 1991, pp. 275–276).

These views have been elaborated on: "Universal [personality] structure does not by itself imply that 'person-ality' as understood within a European-American framework is a universal aspect of human behaviour . . . nor does it imply that the variability that appears as an obvious feature of human life is a function of an internal package of attributes called 'personality'" (Markus & Kitayama, 1998, p. 67). Finally, cultural anthropologist Lawrence Hirschfeld argues that "in many, perhaps most, cultures there is a marked absence of discourse that explains human behaviour in terms of transsituationally stable motivational (or intentional) properties captured by explanations of trait and disposition" (Hirschfeld, 1995, p. 315).

What is reflected in all these quotations is a fundamental challenge to personality psychology—whether the core concept of traits is universal or, instead, is a local concept applicable only in Western cultures. The most extreme of these perspectives suggests that the very notion of personality, as an internal set of psychological characteristics, is an arbitrary construction of Western culture (Church, 2000). If this extreme position were really true, then any attempt to identify and measure personality traits in non-Western cultures would be doomed to failure (Church, 2000). At the other extreme is the position that personality traits are universal in their applicability and that precisely the same personality structure will emerge across cultures. As two personality researchers noted, "The most important dimensions . . . [of] personality judgment are the most invariant and universal dimensions" (Saucier & Goldberg, 2001, p. 851).

The first source of evidence bearing on this debate pertains to the existence of trait terms in other cultures. Many non-Western psychologists have, in fact, described traitlike concepts that are indigenous to non-Western cultures and that appear strikingly like those that appear in Western cultures. Following are some examples: the Filipino concepts of *pakikiramdam* (sensitivity, empathy) and *pakikisama* (getting along with others); the Korean concept of *chong* (human affection); the Japanese concept of *amae* (indulgent dependence); the Chinese concept of *ren qin* (being relationship-oriented); and the Mexican concept of *simpatico* (being harmonious and avoiding conflict) (Church, 2000). Many non-Western cultures, in short, appear to have traitlike concepts embedded in their languages in much the same way that the North American culture and English language do.

A second source of evidence bearing on the debate concerns whether the same factor structure of personality traits is found across cultures. That is, do different cultures have roughly the same broad categories of traits? The trait perspective on personality, of course, does not require the existence of precisely the same traits in all cultures. Indeed, the trait perspective might be extremely useful even if cultures were to differ radically in terms of which trait dimensions they used. Nonetheless, the most powerful support for the trait perspective across cultures would occur if the structure of personality traits were found to be the same across cultures (Church, 2000).

Two approaches have been taken to exploring this issue. In the first approach, which can be labelled the "transport and test" strategy, psychologists have translated existing questionnaires into other languages and then have administered them to native residents in other cultures. This strategy has generated some findings supporting the five-factor model. The five-factor model (extraversion, agreeableness, conscientiousness, neuroticism, and openness) has now been replicated in France, Holland, and the Philippines and in languages from entirely different language families, such as Sino-Tibetan, Hamito-Semitic, Uralic, and Malayo-Polynesian (McCrae et al., 1998). The five-factor model also has been replicated in Spain (Salgado, Moscoso, & Lado, 2003) and in Croatia (Mlacic & Ostendorf, 2005). A study of 13 different countries—from Japan to Slovakia—also found support for the five-factor model (Hendriks et al., 2003).

Perhaps the most impressive was a massive study of 50 different cultures (McCrae et al., 2005b). This study, involving 11,985 participants, had university-age individuals rate someone they knew well using the Revised NEO Personality Inventory. Factor analyses of observer-based ratings yielded the five-factor model, with only minor variations in factor structure across cultures. This study suggests that cross-cultural evidence for the five-factor model is not limited to self-report data, but extends to observer-based data as well. Using the transport and test strategy, the five-factor structure of personality appears to be general across cultures. Table 17.4, for example, shows the factor structure from a Filipino sample.

A more powerful test of generality, however, would come from studies that start out using indigenous personality dimensions first, then testing whether the five-factor structure still emerges. This approach has been tried in Dutch, German, Hungarian, Italian, Czech, and Polish (De Raad et al., 1998). In each case, the trait terms in the language were identified. Although the absolute numbers of personality trait terms varied from language to language—Dutch has 8,690 trait terms, whereas Italian has only 1,337 trait terms—the percentage of words in each language that constituted trait terms was remarkably consistent, averaging 4.4 percent of all dictionary entries. You may recall the lexical hypothesis from Chapter 3, which states that the most important individual differences have been encoded within the natural language.

Table 17.4 Factor Analysis of the Filipino NEO-PI-R					
NEO-PI-R Facet Scale	**N**	**E**	**O**	**A**	**C**
N1: Anxiety	**76**	−08	00	00	06
N2: Angry hostility	**67**	−19	01	−44	−10
N3: Depression	**73**	−23	03	−02	−25
N4: Self-consciousness	**68**	−14	−15	22	−04
N5: Impulsiveness	**40**	20	04	−37	−47
N6: Vulnerability	**70**	−22	−23	04	−30
E1: Warmth	−21	**69**	17	28	08
E2: Gregariousness	−29	**65**	−02	07	04
E3: Assertiveness	−28	**42**	23	−29	35
E4: Activity	−15	**51**	10	−24	25
E5: Excitement seeking	−08	**51**	26	−29	−12
E6: Positive emotions	−16	**66**	14	15	01
O1: Fantasy	16	27	**47**	−06	−27
O2: Aesthetics	14	20	**65**	14	22
O3: Feelings	30	32	**53**	03	12
O4: Actions	−39	−03	**46**	01	04
O5: Ideas	−04	−01	**69**	01	30
O6: Values	−13	−06	**62**	−05	−16
A1: Trust	−20	41	09	**52**	−10
A2: Straightforwardness	−03	−22	−02	**57**	10
A3: Altruism	−12	27	13	**65**	31
A4: Compliance	−20	−10	−09	**75**	12
A5: Modesty	18	−27	−03	**55**	−13
A6: Tender-mindedness	22	27	09	**49**	20
C1: Competence	−38	22	16	−10	**69**
C2: Order	−04	−15	−08	10	**73**
C3: Dutifulness	−08	12	07	21	**69**
C4: Achievement striving	−12	06	01	11	**83**
C5: Self-discipline	−24	02	00	07	**81**
C6: Deliberation	−27	−20	03	24	**65**

Note: N = 696. Decimal points are omitted; loadings greater than 40 in absolute magnitude are given in boldface; N = Neuroticism, E = Extraversion, O = Openness, A = Agreeableness, C = Conscientiousness.

Source: McCrae, Costa, del Pilar, et al., 1998.

The next step in the De Raad and colleagues study was to reduce this list to a manageable number of several hundred trait terms, identified as indigenous to each culture, which could then be tested in each culture. Factor analyses of each sample within each culture showed that there was tremendous replicability of four of the five factors of the five-factor model: extraversion (*talkative, sociable versus shy, introverted*), agreeableness (*sympathetic, warm versus unsympathetic, cold*), conscientiousness (*organized, responsible versus disorganized, careless*), and emotional stability (*relaxed, imperturbable versus moody, emotional*).

Despite cross-cultural agreement on these four factors, this study found some differences in what constituted the fifth factor, as noted in Chapter 3. In some cultures, such as Polish and German, the fifth factor resembled the American fifth factor (openness to experience or intellect-openness), with *intelligent* and *imaginative* anchoring one end and *dull* and *unimaginative* anchoring the other end. One study conducted in the Philippines also found a replicated five-factor model, including the fifth factor resembling intellect–openness, although there are a few indigenous constructs that are less successfully subsumed by the Big Five, such as *social curiosity, obedience,* and *capacity for understanding* (Katigbak et al., 2002). Other languages, however, revealed different fifth factors. In Dutch, for example, the fifth factor seemed more like a dimension of political orientation, ranging from *conservative* at one end to *progressive* at the other. In Hungarian, the fifth factor seemed to be one of truthfulness, with *just, truthful,* and *humane* anchoring one end and *greedy, hypocritical,* and *pretending* at the other (De Raad et al., 1998). The fifth factor, in summary, appeared to be somewhat variable across cultures.

Cross-cultural research using the lexical approach, as you may recall from Chapter 3, has found compelling evidence for *six* factors, rather than five (Ashton et al., 2004; Saucier et al., 2005). The new sixth factor, honesty–humility, represents a major discovery across cultures, lending support to the new HEXACO model of personality (Ashton & Lee, 2010). By starting with the natural language within each culture, these researchers were able to capture an important dimension of personality that may have been bypassed using the "transport and test" research strategy.

Research has of course suggested a few other cross-cultural variations on the five-factor model of personality. Studies using the Cross-Cultural (Chinese) Personality Assessment Inventory (CPAI; Cheung et al., 2001) have supported a four-factor model in Chinese and Eastern cultures consisting of dependability, social potency, individualism/accommodation, and **interpersonal relatedness**. According to factor analyses, the first three traits in this model correspond to the Big Five traits of emotional stability, extraversion, and agreeableness, respectively. The interpersonal relatedness factor, however, appears to tap something unique in Chinese and other Eastern cultures. Specifically, it includes traits involving harmony and reciprocity in relationships that are less important to personality within Western populations of European origins (Cheung et al., 2001).

A large study of over 600 members of the Tsimane Indigenous people in the Bolivian Amazon, a truly traditional foraging-farming community, suggested only two principal personality factors: socially beneficial behaviour, also known as *prosociality*, and *industriousness* (Gurven et al., 2013). Despite a notable scientific consensus on the universality of the five-factor model, studies such as these suggest that some variation may nevertheless exist, and that this variation may depend on factors such as degree of collectivism and the structure of the society itself.

Further indigenous tests are needed to determine the extent to which the five-factor trait model of personality structure is universal. Based on the existing data, however, we can conclude that the truth is somewhere between the extreme positions outlined at the beginning of this section and closer to those that argue for universality. Trait terms appear to be present in all languages. Factor structures based on instruments developed in North America, and then translated and transported to other cultures, show great similarity across cultures. Using the more rigorous standard of instruments developed indigenously, four of the five factors emerge consistently across cultures. The fifth factor is somewhat variable across cultures and therefore may reflect an important lack of universality of personality trait structure. And a sixth factor, honesty–humility, has been revealed by at least some studies using the indigenous strategy.

 Concept Check

What are cultural universals? Provide one example from the emotional domain.

What is one possible exception to the common five factors that has emerged from cross-cultural research?

Summary and Evaluation

People living in different cultures differ in key personality traits, such as self-concept, prevailing levels of aggressiveness, and the moral values they hold. The differences are called cultural variations—patterns of local within-group similarity and between-group difference.

There are two major approaches to examining cultural variations. The first, evoked culture, involves the capabilities present in all people that are elicited only in some cultural contexts. Evoked cooperation provides one example—people tend to share food when there is high variability in success at obtaining it. Presumably, all people have the capacity to cooperate and share, but these dispositions are evoked only in certain cultural circumstances. Evoked aggression provides a second example of evoked culture. All people have the capacity to be aggressive at times; however, if one grows up in a culture of honour, then aggression is more likely to be evoked in response to public insults.

The second major way of conceptualizing cultural variants is called transmitted culture—representations originally in the mind of one or more people that are transmitted to the minds of other people. Three examples of cultural variants that appear to be forms of transmitted culture are differences in moral values, self-construal, and levels of self-enhancement. Patterns of morality, such as whether it is considered appropriate to disobey one's parents or to eat beef, are specific to certain cultures. These moral values appear to be transmitted from person to person within the culture. Cultural differences in self-construal are another example of transmitted culture. Many Asian cultures, as well as Indigenous cultures around the world, appear to foster self-concepts that are highly interdependent and contextual, emphasizing the embeddedness of the self within the group. Western and European cultures (including the United States and Canada generally), in contrast, appear to promote a self-concept that is more independent, stressing the separateness of the person from the group.

The cross-cultural work on interdependence–independence has been criticized on several grounds. First, the magnitudes of effect are sometimes quite small. Second, the dichotomies may be overly simplistic because they ignore the context specificity of the tendencies (e.g., North Americans might be independent at work and interdependent at home with their families) as well as individual differences within culture (e.g., some Koreans are more individualistic, others more collectivistic). Nonetheless, some cultural differences are real and must be explained. Most researchers have assumed that these differences are instances of transmitted culture. An alternative explanation proposes that all humans have evolved psychological mechanisms capable of acting both individualistically and collectively, as well as a mechanism that allows them to switch from one mode to the other, depending on the fitness advantages. This fascinating fusion of evolutionary psychology and cultural psychology holds much promise.

The culture in which we reside appears to influence our self-concepts. Using a procedure known as the Twenty Statements Test, researchers have found that North Americans tend to describe themselves using abstract internal characteristics, such as "I am smart," "I am dependable," and "I am friendly." Asians, in contrast, tend to define themselves more often using social roles, such as "I am the son of . . ." or "I am Liu's friend." These differences in self-concept appear to be examples of transmitted culture, passed down from person to person through the generations. It's important to keep in mind that these cultural differences are a matter of degree. People in collectivist cultures use some global traits to describe themselves, and people in individualist cultures use some relational terms to describe themselves.

Cultural identity refers to a person's sense of belonging to a specific culture or group, and it plays an essential role in the psychological well-being of Indigenous people of Canada. Clarity and consistency of both self-concept and cultural identity are critical factors in the maintenance of self-esteem, particularly for a culture which relies heavily on a narrative oral history.

Another reliable cultural difference pertains to self-enhancement, or the tendency to view oneself using positive or socially valued attributes. Korean and Japanese respondents are more likely than North American respondents to endorse negative statements about themselves, such as "I am lazy" or "I am a somewhat selfish person." North Americans, in contrast, tend to endorse more positive statements about themselves, such as "I'm a hard worker" or "I'm quite creative." These differences in self-enhancement also appear to be examples of transmitted culture.

In addition to cultural variations, some elements of personality appear to be culturally universal. One example of a cultural universal is people's beliefs about the personality traits that characterize men and women. Worldwide, people tend to regard men as having personalities that are more active, loud, adventurous, obnoxious, aggressive, opinionated, arrogant, coarse, and conceited. Women, in contrast, are regarded as having personalities that are more affectionate, modest, nervous, appreciative, patient, changeable, charming, fearful, and forgiving.

Another cultural universal appears to be the experience and recognition of specific emotional states, such as fear, anger, happiness, sadness, disgust, and surprise. People from Italy to Sumatra can recognize and describe these emotions when presented with photographs of others expressing them, even if the photographs are of people from other cultures.

Finally, there is some evidence that the structure of personality traits, as represented by the five-factor model of personality, may be universal, at least for four of the five traits—extraversion, agreeableness, conscientiousness, and emotional stability. There is also evidence for the five-factor model using the "transport and test" strategy model of personality, using observer-based data from 50 cultures. Nonetheless, studies that begin with the natural language within each culture, using the lexical strategy to identify important trait terms, have discovered other key traits. For instance, studies in Eastern cultures have suggested *interpersonal relatedness* as a meaningful trait that is not addressed in the five-factor model. The newly discovered *honesty–humility* factor, part of the HEXACO model, also attests to the importance of cross-cultural research.

 Concept Check

Overall, how much does personality seem to vary by culture? In your response, discuss the role of independence (individualism) and interdependence (collectivism).

Overall, how similar are cultures in personality? Do cultures have distinctive personality profiles?

Key Terms

cultural variations

cultural personality
  psychology

evoked culture

egalitarianism

culture of honour

conformity

authoritarianism

transmitted culture

self-construal

interdependence

independence

individualistic

collectivistic

holistic

analytic

acculturation

metapersonal self-construal

cultural identity

self-enhancement

within-culture variations

historical era

cultural universals

Whorfian hypothesis of
  linguistic relativity

interpersonal relatedness

PART SIX

The Adjustment Domain

This domain is different from the others discussed in the book so far. The first five domains each referred to a collection of specific explanations of personality. That is, each gave a perspective on, and a collection of knowledge about, the causes of personality and individual differences. In this last domain—the adjustment domain—we examine some of the consequences of personality. We focus on adjustment because, in many ways, personality functions to help us adjust to the challenges and demands of life, albeit in a unique way for each of us. We focus on two important outcomes in this domain: physical health and mental health.

Day by day, all of us are adjusting to the demands of life and reacting to life events. Some of us might even think there is too much stress in our lives. However, stress is not necessarily "out there" in our lives; rather, stress mostly refers to how we respond to life events. How we perceive and interpret some event determines whether we feel it as stressful. The tendency to interpret events in a way that evokes a stress response is influenced by our personalities, among other psychological variables. Personality plays a key role in how we appraise and interpret events and cope, adapt, and adjust to the ebb and flow in our day-to-day lives. Moreover, some people display patterns of behaviour, emotion, and interpersonal relations that create problems for them and for those around them. These problematic personality profiles form the collection of personality disorders diagnosed by clinicians. These two areas—coping with stress and disorders of personality—define the adjustment domain because they refer to how effectively people interact with and cope with challenges from the environment.

Considerable evidence has accumulated that personality is associated with important health outcomes, including heart disease. Psychologists have developed several theories for how and why these relationships exist, as well as offering ways to change health-harming behaviour patterns. Personality is also associated with a variety of health-related behaviours such as smoking, drinking, and risk taking. Some research has even demonstrated that personality is correlated with how long we live (Peterson, 1995, 2000).

In addition to maintaining health and coping with stress, many of the important problems in living can be traced to personality. In this domain of knowledge there is the concept of disorder, the idea that certain personality profiles can be so abnormal or problematic that they create clear difficulties in the person's life, particularly in terms of work and social relationships. Certain personality features related to poor adjustment and poor outcomes in life are described as personality disorders. We devote an entire chapter to personality disorders, such as antisocial and narcissistic personality disorders. We believe that an understanding of "normal" personality functioning can be enhanced by examining what can go wrong with personality. This is similar to the field of medicine, in which an understanding of normal physiological functioning is often illuminated by the study of disorders and disease. We begin our coverage of the adjustment domain with the topics of stress, coping, adjustment, and health.

CHAPTER 18

Stress, Coping, Adjustment, and Health

The Adjustment Domain

For much of history, humans have been battling microbes in an effort to overcome disease and illness. The list of germ-borne illnesses is long, with many epidemics throughout history. For example, in 1520, the Spanish conquistadors landed in Mexico with several slaves brought from Spanish Cuba. One of the slaves had smallpox. The illness spread to the native Aztec tribes, who had no immunity to smallpox. It quickly killed half of the Aztec people, including their emperor, Cuitlahuac. Aided by the microbe that causes smallpox, the Spanish had no trouble conquering all of Mexico. Imagine how helpless the Aztecs must have felt as the mysterious disease killed *only* them, sparing the Spaniards, who had developed immunity. The Aztecs must have thought the Spaniards were invincible. The native population of Mexico, estimated at 20 million when the Spaniards arrived, fell to 1.6 million in less than 100 years (Diamond, 1999).

The world is currently experiencing another epidemic of an infectious disease: HIV, which causes AIDS. The microbe that causes HIV/AIDS resides in bodily fluids and passes from person to person when bodily fluids containing the microbe are exchanged. A cure for HIV/AIDS has not yet been discovered, nor is there a vaccine that will prevent the spread of HIV. The explosive spread of this infectious disease has surprised even medical researchers. Although it is a concern in Canada, the AIDS epidemic is far worse in Africa, which is home to about 14.5 percent of the world population yet contains 69 percent of all people in the world living with HIV and accounted for 72 percent of all AIDS deaths in 2009 (United Nations, 2010). The HIV rate in Swaziland is

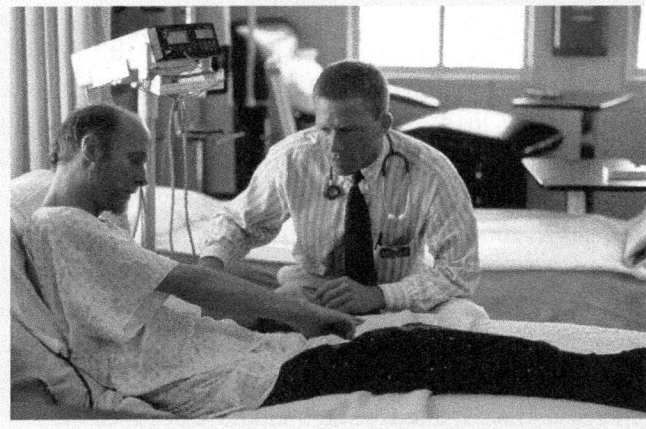

A terminal patient in an advanced stage of AIDS. Although AIDS is caused by a virus, HIV, its transmission often occurs through specific behaviours.
©David Weintraub/Science Source

unprecedented, at over 25 percent of the adult population, reducing the average life expectancy in that country to 32 years, the lowest in the world.

The current epidemic of HIV/AIDS illustrates a very important distinction; although its cause is a virus, its transmission most often occurs through specific behaviours. For example, unsafe sex practices (e.g., not using condoms) greatly increase the likelihood of transmitting HIV. Another high-risk behaviour is the sharing of intravenous needles during drug use. While medical researchers search for a vaccination and cure, psychologists are searching for the best ways to change people's high-risk behaviour.

This is only one example of the importance of behaviour in understanding illness. In earlier centuries, most of the serious illnesses that afflicted humans were caused by microbe infection, including such diseases as tuberculosis, influenza, leprosy, polio, bubonic plague, cholera, smallpox, malaria, measles, rabies, and diphtheria. As modern medicine developed effective vaccines, these microbial diseases pretty much disappeared as major causes of death (at least in Canada and other developed nations). Today, many of the leading causes of death and disease are related not to microbes as much as to lifestyle factors, such as smoking, poor diet, inadequate exercise, and stress. In other words, now that we are curing microbial infections, behavioural factors have emerged as important contributors to the development of illness.

The realization that psychological and behavioural factors can have important health consequences has given rise to the field of **health psychology**. Researchers in this area of psychology study the relationship between the mind and the body, as well as the ways in which these two components respond to challenges from the environment (e.g., stressful events, germs) to produce either illness or health. Many of the psychological variables of interest have to do with stable patterns of behaviour—for example, whether a person copes well with stress, exercises some or not at all, sleeps seven to eight hours each night, drinks alcohol only in moderation, routinely wears a seat belt, keeps his or her weight at a desirable level, avoids drugs, practises safe sex, and avoids unnecessary risks. Researchers find that such behaviours are correlated with life expectancy. In fact, in North America, researchers suggest that lifestyle contributes to more than half of all premature deaths—that is, death before age 65 (Loef & Walach, 2012).

Personality can have an impact on health in many ways, and personality psychologists are developing new methodological approaches to the study of this link. Current research is based on detailed models of the mechanisms underlying the links between personality and health (Smith & Spiro, 2002; Smith, Williams, & Segerstrom, 2015). Lifespan studies show that personality can have lifelong effects on health, though the effects differ depending on the traits being considered (Aldwin et al., 2001) or the specific health outcomes under investigation, such as the coronary-prone personality characterized by hostility and aggressiveness (Eysenck, 2000). The Big Five trait of conscientiousness has been reliably associated with numerous positive health outcomes, including better health behaviours and a longer life expectancy (Bogg & Roberts, 2004; Taylor et al., 2009). There is also evidence that good health and longevity are more likely in cases of higher extraversion, higher agreeableness, and higher openness to experience (e.g., Graham et al., 2017; Taylor et al., 2009). With regards to neuroticism, higher stress reactivity and negative emotion underscore the increased risk of disease and premature death associated with high levels of this trait (Gale et al., 2017).

In this chapter, we focus on the portion of the field of health psychology that concerns personality and individual differences. Some main research questions in this area are the following: "Are some people more likely than others to become ill?" "Do some people recover faster?" "Are some people better able than others to tolerate stress?" Understanding the nature and consequences of such differences among people is the focus of this chapter. We begin by discussing various ways of thinking about how personality influences health.

Models of the Personality–Illness Connection

Researchers have proposed several ways of thinking about how personality can relate to health. These models can take the form of diagrams of key variables, with the causal relations among those variables depicted by arrows. Models are useful to researchers in guiding their thinking about specific variables and especially in thinking about how those variables influence one another (Smith, 2006; Wiebe & Smith, 1997). In most of the models we will discuss, one variable—stress—will be important. **Stress** is the subjective feeling produced by events that are uncontrollable or threatening. It is important to realize that stress is a *response* to the perceived demands of a situation. Stress is not *in* the situation; it does not exist outside of a person.

An early model of the personality health relationship, called the **interactional model**, is depicted in Figure 18.1(a). This model suggests that objective events happen to people, but personality factors determine the impact of those events by influencing people's ability to cope. In this model, personality has its effect on coping responses—that is, on how people respond to the event. It is called the interactional model because personality is assumed to moderate (influence) the relationship between stress and illness. Events such as exposure to microbes or chronic stress cause illness, but personality factors make a person more or less vulnerable to those events. For example, if a person were infected with a cold virus but had a hard-driving, competitive personality, such that the person would not rest, would not take time off from work, and would not do other behaviours necessary to quickly recover from a cold, this person could become very ill, perhaps with the cold turning into pneumonia, because the person's personality influenced how well they coped with the viral infection.

Although the interactional model was useful in early research, health psychologists soon identified many limitations. One problem was that researchers were unable to identify stable coping responses that were

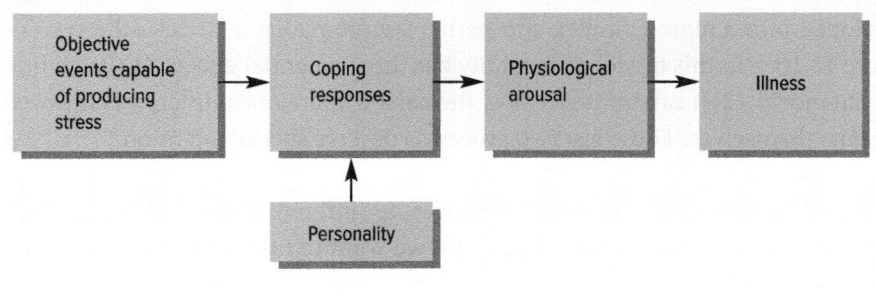

(a)

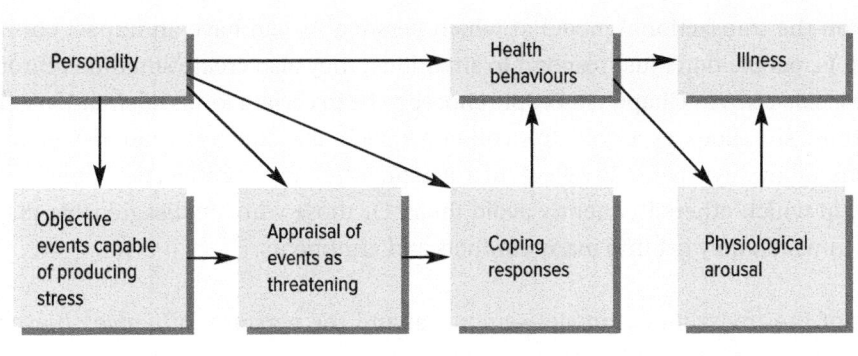

(b)

(c)

FIGURE 18.1 Three models specifying the role of personality in moderating the effects of stress on illness: (a) the interactional model, which specifies that personality influences how people cope; (b) the transactional model, which specifies that personality influences how people cope, as well as how they appraise and influence situations; and (c) the health behaviour model, which specifies that personality influences how people cope, appraise, and influence situations, as well as the likely health behaviours that people practise.

consistently adaptive or maladaptive for any single person (Lazarus, 1991). Subsequently, the interactional model was developed into a more complex and perhaps more realistic model—the **transactional model**, depicted in Figure 18.1(b). In this model, personality has three potential effects: (1) it can influence coping, as in the interactional model; (2) it can influence how the person appraises or interprets the events; and (3) it can influence the events themselves. These last two processes deserve special attention.

We stated above that "personality is assumed to moderate (influence) the relationship between stress and illness." Because moderation is an important concept, we want to take some time to explain what this term means. A variable is called a **moderator** if it influences the direction or degree of relationship between two other variables. So, for example, if stress is correlated with illness, yet this correlation is stronger for some people compared to others (say those high in neuroticism), then we would say that the personality trait of neuroticism is a moderator of the relationship between stress and illness. Examples of moderator effects are common in personality and health. For example, a strong predictor of whether a person will use illegal drugs is if they have friends who use illegal drugs (self use and peer use is correlated). However, for people low on the personality trait of sensation seeking, this correlation is not found, and so the trait of sensation seeking is said to moderate the relationship between own use and peer use of illegal drugs (Marschall-Levesque et al., 2014). A moderator is sometimes thought of as a risk multiplier; in this case, the trait of high sensation seeking multiplies the risk of having peers who use drugs on the probability that the person will themselves use drugs.

In the transactional model, it is not the event itself that causes stress but how the event is appraised, or interpreted, by the person. You will recall from Chapter 12 that interpretation is important in determining behaviour. An event, such as getting stuck in traffic on the way to a job interview, can happen to two people, yet the two people can interpret the event differently and thus experience it differently. One person might interpret getting stuck as a major frustration and hence might respond with a great deal of worry, stress, and anxiety. The other might interpret getting stuck in traffic as an opportunity to relax, enjoy some music on the radio, and do some planning on how to reschedule the job interview. This person does not experience the same level of stress.

The third point on the transactional model at which personality can have an impact consists of the events themselves. That is, people don't just respond to situations; they also create situations through their choices and actions, as we discussed in Chapter 4. People choose to be in certain kinds of situations; they evoke certain responses from those situations, especially from other people in the situations; and they manipulate the people in those situations, all in ways that may reflect their personalities. For example, those high in neuroticism may create situations in which others frequently avoid them. Or those who are disagreeable may create interpersonal situations in which they get into many conflicts and arguments.

These two parts of the transactional model—appraisal and the person's influence on events—are why the model is called transactional. These two elements of the model imply that stressful events don't just influence people; people also influence events. And this influence comes about through the appraisal of events, as well as the selection and modification of events. This reciprocal influence of people and events makes this a more complicated, though perhaps more realistic, model of how the process actually works.

A third model, the **health behaviour model**, adds another factor to the transactional model. It is important to realize that so far the three models are simply extensions of the theme that personality influences the stress–illness link. In this model, which is depicted in Figure 18.1(c), personality does not directly influence the relationship between stress and illness. Instead, in this model, personality affects health indirectly through health-promoting or health-degrading behaviours. Everyone knows that poor health behaviours, such as consuming too much sugar, smoking, and practising unsafe sex, increase the risk of developing certain illnesses. This model suggests that personality influences the degree to which a person engages in various health-promoting or health-degrading behaviours. For example, individuals who are low in the trait of conscientiousness engage in a variety of health-damaging behaviours, including smoking, unhealthy eating habits, dangerous driving, and lack of exercise (Bogg & Roberts, 2004).

Conscientiousness is reliably related to good health (e.g., Hill & Roberts, 2011) and even predicts that one will live a longer life (e.g., Hill et al., 2011; Turiano et al., 2015). As a personality trait, conscientiousness is manifest in such behaviours as making lists before grocery shopping, keeping a calendar to plan activities, keeping one's work area neat and tidy, using a to-do list, and dressing up for special occasions. A list of several hundred behavioural indicators of conscientiousness can be found in Jackson and colleagues (2010). Why is it that conscientiousness predicts positive health outcomes? Researchers conclude that conscientious people are also conscientious about their health behaviours. They tend to floss and brush regularly, take regular exercise, watch their diets, and adhere to other behaviours that are linked to better health. Conscientiousness appears to affect health primarily through a *mediating* mechanism described by the health behaviour model (Hampson et al., 2006). Interestingly, harmful health behaviours such as drinking and smoking are more likely to be reported by those high in neuroticism as well as those high in extraversion (Hampson et al., 2006).

Mediation is similar to moderation, in that both describe specific ways that three variables are related to one another. Mediation is different, however, in that it specifies that the effect of one variable on another "goes through" a third variable. So, for example, the effect of conscientiousness on longevity goes through, or is due to, specific health behaviours. Mediation is a way of understanding the observed relationship (i.e., that conscientiousness is correlated with longevity) by specifying the underlying mechanism or process captured by the mediator variable (i.e., health behaviour). Turiano and colleagues (2015) used a national sample of over 6,000 people over a 14-year period, and found that Conscientiousness predicted a 13 percent reduction in mortality in the time period. Moreover, when health behaviours were examined as mediators, they found that heavy drinking, smoking, and greater waist circumferences (all negatively related to conscientiousness) significantly mediated the conscientiousness-mortality association. Findings such as these show how mediation can be a powerful way to explain how personality effects might work.

A fourth model of the link between personality and health, the **predisposition model**, is shown in Figure 18.2(a). The previous three models were all variations on the same theme that personality influences the relationship between stress and illness either directly (interactional and transactional models) or indirectly (health behaviour model). The fourth model is completely different and holds that personality and illness are both expressions of an underlying predisposition. This model is a very simple conception, suggesting that associations exist between personality and illness because of a third variable, which is causing them both. For example, enhanced sympathetic nervous system reactivity may be the cause of subsequent illnesses, *as well as* the cause of the behaviours and emotions that lead a person to be called neurotic. The predisposition model has not been the topic of much systematic study, though it seems likely that this model will guide investigators interested in the genetic basis of illnesses. It may well turn out that some genetic predispositions are expressed both in terms of a stable individual difference and in terms of susceptibility to specific illnesses (Bouchard et al., 1990). For example, there is evidence of a genetic cause of novelty seeking (associated with the dopamine receptor gene DRD4) which may also cause, or make a person more likely to develop, an addiction to drugs (Cloninger, 1999; Mallard et al., 2016; Ptáček et al., 2011). Consequently, the correlation between the

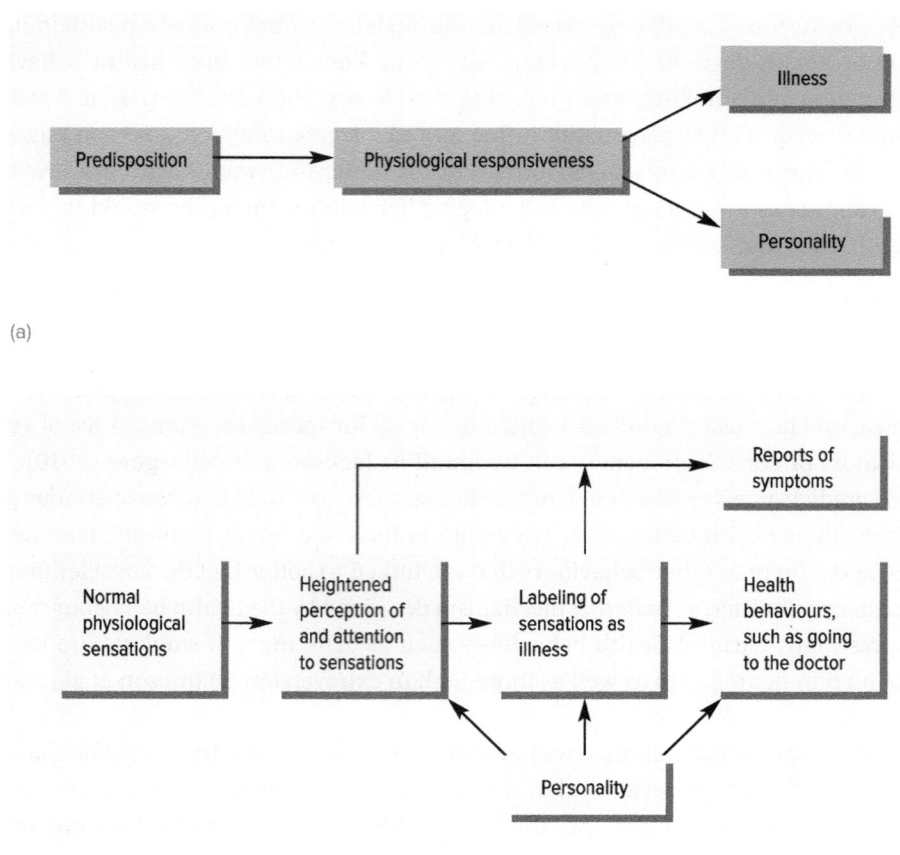

(a)

(b)

FIGURE 18.2 Additional models of the relationship between personality and health: (a) the predisposition model, which holds that personality and health are related due to a common predisposition; and (b) the illness behaviour model, which specifies how personality might influence whether a person would seek medical attention or report illness symptoms.

novelty-seeking personality trait and substance abuse (including substances such as alcohol and cocaine) may be due to the fact that these two variables are both independently caused by a third variable—genes. This simple model may be useful as the human genome project (see Chapter 6) progresses from mapping the genome to understanding what specific genes control.

The final model for our consideration—called the **illness behaviour model**—is not a model of illness per se, but rather a model of illness behaviour. Illness itself is defined as the presence of an objectively measurable abnormal physiological process, such as fever, high blood pressure, or a tumour. Illness behaviour, on the other hand, is the action that people take when they think they have an illness, such as complaining to others about their symptoms, going to a doctor, taking the day off from school or work, or taking medication. Illness behaviours are related to actual illnesses, but not perfectly. Some individuals may tough out an illness, stoically refusing to engage in illness behaviours (e.g., refusing to take the day off from work when ill). Other people engage in all sorts of illness behaviours even in the absence of actual illness.

Figure 18.2(b) portrays the illness behaviour model. It suggests that personality influences the degree to which a person perceives and pays attention to bodily sensations and the degree to which the person interprets and labels those sensations as an illness. The way in which a person perceives and labels those sensations, then, influences the person's illness behaviours, such as reporting the symptoms and going to a doctor. As discussed in Chapter 13, the personality trait of neuroticism is associated with a tendency to complain about physical symptoms, and high neuroticism has been associated with over-using medical services (Cuijpers et al., 2010); though in certain conditions or states of poor health, neuroticism may serve a protective function by leading people to keep up with medical appointments (Gale et al., 2017). Self-reports of physical symptoms and illness behaviours may be influenced by factors other than actual illness, however, and these reports and behaviours are determined by how the person perceives and labels bodily sensations.

It is important to note that these models linking personality to physical health are not mutually exclusive. That is, they may all apply, depending on the personality trait and the illness under consideration. For example, hostility may relate to heart disease because it is a manifestation of the same underlying process (the predisposition model), conscientiousness may relate to illness through specific health behaviours (the health behaviour model), and neuroticism may relate to ill health through its effects on stress appraisal and stress exposure (the transactional model) (Roberts et al., 2007). Personality may influence health through all these different mechanisms, and the various models of the relationships between personality and health give researchers the tools to think clearly about the possibilities.

Most of the models of personality and illness contain one important variable—the concept of stress. Stress is an important but also a very much misunderstood phenomenon.

 Concept Check

Provide two different examples of how personality can interact with stress to impact health.

What is the predisposition model of personality–illness connection? Provide an example.

The Concept of Stress

Imagine that you have an important exam coming up in one of your classes. You've waited until two nights before the exam to start studying. When you finally decide to start studying and begin looking for your class notes, you realize that you left them at your parents' place when you were visiting last weekend. You start to panic and finally call your parents, and your dad agrees to scan them into a PDF and e-mail them to you in the morning. You are pretty anxious now and cannot fall asleep for several hours after you go to bed. The next day you are tired from not sleeping well. The class notes arrive, but you have other classes during the day, so you will have to study later. That night, as you are getting ready to study, your roommate reminds you of the party he has planned for the evening, which you had forgotten about. Now you have to go somewhere else to study— an unfamiliar environment, such as the library. You rush to the library and settle into a secluded area to study. Although it is quiet in the library, you are so tired and anxious that you cannot seem to concentrate on the material. At midnight the library closes, and you rush back to your apartment. The party is still going, and it continues until 2:00 in the morning. Meanwhile, you are impatiently trying to study in your room but are distracted by the people and the music. Finally, you feel so overloaded, you just give up and go to bed after the people leave. But even now you can't sleep. You are anxious and frustrated and feeling totally unprepared for the important exam you have in the morning. In fact, you see that the exam will be held in just a few hours. Things are out of your control. You notice that you have a painful headache, and even though you are lying in your bed, your heart is pounding and the palms of your hands are sweaty. You are not sure what to do. You want to study, but you also know it would be good to sleep a few hours. And you cannot seem to do either.

This is stress. It is a feeling of being overwhelmed by events that you cannot seem to control. Events that cause stress are called **stressors**, and they appear to have several common attributes:

Studying for an exam can be stressful or not, depending on whether the situation controls you or you control the situation. Stress occurs when events seem uncontrollable and threatening. Taking control by keeping up with homework, planning each day, and preparing in a timely fashion can make studying less stressful.
©Caia Image/Image Source/Tom Merton

1. Stressors are extreme, in the sense that they produce a state of feeling overwhelmed or overloaded, that one just cannot take it much longer.
2. Stressors often produce opposing tendencies, such as wanting and not wanting an activity or object—as in wanting to study but also wanting to put it off as long as possible.
3. Stressors are uncontrollable, outside our power to influence, such as an exam we cannot avoid.

The Stress Response

When a stressor appears, people typically experience a pattern of emotional and physiological reactions. For example, if someone were to startle you by honking a car horn as you walked in front of the car, you would experience some startle: your heart would beat faster and your blood pressure would go up, and your palms and the soles of your feet would begin to sweat. This pattern of reaction is called the fight-or-flight response. This physiological response is controlled by an increase of sympathetic nervous system activity (see Chapter 7 for more details on nervous system responses). The increase in heart rate and blood pressure prepares you for action, such as fighting or running away. The sweaty palms and feet are perhaps a preparation for holding a weapon or running away. This physiological response is usually very brief, and if the stressor is as minor as someone honking a car horn to see you jump, then perhaps you return to your normal state in a minute or less.

If, however, a person is exposed to a particular stressor day in and day out, then this physiological fight-or-flight response is just the first step in a chain of events termed the **general adaptation syndrome (GAS)** by Hans Selye (1976), a Canadian scientist and pioneer in stress research. Selye proposed that the GAS followed a stage model, as depicted in Figure 18.3. The first stage, called the **alarm stage**, consists of the fight-or-flight response of the sympathetic nervous system and the associated peripheral nervous system reactions. These include the release of hormones that prepare the body for challenge. If the stressor continues, then the next stage begins, the **resistance stage**. The body is using its resources at an above average rate, even though the immediate fight-or-flight response has subsided. At this point, stress is being resisted, but it is taking a lot of effort and energy. If the stressor remains constant, the person eventually enters the third stage, the **exhaustion stage**. Selye felt that this was the stage in which a person is most susceptible to illness and disease, as physiological resources are depleted.

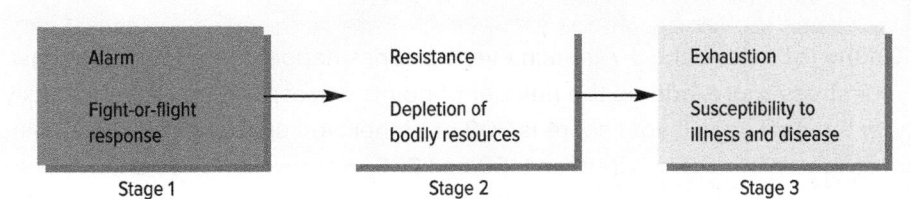

Alarm	Resistance	Exhaustion
Fight-or-flight response	Depletion of bodily resources	Susceptibility to illness and disease
Stage 1	Stage 2	Stage 3

FIGURE 18.3 The three stages of the general adaptation syndrome proposed by Selye.

Major Life Events

What are some common stressors, events that are likely to evoke stress in most people? Holmes and Rahe (1967) studied various **major life events**, those events that require people to make major adjustments in their lives. In their research, Holmes and Rahe wanted to estimate the potential stress value of a wide variety of life events. They started with a long list of events such as the death of a family member, loss of a job, or being arrested. They then had a large number of subjects rate each of the events according to how much stress each was likely to provoke. Each event was then associated with so many points; by counting up the events a person had experienced and adding up the stress points for all of those events, a good estimate of the amount of stress experienced by that person could be obtained.

In Table 18.1 we present a student version of the stressful event schedule based on the original Holmes and Rahe research. It has been modified for teaching purposes to apply to university- and college-age adults and should be considered a rough indication of stress levels. In this scale, the number following the event refers to the stress "points" associated with that event. You can see that death of a close family member, death of a friend, and divorce of parents are the events likely to evoke the most stress. Interestingly, getting married is also likely to be stressful, as are other "positive" events, such as starting university or making some major achievement. This highlights the fact that stress is the subjective response to an event and that even though an event is positive, it may have the three characteristics associated with stressors: intensity, conflict, and uncontrollability.

If you take the Student Stress Test in Table 18.1 and turn out to have high levels of stress, there are several things you can do. First, monitor for early signs of stress, such as recurring stomachaches or headaches. Avoid negative thinking, pessimism, or catastrophizing. Arm your body against stress by eating nutritiously and getting enough sleep and exercise. Practise a relaxation technique regularly. Turn to friends and relatives for support when you need it.

In their initial research, Holmes and Rahe tallied up the stress points that each of the research participants had accumulated in the prior year. They found that the people with the most stress points were also the most likely to have a serious illness during that year. This research was among the first systematic demonstrations that elevated stress—a psychological phenomenon—was associated with elevated risk for a number of illnesses. These findings persuaded medical researchers to take seriously the notion that factors other than microbes and organ malfunctions contribute to illness. Researchers following Holmes and Rahe have consistently found linkages between major life events and illness (reviewed in Schwarzer & Luszczynska, 2013).

Other researchers have taken a more experimental approach to see if stress is related to susceptibility to disease. For example, Cohen, Tyrrell, and Smith (1997) obtained reports of stressful life events for a group of volunteers

Table 18.1 The Student Stress Test

Directions: On the list below, check off each event that has happened to you in the past year. To determine your stress score, add up the number of points corresponding to the events you have experienced in the past year. If your score is 300 or higher, you are at risk for developing a health problem from stress. If your score is between 150 and 300, you have a 50–50 chance of experiencing a health problem in the next few years if the stress persists. If your score is below 150, you have a relatively low risk of a serious health change due to stress (DeMeuse, 1985; Insel & Roth, 1985).

STUDENT STRESS SCALE

1.	Death of a close family member	100
2.	Death of a close friend	73
3.	Divorce between parents	65
4.	Jail term	63
5.	Major personal injury or illness	63
6.	Marriage	58
7.	Fired from job	50
8.	Failed important course	47
9.	Change in health of a family member	45
10.	Pregnancy	45
11.	Sexual problems	44
12.	Serious argument with a close friend	40
13.	Change in financial status	39
14.	Change of major at college or university	39
15.	Trouble with parents	39
16.	New girl- or boyfriend	38
17.	Increased workload	37
18.	Outstanding personal achievement	36
19.	First quarter/semester in college or university	35
20.	Change in living conditions	31
21.	Serious argument with instructor	30
22.	Lower grades than expected	29
23.	Change in sleeping habits	29
24.	Change in social activities	29
25.	Change in eating habits	28
26.	Chronic car trouble	26
27.	Change in number of family occasions	26
28.	Too many missed classes	25
29.	Change of college or university	24
30.	Dropped more than one class	23
31.	Minor traffic violations	20
	TOTAL	

Source: Based on "The Social Adjustment Rating Scale," by T. H. Holmes and R. H. Rahe, 1967, *Journal of Psychosomatic Research,* vol. 11, pp. 213–217.

and were able to score each participant along the lines of Holmes and Rahe's criteria for stressful points for various events. With the permission of the participants, these researchers then tried to infect half the participants with a cold by giving them nose drops containing the cold virus. The other half of the research participants were given plain nose drops; they served as the control group in this experiment. What happened? The participants with more negative life events in the previous year, who indicated they were experiencing a lot of life stress, were more likely to develop a cold after being given the cold virus than were the participants with fewer stressors in their lives, who were more resistant to the cold virus. The researchers interpreted this finding as consistent with the general adaptation syndrome: people under chronic stress eventually deplete bodily resources and become vulnerable to microbial infections.

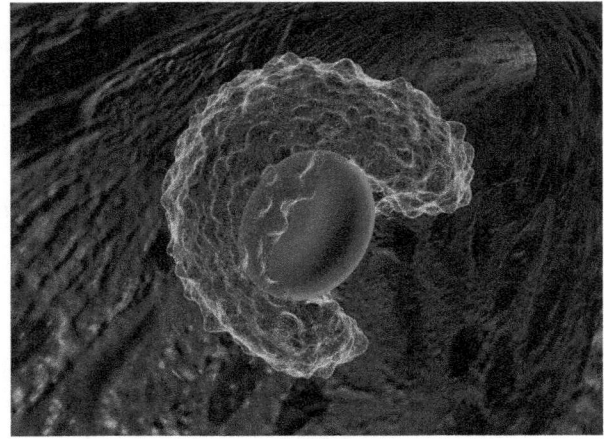

Illustration detail of a macrophage cell engulfing a particle, probably a leukemia-related pathogen.
©Purestock/SuperStock

What is missing in the Holmes and Rahe approach is the individual's subjective appraisals of different events. Nevertheless, the relationship between increased stress and lowered resistance to viral and bacterial infection has been demonstrated repeatedly using multiple approaches (Salleh, 2008; Morey et al., 2015). Currently, most researchers interpret such findings as illustrating the effects of stress on the immune system. That is, stress is thought to lower the functional ability of the immune system to mount an effective response to the presence of microbes, thereby leading to lowered immunity to infection and resulting illness (Marsland et al., 2001; Miller & Cohen, 2001; Morey et al., 2015).

Daily Hassles

Major life events are, thankfully, fairly infrequent in our lives. It seems that the major sources of stress in most people's lives are what are termed **daily hassles** (Delongis, Folkman, & Lazarus, 1988; Lazarus, 1991). Although only minor, daily hassles can be chronic and repetitive. Examples of daily hassles include having too much to do all the time, having to fight the crowds while shopping, getting stuck regularly in heavy traffic, having to wait in lines all the time, having an unpleasant boss at work, and having to worry over money. Such daily hassles can be chronically irritating, though they do not initiate the same general adaptation syndrome evoked by some major life events. The results of research on daily hassles have shown that, similar to major life events, people with a lot of minor stressors in their lives suffer more than expected from psychological and physical symptoms. The top 10 most common daily hassles are listed in Table 18.2.

Varieties of Stress

Stress is a physical and psychological response to perceived demands and pressures. In the stress response, people mobilize physical and emotional resources to cope with the demands and pressures. Psychologists distinguish among four varieties of stress:

- **Acute stress** is what most people associate with the term *stress*. Acute stress results from the sudden onset of demands and is experienced as tension headaches, emotional upsets, gastrointestinal

Table 18.2 The 10 Most Commonly Experienced Daily Hassles	
Hassles	**Percentage***
Concerns about weight	52%
Health of a family member	48
Rising prices of common goods	43
Home maintenance	43
Too many things to do	39
Misplacing or losing things	38
Yard work or outside home maintenance	38
Property, investment, or taxes	37
Crime	37
Physical appearance	36

*Over a nine-month period, these percentages represent the average percentages of people indicating that the hassle was a significant source of stress.

Source: Adapted from Kanner et al., 1981.

disturbances, feelings of agitation, and pressure. A single episode of acute stress can have a significant impact on an individual, yet the effects are not always obvious to bystanders. For example, experimental research by Frances Chen of the University of British Columbia demonstrated an effect of acute social stress on children's emotional processing in the lab (Chen et al., 2014). Very often, it is our emotions and our ability to manage them that become most impaired by experiences of stress.

- **Episodic acute stress** is more serious, in the sense that it refers to repeated episodes of acute stress, such as a weekend job that is stressful or having to meet a deadline each month. Episodic acute stress can lead to migraines, hypertension, stroke, anxiety, depression, or serious gastrointestinal distress.

- **Traumatic stress** refers to a massive instance of acute stress, the effects of which can reverberate for years or even a lifetime (e.g., Bunce, Larsen, & Peterson, 1995). Traumatic stress differs from acute stress mainly in terms of the symptoms associated with the stress response. This collection of symptoms, called **posttraumatic stress disorder (PTSD)**, is a syndrome that occurs in some people after experiencing or witnessing life-threatening events, such as in military combat, natural disasters, terrorist incidents, serious accidents, or violent personal assaults such as rape. For instance, many Americans experienced

On September 11, 2001, many people in and around the World Trade Center in New York City experienced traumatic stress. Some of them went on to develop posttraumatic stress disorder.

©Doug Kanter/AFP/Getty Images

symptoms of PTSD following the September 11 terrorist attacks on the World Trade Center in New York in 2001. For some individuals involved, including emergency workers, PTSD symptoms have lasted a decade or longer (Lowell et al., 2018). In fact those who work regularly in high-stress emergency situations, like paramedics, experience PTSD at much higher rates than other occupations (e.g., King & DeLongis, 2014). People who suffer from PTSD often relive the experience through nightmares or intense flashbacks, have difficulty sleeping, have physical complaints, have flattened emotions, and feel detached or estranged from others. These symptoms can be severe enough and last long enough to significantly impair the person's daily life, such as having trouble with personal relationships or difficulty holding down a job.

- **Chronic stress** is another serious form of stress. It refers to stress that does not end. Day in and day out, chronic stress grinds us down until our resistance is gone. Serious systemic illnesses, such as diabetes, decreased immune system functioning, or cardiovascular disease, can result from chronic stress.

Health psychologists believe that stress has **additive effects**; that is, the effects of stress add up and accumulate in a person over time. Stress affects each person differently. We each perceive demands and pressures differently and have different resources or coping skills. Such individual differences in the stress process form a core issue for psychologists who study personality and health.

Primary and Secondary Appraisal

Not all people respond to stressors in the same way. Two people can experience the same event, yet one is devastated and completely overwhelmed, whereas the other accepts the event as a challenge and is mobilized into positive action. Differences among people in how they respond to the same event are possible because stress is not "out there" in the environment. Rather, stress is in the *subjective reaction* of the person to potential stressors (Lazarus & Folkman, 1984). This is worth emphasizing, because many people refer to an event as stressful, as if stress were a characteristic of the event. Instead, stress is actually the response to that event. For example, two people are taking the same organic chemistry course; they take the same exam, and they both fail. One person may be very stressed by this event, whereas the other may take it in stride and not feel at all stressed by the failure. How can the same event happen to two people, yet one responds with stress and the other does not?

According to psychologist Richard Lazarus (1991), in order for stress to be evoked for a person, two cognitive events must occur. The first cognitive event, which Lazarus called **primary appraisal**, involves the perception that the event is a threat to one's personal goals or is demanding in some way. The second necessary cognitive event, **secondary appraisal**, involves the determination that one does not have the resources to cope with the demands of the threatening event. If either of these appraisals is absent—if the person does not perceive the event as threatening, or if the person feels they have plenty of resources for coping with the threat—then stress is not evoked. For example, if an event, such as an upcoming exam, is perceived as threatening to someone's goals, yet the person feels they have the resources demanded by that event (i.e., the person has been studying and otherwise preparing for the exam), then the person might experience the event more as a challenge than as stress. Alternatively, the person might feel they do not have the resources demanded by the event (secondary appraisal) but might not think that the event is important to their long-term goals (primary appraisal) and so might not respond with stress.

Many personality traits, including the Big Five, have been linked to stress appraisal. Not surprisingly, neuroticism is highly correlated with stress appraisal and stress reactivity. People high in neuroticism are more likely to appraise events as threats (rather than challenges to be overcome), and they tend to describe and interpret stressful events as more severe and threatening compared to those lower in neuroticism. People high in extraversion, on the other hand, are less likely to perceive events as stressful and when they do, they are more likely to appraise them as challenges to be overcome (Bolger & Zuckerman, 1995; Roberts et al., 2007; Schneider et al., 2012). Though to a less significant degree, high levels of agreeableness, conscientiousness, and openness have also been associated with lower stress appraisal (Schneider et al., 2012; Soliemanifar et al., 2018).

What might lead some individuals to consistently avoid the stress response? What are some of the strategies that people use to overcome stress and the accompanying anxiety and feelings of being overwhelmed? Next we consider several personality dimensions that have been associated with resistance to stress.

 Concept Check

Name and describe three different varieties of stress. What is an example of each type?

What two cognitive events account for many of the individual differences in how people interpret potentially stressful situations?

Coping Strategies and Styles

Everyone has unpleasant events happen to them. We all have temporary setbacks, losses, and frustrations in our day-to-day lives. However, some people seem to cope better, to get over stressful events more quickly, or to somehow see such events as challenges rather than as sources of stress. One personality dimension that has been studied in relation to stress is explanatory style.

Explanatory Style

Explanatory style (also referred to as attributional style) is a dispositional way of explaining the causes of events. One way to examine explanatory style is to ask the question "Where does a person typically place the blame when things go wrong?" As introduced in Chapter 12, the three important dimensions of attribution are external versus internal, unstable versus stable, and specific versus global. Various measures have been developed for assessing people's typical explanatory style. One such measure is the Attributional Style Questionnaire (ASQ), developed by psychologist Chris Peterson[1] and his colleagues (1982). However, another very useful technique for scoring explanatory style is by analyzing the content of people's written or spoken explanations. People often spontaneously provide explanations for events in their everyday conversations or writings. It is possible to find these explanations in verbatim material and to rate them along the attributional dimensions of internality, stability, and globality. This technique for measuring explanatory style was also developed by Peterson and his colleagues (1992), who called it the Content Analysis of Verbatim Explanations (CAVE).

---

[1] While completing the 5th US edition of this textbook, Chris Peterson passed away suddenly in Ann Arbor, Michigan. Chris was a friend to some of us, and we will miss him. More importantly, the field of personality psychology has lost a creative and consistent contributor, one who was fascinated with the distinctly human part of human nature.

 Exercise

Find an online news story or blog post in which a person is explaining an event—perhaps a story about an accident, a natural disaster, or some sporting event. Analyze the story, paying particular attention to quotes from various people, to find examples of each of the three dimensions of explanatory style:

- **Internal versus external**
- **Stable versus unstable**
- **Global versus specific**

Come up with a characterization of the views on this event in terms of how people attribute responsibility.

The CAVE technique has the advantage of allowing the researcher to study participants who are either not available or not willing to participate in typical research, provided that such participants have made public some material containing causal explanations (Peterson, Seligman, & Vaillant, 1988). For example, political speeches often contain explanations for a great many events. And movie stars often do interviews that contain explanations for events in their lives. Psychotherapy tapes can be analyzed with CAVE, as they often contain persons' attributions for why things happened to them. Similarly, song lyrics, children's stories, descriptions of sports events, and myths and religious texts all contain explanations for events that can be rated for how internal, stable, and global they are.

Peterson, who has done a great deal of research on explanatory style, now prefers the term *optimism* to refer to this individual difference construct (Peterson, 2000). People who make stable, global, and internal explanations for bad events are seen as pessimists, whereas those who make unstable, specific, and external explanations for bad events are seen as optimists. Optimism/pessimism is viewed as a traitlike dimension along which people differ.

Optimism has several different definitions, and distinctions can be made among the different underlying constructs (Peterson & Chang, 2003). For example, the optimism construct employed by Peterson and colleagues (e.g., Peterson & Steen, 2002) refers to an explanatory style for bad events being due to unstable, specific, and external causes. However, a slightly different definition of optimism is offered by Scheier and Carver (1992; Carver & Scheier, 2000). These researchers emphasize **dispositional optimism** as the expectation that good events will be plentiful in the future, and that bad events will be rare in the future. For example, optimists are likely to believe that they will achieve success in most areas of their lives. This definition emphasizes not explanatory style but expectations for the future.

Another concept related to optimism, called self-efficacy, was developed by Bandura (1986). As discussed in Chapter 12, self-efficacy is the belief that one can engage in the behaviours necessary to achieve a desired outcome. Self-efficacy is also the confidence one has in the ability to perform the actions needed to achieve a specific outcome. For example, someone's belief and confidence that he or she can climb Mt. Everest—this subjective feeling, the positive expectation about performing the behaviours necessary to climb the mountain—is self-efficacy.

Finally, a fourth concept related to optimism concerns perceptions of risk. Imagine being asked to estimate the probability of various events happening to you, using a scale from 0 to 100; 0 means "it will never happen to me" and 100 means "it is certain to happen to me." The events you are asked to estimate are such things as dying in a plane crash, being diagnosed with cancer, having a heart attack, and being hit by lightning. Optimists perceive that they are at lower risk for such negative events than the average person is. What is interesting, however, is that most people generally underestimate their risks, with the average person rating his or her risk as below what is the true probability. This has been referred to as the **optimistic bias**, and it may actually lead people in general to ignore or minimize the risks inherent in life or to take more risks than they should. Nevertheless, people differ dramatically from each other in their perceptions of the risks associated with everyday life, with pessimistic individuals overestimating the risks, relative to optimistic individuals.

Optimism and Health

Many researchers using various definitions of optimism have been examining the correlation between this individual difference and health for decades. Research on optimism and health was recently subjected to a large meta-analysis by Rasmussen, Scheier, and Greenhouse (2010). As a summary, optimism was shown to predict good health as measured by self-report (subjective perceptions of health), objective measures of physical health, survival time after heart attacks, immune system functioning, better cancer outcomes, and longer life. Moreover, optimism appears to have some of its positive effects on health by influencing good health behaviours. In another meta-analysis, optimistic people were less likely to smoke cigarettes and more likely to exercise and eat a healthy diet (Boehm et al., 2018).

As with much personality research, the typical correlations between optimism and health or health behaviours tend to run between .20 and .30, with researchers typically describing effect sizes as modest. Interestingly, the association between optimism and subjective health appears greater than that between optimism and objective measures (Boehm et al., 2018; Rasmussen et al., 2010). Moreover, because this research is correlational, the causal mechanisms involved in the health–optimism link are not well understood. For example, optimism may relate to a lower likelihood of becoming ill, to developing an illness of a lesser severity, to a faster recovery, or to a decreased likelihood of relapse.

As an in-depth example of research on optimism and health, let's look at a study by Peterson, Seligman, and colleagues (1998). This study examined more than 1,000 individuals over almost a 50-year period. The researchers found that the participants who scored in the more pessimistic direction were more likely to die at an earlier age than the optimistic participants were. Because Peterson and colleagues had such a large sample, the researchers were able to look at various causes of death to see where optimists and pessimists most differed. The researchers thought that the biggest differences might be in deaths due to cancer and heart disease, and they predicted that pessimists would have more of these lethal medical problems. This was not the case, however. The researchers found that the real difference between the optimists and pessimists, in terms of the causes of death, was in the frequency of accidents and violent deaths, with pessimists having more accidental deaths and deaths due to violent causes, resulting in a generally shorter life span, on average, than that of the optimists. This effect was especially strong for the men in this sample.

It seems that pessimists, especially male pessimists, have a habit of being in the wrong place at the wrong time. This research does not actually tell us specifically what the participants were doing when they accidentally or violently died. However, it seems likely that they were in the wrong situation, and moreover it is likely that pessimists, especially males, frequently choose to be in the wrong situation. An anecdote told by Peterson and Bossio (2001) is about a person who says, "I broke my nose in two places," and someone responds, "Well,

I'd stay out of those two places if I were you." Pessimists, it appears, are frequently in those wrong places. This result has been replicated, with pessimistic explanatory style correlating with the frequency of occurrence of accidents (Peterson & Bossio, 2001). The link between pessimism and a greater likelihood of mishaps appeared to be due to a preference for potentially hazardous situations and activities on the part of pessimists. Perhaps pessimists are motivated to escape their gloomy moods by choosing exciting but risky situations and activities.

Because of optimism's apparent health benefits, psychologist Marty Seligman and his colleagues are attempting to develop therapeutic ways to increase people's level of optimism (2002; Seligman & Peterson, 2003). In particular, Seligman has introduced a "pessimism prevention" program for use in elementary schools, the details of which can be found in Weissberg, Kumpfer, and Seligman (2003). The program teaches cognitive and social problem-solving skills that are based on optimistic principles. It has been found to be effective at preventing symptoms of depression in low-income minority middle-school students (Cardemil, Reivich, & Seligman, 2002) and mainland Chinese adults (Yu & Seligman, 2002).

Generally speaking, positive emotions have consistently been shown to play an adaptive role in our encounters with stress, and in our ability to manage it effectively. Although being optimistic is one approach, it isn't the only one described by psychologists. We explore a number of ways to maintain positive emotions and better manage stress in A Closer Look: The Role of Positive Emotions in Coping with Stress.

 **A Closer Look**

The Role of Positive Emotions in Coping with Stress

The vast majority of the research on personality and health focuses on negative emotions and how they contribute to stress and illness. However, in recent years, some researchers have taken an interest in positive emotions and appraisals, as well as how these can have a protective function (for a review, see Tedeschi, Park, & Calhoun, 1998). The general hypothesis is that positive emotions and positive appraisals may lead to a reduced impact of stress on health (Lyubomirsky, 2001).

Several decades ago, Lazarus, Kanner, and Folkman (1980) speculated that positive emotions played three important roles in the stress process: (1) they may sustain coping efforts; (2) they may provide a break from stress; and (3) they may give people time and opportunity to restore depleted resources, including the restoration of social relationships. However, no one in health psychology gave serious attention to these ideas for almost two decades.

Psychologist Barbara Fredrickson has led the way in the search for the effects of positive emotions on stress and illness. She has proposed a "broaden and build model" of positive emotions, suggesting that positive emotions broaden the scope of attention, cognition, and action. This helps the person see more options in stressful situations, think about alternatives, and try different ways of coping with the stress. The "build" part of her model suggests that positive emotions help a person build up reserves of energy, as well as build up social resources, especially in terms of how positive emotions help a person build a social support network. She proposes that positive emotions are important in facilitating adaptive coping and adjustment to stress (Fredrickson, 1998, 2000). In experimental research, Fredrickson and Levenson (1998) found that the experience of positive emotions, following a period of acute stress, facilitated recovery from that stress. Specifically, these researchers examined cardiovascular reactivity to anxiety and threat manipulations, and they found that the participants who underwent a positive emotion following this stress showed faster heart rate and blood pressure recovery than did the participants who did not get the positive mood induction.

Psychologists Susan Folkman and Judith Moskowitz (2000) have built on Fredrickson's ideas and have suggested several important mechanisms in determining whether people will experience positive emotions during periods of severe stress. They give examples of these positive coping mechanisms from their study of gay men who were caregivers of partners dying from AIDS. Caring for someone with a chronic debilitating disease, such as AIDS or Alzheimer's disease, can be extremely stressful and often leads the caregiver to suffer physical costs from the stress and strain. From their study of caregivers, Folkman and Moskowitz identified three coping mechanisms that are capable of generating positive emotion during stress, as opposed to coping strategies that mainly provide relief from negative emotions.

The first positive coping strategy is called **positive reappraisal**, a cognitive process whereby a person focuses on the good in what is happening or has happened. Forms of this positive coping strategy include seeing opportunities for personal growth and seeing how one's own efforts can benefit other people. By changing how they interpret what is happening to them, people actually change the meaning of situations such that the adversity, in fact, gives them strength. In their study of caregivers, Folkman and Moskowitz found that the caregivers who were able to positively reappraise the situation (e.g., "I will emerge from this challenge a stronger and better person") showed better adjustment both during caregiving and even after the death of their partners (Moskowitz et al., 1996).

The second positive coping strategy identified by Folkman and colleagues (1997) is **problem-focused coping**, using thoughts and behaviours to manage or solve the underlying cause(s) of the stress. It has typically been assumed that this strategy is useful in situations in which a person has some control over the outcomes. However, Folkman and Moskowitz note how this strategy can be useful in situations that, on the surface, appear uncontrollable. In the caregiver study, many of the caregivers were caring for partners who were dying, a situation that could not be stopped, reversed, or even slowed. However, even in these seemingly uncontrollable conditions, some caregivers were able to focus on the things they could control. For example, many created "to-do" lists of little things, such as getting prescriptions filled, administering medications, and changing their partners' bed linens. Keeping such lists, and ticking off the completed items, gave the caregivers opportunities to feel effective and in control in an otherwise overwhelming situation. In short, focusing on solving problems, even little ones, can give a person a positive sense of control even in the most stressful and uncontrollable circumstances.

The third positive coping mechanism is called **creating positive events** and is defined as creating a positive time-out from the stress. This can be done in a number of ways. Often, all it takes is a moment to pause and reflect on something positive, such as a compliment received, a pleasing or humorous memory, or a sunset. These sorts of time-outs can give a person a momentary respite from the chronic stress. Many of the caregivers took time to remember positive events or to plan positive events, such as taking their partners for scenic drives. Some of the caregivers reported using humour to find some positive relief. It has long been thought that humour can be a tension reducer and that it may contribute to mental and physical health (Menninger, 1963).

This focus on positive emotions and their role in health and illness is relatively new, and the research is in very early stages. Many of the early findings are intriguing but also raise new questions for research. For example, do different kinds of positive emotions—such as excitement, happiness, or contentment—play different roles in the stress process? Are the positive emotions most helpful in coping with particular kinds of stress? And, finally, of particular interest to personality psychologists are questions about differences among people in the ability to generate positive emotions while coping with stress

(Affleck & Tennen, 1996). Who are the people who can generate humour, for example, during periods of coping? Are specific personality traits, such as extraversion or optimism, uniquely related to positive emotion coping styles? Can psychologists develop brief and targeted interventions to increase positive affect for persons experiencing serious life stress? Preliminary studies suggest that positive affect interventions are feasible and may be effective at helping people cope with stress (Moskowitz, 2011). These important questions point the way for personality researchers of the future, who will undertake the necessary studies to understand why it is that some people manage to survive disaster, hardship, and misfortune with some degree of positivity.

Management of Emotions and Disclosure

Sometimes we have emotions, and sometimes emotions have us. Emotions, especially negative ones, can be particularly difficult to control. Nevertheless, we can try to inhibit the expression of negative emotions, especially under certain circumstances. Imagine that your team just lost an important championship, and you are really unhappy, distressed, and in an irritable mood, angry at the referees and disappointed by your team. However, you have an important exam tomorrow, so you must inhibit your distracting unpleasant emotions and concentrate on studying. You can think of similar examples of **emotional inhibition**, such as controlling your anxiety or hiding the fact that you are disappointed. For example, have you ever received a gift you really didn't like? Perhaps you suppressed your disappointment and replaced it with some positive false emotions, smiled, and said, "Thanks a lot; I really wanted one of those."

We all have to cover up such disappointments once in a while. But what about people who routinely suppress their emotions, who keep everything inside? What are the consequences of chronically inhibiting one's emotions? Some theorists suggest that emotional inhibition leads to undesirable consequences. For example, Sigmund Freud (see Chapter 9) believed that most psychological problems were the result of inhibited negative emotions and motivations. That is, repression and the other defence mechanisms are ways of preventing an unacceptable emotion from surfacing and being directly experienced and expressed. The early psychoanalysts saw this suppression of emotion, the pushing of unacceptable desires or urges into the unconscious, as the root of all psychological problems. Psychoanalytic therapy, or the talking cure, was designed to bring unconscious emotion into conscious awareness, so that it could be experienced and expressed in a mature manner. Moreover, the therapeutic relationship was seen as a place to experience and express emotions that had long been inhibited. There are other therapies that might be called "expressive therapies" because their goal is to get the person to release inhibited emotions.

Other theorists see emotional inhibition more positively. From a developmental perspective, the ability to inhibit emotions is acquired at an early age, at around 3 years, and is seen as a major developmental achievement. This is when children, though sad, are able to stop themselves from crying or, when angry, can inhibit themselves from striking back (Kopp, 1989; Thompson, 1991). The ability to inhibit negative emotion is seen as a very useful skill to learn in childhood. Children need to learn to control temper outbursts, such as the urge to hit someone who takes a toy from them. We have all seen adults who don't do a very good job of controlling disappointment or frustration, and their behaviour (e.g., an adult temper tantrum) is often seen as childish. Some people are, however, very good at inhibiting negative emotions, even strong emotions.

What do research psychologists know about the effects of chronically inhibited emotion? Surprisingly, there have been only a few well-done studies that directly address this question. For example, psychologists

James Gross and Robert Levenson (1993, 1997; Gross, 2002) designed studies in which some of the participants were asked to suppress the expression of any emotions they were feeling while they watched a video designed to evoke the emotions of happiness (a comedy routine), then sadness (scenes from the funeral of a child, showing a distraught and highly emotional mother). Half of the participants were randomly assigned to the suppression condition, in which they were told, "If you have any feelings as you watch the [video,] please try your best not to let those feelings show. In other words, try to behave in a way that a person watching you would not know you were feeling anything at all." The other half of the participants were assigned to the no-suppression condition, in which they were simply told to watch the video and were given no instructions to inhibit their emotions.

While the participants watched the video, the researchers recorded them to determine how much they expressed their emotions while watching it. The researchers also collected several physiological measures, such as those we discussed in Chapter 7. They also asked the participants to report on their feelings after each segment of the video.

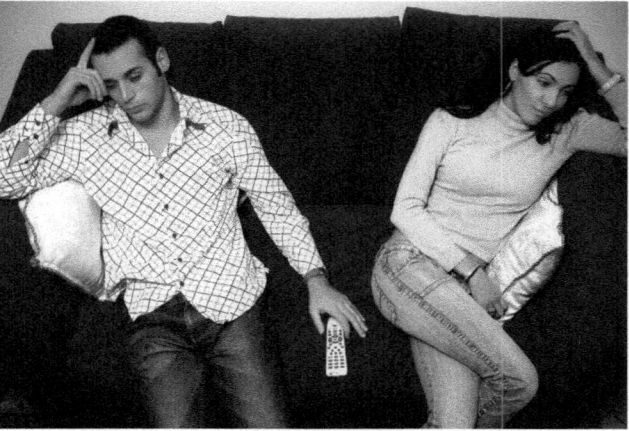

Canadian research on coping has underscored the importance of relationship-focused coping strategies when dealing with interpersonal stress. When spouses or partners respond to each other by being empathic and understanding, conflict is more likely to be reduced and marital satisfaction improves over time. Individuals high on neuroticism tend to engage in less adaptive relationship-focused responses, such as confrontation.
©Ingram Publishing

Results showed that the participants who were instructed to suppress their emotions showed increased levels of physiological arousal, even before the video began, compared with the no-suppression participants. This widespread physiological arousal was interpreted as indicating that the participants were preparing for the effort necessary to suppress their emotions. The suppression participants also showed heightened physiological activity during the video, indicating increased sympathetic nervous system arousal, compared with the no-suppression participants. The researchers suggested that suppression of emotion takes effort and exerts physiological costs above and beyond the emotional arousal. The participants in the suppression condition showed less *outward* expression of emotion than did the control participants, as you would imagine. For example, the facial expressions of the suppression participants displayed little emotion, suggesting that they were, in fact, inhibiting the outward expression of their emotions, as instructed. As for the self-report, the suppression participants reported slightly less amusement in the amusement condition, but not less sadness in the sadness condition, compared with the no-suppression participants.

In an interesting line of research on emotion, Gross and colleagues (Ochsner et al., 2002) attempted to locate the emotional control centre in the brain. They used fMRI to scan participants' brains while the participants tried to reinterpret a highly negative scene in unemotional terms. They found that several brain areas were associated with the successful regulation of negative emotions. These areas were mainly in the prefrontal cortex of the brain. This frontal part of the brain, which is also involved in planning and executive control, appears to be active when people are controlling their emotions. Interestingly, this is the area that was destroyed in the case of Phineas Gage, discussed in Chapter 7. Recall that Mr. Gage, after his accident, had difficulty controlling his negative emotions, took up cursing in public, was quick to anger, and frequently insulted people.

Sometimes it is necessary to inhibit feelings. Perhaps you do not want to hurt someone's feelings; perhaps you do not want to antagonize someone in a position of power; or perhaps you do not want to anger someone who is already acting aggressively (Larsen & Prizmic, 2004). For example, your boss may be upset with you for the wrong reason, and you may feel angry toward her. However, you cannot act out that anger because she is your boss and has a lot of power over you in terms of raises, workload, and working conditions. Quite simply, there are some situations in life in which it is wise to choose to hide feelings.

However, problems can arise when emotional inhibition becomes chronic, when a person routinely hides emotions. Someone who characteristically inhibits the free expression of emotion may experience greater stress and suffer the effects of chronic sympathetic nervous system arousal. For example, people who keep their negative emotions to themselves are more likely than expressive individuals to report poor physical health and display evidence of a suppressed immune system (Slatcher & Pennebaker, 2007). Cancer patients who express their negative emotions, and who emotionally fight their disease, sometimes live longer than patients who accept their situation, inhibit their emotions, and quietly accept their treatment (Levy, 1990; Levy & Heiden, 1990).

Other studies suggest that emotional expressiveness is good for our psychological health and general adjustment. King and Emmons (1990) had participants keep daily records of how they were feeling each day for three consecutive weeks. The participants completed a questionnaire measure of emotional expressiveness. The researchers found that emotional expressiveness correlated with higher levels of happiness over the three weeks, as well as with lower levels of anxiety and guilt. Indeed a great deal of literature has supported both mental and physical health benefits associated with emotionally expressive writing (Baikie & Wilhelm, 2005).

Disclosure

Related to emotional expressiveness is the topic of **disclosure**, or telling someone about a private aspect of oneself. Many theorists have suggested that keeping things to ourselves, not opening up to other people, may be a source of stress and ultimately may lead to psychological distress and physical disease. These theorists have further argued that being open to others with our feelings may be curative, that talk therapy may work in part because through it we uncover secrets and reveal what we have been keeping to ourselves.

Psychologist James Pennebaker has been a pioneer in researching the effects of disclosure. In a typical study, he asks participants to think of an upsetting or traumatic event that has happened to them, something they have not discussed with anyone. He asks them to write down these secrets. People write about many different unpleasant events, such as various embarrassing moments, sexual indiscretions, illegal or immoral behaviours, humiliations, and so on. It is interesting that *all* participants quickly come up with a secret that they have been keeping. This suggests that probably all of us have some secrets.

Pennebaker argues that *not* discussing traumatic, negative, or upsetting events can lead to problems. It takes physical energy, he says, to inhibit the thoughts and feelings associated with such events. In other words, it is not easy to keep a secret to ourselves, and keeping something in, especially if it is a major trauma, is upsetting and takes a lot of energy. Over time, this stress builds and, like all stress, can increase the likelihood of stress-related problems, such as trouble sleeping, irritability, physical symptoms (e.g., stomachaches and headaches), and even illness resulting from lowered immune system functioning. Telling the secret (or simply writing about it), according to Pennebaker, relieves this stress.

Pennebaker and his colleagues have conducted many studies on the topic of disclosure. In one study (Pennebaker, 1990), participants were postsecondary students who were randomly assigned to one of two groups. One group was asked to recall and write about an experience that they found distressing. The other group was asked to write about a trivial topic, such as what they normally ate for breakfast. The students wrote about their assigned topic for 15 minutes each night for four consecutive nights. The participants writing about the traumatic event reported feeling more distress and discomfort while writing, and measures of blood pressure taken while writing suggested they were feeling more stress than was the trivial topic group. Six months later, the participants were contacted again and a health history was obtained. Students who had written about a trauma for those four days had had fewer illnesses in the subsequent six months, compared with the students who had written about trivial topics. Moreover, student records from the health services showed that the participants who had written about trauma had indeed gone to the campus health centre less often than the participants who had written about trivial topics. Interestingly, just the act of writing about an upsetting event, even if no one ever reads the writing, may have a beneficial effect on health.

Physical and mental health benefits of written emotional disclosure have also been observed in cancer patients (Cepeda et al., 2008), individuals diagnosed with eating disorders (Weber et al., 2006), and those with post-traumatic stress disorder (Sloan et al., 2015). Other studies have shows that people who keep unpleasant information about themselves a secret are more likely to develop anxiety or depression than are those who tell someone (Larson & Chastain, 1990). Often, psychotherapists will ask their clients, especially those who have experienced a trauma or another extreme event, to talk or write about that trauma. Some psychologists even recommend keeping a diary of the events in one's life and how one is reacting to those events. Such a daily self-disclosure helps put one's feelings into perspective and make some sense out of the events in one's life. One study, designed to test how little disclosure is necessary to still achieve health benefits, found that two minutes of writing on two consecutive days produced measurable health benefits assessed four to six weeks later (Burton & King, 2008).

> **❓ Exercise**
>
> **Try conducting a small experimental test of Pennebaker's hypothesis that disclosing secrets, even in writing, is associated with better health. Keep a record of your health every day for two weeks. Record each day whether you have a stomachache, a headache, muscle aches, a sore throat, or a runny nose. After this baseline period of recording your health, try keeping a diary each day for two weeks, writing down and describing all the stresses you experience each day and reflecting on how these make you feel. Pay attention to any difficulties, stress, or even embarrassing or trying moments. When the two weeks are over, stop keeping the diary and begin recording your daily health again. Although this is not a true experiment (you are both the subject and the experimenter, which is not done in true experiments), you can nevertheless get a feel for how research on this topic is done, and you might see a change in your health for the better as a function of keeping a diary.**

How does disclosure work to promote healthy adjustment? Pennebaker's first theory of the mechanism concerned the relief that results from telling a secret. In other words, keeping the information inside takes effort and is stressful, and disclosing that information removes the effort and relieves the stress (Niederhoffer & Pennebaker, 2002). This explanation basically argues that disclosure reduces the cost of having to inhibit this information. Pennebaker (2003a) later proposed a second explanation for how disclosure promotes adjustment. This explanation concerns how writing about an event allows a person to reinterpret and reframe the meaning of that event. In other words, a person writing or talking about a past traumatic event can try to better understand that event, search for some positive meaning in the event, and integrate that event into their current situation. Both processes—relief from inhibition and reinterpretation of the event—may be occurring, and so both explanations may be correct. Indeed, Pennebaker (2003b) has speculated that this combination may be the basic ingredient that underlies most forms of successful talking therapy.

There is considerable evidence that expressing our emotions in words can produce some stress-alleviating effects. Moreover, it appears that it does not matter how we put our feelings into words—whether we talk to a trusted friend or relative, go to a professional psychotherapist, have a discussion with our significant other, or write it in a diary. Although generally effective, disclosure is but one of many ways to cope with stress within a social or interpersonal context. We review additional methods of relationship-oriented coping in Highlight On Canadian Research: Coping in a Social Context: Relationship-Focused Coping and the Role of Personality.

 ## Highlight on Canadian Research

Coping in a Social Context: Relationship-Focused Coping and the Role of Personality

Richard Lazarus and his colleagues originally proposed two categories of coping to describe the various ways in which people manage stress. These included problem-focused coping strategies, which involve efforts to deal with a threat or demand head on, and **emotion-focused coping**, efforts aimed at managing the emotional effects of stress (Lazarus & Folkman, 1984). Making a list of "pros and cons" when faced with a tough decision is an example of problem-focused coping. In contrast, attempting to deal with feelings of fear and anxiety by engaging in such strategies as denial and avoidance would constitute emotion-focused coping. Although this is one of many methods for classifying and organizing coping strategies, it has retained the support of many psychologists and researchers for decades.

More recently, Canadian researchers at the University of British Columbia have provided support for a third category of coping: **relationship-focused coping**. Anita DeLongis and her colleagues proposed relationship-focused coping as an extension to traditional problem-focused and emotion-focused functions. Relationship-focused coping efforts involve the regulation and maintenance of social relationships during stressful events. Common relationship-focused strategies that tend to be more adaptive include empathy, compromise, and support (DeLongis & O'Brien, 1990). For instance, responding to a partner in an empathic and understanding way while also considering their perspective has been shown to minimize conflict during laboratory interactions between spouses. Such relationship-focused strategies seem to also predict lower levels of next-day marital tension, indicating that there's a lasting effect. It was recognized early on that managing relationships is just as important as managing one's emotions or the problem itself during stressful times. In research, findings have shown that the consideration of relationship-focused coping strategies significantly improves the predictive value of models of coping. In other words, researchers can be more accurate in their estimation of the outcomes of stress when this third coping category is examined (O'Brien & DeLongis, 1996). Of course, as is true of all categories of coping, many strategies tend to be more or less adaptive than others. Withdrawal, confrontation, and blame are examples of negative forms of relationship-focused coping. In committed relationships and in marriage, withdrawing from one's partner and isolating oneself seems to be especially harmful to both short-term and long-term functioning of the relationship (DeLongis & Holtzman, 2005; King & DeLongis, 2013; King & DeLongis, 2014).

Research by DeLongis and her colleagues has further suggested that this behaviour, *interpersonal withdrawal*, is more common among individuals who are high on neuroticism (Lee-Baggley et al., 2005). As we have previously reviewed in this text, neuroticism is characterized by a tendency to experience greater negative affect, including anxiety, depression, hostility, and self-consciousness. In regards to stress perception and reactivity, individuals higher on neuroticism generally describe stressful events as more threatening and demanding. This includes stressful experiences of an interpersonal or relational nature, such as conflict. To date, studies of coping have suggested an increased likelihood of people high on neuroticism to engage in emotion-focused coping strategies that involve hostility, passivity, and indecisiveness, such as rumination (McCrae & Costa, 1987). This reflects not only the quality of the emotions experienced by people high on neuroticism, but also the accompanying emotional variability and unpredictability.

In examining the role of neuroticism in relationship-focused coping, DeLongis and colleagues observed less frequent use of adaptive strategies like compromise and more frequent use of maladaptive strategies like confrontation and blame. This is not surprising given the nature of neuroticism. However, the results can be quite problematic for relationships, and for partners of people high in neuroticism. In marital relationships, those high in neuroticism tend to make more negative attributions, responding less constructively to spousal tension (Karney et al., 1994) and experiencing more negative social interactions (Davey et al., 2001). This means that daily relationship functioning is already compromised when one or more partners is high on this Big Five trait. When individuals high on neuroticism then attempt to address issues or manage stress with their partner, as in relationship-focused coping, things may indeed worsen. It is important that psychology researchers and clinicians continue to identify specific adaptive strategies in which to engage during relationship conflict.

Hardiness and Resilience

An important consideration in the association between personality and coping is how people tend to cope with stress overall. In other words, looking at a person's life in its entirety, do they tend to deal fairly well with stress? Do they overcome things relatively quickly? Or do they suffer more from some of the long-term effects of stress, often taking longer to recover from negative experiences? To help summarize individual differences in this regard, psychologists have described what they call a **hardy personality** (Kobasa, 1979). People with hardy personalities are better able to "resist" the negative effects of stress and cope more effectively over time. Hardiness has been suggested to involve three main traits:

- *Control.* Hardy people see themselves as being in control of their lives, rather than being controlled by external factors.
- *Commitment.* Hardy people are involved with the world around them, set goals that they pursue, and have a strong sense of purpose.
- *Challenge.* Hardy people see challenges as problems to be overcome rather than as threats or stressors.

Psychological resilience is very similar to the notion of hardiness. It refers to positive adaptation and successful coping after a stressful or adverse situation (Hopf, 2010). Although it is difficult to reduce to a single quality or trait, some people tend to be more resilient over time. In other words, they tend to cope with stress more effectively overall and recover faster, often without experiencing any lasting impact on their health or well-being. As a broad personality trait, Major and colleagues (1998) suggest that resilience involves three main aspects of personality: *high self-esteem*, *high optimism*, and a sense of *personal control* in life. Interestingly, it has been suggested by some psychologists that most people are pretty resilient; that as a species we are able to deal relatively effectively with the stress we encounter in our daily lives, even when it is traumatic in nature (Bonanno & Diminich, 2013). Though a number of other factors have been associated with resilience and hardiness, social support appears to be quite important, such that people who perceive being well supported are more resilient than those who do not (Southwick et al., 2016).

As demonstrated in a meta-analysis by Oshio and colleagues (2018), resilience is further associated with lower neuroticism and higher levels of extraversion, agreeableness, conscientiousness, and openness to experience. Similar associations have been observed between the Big Five traits and hardiness (Eschleman, Bowling, & Alarcon, 2010). Certain levels of key personality traits seem to be more or less helpful when it comes to coping with stress. High neuroticism, low extraversion, low agreeableness, low conscientiousness, and low openness have each been associated with less effective coping. And people high in neuroticism tend to engage in a greater variety of unsuccessful coping strategies over time (Lee-Baggley et al., 2005). Perhaps not surprisingly, those high in conscientiousness tend to engage in more active, problem-focused coping, while those higher in extraversion and agreeableness use their relationships more during stress, are more likely to seek support, and display higher positive reappraisal. Higher openness to experience is also associated with positive reappraisal, as well as the use of humour during stressful times (Lee-Baggley et al., 2005). Personality appears to be related to coping in a variety of ways.

 Concept Check

What are two key behaviours or factors in personality that are associated with effective coping?

How would you describe a "hardy" personality? What is the association between resilience and the Big Five traits?

Type A Personality and Cardiovascular Disease

Cardiovascular disease is the second leading cause of death in Canada, beaten only by cancer (Statistics Canada, 2018). Due to the related disability and impact on life expectancy, health professionals have long been interested in identifying factors that put people at risk for this disease. Known risk factors for developing cardiovascular disease include high blood pressure, obesity, smoking, family history of heart disease, inactive lifestyle, and high cholesterol. In the 1970s, physicians began to consider a new risk factor, a specific personality trait. As mentioned in Chapter 13, this grew out of the observation by some physicians that the patients who had had heart attacks often behaved differently, and they seemed to have different personalities compared with other patients. The heart attack patients were often more competitive and aggressive, more active and energetic in their actions and speaking, and more ambitious and driven (Friedman & Rosenman, 1974). They called this collection of behaviours the Type A personality.

Before examining some of the research findings on Type A, let us look at a few misconceptions. Although researchers often refer to Type A and Type B individuals, it is not true that people come in these two distinct categories. Biological sex is an example of a categorical variable; blood type is another. However, very few personality traits are so strictly categorical. Instead, most are dimensional, ranging from one extreme to the other, with most people falling somewhere around the middle. The Type A/Type B distinction is like this, with Type As defining one end and Type Bs the other, and a large number of people in the middle, who are not clearly A or B. Thus, the Type A personality variable is a trait, or disposition, as discussed in Chapter 3. It is distributed normally, as in Figure 18.4(a), not as a category variable. Psychologists describe normally distributed traits by reference to one end (e.g., Type A). However, by describing the characteristics of people at one end, it is implied that people at the low end (so-called Type B) have the opposite characteristics.

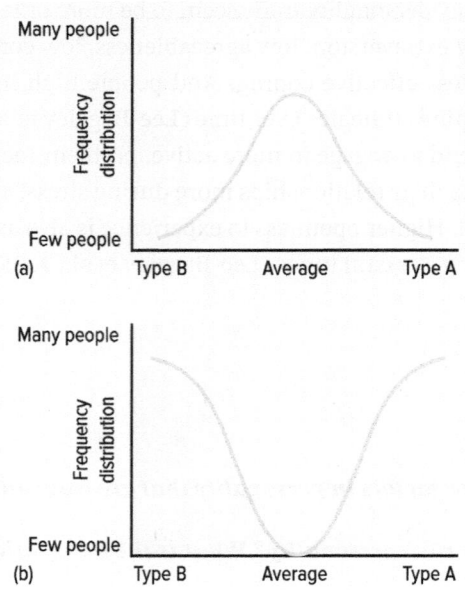

FIGURE 18.4 Type A and Type B are not really types at all and do not refer to categories of people. Rather, *Type A* refers to a normal distribution of people, anchored at one end by individuals showing a lot of Type A behaviour and at the other end by individuals showing very little (a). Most people, however, are in the middle, or average, range. This is the case with almost all personality traits. A true type, or categorical variable, would be distributed as in (b), with most people at one end or the other and very few people in the middle. This is not the case with the Type A personality.

Another misconception is that Type A is a single trait; in actuality, Type A is a syndrome of several traits. More specifically, it is a collection of three subtraits, which together make up the Type A personality. One of these three subtraits is **competitive achievement motivation**. Type A individuals like to work hard and achieve goals. They like recognition, power, and the defeat of obstacles. And they feel that they are at their best when competing with others. For example, a person who shows up at a charity bike-a-thon ready for the Tour de France bicycle race is exhibiting competitive achievement motivation. **Time urgency** is the second subtrait of the Type A behaviour pattern. Type A individuals hate wasting time. They are always in a hurry and feel under pressure to get the most done in the least amount of time. Often, they do two things at once, such as eat while reading a book. Red lights are their enemies, and they hate to wait in line for anything. The third subtrait of Type A is **hostility**. When blocked from attaining their goals, which is the definition of **frustration**, Type A people can be hostile and aggressive. They get frustrated easily, and this frustration can make them act in an unfriendly or even malicious manner. The person you see yelling and pounding on a vending machine is perhaps displaying the hostile component of his Type A personality style.

Early studies of the Type A personality found that it was an independent risk factor for developing cardiovascular disease. An independent risk factor operates independently from other known risk factors, such as being overweight or smoking. Thus, for example, it is not true that Type A people necessarily smoke more and that their smoking causes heart disease. Instead, the Type A personality is independent of smoking, and someone who is Type A and smokes is at more of a risk for heart disease than someone who just smokes or who is just Type A. In fact, one study found that the Type A personality was a better predictor of heart disease than the person's history of smoking or the person's cholesterol level (Jenkins, Zyzanski, & Rosenman, 1976).

Physicians conducted most of the early studies of Type A personality, and to measure this personality variable they developed a structured interview. Standard questions were asked, and the

Frequently doing two activities at once is a component of the Type A personality. Time urgency, however, is not the part of Type A that is most associated with heart disease.
©Fancy/SuperStock

interviewer noted the participants' answers and how they reacted to the questions. In fact, the interviewer was very interested in the behaviour of the participants. For example, what was the tempo of their speech? Did they frequently interrupt the interviewer or put words in the interviewer's mouth? Did they fidget during the interview? Did they make frequent and vigorous gestures with their hands and heads? In one part of the interview, the interviewer tries to aggravate the participants by talking very slowly. Type A people are especially aggravated when other people talk slowly, and they interrupt, talk out of turn, or finish sentences for people in order to speed them up.

As research on Type A personality gained momentum in the 1980s, researchers tried to devise a more efficient measure. Interviews are slow; they can measure only one person at a time, and it takes one interviewer to measure each participant. In short, interviewing is a relatively expensive and time-consuming way to measure any personality variable. Questionnaires are much cheaper because they are generally faster, they can be given to whole groups of participants, and one person can assess 100 or more subjects at a time. Thus, researchers in this area put some effort into developing a questionnaire measure for Type A personality. One of the most widely used questionnaire measures of Type A personality is the Jenkins Activity Survey. It contains questions that tap into each of the three components of the Type A syndrome— for example, "My work improves as the deadline approaches," "I have been told that I eat too fast," and "I enjoy a good competition."

Early researchers using the structured interview often found a relationship between Type A personality and risk for heart attack and cardiovascular disease. Later research, mostly using the Jenkins questionnaire, often failed to replicate this finding. This puzzled researchers for several years. Some wondered if Type A personality was a risk factor for heart attacks at one time, but then things changed so that it no longer was a risk factor. Other psychologists began to take a close look at the studies, searching for a reason why some found a relationship but others didn't. Quickly the pattern emerged that the studies using the questionnaire measure were less likely to find a relationship between Type A and heart disease than the studies using the structured interview (Suls & Wan, 1989; Suls, Wan, & Costa, 1996). Researchers have concluded that the questionnaire measure taps into different aspects of Type A behaviour than does the structured interview measure. Apparently, the structured interview gets more at the lethal component of Type A. But which part of the Type A behaviour pattern is the most lethal, the part that is most related to heart disease?

Hostility: The Lethal Component of the Type A Behaviour Pattern

You will recall that the Type A personality really is a syndrome, a collection of three subtraits, which often, but not always, occur together in the same individuals. For example, a person could have time urgency and high achievement motive, but not have the hostility component. When the interview measure of Type A was developed by physicians, it tended to emphasize the assessment of hostility and aggression. For example, it assessed whether the participants got frustrated when the physicians talked slowly, whether they swore during the interview, or whether they actively gestured or pounded the table. Later, when questionnaire measures were developed, more of an emphasis was placed on the time urgency and achievement components. For example, did the participants say they were always in a hurry, that they worked better as deadlines got closer, or that they achieved more than their peers?

As researchers began to use questionnaires more and more (because they were faster, easier, and cheaper to administer than the interviews), evidence began to accumulate, showing that general Type A personality did not predict heart disease. Researchers then compared the interviews with the questionnaires and learned that the interview method tapped more of the hostility component than the questionnaire method. As such, researchers began testing the hypothesis that it was really the more specific trait of hostility, rather than the general syndrome of Type A personality, that was the better predictor of heart disease.

What do researchers mean by the trait of hostility? People high in hostility are not necessarily violent or outwardly aggressive. They are not necessarily even assertive or demanding of others. Instead, such people are likely to react disagreeably to disappointments, frustrations, and inconveniences. Frustration can be understood as the subjective feeling that comes when you are blocked from an important goal. For example, you want a cold drink from the vending machine and it takes your money but does not give you the drink you request. This is frustrating. A hostile person reacts to such frustrations with disagreeable behaviour, attacking the machine or swearing and kicking the garbage can before walking away angrily. Hostile people are easily irritated, even by small frustrations, such as when they misplace their car keys or have to wait in line at the grocery store. In such situations, hostile people can become visibly upset, sometimes becoming rude and uncooperative or even antagonistic.

Several studies have now established that hostility is a strong predictor of cardiovascular disease (see meta-analysis by Chida & Steptoe, 2009). In fact, psychologists Dembrowski and Costa (1987) demonstrated that even a questionnaire measure of the specific trait of hostility is a better predictor of artery disease than are questionnaire measures of Type A. Recent studies have also shown that hostility is associated with systemic inflammation, as indicated by elevated blood leukocyte counts, also known as white blood cell counts (Surtees et al., 2003). Physicians have long known that chronic inflammation is related to risk for coronary disease, and so have recommended that people at risk take an Aspirin a day, because Aspirin reduces inflammation. Chronic inflammation may be the pathway whereby hostility is linked to the health endpoint of cardiovascular disease.

The good news about this research is that not everything about being Type A is bad for the heart and arteries. Given that hostility is apparently the lethal component, can we envision a "healthy" version of the Type A personality? It's okay to strive for success and achievement, but one should avoid being hostile and aggressive along the way. It's okay to be in a hurry and strive to get as much done as possible, but one should avoid getting frustrated and angry when it becomes difficult to accomplish everything. And it's okay to enjoy a competition as long as it's friendly, not hostile. It may even be good therapy to get into the longest and slowest line at the store and just try to relax, take it easy, and not feel hostile or angry in such situations (Wright, 1988). Davidson and colleagues (2007) estimate that brief hostility-management therapy can result in cost savings for hospitals by reducing hospitalization expenses associated with coronary care.

How the Arteries Are Damaged by Hostile Type A Behaviour

How does Type A behaviour, particularly the hostility component, produce its toxic effects on the heart and arteries? Strong feelings of hostility and aggression produce the fight-or-flight response. Part of this response is an increase in blood pressure, accompanied by a constriction of the arteries, plus an increase in heart rate and in the amount of blood pumped out with each heartbeat. In short, the person's body suddenly pumps more blood through smaller arteries. These changes can produce wear and tear on the inside lining of the arteries, causing microscopic tears and abrasions. These abrasions then become sites at which cholesterol and fat can become attached. In addition to this mechanical wear and tear on the artery walls, stress hormones released into the blood

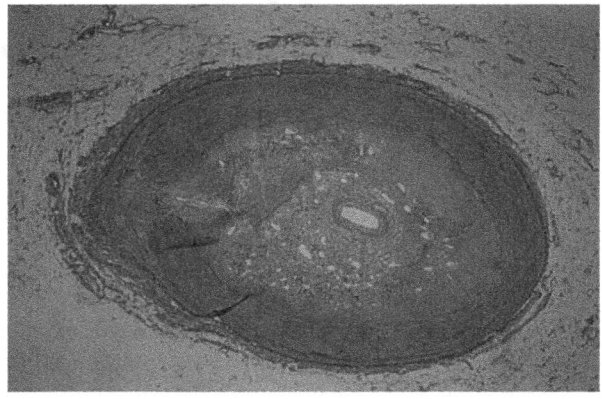

A cross-section of a human coronary artery, the artery that feeds the heart muscle itself, showing extreme arteriosclerosis. Here, the artery diameter has narrowed dramatically by the buildup of plaque on the inside artery wall.
©Martin M. Rotker/Science Source

during the fight-or-flight response may lead to artery damage and subsequent buildup of fatty deposits on the artery walls. As these fat molecules build up on the inside of the arteries, the arteries become progressively narrower. This is called **arteriosclerosis**, or hardening or blocking of the arteries. When the arteries that feed the heart muscle itself become blocked, the subsequent shortage of blood to the heart is called a heart attack.

In summary, research on the Type A personality has taken some interesting twists and turns. It all began with a couple of cardiologists noticing certain personality differences between heart attack patients and other medical patients. This led them to define the Type A personality as consisting of three characteristics: competitive achievement motivation, time urgency, and hostility. After several decades of research, psychologists have found that hostility is the most toxic component of the Type A personality, and most research on cardiovascular disease and personality today is focusing on specific traits. Understanding how hostility develops and is maintained, how exactly it damages the arteries, how it is evoked by specific situations, and how it can be overcome or managed are all important questions for future personality researchers.

Research on personality and heart disease has revealed that in addition to hostility and Type A, there is also a Type D or "distressed" personality that increases the risk of cardiovascular disease. Read more about the Type D personality in A Closer Look: Type D Personality and Heart Disease.

 ## A Closer Look

Type D Personality and Heart Disease

The Type A trait, and especially the hostility component, shows a modest correlation with the risk of developing coronary artery disease. Researchers have nevertheless been examining other personality factors that might relate to heart disease, especially in terms of how quickly the disease progresses or the survival rate after suffering a heart attack. Many people have early-stage indicators of heart problems, such as high blood pressure, minor artery blockage, or even progressive heart failure. Some of these people, but not all, will go on to full-blown heart attacks or death from their heart disease. Researchers are asking whether specific personality factors, other than Type A, predict the progression of heart disease once it has started.

A trait receiving a good deal of attention currently is called **Type D personality**, or "distressed" personality (e.g., Denollet, 2000). Just like Type A, the Type D trait is not truly a type; instead, it refers to a dimension along which individuals differ. In the case of Type D, it refers to two underlying traits. One of the traits is *negative affectivity*, defined as the tendency to frequently experience negative emotions across time and situations, including such unpleasant emotions as tension, worry, irritability, and anxiety. It is very similar to the trait of neuroticism and includes, in addition to a high frequency of negative emotions, a negative view of oneself, a tendency to complain, and finding oneself reacting more than usual to stressful situations. The second trait underlying the Type D construct is *social inhibition*, or the tendency to inhibit the expression of emotions, thoughts, and behaviours in social interactions. People high on social inhibition feel insecure or apprehensive in the company of others and worry about social evaluation and being the target of disapproval from others. Consequently, they inhibit themselves when around others and keep people at a distance. They are less likely to seek social support when they have problems. They also appear to have difficulties identifying emotions and describing their feelings to others (Epifanio et al., 2018).

Denollet (2005) published a brief 14-item self-report personality questionnaire to measure the Type D construct. Items that assess the negative affectivity part of this construct include "I often make a fuss about unimportant things," "I am often in a bad mood," and "I often find myself worrying about something." Items that assess the social inhibition component of Type D include "I find it hard to start a conversation," "I often feel inhibited in social interactions," and "When socializing, I don't find the right things to talk about." Because this scale is short and convenient to use, its publication has stimulated research on the Type D personality dimension.

Research on Type D suggests that these two traits—negative affectivity and social inhibition—act synergistically to put cardiac patients at risk for further adverse cardiac events (Denollet et al., 2006). This means that high levels of *both* traits have to be found in the same person to put that individual at risk for further cardiac problems. For example, Denollet and colleagues (2003) studied 400 cardiac outpatients (aged 31–79 years) who had some degree of coronary artery blockage. These patients were followed up 6 to 10 years later to determine survival status. During this time, 38 patients had died, mostly of cardiac disease. Patients who were high on the Type D trait were about four times more likely to die during this follow-up time period compared to the cardiac patients low on the Type D trait.

Kupper and Denollet (2007) reviewed several studies conducted by Denollet and colleagues showing that among people with coronary artery disease, the Type D personality dimension is associated with poorer health outcomes, such as increased mortality and faster progression of the disease. A meta-analysis of 15 studies concluded that Type D personality has a small though reliable association with major adverse cardiac events (O'Dell et al., 2011), a conclusion that was reiterated in a review by Kupper and Denollet (2018). Pelle and colleagues (2008), for instance, examined 368 patients with coronary artery disease who were undergoing a program in cardiac rehabilitation (e.g., prescribed exercises, stress management techniques, improving diet, weight loss, and smoking cessation). Most patients showed some improvement in health after completing the cardiac rehabilitation program. However, patients high on the Type D dimension had poorer health status after the rehabilitation program than did patients low on Type D.

Given that cardiac patients high on the Type D personality dimension show greater risk for poor outcomes than patients who are low on this dimension, an important question concerns the mechanism underlying this effect: How is it that the personality trait increases the risk for negative outcomes? Ongoing research is attempting to answer this question, and two mechanisms appear to be likely candidates. One mechanism involves disturbances in the brain's stress response, with high Type D individuals showing an exaggerated stress response evidenced by higher levels of cortisol in their blood. **Cortisol**, often referred to as the "stress hormone," is released during the stress response and if high levels occur over time, it can increase inflammation in the arteries, leading to the buildup of blockages in the arteries (Whitehead et al., 2007). The association between Type D and physical health is mediated by measures of inflammatory burden (Mommersteeg et al., 2012).

A second mechanism whereby the Type D personality dimension may result in poorer outcomes for cardiac patients is through lifestyle factors, including health-related behaviours and social support. For example, Williams and colleagues (2008) found that Type D subjects were less likely to eat sensibly, spent less time outdoors, were more bothered by events in their daily lives, and were less likely to get medical checkups than those who are low on the Type D scale. Just as important, people with the Type D personality dimension reported lower levels of perceived social support compared to non-Type D individuals. Other findings suggest that the Type D trait may affect health through poorer health behaviours and lower social support (Gilmour & Williams, 2012). Understanding if and how personality affects cardiac health is an active and exciting area of research.

 Concept Check

Define Type A personality. Which aspect of Type A is most associated with cardiovascular disease?

In contrast to Type A, what is Type D personality?

Summary and Evaluation

This chapter focused on the part of personality psychology related to physical adjustment and health. We began with several models of the personality and illness link. We then examined the concept of stress as the subjective reaction to extreme events, which often involve conflicting feelings, and over which one has little or no control. The stress response comes in four distinct varieties: acute, episodic acute, chronic, and traumatic. Traumatic stress can evolve into a disorder, called posttraumatic stress disorder, in which the person experiences nightmares or flashbacks, difficulties sleeping and other somatic problems, and feelings of being detached from reality or estranged from other people. It is important to realize that stress is not in the event but in how one appraises the event. Primary appraisal concerns an evaluation of how threatening the event is with respect to a person's goals and desires. Secondary appraisal concerns an evaluation of the person's own resources for meeting the challenge of the threatening event. Both of these appraisals are important for understanding how events come to elicit the stress response. Research is exploring the role of positive emotions in coping with chronic stress.

Much of the work on personality and stress began with a focus on major life events, such as losing a loved one or getting fired from one's job. Although serious, such events are relatively rare. More insidious are daily hassles, the relatively minor but frequent frustrations and disappointments of daily life. Stress researchers have begun to focus on these daily stressors in terms of their impact on health.

Personality psychologists have been concerned with understanding why some people appear more resistant to stress than others. That is, some people appear to take frustration and disappointment more in stride and do not suffer the deleterious health consequences often associated with chronic stress. One personality dimension in this regard is optimism, which has a wealth of findings associating it with stress resistance, good health, competent immune functioning, and longer life expectancy. Psychologists are developing grade school programs to train people to be more optimistic. Some related personality characteristics associated with generally better health prognosis are emotional expressivity and personal disclosure. Certain people tend to be more resilient overall (what is sometimes referred to as hardiness), better able to cope effectively and resist the long-term effects of stress on health.

This chapter also focused on a specific disease, cardiovascular disease, the second leading cause of death in Canada. We covered the history of the search for a personality dimension that might be a risk factor for developing heart disease. Type A personality provides an interesting example of progressive research, in which findings are gradually refined until the field becomes more and more certain about an effect. In the case of Type A personality, most researchers now agree that the hostility component is most associated with the tendency to develop heart disease. Fortunately, people can be competitive workaholics and strive to do more and more in less and less time, just as long as they do not have the hostile part of the Type A syndrome.

 Concept Check

In your own words, summarize the main ways in which personality is associated with health. In your response, consider the Big Five personality traits.

How is stress defined by psychologists, and what is the role of personality in various aspects of stress?

Key Terms

health psychology

stress

interactional model

transactional model

moderator (or moderation)

health behaviour model

predisposition model

illness behaviour model

stressors

general adaptation syndrome (GAS)

alarm stage

resistance stage

exhaustion stage

major life events

daily hassles

acute stress

episodic acute stress

traumatic stress

posttraumatic stress disorder (PTSD)

chronic stress

additive effects

primary appraisal

secondary appraisal

dispositional optimism

optimistic bias

positive reappraisal

problem-focused coping

creating positive events

emotion-focused coping

relationship-focused coping

emotional inhibition

disclosure

hardy personality

psychological resilience

competitive achievement
 motivation

time urgency

hostility

frustration

Type D personality

cortisol

arteriosclerosis

Disorders of Personality

The Adjustment Domain

Ashley Smith (January 29, 1988–October 19, 2007) grew up in New Brunswick where, by all accounts, she had a typical childhood, enjoying the outdoors and riding her bicycle often. In 2001, when Ashley was 13 years old, her parents noticed a change in her personality. Ashley became disruptive and defiant. She was suspended from school for bullying and then harassed a teacher from the school, making angry phone calls, following the teacher home, and repeatedly banging on the teacher's door. By the age of 15, Ashley had committed several assaults and was admitted to the Pierre Caissie Centre in Moncton, a facility that specializes in treating young people with behaviour problems. While there, Ashley was diagnosed with attention-deficit/hyperactivity disorder (ADHD), a learning disorder, and borderline personality disorder. Although the original plan was for Ashley to spend 34 days at the centre, she was discharged after only 21 days because she had extreme difficulty interacting with staff and peers, was rude and intimidating, and was verbally aggressive.

Soon after this discharge Ashley was sentenced to one month at the New Brunswick Youth Centre (NBYC), a juvenile detention centre, for assault and trespassing. Ashley was so disruptive and aggressive that she was placed in restraints and was segregated from other inmates. She would spend the next several years in and out of NBYC; each time she was released she would commit a crime within a few days and be put back in custody. Despite a standing policy not to keep residents isolated for more than five days, Ashley was never released into the general population because of concern that she would harm other residents. Between 2002 and 2005, Ashley was involved in more than 800 incidents at NBYC related to defiance and aggression. In 2006, she turned 18 years old and was moved to an adult prison in St. John's, Newfoundland. Ashley's aggressive and defiant behaviour continued, and she was moved from prison to prison frequently in an attempt to keep her in constant segregation from other prisoners. Between 2002 and 2007, Ashley made over 150 attempts to harm herself, and on October 19, 2007, she died by self-strangulation. The jury presiding over a 2012

Ashley Smith was 19 years old when she died by self-inflicted strangulation in the Grand Valley Institution for Women in Kitchener, Ontario, on October 19, 2007. A psychiatrist who testified at the coroner's inquest that followed her death reported that Ashley Smith met all 10 of the diagnostic criteria for antisocial personality disorder.
©The Canadian Press/Geoff Robins

inquest into Ashley Smith's death determined that she died by homicide, not suicide, because her guards saw her hanging in her cell on a video monitor and chose not to intervene. The jury also concluded that Corrections Canada needed to try to better serve female inmates with mental health problems and recommended a complete ban on solitary confinement.

During the inquest, a psychiatrist testified that Ashley Smith met 10 out of 10 criteria for antisocial personality disorder. The criteria included having a conduct disorder before the age of 15, being at least 18 years of age, repeating behaviours that are grounds for an arrest, deceitfulness, impulsivity, irritability and aggressiveness, reckless disregard for the safety of others, consistent irresponsibility, lack of remorse, and not displaying schizophrenia or manic episodes. Ashley also met four out of eight criteria for borderline personality disorder. She had persistent instability in her interpersonal relationships, she had repeated suicidal behaviour, she was emotionally unstable, and she had inappropriate levels of anger that were uncontrollable.

Ashley Smith's antisocial and borderline personality disorders made it impossible for her to relate to others in a constructive way. As a result, Ashley had extremely low self-esteem, and this self-hatred led to self-harming behaviour that ultimately ended her life. Although Ashley Smith's case is well known because of media interest surrounding the inquests that followed her death, her behaviours are not unusual for individuals who are incarcerated. The psychiatrist who assessed Ashley reported that none of her behaviours were unique or unusual and that many women currently incarcerated in Canada have mental illnesses that are similar to those observed in Ashley Smith.

The Building Blocks of Personality Disorders

Many of the topics we have covered in previous chapters come together in helping to describe and understand the various personality disorders. The symptoms of personality disorders can be seen as maladaptive variations within several of the domains we have covered. These include traits, emotions, cognitions, motives, interpersonal behaviour, and self-concepts. The 10 personality disorders we present in this chapter are built on the foundation of these broader concepts, and so we briefly will discuss the relevance of each to this chapter.

Traits of personality describe consistencies in behaviour, thought, or action and represent meaningful differences among people, as we described in Chapter 3. Personality disorders can be thought of as maladaptive variations or combinations of normal personality traits. Widiger and colleagues describe how extremes on either end of specific trait dimensions can be associated with personality disorders (Widiger, Costa, & McCrae, 2002a; Widiger et al., 2002b; Widiger & Costa, 2012). For example, a person with extremely low levels of trust and extremely high levels of hostility might be disposed to paranoid personality disorder. A person very low on sociability but very high on anxiety might be prone to avoidant personality disorder. A person with the opposite combination—extremely high on sociability and low on anxiety—might be prone to histrionic personality disorder. Thus, the concept of traits, such as the five-factor model of traits, can be especially useful for describing personality disorders (Gore & Widiger, 2013; Trull & McCrae, 2002).

Motivation is a second basic building block of personality that is important to understanding personality disorders. Motives describe what people want and why they behave in particular ways. In the intrapsychic domain, Chapters 9 to 11, we discussed several different kinds of motives, ranging from the sexual and aggressive basis of Freud's theory to modern research on the need for intimacy, achievement, and power. A common theme in several personality disorders concerns maladaptive variations on these common motives, especially needs for power and intimacy. One important variation concerns an extreme lack of motivation for intimacy, which is seen in certain personality disorders. Another theme is an exaggerated need for power over others, which, at an extremely high level, can result in a maladaptive personality disorder. Other motives can be involved in personality disorders, such as the extreme need to be superior and receive the praise of others that is found in narcissistic personality disorder. People with obsessive-compulsive personality disorder might be seen as having an extremely high motivation for order and devotion to detail.

Cognition also provides a basis for understanding personality disorders. As covered in Chapter 12, cognition consists of mental activity involved in perceiving, interpreting, and planning. These processes can become distorted in personality disorders. Some disorders involve routine and consistent misinterpretations of the intentions of others. Personality disorders typically involve an impairment of social judgment, such as when those with paranoid personality disorder think others are out to get them, or when those with histrionic personality disorder think others actually like being with them. People with borderline personality disorder may misinterpret innocent comments as signs of abandonment or criticism or rejection. In various ways, each of the personality disorders involves some distortion in the perception of other people and altered social cognition.

Emotion is another area that is important to understanding personality disorders. We discussed normal range individual differences in emotion in Chapter 13. With several personality disorders there is extreme variation in experienced emotions. Some disorders involve extreme volatility in emotions (e.g., borderline), whereas other disorders involve extremes of specific emotions, such as anxiety (avoidant personality disorder), fear (paranoid personality disorder), or rage (narcissistic personality disorder). Most personality disorders have an emotional core that is an important component to understanding that disorder.

As described in Chapter 14, self-concept is a person's own collection of self-knowledge—one's understanding of oneself. In most personality disorders, there is some distortion in self-concept. Most of us are able to build and maintain a stable and realistic image of ourselves; we know our own opinions, we know what we value, and we know what we want out of life. With many of the disorders, there is a lack of stability in self-concept, such that individuals may feel they have no "core" or they have trouble making decisions or need constant reassurance from others. Self-esteem is also an important part of the self, and some disorders are associated with extremely high (e.g., narcissism) or extremely low (e.g., dependent personality disorder) levels of self-esteem. The self provides an important perspective on understanding personality disorders.

Social relationships are frequently disturbed or maladaptive in personality disorders. Thus, the material we covered in the social and cultural domain, Chapters 15 through 17, is important for understanding and describing personality disorders. For example, a successful sexually intimate relationship with another person involves knowing when sexual behaviour is appropriate and expected and when it is inappropriate and unwanted. Problems with intimacy, either staying too distant from others or becoming too intimate too quickly, are frequent features of several personality disorders. An important element of interpersonal skill involves empathy, knowing how another person is feeling. Most personality disorders involve a deficit in empathy, such that the disordered person either misinterprets others or does not care about the feelings of others. Many disorders involve what might be called poor social skills. For instance, a person with schizoid personality disorder may stare at people without starting a conversation, while someone with histrionic personality disorder may behave in an inappropriately flirtatious manner.

Biology can also form the building blocks of several of the personality disorders. The material covered in the biological domain, Chapters 6 through 8, is thus relevant. Some of the personality disorders have been found to have a genetic component. Others have been studied via physiological components, such as examining the brain functioning of antisocial individuals. There has even been an evolutionary theory proposed to explain the existence of personality disorders (Millon, 2000a).

Most personality textbooks do not cover personality disorders. We feel, however, that understanding how something can become dysfunctional can tell us a lot about how it works normally. We also believe that the concept of personality disorders helps to tie together the various components and domains of personality. As such, it is a fitting topic with which to end this book.

The Concept of Disorder

Today, a psychological **disorder** is a pattern of behaviour or experience that is distressing and painful to the person, that leads to disability or impairment in important life domains (e.g., problems with work, marriage or relationship difficulties), and that is associated with increased risk for further suffering, loss of function, death, or confinement (American Psychiatric Association, 2013). The idea that something can go wrong with a person's personality has a long history. Some of the earliest writings in medical psychiatry included classifications and descriptions of personality and mental disorders (e.g., Kraeplin, 1913; Kretschmer, 1925).

A very early concept derived by French psychiatrist Philippe Pinel was *manie sans delire,* or madness without loss of reason. This was applied to individuals who demonstrated disordered behaviour and emotions but who did not lose contact with reality (Morey, 1997). A related concept, popular in the early 1900s, was called "moral insanity," to emphasize that the person did not suffer any impairment of intellect, but rather was impaired in terms of feelings, temperament, or habits. An influential psychiatrist named Kurt Schneider (1958) proposed the term *psychopathic personality* to refer to behaviour patterns that caused the person and the community to suffer. Schneider also emphasized statistical rarity, along with behaviours that have an adverse impact on the person and the community in which that person lives. This definition highlights the notion that all forms of personality disorder involve impaired social relationships; other people suffer as much as or more than the person with the disorder.

A disorder is a conceptual entity that, although abstract, is nevertheless useful. It helps to guide thinking about the distinction between what is normal and what is abnormal, or pathological. The field of **abnormal psychology** is the study of the various mental disorders, including thought disorders, emotional disorders, and personality disorders. In this chapter, we focus on disorders of personality and the ways in which they affect functioning.

What Is Abnormal?

There are many ways to define **abnormal**. One simple definition is that whatever is different from normal is abnormal. This is a statistical definition in the sense that researchers can statistically determine how often something occurs and, if it is rare, call it abnormal. In this sense, colour blindness or polydactyly (having more than 10 fingers) is considered abnormal. Another definition of abnormal is a social definition based on what society tolerates (Shoben, 1957). If we define the term in this sense, behaviours that society deems unacceptable are labelled as abnormal. In this sense, incest and child abuse are both considered abnormal. Both the statistical and the social definitions of abnormality suffer from changing times and changing social or cultural norms (Millon, 2000a, 2000b). Behaviours deemed offensive or socially inappropriate 20 years ago might be acceptable today. For example, 40 years ago, homosexuality was considered to be both rare and socially unacceptable, a form of abnormal behaviour, or even a mental illness. Today, being gay or lesbian is no longer considered abnormal (American Psychiatric Association, 2013) and is protected under civil rights laws in Canada. Thus, the statistical and social definitions of abnormality are always somewhat tentative as society evolves.

Psychologists have consequently looked to other ways of identifying what is abnormal in behaviour and experience. They have looked within individuals, inquiring about subjective feelings, such as anxiety, depression, dissatisfaction, and feelings of loneliness. They have looked at how people think and experience themselves and their worlds. Psychologists have found that some people have disorganized thoughts, disruptive perceptions, or unusual beliefs and attitudes that do not match their circumstances. They have identified ways in which people fail to get along with one another and ways people have trouble living in the community. They have analyzed patterns of behaviour that represent ineffective efforts at coping or that put people at higher risk for other problems, behaviours that harm more than help. From a psychological perspective, any of these may be considered abnormal.

Combining all these approaches to abnormality (statistical, social, and psychological), psychologists and psychiatrists have developed the field of **psychopathology**, or the study of mental disorders. The diagnosis of mental disorders is both a scientific discipline and an important part of the clinical work of many psychiatrists and psychologists. Knowing how to define and how to identify a disorder is the first step in devising treatment or in designing research on that disorder.

The *Diagnostic and Statistical Manual of Mental Disorders*

The most widely used system for diagnosing mental disorders, including personality disorders, is the *Diagnostic and Statistical Manual of Mental Disorders*, published by the American Psychiatric Association (APA) and currently in its fifth edition (called the *DSM-5*). The *DSM-5* sets the standard for diagnoses, and its system is the one taught by almost all psychiatry and psychology doctoral training programs, the one that appears in hospital records systems, and the one most insurance companies demand for reimbursement purposes in both the United States and Canada.

Because society's standards change over time and because new research accumulates, the *DSM* undergoes revision from time to time. The current version—the *DSM-5*—was published in 2013. The APA began working on this revision a decade earlier and appointed various working groups of experts to assist in each broad area of mental disorders. The personality disorders working group consisted of active personality psychologists and psychiatrists. During the decade they worked on the revision for *DSM-5*, the personality disorders working group considered several broad changes to personality disorders that might be incorporated into *DSM-5*.

One change the personality disorders working group considered was to make diagnosis less categorical and more dimensional. The previous edition—*DSM-IV*—was based on a **categorical view** of personality disorders; one either had the disorder or did not have the disorder. The categorical view held that there is a qualitative break between people who are, for example, antisocial and people who are not. And this concept was applied to all the personality disorders, viewing disorders as distinct and qualitatively different from normal extremes on each personality trait.

In contrast to this categorical view is the **dimensional view** of personality disorders. In the dimensional view, each disorder is seen as a continuum, ranging from normality at one end to severe disability or disturbance at the other. According to this view, people with and without the disorder differ in degree only. For example, part of being antisocial is disregarding the rights of others. But there are degrees to which this disregard can manifest in behaviour. For example, some people might simply be aloof and unconcerned about the feelings of others. Farther out on this dimension, a person might lack a desire to help others, being both aloof and uncaring. Even farther out on this dimension is the person who actively hurts or takes advantage of others. And finally, at the greatest extreme of disregard for others, is the person who takes pleasure in harming or terrorizing people.

The dimensional view implies that certain patterns of behaviour, in various amounts, comprise each of the personality disorders. It is only at the extreme ends of the dimensions that the person becomes a problem to themselves and to others. Moreover, extremes of different personality traits can combine in ways that create unique forms of disorder. Modern personality theorists (e.g., Costa & Widiger, 1994, 2002; Widiger, 2000) have argued that the dimensional view provides a more reliable and meaningful way to describe the personality disorders.

As the *DSM-5* revision work progressed, the personality disorders working group considered this, and several other, changes to the way personality disorders are defined and diagnosed. The top personality psychologists and psychiatrists were involved, many meetings were held, data were collected, public input was solicited and obtained, and many proposals were written and considered. However, to make a long story very short, the final outcome of the revision effort was the decision, on the part of the APA Board of Trustees, to make no changes to the way personality disorders are defined. The *DSM-5* therefore maintains the categorical model of personality disorders and retains the criteria for 10 specific personality disorders that were described in the previous edition. The *DSM-5* does contain a section—Section III—that describes issues in need further research. It is in this section, essentially an appendix to the *DSM-5*, where the dimensional model of personality disorders is detailed and a call for further research on the utility of viewing personality disorders as dimensions rather than distinct categories is issued. Later in this chapter we explore the 10 personality disorders included in the *DSM-5*, but first we consider the general notion of "personality disorder."

What Is a Personality Disorder?

A **personality disorder** is an enduring pattern of experience and behaviour that differs greatly from the expectations of the individual's culture (*DSM-5*). As discussed in Chapter 3, traits are patterns of experiencing, thinking about, and interacting with oneself and the world. Traits are observed in a wide range of social and personal situations. For example, a person who is high in conscientiousness is hardworking and persevering. If a trait becomes maladaptive and inflexible and causes significant impairment or distress, then it is considered to be a personality disorder. For example, if conscientiousness were so high that one checked the locks on the door 10 times each night and checked every appliance in the house 5 times before leaving in the morning, then we might consider the possibility of a disorder.

The essential features of a personality disorder, according to the *DSM-5*, are presented in Table 19.1. A personality disorder is usually manifest in more than one of the following areas: in how people think, in how they feel, in how they get along with others, or in their ability to control their own behaviour. The pattern is rigid

---

Table 19.1   General Criteria for Personality Disorders

1. A personality disorder shows an enduring pattern of inner experience and behaviour that deviates markedly from the expectations of the individual's culture. This pattern is manifest in two or more of the following areas:
   - Cognition (i.e., ways of perceiving and interpreting the self, others, and events)
   - Affectivity (i.e., the range, intensity, ability, and appropriateness of emotional responses)
   - Interpersonal functioning
   - Impulse control
2. The enduring pattern is inflexible and pervasive across a broad range of personal and social situations.
3. The enduring pattern leads to clinically significant distress or impairment in social, occupational, or other important areas of functioning.
4. The pattern is stable and of long duration, and its onset can be traced back to adolescence or early adulthood.
5. The enduring pattern is not better accounted for as a manifestation or consequence of another mental disorder.
6. The enduring pattern is not due to the direct physiological effects of a substance (e.g., a drug of abuse, a medication) or a general medical condition, such as head trauma.

Source: American Psychiatric Association, 2013.

and is displayed across a variety of situations, leading to distress or problems in important areas in life, such as at work or in relationships. For example, an overly conscientious man might drive his partner crazy with his constant checking of his household appliances. The pattern of behaviour that defines the personality disorder typically has a long history in the person's life and can often be traced back to manifestations in adolescence or even childhood. To be classed as a personality disorder, the pattern must not result from drug abuse, medication, or a medical condition, such as head trauma.

Culture, Age, and Gender: The Effect of Context

A person's social, cultural, and ethnic background must be taken into account whenever there is a question about personality disorders. Immigrants, for example, often have problems fitting into a new culture. People who originate in a different culture often have customs, habits, expressions, and values that are at odds with, or that create social problems within, a new culture. For example, North American culture is very individualistic overall (as we reviewed in Chapter 17), and it values and rewards individuals for standing out from the crowd. To societies that are more collectivistic and value fitting in with the group, efforts to stand out from the crowd might be interpreted as self-centred and individualistic in an unwanted sense. Indeed, North America has been called a narcissistic culture; therefore, efforts to draw attention to the self are not socially abnormal in this society.

Before judging that a behaviour is a symptom of a personality disorder, we must first become familiar with a person's cultural background, especially if it is different from the majority culture. A study of immigrants to Norway found that many exhibited adjustment problems that might have appeared to be personality disorders (Sam, 1994). Many young male immigrants, for example, exhibited antisocial behaviours. These behaviours tended to diminish as the immigrants acculturated to their new social environment.

Age also is relevant to judgments about personality disorder. Adolescents, for example, often go through periods of instability that may include identity crises (see Chapter 14), a symptom that is often associated with certain personality disorders. Most adolescents experiment with various identities yet do not have a personality disorder. For this reason, the American Psychiatric Association (2013) cautions against diagnosing personality disorders in persons under age 18. Also, adults who undergo severe loss, such as the death of a spouse or the loss of a job, sometimes undergo periods of instability or impulsive behaviour that may look like a personality disorder. For example, a person who has experienced such a traumatic event may become violent or may impulsively enter into sexual relationships. A person's age and life circumstances must therefore be considered to be sure that the person is not simply going through a developmental stage or reacting to a traumatic life event.

Finally, gender is another context in which to frame our understanding of personality disorders. Certain disorders, such as the antisocial personality disorder, are diagnosed much more frequently in men than women. Other personality disorders are diagnosed more frequently in women than men. These gender differences may reflect underlying gender differences in how people cope. For example, in a study of more than 2,000 individuals, Huselid and Cooper (1994) found that males exhibit externalizing problems, such as fighting and vandalism, whereas females tend to exhibit relatively more internalizing problems, such as depression and self-harm. Similar findings were obtained by Kavanagh and Hops (1994). These differences in how men and women cope with problems most likely contribute to gender differences in the behaviours associated with the personality disorders. Psychologists need to be careful not to look for evidence of certain kinds of disorders just because of a person's gender.

 Exercise

In this chapter, you will read about specific personality disorders. For each, try to think of examples of how culture, gender, or age might influence whether a person's behaviour is seen as evidence of a disorder. For example, are people from low socioeconomic groups likely to be seen by others as having particular disorders? How does this correspond to the topic of stereotypes and prejudice? How does this fit with the use of "profiles" by police and other law enforcement agencies?

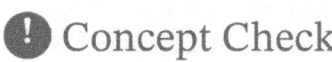 Concept Check

What is the difference between a categorical view and a dimensional view of mental disorders?

What is a personality disorder? List the key general criteria as outlined in the DSM-5.

Specific Personality Disorders

The following sections describe specific personality disorders, including the criteria for diagnosing someone as possessing each disorder. We focus this material on describing the characteristics of each personality disorder and by giving examples. We also organize the personality disorders according to the three clusters used in the DSM-5, which highlight some of the conceptual similarities among the disorders.

Cluster A. The Eccentric Cluster: Ways of Being Different

This cluster of personality disorders contains traits that combine to make people ill at ease socially and appear or act in highly abnormal ways. Most of the oddness in these disorders has to do with how the person interacts with others. Some people have no interest in others; some are extremely uncomfortable with others; and some are suspicious of others. When carried to extremes, these interpersonal styles form the three personality disorders known as the schizoid, schizotypal, and paranoid personalities.

Schizoid personality disorder and **schizotypal personality disorder** both take their root from schizophrenia and are closely tied to the history of this diagnostic category. *Schizophrenia* literally means cutting the mind off from itself and from reality. It is a serious mental illness that involves hallucinations, delusions, and perceptual aberrations. The personality disorders of schizoid and schizotypal exhibit some low-grade nonpsychotic symptoms of schizophrenia. For example, the person with schizotypal is eccentric and is interested in odd and unusual beliefs, whereas the person with schizoid displays social apathy. Individuals with schizophrenia display both of these characteristics *plus* delusions or hallucinations. Thus these personality disorders have much in common with this more severe mental illness. In the case of schizotypal disorders, individuals are likely to possess the genotype that makes them vulnerable to schizophrenia. A large proportion of family members of those with schizophrenia exhibit odd and unusual behaviours that would contribute to a diagnosis of schizotypal personality disorder.

Schizoid Personality Disorder

The schizoid personality is split off (schism), or *detached,* from normal social relations. The person with schizoid personality disorder simply appears to have no need or desire for intimate relationships or even friendships. Family life usually does not mean much to such people, and they do not obtain satisfaction from being part of a group. They have few or no close friends, and they would rather spend time by themselves than with others. They typically choose hobbies that can be done and appreciated alone, such as playing video games. They also typically choose solitary jobs, often with mechanical or abstract tasks, such as machinists or computer programmers. Usually, the schizoid personality experiences *little pleasure* from bodily or sensory experiences, such as eating or having sex. The person's emotional life is typically constricted.

At best, the person with schizoid personality disorder appears indifferent to others, neither bothered by criticism nor buoyed by compliments. "Bland" would be one description of such a person's emotional life. Often, the individual does not respond to social cues and so appears *inept* or *socially clumsy.* For example, such a person may walk into a room where there is another person and simply stare at that person, apparently not motivated to start a conversation. Sometimes the person with schizoid personality disorder is *passive* in the face of unpleasant happenings and does not respond effectively to important events. Such a person may appear directionless.

✐ Application

The case of Roger, a research assistant with schizoid personality disorder. **Roger was an undergraduate who had volunteered to help out in the laboratory of one of his psychology professors. He was responsible, showing up on time and doing the work he was given. However, he seemed detached from the work, never getting too excited or appearing to be even interested, though he volunteered to work for several semesters. Roger often worked in the lab at night. On several occasions, some of the graduate students complained to the professor that Roger was "staring" at them. When pressed for details, these students said that, when they left their office doors open, they would sometimes turn around and find Roger standing in the doorway, looking at them. Several female graduate students complained that he was "spooky" and kept their office doors locked.**

Roger lived with his younger brother, who also went to the same university. The brother apparently handled all the daily chores, such as dealing with the landlord, buying groceries, and arranging for utilities. Roger thus had a protected life and spent most of his time studying, reading, or exploring the Internet. In class, he never talked or participated in discussion. Outside of class, he appeared to have no friends, nor did he participate in any extracurricular activities. The professor he worked for thought he might be on medication but, after inquiring, learned that Roger took no medication. After graduating with a degree in psychology, Roger returned to live with his parents. He remodelled the space above his parents' garage and has been living there, rent-free, for the past 15 years. Every few years, he e-mails his professor with an update on his rather stable life, although the professor's return e-mails bounce back with the message that "no such e-mail address exists." Apparently, Roger has found a way to keep his e-mail address secret.

People from some cultures react to stress in a way that looks like schizoid personality disorder. That is, without actually having the disorder, some people under stress may appear socially numb and passive. For example, people who move out of extremely rural environments into large cities may react in a schizoid fashion for several weeks or months. Such a person, overwhelmed by noise, lights, and overcrowding, may prefer to be alone, have constricted emotions, and manifest other deficits in social skills. Also, people who emigrate from other countries are sometimes seen as cold, reserved, or aloof. For example, people who emigrated from Southeastern Asia during the 1970s and 1980s were sometimes seen as being hostile or cold by people in mainstream urban American culture. These are cultural differences and should not be interpreted as personality disorders.

Schizotypal Personality Disorder

Whereas the person with schizoid personality disorder is indifferent to social interaction, the person with schizotypal personality disorder is acutely uncomfortable in social relationships. Those with schizotypal are *anxious in social situations,* especially if those situations involve strangers. They also feel that they are different from others or that they do not fit in with the group. Interestingly, when such individuals have to interact with a group, they do not necessarily become less anxious as they become more familiar with the group. For example, while attending a group function, those with schizotypal personality disorder will not become less anxious as time wears on, but instead will become more and more tense.

The famous surrealist painter Salvador Dali displayed many of the characteristics associated with the schizotypal personality disorder.
©IanDagnall Computing/Alamy Stock Photo

This is because they tend to be *suspicious of others* and are not prone to trust others or to relax in their presence.

Another characteristic of people with schizotypal personalities is that they are *odd* and *eccentric.* It is not unusual for them to harbour many superstitions such as believing in ESP and many other psychic or paranormal phenomena that are outside of the norms for their culture. They may believe in magic or that they possess some magical or extraordinary power, such as the ability to control other people or animals with their thoughts. They may have *unusual perceptions* that border on hallucinations, such as feeling that other people are looking at them or hearing murmurs that sound like their names.

Because of their suspiciousness of others, social discomfort, and general oddness, individuals with schizotypal personality disorder have difficulty with social relationships. They often violate common social conventions in such ways as not making eye contact, dressing in unkempt clothing, and wearing clothing that does not go together. In many ways, the person simply does not fit into the social group.

Due to their similarity in terms of avoiding social relations, the characteristics of schizoid and schizotypal personality disorders are presented together in Table 19.2. Some beliefs and thoughts (mostly concerned with other people) which characterize individuals with these disorders are also listed.

Mason, Claridge, and Jackson (1995) published a questionnaire for assessing schizotypal traits and validated it in several British samples. One of the scales contains items that get at the presence of *unusual experiences:* "Are your thoughts sometimes so strong you can almost hear them? Have you sometimes had the feeling of gaining or losing energy when certain people look at you or touch you? Are you so good at controlling others

Table 19.2 Characteristics of Schizoid and Schizotypal Personality Disorders

Schizoid

Detached from normal social relationships

Pleasureless life

Inept or socially clumsy

Passive in the face of unpleasant events

Schizotypal

Anxious in social relations and avoids people

"Different" and nonconforming

Suspicious of others

Eccentricity of beliefs, such as in ESP or magic

Unusualness of perceptions and experiences

Disorganized thoughts and speech

Typical Thoughts or Beliefs Associated with the Schizoid and Schizotypal Personalities

"I hate being tied to other people."

"My privacy is more important to me than being close to others."

"It's best not to confide too much in others."

"Relationships are always messy."

"I manage best on my own and set my own standards."

"Intimate relations are unimportant to me."

that it sometimes scares you?" Another scale contains items that assess *cognitive disorganization:* "Do you ever feel that your speech is difficult to understand because the words are all mixed up and don't make any sense? Do you frequently have difficulty starting to do things?" Another set of items measures the *tendency to avoid people:* "Are you much too independent to really get involved with people? Can you usually let yourself go and enjoy yourself at a party?" And, finally, there is a scale for assessing the *nonconformity* aspect of schizotypy: "Do you often feel like doing the opposite of what people suggest, even though you know they are right? Would you take drugs that might have strange or dangerous effects?"

 Exercise

Many famous people have been odd or eccentric. Artists (e.g., Salvador Dali), writers (e.g., Tennessee Williams), musicians, film stars, and even politicians have exhibited some fairly eccentric behaviours. Can you think of examples of public figures who have displayed odd beliefs or actions recently? Would they fit the rest of the characteristics of the schizotypal personality?

Paranoid Personality Disorder

Whereas the personal with schizotypal personality disorder is uncomfortable with others, the person with paranoid personality disorder is extremely *distrustful of others* and sees others as a constant threat. Such individuals assume that others are out to exploit and deceive them, even though there is no good evidence to support this assumption. Individuals feel that they have been injured by others and are preoccupied with doubts about the motivations of others.

People with this personality typically do not reveal personal information to others, fearing that the information will be used against them. Their reaction to others is "Mind your own business." The paranoid person often *misinterprets social events*. For example, someone makes an off-hand comment and the paranoid interprets it as a demeaning or threatening remark (e.g., wondering, "What did he mean by *that*?"). Those with this disorder are constantly on the lookout for hidden meanings and disguised motivations in the comments and behaviours of others.

A person with **paranoid personality disorder** often holds *resentments toward others* for slights or perceived insults. Such a person is reluctant to forgive and forget even minor altercations. Individuals often become involved in legal disputes, suing others for the slightest reasons. Sometimes they plead with those in power to intervene on their behalf, such as writing to congresspersons or calling the local police chief day after day.

Pathological jealousy is a common manifestation of paranoid personality disorder. For example, a pathologically jealous woman suspects that her husband or partner is unfaithful, even though there is no objective evidence of infidelity. She may go to great lengths to find support for her jealous beliefs. She may restrict the activities of her partner or constantly question him as to his whereabouts. She may not believe her partner's accounts of how he spent his time or believe his claims of faithfulness.

People with paranoid personality disorder are at risk of harming those who threaten their belief systems. Their *argumentative and hostile nature* may provoke others to a combative response. This hostile response from others, in turn, validates the paranoids' original suspicion that others are out to get them. Their extreme suspiciousness and the unreasonableness of their beliefs make people with this disorder particularly difficult in social relations. Table 19.3 presents the main characteristics of the paranoid personality disorder, along with some examples of beliefs and thoughts commonly found among individuals with this disorder.

Table 19.3   Characteristics of Paranoid Personality Disorder
Is distrustful of others
Misinterprets social events as threatening
Harbours resentments toward others
Is prone to pathological jealousy
Is argumentative and hostile
Typical Thoughts or Beliefs Associated with the Paranoid Personality
"Get them before they get you."
"Other people always have ulterior motives."
"People will say one thing but do another."
"Don't let them get away with anything."
"I have to be on guard all the time."
"When people act friendly toward you, it is probably because they want something. Watch out!"

Cluster B. The Erratic Cluster: Ways of Being Unstable and Emotional

People who are diagnosed with disorders belonging to the erratic group tend to have trouble with emotional control and to have specific difficulties getting along with others. People with one of these disorders often appear dramatic and emotional and are unpredictable. This group consists of four disorders: *antisocial, borderline, histrionic,* and *narcissistic* personality disorders.

Antisocial Personality Disorder

Antisocial individuals show a general disregard for others and care very little about the rights, feelings, or happiness of other people. Antisocial people have also been referred to as *sociopaths* or *psychopaths* (Zuckerman, 1991a). Adults with this disorder typically had a childhood that was fraught with behavioural problems. Such early childhood behavioural problems generally take the form of violating the rights of others (such as minor thefts) and breaking age-related social norms (such as smoking at an early age or fighting with other children). Other common childhood behavioural problems include behaving aggressively or cruelly toward animals, threatening and intimidating younger children, destroying property, lying, and breaking rules. Behavioural problems in childhood are often first noticed in school, but such children also come to the attention of the police and truant officers. Sometimes even very young children, during an argument with another child, use a weapon that can cause serious physical harm, such as a baseball bat or a knife.

Once childhood behavioural problems become an established pattern, the possibility of **antisocial personality disorder** becomes more likely (American Psychiatric Association, 2013). As a child with behavioural problems grows up, the problems tend to worsen as the child develops physical strength, cognitive power, and sexual maturity. Minor problems, such as lying, fighting, and shoplifting, evolve into more serious ones, such as breaking and entering and vandalism. Severe aggression, such as rape or cruelty to a theft victim, might also follow. Some children with these behavioural problems rapidly develop to a level of dangerous and even sadistic behaviour. For example, we sometimes hear in the news about preteen children (usually male) who murder other children in cold blood and without remorse. In one study, children who grew into severe delinquency as teenagers were already identifiable by kindergarten teachers' ratings of impulsiveness and antisocial behaviour at age five (Tremblay et al., 1994). Studies of children ages 6–13 also find that some children exhibit a syndrome of antisocial behaviours, including impulsivity, behavioural problems, callous social attitudes, and lack of feelings for others (Douglas & Guy, 2008).

If a child exhibits no signs of conduct problems by age 16, it is unlikely that they will develop antisocial personality as an adult. Moreover, even among children *with* conduct problems, the majority simply grow out of them by early adulthood (American Psychiatric Association, 2013). However, some children with conduct problems go on to develop full-blown antisocial personality disorder in adulthood. Children with earlier-onset conduct problems (e.g., by age six or seven) are much more likely to grow into antisocial personality disorder as an adult than are children who displayed a few conduct problems in high school (Laub & Lauritsen, 1994).

The antisocial adult continues with the same sorts of conduct problems started in childhood, but on a much grander scale. The term *antisocial* implies that the person has a *lack of concern for social norms*. Individuals with antisocial personality disorder have very little respect for laws and may repeatedly engage in acts that are grounds for arrest, such as harassing others, fighting, destroying property, and stealing. "Cold-hearted" is a good description of their interactions with others. Individuals may manipulate and deceive others to gain rewards or pleasure (e.g., money, power, social advantage, or sex).

Repeated lying is another feature of the antisocial personality. The pattern of lying starts early in life with minor deceptions and grows into a pattern of deceitfulness. Lying becomes a common part of social interaction for the antisocial personality. Some make a living conning others out of money. "Getting one over" on people, especially authorities, through deception may even be pleasurable to the antisocial person.

Another common characteristic of the antisocial personality is *impulsivity,* which is often manifested as a failure to plan ahead. The antisocial person might start a chain of behaviour without a clear plan or sequence in mind; for example, the person might enter a gas station and decide on the spot to rob the attendant, even without a planned getaway. Prisoners with antisocial personalities often complain that their lack of planning led to their arrest, and they are often more remorseful about getting caught than about committing the crime.

A more common form of impulsivity is to simply make everyday decisions without much forethought or without considering consequences. For example, an antisocial man might leave his wife and baby for several days without calling to say where he is. This often results in trouble in relationships and trouble in employment settings. Generally, antisocial individuals change jobs often, change relationships often, and move often.

Those with antisocial personality disorder also tend to be *easily irritated* and to respond to even minor frustrations with aggression. Losing some coins in a vending machine might be all it takes for such a person to fly into a rage. Antisocial individuals tend to be *assaultive,* particularly to those around them, such as spouses or children. Fights and physical attacks are common. *Recklessness* is another characteristic, such that individuals show little regard for their own safety or that of others. Driving while intoxicated or speeding is indicative of recklessness, as is having unprotected sex with multiple partners. Individuals with antisocial personality disorder who are both highly irritable and highly impulsive are at heightened risk for engaging in suicide-related behaviours (Douglas et al., 2008).

Irresponsibility is another key feature of the antisocial personality. Individuals with antisocial personality disorder get bored easily and find monotony or routine to be stressful. A person may, for example, decide on the spur of the moment to abandon their job, with no plan for getting another right away. Repeated unexplained absences from work are a common sign of the antisocial character. Irresponsibility in financial matters is also common, with the antisocial person often running up unpayable debts, or borrowing money from one person to pay a debt owed to another, staying one step ahead of the bill collector. Such a person may squander the money needed for groceries or gamble away the family savings.

Lack of remorse and guilt feelings, as well as indifference to the suffering of others, are the hallmarks of the antisocial mind. The person with antisocial personality disorder can be ruthless, without the normal levels of human compassion, charity, or social concern. Table 19.4 summarizes the key characteristics of antisocial personality disorder. Also included are typical beliefs or thoughts that someone with this disorder might have.

A concept related to antisocial personality disorder is *psychopathy,* which was a term coined toward the middle of the twentieth century (Cleckley, 1941) to describe people who are superficially charming and intelligent, but are also deceitful, unable to feel remorse or care for others, impulsive, and lacking in shame, guilt, and fear. Psychopathy and antisocial personality are similar notions but there are important distinctions, so they should not be used interchangeably. The antisocial personality designation places emphasis on observable behaviours, such as chronic lying, repeated criminal behaviour, and conflicts with authority.

Application

A possible case of antisocial personality disorder. Conrad Black (b. 1944) was a Canadian citizen until 1999 and once controlled Hollinger International, the third-largest newspaper consortium in the world. Conrad Black is also well known for being convicted of fraud in 2007, for which he served 37 months in prison. Although he had many friends and an active social life, Conrad Black seems to meet seven of the ten criteria for antisocial personality disorder. As a child Black was expelled from three different private schools for academic misconduct and insubordination, suggesting a conduct disorder before the age of 15. Over the course of his adult life, Black was charged with embezzling $80 million from Hollinger International (for which he served prison time) and for lesser crimes related to his financial

Conrad Black exhibits several characteristics consistent with antisocial personality disorder. He has repeatedly made unethical business decisions that have hurt other people and refuses to accept responsibility for his own actions. When confronted with evidence of his crimes Black invariably responds with angry words and typically mocks and insults his accusers while showing a lack of remorse.
©Mug Shot/Alamy Stock Photo

dealings, including securities fraud. Black misled shareholders of his company and is thought to have coerced two elderly widows into selling him companies for much less than the companies were actually worth. When accused of inappropriate behaviour, Conrad Black has responded with aggression and anger, writing scathing newspaper articles directed at his accusers. Black has reportedly spent lavishly on company accounts and gone back on agreements made with businesses with which he worked. The case of Conrad Black demonstrates that even people who hold esteemed positions within society may show signs of antisocial personality disorder.

The psychopathy designation places emphasis on more subjective characteristics, such as the incapacity to feel guilt, a high degree of superficial charm, or having callous social attitudes. The distinction can get blurred, because the *DSM-5* also includes a subjective criterion, "lack of remorse," in its definition of antisocial personality disorder. However, the concept of psychopathy is mainly a research construct, pioneered by the scientific work of Canadian psychologist Robert Hare. He developed a measure of the construct called the Psychopathy Checklist, which contains two major clusters of symptoms. One cluster refers to emotional and interpersonal traits, such as incapacity for fear, superficial charm, lack of empathy and care for others, being egocentric, and having callous social attitudes and shallow emotions. The second cluster assesses the social deviance associated with an antisocial lifestyle, such as being impulsive, displaying poor self-control, possessing a high need for excitement, and having early and chronic behavioural problems. The major distinction between psychopathy and antisocial personality disorder mainly lies in the first cluster of emotional and interpersonal traits that define psychopathy. Consequently, most extreme psychopaths would meet criteria for a diagnosis of antisocial personality disorder, but not all people with antisocial personality disorder are psychopaths (if they don't have the subjective characteristics of superficial charm, egocentricity, lack of empathy, and shallow emotions). Two theories of the origins of psychopathy are discussed in A Closer Look: Theories of the Psychopathic Mind.

Table 19.4   Characteristics of Individuals with Antisocial Personality Disorder
Fails to conform to social norms, e.g., breaks the law
Repeated lying or conning others for pleasure or profit
Impulsivity
Irritable and aggressive, e.g., frequent fights
Reckless disregard for safety of others and self
Irresponsible, e.g., truant from school, cannot hold a job
Lack of remorse, e.g., indifferent to pain of others, rationalizes having hurt or mistreated others
Typical Thoughts Associated with the Antisocial Personality
"Laws don't apply to me."
"I'll say whatever it takes to get what I want."
"I think I'll skip work today and go to the racetrack."
"That guy I beat up deserved every bit of it."
"She had it coming, she asked for it . . ."
"I'm the one you should feel sorry for here . . ."

One interesting concept is the notion of the "successful" psychopath. Certainly there are some features of psychopathy that may be adaptive in some circumstances, such as interpersonal charm and charisma, fearlessness, and a willingness to take calculated risks. Some psychologists have speculated that these features of psychopathy may facilitate success in certain professions, such as financial consulting, politics, and contact sports. A recent review of research on the "successful" psychopath (Lilienfeld, Watts, & Smith, 2015) concluded that it is a controversial and elusive concept, fraught with alternative interpretations, and requires additional research to determine if a positive manifestation of psychopathy can exist without the truly maladaptive and negative elements. Nevertheless, various surveys of psychopathy in business and corporate settings have suggested that between 4 percent and 20 percent of individuals could be described as psychopaths (Brooks & Fritzon, 2016).

 Exercise

For the next week, read through at least one online news outlet each day. Look for stories on people who might be good examples of antisocial personality disorder, such as murderers, white-collar criminals, and con artists. Look for evidence from the person's life and actual behaviours that match the characteristics of antisocial personality listed in Table 19.4.

When evaluating antisocial personality profile, it is good to keep in mind the social and environmental contexts in which some people live. Psychologists have expressed concern that the *antisocial* label is sometimes applied to people who live in settings where socially undesirable behaviours (such as fighting) are viewed as protective. For example, in a high-crime area, some of the antisocial attitudes may safeguard people against being victimized. Thus, the term *antisocial* should be used only when the behaviour pattern is indicative of dysfunction and is not simply a response to the immediate social context. For example, youths who emigrate from war-ravaged countries, where aggressive behaviours are necessary to survive each day, should not be considered antisocial. The economic and social contexts must be taken into account when deciding whether undesirable behaviours are signs of dysfunction.

 A Closer Look

Theories of the Psychopathic Mind

Here we compare two theories about the origins of psychopathy: a biological explanation and a social learning explanation. Many psychologists have argued that psychopathy is caused by a biological deficit or abnormality (e.g., Cleckley, 1988; Fowles, 1980; Gray, 1987a, 1987b). Research along these lines has focused on the idea that psychopaths are deficient in their ability to experience fear (Lykken, 1982). Being deficient in fear would help explain why psychopaths do not learn as well from punishment as from reward (Newman, 1987). Psychopaths may pursue a career in crime and lawlessness because, in part, they are simply not afraid of the punishment because they are insensitive to fear.

The theory of Jeffrey Gray (1990) has been influential to a number of researchers looking for a biological explanation of psychopathy. Recall from Chapter 7 that Gray proposed a system in the brain that is responsible for inhibiting behaviour. The behavioural inhibition system (BIS) acts as a psychological brake, responsible for interrupting ongoing behaviour when cues of punishment are present. According to Gray, the BIS is the part of the brain that is especially sensitive to signals of punishment coming from the environment. People who sense that a punishment is likely to occur typically stop what they are doing and look for ways to avoid the punishment.

Researchers are beginning to examine the emotional lives of psychopaths, especially with respect to their experience of anxiety and other negative emotions. Psychologist Chris Patrick and his colleagues are following an interesting line of research. One study examined a group of prisoners, all of whom were convicted of sexual offences (Patrick, Bradley, & Lang, 1993). Even in this group of severe offenders, some individuals were more psychopathic than others, as measured by Hare's Psychopathy Checklist (Hare, Hart, & Harpur, 1991). Patrick and his colleagues had the prisoners look at unpleasant pictures (e.g., injured people, threatening animals) to try to bring about feelings of anxiety. While they were looking at the pictures, the prisoners were startled by random bursts of a loud noise. People typically blink their eyes when they are startled by a loud noise. Moreover, a person who is in an anxious or fearful state when startled will blink faster and harder than a person in a normal emotional state. This means that eye-blink speed when startled may be an objective physiological measure of how anxious or fearful a person is feeling. That is, the **eye-blink startle method** may allow researchers to measure how anxious individuals are without actually having to ask them.

The results from this study of prisoners showed that the more psychopathic offenders displayed *less* of the eye-blink effect when startled, indicating that they were experiencing relatively *less* anxiety to the same unpleasant pictures. However, when *asked* about how distressing the pictures were, both the psychopaths and the nonpsychopaths reported that the pictures were distressing. Overall, these results suggest that psychopaths will say that they are feeling anxious or distressed, yet direct nervous system measures suggest that they are actually *experiencing* less anxiety than nonpsychopaths in the same situation.

In another study, Patrick, Cuthbert, and Lang (1994) again used a group of prisoners who differed from each other in terms of antisocial behaviours. This time, the prisoners were asked to imagine fearful scenes such as having to undergo an operation. The low- and high-antisocial prisoners did not differ in terms of their self-reports of fear and anxiety—all reported more of these emotions in response to the fear images than in response to neutral images such as walking across the yard. Large differences, however, were found in their *physiological* responses to the fear images. The less antisocial prisoners were more aroused by the fear imagery than were the antisocial subjects. In other words, the antisocial prisoners displayed a deficit in fear responding when their fear responses were assessed with physiological measures, which are less susceptible to being faked than the self-report measures. These results are consistent with the idea that the psychopath is deficient in the ability to experience fear and anxiety. In a review of the literature, Patrick (1994) argued that the core problem with psychopaths is a deficit in the fear response. As a consequence, the psychopath is not motivated to interrupt ongoing behaviour in order to avoid punishment or other unpleasant consequences.

Other researchers have de-emphasized biological explanations for psychopathy and argue instead that the emotional unresponsiveness of the psychopath is learned (Levenson, Kiehl, & Fitzpatrick, 1995). The observed fearlessness of the psychopath may be the result of a desensitization process. If a person is repeatedly exposed to violence or other antisocial behaviour (such as childhood abuse or gang activities), they may become desensitized to such behaviours. That is, the callous disregard for others—the hallmark of psychopathy—may result from desensitization, a well-known form of learning. A prospective study of more than 400 victims of childhood abuse found that, compared with a control group, the abused children had significantly higher rates of psychopathy 20 years later (Luntz & Widom, 1994). By being victims of abuse, the argument goes, people learn that abusing others is a means of achieving power and control and obtaining what they want. Many psychopaths are motivated by interpersonal dominance and appear to enjoy having power over others. This can sometimes be seen in board meetings of corporations, in police stations, in politics, and wherever else one person has an opportunity to bully others. The point of this research, however, is that people who grow up to be bullies were themselves frequently bullied and abused as children.

This is the kind of photo used in the study by psychologist Chris Patrick, who found that psychopaths did not exhibit the normal fear response to such threatening stimuli.
©Taras Verkhovynets/Shutterstock

Levenson (1992) has used results such as these to argue for a social learning model of psychopathy. He holds that at some point people decide to engage in antisocial behaviour because they have learned from observing others that this is one way to get what they want.

Psychologists are currently debating the relative merits of viewing psychopathy as biological or as learned. Whatever the cause of psychopathy, the frequency and severity of antisocial behaviours almost always decrease as a person ages. It has been said that the best therapy for the psychopath is to grow older while in prison. The incidence of antisocial behaviours dramatically decreases in individuals age 40 and older (*DSM-5*). It has been widely known that, among criminals, those who make it to their fourth decade are much less likely to be rearrested for antisocial acts than are those in their twenties or thirties. For example, a study of 809 male prison inmates aged 16–69 found that deviant social behaviours, impulsivity, and antisocial acts were much less prevalent in the older prisoners (Harpur & Hare, 1994). There was less of an age decline in antisocial beliefs and callous social attitudes. Thus, although older psychopaths still don't care much about other people or their feelings, they nevertheless are less likely to impulsively act out these beliefs or to engage in actual antisocial behaviours.

Borderline Personality Disorder

The lives of people with **borderline personality disorder** are marked by *instability*. Their relationships are unstable, their behaviour is unstable, their emotions are unstable, and even their images of themselves are unstable. Let's consider each of these, starting with relationships.

The relationships of borderline individuals tend to be intense, emotional, and potentially violent. They suffer from strong fears of abandonment. If such individuals sense separation or rejection in an important relationship, profound changes in their self-image and in how they behave may result, such as becoming very angry at other people. Borderline individuals show marked difficulties in their relationships. When others leave them, they feel strong abandonment fears and sometimes become angry or *aggressive*. Sometimes, in their efforts to manipulate people back into their relationships, they engage in *self-mutilating behaviour* (burning or cutting themselves) or suicide attempts. A study of 84 hospital patients with a diagnosis of borderline personality disorder found that 72 percent had a history of attempting suicide (Soloff, Lis, Kelly, & Cornelius, 1994). In fact, among this sample, the average borderline patient had attempted suicide on at least three occasions. Recent research suggests that greater impairments in emotional perception in individuals with borderline personality disorder increase the risk for self-harm (Williams et al., 2015). We explore this further in Highlight on Canadian Research: Ambiguous Facial Expressions and Borderline Personality Disorder.

 # Highlight on Canadian Research

Ambiguous Facial Expressions and Borderline Personality Disorder

Researchers have long suspected that the misinterpretation of emotional cues is central to borderline personality disorder (BPD) (Linehan, 1995). Alexander Daros, Amanda Uliaszek, and Anthony Ruocco of the University of Toronto tested this hypothesis by comparing performance on the Penn Emotional Acuity Test (PEAT) in females with BPD and IQ and age-matched nonpsychiatric controls. The PEAT involves presenting an individual with 40 pictures of faces conveying neutral, happy, or sad expressions and asking the individual to rate the emotional expression on each face. The pictures conveying happiness and sadness differ in the intensity of their emotional expression: some convey mild emotion, others moderate emotion, and some prototypical emotions. Faces must be rated as *very sad, moderately sad, mildly sad, neutral, mildly happy, moderately happy*, or *very happy*. Both response time and accuracy are recorded as individuals complete the PEAT.

Daros, Uliaszek, and Ruocco (2014) found that both individuals with BPD and nonpsychiatric controls classified intense emotional expressions quickly and accurately. However individuals with BPD were less accurate than controls when asked to classify facial expressions that were neutral or mildly sad. When the facial expression was neutral, individuals with BPD tended to classify the face as conveying an emotion, although they were equally likely to classify the neutral face as happy or sad. When the facial expression was mildly sad, individuals with BPD were more likely to classify it as more intensely sad. Despite the difference in accuracy, response times to the faces were similar for individuals with BPD and controls. Daros and colleagues (2014) suggest that individuals with BPD may misperceive facial expressions conveying little or no emotional content as conveying an emotion, which may in turn contribute to the symptoms of the disorder. The researchers speculate that treatment that encourages individuals with BPD to be more mindful of their reactions to ambiguous facial expressions may be beneficial.

The relationships of borderline individuals are unpredictable and intense. They may go from idealizing the other to ridiculing the other. They are prone to sudden shifts in their views of relationships, behaving at one time in a caring manner and at another time in a punishing and cruel manner. They may go from being submissive to being an avenger for past wrongs. The 1987 Oscar-nominated movie *Fatal Attraction* contains a character with several features of the borderline personality disorder.

Borderline people also have *shifting views of themselves*. Their values and goals are shallow and change easily. Their opinions may change suddenly. They may experiment with different kinds of friends or with different sexual orientations. Usually, they view themselves as, at heart, evil or bad. Self-harming acts are common and increase when others threaten to leave or demand that the person with borderline personality disorder assume some new responsibilities.

Strong emotions are common in the borderline personality, including panic, anger, and despair. Mostly, these emotions are caused by interpersonal events, especially abandonment or neglect. When stressed by others, the borderline person may lash out, becoming bitter, sarcastic, or aggressive. Periods of anger are often followed by shame, guilt, and feelings of being evil or bad. Borderline people often complain of feeling empty. They also have a way of undermining their own best efforts, such as dropping out of a training program just before finishing or destroying a caring relationship just when it starts going smoothly.

People with borderline personality disorder are characterized by huge vacillations in both mood and feelings about the self and others. They can shift quickly from loving another to hating that same person. They are very demanding on their friends, relatives, lovers, and therapists because they are manipulative. For example, they may threaten or even try suicide when they don't get their way. They are very sensitive to cues that others may abandon or leave them. In particular, people with borderline personality disorder tend to have difficulty correctly identifying neutral facial expressions, which may lead to inaccurate inferences about what others are thinking and feeling (Daros, Uliaszek, & Ruocco, 2014).

Table 19.5 lists the major features of borderline personality disorder, along with examples of beliefs and thoughts that those with this disorder might commonly have. People with borderline personality disorder, compared with those without, have a higher incidence rate of childhood physical or sexual abuse, neglect, or early parental loss. Many researchers believe that borderline disorder is caused by an early loss of love from parents, as may happen in parental death, abuse, severe neglect, or parental drug or alcohol abuse (Kuo, Khoury, Metcalfe, Fitzpatrick, & Goodwill, 2015; Millon et al., 2000). Early loss may affect a child's capacity to form relationships. Children in such circumstances may come to believe that others are not to be trusted. Individuals with borderline personality disorder have also been shown to have difficulty accurately recalling events from the past, which may contribute to their seemingly erratic behaviour (Ruocco & Bahl, 2014). We illustrate one example of how Hollywood explores this disorder in A Closer Look: Does Anakin Skywalker Suffer from Borderline Personality Disorder? Although individuals have difficulty with relationships, they may form stable relationships if given enough structure and support. If they find someone who is accepting and stable, who is diplomatic, who meets their expectations for commitment, and who is caring and can defuse trouble as it occurs, then the borderline personality may experience a satisfying relationship. Recent

Table 19.5   Characteristics of Borderline Personality Disorder
Instability of relationships, emotions, and self-image
Fears of abandonment
Aggressiveness
Proneness to self-harm
Strong emotions
Typical Thoughts or Beliefs Associated with the Borderline Personality
"I'm nothing without you."
"I'll just die if you leave me."
"If you go, I'll kill myself."
"I hate you, I hate you, I HATE YOU."
"I love you so much that I'll do anything or be anything for you."
"I feel empty inside, as if I don't know who I am."

 A Closer Look

Does Anakin Skywalker Suffer from Borderline Personality Disorder?

French researcher Eric Bui was working on his graduate degree around the time that two Star Wars prequels, *Attack of the Clones* (2002) and *Revenge of the Sith* (2005), were released. While watching these movies, Bui noticed that Anakin Skywalker (who eventually becomes Darth Vader) exhibited many of the traits typically associated with borderline personality disorder (BPD). Bui notes that Anakin's life history was similar to many people with BPD: his father was absent and he was separated from his mother from an early age. In addition, Anakin's omnipotent and impulsive behaviour as a child, combined with dysfunctional relationships, mirrors that of many people with BPD. Finally, Anakin fulfills six out of nine of the DSM criteria for BPD. First, he is impulsive and can't control his anger. Second, he can't decide if he idealizes his mentors or hates them. Third, he is so afraid of being abandoned by his wife that he betrays his friends to secure the relationship. Fourth, he experiences dissociative episodes following stressful events. Fifth, he acts out violently. And sixth, he clearly has an identity disturbance which culminates in him turning to the dark side and changing his name. Bui thus concludes that Anakin Skywalker possesses both the psychodynamic and criteriological features of BPD (Bui, Rodgers, Chabrol, Birmes, & Schmitt, 2011).

In the movies Attack of the Clones *and* Revenge of the Sith, *Anakin Skywalker exhibits six out of nine criteria for borderline personality disorder; only five criteria need to be met for a diagnosis of BPD.*
©Moviestore collection Ltd/Alamy Stock Photo

research has also suggested that with the right treatment and therapy, many people with borderline personality disorder appear to experience a remission of symptoms and are able to leave fulfilling and productive lives (Gunderson et al., 2011).

Histrionic Personality Disorder

The hallmarks of **histrionic personality disorder** are *excessive attention seeking* and *emotionality*. Often such individuals are overly dramatic, preferring to be the centre of attention. They may appear charming or even flirtatious. Many are inappropriately seductive or provocative. And this *sexually provocative* behaviour is often undirected and occurs in inappropriate settings, such as in professional settings. Physical appearance is often very important to histrionic individuals, and they work to impress others and obtain compliments. Often, however, they overdo it and appear gaudy or flamboyant (e.g., histrionic women may wear way too much makeup).

Individuals with histrionic personality disorder express their opinions frequently and dramatically. However, their *opinions are shallow* and easily changed. Such a person may say, for example, that some political official is a great and wonderful leader yet be unable to give any supporting details or actual examples of leadership. Such individuals prefer impressions to facts and often act on intuition (Millon et al., 2000). They may *display strong emotions in public,* sometimes to the embarrassment of friends and family. They may throw temper tantrums over minor frustrations or cry uncontrollably over a sentimental little event. To others, their emotions appear insincere and exaggerated, to the point of being theatrical. Histrionic individuals are also highly *suggestible.* Because their opinions are not based on facts, they can be easily swayed. They take up whatever is popular at the time.

Socially, histrionic individuals are difficult to get along with, due to their *excessive need for attention.* They may become upset and act impulsively when not given the attention they think they deserve. Such individuals may use suicidal gestures and threats to get attention from others and to manipulate others into caring for them. Their seductiveness may put them at risk for sexual victimization. Other social difficulties arise out of their shallow emotional style. That is, they crave excitement and novelty, and although they may start relationships or projects with great enthusiasm, their interest does not last long. They may forgo long-term gains to make way for short-term excitement. Histrionic traits are maladaptive because they can interfere with relationships and cause difficulties with the individual being a productive member of society.

Table 19.6 lists the main characteristics of histrionic personality disorder, along with typical beliefs and thoughts people with this disorder might have. As with all personality disorder criteria, the standards for appropriate behaviour differ greatly among cultures, generations, and genders. Therefore, we must ask whether specific behaviours cause social impairment or distress before concluding that those behaviours are signs or symptoms of histrionic personality disorder. For example, behaviour that is considered seductive in one culture may be viewed as acceptable behaviour in another. A woman from the southern coast of Italy may appear flirtatious in North America, when, in fact, in her culture people are much more friendly and at ease with each other, and teasing flirtation is a common form of interaction. Consider also the culture of gender. The expression of histrionic personality disorder may depend on gender stereotypes. A man with this personality may behave in a "hyper-macho" fashion and attempt to be the centre of attention by boasting of his skills

Table 19.6 Characteristics of Histrionic Personality Disorder
Excessive attention seeking
Excessive and strong emotions
Sexual provocativeness
Shallow opinions
Suggestibility
Strong need for attention
Typical Thoughts or Beliefs Associated with the Histrionic Personality
"Hey, look at me!"
"I am happiest when I am the centre of attention."
"Boredom is the pits."
"I usually go with my intuition; I don't have to think things through."
"I can amuse, impress, or entertain anyone, mainly because I am so interesting and exciting."
"If I feel like doing something, I go ahead and do it."

✐ Application

A case of histrionic personality disorder. Roxann was a student who also worked in the evenings as a dancer at an adult club. She would tell people that this was temporary and that she was different from the other women who worked there. She readily admitted, however, that the job met her two most important needs: money and attention, "two things I cannot live without." Roxann decided to take some psychology courses for self-improvement. She typically showed up to classes dressed to kill and seemed out of place even among students her own age. Once she went to her professor's office yet did not seem to have any direct questions to discuss. Instead, she seemed just to want to talk about herself and her extracurricular job. After this meeting, she was overheard telling other students that she was on a first-name basis with her professor and that he was actually her good friend. In class, she frequently behaved in ways that drew attention to herself, such as sighing loudly when the professor made a point, or blurting out answers to rhetorical questions. Toward the end of the course, Roxann quit going to class and missed the final exam. She e-mailed the professor, saying that she had been experiencing a debilitating condition and frequently had to lie down to avoid fainting. She said she had been to several doctors, but none were able to find any medical basis for her condition. The professor never heard from her again.

in seduction or how much influence and power he has in his workplace. A woman with the histrionic style may express it with hyperfemininity, seeking to be the centre of attention by adorning herself with bright, sexy clothes and wearing lots of gaudy accessories and makeup.

Narcissistic Personality Disorder

The calling cards of **narcissistic personality disorder** are a strong *need to be admired,* a strong sense of *self-importance,* and a *lack of insight into other people's feelings.* Those with this disorder see themselves in a very favourable light, inflating their accomplishments and undervaluing the work of others. They daydream about prosperity, victory, influence, adoration from others, and power. They routinely expect adulation from others, believing that homage is generally long overdue. They exhibit feelings of *entitlement,* believing that they should receive special privileges and respect, even though they have done nothing in particular to earn that special treatment.

A sense of *superiority* also pervades the narcissistic personality. Individuals feel that they are special and should associate only with others who are similarly unique or gifted. Because they associate with special people, their own views of themselves are further enhanced. Such a person may insist on having the best lawyer or attending the best university, viewing him- or herself as unique, different from, and better than everyone else.

People with this personality disorder expect a lot from those around them. They must receive regular praise from others and devoted admiration from those close to them. Many clinically narcissistic individuals prefer as friends those who are socially weak or unpopular so that they will not compete with the narcissist for attention. The narcissistic paradox is that although narcissists have high self-esteem, their *grandiose self-esteem is actually quite fragile.* That is, even though they appear self-confident and strong, they need to prop themselves up with admiration and attention from others. You might think that someone with truly high self-esteem would not have such an unreasonable need for praise and admiration from others. When people with narcissistic personality disorder show up at a party, they expect to be welcomed with great fanfare. When they go to a restaurant or store, they assume that waiters or clerks will rush to their attention. They thus depend on others to verify their self-importance.

To say that narcissists' self-esteem is vulnerable does not mean that they are covering up low self-esteem, but rather that they are exquisitely sensitive to criticism, that they can fly into a rage when they don't get what they think they deserve. Their self-esteem is full-blown and real; narcissists fully expect others to recognize how special, unique, and superior they are, even in the absence of any objective supportive evidence. Their vulnerability is exhibited as a thin-skinned, bristling kind of sensitivity, similar to childish temper tantrums and pouting. Such reactions indicate an inflated self-importance that knows no bounds.

Another social difficulty experienced by individuals with narcissistic personality disorder is an *inability to recognize the needs or desires of others*. In conversation, they tend to talk mostly about themselves—"I" this and "my" that. They use first-person pronouns (*I, me, mine*) more frequently in everyday conversation than does the average person (Raskin & Shaw, 1987). Psychologists Richard Robins and Oliver John (1997) have found that people scoring high on a narcissistic traits evaluate their performances much more positively than those performances are evaluated by others, demonstrating the self-enhancement component of narcissism. People who are in a relationship with a narcissist often complain that they are self-centred, emotionally cold, and unwilling to reciprocate in the normal give-and-take of a relationship.

A final social difficulty that creates problems for the narcissistic personality is the ease with which they become *envious of others*. When hearing of the success or accomplishment of acquaintances, those with narcissistic personality disorder may disparage that achievement. They may feel that they deserve the success more than the those who worked to attain it, and they often disdain others' accomplishments, particularly in public. A veneer of snobbery may hide strong feelings of envy and rage over the successes of others.

Table 19.7 lists the main characteristics of narcissistic personality disorder, along with examples of some typical beliefs and thoughts individuals with this disorder might have. Those with this disorder sometimes reach positions of high achievement, due primarily to their self-confidence and ambition. Nevertheless, their interpersonal lives are usually fraught with the problems that come with feelings of entitlement, an excessive need for praise and recognition, and an impaired recognition of others' needs. They have difficulty maintaining intimate relationships.

Table 19.7   Characteristics of Narcissistic Personality Disorder

Need to be admired

Strong sense of self-importance

Lack of insight into other people's feelings and needs

Sense of entitlement

Sense of superiority

Self-esteem that is strong but paradoxically fragile

Envy of others

Typical Thoughts or Beliefs Associated with the Narcissistic Personality

"I'm special and deserve special treatment."

"The typical rules don't apply to me."

"If others don't give me the praise and recognition I deserve, they should be punished."

"Other people should do my bidding."

"Who are *you* to criticize *me*?"

"I have every reason to expect that I will get the best that life has to offer."

 Exercise

Everyone knows someone who is high in narcissism. Think of the most narcissistic person you know. List five characteristics or behaviours that make you think that this person is a narcissist. How do the acts and characteristics you have listed fit with the symptoms of the narcissistic personality disorder?

Cluster C. The Anxious Cluster: Ways of Being Fearful and Distressed

The final cluster of personality traits consists of patterns of behaviour that are geared toward avoiding anxiety. The disorders in this cluster, like all the other disorders, illustrate the **neurotic paradox**: although a behaviour pattern successfully solves one problem for the person, it may create or maintain another equally or more severe problem.

Avoidant Personality Disorder

The major feature of the **avoidant personality disorder** is a pervasive *feeling of inadequacy* and *sensitivity to criticism* from others. Clearly, no one likes to be criticized. However, people with avoidant personality disorder will go to great lengths to avoid situations in which others may have opportunities to criticize their performance or character, such as in school, at work, or in other group settings. The main reason for this anxiety about performance is an extreme fear of criticism or rejection from others. Such individuals may avoid making new friends or going to new places, through fear of criticism or disapproval. Friends may have to plead and promise lots of support and encouragement in order to get them involved in new activities.

Application

The case of Nadia, university student with avoidant personality disorder. **Nadia is a 21-year-old university student who has gone to the university's psychological clinic with the general complaint that she is uncomfortable in social settings. Because she is so shy and nervous, she keeps her contact with others to a minimum. She is worried about starting new classes next semester and having to be in rooms with total strangers. She is especially worried about her psychology courses, where "they might find out I am a nutcase." She suggests, "They are going to think I am a dysfunctional idiot because I am so shy and I go into a panic at the thought of speaking up in a group of strangers." Nadia adds that she is thinking of switching her major from psychology to computer science. Although she is curious about people, and therefore likes psychology, she nevertheless feels awkward around them. Computers, she thinks, are much easier to get along with.**

Nadia reports that, as a child, she was teased mercilessly by the other children in her school. She remembers withdrawing from others at about this time in her life. She says that in grade school she would try to make herself small and inconspicuous, so others would not notice her. As a teenager, she took some jobs babysitting, but she has never held a real job. At the university, she apparently has no friends, or at least cannot name any. She says she is afraid others will not like her "when they find out what I am really like," so she avoids social contact. In fact, she never once makes eye contact with the interviewer at the clinic.

At the university, Nadia follows a pattern of letting work pile up, then works hard to get it all done. She tries to do a few errands each day, keeps her apartment neat, and goes to the grocery

store twice a month. She describes her life as "not very happy, but at least predictable." She says she enjoys going to chat rooms on the Internet, but when pressed on this, she confesses that she just watches and has never actually interacted with anyone over the Internet. She likes staying in the background, watching others interact: "when they don't even know I'm there, then I can be pretty sure they are not laughing at me."

Because people with avoidant personalities fear criticism, they may *restrict their activities* to avoid potential embarrassments. For example, an avoidant man may cancel a blind date at the last minute because he can't find just the right clothes to wear. Avoidant individuals cope with anxiety by avoiding the risks of everyday social life. However, by avoiding the anxiety, they create other problems, often in the form of missed opportunities. In addition, avoidant individuals are typically seen by others as meek, quiet, shy, lonely, and solitary.

Individuals with avoidant personality disorder are sensitive to what others think of them. Their feelings are easily hurt, and they appear vulnerable and inhibited in social interactions, withholding their own views, opinions, or feelings out of fear of being ridiculed. They typically have very *low self-esteem* and feel inadequate to many of life's day-to-day challenges. Because of their social isolation, they typically do not have many sources of social support. Even though they typically desire to be involved with others, and may even fantasize about relationships, they tend to avoid intimate contact out of their fear of rejection and criticism. The paradox is that, in avoidantly coping with their social anxiety, they shun the supportive relationships with caring others that could actually help boost their self-esteem. Table 19.8 presents the main features of the avoidant personality disorder, along with several examples of thoughts and beliefs that might occur in someone with this disorder.

Table 19.8 Characteristics of Avoidant Personality Disorder
Feelings of inadequacy
Sensitive to criticism
Activities are restricted to avoid embarrassment
Low self-esteem
Typical Thoughts or Beliefs Associated with the Avoidant Personality
"I am socially inept and undesirable."
"I wish you would like me, but I think you really hate me."
"I can't stand being criticized; it makes me feel so unpleasant."
"I must avoid unpleasant situations at all costs."
"I don't want to attract attention to myself."
"If I ignore a problem, it will go away."

Dependent Personality Disorder

Whereas the person with avoidant personality disorder avoids others to an extreme, the person with dependent personality disorder seeks out others to an extreme. The hallmark of **dependent personality disorder** is an *excessive need to be taken care of,* to be nurtured, coddled, and told what to do. Individuals with dependent personality disorder act in *submissive* ways so as to encourage others to take care of them or take charge of the situation. Such individuals need lots of encouragement and advice from others and would much rather turn over responsibility for their decisions to someone else. Where should they live, what schools should they attend, what courses should they take, with whom should they make friends? The dependent personality has great difficulty making such decisions, and *seeks out reassurance from others.* However, such a person tends to seek advice about even minor decisions, such as whether to carry an umbrella today, what colour clothes to wear, and what entree to order at a restaurant. The dependent person *rarely takes the initiative.*

Because of their fear of losing the help and advice of others, people with dependent personality disorder *avoid disagreements* with those on whom they are dependent. Because of their extreme need for support, dependent personalities might even agree with decisions or opinions that they feel are wrong to avoid angering the people on whom they depend.

Because of their low self-confidence and need for constant reassurance, individuals with dependent personality disorder may *not work well independently.* They may wait for others to start projects or may need direction often during a task. They may demonstrate how inept they are, so as to trick others into assisting them. They may avoid becoming proficient at a task, so as to keep others from seeing that they are competent to work by themselves. It is too bad that a person who relies on others to solve problems may never learn the skills of living or working independently.

Those with dependent personalities *may tolerate extreme circumstances to obtain reassurance and support from others.* Such people may submit to unreasonable demands, may tolerate abuse, or may stay in a distorted relationship. People who believe that they are unable to take care of themselves may tolerate a lot of abuse in order to maintain bonds with people who will take care of them. The unfortunate aspect of the dependent personality is that by giving over responsibility and depending on other people, dependent individuals may never discover that they can take care of themselves. Table 19.9 presents the main characteristics of dependent personality disorder along with associated beliefs and thoughts that individuals with this disorder might have.

Table 19.9 Characteristics of Dependent Personality Disorder

Has an excessive need to be taken care of

Is submissive

Seeks reassurance from others

Rarely takes initiative and rarely disagrees with others

Does not work well independently

May tolerate abuse from others to obtain support

Typical Thoughts or Beliefs Associated with the Dependent Personality

"I am weak and need support."

"The worst possible thing would be to be abandoned and left alone."

"I must not offend those on whom I depend."

"I must be submissive to obtain their help."

"I need help making decisions."

"I hope someone will tell me what to do."

✎ Application

Degrading and abusive relationships—the way out. A common tactic of keeping people in relationships is to convince them that no one else would want them. This is commonly seen in dysfunctional marriages, in which, for example, the husband degrades the wife constantly. This form of psychological abuse may take the form of constantly pointing out her shortcomings, insulting her appearance or abilities, or pointing to weaknesses. Often, a man who is insecure in his relationship and worried that his mate will leave him will try to lower the self-esteem of his partner so that she will think she cannot do any better. Some men resort to physical abuse. Although the degradation and violence can go from female to male, the more common pattern is for the male to degrade the female.

After undergoing long periods of degradation and psychological abuse, many women do experience a decrease in self-esteem. A woman in this situation may begin to depend more and more on the man for reassurance. She will do whatever she can to avoid making him angry or starting him on one of his bouts of insulting her. She takes no initiative in any decisions about the relationship or the living arrangements and defers every decision to him. If he catches her taking the initiative, he may punish her by again going into a bout of degrading her. She tolerates it in order to obtain the minimal reassurance and support this relationship gives her. Moreover, she is firmly persuaded by him that she cannot find anyone better. Essentially, he psychologically batters her into dependency.

People who are in such abusive relationships, either psychologically or physically, need to realize that they do not have to tolerate such treatment, that they are not the degraded human beings their spouses are portraying them as. The first step is to be empowered to make their own decisions. Often, the first decision is to leave the abusive person and go to a safe place such as a women's shelter or a protective relative. People in abusive relationships have to realize that they can take the initiative. Typically, once this difficult decision is made, others come more easily, and these people can get back on track toward taking care of their own lives.

Obsessive-Compulsive Personality Disorder

Individuals with obsessive-compulsive personality disorder are *preoccupied with order* and *strive to be perfect.* The high need for order can manifest itself in the person's attention to details, however trivial, and fondness for rules, rituals, schedules, and procedures. Such people may, for example, plan out which clothes they will wear every day of the week or clean their apartments every Saturday and Wednesday from 5 until 7 p.m. People with **obsessive-compulsive personality disorder** *hold very high standards for themselves.* However, they may work so hard at being perfect that they are never satisfied with their work. For example, a student might never turn in a research paper because it is never quite perfect enough. The desire for perfection can actually stifle a person's productivity.

Another characteristic is a *devotion to work at the expense of leisure and friendships.* Individuals with obsessive-compulsive personality disorder tend to work harder than they need to. They may work at night and on weekends and rarely take time off. In his book on adult personality development, George Vaillant (1977) saw it as a sign of positive mental adjustment when his adult subjects reported taking at least a one-week vacation each year. Those with obsessive-compulsive personality disorder tend not to meet this criterion for adjustment. When they do take time off for recreation, they prefer serious tasks such as stamp collecting or chess. For hobbies, they pick very demanding tasks or activities that require great attention to detail, such as cross-stitch sewing or computer programming. Even their play looks a lot like work.

The person with obsessive-compulsive personality disorder may also appear *inflexible* with regard to ethics and morals. Such individuals set high principles for themselves and tend to follow the letter of the law. They are highly conscientious and expect others to be that way as well. There is usually only one right way to do something—their way. They often have trouble working with others because they are reluctant to delegate tasks; "If you want something done right, you have to do it yourself" is a common complaint. They become irritated when others don't take their work seriously as they do.

A few other odd characteristics are often present in the obsessive-compulsive personality. One is the preference to hang on to worn-out or useless things; many people with obsessive-compulsive personality disorder have trouble throwing things away. Many are *miserly or stingy,* hoarding their money and resources. And finally, along with being inflexible, individuals can be frustratingly *stubborn.* They may stubbornly insist, for example, that they cannot complete their work because of the imperfections of others. As you might imagine, they often cause difficulties for others at the workplace. Table 19.10 presents the essential features of obsessive-compulsive personality disorder, along with some typical beliefs and thoughts that characterize individuals with this disorder.

Table 19.10   Characteristics of Obsessive-Compulsive Personality Disorder
Preoccupied with order
Perfectionistic
Devoted to work, seeking little leisure time or friendship
Frequently miserly or stingy
Rigid and stubborn
Typical Thoughts or Beliefs Associated with the Obsessive-Compulsive Personality
"I believe in order, rules, and high standards."
"Others are irresponsible, casual, and self-indulgent."
"Details are important; flaws and mistakes are intolerable."
"My way is the only right way to do things."
"If you can't do it perfectly, don't do it at all."
"I have only myself to depend on."

There is another disorder—*obsessive-compulsive disorder* (OCD)—that is often confused with obsessive-compulsive personality disorder (OCPD). OCD is an anxiety disorder that is, in several ways, more serious and debilitating than OCPD. In OCD a pattern of unwanted and intrusive thoughts is recurrent and troubling to the person, such as the persistent thought that one may harm someone. In addition, OCD is characterized by the presence of ritualistic behaviours, such as frequent hand washing or the tendency to repeat actions a set number of times (e.g., having to touch an object three times before leaving a room, or repeating words to oneself three times). Obsessive-compulsive personality disorder, on the other hand, really involves a collection of traits, such as excessive need for order or extremely high conscientiousness.

Nevertheless, people with OCPD are at risk for developing OCD as well as other kinds of anxiety disorders (Oltmanns & Emery, 2004).

Many of the characteristics of obsessive-compulsive personality can be adaptive in some respects. For example, wanting to perform a task as perfectly as possible is, up to a point, desirable and rewarded. Holding one's opinions firm is, up to a point, desirable and indicates character. Keeping everything neat and orderly is, up to a point, useful. How can one tell, however, when some of these characteristics and behaviours indicate an obsessive-compulsive personality? How can we tell the difference between a high level of conscientiousness and the disorder of obsessive-compulsiveness? The clearest way to know when obsessiveness is becoming a disorder is when this pattern of behaviour starts to interfere with a person's ability to be productive or to maintain satisfying relationships. In the case study of Rita presented below, you'll see that her obsessive and compulsive personality led her to behave in ways that seriously interfered with both of these aspects of her life.

 Application

The case of Rita, who has obsessive-compulsive personality disorder. Rita was a 39-year-old computer programmer who had been married for 18 years. She was always orderly and kept a very neat house. It was so neat, in fact, that she noticed when the books were in the wrong order on the bookshelves or if a knick-knack had been moved on a table or shelf. She vacuumed the house every day, whether it needed it or not. This resulted in the need for a new vacuum cleaner almost every year. Her husband thought this odd but concluded that she simply had a low threshold for what counted as dirty. She was constantly nagging him or angry at him because he did not seem to care as much as her that things be so neat, clean, and orderly. They did not have children because, according to Rita, children would be too much additional work for her, and she certainly could not count on her husband to do anything right in terms of taking care of children or the house. Besides, children would disrupt the order and neatness of her life.

Over the years, Rita added to her list of things she needed to do each day but never took anything off the list. In addition to vacuuming, she added dusting each day. Then she added cleaning the sinks with strong cleaners each day. She had to get up earlier in the mornings to get all of this cleaning done before work.

Her boss often complained that she was slow. The boss did not appreciate the fact that Rita checked her work over and over again before turning it in. Rita also had difficulties working as part of a team because none of the other workers met her standards. They did not check their work often enough, she thought, and were sloppy and imprecise. Her boss eventually had to isolate her and give her independent work because she could not get along with her co-workers.

Before leaving the house each morning, Rita checked the windows and doors, the gas, the water faucets, and all the light fixtures. After a few months of this, one check was not sufficient, and she began to check everything twice. Her husband complained about this, so she started making him wait in the car while she checked each sink, light, door, window, and so on. Her husband dutifully waited each day, but as the months went on, the wait grew longer and longer. He was now sitting in the car for an hour each morning, waiting for Rita to finish checking everything in the house. One morning, after checking the house thoroughly, she went outside to find that her husband had left without her. That afternoon she received an e-mail from him saying that he could not take it any longer and had decided to divorce her.

> ⓘ Concept Check
>
> *In your own words, summarize the main features of the three clusters of personality disorders. Within each cluster, what are some of the common traits of the disorders?*
>
> *Compare and contrast (a) schizoid and schizotypal personality disorders; (b) dependent and avoidant personality disorders.*
>
> *What is antisocial personality disorder? How is it similar to, and different from, the concept of psychopathy?*

Prevalence of Personality Disorders

Figure 19.1 indicates the prevalence rates of the 10 personality disorders. **Prevalence** is a term that refers to the total number of cases that are present within a given population during a particular period of time. The data in Figure 19.1 are based on summaries of several community samples (Mattia & Zimmerman, 2001) and refer to prevalence rates at the time of sampling (e.g., at any given time, how many people are diagnosable with paranoid personality disorder?). These results show that obsessive-compulsive personality disorder is the most common, at just over 4 percent prevalence rate. The next most common are schizotypal, histrionic, and dependent personality disorders, approximately 2 percent prevalence each. The least common is narcissistic personality disorder, affecting only 0.2 percent of the population. However, these diagnoses were all based on interviews, and it may be that those with narcissistic personality disorder are least likely to admit to the more disordered features of their condition. In fact, Oltmanns and colleagues have shown that self-reports of narcissism correlate weakly

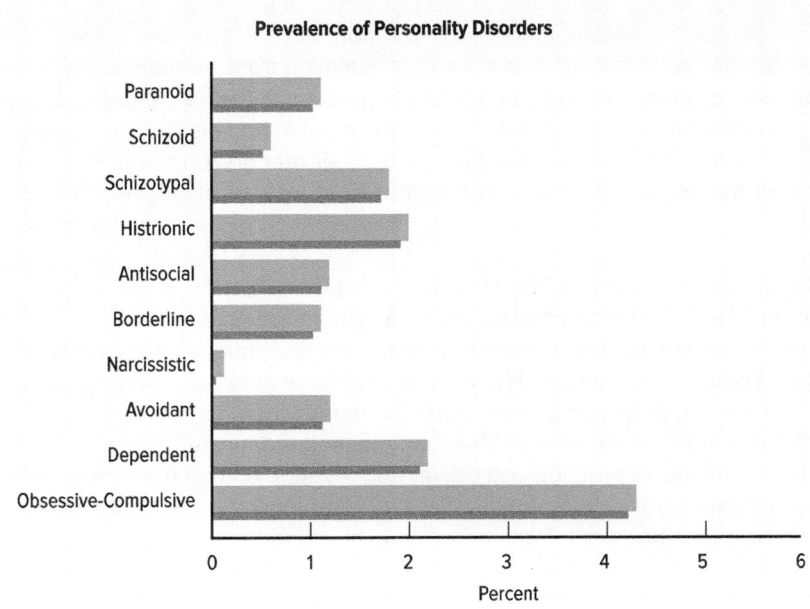

FIGURE 19.1 Estimates of the prevalence of personality disorders.

with peer reports of narcissism, even though with most other personality traits there are modest to substantial correlations between self-report and peer report (Clifton, Turkheimer, & Oltmanns, 2004; Klonsky, Oltmanns, & Turkheimer, 2002; Oltmanns et al., 2004). These findings suggest that, because the data in Figure 19.1 are based on self-report through structured interviews, they may actually underestimate the prevalence of some of the disorders, especially narcissism. The *DSM-5* further reports that narcissistic personality disorder may be one of the most common of the ten (American Psychiatric Association, 2013).

The total prevalence rate for having at least one personality disorder is estimated to be 15 percent (American Psychiatric Association, 2013). That is, at any given time, approximately 15 percent of the population is diagnosable with a personality disorder of one or more types. This brings up the issue of comorbidity. A substantial proportion, between 25 and 50 percent, of the people who meet the criteria for a diagnosis on one personality disorder will also meet the criteria for diagnosis on another personality disorder (Oltmanns & Emery, 2004). Many of the personality disorders contain common features. For example, several disorders involve social isolation, including schizotypal, schizoid, avoidant, and, in many cases, obsessive-compulsive disorder. Uninhibited and irresponsible behaviour is one of the criteria for a diagnosis of borderline, histrionic, and antisocial personality disorders. As such, differential diagnoses are often challenging in personality disorders. A **differential diagnosis** is one in which, out of two or more possible diagnoses, the clinician searches for evidence in support of one diagnostic category over all the others. For illustrative purposes, we explore a case of comorbidity in A Closer Look: The Unabomber: Comorbidity of Personality Disorders.

 A Closer Look

The Unabomber: Comorbidity of Personality Disorders

In 1996, Theodore Kaczynski was arrested for murder in a long line of bombings. He had been mailing bombs to unsuspecting university professors and scientists (hence his FBI code name—Unabomber) for 17 years. Many of his targets were computer scientists, but he did injure one psychology professor with a mail bomb (Professor James McConnell at the University of Michigan). Police knew the bombs were all from the same person, but they had no idea of his motives or why he was targeting university professors. After a 17-year period of anonymous killing and maiming from a distance, he decided to make the nature of his grievances clear. He sent several taunting letters to the FBI, and a long rambling manifesto to the *Washington Post* and *The New York Times*, which published his diatribe against technology and modern society. This was his undoing. Kaczynski's brother recognized the nature of the complaints in the manifesto and notified the police, who arrested Kaczynski at his isolated 10-by-12-foot shack in Montana.

A reporter—Maggie Scarf—writing in *The New Republic* (June 10, 1996, p. 20), presented her view that Ted Kaczynski most likely had a narcissistic personality disorder. Scarf used the *DSM-IV* description of narcissistic disorder to explain Kaczynski's behaviour. For example, as an undergraduate at Harvard, Kaczynski isolated himself so severely that none of his classmates can remember anything about him. He saw himself as a misunderstood genius whom the world would one day recognize. As a mathematics graduate student at the University of Michigan, he isolated himself even more. In his isolation he probably nurtured fantasies of prestige and power and revenge on those who refused to praise him. As a promising young professor of mathematics at U.C.–Berkeley, he suddenly bolted from his faculty position in 1969. No one, apparently, was recognizing his superiority. People did not realize, as he did, that he possessed a phenomenal intellect and superior vision of how everything worked. His colleagues were fools, he must have concluded, because they could not see his obvious superiority. His students, however, complained loudly about his teaching style. In their course evaluations, they indicated that his lectures were boring and useless and that he ignored questions from the students. They too must be fools, Kaczynski probably concluded.

In her article Scarf argued that when Kaczynski struck out at society, he was really saying, "I'm special and I deserve your respect." When he began taunting the police to try to capture him, he was really saying, "I am so extraordinary that I operate with impunity; you haven't been able to catch me for 17 years and you never will." Finally, when he gave his manifesto to the world, he was really saying, "You had better realize you are dealing with someone unprecedented in the history of the human race. I am so clever and powerful and smart that I will tell you all the problems with the world and how to fix them, and if you ignore my commands you do so at your own risk." His entire ranting manifesto is easily located on the World Wide Web by entering "Unabomber" in a search engine.

Scarf is a journalist, not a psychologist, so her diagnosis is based on her speculation. Kaczynski certainly does have some features of the narcissistic personality disorder, but most narcissists are not serial murderers. What other possible clues might we have to his abnormal behaviour? It turns out that the entire text of the court-appointed psychiatrist's report on Ted Kaczynski is available at http://www .paulcooijmans.com/psychology/unabombreport.html (as of August 2019). This report, prepared by government-appointed psychiatrist Sally Johnson, provides another perspective on Kaczynski. While at Harvard, Kaczynski was involved in a study by Henry Murray, whom we discussed in Chapter 11. Personality test results from his undergraduate days at Harvard indicate that he was extremely introverted and somewhat depressive, even at that early age. During his psychological evaluation 30 years later, the main finding was that he suffered from schizophrenia, paranoid type, which is a severe mental illness. However, he also had an IQ of 136, which puts him in the top 1 percent of the population. As for personality disorders, the psychiatrist concluded that Kaczynski had paranoid personality disorder along with many features of the avoidant and antisocial personality disorders as well. The following is a quote from her official report:

Mr. Kaczynski is also diagnosed as suffering from a Paranoid Personality Disorder with Avoidant and Antisocial Features. Review of his developmental history, adolescence and early adult life draws a picture consistent with the symptomatology associated with this type of personality disorder. Consistent with this type of personality disordered function, Mr. Kaczynski historically has shown pervasive distrust of others such that their motives are interpreted as malevolent. Symptoms consistent with Paranoid Personality Disorders that are evident in Mr. Kaczynski's presentation include that he suspects, without sufficient basis, that others are exploiting, harming, or deceiving him; that he reads demeaning or threatening meanings into benign remarks or events; that he persistently bears grudges and is unforgiving of insults, injuries or slights; and that he perceives attacks on his character or reputation that are not apparent to others, and is quick to react angrily or to counterattack.

In addition to meeting the criteria for Paranoid Personality Disorder, Mr. Kaczynski also has features of two other personality disorder types. Support for Avoidant Personality Disorder Traits includes that he has demonstrated a pervasive pattern of social inhibition, feelings of inadequacy and hypersensitivity to negative evaluations, beginning in his early life. Consistent with this, he has shown restraint within intimate relationships because of his fear of being shamed or ridiculed; he has been preoccupied with being criticized or rejected in social situations; and is inhibited in new interpersonal situations because of feelings of inadequacy. Consistent with Antisocial Personality Disorder Traits is his pervasive pattern of disregard for and violation of the rights of others. This includes his failure to conform to social norms with respect to lawful behaviours, as indicated by repeatedly performing acts that are grounds for arrest. This description is based on his own account of his behaviour in his writings and interviews. Also consistent with his Antisocial Personality Traits is the characteristic of deceitfulness, as indicated by his persistent and elaborate efforts to conceal his behaviours. He has demonstrated a reckless regard for the safety of others. He demonstrates a lack of remorse as indicated in his writings by being indifferent to having hurt, mistreated, or stolen from others. Mr. Kaczynski falls short of carrying a diagnosis of Antisocial Personality Disorder in that he does not have evidence of a conduct disorder before the age of 15. (Excerpted from the report of Sally C. Johnson, M.D., Chief Psychiatrist, Associate Warden of Health Services, Federal Correctional Institution, Butner, North Carolina, January, 1996.)

Kaczynski shows features of at least four different personality disorders, with the prominent personality disorder being paranoid personality disorder. This disorder occurred along with paranoid schizophrenia, which involves delusions and elaborate belief systems. The presence of two or more disorders in one person is called *comorbidity*. Comorbidity can occur when two or more personality disorders exist, or when two or more disorders of any type coexist in the same person. Comorbidity is fairly common, and it makes for difficulty in diagnosing disorders (Krueger & Markon, 2006).

Former University of California at Berkeley math professor Theodore Kaczynski was convicted in several of the "Unabomber" attacks, which occurred over a 17-year period. Kaczynski displays characteristics associated with a number of personality disorders.
©Reuters/Corbis

Gender Differences in Personality Disorders

The overall prevalence rate for personality disorders is fairly equal in men and women. A few specific disorders, however, show a tendency to be more prevalent in men or in women. The one disorder with the most disparate gender distribution is antisocial personality disorder, which occurs in men with a prevalence rate of about 4.5 percent and in women at only about a 0.8 percent prevalence rate. As such, about 1 out of every 20 adult men has antisocial personality disorder, whereas it is less than 1 in 100 for women (Oltmanns & Emery, 2004).

A few other personality disorders show tendencies to be more common among men or among women. Borderline and dependent personality disorders may be somewhat more prevalent in women than men, though the evidence is not strong. Paranoid and obsessive-compulsive personality disorder may be more common in men than women, but the difference is not large. One important issue concerns gender biases in diagnoses. For example, in dependent personality disorder, a few of the distinguishing traits might be viewed as traditionally feminine characteristics, such as putting others' needs ahead of one's own or being unassertive. Consequently, if the criteria for this disorder are based on feminine stereotypes, then it might be relatively easier for women than men to meet the criteria for this diagnosis, even if a particular woman is not suffering significant impairment from those particular traits. Clinicians need to be aware of how stereotypes affect the ways they diagnose their clients.

A related issue is gender differences in the manifestation of the different disorders. For example, in histrionic personality disorder a main issue concerns excessive attention seeking. A woman might pursue this through hyperfemininity, perhaps even being sexually seductive. A male might pursue this through hypermasculinity, perhaps through shows of strength and bragging about accomplishments. Each is engaging in excessive attention seeking but doing it in ways that are gender stereotyped.

 Concept Check

How prevalent are personality disorders overall? Why is it important to consider comorbidity when answering this question?

How should issues related to gender be considered in the diagnosis of personality disorders?

Dimensional Model of Personality Disorders

As hinted at the beginning of this chapter, modern theorists are arguing for a dimensional, as opposed to a categorical, view of personality disorders. In the dimensional model of personality, the only distinctions made between normal personality traits and disorders are in terms of extremity, rigidity, and maladaptiveness. For example, Widiger (1997) argues that disorders simply are maladaptive variants and combinations of normal-range personality traits. The personality traits most studied as sources of disorders are the five traits of the five-factor model, which we reviewed in Chapter 3. Costa and Widiger (1994) edited an influential book supporting the idea that the Big Five traits provide a useful framework for understanding disorders. Widiger (1997) presents data arguing that, for example, borderline personality disorder is extreme neuroticism, and schizoid disorder is extreme introversion accompanied by low neuroticism (emotional stability). Extreme introversion accompanied by extremely high neuroticism, on the other hand, results in avoidant personality disorder. Histrionic disorder is characterized as extreme extraversion. Obsessive-compulsive disorder is a maladaptive form of extreme conscientiousness. Schizotypal personality disorder is a complex combination of introversion, high neuroticism, low agreeableness, and extreme openness.

The dimensional view is somewhat like chemistry: Add a little of this trait and some of that trait, amplify to extremely high (or low) levels, and the result is a specific disorder. Dimensional models may have certain advantages, such as accounting for why people in the same diagnostic category can be so different from each other in how they express the disorder. In addition, the dimensional model allows for a person to have multiple disorders of personality. The dimensional model also explicitly acknowledges that the distinction between what is normal and what is abnormal is more a matter of degree than a clear and qualitative break. One line of research is currently underway to develop measures of the Five Factor Model that have higher precision at the tails of the distributions; that is, at the extremely high and extremely low ends (Miller & Lynam, 2015; Samuel & Gore, 2012). The original measures of the Five Factor Model were developed with the greatest precision in the middle of the distribution, which is where most people fall (picture a normal curve, with its bell-shaped distribution). However, if one is interested in the extreme ends of these personality traits, then new measures will need to be developed that have more adequate discrimination and accuracy in measuring the extremes.

As mentioned above, the American Psychiatric Association has decided to continue its application of a categorical view in the definition and diagnosis of personality disorders. The decade of work that went into revising the *DSM-IV* into the *DSM-5* has amounted to essentially "no change" to the way we understand personality disorders. The report of the personality disorders working group does, however, appear in Section III the *DSM-5*. It offers guidelines for the definition and measurement of personality disorders along more dimensional lines.

Notably, the newly proposed guidelines recommend maintaining only six of the original personality disorders: schizotypal, antisocial, borderline, narcissistic, avoidant, and obsessive-compulsive. The remaining four have been recommended for removal because, according to the working group's conclusions, they are neither prevalent enough nor distinct enough from the other disorders to warrant their own diagnostic classification. Any personality disorders observed by clinicians that are not addressed by the primary six disorders could then be diagnosed as a *personality disorder–trait specified*. In addition to identifying whether a patient meets the criteria for one of the six personality disorders, the individual should then be evaluated according to five trait domains. It is this inclusion of trait domains that best approximates a dimensional approach to mental disorders in the recommended approach. The five trait domains are *negative affect* (negative emotions, such as those in high neuroticism), *detachment* (social withdrawal or avoidance), *antagonism* (being deceitful or manipulative, as in low agreeableness), *disinhibition* (impulsiveness and low conscientiousness), and *psychoticism* (including bizarre thoughts and experiences). Determining the degree to which a patient is characterized by each of these trait domains can provide further clarity as to how to best approach treatment (American Psychiatric Association, 2013). Future research will help determine the viability of this newly proposed system for diagnosing personality disorders.

The APA has also changed the numbering system for the *DSM* to numerical rather than roman numbers so that they can introduce more frequent though smaller updates with decimals, similar to software updates—for example *DSM-5.1, DSM-5.2,* and so on. Perhaps one of the minor updates in the future will concern how personality disorders are conceptualized as dimensional rather than categorical.

 Concept Check

Briefly describe the recommended changes to the diagnosis of personality disorders as they appear in Section III of the DSM-5.

Causes of Personality Disorders

The material covered in this chapter so far has been mainly descriptive, drawing from and expanding on the diagnostic criteria in the *DSM-5*. Abnormal psychology is a strongly descriptive science, and efforts are mainly to develop classification systems and taxonomies of disorders. This does not mean, however, that there are no attempts to understand how personality disorders develop or what causes one person to have a particular disorder. Researchers generally examine both biological and environmental factors that contribute to the development of personality disorders (Nigg & Goldsmith, 1994). For example, it is clear that those who suffer with borderline personality disorder experienced poor attachment relationships in childhood (Kernberg, 1975, 1984; Nigg & Goldsmith, 1994), and that many individuals were the target of sexual abuse in childhood (Westen, 1990). There is abundant evidence that most people with borderline personality disorder grew up in chaotic homes, with a lot of exposure to the impulsive behaviour of adults (Millon, 2000b).

It appears that genetic factors play little role in borderline personality disorder. Instead, most of the evidence implicates loss of, or neglect by, the parents in early childhood (Guzder et al., 1996).

When it comes to schizotypal personality disorder, the evidence is more in line with genetic causes. A variety of family, twin, and adoption studies suggest that schizotypal disorder is genetically similar to schizophrenia (Nigg & Goldsmith, 1994). Moreover, the first-degree relatives of those with schizophrenia are much more likely to exhibit features of schizotypal personality disorder than those in the general population. However, prevalence rates for paranoid and avoidant personality disorders were also elevated among the relatives of the schizophrenia patients, suggesting that these disorders may be genetically related to schizophrenia (Kendler et al., 1993).

Antisocial personality disorder also has several explanatory theories. For example, many antisocial individuals were themselves abused and victimized as children (Pollock et al., 1990), leading to social learning and psychoanalytic theories of the cause of this disorder. A high proportion of antisocial people also abuse multiple illegal drugs or alcohol, leading some researchers to propose that biological changes associated with drug abuse are responsible for antisocial behaviour. There are also clear familial trends suggesting that antisocial personality disorder is due, in part, to genetic causes (Lykken, 1995). Others have proposed learning theories of antisocial personality disorder, due mainly to research showing that such individuals are deficient in learning through punishment (e.g., Newman, 1987).

The neurological underpinnings of antisocial and psychopathic traits are also being investigated. A useful model here is the triarchic model, which characterizes psychopaths in terms of three distinguishable components: boldness, meanness, and lack of inhibition (Patrick, Drislane, & Strickland, 2012). A new measure of this triarchic model provides better coverage of these three components than previous inventories (Drislane, Patrick, & Arsal, 2014). Moreover, this new measure correlates with neuroscience findings in quite sensible ways. For example, "boldness" is related to an underreactivity in the brain's defensive motivational system. The "lack of inhibition" component is related to deficits in the frontal cortical regions involved in self-regulation, cognitive control, and moral reasoning. Both of these components—boldness and lack of inhibition—are also associated with brain circuits that process rewards (Seara-Cardoso & Viding, 2015). The third component—"meanness"—is thought to be related to dysfunction in brain systems important to empathy, perspective taking, and perhaps even to lower levels of oxytocin, and neurochemical related to social bonding.

Explanations of the other personality disorders also follow this pattern. There are biological explanations, learning explanations, psychodynamic explanations, and cultural explanations. There may be some truth to each of these views, that personality disorders, like normal-range personality variables, have multiple causes. Moreover, it is very difficult to separate biology from learning, to separate nature from nurture. For example, an individual's early experiences—such as with an abusive parent—may lead to neurological changes in certain brain centres, such as the abnormalities in the hypothalamus and pituitary functioning (e.g., Mason et al., 1994). Consequently, it does not make sense to speak of early childhood abuse as a strictly experiential or learning factor when biological changes can follow from such abusive experiences.

Most of the research on personality disorders is descriptive or correlational. True experiments, where people would be randomly assigned to either have or not have a disorder, are impossible. Because the research is mostly correlational, it cannot pin down the causal direction of relationships that are identified. For example, suppose people with a specific disorder are found to have a high level of a particular neurotransmitter in their system. From these results we know something descriptive, but we don't know whether having a high level of that neurotransmitter causes the disorder, or whether having the disorder causes high levels of the neurotransmitter (or whether a third unknown variable causes both the neurotransmitter changes and the disorder). Consequently, when you read the literature on the "causes" of personality disorders, much of the evidence has to be interpreted with caution because correlational data can rarely prove causality (as we discussed in Chapter 2).

Clearly, biology and experience are tightly intermingled, making it difficult to attribute a disorder to only one kind of cause. Efforts to reduce the cause of personality disorders to one factor—say, genetics—are likely to be an oversimplification. Thus, we have to be comfortable with the notion that something as complicated as human personality—and its disorders—has multiple causes. Table 19.11 presents all of the personality disorders along with descriptions of self-concept, emotional life, behaviour, and social relations of those who have the disorder. Alexithymia, a personality trait associated with emotional awareness and maturity, also seems to be associated with certain personality disorders. We discuss it further in A Closer Look: Alexithymia.

Table 19.11 The Personality Disorders Described According to Unique Characteristics Associated with Self-Concept, Emotional Life, Behaviour, and Social Relations

Specific Disorders	Self-Concept	Emotion	Behaviour	Social Relations
Antisocial Personality	Self as unfettered by rules	Lack of remorse, quick-tempered, easily irritated, aggressive	Reckless, impulsive, irresponsible	Callous and indifferent to rights of others
Borderline Personality	Self as vague, diffuse, changing, unstable, with no strong feeling of identity	Unstable, intense, with anger, shame, and guilt	Unpredictable, perhaps harmful to self or others	Intense, volatile, unstable, fearing abandonment
Histrionic Personality	Self as desirable and charming	Flamboyant in public displays	Attention seeking, extravagant	Attention seeking
Narcissistic Personality	Self as unique, admirable, special	Feelings of entitlement, vengeful when not recognized	Self-displaying, admiration seeking	Envious, lacking in empathy
Schizoid Personality	Self as loner, without ambition	Bland, taking little pleasure in life	Passive	Detached, socially inept, having no or few friends
Schizotypal Personality	Self as different from others, special	Uncomfortable, suspicious	Odd, eccentric with unusual beliefs	Socially anxious, avoiding others
Paranoid Personality	Self as victim	Feels threatened, argumentative, jealous	Distrustful, self-protective, resentful	Sensitive, prone to misinterpretations, with many enemies

Specific Disorders	Self-Concept	Emotion	Behaviour	Social Relations
Avoidant Personality	Self as inadequate	Frequently embarrassed, fearing criticism and rejection	Quiet, shy, solitary	Withdrawing, sensitive to criticism
Dependent Personality	Self as needy, lacking self-direction	Meek, indecisive	Reassurance seeking, rarely taking initiative	Submissive, needs nurturance, avoids conflict
Obsessive-Compulsive Personality	Self as rigid, with high standards and expectations	Easily irritated, stubborn, without much pleasure	Workaholic, likes repetition, details	No time for friends, others don't meet standards

 **A Closer Look**

Alexithymia

Alexithymia, which translates from the Greek to "no words for emotions" is a personality construct characterized by difficulty identifying feelings, difficulty describing feelings to other people, and an externally bound cognitive style (Watters, Taylor, & Bagby, 2015). Alexithymia has been studied extensively by Michael Bagby and Graeme Taylor of the University of Toronto and James Parker of Trent University. Bagby, Taylor, and Parker have demonstrated that alexithymia is a stable personality trait observed in about 10 percent of the population. People with alexithymia not only have difficulty identifying and controlling emotion, but also show a marked deficit in experiencing positive emotions and empathy. Alexithymia is negatively correlated with emotional intelligence and people with alexithymia often develop schizotypal, dependent, and avoidant personality disorders (Parker, Taylor, & Bagby, 2001). Alexithymia is also observed in more than half of people diagnosed with anorexia nervosa, substance use disorder, and major depression. People with alexithymia are also prone to a variety of medical disorders including hypertension, inflammatory bowel disease, migraine, and fibromyalgia (Taylor, Bagby, & Parker, 1999). Researchers believe that an inability to identify emotions (and hence control them) leads people with alexithymia to experience prolonged periods of elevated autonomic nervous system activation, which in turn causes a variety of psychosomatic physical symptoms. Alexithymia not only increases the risk for developing psychological and psychosomatic medical problems, it also makes these disorders difficult to treat through psychotherapy because people with alexithymia have such difficulty describing and modulating their emotional responses. In fact, psychotherapy often exacerbates psychosomatic illnesses and substance use among people with alexithymia (Taylor, Bagby, & Parker, 1999).

Concept Check

How would you summarize the likely causes of personality disorders? In your response, use borderline personality disorder and antisocial personality disorder as examples.

Summary and Evaluation

We began this chapter with a discussion of how disorders of personality draw on almost all the other topics studied so far. The concept of disorder relies on making a distinction between what is normal and what is abnormal. There are several definitions of abnormality. One is statistical and relies on how frequently a condition appears among a population of people. Another definition is sociological and has to do with how much a society tolerates particular forms of behaviour. A psychological definition emphasizes to what extent a behaviour pattern causes distress for the person or for others. For example, is the behaviour associated with disorganization in the person's own thoughts, emotions, or social relations? The hallmark of the psychological definition of abnormal is anything that prevents a person from having satisfying relationships or from carrying on productive work. Most of the personality disorders result in problems with relationships because they impair the person's ability to get along with others. Many of the disorders also impair the person's ability to engage in productive work. We saw that all of the personality disorders refer to symptoms that cause problems with relationships or with work, or both.

Personality disorders are enduring patterns of experience and behaviour that differ greatly from the norm and the expectations of the individual's social group. Disorders typically show up in abnormalities in how people think, in how they feel, in how they get along with others, or in their ability to control their own actions. The patterns are typically displayed across a variety of situations, leading to distress, for either themselves or others, in important areas in life, such as at work or in relations with others. Personality disorders typically have a long history in a person's life and can often be traced back to adolescence or childhood.

In this chapter, we covered the 10 personality disorders contained in the *DSM-5*. We organized these 10 disorders into three clusters: the eccentric cluster (disorders pertaining to ways of being odd), the erratic cluster (disorders pertaining to ways of being unpredictable or violent), and the anxious cluster (disorders pertaining to ways of being nervous or distressed). Each disorder consists of a unique combination of ways of thinking, experiencing, and acting. Future research is likely to emphasize the dimensional view of personality disorders, which sees disorders as simply extreme levels of normal personality traits, or combinations of extreme levels of various traits.

 Concept Check

Think about the concept of disorder, and what it means to have a personality that is "disordered." Do you believe that extreme manifestations of traits as seen in personality disorders should be considered disorders? Why or why not?

Choose one personality disorder from each of the three clusters, and summarize the following: main symptoms or characteristics, prevalence, and causes.

Key Terms

disorder

abnormal psychology

abnormal

psychopathology

categorical view

dimensional view

personality disorder

schizoid personality disorder

schizotypal personality
  disorder

paranoid personality
  disorder

antisocial personality
  disorder

eye-blink startle method

borderline personality
  disorder

histrionic personality
  disorder

narcissistic personality
  disorder

neurotic paradox

avoidant personality
  disorder

dependent personality
  disorder

obsessive-compulsive
  personality disorder

prevalence

differential diagnosis

CHAPTER 20

Summary and Future Directions

Current Status of the Field

Domains of Knowledge: Where We've Been, Where We're Going
Dispositional Domain
Biological Domain
Intrapsychic Domain
Cognitive/Experiential Domain
Social and Cultural Domain
Adjustment Domain

Integration: Personality in the Twenty-First Century

Conclusion

After having read the first 19 chapters of this book, you should be able to provide some insight the next time someone asks, "Why does that person behave that way?" Why do the things people do sometimes seem like a mystery? Personality psychology seeks to open this mystery to scientific investigation. If you are fascinated by the variety of human behaviour, by the clever or silly things that people do, by the ways people solve or create problems for themselves, or by the variety of potential explanations for people's behaviour, then you have something in common with personality psychologists—a deep curiosity about human nature.

Understanding the whole of human nature may seem like an impossible mission, and it is quite a challenge, yet this is the ultimate goal of personality psychology. Psychologist Charles Carver (1996) said that "personality is a topic that's just too large to hold in the mind at once" (p. 330). When confronted with a large and difficult task, it is sometimes useful to

Understanding the whole behind all the parts is the ultimate goal of personality psychology.
Yale University Art Gallery

partition the task into smaller, more manageable domains. This is the approach taken by modern medical science. Medical researchers specialize—there are dermatologists who focus on the skin, heart specialists, lung specialists, and so on. This is the approach we have taken in this book, based on the assumption that progress can be made in understanding human personality by focusing on each of the major domains of functioning. Clearly, these domains of functioning are associated with one another, just as there are important connections between the heart and the skin (e.g., the heart pumps blood that nourishes skin cells). A full understanding of human personality will eventually require not merely understanding each domain of functioning, but also understanding the ways in which the domains are connected and integrated with each other to form the whole functioning person. We have highlighted these links where such knowledge exists, such as the fascinating links between culture and evolutionary biology (Chapter 17).

Current Status of the Field

This is an exciting time for the field of personality psychology. Advances have led to some consensus regarding the nature, structure, and development of personality, resulting in several decades of sustained growth. The field is thriving. One hallmark that a field is hitting its stride is the existence of a handbook. Personality psychology has several handbooks (e.g., Buss & Hawley, 2011; Mikulincer et al., 2015), as well as handbooks on personality disorders (e.g., Livesley & Larstone, 2018). Another indicator that a field is thriving is the existence of professional societies dedicated to its improvement. In personality psychology there are several societies, including the Society for Personality and Social Psychology, the European Society of Personality Psychology, and the Association for Research in Personality. This latter society, founded in 2001, is devoted especially to the interdisciplinary study of personality. It promotes scientific research on personality through an annual conference and through the official scientific journal of the association, the *Journal of Research in Personality*.

Personality psychologists doing research today typically focus on specific components of personality, such as self-esteem; specific traits, such as extraversion or agreeableness; or specific processes, such as the unconscious processing of information. This is the direction toward which the field of personality psychology has shifted over the past 100 years. The early personality theorists, such as Sigmund Freud, constructed theories about the whole person. These grand theories focused on universal properties of human nature, such as Freud's theory that all behaviour is motivated by sexual or aggressive impulses.

Starting about 50 years ago, personality psychologists began turning away from grand theories of personality. In their place, personality psychologists began constructing mini-theories of specific parts of personality. They began to focus on distinct components of the whole person. This allowed psychologists to focus their research on very specific questions. For example, how do people develop and maintain self-esteem? In what ways do high and low self-esteem persons differ from each other? How might a person with low self-esteem increase self-esteem? Certainly, self-esteem is only part of personality. Nevertheless, understanding self-esteem contributes to knowledge about the whole person.

The whole of personality is the sum of its parts and the connections among those parts. Understanding the parts is required for an understanding of the whole. Most of the research in personality today is on specific parts of the proverbial elephant. When these parts are put together—from the dispositional to the biological, to the intrapsychic, to the cognitive/experiential, to the social and cultural, to the adjustment domains—then we have the foundation for understanding the whole personality.

To the extent that understanding the whole elephant requires understanding all of its parts, then the blind men, working together, could begin to assemble a reasonable understanding of the whole elephant. They could communicate to each other and work together to build a reasonable understanding of what a whole elephant is like. They could be systematic in their approach to the elephant, using diverse methods and approaches and communicating clearly with each other about how they see the elephant. Personality psychologists are like these blind men in that they typically focus only on one domain of personality at a time. However, personality psychologists do an excellent job of working together. Many psychologists working in one domain are aware of what is going on in other domains. We can get an idea of the whole by knowing the diverse domains of knowledge about human nature.

All of the contemporary research and theorizing appears to fit into the six major domains of knowledge. Because they formed the basic structure of this book, let's briefly review each domain with some considerations for the future of personality theory and research.

Domains of Knowledge: Where We've Been, Where We're Going

Each of the six domains of knowledge represents a specialty within the field of personality psychology. When any field of knowledge grows large and complex, workers in that field are forced to specialize. For example, there once was a time when the field of medicine was simpler and more limited than it is now, and all doctors were general practitioners. The knowledge base of medicine was small enough so that each practitioner could generally master all of it. Today the field of medicine is so large and complicated that no one person can know it all, so most doctors today are specialists. Personality psychology is much the same—a field in which people tend to specialize in one of the six domains of knowledge outlined in this book. In the remainder of this chapter, we review the main features of each of these domains of knowledge, ending with some predictions about likely developments in each domain.

Dispositional Domain

The dispositional domain concerns the aspects of personality that are stable and that make people different from each other. For example, some people are outgoing and talkative; others are introverted and shy. Some are emotionally reactive and moody; others are calm and cool. Some people are conscientious and reliable; others are undependable. There are many ways in which people differ from one another, and many of these differences can be described as personality traits.

Major questions for psychologists working in this domain include these: How many personality traits exist? How can we discover and measure them? How do personality traits develop? and How do traits interact with situations to produce behaviours?

Trait psychologists will continue to focus on the interaction of persons and situations. Psychologists have realized that behaviours always occur within a context. A formulation offered by psychologists Shoda and Mischel (1996) is the idea of "if . . . then . . ." relations. Shoda and Mischel argue that personality is a specific pattern of "if . . . then . . ." relationships. For example, if an adolescent is aggressive, it means that certain behaviours (e.g., verbal insults) are likely to occur if certain situations are created (e.g., teased by a peer). Individuals may be characterized by distinct profiles of "if . . . then . . ." relationships. What are the conditions under which a particular person will become depressed, angry, or frustrated? Each person has a distinct psychological signature in terms of specific "if . . . then . . ." relationships: The person will do behaviour *A* when situation *Z* occurs, but behaviour *B* when situation *Z* does not occur. Two people may be equally high on aggressiveness, but the situations that trigger their aggression may be different. This is one formulation of person-by-situation interaction.

Personality psychologists will likely refine their understanding of the conditions or situations under which certain behaviours, such as arguing, will be evoked in people with certain traits, such as hostility.
©Jamie Grill/Getty Images

A major emphasis of the dispositional domain concerns the accurate measurement of traits and abilities. The dispositional domain emphasizes quantitative techniques for measuring personality. This trend will probably continue, with trait psychologists developing new methods for measuring personality characteristics, as well as new statistics for evaluating personality research. Future developments in measurement theory are likely to have an impact on how measures of personality traits are developed and evaluated. For example, efforts are underway that will allow test makers to assess the accuracy and validity of individual items on a personality test. Other statistical developments are enabling personality researchers to examine causal connections between variables, even in the absence of experimental procedures. Continued progress in statistics, measurement, and testing will be a major part of the dispositional domain of the future.

Different trait theories are associated with different procedures for identifying the most important individual differences. Some use the lexical strategy—starting with the thousands of trait terms embedded within language. Others use statistical techniques to identify important individual differences. The future will see cooperation among these researchers to test whether specific trait structures are found using different procedures. Indeed, the search will continue for other traits not yet identified by these strategies. The recent discovery of a sixth factor, *Honesty–Humility*, obtained from extensive cross-cultural research, represents an exciting new discovery in the dispositional domain. It is also an example of the pivotal role being played by Canadian researchers in the field.

Biological Domain

The core assumption of biological approaches to personality is that humans are biological systems. This domain concerns the factors within the body that influence or are related to personality as well as the evolutionary causal processes responsible for creating those bodily mechanisms. This domain is not any more fundamental than the other domains, nor is knowledge about this domain any closer to the truth about personality than is the knowledge in other domains. The biological domain simply contains the physical elements and biological systems that influence or are influenced by behaviours, thoughts, feelings, and desires. Biological processes may give rise to observable individual differences, or they may simply correlate with observable individual differences. In addition, biological differences among people cause personality differences (as in the biological theory of extraversion) or may be the result of personality differences (as in heart disease being the long-term consequence of the hostile Type A personality style).

One area of research that is likely to be active in the future concerns the psychology of approach and avoidance. Many current researchers on biological bases of behaviour recognize two tendencies that underlie human behaviour and emotion: (1) the tendency to feel positive emotions and to approach, and (2) the tendency to feel negative emotions and to avoid or withdraw. Much of the research reviewed in Chapter 7 concerns examples of this theme. Some examples include the work on separate brain areas associated with positive and negative emotions, Grey's theory about behavioural approach and behavioural inhibition, and the work on sensitivity to reward and punishment. These areas of research will most likely further converge, and the motives to approach and to avoid will become prominent themes in personality psychology.

Another major physical element within the body that influences personality is genes. Our genetic makeup contributes to whether we are tall or short, have blue eyes or brown eyes, or tend toward being skinny or overweight. It also appears that our genetic makeup influences behaviour patterns associated with personality, such as how active we are, whether we are aggressive, and whether we like to be with others or prefer to spend time by ourselves. Understanding how genetic factors contribute to personality falls squarely within the biological domain.

Behavioural genetics research has come a long way from the simple nature versus nurture question. Most of the major personality traits are now known to show some moderate amount of heritability (in the range of .40 to .60). With 40 to 60 percent of the variance in these traits due to genetic differences, that leaves a significant amount of variance due to either measurement error or the environment. The environment can be broken down into shared and nonshared components. The shared environment is what siblings have in common, such as the same parents, the (presumably) same parental rearing style, the same schools and religious institutions, and so on. The nonshared environment consists of such factors as different friends or peers outside the family, different teachers, different parental treatment, and random factors, such as accidents and illnesses. Researchers are pinpointing shared and nonshared environmental factors that appear important to personality. Thus, we see the counterintuitive scenario in which genetics researchers are also examining environmental influences.

Twin and adoption studies, the primary methods of behavioural genetics, use indirect methods that only estimate the genetic component of traits by assessing the resemblance of relatives. Other researchers concentrate on genetics at the molecular level, attempting to identify the DNA markers of genetic differences among individuals. Already, researchers have begun to focus these molecular techniques on the search for genes related to alcoholism, certain cognitive abilities, criminality, and impulse control. It is likely that researchers will find that genes are responsible for synthesizing specific neurotransmitters, and those neurotransmitters are in turn related to specific traits. Personality psychologists team with molecular geneticists to locate specific genes, as well as interactions among genes and between genes and environments, that will relate to personality dimensions (Plomin & Davis, 2009). Nonetheless, the genetic factors in

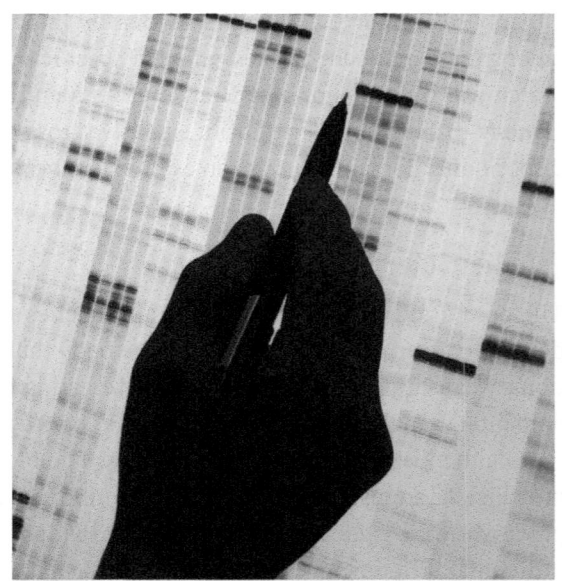

A technician works with DNA sequence information.
©Don Farrall/Getty Images

personality are turning out to be much more complicated than initially envisioned. Hundreds of genes contribute in small ways to explaining each personality dimension, defying simple, single-gene explanations. Perhaps we should not be surprised that human nature is so fascinatingly complex.

The biological domain also includes evolutionary perspectives on personality. From the perspective of evolutionary psychology, personality can be analyzed at three levels: human nature, sex differences, and individual differences. At each of these levels, an evolutionary perspective poses two related questions: What adaptive problems have humans confronted over the long expanse of human evolutionary history? What psychological solutions have evolved in response to these adaptive problems?

Because adaptive problems tend to be specific—for example, the problem of food selection differs from the problem of mate selection—the psychological solutions also tend to be specific. Thus, an evolutionary perspective leads us to expect that personality will be quite complex, consisting of a large collection of evolved psychological mechanisms, each corresponding to a specific adaptive problem. Specific mate preferences, jealousy, fears and phobias, altruistic feelings toward kin, and dozens more all may be parts of evolved psychological mechanisms, according to the evolutionary perspective. This perspective, however, does not claim that humans are optimally adapted, or even well adapted, to the conditions of modern living. Given the slow pace of evolution, we possess Stone Age brains inhabiting a New Age world of the Internet, global travel, and modern medical advancements. Thus, problems can arise when large discrepancies exist between the ancient world in which our adaptations evolved and the modern world that we have created.

The evolutionary perspective will continue to gain in importance, although it will not supplant other perspectives (Buss & Hawley, 2011). Instead, evolutionary psychology will add a new layer of questions and hence a necessary layer of insight when these questions are answered empirically. Perhaps most critically, an evolutionary perspective asks, "What is the adaptive function of each psychological mechanism?" Posing questions about adaptive function will likely result in the discovery that human personality is even more complex and contains even more psychological mechanisms about which we are currently unaware. Rather than being motivated merely by sex and aggression, as Freud envisioned, humans will be found to be motivated by a dozen or more drives. But it should not surprise us that human personality will turn out to be so complex. After all, if personality were really simple, consisting of a small number of easily understood psychological mechanisms, then this book would be a lot shorter than it is.

Intrapsychic Domain

The intrapsychic domain concerns the factors within the mind that influence behaviour, thoughts, and emotions. The pioneer of this domain was Sigmund Freud, though new perspectives have advanced beyond his original ideas. This domain deals with the basic psychological mechanisms of personality, many of which operate outside the realm of conscious awareness. Theories within this domain often start with fundamental assumptions about the motivational system—for example, the sexual and aggressive forces that Freud presumed energized much of human activity. Research has shown that motives, even those outside of awareness, can be powerful and that their manifestations in actual behaviour can be studied empirically. The intrapsychic domain also includes defence mechanisms, such as repression, denial, and projection, some of which have been examined in laboratory studies.

In this book, the ideas and contributions of psychoanalysis were divided into two areas: classical psychoanalytic theory, as put forward by Freud and his disciples; and contemporary psychoanalytic theory, consisting of extensions of and changes to these basic ideas. For example, newer views emphasize social crises rather than sexual conflict as the tasks of personality development. Modern views in psychoanalysis also emphasize the importance of internalized representations of important relationships. These views retain the notion that childhood is crucial to understanding the adult personality, but the emphasis is now on relationships, such as the attachment between an infant and the primary caregiver.

A fundamental assumption of psychologists working in the intrapsychic domain is that there are areas of the mind that are outside of awareness. Within each person, there is a part of the mind that even the individual does not know about, called the unconscious. In classical psychoanalysis, the unconscious mind is thought to have a life of its own. It has its own motivation, its own will, and its own energy. It can interfere with the functions of the rest of the mind. In fact, it is thought to be the source of all psychological problems. Modern research on motives (e.g., the power motive, achievement motive, and intimacy motive) also draws on the notion that motive forces can operate outside of conscious awareness.

Psychologists will continue to be interested in unconscious psychological processes. Many psychologists view the unconscious as an automatic information-processing mechanism, which can influence conscious awareness. And they have developed impressive methods for studying the unconscious, such as priming and subliminal exposure. We are on the verge of learning a great deal about just how much cognitive activity occurs outside of awareness and the extent to which these unconscious thoughts influence behaviour.

Cognitive/Experiential Domain

The cognitive/experiential domain focuses on subjective experiences and other mental processes, such as thoughts, feelings, beliefs, and desires about oneself and others. One of the central concepts in this domain is the self. Some aspects of the self describe how we view ourselves: our knowledge of ourselves, our images of past selves, and our images of possible future selves. Do we see ourselves as good or as evil? Are our past successes or past failures prominent in our self-views? Do we envision ourselves in a positive future? Psychologists will continue to focus their attention on self-concept and identity, better understanding the role of complex social and cultural factors such as gender and culture. Researchers will inevitably also learn more about what it means to be authentic and to live according to one's true self.

A modern metaphor informing personality psychology is the information-processing, or computer, metaphor. Humans take in sensory information; process it through an elaborate cognitive system, which selects and modifies from

Canadian actor Keanu Reeves, who plays aggressive and outgoing characters in many of his movies, leads a very different private life. Often considered one of Hollywood's greatest outcasts, Reeves is a self-proclaimed introvert who prefers solitude to the limelight. The development of the self and social identity, especially in complex and contradictory lives, will continue to fascinate personality psychologists.

the vast array of information available; then store it in memories, which do not bear a one-to-one relationship with the original events. At every step along the way—from attention and perception to memory and recall—there are opportunities for personality to influence the process. Psychologists will continue to take seriously the notion that people construct their experiences. Understanding how this works, and what it says about personality, will be one objective in this domain.

A somewhat different aspect of the cognitive/experiential domain pertains to the goals people strive for. This tradition approaches personality through the personal projects that individuals are trying to accomplish. Goal concepts will continue to be important within personality psychology. Goals have cognitive, emotional, and behavioural components. Goals are often individual expressions of social or institutional norms or standards, so the goal concept may be one route whereby psychologists can study relationships between individuals and broader social systems.

Yet another aspect of subjective experience entails emotions. Is a person habitually happy or sad? What makes a person angry or fearful? The joy, the sadness, feelings of triumph, and feelings of despair are essential elements in our subjective experience subsumed by the cognitive-experiential domain. If you want to learn what is important to people, really important, ask about their emotions. When was the last time they were angry? What makes them sad? What do they fear? Emotions will continue to be important concepts in personality psychology.

Social and Cultural Domain

One of the novel features of this book is an emphasis on the social and cultural aspects of personality. Personality is not something that merely resides within the heads, nervous systems, and genes of individuals. Rather, personality affects, and is affected by, the significant others in our lives.

Humans are not passive recipients of their environments, and personality plays a key role in social interaction. We selectively enter some interpersonal environments and selectively avoid others. We actively choose our mates and friends. We evoke reactions from others, sometimes quite unintentionally. And we actively influence or manipulate those occupying our social worlds. Personality influences these processes of selection, evocation, and manipulation. Emotionally unstable individuals, for example, tend to choose similarly unstable people as romantic partners; they evoke predictable forms of anger in those partners through their moodiness; and they more often use the "silent treatment" as a tactic for influencing their partners. Personality, in short, expresses itself through our social selections, evocations, and manipulations.

One important social sphere concerns gender. Personality may operate differently for men than for women in some domains. An essential part of our identity is gender. Much of what we call gender may have its origins in culture, in how society makes up different rules, roles, and expectations for men and women. Other aspects of gender may lie in evolved behaviour patterns that represent adaptations to different pressures that faced men and women in the past. Although gender differences will continue to be of interest to personality psychologists, the study of gender identity and expression will become increasingly important as social and political factors continue to evolve, in Canada and around the world. In an effort to better understand gender, it is likely that personality psychologists will enlist the help of specialists from other disciplines, such as anthropologists, sociologists, and biopsychologists.

At the cultural level, it is clear that groups differ from one another. Some cultures are individualistic: people prefer to make their own decisions and to be responsible primarily for themselves. Other cultures are more collectivistic or more interdependent: people prefer to see themselves as part of a social group and do not think of their individual needs as more important than their group's needs. Personality differences among these groups may be instances of transmitted culture or evoked culture. Some psychologists assume that they are caused by transmitted culture—ideas, values, and representations passed on from parents and others to children within their culture, down the generations. Other psychologists, however, propose that these are instances of evoked culture. According to this view, everyone may have the evolved capacity to be individualistic and preoccupied with the self. And everyone may also have the evolved capacity to be communal and concerned with the greater good of the group. Which of these capacities any one individual displays may depend on whether one lives in a culture that is highly mobile, with few genetic kin in close proximity (evoking an individualistic proclivity), or highly stable, with many genetic kin in close proximity (evoking a collectivistic proclivity). Another factor in our evoked culture appears to be the historical prevalence of pathogens.

The cultural mosaic of our country makes many of these questions even more interesting—and of greater social relevance—to Canadian researchers and psychologists. Of particular interest to ongoing research is the cultural identity of Indigenous peoples. How can Indigenous communities and individuals maintain a sense of clarity and confidence in their cultural identity over time, particularly when it is at odds with, and challenged by, the general population?

The study of culture, and of cross-cultural differences and similarities, will continue expanding in personality psychology. Our world is increasingly becoming a global community. Diversity is a fact of daily life in many areas. Many of us encounter people from different cultures on a regular basis at our schools, jobs, and communities. There is a growing interdependence among

Interacting with people from different cultures is a fact of daily life in many parts of the world. Understanding how people from different cultures are different from, or similar to, each other will continue to be an important part of personality psychology.
©Tom Carter/PhotoEdit

people from different backgrounds. An important goal of personality psychology will be to understand how cultures shape personality and how specific cultures are different from, or similar to, each other.

Adjustment Domain

Personality plays a key role in how we cope, adapt, and adjust to the ebb and flow of events in our lives. Personality is associated with important health outcomes, such as heart disease. Personality is associated with a variety of health-related behaviours, such as smoking, drinking, and risk taking. Personality is even associated with how long we live. The role of personality in relation to health and well-being will occupy personality psychologists of the future. There has been a shift toward looking at the role of positive emotions, and this emphasis on the positive in psychology is likely to be a part of personality psychology. In addition, several longitudinal studies were started decades ago in various communities around Canada and the United States. Participants in this research are now adults, and researchers are beginning to learn about the long-term effects of lifestyles and personality traits on longevity and health. As the pressures of climate change and global warming increase over the next few decades, personality psychologists may also play a role in understanding human behaviour within this context.

Some important problems in coping and adjustment can be traced to personality disorders. An understanding of "normal" personality functioning can be deepened by examining disorders of personality, and vice versa. Psychologists have more recently applied the trait approach to understanding personality disorders. This is likely to continue to sharpen our understanding of the nature of personality disorders, including their clinical diagnosis and treatment.

Integration: Personality in the Twenty-First Century

The domains of knowledge should be viewed as complementary, not as conflicting. People have many facets, and these facets can be observed and studied from many different perspectives. To say that people have evolved psychological mechanisms to solve social problems does not imply that the principles of psychoanalysis are wrong. Similarly, to say that a portion of the variance in personality traits is due to genetics does not in any way imply that people do not develop or change their personalities in adulthood.

Exciting personality research will occur at the boundaries of domains. Examples include collaborations among brain researchers using functional magnetic resonance imaging (fMRI) technology to conduct brain scans and psychologists studying interpersonal dispositions; collaborations between cultural and evolutionary psychologists to study the causal origins and nature of cultural differences; and collaborations between dispositional researchers and cognitive psychologists to study the information-processing mechanisms underlying stable individual differences. The most interesting work will happen as researchers expand the theories surrounding each domain and try to make connections among domains, or between personality psychology and other scientific fields.

Progress in this century will depend on researchers' willingness and ability to reach across domains. The most exciting progress will occur when researchers, perhaps working on multidisciplinary teams, combine different levels of analysis and different methods in approaching central questions of importance to the field. Building bridges that link domains of knowledge together in new and interesting ways will have the most impact on how human nature is understood.

If we look around the field of personality psychology today, we can find examples of bridges that are already being built among domains. For example, with regard to the topic of approach and avoidance motivation, psychologists are studying this phenomenon through brain activity, exploring the developmental course of these motives, examining cultural differences evoked by predictable environmental factors, and delving into how these traits contribute to disorders. It is likely that centres of research will be models for progress, with groups of diverse scientists—such as trait psychologists, biological psychologists, cultural psychologists, and health psychologists—all working together on questions important to the field of personality psychology. As we move forward in the twenty-first century, the possibilities for increasing our knowledge of human nature are truly exciting. What more will we learn about ourselves and our nature?

Glossary — chapter one

a

abnormal   Broadly defined, the term *abnormal* is based on current levels of societal tolerance. In this sense, behaviours that society deems unacceptable would be labelled as abnormal (e.g., incest and child abuse). Because tolerance levels (e.g., toward homosexuality) can change over time, psychologists have started directing their attention toward people's subjective views and experiences. **Anxiety, depression,** and feelings of loneliness may be linked to disorganized thought patterns, disruptive perceptions, or unusual beliefs. These may inhibit a person's ability to work or socialize, and may all be considered abnormal.

abnormal psychology   The study of the various mental **disorders**, including thought disorders (such as schizophrenia), emotional disorders (such as depression), and personality disorders (such as the antisocial personality).

acculturation   The process of, after arriving in a new culture, adapting to the ways of life and beliefs common in that new culture.

achievement view of intelligence   Associated with educational attainment—how much knowledge a person has acquired relative to others in his or her age cohort.

acquiescence   (also known as *yea saying*) A response set that refers to the tendency to agree with questionnaire items regardless of the content of those items.

action tendencies   Increases in the probabilities of certain behaviours that accompany **emotions**. The activity, or action tendency, associated with fear, for example, is to flee or to fight.

active genotype–environment correlation   Occurs when a person with a particular genotype creates or seeks out a particular environment.

actometer   A mechanical motion-recording device, often in the form of a watch attached to the wrist. It has been used, for example, in research on the activity level of children during several play periods. Motoric movement activates the recording device.

acute stress   Results from the sudden onset of demands or events that seem to be beyond the control of the individual. This type of **stress** is often experienced as tension headaches, emotional upsets, gastrointestinal disturbances, and feelings of agitation and pressure.

adaptations   Inherited solutions to the survival and reproductive problems posed by the **hostile forces of nature**. Adaptations are the primary product of the selective process. An adaptation is a "reliably developing structure in the organism, which, because it meshes with the recurrent structure of the world, causes the solution to an adaptive problem" (Tooby & Cosmides, 1992, p. 104).

adaptive problem   Anything that impedes survival or reproduction. All adaptations must contribute to fitness during the period of time in which they evolve by helping an organism survive, reproduce, or facilitate the reproductive success of genetic relatives. Adaptations emerge from and interact with recurrent structures of the world in a manner that solves adaptive problems and hence aids in reproductive success.

additive effects   The effects of different kinds of **stress** that add up and accumulate in a person over time.

adjacency   In the Wiggins circumplex model, it indicates how close the traits are to each other on the circumference of the circumplex. Those variables that are adjacent or next to each other within the model are positively correlated.

adjustment domain   Personality plays a key role in how we cope, adapt, and adjust to the ebb and flow of events in our day-to-day lives. In addition to health consequences of adjusting to **stress**, certain personality features are related to poor social or emotional adjustment and have been designated as **personality disorders**.

adoption studies   Research that examines the correlations between adopted children and their adoptive parents, with whom they share no **genes**. These correlations are then compared to the correlations between the adopted children and their genetic parents, who had no influence on the **environments** of the children. Differences in these correlations can indicate the relative magnitude of genetic and environment contributions to personality traits.

affect intensity   Larsen and Diener (1987) describe high affect intensity individuals as people who typically experience their **emotions** strongly and are emotionally reactive and variable. Low affect intensity individuals typically experience their emotions only mildly and with only gradual fluctuations and minor reactions.

agency   The tendency towards dominance, competence, and assertiveness; motive to "get ahead" (Abele & Wojciszke, 2018).

aggregation   Adding up or averaging several single observations, resulting in a better (i.e., more reliable) measure of a personality trait than a single observation of behaviour. This approach implies that personality traits refer to average tendencies in behaviour, how people behave on average.

aggressiveness   A tendency to engage in behaviours that cause harm to self or others; a disposition to respond to certain situations with acts of aggression. The opposite of agreeableness.

agreeableness   The second of the personality traits in the **five-factor model**, a model that has proven to be replicable in studies using English-language trait words as items. Some of the key adjective markers for agreeableness are *good natured, cooperative, mild/gentle,* and *not jealous.*

alarm stage   The first stage in Selye's **general adaptation syndrome (GAS)**. Consists of the flight-or-fight response of the sympathetic nervous system and the associated peripheral nervous system reactions. These include the release of hormones, which prepare our bodies for challenge.

alpha press   According to Murray, the notion that there is a real environment, or objective reality that works in tandem with a perceived environment (called *beta press* or reality as it is perceived). In any situation, what one person "sees" may be different from what another "sees." If two people walk down a street and a third person smiles at each of them, one person might "see" the smile as a sign of friendliness while the other person might "see" the smile as a smirk. Objectively (alpha press), it is the same smile; subjectively **(beta press),** it may be a different event for the two people.

alpha wave   A particular type of brain wave that oscillates 8 to 12 times a second. The amount of alpha wave present in a given time period is an inverse indicator of brain activity during that time period. The alpha wave is given off when the person is calm and relaxed. In a given time period of brain wave recording, the more alpha wave activity present the more we can assume that part of the brain was less active.

ambivalent relationship style   According to Hazan and Shaver, adults who are vulnerable and uncertain about relationships. Ambivalent adults become overly dependent and demanding on their partners and friends. They display high levels of neediness in their relationships. They are high-maintenance partners in the sense that they need constant reassurance and attention.

ambivalently attached   Infants, as determined by Ainsworth's strange situation paradigm, who are very anxious about the mother leaving. They often start crying and protesting vigorously before the mother even gets out of the room. While the mother is gone, these infants are difficult to calm. Upon her return, however, these infants behave ambivalently. Their behaviour shows both anger and the desire to be close to the mother; they approach her but then resist by squirming and fighting against being held.

amygdala   A section of the limbic or emotional system of the brain that is responsible for fear.

anal stage   The second stage in Freud's psychosexual stages of development. The anal stage typically occurs between the ages of 18 months and three years. At this stage, the anal sphincter is the source of sexual pleasure, and the child obtains pleasure from first expelling feces and then, during toilet training, from retaining feces. Adults who are compulsive, overly neat, rigid, and never messy are, according to psychoanalytic theory, likely to be fixated at the anal stage.

analytic   To explain an event with the object detached from its context, attributes of objects or people assigned to categories, and a reliance on rules about the categories to explain behaviour. See also **holistic**.

androgynous   In certain personality instruments, the **masculinity** dimension contains items reflecting assertiveness, boldness, dominance, self-sufficiency, and instrumentality. The **femininity** dimension contains items that reflect nurturance, expression of emotions, and empathy. Those persons who scored high on both dimensions are labelled *androgynous*, to reflect the notion that a single person can possess both masculine and feminine characteristics.

anterior cingulate   Located deep toward the centre of the brain, it most likely evolved early in the evolution of the nervous system. In experiments utilizing **fMRI** to trace increased activation of parts of the brain, the anterior cingulate cortex seems to be an area of the brain associated with affect, including social rejection.

antisocial personality disorder   A person suffering from antisocial personality **disorder** has a general disregard for others and cares very little about the rights, feelings, or happiness of other people. Also referred to as a sociopath or psychopath, a person suffering from antisocial personality disorder is easily irritated, assaultive, reckless, irresponsible, glib or superficially charming, impulsive, callous, and indifferent to the suffering of others.

anxiety   An unpleasant, high-arousal emotional state associated with perceived threat. In the psychoanalytic tradition, anxiety is seen as a signal that the control of the ego is being threatened by reality, impulses from the **id**, or harsh controls exerted by the **superego**. Freud identified three different types of anxiety: **neurotic anxiety, moral anxiety**, and objective anxiety. According to Rogers, the unpleasant emotional state of anxiety is the result of having an experience that does not fit with one's self-conception.

apperception   The act of interpreting the environment and perceiving the meaning of what is going on in a situation. The notion that a person's needs influence how he or she perceives the environment, especially when the environment is ambiguous.

aptitude view of intelligence   Considers intelligence less as the product of education and more as an ability to become educated, as the ability or aptitude to learn.

arousability   Recent research suggests that the primary physiological difference between introverts and extraverts lies in the arousability or reactivity of their nervous systems, such that compared to extraverts, introverts are more reactive or easily aroused in response to the same level of moderate stimulation. This leads extraverts to seek out stimulation and introverts to avoid being overstimulated. Research does not support differences in their baseline or resting level of cortical arousal, as Eysenck originally proposed.

arousal level   In Eysenck's original theory of **extraversion**, he held that extraverts had lower levels of resting cortical or brain arousal than introverts, leading them to seek out more stimulation. More recent research suggests that the difference between introverts and extraverts lies in the **arousability** of their nervous systems, such that introverts are more easily aroused in response to moderate levels of stimulation (but do not differ in their baseline or resting level of arousal).

arteriosclerosis   Hardening or blocking of the arteries. When the arteries that feed the heart muscle itself become blocked, the subsequent shortage of blood to the heart is called a heart attack.

ascending reticular activating system (ARAS)   A structure in the brain stem thought to control overall cortical arousal; the structure Eysenck originally thought was responsible for differences between introverts and extraverts.

assortative mating   The phenomenon whereby people partner with people similar to themselves. In addition to personality, people also show assortative mating on a number of physical characteristics, such as height and weight.

attachment   Begins in the human infant when he or she develops a preference for people over objects. Then the preference begins to narrow to familiar persons so that the child prefers to see people he or she has seen before, compared to strangers. Finally, the preference narrows even further so that the child prefers the mother or primary caretaker over anyone else.

attraction similarity theory   States that individuals are attracted to those whose personalities are similar to their own. In other words, "birds of a feather flock together" or "like attracts like." As of 2003, attraction similarity has been proven to be the dominant attraction theory except in biological sex choices (i.e., women tend to be attracted to men and vice versa).

authenticity   The feeling of being aligned or acting in alignment with one's true self.

authoritarianism   A trait marked by blind allegiance to conventional ideas, respect for submission to authority, and belief in aggression towards those who disagree or who are different.

autonomic nervous system (ANS)   That part of the peripheral nervous system that connects to vital bodily structures associated with maintaining life and responding to emergencies (e.g., storing and releasing energy), such as the beating of the heart, respiration, and controlling blood pressure. There are two divisions of the ANS: the sympathetic and parasympathetic branches.

autotelic personality   The tendency to enjoy life and do things for their own sake rather than to achieve some later goal. Individuals with an autotelic personality have a general curiosity and interest in life and tend to be inclined to experience flow states, often seeking them out.

average tendencies   Propensity to display a certain **psychological trait** with regularity. For example, on average, a high-talkative person will start more conversations than a low-talkative person. This idea explains why the principle of **aggregation** works when measuring personality.

avoidant personality disorder The major feature is a pervasive feeling of inadequacy and sensitivity to criticism from others. The avoidant personality will go to great lengths to avoid situations in which others may have opportunities to criticize his or her performance or character, such as school or work or other group settings. Such a person may avoid making new friends or going to new places because of fear of criticism or disapproval.

avoidant relationship style According to Hazan and Shaver, the adult who has difficulty learning to trust others. Avoidant adults remain suspicious of the motives of others, and they are afraid of making commitments. They are afraid of depending on others because they anticipate being disappointed, let down, abandoned, or separated.

avoidantly attached Describes infants in Ainsworth's **strange situation study** avoided the mother when she returned. Infants in this group typically seemed unfazed when the mother left and did not give her much attention when she returned. Avoidant children seem to be aloof from their mothers. Approximately 20 percent of infants fall into this category.

b

balancing selection When genetic variation is maintained by selection because different levels of a personality trait are adaptive in different environments.

Barnum statements Generalities or comments that could apply to anyone. A good example is the astrology column published in daily newspapers.

behavioural activation system (BAS) In Gray's **reinforcement sensitivity theory**, the system that is responsive to incentives, such as cues for reward, and regulates approach behaviour. When some stimulus is recognized as potentially rewarding, the BAS triggers approach behaviour. This system is highly correlated with the trait of **extraversion**.

behavioural inhibition system (BIS) In Gray's **reinforcement sensitivity theory**, the system responsive to cues for punishment, frustration, and uncertainty. The effect of BIS activation is to cease or inhibit behaviour or to bring about avoidance behaviour. This system is highly correlated with the trait of **neuroticism**.

belongingness needs The third level of Maslow's motivation hierarchy. Humans are a very social species, and most people possess a strong need to belong to groups. Being accepted by others and welcomed into a group represents a somewhat more psychological need than the physiological needs or the need for safety.

beta press Murray introduced the notion that there is a real environment (what he called *alpha press* or objective reality) and a perceived environment (called beta press or reality as it is perceived). In any situation, what one person "sees" may be different from what another "sees." If two people walk down a street and a third person smiles at each of them, one person might "see" the smile as a sign of friendliness while the other might "see" the smile as a smirk. Objectively **(alpha press)**, it is the same smile; subjectively (beta press), it may be a different event for the two people.

biological domain The core assumption of these approaches to personality is that humans are, first and foremost, collections of biological systems, and these systems provide the building blocks (e.g., brain, nervous system) for behaviour, thought, and emotion. The term *biological approaches* typically refers to three areas of

research within this general domain: the genetics of personality, the psychophysiology of personality, and the evolution of personality.

bipolarity In the Wiggins circumplex model, traits located at opposite sides of the circle are negatively correlated with each other. Specifying this bipolarity is useful because nearly every interpersonal trait within the personality sphere has another trait that is its opposite.

blindsight Following an injury or stroke that damages the primary vision centre in the brain, a person may lose some or all of their ability to see. In this blindness the eyes still bring information into the brain, but the brain centre responsible for object recognition fails. People who suffer this "cortical" blindness often display an interesting capacity to make judgments about objects that they truly cannot see.

borderline personality disorder The life of the borderline personality is marked by instability. Their relationships are unstable, their emotions are unstable, their behaviour is unstable, and even their image of themselves is unstable. Persons with borderline personality disorder, compared to those without, have a higher incidence rate of childhood physical or sexual abuse, neglect, or early parental loss.

byproducts of adaptations Evolutionary mechanisms that are not adaptations, but rather are byproducts of other adaptations. Our nose, for example, is clearly an adaptation designed for smelling. But the fact that we use our nose to hold up our eyeglasses is an incidental byproduct.

c

Canadian Human Rights Act The act was passed in 1977 with the goal of ensuring equal opportunity to individuals who may be victims of discriminatory practices based on sex, sexual orientation, race, marital status, creed, age, colour, disability, or political or religious belief. The statute helps protect individuals against such discrimination.

cardiac reactivity The increase in blood pressure and heart rate during times of stress. Evidence suggests that chronic cardiac reactivity contributes to coronary artery disease. See also **arteriosclerosis**.

case study method Examining the life of one person in depth can give researchers insights into **personality** that can then be used to formulate a more general theory that is tested in a larger population. They can also provide in-depth knowledge of a particularly outstanding individual. Case studies are useful when studying rare phenomena, such as a person with a photographic memory or a person with multiple personalities—cases for which large samples would be difficult or impossible to obtain.

castration anxiety Freud argued that little boys come to believe that their fathers might make a preemptive Oedipal strike and take away what is at the root of the **Oedipal conflict:** the boy's penis. This fear of losing his penis is called castration anxiety; it drives the little boy into giving up his sexual desire for his mother.

categorical approach Researchers who suggest **emotions** are best thought of as a small number of primary and distinct emotions (anger, joy, anxiety, sadness). Emotion researchers who take the categorical approach have tried to reduce the complexity of emotions by searching for the primary emotions that underlie the great variety of emotion terms. An example of a categorical approach to emotion is that of Paul Ekman, who applies criteria of distinct and universal facial expressions, and whose list of primary emotions contains disgust, sadness, joy, surprise, anger, and fear. See also **dimensional approach**.

categorical view In psychiatry and clinical psychology today, the dominant approach to viewing personality disorders in distinct categories. There is a qualitative distinction made in which people who have a disorder are in one category, whereas people who do not have the disorder are in another category.

causal attribution A person's explanation of the cause of some event.

chronic stress Stress that does not end, like an abusive relationship that grinds the individual down until his or her resistance is eroded. Chronic stress can result in serious systemic diseases such as diabetes, decreased immune system functioning, or cardiovascular disease.

circadian rhythms Many biological processes fluctuate around an approximate 24- to 25-hour cycle. These are called circadian rhythms (*circa* = around; *dia* = day). Circadian rhythms in temporal isolation studies have been found to be as short as 16 hours in one person, and as long as 50 hours in another person (Wehr & Goodwin, 1981).

client-centred therapy In Rogers' approach, clients are never given interpretations of their problem. Nor are clients given any direction about what course of action to take to solve their problem. The therapist makes no attempts to change the client directly. Instead, the therapist tries to create an atmosphere in which the client may change themselves.

cognition A general term referring to awareness and thinking, as well as to specific mental acts such as perceiving, interpreting, remembering, believing, and anticipating.

cognitive approaches Differences in how people think form the focus of cognitive approaches to personality. Psychologists working in this approach focus on the components of cognition, such as how people perceive, interpret, remember, and plan, in their efforts to understand how and why people are different from each other.

cognitive schema A mental concept that helps a person to process incoming information, organize that information, and interpret daily experiences.

cognitive social learning approach A number of modern personality theories have expanded on the notion that personality is expressed in goals and in how people think about themselves relative to their goals. Collectively these theories form an approach that emphasizes the cognitive and social processes whereby people learn to value and strive for certain goals over others.

cognitive triad According to Beck, there are three important areas of life that are most influenced by the depressive cognitive schema. This cognitive triad refers to information about the self, about the world, and about the future.

cognitive unconscious In the cognitive view of the **unconscious**, the content of the unconscious mind is assumed to operate just like thoughts in consciousness. Thoughts are unconscious because they are not in conscious awareness, not because they have been repressed or because they represent unacceptable urges or wishes.

cognitive-experiential domain Focuses on **cognition** and subjective experience, such as **conscious** thoughts, feelings, beliefs, and desires about oneself and others. This domain includes our feelings of self, identity, **self-esteem**, our goals and plans, and our **emotions**.

cohort effects Personality change over time as a reflection of the social times in which an individual or group of individuals live. For example, North American women's trait scores on assertiveness have risen and fallen depending on the social and historical cohort in which they have lived. Jean Twenge has posited that individuals internalize social change and absorb the cultural messages they receive from their culture, all of which, in turn, can affect their personalities.

collectivistic A cultural orientation that focuses on relationships with others, communion, and interdependence.

collective self-esteem An individual's global self-evaluation as a member of social groups or categories.

combinations of Big Five variables "Traits" are often examined in combinations. For example, two people high in extraversion would be very different if one were an extraverted neurotic and the other were extraverted but emotionally stable.

communion The tendency towards interpersonal relatedness, warmth, and caring behaviour; motive to "get along" (Abele & Wojciszke, 2018).

comorbidity The presence of two or more **disorders** of any type in one person.

compatibility and integration across domains and levels A theory that takes into account the principles and laws of other scientific domains that may affect the study's main subject. For example, a theory of biology that violated known principles of chemistry would be judged to be fatally flawed. One of the **five standards for evaluating theories**.

competitive achievement motivation Also referred to as the *need for achievement*, it is a subtrait in the **Type A** behaviour pattern. Type A people like to work hard and achieve goals. They like recognition and overcoming obstacles and feel they are at their best when competing with others.

complementary needs theory Theory of attraction that postulates people are attracted to people whose personality dispositions differ from theirs. In other words, "opposites attract." This is especially true in biological sex choices (i.e., women tend to be attracted to men and vice versa). Other than biological sex choices, the complementary needs theory of attraction has not received any empirical support.

comprehensiveness One of the five **scientific standards used in evaluating personality theories**. Theories that explain more empirical data within a domain are generally superior to those that explain fewer findings.

conditional positive regard According to Rogers, when positive regard must be earned by meeting certain conditions. People behave in specific ways to earn the love and respect and **positive regard** of parents and other significant people in their lives.

conditions of worth According to Rogers, the requirements set forth by parents or significant others for earning their positive regard. Children may become preoccupied with living up to these conditions of worth rather than discovering what makes them happy.

confirmatory bias The tendency to look only for evidence that confirms a previous hunch, and not to look for evidence that might disconfirm a belief.

conformity The tendency to adapt behaviour in response to group pressure

conscientiousness The third of the personality traits in the **five-factor model**, which has proven to be replicable in studies using English-language trait words as items. Some of the key adjective markers for conscientiousness are *responsible, scrupulous, persevering,* and *fussy/tidy*.

conscious That part of the mind that contains all the thoughts, feelings, and images that a person is presently aware of. Whatever a person is currently thinking about is in his or her conscious mind.

conscious goals A person's awareness of what they desire and believe is valuable and worth pursuing. This is the third level of **cognition** that is of interest to personality psychologists, after **perception** and **interpretation**.

consistency Trait theories assume there is some degree of consistency in personality over time. If someone is highly extraverted during one period of observation, trait psychologists tend to assume that they will be extraverted tomorrow, next week, a year from now, or even decades from now.

construct validity A test that measures what it claims to measure, correlates with what it is supposed to correlate with, and does not correlate with what it is not supposed to correlate with.

constructive memory It is accepted as fact that humans have a constructive memory; that is, memory contributes to or influences in various ways (adds to, subtracts from, etc.) what is recalled. Recalled memories are rarely distortion-free, mirror images of the facts.

constructs Concepts or provable hypotheses that summarize a set of observations and convey the meaning of those observations (e.g., gravity).

content (of emotional life) Refers to the characteristic or typical **emotions** a person is likely to experience over time. Someone whose emotional life contains a lot of pleasant emotions is someone who might be characterized as happy, cheerful, and enthusiastic. Thus the notion of *content* leads us to consider the *kinds* of emotions that people are likely to experience over time and across situations in their lives. Compare with **style** of emotional life.

continuity Having an identity means that others can count on you to be reliable in who you are and how you act. Identity has an element of continuity because many of its aspects, such as gender, ethnicity, socioeconomic status, educational level, and occupation, are constant. One of two important features of identity; see also **contrast**.

contrast A person's **social identity** differentiates them from other people. An identity is the combination of characteristics that makes a person unique in the eyes of others. One of two important features of identity; see also **continuity**.

convergent validity Whether a test correlates with other measures that it should correlate with.

core conditions According to Carl Rogers, in client-centred therapy three core conditions must be present in order for progress to occur: (1) an atmosphere of genuine acceptance on the part of the therapist; (2) the therapist must express **unconditional positive regard** for the client; and (3) the client must feel that the therapist understands him or her (empathic understanding).

correlation coefficient Researchers are interested in the direction (positive or negative) and the magnitude (size) of the correlation coefficient. Correlations around .10 are considered small; those around .30 are considered medium; and those around .50 or greater are considered large (Cohen & Cohen, 1975).

correlational method A statistical procedure for determining whether there is a relationship between two variables. In correlational research designs, the researcher is attempting to directly identify the relationships between two or more variables, without imposing the sorts of **manipulations** seen in experimental designs.

cortisol A key **stress** hormone that prepares the body to flee or fight. Increases in cortisol in the blood indicate that the animal has recently experienced stress. If high levels occur over time, it can contribute to a number of negative health effects, including increased inflammation in the arteries.

counterbalancing In some experiments, manipulation is within a single group. For example, participants might get a drug and have their memory tested, then later take a sugar pill and have their memory tested again. In this kind of experiment, equivalence is obtained by counterbalancing the order of the conditions, with half the participants getting the drug first and the sugar pill second, and the other half getting the sugar pill first and the drug second.

creating positive events Creating a positive time-out from **stress**. Folkman and Moskowitz note that humour can have the added benefit of generating positive emotional moments even during the darkest periods of stress.

criterion validity (also referred to as **predictive validity**) Whether a test predicts criteria external to the test.

cross-cultural universality In the **lexical approach**, if a trait is sufficiently important in all cultures so that its members have codified terms within their own languages to describe the trait, then the trait must be universally important in human affairs. In contrast, if a trait term exists in only one or a few languages but is entirely missing from most, then it may be of only local relevance.

cultural context of intelligence Looks at how the definition of intelligent behaviour varies across different cultures. Because of these considerations, intelligence can be viewed as referring to those skills valued in a particular culture.

cultural identity A person's sense of belonging to a particular culture or group.

cultural personality psychology A study that generally has three key goals: (1) to discover the principles underlying the cultural diversity; (2) to discover how human psychology shapes culture; and (3) to discover how cultural understandings in turn shape our psychology (Fiske et al., 1997).

cultural universals Features of personality that are common to everyone in all cultures. These universals constitute the human nature level of analyzing personality and define the elements of personality we share with all or most other people.

cultural variations Within-group similarities and between-group differences, which can be of any sort—physical, psychological, behavioural, or attitudinal. These phenomena are often referred to as cultural variations. Two ingredients are necessary to explain cultural variations: (1) a universal underlying mechanism and (2) environmental differences in the degree to which the underlying mechanism is activated.

culture A set of shared standards for many behaviours. It might contain different standards for males and females, such that girls should be ashamed if they engage in promiscuous sex, whereas boys might be proud of such behaviour, with it being culturally acceptable for them to even brag about such behaviour.

culture of honour Nisbett proposed that the economic means of subsistence of a culture affects the degree to which the group develops what he calls *a culture of honour*. In such cultures, insults are viewed as highly offensive public challenges that must be met with direct confrontation and physical aggression. The theory is that differences in the degree to which honour becomes a central part of the culture rest ultimately with economics, and specifically with the manner in which food is obtained.

d

daily hassles The major sources of **stress** in most people's lives. Although minor, daily hassles can be chronic and repetitive, such as having too much to do all the time, having to fight the crowds while shopping, or having to worry over money. Such daily hassles can be chronically irritating though they do not initiate the same **general adaptation syndrome** evoked by some **major life events**.

Dark Tetrad An expanded version of the Dark Triad, this cluster of malevolent personality traits includes **Machiavellianism, narcissism, subclinical psychopathy,** and **dispositional sadism**.

Dark Triad A cluster of malevolent and socially problematic personality traits including **Machiavellianism, narcissism,** and **subclinical psychopathy**.

deductive reasoning approach The top-down, theory-driven method of empirical research.

defence mechanisms Strategies for coping with anxiety and threats to self-esteem.

defensive pessimism A strategy in which a person expects to do poorly on a task. Individuals who use a defensive pessimism strategy have usually done well on important tasks but lack self-confidence in their ability to handle new challenges. A defensive pessimist controls **anxiety** by preparing for failure ahead of time; they set low expectations for their performance and often focus on worse-case outcomes. This strategy overcomes anticipatory anxiety and transforms it into motivation.

deliberation-without-attention The notion that, when confronted with a decision, if a person can put it out of their conscious mind for a period of time, then the "unconscious mind" will continue to deliberate on it, helping the person to arrive at a "sudden" and often correct decision some time later.

denial A **defence mechanism** that one may resort to when the reality of a particular situation is extremely anxiety provoking. A person in denial insists that things are not the way they seem. Denial can also be less extreme, as when someone reappraises an **anxiety**-provoking situation so that it seems less daunting. Denial often shows up in people's daydreams and fantasies.

density distribution of states Refers to the idea that traits are distributions of states in a person's life over time, and the mean of that distribution is the person's level of the trait.

dependent personality disorder The dependent personality seeks out others to an extreme. The hallmark of the dependent personality is an excessive need to be taken care of, to be nurtured, coddled, and told what to do. Dependent persons act in submissive ways so as to encourage others to take care of them or take charge of the situation. Such individuals need lots of encouragement and advice from others and would much rather turn over responsibility for their decisions to someone else.

depression A psychological disorder whose symptoms include a depressed mood most of the day; diminished interest in activities; change in weight, sleep patterns, and movement; fatigue or loss of energy; feelings of worthlessness; inability to concentrate; and recurrent thoughts of death and suicide. It is estimated to strike 8 percent of the people in Canada at some time in their lives (Canadian Mental Health Association, 2016).

developmental crisis Erikson believed that each stage in personality development represented a conflict, or a developmental crisis, that needed to be resolved before the person advanced to the next stage of development.

diathesis-stress model of depression Suggests that a preexisting vulnerability, or diathesis, is present among people who become depressed. In addition to this vulnerability, a stressful life event must occur in order to trigger the **depression**, such as the loss of a loved one or some other major negative life event. The events must occur together—something bad or stressful has to happen to a person who has a particular vulnerability to depression—in order for depression to occur.

differences among groups Individuals are also members of various groups, such as **culture,** social class, and **gender,** and these groups may differ from one another according to various personality traits. The study of the ways in which groups differ in **personality** from one another (on average) is the study of differences among groups.

differential diagnosis A differential diagnosis is arrived at when, out of two or more possible diagnoses, the clinician searches for evidence in support of one diagnostic category over all the others.

differential gene reproduction Reproductive success relative to others. The **genes** of organisms who reproduce more than others get passed down to future generations at a relatively greater frequency than the genes of those who reproduce less. Because survival is usually critical for reproductive success, characteristics that lead to greater survival get passed along. Because success in mate competition is also critical for reproductive success, qualities that lead to success in same-sex competition or to success at being chosen as a mate get passed along. Successful survival and successful mate competition, therefore, are both part of differential gene reproduction.

differential psychology The name sometimes given to trait psychology due to its emphasis on the study of differences between people. The name distinguishes this subfield from other branches of personality psychology (Anastasi, 1976). Includes the study of other forms of **individual differences** in addition to personality traits, such as abilities, aptitudes, and intelligence.

dimensional approach Another method for understanding the complexity of emotions where researchers gather data by having subjects rate themselves on a wide variety of emotions, then apply statistical techniques (mostly **factor analysis**) to identify the basic dimensions underlying the ratings. Almost all the studies suggest that subjects categorize emotions using just two primary dimensions: how pleasant or unpleasant the emotion is, and how high or low on arousal the emotion is. See also **categorical approach**.

dimensional view The dimensional view approaches a personality disorder as a continuum that ranges from normality at one end to severe disability and disturbance at the other end. According to this view, people with and without the disorder differ in degree only.

directionality problem One reason why correlations can never prove causality. If A and B are correlated, we do not know if A is the cause of B, or if B is the cause of A, or if some third, unknown variable is causing both B and A.

disclosure Telling someone about some private aspect of ourselves. Many theorists have suggested that keeping things to ourselves may be a source of **stress** and ultimately may lead to psychological distress and physical disease.

discriminant validity What a measure should not correlate with.

disorder A pattern of behaviour or experience that is distressing and painful to the person, leads to some disability or impairment in important life domains (e.g., work, marriage, or relationship difficulties), and is associated with increased risk for further suffering, loss of function, death, or confinement.

disparate impact Any employment practice that disadvantages people from a protected group. Most courts define disparity as a difference that is sufficiently large that it is unlikely to have occurred by chance.

displacement A **defence mechanism** that involves generating acceptable reasons for outcomes that might otherwise be unacceptable. The goal is to reduce anxiety by coming up with an explanation for some event that is easier to accept than the "real" reason.

dispositional domain Deals centrally with the ways in which individuals differ from one another. As such, the dispositional domain connects with all the other domains. In the dispositional domain, psychologists are primarily interested in the number and nature of fundamental dispositions, taxonomies of traits, measurement issues, and questions of stability over time and consistency over situations.

dispositional optimism The expectation that in the future good events will be plentiful and bad events will be rare.

dispositional sadism The tendency to gain enjoyment from hurting others. It can occur directly, as in actually causing pain or displeasure in others, or vicariously, through watching movies or playing video games.

distortion A defence mechanism in Rogers's theory of personality; it refers to modifying the meaning of experiences to make them less threatening to the self-image.

dizygotic (DZ) twins (also called fraternal twins) Twins who are not genetically identical. They come from two eggs that were separately fertilized (*di-* means two; so *dizygotic* means "coming from two fertilized eggs"). Such twins share only 50 percent of their genes with their co-twin, the same amount as ordinary brothers and sisters. Fraternal twins can be of the same sex or of the opposite sex.

domain of knowledge A specialty area of science and scholarship, where psychologists have focused on learning about some specific and limited aspect of *human nature*, often with preferred tools of investigation.

domain specific The presumption that adaptations are "designed" by the evolutionary process to solve a specialized **adaptive problem**. Domain specificity implies that selection tends to fashion specific mechanisms for each specific adaptive problem.

dopamine A neurotransmitter that appears to be associated with pleasure. Dopamine appears to function something like the "reward system" and has even been called the "feeling good" chemical (Hamer, 1997).

DRD4 gene A gene located on the short arm of chromosome 11 that codes for a protein called a dopamine receptor. The function of this dopamine receptor is to respond to the presence of **dopamine**, which is a neurotransmitter. When the dopamine receptor encounters dopamine from other neurons in the brain, it discharges an electrical signal, activating other neurons.

dream analysis A technique Freud taught for uncovering the **unconscious** material in a dream by interpreting the content of a dream. Freud called dreams "the royal road to the unconscious."

dynamic The interaction of forces within a person.

e

effect size How large a particular difference is, or how strong a particular correlation is, as averaged over several experiments or studies.

effective polygyny Variances in reproduction between the sexes: most females will have some offspring, whereas a few males will sire many offspring, and some will have none at all.

egalitarianism How much a particular group displays equal treatment of all individuals within that group.

ego The part of the mind that constrains the **id** to reality. According to Freud, it develops within the first two or three years of life. The ego operates according to the reality principle. The ego understands that the urges of the id are often in conflict with social and physical reality, and that direct expression of id impulses must therefore be redirected or postponed.

ego depletion When exertion of self-control results in a decrease of **psychic energy**.

ego psychology Post-Freudian psychoanalysts felt that the ego deserved more attention and that it performed many constructive functions. Erikson emphasized the **ego** as a powerful and independent part of personality, involved in mastering the environment, achieving one's goals, and hence in establishing one's identity. The approach to psychoanalysis started by Erikson was called *ego psychology*.

Electra complex Within the psychoanalytic theory of personality development, the female counterpart to the Oedipal complex; both refer to the **phallic stage** of development.

electrodermal activity (also known as galvanic skin response or **skin conductance**) Electricity will flow across the skin with less resistance if that skin is made damp with sweat. Sweating on the palms of the hands is activated by the sympathetic nervous system, and so electrodermal activity is a way to directly measure changes in the sympathetic nervous system.

electrodes Sensors usually placed on the surface of the skin and linked to a physiological recording machine (often called a polygraph) to measure physiological variables.

electroencephalogram (EEG) A chart or recording of the brain's spontaneously produced small amounts of electricity, measured by electrodes placed on the scalp using an electroencephalograph. EEGs can provide useful information about patterns of activation in different regions of the brain that may be associated with different types of information-processing tasks.

emotional inhibition Suppression of emotional expressions; often thought of as a trait (e.g., some people chronically suppress their emotions).

emotional intelligence An adaptive form of intelligence consisting of the ability to (1) know one's own emotions; (2) regulate those emotions; (3) motivate oneself; (4) know how others are feeling; and (5) influence how others are feeling. Goleman posited that emotional intelligence is more strongly predictive of professional status, marital quality, and salary than traditional measures of intelligence and aptitude.

emotional states Transitory states that depend more on the situation or circumstances a person is in than on the specific person. Emotions as states have a specific cause, and that cause is typically outside of the person (something happens in the environment).

emotional traits Stable personality traits that are primarily characterized by specific emotions. For example, the trait of **neuroticism** is primarily characterized by the emotions of **anxiety** and worry.

emotion-focused coping Efforts to manage emotions generated by a stressful situation.

emotions Defined by their three components: (1) distinct subjective feelings or affects associated with them; (2) emotions are accompanied by bodily changes, mostly in the nervous system, and these produce associated changes in breathing, heart rate, muscle tension, blood chemistry, and facial and bodily expressions; (3) emotions are accompanied by distinct **action tendencies** or increases in the probabilities of certain behaviours.

empathizing Tuning in to other people's thoughts and feelings. See also **empathy**.

empathy In Rogers' client-centred therapy, it is understanding the person from their point of view. Instead of interpreting the meaning behind what the client says (e.g., "You have a harsh **superego** that is punishing you for the actions of your **id**"), the client-centred therapist simply listens to what the client says and reflects it back.

Employment Equity Act This act, in effect since 1986, requires that federally regulated industries in Canada adopt proactive employment practices in order to improve the employment rates of four designated social groups: women, individuals with disabilities, Aboriginal peoples, and visible minorities.

enduring To say that **psychological traits** are enduring is to say that they are relatively stable over time, particularly in adulthood.

environment Can be physical, social, and intrapsychic (within the mind). Which aspect of the environment is important at any moment in time is frequently determined by the personality of the person in that environment.

environmentalist view The belief that personality is determined by socialization practices, such as parenting style and other agents of society.

environmentality The percentage of observed variance in a *group* of individuals that can be attributed to environmental (nongenetic) differences. Generally speaking, the larger the **heritability**, the smaller the environmentality. And vice versa: the smaller the heritability, the larger the environmentality.

episodic acute stress Repeated episodes of **acute stress**, such as having to work at more than one job every day, having to spend time with a difficult in-law, or needing to meet a recurring monthly deadline.

equal environments assumption The assumption that the **environments** experienced by identical twins are no more similar to each other than are the environments experienced by fraternal twins. If they are more similar, then the greater similarity of the identical twins could plausibly be due to the fact that they experience more similar environments rather than the fact that they have more **genes** in common.

Erikson's eight stages of development According to Erikson, there are eight stages of development that last well into adulthood and old age: trust versus mistrust, autonomy versus shame and doubt, initiative versus guilt, industry versus inferiority, identity versus role confusion, intimacy versus isolation, generativity versus stagnation, and integrity versus despair.

esteem needs The fourth level of Maslow's motivation hierarchy. There are two types of esteem: esteem from others and self-esteem, the latter often depending on the former. People want to be seen by others as competent, as strong, and as able to achieve. They want to be respected by others for their achievements or abilities. People also want to feel good about themselves. Much of the activity of adult daily life is geared toward achieving recognition and esteem from others and bolstering one's own self-confidence.

eugenics The notion that the future of the human race can be influenced by fostering the reproduction of people with certain traits and discouraging reproduction among people without those traits or who have undesirable traits.

evocation A form of person–situation interaction discussed by Buss. It is based on the idea that certain personality traits may elicit consistent responses from the **environment**, particularly the social environment.

evoked culture A way of considering culture that concentrates on phenomena that are triggered in different ways by different environmental conditions.

evolutionary byproducts Evolutionary mechanisms that are not adaptations, but rather are byproducts of other adaptations. Our nose, for example, is clearly an adaptation designed for smelling. But the fact that we use our nose to hold up our eyeglasses is an incidental byproduct.

evolutionary noise Random variations that are neutral with respect to selection.

evolutionary-predicted sex differences The theory that predicts that males and females will be the same or similar in all those domains where the sexes have faced the same or similar **adaptive problems** (e.g., both sexes have sweat glands because both sexes have faced the adaptive problem of thermal regulation) and different when men and women have faced substantially different adaptive problems (e.g., in the physical realm, women have faced the problem of childbirth and have therefore evolved adaptations that are lacking in men, such as mechanisms for producing labour contractions through the release of oxytocin into the bloodstream).

exhaustion stage The third stage in Selye's **general adaptation syndrome (GAS)**. Selye felt that this was the stage where we are most susceptible to illness and disease, as our physiological resources are depleted. See also **alarm stage** and **resistance stage**.

expectancy confirmation A phenomenon whereby people's beliefs about the personality characteristics of others cause them to evoke in others actions that are consistent with the initial beliefs. The phenomenon of expectancy confirmation has also been called **self-fulfilling prophecy** and *behavioural confirmation*.

experience sampling People answer some questions, for example about their mood or physical symptoms, every day for several weeks or longer. People are usually contacted electronically ("beeped") one or more times a day at random intervals to complete the measures. Although experience sampling uses self-report as the data source, it differs from more traditional self-report methods in being able to detect patterns of behaviour over time.

experimental methods Typically used to determine causality—to find out whether one variable influences another variable. Experiments involve the manipulation of one variable (the independent variable) and random assignment of subjects to conditions defined by the independent variable.

explanatory style The tendency a person has to employ certain combinations of attributions in explaining events. Whenever someone offers a cause for some event, that cause can be analyzed in terms of the three categories of attributions: internal–external, stable–unstable, and global–specific.

expressiveness The ease with which one can express emotions, such as crying, showing empathy for the troubles of others, and showing nurturance to those in need.

external locus of control Generalized expectancies that events are outside of one's control.

extraversion The first fundamental personality trait in the **five-factor model**, a taxonomy which has proven to be replicable in studies using English-language trait words as items. Some of the key adjective markers for extraversion are *talkative, extraverted, gregarious, assertive, adventurous, open, sociable, forward,* and *outspoken.*

extreme responding A response set that refers to the tendency to give endpoint responses, such as "strongly agree" or "strongly disagree" and avoid the middle part of response scales, such as "slightly agree," "slightly disagree," or "am indifferent."

eye-blink startle method People typically blink their eyes when they are startled by a loud noise. Moreover, a person who is in an anxious or fearful state will blink faster and harder when startled than a person in a normal emotional state. This means that eye-blink speed when startled may be an objective physiological measure of how anxious or fearful a person is feeling. The eye-blink startle method may allow researchers to measure how anxious persons are without actually having to ask them.

f

face validity Whether the test, on the surface, measures what it appears to measure.

factor analysis A commonly used statistical procedure for identifying underlying structure in **personality** ratings or items. Essentially, it identifies groups of items that covary (i.e., go together or correlate) with each other, but tend not to covary with other groups of items. This provides a means for determining which personality variables share some common underlying property or belong together within the same group.

factor loadings Indexes of how much of the variation in an item is "explained" by the factor. Factor loadings indicate the degree to which the item correlates with or "loads on" the underlying factor.

faking The motivated distortion of answers on a questionnaire. Some people may be motivated to "fake good" in order to appear to be better off or better adjusted than they really are. Others may be motivated to "fake bad" in order to appear to be worse off or more maladjusted than they really are.

false consensus effect The tendency many people have to assume that others are similar to them (i.e., extraverts think that many other people are as extraverted as they are). Thinking that many other people share your own traits, preferences, or motivations.

false memories Memories that have been "implanted" by well-meaning therapists or others interrogating a subject about some event.

false negative There are two ways for psychologists to make a mistake when making decisions about persons based on personality tests (e.g., when deciding whether or not to hire a person, to parole a person, or that a person was lying). When trying to decide whether a person's answers are genuine or faked, the psychologist might decide that a truthful person was faking, a false negative.

false positive There are two ways for psychologists to make a mistake when making decisions about persons based on personality tests (e.g., when deciding whether or not to hire a person, to parole a person, or that a person was lying). When trying to decide whether a person's answers are genuine or faked, the psychologist might decide that a person who was faking was actually telling the truth, a false positive.

family studies Research that correlates the degree of genetic overlap among family members with the degree of personality similarity. It capitalizes on the fact that there are known degrees of genetic overlap between different members of a family in terms of degree of relationship.

fear of success Horney coined this phrase to highlight a gender difference in response to competition and achievement situations. Many women, she argued, feel that if they succeed, they will lose their friends. Consequently, many women, she thought, harbour an **unconscious** fear of success. She held that men, on the other hand, feel that they will actually gain friends by being successful and hence are not at all afraid to strive and pursue achievement.

feminine Traits or roles typically associated with being female in a particular **culture**.

femininity A psychological dimension containing traits such as nurturance, empathy, and expression of emotions (e.g., crying when sad). Femininity traits refer to **gender** roles, as distinct from biological **sex**. Two major personality instruments were published in 1974 to assess people using this new conception of gender roles (Bem, 1974; Spence, Helmreich, & Stapp, 1974).

field dependent In Witkin's **Rod and Frame Test (RFT)**, if a participant adjusts the rod so that it is leaning in the direction of the tilted frame, that person is said to be dependent on the visual field. On the other hand, if a participant disregards the external cues and instead uses information from his body in adjusting the rod to upright, he is said to be independent of the field, or **field independent**; appearing to rely on his own sensations, not the **perception** of the field, to make the judgment. This individual difference may have implications in situations where people must extract information from complex sensory fields, such as in multimedia education.

field independent In Witkin's **Rod and Frame Test (RFT)**, if a participant disregards the external cues and instead uses information from his body in adjusting the rod to upright, he is said to be independent of the field, appearing to rely on his own sensations, not the **perception** of the field, to make the judgment. On the other hand, if a participant adjusts the rod so that it is leaning in the direction of the tilted frame, that person is said to be dependent on the visual field, or **field dependent**. This individual difference may have implications in situations where people must extract information from complex sensory fields, such as in multimedia education.

five-factor model A trait taxonomy that has its roots in the **lexical hypothesis**. The first psychologist to use the terms "five-factor model" and "Big Five" was Warren Norman, based on his replications of the factor structure suggesting the following five traits: **surgency** (or **extraversion**), **neuroticism** (or emotional instability), **agreeableness**, **conscientiousness**, and **intellect–openness** to experience (or intellect). The model has been criticized by some for not being comprehensive and for failing to provide a theoretical understanding of the underlying psychological processes that generate the five traits. Nonetheless, it remains heavily endorsed by many personality psychologists and continues to be used in a variety of research studies and applied settings.

fixation According to Freud, if a child fails to fully resolve a conflict at a particular stage of development, he or she may get stuck in that stage. If a child is fixated at a particular stage, he or she exhibits a less mature approach to obtaining sexual gratification. According to Erikson, if a developmental crisis is not successfully and adaptively resolved, personality development could become arrested and the person would continue to have a fixation on that crisis in development.

flow A subjective state that people report when they are completely involved in an activity to the point of forgetting time, fatigue, and everything else but the activity itself. While flow experiences are somewhat rare, they occur under specific conditions; there is a balance between the person's skills and the challenges of the situation, there is a clear goal, and there is immediate feedback on how one is doing.

forced-choice questionnaire Test takers are confronted with pairs of statements and are asked to indicate which statement in the pair is more true of them. Each statement in the pair is selected to be similar to the other in **social desirability**, forcing participants to choose between statements that are equivalently socially desirable (or undesirable), and differ in content.

free association Patients relax, let their minds wander, and say whatever comes into their minds. Patients often say things that surprise or embarrass them. By relaxing the censor that screens everyday thoughts, free association allows potentially important material into **conscious** awareness.

free running A condition in studies of **circadian rhythms** in which participants are deprived from knowing what time it is (e.g., meals are served when the participant asks for them, not at prescheduled times). When a person is free running in time, there are no time cues to influence behaviour or biology.

frequency–dependent selection In some contexts, two or more heritable variants can evolve within a population. The most obvious example is biological sex itself. Within sexually reproducing species, the two sexes exist in roughly equal numbers because of frequency–dependent selection. If one sex becomes rare relative to the other, evolution will produce an increase in the numbers of the rarer sex. Frequency–dependent selection, in this example, causes the frequency of men and women to remain roughly equal. Different personality extremes (e.g., introversion and extraversion) may be the result of frequency dependent selection.

frontal brain asymmetry A different amount of activity in the left and right part of the frontal hemispheres of the brain. Studies using **EEG** measures have linked more relative left brain activity with pleasant emotions and more relative right brain activity with negative emotions.

frustration The high-arousal unpleasant subjective feeling that comes when a person is blocked from attaining an important goal. For example, a thirsty person who just lost his last bit of money in a malfunctioning drink-vending machine would most likely feel frustration.

fully functioning person According to Rogers, someone who is on their way toward **self-actualization**. Fully functioning persons may not actually *be* self-actualized yet, but they are not blocked or sidetracked in moving toward this goal. Such persons are open to new experiences and are not afraid of new ideas. They embrace life to its fullest. Fully functioning individuals are also centred in the present. They do not dwell on the past or their regrets. Fully functioning individuals also trust themselves, their feelings, and their own judgments.

functional analysis In his book *The Expression of the Emotions in Man and Animals*, Charles Darwin proposed a biological basis of emotions and emotional expressions by focusing on the "why" of **emotions** and expressions. Darwin concluded that emotional expressions communicate information from one animal to another about what is likely to happen. For instance, a dog baring its teeth, growling, and bristling the fur on its back is communicating to others that he is likely to attack. If others recognize the dog's communication, they may choose to back away to safety.

functional magnetic resonance imaging (fMRI) A non-invasive imaging technique used to identify specific areas of brain activity. As parts of the brain are stimulated, oxygenated blood rushes to the activated area, resulting in increased iron concentrations in the blood. The fMRI detects these elevated concentrations of iron and prints out colourful images indicating which part of the brain is used to perform certain tasks.

functionality The notion that our psychological mechanisms are designed to accomplish particular adaptive goals.

fundamental attribution error When bad events happen to others, people tend to attribute blame to some characteristic of the person, whereas when bad events happen to oneself, people have the tendency to blame the situation.

g

gender Social and cultural interpretations of what it means to be a man or a woman.

gender differences The distinction between gender and sex can be traced back to Horney. Horney stressed the point that, while biology determines sex, cultural norms determine what is acceptable for typical males and females in that culture. Today we use the terms *masculine* and *feminine* to refer to traits or roles typically associated with being male or female in a particular **culture**, and we refer to differences in such culturally ascribed roles and traits as gender differences. Differences that are ascribed to being a man or a woman per se are, however, called sex differences.

gender identity The personal and psychological conception of oneself as a man, a woman, some combination of the two, or neither

gender schemas Cognitive orientations that lead individuals to process social information on the basis of **sex**-linked associations (Hoyenga & Hoyenga, 1993).

gender stereotypes Beliefs that we hold about how men and women differ or are supposed to differ, which are not necessarily based on reality. Gender stereotypes can have important real-life consequences for men and women. These consequences can damage people where it most counts—in their health, their jobs, their odds of advancement, and their social reputations.

general adaptation syndrome (GAS) According to Selye, the syndrome consists of three stages: when a **stressor** first appears, people experience the **alarm stage**. If the stressor continues, the **resistance stage** begins. If the stressor remains constant, the person eventually enters the third stage, the **stage of exhaustion**.

general intelligence Early on in the study of intelligence, many psychologists thought of intelligence in traitlike terms, as a property of the individual. Individuals were thought to differ from each other in how much intelligence they possessed. Moreover, intelligence was thought of as a single broad factor, often called "g" for general intelligence. This stands in contrast to those views of intelligence as consisting of many discrete factors, such as social intelligence, emotional intelligence, and academic intelligence.

generalizability The degree to which a measure retains its validity across different contexts.

generalized expectancies A person's expectations for reinforcement that hold across a variety of situations (Rotter, 1971, 1990). When people encounter a new situation, they base their expectancies about what will happen on their generalized expectancies about whether they have the abilities to influence events.

genes Packets of DNA that are inherited by children from their parents in distinct chunks. They are the smallest discrete unit that is inherited by offspring intact, without being broken up.

genetic junk The 98 percent of the DNA in human chromosomes that are not protein-coding **genes**. At one time, scientists believed these parts were functionless residue. Recent studies have shown that these portions of DNA may affect everything from a person's physical size to personality, thus adding to the complexity of the human **genome**.

genital stage The final stage in Freud's **psychosexual stage** theory of development. This stage begins around age 12 and lasts through one's adult life. Here the libido is focused on the genitals, but not in the manner of self-manipulation associated with the **phallic stage**. People reach the genital stage with full **psychic energy** if they have resolved the conflicts at the prior stages.

genome The complete set of genes an organism possesses. The human genome contains somewhere between 20,000 and 30,000 genes.

genotype–environment correlation The differential exposure of individuals with different genotypes to different environments.

genotype–environment interaction The differential response of individuals with different genotypes to the same environments.

genotypic variance Genetic variance that is responsible for individual differences in the phenotypic expression of specific traits.

global self-esteem By far the most frequently measured component of self-esteem; defined as "the level of global regard that one has for the self as a person" (Harter, 1993, p. 88). Global self-esteem can range from highly positive to highly negative and reflects an overall evaluation of the self at the broadest level (Kling et al., 1999). Global self-esteem is linked with many aspects of functioning and is commonly thought to be central to mental health.

good theory A theory that serves as a useful guide for researchers, organizes known facts, and makes predictions about future observations.

h

happiness Researchers consider the concept in two complementary ways: in terms of a judgment that life is satisfying, as well as in terms of the predominance of positive compared with negative, **emotions** in one's life (Diener, 2000). It turns out, however, that people's emotional lives and their judgments of how satisfied they are with their lives are highly correlated. People who have a lot of pleasant emotions relative to unpleasant emotions in their lives tend also to judge their lives as satisfying, and vice versa.

hardy personality People with a hardy personality are better able to "resist" the negative effects of **stress** and cope more effectively over time. Hardiness has been suggested to involve three main traits: a sense of control, feeling committed and involved in life, and perceiving events as challenges rather than threats.

harm avoidance The personality trait in Cloninger's **tridimensional personality model** that is associated with low levels of **serotonin**. People low in serotonin are sensitive to unpleasant stimuli or to stimuli or events that have been associated with punishment or pain. Consequently, people low in serotonin seem to expect that harmful and unpleasant events will happen to them, and they are constantly vigilant for signs of such threatening events.

health behaviour model Personality does not directly influence the relation between stress and illness. Instead, personality affects health indirectly, through health-promoting or health-degrading behaviours. This model suggests that personality influences the degree to which a person engages in various health-promoting or health-demoting behaviours.

health psychology Researchers in the area of health psychology study relations between the mind and the body, and how these two components respond to challenges from the environment (e.g., stressful events, germs) to produce illness or health.

heritability A statistic that refers to the proportion of observed variance in a group of individuals that can be explained or "accounted for" by genetic variance (Plomin et al., 2001). It describes the degree to which genetic differences between individuals cause differences in some observed property, such as height, extraversion, or sensation seeking. The formal definition of heritability is the proportion of phenotypic variance that is attributable to **genotypic variance**.

heuristic value An evaluative scientific standard for assessing personality theories. Theories that steer scientists to important new discoveries about personality are superior to those that fail to provide this guidance. One of the **five standards for evaluating theories**.

HEXACO model A recently proposed taxonomy of personality that describes six key traits, extending the five-factor model: **honesty–humility**, emotionality, **extraversion, agreeableness, conscientiousness**, and **openness to experience**.

hierarchy of needs Murray believed that each person has a unique combination of **needs**. An individual's various needs can be thought of as existing at a different level of strength. A person might have a high need for dominance, an average need for intimacy, and a low need for achievement. High levels of some needs interact with the amounts of various other needs within each person.

historical era One type of **within-culture variation** pertains to the effects of historical era on personality. (For example, people who grew up during the great economic depression of the 1930s, for example, might be more anxious about job security or adopt a more conservative spending style.) Disentangling the effects of historical era on personality is an extremely difficult endeavour because most current personality measures were not in use in earlier eras.

histrionic personality disorder The hallmark of this **disorder** is excessive attention seeking and emotionality. Often such persons are overly dramatic and draw attention to themselves, preferring to be the centre of attention or the life of the party. They may appear charming or even flirtatious. Often they can be inappropriately seductive or provocative.

Hogan Personality Inventory (HPI) A questionnaire measure of personality based on the Big Five, or five-factor model, but modified to emphasize the assessment of traits important in the business world, including the motive to get along with others and the motive to get ahead of others.

holistic A way of processing information that involves attention to relationships, contexts, and links between the focal objects and the field as a whole.

Honesty–Humility A trait included in the **HEXACO model** of personality, which describes tendencies to be honest, sincere, trustworthy, and unselfish (versus arrogant, conceited, greedy, and self-important).

hormonal theories Argue that men and women differ not because of the external social environment but because the sexes have different amounts of specific hormones. It is these physiological differences, not differential social treatment, that causes boys and girls to diverge over development.

hostile attributional bias   The tendency to infer hostile intent on the part of others in the face of uncertain or unclear behaviour from others. Essentially, people who are aggressive expect that others will be hostile toward them.

hostile forces of nature   The term used by Darwin describing any event that impedes survival. Hostile forces of nature include food shortages, diseases, parasites, predators, and extremes of weather.

hostility   A tendency to respond to everyday frustrations with anger and aggression, to become irritable easily, to feel frequent resentment, and to act in a rude, critical, antagonistic, and unco-operative manner in everyday interactions (Dembrowski & Costa, 1987). Hostility is a subtrait in the **Type A** behaviour pattern.

human nature   The traits and mechanisms of personality that are typical of our species and are possessed by everyone or nearly everyone.

humanistic tradition   Emphasizes the role of choice in human life, and the influence of responsibility on creating a meaningful and satisfying life. The meaning of any person's life, according to this approach, is found in the choices that people make and the responsibility they take for those choices. The humanistic tradition also emphasizes the human need for growth and realizing one's full potential. In this tradition it is assumed that, if left to their own devices, humans will grow and develop in positive and satisfying directions.

i

id   The most primitive part of the human mind. Freud saw the id as something we are born with and as the source of all drives and urges. The id is like a spoiled child: selfish, impulsive, and pleasure loving. According to Freud, the id operates strictly according to the **plea-sure principle**, which is the desire for immediate gratification.

id psychology   Freud's version of psychoanalysis focused on the **id**, especially the twin instincts of sex and aggression, and how the **ego** and **superego** respond to the demands of the id. Freudian psychoanalysis can thus be called *id psychology*, to distinguish it from later developments that focused on the functions of the ego.

ideal self   The self that a person wants to be.

identification   A developmental process in children. It consists of wanting to become like the same-sex parent. In classic psycho-analysis, it marks the beginning of the resolution of the Oedipal or Electra conflicts and the successful resolution of the phallic stage of psychosexual development. Freud believed that the resolution of the phallic stage was both the beginning of the **superego** and morality and the start of the adult gender role.

identity conflict   According to Baumeister, an incompatibility between two or more aspects of identity. This kind of crisis often occurs when a person is forced to make an important and difficult life decision. Identity conflicts are "approach–approach" conflicts, in that the person wants to reach two mutually contradictory goals. Although these conflicts involve wanting two desirable identities, identity conflicts usually involve intense feelings of guilt or remorse over perceived unfaithfulness to an important aspect of the person's identity.

identity confusion   A period when a person does not have a strong sense of who she or he really is in terms of values, careers, relationships, and ideologies.

identity crisis   Erikson's term refers to the desperation, anxiety, and confusion a person feels when he or she has not developed a strong sense of identity. A period of identity crisis is a common experience during adolescence, but for some people it occurs later in life, or lasts for a longer period. Baumeister suggests that there are two distinct types of identity crises, which he terms identity deficit and identity conflict.

identity deficit   According to Baumeister, when a person has not formed an adequate identity and thus has trouble making major decisions. When people who have an identity deficit look toward their **social identity** for guidance in making decisions (e.g., "What would a person like me do in this situation?"), they find little in the way of a foundation upon which to base such life choices. Identity deficits often occur when a person discards old values or goals.

identity foreclosure   A person does not emerge from a crisis with a firm sense of commitment to values, relationships, or career but forms an identity without exploring alternatives. An example would be young people who accept the values of their parents or their cultural or religious group without question.

idiographic   The study of single individuals, with an effort to observe general principles as they are manifest in a single life over time.

"if ... then ..." propositions   A component of Walter Mischel's theory referring to the notion that, if situation A, the person does X, but if situation B, then the person does Y. Personality leaves its signature, Mischel argues, in terms of the specific situational ingredients that prompt behaviour from the person.

illness behaviour model   Personality influences the degree to which a person perceives and pays attention to bodily sensations, and the degree to which a person will interpret and label those sensations as an illness.

imagination inflation effect   A memory is elaborated upon in the imagination, leading the person to confuse the imagined event with events that actually happened.

implicit motivation   Motives as they are measured in fantasy-based (i.e., TAT) techniques, as opposed to direct self-report mea-sures. The implied **motives** of persons scored, for example, from **TAT** stories, is thought to reveal their unconscious desires and aspirations, their unspoken **needs** and wants. McClelland has argued that implicit motives predict long-term behavioural trends over time, such as implicit **need for achievement** predicting long-term business success.

impulsivity   A personality trait that refers to lowered self-control, especially in the presence of potentially rewarding activi-ties, the tendency to act before one thinks, and a lowered ability to anticipate the consequences of one's behaviour.

inclusive fitness theory   Modern evolutionary theory based on **differential gene reproduction** (Hamilton, 1964). The "inclusive" part refers to the fact that the characteristics that affect reproduction need not affect the personal production of offspring; they can affect the survival and reproduction of genetic relatives as well.

independence   Markus and Kitayama propose that each per-son has two fundamental "cultural tasks" that have to be con-fronted. One such task, agency or independence, involves how you differentiate yourself from the larger group. Independence includes your unique abilities, your personal internal motives and personality dispositions, and the ways in which you sepa-rate yourself from the larger group. See also **interdependence**.

independence training   According to McClelland, certain parental behaviours can promote high achievement motivation and autonomy in their children. Training a child to be independent in different tasks, such as feeding themselves and toilet training, promotes a sense of mastery and confidence in the child.

individual differences Every individual is like some other people (in traits and characteristics, such as **extraversion**) but different from others. The study of all the ways in which individuals can be similar to or different from others, as well as the number, origin, and meaning of such differences, is the study of individual differences.

individualistic A cultural orientation that focuses on uniqueness, independence, **agency** of the individual.

inductive reasoning approach The bottom-up, data-driven method of empirical research.

influential forces **Personality traits** and mechanisms are influential forces that affect our actions, how we view ourselves, how we think about the world, how we interact with others, how we feel, our selection of environments (particularly our social environment), what goals and desires we pursue in life, and how we react to our circumstances. Other influential forces include sociological and economic influences, as well as physical and biological forces.

information processing The transformation of sensory input into mental representations and the manipulation of such representations.

infrequency scale A common method for detecting measurement technique problems within a set of questionnaire items. The infrequency scale contains items that most or all people would answer in a particular way. If a participant answered more than one or two of these unlike the rest of the majority of the participants, a researcher could begin to suspect that the participant's answers do not represent valid information. Such a participant may be answering randomly, may have difficulty reading, or may be marking his or her answer sheet incorrectly.

inhibitory control The ability to control inappropriate responses or behaviours.

insight In **psychoanalysis**, through many interpretations, a patient is gradually led to an understanding of the **unconscious** source of his or her problems. This understanding is called *insight*.

inspection time A variable in intelligence research; the time it takes a person to make a simple discrimination between two displayed objects or two auditory intervals that differ by only a few milliseconds. This variable suggests that brain mechanisms specifically involved in discriminations of extremely brief time intervals represent a sensitive indicator of **general intelligence**.

instincts According to Freud, the strong innate forces that provide *all* the energy in the psychic system. In Freud's initial formulation there were two fundamental categories of instincts: self-preservation instincts and sexual instincts. In his later formulations, Freud collapsed the self-preservation and sexual instincts into one, which he called the *life instinct*.

instrumentality Personality traits that involve working with objects, getting tasks completed in a direct fashion, showing independence from others, and displaying self-sufficiency.

integrity tests Because the private sector cannot legally use polygraphs to screen employees, some companies have developed and promoted questionnaire measures to use in place of the polygraph. These questionnaires are designed to assess whether a person is generally honest or dishonest.

intellect–openness The fifth personality trait in the five-factor model, which has proven to be replicable in studies using English-language trait words as items. Some of the key adjective markers for openness are *creative, imaginative,* and *intellectual*. Those who rate high on openness tend to remember their dreams more and have vivid, prophetic, or problem-solving dreams.

interactional model Objective events happen to a person, but personality factors determine the impact of those events by influencing the person's ability to cope. This is called the interactional model because personality is assumed to moderate (that is, influence) the relation between stress and illness.

interdependence Markus and Kitayama propose that each person has two fundamental "cultural tasks" that have to be confronted. The first is communion or interdependence. This cultural task involves how you are affiliated with, attached to, or engaged in the larger group of which you are a member. Interdependence includes your relationships with other members of the group and your embeddedness within the group. See also **independence**.

internal locus of control The generalized expectancy that reinforcing events are under one's control, and that one is responsible for the major outcomes in life.

internalized In object relations theory, a child will create an unconscious mental representation of his or her mother. This allows the child to have a relationship with this internalized "object" even in the absence of the "real" mother. The relationship object internalized by the child is based on his or her developing relationship with the mother. This image then forms the fundamentals for how children come to view others with whom they develop subsequent relationships.

interpersonal relatedness A personality factor that may be unique to Eastern cultures. It involves traits such as harmony and reciprocity in relationships that are not tapped by conventional measures of the five-factor or Big Five models.

interpersonal traits What people do to and with each other. They include *temperament* traits, such as nervous, gloomy, sluggish, and excitable; *character* traits, such as moral, principled, and dishonest; *material* traits, such as miserly or stingy; *attitude* traits, such as pious or spiritual; *mental* traits, such as clever, logical, and perceptive; and *physical* traits, such as healthy and tough.

interpretation The making sense of, or explaining, various events in the world. One of the three levels of **cognition** that are of interest to personality psychologists. Psychoanalysts offer patients interpretations of the psychodynamic causes of their problems. Through many interpretations, patients are gradually led to an understanding of the unconscious source of their problems.

inter-rater reliability Multiple observers gather information about a person's **personality**, then investigators evaluate the degree of consensus among the observers. When different observers agree with one another, the degree of inter-rater reliability increases. When different raters fail to agree, the measure is said to have low inter-rater reliability.

intersex A general term used to describe a variety of conditions in which a person is born with a reproductive or sexual anatomy that doesn't fit the typical definitions of female or male.

intersexual selection In Darwin's theory, members of one sex choose a mate based on their preferences for particular qualities in that mate. These characteristics evolve because animals that possess them are chosen more often as mates, and their **genes** thrive. Animals that lack the desired characteristics are excluded from mating, and their genes perish.

intrapsychic domain Deals with mental mechanisms of personality, many of which operate outside the realm of conscious awareness. The predominant theory in this domain is Freud's theory of **psychoanalysis**. This theory begins with fundamental assumptions about the instinctual system—the sexual and aggressive forces that are presumed to drive and energize much of human activity. The intrapsychic domain also includes **defence mechanisms** such as **repression, denial,** and **projection**.

intrasexual competition According to Darwin's theory, members of the same sex compete with each other, and the outcome of their contest gives the winner greater sexual access to members of the opposite sex. Two stags locking horns in combat is the prototypical image of this. The characteristics that lead to success in contests of this kind, such as greater strength, intelligence, or attractiveness to allies, evolve because the victors are able to mate more often and hence pass on more genes.

l

latency stage The fourth stage in Freud's **psychosexual stages of development**. This stage occurs from around the age of six until puberty. Freud believed few specific sexual conflicts existed during this time, and was thus a period of psychological rest or latency. Subsequent psychoanalysts have argued that much development occurs during this time, such as learning to make decisions for oneself, interacting and making friends with others, developing an identity, and learning the meaning of work. The latency period ends with the sexual awakening brought about by puberty.

latent content According to Freud, what the elements of a dream actually represent.

learned helplessness Animals (including humans), when subjected to unpleasant and inescapable circumstances, often become passive and accepting of their situation, in effect learning to be helpless. Researchers surmised that if people were in an unpleasant or painful situation, they would attempt to change the situation. However, if repeated attempts to change the situation failed, they would resign themselves to being helpless. Then, even if the situation did improve so that they could escape the discomfort, they would continue to act helpless.

lexical approach The approach to determining the fundamental **personality** traits by analyzing language. For example, a trait adjective that has many synonyms probably represents a more fundamental trait than a trait adjective with few synonyms.

lexical hypothesis (basis for the lexical approach) It states that important **individual differences** have become encoded within the natural language. Over ancestral time, the differences between people that were important were noticed and words were invented to communicate about those differences.

libido Freud postulated humans have a life instinct—a combination of self-preservation and sexual instincts—as well as a fundamental instinct toward destruction—often manifest in aggression toward others. The two instincts were usually referred to as libido, for the life instinct, and **thanatos**, for the death instinct. While the libido was generally considered sexual in nature, Freud also used this term to refer to any need-satisfying, life-sustaining, or pleasure-oriented urge.

life-outcome data (L-data) Information that can be gleaned from the events, activities, and outcomes in a person's life that are available to public scrutiny. For example, marriages and divorces are a matter of public record. Personality psychologists can sometimes secure information about the clubs, if any, a person joins; how many speeding tickets a person has received in the last few years; whether the person owns a handgun. These can all serve as sources of information about **personality**.

Likert-type scale A common rating scale that provides numbers that are attached to descriptive phrases, such as 0 = disagree strongly, 1 = disagree slightly, 2 = neither agree nor disagree, 3 = agree slightly, 4 = strongly agree.

limbic system The part of the brain responsible for emotion and the "flight–fight" reaction. If individuals have a limbic system that is easily activated, we might expect them to have frequent episodes of emotion, particularly those emotions associated with flight (such as anxiety, fear, worry) and those associated with fight (such as anger, irritation, annoyance). Eysenck postulated that the limbic system was the source of the trait of neuroticism.

locus of control A person's **perception** of responsibility for the events in his or her life. It refers to whether people tend to locate that responsibility internally, within themselves, or externally, in fate, luck, or chance. Locus of control research started in the mid-1950s when Rotter was developing his social learning theory.

longitudinal studies Examine the same individuals over time. These types of studies have been conducted spanning as many as four and five decades of life and have examining many different age brackets. Such studies are costly and difficult to conduct, but the information gained about personality development is valuable.

m

Machiavellianism A manipulative strategy of social interaction referring to the tendency to use other people as tools for personal gain. "High Mach" persons tend to tell people what they want to hear, use flattery to get what they want, and rely heavily on lying and deception to achieve their own ends.

major life events According to Holmes and Rahe, these events require that people make major adjustments in their lives. Death or loss of a spouse through divorce or separation are the most stressful events, followed closely by being jailed, losing a close family member in death, or being severely injured.

manifest content According to Freud, what a dream actually contains.

manipulation Researchers conducting experiments use manipulation in order to evaluate the influence of one variable (the manipulated or independent variable) on another (the dependent variable).

masculine Traits or roles typically associated with being male in a particular **culture**.

masculinity Traits that define the cultural roles associated with being male. Two major personality instruments were published in 1974 to assess people using this new conception of gender roles (Bem, 1974; Spence, Helmreich, & Stapp, 1974). The masculinity scales contain items reflecting assertiveness, boldness, dominance, self-sufficiency, and instrumentality. Masculinity traits refer to **gender** roles, as distinct from biological **sex**.

maximalist Those who describe sex differences as comparable in magnitude to **effect sizes** in other areas of psychology, important to consider, and recommend that they should not be trivialized.

mean level change Within a single group that has been tested on two separate occasions, any difference in group averages across the two occasions is considered a mean level change. Using the previous example of political orientation, if the average degree changes, then that population is displaying mean level change.

mean level stability A population that maintains a consistent average level of a trait or characteristic over time. If the average level of liberalism or conservatism in a population remains the same with increasing age, we say that the population exhibits high mean level stability on that characteristic.

mediation A scenario in which the effect of one variable on another "goes through" a third variable. We might observe a relationship between A and B, but these two variables may actually be related because A leads to C, and C in turn leads to B.

metapersonal self-construal A **self-concept** involving definition of the self within a much broader context, such as the global community, humankind, the planet, or the cosmos.

minimalist Those who describe sex differences as small and inconsequential.

modelling By seeing another person engage in a particular behaviour with positive results, the observer is more likely to imitate that behaviour. It is a form of learning whereby the consequences for a particular behaviour are observed, and thus the new behaviour is learned.

moderator (or moderation) A variable that influences the direction or degree of relationship between two other variables.

molecular genetics Techniques designed to identify the specific **genes** associated with specific traits, such as personality traits. The most common method, called the *association method*, identifies whether individuals with a particular gene (or allele) have higher or lower scores on a particular trait measure.

monoamine oxidase (MAO) An enzyme found in the blood that is known to regulate neurotransmitters, those chemicals that carry messages between nerve cells. MAO may be a causal factor in the personality trait of sensation seeking.

monozygotic (MZ) twins Identical twins who come from a single fertilized egg (or zygote, hence *monozygotic*) that divides into two at some point during gestation. Identical twins are always the same sex because they are genetically identical.

mood induction In experimental studies of mood, this is employed as manipulations to determine whether the mood differences (e.g., pleasant versus unpleasant) effect some dependent variable. In studies of personality, mood effects might interact with personality variables. For example, positive mood effects might be stronger for persons high on **extraversion**, and negative mood effects might be stronger for persons high on **neuroticism**.

mood variability Frequent fluctuations in a person's emotional life over time.

moral anxiety Caused by a conflict between the **id** or the **ego** and the **superego**. For example, a person who suffers from chronic shame or feelings of guilt over not living up to "proper" standards, even though such standards might not be attainable, is experiencing moral anxiety.

moratorium The time taken to explore options before making a commitment to an identity. College can be considered a "time out" from life, in which students may explore a variety of roles, relationships, and responsibilities before having to commit to any single life path.

morningness–eveningness The stable differences between persons in preferences for being active at different times of the day. Differences between morning- and evening-types of people appear to be due to differences in the length of their underlying circadian biological rhythms.

motivated unconscious The psychoanalytic idea that information that is **unconscious** (e.g., a repressed wish) can actually motivate or influence subsequent behaviour. This notion was promoted by Freud and formed the basis for his ideas about the unconscious sources of mental disorders and other problems with living. Many psychologists agree with the idea of the unconscious, but there is less agreement today about whether information that is unconscious can have much of an influence on actual behaviour.

motives Internal states that arouse and direct behaviour toward specific objects or goals. A motive is often caused by a deficit, by the lack of something. Motives differ from each other in type, amount, and intensity, depending on the person and his or her circumstances. Motives are based on needs and propel people to perceive, think, and act in specific ways that serve to satisfy those needs.

Multi-Motive Grid Designed to assess motives, it uses 14 pictures representing achievement, power, or intimacy and a series of questions about important motivational states to elicit answers from test subjects. In theory, the **motives** elicited from the photographs would influence how the subject answers the test questions.

multiple intelligences Howard Gardner's theory of multiple intelligences includes several forms: interpersonal intelligence (social skills, ability to communicate and get along with others), intrapersonal intelligence (insight into oneself, one's **emotions** and **motives**), kinesthetic intelligence (the abilities of athletes, dancers, and acrobats), and musical intelligence. There are several other theories proposing multiple forms of intelligence. This position is in contrast to the theory of g or **general intelligence**, which holds that there is only one form of intelligence.

multiple social personalities Each of us displays different sides of ourselves to different people—we may be kind to our friends, ruthless to our enemies, loving toward a spouse, and conflicted toward our parents. Our social personalities vary from one setting to another, depending on the nature of relationships we have with other individuals.

Myers-Briggs Type Indicator (MBTI) One of the most widely used personality tests in the business world. It was developed by a mother–daughter team, Katharine Briggs and Isabel Myers, based on Jungian concepts. The test provides information about personality types by testing for eight fundamental preferences using questions in a "forced-choice" or either/or format. Individuals must respond in one way or another, even if their preferences might be somewhere in the middle. Although the test is not without criticism, it has great intuitive appeal.

n

narcissism A style of inflated self-admiration accompanied by tendencies towards grandiosity, entitlement, dominance, and superiority. High narcissism involves excessive attention-seeking behaviour demonstrated by constant attempts to keep others focused on oneself. Although narcissism can be carried to extremes, narcissistic tendencies can be found in normal range levels. The narcissism trait is distinct from **Narcissistic Personality Disorder**.

narcissistic paradox The fact that, although narcissistic people appear to have high self-esteem, they actually have doubts about their self-worth. While they appear to have a grandiose sense of self-importance, narcissists are nevertheless very fragile and vulnerable to blows to their self-esteem and cannot handle criticism well. They need constant praise, reassurance, and attention from others, whereas a person with truly high self-esteem would not need such constant praise and attention from others.

narcissistic personality disorder The calling card of the narcissistic personality is a strong need to be admired, a strong sense of self-importance, and a lack of insight into other people's feelings. Narcissists see themselves in a very favourable light, inflating their accomplishments and undervaluing the work of others. Narcissists daydream about prosperity, victory, influence, adoration from others, and power. They routinely expect adulation from others, believing that homage is generally long overdue. They exhibit feelings of entitlement, even though they have done nothing in particular to earn that special treatment.

natural selection Darwin reasoned that variants that better enabled an organism to survive and reproduce would lead to more descendants. The descendants, therefore, would inherit the variants that led to their ancestors' survival and reproduction. Through this process, the successful variants were selected, and unsuccessful variants weeded out. Natural selection, therefore, results in gradual changes in a species over time, as successful variants increase in frequency and eventually spread throughout the gene pool, replacing the less successful variants.

naturalistic observation Observers witness and record events that occur in the normal course of the lives of their participants. For example, a child might be followed throughout an entire day, or an observer may record behaviour in the home of the participant. Naturalistic observation offers researchers the advantage of being able to secure information in the realistic context of a person's everyday life, but at the cost of not being able to control the events and behavioural samples witnessed.

nature-nurture debate The ongoing debate as to whether genes or environment are more important determinants of personality.

need for achievement According to McClelland, the desire to do better, to be successful, and to feel competent. People with a high need for achievement obtain satisfaction from accomplishing a task or from the anticipation of accomplishing a task. They cherish the process of being engaged in a challenging task.

need for intimacy McAdams defines the need for intimacy as the "recurrent preference or readiness for warm, close, and communicative interaction with others" (1990, p. 198). People with a high need for intimacy want more intimacy and meaningful human contact in their day-to-day lives than do those with a low need for intimacy.

need for power A preference for having an impact on other people. Individuals with a high need for power are interested in controlling situations and other people.

needs States of tension within a person; as a need is satisfied, the state of tension is reduced. Usually the state of tension is caused by the lack of something (e.g., a lack of food causes a need to eat).

negative affectivity Includes components such as anger, sadness, difficulty, and amount of distress.

negative identity Identities founded on undesirable social roles, such as "gangstas," girlfriends of street toughs, or members of street gangs.

negligent hiring A charge sometimes brought against an employer for hiring someone who is unstable or prone to violence. Employers are defending themselves against such suits, which often seek compensation for crimes committed by their employees. Such cases hinge on whether the employer should have discovered dangerous traits ahead of time, before hiring such a person into a position where he or she posed a threat to others. Personality testing may provide evidence that the employer did in fact try to reasonably investigate an applicant's fitness for the workplace.

neurotic anxiety Occurs when there is a direct conflict between the **id** and the **ego**. The danger is that the ego may lose control over some unacceptable desire of the id. For example, a man who worries excessively that he might blurt out some unacceptable thought or desire in public is beset by neurotic anxiety.

neurotic paradox The fact that people with **disorders** or other problems with living often exhibit behaviours that exacerbate, rather than lessen, their problems. For example, **borderline personality disordered** persons, who are generally concerned with being abandoned by friends and intimate others, may throw temper tantrums or otherwise express anger and rage in a manner that drives people away. The paradox refers to doing behaviours that make their situation worse.

neuroticism (emotional instability) A dimension of **personality** present, in some form, in every major trait theory of personality, including the **five-factor model**. Different researchers have used different terms for neuroticism, such as emotional instability, anxiety-proneness, and **negative affectivity**. Adjectives useful for describing persons high on the trait of **neuroticism** include *moody, touchy, irritable, anxious, unstable, pessimistic,* and *complaining.*

neurotransmitter theory of depression According to this theory, an imbalance of the neurotransmitters at the synapses of the nervous system causes **depression**. Some medications used to treat depression target these specific neurotransmitters. Not all people with depression are treated successfully with drugs. That suggests that there may be varieties of depression; some are biologically based, while others are more reactive to stress, physical exercise, or cognitive therapy.

neurotransmitters Chemicals in the nerve cells that are responsible for the transmission of a nerve impulse from one cell to another. Some theories of personality are based directly on different amounts of neurotransmitters found in the nervous system.

nomothetic The study of general characteristics of people as they are distributed in the population, typically involving statistical comparisons between individuals or groups.

noncontent responding (also referred to as the concept of **response sets**) The tendency of some people to respond to the questions on some basis that is unrelated to the question content. One example is the response set of acquiescence or yea saying. This is the tendency to simply agree with the questionnaire items, regardless of the content of those items.

nonshared environmental influences Features of the **environment** that siblings do not share. Some children might get special or different treatment from their parents, they might have different groups of friends, they might be sent to different schools, or one might go to summer camp while the other stays home each summer. These features are called "nonshared" because they are experienced differently by different siblings.

norepinephrine A neurotransmitter involved in activating the sympathetic nervous system for fight or flight.

novelty seeking One of the personality traits in Cloninger's **tridimensional personality model**, which is based on low levels of **dopamine**. Low levels of dopamine create a drive state to obtain substances or experiences that increase dopamine. Novelty and thrills and excitement can make up for low levels of dopamine, and so novelty-seeking behaviour is thought to result from low levels of this neurotransmitter.

O

object relations theory Places an emphasis on early childhood relationships. While this theory has several versions that differ from each other in emphasis, all the versions have at their core a set of basic assumptions: that the internal wishes, desires, and urges of the child are not as important as his or her developing relationships with significant external others, particularly parents, and that the others, particularly the mother, become internalized by the child in the form of mental objects.

objectifying cognition Processing information by relating it to objective facts. This style of thinking stands in contrast to personalizing cognition.

objective anxiety Fear occurs in response to some real, external threat to the person. For example, being confronted by a large, aggressive-looking man with a knife while taking a shortcut through an alley would elicit objective anxiety (fear) in most people.

objective self-awareness Seeing oneself as an object of others' attention. Often, objective self-awareness is experienced as shyness, and for some people this is a chronic problem. Although objective self-awareness can lead to periods of social sensitivity, this ability to consider oneself from an outside perspective is the beginning of a **social identity**.

observer-report data (O-data) The impressions and evaluations others make of a person with whom they come into contact. For every individual, there are dozens of observers who form such impressions. Observer-report methods capitalize on these sources and provide tools for gathering information about a person's personality. Observers may have access to information not attainable through other sources, and multiple observers can be used to assess each individual. Typically, a more valid and reliable assessment of personality can be achieved when multiple observers are used.

obsessive-compulsive personality disorder The obsessive-compulsive personality is preoccupied with order and strives to be perfect. The high need for order can manifest itself in the person's attention to details, however trivial, and fondness for rules, rituals, schedules, and procedures. Another characteristic is a devotion to work at the expense of leisure and friendships. Obsessive-compulsive persons tend to work harder than they need to.

Oedipal conflict For boys, the main conflict in Freud's **phallic stage**. It is a boy's **unconscious** wish to have his mother all to himself by eliminating the father. (Oedipus is a character in a Greek myth who unknowingly kills his father and marries his mother.)

openness to experience (intellect-openness) The fifth personality trait in the **five-factor model**, which has proven to be replicable in studies using English-language trait words as items. Some of the key adjective markers for openness are *creative, imaginative*, and *intellectual*. Those who rate high on openness tend to remember their dreams more and have vivid, prophetic, or problem-solving dreams.

optimal level of arousal Hebb theorized that people are motivated to reach a level that is "just right" for any given task. If they are underaroused relative to this level, an increase in arousal is rewarding; conversely, if they are overaroused, a decrease in arousal is rewarding.

optimistic bias Most people generally underestimate their risks, with the average person rating his or her risk as below what is the true average. This has been referred to as the optimistic bias, and it may actually lead people in general to ignore or minimize the risks inherent in life or to take more risks than they should.

optimistic explanatory style A style that emphasizes external, temporary, and specific causes of bad events. Opposite of a **pessimistic explanatory style**.

oral stage The first stage in Freud's psychosexual stages of development. This stage occurs during the initial 18 months after birth. During this time, the main sources of pleasure and tension reduction are the mouth, lips, and tongue. Adults who still obtain pleasure from "taking in," especially through the mouth (e.g., people who overeat or smoke or talk too much) might be fixated at this stage.

organized The **psychological traits** and mechanisms for a given person are not simply a random collection of elements; rather, **personality** is coherent because the mechanisms and traits are linked to one another in an organized fashion.

orthogonality Discussed in terms of circumplex models, specifies that traits that are perpendicular to each other on the model (at 90 degrees of separation, or at right angles to each other) are unrelated to each other. In general, the term *orthogonal* is used to describe a zero correlation between traits.

ought self A person's understanding of what others want them to be.

p

pain tolerance The degree to which people can tolerate pain, which shows wide differences between persons. Petrie believed that individual differences in pain tolerance originated in the nervous system. She developed a theory that people with low pain tolerance had a nervous system that amplified or augmented the subjective impact of sensory input. In contrast, people who could tolerate pain well were thought to have a nervous system that dampened or reduced the effects of sensory stimulation.

paranoid personality disorder The paranoid personality is extremely distrustful of others and sees others as a constant threat. Such a person assumes that others are out to exploit and deceive them, even though there is no good evidence to support this assumption. Paranoid personalities feel that they have been injured by other persons and are preoccupied with doubts about the motivations of others. The paranoid personality often misinterprets social events and holds resentments toward others for slights or perceived insults.

parsimony The fewer premises and assumptions a theory contains, the greater its parsimony. This does not mean that simple theories are always better than complex ones. Due to the complexity of the human personality, a complex theory—that is, one containing many premises—may ultimately be necessary for adequate personality theories. One of the **five standards for evaluating theories**.

passive genotype–environment correlation Occurs when parents provide both genes and environment to children, yet the children do nothing to obtain that environment.

peak experience A momentary feeling of extreme wonder, awe, and vision. This is characterized by feelings of euphoria, harmonization, a deep sense of meaning and purpose, and interconnectedness. According to Maslow, they contribute to the **self-actualization** process by providing insight about one's potential.

penis envy The female counterpart of castration anxiety, which occurs during the **phallic stage** of psychosexual development for girls around 3 to 5 years of age.

people–things dimension According to Little, refers to the nature of vocational interests. Those at the "things" end of the dimension like vocations that deal with impersonal tasks—machines, tools, or materials. Examples include carpenter, auto mechanic, building contractor, tool maker, or farmer. Those scoring toward the "people" end of the dimension prefer social occupations that involve thinking about others, caring for others, or directing others. Examples include high school teacher, social worker, or religious counsellor.

percentage of variance Individuals vary or are different from each other, and this variability can be partitioned into percentages that are related to separate causes or separate variables. An example is the percentages of variance in some trait that are related to genetics, the shared environment, and the unshared environment. Another example would be the percentage of variance in happiness scores that are related to various demographic variables, such as income, gender, and age.

perception The process of imposing order on the information our sense organs take in. One of the three levels of **cognition** that are of interest to personality psychologists. Even at the level of perception, what we "see" in the world can be quite different from person to person.

perceptual sensitivity The ability to detect subtle stimuli from the environment.

person–environment interaction A person's interactions with situations include perceptions, selections, evocations, and manipulations. *Perceptions* refer to how we "see" or interpret an environment. *Selection* describes the manner in which we choose situations—such as our friends, our hobbies, our classes, and our careers. *Evocations* refer to the reactions we produce in others, often quite unintentionally. *Manipulations* refer to the ways in which we attempt to influence others.

person–situation interaction Theory which states that one has to take into account both particular situations (e.g., frustration) and personality traits (e.g., hot temper) when understanding a behaviour.

personal constructs In Kelly's theory, beliefs or concepts that summarize a set of observations or version of reality, unique to an individual, which that person routinely uses to interpret and predict events.

personal project A set of relevant actions intended to achieve a goal that a person has selected. Psychologist Brian Little believes that personal projects make natural units for understanding the working of personality because they reflect how people face up to the serious business of navigating through daily life.

personality The set of **psychological traits** and mechanisms within the individual that are organized and relatively enduring and that influence his or her interactions with, and adaptations to, the environment (including the **intrapsychic**, physical, and social **environment**).

personality coherence Changes in the manifestations of personality variables over time, even as the underlying characteristics remain stable. The notion of personality coherence includes both elements of continuity and elements of change: continuity in the underlying trait but change in the outward manifestation of that trait. For example, an emotionally unstable child might frequently cry and throw temper tantrums, whereas as an adult such a person might frequently worry and complain. The manifestation might change, even though the trait stays stable.

personality development The continuities, consistencies, and stabilities in people over time, and the ways in which people change over time.

personality disorder An enduring pattern of experience and behaviour that differs greatly from the expectations of the individual's **culture**. The **disorder** is usually manifest in more than one of the following areas: the way a person thinks, feels, gets along with others, or controls personal behaviour. To be classed as a personality disorder, the pattern must *not* result from drug abuse, medication, or a medical condition such as head trauma.

personality-descriptive nouns As described by Saucier, nouns differ in their content emphases from personality taxonomies based on adjectives and may be more precise. In Saucier's 2003 work on personality nouns, he discovered eight factors, including "Dumbbell," "Babe/Cutie," "Philosopher," "Lawbreaker," "Joker," and "Jock."

personalizing cognition Processing information by relating it to a similar event in your own life. This style of processing information occurs when people interpret a new event in a personally relevant manner. For example, they might see a car accident and start thinking about the time they were in a car accident.

personnel selection Employers sometimes use personality tests to select people especially suitable for a specific job. Alternatively, the employer may want to use personality assessments to deselect, or screen out, people with specific traits. In both cases an employer is concerned with selecting the right person for a specific position from among a pool of applicants.

perspective taking A final unfolding of the **self-concept** during the teen years is the ability to take the perspectives of others, or to see oneself as others do, to step outside of one's self and imagine how one appears to other people. This is why many teenagers go through a period of extreme self-consciousness, focusing much of their energy on how they appear to others.

pessimistic explanatory style Emphasizes internal, stable, and global causes for bad events and puts a person at risk for feelings of helplessness and poor adjustment. It is the opposite of an **optimistic explanatory style**.

phallic stage The third stage in Freud's psychosexual stages of development. It occurs between three and five years of age, during which time the child discovers that he has (or she discovers that she does not have) a penis. This stage also includes the awakening of sexual desire directed, according to Freud, toward the parent of the opposite sex.

phenotypic variance Observed individual differences, such as in height, weight, or personality.

physiological needs The base of Maslow's need hierarchy. These include those needs that are of prime importance to the immediate survival of the individual (the need for food, water, air, sleep) as well as to the long-term survival of the species (the need for sex).

physiological systems Organ systems within the body; for example, the nervous system (including the brain and nerves), the cardiac system (including the heart, arteries, and veins), and the musculoskeletal system (including the muscles and bones which make all movements and behaviours possible).

pleasure principle The desire for immediate gratification. The **id** operates according to the pleasure principle; therefore, it does not listen to reason, does not follow logic, has no values or morals (other than immediate gratification), and has very little patience.

positive illusions Some researchers believe that part of being happy is to have positive illusions about the self—an inflated view of one's own characteristics as a good, able, and desirable person—as this characteristic appears to be part of emotional well-being according to Taylor.

positive reappraisal A cognitive process whereby a person focuses on the good in what is happening or has happened to them. Folkman and Moskowitz note that forms of this positive coping strategy include seeing opportunities for personal growth or seeing how one's own efforts can benefit other people.

positive regard According to Rogers, all children are born wanting to be loved and accepted by their parents and others. He called this inborn need the desire for positive regard.

positive self-regard According to Rogers, people who have received positive regard from others develop a sense of positive self-regard; they accept themselves, even their own weaknesses and shortcomings. People with high positive self-regard trust themselves, follow their own interests, and rely on their feelings to guide them to do the right thing.

possible selves This concept can be viewed in a number of ways, but two are especially important. The first pertains to the desired self—the person we wish to become. The second pertains to our feared self—the sort of person we do not wish to become.

postmodernism In personality psychology, the notion that reality is a **construct**, that every person and culture has its own unique version of reality, and that no single version of reality is more valid or more privileged than another.

posttraumatic stress disorder (PTSD) A syndrome that occurs in some individuals after experiencing or witnessing life-threatening events, such as military combat, natural disasters, terrorist attacks, serious accidents, or violent personal assaults (e.g., rape). Those who suffer from PTSD often relive the trigger experience for years through nightmares or intense flashbacks; have difficulty sleeping; report physical complaints; have flattened emotions; and feel detached or estranged from others. These symptoms can be severe and last long enough to significantly impair the individual's daily life, health, relationships, and career.

power stress According to David McClelland, when people with a high **need for power** do not get their way, or when their power is challenged or blocked, they are likely to show strong stress responses. This **stress** has been linked to diminished immune function and increased illness in **longitudinal studies**.

preconscious Any information that a person is not presently aware of, but that could easily be retrieved and made **conscious**, is found in the preconscious mind.

predictive validity (also referred to as **criterion validity**) Whether a test predicts criteria external to the test.

predisposition model In health psychology, this model suggests that associations may exist between personality and illness because a third variable is causing them both.

prefrontal cortex Area of the brain found to be highly active in the control of **emotions**. Many people who have committed violent acts exhibit a neurological deficit in the frontal areas, portions of the brain assumed to be responsible for regulating negative emotions.

press Need-relevant aspects of the environment according to Henry Murray. A person's need for intimacy, for example, won't affect that person's behaviour without an appropriate environmental press (such as the presence of friendly people).

prevalence The total number of cases that are present within a given population during a particular period of time.

prevention focus The other focus of self-regulation where the person is concerned with protection, safety, and the prevention of negative outcomes and failures. Behaviours with a prevention focus are characterized by vigilance, caution, and attempts to prevent negative outcomes. See also **promotion focus**.

primary appraisal According to Lazarus, in order for stress to be evoked for a person, two cognitive events must occur. The first cognitive event, called the *primary appraisal*, is for the person to perceive that the event is a threat to his or her personal goals. See also **secondary appraisal**.

primary process thinking Thinking without the logical rules of **conscious** thought or an anchor in reality. Dreams and fantasies are examples of primary process thinking. Although primary process thought does not follow the normal rules of reality (e.g., in dreams people might fly or walk through walls), Freud believed there were principles at work in primary process thought and that these principles could be discovered.

priming Technique to make associated material more accessible to **conscious** awareness than material that is not primed. Research using subliminal primes demonstrates that information can get into the mind, and have some influence on it, without going through conscious experience.

private self-concept The development of an inner, private self-concept is a major but often difficult development in the growth of the **self-concept**. It may start out with children developing an imaginary friend, someone only they can see or hear. This imaginary friend may actually be children's first attempt to communicate to their parents that they know there is a secret part, an inner part, to their understanding of their self. Later, children develop the full realization that only they have access to their own thoughts, feelings, and desires, and that no one else can know this part of them unless they choose to tell them.

problem-focused coping Thoughts and behaviours that manage or solve the underlying cause of stress. Folkman and Moskowitz note that focusing on solving problems, even little ones, can give a person a positive sense of control even in the most stressful and uncontrollable circumstances.

projection A **defence mechanism** based on the notion that sometimes we see in others those traits and desires that we find most upsetting in ourselves. We literally "project" (i.e., attribute) our own unacceptable qualities onto others.

projective hypothesis The idea that what a person "sees" in an ambiguous figure, such as an inkblot, reflects his or her personality. People are thought to project their own personalities into what they report seeing in such an ambiguous stimulus.

projective techniques A person is presented with an ambiguous stimulus and is then asked to impose some order on the stimulus, such as asking what the person sees in an inkblot. What the person sees is interpreted to reveal something about his or her personality. The person presumably "projects" his or her concerns, conflicts, traits, and ways of seeing or dealing with the world onto the ambiguous stimulus. The most famous projective technique for assessing personality is the Rorschach inkblot test.

promotion focus   One focus of self-regulation whereby the person is concerned with advancement, growth, and accomplishments. Behaviours with a promotion focus are characterized by eagerness, approach, and "going for the gold." See also **prevention focus**.

psychic energy   According to Sigmund Freud, a source of energy within each person that motivates him or her to do one thing and not another. In Freud's view, it is this energy that motivates all human activity.

psychoanalysis   A theory of personality and a method of psychotherapy (a technique for helping individuals who are experiencing some mental **disorder** or even relatively minor problems with living). It can be thought of as a theory about the major components and mechanisms of personality, as well as a method for deliberately restructuring personality.

psychological mechanisms   Similar to traits, except that mechanisms refer more to the *processes* of personality. For example, most personality mechanisms involve some information-processing activity. A psychological mechanism may make people more sensitive to certain kinds of information from the **environment** (input), may make them more likely to think about specific options (decision rules), or may guide their behaviour toward certain categories of action (outputs).

psychological resilience   The tendency towards positive adaptation or successful coping after a stressful or adverse situation.

psychological traits   Characteristics that describe ways in which people are unique or different from or similar to each other. Psychological traits include all sorts of aspects of persons that are psychologically meaningful and are stable and consistent aspects of personality.

psychological types   A term growing out of Carl Jung's theory implying that people come in distinct categories of personality, for example "extraverted types." This view is not widely endorsed by academic or research-oriented psychologists because most personality traits are normally distributed in the population and are best conceived as dimensions of difference, not categories.

psychopathology   The study of mental disorders that combines statistical, social, and psychological approaches to diagnosing individual abnormality.

psychopathy   A term often used synonymously with the **antisocial personality disorder**. It is used to refer to individual differences in antisocial characteristics.

psychosexual stage theory   According to Freud, all persons pass through a set series of stages in personality development. At each of the first three stages, young children must face and resolve specific conflicts, which revolve around ways of obtaining a type of sexual gratification. Children seek sexual gratification at each stage by investing libidinal energy in a specific body part. Each stage in the developmental process is named after the body part in which sexual energy is invested.

psychosocial conflicts   As posited by Erik Erikson, these occur throughout a person's lifetime and contribute to the ongoing development of personality. He defined them as the crises of learning to trust our parents, learning to be autonomous from them, and learning from them how to act as an adult.

r

race or gender norming   Activities that involve developing different standards for different ethnic groups or genders based on data obtained from large samples of people. The application of these normative data in employment testing scenarios is discriminatory and employers should avoid tests of this sort in favour of personality tests with standard norms applied equally to all applicants.

random assignment   Assignment in an experiment that is conducted randomly. If an experiment has manipulation between groups, random assignment of participants to experimental groups helps ensure that each group is equivalent.

rank order   Maintaining one's relative position within a group over time. Between ages 14 and 20, for example, most people become taller. But the rank order of heights tends to remain fairly stable because this form of development affects all people pretty much the same. The tall people at 14 fall generally toward the tall end of the distribution at age 20. The same can apply to personality traits. If people tend to maintain their position on dominance or extraversion relative to the other members of the group over time, then we say that there is high rank order stability to the personality characteristic. Conversely, if people fail to maintain their rank order, we say that the group has displayed rank order instability or rank order change.

rank order change   The change of individual position within the group.

rank order stability   The maintenance of individual position within the group.

rationalization   A defence mechanism that involves generating acceptable reasons for outcomes that might otherwise be unacceptable. The goal is to reduce anxiety by coming up with an explanation for some event that is easier to accept than the "real" reason.

reaction formation   A **defence mechanism** that attempts to stifle the expression of an unacceptable urge; a person may continually display a flurry of behaviour that indicates the opposite impulse. Reaction formation makes it possible for psychoanalysts to predict that sometimes people will do exactly the opposite of what you might otherwise think they would do. It also alerts us to be sensitive to instances when a person is doing something in excess. One of the hallmarks of reaction formation is excessive behaviour.

reactive genotype–environment correlation   Occurs when parents (or others) respond to children differently depending on their genotype.

reactively heritable   Traits that are secondary consequences of heritable traits.

reality principle   In psychoanalysis, it is the counterpart of the **pleasure principle**. It refers to guiding behaviour according to the demands of reality and relies on the strengths of the **ego** to provide such guidance.

reciprocal causality   The notion that causality can move in two directions; for example, helping others can lead to happiness, and happiness can lead one to be more helpful to others.

reducer/augmenter theory   From Petrie's research on **pain tolerance**, refers to the dimension along which people differ in their reaction to sensory stimulation; some appear to reduce sensory stimulation, some appear to augment stimulation.

reinforcement sensitivity theory   Gray's biological theory of personality. Based on recent brain function research with animals, Gray constructed a model of human personality based on two hypothesized biological systems in the brain: the **behavioural activation system** (which is responsive to incentives, such as cues for reward, and regulates approach behaviour) and the **behavioural inhibition system** (which is responsive to cues for punishment, **frustration**, and uncertainty).

relationship-focused coping   Efforts to maintain and manage social relationships during stressful periods.

reliability The degree to which an obtained measure represents the "true" level of the trait being measured. For example, if a person has a "true" IQ of 115, then a perfectly reliable measure of IQ will yield a score of 115 for that person. Moreover, a truly reliable measure of IQ would yield the same score of 115 each time it was administered to the person. Personality psychologists prefer reliable measures so that the scores accurately reflect each person's true level of the **personality** characteristic being measured.

repeated measurement A way to estimate the reliability of a measure. There are different forms of repeated measurement, and hence different versions of reliability. A common procedure is to repeat the same measurement over time, say at an interval of a month apart, for the same sample of people. If the two tests are highly correlated between the first and second testing, yielding similar scores for most people, then the resulting measure is said to have high test-retest reliability.

repression One of the first **defence mechanisms** discussed by Freud; refers to the process of preventing unacceptable thoughts, feelings, or urges from reaching **conscious** awareness.

resistance When a patient's defences are threatened by a probing psychoanalyst, the patient may unconsciously set up obstacles to progress. At this stage of **psychoanalysis**, it signifies that important **unconscious** material is coming to the fore. The resistance itself becomes an integral part of the interpretations the analyst offers to the patient.

resistance stage The second stage in Selye's **general adaptation syndrome (GAS)**. Here the body is using its resources at an above-average rate, even though the immediate fight-or-flight response has subsided. **Stress** is being resisted, but the effort is making demands on the person's resources and energy. See also **alarm stage**.

response sets (sometimes referred to as **noncontent responding**) The tendency of some people to respond to the questions on some basis that is unrelated to the question content. One example is the response set of acquiescence or yea saying. This is the tendency to simply agree with the questionnaire items, regardless of the content of those items.

responsibility training Life experiences that provide opportunities to learn to behave responsibly, such as having younger siblings to take care of while growing up. Moderates the gender difference in impulsive behaviours associated with **need for power**.

restricted sexual strategy According to Gangestad and Simpson (1990), a woman seeking a high-investing mate would adopt a restricted sexual strategy marked by delayed intercourse and prolonged courtship. This would enable her to assess the man's level of commitment, detect the existence of prior commitments to other women and/or children, and simultaneously signal to the man the woman's sexual fidelity and, hence, assure him of his paternity of future offspring.

reward dependence The personality trait in Cloninger's **tridimensional personality model** associated with low levels of **norepinephrine**. People high on this trait are persistent; they continue to act in ways that produce reward. They work long hours, put a lot of effort into their work, and will often continue striving after others have given up.

right to privacy This is perhaps the largest issue of legal concern for employers using personality testing. The right to privacy in employment settings grows out of the broader concept of the right to privacy. Cases that charge an invasion-of-privacy claim against an employer can be based on the Canadian Charter of Rights and Freedoms.

rite of passage Some cultures and religions institute a rite of passage ritual, usually around adolescence, which typically is a ceremony that initiates a child into adulthood. After such ceremonies, the adolescent is sometimes given a new name, bestowing a new adult identity.

Rod and Frame Test (RFT) An apparatus devised by Witkin to research the cues that people use in judging orientation in space. The participant sits in a darkened room and is instructed to watch a glowing rod surrounded by a glowing square frame. The experimenter can adjust the tilt of the rod, the frame, and the participant's chair. The participant's task is to adjust the rod by turning a dial so that the rod is perfectly upright. To do this accurately, the participant has to ignore cues in the visual field in which the rod appears. This test measures the personality dimension of field dependence–independence.

rumination Repeatedly focusing on one's symptoms or distress (e.g., "Why do I continue to feel so bad about myself?" or "Why doesn't my boss like me?"). Rumination is a key contributor to women's greater experience of depressive symptoms.

S

safety needs The second to lowest level of Maslow's need hierarchy. These needs have to do with shelter and security, such as having a place to live and being free from the threat of danger. Maslow believed that building a life that was orderly, structured, and predictable also fell under safety needs.

schizoid personality disorder The schizoid personality is split off (schism) or detached from normal social relations. The schizoid person simply appears to have no need or desire for intimate relationships or even friendships. Family life usually does not mean much to such people, and they do not obtain satisfaction from being part of a group. They have few or no close friends, and they would rather spend time by themselves than with others.

schizotypal personality disorder Whereas the schizoid person is indifferent to social interaction, the schizotypal personality is acutely uncomfortable in social relationships. Schizotypes are anxious in social situations, especially if those situations involve strangers. Schizotypal persons also feel that they are different from others, or that they do not fit in with the group. They tend to be suspicious of others and are seen as odd and eccentric.

scientific standards for evaluating personality theories The five key standards are **comprehensiveness, heuristic value, testability, parsimony, and compatibility and integration across domains and levels**.

secondary appraisal According to Lazarus, in order for stress to be evoked for a person, two cognitive events must occur. The second necessary cognitive event, called the *secondary appraisal*, is when the person concludes that he or she does not have the resources to cope with the demands of the threatening event. See also **primary appraisal**.

secondary process thinking The **ego** engages in secondary process thinking, which refers to the development and devising of strategies for problem solving and obtaining satisfaction. Often this process takes into account the constraints of physical reality, about when and how to express some desire or urge. See **primary process thinking**.

secure relationship style In Hazan and Shaver's secure relationship style, the adult has few problems developing satisfying friendships and relationships. Secure people trust others and develop bonds with others.

securely attached Describes the infants in Ainsworth's **strange situation study** who endured the separation from their mothers or caregivers and went about exploring the room, waiting patiently, or even approaching the stranger and sometimes wanting to be held by the stranger. When the mother returned, these infants were glad to see her, typically interacted with her for a while, then went back to exploring the new environment. They seemed confident the mother would return. Approximately 66 percent of infants fall into this category.

selective breeding One method of doing behaviour genetic research. Researchers might identify a trait and then see if they can selectively breed animals to possess that trait. This can occur only if the trait has a genetic basis. For example, dogs that possess certain desired characteristics, such as a sociable disposition, might be selectively bred to see if this disposition can be increased in frequency among offspring. Traits that are based on learning cannot be selectively bred for.

selective placement If adopted children are placed with adoptive parents who are similar to their birth parents, this may inflate the correlations between the adopted children and their adoptive parents. In this case, the resulting inflated correlations would artificially inflate estimates of environmental influence because the correlation would appear to be due to the **environment** provided by the adoptive parent. There does not seem to be selective placement, and so this potential problem is not a problem in actual studies (Plomin et al., 1990).

self-actualization need As defined by Maslow, it is becoming "more and more what one idiosyncratically is, to become everything that one is capable of becoming" (1970, p. 46). This need sits at the pinnacle of Maslow's need hierarchy. Maslow was concerned with describing self-actualization; the work of Carl Rogers was focused on how people achieve self-actualization.

self-attributed motivation (or explicit motivation) Primarily a person's **self-awareness** of their own conscious motives according to McClelland. These self-attributed motives reflect a person's conscious awareness about what is important to them. As such, they represent part of the individual's conscious self-understanding. McClelland has argued that self-attributed motives predict responses to immediate and specific situations and to choice behaviours and attitudes. See **implicit motivation**.

self-awareness The capacity for introspection; the ability to recognize oneself as an individual separate from other individuals and the environment.

self-complexity The view that each of us has many roles and many aspects to our self-concepts. However, for some of us, our self-concepts are rather simple, being made up of just a few large categories. Other people may have a more complex or differentiated **self-concept**. For people with high self-complexity, a failure in any one aspect of the self (such as a relationship that breaks apart) is buffered because there are many other aspects of the self that are unaffected by that event. However, for persons low in self-complexity, the same event might be seen as devastating because they define themselves mainly in terms of this one aspect.

self-concept The way a person sees, understands, and defines himself or herself.

self-concept differentiation The tendency to see oneself as having different traits across different social roles.

self-construal The grounds for self-definition; the extent to which the self is defined independently of others or interdependently with others.

self-efficacy A concept related to optimism and developed by Bandura. The belief that one can behave in ways necessary to achieve some desired outcome. Also refers to the confidence one has in one's ability to perform the actions needed to achieve some specific outcome.

self-enhancement The tendency to describe and present oneself using positive or socially valued attributes, such as kind, understanding, intelligent, and industrious. Tendencies toward self-enhancement tend to be stable over time, and hence are enduring features of personality (Baumeister, 1997).

self-esteem A general evaluation of one's **self-concept** along a good–bad or like–dislike dimension. It involves both cognitive and affective components, reflecting how one thinks and feels about various aspects of the self.

self-esteem variability An individual difference characteristic referring to how much a person's self-esteem fluctuates or changes over time. It is uncorrelated with mean level of self-esteem.

self-fulfilling prophecy The tendency for a belief to become reality. For example, a person who thinks he or she is a "total failure" will often act like a total failure and may even give up trying to do better, thus creating a self-fulfilling prophecy.

self-guides The **ideal self** and the **ought self** provide the standards that one uses to organize self-relevant information and motivate appropriate behaviours.

self-handicapping Situations in which people deliberately do things that increase the probability that they will fail.

self-report data (S-data) Information a person verbally reveals about themselves, often based on a questionnaire or interview. Can be obtained through a variety of means, including interviews that pose questions to a person, periodic reports by a person to record the events as they happen, and questionnaires of various sorts.

self-schema The specific knowledge structure, or cognitive representation, of the self-concept. Self-schemas are the network of associated building blocks of the **self-concept**.

self-serving bias The common tendency for people to take credit for success yet to deny responsibility for failure.

self-transcendence Dedicating oneself to a higher goal and/or helping others to self-actualize. This was considered the ultimate expression of **self-actualization** by Abraham Maslow.

sensation seeking A dimension of personality postulated to have a physiological basis. It refers to the tendency to seek out thrilling and exciting activities, to take risks, and to avoid boredom.

sensory deprivation Often done in a sound-proof chamber containing water in which a person floats, in total darkness, such that sensory input is reduced to a minimum. Researchers use sensory deprivation chambers to see what happens when a person is deprived of sensory input.

separation anxiety The agitation and distress children experience when separated from their mother (or primary caretaker). Most primates exhibit separation anxiety.

serotonin A neurotransmitter that plays a role in **depression** and other mood disorders. Drugs such as Prozac, Zoloft, and Paxil block the reuptake of serotonin, leaving it in the synapse longer, leading depressed persons to feel less depressed.

sex Whether an individual is biologically considered male, female, or **intersex** according to specific anatomy or physiology.

sex differences An average difference between women and men on certain characteristics such as height, body fat distribution, or personality characteristics, with no prejudgment about the cause of the difference.

sexual orientation One's sexual or romantic attraction to the same or opposite gender.

sexual selection The evolution of characteristics because of their mating benefits rather than because of their survival benefits. According to Darwin, sexual selection takes two forms: **intrasexual competition** and **intersexual selection**.

sexually dimorphic Species that show high variance in reproduction within one sex tend to be highly different in size and structure. The more intense the effective polygyny, the more dimorphic the sexes are in size and form (Trivers, 1985).

shared environmental influences Features of the **environment** that siblings share; for example, the number of books in the home, the presence or absence of a TV or computer, quality and quantity of the food in the home, the values and attitudes of the parent, and the schools, church, synagogue, or temple the parents send the children to.

shyness A tendency to feel tense, worried, or anxious during social interactions, or even when anticipating a social interaction (Addison & Schmidt, 1999). Shyness is a common phenomenon, and more than 90 percent of the population reports experiencing shyness at some point during their lives (Zimbardo, 1977). Some people, however, seem to be dispositionally shy—they tend to feel awkward in most social situations and so tend to avoid situations in which they will be forced to interact with people.

situational selection A form of interactionism that refers to the tendency to choose or select the situations in which one finds oneself. In other words, people typically do not find themselves in random situations in their natural lives. Instead, they select or choose the situations in which they will spend their time.

situational specificity The view that behaviour is determined by aspects of the situation, such as reward contingencies.

situationism A theoretical position in personality psychology that states that situational differences, rather than underlying personality traits, determine behaviour. For example, how friendly a person will be or how much need for achievement a person displays will depend on the situation, not the traits a person possesses.

Six Factor Personality Questionnaire (SFPQ) A personality test that measures standard broad traits of **extraversion, agreeableness**, and **openness to experience**. Additionally, it measures a broad trait of independence and divides **conscientiousness** into two distinct factors. The SFPQ is commonly employed by the RCMP in Canada.

skin conductance The degree to which the skin carries (or conducts) electricity, which depends on the amount of water present in the skin. See also **electrodermal activity**.

social and cultural domain Personality affects, and is affected by, the social and cultural context in which it is found. Different cultures may bring out different facets of our personalities in manifest behaviour. The capacities we display may depend to a large extent on what is acceptable in and encouraged by our **culture**. At the level of **individual differences** within cultures, personality plays itself out in the social sphere. One important social sphere concerns relationships between men and women.

social anxiety Discomfort related to social interactions, or even to the anticipation of social interactions. Socially anxious persons appear to be overly concerned about what others will think. Baumeister and Tice propose that social anxiety is a species-typical adaptation that functions to prevent social exclusion.

social attention The goal and payback for **surgent** or **extraverted** behaviour. By being the centre of attention, the extravert seeks to gain the approval of others and, in many cases, through tacit approval controls or directs others.

social categories The cognitive component that describes the ways individuals classify other people into groups, such as "cads" and "dads." This cognitive component is one aspect of stereotyping.

social comparison Occurs when people compare their skills and abilities with others.

social desirability Socially desirable responding refers to the tendency to answer items in such a way as to come across as socially attractive or likable. People responding in this manner want to make a good impression, to appear to be well adjusted, to be a "good citizen."

social identity Refers to the social aspects of the self, that part of ourselves we use to create an impression, to let other people know who we are and what can be expected from us. Identity is different from the **self-concept** because identity refers mainly to aspects of the self that are socially observable or publicly available outward, such as ethnicity or gender or age. Nevertheless, the social aspects of identity can become important aspects of the self-concept.

social learning theory A general theoretical view emphasizing the ways in which the presence of others influences people's behaviour, thoughts, or feelings. Often combined with learning principles, the emphasis is on how people acquire beliefs, values, skills, attitudes, and patterns of behaviour through social experiences.

social power Horney, in reinterpreting Freud's concept of **penis envy**, taught that the penis was a symbol of social power rather than an organ that women actually desired. Horney wrote that girls realize at an early age, that they are being denied social power because of their gender. She argued that girls did not really have a secret desire to become boys. Rather, she taught, girls desire the social power and preferences given to boys in the culture at that time.

social role theory The theory states that sex differences originate because men and women are distributed differentially into occupational and family roles. Men, for example, are expected to assume the breadwinning role. Women are expected to assume the housewife role. Over time, children presumably learn the behaviours that are linked to these roles.

socialization theory The notion that boys and girls become different because boys are reinforced by parents, teachers, and the media for being "masculine," and girls for being "feminine." This is probably the most widely held theory of **sex** differences in personality.

sociosexual orientation According to Gangestad and Simpson's theory, men and women will pursue one of two alternative sexual relationship strategies. The first mating strategy entails seeking a single committed relationship characterized by monogamy and tremendous investment in children. The second sexual strategy is characterized by a greater degree of promiscuity, more partner switching, and less investment in children.

specific expectancies Recent researchers have developed specific locus of control scales for specific categories of events. This approach emphasizes **locus of control** in discrete areas of life, such as health locus of control.

spreading activation Roediger and McDermott applied the spreading activation model of memory to account for **false memories**. This model holds that mental elements (like words or images) are stored in memory along with associations to other elements in memory. For example, *doctor* is associated with *nurse* in most people's memories because of the close connection or similarity between these concepts. Consequently, a person recalling some medical event might falsely recall a nurse rather than a doctor doing something.

stability coefficients The correlations between the same measures obtained at two different points in time. Also called test-retest reliability coefficients.

stage model of development Implies that people go through stages in a certain order, and that a specific issue characterizes each stage.

state levels Refers to a person's momentary amount of a specific **need** or emotion, which can fluctuate with specific circumstances. A concept that can be applied to motives and emotions. The **TAT** can be used to assess state levels.

statistical approach Having a large number of people rate themselves on certain items, and then employing a statistical procedure to identify groups or clusters of items that go together. The goal of the statistical approach is to identify the major dimensions or "coordinates" of the **personality** map.

statistically significant Refers to the probability of finding the results of a research study by chance alone. The generally accepted level of statistical significance is 5 percent, meaning that, if a study were repeated 100 times, the particular result reported would be found by chance only 5 times.

strange situation procedure Developed by Ainsworth and her colleagues for studying separation anxiety and for identifying differences between children in how they react to separation from their mothers. In this procedure, a mother and her baby come into a laboratory room. The mother sits down and the child is free to explore the room. After a few minutes an unfamiliar though friendly adult enters the room. The mother gets up and leaves the baby alone with this adult. After a few minutes, the mother comes back into the room and the stranger leaves. The mother is alone with the baby for several more minutes. All the while, the infant is being videotaped so that his or her reactions can later be analyzed.

stress The subjective feeling that is produced by uncontrollable and threatening events. Events that cause stress are called *stressors*.

stressors Events that cause **stress**. They appear to have several common attributes: (1) stressors are extreme in some manner, in the sense that they produce a state of feeling overwhelmed or overloaded, that one just cannot take it much longer; (2) stressors often produce opposing tendencies in us, such as wanting and not wanting some activity or object, as in wanting to study but also wanting to put it off as long as possible; and (3) stressors are uncontrollable, outside of our power to influence, such as the exam that we cannot avoid.

strong situation Certain situations that prompt similar behaviour from everyone.

structured Questions used to collect self-report data that force people to choose from a limited set of answers provided by the researcher. Unlike unstructured or open-ended questions, respondents must choose which response best describes them.

style (of emotional life) How emotions are experienced. For example, saying that someone is high on mood variability is to say something about the style of their emotional life, that their emotions change frequently. Compare with the **content** of emotional life.

subclinical psychopathy The tendency towards high **impulsivity** and thrill-seeking behaviour, along with low **empathy** and **anxiety**, which together are associated with selfish and antisocial (or socially disruptive) behaviour. It is distinct from Antisocial Personality Disorder, **psychopathy**, and sociopathy. The term "subclinical" underscores that it exists within a normal range in the population, like most other traits, and does not reflect a clinical diagnosis.

sublimation A **defence mechanism** that refers to the channelling of unacceptable sexual or aggressive instincts into socially desired activities. For Freud, sublimation is the most adaptive defence mechanism. A common example is going out to chop wood when you are angry rather than acting on that anger or even engaging in other, less adaptive defence mechanisms such as **displacement**.

subliminal perception Perception that bypasses **conscious** awareness, usually achieved through very brief exposure times, typically less than 30 milliseconds.

superego That part of personality that internalizes the values, morals, and ideals of society. The superego makes us feel guilty, ashamed, or embarrassed when we do something wrong, and makes us feel pride when we do something right. The superego sets moral goals and ideals of perfection and is the source of our judgments that something is good or bad. It is what some people refer to as *conscience*. The emotion of guilt is the main tool of the superego in enforcing right and wrong.

surgency A cluster of behaviours including approach behaviour, high activity, and impulsivity.

symbols Psychoanalysts interpret dreams by deciphering how unacceptable impulses and urges are transformed by the **unconscious** into symbols in the dream. (For example, parents may be represented as a king and queen; children may be represented as small animals.)

synonym frequency In the **lexical approach**, if an attribute has not merely one or two trait adjectives to describe it, but rather six, eight, or ten words, then it is a more important dimension of **individual difference**.

systemizing The drive to comprehend how things work, how systems are built, and how inputs into systems produce outputs.

t

taxonomy A technical name given to a classification scheme—the identification and naming of groups within a particular subject field.

telemetry The process by which electrical signals are sent from **electrodes** to a polygraph using radio waves instead of wires.

temperament Individual differences that emerge very early in life, are likely to have a heritable basis, and are often involved in behaviours linked with emotionality or **arousability**.

tender-mindedness A nurturant proclivity, having empathy for others, and being sympathetic with those who are downtrodden.

test data (T-data) A common source of **personality**-relevant information comes from standardized tests (T-data). In these measures, participants are placed in a standardized testing situation to see if different people react or behave differently to an identical situation. Taking a standardized test or exam would be one example of T-data as a measure used to predict success in school.

testability The capacity to render precise predictions that scientists can test empirically. Generally, the testability of a theory is dependent upon the precision of its predictions. If it is impossible to test a theory empirically, the theory is generally discarded. One of the **five standards for evaluating theories**.

thanatos Freud postulated that humans have a fundamental instinct toward destruction—often manifest in aggression toward others—and a life instinct—a combination of self-preservation and sexual instincts. The two instincts were usually referred to as thanatos, for the death instinct, and **libido**, for the life instinct. While thanatos was considered to be the death instinct, Freud also used this term to refer to any urge to destroy, harm, or aggress against others or oneself.

Thematic Apperception Test (TAT) Developed by Murray and Morgan, this is a projective assessment technique that consists of a set of black and white ambiguous pictures. The person is shown each picture and is told to write a short story interpreting what is happening in each picture. The psychologist then codes the stories for the presence of imagery associated with particular motives. The TAT remains a popular personality assessment technique today.

theoretical approach This approach to identifying important dimensions of **individual differences** starts with a theory, which then determines which variables are important. The theoretical strategy dictates in a specific manner which variables are important to measure.

theoretical bridge The connection between two different variables (for instance, dimensions of personality and physiological variables).

theoretical constructs Hypothetical internal entities useful in describing and explaining differences between people.

theories and beliefs Beliefs are often personally useful and crucially important to some people, but they are based on leaps of faith, not on reliable facts and systematic observations. Theories, on the other hand, are based on systematic observations that can be repeated by others and that yield similar conclusions.

third variable problem One reason why correlations can never prove causality could be that two variables are correlated because some third, unknown variable is causing both.

time urgency A subtrait in the **Type A** personality. Type A people hate wasting time. They are always in a hurry and feel under pressure to get the most done in the least amount of time. Often they do two things at once, such as eat while reading a book. Waiting is stressful for them.

trait levels Refers to a person's average tendency, or his or her set point, on the specific motive or emotion. The idea is that people differ from each other in their typical or average amount of specific **motives** or emotions. A concept that can be applied to motives and emotions. **TAT** can be used to assess trait levels.

trait-descriptive adjectives Words that describe traits, the attributes of a person that are reasonably characteristic of the individual and perhaps even enduring over time.

transactional model In this model of personality and health, personality has three potential effects: (1) it can influence coping, as in the **interactional model**; (2) it can influence how the person appraises or interprets the events; and (3) it can influence exposure to the events themselves.

transference A term from **psychoanalytic therapy**. It refers to the patient reacting to the analyst as if he or she were an important figure from the patient's own life. The patient displaces past or present (negative and positive) feelings toward someone from his or her own life onto the analyst. The theory is that the interpersonal problems between a patient and the important people in his or her life will be reenacted in the therapy session with the analyst. This is a specific form of the mechanism of **evocation**, as described in the material on person-situation interaction.

transmitted culture Representations originally in the mind of one or more persons that are transmitted to the minds of other people. Three examples of cultural variants that appear to be forms of transmitted culture are differences in moral values, **self-concept**, and levels of self-enhancement. Specific patterns of morality, such as whether it is considered appropriate to eat beef or wrong for a wife to go to the movies without her husband, are specific to certain cultures. These moral values appear to be transmitted from person to person within the culture.

traumatic stress A massive instance of acute stress, the effects of which can reverberate within an individual for years or even a lifetime. It differs from **acute stress** mainly in terms of its potential to lead to **posttraumatic stress disorder**.

tridimensional personality model Cloninger's theory that ties three specific personality traits to levels of the three neurotransmitters. The first trait is called **novelty seeking** and is based on low levels of **dopamine**. The second personality trait is **harm avoidance**, which he associates with low levels of **serotonin**. The third trait is **reward dependence**, which Cloninger sees as related to low levels of **norepinephrine**.

true self The real and authentic version you

trust The proclivity to cooperate with others, giving others the benefit of the doubt, and viewing one's fellow human beings as basically good at heart.

twin studies Research that estimates **heritability** by gauging whether identical twins, who share 100 percent of their genes, are more similar to each other than fraternal twins, who share only 50 percent of their genes. Twin studies, and especially studies of twins reared apart, have received tremendous media attention.

Type A personality In the 1960s, cardiologists Friedman and Rosenman began to notice that many of their coronary heart disease patients had similar personality traits—they were competitive, aggressive workaholics, were ambitious overachievers, were often hostile, were almost always in a hurry, and rarely relaxed or took it easy. Friedman and Rosenman referred to this as the *Type A personality*, formally defined as "an action-emotion complex that can be observed in any person who is aggressively involved in a chronic, incessant struggle to achieve more and more in less and less time, and if required to do so, against the opposing efforts of other things or other persons" (1974, p. 37). As assessed by personality psychologists, Type A refers to a syndrome of several traits: (1) achievement motivation and competitiveness; (2) **time urgency**; and (3) **hostility** and **aggressiveness**.

Type D personality A dimension along which individuals differ on two underlying traits: (1) **negative affectivity**, or the tendency to frequently experience negative emotions across time and situations (e.g., tension, worry, irritability, and **anxiety**); and (2) social inhibition, or the tendency to inhibit the expression of emotions, thoughts, and behaviours in social interactions. People high on both of these traits are said to have the Type D personality, which places them at risk for poor outcomes once they develop cardiac disease.

U

unconditional positive regard The receipt of affection, love, or respect without having done anything to earn it. For example, a parent's love for a child should be unconditional.

unconscious The unconscious mind is that part of the mind about which the **conscious** mind has no awareness.

unrestricted mating strategy According to Gangestad and Simpson (1990), a woman seeking a man for the quality of his **genes** is not interested in his level of commitment to her. If the man is pursuing a short-term sexual strategy, any delay on the woman's part may deter him from seeking sexual intercourse with her, thus defeating the main adaptive reason for her mating strategy.

unstructured Questions used to collect self-report data that allow people to offer open-ended responses rather than force them to choose from a limited set of answers. In other words, unstructured questions allow respondents to answer in any way they like.

V

valence The quality of an **emotion** is categorized as either pleasant (positive) or unpleasant (negative).

validity The extent to which a test measures what it claims to measure.

validity coefficients The correlations between a trait measure and measures of different criteria that should relate to the trait. An example might be the correlation between a self-report measure of agreeableness, and the person's roommate reports of how agreeable they are.

violation of desire According to this theory of conflict between the sexes, breakups should occur more frequently when one's desires are violated than when they are fulfilled (Buss, 2003). Following this theory, we would predict that people married to others who lack desired characteristics, such as dependability and emotional stability, will more frequently dissolve the marriage.

W

Whorfian hypothesis of linguistic relativity In 1956, Whorf proposed the theory that language creates thought and experience. According to this hypothesis, the ideas that people can think and the emotions they feel are constrained by the need locate words that happen to exist in their language and culture and with which they use to express them.

wish fulfillment If an urge from the **id** requires some external object or person, and that object or person is not available, the id may create a mental image or fantasy of that object or person to satisfy its needs. Mental energy is invested in that fantasy and the urge is temporarily satisfied.

within the individual The important sources of **personality** reside within the individual—that is, people carry the sources of their personality inside themselves—and hence are stable over time and consistent over situations.

within-culture variations Variations within a particular culture that can arise from several sources, including differences in growing up in various socioeconomic classes, differences in historical era, or differences in the racial context in which one grows up.

working models The prototype for later adult relationships, according to Bowlby, based on the early experiences and reactions of the infant to the parents, particularly the mother. Working models are internalized in the form of unconscious expectations about relationships.

X

xenophobia The fear of strangers. Characteristics that were probably adaptive in ancestral environments, such as xenophobia, are not necessarily adaptive in modern environments. Some of the personality traits that make up human nature may be vestigial adaptations to an ancestral environment that no longer exists.

References

Abe, J. A. A. (2005). The predictive validity of the five-factor model of personality with preschool age children: A nine year follow-up study. *Journal of Research in Personality, 39,* 423–442.

Abele, A. E., and Wojciszke, B. (Eds.). (2018). *Current issues in social psychology: Agency and communion in social psychology* (1st ed.). New York, NY: Routledge.

Abelson, R. P. (1985). A variance explanation paradox: When a little is a lot. *Psychological Bulletin, 97,* 129–133.

Abrahamson, A. C., Baker, L. A., and Caspi, A. (2002). Rebellious teens? Genetic and environmental influences on the social attitudes of adolescents. *Journal of Personality and Social Psychology, 83*(6), 1392–1408.

Acar, S., and Runco, M. A. (2012). Psychoticism and creativity: A meta-analytic review. *Psychology of Aesthetics, Creativity, and the Arts, 6,* 341–350.

Ackerman, J. M., and Bargh, J. A. (2010). The purpose-driven life: Commentary on Kenrick et al. (2010). *Perspectives on Psychological Science, 5,* 323–326.

Aczel, B., Lukacs, B., Komlos, J., and Aitken, M. R. F. (2011). Unconscious intuition or conscious analysis? Critical questions for the deliberation-without-attention paradigm. *Judgment and Decision Making, 6,* 351–358.

Adan, A. (1991). Influence of morningness-eveningness preference in the relationship between body temperature and performance: A diurnal study. *Personality and Individual Differences, 12,* 1159–1169.

Adan, A. (1992). The influence of age, work schedule and personality on morningness dimension. *International Journal of Psychophysiology, 12,* 95–99.

Addison, T. L., and Schmidt, L. A. (1999). Are women who are shy reluctant to take risks? Behavioral and psychophysiological correlates. *Journal of Research in Personality, 33,* 352–357.

Affleck, G., and Tennen, H. (1996). Construing benefits from adversity: Adaptational significance and dispositional underpinnings. *Journal of Personality, 64,* 899–922.

Ahlenius, H., and Tännsjö, T. (2012). Chinese and Westerners respond differently to the trolley dilemmas. *Journal of Cognition and Culture, 12,* 195–201.

Ahmadian, S., Azarshahi, S., & Paulhus, D. L. (2017). Explaining Donald Trump via communication style: Grandiosity, informality, and dynamism. *Personality and Individual Differences, 107,* 49–53.

Aigner, M., Eher, R., Fruenhwald, S., Frottier, P., Gutierrez-Lobos, K., and Dwyer, S. M. (2000). Brain abnormalities and violent behavior. *Journal of Psychology and Human Sexuality, 11,* 57–64.

Ainsworth, M. D. (1979). Infant-mother attachment. *American Psychologist, 34,* 932–937.

Ainsworth, M. D., Bell, S. M., and Stayton, D. J. (1972). Individual differences in the development of some attachment behaviors. *Merrill-Palmer Quarterly, 18,* 123–143.

Ainsworth, M. D., and Bowlby, J. (1991). An ethological approach to personality development. *American Psychologist, 46,* 333–341.

Aknin, L. B., Barrington-Leigh, C. P., Dunn, E. W., Helliwell, J. F., Burns, J., Biswas-Diener, R., . . . Norton, M. I. (2013). Prosocial spending and well-being: Cross-cultural evidence for a psychological universal. *Journal of Personality and Social Psychology, 104*(4), 635–652.

Aknin, L. B., Norton, M. I., and Dunn, E. W. (2009). From wealth to well-being? Money matters, but less than people think. *The Journal of Positive Psychology, 4*(6), 523–527.

Albert, P. R. (2015). Why is depression more prevalent in women? *Journal of Psychiatry & Neuroscience, 40,* 219–221.

Aldwin, C. M., Spiro, A., III, Levenson, M. R., and Cupertino, A. P. (2001). Longitudinal findings from the normative aging study: III. Personality, individual health trajectories, and mortality. *Psychology and Aging, 16,* 450–465.

Alexander, G., Wilcox, T., and Woods, R. (2008). Sex differences in infants' interest in toys. *Archives of Sexual Behavior, 38,* 427–433.

Alexander, R. D., Hoodland, J. L., Howard, R. D., Noonan, K. M., and Sherman, P. W. (1979). Sexual dimorphisms and breeding systems in pinnipeds, ungulates, primates, and humans. In N. A. Chagnon and W. Irons (Eds.), *Evolutionary biology and human social behavior.* North Scituate, MA: Duxbury Press.

Algom, D., Chajut, E., and Lev, S. (2004). A rational look at the emotional Stroop phenomenon: A generic slowdown, not a Stroop effect. *Journal of Experimental Psychology: General, 133,* 323–338.

Allan, B., and Smylie, J. (2015). *First peoples, second class treatment. The role of racism in the health and well-being of Indigenous peoples in Canada.* Toronto: Well Living House for Wellesley Institute.

Allemand, M., Zimprich, D., and Hertzon, C. (2007). Cross-sectional age differences and longitudinal age changes in middle adulthood and old age. *Journal of Personality, 75,* 323–358.

Allemand, M., Gomez, V., and Jackson, J. J. (2010). Personality trait development in midlife: Exploring the impact of psychological turning points. *European Journal of Aging, 7,* 147–155.

Allik, J. (2012). National differences in personality. *Personality and Individual Differences, 53,* 114–117.

Allik, J., and Realo, A. (2009). Editorial: Personality and culture. *European Journal of Personality, 23,* 149–152.

Allport, G. W. (1937). *Personality: A psychological interpretation.* New York: Holt, Rinehart and Winston.

Allport, G. W. (1961). *Pattern and growth in personality.* New York: Holt, Rinehart and Winston.

Allport, G. W., and Odbert, H. S. (1936). Trait-names: A psycho-lexical study. *Psychological Monographs, 47* (1, Whole No. 211).

Almagor, M., Tellegen, A., and Waller, N. G. (1995). The big seven model: A cross-cultural replication and further exploration of the basic dimensions of natural language trait descriptors. *Journal of Personality and Social Psychology, 69,* 300–307.

Alston, W. P. (1975). Traits, consistency and conceptual alternatives for personality theory. *Journal for the Theory of Social Behavior, 5,* 17–48.

Amelang, M., Herboth, G., and Oefner, I. (1991). A prototype strategy for the construction of a creativity scale. *European Journal of Personality, 5,* 261–285.

American Psychiatric Association. (2013). *Diagnostic and statistical manual of mental disorders* (5th ed.). Washington, DC: Author.

American Psychological Association. (2018). A glossary: Defining transgender terms. *Monitor on Psychology, 49,* 32.

Anastasi, A. (1976). *Psychological testing.* New York: Macmillan.

Andersen, S., Ertac, S., Gneezy, U., List, J. A., and Maximiano, S. (2013). Gender, competitiveness, and socialization at a young age: Evidence from a matrilineal and a patriarchal society. *The Review of Economics and Statistics, 95,* 1438–1443.

Anderson, C., and Kilduff, G. J. (2009). Why do dominant personalities attain influence in face-to-face groups? The competence-signaling effects of trait dominance. *Journal of Personality and Social Psychology, 96,* 491–503.

Ando, J., Ono, Y., Yoshimura, K., Onoda, N., Shinohara, M., Kanba, S., and Asai, M. (2002). The genetic structure of Cloninger's seven-factor model of temperament and character in a Japanese sample. *Journal of Personality, 70, 5,* 583–610.

Andrews, J. D. W. (1967). The achievement motive in two types of organizations. *Journal of Personality and Social Psychology, 6,* 163–168.

Andrews, P. W., and Thomson Jr., J. A. (2009). The bright side of being blue: Depression as an adaptation for analyzing complex problems. *Psychological Review, 116*(3), 620.

Angleitner, A., and Demtroder, A. I. (1988). Acts and dispositions: A reconsideration of the act frequency approach. *European Journal of Psychology, 2,* 121–141.

Angleitner, A., Buss, D., and Demtröder, A. I. (1990). A cross-cultural comparison using the act frequency approach (AFA) in West Germany and the United States. *European Journal of Personality, 4,* 187–207.

Anglim, J., Knowles, E. R. V., Dunlop, P. D., and Marty, A. (2017). HEXACO Personality and Schwartz's Personal Values: A facet-level analysis. *Journal of Research in Personality, 68,* 23–31.

Anusic, I., Lucas, R. E., and Donnellan, M. B. (2012). Cross-sectional age differences in personality: Evidence from nationally representative samples from Switzerland and the United States. *Journal of Research in Personality, 46,* 116–120.

Apostolou, M., Zacharia, M., and Frantzides, N. (2015). Children's tactics of mate choice manipulation: Exploring sex differences and personality effects. *Personality and Individual Differences, 80,* 6–11.

References

Archer, J. (2009). Does sexual selection explain human sex differences in aggression? *Behavioral and Brain Sciences, 32,* 249–311.

Archer, J., and Thanzami, V. (2009). The relation between mate value, entitlement, physical aggression, size and strength among a sample of young Indian men. *Evolution and Human Behavior, 30,* 315–321.

Areepattamannil, S., Freeman, J. G., and Klinger, D. A. (2011). Intrinsic motivation, extrinsic motivation, and academic achievement among Indian adolescents in Canada and India. *Social Psychology of Education, 14*(3), 427–439.

Arnocky, S., Stroink, M., and DeCicco, T. (2007). Self-construal predicts environmental concern, cooperation, and conservation. *Journal of Environmental Psychology, 27*(4), 255–264.

Aron, A., Aron, E. N., Tudor, M., and Nelson, G. (2004). Close relationships as including other in the self. In H. T. Reis and C. E. Rustbult (Eds.), *Close relationships: Key readings* (pp. 365–379). Philadelphia: Taylor and Francis.

Aschoff, J. (1965). Circadian rhythms in man. *Science, 143,* 1427–1432.

Asendorpf, J. B., and Scherer, K. R. (1983). The discrepant repressor: Differentiation between low anxiety, high anxiety, and repression of anxiety by autonomic-facial-verbal patterns of behavior. *Journal of Personality and Social Psychology, 45,* 1334–1346.

Asendorpf, J. B., and Van Aken, M. A. G. (2003). Validity of five personality judgments in childhood: A 9-year longitudinal study. *European Journal of Personality, 32,* 649–656.

Ashmore, R. D. (1990). Sex, gender, and the individual. In L. A. Pervin (Ed.), *Handbook of personality: Theory and research* (pp. 486–526). New York: Guilford Press.

Ashton, M. C. (2007). Self-reports and stereotypes: A comment on McCrae et al. *European Journal of Personality, 21,* 983–986.

Ashton, M. C., and Lee, K. (2005). A defense of the lexical approach to the study of personality. *European Journal of Personality, 19,* 5–24.

Ashton, M. C., and Lee, K. (2007). Empirical, theoretical, and practical advantages of the HEXACO model of personality structure. *Personality and Social Psychology Review, 11,* 150–166.

Ashton, M. C., and Lee, K. (2008). The prediction of honesty–humility-related criteria by the HEXACO and five-factor models of personality. *Journal of Research in Personality, 42,* 1216–1228.

Ashton, M. C., and Lee, K. (2010). On the cross-language replicability of personality factors. *Journal of Research in Personality, 44,* 436–441.

Ashton, M. C., Lee, K., and de Vries, R. E. (2014). The HEXACO honesty–humility, agreeableness, and emotionality factors: A review of research and theory. *Personality and Social Psychology Review, 18,* 139–152.

Ashton, M. C., Lee, K., and Goldberg, L. R. (2004). A hierarchical analysis of 1,710 English personality-descriptive adjectives. *Journal of Personality and Social Psychology, 87,* 707–721.

Ashton, M. C., Lee, K., and Paunonen, S. V. (2002). What is the central feature of extraversion? Social attention versus reward sensitivity. *Journal of Personality and Social Psychology, 83*(1), 245–252.

Assor, A. (1989). The power motive as an influence on the evaluation of high and low status persons. *Journal of Research in Personality, 23,* 55–69.

Augustine, A. A., Larsen, R. J., Walker, M. S., and Fisher, E. B. (2008). Personality predictors of the time course for lung cancer onset. *Journal of Research in Personality, 42,* 1448–1455.

Averill, J. R. (1975). A semantic atlas of emotional concepts. *Catalog of Selected Documents in Psychology, 5,* 30.

Azar, B. (2002). Searching for genes that explain our personalities. *American Psychological Association Monitor, 33,* 44.

Back, M. D., Schmukle, S. C., and Egloff, B. (2008). How extraverted is honey. bunny77@hotmail.de? Inferring personality from email addresses. *Journal of Research in Personality, 42,* 1116–1122.

Bagby, R. M., Vachon, D. D., Bulmash, E. L., Toneatto, T., Quilty, L. C., and Costa, P. T. (2007). Pathological gambling and the five-factor model of personality. *Personality and Individual Differences, 43,* 873–880.

Baikie, K., and Wilhelm, K. (2005). Emotional and physical health benefits of expressive writing. *Advances in Psychiatric Treatment, 11*(5), 338–346.

Bailey, J. M., Dunne, M. P., and Martin, N. G. (2000). Genetic and environmental influences on sexual orientation and its correlates in an Australian twin sample. *Journal of Personality and Social Psychology, 78,* 524–536.

Bailey, S. L., and Heitkemper, M. M. (1991). Morningness–eveningness and early-morning salivary cortisol levels. *Biological Psychology, 32,* 181–192.

Bailey, J. M., Kirk, K. M., Zhu, G., Dunne, M. P., and Martin, N. G. (2000). Do individual differences in sociosexuality represent genetic or environmentally contingent strategies? Evidence from the Australian Twin Registry. *Journal of Personality and Social Psychology, 78,* 537–545.

Bailey, J. M., Pillard, R. C., Neale, M. C., and Agyei, Y. (1993). Heritable factors influence sexual orientation in women. *Archives of General Psychiatry, 50,* 217–223.

Bailis, D. S., Chipperfield, J. G., and Helgason, T. R. (2008). Collective self-esteem and the onset of chronic conditions and reduced activity in a longitudinal study of aging. *Social Science & Medicine, 66*(8), 1817–1827.

Bakan, D. (1966). *The duality of human existence: Isolation and communion in Western man.* Boston: Beacon

Baker, R. A. (1992). *Hidden memories.* Buffalo, NY: Prometheus Books.

Bakker, A. B., Van Der Zee, K. I., Lewig, K. A., and Dollard, M. F. (2006). The relationship between the Big Five personality factors and burnout: A study among volunteer counselors. *The Journal of Social Psychology, 146,* 31–50.

Balliet, D., Li, N. P., Macfarlan, S. J., and Van Vugt, M. (2011). Sex differences in cooperation: A meta-analytic review of social dilemmas. *Psychological Bulletin, 137,* 881–909.

Bandura, A. (1977). *Social learning theory.* Englewood Cliffs, NJ: Prentice Hall.

Bandura, A. (1986). The explanatory and predictive scope of self-efficacy theory. *Journal of Social and Clinical Psychology, Special Issue: Self-efficacy theory in contemporary psychology, 4,* 359–373.

Bandura, A. (1989). Human agency in social cognitive theory. *American Psychologist, 44,* 1175–1184.

Bandura, A. (1997). *Self-efficacy: The exercise of control.* New York: Freeman.

Barelds, D. P. H. (2005). Self and partner personality in intimate relationships. *European Journal of Personality, 19,* 501–518.

Barelds, D. P. H., and Dijkstra, P. (2011). Positive illusions about a partner's personality and relationship quality. *Journal of Research in Personality, 45,* 37–43.

Barenbaum, N. B., and Winter, D. G. (2003). Personality. In D. K. Freedheim (Ed.), *Handbook of psychology: History of psychology* (pp. 177–203). New York: Wiley.

Bargh, J. A. (2005). Bypassing the will: Toward demystifying the nonconscious control of social behavior. In R. R. Hassin, J. S. Uleman, and J. A. Bargh (Eds.), *The new unconscious* (pp. 37–60). New York: Oxford University Press.

Bargh, J. A. (2006a). *The new unconscious.* New York: Oxford University Press.

Bargh, J.A. (2006b). *Social psychology and the unconscious: The automaticity of higher mental processes.* Philadelphia: Psychology Press.

Bargh, J. A. (2008). Free will is un-natural. In J. Baer, J. C. Kaufman, and R. F. Baumeister (Eds.), *Are we free? Psychology and free will* (pp. 128–154). New York: Oxford University Press.

Bargh, J. A., and Morsella, E. (2008). The unconscious mind. *Perspectives on Psychological Science, 3,* 73–79.

Bargh, J. A., and Morsella, E. (2010). Unconscious behavioral guidance systems. In C. R. Agnew, D. E. Carlston, W. G. Graziano, and J. R. Kelly (Eds.), *Then a miracle occurs: Focusing on behavior in social psychological theory and research* (pp. 89–118). New York, NY: Oxford University Press.

Baron, M. (1993). Genetics and human sexual orientation. *Biological Psychology, 33,* 759–761.

Bar-On, R. (2001). Emotional intelligence and self-actualization. In J. Ciarrochi and J. P. Forgas (Eds.), *Emotional intelligence in everyday life: A scientific inquiry* (pp. 82–97). Philadelphia, PA: Psychology Press.

Baron, R. A. (1977). *Human aggression.* New York: Plenum Press.

Barrick, M. R., and Mount, M. K. (1991). The Big Five personality dimensions and job performance: A meta-analysis. *Personnel Psychology, 44,* 1–25.

Barron, J. W., Eagle, M. N., and Wolitzky, D. L. (1992). *Interface of psychoanalysis and psychology.* Washington, DC: American Psychological Association.

Bass, E., and Davis, L. (1988). *The courage to heal: A guide for women survivors of child sexual abuse.* New York: Perennial Library/Harper and Row.

Baron-Cohen, S., Richler, J., Bisarya, D., Gurunathan, N., and Wheelwright, S. (2003). The systemizing quotient: an investigation of adults with Asperger syndrome or high-functioning autism, and normal sex differences. *Philosophical transactions of the Royal Society of London. Series B, Biological sciences, 358,* 361–374.

Bastone, L. M., and Wood, H. A. (1997). Individual differences in the ability to decode emotional facial expressions. *Psychology: A Journal of Human Behavior, 34,* 32–36.

Battiste, M. (1998). Enabling the autumn seed: Toward a decolonized approach to aboriginal knowledge, language, and education. *Canadian Journal of Native Education, 22*(1), 16–27.

Battle, J. (1979). Self-esteem of students in regular and special classes. *Psychological Reports, 44*, 212–214.

Bauer, G. R., Scheim, A. I., Pyne, J., Travers, R., and Hammond, R. (2015). Intervenable factors associated with suicide risk in transgender persons: A respondent driven sampling study in Ontario, Canada. *BioMed Central Public Health, 15*, 1–15.

Bauer, J. J., Schwab, J. R., and McAdams, D. P. (2011). Self-actualizing: Where ego development finally feels good? *The Humanistic Psychologist, 39*, 121–136.

Baughman, H. M., Dearing, S., Giammarco, E., and Vernon, P. A. (2012). Relationship between bullying behaviours and the Dark Triad: A study with adults. *Personality and Individual Differences, 52*, 571–575.

Baumeister, R. F. (1986). *Identity: Cultural change and the struggle for self.* New York: Oxford University Press.

Baumeister, R. F. (1988). Should we stop studying sex differences altogether? *American Psychologist, 43*, 1092–1095.

Baumeister, R. F. (1991). The self against itself: Escape or defeat? In R. C. Curtis (Ed.), *The relational self: Theoretical convergences in psychoanalysis and social psychology* (pp. 238–256). New York: Guilford Press.

Baumeister, R. F. (1997). Identity, self-concept, and self-esteem: The self lost and found. In R. Hogan, J. Johnson, and S. Briggs (Eds.), *Handbook of personality psychology* (pp. 681–711). New York: Academic Press.

Baumeister, R. F., Bratslavsky, E., Muraven, M., and Tice, D. M. (1998). Ego depletion: Is the active self a limited resource? *Journal of Personality and Social Psychology, 74*, 1252–1265.

Baumeister, R. F., Campbell, J. D., Krueger, J. I., and Vohs, K. D. (2003). Does high self-esteem cause better performance, interpersonal success, happiness, or healthier lifestyles? *Psychological Science in the Public Interest, 4*, 1–44.

Baumeister, R. F., Dale, K., and Sommer, K. L. (1998). Freudian defense mechanisms and empirical findings in modern social psychology: Reaction formation, projection, displacement, undoing, isolation, sublimation, and denial. *Journal of Personality, 66*, 1061–1081.

Baumeister, R. F., and Leary, M. R. (1995). The need to belong: Desire for interpersonal attachments as a fundamental human motivation. *Psychological Bulletin, 117*, 497–529.

Baumeister, R. F., and Muraven, M. (1996). Identity as adaptation to social, cultural and historical context. *Journal of Adolescence, 19*, 405–416.

Baumeister, R. F., and Tice, D. M. (1990). Anxiety and social exclusion. *Journal of Social and Clinical Psychology, 9*, 165–195.

Baumeister, R. F., and Tice, D. M. (2006). Self-esteem and responses to success and failure: Subsequent performance and intrinsic motivation. *Journal of Personality, 53*, 450–467.

Baumeister, R. F., Tice, D. M., and Hutton, D. G. (1989). Self-presentational motivations and personality differences in self-esteem. *Journal of Personality, 57*, 547–579.

Baumeister, R. F., and Vohs, K. (2004). *Handbook of self-regulation.* New York: Guilford Press.

Baumeister, R. F., Vohs, K. D., and Tice, D. M. (2007). The strength model of self-control. *Current Directions in Psychological Science, 16*, 396–403.

Beauducel, A., Debener, S., Brocke, B., and Kayser, J. (2000). On the reliability of augmenting/reducing: Peak amplitudes and principal component analysis of auditory evoked potentials. *Journal of Psychophysiology, 14*, 226–240.

Beauregard, M., Levesque, J., and Bourgouin, P. (2001). Neural correlates of conscious self-regulation of emotion. *Journal of Neuroscience, 21*, RC165 (1–6).

Beck, A. T. (1976). *Cognitive therapy and the emotional disorders.* New York: International Universities Press.

Beer, J. S., and Lombardo, M. V. (2007a). Insights into Emotion Regulation from Neuropsychology. In J. J. Gross (Ed.), Handbook of emotion regulation (pp. 69–86). New York, NY, US: The Guilford Press.

Beer, J. S., and Lombardo, M. V. (2007b). Patient and neuroimaging methods. In R. W. Robins, R. C. Fraley, and R. F. Krueger (Eds.), *Handbook of research methods in personality psychology* (pp. 360–369). New York: Guilford Press.

Belle, D., Doucet, J., Harris, J., Miller, J., and Tan, E. (2000). Who is rich? Who is happy? *American Psychologist, 55*, 116–117.

Belsky, J. (2000). Conditional and alternative reproductive strategies: Individual differences in susceptibility to rearing experience. In J. Rodgers, D. Rowe, and W. Miller (Eds.), *Genetic influences on human fertility and sexuality: Theoretical and empirical contributions from the biological and behavioral sciences* (pp. 127–146). Boston: Kluwer.

Belsky, J. (2012). The development of human reproductive strategies: Progress and prospects. *Current Directions in Psychological Science, 21*, 310–316.

Belsky, J., Steinberg, L., and Draper, P. (1991) Childhood experience, interpersonal development, and reproductive strategy: and evolutionary theory of socialization. *Child Development, 62*(4), 647–670.

Bem, D. J. (1996). Exotic becomes erotic: A developmental theory of sexual orientation. *Psychological Review, 103*, 320–333.

Bem, S. L. (1974). The measurement of psychological androgyny. *Journal of Consulting and Clinical Psychology, 42*, 153–162.

Bem S. L. (1981). Gender schema theory: a cognitive account of sex typing. *Psychological Review, 88*, 354–364.

Benet-Martinez, V., Donnellan, M. B., Fleeson, W., Fraley, R. C., Gosling, S. D., King, L. A., Robins, R. W., and Funder, D. C. (2015). Six visions for the future of personality psychology. In L. Cooper and R. J. Larsen (Eds.), *Handbook of personality and social psychology: Personality processes and individual differences.* Washington, DC: American Psychological Association.

Benjamin, J., Li, L., Patterson, C., Greenberg, B. D., Murphy, D. L., and Hamer, D. H. (1996). Population and familial association between the D4 dopamine receptor gene and measures of novelty seeking. *Nature Genetics, 12*, 81–84.

Bensch, D., Paulhus, D. L., Stankov, L., & Ziegler, M. (2017). Teasing apart overclaiming, overconfidence, and socially desirable responding. *Assessment, 26*(3), 351–363. doi: 10.1177/1073191117700268

Berant, E. (2009). Attachment styles, the Rorschach, and the Thematic Apperception Test: Using traditional projective measures to assess aspects of attachment. In J. J. Obegi and E. Berant (Eds.), *Attachment theory and research in clinical work with adults* (pp. 181–206). New York, NY: Guilford Press.

Berenbaum, S. A., and Snyder, E. (1995). Early hormonal influences on childhood sex-typed activity and playmate preferences: Implications for the development of sexual orientation. *Developmental Psychology, 31*, 31–42.

Berman, S., Ozkaragoz, T., Yound, R. M., and Noble, E. P. (2002). D2 dopamine receptor gene polymorphism discriminates two kinds of novelty seeking. *Personality and Individual Differences, 33*, 867–882.

Bernhardt, P. C., Dabbs, J. M., Jr., Fielden, J., and Lutter, C. (1998). Testosterone changes during vicarious experiences of winning and losing among fans at sporting events. *Physiology and Behavior, 65*, 59–62.

Bernstein, D. M., and Loftus, E. F. (2009). How to tell if a particular memory is true or false. *Perspectives on Psychological Science, 4*, 370–374.

Berry, D. S., and Miller, K. M. (2001). When boy meets girl: Attractiveness and the five-factor model in opposite-sex interactions. *Journal of Research in Personality, 35*, 62–77.

Berry, C. M., Sackett, P. R., and Wiemann, S. (2007). A review of recent developments in integrity test research. *Personnel Psychology, 60*, 271–301.

Birley, A. J., Gillespie, N. A., Heath, A. C., Sullivan, P. F., Boomsma, D. I., and Martin, N. G. (2006). Heritability and nineteen-year stability of long and short EPQ-R Neuroticism scales. *Personality and Individual Differences, 40*, 737–747.

Bjork, R. A., and Druckman, D. (1991). *In the mind's eye: Enhancing human performance.* Washington, DC: National Academy Press.

Björkqvist, K. (2018). Gender differences in aggression. *Current Opinion in Psychology, 19*, 39–42.

Black, J. (2000). Personality testing and police selection: Utility of the Big Five. *New Zealand Journal of Psychology, 29*, 2–9.

Blakemore, J., and Centers, R. E. (2005). Characteristics of boys' and girls' toys. *Sex Roles, 53*, 619–633.

Blasberg, S. A., Rogers, K. H., & Paulhus, D. L. (2014). The Bidimensional Impression Management Index (BIMI): Measuring agentic and communal forms of impression management. *Journal of Personality Assessment, 96*, 523–531.

Bleidorn, W., Arslan, R. C., Denissen, J. J. A., Rentfrow, P. J., Gebauer, J. E., Potter, J., and Gosling, S. D. (2016). Age and gender differences in self-esteem: A cross-cultural window. *Journal of Personality and Social Psychology, 111*, 396–410.

Bleske-Rechek, A. L., and Buss, D. M. (2001). Opposite-sex friendship: Sex differences and similarities in initiation, selection, and dissolution. *Personality and Social Psychology Bulletin, 27, 10*, 1310–1323.

Bleske-Rechek, A., Remiker, M. W., and Baker, J. P. (2008). Narcissistic men and women think they are so hot—but they are not. *Personality and Individual Differences, 45*, 420–424.

Blinkhorn, V., Lyons, M., and Almond, L. (2015). The ultimate femme fatale? Narcissism predicts serious and aggressive sexually coercive behaviour in females. *Personality and Individual Differences, 87,* 219–223.

Block, J. (1971). *Lives through time.* Berkeley, CA: Bancroft Books.

Block, J. (1977). Advancing the psychology of personality: Paradigmatic shift or improving the quality of research. In D. Magnusson and N. S. Endler (Eds.), *Personality at the crossroads* (pp. 37–63). Hillsdale, NJ: Erlbaum.

Block, J. (1989). Critique of the act frequency approach to personality. *Journal of Personality and Social Psychology, 56,* 234–245.

Block, J. (1995). Going beyond the five factors given: Rejoinder to Costa and McCrae (1995) and Goldberg and Saucier (1995). *Psychological Bulletin, 117,* 226–229.

Block, J. H., and Block, J. (1980). *The California Child Q-Set.* Palo Alto, CA: Consulting Psychologists Press.

Block, J. (2010). The five-factor framing of personality and beyond: Some ruminations. *Psychological Inquiry, 21,* 2–25.

Block, J., and Robbins, R. W. (1993). A longitudinal study of consistency and change in self-esteem from early adolescence to early adulthood. *Child Development, 64,* 909–923.

Block, J. H. (1983). Differential premises arising from differential socialization of the sexes: Some conjectures. *Child Development, 54,* 1335–1354.

Blonigen, D. M., Carlson, M. D., Hicks, B. M., Kreuger, R. F., and Iacono, W. G. (2008). Stability and change in personality traits from late adolescence to early adulthood: A longitudinal twin study. *Journal of Personality, 76,* 229–266.

Blonigen, D. M., Carlson, S. R., Krueger, R. F., and Patrick, C. J. (2003). A twin study of self-reported psychopathic personality traits. *Personality and Individual Differences, 35,* 179–197.

Blonigen, D. M., Hicks, B. M., Krueger, R. F., Patrick, C. J., and Iacono, W. G. (2006). Continuity and change in psychopathic traits as measured via normal-range personality: A longitudinal–biometric study. *Journal of Abnormal Psychology, 115*(1), 85.

Bochner, S. (1994). Cross-cultural differences in the self-concept: A test of Hofstede's individualism/collectivism distinction. *Journal of Cross-Cultural Psychology, 25,* 273–283.

Bockting, W. O., Miner, M. H., Swinburne Romine, R. E., Hamilton, A., and Coleman, E. (2013). Stigma, mental health, and resilience in an online sample of the US transgender population. *American Journal of Public Health, 103*(5), 943–951.

Boehm, J. K., Chen, Y., Koga, H., Mathur, M. B., Vie, L. L., and Kubzansky, L. D. (2018). Is optimism associated with healthier cardiovascular-related behavior?: Meta-analyses of 3 health behaviors. *Circulation Research, 122*(8), 1119–1134. doi: 10.1161/CIRCRESAHA.117.310828

Bogg, T. (2008). Conscientiousness, the transtheoretical model of change, and exercise: A neo-socioanalytic integration of trait and social-cognitive frameworks in the predictions of behavior. *Journal of Personality, 76,* 775–802.

Bogg, T., and Roberts, B. W. (2004). Conscientiousness and health behaviors: A meta-analysis of the leading behavioral contributors to mortality. *Psychological Bulletin, 130,* 887–919.

Bolger, N., and Zuckerman, A. (1995). A framework for studying personality in the stress process. *Journal of Personality and Social Psychology, 69*(5), 890–902 .

Bolkan, C., Hooker, K., and Coehlo, D. (2015). Possible selves and depressive symptoms in later life. *Research On Aging, 37*(1), 41–62.

Bonanno, G. A. (1990). Repression, accessibility, and the translation of private experience. *Psychoanalytic Psychology, 7,* 453–473.

Bonanno, G. A., and Diminich, E. D. (2013). Annual Research Review: Positive adjustment to adversity—trajectories of minimal-impact resilience and emergent resilience. *Journal of Child Psychology and Psychiatry, and Allied Disciplines, 54*(4), 378–401.

Bonanno, G. A., Wortman, C. B., Lehman, D. R., Tweed, R. G., Haring, M., Sonnega, J., Carr, D., and Nesse, R. M. (2002). Resilience to loss and chronic grief: A prospective study from preloss to 18-months postloss. *Journal of Personality and Social Psychology, 83*(5), 1150–1164.

Bono, J. E., Boles, T. L., Judge, T. A., and Lauver, K. J. (2002). The role of personality in task and relationship conflict. *Journal of Personality, 70,* 311–344.

Boomsma, D. I., Koopmans, J. R., Van Doornen, L.J.P., and Orlebeke, J. M. (1994). Genetic and social influences on starting to smoke: A study of Dutch adolescent twins and their parents. *Addiction, 89,* 219–226.

Borkenau, P., Riemann, R., Angleitner, A., and Spinath, F. M. (2001). Genetic and environmental influences on observed personality: Evidence from the German observational study of adult twins. *Journal of Personality and Social Psychology, 80*(4), 655–668.

Bornstein, R. F. (1999). Source amnesia, misattribution, and the power of unconscious perceptions and memories. *Psychoanalytic Psychology, 16,* 155–178.

Bornstein, R. F. (2005). The dependent patient: Diagnosis, assessment, and treatment. *Professional Psychology: Research and Practice, 36,* 82–89.

Botwin, M. D., and Buss, D. M. (1989). Structure of act-report data: Is the five-factor model of personality recaptured? *Journal of Personality and Social Psychology, 56,* 988–1001.

Botwin, M. D., Buss, D. M., and Shackelford, T. K. (1997). Personality and mate preferences: Five factors in mate selection and marital satisfaction. *Journal of Personality, 65*(1), 107–136. doi: 10.1111/j.1467-6494.1997.tb00531.x

Bouchard, T. J., and Loehlin, J. C. (2001). Genes, evolution, and personality. *Behavior Genetics, 31,* 243–273.

Bouchard, T. J., Lykken, D. T., McGue, M., and Segal, N. L. (1990). Sources of human psychological differences: The Minnesota study of twins reared apart. *Science, 250,* 223–228.

Bouchard, T. J., and McGue, M. (1990). Genetic and rearing environmental influences on adult personality: An analysis of adopted twins reared apart. *Journal of Personality, 58,* 263–292.

Bouzenita, A. I., and Boulanouar, A. W. (2016). Maslow's hierarchy of needs: An Islamic critique. *Intellectual Discourse, 24*(1), 59–81.

Bowlby, J. (1969a). *Attachment and loss: Vol. 1: Attachment.* New York: Basic Books.

Bowlby, J. (1969b). *Attachment and loss: Vol. 2: Separation, anger, and anxiety.* New York: Basic Books.

Bowlby, J. (1980). *Attachment and loss: Vol. 3: Loss, sadness, and depression.* New York: Basic Books.

Bowlby, J. (1988). *A secure base: Parent-child attachment and healthy human development.* New York: Basic Books.

Boyce, C. J., Wood, A. M., and Brown, G. D. A. (2010). The dark side of conscientiousness: Conscientious people experience greater drops in life satisfaction following unemployment. *Journal of Personality, 44,* 535–539.

Boyle, G. J. (1995). Myers-Briggs Type Indicator (NBTI): Some psychometric limitations. *Australian Psychologist, 30,* 71–74.

Bradberry, T. (2007). *The personality code.* New York: Putnam.

Brand, C. R., and Egan, V. (1989). The "Big Five" dimensions of personality? Evidence from ipsative, adjectival self-attributions. *Personality and Individual Differences, 10,* 1165–1171.

Branje, S. J. T., van Lieshout, C. F. M., and Geris, J. R. M. (2006). Big Five personality development in adolescence and adulthood. *European Journal of Personality, 21,* 45–62.

Braun, K. A., Ellis, R., and Loftus, E. F. (2002). Make my memory: How advertising can change our memories of the past. *Psychology and Marketing, 19,* 1–23.

Brebner, J. (2003). Gender and emotions. *Personality and Individual Differences, 34,* 387–394.

Brebner, J., and Cooper, C. (1978). Stimulus- or response-induced excitation: A comparison of the behavior of introverts and extraverts. *Journal of Research in Personality, 12,* 306–311.

Bredemann, T. M. (2012). Estrogen increases stress resilience and hippocampal synaptic physiology in the learned helplessness model of depression in female rats. *Dissertation Abstracts International: Section B: The Sciences and Engineering, 72*(12-B), 7734.

Brennan, K. A., and Shaver, P. R. (1993). Attachment styles and parental divorce. *Journal of Divorce and Remarriage, 21,* 161–175.

Brennan, P. A., and Raine, A. (1997). Biosocial bases of antisocial behavior: Psychophysiological, neurological, and cognitive factors. *Clinical Psychology Review Special Issue: Biopsychosocial Conceptualizations of Human Aggression, 17,* 589–604.

Brescoll, V. L. (2016). Leading with their hearts? How gender stereotypes of emotion lead to biased evaluations of female leaders. *The Leadership Quarterly, 27,* 415–428.

Bretherton, I., and Main, M. (2000). Obituary: Mary Dinsmore Salter Ainsworth (1913–1999). *American Psychologist, 55,* 1148–1149.

Brickman, P., Coates, D., and Janoff-Bulman, R. J. (1978). Lottery winners and accident victims: Is happiness relative? *Journal of Personality and Social Psychology, 36,* 917–927.

Brody, J. E. (1996, March 27). Personal health. *The New York Times,* Section B.

Broesch, T., Callaghan, T., Henrich, J., Murphy, C., and Rochat, P. (2011). Cultural variations in children's mirror self-recognition. *Journal of Cross-Cultural Psychology, 42*(6), 1018–1029.

Brooks, N., and Fritzon, K. (2016). Psychopathic personality characteristics amongst high functioning populations. *Crime Psychology Review, 2*, 1–21.

Brose, L. A., Rye, M. S., Lutz-Zois, C., and Ross, S. R. (2005). Forgiveness and personality traits. *Personality and Individual Differences, 39*, 35–46.

Brown, D. E. (1991). *Human universals.* New York: McGraw-Hill.

Brown J. D. (2012). Understanding the better than average effect: Motives (still) matter. *Personality and Social Psychology Bulletin, 38*, 209–219.

Brown, J. D., and Dutton, K. A. (1995). The thrill of victory, the complexity of defeat: Self-esteem and people's emotional reactions to success and failure. *Journal of Personality and Social Psychology, 68*, 712–722.

Brown, J. D., and Smart, S. A. (1991). The self and social conduct: Linking self-representations to prosocial behavior. *Journal of Personality and Social Psychology, 60*, 368–375.

Brown, R. P., and Zeigler-Hill, V. (2004). Narcissism and the non-equivalence of self-esteem measures: A matter of dominance. *Journal of Research in Personality, 38*, 585–592.

Bruce, J., Davis, E. P., Gunnar, M. R. (2002). Individual differences in children's cortisol response to the beginning of a new school year. *Psychoneuroendocrinology, 27*, 635–650.

Bruch, M. A., and Hynes, M. J. (1987). Heterosexual anxiety and contraceptive behavior. *Journal of Research in Personality, 21*, 343–360.

Bruggemann, J. M., and Barry, R. J. (2002). Eysenck's P as a modulator of affective and electrodermal responses to violent and comic film. *Personality and Individual Differences, 32*, 1029–1048.

Brummett, B. H., Babyak, M. A., Williams, R. B., Barefoot, J. C., Costa, P. T., and Siegler, I. C. (2006). NEO personality domains and gender predict levels and trends in body mass index over 14 years during midlife. *Journal of Research in Personality, 40*, 222–236.

Buckels, E. E., Jones, D. N., and Paulhus, D. L. (2013). Behavioral confirmation of everyday sadism. *Psychological Science, 24*, 2201–2209.

Buckels, E. E., Trapnell, P. D., and Paulhus, D. L. (2014). Trolls just want to have fun. *Personality and Individual Differences, 67*, 97–102.

Buday, S. K., Stake, J. E., and Peterson, Z. D. (2012). Gender and the choice of a science career: The impact of social support and possible selves. *Sex Roles, 66*, 197–209.

Buerkle, J. V. (1960). Self attitudes and marital adjustment. *Merrill-Palmer Quarterly, 6*, 114–124.

Buffardi, L. E., and Campbell, W. K. (2008). Narcissism and social networking Web sites. *Personality and Social Psychology Bulletin, 34*, 1303–1314.

Buhrmester, M., Blanton, H. and Swann, W. (2010). Implicit self-esteem: Nature, measurement, and a new way forward. *Journal of Personality and Social Psychology, 100*, 365–385.

Bui, E., Rodgers, R., Chabrol, H., Birmes, P., and Schmitt, L. (2011). Is Anakin Skywalker suffering from borderline personality disorder? *Psychiatry Research,185*(1), 299.

Bullock, W. A., and Gilliland, K. (1993). Eysenck's arousal theory of introversion-extraversion: A converging measures investigation. *Journal of Personality and Social Psychology, 64*, 113–123.

Bunce, S. C., Larsen, R. J., and Peterson, C. (1995). Life after trauma: Personality and daily life experiences of traumatized persons. *Journal of Personality, 63*, 165–188.

Burack, J. A., Gurr, E., Stubbert, E., and Weva, V. (2019). Personality development among Indigenous youth in Canada: Weaving together universal and community-specific perspectives. *New Ideas in Psychology, 53*, 67–74.

Burke, R. J., Matthiesen, S. B., and Pallesen, S. (2006). Personality correlates of workaholism. *Personality and Individual Differences, 40*, 1223–1233.

Burns, M. O., and Seligman, M. E. (1989). Explanatory style across the life span: Evidence for stability over 52 years. *Journal of Personality and Social Psychology, 56*, 471–477.

Burnstein, E., Crandall, C., and Kitayama, S. (1994). Some neo-Darwinian decision rules for altruism: Weighing cures for inclusive fitness as a function of the biological importance of the decision. *Journal of Personality and Social Psychology, 67*, 773–789.

Burt, S. A. (2009). A mechanistic explanation of popularity: Genes, rule breaking, and evocative gene-environment correlations. *Journal of Personality and Social Psychology, 96*, 783–794.

Burt, S. A., McGue, M., Iacono, W., Comings, D., and MacMurray, J. (2002). An examination of the association between DRD4 and DRD2 polymorphisms and personality traits. *Personality and Individual Differences, 33*, 849–859.

Burton, C. M., and King, L. A. (2008). Effects of (very) brief writing on health: The two-minute miracle. *British Journal of Health Psychology, 13*, 9–14.

Bush, G., Luu, P., and Posner, M. I. (2000). Cognitive and emotional influences in anterior cingulated cortex. *Trends in Cognitive Sciences, 4*, 215–222.

Bushman, B., and Baumeister, R. (1998). Threatened egotism, narcissism, self-esteem, and direct and displaced aggression: Does self-love or self-hate lead to violence? *Journal of Personality and Social Psychology, 75*, 219–229.

Bushman, B. J., Bonacci, A. M., van Dijk, M., and Baumeister, R. F. (2003). Narcissism, sexual refusal and aggression: Testing a narcissistic reactance model of sexual coercion. *Journal of Personality and Social Psychology, 84*(5), 1027–1040.

Buss, A. H. (1989). Personality as traits. *American Psychologist, 44*, 1378–1388.

Buss, D. M. (1981). Predicting parent-child interactions from children's activity level. *Developmental Psychology, 17*, 59–65.

Buss, D. M. (1984). Toward a psychology of person-environment (PE) correlation: The role of spouse selection. *Journal of Personality and Social Psychology, 47*, 361–377.

Buss, D. M. (1987). Selection, evocation, and manipulation. *Journal of Personality and Social Psychology, 53*, 1214–1221.

Buss, D. M. (1989). Sex differences in human mate preferences: Evolutionary hypotheses tested in 37 cultures. *Behavioral and Brain Sciences, 12*, 1–49.

Buss, D. M. (1990). The evolution of anxiety and social exclusion. *Journal of Social and Clinical Psychology, 9*, 196–201.

Buss, D. M. (1991a). Conflict in married couples: Personality predictors of anger and upset. *Journal of Personality, 59*(4), 663–688.

Buss, D. M. (1991b). Evolutionary personality psychology. *Annual Review of Psychology.* Palo Alto, CA: Annual Reviews, Inc.

Buss, D. M. (1992). Manipulation in close relationships: Five personality factors in interactional context. *Journal of Personality, 60*, 477–499.

Buss, D. M. (1993). Strategic individual differences: The role of personality in creating and solving adaptive problems. In J. Hettema and I. Deary (Eds.), *Social and biological approaches to personality* (pp. 175–189) New York: Wiley.

Buss, D. M. (1995a). Evolutionary psychology: A new paradigm for psychological science. *Psychological Inquiry, 6*, 1–49.

Buss, D. M. (1995b). Psychological sex differences: Origins through sexual selection. *American Psychologist, 50*, 164–168.

Buss, D. M. (1996). Social adaptation and five major factors of personality. In J. S. Wiggins (Ed.), *The five-factor model of personality: Theoretical perspectives* (pp. 180–207). New York: Guilford Press.

Buss, D. M. (2000a). *The dangerous passion: Why jealousy is as necessary as love and sex.* New York: Free Press.

Buss, D. M. (2000b). The evolution of happiness. *American Psychologist, 55*, 15–23.

Buss, D. M. (2003). Sexual strategies: A journey into controversy. *Psychological Inquiry, 14*(3–4), 219–226.

Buss, D. M. (2005a). *The handbook of evolutionary psychology.* New York: Wiley.

Buss, D. M. (2005b). *The murderer next door: Why the mind is designed to kill.* New York: Penguin.

Buss, D. M. (2009a). The great struggles of life: Darwin and the emergence of evolutionary psychology. *American Psychologist, 64*, 140–148.

Buss, D. M. (2009b). How can evolutionary psychology successfully explain personality and individual differences? *Perspectives in Psychological Science, 5*.

Buss, D. M. (2011). Personality and the adaptive landscape: The role of individual differences in creating and solving social adaptive problems. In D. M. Buss and P. Hawley (Eds.), *The evolution of personality and individual differences* (pp. 29–60). New York: Oxford University Press.

Buss, D. M. (2012). *Evolutionary psychology: The new science of the mind* (4th ed.). Boston: Allyn & Bacon.

Buss, D. M. (2016). *The evolution of desire: Strategies of human mating* (Revised and updated ed.). New York: Basic Books.

Buss, D. M., Abbott, M., Angleitner, A., Asherian, A., Biaggio, A., et al. (1990). International preferences in selecting mates: A study of 37 cultures. *Journal of Cross-Cultural Psychology, 21*(1), 5–47.

Buss, D. M., and Barnes, M. L. (1986). Preferences in human mate selection. *Journal of Personality and Social Psychology, 50*, 559–570.

Buss, D. M., Block, J. H., and Block, J. (1980). Preschool activity level: Personality correlates and developmental implications. *Child Development, 51*, 401–408.

Buss, D. M., and Chiodo, L. M. (1991). Narcissistic acts in everyday life. *Journal of Personality, 59, 2*, 179–215.

Buss, D. M., and Craik, K. H. (1983). The act frequency approach to personality. *Psychological Review, 90*, 105–126.

Buss, D. M., and Duntley, J. D. (2006). The evolution of aggression. In M. Schaller, D. T. Kenrick, and J. A. Simpson (Eds.), *Evolution and social psychology* (pp. 263–286). New York: Psychology Press.

Buss, D. M., Gomes, M., Higgins, D. S., and Lauterbach, K. (1987). Tactics of manipulation. *Journal of Personality and Social Psychology, 52*, 1219–1229.

Buss, D. M., and Greiling, H. (1999). Adaptive individual differences. *Journal of Personality, 67*, 209–243.

Buss, D. M., and Hawley, P. (2011). *The evolution of personality and individual differences.* New York: Oxford University Press.

Buss, D. M., Larsen, R. J., Semmelroth, J., and Westen, D. (1992). Sex differences in jealousy: Evolution, physiology, and psychology. *Psychological Science, 3*, 251–255.

Buss, D. M., and Schmitt, D. P. (1993). Sexual strategies theory: An evolutionary perspective on human mating. *Psychological Review, 100*, 204–232.

Buss, D. M., and Schmitt, D. P. (2011). Evolutionary psychology and feminism. *Sex Roles, 64*, 768–787.

Buss, D. M., Shackelford, T. K., Kirkpatrick, L. A., Choe, J., Hasegawa, M., Hasegawa, T., and Bennett, K. (1999). Jealousy and the nature of beliefs about infidelity: Tests of competing hypotheses about sex differences in the United States, Korea, and Japan. *Personal Relationships, 6*, 125–150.

Buss, K. A., Schumacher, J. R. M., Dolski, I., Kalin, N. H., Goldsmith, H. H., and Davidson, R. J. (2003). Right frontal brain activity, cortisol, and withdrawal behavior in 6-month-old infants. *Behavioral Neuroscience, 117*, 11–20.

Butkovic, A., and Bratko, D. (2007). Family study of manipulation tactics. *Personality and Individual Differences, 43*, 791–801.

Butler, A. C., Hokanson, J. E., and Flynn, H. A. (1994). A comparison of self-esteem lability and low trait self-esteem as vulnerability factors for depression. *Journal of Personality and Social Psychology, 66*, 166–177.

Button, T. M. M., Stallings, M. C., Rhee, S. H., Corley, R. P., and Hewitt, J. K. (2011). The etiology of stability and change in religious values and religious attendance. *Behavior Genetics, 41*, 201–210.

Buunk, B., Angleitner, A., Oubaid, V., and Buss, D. M. (1996). Sexual and cultural differences in jealousy: Tests from the Netherlands, Germany, and the United States. *Psychological Science, 7*, 359–363.

Byrnes, J. P., Miller, D. C., and Schafer, W. D. (1999). Gender differences in risk taking: A meta-analysis. *Psychological Bulletin, 125*, 367–383.

Cafferty, T. P., Davis, K. E., Medway, F. J., O'Hearn, R. E., and Chappell, K. D. (1994). Reunion dynamics among couples separated during Operation Desert Storm: An attachment theory analysis. In K. Bartholomew and D. Perlman (Eds.), *Attachment processes in adulthood* (pp. 309–330). Philadelphia, PA: Jessica Kingsley.

Cai, H., Kwan, V. S. Y., and Sedikides, C. (2012). A sociocultural approach to narcissism: The case of modern China. *European Journal of Personality, 26*, 529–535.

Cammaerts, M.-C., and Cammaerts, R. (2015). Are ants (hymenoptera, formicidae) capable of self recognition? *Journal of Science, 5*(7), 521–532.

Campbell, J. B., and Hawley, C. W. (1982). Study habits and Eysenck's theory of extraversion-introversion. *Journal of Research in Personality, 16*, 139–146.

Campbell, W. K., and Foster, C. A. (2002). Narcissism and commitment in romantic relationships: An investment model analysis. *Personality and Social Psychology Bulletin, 28*(4), 484–495.

Campbell, W. K., Rudich, E. A., and Sedikides, C. (2002). Narcissism, self-esteem, and the positivity of self-views: Two portraits of self-love. *Personality and Social Psychology Bulletin, 28*(3), 358–368.

Canadian Mental Health Association. (2016). *Fast facts about mental illness.* Retrieved from http://www.cmha.ca/media/fast-facts-about-mental-illness/.

Canli, T. (2008). Toward a neurogenetic theory of neuroticism. In D. W. Pfaff and B. L. Kieffer (Eds.), *Molecular and biophysical mechanisms of arousal, alertness, and attention* (pp. 153–174). Malden: Blackwell.

Canli, T., and Amin, Z. (2002). Neuroimaging of emotion and personality: Scientific evidence and ethical considerations. *Brain and Cognition, 50*, 414–431.

Canli, T., Zuo, Z., Kang, E., Gross, J., Desmond, J. E., and Gabrielil, J. D. (2001). An fMRI study of personality influences on brain reactivity to emotional stimuli. *Behavioral Neuroscience, 115*, 33–42.

Cantor, N. (1990). From thought to behavior: "Having" and "doing" in the study of personality and cognition. *American Psychologist, 45*, 735–750.

Caprara, G. V., Alessandri, G., De Giunta, L., Panerai, L., and Eisenberg, N. (2010). The contribution of agreeableness and self-efficacy beliefs to prosociality. *European Journal of Personality, 24*, 36–55.

Caprara, G. V., Barbaranelli, C., Consiglio, C., Picconi, L., and Zimbardo, P. G. (2003). Personalities of politicians and voters: Unique and synergistic relationships. *Journal of Personality and Social Psychology, 84*(4), 849–856.

Caprara, G. V., and Perugini, M. (1994). Personality described by adjectives: Generalizability of the Big Five to the Italian lexical context. *European Journal of Psychology, 8*, 357–369.

Caputi, P. (2012). An introduction to grid-based methods. In P. Caputi, L. L. Viney, B. M. Walker, and N. Crittenden (Eds.), *Personal construct methodology* (pp. 149–158). Hoboken, NJ: John Wiley & Sons.

Cardemil, E. V., Reivich, K. J., and Seligman, M. E. P. (2002). The prevention of depressive symptoms in low-income minority middle school students. *Prevention and Treatment, 5*, np.

Carli, V., and Durkee, T. (2016). Pathological use of the Internet. In D. Mucic, D. M. Hilty, D. Mucic, D. M. Hilty (Eds.), *e-Mental health* (pp. 269–288). Cham, Switzerland: Springer International Publishing.

Carlo, G., Okun, M. A., Knight, G. P., and de Guzman, M. R. T. (2005). The interplay of traits and motives on volunteering: Agreeableness, extraversion and prosocial value motivation. *Personality and Individual Differences, 38*, 1293–1305.

Carpenter, C. J. (2012). Narcissism on Facebook: Self-promotional and anti-social behavior. *Personality and Individual Differences, 52*, 482–486.

Carrasco, M., Barker, E. D., Trembley, R. E., and Vitaro, J. (2006). Eysenck's personality dimensions as predictors of male adolescent trajectories of physical aggression, theft, and vandalism. *Personality and Individual Differences, 41*, 1309–1320.

Carron, A. V., Shapcott, K. M., and Martin, L. J. (2014). The relationship between team explanatory style and team success. *International Journal of Sport And Exercise Psychology, 12*(1), 1–9.

Carter, R. (1999). *Mapping the mind.* Berkeley: University of California Press.

Carver, C. S. (1996). Emergent integration in contemporary personality psychology. *Journal of Research in Personality, 30*, 319–334.

Carver, C. S., and Scheier, M. F. (2000). Autonomy and self regulation. *Psychological Inquiry, 11*, 284–291.

Carver, C. S., Sutton, S. K., and Scheier, M. F. (1999). Action, emotion, and personality: Emerging conceptual integration. *Personality and Social Psychology Bulletin, 26*, 741–751.

Carver, C. S., and White, T. L. (1994). Behavioral inhibition, behavioral activation, and affective responses to impeding reward and punishments: The BIS/BAS scales. *Journal of Personality and Social Psychology, 67*, 319–333.

Cashden, E. (1980). Egalitarianism among hunters and gatherers. *American Anthropologist, 82*, 116–120.

Caspi, A., Elder, G. H., Jr., and Bem, D. J. (1987). Moving against the world: Life-course patterns of explosive children. *Developmental Psychology, 23*, 308–313.

Caspi, A., Harrington, H., Milne, B., Amell, J. W., Theodore, R. F., and Moffitt, T. E. (2003). Children's behavioral styles at age 3 are linked to their adult personality traits at age 26. *Journal of Personality, 71*, 495–513.

Caspi, A., and Herbener, E. S. (1990). Continuity and change: Assortative mating and the consistency of personality in adulthood. *Journal of Personality and Social Psychology, 58*, 250–258.

Caspi, A., Roberts, B. W., and Shiner, R. L. (2005). Personality development: Stability and change. *Annual Review of Psychology, 56*, 453–458.

Caspi, A., Sugden, K., Moffitt, T., Taylor, A., Craig, I. W., Harringon, H., et al. (2003). Influence of life stress on depression: Moderation by a polymorphism in the 5-HTT gene. *Science, 301*, 386–389.

Cassidy, J., and Shaver, P. (1999). *Handbook of attachment: Theory, research, and clinical applications.* New York: Guilford Press.

Cattell, R. B. (1943). The description of personality: Basic traits resolved into clusters. *Journal of Abnormal and Social Psychology, 38*, 476–507.

Cattell, R. B. (1973). *Personality and mood by questionnaire.* San Francisco: Jossey-Bass.

Cattell, R. B., Eber, H. W., and Tatsouoka, M. M. (1970). *Handbook for the 16 PF.* Champaign, IL: Institute for Personality and Ability Testing.

Cepeda, M. S., Miranda, N, Sanchez, R., Rodriguez, C. H., Restrepo, A. E., Ferrer, L. M., Linares, R. A., and Carr, D. B. (2008). Emotional disclosure through patient narrative may improve pain and well-being: results of a randomized controlled trial in patients with cancer pain. *Journal of Pain and Symptom Management, 35*(6), 623–631.

Chabrol, H., Leeuwen, N.V., Rodgers, R., & Sejourne, N. (2009). Contributions of psychopathic, narcissistic, Machiavellian, and sadistic personality traits to juvenile delinquency. *Personality and Individual Differences, 47*, 734–739.

Chagnon, N. (1983). *Yanomamö: The fierce people* (3rd ed.). New York: Holt, Rinehart and Winston.

Chagnon, N. (1988). Life histories, blood revenge, and warfare in a tribal population. *Science, 239,* 985–992.

Chamorro-Premuzic, T., and Furnham, A. (2003a). Personality predicts academic performance: Evidence from two longitudinal university samples. *Journal of Research in Personality, 37,* 319–338.

Chamorro-Premuzic, T., and Furnham, A. (2003b). Personality traits and academic examination performance. *European Journal of Personality, 17,* 237–250.

Chan, W., McCrae, R. R., De Fruyt, F., Jussim, L., Löckenhoff, C. E., De Bolle, M., . . . and Nakazato, K. (2012). Stereotypes of age differences in personality traits: Universal and accurate? *Journal of Personality and Social Psychology, 103*(6) 1050–1066.

Chandler, M. J., Lalonde, C. E., and Sokol, B. (2000). Continuities of selfhood in the face of radical developmental and cultural change. In L. Nucci, G. Saxe, E. Turiel (eds.), *Culture, Thought, and Development* (pp. 65–84). Mahwah, NJ: Erlbaum.

Chang, L., Zhang, S., Poo, M-M., and Gong, N. (2017). Spontaneous expression of mirror self-recognition in monkeys after learning precise visual-proprioceptive association for mirror images. *Proceedings of the National Academy of Sciences, 114*(12), 3258–3263.

Chapman, B. P., and Goldberg, L. R. (2011). Replicability and 40-year predictive power of childhood ARC types. *Journal of Personality and Social Psychology, 101,* 593–606.

Charles, S. T., Reynolds, C. A. and Gatz, M. (2001). Age-related differences and change in positive and negative affect over 23 years. *Journal of Personality and Social Psychology, 80*(1), 136–151.

Chavira, D. A., Stein, M. B., and Malcarne, V. L. (2002). Scrutinizing the relationship between shyness and social phobia. *Journal of Anxiety Disorders, 16,* 585–598.

Cheek, J. M. (1983). *The revised Cheek and Buss Shyness Scale.* Unpublished manuscript, Department of Psychology, Wellesley College, Wellesley, MA.

Cheek, J. M. (1989). *Conquering shyness.* New York: Dell.

Cheek, J. M., and Buss, A. H. (1981). Shyness and sociability. *Journal of Personality and Social Psychology, 41,* 330–339.

Cheek, J. M., and Krasnoperova, E. N. (1999). Varieties of shyness in adolescence and adulthood. In L. A. Schmidt and J. Schulkin (Eds.), *Extreme fear, shyness, and social phobia: Origins, biological mechanisms, and clinical outcomes* (pp. 224–250). London: Oxford University Press.

Cheek, J. M., and Melchior, L. A. (1990). Shyness, self-esteem, and self-consciousness. In H. Leitenberg (Ed.), *Handbook of social and evaluation anxiety* (pp. 47–82). New York: Plenum Press.

Chen, C., Burton, M., Greenberger, E., and Dmitrieva, J. (1999). Population migration and the variation of dopamine D4 receptor (DRD4) allele frequencies around the globe. *Evolution and Human Behavior, 20,* 309–324.

Chen, F. F., and West, S. G. (2008). Measuring individualism and collectivism: The importance of considering differential components, reference groups, and measurement invariance. *Journal of Research in Personality, 42,* 259–294.

Chen, F. S., and Johnson, S. C. (2012). An oxytocin receptor gene variant predicts attachment anxiety in females and autism-spectrum traits in males. *Social Psychological and Personality Science, 3,* 93–99.

Chen, F. S., Schmitz, J., Domes, G., Tuschen-Caffier, B., and Heinrichs, M. (2014). Effects of acute social stress on emotion processing in children. *Psychoneuroimmunology, 40,* 91–95.

Chen, S., Su, X., and Wu, S. (2012). Need for achievement, education, and entrepreneurial risk-taking behavior. *Social Behavior and Personality, 40,* 1311–1318.

Cheng, H., and Furnham, A. (2003). Personality, self-esteem, and demographic predictions of happiness and depression. *Personality and Individual Differences, 34,* 921–942.

Cheung, F. M., Leung, K., Zhang, J. X., Sun, H. F., Gan, Y. G., Song, W. Z., and Xie, D. (2001). Indigenous Chinese personality constructs: Is the five-factor model complete? *Journal of Cross-Cultural Psychology, 32,* 407–433.

Chida, Y., and Steptoe, A. (2009). The association of anger and hostility with future coronary heart disease: A meta-analytic review of prospective evidence. *Journal of the American College of Cardiology, 53,* 774–778.

Chioqueta, A. P., and Stiles, T. C. (2005). Personality traits and the development of depression, hopelessness, and suicidal ideation. *Personality and Individual Differences, 38,* 1283–1291.

Chodorow, N. J. (1989). *Feminism and psychoanalytic theory.* New Haven, CT: Yale University Press.

Choi, J. K., and Ji, Y. G. (2015). Investigating the importance of trust on adopting an autonomous vehicle. *International Journal of Human-Computer Interaction, 31*(10), 692–702.

Christ, S. E., White, D., Brunstrom, J. E., and Abrams, R. A. (2003). Inhibitory control following perinatal brain injury. *Neuropsychology, 17,* 171–178.

Christie, R., and Geis, F. L. (1970). *Studies in Machiavellianism* (pp. 53–76). New York: Academic Press.

Chu, S. W., and Clark, L. (2015) Cognitive and neurobiological aspects of problem gambling: Relevance to treatment. *Canadian Journal of Addiction, 6,* 62–71.

Church, A. T. (2000). Culture and personality: Toward an integrated cultural trait psychology. *Journal of Personality, 68,* 651–703.

Church, A. T. (2009). Prospects for an integrated trait and cultural psychology. *European Journal of Personality, 23,* 153–182.

Church, A. T., Katigbak, M. S., Mazuera Arias, R., Rincon, B. C., Vargas-Flores, J. D. J., Ibáñez-Reyes, J., . . . and Ortiz, F. A. (2014). A four-culture study of self-enhancement and adjustment using the social relations model: Do alternative conceptualizations and indices make a difference? *Journal of Personality and Social psychology, 106,* 997–1014.

Church, A. T., Katigbak, M. S., Miramontes, L. G., del Prado, A. M., and Cabrera, H. F. (2007). Culture and the behavioural manifestations of traits: An application of the act frequency approach. *European Journal of Personality, 21,* 389–417.

Clapper, R. L. (1990). Adult and adolescent arousal preferences: The revised reducer augmenter scale. *Personality and Individual Differences, 11,* 1115–1122.

Clapper, R. L. (1992). The reducer-augmenter scale, the revised reducer augmenter scale, and predicting late adolescent substance use. *Personality and Individual Differences, 13,* 813–820.

Claridge, G. S., Donald, J., and Birchall, P. M. (1981). Drug tolerance and personality: Some implications for Eysenck's theory. *Personality and Individual Differences, 2,* 153–166.

Clark, L., Stokes, P. R., Wu, K., Michalczuk, R., Benecke, A., Watson, B. J., Egerton, A., Piccini, P., Nutt, D. J., Bowden-Jones, H., and Lingford-Hughes, A. R. (2012). Striatal dopamine D2/D3 receptor binding in pathological gambling is correlated with mood-related impulsivity. *NeuroImage, 63,* 40–46.

Claxton, A., O'Rourke, N., Smith, J. Z., and DeLongis, A. (2012). Personality traits and marital satisfaction within enduring relationships: An intra-couple discrepancy approach. *Journal of Social and Personal Relationships, 29,* 375–396.

Cleckley, H. (1941). *The mask of sanity: An attempt to reinterpret the so-called psychopathic personality.* Oxford, England: Mosby.

Cleckley, H. (1988). *The mask of sanity.* Augusta, GA: Emily S. Cleckley.

Cleveland, H. H., Udry, J. R., and Chantala, K. (2001). Environmental and genetic influences on sex-types behaviors and attitudes of male and female adolescents. *Personality and Social Psychology Bulletin, 27*(12), 1587–1598.

Clewley, N., Chen, S. Y., and Liu, X. (2011). Mining learning preferences in Web-based instruction: Holists vs. serialists. *Journal of Educational Technology and Society, 14,* 266–277.

Clifton, A., Turkheimer, E., and Oltmanns, T. F. (2004). Contrasting perspectives on personality problems: Descriptions from the self and others. *Personality and Individual Differences, 36,* 1499–1514.

Cloninger, C. R. (1986). A unified biosocial theory of personality and its role in the development of anxiety states. *Psychiatric Developments, 3,* 167–226.

Cloninger, C. R. (1987). A systematic method for clinical description and classification of personality variants: A proposal. *Archives of General Psychiatry, 44,* 573–588.

Cloninger, C. R. (1999). *Personality and psychopathology.* Washington, DC: American Psychiatric Press.

Cloninger, C. R., Sigvardsson, S., and Bohman, M. (1988). Childhood personality predicts alcohol abuse in young adults. *Alcoholism Clinical and Experimental Research, 12,* 494–505.

Cloninger, C. R., Svrakic, D. M., and Przybeck, T. R. (1993). A psychobiological model of temperament and character. *Archives of General Psychiatry, 50,* 975–990.

Clower, C. E., and Bothwell, R. K. (2001). An exploratory study of the relationship between the Big Five and inmate recidivism. *Journal of Research in Personality, 35,* 231–237.

Coan, J. A., and Gottman, J. M. (2007). Sampling, experimental control, and generalizability in the study of marital process models, *Journal of Marriage and Family, 69,* 73–80.

Cohen, J. (1977). *Statistical power analysis for the behavioral sciences.* San Diego, CA: Academic Press.

Cohen, J., and Cohen, P. (1975). *Applied multiple regression/correlation analysis for the behavioral sciences.* Hillsdale, NJ: Erlbaum.

Cohen, S., Tyrrell, D. A. J., and Smith, A. P. (1997). Psychological stress in humans and susceptibility to the common cold. In T. W. Moller (Ed.), *Clinical disorders and stressful life events* (pp. 217–235). Madison, CT: International Universities Press.

Coleman, R. (1992). *Lennon: The definitive biography.* New York: Perennial.

Collins, J. N. (1994). Some fundamental questions about scientific thinking. *Research in Science and Technological Education, 12,* 161–173.

Colzato, L. S., Ozturk, A., and Hommel, B. (2012). Meditate to create: the impact of focused-attention and open-monitoring training on convergent and divergent thinking. *Frontiers in Psychology, 3,* 116.

Confer, J. C., Easton, J. E., Fleischman, D. S., Goetz, C., Lewis, D. M., Perilloux, C., and Buss, D. M. (2010). Evolutionary psychology: Controversies, questions, prospects, and limitations. *American Psychologist, 65,* 110–126.

Conley, J. J. (1984a). The hierarchy of consistency: A review and model of longitudinal findings on adult individual differences in intelligence, personality, and self-opinion. *Personality and Individual Differences, 5,* 11–25.

Conley, J. J. (1984b). Longitudinal consistency of adult personality: Self-reported psychological characteristics across 45 years. *Journal of Personality and Social Psychology, 47,* 1325–1333.

Conley, J. J. (1985). Longitudinal stability of personality traits: A multitrait-multimethod-multioccasion analysis. *Journal of Personality and Social Psychology, 49,* 1266–1282.

Conley, J. J., and Angelides, M. (1984). *Personality antecedents of emotional disorders and alcohol abuse in men: Results of a forty-five-year prospective study.* Unpublished manuscript: Wesleyan University, Middletown, CT.

Connelly, B. S., and Hülsheger, U. R. (2012). A narrower scope or a clearer lens for personality? Examining sources of observers' advantages over self-reports for predicting performance. *Journal of Personality, 80,* 603–631.

Connelly, B. S., and Ones, D. S. (2010). Another perspective on personality: Meta-analytic integration of observers' accuracy and predicative validity. *Psychological Bulletin, 136,* 1092–1122.

Connolly, I., and O'Moore, M. (2003). Personality and family relations of children who bully. *Personality and Individual Differences, 35,* 559–567.

Conrad, M. A. (2006). Aptitude is not enough: How personality and behavior predict academic performances. *Journal of Research in Personality, 40,* 339–346.

Conroy-Beam, D., Goetz, C. D., & Buss, D. M. (2016). What predicts romantic relationship satisfaction and mate retention intensity: Mate preference fulfillment or mate value discrepancies? *Evolution and Human Behavior, 37.* doi: 10.1016/j.evolhumbehav.2016.04.003

Cooper, M. L., Wood, P. K., Orcutt, H. K., and Albino, A. (2003). Personality and the predisposition to engage in risky or problem behaviors during adolescence. *Journal of Personality and Social Psychology, 84*(2), 390–410.

Cooper, S. H. (1998). Changing notions of defense within psychoanalytic theory. *Journal of Personality, 66,* 947–965.

Cooper, W. E. (1992). William James's theory of the self. *Monist 75*(4), 504–520.

Coplan, R. J., Ooi, L. L., and Nocita, G. (2015). When one is company and two is a crowd: Why some children prefer solitude. *Child Development Perspectives, 9*(3), 133–137.

Coplan, R. J., Prakash, K., O'Neil, K., and Armer, M. (2004). Do you "want" to play? Distinguishing between conflicted shyness and social disinterest in early childhood. *Developmental Psychology, 40*(2), 244–258.

Corcoran, D. W. J. (1964). The relation between introversion and salivation. *American Journal of Psychology, 77,* 298–300.

Correa, T., Hinsley, A. W., and Gil de Zúñiga, H. (2010). Who interacts on the Web?: The intersection of users' personality and social media use. *Computers in Human Behavior, 26,* 247–253.

Cosmides, L., and Tooby, J. (1992). Cognitive adaptations for social exchange. In J. Barkow, L. Cosmides, and J. Tooby (Eds.), *The adapted mind* (pp. 163–228). New York: Academic Press.

Costa, P. T., and McCrae, R. R. (1980). Influence of extraversion and neuroticism on subjective well-being: Happy and unhappy people. *Journal of Personality and Social Psychology, 38,* 668–678.

Costa, P. T., and McCrae, R. R. (1985). Hypochondriasis, neuroticism, and aging: When are somatic complaints unfounded? *American Psychologist, 40,* 19–28.

Costa, P. T., Jr., and McCrae, R. R. (1988). Personality in adulthood: A six-year longitudinal study of self-reports and spouse ratings on the NEO Personality Inventory. *Journal of Personality and Social Psychology, 54,* 853–863.

Costa, P. T., Jr., and McCrae, R. R. (1989). *The NEO-PI/NEO-FFI manual supplement.* Odessa, FL: Psychological Assessment Resources.

Costa, P. T., Jr., and McCrae, R. R. (1992). Trait psychology comes of age. In T. B. Sonderegger (Ed.), *Nebraska symposium on motivation: Psychology and aging* (pp. 169–204). Lincoln: University of Nebraska Press.

Costa, P. T., Jr., and McCrae, R. R. (1994). Set like plaster? Evidence for the stability of adult personality. In T. F. Heatherton and J. L. Weinberger (Eds.), *Can personality change?* Washington, DC: American Psychological Association.

Costa, P. T., Jr., and McCrae, R. R. (1995). Solid ground in the wetlands of personality: A reply to Block. *Psychological Bulletin, 117,* 216–220.

Costa, P. T., Jr., and McCrae, R. R. (2005). The NEO-PI-3: A more readable revised NEO personality inventory. *Journal of Personality, 84,* 261–270.

Costa, P. T., McCrae, R. R., and Zonderman, A. B. (1987). Environmental and dispositional influences on well-being: Longitudinal follow-up of an American national sample. *British Journal of Psychology, 78,* 299–306.

Costa, P. T., Terracciano, A., and McCrae, R. R. (2001). Gender differences in personality traits across cultures: Robust and surprising findings. *Journal of Personality and Social Psychology, 81,* 322–331.

Costa, P. T., and Widiger, T. A. (Eds.). (1994). *Personality disorders and the five-factor model of personality.* Washington, DC: American Psychological Association.

Costa, P. T., and Widiger, T. A. (Eds.). (2002). *Personality disorders and the five-factor model of personality* (2nd ed.). Washington, DC: American Psychological Association.

Coutts, L. M. (1990). Police hiring and promotion: Methods and outcomes. *Canadian Police College Journal, 14,* 98–122.

Cox, K., and McAdams, D. P. (2012). The transforming self: Service narratives and identity change in emerging adulthood. *Journal of Adolescent Research, 27,* 18–43.

Craik, K. H. (1986). Personality research methods: An historical perspective. *Journal of Personality, 54,* 18–51.

Craik, K. H. (2008). *Reputation: A network analysis.* New York: Oxford University Press.

Cramer, P. (1991). *The development of defense mechanisms: Theory, research, and assessment.* New York: Springer-Verlag.

Cramer, P. (2000). Defense mechanisms in psychology today: Further processes for adaptation. *American Psychologist, 55,* 637–646.

Cramer, P. (2002). Defense mechanisms, behavior, and affect in young adulthood. *Journal of Personality, 70,* 103–126.

Cramer, P. (2012). Psychological maturity and change in adult defense mechanisms. *Journal of Research in Personality, 46,* 306–316.

Cramer, P., and Davidson, K. (1998). Defense mechanisms in contemporary personality research. *Special Issue of the Journal of Personality, 66.*

Crandall, V., Dewey, R., Katkovsky, W., and Preston, A. (1964). Parents' attitudes and behaviors and grade-school children's academic achievements. *Journal of Genetic Psychology, 104,* 53–66.

Crandall, V. C., Katkovsky, W., and Crandall, V. J. (1965). Children's belief in their own control of reinforcements in intellectual-academic achievement situations. *Child Development, 36,* 91–109.

Crocker, J., and Luhtanen, R. (1990). Collective self-esteem and ingroup bias. *Journal of Personality and Social Psychology, 58,* 60–67.

Crocker, J., and Major, B. (1989). Social stigma and self-esteem: The self-protective properties of stigma. *Psychological Review, 96,* 608–630.

Cronbach, L. J., and Gleser, G. C. (1965). *Psychological tests and personnel decisions.* Urbana: University of Illinois Press.

Cronbach, L. J., and Meehl, P. E. (1955). Construct validity in psychological tests. *Psychological Bulletin, 52,* 281–302.

Cross, C. P., Copping, L. T., and Campbell, A. (2011). Sex differences in impulsivity: A meta-analysis. *Psychological Bulletin, 137,* 97–130.

Cross, S. E., Kanagawa, C., Markus, H. R., and Kitayama, S. (1995). *Cultural variation in self-concept.* Unpublished manuscript, Iowa State University, Ames, IA.

Crowne, D. P., and Marlowe, D. (1964). *The approval motive: Studies in evaluation dependence.* New York: Wiley.

Cruce, S. E., Pashak, T. J., Handal, P. J., Munz, D. C., and Gfeller, J. D. (2012). Conscientious perfectionism, self-evaluative perfectionism, and the five-factor model of personality traits. *Personality and Individual Differences, 53,* 268–273.

Cruz, M., and Larsen, R. J. (1995). Personality correlates of individual differences in electrodermal lability. *Journal of Social Behavior and Personality, 23,* 93–104.

Csikszentmihalyi, M. (1997). *Finding flow.* New York: Basic.

Csikszentmihalyi, M. (1999). If we are so rich, why aren't we happy? *American Psychologist, 54,* 821–827.

Csikszentmihalyi, M. (2000). *Beyond boredom and anxiety* (25th anniversary ed.). San Francisco: Jossey-Bass. (Original work published 1975.)

Csikszentmihalyi, M., Abuhamdeh, S., and Nakamura, J. (2005). Flow. In A. J. Elliot and C. S. Dweck (Eds.), *Handbook of competence and motivation* (pp. 598–608). New York: Guilford Press.

Cuijpers, P., Smit, F., Penninx B. W. J. H., de Graaf, R., ten Have, M., and Beekman, A. T. F. (2010). Economic costs of neuroticism: A population-based study. *Archives of General Psychiatry, 67*(10), 1086–1093.

Cutler, S. S., Larsen, R. J., and Bunce, S. C. (1996). Repressive coping style and the experience and recall of emotion: A naturalistic study of daily affect. *Journal of Personality, 65,* 379–405.

Dabbs, J. M., Jr., and Dabbs, M. G. (2000). *Heroes, rogues and lovers: Testosterone and behavior.* New York: McGraw-Hill.

Dabbs, J. M., Jr., and Hargrove, M. F. (1997). Age, testosterone, and behavior among female prison inmates. *Psychosomatic Medicine, 59,* 477–480.

Dabbs, J. M., Jr., Hargrove, M. F., and Heusel, C. (1996). Testosterone differences among college fraternities: Well-behaved vs. rambunctious. *Personality and Individual Differences, 20,* 157–161.

Dale, A. L., and DeCicco, T. L. (2014). Examining the storytelling method of dream interpretation with Canadian soldiers. *Imagination, Cognition and Personality, 33*(4), 367–381.

Dalgleish, T. (1995). Performance on the emotional Stroop task in groups of anxious, expert, and control subjects: A comparison of computer and card presentation formats. *Cognition and Emotion, 9,* 341–362.

Daly, M., and Wilson, M. (1988). *Homicide.* New York: Aldine de Gruyter.

Damasio, A. R. (1994). *Descartes' error: Emotion, reason, and the human brain.* New York: Avon Books.

Danner, D. D., Snowdon, D. A., and Friesen, W. V. (2001). Positive emotions in early life and longevity: Findings from the nun study. *Journal of Personality and Social Psychology, 80,* 804–813.

Daros, A. R., Uliaszek, A. A., and Ruocco, A. C. (2014). Perceptual biases in facial emotion recognition in borderline personality disorder. *Personality Disorders: Theory, Research, and Treatment, 5*(1), 79.

Darwin, C. (1859) *The origin of species.* London: Murray.

Darwin, C. (1872/1965). *The expression of the emotions in man and animals.* Chicago: University of Chicago Press.

Davey, A., Fincham, F. D., Beach, S. R. H., and Brody, G. H. (2001). Attributions in marriage: Examining the entailment model in dyadic context. *Journal of Family Psychology, 15,* 721–734.

Davidson, K. W., Gidron, Y., Mostofsky, E., and Trudeau, K. J. (2007). Hospitalization cost offset of a hostility intervention for coronary heart disease patients. *Journal of Consulting and Clinical Psychology, 75,* 657–662.

Davidson, R. J. (1991). Cerebral asymmetry and affective disorders: A developmental approach. In D. Cicchetti and S. L. Toth (Eds.), *Internalizing and externalizing expressions of dysfunction: Rochester Symposium on Developmental Psychopathology* (Vol. 2, pp. 123–154). Hillsdale, NJ: Erlbaum.

Davidson, R. J. (1993). The neuropsychology of emotion and affective style. In M. Lewis and J. M. Haviland (Eds.), *Handbook of emotions* (pp. 143–154). New York: Guilford Press.

Davidson, R. J. (2003). Affective neuroscience and psychophysiology: Toward a synthesis. *Psychophysiology, 40,* 655–665.

Davidson, R. J., Ekman, P., Saron, C. D., Senulis, J. A., and Friesen, W. V. (1990). Approach/withdrawal and cerebral asymmetry: Emotional expression and brain physiology. I. *Journal of Personality and Social Psychology, 58,* 330–341.

Davidson, R. J., Kabat-Zinn, J., Schumacher, J., Rosenkranz, M., Muller, D., Santorelli, S. F., Urbanowski, F., Harrington, A., Bonus, K., and Sheridan, J. F. (2003). Alterations in brain and immune function produced by mindfulness meditation. *Psychosomatic Medicine, 65,* 564–570.

Davidson, R. J., Scherer, K. R., and Goldsmith, H. H. (2003). *Handbook of affective sciences.* New York: Oxford University Press.

Davis, A. C., and Stroink, M. L. (2016). Within-culture differences in self-construal, environmental concern, and proenvironmental behavior. *Ecopsychology, 8*(1), 64–73.

Davis, M. H., Luce, C., and Kraus, S. J. (1994). The heritability of characteristics associated with dispositional empathy. *Journal of Personality, 62,* 369–391.

Davis, M. H., Mitchell, K. V., Hall, J. A., Lothert, J., Snapp, T., and Meyer, M. (1999). Empathy, expectations, and situational preferences: Personality influences on the decision to participate in volunteer helping behaviors. *Journal of Personality, 67,* 469–503.

Davis, P. J. (1987). Repression and the inaccessibility of affective memories. *Journal of Personality and Social Psychology, 53,* 585–593.

Davis, P. J., and Schwartz, G. E. (1987). Repression and the inaccessibility of affective memories. *Journal of Personality and Social Psychology, 52,* 155–162.

De Bolle, M., De Fruyt, F., McCrae, R. R., Löckenhoff, C. E., Costa Jr., P. T., Aquilar-Vafaie, M. E., . . . Avdeyeva, T. V. et al. (2015). The emergence of sex differences in personality traits in early adolescence: A cross-sectional, cross-cultural study. *Journal of Personality and Social Psychology, 108*(1), 171–185.

De Raad, B. (1998). Five big, big five issues: Rationale, content, structure, status, and crosscultural assessment. *European Psychologist, 3,* 113–124.

De Raad, B., and Barelds, D. P. H. (2008). A new taxonomy of Dutch personality traits based on a comprehensive and unrestricted list of descriptors. *Journal of Personality and Social Psychology, 94,* 347–364.

De Raad, B., Barelds, D. P. H., Levert, E., Ostendof, F., Mlacic, B., De Blas, L., Hrebickova, M., et al. (2010). Only three factors of personality description are fully replicable across languages: A comparison of 14 trait taxonomies. *Journal of Personality and Social Psychology, 98,* 1060–1173.

De Raad, B., Perugini, M., Hrebickova, M., and Szarota, P. (1998). Lingua Franca of personality: Taxonomies and structures based on the psycholexical approach. *Journal of Cross-Cultural Psychology, 29,* 212–232.

De Vries, J., and Van Heck, G. L. (2002). Fatigue: Relationships with basic personality and temperament dimensions. *Personality and Individual Differences, 33,* 1311–1324.

Del Giudice, M., and Belsky, J. (2001). The development of life history strategies: Toward a multi-stage theory. In D. M. Buss and P. Hawley (Eds.), *The evolution of personality and individual differences.* New York: Oxford University Press.

del Prado, A. M., Church, A. T., Katigbak, M. S., Miramontes, L. G., Whitty, M. T., Curtis, G. J., et al. (2007). Culture, method, and the content of self-concepts: Testing trait, individual-self primacy, and cultural psychology perspectives. *Journal of Research in Personality, 41,* 1119–1160.

DeAngelis, T. (1991). Honesty tests weigh in with improved ratings. *APA Monitor, 22,* 6.

Deaner, R. O., Goetz, S. M. M., Shattuck, K., and Schnotala, T. (2012). Body weight, not facial width-to-height ratio, predicts aggression in pro hockey players. *Journal of Research in Personality, 46,* 235–238.

Deaux, K. (1984). From individual differences to social categories: Analysis of a decade's research on gender. *American Psychologist, 39,* 105–116.

Deaux, K., and LaFrance, M. (1998). Gender. In D. T. Gilbert, S. T. Fiske, and G. Lindzey (Eds.), *The handbook of social psychology* (vol. 1, 4th ed., pp. 788–827). Boston: McGraw-Hill.

DeCicco, T. L. (2007). What is the story telling? Examining discovery with the storytelling method (TSM) and testing with a control group. *Dreaming, 17*(4), 227–238.

DeCicco, T. L., and Higgins, H. (2009). Dreams of recovering alcoholics: Mood, dream content, discovery, and the storytelling method of dream interpretation. *International Journal of Dream Research, 2*(2), 45–51.

DeCicco, T. L., and Stroink, M. L. (2007). A third model of self-construal: The metapersonal self. *International Journal of Transpersonal Studies, 26,* 82–104.

DeCicco, T. L., Lyons, T., Pannier, W., Wright, C., and Clarke, J. (2010). Exploring the dreams of women with breast cancer: Content and meaning of dreams. *International Journal of Dream Research, 3*(2), 104–110.

Decuyper, M., De Bolle, M., and De Fruyt, F. (2012). Personality similarity, perceptual accuracy, and relationship satisfaction in dating and married couples. *Personal Relationships, 19,* 128–145.

Deiner, C. I., and Dweck, C. S. (1978). An analysis of learned helplessness: Continuous changes in performance, strategy, and achievement cognitions following failure. *Journal of Personality and Social Psychology, 36,* 451–462.

Deiner, C. I., and Dweck, C. S. (1980). An analysis of learned helplessness (II): The processing of success. *Journal of Personality and Social Psychology, 39,* 940–952.

Delfour, F., and Marten, K. (2001). Mirror image processing in three marine mammal species: killer whales (Orcinus orca), false killer whales (Pseudorca crassidens) and California sea lions (Zalophus californianus). *Behavioural Processes, 53*(3), 181–190.

DeLongis, A., and Holtzman, S. (2005). Coping in context: The role of stress, social support, and personality in coping. *Journal of Personality, 73,* 1633–1656.

DeLongis, A., and O'Brien, T. B. (1990). An interpersonal framework for stress and coping: An application to the families of Alzheimer's patients. In M. A. P. Stephens, J. H. Crowther, S. E. Hobfoll, and D. L. Tennenbaum (Eds.), *Stress and coping in later life families* (pp. 221–239). Washington, DC: Hemisphere Publishers.

DeLongis, A., Folkman, S., and Lazarus, R. S. (1988). The impact of daily stress on health and mood: Psychological and social resources as mediators. *Journal of Personality and Social Psychology, 54,* 986–995.

DeLongis, A., Nathanson, C., Paulhus, D.L. (2011). Revenge: Who, when, and why. Unpublished manuscript, University of British Columbia, Vancouver, Canada.

Dembrowski, T. M., and Costa, P. T. (1987). Coronary-prone behavior: Components of the Type A pattern and hostility. *Journal of Personality, 55,* 211–235.

Demerath, P. (2001). The social cost of acting "extra": Students' moral judgments of self, social relations, and academic success in Papua New Guinea. *American Journal of Education, 108,* 3.

DeMeuse, K. (1985). The relationship between life events and indices of classroom performance. *Teaching of Psychology, 12,* 146–149.

Denissen, J. J. A., and Penke, L. (2008a). Motivational individual reaction norms underlying the five-factor model of personality: First steps toward a theory-based conceptual framework. *Journal of Research in Personality, 42,* 1285–1302.

Denissen, J. J. A., and Penke, L. (2008b). Neuroticism predicts reactions to cues of social exclusion. *European Journal of Personality, 22,* 497–517.

Denissen, J., Penke, L., Schmitt, D. P., and van Aken, M. (2008). Self-esteem reactions to social interactions: Evidence for sociometer mechanisms across days, people, and nations. *Journal of Personality and Social Psychology, 95,* 181–196.

Denollet, J. (2000). Type D personality: A potential risk factor refined. *Journal of Psychosomatic Research, 49,* 255–266.

Denollet, J. (2005). DS14: Standard assessment of negative affectivity, social inhibition, and Type D personality. *Psychosomatic Medicine, 67,* 89–97.

Denollet, J., Conraads, V. M., Brutsart, D. L., De Clerck, L. S., Stevens, W. J., and Brints, C. J. (2003). Cytokines and immune activation in systolic heart failure: The role of Type D personality. *Brain, Behavior, and Immunity, 17,* 304–309.

Denollet, J., Pedersen, S. S., Ong, A. T., Erdman, R. A., Serruys, P. W., and van Domburg, R. T. (2006). Social inhibition modulates the effects of negative emotions on cardiac prognosis following percutaneous coronary intervention in the drug-eluting stent era. *European Heart Journal, 27,* 171–177.

DePaulo, B. (2006). *Singled out: How singles are stereotyped, stigmatized, and ignored, and still live happily ever after.* New York: St. Martin's Press.

DePaulo, B. M., Kenny, D. A., Hoover, C. W., Webb, W., and Oliver, P. V. (1987). Accuracy of person perception: Do people know what kinds of impressions they convey? *Journal of Personality and Social Psychology, 52,* 303–315.

Depue, R. A. (1996). A neurobiological framework for the structure of personality and emotion: Implications for personality disorders. In J. Clarkin and M. Lenzenweger (Eds.), *Major theories of personality disorders* (pp. 347–390). New York: Guilford Press.

Depue, R. A. (2006). Interpersonal behavior and the structure of personality: Neurobehavioral foundations of agentic extraversion and affiliation. In T. Canli (Ed.), *Biology of personality and individual differences* (pp. 60–92). New York: Guilford Press.

Depue, R. A., and Collins, P. F. (1999). Neurobiology of the structure of personality: Dopamine, facilitation of incentive motivation, and extraversion. *Behavioral and Brain Sciences, 22,* 491–517.

DeSteno, D. A., and Salovey, P. (1996). Evolutionary origins of sex differences in jealousy: Questioning the "fitness" of the model. *Psychological Science, 7,* 367–372.

Devos, G., Clark, L., Maurage, P., and Billieux, J. (2015). Reduced inhibitory control predicts persistence in laboratory slot machine gambling. *International Gambling Studies, 15,* 408–421.

DeWall, C. N., Baumeister, R. F., Stillman, T. F., and Gailliot, M. T. (2007). Violence restrained: Effects of self-regulatory capacity and its depletion on aggressive behavior. *Journal of Experimental Social Psychology, 33,* 1547–1558.

DeWall, C. N., Buffardi, L. E., Bosner, I., and Campbell, W. K. (2011). Narcissism and implicit attention seeking: Evidence from linguistic analyses of social networking and online presentation. *Personality and Individual Differences, 51,* 57–62.

DeYoung, C. G. (2010). Personality neuroscience and the biology of traits. *Social and Personality Psychology Compass, 4,* 1165–1180.

DeYoung, C. G., Grazioplene, R. G., and Peterson, J. B. (2012). From madness to genius: The openness/intellect trait domain as a paradoxical simplex. *Journal of Research in Personality, 46,* 63–78.

DeYoung, C. G., Hirsh, J. B., Shane, M.S., Rajeevan, N., and Gray, J. R. (2010). Testing predictions from personality neuroscience: Brain structure and the big five. *Psychological Science, 21,* 820–828.

DeYoung, C. G., Shamosh, N. A., Green, A. E., Braver, T. S., and Gray, J. R. (2009). Intellect as distinct from openness: Differences revealed by fMRI of working memory. *Journal of Personality and Social Psychology, 97,* 883–892.

Di Blas, L. (2005). Personality-relevant attribute-nouns: A taxonomic study in the Italian language. *European Journal of Personality, 19,* 537–557.

Di Blas, L. (2007). A circumplex model of interpersonal attributes in middle childhood. *Journal of Personality, 75,* 863–897.

Diamond, J. (1999). *Guns, germs, and steel.* New York: Norton.

Diener, E. (2000). Subjective well-being: The science of happiness and a proposal for a national index. *American Psychologist, 55,* 34–43.

Diener, E., and Biswas-Diener, R. (2002). Will money increase subjective well-being? A literature review and guide to needed research. *Social Indicators Research, 57,* 119–169.

Diener, E., and Biswas-Diener, R. (2008). *Happiness: Unlocking the mysteries of psychological wealth.* Malden, MA: Blackwell.

Diener, E., and Diener, M. (1995). Cross-cultural correlates of life satisfaction and self-esteem. *Journal of Personality and Social Psychology, 68,* 653–663.

Diener, E., Diener, M., and Diener, C. (1995). Factors predicting the subjective well-being of nations. *Journal of Personality and Social Psychology, 69,* 851–864.

Diener, E., Emmons, R. A., Larsen, R. J., and Griffin, S. (1985). The Satisfaction with Life Scale. *Journal of Personality Assessment, 49,* 71–75.

Diener, E., Ng, W., Harter, J., and Arora, R. (2010). Wealth and happiness across the world: Material prosperity predicts life evaluation, whereas psychosocial prosperity predicts positive feeling. *Journal of Personality and Social Psychology, 99,* 52–61.

Diener, E., Horowitz, J., and Emmons, R. A. (1985). Happiness of the very wealthy. *Social Indicators Research, 16,* 263–274.

Diener, E., and Larsen, R. J. (1984). Temporal stability and cross-situational consistency of affective, behavioral, and cognitive responses. *Journal of Personality and Social Psychology, 47,* 871–883.

Diener, E., Larsen, R. J., and Emmons, R. A. (1984). Person X situation interactions: Choice of situations and congruence response models. *Journal of Personality and Social Psychology, 47,* 580–592.

Diener, E., Larsen, R. J., Levine, S., and Emmons, R. A. (1985). Intensity and frequency: Dimensions underlying positive and negative affect. *Journal of Personality and Social Psychology, 48,* 1253–1265.

Diener, E., Lucas, R. E., and Larsen, R. J. (2003). Measuring positive emotions. In C. R. Snyder, and S. J. Lopez (Eds.), *The handbook of positive psychological assessment* (pp. 201–218). Washington, DC: American Psychological Association.

Diener, E., Oishi, S., and Lucas, R. E. (2003). Personality, culture, and subjective well-being: Emotional and cognitive evaluations of life. *Annual Review of Psychology, 54,* 403–425.

Diener, E., Sandvik, E., Seidlitz, L., and Diener, M. (1993). The relationship between income and subjective well-being: Relative or absolute? *Social Indicators Research, 28,* 195–223.

Diener, E., and Seligman, M. E. P. (2002). Very happy people. *Psychological Science, 13,* 80–83.

Diener, E., Suh, E. M., Lucas, R. E., and Smith, H. L. (1999). Subjective well-being: Three decades of progress. *Psychological Bulletin, 125,* 276–302.

Digman, J. M., and Inouye, J. (1986). Further specification of the five robust factors of personality. *Journal of Personality and Social Psychology, 50,* 116–123.

Dijksterhuis, A., Bos, M. W., Nordgren, L. F., and van Baaren, R. B. (2006). On making the right choice: The deliberation-without-attention effect. *Science, 311,* 1005–1007.

Dijkstra, P., and Barelds, D. P. H. (2008). Self and partner personality and responses to relationship threat. *Journal of Research in Personality, 42,* 1500–1511.

Dill, K. E., Anderson, C. A., Anderson, K. B., and Deuser, W. E. (1999). Effects of aggressive personality on social expectations and social perceptions. *Journal of Research in Personality, 31,* 272–292.

Dixon, W. A., Mauzey, E. D., and Hall, C. R. (2003). Physical activity and exercise: Implications for counselors. *Journal of Counseling and Development, 81,* 502–505.

Dobbs, D. (2013). Restless genes. *National Geographic, 223*(1), 44–57.

Dodge, K. A., and Coie, J. D. (1987). Social-information-processing factors in reactive and proactive aggression in children's peer groups. *Journal of Personality and Social Psychology, 53,* 1146–1158.

Donahue, E. M., Robins, R. W., Roberts, B. W., and John, O. P. (1993). The divided self: concurrent and longitudinal effects of psychological adjustment and social roles on self-concept differentiation. *Journal of Personality and Social Psychology, 64*(5), 834–846.

Donhauser, P. W., Rösch, A. G., and Schultheiss, O. C. (2015). The implicit need for power predicts recognition speed for dynamic changes in facial expressions of emotion. *Motivation and Emotion, 39*(5), 714–721.

Donnellan, M. B., Kenny, D. A., Trzesniewski, K. H., Lucas, R. E., and Conger, R. D. (2012). Using trait-state models to evaluate the longitudinal consistency of global self-esteem from adolescence to adulthood. *Journal of Research in Personality, 46,* 634–645.

Donnellan, M. B., Larsen-Rife, D., and Conger, R. D. (2005). Personality, family history, and competence in early adult romantic relationships. *Journal of Personality and Social Psychology, 88,* 562–576.

Dorros, S. M., Hanzal, A., and Segrin, C. (2008). What does sex, personality, and relationship satisfaction have to do with it? Finding the best predictor of positive reactions to intimate and nonintimate touch from a relational partner. *Journal of Research in Personality, 42,* 1067–1073.

Douglas, K. S., and Guy, L. S. (2008). Antisocial personality disorder. In B. Cutler (Ed.), *Encyclopedia of psychology and law.* Thousand Oaks, CA: Sage.

Douglas, K. S., Lilienfeld, S. O., Skeem, J. L., Poythress, N. G., Edens, J. F., and Patrick, C. J. (2008). Relation of antisocial and psychopathic traits to suicide-related behavior among offenders. *Law and human behavior, 32*(6), 511.

Dreber, A., Apilcella, C. L., Eisenberg, D. T. A., Garcia, J. R., Zamore, R. S., Lum, J. K., and Campbell, B. (2009). The 7R polymorphism in the dopamine receptor D4 gene (DRD4) is associated with financial risk taking in men. *Evolution and Human Behavior, 30,* 85–92.

Drislane, L. E., Patrick, C. J., and Arsal, G. (2014). Clarifying the content coverage of differing psychopathy inventories through reference to the Triarchic Psychopathy Measure. *Psychological Assessment, 26*(2), 350–362.

Dubbert, Patricia M. (2002). Physical activity and exercise: Recent advances and current challenges. *Journal of Consulting and Clinical Psychology Special Issue: Behavioral medicine and clinical health psychology, 70,* 526–536.

Duckworth, A. L., Peterson, C., Matthews, M. D., and Kelly, D. R. (2007). Grit: Perseverance and passion for long-term goals. *Journal of Personality and Individual Differences, 92,* 1087–1101.

Dudley, N. M., Orvis, K. A., Lebiecki, J. E., and Cortina, J. M. (2006). A meta-analytic investigation of conscientiousness in the prediction of job performance: Examining the intercorrelations and the incremental validity of narrow traits. *Journal of Applied Psychology, 91,* 40–57.

Dunbar, R. I. M. (1993). Coevolution of neocortical size, group size, and language in humans. *Behavioral and Brain Sciences, 16,* 681–735.

Dunn, E. W., Aknin, L. B., and Norton, M. I. (2008). Spending money on others promotes happiness. *Science, 319,* 1687–1688.

Durand, G. (2017). Using the HEXACO model of personality to test the validity of the Durand Adaptive Psychopathic Traits Questionnaire. *Preprints 2017, 2017060065.* doi: 10.20944/preprints201706.0065.v1

Dutton, D. G., Saunders, K., Starzomski, A., and Bartholomew, K. (1994). Intimacy-anger and insecure attachment as precursors of abuse in intimate relationships. *Journal of Applied Social Psychology, 24,* 1367–1386.

Dweck, C. S. (1999). Caution—praise can be dangerous. *American Educator, 23,* 4–9.

Dweck, C. S. (2002). Beliefs that make smart people dumb. In R. J. Sternberg (Ed.), *Why smart people can be so stupid* (pp. 24–41). New Haven, CT: Yale University Press.

Dweck, C. S. (2006). *Mindset.* New York: Random House.

Dweck, C. S., Chiu, C., and Hong, Y. (1995). Implicit theories and their role in judgments and reactions: A world from two perspectives. *Psychological Inquiry, 6,* 267–285.

Dweck, C. S., and Master, A. (2009). Self-theories and motivation: Students' beliefs about intelligence. In K. R. Wenzel, A. Wigfield, K. R. Wenzel, A.

Wigfield (Eds.), *Handbook of motivation at school* (pp. 123–140). New York, NY, US: Routledge/Taylor & Francis Group.

Eagly, A. H. (1987). *Sex differences in social behavior: A social-role interpretation.* Hillsdale, NJ: Erlbaum.

Eagly, A. H. (1995). The science and politics of comparing women and men. *American Psychologist, 50,* 145–158.

Eagly, A., and Wood, W. (1999). A social role interpretation of sex differences in human mate preferences. *American Psychologist, 54,* 408–423.

Easterlin, R. A. (1974). Does economic growth improve the human lot: Some empirical evidence. In P. A. David and W. R. Levin (Eds.), *Nations and households in economic growth* (pp. 98–125). Palo Alto, CA: Stanford University Press.

Ebstein, R., Novick, O., Umansky, R., Priel, B., Osher, Y., Blaine, D., Bennett, E. R., Nemanov, L., Katz, M., and Belmaker, R. H. (1996). Dopamine D4 receptor (D4DR) exon III polymorphism associated with the human personality trait of novelty seeking. *Nature Genetics, 12,* 78–80.

Edwards, D. A., Wetzel, K., and Wyner, D. R. (2006). Intercollegiate soccer: Saliva cortisol and testosterone are elevated during competition, and testosterone is related to status and social connectedness with teammates. *Physiology and Behavior, 30,* 135–143.

Egan, S., and Stelmack, R. M. (2003). A personality profile of Mount Everest climbers. *Personality and Individual Differences, 34,* 1491–1494.

Eid, M., and Larsen, R. J. (2008). *The science of subjective well-being.* New York: Guilford Press.

Eisenberg, D. T. A., Campbell, B., Gray, P. B., and Soronson, M. D. (2008). Dopamine receptor genetic polymorphisms and body composition in undernourished pastoralists: An exploration of nutrition indices among nomadic and recently settled Ariaal men of northern Kenya. *BMC Evolutionary Biology, 8,* 173.

Eisenberg, N., Guthrie, I. K., Cumberland, A., Murphy, B. C., Shepard, S. A., Zhou, Q., and Carlo, G. (2002). Prosocial development in early adulthood: A longitudinal study. *Journal of Personality and Social Psychology, 82*(6), 993–1006.

Eisenberger, N. I. (2012). The pain of social disconnection: Examining the shared neural underpinnings of physical and social pain. *Nature Reviews Neuroscience, 13*(6), 421–434.

Ekman, P. (1973). Cross-cultural studies of facial expression. In P. Ekman (Ed.), *Darwin and facial expression: A century of research in review* (pp. 169–222). New York: Academic Press.

Ekman, P. (1992a). An argument for basic emotions. *Cognition and Emotion, 6,* 169–200.

Ekman, P. (1992b). Facial expressions of emotion: New findings, new questions. *Psychological Science, 3,* 34–38.

Ekman, P. (1999). In T. Dalgleish and M. Power (Eds.), *Handbook of Cognition and emotion.* Sussex, UK: John Wiley & Sons.

Ekman, P., Friesen, W. V., and Ellsworth, P. (1972). *Emotion in the human face: Guidelines for research and an integration of findings.* New York: Pergamon Press.

Ekman, P., Friesen, W. V., O'Sullivan, M., Chan, A., Diacoyanni-Tarlatzis, I., Heider, K., Krause, R., et al. (1987). Universals and cultural differences in the judgments of facial expressions of emotions. *Journal of Personality and Social Psychology, 53,* 712–717.

Elder, G. H., and Clipp, E. C. (1988). Wartime losses and social bonding: Influence across 40 years in men's lives. *Psychiatry, 51,* 117–198.

Elfenbein, H. H., Curhan, J. R., Eisenkraft, N., Shirako, A., and Baccaro, L. (2008). Are some negotiators better than others? Individual differences in bargaining outcomes. *Journal of Research in Personality, 42,* 1463–1475.

Elkins, I. J., King, S. M., McGue, M., and Iacono, W. G. (2006). Personality traits and the development of nicotine, alcohol, and illicit drug disorders: Prospective links from adolescence to young adulthood. *Journal of Abnormal Psychology, 115,* 26–39.

Elliot, A. J., and Dweck, C. S. (2005). *Handbook of competence and motivation.* New York: Guilford Press.

Elliot, A. J., and Reis, H. T. (2003). Attachment and exploration in adulthood. *Journal of Personality and Social Psychology, 85,* 317–331.

Ellis, B. J., Simpson, J. A., and Campbell, L. (2002). Trait-specific dependence in romantic relationships. *Journal of Personality, 70,* 611–660.

Ellis, L., and Bonin, S. L. (2003). Genetics and occupation-related preferences. Evidence from adoptive and nonadoptive families. *Personality and Individual Differences, 35,* 929–937.

Else-Quest, N. M., Hyde, J. S., Goldsmith, H. H., and Van Hulle, C. A. (2006). Gender differences in temperament: A meta-analysis. *Psychological Bulletin, 132,* 33–72.

Emmerich, A. I., and Rigotti, T. (2017). Reciprocal relations between work-related authenticity and intrinsic motivation, work ability and depressivity: A two-wave study. *Frontiers in Psychology, 8*, 307. doi:10.3389/fpsyg.2017.00307

Emmons, R. A. (1987). Narcissism: Theory and measurement. *Journal of Personality and Social Psychology, 52*, 11–17.

Emmons, R. A. (1989). The personal striving approach to personality. In L. Pervin et al. (Eds.), *Goal concepts in personality and social psychology* (pp. 87–126). Hillsdale, NJ: Erlbaum.

Endendijk, J. E., Groeneveld, M. G., Bakermans-Kranenburg, M. J., and Mesman, J. (2016). Gender-differentiated parenting revisited: Meta-analysis reveals very few differences in parental control of boys and girls. *PLoS ONE, 11*(7), e0159193. doi: 10.1371/journal.pone.0159193

Endler, N. S. (1977). The role of person by situation interactions in personality theory. In I. C. Uzgiris and F. Weismann (Eds.), *The structuring of experience.* New York: Plenum Press.

Endler, N. S., and Magnusson, D. (1976). Toward an interactional psychology of personality. *Psychological Bulletin, 83*, 956–974.

Engelhard, I. M., van den Hout, M. A., and Kindt, M. (2003). The relationship between neuroticism, pre-traumatic stress, and post-traumatic stress: A prospective study. *Personality and Individual Differences, 35*, 381–388.

Entwisle, D. R. (1972). To dispel fantasies about fantasy-based measures of achievement motivation. *Psychological Bulletin, 77*, 377–391.

Epifanio, M. S., Ingoglia, S., Alfano, P., Lo Coco, G., and La Grutta, S. (2018). Type D personality and alexithymia: Common characteristics of two different constructs. Implications for research and clinical practice. *Frontiers in Psychology, 9*, 106. doi:10.3389/fpsyg.2018.00106.

Epstein, S. (1979). The stability of behavior: I. On predicting most of the people much of the time. *Journal of Personality and Psychology, 37*, 1097–1126.

Epstein, S. (1980). The stability of behavior: II. Implications for psychological research. *American Psychologist, 35*, 790–806.

Epstein, S. (1983). Aggregation and beyond: Some basic issues on the prediction of behavior. *Journal of Personality, 51*, 360–392.

Erdelyi, M. H., and Goldberg, B. (1979). Let's not sweep repression under the rug: Toward a cognitive psychology of repression. In J. G. Kihlstrom and F. J. Evans (Eds.), *Functional disorders of memory* (pp. 355–402). Hillsdale, NJ: Erlbaum.

Erdheim, J., Wang, M., and Zickar, M. J. (2006). Linking the Big Five personality constructs to organizational commitment. *Personality and Individual Differences, 41*, 959–970.

Erikson, E. H. (1963). *Childhood and society* (2nd ed.). New York: Norton. (Original work published 1950.)

Erikson, E. H. (1968). *Identity: Youth and crisis.* New York: Norton.

Erikson, E. H. (1975). *Life history and the historical moment.* New York: Norton.

Eschleman, K. J., Bowling, N. A., and Alarcon, G. M. (2010). A meta-analytic examination of hardiness. *International Journal of Stress Management, 17*(4), 277–307.

Evans, C. A., Nelson, L. J., and Porter, C. L. (2009). Making sense of their world: Sensory reactivity and novelty awareness as aspects of temperament and correlates of social behaviours in early childhood. *Dissertation Abstracts International: Section B: The Sciences and Engineering, 69*(10-B), 6450.

Exline, J. J., Baumeister, R. F., Bushman, B. J., Campbell, W. K., and Finkel, E. J. (2004). Too proud to let go: Narcissistic entitlement as a barrier to forgiveness. *Journal of Personality and Social Psychology, 87*, 894–912.

Exline, R. V., Thiabaut, J., Hickey, C. B., and Gumpart, P. (1970). Visual interaction in relation to expectations, and situational preferences: Personality influences on the decision to participate in volunteer helping behaviors. *Journal of Personality, 67*, 470–503.

Eysenck, H. J. (1967). *The biological basis of personality.* Springfield, IL: Charles C Thomas.

Eysenck, H. J. (Ed.). (1981). *A model for personality.* Berlin: Springer-Verlag.

Eysenck, H. J. (1985). *The decline and fall of the Freudian empire.* London: Viking Press.

Eysenck, H. J. (1990). Biological dimensions of personality. In L. Pervin (Ed.), *Handbook of personality theory and research* (pp. 244–276). New York: Guilford Press.

Eysenck, H. J. (1991). Biological dimensions of personality. In L. A. Pervin (Ed.), *Handbook of personality* (pp. 244–276). New York: Guilford Press.

Eysenck, H. J. (2000). Personality as a risk factor in cancer and coronary heart disease. In D. T. Kenny and J. G. Carlson (Eds.), *Stress and health:*

Research and clinical applications (pp. 291–318). Amsterdam, Netherlands: Harwood Academic.

Eysenck, H. J., and Eysenck, M. W. (1985). *Personality and individual differences: A natural science approach.* New York: Plenum Press.

Eysenck, H. J., and Eysenck, S. B. (1967). On the unitary nature of extraversion. *Acta Psychologica, 26*, 383–390.

Eysenck, H. J., and Eysenck, S. B. G. (1972). *Manual of the Eysenck Personality Questionnaire.* San Diego: Educational and Industrial Testing Service.

Eysenck, H. J., and Eysenck, S. B. G. (1975). *Eysenck personality questionnaire manual.* San Diego: Educational and Industrial Testing Service.

Eysenck, S. B. G., Eysenck, H. J., and Barrett, P. (1985) A revised version of the Psychoticism scale. *Personality and Individual Differences, 6*, 21–29.

Fagot, B. I., and Leinbach, M. D. (1987). Socialization of sex roles within the family. In D. B. Carter (Ed.), *Current conceptions of sex roles and sex typing.* New York: Praeger.

Falk, C. F., and Heine, S. J. (2015). What is implicit self-esteem, and does it vary across cultures? *Personality and Social Psychology Review, 19*(2), 177–198.

Falk, C. F., Heine, S. J., Yuki, M., and Takemura, K. (2009). Why do Westerners self-enhance more than East Asians? *European Journal of Personality, 23*, 183–203.

Feingold, A. (1994). Gender differences in personality: A meta-analysis. *Psychological Bulletin, 116*, 429–456.

Fenichel, O. (1945). *The psychoanalytic theory of neurosis.* New York: Norton.

Fetchenhauer, D., Groothuis, T., and Pradel, J. (2010). Not only states but traits—Humans can identify permanent altruistic dispositions in 20 s. *Evolution and Human Behavior, 31*, 80–86.

Figueredo, A. J., de Baca, T. C., and Woodley, M. A. (2012). The measurement of Human Life History strategy. *Personality and Individual Differences, 55*, 251–255.

Figueredo, A. J., Sefcek, J. A., and Jones, D. N. (2006). The ideal romantic personality. *Personality and Individual Differences, 41*, 431–441.

Figueredo, A. J., Sefcek, J. S., Vasquez, G., Brumbach, B. H., King, J. E., and Jacobs, W. J. (2005a). Evolutionary personality psychology. In D. M. Buss (Ed.), *The handbook of evolutionary psychology* (pp. 851–877). New York: Wiley.

Figueredo, A. J., Vasquez, G., Brumbach, B. H., Sefcek, J. A., Kirsner, B. R., and Jacobs, W. J. (2005b). The K-factor: Individual differences in life history strategy. *Personality and Individual Differences, 39*, 1349–1360.

Fineman, S. (1977). The achievement motive and its measurement: Where are we now? *British Journal of Psychology, 68*, 1–22.

Finger, F. W. (1982). Circadian rhythms: Implications for psychology. *New Zealand Psychologist, 11*, 1–12.

Fink, B., Weege, B., Pham, M. N., and Shackelford, T. K. (2016). Handgrip strength and the Big Five personality factors in men and women. *Personality and Individual Differences, 88*, 175–177.

Fiske, A. P. (2002). Using individualism and collectivism to compare cultures: A critique of the validity and measurement of the constructs. *Psychological Bulletin, 128*, 78–88.

Fiske, A. P., Kitayama, S., Markus, H., and Nisbett, R. E. (1997). The cultural matrix of social psychology. In D. Gilbert, S. Fiske, and G. Lindzey (Eds.), *Handbook of social psychology* (3rd ed.). New York: McGraw-Hill.

Fiske, D. W. (1949). Consistency of the factorial structures of personality ratings from different sources. *Journal of Abnormal and Social Psychology, 44*, 329–344.

Fitzgerald, C. J., and Colarelli, S. M. (2009). Altruism and reproductive limitations. *Evolutionary Psychology, 7*(2), 234–252.

Flanagan, T. D., Iarocci, G., D'Arrisso, A., Mandour, T., Tootoosis, C., Robinson, S. W., & Burack, J.A. (2011). Reduced ratings of physical and relational aggression for youths with a strong cultural identity: evidence from the Naskapi people. *The Journal of Adolescent Health, 49*, 155–159.

Flanders, J. L., Leo, V., Paquette, D., Pihl, R. O., and Séguin, J. R. (2009). Rough-and-tumble play and the regulation of aggression: An observational study of father-child play dyads. *Aggressive Behavior, 35*, 285–295.

Fleeson, W. (2001). Toward a structure- and process-integrated view of personality: Traits as density distributions of states. *Journal of Personality and Social Psychology, 80*, 1011–1027.

Fleeson, W., and Gallagher, P. (2009). The implications of Big Five standing for the distribution of trait manifestation in behavior: Fifteen experience-sampling studies and a meta-analysis. *Journal of Personality and Social Psychology, 97*, 1097–1114.

Fleeson, W., and Noftle, E. E. (2012). Personality research. In M. R. Mehl and T. S. Conner (Eds.), *Handbook of research methods for studying daily life* (pp. 525–538). New York, NY: Guilford Press.

Fleeson, W., Malanos, A. B., and Achille, N. M. (2002). An intraindividual process approach to the relationship between extraversion and positive affect: Is acting extraverted as "good" as being extraverted? *Journal of Personality and Social Psychology, 83*(6), 1409–1422.

Fleeson, W., and Wilt, J. (2010), The Relevance of Big Five Trait Content in Behavior to Subjective Authenticity: Do High Levels of Within-Person Behavioral Variability Undermine or Enable Authenticity Achievement?. *Journal of Personality, 78,* 1353–1382.

Fletcher, G.J.O., Tither, J. M., O'Loughlin, C., Friesen, M., and Overall, N. (2004). Warm and homely or cold and beautiful? Sex differences in trading off traits in mate selection. *Personality and Social Psychology Bulletin, 30,* 659–672.

Flett, G. L., Blankstein, K. R., and Hewitt, P. L. (1991). Factor structure of the Short Index of Self-Actualization. *Journal of Social Behavior and Personality Special Issue: Handbook of self-actualization, 6,* 321–329.

Floderus-Myrhed, B., Pedersen, N., and Rasmuson, I. (1980). Assessment of heritability for personality based on a short form of the Eysenck Personality Inventory: A study of 12,898 twin pairs. *Behavior Genetics, 10,* 153–162.

Flynn, F. J. (2005). Having an open mind: The impact of openness to experience on interracial attitudes and impression formation. *Journal of Personality and Social Psychology, 88,* 816–826.

Flynn, J. R. (1984). The mean IQ of Americans: Massive gains 1932 to 1978. *Psychological Bulletin, 95,* 29–51.

Flynn, J. R. (2007). *What is intelligence? Beyond the Flynn effect.* New York: Cambridge University Press.

Flynn, J. R. (2012). *Are we getting smarter? Rising IQ in the twenty-first century.* New York, NY: Cambridge University Press.

Foa, U. G., and Foa, E. B. (1974). *Societal structures of the mind.* Springfield, IL: Charles C Thomas.

Fodor, E. M. (1985). The power motive, group conflict, and physiological arousal. *Journal of Personality and Social Psychology, 49,* 1408–1415.

Fodor, E. M. (2009). Power motivation. In M. R. Leary, R. H. Hoyle, M. R. Leary, R. H. Hoyle (Eds.), *Handbook of individual differences in social behavior* (pp. 426–440). New York, NY, US: Guilford Press.

Folkman, S., and Moskowitz, J. T. (2000). Stress, positive emotion, and coping. *Current Directions in Psychological Science, 9,* 115–118.

Folkman, S., Moskowitz, J. T., Ozer, E. M., and Park, C. L. (1997). Positive meaningful events and coping in the context of HIV/AIDS. In B. H. Gottlieb (Ed.), *Coping with chronic stress* (pp. 293–314). New York: Plenum Press.

Fordyce, M. W. (1978). *Prospectus: The self-descriptive inventory.* Unpublished manuscript, Edison Community College, Fort Myers, FL.

Fordyce, M. W. (1988). A review of results on the happiness measures: A 60-second index of happiness and mental health. *Social Indicators Research, 20,* 355–381.

Forest, A. L., and Wood, J. V. (2012). When social networking is not working: Individuals with low self-esteem recognize but do not reap the benefits of self-disclosure on Facebook. *Psychological Science, 23*(3), 295–302.

Foster, J. D., and Campbell, W. K. (2005). Narcissism and resistance to doubts about romantic partners. *Journal of Research in Personality, 39,* 550–557.

Fowles, D. C. (1980). The three arousal model: Implications of Gray's two-factor learning theory for heart rate, electrodermal activity, and psychopathy. *Psychophysiology, 17,* 87–104.

Fowles, D. C. (1987). Application of a behavioral theory of motivation to the concepts of anxiety and impulsivity. *Journal of Research in Personality, 21,* 417–435.

Fowles, D. C. (2006). Jeffrey Gray's contributions to theories of anxiety, personality, and psychopathology. In T. Canli (Ed.), *Biology of personality and individual differences* (pp. 7–34). New York: Guilford Press.

Fox, N. A., Bell, M. A., and Jones, N. A. (1992). Individual differences in response to stress and cerebral asymmetry. *Developmental Neuropsychology, 8,* 165–184.

Fox, N. A., and Calkins, S. D. (1993). Multiple-measure approaches to the study of infant emotion. In M. Lewis and J. M. Haviland (Eds.), *Handbook of emotions* (pp. 167–185). New York: Guilford Press.

Fox, N. A., and Davidson, R. J. (1986). Taste-elicited changes in facial signs of emotion and the asymmetry of brain electrical activity in human newborns. *Neuropsychologia, 24,* 417–422.

Fox, N. A., and Davidson, R. J. (1987). Electroencephalogram asymmetry in response to the approach of a stranger and maternal separation. *Developmental Psychology, 23,* 233–240.

Fox, N. A., and Polak, C. P. (2004). The role of sensory reactivity in understanding infant temperament. In R. DelCarmen-Wiggins and A.

Carter (Eds.), *Handbook of infant, toddler, and preschool mental health assessment* (pp. 105–119). New York, NY: Oxford University Press.

Fraley, R. C. (2002a). Attachment stability from infancy to adulthood: Meta-analysis and dynamic modeling of developmental mechanisms. *Personality and Social Psychology Review, 6,* 123–151.

Fraley, R. C. (2002b). Introduction to the special issue: The psychodynamics of adult attachments—Bridging the gap between disparate research traditions. *Attachment and Human Development Special Issue: The psychodynamics of adult attachments—Bridging the gap between disparate research traditions, 4,* 131–132.

Fraley, R. C. (2007). A connectionist approach to the organization and continuity of working models of attachment. *Journal of Personality, 75,* 1157–1180.

Fraley, R. C., Roisman, G. I., and Haltigan, J. D. (2013). The legacy of early experiences in development: Formalizing alternative models of how early experiences are carried forward over time. *Developmental Psychology, 49,* 109–126.

Fraley, R. C., and Tancredy, C. M. (2012). Twin and sibling attachment in a nationally representative sample. *Personality and Social Psychology Bulletin, 38,* 308–316.

Fraley, R. C., Vicary, A. M., Brumbaugh, C. C., and Roisman, G. I. (2011). Patterns of stability in adult attachment: An empirical test of two models of continuity and change. *Journal of Personality and Social Psychology, 101,* 974–992.

Fransella, F. (2003). *International handbook of personal construct psychology.* New York: Wiley.

Fransella, F., and Neimeyer, R. A. (2003). George Alexander Kelly: The man and his theory. In F. Fransella (Ed.), *International handbook of personal construct psychology* (pp. 21–31). New York: Wiley.

Fraser, S. (1995). *The bell curve wars: Race, intelligence, and the future of America.* New York: Basic Books.

Fredrickson, B. L. (1998). What good are positive emotions? *Review of General Psychology, 2,* 300–319.

Fredrickson, B. L. (2000). Cultivating positive emotions to optimize health and well-being. *Prevention and Treatment, 3*(1). doi: 10.1037/1522-3736.3.1.31a

Fredrickson, B. L., and Levenson, R. W. (1998). Positive emotions speed recovery from the cardiovascular sequelae of negative emotions. *Cognition and Emotion, 12,* 191–220.

Freeman, D. (1983). *Margaret Mead and Samoa: The making and unmaking of an anthropological myth.* Cambridge, MA: Harvard University Press.

Freshwater, S. M., and Golden, C. J. (2002). Personality changes associated with localized brain injury in elderly populations. *Journal of Clinical Geropsychology, 8,* 251–277.

Freud, A. (1936/1992). The ego and mechanisms of defense. In Vol. 2 of *The writings of Anna Freud.* New York: International Universities Press.

Freud, S. (1900/1913). *The interpretation of dreams.* New York: Macmillan.

Freud, S. (1915/1957). The unconscious. In J. Strachey (Ed. and Trans.), *The standard edition of the complete psychological works of Sigmund Freud* (vol. 14, pp. 166–204). London: Hogarth Press.

Freud, S. (1916/1947). *Leonardo da Vinci, a study in psychosexuality.* New York: Random House.

Frideres, J. (2008). Aboriginal identity in the Canadian context. *The Canadian Journal of Native Studies, XXVIII*(2), 313–342.

Friedman, H. S., Tucker, J. S., Schwartz, J. E., Tomlinson-Keasey, C., and Martin, L. R., et al. (1995). Psychosocial and behavioral predictors of longevity. *American Psychologist, 50,* 69–78.

Friedman, M., and Rosenman, R. H. (1974). *Type A behavior and your heart.* New York: Knopf.

Frijda, N. H. (1986). *The emotions.* New York: Cambridge University Press.

Frisell, T., Pawitan, Y., Langstrom, N., and Lichtenstein, P. (2012). Heritability, assortative mating and gender differences in violent crime: Results from a total population sample using twin, adoption, and sibling models. *Behavior Genetics, 42,* 3–18.

Frodi, A., Macauley, J., and Thome, P. R. (1977). Are women always less aggressive than men? A review of the experimental literature. *Psychological Bulletin, 84,* 634–660.

Fryberg, S. A., and Markus, H. R. (2003). On being American Indian: Current and possible selves. *Self and Identity, 2,* 325–344.

Funder, D. C. (2006). Towards a resolution of the personality triad: Persons, situations, and behaviors. *Journal of Research in Personality, 40,* 21–34.

Furnham, A. (1982). Psychoticism, social desirability, and situation selection. *Personality and Individual Differences, 3,* 43–51.

Furnham, A., Richards, S. C., and Paulhus, D. L. (2013). The Dark Triad of personality: A 10-year review. *Social and Personality Compass, 7,* 199–216.

Furr, R. M. (2009). Personality psychology as a truly behavioural science. *European Journal of Personality, 23,* 369–401.

Gable, S. L., and Nezlak, J. B. (1998). Level and instability of day-to-day psychological well-being and risk for depression. *Journal of Personality and Social Psychology, 74,* 129–138.

Gabriel, S., and Gardner, W. L. (1999). Are there "his" and "hers" types of interdependence? The implications of gender differences in collective versus relational interdependence for affect, behavior, and cognition. *Journal of Personality and Social Psychology, 77,* 642–655.

Gailliot, M. T., and Baumeister, R. F. (2007). Self-regulation and sexual restraint: Dispositionally and temporarily poor self-regulatory abilities contribute to failures at restraining sexual behavior. *Personality and Social Psychology Bulletin, 33,* 173–186.

Gale, A. (1983). Electroencephalographic studies of extraversion-introversion: A case study in the psychophysiology of individual differences. *Personality and Individual Differences, 4,* 371–380.

Gale, A. (1986). Extraversion-introversion and spontaneous rhythms of the brain: Retrospect and prospect. In J. Strelau, F. Farley, and A. Gale (Eds.), *The biological basis of personality and behavior* (vol. 2). Washington, DC: Hemisphere.

Gale, A. (1987). The psychophysiological context. In A. Gale and B. Christie (Eds.), *Psychophysiology and the electronic workplace* (pp. 17–32). Chichester, England, UK: Wiley.

Gale, C. R., Batty, G. D., and Deary, I. J. (2008). Locus of control at age 10 years and health outcomes and behaviors at age 30 years: The 1970 British cohort study. *Psychosomatic Medicine, 70,* 397–403.

Gale, C. R., Čukić, I., Batty, G. D., McIntosh, A. M., Weiss, A., and Deary, I. J. (2017). When is higher neuroticism protective against death? Findings from UK Biobank. *Psychological Science, 28*(9), 1345–1357.

Galic, Z., Jerneic, Z., and Kovacic, M. P. (2012). Do applicants fake their personality questionnaire responses and how successful are their attempts? A case of military pilot cadet selection. *International Journal of Selection and Assessment, 20,* 229–241.

Gallo, L. C., and Smith, T. W. (1999). Patterns of hostility and social support: Conceptualizing psychosocial risk factors as characteristics of the person and the environment. *Journal of Research in Personality, 33,* 281–310.

Gallup, A. C., O'Brien, D. T., White, D. D., and Wilson, D. S. (2009). Peer victimization in adolescence has different effects on the sexual behavior of male and female college students. *Personality and Individual Differences, 46,* 611–615.

Gallup, G. G. (1977a). Self-recognition in primates: A comparative approach to the bidirectional properties of consciousness. *American Psychologist, 32,* 329–338.

Gallup, G. G. (1977b). Absences of self-recognition in a monkey (*Macaca fascicularis*) following prolonged exposure to a mirror. *Developmental Psychobiology, 10,* 281–284.

Gallup, G. G., Jr., Anderson, J. R., and Shillito, D. J. (2002). The mirror test. In M. Bekoff, C. Allen, & G. M. Burghardt (Eds.), *The cognitive animal: Empirical and theoretical perspectives on animal cognition* (pp. 325–333). Cambridge, MA, US: MIT Press.

Gambrel, P. A., and Cianci, R. (2003). Maslow's hierarchy of needs: Does it apply in a collectivist culture? *Journal of Applied Management and Entrepreneurship, 8*(2), 143–161.

Gangestad, S. W., and Cousins, A. J. (2002). Adaptive design, female mate preferences, and shifts across the menstrual cycle. *Annual Review of Sex Research.*

Gangestad, S. W., and Simpson, J. A. (1990). Toward an evolutionary history of female sociosexual variation. *Journal of Personality, 58,* 69–96.

Gangestad, S. W., and Thornhill, R. (2008). Human oestrus. *Proceedings of the Royal Society of London, B, 275,* 991–1000.

Garbarino, E., Slonim, R., and Sydnor, J. (2011). Digit ratios (2D:4D) as predictors of risky decision making for both sexes. *Journal of Risk and Uncertainty, 42,* 1–26.

Garber, J., and Seligman, M. E. P. (1980). *Human helplessness: Theory and applications.* New York: Academic Press.

Gardner, H. (1983). *Frames of mind: The theory of multiple intelligences.* New York: Basic Books.

Gardner, H. (1999). *Intelligence reframed: Multiple intelligences for the 21st century.* New York: Basic Books.

Gardner, W. I., and Martinko, M. J. (1996). Using the Myers-Briggs Type Indicator to study managers: A literature review and research agenda. *Journal of Management, 22,* 45–83.

Gauguin, P. (1985). *Noa Noa: The Tahitian Journal.* Mineola, NY: Dover.

Geen, R. (1984). Preferred stimulation levels in introverts and extraverts: Effects on arousal and performance. *Journal of Personality and Social Psychology, 46,* 1303–1312.

Geer, J. H., and Head, S. (1990). The sexual response system. In J. T. Cacioppo and L. G. Tassinary (Eds.), *Principles of psychophysiology* (pp. 599–630). Cambridge, UK: Cambridge University Press.

Geis, F. L., and Moon, T. H. (1981). Machiavellianism and deception. *Journal of Personality and Social Psychology, 41,* 766–775.

Geist, C., and Ruppanner, L. (2018). Mission impossible? New housework theories for changing families. *Journal of Family Theory & Review, 10,* 242–262.

Gelade, G. A. (2008). IQ, cultural values, and the technological achievement of nations. *Intelligence, 36,* 711–718.

George, C., and Solomon, J. (1996). Representational models of relationships: Links between caregiving and attachment. *Infant Mental Health Journal, 17,* 198–216.

Gergen, K. J. (1992). Toward a postmodern psychology. In S. Kvale (Ed.), *Psychology and postmodernism* (pp. 17–30). London: Sage.

Gerson, M. W., and Fernandez, N. (2013). PATH: A program to build resilience and thriving in undergraduates. *Journal of Applied Social Psychology, 43*(11), 2169–2184.

Gewertz, D. (1981). A historical reconsideration of female dominance among the Chambri of Papua New Guinea. *American Ethnologist, 8,* 94–106.

Gibbs, W. (2003). The unseen genome: Gems among the junk. *Scientific American, 289,* 49.

Gigy, L. L. (1980). Self-concept in single women. *Psychology of Women Quarterly, 5,* 321–340.

Gil de Zúñiga, H., Diehl, T., Huber, B., and Liu, J. (2017). Personality traits and social media use in 20 countries: How personality relates to frequency of social media use, social media news use, and social media use for social interaction. *Cyberpsychology, Behavior, and Social Networking, 20,* 540–552.

Gilligan, C., Lyons, N. P., and Hammer, T. J. (1990). *Making connections: The relational worlds of adolescent girls at Emma Willard School.* Cambridge, Massachusetts: Harvard University Press.

Gilmour, J., and Williams, L. (2012). Type D personality is associated with maladaptive health-related behaviours. *Journal of Health Psychology, 17,* 471–478.

Giluk, T. L., and Postlethwaite, B. E. (2015). Big Five personality and academic dishonesty: A meta-analytic review. *Personality and Individual Differences, 72,* 59–67.

Gladden, P. R., Figueredo, A. J., and Jacobs, W. J. (2009). Life history strategy, psychopathic attitudes, personality, and general intelligences. *Personality and Individual Differences, 46,* 270–275.

Gladwell, M. (2008). *Outliers: The story of success.* New York: Little, Brown.

Glick, P., Wilkerson, M., and Cuffe, M. (2015). Masculine identity, ambivalent sexism, and attitudes toward gender subtypes: Favoring masculine men and feminine women. *Social Psychology, 46,* 210–217.

Gneezy, U., and Rustichini, A. (2004). Gender and competition at a young age. *American Economic Review Papers and Proceedings, 94,* 377–381.

Godley, J. (2018). Everyday discrimination in Canada: Prevalence and patterns. *Canadian Journal of Sociology, 43,* 111–142.

Gold, N., Colman, A. M., and Pulford, B. D. (2014). Cultural differences in responses to real-life and hypothetical trolley problems. *Judgment and Decision Making, 9,* 65–76.

Goldberg, J., Matte, N., MacMillan, M., and Hudspith, M. (2003). *VCHA/community survey: Gender transition and crossdressing services—final report.* Vancouver: Vancouver Coastal Health Authority.

Goldberg, L. R. (1981). Language and individual differences: The search for universals in personality lexicons. In L. Wheeler (Ed.), *Review of personality and social psychology* (vol. 2, pp. 141–165). Beverly Hills, CA: Sage.

Goldberg, L. R. (1990). An alternative "description of personality": The Big-Five factor structure. *Journal of Personality and Social Psychology, 59,* 1216–1229.

Goldberg, L. R., and Saucier, G. (1995). So what do you propose we use instead? A reply to Block. *Psychological Bulletin, 117,* 221–225.

Goldey, K. L., and van Anders, S. M. (2012). Sexual arousal and desire: Interrelations and responses to three modalities of sexual stimuli. *Journal of Sexual Medicine, 9,* 2315–2329.

Golding, S. L. (1978). Toward a more adequate theory of personality: Psychological organizing principles. In H. London (Ed.), *Personality: A new look at metatheories* (pp. 69–96). New York: Wiley.

Goldsmith, H. H., Aksan, N., and Essex, M. (2001). Temperament and socioemotional adjustment to kindergarten: A multi-informant perspective. In T. Wachs and G. A. Kohnstamm (Eds.), *Temperament in context* (pp. 103–138). Mahwah, NJ: Erlbaum.

Goldsmith, H. H., and Rothbart, M. K. (1991). Contemporary instruments for assessing early temperament by questionnaire and in the laboratory. In J. Strelau and A. Angleitner (Eds.), *Explorations in temperament.* New York: Plenum Press.

Goleman, D. (1995). *Emotional intelligence: Why it can matter more than IQ.* New York: Bantam.

Gomez, R., Cooper, A., and Gomez, A. (2000). Susceptibility to positive and negative mood states: A test of Eysenck's, Ray's, and Newman's theories. *Personality and Individual Differences, 29,* 351–365.

Goodman, G., and Kaufman, J. C. (2014). Gremlins in my head: Predicting stage fright in elite actors. *Empirical Studies of the Arts, 32*(2), 133–148.

Gordon, R. A. (1997). Everyday life as an intelligence test: Effects of intelligence and intelligence context. *Intelligence, 24,* 203–320.

Gore, W. L., and Widiger, T. A. (2013). The DSM-5 dimensional trait model and five-factor models of general personality. *Journal of Abnormal Psychology, 122*(3), 816.

Gosling, S. D., John, O. P., Craik, K. H., and Robins, R. W. (1998). Do people know how they behave? Self-reported act frequencies compared with on-line codings by observers. *Journal of Personality and Social Psychology, 74,* 1337–1349.

Gosling, S. D., Ko, S. J., Mannarelli, T., and Morris, M. E. (2002). A room with a cue: Personality judgments based on offices and bedrooms. *Journal of Personality and Social Psychology, 82,* 379–398.

Gosling, S. D., Kwan, V. S. Y., and John, O. P. (2003). A dog's got personality: A cross-species comparative approach to evaluating personality judgments. *Journal of Personality and Social Psychology, 85,* 1161–1169.

Gottman, J. (1994). *Why marriages succeed or fail.* New York: Simon and Schuster.

Gottman, J., Levenson, R., and Woodin, E. (2001). Facial expressions during marital conflict. *Journal of Family Communication, 1,* 37–57.

Gottman, J. M., and Silver, N. (1999). *The seven principles for making marriage work.* New York: Three Rivers Press.

Gough, H. G. (1957/1987). *California Psychological Inventory: Administrator's guide.* Palo Alto, CA: Consulting Psychologists Press.

Gough, H. G. (1980). *The Adjective Check List manual.* Palo Alto, CA: Consulting Psychologists Press.

Gough, H. G. (1996). *California psychological inventory manual* (3rd ed.). Palo Alto, CA: Consulting Psychologists Press.

Graham, E. K., Rutsohn, J. P., Turiano, N. A., Bendayan, R., Batterham, P. J., Gerstorf, D., . . . Herd, P., Hofer, S. M., and Mroczek, D. K. (2017). Personality predicts mortality risk: An integrative data analysis of 15 international longitudinal studies. *Journal of Research in Personality, 70,* 174–186.

Grano, N., Virtanen, M., Vahtera, J., Elovainio, M., and Kivimaki, M. (2004). Impulsivity as a predictor of smoking and alcohol consumption. *Personality and Individual Differences, 37,* 1693–1700.

Granqvist, P., Mikulincer, M., Gewirtz, V., and Shaver, P. R. (2012). Experimental findings on God as an attachment figure: Normative processes and moderating effects of internal working models. *Journal of Personality and Social Psychology, 103,* 804–818.

Grant, H., and Higgins, E. T. (2003). Optimism, promotion pride, and prevention pride as predictors of quality of life. *Personality and Social Psychology Bulletin, 29,* 1521–1532.

Grant, J. D., and Grant, J. (1996). Officer selection and the prevention of abuse of force. In W. Geller and H. Toch (Eds.), *Police violence: Understanding and controlling police abuse of force* (pp. 150–164). New Haven, CT: Yale University Press.

Gray, J. (1990). Brain systems that mediate both emotion and cognition. *Motivation and Emotion, 4,* 269–288.

Gray, J. A. (1972). *The psychology of fear and stress.* New York: McGraw-Hill.

Gray, J. A. (1975). *Elements of a two-process theory of learning.* Oxford, England: Academic Press.

Gray, J. A. (1982). *The neuropsychology of anxiety.* Oxford, England: Oxford University Press.

Gray, J. A. (1987a). *The psychology of fear and stress.* Cambridge, England: Cambridge University Press.

Gray, J. A. (1987b). Perspectives on anxiety and impulsivity: A commentary. *Journal of Research in Personality, 21,* 493–509.

Gray, J. A. (1991). The neuropsychology of temperament. In J. Strelau and A. Angleitner (Eds.), *Explorations in temperament: International perspectives on theory and measurement* (pp. 105–128). New York: Plenum Press.

Grayson, D. K. (1993). Differential mortality and the Donner Party disaster. *Evolutionary Anthropology, 2,* 151–159.

Graziano, W. G., (2003). Personality development: An introduction toward process approaches to long-term stability and change in persons. *Journal of Personality, 71,* 893–903.

Graziano, W. G., and Tobin, R. M. (2002). Agreeableness: Dimension of personality or social desirability artifact? *Journal of Personality, 70,* 695–727.

Greaves, L., Johnson, J., Qu, A., Okoli, C. T. C., Hemsing, N., and Barney, L. (2012). Gender identity, ethnic, identity, and smoking among First Nations adolescents. *Journal of Aboriginal Health, March 2012,* 37–46.

Green, J. (2009). The complexity of Indigenous identity formation and politics in Canada: Self-determination and decolonisation. *International Journal of Critical Indigenous Studies, 2*(2), 36–46.

Greenberg, D. M., Müllensiefen, D., Lamb, M. E., and Rentfrow, P. J. (2015). Personality predicts musical sophistication. *Journal of Research in Personality, 58,* 154–158.

Greenberg, J. R., and Mitchell, S. (1983). *Object relations in psychoanalytic theory.* Cambridge, MA: Harvard University Press.

Greenwald, A. G., and Farnham, S .D. (2000). Using the Implicit Association Test to measure self-esteem and self-concept. *Journal of Personality and Social Psychology, 79,* 1022–1038.

Gregg, A. P., and Sedikides, C. (2010). Narcissistic fragility: Rethinking its links to explicit and implicit self-esteem. *Self and Identity, 9,* 142–161.

Gregory, T., Nettelbeck, T., Howard, S., and Wilson, C. (2008). Inspection time: A biomarker for cognitive decline. *Intelligence, 36,* 664–671.

Greiling, H., and Buss, D. M. (2000). Women's sexual strategies: The hidden dimension of extra-pair mating. *Personality and Individual Differences, 28,* 929–963.

Griskevicius, V., Tybur, J. M., Gangestad, S. W., Perea, E. F., Shapiro, J. R., and Kenrick, D. T. (2009). Aggress to impress: Hostility as an evolved context-dependent strategy. *Journal of Personality and Social Psychology, 96,* 980–994.

Gross, J. J. (2002). Emotion regulation: Affective, cognitive, and social consequences. *Psychophysiology, 39,* 281–291.

Gross, J. J., and Levenson, R. W. (1993). Emotional suppression: Physiology, self-report, and expressive behavior. *Journal of Personality and Social Psychology, 64,* 970–986.

Gross, J. J., and Levenson, R. W. (1997). Hiding feelings: The acute effects of inhibiting positive and negative emotions. *Journal of Abnormal Psychology, 106,* 95–103.

Gross, J. J., Sutton, S. K., and Ketelaar, R. (1998). Relations between affect and personality: Support for the affect-level and affective reactivity views. *Personality and Social Psychology Bulletin, 24,* 279–288.

Grosskurth, P. (1991). *The secret ring: Freud's inner circle and the politics of psychoanalysis.* Reading, MA: Addison-Wesley.

Guay, F., Ratelle, C. F., and Chanal, J. (2008). Optimal learning in optimal contexts: The role of self-determination in education. *Canadian Psychology, 49,* 233–240.

Gunderson, E. A., Gripshover, S. J., Romero, C., Dweck, C. S., Goldin-Meadow, S., and Levine, S. C. (2013). Parent praise to 1- to 3-year-olds predicts children's motivational frameworks 5 years later. *Child Development, 84*(5), 1526–1541.

Gunderson, J. G., et al. (2011). Ten-year course of borderline personality disorder: psychopathology and function from the Collaborative Longitudinal Personality Disorders study. *Archives of General Psychiatry, 68*(8), 827–837.

Güngör, D., Bornstein, M. H., Leersnyder, J. D., Cote, L., Ceulemans, E., and Mesquita, B. (2013). Acculturation of personality: A three-culture study of Japanese, Japanese Americans, and European Americans. *Journal of Cross-Cultural Psychology, 44*(5), 701–718.

Gurven, M., von Rueden, C., Massenkoff, M., Kaplan, H., and Lero Vie, M. (2013). How universal is the Big Five? Testing the five-factor model of personality variation among forager-farmers in the Bolivian Amazon. *Journal of Personality and Social Psychology, 104*(2), 354–370.

Guzder, J., Paris, J., Zelkowitz, P., and Marchessault, K. (1996). Risk factors for borderline personality in children. *Journal of the American Academy of Child and Adolescent Psychiatry, 35,* 26–33.

Hacher, S. L., Nadeau, M. S., Walsh, L. K., and Reynolds, M. (1994). The teaching of empathy for high school and college students: Testing Rogerian methods with the Interpersonal Reactivity Index. *Adolescence, 29,* 961–974.

Hagerty, M. R. (1999). Testing Maslow's hierarchy of needs: National quality-of-life across time. *Social Indicators Research, 46,* 249–271.

Hair, E. C., and Graziano, W. G. (2003). Self-esteem, personality, and achievement in high school: A prospective longitudinal study in Texas. *Journal of Personality, 71,* 971–994.

Hald, G. M., and Hogh-Olesen, H. (2010). Receptivity to sexual invitations from strangers of the opposite gender. *Evolution and Human Behavior, 31,* 453–458.

Hall, C., Smith, K., and Chia, R. (2008). Cognitive and personality factors in relation to timely completion of a college degree. *College Student Journal, 42,* 1087–1098.

Hall, J. A. (1984). *Nonverbal sex differences.* Baltimore: Johns Hopkins University Press.

Hamer, D. (1997). The search for personality genes: Adventures of a molecular biologist. *Current Directions in Psychological Science, 6,* 111–114.

Hamer, D., and Copeland, P. (1994). *The science of desire: The search for the gay gene and the biology of behavior.* New York: Simon and Schuster.

Hamilton, L. D., Rellini, A. H., and Meston, C. M. (2008). Cortisol, sexual arousal, and affect in response to sexual stimuli. *Journal of Sexual Medicine, 5,* 2111–2118.

Hamilton, W. D. (1964). The evolution of social behavior. *Journal of Theoretical Biology, 7,* 1–52.

Hamm, A. O., Weike, A. I., Schupp, H. T., Treig, T., Dressel, A., and Kessler, C. (2003). Affective blindsight: Intact fear conditioning to a visual cue in a cortically blind patient. *Brain, 126*(2), 267–275.

Hammack, S. E., Cooper, M. A., and Lezak, K. R. (2012). Overlapping neurobiology of learned helplessness and conditioned defeat: Implications for PTSD and mood disorders. *Neuropharmacology, 62,* 565–575.

Hampshire, S. (1953). Dispositions. *Analysis, 14,* 5–11.

Hampson, S. E., Andrews, J. A., Barckley, M., and Peterson, M. (2007). Trait stability and continuity in childhood: Relating sociability and hostility to the five-factor model of personality. *Journal of Research in Personality, 41,* 507–523.

Hampson, S. E., Goldberg, L. R., Vogt, T. M., and Dubanoski, J. P. (2006). Forty years on: Teachers' assessments of children's personality traits predict self-reported health behaviors and outcomes at midlife. *Health Psychology, 25,* 57–64.

Hampson, S. E., Severson, H. H., Burns, W. J., Slovic, P., and Fisher, K. J. (2001). Risk perception, personality factors and alcohol use among adolescents. *Personality and Individual Differences, 30,* 167–181.

Hango, D., and Moyser, M. (2018). Insights on Canadian society: Harassment in Canadian workplaces. *Center for Gender, Diversity, and Inclusion Statistics. Statistics Canada, Catalogue no. 75-006-X.*

Hanley, A. W., Baker, A. K., and Garland, E. L. (2017). Self-interest may not be entirely in the interest of the self: Association between selflessness, dispositional mindfulness and psychological well-being. *Personality and Individual Differences, 117,* 166–171.

Hansen, C. H., Hansen, R. D., and Shantz, D. W. (1992). Repression at encoding: Discrete appraisals of emotional stimuli. *Journal of Personality and Social Psychology, 63,* 1026–1035.

Hansen, R. D., and Hansen, C. H. (1988). Repression of emotionally tagged memories: The architecture of less complex emotions. *Journal of Personality and Social Psychology, 55,* 811–818.

Harden, K. P., & Tucker-Drob, E. M. (2011). Individual differences in the development of sensation seeking and impulsivity during adolescence: Further evidence for a dual systems model. *Developmental Psychology, 47*(3), 739–746.

Hare, R. D., Hart, S. D., and Harpur, T. J. (1991). Psychopathy and the DSM-IV criteria for antisocial personality disorder. *Journal of Abnormal Psychology Special Issue: Diagnosis, dimensions, and DSM-IV: The science of classification, 100,* 391–398.

Hardison, H. G., and Neimeyer, R. A. (2012). Assessment of personal constructs: Features and functions of constructivist techniques. In P. Caputi, L. L. Viney, B. M. Walker, and N. Crittenden (Eds.), *Personal construct methodology* (pp. 3–51). Hoboken, NJ: John Wiley & Sons.

Harenski, C. L., Kim, S. H., and Hamann, S. (2009). Neuroticism and psychopathy predict brain activation during moral and nonmoral emotion regulation. *Cognitive, Affective and Behavioral Neuroscience, 9,* 1–15.

Hargrave, G. E., and Hiatt, D. (1989). Use of the California Psychological Inventory in law enforcement officer selection. *Journal of Personality Assessment, 53,* 267–277.

Haring, M. J., Stock, W. A., and Okun, M. A. (1984). A research synthesis of gender and social class as correlates of subjective well-being. *Human Relations, 37,* 645–657.

Harlow, H. F. (1958). The nature of love. *American Psychologist, 13,* 673–685.

Harlow, H. F., and Suomi, S. J. (1971). Production of depressive behaviors in young monkeys. *Journal of Autism and Childhood Schizophrenia, 1,* 246–255.

Harlow, H. F., and Zimmermann, R. R. (1959). Affectionate responses in the infant monkey. *Science, 130,* 421–432.

Harpending, H., and Cochran, G. (2002). In our genes. *Proceedings of the National Academy of Sciences of the United States of America, 99,* 10–12.

Harpur, T. J., and Hare, R. D. (1994). Assessment of psychopathy as a function of age. *Journal of Abnormal Psychology, 103,* 604–609.

Harrell, W. A., and Hartnagel, T. (1976). The impact of Machiavellianism and the trustfulness of the victim on laboratory theft. *Sociometry, 39,* 157–165.

Harris, C. R. (2002). Sexual and romantic jealousy in heterosexual and homosexual adults. *Psychological Science, 13*(1), 7–12.

Harris, C. R. (2003). A review of sex differences in sexual jealousy, including self-report data, psychophysiological responses, interpersonal violence, and morbid jealousy. *Personality and Social Psychology Review, 7*(2), 102–128.

Harris, J. R. (2007). *No two alike: Human nature and human individuality.* New York: Norton.

Hart, C. M., Ritchie, T. D., Hepper, E. G., and Gebauer, J. E. (2015). The Balanced Inventory of Desirable Responding short form (BIDR-16). *SAGE Open.* doi:10.1177/2158244015621113.

Hart, J., and Graether, M. (2018). Something's going on here: Psychological predictors of belief in conspiracy theories. *Journal of Individual Differences, 39*(4), 229–237.

Harter, S. (1993). Causes and consequences of low self-esteem in children and adolescents. In R. Baumeister (Ed.), *Self- esteem: The puzzle of low self-regard* (pp. 87–111). New York: Plenum Press.

Hartshorne, H., and May, M. A. (1928). *Studies in the nature of character: Vol. 1. Studies in deceit.* New York: Macmillan.

Haslam, C., and Montrose, V. T. (2015). Should have known better: The impact of mating experience and the desire for marriage upon attraction to the narcissistic personality. *Personality and Individual Differences, 82,* 188–192.

Hassabis, D., Spreng, R. N., Rusu, A. A., Robbins, C. A., Mar, R. A., and Schacter, D. L. (2014). Imagine all the people: How the brain creates and uses personality models to predict behavior. *Cerebral Cortex, 24,* 1979–1987.

Hawes, S. W., Perlman, S. B., Byrd, A. L., Raine, A., Loeber, R., and Pardini, D. A. (2016). Chronic anger as a precursor to adult antisocial personality features: The moderating influence of cognitive control. *Journal of Abnormal Psychology, 125*(1), 64–74.

Hazan, C., and Shaver, P. R. (1987). Romantic love conceptualized as an attachment process. *Journal of Personality and Social Psychology, 52,* 511–524.

Hazan, C., and Shaver, P. R. (1994). Attachment as an organizational framework for research on close relationships. *Psychological Inquiry, 5,* 1–22.

Heath, A. C., Bucholz, K. K., Dinwiddie, S. H., Madden, P. A. F., and Slutske, W. W. (1994). *Pathways from the genotype to alcoholism risk in women.* Paper presented at the annual meeting of the Behavioral Genetics Association, Barcelona, Spain.

Heaven, P. C. L., Crocker, D., Edwards, B., Preston, N., Ward, R., and Woodbridge, N. (2003). Personality and sex. *Personality and Individual Differences, 35,* 411–419.

Hebb, D. O. (1955). Drives and the CNS (conceptual nervous system). *Psychological Review, 62,* 243–259.

Heckhausen, H. (1982). The development of achievement motivation. In W. W. Hartup (Ed.), *Review of child development research* (vol. 6, pp. 600–668). Chicago: University of Chicago Press.

Heidemeier, H., and Göritz, A. S. (2013). Perceived control in low-control circumstances: Control beliefs predict a greater decrease in life satisfaction following job loss. *Journal of Research in Personality, 47,* 52–56.

Heine, S. J., and Lehman, D. R. (1995). Cultural variation in unrealistic optimism: Does the West feel more invulnerable than the East? *Journal of Personality and Social Psychology, 68,* 595–607.

Helson, R., & Picano, J. (1990). Is the traditional role bad for women? *Journal of Personality and Social Psychology, 59*(2), 311–320. doi: 10.1037/0022-3514.59.2.311

Helson, R., and Stewart, A. (1994). Personality change in adulthood. In T. F. Heatherton and J. L. Weinberger (Eds.), *Can personality change?* Washington, DC: American Psychological Association.

Henderson, L., and Zimbardo, P. (2000). *The Henderson Zimbardo Shyness Questionnaire: A new scale to measure chronic shyness.* Berkeley, CA: The Shyness Institute.

Henderson, L., and Zimbardo, P. (2001a). Shyness as a clinical condition: The Stanford model. In W. R. Crozier and L. E. Alden (Eds.), *International handbook of social anxiety: Concepts, research and interventions relating to the self and shyness* (pp. 431–447). New York: Wiley.

Henderson, L., and Zimbardo, P. (2001b). Shyness, social anxiety, and social phobia. In S. G. Hofmann and P. M. DiBartolo (Eds.), *From social anxiety to social phobia: Multiple perspectives* (pp. 46–85). Needham Heights, MA: Allyn and Bacon.

Henderson, N. D. (1982). Human behavioral genetics. *Annual Review of Psychology, 33,* 403–440.

Hendriks, A. A. J., Perugini, M., Angleitner, A., Ostendorf, F., Johnson, J. A., De Fruyt, F., Hrebickova, M., et al. (2003). The five-factor personality inventory: Cross-cultural generalizability across 13 countries. *European Journal of Personality, 17,* 347–373.

Hennig, K. H., and Walker, L. J. (2008). The darker side of accommodating others: Examining the interpersonal structure of maladaptive constructs. *Journal of Research in Personality, 42,* 2–21.

Henrich, J. (2015). *The secret of our success: How culture is driving human evolution, domesticating our species, and making us smarter.* Princeton, NJ: Princeton University Press.

Henrich, J., Heine, S. J., and Norenzayan, A. (2010). The weirdest people in the world? *Behavioral and Brain Sciences, 33,* 61–135.

Herbert, T. B., and Cohen, S. (1993). Depression and immunity: A meta-analytic review. *Psychological Bulletin, 113,* 472–486.

Herrington, J. D., Koven, N. S., Miller, G. A., and Heller, W. (2006). Mapping the neural correlates of dimensions of personality, emotion, and motivation. In T. Canli (Ed.), *Biology of personality and individual differences* (pp. 133–156). New York: Guilford Press.

Herrnstein, R., and Murray, C. (1994). *The bell curve: Intelligence and class structure in American life.* New York: Free Press.

Herzog, A. R., Franks, X., Markus, H. R., and Holmberg, X. (1995). *The American self in its sociocultural variations.* Unpublished manuscript.

Herzog, T. R., Williams, D. M., and Weintraub, D. J. (1985). Meanwhile, back at personality ranch: The augmenters and reducers ride again. *Journal of Personality and Social Psychology, 48,* 1342–1352.

Hess, N., Helfrecht, C., Hagen, E., Sell, A., and Hewlett, B. (2010). Interpersonal aggression among Aka hunter-gatherers of the Central African Republic: Assessing the effects of sex, strength, and anger. *Human Nature, 21,* 330–354.

Hibbard, S., Porcerelli, J., Kamoo, R., Schwartz, M., Abell, S. (2010). Defense and object relational maturity on Thematic Apperception Test Scales indicate levels of personality organization. *Journal of Personality Assessment, 92,* 241–253.

Higgins, E. T. (1987). Self-discrepancy: A theory relating self to affect. *Psychological Review, 94,* 319–340.

Higgins, E. T. (1996). The "self digest": Self-knowledge serving self-regulatory functions. *Journal of Personality and Social Psychology, 71,* 1062–1083.

Higgins, E. T. (1997). Beyond pleasure and pain. *American Psychologist, 52,* 1280–1300.

Higgins, E. T. (1999). Persons and situations: Unique explanatory principles or variability in general principles? In D. Cervone and Y. Shoda (Eds.), *The coherence of personality* (pp. 61–93). New York: Guilford Press.

Higgins, E. T. (2012). Regulatory focus theory. In P. A. M. Van Lange, A. W. Kruglanski, and T. E. Higgins (Eds.), *Handbook of theories of social psychology* (pp. 483–504). Thousand Oaks, CA: Sage.

Higgins, E. T., Friedman, R. S., Harlow, R. E., Idson, L. C., Ayduk, O. N., and Taylor, A. (2001). Achievement orientations from subjective histories of success: Promotion pride versus prevention pride. *European Journal of Social Psychology, 31,* 3–23.

Higgins, E. T., Shah, J., and Friedman, R. (1997). Emotional responses to goal attainment: Strength of regulatory focus as moderator. *Journal of Personality and Social Psychology, 72,* 515–525.

Hill, P. L., and Roberts, B. W. (2011). The role of adherence in the relationship between conscientiousness and perceived health. *Health Psychology, 30,* 797–804.

Hill, P. L., Turiano, N., Hurd, M. D., Mroczek, D. K., and Roberts, B. W. (2011). Conscientiousness and longevity: An examination of possible mediators. *Health Psychology, 30,* 536–541.

Hiroto, D. S., and Seligman, M. E. P. (1975). Generality of learned helplessness in man. *Journal of Personality and Social Psychology, 102,* 311–327.

Hirschfeld, L. A. (1995). Anthropology, psychology, and the meaning of social causality. In D. Sperber, D. Premack, and A. J. Premack (Eds.), *Causal cognition: A multidisciplinary debate* (pp. 313–344). Oxford, England: Clarendon Press.

Hirsh, J. B. (2015). Extraverted populations have lower savings rates. *Personality and Individual Differences, 81,* 162–168.

Hirsh, J. B., and Peterson, J. B. (2008). Predicting creativity and academic success with a "fake-proof" measure of the Big Five. *Journal of Research in Personality, 42,* 1323–1333.

Hirsh, J. B., and Peterson, J. B. (2009). Extraversion, neuroticism, and the prisoner's dilemma. *Personality and Individual Differences, 46,* 254–256.

Hirsh, J. B., and Peterson, J. B. (2009). Extraversion, neuroticism, and the prisoner's dilemma. *Personality and Individual Differences, 46*(2), 254–256.

Hirsh, S. K., and Kummerow, J. M. (1990). *Introduction to type in organizations* (2nd ed.). Palo Alto, CA: Consulting Psychologists Press.

Hodson, G., Book, A., Visser, B.A., Volk, A.A., Ashton, M.C., and Lee, K. (2018). Is the Dark Triad common factor distinct from low Honesty-Humility? *Journal of Research in Personality, 73,* 123–129.

Hofer, J., Bond, M. H., and Li, M. (2010). The implicit power motive and sociosexuality in men and women: Pancultural effects of responsibility. *Journal of Personality and Social Psychology, 99,* 380–394.

Hofstede, G. (2001). *Culture's consequences: Comparing values, behaviors, institutions, and organizations across nations.* Thousand Oaks, CA: Sage Publications.

Hoffman, R. M., & Borders, L. D. (2001). Twenty-five years after the Bem Sex-Role Inventory: A reassessment and new issues regarding classification variability. *Measurement and Evaluation in Counseling and Development, 34,* 39–55.

Hoffman, W., Baumeister, R. F., Forster, G., and Vohs, K. E. (2012). Everyday temptations: An experience sampling study of desire, conflict, and self-control. *Journal of Personality and Social Psychology, 102,* 1318–1335.

Hoffmann, W., Vohs, K. D., and Baumeister, R. F. (2012). What people desire, feel conflicted about, and try to resist in everyday life. *Psychological Science, 23,* 582–588.

Hogan, J., and Holland, B. (2003). Using theory to evaluate personality and job performance relations. *Journal of Applied Psychology, 88,* 100–112.

Hogan, R. (1983). A socioanalytic theory of personality. In M. Page and R. Dienstbier (Eds.), *Nebraska Symposium on Motivation, 1982* (pp. 55–89). Lincoln: University of Nebraska Press.

Hogan, R. (2005). In defense of personality measurement: New wine for old whiners. *Human Performance, 18,* 331–341.

Hogan, R., and Hogan, J. (2002). The Hogan personality inventory. In B. de Raad and M. Perugini (Eds.), *Big Five assessment* (pp. 329–346). Ashland, OH: Hogrefe & Huber Publishers.

Hokanson, J. E., Burgess, M., and Cohen, M. F. (1963). Effect of displaced aggression on systolic blood pressure. *Journal of Abnormal and Social Psychology, 67,* 214–218.

Holland, A. S., Fraley, R. C., and Roisman, G. I. (2012). Attachment styles in dating couples: Predicting relationship functioning over time. *Personal Relationships, 19,* 234–246.

Hollmann, E. (2001). *Paul Gaugin: Images from the South Seas.* New York: Prestel USA.

Holmes, D. (1990). The evidence for repression: An examination of sixty years of research. In J. Singer (Ed.), *Repression and dissociation: Implications for personality, theory, psychopathology, and health* (pp. 85–102). Chicago: University of Chicago Press.

Holmes, T. H., and Rahe, R. H. (1967). The Social Readjustment Rating Scale. *Journal of Psychosomatic Research, 11,* 213–218.

Holroyd, K. A., and Coyne, J. (1987). Personality and health in the 1980s: Psychosomatic medicine revisited? *Journal of Personality, 55,* 359–375.

Holtzman, N. S., and Strube, M. J. (2010). Narcissism and attractiveness. *Journal of Research in Personality, 44,* 133–136.

Honekopp, J. (2011). Relationships between digit ratio 2D:4D and self-reported aggression and risk taking in an online study. *Personality and Individual Differences, 51,* 77–80.

Hong, R. Y., and Paunonen, S. V. (2009). Personality traits and health-risk behaviours in University students. *European Journal of Personality, 23,* 675–696.

Honomichl, R. D., and Donnellan, M. B. (2012). Dimensions of temperament in preschoolers predict risk taking and externalizing behaviors in adolescents. *Social Psychological and Personality Science, 3,* 14–22.

Hooper, J. L., White, V. M., Macaskill, G. T., Hill, D. J., and Clifford, C. A. (1992). Alcohol use, smoking habits and the Junior Eysenck Personality Questionnaire in adolescent Australian twins. *Acta Genetica Med. Gemellol. 41,* 311–324.

Hoover, E. (2013). Colleges seek "noncognitive" gauges of applicants. *The Chronicle of Higher Education, 56,* 1.

Hopf, S. M. (2010). *Risk and resilience in children coping with parental divorce.* Dartmouth Undergraduate Journal of Science.

Hopkins, A. B. (1996). *So ordered: Making partner the hard way.* Amherst: University of Massachusetts Press.

Hopwood, C. J., Ansell, E .B., Pincus, A. L., Wright, A. G. C., Lukowitsky, M. R., and Roche, M. J. (2011). The circumplex model of interpersonal sensitivities. *Journal of Personality, 79,* 707–739.

Horita, Y., and Takezawa, M. (2018). Cultural differences in strength of conformity explained through pathogen stress: A statistical test using Hierarchical Bayesian Estimation. *Frontiers in Psychology, 9,* 1921. doi:10.3389/fpsyg.2018.01921

Hormuth, S. E. (1986). The sampling of experiences in situ. *Journal of Personality, 54,* 262–293.

Horne, J. A., and Ostberg, O. (1976). A self-assessment questionnaire to determine morningness–eveningness in human circadian rhythms. *International Journal of Chronobiology, 4*(2), 97–110.

Horne, J. A., and Ostberg, O. (1977). Individual differences in human circadian rhythms. *Biological Psychology, 5,* 179–190.

Horne, R. M., Johnson, M. D., Galambos, N. L. and Krahn, H. J. (2018). Time, money, or gender? Predictors of the division of household labour across life stages. *Sex Roles, 78,* 731–743.

Horney, K. (1937). *The neurotic personality of our time.* New York: Norton.

Horney, K. (1939). *New ways in psychoanalysis.* New York: Norton.

Horney, K. (1945). *Our inner conflicts: A constructive theory of neurosis.* New York: Norton.

Horney, K. (1950). *Neurosis and human growth: The struggle toward self-realization.* New York: Norton.

Horsburgh, V. A., Schermer, J. A., Veselka, L., and Vernon, P. A. (2009). A behavioural genetic study of mental toughness and personality. *Personality and Individual Differences, 46,* 100–105.

Horton, R. S., and Sedikides, C. (2009). Narcissistic responding to ego threat: When the status of the evaluator matters. *Journal of Personality, 77,* 1493–1526.

Hotard, S. R., McFatter, R. M., McWhirter, R. M., and Stegall, M. E. (1989). Interactive effects of extraversion, neuroticism, and social relationships on subjective well-being. *Journal of Personality and Social Psychology, 57,* 321–331.

Howard, A., and Bray, D. (1988). *Managerial lives in transition: Advancing age and changing times.* New York: Guilford Press.

Hoyenga, K. B., and Hoyenga, K. T. (1993). *Gender-related differences: Origins and outcomes.* Boston: Allyn and Bacon.

Hsu, F. K. L. (1985). The self in cross-cultural perspective. In J. J. Marsella, G. De Vos, and F. L. K. Hsu (Eds.), *Culture and self* (pp. 24–55). London: Tavistock.

Hua, H., and Epley, C. H. (2012). Putting the "personal" into personal construct theory. *Journal of Constructivist Psychology, 25,* 269–273.

Hudson, N. W., and Fraley, R. C. (2015). Volitional personality trait change: Can people choose to change their personality traits? *Journal of Personality and Social Psychology, 109*(3), 490–507.

Hudson, N. W., and Fraley, R. C. (2017). Volitional personality change. In *Personality development across the lifespan* (pp. 555–571). Elsevier Inc.

Hudziak, J. J., van Beijsterveldt, C. E. M., Bartels, M., Rietveld, J. J. J., Rettew, D. C., Derks, E. M., and Boomsma, D. I. (2003). Individual differences in aggression: Genetic analyses by age, gender, and informant in 3-, 7-, and 10-year-old Dutch twins. *Behavior Genetics, 33,* 575–589.

Humbad, M. N., Donnellan, M. B., Iacono, W. G., McGue, M., and Burt, S. A. (2010). Is spousal similarity for personality a matter of convergence or selection? *Personality and Individual Differences, 49,* 827–830.

Hunsley, J., Lee, C. M., and Wood, J. M. (2003). Controversial and questionable assessment techniques. In S. O. Lilienfeld, S. J. Lynn, and J. M. Lohr (Eds.), *Science and pseudoscience in clinical psychology* (pp. 39–76). New York: Guilford Press.

Hunt, E., and Wittmann, W. (2008). National intelligence and national prosperity. *Intelligence, 36,* 1–9.

Huprich, S. K. (2008). TAT oral dependency scale. In S. R. Jenkins (Ed.), *A handbook of clinical scoring systems for thematic apperceptive techniques* (pp. 385–398). Mahwah, NJ: Erlbaum.

Huselid, R. F., and Cooper, M. L. (1994). Gender roles as mediators of sex differences in expressions of pathology. *Journal of Abnormal Psychology, 103,* 595–603.

Hyde, J. S. (1986). Gender differences in aggression. In J. S. Hyde and M. C. Linn (Eds.), *The psychology of gender: Advances through meta-analysis.* Baltimore: Johns Hopkins University Press.

Hyde, J. S. (2005). The gender similarities hypothesis. *American Psychologist, 60,* 581–592.

Hyde, J. S. (2014). Gender similarities and differences. *Annual Review of Psychology, 65,* 373–398.

Hyde, J. S., and Plant, E. A. (1995). Magnitude of psychological gender differences: Another side to the story. *American Psychologist, 50,* 159–161.

Hyman, I. E., and Loftus, E. F. (2002). False childhood memories and eyewitness memory errors. In M. L. Eisen (Ed.), *Memory and suggestibility in the forensic interview* (pp. 63–84). Mahwah, NJ: Erlbaum.

Ickes, W., Snyder, M., and Garcia, S. (1997). Personality influences on the choice of situations. In R. Hogan, J. A. Johnson, and S. Briggs (Eds.), *Handbook of personality psychology* (pp. 165–195). San Diego: Academic Press.

Indigenous and Northern Affairs Canada. (2010). Highlights from the Report of the Royal Commission on Aboriginal Peoples. Retrieved March 6, 2019, from https://www.aadnc-aandc.gc.ca/eng/1100100014597/1100100014637.

Inglehart, R. (1990). *Culture shift in advanced industrial society.* Princeton, NJ: Princeton University Press.

Insel, P., and Roth, W. (1985). *Core concepts in health* (4th ed.). Palo Alto, CA: Mayfield.

Ip, G. W. M., and Bond, M. H. (1995). Culture, values, and the spontaneous self-concept. *Asian Journal of Psychology, 1,* 30–36.

Irwin, M. (2002). Psychoneuroimmunology of depression: Clinical implications. *Brain, Behavior, and Immunity, 16,* 1–16.

Ishihara, K., Miyake, S., Miyasita, A., and Miyata, Y. (1992). Morningness-eveningness preference and sleep habits in Japanese office workers of different ages. *Chronobiologia, 19,* 9–16.

Ishihara, K., Saitoh, T., and Miyata, Y. (1983). Short-term adjustment of oral temperature of 8-hour advanced-shift. *Japanese Psychological Research, 25,* 228–232.

Ishikawa, S. S., Raine, A., Lencz, T., Bihrle, S., and LaCasse, L. (2001). Increased height and bulk in antisocial personality disorder and its subtypes. *Psychiatry Research, 105,* 211–219.

Izard, C. E. (1960). Personality similarity, positive affect and interpersonal attraction. *Journal of Abnormal and Social Psychology, 61,* 484–485.

Izard, C. E. (1977). *Human emotions.* New York: Plenum Press.

Jackson, D. N. (1967). *Personality research form manual.* Goshen, NY: Research Psychologists Press.

Jackson, D. N., and Messick, S. (1967). *Problems in human assessment.* New York, McGraw-Hill.

Jackson, D. N., Paunonen, S. V., and Tremblay, P. F. (2000). *Six Factor personality questionnaire manual.* Port Huron, MI: Sigma Assessment Systems.

Jackson, J. J., Bogg, T., Walton, K. E., Wood, D., Harms, P. D., Lodi-Smith, J., Edmonds, G. W., and Roberts, B. W. (2009). Not all conscientiousness scales change alike: A multimethod, multisample study of age differences in the facets of conscientiousness. *Journal of Personality and Social Psychology, 96,* 446–459.

Jackson, J. J., Hill, P. L., Payne, B. R., Roberts, B. W., and Stine-Morrow, E. A. (2012). Can an old dog learn (and want to experience) new tricks? Cognitive training increases openness to experience in older adults. *Psychology and Aging, 27*(2), 286–292.

Jackson, J. J., Wood, D., Bogg, T., Walton, K. E., Harms, P. D., and Roberts, B. W. (2010). What do conscientious people do? Development and validation of the Behavioral Indicators of Conscientiousness (BIC). *Journal of Research in Personality, 44,* 501–511.

Jackson, S. A., and Marsh, H. (1996). Development and validation of a scale to measure optimal experience: The Flow State Scale. *Journal of Sport & Exercise Psychology, 18*(1), 17–35.

Jackson, T., Towson, S., and Narduzzi, K. (1997). Predictors of shyness: A test of variables associated with self-presentational models. *Social Behavior and Personality, 25*(2), 149–154.

Jacoby, R., and Glauberman, N. (1995). *The bell curve debate: History, documents, opinions.* New York: Random House.

Jadva, V., Hines, M., and Golombok, S. (2010). Infants' preferences for toys, colors, and shapes: Sex differences and similarities. *Archives of Sexual Behavior, 39,* 1261–1273.

Jakobwitz, S., and Egan, V. (2006). The dark triad and normal personality traits. *Personality and Individual Differences, 40,* 331–339.

James, W. (1884). What is an emotion? *Mind, 9,* 188–205.

James, W. (1891). *The principles of psychology (Vol. 1).* London: Macmillan.

James, W. (1999). *The varieties of religious experience.* New York: The Modern Library. (Original work published 1902).

Jang, K. L., Dick, D. M., Wolf, H., Livesley, W. J., and Paris, J. (2005). Psychosocial adversity and emotional instability: An application of gene–

environment interaction models. *European Journal of Personality, 19,* 359–372.

Jang, K. L., Livesley, W. J., Angleitner, A., Riemann, R., and Vernon, P. A. (2002). Genetic and environmental influences on the covariance of facets defining the domains of the five-factor model of personality. *Personality and Individual Differences, 33,* 83–101.

Jehn, A. (2014). The happiness and income correlation in Canada. *Studies by Undergraduate Researchers at Guelph, 7*(2), 13–17.

Jenkins, S. R. (1994). Need for power and women's careers over 14 years: Structural power, job satisfaction, and motive change. *Journal of Personality and Social Psychology, 66,* 155–165.

Jenkins, C. D., Zyzanski, S. J., and Rosenman, R. H. (1976). Risk of new myocardial infarction in middle age men with manifest coronary heart disease. *Circulation, 53,* 342–347.

Jensen, A. R. (2011). The theory of intelligence and its measurement. *Intelligence, 39,* 171–177.

Jensen-Campbell, L. A., Adams, R., Perry, D. G., Workman, K. A., Furdella, J. Q., and Egan, S. K. (2002). Agreeableness, extraversion, and peer relations in early adolescence: Winning friends and deflecting aggression. *Journal of Research in Personality, 36,* 224–251.

Jensen-Campbell, L. A., Gleason, K. A., Adams, R., and Malcolm, K. T. (2003). Interpersonal conflict, agreeableness, and personality development. *Journal of Personality, 71,* 1059–1085.

Jensen-Campbell, L. A., and Graziano, W. G. (2001). Agreeableness as a moderator of interpersonal conflict. *Journal of Personality, 69,* 323–362.

Jerskey, B. A., Panizzon, M. S., Jacobson, K. C., Neale, M. C., Grant, M. D., Schultz, M., Eisen, S., et al. (2010). Marriage and divorce: A genetic perspective. *Personality and Individual Differences, 49,* 473–478.

Johansen, H., Nair, C., and Taylor, G. (1998). Variations in angioplasty and bypass surgery. *Statistics Canada Health Reports, 10,* 63–76.

John, O. P. (1990). The "Big Five" factor taxonomy: Dimensions of personality in the natural language and questionnaires. In L. A. Pervin (Ed.), *Handbook of personality* (pp. 66–100). New York: Guilford Press.

John, O. P., and Naumann, L. (2010). Surviving two critiques by Block? The resilient Big Five have emerged as the paradigm for personality trait psychology. *Psychological Inquiry, 21,* 44–49.

John, O. P., Naumann, L. P., and Soto, C. J. (2008). Paradigm shift to the integrative Big Five trait taxonomy: History, measurement, and conceptual issues. In O. P. John, R. W. Robins, and L. A. Pervin (Eds.), *Handbook of personality* (pp. 114–158). New York: Guilford Press.

Johnson, J., Prior, S., and Artuso, M. (2000). Field dependence as a factor in second language communicative production. *Language Learning, 50*(3), 529–567.

Johnson, M. K., Rowatt, W. C., and Petrini, L. (2011). A new trait on the market: Honesty-humility as a unique predictor of job performance. *Personality and Individual Differences, 50,* 857–862.

Johnson, W. (2007). Genetic and environmental influences on behavior: Capturing all the interplay. *Psychological Review, 114,* 423–440.

Johnson, W., and Deary, I. J. (2011). Placing inspection time, reaction time, and perceptual speed in the broader context of cognitive ability: The VPR model in the Lothian Birth Cohort 1936, *Intelligence, 39,* 405–417.

Johnson, W., Hicks, B. M., McGue, M., and Iacono, W. G. (2007). Most of the girls are alright, but some aren't: Personality trajectory groups from ages 14–24 and some associations with outcomes. *Journal of Personality and Social Psychology, 93,* 266–284.

Johnson, W., McGue, M., and Krueger, R. F. (2005). Personality stability in late adulthood: A behavior genetic analysis. *Journal of Personality, 73,* 523–551.

Johnson, W., McGue, M., Krueger, R. F., and Bouchard, T. J., Jr. (2004). Marriage and personality: A genetic analysis. *Journal of Personality and Social Psychology, 86,* 285–294.

Johnson, W., Penke, L., and Spinath, F. M. (2011). Heritability in the era of molecular genetics: Some thoughts for understanding genetic influences on behavioural traits: Understanding heritability. *European Journal of Personality, 25,* 254–266.

Jokela, M. (2009). Personality predicts migration within and between U.S. states. *Journal of Research in Personality, 43,* 79–83.

Jonason, P. K., Garcia, J. R., Webster, G. D., Li, N. P., and Fisher, H. E. (2015). Relationship deal breakers traits people avoid in potential mates. *Personality and Social Psychology Bulletin, 41*(12), 1697–1711.

Jonason, P. K., and Webster, G. D. (2012). A protean approach to social influence: Dark Triad personalities and social influence tactics. *Personality and Individual Differences, 52,* 521–526.

Jones, A., and Crandall, R. (1986). Validation of a short index of self-actualization. *Personality and Social Psychology Bulletin, 12,* 63–73.

Jones, D. N., and Paulhus, D. L. (2010). Different provocations trigger aggression in narcissists and psychopaths. *Social Psychological and Personality Science, 1,* 12–18.

Jordan, C. H., Spencer, S. J., Zanna, M. P., Hoshino-Browne, E., and Correll, J. (2003). Secure and defensive high self-esteem. *Journal of Personality and Social Psychology, 85,* 969–978.

Judge, T., and Larsen, R. J. (2001). Dispositional sources of job satisfaction: A review and theoretical extension. *Organizational Behavior and Human Decision Processes, 86,* 67–98.

Jung, I., Lee, H., and Cho, B. (2004). Persistent psychotic disorder in an adolescent with a past history of butane gas dependence. *European Psychiatry, 19,* 519–520.

Kachel, S., Steffens, M. C., and Niedlich, C. (2016). Traditional masculinity and femininity: Validation of a new scale assessing gender roles. *Frontiers in Psychology, 7,* 956.

Kagan, J. (1981). *The second year: The emergence of self-awareness.* Cambridge, MA: Harvard University Press.

Kagan, J. (1994). *Galen's prophecy: Temperament in human nature.* New York: Basic Books.

Kagan, J. (1999). Born to be shy? In R. Conlan (Ed.), *States of mind* (pp. 29–51). New York: Wiley.

Kagan, J., and Moss, H. (1962). *Birth to maturity: A study in psychological development.* New York: Wiley.

Kagan, J., and Snidman, N. (1991). Infant predictors of inhibited and uninhibited profiles. *Psychological Science, 2,* 40–44.

Kahan, D., Peters, E., & Dawson, E. C., & Slovic, P. (2017). Motivated numeracy and enlightened self-government. *Behavioural Public Policy, 1,* 54–86.

Kajonius, P. J., and Johnson, J. (2018). Sex differences in 30 facets of the five factor model of personality in the large public (N = 320, 128). *Personality and Individual Differences, 129,* 126–130.

Kamakura, T., Ando, J., and Ono, Y. (2007). Genetic and environmental effects on the stability and change in self-esteem during adolescence. *Personality and Individual Differences, 42,* 181–190.

Kamble, S., Shackelford, T. K., Pham, M., and Buss, D. M. (2014). Indian mate preferences: Continuity, sex differences, and cultural change across a quarter of a century. *Personality and Individual Differences, 70,* 150–155.

Kammrath, L. K., and Scholer, A. A. (2011). The Pollyanna myth: How highly agreeable people judge positive and negative relational acts. *Personality and Social Psychology Bulletin, 37,* 1172–1184.

Kandler, C., Bleidorn, W., Spinath, F. M., and Riemann, R. (2010). Sources of cumulative continuity in personality: A longitudinal multiple-rater twin study. *Journal of Personality and Social Psychology, 98,* 995–1008.

Kanner, Allen D., Feldman, S., and Weinberger, D. A. (1991). Uplifts, hassles, and adaptational outcomes in early adolescents. In A. Monat and R. S. Lazarus (Eds.), *Stress and coping: An anthology* (3rd ed.) (pp. 158–181). New York: Columbia University Press.

Kaplan, H., and Hill, K. (1985). Food-sharing among Ache foragers: Tests of evolutionary hypotheses. *Current Anthropology, 26,* 223–246.

Karney, B. R., and Bradbury, T. N. (1997). Neuroticism, marital interaction, and the trajectory of marital satisfaction. *Journal of Personality and Social Psychology, 72,* 1075–1092.

Karney, B. R., Bradbury, T. N., Fincham, F. D., and Sullivan, K. T. (1994). The role of negative affectivity in the association between attributions and marital satisfaction. *Journal of Personality and Social Psychology, 66,* 413–424.

Katigbak, M. S., Church, A. T., Guanzon-Lapena, M. A., Carlota, A. J., and del Pilar, G. H. (2002). Are indigenous personality dimensions culture-specific? Philippine inventories and the five-factor model. *Journal of Personality and Social Psychology, 82*(1), 89–101.

Kaufman, S. B. (2018). Self-actualizing people in the 21st Century: Integration with contemporary theory and research on personality and well-being. *Journal of Humanistic Psychology,* November 7, 2018. doi: 10.1177/0022167818809187

Kaufman, S. B., Quilty, L. C., Grazioplene, R. G., Hirsh, J. B., Gray, J. R., Peterson, J. B., and DeYoung, C. G. (2016). Openness to experience and intellect differentially predict creative achievement in the arts and sciences. *Journal of Personality, 82,* 248–258.

Kavanagh, K., and Hops, H. (1994). Good girls? Bad boys? Gender and development as contexts for diagnosis and treatment. *Advances in Clinical Child Psychology, 16,* 45–79.

Kelly, E. L., and Conley, J. J. (1987). Personality and compatibility: A prospective analysis of marital stability and marital satisfaction. *Journal of Personality and Social Psychology, 52,* 27–40.

Kelly, G. A. (1955). *The psychology of personal constructs* (vols. 1 and 2). London: Routledge.

Kelley, H. H. (1992). Common-sense psychology and scientific psychology. In M. R. Rosensweig and L. W. Porter (Eds.), *Annual review of psychology* (vol. 43, pp. 1–23). Palo Alto, CA: Annual Reviews.

Keltikangas-Järvinen, L., Elovainio, M., Kivimäki, M., Lichtermann, D., Ekelund, J., and Leena Peltonen, L. (2003). Association between the Type 4 dopamine receptor gene polymorphism and novelty seeking. *Psychosomatic Medicine, 65,* 471–476.

Kendler, K. S., McGuire, M., Gruenberg, A. M., O'Hare, A., Spellman, M., and Walsh, D. (1993). The Roscommon Family Study III: Schizophrenia-related personality disorders in relatives. *Archives of General Psychiatry, 50,* 781–788.

Kendler, R. S., Heath, A. C., Neale, M. C., Kessler, R. C., and Eaves, L. J. (1992). A population-based twin study of alcoholism in women. *Journal of the American Medical Association, 268,* 1877–1882.

Kenrick, D. T., Griskevicius, V., Neuberg, S. L., and Schaller, M. (2010). Renovating the pyramid of needs: Contemporary extensions built upon ancient foundations. *Perspectives on Psychological Science, 5,* 292–314.

Kenrick, D. T., and Luce, C. L. (2004). *The functional mind: Readings in evolutionary psychology.* Boston: Allyn and Bacon.

Kerkhof, G. A. (1985). Inter-individual differences in the human circadian system: A review. *Biological Psychology, 20,* 83–112.

Kernberg, O. (1975). *Borderline conditions and pathological narcissism.* New York: Jason Aronson.

Kernberg, O. F. (1984). *Severe personality disorders.* New Haven, CT: Yale University Press.

Kernis, M. H., and Goldman, B. M. (2006). A multicomponent conceptualization of authenticity: Theory and research. In M. P. Zanna (Ed.), *Advances in experimental social psychology* (Vol. 38, pp. 283–357). San Diego, CA: Elsevier Academic Press.

Kernis, M. H., Grannemann, B. D., and Barclay, L. C. (1992). Stability of self-esteem: Assessment, correlates, and excuse making. *Journal of Personality, 60,* 621–643.

Kernis, M. H., Grannemann, B. D., and Mathis, L. C. (1991). Stability of self-esteem as a moderator of the relation between level of self-esteem and depression. *Journal of Personality and Social Psychology, 61,* 80–84.

Kesebir, S., Graham, J., Oishi, S. (2010). A theory of human needs should be human-centered, not animal-centered: Commentary on Kenrick et al. (2010). *Perspectives on Psychological Science, 5,* 315–319.

Ketelaar, T. (1995). *Emotion as mental representations of fitness affordances: I. Evidence supporting the claim that the negative and positive emotions map onto fitness costs and benefits.* Paper presented at the annual meeting of the Human Behavior and Evolution Society, Santa Barbara.

Kihlstrom, J. F. (1999). The psychological unconscious. In L. A. Pervin and O. P. John (Eds.), *Handbook of personality: Theory and research* (pp. 424–442). New York: Guilford Press.

Kihlstrom, J. F. (2003a). Freud is dead weight on psychology. In E. E. Smith, S. Nolen-Hoeksema, B. L. Fredrickson, G. R. Loftus, D. J. Bem, and S. Maren, *Introduction to psychology* (p. 487). Belmont, CA: Wadsworth/Thomson Learning.

Kihlstrom, J. F. (2003b). Hypnosis and memory. In J. F. Byrne (Ed.), *Learning and memory* (2nd ed., pp. 240–242). Farmington Hills, MI: Macmillan.

Kihlstrom, J. F., Barnhardt, T. M., and Tataryn, D. J. (1992). The psychological unconscious: Found, lost, and regained. *American Psychologist, 47,* 788–791.

Kim, E. (2002). Agitation, aggression, and disinhibition syndromes after traumatic brain injury. *NeuroRehabilitation, 17,* 297–310.

Kim, K., Smith, P. K., and Palermiti, A. (1997). Conflict in childhood and reproductive development. *Evolution and Human Behavior, 18,* 109–142.

Kim-Cohen, J., Caspi, A., Taylor, A., Williams, B., Newcombe, R., Craig, I. W., et al. (2006). MAOA, maltreatment, and gene-environment interaction predicting children's mental health: New evidence and a meta-analysis. *Molecular Psychiatry, 11,* 903–913.

Kimura, D. (2002). Sex hormones influence human cognitive pattern. *Neuroendocrinology Letters, 23* (Suppl. 4), 67–77.

King, D. B., DeCicco, T. L., and Humphreys, T. P. (2009). Investigating sexual dream imagery in relation to daytime sexual behaviours and fantasies among Canadian university students. *The Canadian Journal of Human Sexuality, 18*(3), 135–146.

King, D. B., and DeLongis, A. (2013). Dyadic coping with stepfamily conflict: Demand and withdraw responses between husbands and wives. *Journal of Social and Personal Relationships, 30*(3), 198–206.

King, D. B., and DeLongis, A. (2014). When couples disconnect: Rumination and withdrawal as maladaptive responses to everyday stress. *Journal of Family Psychology, 28*(4), 460–469.

King, L. A. (1995). Wishes, motives, goals, and personal memories: Relations and correlates of measures of human motivation. *Journal of Personality, 63,* 985–1007.

King, L. A., and Emmons, R. A. (1990). Conflict over emotional expression: Psychological and physical correlates. *Journal of Personality and Social Psychology, 58,* 864–877.

King, L. A., and Hicks, J. A. (2012). Positive affect and meaning in life: The intersection of hedonism and eudaimonia. In P. T. P Wong (Ed.), *The human quest for meaning: Theories, research and applications* (2nd ed., pp. 125–141). New York, NY: Routledge/Taylor & Francis Group.

Kingsbury, M., and Coplan, R. J. (2016). RU mad @ me? Social anxiety and interpretation of ambiguous text messages. *Computers in Human Behavior, 54,* 368–379.

Kintz, B. L., Delprato, D. J., Mettee, D. R., Parsons, D. E., and Schappe, R. H. (1965). The experimenter effect. *Psychological Bulletin, 63,* 223–232.

Kipnis, D. (1971). *Character structure and impulsiveness.* New York: Academic Press.

Kircaburun, K., Jonason, P.K., & Griffiths, M.D. (2018). The Dark Tetrad traits and problematic social media use: The mediating role of cyberbullying and cyberstalking. *Personality and Individual Differences, 135,* 264–269.

Kirmayer, L. J., Brass, G. M., and Tait, C. L. (2000). The mental health of Aboriginal peoples: Transformations of identity and community. *The Canadian Journal of Psychiatry, 45*(7), 607–616.

Kjærgaard, A., Leon, G. R., and Venables, N. C. (2015). The 'right stuff' for a solo sailboat circumnavigation of the globe. *Environment And Behavior, 47*(10), 1147–1171.

Kling, K. C., Hyde, J. S., Showers, C. J., and Buswell, B. N. (1999). Gender differences in self-esteem: A meta-analysis. *Psychological Bulletin, 125,* 470–500.

Klinger, E. (1977a). The nature of fantasy and its clinical uses. *Psychotherapy: Theory, Research, and Practice, 14,* 223–231.

Klinger, E. (1977b). *Meaning and void: Inner experience and the incentives in people's lives.* Minneapolis: University of Minnesota Press.

Klonsky, E. D., Oltmanns, T. F., and Turkheimer, E. (2002). Informant reports of personality disorder: Relation to self-reports and future research directions. *Clinical Psychology: Science and Practice, 9,* 300–311.

Kluckhohn, C., and Murray, H. A. (1948). *Personality in nature, society, and culture.* New York: Knopf.

Knutson, B., and Bhanji, J. (2006). Neural substrates for emotional traits? In T. Canli (Ed.), *Biology of personality and individual differences* (pp. 116–132). New York: Guilford Press.

Knutson, B., Wolkowitz, O. M., Cole, S. W., Chan, T., Moore, E. A., Johnson, R. C., Terpestra, J., et al. (1998). Selective alteration of personality and social behavior by serotonergic intervention. *American Journal of Psychiatry, 155,* 373–378.

Kobasa, S. C. (1979). Stressful life events, personality, and health: An inquiry into hardiness. *Journal of Personality and Social Psychology. 52,* i-ii.

Koenig, L. B., McGue, M., Krueger, R. F., and Bouchard, T. J., Jr. (2005). Genetic and environmental influences on religiousness ratings. *Journal of Personality, 73,* 471–488.

Koestner, R., and McClelland, D. C. (1990). Perspectives on competence motivation. In L. A. Pervin (Ed.), *Handbook of personality: Theory and research* (pp. 527–548). New York: Guilford Press.

Koestner, R., Otis, N., Powers, T. A., Pelletier, L., and Gagnon, H. (2008). Autonomous motivation, controlled motivation, and goal progress. *Journal of Personality, 76*(5), 1201–1230.

Kofman, S. (1985). *The enigma of woman: Woman in Freud's writings.* Ithaca, NY: Cornell University Press.

Koh, J-B, and Wong, J. S. (2015). Survival of the fittest and the sexiest: Evolutionary origins of adolescent bullying. *Journal of Interpersonal Violence, 32*(17), 2668–2690. doi: 0886260515593546.

Kohda, M., Takashi, H., Takeyama, T., Awata, S., Tanaka, H., Asai, J., & Jordan, A. (2018, August). Cleaner wrasse pass the mark test. What are the implications for consciousness and self-awareness testing in animals? *BioRxiv: The Preprint Server for Biology.* doi: 10.1101/397067

Kohn, M. L., Naoi, A., Schoenbach, C., Schooler, C., and Slomczynski, K. M. (1990). Position in the class structure and psychological functioning in the United States, Japan, and Poland. *American Journal of Sociology, 95,* 964–1008.

Kohut, H. (1977). *The restoration of the self.* Madison, CT: International Universities Press.

Kollmayer, M., Schultes, M., Schober, B., Hodosi, T., and Spiel, C. (2018). Parents' judgments about the desirability of toys for their children: Associations with gender role attitudes, gender-typing of toys, and demographics. *Sex Roles, 79,* 329–341.

Koltko-Rivera, M. (2006). Rediscovering the later version of Maslow's hierarchy of needs: Self-transcendance and opportunities for theory, research, and unification. *Review of General Psychology, 10*(4), 302–317.

Konrath, S. H., O'Brien, E. H., and Hsing, C. (2011). Changes in dispositional empathy in American college students over time: A meta-analysis. *Personality and Social Psychology Review, 15,* 180–198.

Koole, S. L., Jager, W., van den Berg, A. E., Vlek, C.A.J., and Hofstee, W. K. B. (2001). On the social nature of personality: Effects of extraversion, agreeableness, and feedback about collective resource use on cooperation in a resource dilemma. *Personality and Social Psychology Bulletin, 27*(3), 289–301.

Koopmans, J. R., and Boomsma, D. I. (1993). Bivariate genetic analysis of the relation between alcohol and tobacco use in adolescent twins. *Psychiatric Genetics, 3,* 172.

Kopp, C. B. (1989). Regulation of distress and negative emotions: A developmental view. *Developmental Psychology, 25,* 343–354.

Kosslyn, S. M., Cacioppo, J. T., Davidson, R. J., Hugdahl, K., Lovallo, W. R., Spiegel, D., and Rose, R. (2002). Bridging psychology and biology: The analysis of individuals in groups. *American Psychologist, 57,* 341–351.

Kosslyn, S. M., and Rosenberg, R. S. (2004). *Psychology: The brain, the person, the world.* Boston: Allyn and Bacon.

Kotelnikova, Y., and Tackett, J. L. (2009). Personality correlates of cross-cultural differences in childhood psychopathology. *Journal of Undergraduate Life Sciences, 3,* 10–13.

Kotov, R., Gamez, W., Schmidt, F., and Watson, D. (2010). Linking "big" personality traits to anxiety, depressive, and substance use disorders: A meta-analysis. *Psychological Bulletin, 136,* 768–821.

Kotter-Gruhn, D., Wiest, M., Zurek, P. P., and Scheibe, S. (2009). What is it we are longing for? Psychological and demographic factors influencing the contents of Sehnsucht (life longings). *Journal of Research in Personality, 43,* 428–437.

Kowalski, R. M., and Brown, K. J. (1994). Psychosocial barriers to cervical cancer screening: Concerns with self-presentation and social evaluation. *Journal of Applied Social Psychology, 24,* 941–958.

Kraeplin, E. (1913). *Psychiatrie: Ein Lehrbuch* (8th ed.). Leipzig: Barth.

Krasno, J. (2015). William Jefferson Clinton: Promise, persistence, and the will to be adored. In J. Krasno, S. LaPides, J. Krasno, S. LaPides (Eds.), *Personality, political leadership, and decision making: A global perspective* (pp. 295–318). Santa Barbara, CA, US: Praeger/ABC-CLIO.

Krems, A. J., Kenrick, D. T., and Neel, R. (2017). Individual perceptions of self-actualization: What functional motives are linked to fulfilling one's full potential? *Personality and Social Psychology Bulletin, 43*(9), 1337–1352. doi: 10.1177/0146167217713191

Kretschmer, E. (1925). *Physique and character.* London: Kegan Paul.

Krueger, J. I., Hasman, J. F., Acevedo, M., and Villano, P. (2003). Perceptions of trait typicality in gender stereotypes: Examining the role of attribution and categorization processes. *Personality and Social Psychology Bulletin, 29*(1), 108–116.

Krueger, R. F., and Markon, K. E. (2006). Reinterpreting comorbidity: A model-based approach to understanding and classifying psychopathology. *Annual Review of Clinical Psychology, 2,* 111–133.

Krueger, R. F., Markon, K. E., and Bouchard, T. J., Jr. (2003). The extended genotype: The heritability of personality accounts for the heritability of recalled family environments in twins reared apart. *Journal of Personality, 71*(5), 809–834.

Krueger, R. F., South, S., Johnson, W., and Iacono, W. (2008). The heritability of personality is not always 50%: Gene-environment interactions and correlations between personality and parenting. *Journal of Personality, 76,* 1485–1522.

Krug, S. E. (1981). *Interpreting 16 PF profile patterns.* Champaign, IL: Institute for Personality and Ability Testing.

Kuhl, J., and Kazén, M. (2008). Motivation, affect, and hemispheric asymmetry: Power versus affiliation. *Journal of Personality and Social Psychology, 95,* 456–469.

Kuhn, M., and McPartland, T. S. (1954). An empirical investigation of self-attitudes. *American Sociological Review, 19,* 68–76.

Kuo, J. R., Khoury, J. E., Metcalfe, R., Fitzpatrick, S., and Goodwill, A. (2015). An examination of the relationship between childhood emotional abuse and borderline personality disorder features: The role of difficulties with emotion regulation. *Child Abuse & Neglect, 39,* 147–155.

Kupper, N., and Denollet, J. (2007). Type D personality as a prognostic factor in heart disease: Assessment and mediating mechanisms. *Journal of Personality Assessment, 89,* 265–276.

Kupper, N., and Denollet, J. (2018). Type D personality as a risk factor in coronary heart disease: A review of current evidence. *Current Cardiology Reports, 20*(11), 104. doi:10.1007/s11886-018-1048-x

Kurman, J. (2001). Self-enhancement: Is it restricted to individualistic cultures? *Personality and Social Psychology Bulletin, 27*(12), 1705–1716.

Kushlev, K., Dunn, E., & Lucas, R. E. (2015). Higher income is associated with less daily sadness but not more daily happiness. *Social Psychological and Personality, 6*(5), 483–489.

Kwapil, T. R., Wrobel, M. J., and Pope, C. A. (2002). The five-factor personality structure of dissociative experiences. *Personality and Individual Differences, 32,* 431–443.

Kwon, P., Campbell, D. G., and Williams, M. G. (2001). Sociotropy and autonomy: Preliminary evidence for construct validity using TAT narratives. *Journal of Personality Assessment Special Issue: More data on the current Rorschach controversy, 77,* 128–138.

Kyl-Heku, L., and Buss, D. M. (1996). Tactics as units of analysis in and personality psychology: An illustration using tactics of hierarchy negotiation. *Personality and Individual Differences, 21,* 497–517.

Laham, S. M., Gonsalkorale, K., and von Hippel, W. (2005). Darwinian grandparenting: Preferential investment in more certain kin. *Personality and Social Psychology Bulletin, 31,* 63–72.

Lajunen, T. (2001). Personality and accident liability: Are extraversion, neuroticism and psychoticism related to traffic and occupational fatalities? *Personality and Individual Differences, 31,* 1365–1373.

Lalonde, C. E. (2006). Identity formation and cultural resilience in Aboriginal communities. In R. J. Flynn, P. Dudding, and J. Barber (Eds.), *Promoting resilient development in young people receiving care: International perspectives on theory, research, practice & policy* (pp. 52–71). Ottawa, Ontario: University of Ottawa Press.

Lalumiere, M. L., Chalmers, L. J., Quinsey, V. L., and Seto, M. C. (1996). A test of the mate deprivation hypothesis of sexual coercion. *Ethology and Sociobiology, 17,* 299–318.

Lalumiere, M. L., Harris, G. T., and Rice, M. E. (2001). Psychopathy and developmental instability. *Evolution and Human Behavior, 22,* 75–92.

Langens, T. A. (2001). Predicting behavior change in Indian businessmen from a combination of need for achievement and self-discrepancy. *Journal of Research in Personality, 35,* 339–352.

Langens, T. A., and Schmalt, H. D. (2008). Motivational traits: New directions and measuring motives with the multi-motive grid (MMG). In G. J. Boyle, G. Matthews, and D. H. Saklofske (Eds.), *The SAGE handbook of personality theory and assessment, vol. 1: Personality theories and Models* (pp. 523–544). Thousand Oaks, CA: Sage.

Langevin, R., Bain, J., Wortzman, G., and Hucker, S. (1988). Sexual sadism: Brain, blood, and behavior. *Annals of the New York Academy of Science, 528,* 163–171.

Langford, P. H. (2003). A one-minute measure of the Big Five? Evaluating and abridging Shafer's (1999) Big Five markers. *Personality and Individual Differences, 35,* 1127–1140.

Langner, C. A., and Winter, D. G. (2001). The motivational basis of concessions and compromise: Archival and laboratory studies. *Journal of Personality and Social Psychology, 81,* 711–727.

Lanning, K. (1994). Dimensionality of observer ratings on the California Adult Q-set. *Journal of Personality and Social Psychology, 67*(1), 151.

Larsen, R. J. (1984). Theory and measurement of affect intensity as an individual difference characteristic. *Dissertation Abstracts International, 45, 7-B.* (UMI No. 2297).

Larsen, R. J. (1985). Individual differences in circadian activity rhythm and personality. *Personality and Individual Differences, 6,* 305–311.

Larsen, R. J. (1987). The stability of mood variability: A spectral analytic approach to daily mood assessments. *Journal of Personality and Social Psychology, 52,* 1195–1204.

Larsen, R. J. (1989). A process approach to personality: Utilizing time as a facet of data. In D. Buss and N. Cantor (Eds.), *Personality psychology: Recent trends and emerging directions* (pp. 177–193). New York: Springer-Verlag.

Larsen, R. J. (1991). Personality and emotion. In V. Derlega, B. Winstead, and W. Jones (Eds.), *Contemporary research in personality* (pp. 407–432). Chicago: Nelson-Hall.

Larsen, R. J. (1992). Neuroticism and selective encoding and recall of symptoms: Evidence from a combined concurrent-retrospective study. *Journal of Personality and Social Psychology, 62,* 480–488.

Larsen, R. J. (2000a). Toward a science of mood regulation. *Psychological Inquiry, 11,* 129–141.

Larsen, R. J. (2000b). Maintaining hedonic balance. *Psychological Inquiry, 11,* 218–225.

Larsen, R. J. (2009). Affect intensity. In M. R. Leary and R. H. Hoyle (Eds.), *Handbook of individual differences in social behaviors* (pp. 241–254). New York: Guilford Press.

Larsen, R. J., Billings, D., and Cutler, S. (1996). Affect intensity and individual differences in cognitive style. *Journal of Personality, 64,* 185–208.

Larsen, R. J., Chen, B., and Zelenski, J. (2003). *Responses to punishment and reward in the emotion Stroop paradigm: Relations to BIS and BAS.* Unpublished manuscript.

Larsen, R. J., and Cowan, G. S. (1988). Internal focus of attention and depression: A study of daily experience. *Motivation and Emotion, 12,* 237–249.

Larsen, R. J., and Diener, E. (1985). A multitrait-multimethod examination of affect structure: Hedonic level and emotional intensity. *Personality and Individual Differences, 6,* 631–636.

Larsen, R. J., and Diener, E. (1987). Affect intensity as an individual difference characteristic: A review. *Journal of Research in Personality, 21,* 1–39.

Larsen, R. J., and Diener, E. (1992). Problems and promises with the circumplex model of emotion. *Review of Personality and Social Psychology, 13,* 25–59.

Larsen, R. J., Diener, E., and Cropanzano, R. S. (1987). Cognitive operations associated with individual differences in affect intensity. *Journal of Personality and Social Psychology, 53,* 767–774.

Larsen, R. J., Diener, E., and Emmons, R. A. (1986). Affect intensity and reactions to daily life events. *Journal of Personality and Social Psychology, 51,* 803–814.

Larsen, R. J., Diener, E., and Lucas, R. (2002). Emotion: Models, measures, and individual differences. In R. Lord, R. Klimoski, and R. Kanfer (Eds.), *Emotions at work* (pp. 64–106). San Francisco: Jossey-Bass.

Larsen, R. J., and Fredrickson, B. L. (1999). Measurement issues in emotion research. In D. Kahneman, E. Diener, and N. Schwarz (Eds.), *Understanding quality of life: Scientific perspectives on enjoyment and suffering* (pp. 40–60). New York: Sage.

Larsen, R. J., and Kasimatis, M. (1990). Individual differences in entrainment of mood to the weekly calendar. *Journal of Personality and Social Psychology, 58,* 164–171.

Larsen, R. J., and Ketelaar, T. (1989). Extraversion, neuroticism, and susceptibility to positive and negative mood induction procedures. *Personality and Individual Differences, 10,* 1221–1228.

Larsen, R. J., and Ketelaar, T. (1991). Personality and susceptibility to positive and negative emotional states. *Journal of Personality and Social Psychology, 61,* 132–140.

Larsen, R. J., Mercer, K. A., and Balota, D. A. (2006). Lexical characteristics of words used in emotion Stroop tasks. *Emotion, 6,* 62–72.

Larsen, R. J., and Prizmic, Z. (2004). Affect regulation. In R. Baumeister and K. Vohs (Eds.), *Handbook of self-regulation research* (pp. 40–60). New York: Guilford Press.

Larsen, R. J., and Prizmic, Z. (2006). Multimethod measurement of emotion. In M. Eid and E. Diener (Eds.), *Handbook of measurement: A multimethod perspective* (pp. 337–352). Washington, DC: American Psychological Association.

Larsen, R. J., and Zarate, M. A. (1991). Extending reducer/augmenter theory into the emotion domain: The role of affect in regulating stimulation level. *Personality and Individual Differences, 12,* 713–723.

Larson, D. G., and Chastain, R. L. (1990). Self-concealment: Conceptualization, measurement, and health implications. *Journal of Social and Clinical Psychology, 9,* 439–455.

Lassek, W. D., and Gaulin, S. J. C. (2009). Costs and benefits of fat-free muscle mass in men: Relationship to mating success, dietary requirements, and native immunity. *Evolution and Human Behavior, 30,* 322–328.

Lassiter, G. D., Lindberg, M. J., Gonzalez-Vallejo, C., Bellezza, F. S., and Phillips, N. D. (2009). The deliberation-without-attention effect: Evidence for an artifactual interpretation. *Psychological Science, 20,* 671–675.

Laub, J. H., and Lauritsen, J. L. (1994). The precursors of criminal offending across the life course. *Federal Probation, 58,* 51–57.

Laws, V. L., and Rivera. L. M. (2012). The role of self-image concerns in discrepancies between implicit and explicit self-esteem. *Personality and Social Psychology Bulletin, 38,* 1453–1466.

Lawton, M. P., Moss, M. S., Winter, L., and Hoffman, C. (2002). Motivation in later life: Personal projects and well-being. *Psychology and Aging, 17,* 539–547.

Lay, C., and Verkuyten, M. (1999). Ethnic identity and its relation to personal self-esteem: A comparison of Canadian-born and foreign-born Chinese adolescents. *The Journal of Social Psychology, 139*(3), 288–299.

Lazarus, R. S. (1991). *Emotion and adaptation.* Oxford, England: Oxford University Press.

Lazarus, R. S., and Folkman, S. (1984). *Stress, appraisal and coping.* New York: Springer.

Lazarus, R. S., Kanner, A. D., and Folkman, S. (1980). Emotions: A cognitive-phenomenological analysis. In R. Plutchik and H. Kellerman (Eds.), *Theories of emotion* (pp. 189–217). New York: Academic Press.

Leary, M. R., and Kowalski, R. M. (1995). *Social anxiety.* New York: Guilford Press.

Le Boeuf, B. J., and Reiter, J. (1988). Lifetime reproductive success in northern elephant seals. In T. H. Clutton-Brock (Ed.), *Reproductive success* (pp. 344–362). Chicago: University of Chicago Press.

Lee, B. W., and Leeson, P. C. (2015). Online gaming in the context of social anxiety. *Psychology of Addictive Behaviors, 29*(2), 473–482.

Lee, C., Corte, C., Stein, K. F., Finnegan, L., McCreary, L. L., and Park, C. G. (2015). Expected problem drinker possible self: Predictor of alcohol problems and tobacco use in adolescents. *Substance Abuse, 36*(4), 434–439.

Lee, D., Kelley, K. R., and Edwards, J. K. (2006). A closer look at relationships among trait procrastination, neuroticism, and conscientiousness. *Personality and Individual Differences, 40,* 27–37.

Lee, K., and Ashton, M. C. (2008). The HEXACO personality factors in the indigenous personality lexicons of English and 11 other languages. *Journal of Personality, 76,* 1011–1054.

Lee, K., Ogunfowora, B., and Ashton, M. C. (2005). Personality traits beyond the Big Five: Are they within the HEXACO space? *Journal of Personality, 73,* 1437–1463.

Lee-Baggley, D., Preece, M., and DeLongis, A. (2005). Coping with interpersonal stress: Role of the Big Five traits. *Journal of Personality, 73,* 1141–1180.

Lee-Ross, D. (2015). Personality characteristics of the self-employed: A comparison using the world values survey data set. *Journal of Management Development, 34*(9), 1094–1112.

Leeuwis, F. H., Koot, H. M., Creemers, D. M., & van Lier, P. C. (2015). Implicit and explicit self-esteem discrepancies, victimization and the development of late childhood internalizing problems. *Journal of Abnormal Child Psychology, 43*(5), 909–919.

Lee-Won, R. J., Herzog, L., and Park, S. G. (2015). Hooked on Facebook: The role of social anxiety and need for social assurance in problematic use of Facebook. *Cyberpsychology, Behavior, and Social Networking, 18*(10), 567–574.

Lei, C., Wang, Y., Shackelford, T. K., and Buss, D. M. (2011). Chinese mate preferences: Cultural evolution and continuity across a quarter century. *Personality and Individual Differences, 50,* 678–683.

Leikas, S., Lönnqvist, J., and Verkasalo, M. (2012). Persons, situations, and behaviors: Consistency and variability of different behaviors in four interpersonal situations. *Journal of Personality and Social Psychology, 103,* 1007–1022.

Leopold, D. A. (2012). Primary visual cortex: Awareness and blindsight. *Annual Review of Neuroscience, 35,* 91–109.

LeVay, S. (1991). A difference in hypothalamic structure between heterosexual and homosexual men. *Science,* pp. 1034–1037.

LeVay, S. (1993). *The sexual brain.* Cambridge, MA: MIT Press.

LeVay, S. (1996). *Queer science: The use and abuse of research into homosexuality.* Cambridge, MA: MIT Press.

Levenson, M. R. (1992). Rethinking psychopathy. *Theory & Psychology, 2*(1), 51–71.

Levenson, M. R., Kiehl, K. A., and Fitzpatrick, C. M. (1995). Assessing psychopathic attributes in a noninstitutionalized population. *Journal of Personality and Social Psychology, 68,* 151–158.

Levenson, R. W. (1983). Personality research and psychophysiology: General considerations. *Journal of Research in Personality, 17,* 1–21.

Levenson, R. W. (2003). Autonomic specificity and emotion. In R. J. Davidson, K. R. Scherer, and H. H. Goldsmith (Eds.), *Handbook of affective science* (pp. 212–224). New York: Oxford University Press.

Levesque, J., Fanny, E., and Joanette, Y. (2003). Neural circuitry underlying voluntary suppression of sadness. *Biological Psychiatry 53,* 502–510.

Levy, B. R., Slade, M. D., and Ranasinghe, P. (2009). Causal thinking after a tsunami wave: Karma beliefs, pessimistic explanatory style and health among Sri Lankan survivors. *Journal of Religion and Health, 48*(1), 38–45.

Levy, S. M. (1990). Psychosocial risk factors and cancer progression: Mediating pathways linking behavior and disease. In K. D. Craig and S. M. Weiss (Eds.), and *Health enhancement, disease prevention, and early intervention: Biobehavioral perspectives* (pp. 348–369). New York: Springer.

Levy, S. M., and Heiden. L. A. (1990). Personality and social factors in cancer outcome. In H. S. Friedman (Ed.), *Personality and disease* (pp. 254–279). New York: Wiley.

Lewis, M., and Ramsay, D. (2004). Development of self-recognition, personal pronoun use, and pretend play during the second year. *Child Development, 75,* 1821–1831.

Li, N. P., Valentine, K. A., and Patel, L. (2011). Mate preferences in the U.S. and Singapore: A cross-cultural test of the mate preference priority model. *Personality and Individual Differences, 50,* 291–294.

Lieberman, D., and Lobel, T. (2012). Kinship on the Kibbutz: Coresidence duration predicts altruism, personal sexual aversions and moral attitudes among communally reared peers. *Evolution and Human Behavior, 33*(1), 26–34.

Likert, R. (1932). A technique for the measurement of attitudes. *Archives of Psychology, 140,* 1–55.

Lilienfeld, S. O. (2002). When worlds collide: Social science, politics and the Rind et al. (1998) child abuse meta-analysis. *American Psychologist, 57,* 177–187.

Lilienfeld, S. O., Watts, A. L., and Smith, S. F. (2015). Successful psychopathy: A scientific status report. *Current Directions in Psychological Science, 24*(4), 298–303.

Lindo, J., Huerta-Sánchez, E., Nakagome, S., Rasmussen, M., Petzelt, B., Mitchell, J., ... Malhi, R. S. (2016). A time transect of exomes from a Native American population before and after European contact. *Nature Communications, 7,* 13175.

Linehan, M. (1995). *Understanding borderline personality disorder: The dialectical approach.* New York, NY: Guilford Press.

Linville, P. W. (1987). Self-complexity as a cognitive buffer against stress-related illness and depression. *Journal of Personality and Social Psychology, 52,* 663–676.

Lippa, R. (1998). Gender-related individual differences and the structure of vocational interests: The importance of the people–things dimension. *Journal of Personality and Social Psychology, 74,* 996–1009.

Lishman, W. A. (1972). Selective factors in memory. Part 1: Age, sex, and personality attributes. *Psychological Medicine, 2,* 121–138.

Little, A. C., Burt, D. M., and Perrett, D. I. (2006). Assortative mating for perceived facial personality traits. *Personality and Individual Differences, 40,* 973–984.

Little, B. R. (1972a). *Person–thing orientation: A provisional manual for the T-P scale.* Oxford, England: Oxford University, Department of Experimental Psychology.

Little, B. R. (1972b). Psychological man as scientist, humanist, and specialist. *Journal of Experimental Research in Personality, 6,* 95–118.

Little, B. R. (1999). Personality and motivation: Personal action and the cognitive revolution. In L. A. Pervin and O. P. John (Eds.), *Handbook of personality: Theory and research* (pp. 501–524). New York: Guilford Press.

Little, B. R. (2007). Prompt and circumstance: The generative contexts of personal projects analysis. In B. Little, K. Salmela-Aro, and S. D. Phillips (Eds.), *Personal project pursuit: Goals, action, and human flourishing* (pp. 3–49). Mahwah, NJ: Erlbaum.

Little, B. R. (2011). Personal projects and motivational counseling: The quality of lives reconsidered. In W. M. Cox and E. Klinger (Eds.), *Handbook of motivational counseling: Goal-based approaches to assessment and intervention with addiction and other problems* (2nd ed.). New York: Wiley-Blackwell.

Little, B. R., and Gee, T. L. (2007). The methodology of personal projects analysis: Four modules and a funnel. In B. Little, K. Salmela-Aro, and S. D. Phillips (Eds.), *Personal project pursuit: Goals, action, and human flourishing* (pp. 51–94). Mahwah, NJ: Erlbaum.

Little, B. R., Lecci, L., and Watkinson, B. (1992). Personality and personal projects: Linking Big Five and PAC units of analysis. *Journal of Personality, 60,* 501–525.

Little, B. R., Salmela-Aro, K., and Phillips, S. D. (2007). *Personal project pursuit: Goals, action, and human flourishing.* Mahwah, NJ: Erlbaum.

Liu, S. Y., Wrosch, C., Miller, G. E., and Pruessner, J. C. (2014). Self-esteem change and diurnal cortisol secretion in older adulthood. *Psychoneuroendocrinology, 41,* 111–120.

Livesley, W. J., and Larstone, R. (2018). *Handbook of personality disorders: Theory, research, and treatment* (2nd. ed.). New York: Guilford Press.

Löckenhoff, C. E., Chan, W., McCrae, R. R., De Fruyt, F., Jussim, L., De Bolle, M., Costa, P., . . . Nansubuga, F., Miramontez, D. R., and Terracciano, A. (2014). Gender stereotypes of personality: Universal and accurate? *Journal of Cross-Cultural Psychology, 45*(5), 675–694. doi: 10.1177/0022022113520075

Loef, M., and Walach, H. (2012). The combined effects of healthy lifestyle behaviors on all cause mortality: A systematic review and meta-analysis. *Preventive Medicine, 55*(3), 163–170.

Loehlin, J. C. (2010). Is there an active gene-environment correlation in adolescent drinking behavior? *Behavior Genetics, 40,* 447–451.

Loehlin, J. C. (2012). The differential heritability of personality item clusters. *Behavior Genetics, 42,* 500–507.

Loehlin, J. C., Neiderhiser, J. M., and Reiss, D. (2003). The behavior genetics of personality and the NEAD Study. *Journal of Research in Personality, 37,* 373–387.

Loehlin, J. C., and Nichols, R. C. (1976). *Heredity, environment and personality.* Austin: University of Texas Press.

Loftus, E. F. (1992). When a lie becomes memory's truth: Memory distortion after exposure to misinformation. *Current Directions in Psychological Science, 1,* 121–123.

Loftus, E. F. (1993). The reality of repressed memories. *American Psychologist, 48,* 518–537.

Loftus, E. F. (2000). Remembering what never happened. In E. Tulving (Ed.), *Memory, consciousness, and the brain: The Tallinn Conference* (pp. 106–118). Philadelphia, PA: Psychology Press.

Loftus, E. F. (2003). Memory in Canadian courts of law. *Canadian Psychology, 44,* 207–212.

Loftus, E. F. (2011). Intelligence gathering post-9/11. *American Psychologist, 66,* 532–541.

London, H., and Exner, J. E., Jr. (Eds.). (1978). *Dimensions of personality.* New York: Wiley.

Lönnqvist, J. E., Itkonen, J. V., Verkasalo, M., and Poutvaara, P. (2014). The five-factor model of personality and degree and transitivity of Facebook social networks. *Journal of Research in Personality, 50,* 98–101.

Lounsbury, J. W., Sundstrom, E., Loveland, James M., and Gibson, L. W. (2003). Intelligence, "Big Five" personality traits, and work drive as predictors of course grade. *Personality and Individual Differences, 35,* 1231–1239.

Low, B. (1989). Cross-cultural patterns in the training of children: An evolutionary perspective. *Journal of Comparative Psychology, 103,* 311–319.

Lowell, A., Suarez-Jimenez, B., Helpman, L., Zhu, X., Durosky, A., Hilburn, A., Schneier, F., Gross, R., ... Neria, Y. (2017). 9/11-related PTSD among highly exposed populations: a systematic review 15 years after the attack. *Psychological Medicine, 48*(4), 537–553.

Lowenstein, L. F. (2002). Ability and personality changes after brain injuries. *Criminal Lawyer, 120,* 5–8.

Lowry, P. E. (1997). The assessment center process: New directions. *Journal of Social Behavior and Personality, 12,* 53–62.

Lucas, R. E. (2007). Personality and the pursuit of happiness. *Social and Personality Psychology Compass, 1,* 168–182.

Lucas, R. E., and Baird, B. M. (2004). Extraversion and emotional reactivity. *Journal of Personality and Social Psychology, 86,* 473–485.

Lucas, R. E., Le, K., and Dyrenforth, P. S. (2008). Explaining the extraversion/positive affect relation: Sociability cannot account for extraverts' greater happiness. *Journal of Personality, 76,* 385–414.

Lucas, R. E., and Schimmack, U. (2009). Income and well-being: How big is the gap between the rich and the poor? *Journal of Research in Personality, 43,* 75–78.

Ludtke, O., Trautwein, U., and Husemann, N. (2009). Goal and personality trait development in a transitional period: Assessing change and stability in personality development. *Personality and Social Psychology Bulletin, 35,* 428–441.

Lukaszewski, A. W., and Roney, J. (2010). Kind toward whom? Mate preferences for personality traits are target-specific. *Evolution and Human Behavior, 31,* 28–38.

Lukaszewski, A. W., and Roney, J. (2011). The origins of extraversion: Joint effects of facultative calibration and genetic polymorphism. *Personality and Social Psychology Bulletin, 37,* 409–421.

Lund, O. C. H., Tamnes, C. K., Moestue, C., Buss, D. M., and Vollrath, M. (2006). Tactics of hierarchy negotiation. *Journal of Research in Personality, 41,* 25–44.

Luntz, B. K., and Widom, C. S. (1994). Antisocial personality disorder in abused and neglected children grown up. *American Journal of Psychiatry, 151,* 670–674.

Luo, S., Chen, H., Yue, G., Zhang, G., Zhaoyang, R., and Xu, D. (2008). Predicting marital satisfaction from self, partner, and couple characteristics: Is it me, you, or us? *Journal of Personality, 76,* 1231–1266.

Luo, S., and Klohnen, E. C. (2005). Assortative mating and marital quality in newlyweds: A couple-centered approach. *Journal of Personality and Social Psychology, 88,* 304–326.

Lykken, D. T. (1982, September). Fearlessness. *Psychology Today,* pp. 6–10.

Lykken, D. T. (1995). *The antisocial personalities.* Hillsdale, NJ: Erlbaum.

Lynn, R. (2008). *The global bell curve: Race, IQ and inequality worldwide.* Augusta, GA: Washington Summit.

Lynn, R., and Harvey, J. (2008). The decline of the world's IQ. *Intelligence, 36,* 112–120.

Lynn, S. J., Lock, T., Loftus, E. F., Krackow, E., and Lilienfeld, S. O. (2003). The remembrance of things past: Problematic memory recovery techniques in psychotherapy. In S. O. Lilienfeld and S. J. Lynn (Eds.), *Science and pseudoscience in clinical psychology* (pp. 205–239). New York: Guilford Press.

Lytton, H., Martin, N. G., and Eaves, L. (1977). Environmental and genetical causes of variation in ethological aspects of behavior in two-year-old boys. *Social Biology, 24,* 200–211.

Lyubomirsky, S. (2001). Why are some people happier than others? The role of cognitive and motivational processes in well-being. *American Psychologist, 56,* 239–249.

Lyubomirsky, S., King, L., and Diener, E. (2005). The benefits of frequent positive affect: Does happiness lead to success? *Psychological Bulletin, 131,* 803–855.

MacAndrew, C., and Steele, T. (1991). Gray's behavioral inhibition system: A psychometric examination. *Personality and Individual Differences, 12,* 157–171.

Maccoby, E. E., and Jacklin, C. N. (1974). *The psychology of sex differences.* Stanford, CA: Stanford University Press.

MacDonald, G., and Leary, M. R. (2005). Why does social exclusion hurt? The relationship between social and physical pain. *Psychological Bulletin, 131,* 202–223.

Machiavelli, N. (1966). *The prince.* New York: Bantam. (Original work published 1513.)

MacLaren, V. V., Best, L. A., Dixon, M. J., and Harrigan, K. A. (2011). Problem gambling and the five factor model in university students. *Personality and Individual Differences, 50,* 335–338.

MacLean, K. A., Johnson, M. W., and Griffiths, R. R. (2011). Mystical experiences occasioned by the hallucinogen psilocybin lead to increases in the personality domain of openness. *Journal of Psychopharmacology, 25,* 1453–1461.

Macmillan, M. B. (2000). Restoring Phineas Gage: A 150th retrospective. *Journal of the History of the Neurosciences, 9,* 42–62.

MacNab, B., Worthley, R., Brislin, R., Galperin, B. L., and Lituchy, T. R. (2007). National homogeneity vs. regional specificity: An examination of the Canadian cultural mosaic and whistle-blowing. *Canadian Journal of Regional Science, Summer 2007,* 293–312.

Major, B., and O'Brien, L. T. (2015). The social psychology of stigma. *Annual Reviews in Psychology, 56,* 393–421.

Major, B., Richards, C., Cooper, M. L., Cozzarelli, C., and Zubek, J. (1998). Personal resilience, cognitive appraisals, and coping: An integrative model of adjustment to abortion. *Journal of Personality and Social Psychology, 74*(3), 735–752.

Makridakis, S., and Moleskis, A. (2015). The costs and benefits of positive illusions. *Frontiers in Psychology, 6,* 859. doi: 10.3389/fpsyg.2015.00859.

Malcolm, J. (1981). *Psychoanalysis: The impossible profession.* New York: Knopf.

Maleva, V., Westcott, K., McKellop, M., McLaughlin, R., Widman, D., and College, J. (2014). Optimism and college grades: Predicting GPA from explanatory style. *Psi Chi Journal of Psychological Research, 19*(3), 129–135.

Mallard, T. T., Doorley, J. D., Esposito-Smythers, C. L., and McGeary, J. E. (2016). Dopamine D4 receptor VNTR polymorphism associated with greater risk for substance abuse among adolescents with disruptive behavior disorders: Preliminary results. *The American Journal on Addictions, 25*(1), 56–61 .

Malone, J. C., Weston, D., and Levendosky, A. (2011). Personalities of adults with traumatic childhood separations. *Journal of Clinical Psychology, 67,* 1259–1282.

Malouff, J. M., Thorsteinsson, E. B., Schutte, N. S., Bhullar, N., and Rooke, S. E. (2010). The five-factor model of personality and relationship satisfaction of intimate partners: A meta-analysis. *Journal of Research in Personality, 44,* 124–127.

Maltby, J., Wood, A. M., Day, L., Kon, T. W. H., Colley, A., and Linley, P. A. (2008). Personality predictors of levels of forgiveness two and a half years after the transgression. *Journal of Research in Personality, 42,* 1088–1094.

Maltby, J., Wood, A., Day, L., and Pinto, D. (2012). The position of authenticity within extant models pf personality. *Personality and Individual Differences, 52*(3), 269–273.

Marangoni, C., Garcia, S., Ickes, W., and Teng, G. (1995). Empathic accuracy in a clinically relevant setting. *Journal of Personality and Social Psychology, 68,* 854–869.

March, E., Grieve, R., Marrington, J., and Jonason, P. K. (2017). Trolling on Tinder® (and other dating apps): Examining the role of the Dark Tetrad and impulsivity. *Personality and Individual Differences, 110,* 139–143.

Marcia, J. E. (1966). Development and validation of ego-identity status. *Journal of Personality and Social Psychology, 3,* 551–558.

Marcia, J. E. (2002). Identity and psychosocial development in adulthood. *Identity, 2,* 7–28.

Markey, C. N., Markey, P. M., and Tinsley, B. J. (2003). Personality, puberty, and preadolescent girls' risky behaviors: Examining the predictive value of the five-factor model of personality. *Journal of Research in Personality, 37,* 405–419.

Markey, P. M., and Markey, C. N. (2007). The interpersonal meaning of sexual promiscuity. *Journal of Research in Personality, 41,* 1199–1212.

Markus, H. (1983). Self-knowledge: An expanded view. *Journal of Personality, 51,* 543–565.

Markus, H., and Nurius, P. (1986). Possible selves. *American Psychologist, 41,* 954–969.

Markus, H., and Nurius, P. (1987). Possible selves: The interface between motivation and the self concept. In K. Yardley and T. Honness (Eds.), *Self and identity: Psychosocial perspectives* (pp. 157–172). Chichester, England: Wiley.

Markus, H. R., and Kitayama, S. (1991). Culture and the self: Implications for cognition, emotion, and motivation. *Psychological Review, 98,* 224–253.

Markus, H. R., and Kitayama, S. (1994). A collective fear of the collective: Implications for selves and theories of selves. *Personality and Social Psychology Bulletin, 20,* 568–579.

Markus, H. R., and Kitayama, S. (1998). The cultural psychology of personality. *Journal of Cross-Cultural Psychology, 29,* 63–87.

Marschall-Lévesque, S., Castellanos-Ryan, N., Vitaro, F., and Séguin, J. R. (2014). Moderators of the association between peer and target adolescent substance use. *Addictive Behaviors, 39*(1), 48–70.

Marshall, T. C., Lefringhausen, K., and Ferenczi, N. (2015). The Big Five, self-esteem, and narcissism as predictors of the topics people write about in Facebook status updates. *Personality and Individual Differences 85,* 35–40.

Marsland, A. L., Cohen, S., Rabin, B. S., and Manuck, S. B. (2001). Associations between stress, trait negative affect, acute immune reactivity, and antibody response in hepatitis B injection in healthy young adults. *Health Psychology, 20,* 4–11.

Marten, K., and Psarakos, S. (1994). Evidence of self-awareness in the bottlenose dolphin (Tursiops truncatus). In S. T. Parker, R. W. Mitchell, & M. L. Boccia (Eds.), *Self-awareness in animals and humans: Developmental perspectives* (pp. 361–379). New York, NY, US: Cambridge University Press.

Martin, M., Ward, J. C., and Clark, D. M. (1983). Neuroticism and the recall of positive and negative personality information. *Behavior Research and Therapy, 21,* 495–503.

Martinelli, A. Ackermann, K., Bernhard, A.,Freitag, C.M., and Schwenck, C. (2018). Hostile attribution bias and aggression in children and adolescents: A systematic literature review on the influence of aggression subtype and gender. *Aggression and Violent Behavior, 39,* 25–32.

Martins, A., and Calheiros, M. M. (2012). Construction of a self-complexity scale for adolescents. *Psychological Assessment, 24,* 973–982.

Maslow, A. H. (1964). *Religions, values, and peak experiences.* London: Penguin Books Limited.

Maslow, A. H. (1968). *Toward a psychology of being* (2nd ed.). New York: Harper and Row. (Original work published 1954.)

Maslow, A. H. (1970). *Motivation and personality.* New York: Harper and Row. (Original work published 1954.)

Maslow, A. H. (1971). *The farther reaches of human nature.* New York: Viking Press.

Maslow, A. H. (1987). *Motivation and personality.* New York: Harper and Row. (Original work published 1954.)

Maslow, A. H., and Hoffman, E. (1996). *Future visions: The unpublished papers of Abraham Maslow.* Thousand Oaks, CA: Sage.

Mason, A., and Blankenship, V. (1987). Power and affiliation motivation, stress, and abuse in intimate relationships. *Journal of Personality and Social Psychology, 52,* 203–210.

Mason, J., Southwick, S., Yehuda, R., Wang, S., Riney, S., Bremner, D., Johnson, D., Lubin, H., Blake, D., and Zhou, G. (1994). Elevation of serum free triiodothyronine, total triiodothyronine, thyroxine-binding globulin, and total thyroxine levels in combat-related posttraumatic stress disorder. *Archives of General Psychiatry, 51,* 629–641.

Mason, O., Claridge, G., and Jackson, M. (1995). New scales for the assessment of schizotypy. *Personality and Individual Differences, 18,* 7–13.

Masson, J. M. (1984). *The assault on truth: Freud's suppression of the seduction theory.* New York: Farrar, Straus and Giroux.

Masuda, T., and Nisbett, R. E. (2001). Attending holistically versus analytically: Comparing the context sensitivity of Japanese and Americans. *Journal of Personality and Social Psychology, 81*(5), 922–934.

Matsumoto, D. (1999). Culture and self: An empirical assessment of Markus and Kitayama's theory of independent and interdependent self-construals. *Asian Journal of Social Psychology, 2,* 289–310.

Matthews, G. (2000). Attention, automaticity, and affective disorder. *Behavior Modification, 24,* 69–93.

Matthews, G., Derryberry, D., and Siegle, G. J. (2000). Personality and emotion: Cognitive science perspectives. In S. E. Hampson (Ed.), *Advances in personality psychology* (vol. 1, pp. 199–237). Philadelphia: Taylor and Francis.

Matthews, G., and Gilliland, K. (1999). The personality theories of H. J. Eysenck and J. A. Gray: A comparative review. *Personality and Individual Differences, 26,* 583–626.

Matthews, G., and Oddy, K. (1993). Recovery of major personality dimensions from trait adjective data. *Personality and Individual Differences, 15,* 419–431.

Matthews, L. J., and Butler, P. M. (2011). Novelty-seeking DRD4 polymorphisms are associated with human migration distance out-of-Africa after controlling for neutral population gene structure. *American Journal of Physical Anthropology, 145*(3), 382–389.

Mattia, J. I., and Zimmerman, M. (2001). Epidemiology. In W. J. Livesley (Ed.), *Handbook of personality disorders: Theory, research and treatment.* New York: Guilford Press.

Maynard Smith, J. (1982). *Evolution and the theory of games.* Cambridge, England: Cambridge University Press.

McAdams, D. P. (1990). Motives. In V. Derlega, B. Winstead, and W. Jones (Eds.), *Contemporary research in personality* (pp. 175–204). Chicago: Nelson-Hall.

McAdams, D. P. (1992). The five-factor model in personality: A critical appraisal. *Journal of Personality, 60,* 329–361.

McAdams, D. P. (1999). Personal narratives and the life story. In L. A. Pervin and O. P. John (Eds.), *Handbook of personality: Theory and research* (2nd ed., pp. 478–500). New York: Guilford Press.

McAdams, D. P. (2008). Personal narratives and the life story. In O. John, R. Robins, and L. A. Pervin, *Handbook of personality: Theory and research* (pp. 241–261). New York: Guilford Press.

McAdams, D. P. (2011). Narrative identity. In S. J. Schwartz, K. Luyckx, and V. L. Vignoles (Eds.), *Handbook of identity theory and research* (vols. 1 & 2, pp. 99–115). New York, NY: Springer Science + Business Media.

McAdams, D. P., and Bryant, F. B. (1987). Intimacy motivation and subjective mental health in a nationwide sample. *Journal of Personality, 55,* 395–413.

McAdams, D. P., and Vaillant, G. E. (1982). Intimacy motivation and psychosocial adjustment: A longitudinal study. *Journal of Personality Assessment, 46,* 586–593.

McCarley, N. G., and Clarskadon, T. G. (1983). Test-retest reliabilities of the scales and subscales of the Myers-Briggs Type Indicator and of criteria for clinical interpretive hypotheses involving them. *Research in Psychological Type, 6,* 24–36.

McClelland, D. C. (1958). Risk-taking in children with high and low need for achievement. In J. W. Atkinson (Ed.), *Motives in fantasy, action, and society* (pp. 306–327). Princeton, NJ: Van Nostrand.

McClelland, D. C. (1965). N achievement and entrepreneurship: A longitudinal study. *Journal of Personality and Social Psychology, 1,* 389–392.

McClelland, D. C. (1979). Inhibited power motivation and high blood pressure in men. *Journal of Abnormal Psychology, 88,* 182–190.

McClelland D. C. (1982). The need for power, sympathetic activation, and illness. *Motivation and Emotion, 6,* 31–41.

McClelland, D. C. (1985). How motives, skills, and values determine what people do. *American Psychologist, 40,* 812–825.

McClelland, D. C., Alexander, C., and Marks, E. (1982). The need for power, stress, immune function, and illness among male prisoners. *Journal of Abnormal Psychology, 91,* 61–70.

McClelland, D. C., and Jemmott, J. B. (1980). Power motivation, stress, and physical illness. *Journal of Human Stress, 6,* 6–15.

McClelland, D. C., Koestner, R., and Weinberger, J. (1989). How do self-attributed and implicit motives differ? *Psychological Review, 96,* 690–702.

McClelland, D. C., and Pilon, D. A. (1983). Sources of adult motives in patterns of parent behavior in early childhood. *Journal of Personality and Social Psychology, 44,* 564–574.

McConnell, A. R., Strain, L. M., Brown, C. M., and Rydell, R. J. (2009). The simple life: On the benefits of low self-complexity. *Personality and Social Psychology Bulletin, 35,* 823–835.

McCoul, M. D., and Haslam, N. (2001). Predicting high risk sexual behaviour in heterosexual and homosexual men: The roles of impulsivity and sensation seeking. *Personality and Individual Differences, 31,* 1303–1310.

McCrae, R. R., and Costa, P. T., Jr. (1985). Updating Norman's "adequate taxonomy": Intelligence and personality dimensions in natural language and questionnaires. *Journal of Personality and Social Psychology, 49,* 710–721.

McCrae, R. R., and Costa, P. T., Jr. (1987). Validation of the five-factor model of personality across instruments and observers. *Journal of Personality and Social Psychology, 52,* 81–90.

McCrae, R. R., and Costa, P. T. (1991). Adding *liebe und arbeit*: The full five-factor model and well-being. *Personality and Social Psychology Bulletin, 17,* 227–232.

McCrae, R. R., and Costa, P. T., Jr. (1997). Personality trait structure as a human universal. *American Psychologist, 52,* 509–516.

McCrae, R. R., and Costa, P. T., Jr. (1999). A five-factor theory of personality. In L. A. Pervin and O. John (Eds.), *Handbook of personality: Theory and research* (2nd ed.). New York: Guilford Press.

McCrae, R. R., and Costa, P. T., Jr. (2008). The five factor theory of personality. In O. P. John, R. W. Robins, and L. A. Pervin (Eds.), *Handbook of personality* (pp. 159–181). New York: Guilford Press.

McCrae, R. R., Chan, W., Jussim, L., De Fruyt, F., Löckenhoff, C. E., De Bolle, M., Costa, P. T., Jr., . . . Avdeyeva, T. V., Pramila, V. S., and Terricciano, A. (2013). The inaccuracy of national character stereotypes. *Journal of Research in Personality, 47*(6), 831–842. doi: 10.1016/j.jrp.2013.08.006

McCrae, R. R., Costa, P. T., Jr., del Pilar, G. H., Rolland, J., and Parker, W. D. (1998). Cross-cultural assessment of the five-factor model: The Revised NEO Personality Inventory. *Journal of Cross-Cultural Psychology, 29,* 171–188.

McCrae, R. R., Costa, P. T., Jr., Terracciano, A., Parker, W. D., Mills, C. J., De Fruyt, F., and Mervielde, I. (2002). Personality trait development from age 12 to age 18: Longitudinal, cross-sectional, and cross-cultural analyses. *Journal of Personality and Social Psychology, 83,* 1456–1468.

McCrae, R. R., and John, O. P. (1992). An introduction to the five-factor model and its applications. *Journal of Personality, 60,* 175–215.

McCrae, R. R., Terracciano, A., and 78 Members of the Personality Profiles of Cultures Project. (2005a). Personality profiles of cultures: Aggregate personality traits. *Journal of Personality and Social Psychology, 89,* 407–425.

McCrae, R. R., Terracciano, A., and 78 Members of the Personality Profiles of Cultures Project. (2005b). Universal features of personality traits from the observer's perspective: Data from 50 cultures. *Journal of Personality and Social Psychology, 88,* 547–561.

McCullough, M. E., Bellah, C. G., Kilpatrick, S. D., and Johnson, J. L. (2001). Vengefulness: Relationships with forgiveness, rumination, well-being, and the Big Five. *Personality and Social Psychology Bulletin, 27*(5), 601–610.

McCullough, M. E., Emmons, R. A., Kilpatrick, S. D., and Mooney, C. N. (2003). Narcissists as "victims": The role of narcissism in the perception of transgressions. *Personality and Social Psychology Bulletin, 29*(7), 885–893.

McDaniel, M. J., Beier, M. E., Perkins, A. W., Goggin, S., and Frankel, B. (2009). An assessment of fakeability of self-report and implicit personality measures. *Journal of Research in Personality, 43,* 682–685.

McDaniel, S. R., and Zuckerman, M. (2003). The relationship of impulsive sensation seeking and gender to interest and participation in gambling activities. *Personality and Individual Differences, 35,* 1385–1400.

McDougall, P., and Vaillancourt, T. (2015). Long-term adult outcomes of peer victimization in childhood and adolescence: Pathways to adjustment and maladjustment. *American Psychologist, 70*(4), 300–310.

McGrath, R. E., and Carroll, E. J. (2012). The current status of "projective" "tests." In H. Cooper, P. M. Camic, D. L. Long, A. T. Panter, D. Rindskopf, and K. J. Sher (Eds.), *APA handbook of research methods in psychology, vol. 1: Foundations, planning, measures, and psychometrics* (pp. 329–348). Washington, DC: American Psychological Association.

McGue, M. (2010). The end of behavioral genetics? *Behavior Genetics, 40,* 284–296.

McHoskey, J. W. (2001). Machiavellianism and sexuality: On the moderating role of biological sex. *Personality and Individual Differences, 31,* 779–789.

McLoyd, V. S. (1998). Socioeconomic disadvantage and child development. *American Psychologist, 53,* 188–204.

Mead, M. (1928). *Coming of age in Samoa.* New York: Morrow.

Mead, M. (1935). *Sex and temperament in three primitive societies.* New York: Morrow.

Mealey, L. (1995). The sociobiology of sociopathy: An integrated evolutionary model. *Behavioral and Brain Sciences, 18,* 523–599.

Mecacci, L., Scaglione, M. R., and Vitrano, I. (1991). Diurnal and monthly variations of temperature and self-reported activation in relation to sex and circadian typology. *Personality and Individual Differences, 12,* 819–824.

Medd, K. D. (2010). *An application of Hofstede's Values Survey Module with Aboriginal and Non-Aboriginal governments in Canada (unpublished doctoral dissertation).* Carleton University, Ottawa, Ontario.

Megargee, E. I. (1969). Influence of sex roles on the manifestation of leadership. *Journal of Applied Psychology, 53,* 377–382.

Mehl, M. R., and Pennebaker, J. W. (2003). The social dynamics of a cultural upheaval: Social interactions surrounding September 11, 2001. *Psychological Science, 14,* 579–585.

Menninger, K. (1963). *The vital balance: The life process in mental health and illness.* New York: Viking Press.

Messick, S. (1994). The matter of style: Manifestations of personality in cognition, learning, and teaching. *Educational Psychologist, 29,* 121–136.

Meston, C. M., Heiman, J. R., Trapnell, P. D., and Paulhus, D. L. (1998). Socially desirable responding and sexuality self-reports. *Journal of Sex Research, 35,* 148–157.

Michalos, A. C. (1991). *Global report on student well-being. Vol. 1: Life satisfaction and happiness.* New York: Springer-Verlag.

Mike, A., Jackson, J. J., and Oltmanns, T. F. (2014). The conscientious retiree: The relationship between conscientiousness, retirement, and volunteering. *Journal of Research in Personality, 52,* 68–77.

Mikulincer, M., and Florian, V. (1995). Appraisal and coping with a real-life stressful situation: The contribution of attachment styles. *Personality and Social Psychology Bulletin, 69,* 1203–1215.

Mikulincer, M., Florian, V., and Weller, A. (1993). Attachment styles, coping strategies, and posttraumatic psychological distress: The impact of the Gulf War in Israel. *Journal of Personality and Social Psychology, 64,* 817–826.

Mikulincer, M., Shaver, P. R., Cooper, M. L., and Larsen, R. J. (Eds.). (2015). *APA handbooks in psychology. APA handbook of personality and social psychology, Vol. 4. Personality processes and individual differences.* Washington, DC, US: American Psychological Association.

Milan, A. (2013). Marital status: Overview, 2011. Statistics Canada. Retrieved from http://www.statcan.gc.ca/pub/91-209-x/2013001/article/11788-eng.htm.

Milin, R., Loh, E. A., and Wilson, A. (1992). Drug preference, reported drug experience, and stimulus sensitivity. *American Journal on Addictions, 1,* 248–256.

Miller, A. L. (2007). Creativity and cognitive style: The relationship between field-dependence-independence, expected evaluation, and creative performance. *Psychology of Aesthetics, Creativity, and the Arts, 1,* 243–246.

Miller, G. E., and Cohen, S. (2001). Psychological interventions and the immune system: A meta-analytic review and critique. *Health Psychology, 20,* 47–63.

Miller, J. D., and Lynam, D. R. (2015). Understanding psychopathy using the basic elements of personality. *Social and Personality Psychology Compass, 9*(5), 223–237.

Miller, J. D., Lynam, D., Zimmerman, R. S., Logan, T. K., Leukefeld, C., and Clayton, R. (2004). The utility of the five factor model in understanding risky sexual behavior. *Personality and Individual Differences, 36,* 1611–1626.

Miller, J. L., Schmidt, L. A., Vaillancourt, T., McDougall, P., and Laliberte, M. (2006). Neuroticism and introversion: A risky combination for disordered eating among a non-clinical sample of undergraduate women. *Eating Behaviors, 7*(1), 69–78.

Miller, L. C., and Fishkin, S. A. (1997). On the dynamics of human bonding and reproductive success: Seeking windows on the adapted-for human-environmental interface. In J. Simpson and D. T. Kenrick (Eds.), *Evolutionary social psychology* (pp. 197–235). Hillside, NJ: Erlbaum.

Miller, P. C., Lefcourt, H. M., and Ware, E. E. (1983). The construction and development of the Miller Marital Locus of Control scale. *Canadian Journal of Behavioral Science, 15,* 266–279.

Miller, T. W. K., Smith, T. W., Turner, C. W., Guajardo, M. L., and Hallet, A. J. (1996). A meta-analytic review of research on hostility and physical health. *Psychological Bulletin, 119,* 322–348.

Millon, T. (1990). *Toward a new personology: An evolutionary model.* New York: Wiley-Interscience.

Millon, T. (1999). Reflections on psychosynergy: A model for integrating science, theory, classification, assessment, and therapy. *Journal of Personality Assessment, 72,* 437–456.

Millon, T. (2000a). Reflections of the future of DSM Axis II. *Journal of Personality Disorders, 14,* 30–41.

Millon, T. (2000b). Sociocultural conceptions of the borderline personality. *Psychiatric Clinics of North America Special Issue: Borderline Personality Disorder, 23,* 123–136.

Millon, T., Davis, R., Millon, C., Escovar, L., and Meagher, S. (2000). *Personality disorders: Current concepts and classical foundations.* New York: Wiley.

Mischel, W. (1968). *Personality and assessment.* New York: Wiley.

Mischel, W. (1984). Convergences and challenges in the search for consistency. *American Psychologist, 39,* 351–364.

Mischel, W. (1990). Personality dispositions revisited and revised: A view after three decades. In L. Pervin (Ed.), *Handbook of personality: Theory and research* (pp. 111–134). New York, Guilford Press.

Mischel, W. (2000). A cognitive-affective system theory of personality: Reconceptualizing situations, dispositions, dynamics, and invariance in personality structure. In E. T. Higgins and A. W. Kruglanski (Eds.), *Motivational science: Social and personality perspectives* (pp. 150–176). New York: Psychology Press.

Mischel, W. (2004). Toward an integrative science of the person. *Annual Review of Psychology, 55,* 1–22.

Mischel, W., and Peake, P. K. (1982). Beyond déjà vu in the search for cross-situational consistency. *Psychological Review, 89,* 730–755.

Mischel, W., and Shoda, Y. (2010). The situated person. In B. Mesquita, L. F. Barrett, and E. R. Smith (Eds.), *The mind in context* (pp. 149–173). New York: Guilford.

Mischel, W., Shoda, Y., and Mendoza-Denton, R. (2002). Situation-behavior profiles as a locus of consistency in personality. *Current Directions in Psychological Science, 11,* 50–54.

Mittler, P. (1971). *The study of twins.* Harmondsworth, England: Penguin Books.

Mlacic, B., and Ostendorf, F. (2005). Taxonomy and structure of Croatian personality-descriptive adjectives. *European Journal of Personality, 19,* 117–152.

Moffitt, T. E. (2005). The new look of behavioral genetics in developmental psychopathology: Gene-environment interplay in antisocial behaviors. *Psychological Bulletin, 131,* 533–554.

Mommersteeg, P. M. C., Pelle, A. J., Ramakers, C., Szabó, B. M., Denollet, J., and Kupper, N. (2012). Type D personality and course of health status over 18 months in outpatients with heart failure: Multiple mediating inflammatory biomarkers. *Brain, Behavior, and Immunity, 26,* 301–310.

Monk, T. H., and Leng, V. C. (1986). Interactions between inter-individual and inter-task differences in the diurnal variation of human performance. *Chronobiology International, 3,* 171–177.

Monk, T. H., Leng, V. C., Folkard, S., and Weitzman, E. D. (1983). Circadian rhythms in subjective alertness and core body temperature. *Chronobiologia, 10,* 49–55.

Moon, J. H., Lee, E., Lee, J. A., Choi, T. R., and Sung, Y. (2016). The role of narcissism in self-promotion on Instagram. *Personality and Individual Differences, 101,* 22–25.

Moore, M., Schermer, J. A., Paunonen, S.V., and Vernon, P. A. (2010). Genetic and environmental influences on verbal and nonverbal measures of the Big Five. *Personality and Individual Differences, 48,* 884–888.

Moretti, R. J., and Rossini, E. D. (2004). The Thematic Apperception Test (TAT). In M. J. Hilsenroth and E. L. Segal (Eds.), *Comprehensive handbook of psychological assessment, Vol. 2: Personality assessment* (pp. 356–371). Hoboken, NJ: Wiley.

Morey, J. N., Boggero, I. A., Scott, A. B., and Segerstrom, S. C. (2015). Current directions in stress and human immune function. *Current Opinion in Psychology, 5,* 13–17.

Morey, L. C. (1997). Personality diagnosis and personality disorders. In R. Hogan, J. A. Johnson, and S. R. Briggs (Eds.), *Handbook of personality psychology* (pp. 919–946). San Diego: Academic Press.

Morgan, C. D., and Murray, H. A. (1935). A method of investigating fantasies. *Archives of Neurological Psychiatry, 34,* 289–306.

Morgan, C. A., Southwick, S., Steffian, G., Hazlett, G. A., and Loftus, E. F. (2012). Misinformation can influence memory for recently experienced, highly stressful events. *International Journal of Law and Psychiatry, 36*, 11–17.

Morissette, R., Picot, G., and Lu, Y. (2013). The evolution of Canadian wages over the last three decades. *Analytical Studies Branch Research Paper Series. Statistics Canada, Catalogue no. 11F0019M — No. 347.*

Moskowitz, D. S. (1993). Dominance and friendliness: On the interaction of gender and situation. *Journal of Personality, 61*, 387–409.

Moskowitz, D. S., Suh, E. J., and Desaulniers, J. (1994). Situational influences on gender differences in agency and communion. *Journal of Personality and Social Psychology, 66*, 753–761.

Moskowitz, J. T. (2011). Coping interventions and the regulation of positive affect. In S. Folkman (Ed.), *The Oxford handbook of stress, health, and coping* (pp. 407–427). New York, NY: Oxford University Press.

Moskowitz, J. T., Folkman, S., Collette, L., and Vittinghoff, E. (1996). Coping and mood during AIDS-related caregiving and bereavement. *Annals of Behavioral Medicine, 18*, 49–57.

Moss-Racusin, C. A., and Good, J. J. (2015). Measure of a man: Outcomes of gender stereotyping for men and masculinity. *Social Psychology, 46*, 179–181.

Mower, O. H. (1960). *Learning theory and behavior.* New York: Wiley.

Mroczek, D. K., and Spiro, A., III. (2003). Modeling intraindividual change in personality traits: Findings from the Normative Aging Study. *Journals of Gerontology Series B-Psychological Sciences & Social Sciences, 58B*, P153–P165.

Mroczek, D. K., Spiro, A., III., and Turiano, N. A. (2009). Do health behaviors explain the effect of neuroticism on mortality? Longitudinal findings from the VA Normative Aging Study. *Journal of Research in Personality, 43*, 653–659.

Mufson, D. W., and Mufson, M. A. (1998). Predicting police officer performance using the Inwald Personality Inventory: An illustration from Appalachia. *Professional Psychology: Research and Practice, 29*, 59–62.

Multon, K. D., Brown, S. D., and Lent, R. W. (1991). Relation of the self-efficacy beliefs to academic outcomes: A meta-analytic investigation. *Journal of Counseling Psychology, 38*, 30–38.

Munafo, M. R., Yalcin, B., Willis-Owen, S. A., and Flint, J. (2008). Association of the dopamine D4 receptor (DRD4) gene and approach-related personality traits: Meta-analysis and new data. *Biological Psychiatry, 63*, 197–206.

Murdock, G. P. (1980). *Theories of illness: A world survey.* Pittsburgh: University of Pittsburgh Press.

Murray, D. R., Schaller, M., and Suedfeld, P. (2013). Pathogens and politics: Further evidence that parasite prevalence predicts authoritarianism. *PLoS ONE, 8*(5), e62275. doi: 10.1371/journal.pone.0062275.

Murray, D. R., Trudeau, R., and Schaller, M. (2011). On the origins of cultural differences in conformity: Four tests of the pathogen prevalence hypothesis. *Personality and Social Psychology Bulleti.n, 37*, 318–329.

Murray, G., Allen, N.B., and Trinder, J. (2002). Longitudinal investigation of mood variability and neuroticism predicts variability in extended states of positive and negative affect. *Personality and Individual Differences, 33*, 1217–1228.

Murray, H. A. (1933). The effect of fear upon estimates of the maliciousness of other personalities. *Journal of Social Psychology, 4*, 310–329.

Murray, H. A. (1938). *Explorations in personality.* New York: Oxford University Press.

Murray, H. A. (1967). Autobiography (the case of Murr). In E. G. Boring and G. Lindzey (Eds.), *History of psychology in autobiography* (vol. 5, pp. 285–310). New York: Appleton-Century-Crofts.

Murstein, B. I. (1976). *Who will marry whom? Theories and research in marital choice.* New York: Springer.

Mushquash, C., Stewart, S., Mushquash, A., Comeau, N., and McGrath, P. (2014). Personality traits and drinking motives predict alcohol misuse among Canadian Aboriginal youth. *International Journal of Mental Health and Addiction, 12*(3), 270–282.

Myers, D. G. (1993). *The pursuit of happiness.* New York: Avon Books.

Myers, D. G. (2000). The funds, friends, and faith of happy people. *American Psychologist, 55*, 56–67.

Myers, D. G., and Diener, E. (1995). Who is happy? *Psychological Science, 6*, 10–19.

Myers, I. B., McCaulley, M. H., Quenk, N. L., and Hammer, A. L. (1998). *Manual: A guide to the development and use of the Myers-Briggs Type Indicator.* Palo Alto: Consulting Psychologists Press.

Myrseth, H., Pallesen, S., Molde, H., Johnsen, B. H., and Lorvik, I. M. (2009). Personality factors as predictors of pathological gambling. *Personality and Individual Differences, 47*, 933–937.

Na, J., and Choi, I. (2009). Culture and first-person pronouns. *Personality and Social Psychology Bulletin, 35*, 1492–1499.

Nasby, W., and Read, N. W. (1997). The life voyage of a solo circumnavigator: Integrating theoretical and methodological perspectives. *Journal of Personality, 65*, 785–1068.

Nash, M. R. (1987). What, if anything, is regressed about hypnotic age regression: A review of the empirical literature. *Psychological Bulletin, 102*, 42–52.

Nash, M. R. (1988). Hypnosis as a window on regression. *Bulletin of the Menninger Clinic, 52*, 383–403.

Nash, M. R. (1999). The psychological unconscious. In V. J. Derlega, B. A. Winstead, and W. H. Jones (Eds.), *Personality: Contemporary theory and research* (pp. 197–228). Chicago: Nelson-Hall.

Nash, M. R. (2001). The truth and the hype of hypnosis. *Scientific American* (July), 47–55.

Nathanson, C., Paulhus, D. L., and Williams, K. M. (2006). Personality and misconduct correlates of body modification and other cultural deviance markers. *Journal of Research in Personality, 40*, 779–802.

National Inquiry into Missing and Murdered Indigenous Women and Girls (2019). *Reclaiming power and place: The final report of the National Inquiry into Missing and Murdered Indigenous Women and Girls.* Retrieved June 17, 2019, from https://www.mmiwg-ffada.ca/final-report.

Neisser, U. (1998). *The rising curve: Long-term gains in IQ and related measures.* Washington, DC: American Psychological Association.

Nelson, E., Hoffman, C. L., Gerald, M. S., and Schultz, S. (2010). Digit ratio (2D:4D) and dominance rank in female rhesus macaques (*Macaca mulatta*). *Behavioral Ecology and Sociobiology, 64*, 1001–1009.

Nettle, D. (2006). The evolution of personality variation in humans and other animals. *American Psychologist, 61*, 622–631.

Nettle, D., and Liddle, B. (2008). Agreeableness is related to socio-cognitive, but not socio-perceptual, theory of mind. *European Journal of Personality, 22*, 323–335.

Nevis, E. C. (1983). Using an American perspective in understanding another culture: Toward a hierarchy of needs for the People's Republic of China. *Journal of Applied Behavioral Science, 19*, 249–264.

Newman, J. P. (1987). Reaction to punishment in extraverts and psychopaths: Implications for the impulsive behavior of disinhibited individuals. *Journal of Research in Personality, 21*, 464–480.

Newman, J. P., Widom, C. S., and Nathan, S. (1985). Passive avoidance and syndromes of disinhibition: Psychopathy and extraversion. *Journal of Personality and Social Psychology, 48*, 1316–1327.

Newman, L. C., and Larsen, R. J. (2011). *Taking sides: Clashing views in personality psychology.* New York: McGraw-Hill.

Newman, P. R., and Newman, B. M. (1988). Differences between childhood and adulthood: The identity watershed. *Adolescence, 23*, 551–557.

Neyer, F. J. (2006). Editorial: EJP special edition on personality change. *European Journal of Personality, 20*, 419–420.

Neyer, F. J., and Lehnart, J. (2007). Relationships matter in personality development: Evidence from an 8-year longitudinal study across young adulthood. *Journal of Personality, 75*, 535–568.

Neyer, F. J., and Voigt, D. (2004). Personality and social network effects on romantic relationships: A dyadic approach. *European Journal of Personality, 18*, 279–299.

Nicolaou, A., and Xistouri, X. (2011). Field dependence/independence cognitive style and problem posing: An investigation with sixth grade students. *Educational Psychology, 31*, 611–627.

Niederhoffer, K. G., and Pennebaker, J. W. (2002). Sharing one's story: On the benefits of writing or talking about emotional experience. In C. R. Snyder and S. J. Lopez (Eds.), *Handbook of positive psychology* (pp. 573–583). London: Oxford University Press.

Niederle, M., and Vesterlund, L. (2005). *Do women shy away from competition? Do men compete too much?* Working paper # 11474, National Bureau of Economic Research, Cambridge, MA.

Nietzsche, F. (1891/1969). *Thus spoke Zarathustra: A book for everyone and no one.* Translated with an introduction by R. J. Hollingdale. New York: Penguin Books.

Nigg, J. T., and Goldsmith, H. H. (1994). Genetics of personality disorders: Perspectives from personality and psychopathology research. *Pathological Bulletin, 115*, 346–380.

Nisbet, R., and Cohen, D. (1996). *Culture of honor.* Boulder, CO: Westview Press.

Nisbett, R. E. (1993). Violence and U.S. regional culture. *American Psychologist, 48*, 441–449.

Nisbett, R. E., Peng, K., Choi, I., and Norenzayan, A. (2001). Culture and systems of thought: Holistic vs. analytic cognition. *Psychological Review, 108*, 291–310.

Niv, S., Tuvbld, C., Raine, A., Want, P., and Baker, L. A. (2012). Heritability and longitudinal stability of impulsivity in adolescence. *Behavior Genetics, 42,* 378–392.

Noftle, E. E., and Robins, R. W. (2007). Personality predictors of academic outcomes: Big Five correlates of GPA and SAT scores. *Journal of Personality and Social Psychology, 93,* 116–130.

Nolen-Hoeksema, S., Larson, J., and Grayson, C. (1999). Explaining gender differences in depressive symptoms. *Journal of Personality and Social Psychology, 77,* 1061–1072.

Norem, J. K. (1995, June). The power of negative thinking: Interview with psychology professor Julie Norem. *Men's Health, 10,* p. 46.

Norem, J. K. (1998). Why should we lower our defenses about defense mechanisms? *Journal of Personality Special Issue: Defense mechanisms in contemporary personality research, 66,* 895–917.

Norem, J. K. (2001). Defensive pessimism, optimism, and pessimism. In E. Change (Ed.), *Optimism and pessimism: Implications for theory, research, and practice* (pp. 77–100). Washington, DC: American Psychological Association.

Norman, W. T. (1963). Toward an adequate taxonomy of personality attributes: Replicated factor structure in peer nomination personality ratings. *Journal of Abnormal Psychology, 66,* 574–583.

Norman, W. T. (1967). *2800 personality trait descriptors: Normative operating characteristics in a university population.* Ann Arbor: Department of Psychology, University of Michigan.

Nudelman, A. E. (1973). Bias in the Twenty-Statements Test: Administration time, incomplete protocols, and intelligence. *Psychological Reports, 33,* 524–526.

Nusbaum, E. C., and Silva, P. J. (2011). Are openness and intellect distinct aspects of Openness to Experience? A test of the O/I model. *Personality and Individual Differences, 51,* 571–574.

Nusbaum, E. C., and Silvia, P. J. (2011). Are intelligence and creativity really so different? Fluid intelligence, executive processes, and strategy use in divergent thinking. *Intelligence, 39,* 36–45.

Oatley, K., and Johnson-Laird, P. N. (1987). Towards a cognitive theory of emotions. *Cognition and Emotion, 1,* 29–50.

O'Brien, T. B., and DeLongis, A. (1996). The interactional context of problem-, emotion- and relationship-focused coping: The role of the Big Five personality factors. *Journal of Personality, 64,* 775–813.

Ochsner, K. N., Bunge, S. A., Gross, J. J., and Gabrieli, J. D. E. (2002). Rethinking feelings: An fMRI study of the cognitive regulation of emotion. *Journal of Cognitive Neuroscience, 14,* 1215–1229.

O'Connell, M., and Sheikh, H. (2011). "Big Five" personality dimensions and social attainment: Evidence from beyond the campus. *Personality and Individual Differences, 50,* 828–833.

O'Connor, M. C., and Paunonen, S. V. (2007). Big Five personality predictors of post-secondary academic performance. *Personality and Individual Differences, 43,* 971–990.

Ode, S., Robinson, M. D., and Wilkowski, B. M. (2008). Can one's temper be cooled? A role for agreeableness in moderating neuroticism's influence on anger and aggression. *Journal of Research in Personality, 42,* 295–311.

O'Dell, K. R., Masters, K. S., Spielmans, G. I., and Maisto, S. A. (2011). Does type-D personality predict outcomes among patients with cardiovascular disease? A meta-analytic review. *Journal of Psychosomatic Research, 71,* 199–206.

Oerlemans, W. G., and Bakker, A. B. (2014). Why extraverts are happier: A day reconstruction study. *Journal of Research in Personality, 50,* 11–22.

Ofshe, R. J. (1992). Inadvertent hypnosis during interrogation: False confession due to dissociative states: Misidentified multiple personality and the satanic cult hypothesis. *International Journal of Clinical and Experimental Hypnosis, 40,* 125–156.

Oishi, S., Talhelm, T., and Lee, M. (2015). Personality and geography: Introverts prefer mountains. *Journal of Research in Personality, 58,* 55–68.

Olino, T. M., Durbin, C. E., Klein, D. N., Hayden, E. P., and Dyson, M. W. (2013). Gender differences in young children's temperament traits: Comparisons across observational and parent-report methods. *Journal of Personality, 81*(2), 119–129.

Olsson, M., and Martiny, S. E. (2018). Does exposure to counterstereotypical role models influence girls' and women's gender stereotypes and career choices? A review of social psychological research. *Frontiers in Psychology, 9,* 2264.

Olson, J. (2002). *"I": The creation of a serial killer.* New York: St. Martin's Paperbacks.

Olson, J. M., Vernon, P. A., Harris, J. A., and Jang, K. L. (2001). The heritability of attitudes: A study of twins. *Journal of Personality and Social Psychology, 80,* 845–860.

Olson, K. R., Key, A. C., and Eaton, N. R. (2015). Gender cognition in transgender children. *Psychological Science, 26*(4), 467–474. doi: 10.1177/0956797614568156

Oltmanns, T. F., and Emery, R. E. (2004). *Abnormal psychology* (4th ed.). Upper Saddle River, NJ: Prentice Hall.

Oltmanns, T. F., Friedman, J. N., Fiedler, E. R., and Turkheimer, E. (2004). Perceptions of people with personality disorders based on thin slices of behavior. *Journal of Research in Personality, 38,* 216–229.

Olweus, D. (1978). *Bullies and whipping boys.* Washington, DC: Hemisphere.

Olweus, D. (1979). Stability of aggressive reaction patterns in males: A review. *Psychological Bulletin, 86,* 852–875.

Olweus, D. (2001). *Olweus' core program against bullying and antisocial behavior: A teacher handbook.* Research Center for Health promotion (Hemil Center). Bergen, Norway.

O'Neill, L. (2017). An ally in Northern community health: Respectful engagement in healing relationships. In S. L. Stewart, R. Moodley, & A. Hyatt (Eds.), *Indigenous cultures and mental health counselling: Four directions for integration with counselling psychology* (pp. 171–181). New York, NY: Routledge/Taylor & Francis Group.

O'Neill, T. A., and Paunonen, S. V. (2013). Breadth in personality assessment: Implications for the understanding and prediction of work behavior. In N. D. Christiansen and R. P. Tett (Eds.), *Handbook of personality at work* (pp. 299–333). New York, NY: Routledge.

Ones, D. S., and Viswesvaran, C. (1998). Integrity testing in organizations. *Monographs in Organizational Behavior and Industrial Relations, 23,* 243–276.

Ong, E. Y. L., Ang, R. P., Ho, J.C.M., Lim, J. C. Y., Goh, D. H., Lee, C. S., and Chua, A. Y. K. (2011). Narcissism, extraversion and adolescents' self-presentation on Facebook. *Personality and Individual Differences, 50,* 180–185.

Oniszczenko, W., Zawadzki, B., Strelau, J., Reimann, R., Angleitner, A., and Spinath, F. M. (2003). Genetic and environmental determinants of temperament: A comprehensive study based on Polish and German samples. *European Journal of Personality, 17,* 207–220.

Ortony, A., and Turner, T. J., (1990). What's basic about basic emotions. *Psychological Review, 97,* 315–331.

Osgood, C. E., Suci, G. J., and Tannenbaum, P. H. (1957). *The measurement of meaning.* Urbana: University of Illinois Press.

Oshio, A., Taku, K., Hirano, M., and Saeed, G. (2018). Resilience and Big Five personality traits: A meta-analysis. *Personality and Individual Differences, 127,* 54–60.

Osmon, D. C., and Jackson, R. (2002). Inspection time and IQ: Fluid or perceptual aspects of intelligence? *Intelligence, 30,* 119–128.

Ostendorf, F. (1990). *Language and personality structure: Towards the validity of the five-factor model of personality.* Regensburg, Germany: Roderer-Verlag.

Ostrov, J. M., and Godleski, S. A. (2010). Toward an integrated gender-linked model of aggression subtypes in early and middle childhood. *Psychological Review, 117,* 233–242.

Ottoni, G. L., Antoniolli, E., and Lara, D. R. (2011). The Circadian Energy Scale (CIRENS): Two simple questions for a reliable chronotype measurement based on energy. *Chronobiology International, 28,* 229–237.

Oughton, J. M., and Reed, W. M. (1999). The influence of learner differences on the construction of hypermedia concepts: A case study. *Computers in Human Behavior, 15,* 11–50.

Oyserman, D., Coon, H. M., and Kemmelmeier, M. (2002a). Rethinking individualism and collectivism: Evaluation of theoretical assumptions and meta-analyses. *Psychological Bulletin, 128*(1), 3–72.

Oyserman, D., Coon, H. M., and Kemmelmeier, M. (2002b). Cultural psychology, a new look: Reply to Bond (2002), Fiske (2002), Kitayama (2002), and Miller (2002). *Psychological Bulletin, 128*(1), 110–117.

Oyserman, D., and Markus, H. (1990). Possible selves in balance: Implications for delinquency. *Journal of Social Issues, 46,* 141–157.

Ozer, D. J., and Benet-Martinez, V. (2006). *Annual Review of Psychology, 57,* 401–421.

Ozer, D. J., and Buss, D. M. (1991). Two views of behavior: Agreement and disagreement in married couples. In A. Stewart, J. Healy, and D. Ozer (Eds.), *Perspectives in personality psychology* (pp. 93–108). London: Jessica Kingsley.

Palys, T. S., and Little, B. R. (1983). Perceived life satisfaction and the organization of personal project systems. *Journal of Personality and Social Psychology, 44,* 1221–1230.

Panksepp, J. (2005). Why does separation distress hurt? Comment on MacDonald and Leary (2005). *Psychological Bulletin, 131,* 224–230.

Paradis, C. M., Horn, L., Lazar, R. M., and Schwartz, D. W. (1994). Brain dysfunction and violent behavior in a man with a congenital subarachnoid cyst. *Hospital and Community Psychiatry, 45,* 714–716.

Park, S. W., and Colvin, C. R. (2015). Narcissism and other-derogation in the absence of ego threat. *Journal of Personality, 83*(3), 334–345. doi: 10.1111/jopy.12107

Parker, J., Taylor, G., and Bagby R. M. (2001). The relationship between emotional intelligence and alexithymia. *Personality and Individual Differences, 30,* 107–115.

Parkes, K. R., and Razavi, T. D. B. (2004). Personality and attitudinal variables as predictors of voluntary union membership. *Personality and Individual Differences, 37,* 333–347.

Patrick, C. J. (1994). Emotion and psychopathy: Startling new insights. *Psychophysiology, 31,* 319–330.

Patrick, C. J. (Ed.). (2005). *The handbook of psychopathy.* New York: Guilford Press.

Patrick, C. J., Bradley, M. M., and Lang, P. J. (1993). Emotion in the criminal psychopath: Startle reflex modulation. *Journal of Abnormal Psychology, 102,* 82–92.

Patrick, C. J., Cuthbert, B. N., and Lang, P. J. (1994). Emotion in the criminal psychopath: Fear image processing. *Journal of Abnormal Psychology, 103,* 523–534.

Patrick, C. J., Drislane, L. E., & Strickland, C. (2012). Conceptualizing psychopathy in Triarchic terms: Implications for treatment. *The International Journal of Forensic Mental Health, 11*(4), 253–266.

Patterson, C. H. (2000). *Understanding psychotherapy: Fifty years of client-centred theory and practice.* Ross-on-Wye, England: PCCS Books Ltd.

Patton, D., Barnes, G. E., and Murray, R. P. (1993). Personality characteristics of smokers and ex-smokers. *Personality and Individual Differences, 15,* 653–664.

Paulhus, D. L. (1984). Two component models of socially desirable responding. *Journal of Personality and Social Psychology, 46,* 598–609.

Paulhus, D. L. (1990). Measurement and control of response bias. In J. P. Robinson, P. R. Shaver, and L. Wrightsman (Eds.), *Measures of personality and social-psychological attitudes* (pp. 17–59). San Diego, CA: Academic Press.

Paulhus, D. L. (1998). Intrapsychic and interpersonal adaptiveness of trait self-enhancement: A mixed blessing? *Journal of Personality and Social Psychology, 74,* 812–820.

Paulhus, D. L. (2002). Socially desirable responding: The evolution of a construct. In H. I. Braun, D. N. Jackson, and D. E. Wiley (Eds.), *The role of constructs in psychological and educational measurement* (pp. 49–69). Mahwah, NJ: Erlbaum.

Paulhus, D. L., and Vazire, S. (2007). The self-report method. In R. W. Robins, R. C. Fraley, and R. F. Krueger (Eds.), *Handbook of Research Methods in Personality Psychology* (pp. 224–239). New York: Guilford.

Paulhus, D. L., and Williams, K. M. (2002). The Dark Triad of personality: Narcissism, Machiavellianism, and psychopathy. *Journal of Research in Personality, 36,* 556–563.

Paunesku, D., Walton, G. M., Romero, C., Smith, E. N., Yeager, D. S., and Dweck, C. S. (2015). Mind-set interventions are a scalable treatment for academic underachievement. *Psychological Science, 26*(6), 784–793.

Paunonen, S. V. (1998). Hierarchical organization of personality and prediction of behavior. *Journal of Personality and Social Psychology, 74,* 538–556.

Paunonen, S. V. (2002). *Design and construction of the Supernumerary Personality Inventory* (Research Bulletin 763). London, Ontario: University of Western Ontario.

Paunonen, S. V. (2003). Big Five factors of personality and replicated predictions of behavior. *Journal of Personality and Social Psychology, 84*(2), 411–424.

Paunonen, S. V., and Ashton, M. C. (1998). The structured assessment of personality across cultures. *Journal of Cross-Cultural Psychology, 29,* 150–170.

Paunonen, S. V., and Ashton, M. C. (2001a). Big Five predictors of academic achievement. *Journal of Research in Personality, 35,* 78–90.

Paunonen, S. V., and Ashton, M. C. (2001b). Big Five factors and facets and the prediction of behavior. *Journal of Personality and Social Psychology, 81*(3), 524–539.

Paunonen, S. V., Haddock, G., Forsterling, F., and Keinonen, M. (2003). Broad versus narrow personality measures and the prediction of behaviour across cultures. *European Journal of Personality, 17,* 413–433.

Paunonen, S. V., and Hong, R. Y. (2015). On the properties of personality traits. In M. Mikulincer, P. R. Shaver, M. L. Cooper, and R. J. Larsen (Eds.), *APA handbooks in psychology. APA handbook of personality and social psychology, Volume 4: Personality processes and individual differences* (pp. 233–259). Washington, DC: American Psychological Association.

Paunonen, S. V., and Nicol, A. A. M. (2001). The personality hierarchy and the prediction of work behaviors. In R. Hogan and B. W. Roberts (Eds.), *Personality psychology in the workplace* (pp. 161–191). Washington, DC: American Psychological Association.

Paunonen, S. V., and O'Neil, T. A. (2010). Self-reports, peer ratings, and construct validity. *European Journal of Personality, 24,* 189–206.

Pedersen, N. L. (1993). Genetic and environmental change in personality. In T. J. Bouchard and P. Proping (Eds.), *Twins as a tool of behavioral genetics* (pp. 147–162). West Sussex, England: Wiley.

Pelle, A. J., Erdman, R. A. M., van Domburg, R. T., Spiering, M., Kazemier, M., and Pedersen, S. S. (2008). Type D patients report poorer health status prior to and after cardiac rehabilitation compared to non-Type D patients. *Annals of Behavioral Medicine, 36,* 167–175.

Penke, L., and Asendorpf, J. B. (2008a). Beyond global sociosexual orientations: A more differentiated look at sociosexuality and its effects on courtship and romantic relationships. *Journal of Personality and Social Psychology, 95,* 1113–1135.

Penke, L., and Asendorpf, J. B. (2008b). Evidence for conditional sex differences in emotional but not in sexual jealousy at the automatic level of cognitive processing. *European Journal of Personality, 22,* 3–30.

Penke, L., Denissen, J. J. A., and Miller, G. F. (2007). The evolutionary genetics of personality. *European Journal of Personality, 21,* 549–587.

Pennebaker, J. W. (1990). *Opening up: The healing powers of confiding in others.* New York: Morrow.

Pennebaker, J. W. (2003a). The social, linguistic and health consequences of emotional disclosure. In J. Suls and K. A. Wallston (Eds.), *Social psychological foundations of health and illness* (pp. 288–313). Malden, MA: Blackwell.

Pennebaker, J. W. (2003b). Writing about emotional experiences as a therapeutic process. In P. Salovey and A. J. Rothman (Eds.), *Social psychology of health* (pp. 362–368). New York: Psychology Press.

Perilloux, C., Fleischman, D. S., and Buss, D. M. (2008). The daughter-guarding hypothesis: Parental influence on children's mating behavior. *Evolutionary Psychology, 6,* 217–233.

Perilloux, C., Fleischman, D. S., and Buss, D. M. (2011). Meet the parents: Parent-offspring convergence and divergence in mate preferences. *Personality and Individual Differences, 50,* 253–258.

Perry, V. G. (2008). Giving credit where credit is due: The psychology of credit ratings. *Journal of Behavioral Finance, 9,* 15–21.

Perugini, M., and Richetin, J. (2007). In the land of the blind, the one-eyed man is king. *European Journal of Personality, 21,* 977–981.

Pessant, N., and Zadra, A. (2004). Working with dreams in therapy: What do we know and what should we do? *Clinical Psychology Review, 24,* 489–512.

Petersen, J. L., and Hyde, J. S. (2010). A meta-analytic review of research on gender differences in sexuality, 1993–2007. *Psychological Bulletin, 136,* 21–38.

Peterson, B. E., Winter, D. G., and Doty, R. M. (1994). Laboratory tests of a motivational-perceptual model of conflict escalation. *Journal of Conflict Resolution, 38,* 719–748.

Peterson, C. (1991). The meaning and measurement of explanatory style. *Psychological Inquiry, 2,* 1–10.

Peterson, C. (1995). Explanatory style and health. In G. M. Buchanan and M. E. P. Seligman (Eds.), *Explanatory style* (pp. 233–246). Hillsdale, NJ: Erlbaum.

Peterson, C. (2000). The future of optimism. *American Psychologist, 55,* 44–55.

Peterson, C., and Bossio, L. M. (2001). Optimism and physical well-being. In E. C. Chang (Ed.), *Optimism and pessimism: Implications for theory, research, and practice* (pp. 127–145). Washington, DC: American Psychological Association.

Peterson, C., and Chang, E. C. (2003). Optimism and flourishing. In C. L. Keyes and J. Haidt (Eds.), *Flourishing: Positive psychology and the life well-lived* (pp. 55–79). Washington, DC: American Psychological Association.

Peterson, C., Maier, S. F., and Seligman, M. E. P. (1993). *Learned helplessness: A theory for the age of personal control.* New York: Oxford University Press.

Peterson, C., and Park, N. (2010). What happened to self-actualization? Commentary on Kenrick et al. (2010). *Perspectives on Psychological Science, 5,* 320–322.

Peterson, C., Schulman, P., Castellon, C., and Seligman, M. E. P. (1992). CAVE: Content analysis of verbatim explanations. In C. P. Smith (Ed.), *Motivation and personality: Handbook of thematic content analysis* (pp. 383–392). New York: Cambridge University Press.

Peterson, C., Seligman, M. E. P., and Vaillant, G. E. (1988). Pessimistic explanatory style is a risk factor for physical illness: A thirty-five-year longitudinal study. *Journal of Personality and Social Psychology, 55,* 23–27.

Peterson, C., Seligman, M. E. P., Yurko, K. H., Martin, L. R., and Friedman, H. S. (1998). Catastrophizing and untimely death. *Psychological Science, 9,* 49–52.

Peterson, C., Semmel, A., von Baeyer, C., Abramson, L. Y., Metalsky, G. I., and Seligman, M. E. P. (1982). The Attributional Style Questionnaire. *Cognitive Therapy and Research, 6,* 287–299.

Peterson, C., and Steen, T. A. (2002). Optimistic explanatory style. In C. R. Snyder and S. J. Lopez (Eds.), *Handbook of positive psychology* (pp. 244–256). London: Oxford University Press.

Peterson, J. B., Smith, K. W., and Carson, S. (2002). Openness and extraversion are associated with reduced latent inhibition: Replication and commentary. *Personality and Individual Differences, 33,* 1137–1147.

Petrie, A. (1967). *Individuality in pain and suffering.* Chicago: University of Chicago Press.

Petrill, S. A. (2002). The case for general intelligence: A behavioral genetic perspective. In R. J. Sternberg and E. L. Grigorenko (Eds.), *The general factor of intelligence: How general is it?* (pp. 281–298). Mahwah, NJ: Erlbaum.

Pickering, A. D., Corr, P. J., and Gray, J. A. (1999). Interactions and reinforcement sensitivity theory: A theoretical analysis of Rusting and Larsen (1997). *Personality and Individual Differences, 26,* 357–365.

Pickering, A., Farmer, A., Harris, T., Redman, K., Mahmood, A., Sadler, S., and McGuffin, P. (2003). A sib-pair study of psychoticism, life events and depression. *Personality and Individual Differences, 34,* 613–623.

Piedmont, R. L. (2001). Cracking the plaster cast: Big Five personality change during intensive outpatient counseling. *Journal of Research in Personality, 35,* 500–520.

Piff, P. K., Kraus, M. W., Côté, S., Cheng, B. H., and Keltner, D. (2010). Having less, giving more: The influence of social class on prosocial behavior. *Journal of Personality and Social Psychology, 99*(5), 771–784.

Pilarska, A., and Suchanska, A. (2015). Self-complexity and self-concept differentiation – What have we been measuring for the past 30 years? *Current Psychology, 34,* 723–743.

Pincus, J. H. (2001). *Base instincts: What makes killers kill?* New York: Norton.

Pinker, S. (1997). *How the mind works.* New York: Norton.

Pinker, S. (2012). *The better angels of our nature.* New York: Viking.

Pipher, M. (1994). *Reviving Ophelia: Saving the selves of adolescent girls.* New York: Ballantine Books.

Pittenger, D. J. (2005). Cautionary comments regarding the Myers-Briggs Type Indicator. *Consulting Psychology Journal: Practice and Research, 57,* 210–221.

Plavcan, J. M. (2012). Sexual size dimorphism, canine dimorphism, and male-male competition in primates. *Human Nature, 23,* 45–67.

Plomin, R. (2002). Individual differences research in a postgenomic era. *Personality and Individual Differences, 33,* 909–920.

Plomin, R., and Crabbe, J. (2000). DNA. *Psychological Bulletin Special Issue: Psychology in the 21st Century, 126,* 806–828.

Plomin, R., and Davis, O. S. P. (2009). The future of genetics in psychology and psychiatry: Microarrays, genome-wide association, and non-coding RNA. *Journal of Child Psychology and Psychiatry, 50,* 63–71.

Plomin, R., and DeFries, G. E. (1985). *Origins of individual differences in infancy: The Colorado Adoption Project.* New York: Academic Press.

Plomin, R., DeFries, J. C., and Fulker, D. W. (1988). *Nature and nurture during infancy and early childhood.* New York: Cambridge University Press.

Plomin, R., DeFries, J. C., and Loehlin, J. C. (1977). Genotype–environment interaction and correlation in the analysis of human behavior. *Psychological Bulletin, 84,* 309–322.

Plomin, R., DeFries, J. C., McClern, G. E., and McGuffin, P. (2001). *Behavioral genetics* (4th ed.). New York: Worth.

Plomin, R., DeFries, J. C., McClearn, G. E., and McGuffin, P. (2008). *Behavioral genetics* (5th ed.). New York: Worth.

Plotnik, J. M., de Waal, F. B., and Reiss, D. (2006). Self-recognition in an Asian elephant. *Proceedings of the National Academy of Sciences of the United States of America, 103*(45), 17053–17057.

Plutchik, R. (1980). A general psychoevolutionary theory of emotion. In R. Plutchik and H. Kellerman (Eds.), *Emotion: Theory, research, and experience: Vol. 1: Theories of emotion* (pp. 3–31). New York: Academic Press.

Polderman, T. J. C., Kreukels, B. P. C., Irwig, M. S., Beach, L., . . . Tishelman, A., and Davis, K. (2018). The biological contributions to gender identity and gender diversity: Bringing data to the table. *Behavior Genetics, 48,* 95–108.

Pollock, V. E., Briere, J., Schneider, L., Knop, J., Mednick, S., and Goodwin, D. W. (1990). Childhood antecedents of antisocial behavior: Parental alcoholism and physical abusiveness. *American Journal of Psychiatry, 147,* 1290–1293.

Poropat, A. E. (2009). A meta-analysis of the five-factor model of personality and academic performance. *Psychological Bulletin, 135,* 322–338.

Powell, D. M., Goffin, R. D., and Gellatly, I. R. (2011). Gender differences in personality scores: Implications for differential hiring rates. *Personality and Individual Differences, 50,* 106–110.

Price, M. E., Cosmides, L., and Tooby, J. (2002). Punitive sentiment as an anti-free rider psychological device. *Evolution and Human Behavior, 23,* 203–231.

Prior, H., Schwarz, A., and Güntürkün, O. (2008). Mirror-induced behavior in the magpie (*Pica pica*): Evidence of self-recognition. *Public Library of Science: Biology, 6*(8), 202. doi:10.1371/ journal.pbio.0060202.

Promislow, D. (2003). Mate choice, sexual conflict, and evolution of senescence. *Behavior Genetics, 33,* 191–201.

Ptácek, R., Kuzelová, H., and Stefano, G. B. (2011). Dopamine D4 receptor gene DRD4 and its association with psychiatric disorders. *Medical Science Monitor: International Medical Journal of Experimental and Clinical Research, 17*(9), RA215-RA220.

Pullmann, H., Raudsepp, L., and Allik, J. (2006). Stability and change in adolescents' personality: A longitudinal study. *European Journal of Personality, 20,* 447–459.

Rabbie, J. M., and Horwitz, M. (1969). Arousal of ingroup-outgroup bias by a chance win or loss. *Journal of Personality and Social Psychology, 13,* 269–277.

Rafaeli-Mor, E., and Steinberg, J. (2002). Self-complexity and well-being: A review and research synthesis. *Personality and Social Psychology Review, 6,* 31–58.

Raine, A. (2002). Biosocial studies of antisocial and violent behavior in children and adults: A review. *Journal of Abnormal Child Psychology, 30,* 311–326.

Raine, A., Meloy, J. R., and Bihrle, S. (1998). Reduced prefrontal and increased subcortical brain functioning assessed using positron emission tomography in predatory and affective murderers. *Behavioral Sciences and the Law Special Issue: Impulsive aggression, 16,* 319–332.

Rammsayer, T. H., and Brandler, S. (2002). On the relationship between general fluid intelligence and psychophysical indicators of temporal resolution in the brain. *Journal of Research in Personality, 36,* 507–530.

Rammstedt, B., Goldberg, L. R., and Borg, I. (2010). The measurement equivalence of Big-Five factor markers for persons with different levels of education. *Journal of Research in Personality, 44,* 53–61.

Raskin, J. D. (2001). The modern, the postmodern, and George Kelly's personal construct psychology. *American Psychologist, 56,* 368–369.

Raskin, R., and Hall, C. S. (1979). A narcissistic personality inventory. *Psychological Reports, 45,* 590.

Raskin, R., and Shaw, R. (1987). *Narcissism and the use of personal pronouns.* Unpublished manuscript.

Raskin, R., and Terry, H. (1988). A principle-components analysis of the narcissistic personality inventory and further evidence of its construct validity. *Journal of Personality and Social Psychology, 54,* 890–902.

Rasmussen, H. N., Scheier, M. F., and Greenhouse, J. B. (2009). Optimism and physical health: a meta-analytic review. *Annals of behavioral medicine: A Publication of the Society of Behavioral Medicine, 37*(3), 239–256.

Rattan, A., Good, C., and Dweck, C. S. (2012). "It's OK—Not everyone can be good at math": Instructors with an entity theory comfort (and demotivate) students. *Journal of Experimental Social Psychology, 48,* 731–737.

Rattan, A., Savani, K., Chugh, D., and Dweck, C. S. (2015). Leveraging mindsets to promote academic achievement: Policy recommendations. *Perspectives on Psychological Science, 10*(6), 721–726.

Rauthmann, J., and Denissen, J. J. A. (2011). I often do it vs. I like doing it: Comparing a frequency- and valency-approach to extraversion. *Personality and Individual Differences, 50,* 1283–1288.

Rawlings, D. (2003). Personality correlates of liking for "unpleasant" paintings and photographs. *Personality and Individual Differences, 34,* 395–410.

Reidy, D. E., Zeichner, A., Foster, J. D., and Martinez, M. A. (2008). Effects of narcissistic entitlement and exploitativeness on human physical aggression. *Personality and Individual Differences, 44,* 685–875.

Renner, W., Kandler, C., Bleidorn, W., Riemann, R., Angleitner, A., Spinath, F. M., and Menschik-Bendele, J. (2012). Human values: Genetic and environmental effects on five lexically derived domains and their facets. *Personality and Individual Differences, 52,* 89–93.

Retail Council of Canada. (2012). Securing the bottom line: Canadian retail security survey 2012. Retrieved from http://www.pwc.com/ca /retailsecuritysurvey.

Revelle, W., Humphreys, M. S., Simon, L., and Gilliland, K. (1980). The interactive effect of personality, time of day, and caffeine: A test of the arousal model. *Journal of Experimental Psychology: General, 109,* 1–31.

Rhee, E., Uleman, J., Lee, H., and Roman, R. (1995). Spontaneous self-descriptions and ethnic identities in individualistic and collectivist cultures. *Journal of Personality and Social Psychology, 69,* 142–152.

Rheingold, H. L., and Cook, K. V. (1975). The contents of boys' and girls' rooms as an index of parents' behavior. *Child Development, 46,* 459–463.

Rhodenwalt, F., and Morf, C. (1998). On self-aggrandizement and anger: A temporal analysis of narcissism and affective reactions to success and failure. *Journal of Personality and Social Psychology, 74,* 672–685.

Richards, Z., and Hewstone, M. (2001). Subtyping and subgrouping: Processes for the prevention and promotion of stereotype change. *Personality and Social Psychology Review, 5,* 52–73.

Richardson, J. A., and Turner, T. E. (2000). Field dependence revisited I: Intelligence. *Educational Psychology, 20,* 255–270.

Richardson, M., and Abraham, C. (2009). Conscientiousness and achievement motivation predict performance. *European Journal of Personality, 23,* 589–605.

Ridley, M. (1999). *Genome: The autobiography of a species in 23 chapters.* New York: HarperCollins.

Rind, B., Tromovitch, P., and Bauserman, R. (1998). A meta-analytic examination of assumed properties of child sexual abuse using college samples. *Psychological Bulletin, 124,* 22–53.

Rindermann, H. (2008). Relevance of education and intelligence at the national level for the economic welfare of people. *Intelligence, 36,* 127–142.

Ritter, V., Leichsenring, F., Strauss, B. M., and Stangier, U. (2013). Changes in implicit and explicit self-esteem following cognitive and psychodynamic therapy in social anxiety disorder. *Psychotherapy Research, 23*(5), 547–558.

Ritts, V., and Patterson, M. L. (1996). Effects of social anxiety and action identification on impressions and thoughts in interaction. *Journal of Social and Clinical Psychology, 15,* 191–205.

Ritvo, L. B. (1990). *Darwin's influence on Freud: A tale of two sciences.* New Haven, CT: Yale University Press.

Roberts, B. W., Caspi, A., and Moffitt, T. E. (2001). The kids are alright: Growth and stability in personality development from adolescence to adulthood. *Journal of Personality and Social Psychology, 81*(4), 670–683.

Roberts, B. W., Caspi, A., and Moffitt, T. E. (2003). Work experiences and personality development in young adulthood. *Journal of Personality and Social Psychology, 84*(5), 582–593.

Roberts, B. W., and DelVecchio, W. F. (2000). The rank-order consistency of personality traits from childhood to old age: A quantitative review of the longitudinal studies. *Psychological Bulletin, 126,* 3–25.

Roberts, B. W., Kuncel, N. R., Shiner, R., Caspi, A., and Goldberg, L. R. (2007). The power of personality: The comparative validity of personality traits, socioeconomic status, and cognitive ability for predicting important life outcomes. *Perspectives on Psychological Science, 2,* 313–345.

Roberts, B. W., Walton, K. R., and Viechtbauer, W. (2006). Patterns of mean-level change in personality traits across the life course: A meta-analysis of longitudinal studies. *Psychological Bulletin, 132,* 1–25.

Roberts, J. E., and Monroe, S. M. (1992). Vulnerable self-esteem and depressive symptoms: Prospective findings comparing three alternative conceptualizations. *Journal of Personality and Social Psychology, 62,* 804–812.

Roberts, W. B., and Robins, R. W. (2004). Person-environment fit and its implications for personality development: A longitudinal study. *Journal of Personality, 72,* 89–110.

Robins, R. W., and Beer, J. S. (2001). Positive illusions about the self: Short-term benefits and long-term costs. *Journal of Personality and Social Psychology, 80*(2), 340–352.

Robins, R. W., Caspi, A., and Moffitt, T. E. (2002). It's not just who you're with, it's who you are: Personality and relationship experiences across multiple relationships. *Journal of Personality, 70,* 925–964.

Robins, R. W., Fraley, R. C., Roberts, B. W., and Trzesniewski, K. H. (2001). A longitudinal study of personality change in young adulthood. *Journal of Personality, 69*(4), 617–640.

Robins, R. W., and John, O. P. (1997). Self-perception, visual perspective, and narcissism: Is seeing believing? *Psychological Science, 8,* 37–42.

Robins, R. W., Noftle, E. E., Trzesniewski, K. H., and Roberts, B. W. (2005). Do people know how their personality has changed? Correlates of perceived and actual personality change in young adulthood. *Journal of Personality, 73,* 489–521.

Robins, R. W., Trzesniewski, K. H., Tracy, J. L., Gosling, S. D., and Potter, J. (2002). Global self-esteem across the life span. *Psychology of Aging, 17,* 423–434.

Roediger, H. L., Balota, D. A., and Watson, J. M. (2001). Spreading activation and arousal of false memories. In Henry L. Roediger, III and James S. Nairne (Eds.), *The nature of remembering: Essays in honor of Robert G. Crowder* (pp. 95–115). Washington, DC: American Psychological Association.

Roediger, H. L., and McDermott K. B. (1995). Creating false memories: Remembering words not presented in lists. *Journal of Experimental Psychology: Learning, Memory, and Cognition, 21,* 803–814.

Roediger, H. L., McDermott, K. B., and Robinson, K. J. (1998). The role of associative processes in creating false memories. In M. A. Conway, S. E. Gathercole, and C. Cornoldi (Eds.), *Theories of memory II* (pp. 187–246). Hove, Sussex, England: Psychological Press.

Rogers, C. R. (1957). The necessary and sufficient conditions of therapeutic personality change. *Journal of Consulting Psychology, 21,* 95–103.

Rogers, C. R. (1975). Empathic: An unappreciated way of being. *The Counseling Psychologist, 5,* 2–10.

Rogers, C. R. (2002). *Carl Rogers: The quiet revolutionary, an oral history.* Roseville, CA Penmarin Books.

Rogness, G. A., and McClure, E. B. (1996). Development and neurotransmitter-environment interactions. *Development and Psychopathology, 8,* 183–199.

Romero, C., Master, A., Paunesku, D., Dweck, C. S., and Gross, J. J. (2014). Academic and emotional functioning in middle school: The role of implicit theories. *Emotion, 14*(2), 227–234.

Romero, E., Luengo, M. T., Carrillo-de-la-Pena, T., and Otero-Lopez, J. M. (1994). The act frequency approach to the study of impulsivity. *European Journal of Personality, 8,* 119–134.

Rosch, E. (1975). Cognitive reference points. *Cognitive Psychology, 7,* 532–547.

Rose, R. J. (1995). Genes and behavior. *Annual Review of Psychology, 46,* 625–654.

Rosenbaum, R. S., Kohler, S., Schacter, D. L., Moscovitch, M., Westmacott, R., Black, S. E., Gao, F., and Tulving, E. (2005). The case of K. C.: Contributions of a memory-impaired person to memory theory. *Neuropsychologia, 43,* 989–1021.

Rosenzweig, S. (1986). Idiodynamics vis-à-vis psychology. *American Psychologist, 41,* 241–245.

Rosenzweig, S. (1994). *The historic expedition to America (1909): Freud, Jung, and Hall the king-maker.* St. Louis, MO: Rana House.

Rosenzweig, S. (1997). "Idiographic" vis-à-vis "idiodynamic" in the historical perspective of personality theory: Remembering Gordon Allport, 1897–1997. *Journal of the History of the Behavioral Sciences, 33,* 405–419.

Ross, K. M., Liu, S., Tomfohr, L. M., and Miller, G. E. (2013). Self-esteem variability predicts arterial stiffness trajectories in healthy adolescent females. *Health Psychology, 32*(8), 869–876.

Ross, L., Greene, D., and House, P. (1977). The false consensus effect: An egocentric bias in social perception and attribution processes. *Journal of Experimental Social Psychology, 13,* 279–301.

Ross, M., Xun, W. Q., and Wilson, A. E. (2002). Language and the bicultural self. *Personality and Social Psychology Bulletin, 28,* 1040–1050.

Ross, S. R., Canada, K. E., and Rausch, M. K. (2002). Self-handicapping and the five factor model of personality: Mediation between neuroticism and conscientiousness. *Personality and Individual Differences, 32,* 1173–1184.

Rothbart, M. K. (1981). Measurement of temperament in infancy. *Child Development, 52,* 569–578.

Rothbart, M. K. (1986). Longitudinal observation of infant temperament. *Developmental Psychology, 22,* 356–365.

Rothbart, M. K., and Hwang, J. (2005). Temperament. In A. J. Elliot and C. S. Dweck (Eds.), *Handbook of competence & motivation* (pp. 167–184). New York: Guilford.

Rotter, J. B. (1971). Generalized expectancies for interpersonal trust. *American Psychologist, 26,* 443–452.

Rotter, J. B. (1982). *The development and application of social learning theory.* New York: Praeger.

Rotter, J. B. (1990). Internal versus external control of reinforcement: A case history of a variable. *American Psychologist, 45,* 489–493.

Rowe, D. C. (2001). *Biology and crime.* New York: Roxbury.

Royal Canadian Mounted Police. (2016). *Careers.* Retrieved from http://www.rcmp-grc.gc.ca/en/careers.

Rozin, P. (2003). Five potential principles for understanding cultural differences in relation to individual differences. *Journal of Research in Personality, 37,* 273–283.

Ruchkin, V. V., Koposov, R. A., Eisemann, M., and Hagglof, B. (2002). Alcohol use in delinquent adolescents from Northern Russia: The role of personality, parental rearing and family history of alcohol abuse. *Personality and Individual Differences, 32*, 1139–1148.

Rule, A. (2000). *The stranger beside me.* New York: Norton.

Runyon, W. M. (1983). Idiographic goals and methods in the study of lives. *Journal of Personality, 51*, 413–437.

Ruocco, A. C., and Bahl, N. (2014). Material-specific discrepancies in verbal and visual episodic memory in borderline personality disorder. *Psychiatry Research, 220*(1), 694–697.

Rushton, J. P. (1985). Differential K theory: The sociobiology of individual and group differences. *Personality and Individual Differences, 6*, 441–452.

Rushton, J. P., Cons, T. A., and Hur, Y-M. (2008). The genetics and evolution of the general factor of personality. *Journal of Research in Personality, 42*, 1173–1185.

Russell, V. M., and McNulty, J. K. (2011). Frequent sex protects intimates from the negative implications of their neuroticism. *Social Psychological and Personality Science, 2*, 220–227.

Rusting, C. L., and Larsen, R. J. (1997). Extraversion, neuroticism, and susceptibility to positive and negative affect: A test of two theoretical models. *Personality and Individual Differences, 22*, 607–612.

Rusting, C. L., and Larsen, R. J. (1998a). Diurnal patterns of unpleasant mood: Associations with neuroticism, depression, and anxiety. *Journal of Personality, 66*, 85–103.

Rusting, C. L., and Larsen, R. J. (1998b). Personality and cognitive processing of affective information. *Personality and Social Psychology Bulletin, 24*, 200–213.

Rusting, C. L., and Larsen, R. J. (1999). Clarifying Gray's theory of personality: A response to Pickering, Corr, and Gray. *Personality and Individual Differences, 26*, 367–372.

Ryan, R. M., and Deci, E. L. (2000). Self-determination theory and the facilitation of intrinsic motivation, social development, and well-being. *American Psychologist, 55*, 68–78.

Ryff, C., Lee, Y., and Na, K. (1995). *Through the lens of culture: Psychological well-being at mid-life.* Unpublished manuscript, University of Michigan, Ann Arbor.

Sagie, A., and Elizur, D. (1999). Achievement motive and entrepreneurial orientation: A structural analysis. *Journal of Organizational Behavior, 20*, 375–387.

Sakuta, A., and Fukushima, A. (1998). A study on abnormal findings pertaining to the brain in criminals. *International Medical Journal, 5*, 283–292.

Salgado, J. F., Moscoso, S., and Lado, M. (2003). Evidence of cross-cultural invariant of the Big Five personality dimensions in work settings. *European Journal of Personality, 17*, S67–S76.

Salleh, M. R. (2008). Life event, stress and illness. *The Malaysian Journal of Medical Sciences, 15*(4), 9–18.

Salovey, P., and Mayer, J. D. (1990). Emotional intelligence. *Imagination, Cognition, and Personality, 9*, 185–211.

Sam, D. L. (1994). The psychological adjustment of young immigrants in Norway. *Scandinavian Journal of Psychology, 35*, 240–253.

Samuel, D. B., and Gore, W. L. (2012). Maladaptive variants of conscientiousness and agreeableness. *Journal of Personality, 80*(6), 1669–1696.

Sandvik, E., Diener, E., and Seidlitz, L. (1993). Subjective well-being: The convergence and stability of self-report and non-self-report measures. *Journal of Personality, 61*, 317–342.

Santayana, G. (1905/1980). *Reason in common sense: The life of reason, vol. 1.* New York, NY: Dover.

Sapienza, P., Zingales, L., and Maestripieri, D. (2009). Gender differences in financial risk aversion and career choices are affected by testosterone. *Proceedings of the National Academy of Science, USA, 106*, 15268–15273.

Sapolsky, R. M. (1987). Stress, social status, and reproductive physiology in free-living baboons. In D. Crews (Ed.), *Psychobiology of reproductive behavior: An evolutionary perspective.* Englewood Cliffs, NJ: Prentice Hall.

Saroglou, V. (2002). Religion and the five factors of personality: A meta-analytic review. *Personality and Individual Differences, 32*, 15–25.

Satterfield, J. H., and Schelle, A. M. (1984). Childhood brain function differences in delinquent and non-delinquent hyperactive boys. *Electroencephalography and Clinical Neurophysiology, 57*, 199–207.

Saucier, G. (2003). Factor structure of English-language personality type-nouns. *Journal of Personality and Social Psychology, 85*(4), 695–708.

Saucier, G. (2009). Recurrent personality dimensions in inclusive lexical studies: Indications for a Big Six structure. *Journal of Personality, 77*, 1577–1614.

Saucier, G. (2010). The structure of social effects: Personality as impact on others. *European Journal of Personality, 24*, 222–240.

Saucier, G., Georgiades, S., Tsaousis, I., and Goldberg, L. R. (2005). The factor structure of Greek personality adjectives. *Journal of Personality and Social Psychology, 5*, 856–875.

Saucier, G., and Goldberg, L. R. (1996). The language of personality: Lexical perspectives on the five-factor model. In J. S. Wiggins (Ed.), *The five-factor model of personality: Theoretical perspectives* (pp. 21–50). New York: Guilford Press.

Saucier, G., and Goldberg, L. R. (1998). What is beyond the Big Five? *Journal of Personality, 66*, 495–524.

Saucier, G., and Goldberg, L. R. (2001). Lexical studies of indigenous personality factors: Premises, products, and prospects. *Journal of Personality, 69*(6) 847–879.

Sauter, D. A., Eisner, F., Ekman, P., and Scott, S. K. (2010). Cross-cultural recognition of basic emotions through nonverbal emotional vocalizations. *Proceedings of the National Academy of Sciences, 107*(6), 2408–2412.

Scarf, M. (1996). The mind of the Unabomber. *The New Republic,* June 10, 1996, p. 20.

Scarr, S. (1968). Environmental bias in twin studies. *Eugenics Quarterly, 15*, 34–40.

Scarr, S., and Carter-Saltzman, L. (1979). Twin method: Defense of a critical assumption. *Behavior Genetics, 9*, 527–542.

Scarr, S. and McCartney, K. (1983). How people make their own environments: A theory of genotype → environment effects. *Child Development, 54*(2), 424–435. doi: 10.2307/1129703

Schaffhuser, K., Allemand, M., and Martin, M. (2014). Personality traits and relationship satisfaction in intimate couples: Three perspectives on personality. *European Journal of Personality, 28*(2), 120–133.

Schaller, M., and Murray, D. R. (2008). Pathogens, personality, and culture: Disease prevalence predicts worldwide variability in sociosexuality, extraversion, and openness to experience. *Journal of Personality and Social Psychology, 95*(1), 212–221.

Schaller, M., Neuberg, S. L., Griskevicius, V., and Kenrick, D. T. (2010). Pyramid power: A reply to commentaries. *Perspectives on Psychological Sciences, 5*, 335–337.

Scheier, M. F., and Carver, C. S. (1992). Effects of optimism on psychological and physical well-being: Theoretical overview and empirical update. *Cognitive Therapy and Research, 16*, 201–228.

Schermer, J. A., Vernon, P. A., Maio, G. R., and Jang, K. L. (2011). A behavior genetic study of the connection between social values and personality. *Twin Research and Human Genetics, 14*, 233–239.

Schinka J. A., Letsch, E. A., and Crawford, F. C. (2002). DRD4 and novelty seeking: Results of meta-analyses. *American Journal of Medical Genetics, 114*, 643–648.

Schiraldi, G. (2007). *10 simple solutions for building self-esteem.* Oakland, CA: New Harbinger.

Schmalt, H. (1999). Assessing the achievement motive using the grid technique. *Journal of Research in Personality, 33*, 109–130.

Schmidt, L. A., and Fox, N. A. (1995). Individual differences in young adults' shyness and sociability: Personality and health correlates. *Personality and Individual Differences, 19*, 455–462.

Schmidt, L. A., Fox, N. A., Rubin, K. H., Hu, S., and Hamer, D. H. (2002). Molecular genetics of shyness and aggression in preschoolers. *Personality and Individual Differences, 33*, 227–238.

Schmitt, D. P. (2004). The Big Five related to risky sexual behavior across 10 world regions: Differential personality associations of sexual promiscuity and relationship infidelity. *European Journal of Personality, 18*, 301–319.

Schmitt, D. P., and Buss, D. M. (2000). Sexual dimensions of person description: Beyond or subsumed by the Big Five? *Journal of Research in Personality, 34*, 141–177.

Schmitt, D. P., and Buss, D. M. (2001). Human mate poaching: Tactics and temptations for infiltrating existing relationships. *Journal of Personality and Social Psychology, 80*, 894–917.

Schmitt, D. P., Jonason, P. K., Byerley, G. J., Flores, S. D., Illbeck, B. E., O'Leary, K. N., and Qudrat, A. (2012). A reexamination of sex differences in sexuality: New studies reveal old truths. *Current Directions in Psychological Science, 21*, 135–139.

Schmitt, D. P., Long, A. E., McPhearson, A., O'Brien, K. , Remmert, B., and Shah, S. H. (2017). Personality and gender differences in global perspective. *International Journal of Psychology, 52*, 45–56.

Schmitt, D. P., Realo, A., Voracek, M., & Allik, J. (2008). Why can't a man be more like a woman? Sex differences in Big Five personality traits across 55 cultures. *Journal of Personality and Social Psychology, 94*(1), 168–182.

Schmitt, D. P., Youn, G., Bond, B., Brooks, S., Frye, H., Johnson, S., Klesman, J., et al. (2009). When will I feel love? The effects of culture, personality, and gender on the psychological tendency to love. *Journal of Research in Personality, 43,* 830–846.

Schmutte, P. S., Lee, Y. H., and Ryff, C. D. (1995). *Reflections on parenthood: A cultural perspective.* Unpublished manuscript, Madison: University of Wisconsin.

Schneider, K. (1958). *Psychopathic personalities.* London: Cassell.

Schneider, T.R., Rench, T.A., Lyons, J.B., and Riffle, R.R. (2012). The influence of neuroticism, extraversion and openness on stress responses. *Stress and Health: Journal of the International Society for the Investigation of Stress, 28*(2), 102–110.

Scholer, A. A., and Higgins, E. T. (2011). Promotion and prevention systems: Regulatory focus dynamics within self-regulatory hierarchies. In K. D. Voys and R. F. Baumeister (Eds.), *Handbook of self-regulation: Research, theory, and applications* (2nd ed., pp. 143–161). New York, NY: Guilford Press.

Schüler, J., Sheldon, K. M., and Fröhlich, S. M. (2010). Implicit need for achievement moderates the relationship between competence need satisfaction and subsequent motivation. *Journal of Research in Personality, 44,* 1–12.

Schultheiss, O. C., and Brunstein, J. C. (2001). Assessment of implicit motives with a research version of the TAT: Picture profiles, gender differences, and relations to other personality measures. *Journal of Personality Assessment Special Issue: More data on the current Rorschach controversy, 77,* 71–86.

Schultheiss, O. C., Liening, S., and Schad, D. (2008). The reliability of a Picture Story Exercise measure of implicit motives: Estimates of internal consistency, retest reliability, and ipsative stability. *Journal of Research in Personality, 42,* 1560–1571.

Schultheiss, O. C., and Pang, J. S. (2007). Measuring implicit motives. In R. W. Robins, R. C. Fraley, and R. Krueger (Eds.), *Handbook of research methods in personality psychology* (pp. 322–344). New York: Guilford Press.

Schwartz, C. E., Wright, C. I., Shin, L. M., Kagan, J., and Rauch, S. L. (2003). Inhibited and uninhibited infants "grown up": Adult amygdalar response to novelty. *Science, 300,* 1952–1953.

Schwartz, S. H., and Rubel, T. (2005). Sex differences in value priorities: Cross-cultural and multimethod studies. *Journal of Personality and Social Psychology, 89,* 1010–1028.

Schwarzer, R., and Luszczynska, A. (2013). Stressful life events. In A. M. Nezu, C. M. Nezu, P. A. Geller, and I. B. Weiner (Eds.), *Handbook of psychology, vol. 9: Health psychology* (2nd ed., pp. 29–56). Hoboken, NJ: John Wiley & Sons.

Schwerdtfeger, A. (2007). Individual differences in auditory, pain, and motor stimulation: The case of augmenting/ reducing. *Journal of Individual Differences, 28,* 165–177.

Schwerdtfeger, A., and Baltissen, R. (1999). Augmenters vs. reducers: Cortical and autonomic reactivity in response to increasing stimulus intensity. *Zeitschrift fuer Differentielle und Diagnostische Psychologie, 20,* 247–262.

Schwerdtfeger, A., and Baltissen, R. (2002). Augmenting-reducing paradox lost? A test of Davis et al.'s (1983) hypothesis. *Personality and Individual Differences, 32,* 257–271.

Schwerdtfeger, A., Heims, R., and Heer, J. (2010). Digit ratio (2D:4D) is associated with traffic violations for male frequent car drivers. *Accident Analysis and Prevention, 42,* 269–274.

Scott, W. A., and Johnson, R. C. (1972). Comparative validities of direct and indirect personality tests. *Journal of Consulting and Clinical Psychology, 38,* 301–318.

Sear, R., and Mace, R. (2008). Who keeps children alive? A review of the effects of kin on child survival. *Evolution and Human Behavior, 29,* 1–18.

Seara-Cardoso, A., and Viding, E. (2015). Functional neuroscience of psychopathic personality in adults. *Journal of Personality, 83*(6), 723–737.

Segal, N. L. (1999). *Entwined lives: Twins and what they tell us about human behavior.* New York: Plume.

Seidlitz, L., and Diener, E. (1993). Review of the Satisfaction with Life Scale. *Psychological Assessment, 5,* 164–172.

Selfhout, M., Burk, W., Branje, S., Denissen, J., van Aken, M., and Meeus, W. (2010). Emerging late adolescent friendship networks and Big Five personality traits: A social network approach. *Journal of Personality, 78,* 509–538.

Seligman, M., and Hager, J. (1972). *Biological boundaries of learning.* New York: Appleton-Century-Crofts.

Seligman, M. E. P. (1992). *Helplessness: On depression, development, and death.* New York: Freeman.

Seligman, M. E. P. (1994). *What you can change and what you can't.* New York: Knopf.

Seligman, M. E. P. (2002). Positive psychology, positive prevention, and positive therapy. In C. R. Snyder and S. J. Lopez (Eds.), *Handbook of positive psychology* (pp. 3–9) London: Oxford University Press.

Seligman, M. E. P., and Csikszentmihalyi, M. (2000). Positive psychology: An introduction. *American Psychologist, 55,* 5–14.

Seligman, M. E. P., and Peterson, C. (2003). Positive clinical psychology. In L. G. Aspinwall and U. M. Staudinger (Eds.), *A psychology of human strengths: Fundamental questions and future directions for a positive psychology* (pp. 305–317). Washington, DC: American Psychological Association.

Sell, A., Hone, L. S. E., and Pound, N. (2012). The importance of physical strength to human males. *Human Nature, 23,* 30–44.

Sell, A., Tooby, J., and Cosmides, L. (2009). Formidability and the logic of human anger. *Proceedings of the National Academy of Science, 106,* 15073–15078.

Selye, H. (1976). *The stress of life.* New York: McGraw-Hill.

Shackelford, T. K., Goetz, A., Buss, D. M., Euler, H. A., and Hoier, S. (2005). When we hurt the ones we love: Predicting violence against women from men's mate retention. *Personal Relationships, 12,* 447–463.

Shafer, A. B. (2001). The Big Five and sexuality trait terms as predictors of relationships and sex. *Journal of Research in Personality, 35,* 313–338.

Shatz, S. M. (2008). IQ and fertility: A cross-national study. *Intelligence, 36,* 109–111.

Shaver, P. R., and Mikulincer, M. (2012). Attachment theory. In P. A. M. Van Lange, A. W. Kruglanski, and E. T. Higgins (Eds.), *Handbook of theories of social psychology* (vol. 2, pp. 160–179). Thousand Oaks, CA: Sage.

Sheldon, K. M., and Kasser, T. (2001). Getting older, getting better? Personal strivings and psychological maturity across the life span. *Developmental Psychology, 37,* 491–501.

Sheppard, K. E., and Boon, S. D. (2012). Predicting appraisals of romantic revenge: The roles of honest-humility, agreeableness, and vengefulness. *Personality and Individual Differences, 52,* 128–132.

Sheppard, L. D., and Vernon, P. A. (2008). Intelligence and speed of information-processing. *Personality and Individual Differences, 44,* 535–551.

Sherwin, B. B. (1988). Estrogen and/or androgen replacement therapy and cognitive functioning in surgically menopausal women. *Psychoneuroendocrinology, 13,* 345–357.

Shields, S. A. (2002). *Speaking from the heart: Gender and the social meaning of emotion.* Cambridge, U.K.: Cambridge University Press.

Shiner, R. L., Masten, A. S., and Roberts, J. M. (2003). Childhood personality foreshadows adult personality and life outcomes two decades later. *Journal of Personality, 71,* 1145–1170.

Shiner, R. L., Masten, A. S., and Tellegen, A. (2002). A developmental perspective on personality in emerging adulthood: Childhood antecedents and concurrent adaptation. *Journal of Personality and Social Psychology, 83*(5), 1165–1177.

Shneidman, E. S. (1981). *Endeavors in psychology: Selections from the personology of Henry A. Murray.* New York: Harper and Row.

Shoben, E. J. (1957). Toward a concept of the normal personality. *American Psychologist, 12,* 183–189.

Shoda, Y., and Mischel, W. (1996). Toward a unified, intra-individual dynamic conception of personality. *Journal of Research in Personality, 30,* 414–428.

Shoda, Y., Mischel, W., and Wright, J. C. (1994). Intra-individual stability in the organization and patterning of behavior: Incorporating psychological situations into the idiographic analysis of personality. *Journal of Personality and Social Psychology, 67,* 674–687.

Shoda, Y., Wilson, N. L., Chen, J., Gilmore, A. K., and Smith, R. E. (2013). Cognitive-affective processing system analysis of intra-individual dynamics in collaborative therapeutic assessment: Translating basic theory and research into clinical applications. *Journal of Personality, 81*(6), 554–568.

Shoda, Y., Wilson, N. L., Whitsett, D. D., Lee-Dussud, J., and Zayas, V. (2015). The person as a cognitive-affective processing system: Quantitative ideography as an integral component of cumulative science. In M. Mikulincer, P. R. Shaver, M. L. Cooper, R. J. Larsen, M. Mikulincer, P. R. Shaver, ... and R. J. Larsen (Eds.), *APA handbook of personality and social psychology, Volume 4: Personality processes and individual differences* (pp. 491–513). Washington, DC, US: American Psychological Association.

Shultz, J. S. (1993). Situational and dispositional predictions of performance: A test of the hypothesized Machiavellianism X structure interaction among salespersons. *Journal of Applied Social Psychology, 23,* 478–498.

Shweder, R. A. (1991). *Thinking through cultures: Expeditions in cultural psychology.* Cambridge, MA: Harvard University Press.

Shweder, R. A., Mahapatra, M., and Miller, J. G. (1990). Culture and moral development. In J. W. Stigler, R. A. Shweder, and G. Herdt (Eds.), *Cultural psychology: Essays on comparative human development* (pp. 130–204). Cambridge, MA: Cambridge University Press.

Sibley, C. G., Osborne, D., and Duckitt, J. (2012). Personality and political orientation: Meta-analysis and test of a Threat-Constraint Model. *Journal of Research in Personality, 46*(6), 664–677.

Siegel, J. (1997). Augmenting and reducing of visual evoked potentials in high- and low-sensation seeking humans, cats, and rats. *Behavior Genetics, 27,* 557–563.

Siegel, J., and Driscoll, P. (1996). Recent developments in an animal model of visual evoked potential augmenting/reducing and sensation seeking behavior. *Neuropsychobiology, 34,* 130–135.

Siegel, J. M. (1986). The Multidimensional Anger Inventory. *Journal of Personality and Social Psychology, 51,* 191–200.

Silverthorne, C. (2001). Leadership effectiveness and personality: A cross-cultural evaluation. *Personality and Individual Differences, 30,* 303–309.

Simonton, D. K. (1991). Emergence and realization of genius: The lives and works of 120 classical composers. *Journal of Personality and Social Psychology, 61,* 829–840.

Simpson, J. A., and Gangestad, S. W. (1991). Individual differences in sociosexuality: Evidence for convergent and discriminant validity. *Journal of Personality and Social Psychology, 60,* 870–883.

Simpson, J. A., and Rholes, W. S. (1998). *Attachment theory and close relationships.* New York: Guilford Press.

Simpson, J. A., Rholes, W. S., Orinea, M. M., and Grich, J. (2002). Working models of attachment, support giving, and support seeking in a stressful situation. *Personality and Social Psychology Bulletin, 28,* 598–608.

Singh, D., Vidaurri, M., Zambarano, R. J., and Dabbs, J. M., Jr. (1999). Behavioral, morphological, and hormonal correlates to erotic role identification among lesbian women. *Journal of Personality and Social Psychology, 76,* 1035–1049.

Singh, S. (1978). Achievement motivation and entrepreneurial success: A follow-up study. *Journal of Research in Personality, 12,* 500–503.

Six, B., and Eckes, T. (1991). A closer look at the complex structure of gender stereotypes. *Sex Roles, 24,* 64.

Slatcher, R. B., and Pennebaker, J. (2007). Emotional expression and health. In *Cambridge Handbook of Psychology, Health and Medicine, Second Edition* (pp. 84–87). Cambridge University Press.

Slatcher, R. B., and Vazire, S. (2009). Effects of global and contextualized personality on relationship satisfaction. *Journal of Research in Personality, 43,* 624–633.

Sloan, D. M., Sawyer, A. T., Lowmaster, S. E., Wernick, J., and Marx, B. P. (2015). Efficacy of narrative writing as an intervention for PTSD: Does the evidence support its use? *Journal of Contemporary Psychotherapy, 45*(4), 215–225.

Slutske, W. S., Caspi, A., Moffitt, T. E., and Poulton, R. (2005). Personality and problem gambling. *Archives of General Psychiatry, 62,* 769–775.

Slutske, W. S., Eisen, S. A., True, W. R., Lyons, M. J., Goldberg, J., and Tsuang, M. T. (2005). Common genetic vulnerability for pathological gambling and alcohol dependence in men. *Archives of General Psychiatry, 57,* 666–673.

Small, B. J., Hertzog, C., Hultsch, D. F., and Dixon, R. A. (2003). Stability and change in adult personality over 6 years: Findings from the Victoria Longitudinal Study. *The Journals of Gerontology, 58B,* 166–176.

Smillie, L. D., Cooper, A. J., Wilt, J., and Revelle, W. (2012). Do extraverts get more bang for the buck? Refining the affective-reactivity hypothesis of extraversion. *Journal of Personality and Social Psychology, 103,* 306–326.

Smillie, L. D., Yeo, G. B., Furnham, A. F., and Jackson, C. J. (2006). Benefits of all work and no play: The relationship between neuroticism and performance as a function of resource allocation. *Journal of Applied Psychology, 91,* 139–155.

Smith, C. P., and Atkinson, J. W. (1992). *Motivation and personality: Handbook of thematic content analysis.* New York: Cambridge University Press.

Smith, G. M. (1967). Usefulness of peer ratings of personality in educational research. *Educational and Psychological Measurement, 27,* 967–984.

Smith, P., Caputi, P., and Crittenden, N. (2013). Measuring optimism in organizations: Development of a workplace explanatory style questionnaire. *Journal of Happiness Studies, 14*(2), 415–432.

Smith, R. E., and Shoda, Y. (2009). Personality as a cognitive-affective processing system. In P. J. Corr and G. Matthews (Eds.), *The Cambridge handbook of personality psychology* (pp. 473–487). New York, NY: Cambridge University Press.

Smith, R. E., Shoda, Y., Cumming, S. P., and Smoll, F. L. (2009). Behavioral signatures at the ballpark: Intraindividual consistency of adults' situation-behavior patterns and their interpersonal consequences. *Journal of Research in Personality, 43,* 187–195.

Smith, T. W., Williams, P. G., and Segerstrom, S. C. (2015). Personality and physical health. In L. Cooper and R. J. Larsen (Eds.), *Handbook of personality and social psychology: Personality processes and individual differences.* Washington, DC: American Psychological Association.

Smith, T. W. (1979). Happiness: Time trends, seasonal variations, intersurvey differences, and other mysteries. *Social Psychology Quarterly, 42,* 18–30.

Smith, T. W. (2006). Personality as risk and resilience in physical health. *Current Directions in Psychological Science, 15,* 227–231.

Smith, T. W., Pope, M. K., Rhodewalt, F., and Poulton, J. L. (1989). Optimism, neuroticism, coping, and symptom reports: An alternative interpretation of the Life Orientation Test. *Journal of Personality and Social Psychology, 56,* 640–648.

Smith, T. W., and Spiro, A. III. (2002). Personality, health, and aging: Prolegomenon for the next generation. *Journal of Research in Personality, 36,* 363–394.

Smits, I. A. M., Dolan, C. V., Vorst, H. C. M., Wicherts, J. M., and Timmerman, M. E. (2011). Cohort differences in Big Five personality factors over a period of 25 years. *Journal of Personality and Social Psychology, 100,* 1124–1138.

Snyder, J. K., Fessler, D. M. T., Tiokhin, L., Frederick, D. A., Lee, S. W., and Navarrete, C. D. (2011). Trade-offs in a dangerous world: Women's fear of crime predicts preferences for aggressive and formidable mates. *Evolution and Human Behavior, 32,* 127–137.

Snyder, M. (1983). The influence of individuals on situations: Implications for understanding the links between personality and social behavior. *Journal of Personality, 51,* 497–516.

Snyder, M., and Cantor, N. (1998). Understanding personality and social behavior: A functionalist strategy. In D. T. Gilbert, S. T. Fiske, and G. Lindzey (Eds.), *The handbook of social psychology* (vol. 1, 4th ed., pp. 635–679). Boston: McGraw-Hill.

Snyder, M., and Gangestad, S. (1982). Choosing social situations: Two investigations of self-monitoring processes. *Journal of Personality and Social Psychology, 43,* 123–135.

Snyder, M., and Swann, W. B., Jr. (1978). Behavioral confirmation in social interaction: From social perception to social reality. *Journal of Experimental Social Psychology, 14,* 148–162.

Sokolowski, K., Schmalt, H., Langens, T. A., and Puca, R. M. (2000). Assessing achievement, affiliation, and power motives all at once: The Multi-Motive Grid (MMG). *Journal of Personality Assessment, 74,* 126–145.

Soliemanifar, O., Soleymanifar, A., and Afrisham, R. (2018). Relationship between personality and biological reactivity to stress: A review. *Psychiatry Investigation, 15*(12), 1100–1114.

Soloff, P. H., Lis, J. A., Kelly, T., and Cornelius, J. (1994). Risk factors for suicidal behavior in borderline personality disorder. *American Journal of Psychiatry, 151,* 1316–1323.

Somer, O., and Goldberg, L. R. (1999). The structure of Turkish trait-descriptive adjectives. *Journal of Personality and Social Psychology, 76,* 431–450.

Sorokowski, P., Sorokowska, A., Oleszkiewicz, A., Frackowiak, T., Huk, A., and Pisanski, K. (2015). Selfie posting behaviors are associated with narcissism among men. *Personality and Individual Differences, 85,* 123–127.

South, S. C., and Krueger, R. F. (2008). An interactionist perspective on genetic and environmental contributions to personality. *Social and Personality Psychology Compass, 2,* 929–948.

South, S. C., Krueger, R. F., Johnson, W., and Iacono, W. G. (2008). Adolescent personality moderates genetic and environmental influences on relationships with parents. *Journal of Personality and Social Psychology, 94,* 899–912.

South, S. C., Oltmanns, T. F., and Turkheimer, E. (2003). Personality and the derogation of others: Descriptions based on self- and peer report. *Journal of Research in Personality, 37,* 16–33.

Southwick, S. M., Sippel, L., Krystal, J., Charney, D., Mayes, L., and Pietrzak, R. (2016). Why are some individuals more resilient than others: the role of social support. *World Psychiatry: Official Journal of the World Psychiatric Association (WPA), 15*(1), 77–79.

Souza, A. L., Conroy-Beam, D., and Buss, D. M. (2016). Mate preferences in Brazil: Evolved desires and cultural evolution over three decades. *Personality and Individual Differences, 95,* 45–49.

Sowislo, J. F., and Orth, U. (2013). Does low self-esteem predict depression and anxiety? A meta-analysis of longitudinal studies. *Psychological Bulletin, 139,* 213–240.

Spangler, W. D. (1992). Validity of questionnaire and TAT measures of need for achievement: Two meta-analyses. *Psychological Bulletin, 112,* 140–154.

Spanos, N. P., and McLean, J. (1986). Hypnotically created false reports do not demonstrate pseudomemories. *British Journal of Experimental and Clinical Hypnosis, 3,* 167–171.

Spearman, C. (1910). Correlation calculated from faulty data. *British Journal of Psychology, 3,* 271–295.

Specht, J., Egloff, B., and Schmukle, S. C. (2011). Stability and change of personality across the life course: The impact of age and major life events on mean-level and rank-order stability of the Big Five. *Journal of Personality and Social Psychology, 101,* 862–882.

Spence, J. T., Helmreich, R., and Stapp, J. (1974). The Personal Attributes Questionnaire: A measure of sex-role stereotypes and masculinity and femininity. *Journal Supplement Abstract Service Catalog of Selected Documents in Psychology, 4,* 42 (No. 617).

Spiers, A., and Walker, G. J. (2008/2009). The effects of ethnicity and leisure satisfaction on happiness, peacefulness, and quality of life. *Leisure Sciences, 31*(1), 84–99.

Spies, R. A., and Plake, B. S. (2005). *The Sixteenth Mental Measurements Yearbook.* Lincoln, NE: Buros Institute of Mental Measurements.

Spilker, B., and Callaway, E. (1969). Augmenting and reducing in averaged visual evoked responses to sine wave light. *Psychophysiology, 6,* 49–57.

Spinath, F. M., and O'Connor, T. G. (2003). A behavioral genetic study of the overlap between personality and parenting. *Journal of Personality, 71*(5), 785–808.

Spinath, F. M., Wolf, H., Angleitner, A., Borkenau, P., and Riemann, R. (2002). Genetic and environmental influences on objectively assessed activity in adults. *Personality and Individual Differences, 33,* 633–645.

Spotts, E. L., Lichtenstein, P., Pedersen, N., Neiderhiser, J. M., Hansson, K., Cederblad, M., and Reiss, D. (2005). Personality and marital satisfaction: A behavioural genetic analysis. *European Journal of Personality, 19,* 205–227.

Spotts, E. L., Neiderhiser, J. M., Towers, H., Hansson, K., Lichtenstein, P., Cederblad, M., and Pedersen, N. L. (2004). Genetic and environmental influences on marital relationships. *Journal of Family Psychology, 18,* 107–119.

Srivastava, S., John, O. P., Gosling, S. D., and Potter, J. (2003). Development of personality in early and middle adulthood: Set like plaster or persistent change? *Journal of Personality and Social Psychology, 84*(5), 1041–1053.

Stake, J. E., Huff, L., and Zand, D. (1995). Trait self-esteem, positive and negative events, and event specific shifts in self-evaluation and affect. *Journal of Research in Personality, 29,* 223–241.

Statistics Canada. (2001). Family violence in Canada: A statistical profile, 2001. Retrieved from http://www.statcan.gc.ca/pub/85-002-x/2013001/article/11805-eng.pdf.

Statistics Canada. (2009). Number and rate of youth and adults accused by police, by sex and type of crime, 2009. Retrieved from http://www.statcan.gc.ca/pub/89-503-x/2010001/article/11416/tbl/tbl007-eng.htm.

Statistics Canada. (2015). Victims and persons accused of homicide, by age and sex (victims). Retrieved from http://www.statcan.gc.ca/tables-tableaux/sum-som/l01/cst01/legal10a-eng.htm.

Statistics Canada. (2016). National Indigenous Peoples Day...by the numbers. Retrieved March 6, 2019, from https://www.statcan.gc.ca/eng/dai/smr08/2018/smr08_225_2018.

Statistics Canada. (2018). Deaths, causes of death and life expectancy, 2016. Retrieved March 9, 2019, from https://www150.statcan.gc.ca/n1/daily-quotidien/180628/dq180628b-eng.htm.

Steel, P., and Ones, D. S. (2002). Personality and happiness: A national-level analysis. *Journal of Personality and Social Psychology, 83*(3), 767–781.

Steger, M. F., Hicks, B. M., Kashdan, T. B., Krueger, R. F., and Bouchard, T. J., Jr. (2007). Genetic and environmental influences on the positive traits of the values in action classification, and biometric covariance with normal personality. *Journal of Research in Personality, 41,* 524–539.

Stein, A. A. (1976). Conflict and cohesion: A review of the literature. *Journal of Conflict Resolution, 20,* 143–172.

Steinberg, L., Albert, D., Cauffman, E., Banich, M., Graham, S., and Woolard, J. (2008). Age differences in sensation seeking and impulsivity as indexed by behavior and self-report: evidence for a dual systems model. *Developmental Psychology, 44*(6), 1764–1778.

Steiner, M., Allemand, M., and McCullough, M. E. (2012). Do agreeableness and neuroticism explain age differences in the tendency to forgive others? *Personality and Social Psychology Bulletin, 38,* 441–453.

Stelmack, R. M. (1990). Biological basis of extraversion: Psychophysiological evidence. *Journal of Personality, 58,* 293–311.

Stelmack, R. M., and Stalkas, A. (1991). Galen and the humour theory of temperament. *Personality and Individual Differences, 12,* 255–263.

Štěrbová, Z., Bártová, K., Nováková, L. M., Varella, M. A. C., Havlíček, J., and Valentova, J. V. (2017). Assortative mating in personality among heterosexual and male homosexual couples from Brazil and the Czech Republic. *Personality and Individual Differences, 112,* 90–96.

Sternberg, R. J. (1985). *Beyond IQ: A triarchic theory of human intelligence.* New York: Cambridge University Press.

Stewart, K. D., and Bernhardt, P. C. (2010). Comparing Millennials to pre-1987 students and with one another. *North American Journal of Psychology, 12,* 579–602.

Stewart, M. E., Donaghey, C., Deary, I. J., and Ebmeier, K. P. (2008). Suicidal thoughts in young people: Their frequency and relationships with personality factors. *Personality and Individual Differences, 44,* 809–820.

Stewart, M. E., Ebmeier, K. P., and Deary, I. J. (2005). Personality correlates of happiness and sadness: EPQ-R and TPQ compared. *Personality and Individual Differences, 38,* 1085–1096.

Stocker, S. (1997). Don't be shy: Advice for becoming more outgoing. *Prevention,* p. 96.

Stoeber, J., Otto, K., and Dalbert, C. (2009). Perfectionism and the Big Five: Conscientiousness predicts longitudinal increases in self-oriented perfectionism. *Personality and Individual Differences, 47,* 363–368.

Stopfer, J. M., Egloff, B., Nestler, S., and Back, M. D. (2013). Being popular in online social networks: How agentic, communal, and creativity traits relate to judgments of status and liking. *Journal of Research in Personality, 47*(5), 592–598.

Story, L. B., & Repetti, R. (2006). Daily occupational stressors and marital behaviour. *Journal of Family Psychology, 20,* 690–700.

Strauss, K., Griffin, M. A., and Parker, S. K. (2012). Future work selves: How salient hoped-for identities motivate proactive career behaviors. *Journal of Applied Psychology, 97,* 580–598.

Strelan, P. (2007). Who forgives others, themselves, and situations? The roles of narcissism, guilt, self-esteem, and agreeableness. *Personality and Individual Differences, 42,* 259–269.

Stroop, J. R. (1935). Studies of interference in serial verbal reactions. *Journal of Experimental Psychology, 18,* 643–661.

Stucke, T. S., and Baumeister, R. F. (2006). Ego depletion and aggressive behavior: Is the inhibition of aggression a limited resource? *European Journal of Social Psychology, 36,* 1–13.

Su, R., Rounds, J., and Armstrong, P. I. (2009). Men and things, women and people: A meta-analysis of sex differences in interests. *Psychological Bulletin, 135,* 859–884.

Suedfeld, P., Soriano, E., McMurtry, D. L., Paterson, H., Weiszbeck, T. L., and Krell, R. (2005). Erikson's "components of a healthy personality" among Holocaust survivors immediately and 40 years after the war. *International Journal of Aging and Human Development, 60*(3), 229–248.

Suls, J., and Wan, C. K. (1989). The relation between Type A behavior and chronic emotional distress: A meta-analysis. *Journal of Personality and Social Psychology, 57,* 503–512.

Suls, J., Wan, C. K., and Costa, P. T., Jr. (1996). Relationship of trait anger to resting blood pressure: A meta-analysis. *Health Psychology, 14,* 444–456.

Surtees, P., Wainwright, N., Khaw, K. T., Luben, R., Brayne, C., and Day, N. (2003). Inflammatory dispositions: A population-based study of the association between hostility and peripheral leukocyte counts. *Personality and Individual Differences, 35,* 1271–1284.

Sutin, A. R., Ferrucci, L., Zonderman, A. B., and Terracciano, A. (2011). Personality and obesity across the adult life span. *Journal of Personality and Social Psychology, 101,* 579–592.

Sutton, S. K. (2002). Incentive and threat reactivity: Relations with anterior cortical activity. In D. Cervone and W. Mischel (Eds.), *Advances in personality science* (pp. 127–150). New York: Guilford Press.

Sutton, S. K., and Davidson, R. J. (1997). Prefrontal brain asymmetry: A biological substrate of the behavioral approach and inhibition systems. *Psychological Science, 8,* 210–214.

Sverko, B., and Fabulic, L. (1985). Stability of morningness-eveningness: Retest changes after seven years. *Revija za Psihologiju, 15,* 71–78.

Swanbrow, D. (1989, August). The paradox of happiness. *Psychology Today,* pp. 37–39.

Swann, W. B., Langlois, J. H., and Gilbert, L. A. (Eds.). (1999). *Sexism and stereotypes in modern society: The gender science of Janet Taylor Spence.* Washington, DC: American Psychological Association.

Swann, W. R., Jr., and Selye, C. (2005). Personality psychology's comeback and its emerging symbiosis with social psychology. *Personality and Social Psychology Bulletin, 31,* 155–165.

Symons, D. (1979). *The evolution of human sexuality.* New York: Oxford.

Symons, D. (1992). On the use and misuse of Darwinism in the study of human behavior. In J. Barkow, L. Cosmides, and J. Tooby (Eds.), *The adapted mind* (pp. 137–159). New York: Oxford University Press.

Tackett, J. L., Krueger, R. F., Iacono, W. G., and McGue, M. (2008). Personality in middle childhood: A hierarchical structure and longitudinal connections with personality in late adolescence. *Journal of Research in Personality, 42,* 1456–1462.

Tafarodi, R. W., and Ho, C. (2006). Implicit and explicit self-esteem: What are we measuring? *Canadian Psychology, 47*(3), 195–202.

Tafarodi, R. W., Marshall, T. C., and Milne, A. B. (2003). Self-esteem and memory. *Journal of Personality and Social Psychology, 84*(1), 29–45.

Tamir, M., Robinson, M. D., and Solberg, E. C. (2006). You may worry, but can you recognize threats when you see them? Neuroticism, threat identifications, and negative affect. *Journal of Personality, 74,* 1481–1506.

Tamir, Y., and Nadler, A. (2007). The role of personality in social identity: Effects of field-dependence and context on reactions to threat to group distinctiveness. *Journal of Personality, 75,* 927–954.

Tang, A., Santesso, D. L., Segalowitz, S. J., and Schmidt, L. A. (2016). Distinguishing shyness and sociability in children: An event-related potential study. *Journal of Experimental Child Psychology, 142,* 291–311.

Tate, J. C., and Shelton, B. L. (2008). Personality correlates of tattooing and body piercing in a college sample: The kids are alright. *Personality and Individual Differences, 45,* 281–285.

Tate, R. L. (2003). Impact of pre-injury factors on outcome after severe traumatic brain injury: Does post-traumatic personality change represent an exacerbation of premorbid traits? *Neuropsychological Rehabilitation, 3,* 43–64.

Taylor, D. M., and de la Sablonnière, R. (2014). *Towards constructive change in Aboriginal communities: A social psychology perspective.* Montreal, Quebec: McGill-Queen's University Press.

Taylor, D. M., and Usborne, E. (2010). When I Know Who "We" Are, I Can Be "Me": The Primary Role of Cultural Identity Clarity for Psychological Well-Being. *Transcultural Psychiatry, 47*(1), 93–111.

Taylor, G., Bagby, M., and Parker, J. (1999). *Disorders of affect regulation: Alexithymia in medical and psychiatric illness.* Cambridge: Cambridge University Press.

Taylor, M. D., Whiteman, M. C., Fowkes, G. F., Lee, A. J., Allerhand, M. M., and Deary, I.J. (2009). Five Factor Model personality traits and all-cause mortality in the Edinburgh Artery Study cohort. *Psychosomatic Medicine, 71*(6), 631–641.

Taylor, S. E. (1989). *Positive illusions: Self-deception and the healthy mind.* New York: Basic Books.

Taylor, S. E., Kemeny, M. E., Reed, G. M., Bower, J. E., and Gruenewald, T. L. (2000). Psychological resources, positive illusions, and health. *American Psychologist, 55,* 99–109.

Teasdale, T. W., and Owen, D. R. (2008). Secular declines in cognitive test scores: A reversal of the Flynn effect. *Intelligence, 36,* 121–126.

Tedeschi, R. G., Park, C. L., and Calhoun, L. (1998). Posttraumatic growth: Conceptual issues. In R. G. Tedeschi and P. L. Crystal (Eds.), *Posttraumatic growth: Positive changes in the aftermath of crisis* (pp. 1–22). Mahwah, NJ: Erlbaum.

Tellegen, A., Lykken, D. T., Bouchard, T. J., Wilcox, K., Segal, N., and Rich, S. (1988). Personality similarity in twins reared apart and together. *Journal of Personality and Social Psychology, 54,* 1031–1039.

Tellhed, U., Martin, B., and Fredrik, B. (2017). Will I fit in and do well? The importance of social belongingness and self-efficacy for explaining gender differences in interest in STEM and HEED majors. *Sex Roles: A Journal of Research, 77*(1–2), 86–96.

Templer, D. I. (2008). Correlational and factor analytic support for Rushton's differential K life history theory. *Personality and Individual Differences, 45,* 440–444.

Theakston, J. A., Stewart, S. H., Dawson, M. Y., Knowlden-Loewen, S. A. B., and Lehman, D. R. (2004). Big Five personality domains predict drinking motives. *Personality and Individual Differences, 37,* 971–984.

Thielmann, I., and Hilbig, B. E. (2014). Trust in me, trust in you: A social projection account of the link between personality, cooperativeness, and trustworthiness expectations. *Journal of Research in Personality, 50,* 61–65.

Thomas, A. K., Bulevich, J. B., and Loftus, E. F. (2003). Exploring the role of repetition and sensory elaboration in the imagination inflation effect. *Memory and Cognition, 31,* 630–640.

Thompson, E. H., Pleck, H. H., & Ferrera, D. L. (1992). Men and masculinities: Scales for masculinity ideology and masculinity-related constructs. *Sex Roles, 27,* 573–607.

Thompson, R. A. (1991). Emotional regulation and emotional development. *Educational Psychology Review, 3,* 269–307.

Thornhill, R., and Gangestad, S. W. (2008). *The evolutionary biology of human female sexuality.* New York: Oxford University Press.

Thrash, T. M., and Elliot, A. J. (2002). Implicit and self-attributed achievement motives: Concordance and predictive validity. *Journal of Personality, 70,* 729–755.

Thrash, T. M., Elliot, A. J., and Schultheiss, O. C. (2007). Methodological and dispositional predictors of congruence between implicit and explicit need for achievement. *Personality and Social Psychology Bulletin, 33,* 961–974.

Tice, D. M. (1993). The social motivations of people with low self-esteem. In R. F. Baumeister (Ed.), *Self-esteem: The puzzle of low self-regard* (pp. 37–53). New York: Plenum Press.

Tice, D. M., and Baumeister, R. F. (1990). Self-esteem, self-handicapping, and self-presentation: The strategy of inadequate practice. *Journal of Personality, 58,* 443–464.

Tice, D. M., and Bratslavsky, E. (2000). Giving in to feel good: The place of emotion regulation in the context of general self-control. *Psychological Inquiry, 11,* 149–159.

Tjepkema, M. (2002). The health of the off-reserve Aboriginal population. *Health Reports—Supplement, 13,* 1–17.

Tolea, M. I., Terracciano, A., Simonsick, E. M., Metter, E. J., Costa, P. T., Jr., and Ferrucci, L. (2012). Associations between personality traits, physical activity level, and muscle strength. *Journal of Research in Personality, 46,* 264–270.

Tomarken, A. J., Davidson, R. J., and Henriques, J. B. (1990). Resting frontal brain asymmetry predicts affective responses to films. *Journal of Personality and Social Psychology, 59,* 791–801.

Tomkins, S. S. (2008). *Affect, imagery, consciousness: The complete edition* (vols. 1–4). New York: Springer.

Tooby, J., and Cosmides, L. (1990). On the universality of human nature and the uniqueness of the individual: The role of genetics and adaptation. *Journal of Personality, 58,* 17–68.

Tooby, J., and Cosmides, L. (1992). Psychological foundations of culture. In J. Barkow, L. Cosmides, and J. Tooby (Eds.), *The adapted mind* (pp. 19–136). New York: Oxford University Press.

Tooke, J., and Camire, L. (1991). Patterns of deception in intersexual and intrasexual mating strategies. *Ethology and Sociobiology, 12,* 345–364.

Tracy, J. L., and Robins, R. W. (2004). Show your pride: Evidence for a discrete emotion expression.*Psychological Science, 15*(3), 194–197.

Tracy, J. L., and Robins, R. W. (2007a). The psychological structure of pride: A tale of two facets. *Journal of Personality and Social Psychology, 92,* 506–525.

Tracy, J. L., and Robins, R. W. (2007b). The prototypical pride expression: Development of a nonverbal behavioral coding system. *Emotion, 7,* 789–801.

Tracy, J. L., and Robins, R. W. (2008). The nonverbal expression of pride: Evidence for cross-cultural recognition. *Journal of Personality and Social Psychology, 94,* 516–530.

Tremblay, R. E., Pihl, R. O., Vitaro, F., and Dobkin, P. L. (1994). Predicting early onset of male antisocial behavior from preschool behavior. *Archives of General Psychiatry, 51,* 732–739.

Trinkaus, E., and Zimmerman, M. R. (1982). Trauma among the Shanidar Neanderthals. *American Journal of Physical Anthropology, 57,* 61–76.

Trivers, R. (1985). *Social evolution.* Menlo Park, CA: Benjamin/Cummings.

Trivers, R. L. (1972). Parental investment and sexual selection. In B. Campbell (Ed.), *Sexual selection and the descent of man: 1871–1971* (pp. 136–179). Chicago: Aldine.

Trobst, K. K., Herbst, J. H., Masters, H. L., and Costa, P. T. (2002). Personality pathways to unsafe sex: Personality, condom use, and HIV risk behaviors. *Journal of Research in Personality, 36,* 117–133.

Trull, J. J., and McCrae, R. M. (2002). A five-factor perspective on personality disorder research. In P. T. Costa, Jr., and T. A. Widiger (Eds.), *Personality disorders and the five factor model of personality* (2nd ed., pp. 45–58). Washington, DC: American Psychological Association.

Trzesniewski, K. H., Donnellan, M. B., and Robins, R. W. (2003). Stability of self-esteem across the life span. *Journal of Personality and Social Psychology, 84*(1), 205–220.

Tsai, A., Loftus, E., and Polage, D. (2000). Current directions in false-memory research. In D. F. Bjorklund (Ed.), *False-memory creation in children and adults: Theory, research, and implications* (pp. 31–44). Mahwah, NJ: Erlbaum.

Tsaur, S.-H., Yen, C.-H., and Hsiao, S.-L. (2013). Transcendent experience, flow and happiness for mountain climbers. *International Journal of Tourism Research, 15*(4), 360–374.

Tse, D., Lau, V., Perlman, R., and McLaughlin, M. (2018). The development and validation of the Autotelic Personality Questionnaire. *Journal of Personality Assessment.* doi:10.1080/00223891.2018.1491855

Tuerlinckz, F., De Boeck, P., and Lens, W. (2002). Measuring needs with the Thematic Apperception Test: A psychometric study. *Journal of Personality and Social Psychology, 82,* 448–461.

Tupes, E. C., and Christal, R. C. (1961). *Recurrent personality factors based on trait ratings.* USAF ASD Technical Report, No. 61–97, U.S. Air Force, Lackland Air Force Base, TX.

Turiano, N. A., Chapman, B. P., Gruenewald, T. L., and Mroczek, D. K. (2015). Personality and the leading behavioral contributors of mortality. *Health Psychology, 34*(1), 51–60.

Turiano, N. A., Whiteman, S. D., Hampson, S. E., Roberts, B. W., and Mroczek, D. K. (2012). Personality and substance use in midlife: Conscientiousness as a moderator and the effects of trait change. *Journal of Research in Personality, 46,* 295–305.

Turkheimer, E., Pettersson, E., and Horn, E. E. (2014). A phenotypic null hypothesis for the genetics of personality. *Annual Review of Psychology, 65,* 515–540.

Twenge, J. M. (2000). The age of anxiety? Birth cohort change in anxiety and neuroticism, 1952–1993. *Journal of Personality and Social Psychology, 79,* 1007–1021.

Twenge, J. M. (2001a). Changes in women's assertiveness in response to status and roles: A cross-temporal meta-analysis, 1931–1993. *Journal of Personality and Social Psychology, 81,* 133–145.

Twenge, J. M. (2001b). Birth cohort changes in extraversion: A cross-temporal meta-analysis, 1966–1993. *Personality and Individual Differences, 30,* 735–748.

Twenge, J. M., and Kasser, T. (2013). Generational changes in materialism and work centrality, 1976–2007: Associations with temporal changes in societal insecurity and materialistic role-modeling. *Personality and Social Psychology Bulletin, 39,* 883–897.

Twenge, J. M., Konrath, S., Foster, J. D., Campbell, W. K., and Bushman, B. J. (2008). Egos inflating over time: A cross-temporal meta-analysis of the Narcissistic Personality Inventory. *Journal of Personality, 76,* 875–902.

Udry, J. R., and Chantala, K. (2004). Masculinity-femininity guides sexual union formation in adolescence. *Personality and Social Psychology Bulletin, 30,* 44–55.

Uher, R., Caspi, A., Houts, R., Sugden, K., Williams, B., Poulton, R., and Moffitt, T. E. (2011). Serotonin transporter gene moderates childhood maltreatment's effects on persistent but not single-episode depression: Replications and implications for resolving inconsistent results. *Journal of Affective Disorders, 135,* 55–65.

United Nations. (2010). UN AIDS report on the global AIDS epidemic. Retrieved from http://www.unaids.org/globalreport/documents/20101123_GlobalReport_full_en.pdf.

Usborne, E., and Taylor, D. M. (2010). The role of cultural identity clarity for self-concept clarity, self-steem, and subjective well-being. *Personality and Social Psychology Bulletin, 36*(7), 883–897.

Vaidya, J. G., Gray, E. K., Gaig, J. R., Mroczek, D. K., and Watson, D. (2008). Differential stability and individual growth trajectories of Big Five and affective traits during young adulthood. *Journal of Personality, 76,* 267–304.

Vaidya, J. G., Gray, E. K., Haig, J., and Watson, D. (2002). On the temporal stability of personality: Evidence for differential stability and the role of life experiences. *Journal of Personality and Social Psychology, 83*(6), 1469–1484.

Vaillant, G. E. (1994). Ego mechanisms of defense and personality psychopathology. *Journal of Abnormal Psychology, 103,* 44–50.

Valentova, J. V., Štěrbová, Z., Bártová, K., and Varella, M. A. C. (2016). Personality of ideal and actual romantic partners among heterosexual and non-heterosexual men and women: A cross-cultural study. *Personality and Individual Differences, 101,* 160–166.

van Anders, S. M. (2012). Testosterone and sexual desire in healthy women and men. *Archives of Sexual Behavior, 41,* 1471–1484.

van Anders, S. M., Steiger, J., and Goldey, K. L. (2015). Effects of gendered behavior on testosterone in women and men. *Proceedings of the National Academy of Sciences of the United States of America, 112,* 13805-13810.

Van Beijsterveldt, C. E. M., Bartels, M., Hudziak, J. J., and Boomsma, D. I. (2003). Causes of stability of aggression from early childhood to adolescence: A longitudinal genetic analysis of Dutch twins. *Behavior Genetics, 33,* 591–605.

van den Berg, S. M., de Moor, M. H., Verweij, K. J., Krueger, R. F., Luciano, M., Vasquez, A. A., ... & Gordon, S. D. (2016). Meta-analysis of Genome-Wide Association Studies for Extraversion: Findings from the Genetics of Personality Consortium. *Behavior genetics, 46*(2), 170–182.

van den Hurk, P. A., Wingens, T., Giommi, F., Barendregt, H. P., Speckens, A. E., and van Schie, H. T. (2011). On the relationship between the practice of mindfulness meditation and personality: An exploratory analysis of the mediating role of mindfulness skills. *Mindfulness, 2*(3), 194–200.

Van der Linden, D., Figueredo, A. J., de Leeuw, R. N. H., Scholte, R. J. J., and Engels, R. C. M. E. (2012). The general factor of personality (GFP) and parental support: Testing a prediction from Life History Theory. *Evolution and Human Behavior, 33,* 537–546.

Vando, A. (1974). The development of the R-A scale: A paper-and-pencil measure of pain tolerance. *Personality and Social Psychology Bulletin, 1,* 28–29.

Vasquez, K., Durik, A. M., and Hyde, J. S. (2002). Family and work: Implications of adult attachment styles. *Personality and Social Psychology Bulletin, 28,* 874–886.

Vater, A., Moritz, S., and Roepke, S. (2018). Does a narcissism epidemic exist in modern western societies? Comparing narcissism and self-esteem in East and West Germany. *PLOS ONE, 13*(1), e0198386.

Vazire, S. (2010). Who knows what about a person? The self-other knowledge asymmetry (SOKA) model. *Journal of Personality and Social Psychology, 98,* 281–300.

Vazire, S., and Mehl, M. R. (2008). Knowing me, knowing you: The accuracy and unique predictive validity of self and other ratings of daily behavior. *Journal of Personality and Social Psychology, 95,* 1207–1216.

Vazire, S., Naumann, L. P., Rentfrow, P. J., and Gosling, S. D. (2008). Portrait of a narcissist: Manifestations of narcissism in physical appearance. *Journal of Research in Personality, 42,* 1439–1447.

Veale, J. F., Watson, R. J., Peter, T., and Saewyc, E. M. (2017). The mental health of Canadian transgender youth compared with the Canadian population. *Journal of Adolescent Health, 60,* 44–49.

Veenhoven, R. (1988). The utility of happiness. *Social Indicators Research, 20,* 333–354.

Veenhoven, R. (1991a). Questions on happiness: Classical topics, modern answers, blind spots. In F. Strack and M. Argyle (Eds.), *Subjective well-being: An interdisciplinary perspective* (pp. 7–26). Oxford, England: Pergamon Press.

Veenhoven, R. (1991b). Is happiness relative? *Social Indicators Research, 24,* 1–34.

Verbakel, E., and Kalmijn, M. (2014). Assortative mating among Dutch married and cohabiting same-sex and different-sex couples. *Journal of Marriage and Family, 76*(1), 1–12. doi: 10.1111/jomf.12084.

Vernon, P., Villani, V. C., Vickers, L. C., and Harris, J. A. (2008). A behavioral genetic investigation of the Dark Triad and the Big 5. *Personality and Individual Differences, 44,* 445–452.

Veselka, L., Schermer, J. A., and Vernon, P. A. (2012). The Dark Triad and an expanded framework of personality. *Personality and Individual Differences, 53,* 417–425.

Vidacek, S., Kaliterna, L., Radosevic-Vidacek, B., and Folkard, S. (1988). Personality differences in the phase of circadian rhythms: A comparison of morningness and extraversion. *Ergonomics, 31,* 873–888.

Vignoles, V. L., Regalia, C., Manzi, C., Golledtge, J., and Scabini, E. (2006). Beyond self-esteem: Influence of multiple motives on identity construction. *Journal of Personality and Social Psychology, 90,* 308–333.

Vining, D. (1982). On the possibility of the reemergence of a dysgenic trend with respect to intelligence in American fertility differentials. *Intelligence, 6,* 241–264.

Vitaro, F., Arsenault, L., and Tremblay, R. E. (1997). Dispositional predictors of problem gambling in male adolescents. *American Journal of Psychiatry, 154,* 1769–1770.

Vrij, A., van der Steen, J., and Koppelaar, L. (1995). The effects of street noise and field independence on police officers' shooting behavior. *Journal of Applied Social Psychology, 25,* 1714–1725.

Vukasović, T., and Bratko, D. (2015). Heritability of personality: A meta-analysis of behavior genetic studies. *Psychological Bulletin, 141*(4), 769–785.

Wachtel, P. L. (1973). Psychodynamics, behavior therapy, and the implacable experimenter: An inquiry into the consistency of personality. *Journal of Abnormal Psychology, 82,* 324–334.

Wacker, J., Mueller, E. M., and Stemmler, G. (2012). Prenatal testosterone and personality: Increasing the specificity of trait assessment to detect consistent associations with digit ratio (2D:4D). *Journal of Research in Personality,* online first posting. doi:10.1016/j.jrp.2012.10.007.

Wagner, J., Lüdtke, O., Jonkmann, K., and Trautwein, U. (2013). Cherish yourself: Longitudinal patterns and conditions of self-esteem change in the transition to young adulthood. *Journal of Personality and Social Psychology, 104,* 148–163.

Wagstaff, G. F., Vella, M., and Perfect, T. (1992). The effect of hypnotically elicited testimony on jurors' judgments of guilt and innocence. *Journal of Social Psychology, 132,* 591–595.

Wahba, M. A., and Bridwell, L. (1973). Maslow's need hierarchy theory: A review of research. *Proceedings of the Annual Convention of the American Psychological Association (1973).* 571–572.

Wallace, H. M., and Baumeister, R. F. (2002). The performance of narcissists rises and falls with perceived opportunity for glory. *Journal of Personality and Social Psychology, 82*(5), 819–834.

Waller, N. (1994). The importance of nongenetic influences on romantic love styles. *Psychological Science, 9,* 268–274.

Wallston, B. S., and Wallston, K. (1978). Locus of control and health: A review of the literature. *Health Education Monographs, 6,* 107–117.

Wallston, K. A., Wallston, B. S., Smith, S., and Dobbins, C. J. (1989). Perceived control and health. In M. Johnston and T. Marteau (Eds.), *Applications in health psychology* (pp. 5–25). New Brunswick, NJ: Transaction.

Walton, G. M., Paunesku, D., and Dweck, C. S. (2012). Expandable selves. In M. R. Leary and J. P. Tangney (Eds.), *Handbook of self and identity* (2nd ed., pp. 141–154). New York, NY: Guilford Press.

Watson, D. (2000). *Mood and temperament.* New York: Guilford Press.

Watson, D. (2003). To dream, perchance to remember: Individual differences in dream recall. *Personality and Individual Differences, 34,* 1271–1286.

Watson, D., and Clark, L. A. (1984). Negative affectivity: The disposition to experience aversive emotional states. *Psychological Bulletin, 96,* 465–490.

Watson, D., and Humrichouse, J. (2006). Personality development in emerging adulthood: Integrating evidence from self-ratings and spouse ratings. *Journal of Personality and Social Psychology, 91,* 959–974.

Watson, D., and Pennebaker, J. W. (1989). Health complaints, stress, and distress: Exploring the central role of negative affectivity. *Psychological Review, 96,* 234–254.

Watson, D. C. (2001). Procrastination and the five-factor model: A facet level analysis. *Personality and Individual Differences, 30,* 149–158.

Watters, C. A., Taylor, G. J., and Bagby, R. M. (2015, July 13). Illuminating the theoretical components of alexithymia using bifactor modeling and network analysis. *Psychological Assessment.* Advance online publication. http://dx.doi.org/10.1037/pas0000169.

Watts, B. L. (1982). Individual differences in circadian activity rhythms and their effects on roommate relationships. *Journal of Personality, 50,* 374–384.

Weber, M., Davis, K., and McPhie, L. (2006). Narrative therapy, eating disorders and groups: Enhancing outcomes in rural NSW. *Australian Social Work, 59*(4), 391–405.

Wechsler, D. (1949). *The Wechsler Intelligence Scale for Children.* New York: Psychological Corporation.

Wehr, T. A., and Goodwin, F. K. (1981). Biological rhythms and psychiatry. In S. Arieti and H. K. Brodie (Eds.), *American handbook of psychiatry: Advances and new directions* (vol. 7). New York: Basic Books.

Weidman, A. C., Cheng, J. T., and Tracy, J. L. (2018). The psychological structure of humility. *Journal of Personality and Social Psychology, 114,* 153–178.

Weidman, A. C., Tracy, J. L., and Elliot, A. J. (2016). The benefits of following your pride: Authentic pride promotes achievement. *Journal of Personality, 84,* 607–622.

Weinberger, D. S., Schwartz, G. E., and Davidson, R. J. (1979). Low-anxious, high-anxious, and repressive coping styles: Psychometric patterns and behavioral and physiological responses to stress. *Journal of Abnormal Psychology, 88,* 369–380.

Weinberger, J. (2003). Freud's influence on psychology is alive and vibrant. In E. E. Smith, S. Nolen-Hoeksema, B. L. Fredrickson, G. R. Loftus, D. J. Bem, and S. Maren, *Introduction to psychology* (p. 486). Belmont, CA: Wadsworth/Thomson Learning.

Weinberger, J., and McClelland, D. C. (1990). Cognitive versus traditional motivational models: Irreconcilable or complementary? In E. T. Higgins and R. M. Sorrentino (Eds.), *Handbook of motivation and cognition* (vol. 2, pp. 562–597). New York: Guilford Press.

Weinberger, J., and Westen, D. (2007). *RATS, we should have used Clinton: Subliminal priming in political campaigns.* Paper presented at the annual meeting of the International Society of Political Psychology, Portland, Oregon. *USA Online.* Retrieved February 3, 2009, from www.allacademic.com/meta/ p204661_index.html

Weinstein, A., Dorani, D., Elhadif, R., Bukovza, Y., Yarmulnik, A., and Dannon, P. (2015). Internet addiction is associated with social anxiety in young adults. *Annals of Clinical Psychiatry, 27*(1), 4–9.

Weinstock, L. M., and Whisman, M. A. (2006). Neuroticism as a common feature of the depressive and anxiety disorders: A test of the revised integrative hierarchical model in a national sample. *Journal of Abnormal Psychology, 115,* 68–74.

Weisberg, Y. J., DeYoung, C. G., and Hirsh, J. B. (2011). Gender differences in personality across the ten aspects of the Big Five. *Frontiers in Psychology, 2,* 178. doi: 10.3389/fpsyg.2011.00178

Weiser, E. (2015). #Me: Narcissism and its facets as predictors of selfie-posting frequency. *Personality and Individual Differences, 86,* 477–481. doi: 10.1016/j.paid.2015.07.007

Weiss, A., King, J. E., and Enns, R. M. (2002). Subjective well-being is heritable and genetically correlated with dominance in chimpanzees (Pan troglodytes). *Journal of Personality and Social Psychology, 83*(5), 1141–1149.

Weissberg, R. P., Kumpfer, K. L., and Seligman, M. E. P. (2003). Prevention that works for children and youth: An introduction. *American Psychologist Special Issue: Prevention that works for children and youth, 58,* 425–432.

Weisz, E., and Zaki, J. (2017). Empathy-building interventions: A review of existing work and suggestions for future directions. In E. M. Seppala et al. (Eds.), *The Oxford Handbook of Compassion Science* (pp. 205–217). Oxford University Press.

Weller, H. G., Repman, J., Lan, W., and Rooze, G. (1995). Improving the effectiveness of learning through hypermedia-based instruction: The importance of learner characteristics. Special Issue: Hypermedia: Theory, research, and application. *Computers in Human Behavior, 11,* 451–465.

Wertsch, J., and Kanner, B. (1992). A socio-cultural approach to intellectual development. In R. Sternberg and C. A. Berg (Eds.), *Intellectual development* (pp. 328–349). New York: Cambridge University Press.

Wesley-Esquimaux, C. C., and Smolewski, M. (2004). Historic trauma and Aboriginal healing. Ottawa: Aboriginal Healing Foundation. Retrieved from http://www.ahf.ca.

Wessman, A. E., and Ricks, D. F. (1966). *Mood and personality.* New York: Holt, Rinehart, and Winston.

Westen, D. (1990). Psychoanalytic approaches to personality. In L. A. Pervin (Ed.), *Handbook of personality: Theory and research* (pp. 21–65). New York: Guilford Press.

Westen, D. (1992). The cognitive self and the psychoanalytic self: Can we put our selves together? *Psychological Inquiry, 3,* 1–13.

Westen, D. (1998). The scientific legacy of Sigmund Freud: Toward a psychodynamically informed psychological science. *Psychological Bulletin, 124,* 333–371.

Westen, D., and Gabbard, G. O. (2002a). Developments in cognitive neuroscience: I. Conflict, compromise, and connectionism. *Journal of the American Psychoanalytic Association, 50,* 53–98.

Westen, D., and Gabbard, G. O. (2002b). Developments in cognitive neuroscience: II. Implications for theories of transference. *Journal of the American Psychoanalytic Association 50,* 99–134.

Westen, D., Ludolph, P., Misle, B., and Ruffins, S. (1990). Physical and sexual abuse in adolescent girls with borderline personality disorder. *American Journal of Orthopsychiatry, 60,* 55–66.

Westergaard, G. C. and Hyatt, C. W. (1994). The responses of bonobos (Pan paniscus) to their mirror images: Evidence of selfrecognition. *Human Evolution, 9*(4), 273–279.

Wever, R. A. (1979). *The circadian system of man: Results of experiments under temporal isolation.* New York: Springer.

Whalen, P. J., Bush, G., and McNally, R. J. (1998). The emotional counting Stroop paradigm: A functional magnetic resonance imaging probe of the anterior cingulate affective division. *Biological Psychiatry, 44,* 1219–1228.

Wheeler, J. G., George, W. H., and Dahl, B. J. (2002). Sexually aggressive college males: Empathy as a moderator in the "Confluence Model" of sexual aggression. *Personality and Individual Differences, 33,* 759–775.

Wheeler, R. W., Davidson, R. J., and Tomarken, A. J. (1993). Frontal brain asymmetry and emotional reactivity: A biological substrate of affective style. *Psychophysiology, 30,* 82–89.

White, J. K., Hendrick, S. S., and Hendrick, C. (2004). Big Five personality variables and relationship constructs. *Personality and Individual Differences, 37,* 1519–1530.

Whitehead, D. L., Perkins-Porras, L., Strike, P. D., Magid, K., and Steptoe, A. (2007). Cortisol awakening response is elevated in acute coronary syndrome patients with Type D personality. *Journal of Psychosomatic Research, 62,* 419–425.

Whorf, B. L. (1956). *Language, thought, and reality.* Cambridge, MA: MIT Press.

Wicker, F. W., Brown, G., Weihe, J. A., Hagen, A. S., and Reed, J. L. (1993). On reconsidering Maslow: An examination of the deprivation/domination proposition. *Journal of Research in Personality, 27,* 118–133.

Wickman, S. A., and Campbell, C. (2003). An analysis of how Carl Rogers enacted client-centered conversation with Gloria. *Journal of Counseling and Development, 81,* 178–184.

Widiger, T. A. (1997). Personality disorders as maladaptive variants of common personality traits: Implications for treatment. *Journal of Contemporary Psychotherapy Special Issue: Personality disorders, 27,* 265–282.

Widiger, T. A. (2000). Personality disorders in the 21st century. *Journal of Personality Disorders, 14,* 3–16.

Widiger, T. A., Costa, P. T., Jr., and McCrae, R. M. (2002a). A proposal for Axis II: Diagnosing personality disorders using the five-factor model. In P. T. Costa Jr. and T. A. Widiger (Eds.), *Personality disorders and the five-factor model of personality* (2nd ed., 431–456). Washington, DC: American Psychological Association.

Widiger, T. A., Trull, T. J., Clarkin, J. F., Sanderson, C., and Costa, P. T., Jr. (2002b). A description of the *DSM-IV* personality disorders with the five-factor model of personality. In P. T. Costa Jr. and T. A. Widiger (Eds.), *Personality disorders and the five-factor model of personality* (2nd ed., 89–102). Washington, DC: American Psychological Association.

Widiger, T. A., and Costa, P. T. (2012). Integrating normal and abnormal personality structure: The five-factor model. *Journal of Personality, 80*(6), 1471–1506.

Wiebe, D. J., and Smith, T. (1997). Personality and health: Progress and problems in psychosomatics. In R. Hogan, J. Johnson, and S. Briggs (Eds.), *Handbook of personality psychology* (pp. 892–918). San Diego, CA: Academic Press.

Wiggins, J. S. (1973). *Personality and prediction: Principles of personality assessment.* Menlo Park, CA: Addison-Wesley.

Wiggins, J. S. (1979). A psychological taxonomy of trait-descriptive terms: I. The interpersonal domain. *Journal of Personality and Social Psychology, 37,* 395–412.

Wiggins, J. S. (1996). *The five-factor model of personality: Theoretical perspectives.* New York: Guilford Press.

Wiggins, J. S. (2003). *Paradigms of personality assessment.* New York: Guilford Press.

Wiggins, J. S., Phillips, N., and Trapnell, P. (1989). Circular reasoning about interpersonal behaviour: Evidence concerning some untested assumptions underlying diagnostic classification. *Journal of Personality and Social Psychology, 56*(2), 296–305.

Willerman, L. (1979). Effects of families on intellectual development. *American Psychologist, 34,* 923–929.

Willerman, L., Loehlin, J. C., and Horn, J. M. (1992). An adoption and a cross-fostering study of the Minnesota Multiphasic Personality Inventory (MMPI) Psychopathic Deviate scale. *Behavior Genetics, 22,* 515–529.

Williams, D. E., and Page, M. M. (1989). A multi-dimensional measure of Maslow's hierarchy of needs. *Journal of Research in Personality, 23,* 192–213.

Williams, G. E., Daros, A. R., Graves, B., McMain, S. F., Links, P. S., and Ruocco, A. C. (2015). Executive functions and social cognition in highly lethal self-injuring patients with borderline personality disorder. *Personality Disorders: Theory, Research, and Treatment, 6*(2), 107.

Williams, J. E., and Best, D. L. (1982). *Measuring sex stereotypes: A thirty-nation study.* Beverly Hills: Sage.

Williams, J. E., and Best, D. L. (1990). *Measuring sex stereotypes: A multi-nation study.* Newbury Park, CA: Sage.

Williams, J. E., and Best, D. L. (1994). Cross-cultural views of women and men. In W. J. Lonner and R. Malpass (Eds.), *Psychology and culture* (pp. 191–196). Boston: Allyn and Bacon.

Williams, J. M. G., Mathews, A., and MacLeod, C. (1996). The emotional Stroop task and psychopathology. *Psychological Bulletin, 120,* 3–24.

Williams, L., O'Connor, R. C., Howard, S., Hughes, B. M., Johnston, D. W., Hay, J. L., O'Connor, et al. (2008). Type D personality mechanisms of effect: The role of health-related behavior and social support. *Journal of Psychosomatic Research, 64,* 63–69.

Williams, P. G., O'Brien, C. D., and Colder, C. R. (2004). The effects of neuroticism and extraversion on self-assessed health and health-relevant cognition. *Personality and Individual Differences, 37,* 83–94.

Willows, N. D., Ridley, D., Raine, K. D., and Maximova, K. (2013). High adiposity is associated cross-sectionally with low self-concept and body size dissatisfaction among indigenous Cree schoolchildren in Canada. *BMC Pediatrics, 13*(1), 1–7.

Wilson, D. S., Near, D., and Miller, R. R. (1996). Machiavellianism: A synthesis of the evolutionary and psychological literatures. *Psychological Bulletin, 119,* 285–299.

Wilson, M., and Daly, M. (1985). Competitiveness, risk-taking, and violence: The young male syndrome. *Ethology and Sociobiology, 6,* 59–73.

Wilson, M., and Daly, M. (2004). Do pretty women inspire men to discount the future? *Proceedings of the Royal Society of London, B (Suppl.), 271,* S177–S179.

Wilson, M. S., and Sibley, C. G. (2011). 'Narcissism creep?' Evidence for age-related differences in narcissism in the New Zealand general populations. *New Zealand Journal of Psychology, 40,* 89–95.

Winch, R. F. (1954). The theory of complementary needs in mate selection: An analytic and descriptive study. *American Sociological Review, 19,* 241–249.

Wingert, S. (2011). The social distribution of distress and well-being in the Canadian Aboriginal population living off reserve. *The International Indigenous Policy Journal, 2*(1). Retrieved from http://ir.lib.uwo.ca/iipj/vol2/iss1/4.

Winjgaards-de Meij, L., Stroebe, M., Schut, H., Stroebe, W., van den Bout, J., van der Heijden, P., and Dijkstra, I. (2007). Neuroticism and attachment insecurity as predictors of bereavement outcome. *Journal of Research in Personality, 41,* 498–505.

Wink, P., Ciciolla, L., Dillon, M., and Tracy, A. (2007). Religiousness, spiritual seeking, and personality: Findings from a longitudinal study. *Journal of Personality, 75,* 1051–1070.

Winter, D. G. (1973). *The power motive.* New York: Free Press.

Winter, D. G. (1988). The power motive in women—and men. *Journal of Personality and Social Psychology, 54,* 510–519.

Winter, D. G. (1993). Power, affiliation, and war: Three tests of a motivational model. *Journal of Personality and Social Psychology, 65,* 532–545.

Winter, D. G. (1998). A motivational analysis of the Clinton first term and the 1996 presidential campaign. *Leadership Quarterly, 9,* 367–376.

Winter, D. G. (1999). Linking personality and "scientific" psychology: The development of empirically derived Thematic Apperception Test measures. In Gieser and M. I. Stein (Eds.), *Evocative images: The Thematic Apperception Test and the art of projection* (pp. 107–124). Washington, DC: American Psychological Association.

Winter, D. G. (2002). The motivational dimensions of leadership: Power, achievement, and affiliation. In R. E. Riggio and S. E. Murphy (Eds.), *Multiple intelligences and leadership* (pp. 119–138). Mahwah, NJ: Erlbaum.

Winter, D. G., and Barenbaum, N. B. (1985). Responsibility and the power motive in women and men. *Journal of Personality, 53,* 335–355.

Winter, D. G., John, O. P., Stewart, A. J., Klohnen, E. C., and Duncan, L. E. (1998). Traits and motives: Toward an integration of two traditions in personality research. *Psychological Review, 105,* 230–250.

Witkin, H. A. (1973). A cognitive-style perspective on evaluation and guidance. *Proceedings of the Invitational Conference on Testing Problems,* 21–27.

Witkin, H. A. (1977). Role of the field-dependent and field-independent cognitive styles in academic evolution: A longitudinal study. *Journal of Educational Psychology, 69,* 197–211.

Witkin, H. A., Dyk, R. B., Fattuson, H. F., Goodenough, D. R., and Karp, S. A. (1962). *Psychological differentiation: Studies of development.* New York: Wiley.

Witkin, H. A., and Goodenough, D. R. (1977). Field dependence and interpersonal behavior. *Psychological Bulletin, 84,* 661–689.

Witkin, H. A., Lewis, H. B., Hertzman, M., Machover, K., Meissner, P. B., and Wapner, S. (1954). *Personality through perception: An experimental and clinical study.* New York: Harper.

Witkin, H. A., Moore, C. A., Goodenough, D. R., and Cox, P. W. (1977). Field-dependent and field-independent cognitive styles and their educational implications. *Review of Educational Research, 47*(1), 1–64.

Woike, B. A. (1995). Most memorable experiences: Evidence for a link between implicit and explicit motives and social cognitive processes in everyday life. *Journal of Personality and Social Psychology, 68,* 1081–1091.

Wood, A. C., Saudino, K. J., Rogers, H., Asherson, P., and Kuntsi, J. (2007). Genetic influences on mechanically-assessed activity level in children. *Journal of Child Psychology and Psychiatry, 48,* 695–702.

Wood, A. H., and Eagly, A. H. (2010). Gender. In S. Fiske, D. Gilbert, and G. Lindzey (Eds.), *Handbook of Social Psychology* (5th ed., vol. 1, pp. 629–667). New York: Wiley.

Wood, J. J., McLeod, B. D., Sigman, M., Hwang, W. C., and Chu, B. C. (2003). Parenting and childhood anxiety: Theory, empirical findings, and future directions. *Journal of Child Psychology and Psychiatry and Allied Disciplines, 44,* 134–151.

Wood, J. M., Nezworski, M. T., Lilienfeld, S. O., and Garb, H. N. (2003). *What's wrong with the Rorschach? Science confronts the controversial inkblot test.* San Francisco: Jossey-Bass.

Wood, J. M., Nezworski, M. T., and Stejskal, J. W. (1996). The comprehensive system for the Rorschach: A critical examination. *Psychological Science, 7,* 3–10.

Wortman, J., and Wood, D. (2011). The personality traits of liked people. *Journal of Research in Personality, 45,* 519–528.

Wright, D. B., Eaton, A. A., and Skagerberg, E. (2015). Occupational segregation and psychological gender differences: How empathizing and systemizing help explain the distribution of men and women into (some) occupations. *Journal of Research in Personality, 54,* 30–39.

Wright, L. (1988). The Type A behavior pattern and coronary artery disease. *American Psychologist, 43,* 2–14.

Wright Cardinal, S. (2017). *Beyond the Sixties Scoop: Reclaiming Indigenous identity, reconnection to place, and reframing understandings of being Indigenous.* Unpublished doctoral dissertation. University of Victoria, Victoria, British Columbia.

Wu, K. D., and Clark, L. A. (2003). Relations between personality traits and self-reports of daily behavior. *Journal of Research in Personality, 37,* 231–256.

Wu, Y., van Dijk, E., Aitken, M. R. F., and Clark, L. (2016). Missed losses loom larger than missed gains: Electrodermal reactivity to decision choices and outcomes in a gambling task. *Cognitive Affective and Behavioral Neuroscience, 16*(2), 353–361. doi:10.3758/s13415-015-0395-y.

Yarkoni, T. (2015). Neurobiological substrates of personality: A critical overview. In M. L. Cooper and R. J. Larsen (Eds.), *Handbook of personality and social psychology: Vol. 2. Personality processes and individual differences.* Washington, DC: American Psychological Association.

Yeh, C. (1995). *A cultural perspective on interdependence in self and morality: A Japan–U.S. comparison.* Unpublished manuscript, Department of Psychology, Stanford University, Stanford, CA.

Yik, M. S. M., and Russell, J. A. (2001). Predicting the big two of affect from the Big Five of personality. *Journal of Research in Personality, 35,* 247–277.

Young, S. M., and Pinsky, D. (2006). Narcissism and celebrity. *Journal of Research in Personality, 40,* 463–471.

Yu, D. L., and Seligman, M. E. P. (2002). Preventing depressive symptoms in Chinese children. *Prevention and Treatment, 5,* np.

Zagorsky, J. L. (2007). Do you have to be smart to be rich? The impact of IQ on wealth, income, and financial distress. *Intelligence, 35,* 489–501.

Zakriski, A. L., Wright, J. C., and Underwood, M. K. (2005). Gender similarities and differences in children's social behavior: Finding personality in contextualized patterns of adaptation. *Journal of Personality and Social Psychology, 88,* 844–855.

Zeidner, M., Matthews, G., Roberts, R. D., and MacCann, C. (2003). Development of emotional intelligence: Towards a multi-level investment model. *Human Development, 46,* 69–96.

Zeigler-Hill, V., Myers, E. M., and Clark, C. B. (2010). Narcissism and self-esteem reactivity: The role of negative achievement events. *Journal of Research in Personality, 44,* 285–292.

Zelenski, J. M., and Larsen, R. J. (1999). Susceptibility to affect: A comparison of three personality taxonomies. *Journal of Personality, 67,* 761–791.

Zelenski, J. M., and Larsen, R. J. (2000). The distribution of emotions in everyday life: A state and trait perspective from experience sampling data. *Journal of Research in Personality, 34,* 178–197.

Zentner, M. R. (2005). Ideal mate personality concepts and compatibility in close relationships: A longitudinal analysis. *Journal of Personality and Social Psychology, 89,* 242–256.

Zettler, I., and Hilbig, B. E. (2010). Honesty-humility and person-situation interaction at work. *European Journal of Personality, 24,* 569–582.

Zhao, K., & Smillie, L. D. (2014). The role of interpersonal traits in social decision making exploring sources of behavioral heterogeneity in economic games. *Personality and Social Psychology Review, 19*(3), 277–302. doi: 10.1177/1088868314553709.

Zhu, B., Chen, C., Loftus, E .F., He, Q., Chen, C., Lei, X., Lin, C., and Dong, Q. (2012). Brief exposure to misinformation can lead to long-term false memories. *Applied Cognitive Psychology, 26,* 301–307.

Zilcha-Mano, S., Mikulincer, M., and Shaver, P. R. (2012). Pets as safe havens and secure bases: The moderating role of pet attachment orientations. *Journal of Research in Personality, 46,* 571–580.

Zimbardo, P. G. (1977). *Shyness: What it is and what to do about it.* New York: Symphony.

Zuckerman, M. (1974). The sensation seeking motive. In B. Maher (Ed.), *Progress in experimental personality research* (vol. 7, pp. 79–148). New York: Academic Press.

Zuckerman, M. (1978, February). The search for high sensation. *Psychology Today,* February, 38–46.

Zuckerman, M. (1984). Sensation seeking: A comparative approach to a human trait. *Behavioral and Brain Sciences, 7,* 413–471.

Zuckerman, M. (1991a). *Psychobiology of personality.* New York: Cambridge University Press.

Zuckerman, M. (1991b). Sensation-seeking trait. *Encyclopedia of Human Biology, 6,* 809–817.

Zuckerman, M. (2006). Biosocial bases of sensation seeking. In T. Canli (Ed.), *Biology of personality and individual differences* (pp. 37–59). New York: Guilford Press.

Zuckerman, M., and Aluja, A. (2015). Measures of sensation seeking. In G. J. Boyle, D. H. Saklofske, G. Matthews, G. J. Boyle, D. H. Saklofske, and G. Matthews (Eds.), *Measures of personality and social psychological constructs* (pp. 352–380). San Diego, CA, US: Elsevier Academic Press.

Zuckerman, M., and Haber, M. M. (1965). Need for stimulation as a source of stress response to perceptual isolation. *Journal of Abnormal Psychology, 70,* 371–377.

Zuckerman, M., Joireman, J., Kratl, M., and Kuhilan, D. M. (1999). Where do motivational and emotional traits fit within three factor models of personality? *Personality and Individual Differences, 26,* 487–504.

Zuckerman, M., and Kuhlman, D. M. (2000). Personality and risk-taking: Common biosocial factors. *Journal of Personality, 68,* 999–1029.

Chapter Sources

Chapter 3
Table 3.2: *Source:* Adapted from Matthews & Oddy, 1993.

Chapter 4
Table 4.1: *Sources:* Myers et al., 1998; Hirsh & Kummerow, 1990.

Chapter 5
Table 5.1: *Source:* Adapted from Rothbart, 1981.
Figure 5.1: *Source:* Olweus, 1979.

Chapter 6
Table 6.2: *Source:* Bouchard & McGue, 1990; Tellegen et al., 1988.
Figure 6.1: *Source:* Dreber et al. (2009).

Chapter 7
Table 7.2: *Source:* Eysenck, Eysenck, & Barrett, 1985.

Chapter 8
Figure 8.1: *Source:* Adapted from Buss, 1995a.

Chapter 9
Figure 9.2: *Source:* Dijksterhhuis, A., Bos, M. W., Nordgren, L. F., and van Baaren, R. B. (2006). On making the right choice: The deliberation without-attention effect. *Science, 311,* 1005–1007.

Chapter 11
Table 11.1: *Source:* Adapted from *Explorations in personality,* by J. H. Murray, New York, Oxford University Press.
Table 11.3: *Source:* Adapted from Maslow, 1954/1987.

Chapter 13
Table 13.2: *Source:* Diener et al., 1985.

Chapter 15
Table 15.1: *Source:* Adapted from Buss et al. (1990), p. 19, Table 4.
Table 15.2: *Source:* Botwin, Buss, & Shackelford (1997).
Table 15.3: *Source:* Botwin, Buss, & Shackelford (1997).
Table 15.4: *Source:* Botwin, Buss, & Shackelford (1997).
Exercise: Personality Characteristics in Mate Selection *Source:* Buss (1991a).

Chapter 16
Table: *Sources:* For S-Data, see Costa et al. (2001); for O-Data, see McCrae et al. (2005b).
Exercise: The Personal Attributes Questionnaire *Source:* Spence et al. (1974).

Chapter 17
Table 17.3: *Source:* Adapted from Williams & Best, 1994. Cross-cultural views of women and men. In Walter J. Lonner and Roy S. Malpass (Eds.), *Psychology and culture,* 1st edition, p. 193, © 1994. Reprinted by permission of Pearson Education, Inc., Upper Saddle River, New Jersey.

Chapter 19
Figure 19.1: *Source:* Adapted from Epidemiology, by J. I. Mattia and M. Zimmerman, 2001, in *Handbook of Personality Disorders: Theory, Research, and Treatment,* edited by W. J. Livesley, New York: Guilford.

Name Index

Broesch, T., 441
Brooks, N., 618
Brose, L. A., 81
Brown, D. E., 556
Brown, J. D., 453, 455, 459
Brown, K. J., 480
Brown, R. P., 320
Brown, S. D., 393
Bruce, J., 445
Bruch, M. A., 480
Bruggemann, J. M., 69
Brummett, B. H., 78
Brunstein, J. C., 337
Bryant, F. B., 350
Buckels, E. E., 85, 493, 494
Buday, S. K., 447
Buerkle, J. V., 23
Buffardi, L. E., 497
Bui, E., 623
Bulevich, J. B., 306
Bullock, W. A., 203
Bunce, S. C., 281, 580
Burack, J. A., 550
Burgess, M., 283
Burke, R. J., 77
Burns, M. O., 389
Burnstein, E., 238, 239, 239n
Burt, D. M., 475
Burt, S. A., 183, 184
Burton, C. M., 590
Bush, G., 423
Bushman, B. J., 320, 514
Buss, A. H., 93, 444
Buss, D. M., 19, 27, 30, 35, 58, 61, 74, 78, 80, 81, 98, 99, 132, 132n, 147, 150, 177, 182, 236, 237, 242, 244, 245, 246, 247, 253, 254, 255, 256, 258, 420, 472, 475, 476, 479, 483, 487, 488, 489, 496, 509, 511, 512, 514, 525, 529, 530, 539, 553, 645, 649
Buss, K. A., 222
Butkovic, A., 492
Butler, A. C., 144, 460
Butler, P. M., 249
Button, T. M. M., 175
Buunk, B., 245
Byrnes, J. P., 530

C

Cafferty, T. P., 324
Cai, H., 147
Calheiros, M. M., 455
Calhoun, L., 585
Calkins, S. D., 223
Callaway, E., 379
Camire, L., 61
Cammaerts, M.-C., 441

Cammaerts, R., 441
Campbell, A., 509
Campbell, C., 363, 497
Campbell, D. G., 337
Campbell, J. B., 204
Campbell, L., 255
Campbell, W. K., 496
Canada, K. E., 79
Canadian Mental Health Association, 425
Canli, T., 199, 207, 223, 422
Cantor, N., 331, 391, 486
Caprara, G. V., 77, 78
Caputi, P., 382, 390
Cardemil, E. V., 585
Carli, V., 443
Carlo, G., 81
Carpenter, C. J., 496
Carrasco, M., 70
Carroll, E. J., 338
Carron, A. V., 390
Carson, S., 80
Carter, R., 192
Carter-Saltzman, L., 169
Carver, C. S., 208, 222, 583, 644
Cashden, E., 538
Caspi, A., 33–34, 91, 134, 139, 151, 152, 153, 153n, 174, 180, 185, 211, 485
Cassidy, J., 328
Cattell, R. B., 71, 74, 104, 113, 182
Centers, R. E., 525
Cepeda, M. S., 590
Chabrol, H., 85, 493, 623
Chagnon, N., 63, 534–535
Chajut, E., 425
Chamorro-Premuzic, T., 80, 151
Chan, W., 145
Chanal, J., 343
Chandler, M. J., 550
Chang, E. C., 583
Chang, L., 441
Chantala, K., 518
Chapman, B. P., 152
Charles, S. T., 138, 139
Chastain, R. L., 590
Chavira, D. A., 444
Cheek, J. M., 443, 444, 445, 480
Chen, B., 208
Chen, C., 184, 248
Chen, F. F., 547
Chen, F. S., 184, 580
Chen, S., 339
Chen, S. Y., 377–378
Cheng, H., 81
Cheung, F. M., 563
Chia, R., 384
Chida, Y., 596
Chiodo, L. M., 147, 496

Chioqueta, A. P., 79
Chipperfield, J. G., 455–456
Chiu, C., 391, 393
Cho, B., 430
Chodorow, N. J., 297
Choi, J. K., 385
Christ, S. E., 191
Christal, R. C., 74
Christie, R., 490
Chu, S. W., 211
Church, A. T., 58, 61, 535, 547, 552, 560, 561
Cianci, R., 357
Clapper, R. L., 380
Claridge, G. S., 202, 612
Clark, D. M., 423
Clark, L. A., 78, 211, 212, 421
Clarskadon, T. G., 116
Claxton, A., 478, 480
Cleckley, H., 254, 616, 619
Clewley, N., 377–378
Clifton, A., 634
Clipp, E. C., 237
Cloninger, C. R., 215–216, 216–217, 573
Clower, C. E., 78, 492
Coan, J. A., 28
Coates, D., 416
Cochran, G., 184
Coehlo, D., 447
Cohen, D., 539
Cohen, J., 48, 503
Cohen, M. F., 283
Cohen, P., 48
Cohen, S., 200, 424, 577–578, 579
Coie, J. D., 482
Colarelli, S. M., 238
Colder, C. R., 79
Coleman, R., 517
Collins, J. N., 379
Collins, P. F., 217
Colzato, L. S., 146
Confer, J. C., 236
Conger, R. D., 485
Conley, J. J., 91, 149, 150, 422, 480
Connelly, B. S., 22, 26, 27
Connolly, I., 135
Conrad, M. A., 78
Conroy-Beam, D., 479
Cons, T. A., 254
Cook, K. V., 525
Coon, H. M., 547, 548
Cooper, A., 207, 420
Cooper, C., 204
Cooper, M. A., 388
Cooper, M. L., 150, 609
Cooper, S. H., 283
Cooper, W. E, 439
Copeland, P., 176

Coplan, R. J., 443, 444, 453–454
Copping, L. T., 509
Corcoran, D. W. J., 204
Cornelius, J., 621
Corr, P. J., 207
Correa, T., 482
Cosmides, L., 19, 231, 250, 254, 536, 537, 540
Costa, P. T., Jr., 25, 62, 71, 73, 74, 75, 77, 82, 135, 136n, 138n, 416, 417, 424, 429, 501, 507, 508, 509, 510, 527, 592, 595, 596, 604, 607, 637
Cousins, A. J., 530
Coutts, L. M., 112
Cowan, G. S., 427
Cox, K., 312
Coyne, J., 424
Crabbe, J., 184
Craik, K. H., 27, 58, 103
Cramer, P., 281, 285, 295
Crandall, C., 238, 239n
Crandall, R., 356
Crandall, V. C., 345, 385
Crandall, V. J., 385
Crawford, F. C., 216
Crittenden, N., 390
Crocker, J., 413, 455
Cronbach, L. J., 41, 42
Cropanzano, R. S., 372
Cross, C. P., 509
Cross, S. E., 545
Crowne, D. P., 38
Cruce, S. E., 78
Cruz, M., 197
Csikszentmihalyi, M., 355, 388, 416, 420
Cuijpers, P., 575
Cuthbert, B. N., 619
Cutler, S. S., 281, 434

D

Dabbs, J. M., Jr., 200, 529
Dabbs, M. G., 200
Dahl, B. J., 514
Dalbert, C., 78
Dale, A. L., 291
Dale, K., 281
Dalgleish, T., 424–425
Daly, M., 194, 509, 530
Damasio, A. R., 190, 191n
Damasio, T., 191n
Danner, D. D., 151
Daros, A. R., 621, 622
Darwin, C., 19, 228–229, 267, 406, 558–559
Davey, A., 592
Davidson, K., 295
Davidson, K. W., 596

Davidson, R. J., 207, 220–221, 221–222, 222, 223, 279, 404
Davis, A. C., 548
Davis, E. P., 445
Davis, L., 265, 303
Davis, M. H., 364, 481
Davis, O. S. P., 648
Davis, P. J., 280
De Boeck, P., 337
De Bolle, M., 89, 508, 510
De Fruyt, F., 89
de la Sablonnière, R., 549–550, 551
De Raad, B., 77, 83, 561, 563
De Vries, J., 79
de Vries, R. E., 84
Deaner, R. O., 250
DeAngelis, T., 108
Deary, I. J., 81, 384, 399
Deaux, K., 502, 505
Deci, E. L., 144
DeCicco, T. L., 291, 292, 548, 549
Decuyper, M., 89
DeFries, J. C., 167, 170, 181
Deiner, C. I., 393
Del Giudice, M., 250
del Prado, A. M., 547
Delfour, F., 441
DeLongis, A., 85, 579, 581, 591–592
DelVecchio, W. F., 137
Dembrowski, T. M., 429, 596
Demerath, P., 342
Demtröder, A. I., 58, 60
Denissen, J. J. A., 60, 69, 184, 238, 255, 256
Denollet, J., 598
DePaulo, B. M., 316, 445
Depue, R. A., 215, 217
Derryberry, D., 424–425
Desaulniers, J., 526
DeSteno, D. A., 246
Devos, G., 212
DeWall, C. N., 274, 497
DeYoung, C. G., 199, 422, 423
Di Blas, L., 73, 82, 83
Diamond, J., 568
Diener, C., 414
Diener, E., 97, 100, 316, 356, 372, 407, 410, 411, 412, 413, 414, 415, 416, 431, 433, 434, 435
Diener, M., 414, 415
Digman, J. M., 74
Dijksterhuis, A., 271
Dijkstra, P., 479, 480
Dill, K. E., 482
Diminich, E. D., 593
Dixon, W. A., 429
Dobbs, D., 249
Dodge, K. A., 482

Dollard, M. F., 79
Donahue, E. M., 464
Donald, J., 202
Donhauser, P. W., 347
Donnellan, M. B., 137, 147, 152, 450, 485
Dorros, S. M., 81
Doty, R. M., 349
Douglas, K. S., 615, 616
Draper, P., 249
Dreber, A., 184
Driscoll, P., 380
Drislane, L. E., 639
Druckman, D., 117
Dubbert, P. M., 429
Duckworth, A. L., 78
Dudley, N. M., 82
Dunbar, R. I. M., 232, 257
Dunn, E. W., 416, 417
Dunne, M. P., 176
Duntley, J. D., 244
Durand, G., 84
Durik, A. M., 327–328
Durkee, T., 443
Dutton, D. G., 328
Dutton, K. A., 453
Dweck, C. S., 346, 391, 393, 394, 455
Dyrenforth, P. S., 417

E

Eagle, M. N., 296
Eagly, A. H., 96, 502, 505, 508, 520, 526
Easterlin, R. A., 415
Eaves, L., 169
Eber, H. W., 104
Ebmeier, K. P., 81
Ebstein, R., 183
Eckes, T., 520
Edwards, D. A., 529, 531
Edwards, J. K., 78
Egan, S., 81
Egan, V., 77, 85
Egloff, B., 34, 137
Eid, M., 410
Eisen, S. A., 211
Eisenberg, D. T. A., 184, 249, 249f
Eisenberg, N., 137
Eisenberger, N. I., 238
Ekman, P., 240, 241, 405, 406t, 407, 559, 560
Elder, G. H., Jr., 34, 91, 237
Elfenbein, H. H., 30
Elizur, D., 342
Elkins, I. J., 152
Elliot, A. J., 327, 339, 340, 346
Ellis, B. J., 255, 256
Ellis, L., 174

Ellis, R., 306
Ellsworth, P., 406t
Else-Quest, N. M., 506
Emery, R. E., 632, 634, 636
Emmerich, A. I., 449
Emmons, R. A., 97, 320, 356, 391, 434, 589
Endendijk, J. E., 525
Endler, N. S., 93, 96
Engelhard, I. M., 79
Enns, R. M., 173
Entwisle, D. R., 338
Epifanio, M. S., 598
Epley, C. H., 381
Epstein, S., 100
Erdelyi, M. H., 302
Erdheim, J., 77
Erikson, E. H., 311–313, 313f, 314, 315, 317, 462, 463
Eschleman, K. J., 593
Essex, M., 422
Evans, C. A., 380
Exline, R. V., 491, 497
Exner, J. E., Jr., 66
Eysenck, H. J., 38, 67, 177, 202, 203, 203f, 204, 207, 207f, 212, 213, 217, 295, 421, 422, 486, 570
Eysenck, M. W., 203, 204, 421, 486
Eysenck, S. B. G., 38, 67

F

Fabulic, L., 219
Fagot, B. I., 525
Falk, C. F., 459, 552
Fanny, E., 423
Farnham, S. D., 451
Feingold, A., 508, 513
Fenichel, O., 281
Fernandez, N., 390
Fetchenhauer, D., 26
Figueredo, A. J., 254, 255, 476
Fineman, S., 339
Finger, F. W., 218
Fink, B., 77
Fishkin, S. A., 246
Fiske, A. P., 537, 547, 551
Fiske, D. W., 74
Fitzgerald, C. J., 238
Fitzpatrick, C. M., 620
Fitzpatrick, S., 622
Flanagan, T. D., 550
Flanders, J. L., 525
Fleeson, W., 60, 77, 98, 101, 449
Fleischman, D. S., 525
Fletcher, G. J. O., 473
Flett, G. L., 356
Floderus-Myrhed, B., 172
Florian, V., 327

Flynn, F. J., 80
Flynn, H. A., 144, 460
Flynn, J. R., 398
Foa, E. B., 71
Foa, U. G., 71
Fodor, E. M., 347
Folkman, S., 579, 581, 585, 586, 591
Fordyce, M. W., 410f, 420
Forest, A. L., 454
Foster, C. A., 496
Fowles, D. C., 207, 619
Fox, N. A., 221, 223, 480
Fraley, R. C., 148, 324, 325, 326, 327, 328
Frank, R., 191n
Fransella, F., 381, 382
Fraser, S., 399
Fredrickson, B. L., 408, 585
Freeman, D., 556
Freeman, J. G., 343
Freshwater, S. M., 191
Freud, A., 281
Freud, S., 11, 236, 279, 280, 290, 318
Frideres, J., 549
Friedman, H. S., 151
Friedman, M., 593
Friedman, R., 447
Friesen, W. V., 151, 406t
Frijda, N. H., 406t
Frisell, T., 173
Fritzon, K., 618
Frodi, A., 503
Fröhlich, S. M., 339
Fryberg, S. A., 549
Fukushima, A., 430
Fulker, D. W., 170
Funder, D. C., 95
Furnham, A., 80, 81, 84, 85, 151, 481, 493
Furr, R. M., 61

G

Gabbard, G. O., 302
Gable, S. L., 460
Gabriel, S., 514
Gailliot, M. T., 274, 275
Galaburda, A. M., 191n
Gale, A., 203, 204
Gale, C. R., 384, 570, 575
Galic, Z., 105
Gallagher, P., 60
Gallo, L. C., 486
Gallup, A. C., 243
Gallup, G. G., 440–441
Gambrel, P. A., 357
Gangestad, S., 98
Gangestad, S. W., 65, 253, 530

Subject Index